Microsoft
ACCESS 2
BIBLE 2nd Edition

PC WORLD
Microsoft ACCESS 2 BIBLE
2nd Edition

by Cary N. Prague
and
Michael R. Irwin

IDG Books Worldwide, Inc.
An International Data Group Company

Foster City, CA ✦ Chicago, IL ✦ Indianapolis, IN ✦ Braintree, MA ✦ Dallas, TX

PC World Microsoft Access 2 Bible, 2nd Edition

Published by
IDG Books Worldwide, Inc.
An International Data Group Company
919 E. Hillsdale Blvd.
Suite 400
Foster City, CA 94404

Text and art copyright © 1994 by IDG Books Worldwide. All rights reserved. No part of this book may be reproduced or transmitted in any form, by any means (electronic, photocopying, recording, or otherwise) without the prior written permission of the publisher.

Library of Congress Catalog Card No.: 94-75649

ISBN: 1-56884-086-1

Printed in the United States of America

10 9 8 7 6 5 4 3

2D/QR/RS/ZU

Distributed in the United States by IDG Books Worldwide, Inc.

Distributed in Canada by Macmillan of Canada, a Division of Canada Publishing Corporation; by Computer and Technical Books in Miami, Florida, for South America and the Caribbean; by Longman Singapore in Singapore, Malaysia, Thailand, and Korea; by Toppan Co. Ltd. in Japan; by Asia Computerworld in Hong Kong; by Woodslane Pty. Ltd. in Australia and New Zealand; and by Transworld Publishers Ltd. in the U.K. and Europe.

For general information on IDG Books in the U.S., including information on discounts and premiums, contact IDG Books at 800-434-3422 or 415-312-0650.

For information on where to purchase IDG Books outside the U.S., contact Christina Turner at 415-312-0650.

For information on translations, contact Marc Jeffrey Mikulich, Director, Foreign & Subsidiary Rights, at IDG Books Worldwide, 415-312-0650.

For sales inquiries and special prices for bulk quantities, write to the address above or call IDG Books Worldwide at 415-312-0650.

For information on using IDG Books in the classroom, or ordering examination copies, contact Jim Kelly at 800-434-2086

Limit of Liability/Disclaimer of Warranty: The author and publisher have used their best efforts in preparing this book. IDG Books Worldwide, Inc., International Data Group, Inc., PCW Communications, and the author make no representation or warranties with respect to the accuracy or completeness of the contents of this book and specifically disclaim any implied warranties of merchantability or fitness for any particular purpose and shall in no event be liable for any loss of profit or any other commercial damage, including but not limited to special, incidental, consequential, or other damages.

Trademarks: Microsoft Access is a registered trademark of Microsoft Corporation. All brand names and product names used in this book are trademarks, registered trademarks, or trade names of their respective holders. IDG Books Worldwide is not associated with any product or vendor mentioned in this book. PC World is a registered trademark of PCW Communications, Inc.

 is a registered trademark of IDG Books Worldwide, Inc.

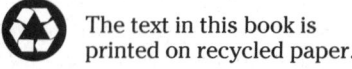 The text in this book is printed on recycled paper.

About the Authors

Cary N. Prague

Cary Prague is a well known author in the database industry, having written over 35 books on personal computer database products including Access, dBASE, Paradox, and R:Base. He is a Contributing Editor of *Access Advisor* Magazine.

He has won many awards for both speaking and writing, including the Computer Press Association's award for Best Software-Specific Book of the Year and many awards for the Best Speaker at major database conferences. Mr. Prague is Director of Information Management for the Managed Care Division of Travelers Insurance Company in Hartford, Connecticut. Formerly, he was Director of Software Productivity where he managed software support and training nationally for 35,000 end users.

Cary is the founder of Cary Prague Books and Software, the world's largest Access add-on software vendor. His current catalog contains many products for Access 2.0, including Access Business Forms Library, Yes! I Can Run My Business With Access, Access Mail Merge Report Wizard, The Envelope Wizard, The Picture Builder Add-On Picture Pack, and The Buttons Bundle.

He is a frequent speaker at national computer conferences and is a 1994 speaker at Microsoft's Database Conference, Digital Consulting's Database World Conference, and Borland's Database Conference and World Tour.

Prague has a Masters Degree in Computer Science from Rensselaer Polytechnic University. He also earned Bachelor of Accounting and MBA degrees from the University of Connecticut. He is a Certified Data Processor.

Michael R. Irwin

Michael Irwin is a well known expert in database integration. Over the past 10 years, he has written many articles for national computer magazines and authored white papers on subjects ranging from PC-based databases to cross-platform database issues. He has written and taught courses on dBASE internationally for Ashton-Tate and Borland on topics ranging from introduction to advanced performance issues. Additionally, he has written and taught a range of database subjects to several government agencies and private corporations. He has also chaired several user groups focusing on xBase databases.

Mr. Irwin is a frequently requested speaker at national computer conferences and in the last year has spoken at over 30 conferences, including Digital Consulting's Database World Conference, Borland's Database Conference, and Borland's World Tour. He is currently a member of Borland's dBASE Roundtable and is Co-Chairman of Borland's Database Conference for 1994.

Having recently retired (June 1992) from the Metropolitan Police Department of Washington, DC, Mr. Irwin and his family have relocated to Cincinnati, Ohio. Prior to retiring, he was a systems analyst and developer specializing in dBASE and cross-platform applications with experience in a wide range of database programs — from simple personnel systems to tracking events for the Presidential Inauguration. Currently, he is a third-party developer specializing in database integration and large-scale database projects.

ABOUT IDG BOOKS WORLDWIDE

Welcome to the world of IDG Books Worldwide.

IDG Books Worldwide, Inc. is a subsidiary of International Data Group, the world's largest publisher of business and computer-related information and the leading global provider of information services on information technology. IDG was founded more than 25 years ago and now employs more than 7,000 people worldwide. IDG publishes more than 220 computer publications in 65 countries (see listing below). More than fifty million people read one or more IDG publications each month.

Launched in 1990, IDG Books Worldwide is today the fastest-growing publisher of computer and business books in the United States. We are proud to have received 3 awards from the Computer Press Association in recognition of editorial excellence, and our best-selling ...For Dummies™ series has more than 12 million copies in print with translations in more than 24 languages. IDG Books, through a recent joint venture with IDG's Hi-Tech Beijing, became the first U.S. publisher to publish a computer book in the People's Republic of China. In record time, IDG Books has become the first choice for millions of readers around the world who want to learn how to better manage their businesses.

Our mission is simple: Every IDG book is designed to bring extra value and skill-building instructions to the reader. Our books are written by experts who understand and care about our readers. The knowledge base of our editorial staff comes from years of experience in publishing, education, and journalism — experience which we use to produce books for the '90s. In short, we care about books, so we attract the best people. We devote special attention to details such as audience, interior design, use of icons, and illustrations. And because we use an efficient process of authoring, editing, and desktop publishing our books electronically, we can spend more time ensuring superior content and spend less time on the technicalities of making books.

You can count on our commitment to deliver high-quality books at competitive prices on topics consumers want to read about. At IDG, we value quality, and we have been delivering quality for more than 25 years. You'll find no better book on a subject than an IDG book.

John Kilcullen
President and CEO
IDG Books Worldwide, Inc.

VIII WINNER Eighth Annual Computer Press Awards 1992

IX WINNER Ninth Annual Computer Press Awards 1993

IDG Books Worldwide, Inc. is a subsidiary of International Data Group, the world's largest publisher of computer-related information and the leading global provider of information services on information technology. International Data Group publishes over 220 computer publications in 65 countries. More than fifty million people read one or more International Data Group publications each month. The officers are Patrick J. McGovern, Founder and Board Chairman; Kelly Conlin, President; Jim Casella, Chief Operating Officer. International Data Group's publications include: **ARGENTINA'S** Computerworld Argentina, Infoworld Argentina; **AUSTRALIA'S** Computerworld Australia, Computer Living, Australian PC World, Australian Macworld, Network World, Mobile Business Australia, Publish!, Reseller, IDG Sources; **AUSTRIA'S** Computerwelt Oesterreich, PC Test; **BELGIUM'S** Data News (CW); **BOLIVIA'S** Computerworld; **BRAZIL'S** Computerworld, Connections, Game Power, Mundo Unix, PC World, Publish, Super Game; **BULGARIA'S** Computerworld Bulgaria, PC & Mac World Bulgaria, Network World Bulgaria; **CANADA'S** CIO Canada, Computerworld Canada, InfoCanada, Network World Canada, Reseller; **CHILE'S** Computerworld Chile, Informatica; **COLOMBIA'S** Computerworld Colombia, PC World; **COSTA RICA'S** PC World; **CZECH REPUBLIC'S** Computerworld, Elektronika, PC World; **DENMARK'S** Communications World, Computerworld Danmark, Computerworld Focus, Macintosh Produktkatalog, Macworld Danmark, PC World Danmark, PC Produktguide, Tech World, Windows World; **ECUADOR'S** PC World Ecuador; **EGYPT'S** Computerworld (CW) Middle East, PC World Middle East; **FINLAND'S** MikroPC, Tietoviikko, Tietoverkko; **FRANCE'S** Distributique, GOLDEN MAC, InfoPC, Le Guide du Monde Informatique, Le Monde Informatique, Telecoms & Reseaux; **GERMANY'S** Computerwoche, Computerwoche Focus, Computerwoche Extra, Electronic Entertainment, Gamepro, Information Management, Macwelt, Netzwelt, PC Welt, Publish, Publish; **GREECE'S** Publish & Macworld; **HONG KONG'S** Computerworld Hong Kong, PC World Hong Kong; **HUNGARY'S** Computerworld SZT, PC World; **INDIA'S** Computers & Communications; **INDONESIA'S** Info Komputer; **IRELAND'S** ComputerScope; **ISRAEL'S** Beyond Windows, Computerworld Israel, Multimedia, PC World Israel; **ITALY'S** Computerworld Italia, Lotus Magazine, Macworld Italia, Networking Italia, PC Shopping Italy, PC World Italia; **JAPAN'S** Computerworld Today, Information Systems World, Macworld Japan, Nikkei Personal Computing, SunWorld Japan, Windows World; **KENYA'S** East African Computer News; **KOREA'S** Computerworld Korea, Macworld Korea, PC World Korea; **LATIN AMERICA'S** GamePro; **MALAYSIA'S** Computerworld Malaysia, PC World Malaysia; **MEXICO'S** Compu Edicion, Compu Manufactura, Computacion/Punto de Venta, Computerworld Mexico, MacWorld, Mundo Unix, PC World, Windows; **THE NETHERLANDS'** Computer! Totaal, Computable (CW), LAN Magazine, Lotus Magazine, MacWorld; **NEW ZEALAND'S** Computer Buyer, Computerworld New Zealand, Network World, New Zealand PC World; **NIGERIA'S** PC World Africa; **NORWAY'S** Computerworld Norge, Lotusworld Norge, Macworld Norge, Maxi Data, Networld, PC World Ekspress, PC World Nettverk, PC World Norge, PC World's Produktguide, Publish& Multimedia World, Student Data, Unix World, Windowsworld; **PAKISTAN'S** PC World Pakistan; **PANAMA'S** PC World Panama; **PERU'S** Computerworld Peru, PC World; **PEOPLE'S REPUBLIC OF CHINA'S** China Computerworld, China Infoworld, China PC Info Magazine, Computer Fan, PC World China, Electronics International, Electronics Today/Multimedia World, Electronic Product World, China Network World, Software World Magazine, Telecom Product World, **PHILIPPINES'** Computerworld Philippines, PC Digest (PCW); **POLAND'S** Computerworld Poland, Computerworld Special Report, Networld, PC World/Komputer, Sunworld; **PORTUGAL'S** Cerebro/PC World, Correio Informatico/Computerworld, MacIn; **ROMANIA'S** Computerworld, PC World, Telecom Romania; **RUSSIA'S** Computerworld-Moscow, Mir - PK (PCW), Sety (Networks); **SINGAPORE'S** Computerworld Southeast Asia, PC World Singapore; **SLOVENIA'S** Monitor Magazine; **SOUTH AFRICA'S** Computer Mail (CIO),Computing S.A.,Network World S.A., Software World; **SPAIN'S** Advanced Systems, Amiga World, Computerworld Espana, Communicaciones World, Macworld Espana, NeXTWORLD, Super Juegos Magazine (GamePro), PC World Espana, Publish; **SWEDEN'S** Attack, ComputerSweden, Corporate Computing, Macworld, Mikrodatorn, Natverk & Kommunikation, PC World, CAP & Design, Datalngenjoren, Maxi Data,Windows World; **SWITZERLAND'S** Computerworld Schweiz, Macworld Schweiz, PC Tip; **TAIWAN'S** Computerworld Taiwan, PC World Taiwan; **THAILAND'S** Thai Computerworld; **TURKEY'S** Computerworld Monitor, Macworld Turkiye, PC World Turkiye; **UKRAINE'S** Computerworld, Computers+Software Magazine; **UNITED KINGDOM'S** Computing /Computerworld, Connexion/Network World, Lotus Magazine, Macworld, Open Computing/Sunworld; **URAGUAY'S** PC World Uraguay; **UNITED STATES'** Advanced Systems, AmigaWorld, Cable in the Classroom, CD Review, CIO, Computerworld, Computerworld Client/Server Journal, Digital Video, DOS World, Electronic Entertainment Magazine (E2), Federal Computer Week, Game Hits, GamePro, IDG Books, Infoworld, Laser Event, Macworld, Maximize, Multimedia World, Network World, PC Letter, PC World, Publish, SWATPro, Video Event; **VENEZUELA'S** Computerworld Venezuela, PC World; **VIETNAM'S** PC World Vietnam.

Dedication

This book is dedicated to Richard Booth, Dick Porell, and Robert Randell, for solving my mid-life crisis through new opportunities, constant change, and most of all, daily challenges

CNP

In remembrance of Richard Irwin, my father

MRI

Credits

VP & Publisher
David Solomon

Managing Editor
Mary Bednarek

Acquisitions Editor
Janna Custer

Production Director
Beth Jenkins

Senior Editors
Tracy L. Barr
Sandra Blackthorn
Diane Graves Steele

Production Coordinator
Cindy L. Phipps

Associate Acquisitions Editor
Megg Bonar

Editorial Assistant
Tamara S. Castleman

Project Editor
Erik Dafforn

Editors
Shawn MacLaren
Andy Cummings
Kezia Endsley
A. Timothy Gallan
Marta Justak Partington
Mary C. Corder

Technical Reviewer
Diana Smith

Production Staff
Tony Augsburger
Valery Bourke
Mary Breidenbach
Chris Collins
Sherry Gomoll
Drew R. Moore
Mark Owens
Dwight Ramsey
Theresa Sanchez-Baker
Kathie Schnorr
Gina Scott

Cover Illustrator
Roy Wiemann

Cover Design
Kavish + Kavish

Proofreader
Henry Lazarek

Indexer
Anne Leach

Book Design
IDG Production Staff

Acknowledgments

When we first saw Access in July of 1992, we were instantly sold on this new generation of database management and access tool. We've both spent the last two years using Access daily. In fact, after two short years, there are estimated to be nearly 2 million Access users worldwide.

Now, we have rewritten this book for all the incredible new features in Access 2.0. We've also written countless systems, designed and brought to market many add-on products for Access, and created the largest Access add-on software and book distributing company in the world. We've served nearly 10,000 customers, our staff has answered thousands of technical support questions, and we've received critical acclaim from readers and reviewers alike. Our first acknowledgment is to all the users of Access who have profited and benefitted beyond everyone's wildest dreams.

There are many people who assisted us in writing this book. We'd like to recognize each of them.

To Christine Capazzi, for running Cary's business, editing his pigeon English, and generally being an incredible help.

To John S. Dranchak for designing the reports in Chapters 21 and 23 and creating the logo for Mountain Animal Hospital.

To Diana Smith, who wrote the original introductory chapters (2, 3, and 5) and also was the technical editor for this book. To her we offer a special thank you.

Thanks to Mary Lynn Maurice for her assistance in Chapters 4 and 6. Again, through her efforts, we were able to shorten the writing time of this project.

To all the folks at Microsoft who dedicated innumerable hours of their lives to us over the last few months — especially David Risher, Access Product Manager and our main technical contact. He put up with constant phone calls and always was as straight with us as he was allowed to be. A special thanks, too, to Scott Fallon.

To our agent, Bill Gladstone.

To the folks at IDG Books: John Kilcullen, President and CEO, who is no dummy, but whose Dummies books are taking the world by storm.

To Janna Custer for her patience and understanding.

To Mary Bednarek, Sandra Blackthorn, and Erik Dafforn. Thanks for the incredible job you did managing the project and editing our book.

In closing, to our wives and children. Although we didn't spend much time with each of you over the last two years, your love and support is what made it possible for us to complete this book. Even though we were remiss on our side of the relationship, you (our wives) were there to offer support and advice when we needed it most. When we became grumpy and argumentative, each of you were there to offer unconditional love. For this, we especially what to thank all of you — Karen, David, Jeffery, Alex, Patricia, Richard Rocco, and Joseph Patrick!

The publisher would like to give special thanks to Patrick J. McGovern, without whom this book would not have been possible.

Contents at a Glance

Introduction 1

Part I: First Things First 7
    Chapter 1: What is Access? 9
    Chapter 2: Installing Access 21
    Chapter 3: Getting Started with Access 31
    Chapter 4: A Review of Database Concepts 43
    Chapter 5: A Hands-On Tour of Access 55
    Chapter 6: A Case Study in Database Design 75

Part II: Basic Database Usage 99
    Chapter 7: Creating Database Tables 101
    Chapter 8: Entering, Changing, Deleting, and Displaying Data 137
    Chapter 9: Creating and Using Simple Data-Entry Forms 175
    Chapter 10: Understanding and Using Simple Queries 199
    Chapter 11: Creating and Printing Simple Reports 231
    Chapter 12: Setting Relationships between Multiple Tables 253

Part III: Using Access in Your Work 275
    Chapter 13: Using Operators, Functions, and Expressions 277
    Chapter 14: Creating Relations and Joins in Queries 305
    Chapter 15: Creating Select Queries 335
    Chapter 16: Understanding Controls and Properties 365
    Chapter 17: Creating and Customizing Data-Entry Forms 401
    Chapter 18: Creating Great-Looking Forms 441
    Chapter 19: Adding Data Validation Controls to Forms 463
    Chapter 20: Using OLE Objects, Pictures, and Graphs 493
    Chapter 21: Creating and Customizing Reports 529
    Chapter 22: Database Publishing and Printing 583
    Chapter 23: Creating Calculations and Summaries in Reports 619

Part IV: Advanced Database Features 657

Chapter 24: Working with External Data 659
Chapter 25: Advanced Select Queries 707
Chapter 26: Creating Action Queries 741
Chapter 27: Advanced Query Topics 769
Chapter 28: Creating and Using Subforms 797
Chapter 29: Creating Mailing Labels and Mail Merge Reports 829

Part V: Applications in Access 859

Chapter 30: An Introduction to Macros and Events 861
Chapter 31: Using Macros in Forms and Reports 889
Chapter 32: Creating Switchboards, Menus, and Dialogs 937
Chapter 33: Next Steps — Modules and Access Basic 987

Appendixes

Appendix A: Microsoft Access Specifications 1001
Appendix B: Mountain Animal Hospital Tables 1005

Index 1011

Disclaimer and Copyright Notice 1042

Installation Instructions for the Companion Disk 1043

Reader Response Card .... back of book

Table of Contents

Introduction 1
   Is This Book for You? 1
      Yes — If you have no database experience 2
      Yes — If you've used other database managers like dBASE or Paradox .. 2
      No — If you want to learn Access Basic programming 2
   Conventions Used in This Book 2
   Icons and Alerts 3
   How This Book Is Organized 4
      Part I: First Things First 4
      Part II: Basic Database Usage 5
      Part III: Using Access in Your Work 5
      Part IV: Advanced Database Features 5
      Part V: Applications in Access 6
      The appendixes and reference material 6

Part I: First Things First 7

Chapter 1: What Is Access? 9
   In This Chapter 9
   Access Is 9
   What Access Offers 11
      True relational database management 12
      Context-sensitive Help and Cue Cards 12
      Ease-of-use Wizards 12
      Importing, exporting, and attaching external files 13
      WYSIWYG forms and reports 14
      Multiple-table queries 14
      Business graphs and charts 15
      DDE and OLE capabilities 17
      Built-in functions 17
      Macros — programming without programming 17
      Modules — Access Basic for database programming 17

Information for Database Users 18
Information for Spreadsheet Users 19
Summary 20

Chapter 2: Installing Access 21

In This Chapter 21
Determining What You Need 22
    Hardware requirements 22
    Software requirements 22
Upgrading to Access 2.0 from Access 1.x 23
Installing Access 23
Converting Access 1.x Files 27
Troubleshooting 28
Summary 29

Chapter 3: Getting Started with Access 31

In This Chapter 31
Starting Access 31
    Starting from the Access icon 31
    Starting from Program Manager 32
    Starting from File Manager 33
    Starting from DOS 34
    Options for starting Access 34
Exiting Access 36
Shortcut Menus 36
Getting Help 37
    Cue Cards 38
    Essentials of on-line help 39
    Searching for help 40
    Help pull-down menus 42
Exiting Help 42
Summary 42

Chapter 4: A Review of Database Concepts 43
In This Chapter 43
What Is a Database? 43
Databases, Tables, Records, Fields, and Values 45
    Databases 45
    Tables 46
    Records and fields 46
    Values 46
Why Use More Than One Table? 47
Database Objects and Views 48
    Datasheets 49
    Queries and dynasets 49
    Data-entry and display forms 51
    Reports 52
Summary 54

Chapter 5: A Hands-On Tour of Access 55
In This Chapter 55
A Tour of the Screen 55
    Using the mouse and keyboard 55
    The Access window 56
    The Database window 57
    Design windows 58
        The toolbox 58
        The palette 59
        The Field List window 59
        The property sheet 60
A Simple Access Session 60
    Opening a database 62
    Opening a table 63
    Displaying a datasheet 64
    Viewing a table design 65
    Displaying a form 66
    Creating a query 68
    Displaying a report 71
Ready for More 74
Summary 74

Chapter 6: A Case Study in Database Design 75

In This Chapter 75
The Seven-Step Method for Design 76
    Step 1: The overall design — from concept to reality 77
    Step 2: Report design — placing your fields 78
        Laying out fields in the report 78
        The pets and owners directory 78
        The Monthly Invoice Report 80
    Step 3: Data design — what fields do you have? 82
        Determining customer information 83
        Determining pet information 83
        Determining visit information 84
        Combining the data 85
    Step 4: Table design and relationships 88
        Setting relations 88
    Step 5: Field design — data-entry rules and validation 89
        Designing field names, types, and sizes 90
        Designing data-entry rules 90
        Designing lookup tables 91
        Creating test data 92
    Step 6: Form design — input 93
        Designing data-entry screens 93
        The customer form 94
        The pets form 94
        The general visit form 96
        The visit details form 96
    Step 7: Automation design — menus 97
Summary 98

Part II: Basic Database Usage 99

Chapter 7: Creating Database Tables 101

In This Chapter 101
Creating the Pets Table 101
Creating a Database 102
The Database Window 104

The Database Window	104
Object buttons	105
The Database window toolbar	105
Controlling Access 2.0 toolbars	106
The Database window command buttons	106
Creating a New Table	107
The table design process	107
The New Table Dialog Box	107
The Table window	109
Using the Table window toolbar	110
Creating Fields	110
Naming a field	110
Specifying a data type	111
Entering a field description	113
Completing the Pets Table	113
Understanding Field Properties	114
Entering field size properties	115
Using formats	116
Text and Memo data type formats	116
Number and Currency data type formats	117
Date/Time data type formats	117
Yes/No data type formats	119
Entering formats	119
Entering input masks	120
The input mask wizard	121
Entering decimal places	122
Creating a caption	122
Setting a default value	123
Understanding data validation	123
Determining the Primary Key	124
Creating a unique key	124
Creating the primary key	125
The Indexes window	125
The Table Properties window	126
Changing a Table Structure	127
Changing a field's location	127
Inserting a new field	127
Deleting a field	127

Changing a field name 129
　　Changing a field size 129
　　Changing a field data type 129
　　　　To Text from other data types 130
　　　　From Text to Number, Currency, Date/Time, or Yes/No 130
　　　　From Currency to Number 130
　　　　From Text to Memo 131
　Printing a Table Design 131
　Saving the Completed Table 131
　Manipulating Tables in a Database Window 132
　　Renaming tables 132
　　Deleting tables 133
　　Copying tables in a database 133
　　Copying a table to another database 134
　Summary 135

Chapter 8: Entering, Changing, Deleting, and Displaying Data 137

　In This Chapter 137
　Understanding Datasheets 138
　The Datasheet Window 139
　　Navigation inside a datasheet 139
　　　The navigation buttons 140
　　　　The datasheet toolbar 141
　Opening a Datasheet 142
　Entering New Data 142
　　Saving the record 144
　　Understanding automatic data type validation 145
　　Using various data-entry techniques 145
　　　Standard text data entry 146
　　　Date/Time data entry 146
　　　Text data entry with data validation 146
　　　Numeric data entry with data validation 146
　　　OLE object data entry 147
　Navigating Records in a Datasheet 148
　　Memo field data entry 148
　　Moving between records 149
　　Finding a specific value 150

Replacing an existing value	152
Changing an existing value	153
Fields that you can't edit	153
Using the Undo Features	154
Copying and Pasting Values	155
Replacing Values without Typing	155
Adding New Records	155
Deleting Records	156
Displaying Records	156
Changing the field order	156
Changing the field display width	158
Changing the record display height	159
Changing display fonts	160
Hiding and showing columns	161
Freezing columns	162
Displaying gridlines	162
Saving the changed layout	162
Saving a record	163
Sorting and filtering records in a datasheet	163
Using the QuickSort feature	163
Displaying the Filter/Sort window	164
Adding a field to the QBE pane	165
Specifying a sort order	167
Specifying filter criteria	167
Displaying the sorted or filtered data	168
Redisplaying all records	168
Changing the Filter/Sort window	168
Printing Records	169
Printing the datasheet	170
Using the Print Preview window	170
Summary	172

Chapter 9: Creating and Using Simple Data-Entry Forms 175

In This Chapter	175
Understanding Data-Entry Forms	175
What types of forms can you create?	176
How do forms differ from datasheets?	178
Creating a form With AutoForm	179

Creating a form With AutoForm	179
Creating a Form with Form Wizards	180
Creating a new form	180
Selecting the form type	181
Choosing the fields	182
Choosing the look of the form	183
Creating a form title	184
Opening the form	185
Using the Form Window	186
The Form toolbar	187
Navigating between fields	187
Moving between records in a form	188
Displaying Your Data with a Form	189
Working with pictures and OLE objects	189
Memo field data entry	191
Switching to a datasheet	191
Working with form records	192
Changing the Design	192
Saving a Record and the Form	193
Printing a Form	195
Using the Print Preview Window	195
Printing a Form Definition	196
Summary	197

Chapter 10: Understanding and Using Simple Queries 199

In This Chapter	199
Understanding Queries	199
What is a query?	200
Types of queries	202
Query capabilities	203
How dynasets work	204
Creating a Query	205
Selecting a table	205
Using the Query window	206
Navigating the Query Design window	207
Using the Query Design toolbar	208
Using the Query Design menu	209
Using the QBE pane of the query design window	211

Selecting Fields 212
    Adding a single field 212
    Adding multiple fields 213
    Adding all table fields 214
        Dragging all fields as a group 215
        Selecting the all-field reference tag 216
Displaying the Dynaset 217
    Working with the datasheet 217
    Changing data in the query datasheet 218
    Returning to the query design 218
Working with Fields 219
    Changing field order 219
    Removing a field 220
    Inserting a field 221
    Changing the field display name 221
    Showing a field 222
Changing the Sort Order 223
    Specifying a sort 223
    Sorting on more than one field 224
Displaying Only Selected Records 225
    Understanding record criteria 225
    Entering simple character criteria 226
    Entering other simple criteria 227
Printing a Query Dynaset 228
Saving a Query 229
Summary 230

Chapter 11: Creating and Printing Simple Reports ... 231

In This Chapter 231
Understanding Reports 231
    What types of reports can you create? 232
        Groups/totals reports 232
        Column reports 233
        Mailing labels 234
    The difference between reports and forms 235
    The process of creating a report 235
        Defining the report layout 235
        Assembling the data 235

Creating a Report with Report Wizards 238
    Creating a new report 238
    Choosing the data source 239
    Choosing the fields 240
    Selecting the Wizard 240
    Selecting the group by: field 241
    Defining the group data 242
    Selecting sort order 242
    Choosing the print effect 243
    Opening the report design 244
    Using the Print Preview window 245
    Viewing the Report Design window 246
    Using sample previews 248
Printing a Report 248
Saving the Report 248
Creating a Report with AutoReport 249
Summary 251

Chapter 12: Setting Relationships between Multiple Tables 253

In This Chapter 253
Tables Used in the Mountain Animal Hospital Database 254
Understanding Keys 255
    Deciding on a primary key 256
    Benefits of a primary key 257
    Creating a primary key 259
    Understanding foreign keys 260
Understanding Relations between Tables 260
    A review of relationships 260
    Understanding the four types of table relationships 261
        The one-to-one relationship 262
        The one-to-many relationship 262
        The many-to-one relationship 262
        The many-to-many relationship 262
Understanding Referential Integrity 263
Creating Relationships 264
    Using the relationships builder tool 264
    Creating a link between tables 266

Specifying relationship options in the relationship dialog box 268
    Specifying the primary table 268
    Enforcing referential integrity 268
Saving the relationships between tables 271
Adding another relationship 271
Deleting an existing relationship 271
Join lines in the Relationships window 272
Creating the relationships for the Mountain Animal Hospital system .. 272
Creating relationships using queries 273
Summary 274

Part III: Using Access in Your Work 275

Chapter 13: Using Operators, Functions, and Expressions 277

In This Chapter 277
Operators 277
    Types of operators 277
    When are operators used? 278
    Mathematical operators 278
        The * (multiplication) operator 279
        The + (addition) operator 279
        The – (subtraction) operator 279
        The / (division) operator 279
        The \ (integer division) operator 280
        The ^ (exponentiation) operator 281
    Relational operators 281
        The = (equal) operator 281
        The <> (not equal) operator 282
        The < (less than) operator 282
        The <= (less than or equal to) operator 282
        The > (greater than) operator 282
        The >= (greater than or equal to) operator 282
    String operators 283
        The & (concatenation) operator 283
        The Like (similar to ...) operator 284

- Boolean (logical) operators 285
  - The And operator 286
  - The Or operator 287
  - The Eqv operator 287
  - The Not operator 288
- Miscellaneous operators 289
  - The Between ... And operator 289
  - The In operator 289
  - The Is (reserved word) operator 290
- Operator precedence 290
  - The mathematical precedence 291
  - The comparison precedence 291
  - The Boolean precedence 291

What Are Functions? 292
- Using functions in Access 293
- Types of functions 294
  - Conversion 294
  - Date/Time 295
  - Financial (SQL) 295
  - Financial (monetary) 295
  - Mathematical 296
  - String manipulation 296
  - Domain 296

What Are Expressions? 297
- The parts of an expression 298
- Creating an expression 299
  - Entering object names 299
  - Entering text 300
  - Entering date/time values 300
  - Expression Builder 300
- Special identifier operators and expressions 300
  - The ! (exclamation) identifier operator 302
  - The . (dot) identifier operator 303

Summary 304

Chapter 14: Creating Relations and Joins in Queries 305

In This Chapter 305
Adding More Than One Table to the Query Window 305
Working with the Table/Query Pane 307
    The join line 307
    Manipulating the Table Design window 308
    Resizing the table/query pane 308
    Moving a table 310
    Removing a table 311
        Adding more tables 311
    Resizing a table design 312
    Creating a database diagram 312
Adding Fields from More Than One Table 313
    Adding a single field 314
    Viewing the table names 314
        Adding multiple fields 315
        Adding all table fields 315
        Selecting all fields with the Asterisk (*) method 316
Understanding the Limitations of Multiple-Table Queries 317
    Updating limitations 317
    Overcoming query limitations 318
        A unique index (primary key) and updatability 318
        Replacing existing data in a query with a one-to-many relationship 319
        Design tips for updating fields in queries 320
        Temporary non-updatability in a one-to-many relationship 320
Creating Query Joins 320
    Joining tables 321
    Deleting joins 323
Understanding Types of Table Joins 324
    Inner joins (equi-joins) 325
    Changing join properties 325
    Inner and outer joins 327
        Displaying an inner join 327
    Creating an outer join 328
    Creating another outer join 330
    Creating a self-join 331
    Creating a Cartesian product 332
Summary 333

Chapter 15: Creating Select Queries 335
In This Chapter 335
Moving Beyond Simple Queries 336
    Using query comparison operators 336
    Understanding complex criteria selection 338
    Using functions in select queries 341
    Referencing fields in select queries 341
Entering Single-Value Field Criteria 342
    Entering character (Text or Memo) criteria 342
    The Like operator and wildcards 344
    Specifying nonmatching values 346
    Entering numeric (Number, Currency, or Counter) criteria 347
    Entering Yes/No (logic) criteria 348
    Entering OLE object criteria 349
Entering Multiple Criteria in One Field 349
    Understanding an Or operation 349
    Specifying multiple values for a field using the Or operator ... 350
    Using the or: cell of the QBE pane 351
    Using a list of values with the In operator 352
    Understanding an And query 352
    Specifying a range using the And operator 353
    Using the Between ... And operator 354
    Searching for Null data 354
Entering Criteria in Multiple Fields 355
    Using And and Or across fields in a query 355
    Specifying And criteria across fields of a query 356
    Specifying Or criteria across fields of a query 358
    Using And and Or together in different fields 358
    A complex query on different lines 359
    A complex query on one line 360
Creating a New Calculated Field in a Query 361
Summary 364

Chapter 16: Understanding Controls and Properties 365
In This Chapter 365
What Is a Control? 367
    The different control types 367
    Understanding bound, unbound, and calculated controls 368

Standards for Using Controls 370
    Label controls 370
    Text box controls 371
    Toggle buttons, option buttons, and checkboxes 372
    Option groups 374
    Buttons in rectangles 374
    List boxes 376
    Combo boxes 376
Creating New Controls 378
    The two ways to create a control 378
        Using the Field List window 378
        Using the toolbox 379
    Dragging a field name from the Field List window 379
    Creating unbound controls with the toolbox 381
Selecting Controls 383
    Deselecting selected controls 384
    Selecting a single control 384
    Selecting multiple controls 384
Manipulating Controls 385
    Resizing a control 385
    Moving a control 386
    Aligning controls 387
    Deleting a control 389
    Attaching a label to a control 390
    Copying a control 391
    Changing the control type 391
What Are Properties? 391
    Viewing a control's properties 392
    Changing a control property 394
    Default properties 395
    Applying default properties to existing controls 396
    Changing default properties 396
    Creating a new template for forms and reports 397
Summary 398

Chapter 17: Creating and Customizing Data-Entry Forms 401

In This Chapter 401
Creating a Standard Data-Entry Form 402
    Assembling the data 402
    Creating a new form and binding it to a query 405
    Defining the form display size 405
    Changing form properties 407
        Changing the title bar text with the Caption property 408
        Setting the various views 408
    Placing fields on the form 411
        Displaying the field list 411
        Selecting the fields for your form 412
        Dragging fields onto your form 413
Working with Label Controls and Text Box Controls 414
    Creating unattached labels 414
    Modifying the text in a label or text control 415
    Modifying the appearance of text in a control 416
    Sizing a text box control or label control 416
    Moving label and text controls 417
    Modifying the appearance of multiple controls 418
    Setting the tab order 420
    Adding multiple-line text box controls for Memo fields 421
    Adding a bound object frame to the form 423
Creating a Form Using Multiple Tables 426
    Adding fields from a second table 426
    Working with attached label and text controls 428
    Creating a calculated field 430
    Changing the updatability of a multiple-table form 431
Creating a Multiple-Page Form 433
    Why use multiple-page forms? 433
    Adding a page break 434
Using Form and Page Headers and Footers 435
    The different types of headers and footers 436
    Creating a form header and footer 437
Printing a Form 438
Converting a Form to a Report 439
Summary 440

Chapter 18: Creating Great-Looking Forms 441

In This Chapter 441
Making a Good Form Look Great 441
    Understanding WYSIWYG 442
    Using the palette 443
    Creating special looks 444
        Standard 445
        Raised 445
        Sunken 446
        Shadowed 446
        Chiseled 446
    Changing the form's background color 446
Enhancing Text-Based Controls 447
    Enhancing label and text box controls 447
    Creating a text shadow 448
    Changing text to a reverse video display 449
    Displaying label or text box control properties 450
Displaying Unbound OLE Objects in Forms 452
Working with Lines and Rectangles 454
Emphasizing Areas of the Form 456
    Adding background color to a control 456
    Sinking controls 457
    Raising controls 457
    Creating a shadow on a rectangle 458
Adding a Background Bitmap 459
Summary 461

Chapter 19: Adding Data-Validation Controls to Forms 463

In This Chapter 463
Creating Data-Validation Expressions 464
    Table-level validation 464
    Form-level validation 466
    Entering a validation expression 466
Creating Choices with Option Buttons 467
    Creating option groups 468
    Creating an option group box 468

Creating Yes/No Options 472
    Creating checkboxes 473
    Creating visual selections with toggle buttons 474
    Adding a bitmapped image to the toggle button 475
Working with List Boxes and Combo Boxes 477
    Understanding the differences between list boxes and combo boxes .. 477
    Settling real-estate issues 477
    Creating a single-column list box 478
    Understanding list box properties 480
    Creating a multiple-column list box 482
    Hiding a column in a list box 484
Creating and Using Combo Boxes 484
    Creating a multiple-column combo box from a query 487
Summary 491

Chapter 20: Using OLE Objects, Pictures, and Graphs 493

In This Chapter 493
Understanding Objects 493
    Types of objects 494
    Using bound and unbound objects 494
    Linking and embedding 494
Embedding Objects 497
    Embedding an unbound object 497
        Pasting an unbound object 497
        Inserting an unbound OLE object 498
        Changing the display of an unbound OLE object 500
    Embedding bound objects 502
        Creating a bound OLE object 502
    Adding a picture to a bound object frame 502
    Editing an embedded object 504
Linking Objects 504
    Linking a bound object 505
Creating a Graph 507
    The different ways to create a graph 508
Embedding a Graph in a Form 508
    Assembling the data 509
    Adding the graph to the form 509

Customizing a Graph 517
    Understanding the Graph window 518
    Working with attached text 519
    Changing the graph type 522
    Changing axis labels 524
    Changing a bar color and pattern 524
    Modifying gridlines 525
    Manipulating three-dimensional graphs 525
Summary 528

Chapter 21: Creating and Customizing Reports 529

In This Chapter 529
Starting with a Blank Form 529
    The Design window toolbar 530
Banded Report Writer Concepts 532
    How sections process data 533
    The report writer sections 534
        Report header section 535
        Page header section 536
        Group header 536
        Detail section 536
        Group footer 537
        Page footer 537
        Report footer 537
Creating a New Report 538
    Eleven tasks to creating a great report 539
    Designing the report 540
    Assembling the data 541
    Creating a new report and binding it to a query 542
    Defining the report page size and layout 544
    Placing fields on the report 547
        Displaying the field list 547
        Selecting the fields for your report 548
        Dragging fields onto your report 549
        Resizing a section 550
    Working with label controls and text 552
        Creating unattached labels 552
        Modifying the appearance of text in a control 552

Working with text boxes and attached label controls 553
    Adding text box controls 553
    Entering an expression in a text control 553
    Sizing a text box control or label control 554
    Changing the size of a label control 555
    Deleting attached label and text controls 557
    Moving label and text controls 557
    Modifying the appearance of multiple controls 563
Changing label and text box control properties 566
Formatting the display of text controls 567
Growing and shrinking text box controls 568
Sorting and grouping data 570
    Creating a group header or footer 573
    Changing the group order 575
    Removing a group header or footer 576
    Hiding a section 577
    Sizing a section 577
Adding page breaks 578
Saving your report 580
Summary 581

Chapter 22: Database Publishing and Printing 583

In This Chapter 583
Database Publishing with Access 584
    Understanding WYSIWYG printing 585
    Using the palette 586
Enhancing Text-Based Controls 588
    Enhancing label controls 588
        Changing text fonts and size 588
        Creating a text shadow 588
    Displaying label or text box control properties 589
    Working with multiple-line text box controls 590
        Displaying multiple lines of text using a text box 590
        Displaying Memo fields in multiple-line text box controls 591
Adding New Controls 592
    Displaying values with option groups and option buttons 593
    Creating the option group 593
        Creating an option group with a calculated control 597

Displaying Yes/No values with checkboxes 600
Displaying values as toggle buttons 602
Displaying bound OLE objects in reports 602
Displaying unbound OLE objects in reports 603
Working with Lines and Rectangles 605
Emphasizing Areas of the Report 607
    Adding background shade 607
    Sinking controls 608
    Raising controls 608
    Creating a shadow on a rectangle 609
    Changing text to a reverse video display 609
Seeing Your Output in Different Ways 610
    Using the Print Preview window 611
    Using sample previews 612
    Printing a report 612
        The Print dialog box 613
        The Print Setup dialog box 614
    Printing the report definition 616
Summary 617

Chapter 23: Creating Calculations and Summaries in Reports 619

In This Chapter 619
Creating a Multilevel Grouping Report with Totals 620
    Designing the Invoice Report 620
    Designing and creating the query for the report 621
    Designing test data 625
    Creating a new report 627
    Creating the sorting orders 628
    Creating the detail section 629
    Creating the detail section controls 630
        Creating calculated controls 631
        Naming controls used in calculations 631
    Testing the detail section 632
    Creating the Pet ID header and footer sections 633
    Creating the Pet ID header controls 634
    Creating the Pet ID footer controls 635

Using concatenation to join text and fields 635
Calculating group summaries 637
Creating the Customer Number header and footer sections 639
Creating the Customer Number header controls 640
Creating the Customer Number footer controls 642
Creating the Visit Date header 646
Creating the page header controls 647
Creating the page footer controls 649
Calculating percentages using totals 650
Calculating running sums 652
Creating a title page in a report header 652
Using the report footer 654
Summary 655

Part IV: Advanced Database Features 657

Chapter 24: Working with External Data 659

In This Chapter 659
Access and External Data 659
Types of external data 660
Methods of working with external data 660
Should you import or attach data? 661
When to import external data 661
When to attach external data 662
Attaching External Data 663
Database connectivity 663
Types of Database Management Systems (DBMSs) 663
Attaching to other Access database tables 665
Attaching to dBASE and FoxPro databases (tables) 667
Access and dBASE/FoxPro indexes 667
Attaching to dBASE IV tables 668
Attaching to dBASE III table with an index 669
Attaching to Paradox tables 669
Access and Paradox index files 669
Attaching to Paradox tables 670
Attaching to Btrieve tables 670
Attaching to SQL database tables 671

Working with Attached Tables	673
Setting view properties	673
Setting relationships	673
Setting links between external tables	673
Using external tables in queries	674
Renaming tables	675
Optimizing attached tables	675
Deleting a linked table reference	676
Viewing or changing information for attached tables	676
Importing External Data	677
Importing other Access objects	678
Importing PC-based database tables	679
Importing a PC-based database	680
Importing Btrieve tables	681
Importing from an ODBC server database	682
Importing spreadsheet data	683
The First Row Contains Field Names option	685
Table Options	685
The Spreadsheet Range option	685
Importing from word processing files	685
Importing text file data	686
Delimited text files	686
Fixed-width text files	686
Importing delimited text files	687
Importing fixed-width text files	688
Creating an Import/Export Setup	688
Creating or editing text file setup specifications	689
Understanding setup options	690
The Specification Name option	691
The File Type option	691
The Text Delimiter option	691
The Field Separator option	692
The Date Order option	692
The Date Delimiter option	693
The Leading Zeros in Dates option	693
The Four Digit Years option	693
The Time Delimiter option	694
The Decimal Separator option	694
The Field Information: (fixed width only) option	694

Setup command buttons 694
Importing a text file (fixed width) 695
Modifying imported table elements 696
Troubleshooting import errors 697
  Import errors for new tables 697
  Import errors for existing tables 697
  The Import Errors table 698
Exporting to External Formats 698
  Exporting objects to other Access databases 699
  Exporting to spreadsheets 699
  Exporting to PC-based databases 700
  Exporting to text files 700
  Exporting to word processor files 701
  Exporting to a Microsoft Word for Windows mail merge data file 701
  Exporting to Btrieve tables 702
  Exporting to an SQL database 703
Moving Data between Windows Applications 704
Summary 705

Chapter 25: Advanced Select Queries 707

In This Chapter 707
Creating Queries That CalculateTotals 708
  Displaying the Total: row in the QBE pane 708
  Removing the Total: row from the QBE pane 710
  The Total: row options 710
    Group By category 711
    Expression category 711
    Total Field Record Limit category 712
    Aggregate category 712
  Performing totals on all records 712
    Performing totals on groups of records 715
    Calculating totals for a single group 715
    Calculating totals for several groups 716
  Specifying criteria for a total query 718
    Specifying criteria for a Group By field 719
    Specifying criteria for an Aggregate Total field 719
    Specifying criteria for a Non-Aggregate Total field 720
  Creating expressions for totals 721

Creating Crosstab Queries 722
    Understanding the crosstab query 722
    Creating the crosstab query 724
    Entering multiple-field row headings 726
    Specifying criteria for a crosstab query 727
        Specifying criteria in a new field 728
        Specifying criteria in a Row Heading field 728
        Specifying criteria in a Column Heading field 729
        Specifying criteria in multiple fields of a crosstab query 730
    Specifying fixed column headings 731
Crosstab Query Wizard 733
Creating a Parameter Query 734
    Understanding the parameter query 734
    Creating a single-parameter query 734
    Running a parameter query 736
    Creating a multiple-parameter query 736
    Viewing the parameter dialog box 738
Summary 740

Chapter 26: Creating Action Queries 741

In This Chapter 741
What Is an Action Query? 741
Uses of Action Queries 742
The Process of Action Queries 743
Viewing the Results of an Action Query 744
    Viewing the query before using update and delete queries 744
    Switching to the result table of a make-table or append query 744
    Reversing action queries 745
Creating an Action Query 745
Creating an Update Action Query to Change Values 746
    Creating a select query before an update action 746
    Converting a select query to an update query 748
    Checking your results 748
Creating a New Table Using a Make-Table Query 750
    Creating the select query 750
    Checking your results 753
Creating a Query to Append Records 754
    Creating the select query for an append query 756

Converting to an append query 758
Checking your results 760
Creating a Query to Delete Records 760
Creating a Cascading Delete query 762
Checking your results 763
Creating Other Queries Using the Query Wizards 763
Find Duplicate Records Wizard 764
Find Unmatched Records Wizard 764
Archive Records Wizard 764
Saving an Action Query 765
Running an Action Query 765
Troubleshooting Action Queries 765
Data-type errors in appending and updating 766
Key violations in action queries 766
Record-locked fields in multiuser environments 766
Text fields 766
Summary 767

Chapter 27: Advanced Query Topics 769

In This Chapter 769
Using Lookup Tables and Joins 769
Using Calculated Fields 776
Finding the Number of Records in a Table or Query 780
Finding the Top (n) Records in a Query 782
SQL Specific Queries 784
Creating union queries 784
Creating pass-through queries 784
Creating data definition queries 785
How Queries Save Field Selections 786
Hiding (not showing) fields 786
Renaming Fields in Queries 787
Hiding and Unhiding Columns in the QBE Pane 788
Query Design Options 790
Setting Query Properties 791
Viewing SQL Statements in Queries 793
Summary 795

Chapter 28: Creating and Using Subforms 797

In This Chapter 797
What Is a Subform? 797
Creating Subforms with the Form Wizard 799
    Creating the form and selecting the Form Wizard 799
    Selecting the subform table or query 800
    Choosing the fields for the main form 801
    Choosing the fields for the subform 802
    Selecting the visual effect 803
    Selecting the form title 803
    Saving and naming the subform 803
    Displaying the form 805
    Displaying the main form design 806
    Displaying the subform design 807
Creating a Simple Subform without Wizards 808
    Creating a form for a subform 809
    Adding the subform to the main form 813
    Linking the form and subform 815
    Adding lookup tables to the subform fields 816
    Creating totals in subforms 824
Summary 827

Chapter 29: Creating Mailing Labels and Mail Merge Reports 829

In This Chapter 829
Creating Mailing Labels 829
    Creating the new report 830
    Choosing the Report Wizard 830
    Creating the mailing label text and fields 831
    Selecting the label size 832
    Selecting the font and color 833
    Displaying the labels in the Print Preview window 835
    Modifying the label design in the Report Design window 836
    Printing labels 839
Creating Snaked Column Reports 840
    Creating the report 841
    Defining the print setup 842
    Printing the snaked column report 844

Creating Mail Merge Reports 845
    Assembling data for a mail merge report 846
    Creating a mail merge report 847
    Creating the page header area 848
    Working with embedded fields in text 850
    Printing the mail merge report 852
Using the Access Mail Merge Wizard for Word for Windows 6.0 853
Summary 857

Part V: Applications in Access 859

Chapter 30: An Introduction to Macros and Events ... 861

In This Chapter 861
Understanding Macros 862
    What is a macro? 862
    When to use a macro 862
The Macro Window 863
    The Action pane 865
    The Argument pane 865
    The Macro window menu bar 866
    The macro design toolbar 867
    Creating a macro 867
    Entering actions and arguments 867
        Selecting actions from the pull-down list 867
        Specifying arguments for actions 868
        Selecting actions by dragging and dropping objects 868
    Adding multiple actions to a macro 870
    Rearranging macro actions 871
    Deleting macro actions 872
    Saving macros 872
    Editing existing macros 872
    Copying macros 873
    Renaming macros 873
Running Macros 874
    Running a macro from the Macro window 874
    Running a macro from the Database window 874
    Running a macro from any window in the database 874
    Running a macro from another macro 875

Using the AutoExec macro 875
Macro Groups 876
    Creating macro groups 876
    Running a macro in a macro group 877
Supplying Conditions for Actions 878
    What is a condition? 878
    Activating the Condition column in a macro 878
    Specifying a condition for a single action 880
    Specifying a condition for multiple actions 881
    Controlling the flow of actions 882
Troubleshooting Macros 882
    The single-step mode 882
    The Action Failed dialog box 883
Understanding Events 884
    What is an event? 884
    How do events trigger actions? 885
    Where to trigger macros 886
Summary 887

Chapter 31: Using Macros in Forms and Reports 889

In This Chapter 889
Types of Macros 889
    Macros for forms 891
    Macros for reports 893
    Macros for hotkeys 893
    Macros for importing and exporting 893
Form-Level Event Macros 894
    Attaching macros to forms 894
    Opening a form with a macro 896
    Attaching a macro to a form 897
    Synchronizing two forms with On Current 898
    Running a macro when closing a form 901
    Confirming a delete with On Delete 904
Control Event Macros 907
    Attaching macros to controls 907
    Clicking on a command button to open a form 911
        Creating a macro to open another form 912
        Relating information from two forms using a macro 913
        Activating a related form using a command button 914

Double-clicking on a field control or its label	915
Double-clicking on a command button	916
Working with Macros on Forms	916
Validating data	916
Displaying a message	916
Canceling events	917
Stopping a macro	917
Going to a specific control	917
Setting values	917
Converting a field to uppercase	918
Assigning values to new records	918
Navigating in forms and records	920
Moving to a specific control	920
Moving to a specific record	920
Moving to a specific page	920
Filtering records	920
Using the ApplyFilter action	921
Using the ShowAllRecords action	922
Running filter macros	922
Finding Records	923
Report Event Macros	925
Opening a report with a macro	926
Report Section Macros	926
Using On Format	927
Using On Print	927
Report Properties	927
Using Format Count	928
Using Print Count	928
Working with macros in reports	929
Underlining data in a report with a macro	929
Hiding data in a report with a macro	932
Filtering records for a report with a macro	932
Importing and Exporting Macros	932
Using command buttons to import or export	932
Creating Hotkeys	933
Changing the default key assignment macro	933
Creating a hotkey combination	934
Using SendKeys syntax for key assignments	934
Creating a hotkey	934
Summary	936

Chapter 32: Creating Switchboards, Menus, and Dialogs 937

In This Chapter 937
What Is a Switchboard? 937
    Using a switchboard 938
    Creating the basic form for a switchboard 939
    Working with command buttons 939
    Creating command buttons 942
        Linking a command button to a macro 947
    The macros for the Mountain Switchboard 948
    Dragging a macro to the form to create a button 950
    Adding a picture to a command button 951
Creating Customized Bar Menus 954
    Defining the drop-down menus 954
        Defining a single-bar drop-down menu 955
        Defining a multiple-bar drop-down menu 956
        Adding options to a drop-down menu 957
    Defining a menu bar 960
    Attaching the menu bar to a form 961
    The Access 2.0 Menu Builder 963
    Running a macro automatically on starting Access 965
Creating a Print Report Dialog Box Form and Macros 966
    Creating a form for a macro 967
    Creating the option group 968
        Creating a list box on the print report form 970
    Creating the print macros 972
    Creating the Print Macro Library 974
        Creating the Show List macro 976
        Entering the Show List macro calls 977
        Creating the Print Preview macro 978
        Creating the Print macro 982
        Creating the Close macro 982
        Entering the Print Preview, Print, and Close macro calls 982
        Sizing the dialog and changing form properties 983
Summary 984

Chapter 33: Next Steps — Modules and Access Basic ... 987

In This Chapter 987
Access Basic Programming 987
Why Use Modules? 988
Modules and Procedures 988
    Sub procedures 989
    Function procedures 989
Creating a Procedure 989
    The declaration section 990
    Creating a new function 991
    Saving a procedure 993
    Compiling the procedures 993
    Saving a module 993
Editing an Existing Procedure 994
    Editing two procedures simultaneously 995
    The immediate window 995
Using a Function Procedure 997
Where Do You Go from Here? 999
Summary 1000

Appendix A: Microsoft Access Specifications 1001

Appendix B: Mountain Animal Hospital Tables 1005

Index 1011

Disclaimer and Copyright Notice 1042

Installation Instructions for the
PC World Microsoft Access 2 Bible, 2nd Edition
Companion Disk 1043

Reader Response Card .... back of book

Introduction

Welcome to the *PC World Microsoft Access 2.0 for Windows Bible* — your personal guide to a powerful, easy-to-use database management system.

This book examines Microsoft Access 2.0. We think that Microsoft Access is an excellent database manager and the best Windows database on the market today. Our goal with this book is to share what we know about Access and, in the process, to help make your work and your life easier.

This book contains everything you need in order to learn Microsoft Access to a fairly advanced level. You'll find that the book starts off with the basics and builds chapter by chapter on topics previously covered. In places where it is essential that you understand previously covered topics, we present the concepts again and review how to perform specific tasks before moving on. Although each chapter is an integral part of the book as a whole, each chapter can also stand on its own. You can read the book in any order you want, skipping from chapter to chapter and from topic to topic. (Note that this book's index is particularly thorough, so you can refer to the index to find the location of a particular topic you're interested in.)

The examples in this book have been well thought out to simulate the types of tables, queries, forms, and reports most people need to create when performing common business activities. There are many notes, tips, and techniques (and even a few secrets) to help you better understand the product.

Although designed to supplement the Microsoft Access documentation, this book can easily substitute for the manuals included with Access. We even created appendixes to be used as reference manuals for common Access functions and macro commands. This book follows a much more structured approach than the Microsoft Access manuals — going into more depth on almost every topic and showing many different types of examples.

Is This Book for You?

We wrote this book for beginning, intermediate, and advanced users of Microsoft Access. With any new product, most users start at the beginning. If, however, you've already read through the Microsoft Access manuals and worked with the North Winds sample files, you may want to start with the later parts of this book. Note, though, that starting at the beginning of a book is usually a good idea so that you don't miss out on the secrets and tips in the early chapters.

We think that this book covers Microsoft Access in detail better than any other book currently on the market. We hope that you will find this book helpful while working with Access and enjoy the innovative style of an IDG book.

Yes — If you have no database experience

If you're new to the world of database management, this book has everything you need to get started with Microsoft Access. It then offers advanced topics for reference and learning.

Yes — If you've used other database managers like dBASE or Paradox

If you're abandoning a character-based database, such as dBASE III PLUS, dBASE IV, Paradox, R:Base, Q&A, Powerbase, Dataease, or Alpha Four, in favor of a more modern graphical product, this book is for you. You'll have a head start because you're already familiar with database managers and how to use them. With Microsoft Access, you will be able to do all the tasks you've always performed with character-based databases — *without* programming or getting lost. This book will take you through each subject step by step.

☐ ## No — If you want to learn Access Basic programming

We had to stop somewhere. The Access Basic language is loosely based on Microsoft's Visual Basic. Many other books are written about just Visual Basic and the Access Basic language. We know that an entire book is needed to properly cover the Access Basic language. Because the macro commands in Access are so powerful, we think that most tasks can be accomplished without programming anyway.

Conventions Used in This Book

The following conventions are used in this book:

▧ When you are instructed to press a *key combination* (press and hold down one key while pressing another key), the key combination is separated by a plus sign. Ctrl+Esc, for example, indicates that you must hold down the Ctrl key and press the Esc key; then release both keys.

Introduction

- *Point the mouse* refers to moving the mouse so that the mouse pointer is on a specific item. *Click* refers to pressing the left mouse button once and releasing it. *Double-click* refers to pressing the left mouse button twice in rapid succession and then releasing it. Right-click refers to pressing the right mouse button once and releasing it. *Drag* refers to pressing and holding down the left mouse button while moving the mouse.

- When you are instructed to select a menu, you can use the keyboard or the mouse. To use the keyboard, press and hold down the Alt key (to activate the menu bar) and then press the underlined letter of the menu name; press Alt+E to select the Edit menu, for example. Or you can use the mouse to click on the word Edit on-screen. Then, from the menu that drops down, you can press the underlined letter of the command you want or click on the command name to select it.

- When you are instructed to select a command from a menu, you will often see the menu and command separated by an arrow symbol. Edit⇨Paste, for example, indicates that you need to select the Edit menu and then choose the Paste command from the menu.

- *Italic* type is used for new terms and for emphasis.

- **Bold** type is used for material you need to type directly into the computer.

- A special typeface is used for information you see on-screen — error messages, expressions, and formulas, for example.

Icons and Alerts

You'll notice special graphic symbols, or *icons,* used in the margins throughout this book. These icons are intended to alert you to points that are particularly important or noteworthy. The following icons are used in this book:

This icon highlights a special point of interest about the topic under discussion.

This icon points to a useful hint that may save you time or trouble.

This icon alerts you that the operation being described can cause problems if you're not careful.

 This icon alerts you to a new feature found in Access 2.0.

 This icon points to a more complete discussion in another chapter of the book.

 This icon points to information that gives you some special insight about the topic under discussion.

Following Along in This Book

This icon highlights information for readers who are following the examples and using the sample files included on the disk accompanying this book.

Sidebars

In addition to noticing the icons used throughout this book, you will also notice material placed in grey boxes. This material offers background information, an expanded discussion, or a deeper insight about the topic under discussion. Some *sidebars* offer nuts-and-bolts technical explanations, and others provide useful anecdotal material.

How This Book Is Organized

This book contains 33 chapters, which are divided into five main parts. In addition, the book contains two appendixes.

Part I: First Things First

Part I consists of the first six chapters of the book. In Chapter 1, you receive background information on Microsoft Access and an overview of its features. Chapter 2 covers installation — what you need in terms of hardware and software and how to get Access running properly. In Chapter 3, you learn how to start and stop Access, plus several techniques for moving between Access and other applications. Chapter 4 provides a review of database concepts for new users of a database product. Chapter 5 is a hands-on test drive of Access, provided to give you a quick look at some of its features. And Chapter 6 is a case study of the up-front design that is necessary for properly implementing a database system; otherwise, you must go through many false starts and redesigns when creating an application. You will design on paper the tables, forms, queries, reports, and menus necessary for creating the application.

Part II: Basic Database Usage

The next six chapters make up Part II. You learn how to create a database table in Chapter 7, and you also examine how to change a database table, including moving and renaming fields without losing data. In Chapter 8, you learn how to enter, display, change, and delete data. Chapter 9 teaches the basics of creating data-entry forms, using Wizards to simplify the creation process; using data-entry forms is also discussed. In Chapter 10, you examine the concept of queries; then you create several queries to examine how data can be rearranged and displayed. Chapter 11 covers the basics of report creation and printing. And in Chapter 12, you create the many tables used in the case study and then learn how to relate multiple tables.

Part III: Using Access in Your Work

Part III contains eleven chapters that go into more depth on creating and using forms, queries, and reports. In Chapter 13, you take a look at how to create the expressions and built-in functions that are so important in forms and reports. In Chapter 14, you learn how to create relations and joins in queries. Chapter 15 discusses basic selection queries, using many examples and pictures. In Chapter 16, you examine the concepts of controls and properties and learn how to manipulate controls in a form. Chapter 17 examines in detail how to create and use data-entry forms. Chapter 18 covers how to use visual effects to create great looking forms and reports that catch the eye and increase productivity. In Chapter 19, you learn how to add complex data validation to tables and data-entry forms. In Chapter 20, the use of pictures, graphs, sound, video, and other OLE objects is explained. And Chapters 21–23 cover reports — from simple controls to complex calculations, summaries, printing, and desktop publishing.

Part IV: Advanced Database Features

This part contains six chapters that present advanced topics on each of the basic tasks of Access. Chapter 24 examines how to import, export, and attach external files, along with copying Access objects to other Access databases. Chapter 25 discusses advanced select query topics, including total, cross-tabulation, top value, and union queries.

Chapter 26 covers action queries, which change data rather than simply display records. Chapter 27 is a compendium of advanced query topics that will leave you amazed at the power of Access. Creating forms and subforms from multiple tables is the subject of Chapter 28; this chapter examines how to create the one-to-many relationship found in many database systems. And this part ends with Chapter 29, which offers a look at additional types of reports not previously covered, including mail merge reports and mailing labels.

Part V: Applications in Access

This part looks at Access as an application environment. Chapter 30 covers the concept of event driven software and how Access uses macros to automate manual processes. This chapter also examines what a macro is, how macros are created, and how to debug macros. Data manipulation, including posting totals and filling in data-entry fields, is explained in Chapter 31. In Chapter 32, you learn how to create button menus known as switchboards, traditional pull-down menus, and dialog boxes. The final chapter, Chapter 33, is an introduction to modules using Access Basic.

The appendixes and reference material

Two appendixes are included in this book. Appendix A presents a series of tables listing Access specifications, including maximum and minimum sizes of many of the controls in Access. Appendix B displays a database diagram of the many database tables used in this book so that you can create your own system.

Part I

First Things First

- 9 **Chapter 1:** What is Access?
- 21 **Chapter 2:** Installing Access
- 31 **Chapter 3:** Getting Started with Access
- 43 **Chapter 4:** A Review of Database Concepts
- 55 **Chapter 5:** A Hands-On Tour of Access
- 75 **Chapter 6:** A Case Study in Database Design

What Is Access?

CHAPTER 1

In This Chapter

- Examining what Access is
- Looking at some of the capabilities of Access
- Understanding how to work with Access if you're already a database user
- Understanding how to work with Access if you're already a spreadsheet user

Before you begin to use a software product, it is important to understand its capabilities and the types of tasks the software is designed to perform. Access is a multifaceted product whose use is bounded only by your imagination.

Access Is . . .

Essentially, Access is a database management system (DBMS). Like other products in this category, Access stores and retrieves data, presents information, and automates repetitive tasks, such as maintaining accounts payable, inventory control, and scheduling. By using Access, you can develop easy-to-use input forms like the one shown in Figure 1-1. You can process your data and run powerful reports.

Access also is a powerful Windows application. This means that, for the first time, the productivity of database management meets the usability of Microsoft Windows. Because both Windows and Access are from Microsoft, the two products work very well together. Access runs on the Windows platform, so all the advantages of Windows are available in Access. You can cut, copy, and paste data from any Windows application to and from Access. You can create a form design in Access and paste it into the report designer. You can link to OLE objects in Excel, Paintbrush, and Word for Windows to turn Access into a true database operating environment.

10   Part I: First Things First

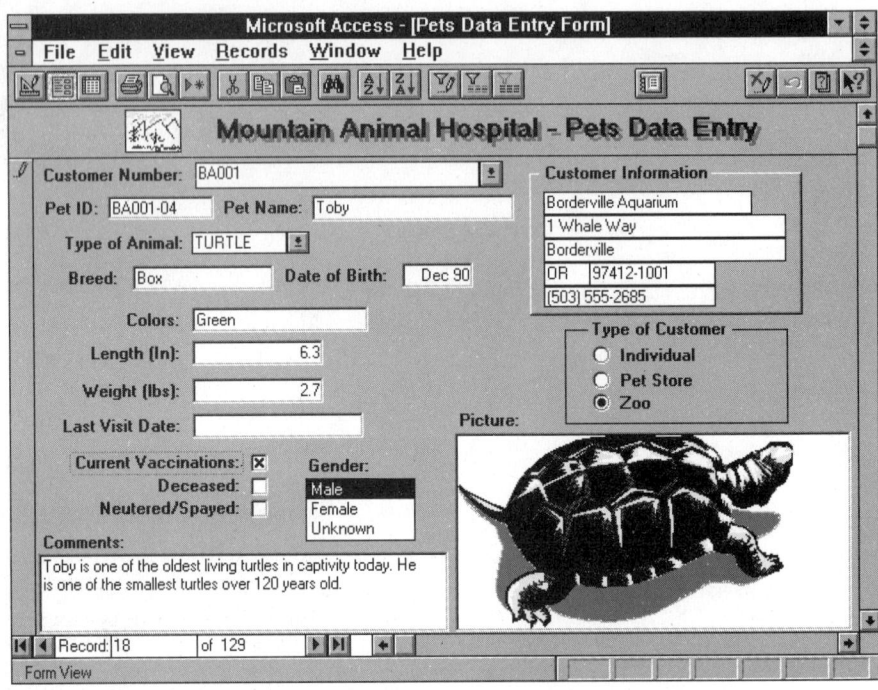

Figure 1-1: A typical Access data-entry form.

However, Access is more than just a database manager. It is a relational database manager that gives you access to all types of data. It lets you use more than one database table at a time to reduce the complexity of your data and make it easier to get your job done. You can link an Access table with a Paradox table and a dBASE table. You can take the results of the link and combine the data with an Excel worksheet quickly and easily.

Microsoft's original marketing for Access is shown in Figure 1-2. This simple figure conveys the message that Access is usable at all levels. Beginning at the lowest level of the hierarchy and moving upward, you see tools listed first. Tools provide the end user with the ability to easily create forms and reports. You can perform simple processing by using expressions to validate data or display a number with a currency symbol. Macros allow for automation without programming, whereas *Access Basic Code* lets the user program complex processes. Finally, a C programmer can write interfaces to other programs and data sources.

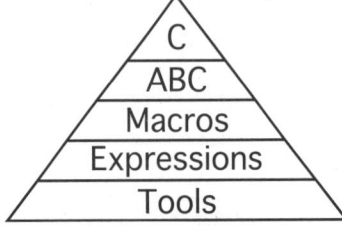

Figure 1-2: The Access usability hierarchy.

The Windows DBMS that defines a new level of usability and access to data

Chapter 1: What Is Access?

Access is a set of tools for end-user database management. Access has a table creator, a form designer, a query manager, and a report writer. Access is also an application development environment. By using macros to automate tasks, you can create user-oriented applications as powerful as those created with programming languages, complete with the buttons, menus, and dialog boxes that you see in Figure 1-3. By programming in Access Basic or C, you can actually create programs as powerful as Access itself. In fact, many of the tools in Access, such as the Wizards, are written in Access Basic.

But simply telling you about what Access can do doesn't begin to cover the material within this book. Access is, by far, the best database management software on the market today. What allows us to say this is the combination of power and usability in Access. In the first 500 pages, you learn how to use Access from an end-user point of view. In the last 500 pages, you will learn Access from the power-user's view. And you examine many topics in a depth that your reference manuals can only begin to touch.

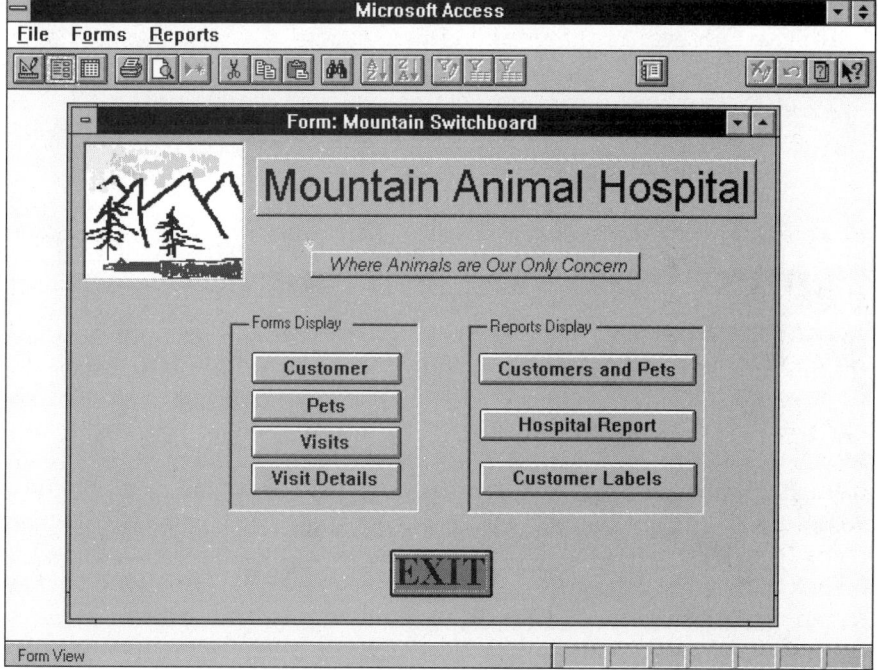

Figure 1-3: A macro switchboard and custom menu.

What Access Offers

The following paragraphs briefly describe some of the key features in Access and will help prepare you for some of the subjects that are covered in this book.

True relational database management

Access provides true relational database management, complete with primary and foreign key definitions, a model for referential integrity, table-level data-validation rules, and both format and default definitions for each field in a table. By implementing full referential integrity at the database engine level, Access prevents inconsistent updates or deletes.

Access supports all the necessary field types, including Text, Number, Currency, Date/Time, Memo, Yes/No, and OLE objects. It also features full null-value support for special processing when values are missing.

The relational processing in Access fills many needs with its flexible architecture. It can be used as a stand-alone database management system, in a file-server configuration, or as a front-end client to products such as SQL server. Through ODBC (Open Database Connectivity), you'll be able to connect to many more external formats, such as Oracle, RdB, Sybase, or even mainframe IBM DB/2.

A complete programmatic support of transaction processing ensures transaction integrity, along with user-level security to assign user and group permissions to view and modify various database objects.

Context-sensitive Help and Cue Cards

For both beginners and experienced users, Microsoft's Help continues to be the best in the industry. In Access, there is context-sensitive Help, so you can press the F1 key whenever you're stuck. Help about the item you are on is instantly displayed. Access also has an easy-to-use table of contents, a search facility, a history log, and bookmarks.

In Access, Microsoft goes one step further and introduces Cue Cards. As you can see in Figure 1-4, Cue Cards provide step-by-step help on-screen alongside the database task you are working on — no more canned tutorials displaying someone else's business.

Ease-of-use Wizards

A wizard lets you turn hours of work into minutes. Wizards ask you questions about content, style, and format and then automatically build the object for you. Access features wizards to design several varieties of forms, reports, graphs, mailing labels, controls, and properties. Figure 1-5 shows a Form Wizard screen. In Access 2.0, you can even customize wizards for use in a variety of tasks.

Chapter 1: What Is Access? **13**

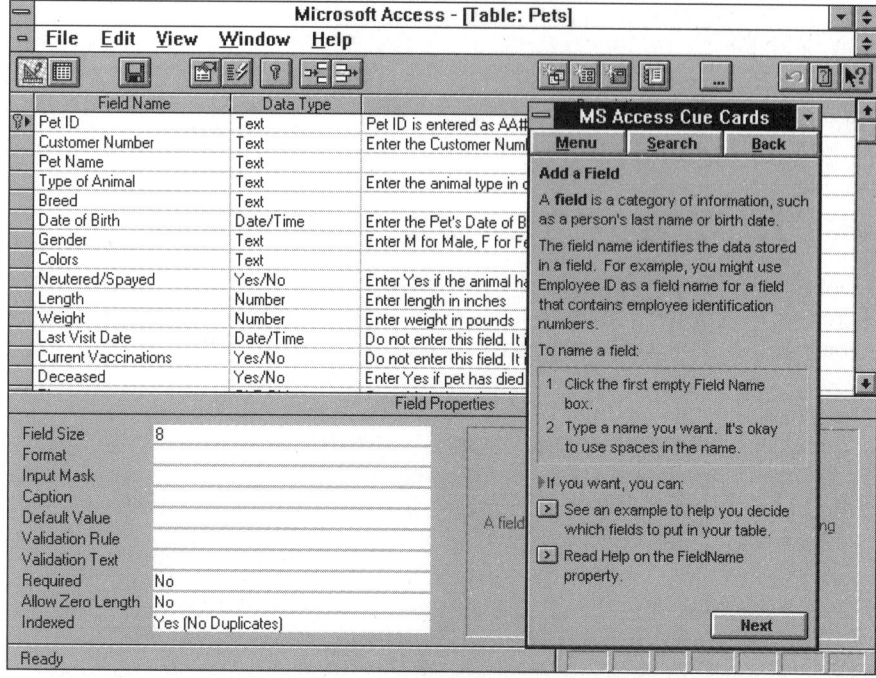

Figure 1-4:
A sample Cue Card session.

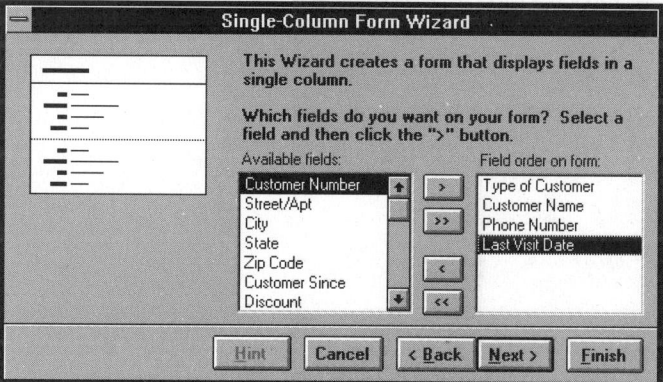

Figure 1-5:
Using a Form Wizard.

Importing, exporting, and attaching external files

Access lets you import from or export to many common formats, including dBASE, Paradox, FoxPro, Lotus 1-2-3, Excel, SQL server Oracle, Btrieve, and many ASCII formats. Whereas importing creates an Access table, exporting an Access table creates a file in the native file format that you are exporting to.

Attaching means that you can simply use external data without creating an Access table. You can attach to dBASE, Paradox 3.5, and SQL data. Attaching to external tables and then relating them to other tables that can include Access, dBASE, Paradox, and SQL server is a very powerful feature.

WYSIWYG forms and reports

The Form and Report Design windows share a common interface and power. Your form or report is designed in a WYSIWYG environment. As you add each control, you see the form take shape as you build your design.

You can add labels, text data fields, option buttons, checkboxes, lines, boxes, colors, shading, and even pictures, graphs, and subforms/subreports to your forms and reports. In addition, you have complete control over the style and presentation of data in a form or report, as shown in Figure 1-6. Forms can have multiple pages, and reports can have many levels of groupings and totals.

You can see your form or report in a page preview mode to let you zoom out and get a bird's-eye view of your form or report. You can also view your report with sample data so that you don't waste valuable time waiting for a large data file to be processed when you're in the design mode.

Most important, the report writer is very powerful. It allows up to ten levels of aggregation and sorting. The report writer performs two passes on the data to let you create reports showing the row percentage of a group total. You can create many types of reports that include mailing labels and mail merge reports.

Multiple-table queries

One of the most powerful features in Access is also the most important. As you can see in Figure 1-7, the Graphical Query by Example (GQBE) window lets you graphically link your tables together. You can even link tables of different file types, such as an Access table and a dBASE table. When linked, your tables act as a single entity that lets you ask questions about your data. You can select specific fields, define sorting orders, create calculated expressions, and enter criteria to select desired records. You can display the results of a query in a datasheet, form, or report.

Additionally, the query can take many forms. You can create queries that calculate totals and display cross tabulations and then make new tables from the results. You can even use a query to update data in tables, delete records, or append one table to another.

Chapter 1: What Is Access?

Figure 1-6:
A database-published report.

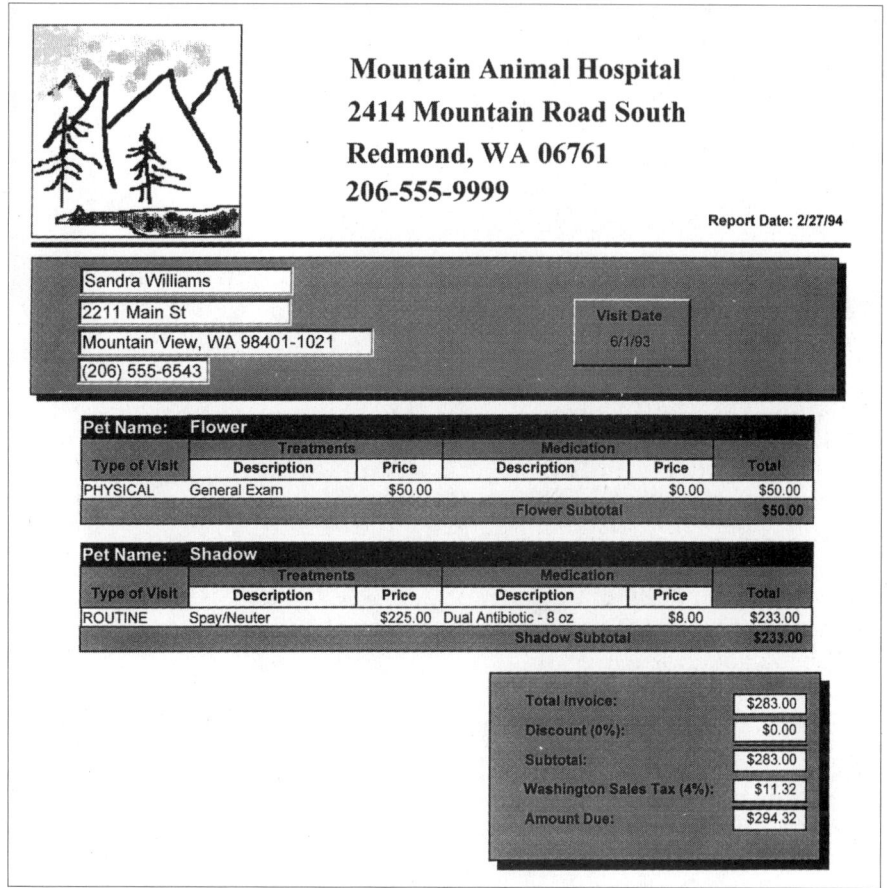

Business graphs and charts

The same graph application found in Microsoft Word, Excel, Powerpoint, and Project is also built into Access. You can create hundreds of types of business graphs and customize the display to your every need. You can create bar charts, column charts, line charts, pie charts, area charts, and high-low-close charts in both two and three dimensions. You can add free-form text, change the gridlines, adjust the color and pattern in a bar, display data values on a bar or pie slice, and even rotate the viewing angle of a chart from within the Access Graph applet.

In addition, you can link your graph with a form to get a powerful graphic data display that changes from record to record in the table. This feature is demonstrated in Figure 1-8.

16 Part I: First Things First

Figure 1-7: A graphical QBE window.

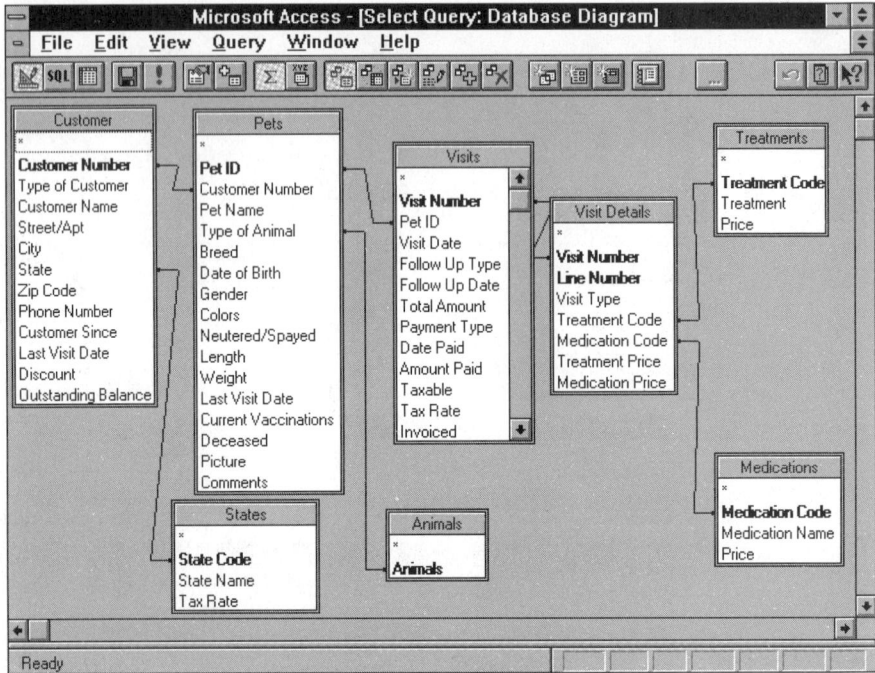

Figure 1-8: A typical form linked to a graph.

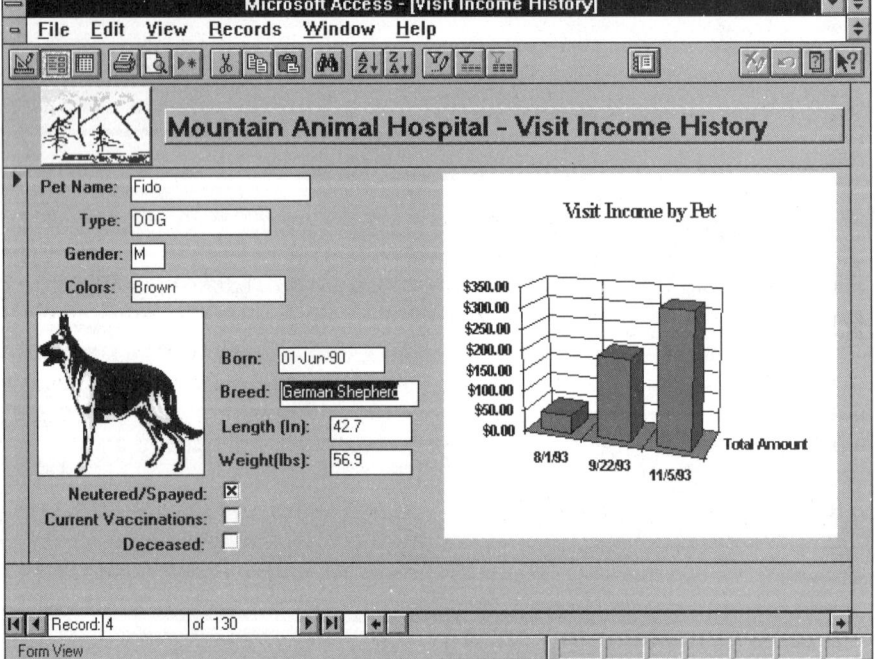

DDE and OLE capabilities

Through the capabilities of DDE (Dynamic Data Exchange) and OLE (Object Linking and Embedding), two of the most important features in Windows 3.1, you can add exciting new objects to your Access forms and reports. Such objects may be sound, pictures, graphs, and even video clips. You can embed OLE objects, such as a bitmap picture, or documents created from word processors, such as Word or WordPerfect, or link to a range of cells in an Excel or 1-2-3 spreadsheet. By linking these objects to records in your tables, you can create dynamic database forms and reports and share information between Windows applications.

Built-in functions

Access contains over one hundred functions in a wide variety of categories that include database, mathematics, business, financial, date, time, and string functions. You can use these functions to create calculated expressions in forms, reports, and queries.

Macros — programming without programming

For nonprogrammers or power users who simply don't want to program, there are macros. Macros let you perform common tasks without user intervention. Nearly 60 macro actions let you manipulate data, create menus and dialog boxes, open forms and reports, and basically automate any task you can imagine. Macros can probably solve 90 percent of your processing problems.

Modules — Access Basic for database programming

Access is a serious development environment with a full-featured programming language. Access Basic features an event-driven programming model. Access Basic Code is a powerful, extensible, structured programming language.

A full-featured IDE (Integrated Development Environment) allows multiple windows for code editing and debugging, automatic syntax checking, breakpoints, and single-step execution.

Access Basic is also fully extensible, featuring call routines in any dynamic link library for the Windows operating system.

Information for Database Users

If you're already a database user, chances are that you're ready to jump right in and start using Access. A word of warning: *This is not your father's Oldsmobile.* You may be an expert in relational database management software such as dBASE, FoxPro, or Paradox, but you probably never used a database under Windows.

You should try to become familiar with Windows software before you jump right in to a database package. Play with Windows Paintbrush or experiment with Word for Windows or Excel. Learn how to use the mouse to click, double-click, select, drag, and drop. Create a graph in Excel, use a Wizard, and try the Help system. All these tasks will make your learning experience much faster when you use Access.

You also need to get used to some new terminology. Table 1-1 lists the Access terminology and its dBASE and Paradox equivalents.

Table 1-1
Access, dBASE, and Paradox Terminology

Microsoft Access	Borland dBASE	Borland Paradox
Database	Catalog	Directory of related files
Table	Database file	Table
Datasheet	BROWSE command	View command
Table Design	MODIFY STRUCTURE	Modify Restructure
Text data type	Character data type	Alphanumeric data type
Primary key	Unique Index	Key field
Index	Index	Tools QuerySpeed
Validation rule	PICTURE/VALID Clause	ValChecks
Query	Query, QBE, View	Query
Form	Screen	Forms
Subform	Multiple File Screen	Multiple-record selection
Open a form	SET FORMAT TO, EDIT	Image PickForm
Find command	LOCATE AND SEEK	Zoom
Data entry command	APPEND	Modify DataEntry
List box, combo box	Pick list	Lookup
Exclusive/shared access	SET EXCLUSIVE ON/OFF	Edit/Coedit mode
Module	Program file	Script

Information for Spreadsheet Users

If you are an Excel expert, you'll find that many things about Access are similar to Excel. First of all, both programs are Windows products, so you should already have experience using the Windows-specific conventions within Access. Access has a spreadsheet view of the data in a table or query, known as a *datasheet*. You'll find that you can resize the rows and columns in much the same way as within Excel worksheets.

Excel has a WYSIWYG drawing capability like Access. Excel shares the same graph applet that Access uses and can create the same types of graphs, as well as perform the same annotation to the graphs. Also, because Access uses graph wizards, perhaps you've also used these.

With Excel, you can query and sort the data. Access goes far beyond this simple capability. However, if you've used the Excel query and sorting menu options, you already are familiar with these concepts.

Summary

In this chapter, you learned about the capabilities of Access and got an idea of the types of tasks Access can accomplish. The following points were introduced:

- Access is a database management system (DBMS).
- You can use Access to store and retrieve data, present information, and automate repetitive tasks.
- Using Access, you can develop easy-to-use input forms, process your data, and run powerful reports.
- Access features Graphical Query By Example (6QBE) for selecting, sorting, and searching data.
- By using Access macros, you can create applications without programming.
- If you are a Paradox or dBASE user, you should make sure that you understand the differences in terminology between Access and the product you are familiar with.
- Spreadsheet and database users should already be familiar with many of the key concepts used in Access.

In the next chapter, you learn how to install Access.

Installing Access

CHAPTER 2

In This Chapter

- What hardware and software you need to run Access
- How to successfully install and run Access on your computer
- How to install the Access 2.0 upgrade
- How to convert Access 1.x databases
- How to handle problems that occur during installation

Access must be installed on your computer before you can use it. The installation is very simple. After you begin the process, you need only to supply the requested disks when prompted. As Access is installed, information about Access is displayed on-screen.

Access is installed in a manner similar to other Windows software products. If your company has a special person or area designated to install and troubleshoot software, you may want to have this person or department install Access for you. This way, your system will be standardized with the other systems in your company.

If you are installing an upgrade to Access 2.0, Access must already be installed on your machine. New installations of Access 2.0 do not require that Access already be on your machine.

Determining What You Need

Access requires specific hardware and software to run. Before you install Access, check to see that your computer meets the minimum requirements needed to run Access.

Hardware requirements

To use Access 2.0, you'll need an IBM or compatible personal computer with an 80386SX or higher processor with 6MB of RAM. To get the best performance from Access, we recommend an 80386DX33 computer with at least 8MB of RAM. With more memory, you'll be able to run more applications simultaneously, and overall performance will be increased. A fast video card is also recommended to display pictures and graphs.

You will also need 19MB of hard disk space for a typical installation. Keep in mind that you will need additional space to store your database files as you create them. If space is a problem, you can always perform a partial installation, or you can delete unwanted files from your hard disk to free up space needed for the installation.

Access requires you to have an EGA monitor as a minimum requirement. However, we recommend using a VGA or better type of display. This setup allows you to view more information on-screen and to get a sharper resolution.

A mouse or some other compatible pointing device is mandatory in order for you to use Access. These devices include track balls and pens.

If you're planning to print from Access, you need to have a printer. Any printer that is supported by Windows works.

Software requirements

Access requires that Microsoft Windows 3.1 be installed on your computer. Windows does *not* come with Access and must be purchased separately. If Windows is not currently installed on your computer, you need to install it before you can continue with the Access installation.

Also, keep in mind that you must be using DOS 3.1 or later in order to install Windows. Any type of DOS will work, including MS-DOS, PC DOS, and DR-DOS. You can also run Access in the Win/OS/2 box of OS/2 2.1.

Upgrading to Access 2.0 from Access 1.x

Before you upgrade to Access 2.0 from Access 1.x, you should think about a few things.

Access 1.x databases must be converted to Access 2.0 format before they are fully usable. And once a database is converted to Access 2.0 format, it cannot be converted back and is unusable by Access 1.0 or 1.1. As an Access 2.0 user, you can open and work with Access 1.x databases; however, you cannot modify any of the objects (forms, reports, queries, and so on).

If you are sharing files with people who use Access 1.1, think about leaving Access 1.1 on your machine and installing Access 2.0 in a separate directory. Then you can create personal files in Access 2.0 but still use Access 1.1 to work with files that are shared with others. You can export Access 2.0 tables to Access 1.1, but you cannot export any other Access objects.

Installing Access

You can now begin to install Access. Be sure that you are in the Windows Program Manager. Insert Disk 1 into drive A and then select Run from the File menu. Windows will display the Run dialog box. Type **A:\SETUP** in the Command Line box, as shown in Figure 2-1, and select OK to begin the installation. This procedure works for new installations and upgrades to Access 2.0.

Figure 2-1:
The Run dialog box.

Because some Windows programs interfere with the Setup program, Access warns you to shut down any applications currently running. You can simply press the OK button to continue setup, or you can press the Exit Setup button to cancel the installation and shut down your applications (you then can run Setup later).

The Setup program now requires some information from you. If you are installing Access for the first time, you are asked to customize your copy of the program by entering your name and, optionally, a company name.

Next, a screen appears with your product ID number. You should write this number down; you'll need it if you call Microsoft Support for help.

Next, Setup wants to know where you want to install Access. The default is C:\ACCESS. If this location is satisfactory, select OK to continue with the installation. If you want to change this directory, simply type in the new drive and directory name. For example, to have Access installed in a subdirectory located on drive D, you type **D:\ACCESS20**. If you type a directory that does not exist, one is created for you.

Setup then takes some time to check for available disk space or existing copies of Access files. When this verification step is completed, Setup asks you to choose what type of installation you want, as you see in Figure 2-2. You can choose from these three options:

1. Typical	This option installs all the Access files into the directory you specify.
2. Complete/custom	This option lets you choose which files you want added. You can install omitted options in the future by rerunning Setup.
3. Laptop (minimum)	This option installs the minimum amount of files needed to run Access. This option is designed for systems with limited hard disk space or for users who do not need all the options provided with Access.

If you choose custom installation, you see the screen that is displayed in Figure 2-3. Setup provides you with a list of options that you can install. At this point, all the options are selected to be installed. To deselect an option, click on the checkbox next to the option you do not want installed. The X in the checkbox will disappear, and the option will not be installed.

Next, indicate which Program Manager group you want to display the Access 2.0 icons. You can choose any existing group or create a new one.

Depending on whether you are upgrading or installing a new version, you may receive messages about converting objects such as graphs.

Setup next determines which disks and files to copy. Depending on the installation type you choose, you may not use all the disks provided.

If there is insufficient disk space to install all the files you select, Setup tells you how much more disk space you need to install all the files you want. You have the choice of trying to continue with the installation, backing up to the preceding screen to change your selections, or cancelling the installation.

Chapter 2: Installing Access

Figure 2-2: Choosing the installation method.

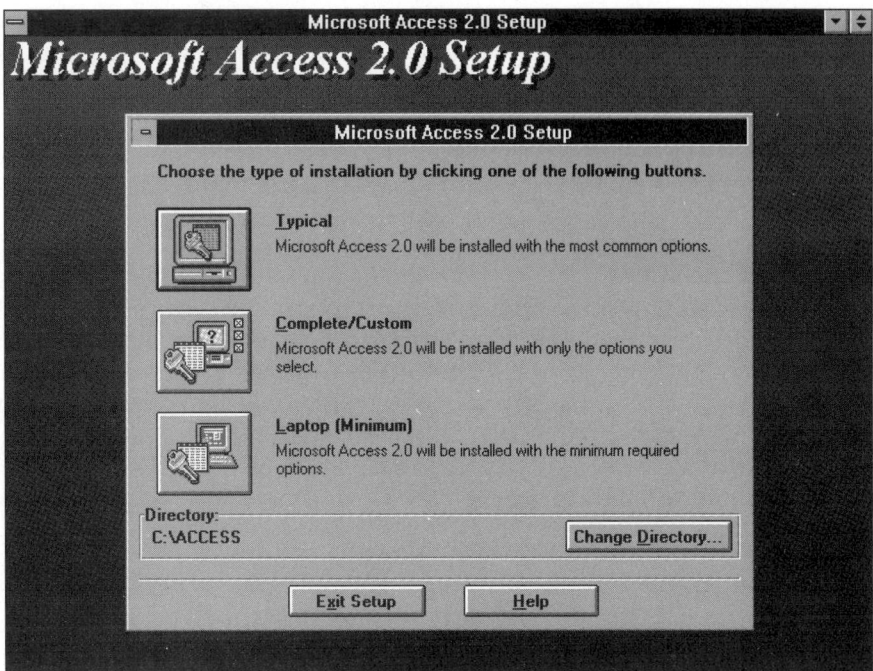

Figure 2-3: The Custom Installation dialog box.

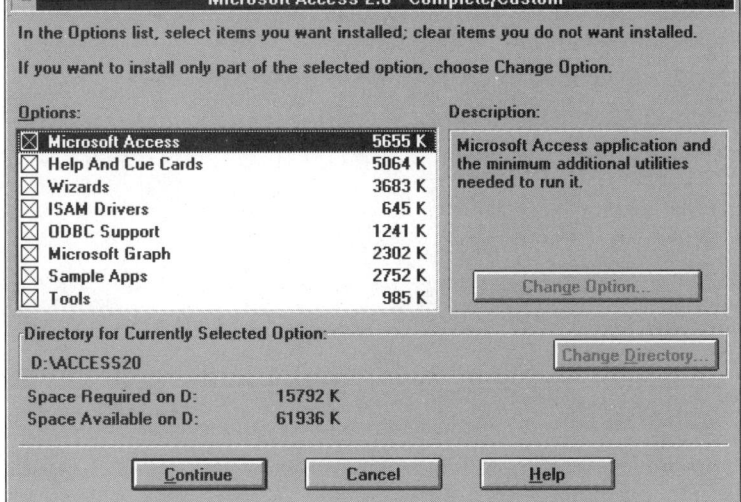

The installation now proceeds, and you are prompted to insert the required disks as needed. This process will take some time — approximately 30–35 minutes for a complete installation, and 10 minutes for an upgrade.

As the installation continues, a series of pictures appear on-screen. These pictures provide some basic information about the various features of Access and how you can use them.

You can test the installation to be sure Access will run. To do this, locate the Microsoft Access icon from the Microsoft Access group, as shown in Figure 2-4. Double-click on the icon and Access should start up. You see a Welcome screen that provides four tutorials you can run to help you get started in using Access. These tutorials are shown in Figure 2-5. The Welcome screen appears every time you start Access. If you don't want to see this screen when you start Access, click inside the checkbox for the option of never viewing the screen again. An X is placed in the box, and the Welcome screen will not reappear when you start Access.

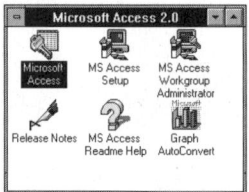

Figure 2-4: The Access icons.

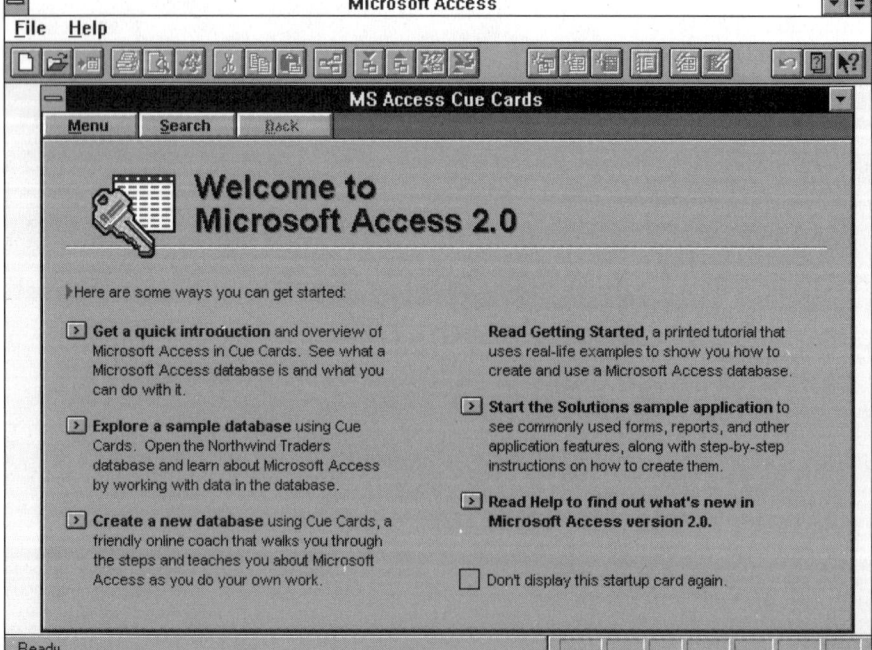

Figure 2-5: The Access Welcome screen.

Converting Access 1.x Files

Access 2.0 can read Access 1.0 or 1.1 database files. You can add, change, and delete data. You can run Access 1.x queries, forms, reports, macros, and even Access BASIC modules. However, you cannot change any objects: tables, queries, forms, reports, macros, and modules. To redesign an Access 1.x object, you must either use Access 1.x or convert the object to Access 2.0.

You convert Access 1.x databases by using File⇨Convert Database... in the Access database window, as shown in Figure 2-6.

No database can be open if you want to see the Convert Database option.

To convert a database, simply select File⇨Convert Database... from the Database window. A standard Windows file selector dialog box appears. You select the database to be converted and give it a new name. The database is converted.

If the database is already in Access 2.0 format, Access tells you so, and the database is not converted.

Figure 2-6: The Database File menu, showing the Convert Database option.

 If you try to convert the database and save it to the same path and name, you get an error message, and the conversion does not take place.

Before you convert a database, check for a few peculiar things that are not converted correctly by the conversion utility:

- If you use Microsoft Access security, you must own the database or be a member of the Admins group that was in effect when the database was created.

- After you convert a database to version 2.0, the attachments of its tables into version 1.x databases are no longer valid. To use the attached tables, you must convert the attaching database as well. You can, however, attach tables from a version 1.x database to a version 2.0 database.

- If an object in a database uses a backquote (') character in the object name, the object does not convert to Access 2.0 format. You should rename the object before converting. Remember that you must change any references in other objects, such as forms and reports, too.

- If you have a control name that includes a right bracket (]) in its name, the form works after conversion. However, you can't create a new control in Access 2.0 that contains a right bracket, and you cannot modify a control that contains a right bracket.

When Access encounters invalid rules when converting your database, the program creates a table in the converted database to supply you with the information needed to help you fix the errors. The table, named ConvertErrors, has five columns: Error, Field, Property, Table, and Unconverted Value.

Troubleshooting

If you run into problems while installing Access, Setup displays a message telling you what the problem may be. Some common problems include lack of disk space and problems reading the floppy disk.

If you receive a message saying that an error has occurred during Setup, you may have run out of disk space. You need to delete some files before proceeding with the installation. You can delete files from the Windows File Manager or from DOS. Remember to be careful not to delete important files. If you find that you have plenty of available disk space, something else has failed in the installation, and you should contact Microsoft Product Support for help.

If your floppy drive has problems reading the installation disks, there may be a problem with your floppy drive. You may want to contact someone to check the floppy drive for you. Then, if you still receive this message and cannot find the problem, call Microsoft Product Support for help in troubleshooting the problem.

Summary

In this chapter, you learned about the equipment you need to install Access, how to install Access, and how to convert Access 1.x databases. The following points were covered:

- You need to have Microsoft Windows 3.1 installed on your system before you can install Access.

- Your system must be capable of running Windows in standard mode or 386 enhanced mode in order to successfully run Access.

- At least 19MB of free hard disk space is needed to fully install Access 2.0.

- If available hard disk space is a problem, you can select minimum installation or custom installation to limit the options that are installed. You can then install omitted options at a later time by rerunning Setup.

- The Access 2.0 upgrade installs over the old Access 1.1 installation, if you want.

- You must convert Access 1.x databases to work with Access 2.0.

Now that you have successfully installed Access, it's time to learn a little bit about how to use this software. Chapter 3 provides information on how to get started using Access.

Getting Started with Access

CHAPTER 3

In This Chapter

- How you can use different ways to start Access
- How to work in other applications without exiting Access
- How to add options to the Access command line
- How to exit Access
- How to get Help
- How to use Cue Cards

After you successfully install Access, you are ready to learn the various ways to start the Access database program. If you haven't installed Access yet, read Chapter 2 before proceeding.

Starting Access

You can start Access in several ways:

- From the Access icon in a program group
- From the Windows Program Manager
- From the File Manager
- From the DOS prompt, if Windows is not already running

Starting from the Access icon

One of your program groups in the Program Manager is called Microsoft Access, as shown in Figure 3-1.

Figure 3-1:
The Microsoft Access program group.

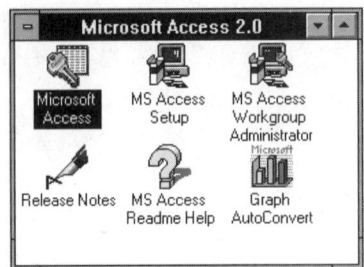

The Program Manager can be customized, so your screen may look different from the one shown here.

If you don't see the Access program group with several icons, the Access group may be minimized to a group icon. Find the group icon labeled Microsoft Access in the Program Manager and double-click it. This action opens up the Access program group, and the icons will now be visible. You can also find a program group by selecting the Window menu in the Windows Program Manager and selecting the Microsoft Access program group.

You can move the Access icon to other program groups. If you don't find the Access icon in the Microsoft Access program group, you may need to open up other program groups to locate the icon. A common place to put the Access program icon is in the Windows Applications group.

When you find the Access icon that looks like a key, you can start Access. The easiest way to start Access is by double-clicking the Access icon. This action automatically launches Access, and you can begin to use the program.

Starting from Program Manager

You can start Access by choosing File→Run... from the Windows Program Manager. A text box is displayed, where you can enter the program name. Enter the program name **MSACCESS** in the text box and press Enter. If you want to launch Access and open the MTNANHSP database file, enter **MSACCESS MTNANHSP** (see Figure 3-2) and press Enter.

Figure 3-2:
Starting Access from the Program Manager.

Chapter 3: Getting Started with Access   33

 You need to specify the correct path when you enter the name.

You probably won't use this method to start Access because it's easier to simply double-click the Access icon to launch Access. But you may want to start Access from the Program Manager if you can't find the Access icon or if you want to load a database file as you open Access.

Starting from File Manager

If you want to load a particular database into Access, you can also start Access from the Windows File Manager by selecting the database file. The Windows File Manager is shown in Figure 3-3 with the MTNANHSP.MDB file selected. This is the File Manager, as you see it in Windows 3.1. If you have Windows 3.0, your screen looks slightly different.

When you find the database file you want to load, you can double-click the filename. Windows then starts Access and opens the database you selected. If you are unsure of which file you should choose, check to see that it has a proper file extension. The file extension is the three-character designation that follows the period in the filename. A Microsoft Access database file has a file extension of MDB.

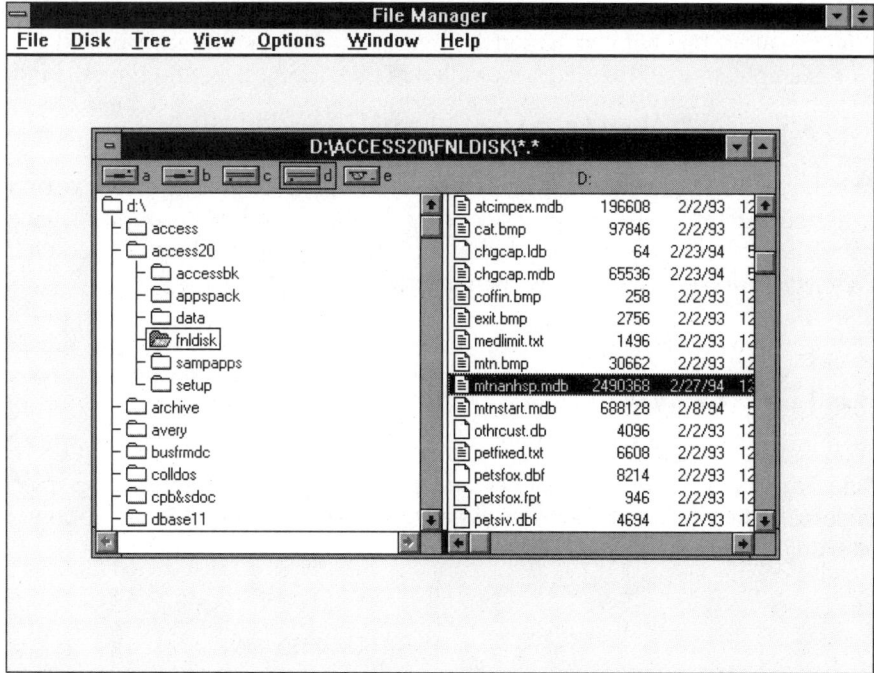

Figure 3-3: The Windows File Manager.

34 Part I: First Things First

If you already have Access running and you double-click a file in the File Manager, another copy of Access will start, which will load the file you selected. You may want to do this if you want more than one database open at a time. Access does not let you open more than one database at a time if you are running only one occurrence of Access.

Starting from DOS

You can start Windows and Access at the same time from the DOS prompt. First, check to make sure that Windows is not already running. To do so, type **EXIT** at the DOS prompt and then press Enter. If you are returned to Windows, then you were in a DOS shell under Windows and Windows was already running. If you get the message `Bad command or file name` when you type **EXIT,** you know that Windows is not running and that you can proceed with the following instructions.

To run Windows and launch Access, type the following at the DOS prompt:

> C:\>**WIN MSACCESS**

The preceding instruction assumes that Access is stored in the directory specified in the path name.

You can also start Windows, launch Access, and load a database all at the same time. For example, to load the database called MTNANHSP.MDB, you type the following:

> C:\>**WIN MSACCESS C:\ACCESS\MTNANHSP.MDB**

When you enter the database name, be sure to precede it with the drive and directory where the database is stored. If Access is the only Windows product you ever run, you may prefer to use this process. Using this method, you will bypass loading Program Manager and go right into loading Access.

Options for starting Access

You can customize how Access starts by adding options to the MSACCESS command line. For example, you can have Access automatically open a database, execute a macro, or supply a user name or password. Table 3-1 identifies the options available for starting Access.

Table 3-1
Access Command Line Options

Option	Function
<DATABASE.MDB>	Opens the specified database.
/Excl	Opens the specified database for exclusive access. To open the database for shared access in a multiuser environment, enter the command line without this option.
/RO	Opens the specified database for read-only access.
/User <user name>	Starts Microsoft Access, using the specified user name.
/Pwd <password>	Starts Microsoft Access, using the specified password.
/Ini <filename>	Starts Access using an alternate initialization file. Normally, MSACC20.INI in your Windows directory is used.
/Compact <filename>	Compacts the database specified.
/Convert <filename>	Converts an Access 1.1 database to version 2.0.
/Repair	Repairs the specified database.
/X <macro>	Starts Microsoft Access and runs the specified macro.
/Cmd	Specifies that what follows on the command line is the value that will be returned by the Access Basic Command function. This option must be the last option on the command line. You can use a semicolon (;) as an alternative to /Cmd.

For example, to have Access automatically execute a macro called MYMACRO, enter the following command in the Command Line box:

C:\ACCESS\MSACCESS.EXE /X MYMACRO

You can create a special macro named AutoExec that runs automatically when you first open a Microsoft Access database (you will learn more about this macro in Part V). You can use this macro to open certain tables or forms every time you enter a database or to perform complex processing, change the menus, hide the database container, or do just about anything you can think of.

 To prevent an AutoExec macro from running, hold down the Shift key as you open the database.

Exiting Access

When you are finished using Access or any application, you should always exit gracefully. Simply turning off your system is not a good method. Doing so can cause problems for you in the future. Windows and your applications use many files while they are running that you may not even be aware of. Turning off your system can cause these files not to be closed properly, which can result in hard disk problems in the near future.

Another reason for exiting gracefully is to ensure that all your data is saved before exiting the application. If you have spent quite a bit of time inputting data and then you turn off your system, accidentally forgetting to save this work, all this unsaved data will be lost! Save yourself time and grief by exiting your applications the correct way.

You can exit Access in several ways:

- Double-click the Control button in the Access title bar.
- From the Access menu, select File➪Exit.
- Press Alt+F4.
- Display the Task List and select Access. Then click on the End Task button. You can use this method to close Access from within another application.

When you exit Access with one of these methods, you may see a message displayed on-screen prompting you to save any changes that you may have made during that session. You can select Yes to save the changes and exit Access. Selecting No will exit Access without saving the changes you made. Cancel stops Access from closing, and you are returned to Access. You can also choose Help for more information on exiting Access.

Shortcut Menus

Access 2.0 introduces the now-popular concept of shortcut menus. By pressing the *right* mouse button while you are on any object, a menu appears that displays menu choices only for the specific object your cursor is on. Figure 3-4 shows a typical shortcut menu. This menu is shown next to the Database Container and contains only options that would pertain to the Database Container. Shortcut menus can be disabled on forms to prevent users from changing them.

Chapter 3: Getting Started with Access   **37**

Figure 3-4: Shortcut menus.

Getting Help

Now that you have learned how to start Access, you may need some help in learning how to use the software. When you start Access, the first thing you see is the cue card screen. This screen provides a few ways to help you get started using Access. You have five options to choose from:

Get a quick introduction	This option gives you an introduction to Access and explains various concepts, such as databases, forms, and tables, and how you can use them.

Explore a sample database	You can open a sample database called Northwind Traders and follow along with Cue Cards to learn how datasheets and forms work, how to view data, how to save and print forms, and how to accomplish various other tasks.

Create a new database	This option uses a concept called Cue Cards to walk you through the steps and teaches you how to use Access as you do your own work.

Start the Solutions sample application	This option shows you commonly used forms, reports, and application features.
Read Help to find out what's new in Microsoft Access 2.0	This option takes you to the Help menu.

If you decide not to use any of these tutorials, simply click on the Close button on the bottom right corner of the Welcome screen. You see the Access screen, where you can create or open a database on your own.

The Welcome screen appears every time you start Access. To stop this screen from appearing each time, click inside the checkbox next to `Don't display this startup card again` on the bottom left corner of the Welcome screen.

Cue Cards

All the tutorials offered on the Welcome screen use a concept called *Cue Cards*. Cue Cards are like an on-line tutor. They provide step-by-step instructions to help you learn Microsoft Access as you create and use your own database. Many of the Cue Card screens provide graphical examples, as shown in Figure 3-5, to make understanding a concept even easier. Cue Cards are also linked to the Help facility within Access, so you can look up information in Help without losing your place in Cue Cards. Or you can use Help to find a Cue Card relating to a question or task that you may need step-by-step instructions for.

You can open Cue Cards from within Access by selecting Help⇨Cue Cards. From here, you can decide what you want to do. You can select a topic and follow along, as a Cue Card explains how to perform a specific task. You often have several alternatives to choose from, and the path you take depends on what you decide to do.

The unique advantage to using Cue Cards is that they remain visible on top of the Access Window, so Access still works, just as if the Cue Cards weren't there. This enables you to perform your work as you follow along with the steps the Cue Card provides you. Although the Cue Cards window cannot be sized, it can be moved or minimized if you need to view what lies underneath it.

Cue Cards are a great way to learn how to create a database and get information on how Access works. We highly suggest that you spend some time learning how to use Cue Cards.

The next section of this chapter focuses on another way to get answers to your questions — through the Help facility.

Figure 3-5: A Cue Card graphical example.

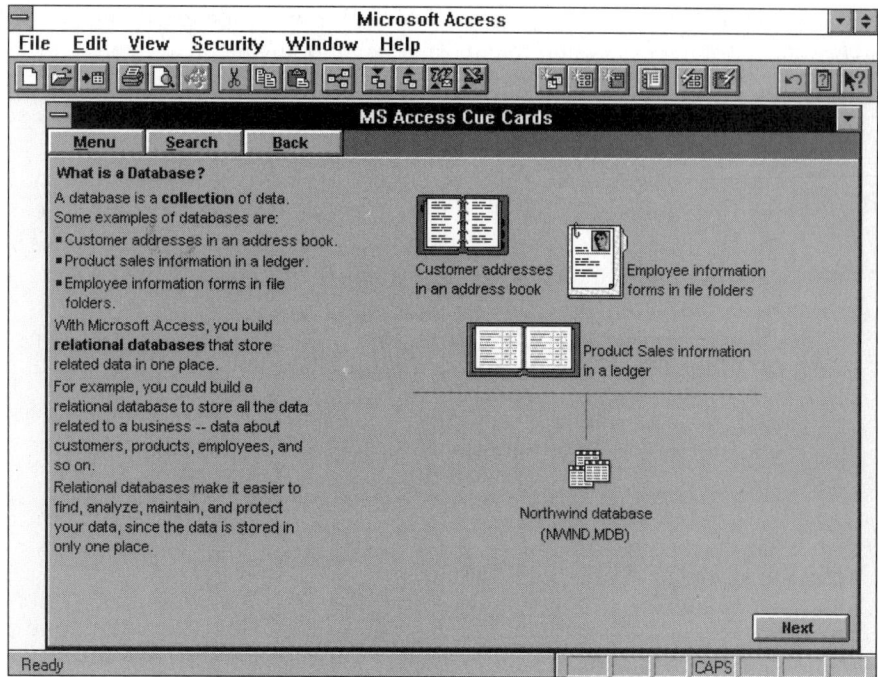

Essentials of on-line help

Getting help in Access is always a keystroke away. There are many easy ways to get help:

- Press the F1 key.
- Click the Help button that resembles a question mark on the Access toolbar.
- Select Help from the Access pull-down menu.
- Select the Help icon, located in the Access program group.
- Press the right mouse button for a shortcut menu.

One way to get help on a specific item is to press Shift+F1. A question mark appears next to the mouse cursor. Simply point and click an item you want help on, and a help screen appears for the item you selected.

If you have a question on the current activity, press F1 to bring up a Help window with specific information on that activity. You can do this because Help is context-sensitive, meaning that it displays information for the activity in progress.

40 Part I: First Things First

You can get help at any time in Access, no matter what you are doing. There is help for every aspect of Access — commands, menus, building macros, Access terms and concepts, and even programming topics. Figure 3-6 shows the Help Table of Contents window that is displayed when you press F1 and if no activity is in progress.

Often, even when you think you're not performing any activity, you may not see the Help Table of Contents screen. Often, the Databases Help screen appears in the Database window. If a different screen appears after you press F1, simply click on the Contents button to display the Help Table of Contents screen.

Suppose that you need help on something not related to your current activity. You can use the Help pull-down menu to search for information on any topic.

Help is a separate program from Access and has its own window. Therefore, you can move, size, minimize, or close the Help window.

Searching for help

The Search menu option lets you search for a specific help topic by entering a key word. When you select this choice, you see the Search dialog box. There are two ways to use the Search dialog box. First, you can enter a key word in the text box. As you begin

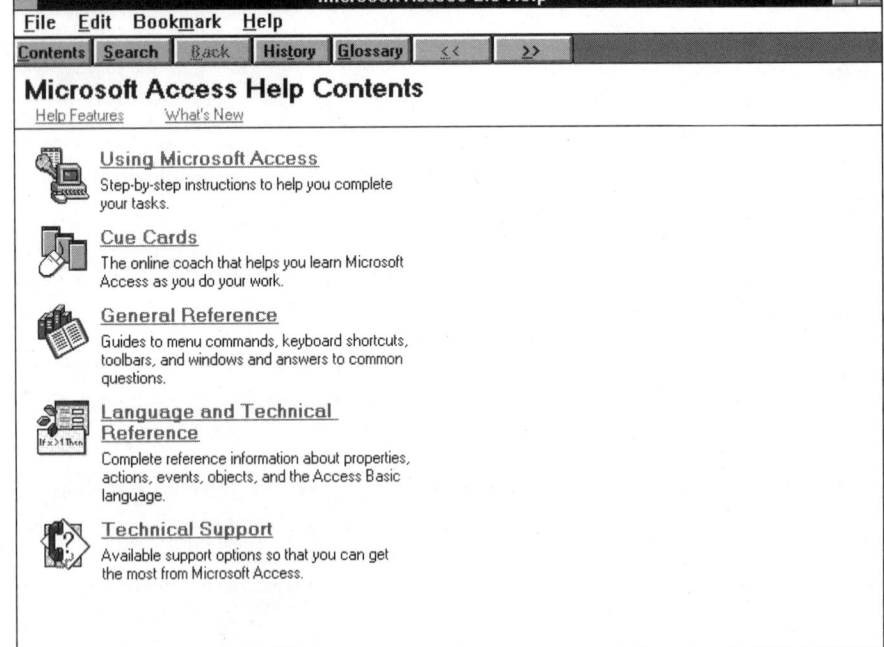
Figure 3-6: The Access Help Table of Contents window.

typing, Help scrolls through the list of available Help topics in the upper list box. You can also use the scroll bar or press Tab and then use the arrow keys or PgUp/PgDn keys to scroll through the list of available topics. When you see a topic you want information on, highlight it and press Enter, or select Show Topics. You'll see a list of relevant topics displayed in the lower list box. You can then select the topic you want to go to and press Enter.

Table 3-2
Help Menu Options

File Menu	
Open	Lets you open a Help file.
Print Topic	Prints the current topic in the Help window. You can print only entire topics.
Print Setup	Sets printer options before printing a topic. You can select a printer and set or change options for the printer. The options available depend on the type of printer selected.
Exit	Quits Help and saves any annotations or bookmarks you created.
Edit Menu	
Copy	Copies the text of the current Help topic to the Clipboard. From the Clipboard, you can paste the text into another application or document.
Annotate	Lets you add text to the current Help topic. Annotations are marked with a Paper Clip icon in front of the topic heading. This is a good way to add your own notes to a Help topic for future reference. You can also copy and paste annotations to other Help topics or into other applications or documents.
Bookmark Menu	
Define...	A bookmark lets you mark a Help screen that you may want to view again by giving it a reference name. The Define command places a bookmark in the current topic or removes a bookmark from any topic. The name you specify for the topic appears on the Bookmark menu.
	A list of bookmark names appears after you define a bookmark. From this list, you can choose the bookmark for the topic you want to display in the Help window.
More	This command appears when you define more than nine bookmarks. You can use the More command to display the complete list of bookmark names you defined.
Help Menu	
How to Use Help	This command lets you display the How to Use Help Contents screen.
Always on Top	This command causes all Help windows to appear on top of other windows. After you choose this command, a shadow appears around the Help window border to let you know that the Help windows are on top.
About Help...	This selection displays the version, mode, and copyright information about Windows.

Help pull-down menus

Help has a pull-down menu bar that enables you to control parts of the Help program itself. Select a command by pointing and clicking on it or press the Alt or F10 key along with the corresponding letter for that command. Table 3-2 lists the menu choices that are available.

Exiting Help

After you are finished using Help, you can exit in several ways:

- Double-clicking the Help Control button
- Choosing Exit from the Help File menu
- Pulling down the Control menu and selecting Close
- Pressing the Alt+F4 key combination

Summary

In this chapter, you learned various ways to start Access and how to exit the program. You learned about the many ways to use the Access Help system. The following points were covered:

- You can start Access in various ways; the easiest and most common method is double-clicking the Access icon.
- You can add options to the Access command line that can automatically open a database, execute a macro, or set a user name or password.
- You should use one of the suggested ways to exit Access. If you exit by turning off your system, the result can be loss of data.
- Cue Cards can provide step-by-step instructions for learning Access and will walk you through the setups needed to create your own database.
- You can press F1 to activate the Help feature, which gives information on how to use Access or a definition of the various concepts used by Access.
- Help appears in a window of its own that can be minimized or resized so that you can keep it open as you work on your database.

In the next chapter, you review basic database concepts as you begin the journey to understanding database management with Access.

A Review of Database Concepts

CHAPTER 4

In This Chapter

- What is a database?
- What are the differences between databases, tables, records, fields, and values?
- Why are multiple tables used in a database?
- What are database objects?

Before you begin to use a database software package, you must understand several basic concepts. The most important concept is that the data is stored in a *black box*, known as a *table*, and that by using the tools of the database, you can retrieve, display, and report the data in any format you want.

What Is a Database?

Database is a computer term for a collection of information concerning a certain topic or business application. Databases let you organize this related information into a logical fashion for easy access and retrieval.

Figure 4-1 shows a conceptual view of a typical manual filing system consisting of people, papers, and filing cabinets. This lighthearted view of a manual database makes the point that *paper* is the key to a manual database system. In a real manual database system, you probably have in/out baskets and some type of formal filing method. You access information manually by opening a file cabinet, taking out a file folder, and finding the correct piece of paper. Paper forms are used for input, perhaps with a typewriter. You find information by manually sorting the papers or copying desired information from many papers onto another piece of paper or even a computer spreadsheet. A calculator or a computer spreadsheet may be used for further analyzing and reporting the data.

Part I: First Things First

Figure 4-1:
A typical manual filing system.

A computer database is nothing more than an automated version of the filing and retrieval functions of a manual paper filing system. Computer databases store information in a structured format that you define. These databases can store data in a variety of forms that range from simple lines of text, such as name and address, to complex data structures that include pictures and even sounds or video images. Data is stored in a precise and known format that enables a database management system (DBMS) to turn the data into useful information through many types of output, such as queries and reports.

Figure 4-2 shows a conceptual view of an automated database management system such as Access. The person uses a computer to access the data stored in *tables.* Data is input to the tables through data-entry *forms* and retrieved by use of a *query.* Queries are used for retrieving only the desired data from the tables. A *report* is then used for outputting the data to the screen or a printer. *Macros* and *modules* are used for automating the process and even allow the creation of menus and dialog boxes.

A *relational* database management system (RDBMS), such as Access, stores data in many related tables, which lets the user ask complex questions from one or more related tables and receive the answers to these questions in the form of information such as forms and reports.

Figure 4-2:
A computer database system.

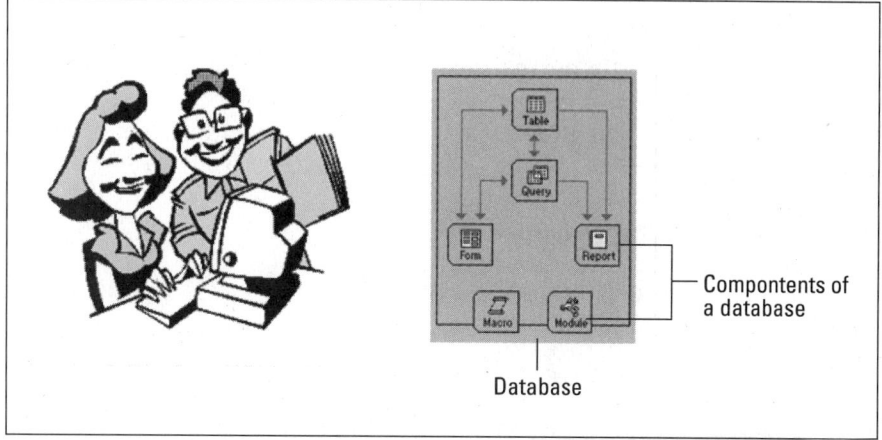

Databases, Tables, Records, Fields, and Values

In Microsoft Access, the terms *database, table, record, field,* and *value* indicate a hierarchy from largest to smallest. Access follows traditional database terminology.

 If you are an experienced dBASE IV user, the term *database* is synonymous with a catalog in the Control Center. A dBASE database file is the same as an Access table.

Databases

In Access, a database is the overall container for the data and associated objects. Database objects include tables, queries, forms, reports, macros, and modules, as shown in Figure 4-2. In some computer software products, the database is the *object* that holds the actual data. In Access, this is called a *table.* Access can work with only one database at a time. However, within a single Access database, you can have hundreds of tables, forms, queries, reports, macros, and modules all stored in a single DOS file with the file extension MDB.

Tables

A *table* is the container for the raw data. When you enter data in Access, the data is stored in a table. A table stores logical groupings of similar data. For example, the data about pets is contained in the Pets table. A table organizes information in rows and columns, which are defined by the table design. Figure 4-3 shows a typical Access table design and *datasheet* (also known as a *browse table* or *table view*), which displays multiple lines of data in neat rows and columns.

The database design defines the types of data contained in each field of the table and the size of each value in the table.

Records and fields

As shown in Figure 4-3, the datasheet is divided into rows called *records* and columns called *fields*. The data shown in the table has columns of similar information, such as Pet Name, Customer Number, Breed, or Date of Birth. These columns of data items are called *fields*. Each field is identified as a certain type of data (Text, Number, Date, and so on) and has a specified length. Each field has a name that identifies these categories of information.

The rows of data within the same table are called *records*. Each row of information is considered a separate entity that can be accessed or sequenced as desired. All the fields of information concerning a certain pet are contained within a specific record.

Values

At the intersection of a row (record) and a column (field) is a *value*. A value is the actual data element. For example, Bobo, the Pet Name of the first record, is one data value. How do you identify the first record? It's the record with the rabbit. But what if there is more than one rabbit? Whereas fields are known by the field name, records are usually known by some unique characteristic of the record. In the Pets table, one field is the Pet ID. The Pet Name is not unique because there could be two pets named Fido in the table. Sometimes, it takes more than one field to find a unique value. Customer Number and Pet Name could be used, but it's possible for one customer to have two pets with the same name. You could use the fields Customer Number, Pet Name, and Type of Animal. But, again, you could theoretically have a customer come in and say, "Hi, my name's Larry; this is my pet snake Darryl, and this is my other pet snake Darryl." So, often a unique identifier is created, such as Pet ID, to identify one record from another without having to look through all the values.

Chapter 4: A Review of Database Concepts

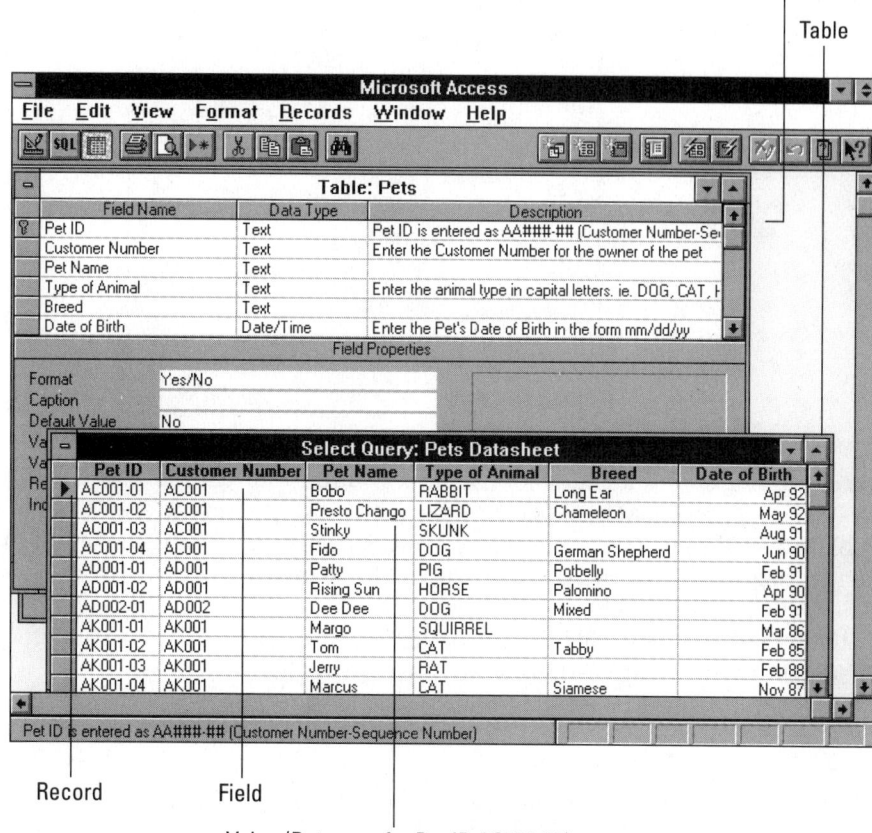

Figure 4-3: A database table design and datasheet.

Why Use More Than One Table?

A database contains one or more *tables*. As previously defined, tables are logical groupings of similar data. Most applications have several related tables to present the information in an efficient manner. An application that uses multiple tables can manipulate data more efficiently than with one large table.

Multiple tables simplify data entry and reporting by decreasing the input of redundant data. For example, by defining two tables for an application that uses customer information, you don't need to store the customer's name and address information every time the customer purchases an item. Figure 4-4 shows a typical table relation. In this example, the Customer table is related to the Pets table. If there were only one table, the customer name and address would have to be repeated for each pet record. By having two tables, the information in the Customer table can be looked up for each pet by use of the common field Customer Number. This way, when a customer address changes, it is changed only in the one record in the Customer table. When the pet information is viewed, the customer address is looked up and is always correct.

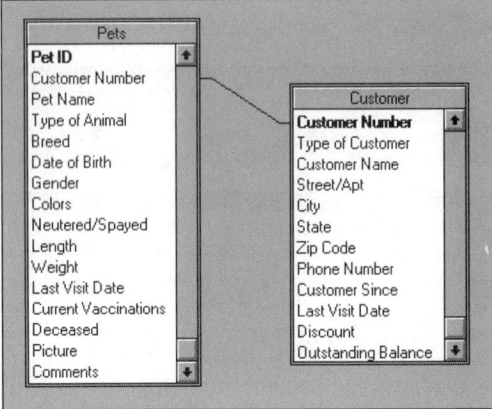

Figure 4-4: Related tables.

By separating your data into multiple tables within your database, you'll find that your system is easier to maintain because all records of a given type are within the same table. You will significantly reduce your design and work time if you invest the extra time to segment your data properly into multiple tables.

Later in this book, you will have the opportunity to work through a case study for the Mountain Animal Hospital that consists of eight tables.

Database Objects and Views

If you are new to databases or even an experienced database user, you should understand some key concepts in Access before starting to use the product. The Access database contains six objects that consist of the data and tools you need to use Access:

Table   Holds the actual data (uses a datasheet to display the raw data)

Query   Lets you search, sort, and retrieve specific data

Form   Lets you enter and display data in a customized format

Report   Lets you display and print formatted data including calculations and totals

Macro   Gives you easy-to-use commands to automate tasks without programming

Module   Programs written in Access Basic

Datasheets

Datasheets are one of the many ways you can view data. Although not a database object, a datasheet displays a list of records from your table in a format commonly known as a browse screen, or table view. A datasheet displays data as a series of rows and columns, comparable to a spreadsheet, as shown in Figure 4-5. A datasheet simply displays the information from a table in its raw form. All fields for all records are displayed in the default mode of this spreadsheet format.

You can scroll through the datasheet by using the directional keys on your keyboard. In addition, you can make changes to the displayed data. You should use caution when making any changes or allowing a user to make any modifications in this format. When you change a record in a datasheet, you are actually changing the data in the underlying table.

Queries and dynasets

You use a *query* to extract information from a database. A query can select and define a group of records that fulfill a certain condition. Queries can be used prior to printing a report so that only the desired data is printed. Forms can also use a query so that only certain records that meet the desired criteria will be displayed. Queries can be used within procedures that change, add, or delete records from the database. An example of a query is when a doctor at Mountain Animal Hospital says, "Show me which pets that

Figure 4-5: A typical datasheet.

Pet ID	Customer Number	Pet Name	Type of Animal	Breed	Date of Birth	Gender
AC001-01	AC001	Bobo	RABBIT	Long Ear	Apr 92	M
AC001-02	AC001	Presto Chango	LIZARD	Chameleon	May 92	F
AC001-03	AC001	Stinky	SKUNK		Aug 91	M
AC001-04	AC001	Fido	DOG	German Shepherd	Jun 90	M
AD001-01	AD001	Patty	PIG	Potbelly	Feb 91	F
AD001-02	AD001	Rising Sun	HORSE	Palomino	Apr 90	M
AD002-01	AD002	Dee Dee	DOG	Mixed	Feb 91	F
AK001-01	AK001	Margo	SQUIRREL		Mar 86	F
AK001-02	AK001	Tom	CAT	Tabby	Feb 85	M
AK001-03	AK001	Jerry	RAT		Feb 88	M
AK001-04	AK001	Marcus	CAT	Siamese	Nov 87	M
AK001-05	AK001	Pookie	CAT	Siamese	Apr 85	F
AK001-06	AK001	Mario	DOG	Beagle	Jul 91	M
AK001-07	AK001	Luigi	DOG	Beagle	Aug 92	M
BA001-01	BA001	Swimmy	DOLPHIN	Bottlenose	Jul 90	F
BA001-02	BA001	Charger	WHALE	Beluga	Oct 90	M
BA001-03	BA001	Daffy	DUCK	Mallard	Sep 83	M
BA001-04	BA001	Toby	TURTLE	Box	Dec 90	M
BA001-05	BA001	Jake	DOLPHIN	Bottlenose	Apr 91	M
BL001-01	BL001	Tiajuana	BIRD	Toucan	Sep 90	F
BL001-02	BL001	Carlos	BIRD	Cockatoo	Jan 91	M
BL001-03	BL001	Ming	BIRD	Humming	Feb 88	F
BL001-04	BL001	Yellow Jacket	BIRD	Canary	Mar 83	F
BL001-05	BL001	Red Breast	BIRD	Robin	Jun 90	M
BL001-06	BL001	Mickey	BIRD	Parrot	May 91	M
BL001-07	Bl001	Sally	BIRD	Parrot	Jul 85	F

Record: 1 of 130

Pet ID is entered as AA###-## (Customer Number-Sequence Number)

we treat are dogs or cats and are located in Idaho, and show them to me sorted by customer name and then pet name." You don't actually ask the questions in English. Rather, you use a method known as *QBE,* which stands for Query By Example. Figure 4-6 shows a typical query screen that asks the doctor's question.

The query works by translating the *instructions* that you enter into the QBE window and retrieving the desired data. In this example, data from both the Customer and Pets tables is first combined by the related field Customer Number, which is the common link between the tables. Then the fields Customer Name, Pet Name, Type of Animal, and State are retrieved. The records are filtered so that only those records where the value of State is ID and the value of Type of Animal is dog or cat are selected. The resulting records are sorted by customer name and then by pet name within the customer names that are alike. Finally, the records are presented in a datasheet.

These selected records are known as a *dynaset* — a *dyna*mic *set* of data that can change according to the raw data in the original tables.

After you run a query, you can use the resulting dynaset in a form to be displayed on-screen in a specified format or to be printed on a report. In this way, you can limit user access to restricted data.

Figure 4-6:
A typical query.

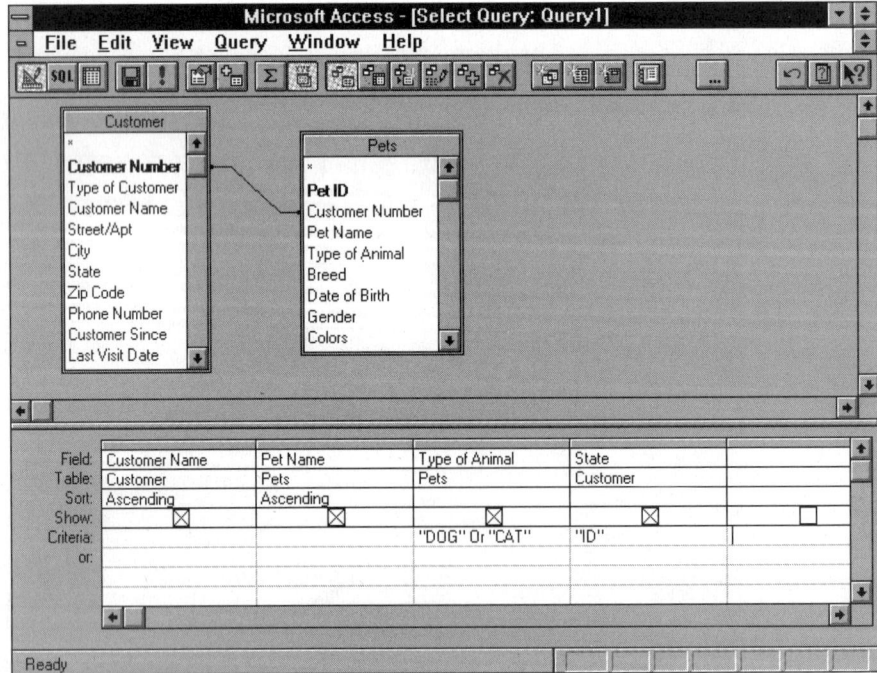

Data-entry and display forms

Data-entry forms help users get information into a database table in a quick, easy, and accurate manner. Data-entry and display forms provide a more structured view of the data than a datasheet. From this structured view, you can view, add, change, or delete database records. Entering data through the data-entry forms is the most common way to get the data into the database table. Figure 4-7 shows a typical form.

You can use data-entry forms to restrict access to certain fields within the table. You can also use these forms to perform validity checks on the data before you accept the data into the database table. Most users prefer to enter information into data-entry forms rather than datasheet tables because the data-entry forms can be made to resemble the paper documents that are familiar to the user. Forms make data entry self-explanatory by guiding the user through the fields of the table being updated.

Display-only screens and forms are solely for inquiry purposes. These forms allow for selective display of certain fields within a given table. In this way, you can limit a user's access to sensitive data, while allowing inquiry into other fields.

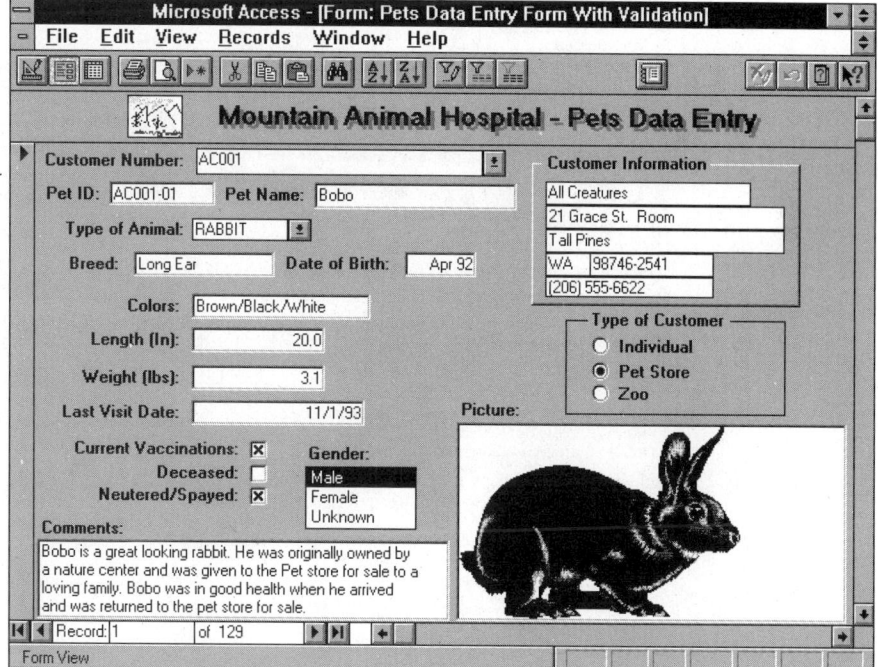

Figure 4-7: A typical data-entry form.

Reports

Reports present your data in printed format. You can create a number of different types of reports within a database management system. For example, your report can list all records in a given table, such as a customer table. You can also create a report that lists only the customers within a given criteria, such as all customers located in Washington. You do this by incorporating a query into your report design. The query creates a dynaset consisting of the records that contain the state code WA.

Reports can combine multiple tables in order to present complex relationships between the tables. An example is printing an invoice. You access the customer table to obtain

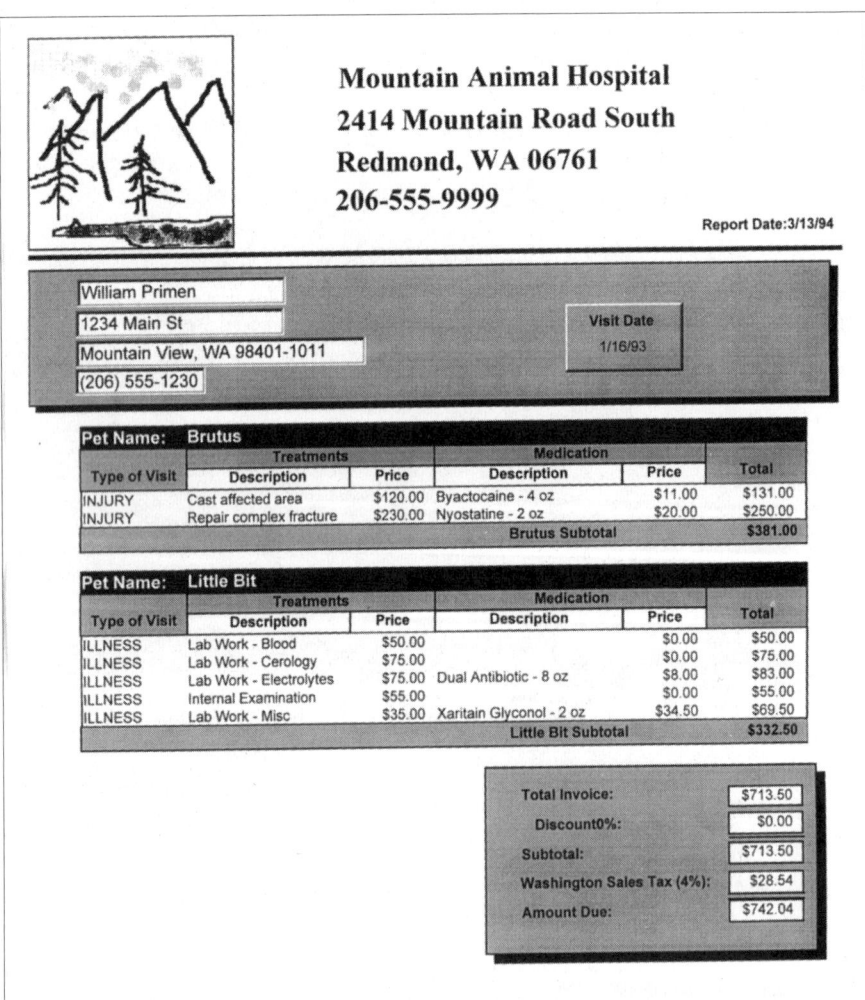

Figure 4-8: A typical invoice report.

Chapter 4: A Review of Database Concepts

the customer name and address and other pertinent customer data. The sales table is also accessed to print the individual line-item information for the products ordered. Totals can be calculated and printed on the invoice form in a specific format. Additionally, output records can be produced into another table that contains summary information about the given invoice. Figure 4-8 shows a typical invoice report.

It is important to keep in mind all the necessary information you want printed when you initially design your database tables. Doing so ensures that the information you require on your various reports is available from within your database tables.

Summary

In this chapter, you learned the most basics concepts of a database and of Access. Throughout this book, new concepts are introduced and thoroughly discussed. If you want to learn more about database concepts when working with multiple tables and about such concepts as primary and foreign keys, referential integrity, and relationships, Chapter 12 covers all these topics in depth. In this chapter, the following points were covered:

- *Database* is a computer term for a collection of information related to a certain topic or business application.
- Databases let you organize this related information into a logical fashion for easy access and retrieval.
- An Access database is a single DOS file with an MDB file extension that holds all the database objects used in Access.
- Database objects include tables, queries, forms, reports, macros, and modules.
- A table contains definitions of each field in the table and holds the raw data.
- A record is a row in the table and is identified by some unique value.
- A field is a column in the table and is identified by a field name.
- The *value* is an element of data and is found at the intersection of a record and field.
- Relational database management systems use more than one table to simplify database reporting and eliminate redundant data.
- A *datasheet* is a spreadsheet-type view of your data. This is also known as a *browse table* or *table view*. The datasheet lets you view raw data in a table.
- A query lets you ask questions of your data by using the Query By Example (QBE) screen to select fields, sort the data, and select only specific records by specified criteria. The result of a query is a *dynaset*. This dynamic set of data can be used with a datasheet, form, or report.
- Forms let you view your data in a more structured format. You can enter data into a form or make the form read-only.
- Reports are used mainly for calculating and summarizing data. Reports are frequently printed.

In the next chapter, you take a guided tour through Access and see how some of these objects are used.

A Hands-On Tour of Access

CHAPTER 5

In This Chapter

- Learning how to navigate the screen by using the mouse, the keyboard, or a combination of the two
- Seeing a brief overview of the basic components found on the Access screen
- Taking a hands-on tour through a simple Access session, where you learn how to open a database and a table, display a form, create a query, and display a report

To use Access, you need to know how to get around the Access screen. In this chapter, you learn that each task you want to complete in Access can probably be accomplished with several different methods. Some tasks have as many as five ways to accomplish the same thing. It's important to understand that the method using the fewest keystrokes or mouse clicks is usually the best method.

A Tour of the Screen

In this book, you learn many terms and see many Access windows and shortcut dialog boxes. It is a good idea to become familiar with these specific terms. If you've used another database software package before Access, you need to be able to translate the terms you already know into the words Microsoft Access uses to refer to the same task or action.

Using the mouse and keyboard

You can navigate the Access screen by using the mouse, the keyboard, or a combination of both. The best way to get around Access is by using a mouse or some other type of pointing device. You'll find that the keyboard is used for entering data and for moving around the various data-entry areas. However, when designing new forms, queries, or reports, you'll find it unproductive to try using only the keyboard. In this book, you learn how to complete tasks by using both the keyboard and mouse. In most cases, however, using the mouse is preferable.

The Access window

The Access window is the center of activity for everything you do in Access. From here, you can have many windows open, each of which displays a different view of your data. Figure 5-1 shows the Access window with a Database window open inside it.

Following are a number of Access window features that you should be familiar with:

Title bar: You know what program is currently active by the name of the program you see displayed in the title bar. The program name Microsoft Access is always displayed here.

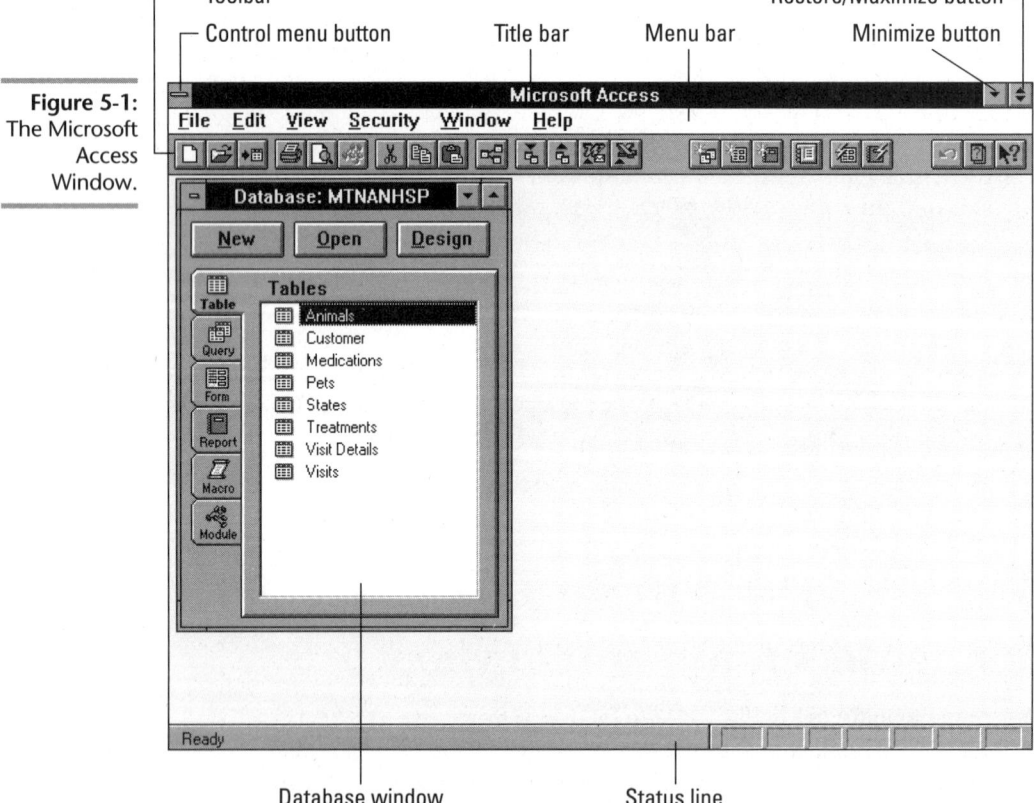

Figure 5-1: The Microsoft Access Window.

Control menu button: You'll find this button on nearly every application window. When you click this button once, a menu appears that lets you do certain tasks, such as move, size, minimize, or close the current application window. When you double-click the Control button, you automatically exit the application.

Minimize button: Clicking this button reduces Access to an icon. Access will still be running, and you can reactivate it by double-clicking the icon.

Restore button: You can click this button to restore the window to its previous size.

Maximize button: This button resizes the Access window to a full-screen view. The maximize button does not appear in Figure 5-1 because Access is already maximized. If Access is not maximized, the Restore button is replaced with the Maximize button, which is identified by the symbol of a single triangle pointing upward.

Menu bar: The menu bar contains several menu choices. When you click one, a menu drops down, offering further choices. The items on the menu bar and the choices you find in each menu will vary in Access, depending on what you are working on.

Toolbar: The toolbar consists of a group of picture buttons just below the menu bar that provide shortcuts for running commands. The buttons on the toolbar vary, depending on what you are working on at the time. The toolbar can be resized and moved by clicking between buttons and moving it around the screen. You can also select View⇨Toolbars to show or hide different toolbars.

Status line: The left side of the status line displays helpful information about what you are doing at the time. In Figure 5-1, the status line simply says `Ready`. The right side of the status line tells you whether certain keyboard settings are active. For example, if you have the Caps Lock on, the word `CAPS` appears in the status line.

Database window: This window appears whenever a database is open; it is the control center of your database. You use the Database window to open the objects that are contained within a database, including tables, queries, forms, reports, macros, and modules.

The Database window

The Database window always displays the name of the open database in the title bar. For example, in Figure 5-1, you see the MTNANHSP database in the title bar. The MTNANHSP database is on the disk that comes with this book and contains all the tables, forms, and other objects that are demonstrated in this book.

The Database window has three basic parts to it. You see a set of six object buttons in a vertical row to the left, a set of three command buttons along the top of the window, and a list of files.

Object buttons: These buttons are located in a vertical row along the left side of the Database window. With these buttons, you can select the type of object you want to work with. For example, selecting the Form button displays a list of forms created for that database. Selecting this button also lets you create a new form or redesign an existing one.

Command buttons: You can use the command buttons, located along the top of the Database window, to place a database object in a different window or view. These buttons let you create, open, or design a database object.

Object list: This list displays existing files for the database object that you select. You can choose a name from the list to display or redesign the object.

The Database window also has a Control button, Minimize button, and Maximize button, which work the same as those mentioned earlier in the chapter.

Design windows

The Database window is just one of several windows that you use for your many tasks in Access. Several other windows that you commonly see are the object design windows, which let you design such objects as tables, queries, forms, reports, macros, and modules. There are also windows that let you view or edit your data in datasheets, forms, and report previews.

Figure 5-2 shows the Database window, along with the Form Design window and several other windows that assist you in designing queries, forms, and reports. These are generally known as design windows. The Form window is shown with several fields displayed. The form that you see in the figure, named Animals, can be used for displaying information about each pet in the Pets table.

In Figure 5-2, you see the four most common design windows: the toolbox, palette, field list, and property windows. Because the Form window is active, you may also notice that the toolbar is different.

The toolbox

Figure 5-2 displays the toolbox in the bottom right portion of the screen. You use the toolbox when you design a form or report. The toolbox is similar to a toolbar, but the

Chapter 5: A Hands-On Tour of Access   **59**

toolbox is initially vertically arranged and can be moved around. The toolbox shown in the figure contains toggle buttons you can select to add objects to a form or report, such as labels, text boxes, option group boxes, and so on. You can move the toolbox or close it when you don't need it. You can also resize it by clicking and dragging the toolbox border.

The palette

The palette is displayed in Figure 5-2 in the bottom left corner of the screen. You can use the palette to change colors of objects and to give their appearance a three-dimensional look if desired. Like with the toolbox, the size of the palette is resizable.

The Field List window

The Field List window displays a list of fields from the currently open table or query dynaset. Field List windows are used in query, form, and report design windows. You can select fields from this window by double-clicking them, and you can drag the fields onto a query, form, or report.

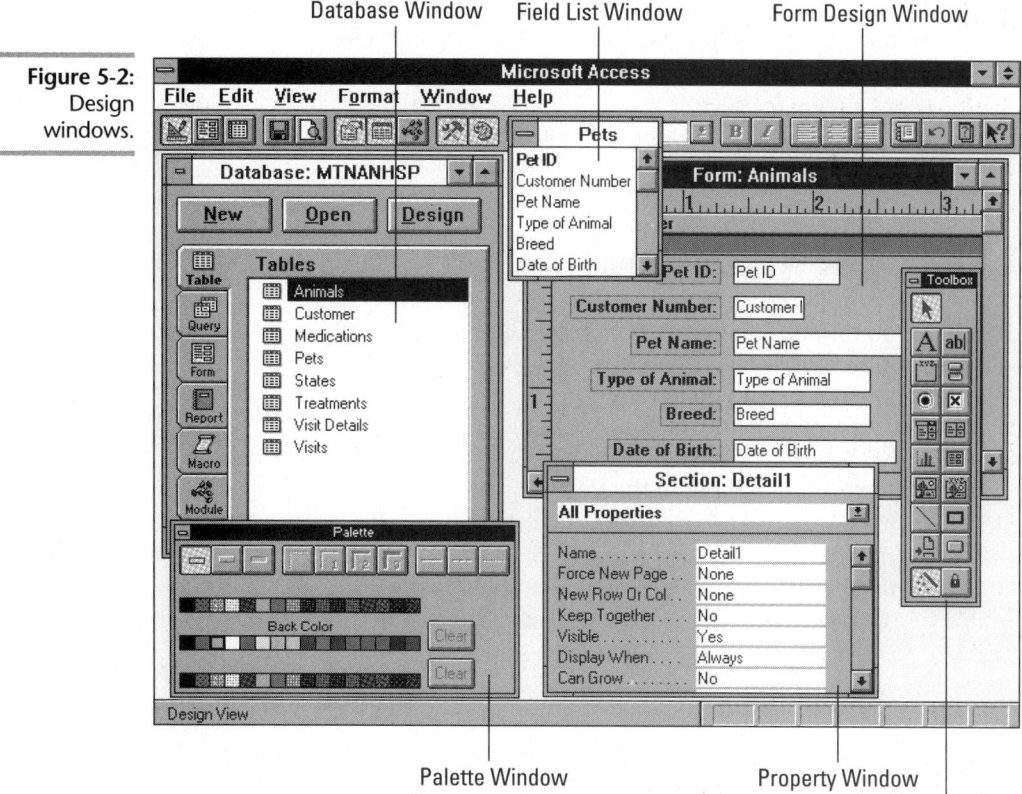

Figure 5-2: Design windows.

The property sheet

In a form or report, each field (called a *control* in Access) has properties that further define the characteristics of the control. The form or report itself and sections of the form or report also have properties. In Figure 5-2 in the lower right-hand area, you see a property sheet displaying the section properties for a form. Usually, a property sheet displays only a portion of the properties available for a specific control, so a vertical scroll bar in the window lets you scroll through the complete list. You can also resize a property sheet and even move it around the screen.

You'll soon see that having many windows open at once, resizing and rearranging them on-screen, helps you use information productively as you create such objects as forms and reports and use the features in Access. Each of the windows is described in detail in the appropriate chapters in this book.

A Simple Access Session

Now that you are familiar with the Access screen, you can go through a simple Access session even before you know more about Access. Before proceeding, make sure that you are ready to follow along on your own computer. Your computer should be on, and Access should be installed. Chapters 2 and 3 showed you how to install and start Access. You can refer to those chapters for details. If you have not done so already, perform the following steps to get ready for this session:

Steps:	Preparing Your Computer
Step 1.	Start your computer. Turn on your computer and start Windows. Type **WIN** at the DOS prompt to start the Windows program if it is not already started.
Step 2.	Start Access. Find the Access icon and double-click on the icon with the left mouse button to start Access. See Chapter 3 if you need further help starting Access.
Step 3.	Maximize the Access window. On the upper right corner of the Access window, you see two grey boxes containing triangles. If the box on the right shows two triangles, Access is already maximized; you can go on to the next section. If the triangle in this box points upward, click on the box to maximize the Access screen. Your screen should now look like the one in Figure 5-3.

Chapter 5: A Hands-On Tour of Access

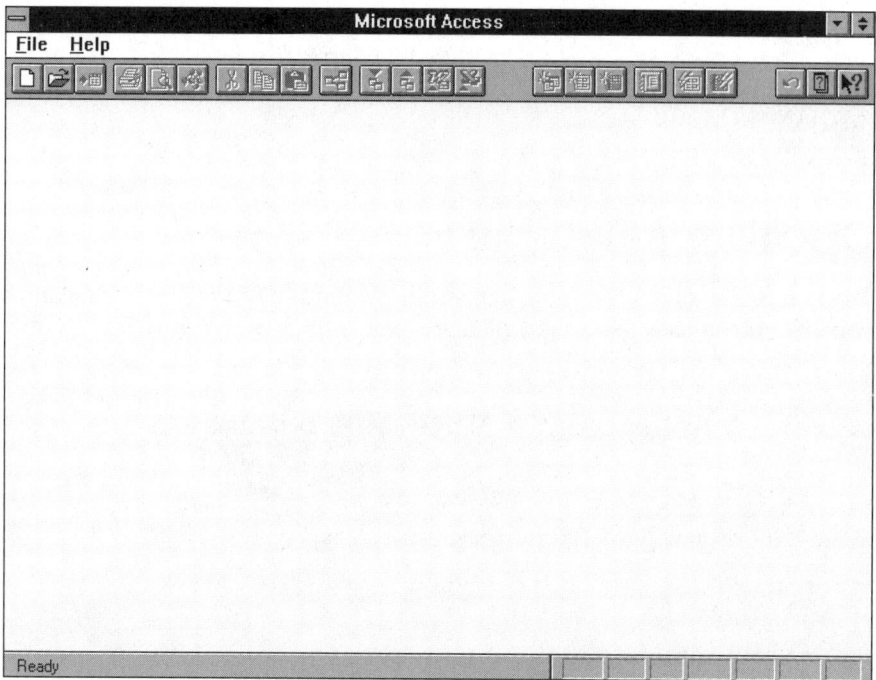

Figure 5-3: The Access window.

The Disk in the Back of the Book

In the back of your book is a disk that contains several files. The disk contains several database files that you'll use throughout the book, as well as some dBASE and Paradox files used in Chapter 24. To use this disk, follow the directions in the back of the book on the pages opposite the disk envelope. Following is a description of the two main database files used in this book:

MTNANHSP.MDB   A database containing all the tables, queries, forms, reports, and macros used in this book

MTNSTART.MDB   A file containing tables only

You can use the MTNSTART database file, beginning with Chapter 8, to create your own queries, forms, and reports. You can use the MTNANHSP database file to see how the Mountain Animal Hospital final application is created and used.

If you haven't used the disk in your book yet, now is a good time to take it out and copy the disk files to the Access directory on your hard disk.

You are now ready to move on. Your goal for this session is to open a database and then perform such simple steps as opening a table, displaying a form, and creating a query. You'll be using the Mountain Animal Hospital database that came with this book (MTNANHSP.MDB).

Opening a database

The first thing you'll want to do is open the Mountain Animal Hospital database. When you first start Access, you see a blank screen, as shown in Figure 5-3. To open the database, follow these steps:

Steps:	**Opening the MTNANHSP.MDB Database**
Step 1.	Select File➪Open Database.
Step 2.	Click the name MTNANHSP and select OK.

A dialog box similar to the one in Figure 5-4 appears, which lists all the databases available in the current directory. If you don't see the MTNANHSP data-base listed, you may have to change the directory Access is looking in. To do so, select the proper drive and directory where you stored this database. After you tell Access where to find the database, the name should appear in the left window of the dialog box.

Access opens the database, and your screen should now look similar to Figure 5-5. You should find the name MTNANHSP at the top of the Database window.

Figure 5-4: The Open Database dialog box.

Chapter 5: A Hands-On Tour of Access

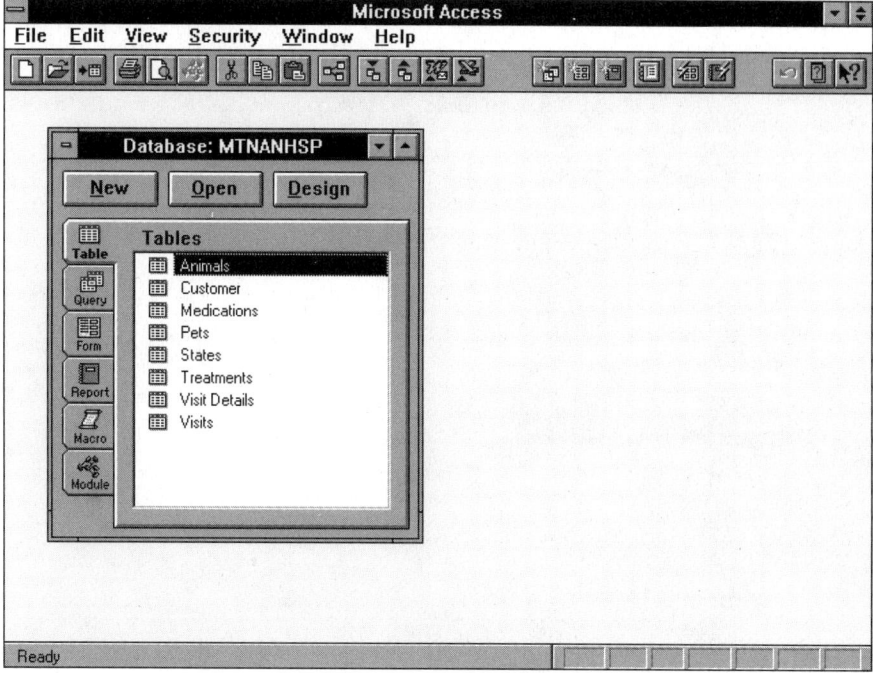

Figure 5-5: The MTNANHSP database opened.

Opening a table

Now that you've opened the database, you'll open a table so that you can view some of the data stored in the Mountain Animal Hospital database. You should open the table named Pets. This table contains information about the various pets that are treated at the hospital, including the pet and customer identifications, type of animal, pet name, breed, gender, height, weight, and so forth. Follow these steps to open the Pets table:

Steps:	Opening the Pets Table
Step 1.	Click the Table object button in the Database window if it is not already selected.
Step 2.	Select the table called Pets.
Step 3.	Select the Open command button found in the top part of the Database window.
Step 4.	Maximize the window by selecting the Maximize button in the top right corner of the window.

Access now opens the Pets table, and your screen should look like Figure 5-6.

Part I: First Things First

Figure 5-6: The Pets table opened.

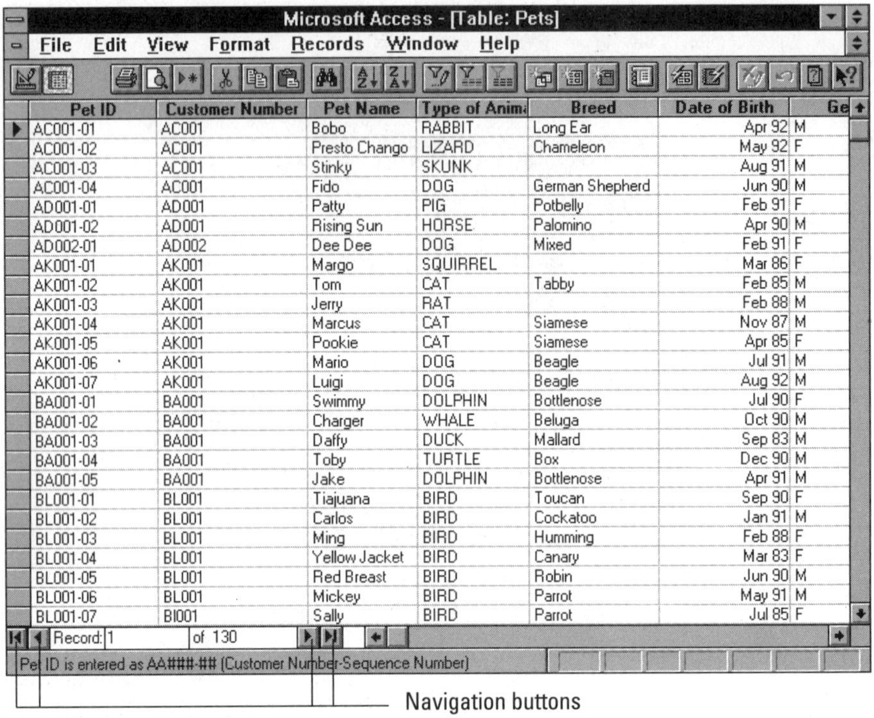

Pet ID	Customer Number	Pet Name	Type of Animal	Breed	Date of Birth	Ge
AC001-01	AC001	Bobo	RABBIT	Long Ear	Apr 92	M
AC001-02	AC001	Presto Chango	LIZARD	Chameleon	May 92	F
AC001-03	AC001	Stinky	SKUNK		Aug 91	M
AC001-04	AC001	Fido	DOG	German Shepherd	Jun 90	M
AD001-01	AD001	Patty	PIG	Potbelly	Feb 91	F
AD001-02	AD001	Rising Sun	HORSE	Palomino	Apr 90	M
AD002-01	AD002	Dee Dee	DOG	Mixed	Feb 91	F
AK001-01	AK001	Margo	SQUIRREL		Mar 86	F
AK001-02	AK001	Tom	CAT	Tabby	Feb 85	M
AK001-03	AK001	Jerry	RAT		Feb 88	M
AK001-04	AK001	Marcus	CAT	Siamese	Nov 87	M
AK001-05	AK001	Pookie	CAT	Siamese	Apr 85	F
AK001-06	AK001	Mario	DOG	Beagle	Jul 91	M
AK001-07	AK001	Luigi	DOG	Beagle	Aug 92	M
BA001-01	BA001	Swimmy	DOLPHIN	Bottlenose	Jul 90	F
BA001-02	BA001	Charger	WHALE	Beluga	Oct 90	M
BA001-03	BA001	Daffy	DUCK	Mallard	Sep 83	M
BA001-04	BA001	Toby	TURTLE	Box	Dec 90	M
BA001-05	BA001	Jake	DOLPHIN	Bottlenose	Apr 91	M
BL001-01	BL001	Tiajuana	BIRD	Toucan	Sep 90	F
BL001-02	BL001	Carlos	BIRD	Cockatoo	Jan 91	M
BL001-03	BL001	Ming	BIRD	Humming	Feb 88	F
BL001-04	BL001	Yellow Jacket	BIRD	Canary	Mar 83	F
BL001-05	BL001	Red Breast	BIRD	Robin	Jun 90	M
BL001-06	BL001	Mickey	BIRD	Parrot	May 91	M
BL001-07	BI001	Sally	BIRD	Parrot	Jul 85	F

Record: 1 of 130

Pet ID is entered as AA###-## (Customer Number-Sequence Number)

Navigation buttons

Displaying a datasheet

When you open the Pets table, you see a datasheet that contains all the data stored in the Pets table. The data is displayed in a column-and-row format. You can move around the datasheet to view the different types of data stored here. Table 5-1 shows how to move around the table window by using the keyboard. You can also use the mouse to navigate throughout the table. Simply click any cell with the left mouse button to move the cursor to that cell. You can also use the mouse to move the elevators to navigate around the table.

You can also move through the table with the mouse by using the navigation buttons found at the bottom left corner of the datasheet window. These are sometimes called VCR buttons. The arrows located at the left and right ends with a vertical line next to them move you to the first or last record of the table. The two arrows to the inside of the outer two arrows move you to the preceding or the next record. Between these arrows are two small rectangles that display the current record number and the number of records. If you know which record you want to move to, you can get there quickly by clicking the mouse on the record number (or by pressing F5), typing the number of the record that you want to move to, and pressing Enter.

 You can also use the GoTo command found in the Records menu to go to the first, last, next, previous, or new record.

Table 5-1
Keyboard Techniques for Moving around the Window

Keyboard Keys	Action
Left- and right-arrow keys	Move left or right one column at a time
Up- and down-arrow keys	Move up or down one row at a time
PgUp and PgDn	Move up or down one screen at a time
Home	Move to the first column of the row the cursor is in
End	Move to the last column of the row the cursor is in
Tab	Move right one column at a time
Shift+Tab	Move left one column at a time
Ctrl+Home	Move to the first column of the first record in the table
Ctrl+End	Move to the last column of the last record in the table

Viewing a table design

Now that you've seen what kind of information is contained in the Pets table and how to navigate around the datasheet, you can look at the design of the table. You first need to be in the Design view to see the design of the Pets table.

To get to the Design view, click on the Design button in the toolbar; it is the first button on the Access toolbar and shows a triangle, ruler, and pencil. The Pets datasheet will disappear and be replaced by the Design window for the Pets table. Figure 5-7 displays the Pets Design window.

Here in the Design view is where the fields for the Pets table were set up. When the Pets table was created, fields that were to be included in the table were added here. Depending on the type of information to be entered in each field, a specific data type is given to each field. Some of the data types that you can choose are Text, Currency, Date/Time, and Memo. A field is also provided for a description of the type of data the field will contain.

The Design window has two parts. In Figure 5-7, you see that the top half of the window lists the field names and field types and a description for each field of the Pets table. Moving around this window is similar to moving around the Pets datasheet.

The bottom half of the Pets Design window displays the field properties. Different properties can be set up for each field in the table. You can use the mouse or the F6 key to move between the top and bottom panes of the Design window.

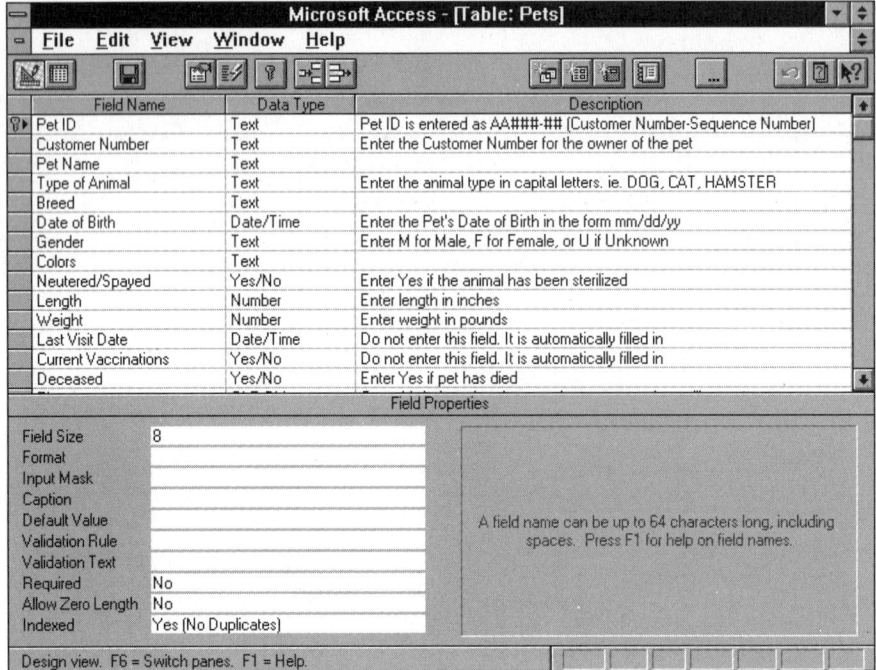

Figure 5-7: The Pets Design window.

The next object you'll display is a form. At this time, you should close the Design window by selecting File➪Close. This selection closes the Table Design window and returns you to the Database window.

Displaying a form

The steps for displaying a form are similar to the steps for opening a table. In this case, you are opening a different type of database object. Follow these steps for opening up the form called Pets:

Steps:	Opening the Pets Form
Step 1.	Click the Form object button in the Database window.
Step 2.	Select the form named Pets.
Step 3.	Click the Open command button at the top of the Database window to open the form.

Chapter 5: A Hands-On Tour of Access 67

 You can also double-click any name to open the form.

The Pets form should look like the one in Figure 5-8.

A form provides another way of displaying or changing data. The Pets form is an example of a simple form. You enter information in each text box just as you enter information in a table. There are some advantages when using a form instead of a datasheet; in a form, you can view more fields on-screen at once, and you can use many data-entry and validation shortcuts. Also notice that you can view the picture of each animal on a form and the contents of the Comments Memo field. You cannot do this when you are using a datasheet.

To see how this form was created, click the Design button located on the Access toolbar (the first button on the left with the triangle, ruler, and pencil). Your form should now look like Figure 5-9.

In Figure 5-9, on the right side of the form is a long, rectangular box containing several buttons. This is the form toolbox. You can move the toolbox anywhere on-screen. The toolbox lets you add controls to the form. A *control* is a graphical object, such as a label, text box, checkbox, or command button that you can place on a form to display data from a field or enhance the look of the form.

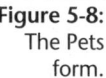

Figure 5-8: The Pets form.

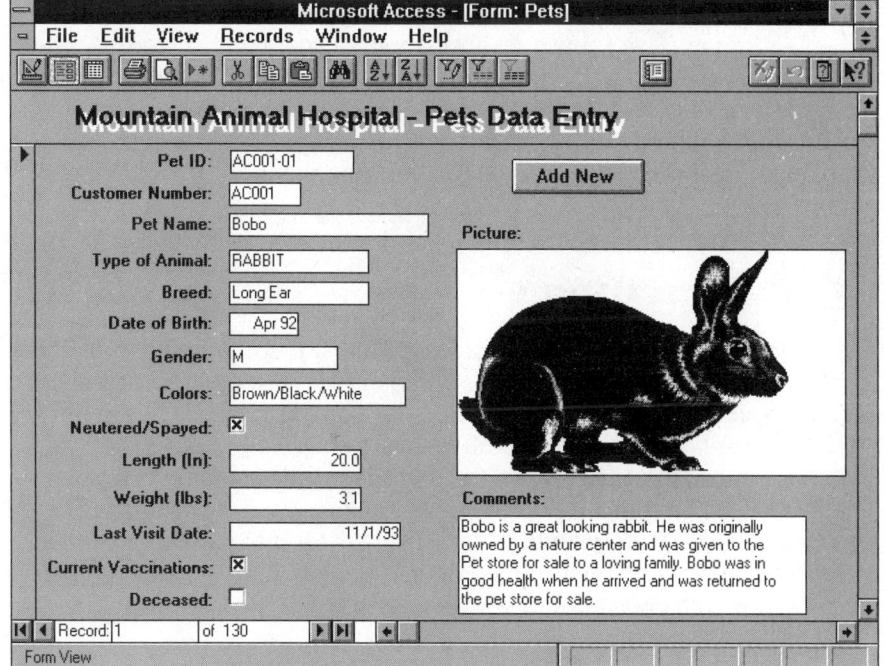

Figure 5-9:
The Pets form Design view.

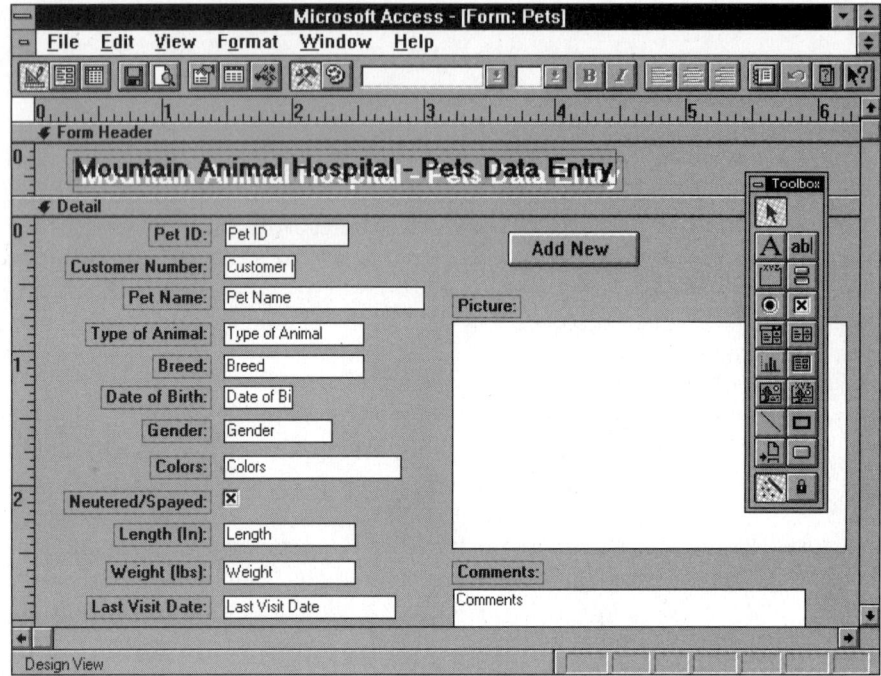

Now that you've seen two different methods of entering data — datasheets and forms — you may have some questions about the data that is stored in the Pets table. You can find the answers to your questions through queries. Before creating a query, you should close the form by selecting File⇨Close. This selection closes both the form and the form toolbox and returns you to the Database window. If you made any changes to the form, Access will prompt you to save your changes before closing the form.

Creating a query

A query lets you ask questions about the data that is stored in your database. The data that is produced by the query can be saved into its own table for future use or printed out as a report. You next learn how to create a simple query by using the Pets table.

Suppose that you want to see only the records in the Pets table in which the type of animal is a dog. You only want to see the pet name, type of animal, and breed. The first step is to create the query and add only the Pets table to it. You can add as many tables as you want to a query, but for this example you add only the Pets table. To create the query and add the Pets table, follow these steps:

Chapter 5: A Hands-On Tour of Access

Steps: Creating a Simple Query

Step 1. Select the Query button from the Database window.

Step 2. Click New to create a new query. Access displays a list of all tables and queries.

Step 3. Press the New Query button in the dialog box.

Step 4. Select Pets by clicking the table name.

Step 5. Select Add.

Step 6. Select Close.

You should now see an empty query window, as shown in Figure 5-10.

The query form consists of two panes. The top pane contains a Field List window of the Pets table fields. You use the Field List window to choose which fields will appear in the query datasheet. The bottom part of the Query screen contains a series of rows and

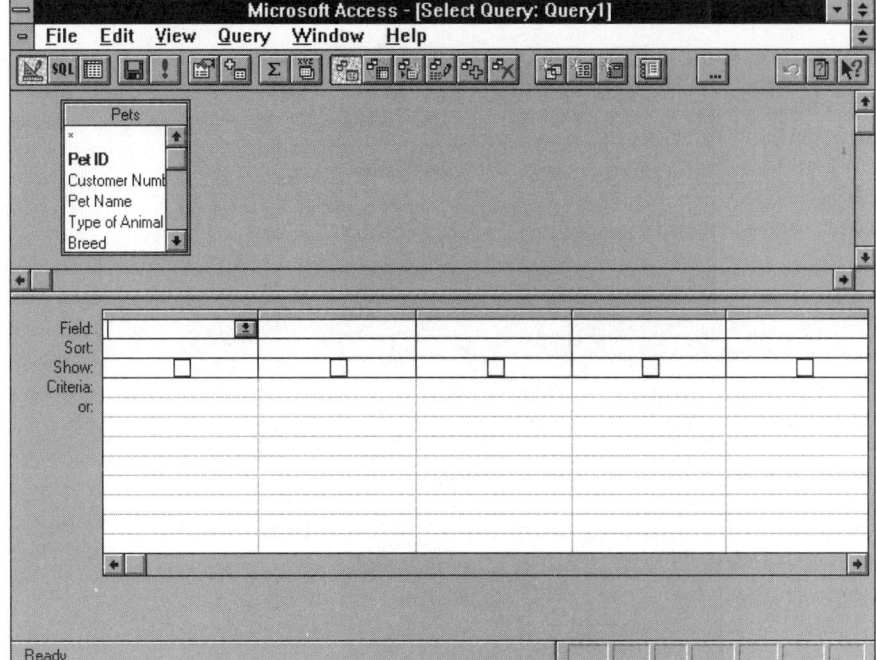

Figure 5-10: The empty query window.

columns. In this pane, you'll ask questions about the fields in your tables. To view the fields Pet Name, Type of Animal, and Breed and to select only the records where the value of Type of Animal is DOG, follow these steps:

Steps: Setting Up a Query

Step 1. Double-click the Pet Name field from the Field List window to add the field to the query.

Step 2. Add the Type of Animal field to the query.

Step 3. Add the Breed field to the query.

Step 4. Press F6 to move to the lower pane and place the cursor on the Criteria: row of the Type of Animal column of the query.

Step 5. Type **DOG** in the cell.

Your query should now look like Figure 5-11. You added the three fields to the query that you want to see in your results. In addition, you want to see only the dogs. Placing the word *DOG* in the criteria range tells Access to find only records where the value of Type of Animal is DOG.

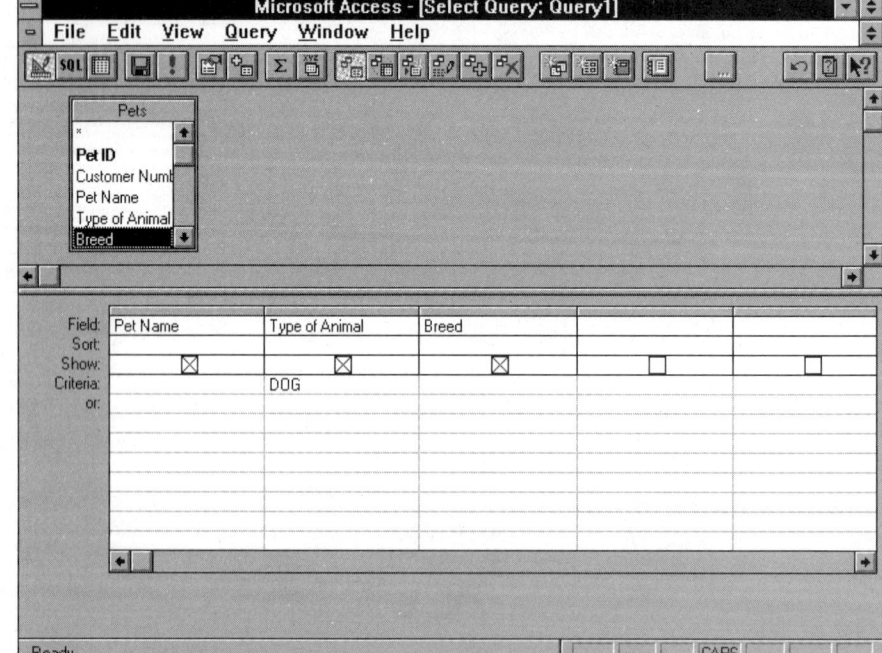

Figure 5-11: The completed query.

Chapter 5: A Hands-On Tour of Access **71**

To run the query, you need to select the Run button. This button shows an exclamation point and is found on the toolbar. After you select this button, Access goes to work to process your query and produce the results in what is called a *dynaset*. Your dynaset should look like the one in Figure 5-12. The dynaset displays the pet name, type of animal, and breed for each pet that is a dog.

The results from a query can be saved and used for creating a report that you can view or print. The next section explains how to display a report. Select File⇒Close to close the query. Select No because you don't want to save the query.

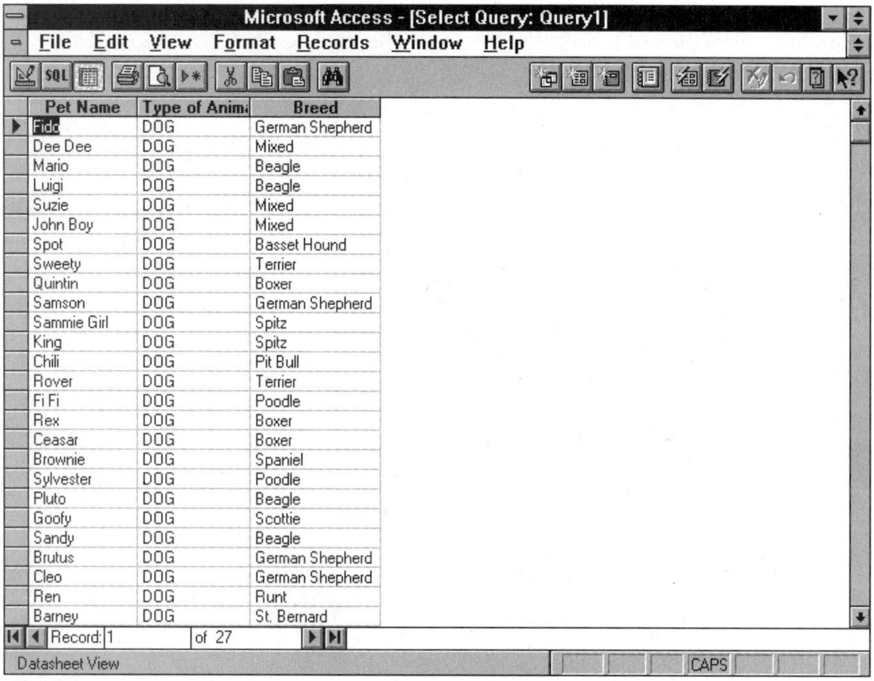

Figure 5-12: The query dynaset.

Pet Name	Type of Animal	Breed
Fido	DOG	German Shepherd
Dee Dee	DOG	Mixed
Mario	DOG	Beagle
Luigi	DOG	Beagle
Suzie	DOG	Mixed
John Boy	DOG	Mixed
Spot	DOG	Basset Hound
Sweety	DOG	Terrier
Quintin	DOG	Boxer
Samson	DOG	German Shepherd
Sammie Girl	DOG	Spitz
King	DOG	Spitz
Chili	DOG	Pit Bull
Rover	DOG	Terrier
Fi Fi	DOG	Poodle
Rex	DOG	Boxer
Ceasar	DOG	Boxer
Brownie	DOG	Spaniel
Sylvester	DOG	Poodle
Pluto	DOG	Beagle
Goofy	DOG	Scottie
Sandy	DOG	Beagle
Brutus	DOG	German Shepherd
Cleo	DOG	German Shepherd
Ren	DOG	Runt
Barney	DOG	St. Bernard

Displaying a report

Queries or tables can be formatted and placed into a report for output to a printer. Next, you view and print a report that was already created. You'll be using a report of all the pets in the Pets table. Follow these steps for displaying and printing this report:

Steps:	**Displaying a Report**
Step 1.	Click the Report button in the Database window.
Step 2.	Select Pet Directory from the file list.

Part I: First Things First

Step 3. Select the <u>P</u>review button.

The report is displayed in the zoomed preview mode. You can display the entire page by clicking the cursor anywhere on-screen (the cursor currently is shaped as a magnifying glass).

Step 4. Click anywhere on the screen to display the entire page.

The report should look like Figure 5-13.

The Pets report shows all the fields from the first record of the Pets table. You can use the PgDn key or the navigation buttons at the bottom left corner of the window to see other pages of the report. The report can also be printed to the Windows printer, or you can return to the Design window to enhance the report.

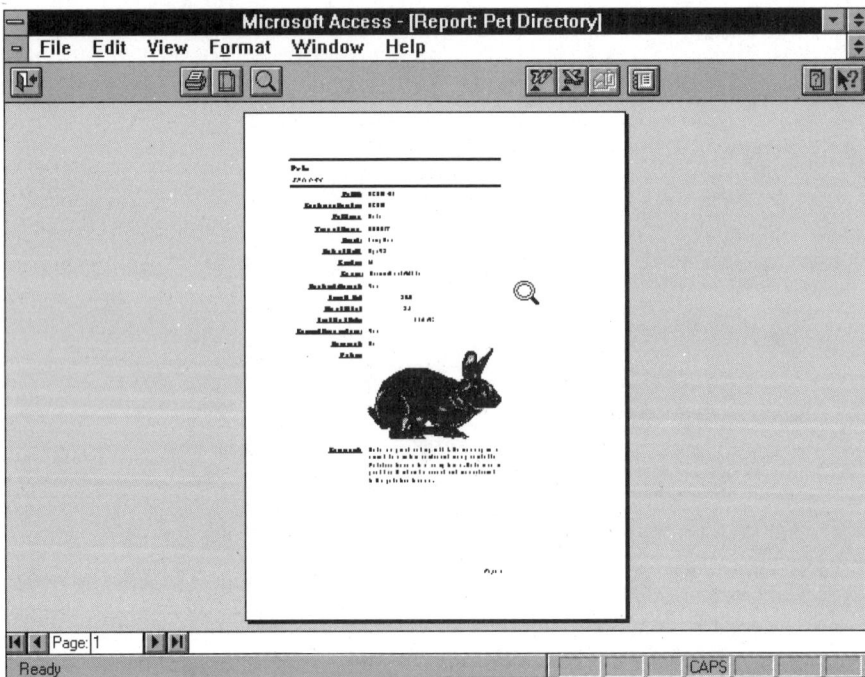

Figure 5-13: The Pets report in print preview mode.

Microsoft Access Product Support

Microsoft offers a variety of no-charge and fee-based support options to help you get the most from Microsoft Access. If you have a question about Access, you can consult

- The printed product documentation
- Cue Cards and Online Help
- The README files that came with your product disks
- Answers to Common Questions, included as a separate icon in your Microsoft Access program group when you installed Access
- Electronic options such as CompuServe forums or the Microsoft Download Bulletin Board

If you can't find the answer in any of these sources, contact Microsoft Product Support Services, which provides product support and technical information. You can call Microsoft Product Support Services at (206) 635-7050 between 6 a.m. and 6 p.m. (Pacific time), Monday through Friday.

For quick information on frequently asked questions, use the Microsoft Access automated telephone support service. You can hear recorded responses to common Access questions. You can also order application notes that will be sent to your fax machine. These services are offered 24 hours a day, 7 days a week, and require a touch-tone telephone.

To reach Fast Tips for Microsoft Access, call (800) 936-4100.

You can contact the Microsoft Product Support Services staff on several CompuServe forums. To get information through CompuServe, do one of the following:

- If you are already a CompuServe member, type **GO MICROSOFT** at any ! prompt, or type **GO MSKB** for Access-specific support.
- For an introductory CompuServe membership kit specifically for users of Microsoft software, call (800) 848-8199 and ask for operator 519.

You can get the latest technical notes and supplementary files covering common Microsoft Access support issues via modem on the Microsoft Download Service at (206) 936-MSDL (1200, 2400, or 9600 baud; no parity; 8 data bits; 1 stop bit). The service is available 24 hours a day, 7 days a week.

Ready for More

You now have experienced many of the different capabilities of Access. If you had problems with this chapter, you should start again from the beginning. Make sure that you follow the directions exactly and don't move on to the next steps until you understand what you were supposed to do. Hopefully, this quick view of Access will make you eager to learn how to use Access in detail. Don't be afraid to experiment. You can always reload the files from the disk in the back of the book. You can't hurt Access or your computer.

Now that you have a basic understanding of the various database objects in Access, you are ready to move on to creating your own tables, forms, queries, and reports. But, before moving on to Part II of this book, you should have an understanding of how to design a database system. In Chapter 6, you learn how some of the tables, forms, queries, reports, and macros are designed. Throughout the book, you will see this design implemented.

Summary

In this chapter, you took a quick tour through Access to learn about the windows you can use. You learned some basic terms that you need as you progress through the book, and you now have some hands-on experience in creating and using forms, reports, and queries. The following points were covered:

- You can navigate through Access by using the mouse or the keyboard.
- The Access Database window contains several menus and a toolbar.
- When you open a database, all the database objects that comprise the database are displayed in the Database window.
- When you open a database table, you see the information stored in the table as a datasheet.
- You can make your data entry easier by creating a form from an existing table.
- You can ask questions about data in a table by assembling a query and creating a view known as a dynaset.
- You can save a query to a report for output to a printer.

A Case Study in Database Design

CHAPTER 6

In This Chapter

- Learn the seven-step design method
- Be introduced to the Mountain Animal Hospital example
- See how to create the overall design of a system
- Learn how to create reports
- Learn how to extract report fields to perform data design
- Design database tables and relationships
- Learn how to design data-entry rules and validation
- Design input forms
- Design menus

The most important lesson to learn as you create a database is good design. Without a good design, you'll be constantly reworking your tables and you may not be able to extract the information you want out of your database. Throughout this book, you learn not only how to use queries, forms, and reports, but also how to design each of these objects before you attempt to create one. Although the entity used in this chapter is fictitious, the concepts are not.

This chapter is not simple to understand. Some of the concepts and ideas in this chapter are fairly complex. If your goal is to get right into Access, you may want to read this chapter later. If you are new to designing and creating tables, you may want to read it before you move on and begin the actual process of creating your tables.

Examples from the Mountain Animal Hospital are used throughout this book to serve as a case study.

Specifically, you design forms and reports that range from simple to complex. Throughout this book, you create each of the forms and reports and much more. You learn how to create simple forms and reports with just a few fields from a single table. Then you learn how to create multiple-page forms and reports that use multiple tables. You create forms and reports that use many types of advanced controls, including option buttons, list boxes, combo boxes, and checkboxes. You create forms and reports that use one-to-many relationships displayed as subforms and subreports. Finally, you learn how to design customer mailing labels and mail merge reports. Most important, you learn how to do data design and create the many tables used by the Mountain Animal Hospital application.

The Seven-Step Method for Design

In order to create database objects such as tables, forms, and reports, you must first complete a series of tasks known as design. The better your design, the better your application. The more you think through your design, the faster you can complete any system. Design is not some necessary evil, nor is its intent to produce voluminous amounts of documentation. The sole intent of design is to enable you to produce a clear-cut path to follow as you implement your design.

Figure 6-1 shows a modified version of this method designed especially for Access.

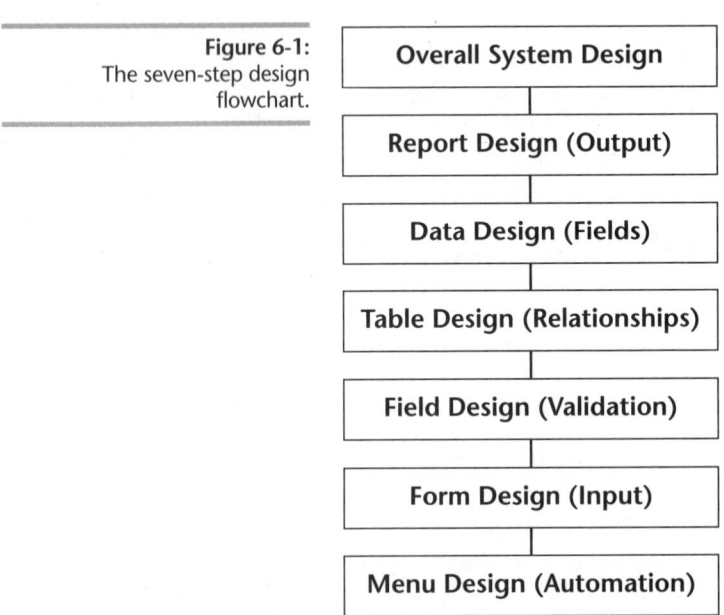

Figure 6-1:
The seven-step design flowchart.

Both the design and the system will teach you almost all there is to know about Access to create and use databases and to create tables, queries, forms, reports, and macros.

As you read through each step, you'll look at the design in terms of the outputs and the inputs. Although you see the actual components of the system (customers, pets, visits, and visit details), remember that the focus of this chapter is how you design each step. As you watch the Mountain Animal Hospital system being designed, pay attention to the design, not the actual system.

Step 1: The overall design — from concept to reality

All software developers and end users face similar problems. The first set of problems you encounter is with gathering requirements. The end user is typically your client, your coworker, or you. It is important to understand the overall needs of the system before you begin to zero in on the details.

The seven-step design method shown in Figure 6-1 can help you create the system you need and at a price (measured in time or dollars) that you can afford. The Mountain Animal Hospital is a medium-size animal hospital that services individuals, pet stores, and zoos across three states. Basically, Mountain Animal Hospital needs to automate several tasks:

- Entering customer information — name, address, and financial history
- Entering pet information — pet name, type, breed, length, weight, picture, and comments
- Entering visit information, details of treatments performed, and medications dispensed
- Asking all types of questions about the information in the database
- Producing a current pets and owners directory
- Producing a monthly invoice report
- Producing mailing labels and mail merge reports

The design process is an iterative procedure. That is, as each new step is finished, all the previous steps must again be looked at to make sure that nothing in the basic design has changed. If you decide when creating a data-entry rule that you need another field not already in the table to validate a field you already defined, you then have to go back and follow each previous step to add the field. You have to be sure to add the field to each report that you want to see the field on. You also have to make sure that it is on an input form that uses the table the field is in. Only then can you use this new field in your system.

Now that you've defined Mountain Animal Hospital's overall systems in terms of what needs to be accomplished, you can begin the next step of report design.

Step 2: Report design — placing your fields

Design work should be broken up into the smallest level of detail that you know of at the time. You should start each new step by reviewing the overall design objectives. In the case of Mountain Animal Hospital, your objectives are to track customers, track pets, keep a record of visits and treatments, produce invoices, create a pets and owners directory, and produce mailing labels.

Laying out fields in the report

When you look at the reports you create in this section, you may wonder, "What comes first — the duck or the egg?" Does the report layout come first, or do you first determine the data items and text that make up the report? Well, actually, these items are conceived together.

It is not important how you lay out the fields in this conception of a report. However, the more time you take now, the easier it will be when you actually create the report. Some people go as far as to place gridlines on the report so they will know the exact location they want each field to occupy on the report. In this example, you can just do it visually.

The pets and owners directory

Mountain Animal Hospital will begin with the tasks of tracking customers and pets. The first report that needs to be developed is one sorted by customer number that shows important customer and pet information. Each customer's name and address are shown along with a listing of the pets the customer has brought into the Mountain Animal Hospital.

The hospital staff has already decided on some of the fields for the customer file. First, of course, is the customer's name and address. The customer name field can be used for an individual's name or for the name of a company. The address consists of the customer's street, city, state, and ZIP code. Then the customer's phone number must also be recorded.

Another field that the hospital will maintain on file and use on the report is the last visit date. This field will be used for letting Mountain Animal Hospital know when it is time to remove a pet from the pets table. Already decided is that a pet will be removed from the table if it hasn't been in for a visit in the last three years. Because the plan is to purge the pets table each year, there is no other way to find this information. Recording the last visit date will also alert Mountain Animal Hospital when an animal is due for its yearly checkup so that reminder notices can be sent out.

With that information in mind, the Mountain Animal Hospital people create the report form design shown in Figure 6-2.

Figure 6-2: The customer and pets report design.

Mountain Animal Hospital Pets and Owners Directory

[Customer Name]
[Street/Apt]
[City] [State] [Zip Code]   Type of Customer: [Type of Customer]
[Phone Number]

	General Information	Physical Attributes
Picture of Animal	Pet ID: [Pet ID]	Length Weight Colors Gender
	Type of Animal: [Type of Animal]	[Length] [Weight] [Colors] [Gender]
	Breed: [Breed]	Status
	Date of Birth: [Date of Birth]	Neutered/Spayed Current Vaccinations Deceased
[Pet Name]	Last Visit: [Last Visit Date]	[Neutered/Spayed] [Current Vaccinations] [Deceased]
[Comments]		

If you want to see how this report is implemented, Chapter 21 teaches you how to create this report. If you want to see how this report is completed with advanced database publishing enhancements, see Chapter 22.

Figure 6-3 shows the final hard-copy printout of this report, to show you the capabilities of Access.

Figure 6-3: The completed Pets and Owners Directory report.

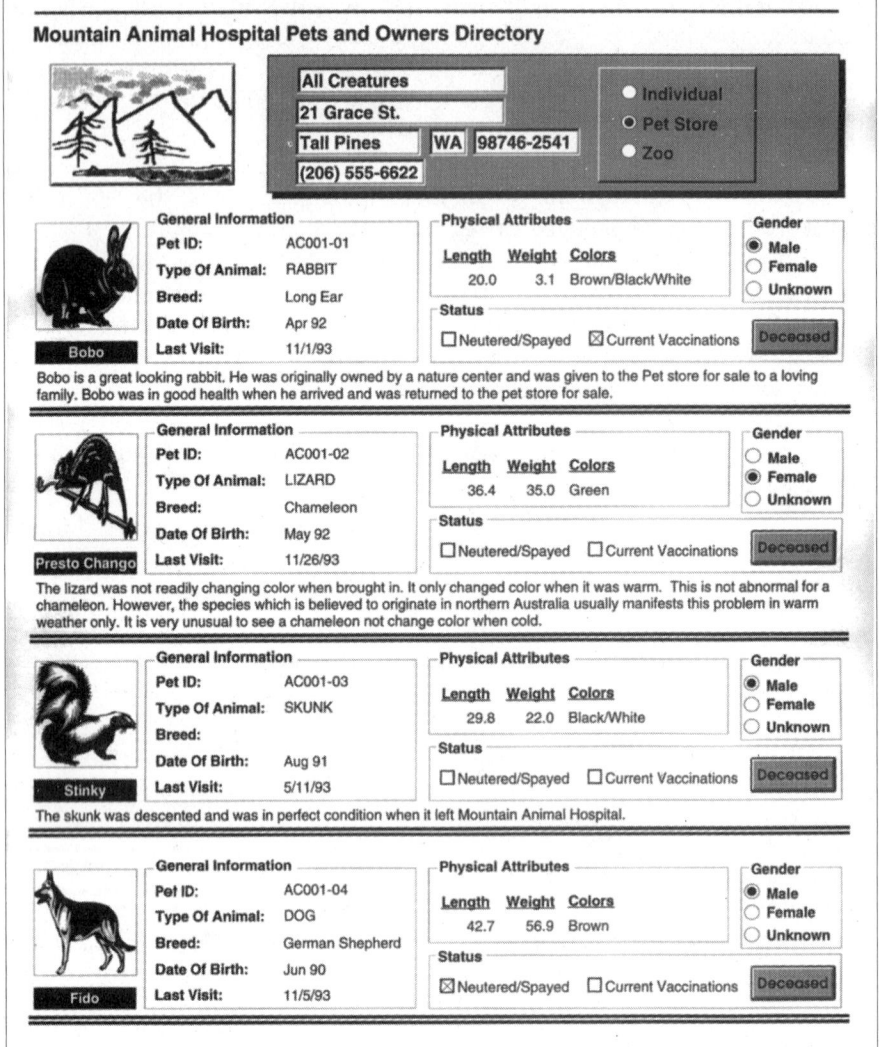

The Monthly Invoice Report

Whereas the Pets and Owners Directory concentrates on information about customers and pets, the Monthly Invoice Report displays information about individual visits by these pets and customers. Mountain Animal Hospital needs to produce a monthly report that lists all the daily visits by each customer and the customer's pets. Figure 6-4 shows the design of this report.

The design of this report shows customer information at the top of the report, and information about the visit is shown in the middle. The middle block appears as many

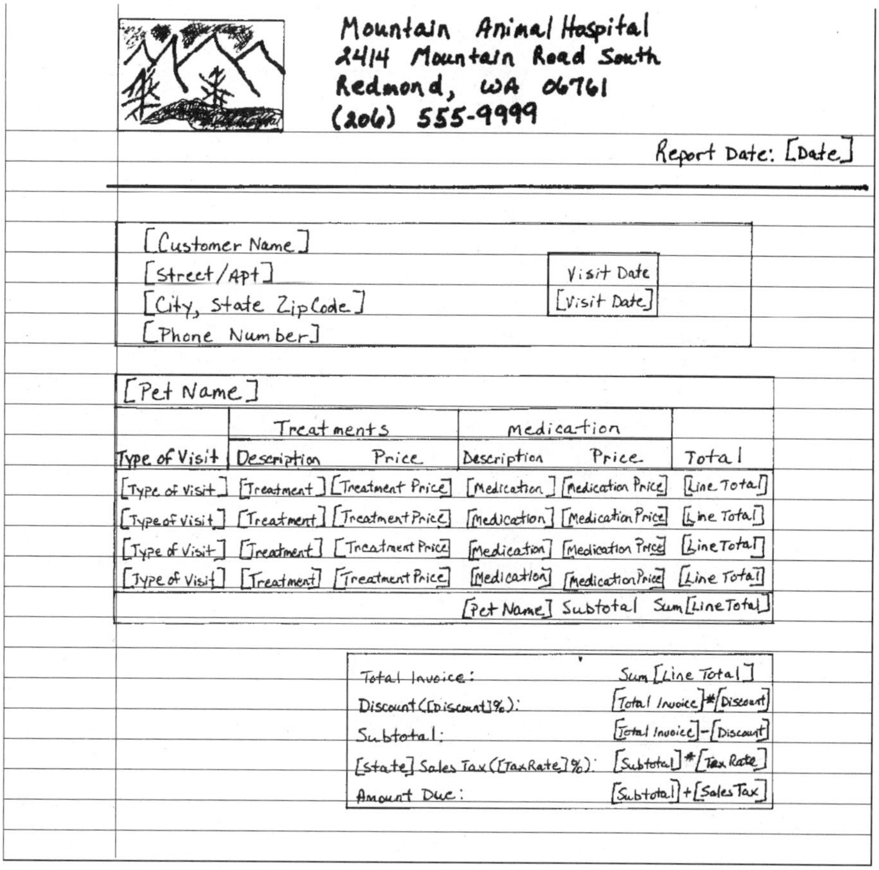

Figure 6-4:
The design for the Monthly Invoice Report.

[Hand-drawn invoice design showing:]

Mountain Animal Hospital
2414 Mountain Road South
Redmond, WA 06761
(206) 555-9999

Report Date: [Date]

[Customer Name]
[Street/Apt]
[City, State ZipCode]
[Phone Number]

Visit Date
[Visit Date]

[Pet Name]

Type of Visit	Treatments		Medication		Total
	Description	Price	Description	Price	
[Type of Visit]	[Treatment]	[Treatment Price]	[Medication]	[Medication Price]	[Line Total]
[Type of Visit]	[Treatment]	[Treatment Price]	[Medication]	[Medication Price]	[Line Total]
[Type of Visit]	[Treatment]	[Treatment Price]	[Medication]	[Medication Price]	[Line Total]
[Type of Visit]	[Treatment]	[Treatment Price]	[Medication]	[Medication Price]	[Line Total]

[Pet Name] Subtotal Sum [Line Total]

Total Invoice: Sum [Line Total]
Discount ([Discount]%): [Total Invoice] * [Discount]
Subtotal: [Total Invoice] - [Discount]
[State] Sales Tax ([TaxRate]%): [Subtotal] * [Tax Rate]
Amount Due: [Subtotal] + [Sales Tax]

---

times as each customer had visits on the same date. If a customer brings three pets to the hospital on the same day, the report shows the middle block of data three times — one for each pet. The middle block contains data about each visit. The prices are totaled for each line, and then the sum of the line totals is shown at the bottom of the block.

Data items in the bottom block are all summarized and calculated fields. These fields aren't stored in a table because they can be calculated whenever necessary. After subtracting the discount from the subtotal, the report shows a taxable amount. If the customer is subject to tax, the tax is calculated based on the current tax rate. Adding the tax to the taxable amount gives the total. This is the amount on the invoice that the customer pays. The final report that is created in Chapter 23 is shown in Figure 6-5.

In reality, you'd design many more reports. However, in the interest of time and pages, the preceding two report designs will suffice.

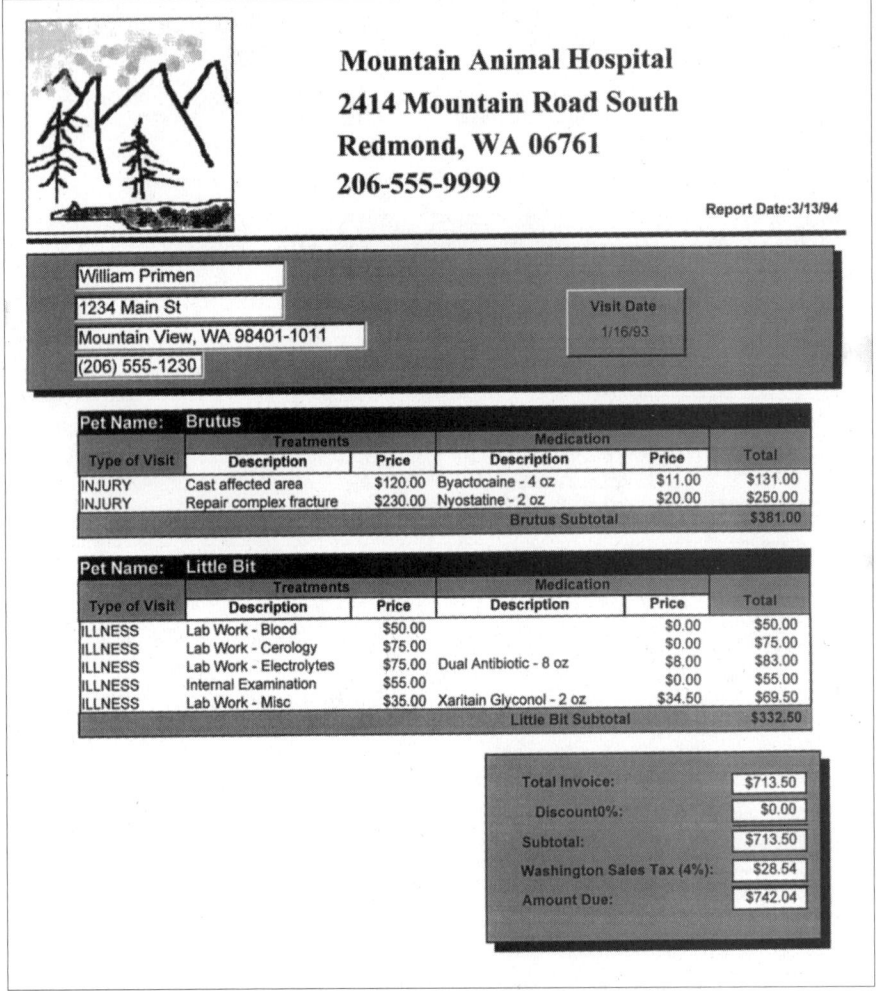

Figure 6-5: The final report for the Mountain Animal Hospital Monthly Invoice Report.

Step 3: Data design — what fields do you have?

Now that you've decided what you want for output, it's time to think about how you'll get the data into a system to make it available for the reports you already defined, as well as for any ad hoc queries. The next step in the design phase is to take an inventory of all the data fields that you need to accomplish the output. One of the best ways to do this task is to take each report and list the data items that are found in the report. As you do so, you should take careful note of the items that are found in more than one report. Make sure that an item with the same name in one report is really the same data item in another report.

Chapter 6: A Case Study in Database Design

Another step is to see whether you can begin to separate the data items into some logical arrangement. Later, you'll have to group these data items into logical table structures and then map them onto data-entry screens that make sense. For example, customer data should be entered as part of a customer table process — not part of a visit entry.

Determining customer information

First, you must look at each report. For the Mountain Animal Hospital customer reports, you start with the customer data and list the data items, as shown in Figure 6-1.

**Table 6-1
Customer Related Data Items Found in the Customer Reports**

Pets and Owners Directory	Monthly Invoice Report
Customer Name	Customer Name
Street	Street
City	City
State	State
ZIP Code	ZIP Code
Phone Number	Phone Number
Type of Customer	
Last Visit Date	
	Discount

As you can see, most of the data fields pertaining to the customer are found in both reports. Only the fields that are used are placed in the table. Fields appearing on both reports are placed on the same lines in the table, which allows you to see more easily which items are in which reports. You can look across a row instead of looking for the same names. Because the related row and the field names are the same, it is easy to make sure that you have all the data items. Although not critical for this small database, easily located items become very important when dealing with large tables.

Determining pet information

After extracting the customer data, you can move on to the pet data. Again, you need to analyze the two reports for data items specific to the pets. Table 6-2 shows a listing of the fields found in the two reports that contain information about the animals. Notice that only one field in the Monthly Invoice Report contains pet information.

Table 6-2
Pet Data Items Found in the Reports

Pets and Owners Directory	Monthly Invoice Report
Pet ID	
Pet Name	Pet Name
Type of Animal	
Breed	
Date of Birth	
Last Visit Date	
Length	
Weight	
Colors	
Gender	
Neutered/Spayed	
Current Vaccinations	
Deceased	
Picture	
Comments	

Determining visit information

Finally, you need to extract information about the visits from the Monthly Invoice Report, as shown in Table 6-3. Only this report is used because the Pets and Owners Directory report does not deal with visit information.

Table 6-3
Extracting Visit Information

Monthly Invoice Report	
Visit Date	Discount
Type of Visit	Tax Rate
Treatment	Total Amount
Treatment Price	
Medication	
Medication Price	
Line Total	

Some of the calculated fields are not listed. However, they can be easily recreated in the report. So, unless a field needs to be specifically stored in a table, it is simply recalculated at the report run time.

Combining the data

Now for the difficult part. You must determine the fields that are needed to create the tables that make up the reports. On examining the multitude of fields and calculations that make up the many documents you have, you begin to see which fields actually belong to the different tables. You already did some preliminary work by arranging the fields into logical groupings. For now, every field you extracted should be included. Later, although some fields will not be placed in any table, others will need to be added for various reasons.

After all the data has been displayed using each report, it is time to consolidate the data by function and then compare the data across functions. You can do this step by first looking at the customer information and creating one set of data items by combining all the different fields. Then you do the same thing for the pet information and the visit information. Table 6-4 shows the comparison of data items from these three groups of information.

Table 6-4
Comparing the Data Items from the Three Groups

Customer Data Items	Pet Data Items	Visits Data Items
Customer Name	Pet ID	Visit Date
Street	Pet Name	Type of Visit
City	Type of Animal	Treatment
State	Breed	Treatment Price
ZIP Code	Date of Birth	Medication
Phone Number	Last Visit Date	Medication Price
Type of Customer	Length	Discount
Last Visit Date	Weight	Tax Rate
Discount	Colors	Total Amount
	Gender	
	Neutered/Spayed	
	Current Vaccinations	
	Deceased	
	Picture	
	Comments	

This is a good start for the beginning of the table definitions for Mountain Animal Hospital. However, there is much more still to do. First, as you learn more about how to perform a data design, you learn that the information in the visits column must be split into two columns. Some of the items are used only once for the visit, and yet other items are used for each detail line in the visit. This is part of a process called *normalization*. One customer has one pet, which has one visit with many visit details. The customer and pet data items each represent one customer or pet. However, the visits have multiple detail lines.

The Visits column is broken into two columns, as shown in Table 6-5. The visit date is no longer a unique field for the second table, which contains multiple items for each visit. Another field will have to be added. You see this in Table 6-6.

When you look at Table 6-5, you may wonder how these two files can be linked together so that Access knows which visit detail information goes with which visit. A unique field needs to do this job. Often, this field is an identification number or code. By adding the same field to each group of information, you can keep like information together. You can create a field called Visit Number and assign it through some consistently chosen methodology. For example, you can create a numeric sequence of year, the day number of the year, and a sequence number. Then the third pet to visit on January 12, 1993, is identified as 1993012-03. The first four digits record the year, the next three digits tell you the number of days since January 1, and then a hyphen separates the date from a sequence number. This field must be added to both columns for the Visits and Visit Details tables. Then you can tie the two files together.

Table 6-5
Dividing the Visits Information

Visits	Visit Details
Visit Date	Visit Date
	Type of Visit
	Treatment
	Treatment Price
	Medication
	Medication Price
Discount	
Tax Rate	
Total Amount	

There is one more identification number to assign. The Visit Details table does not have a *unique* identifier. It does have a partially unique identifier. The Visit Number identifier is unique for an individual visit but not for a visit that has multiple detail lines. A common practice is to simply assign a sequential number for each visit detail, as, for example, 001, 002, 003, and so on.

 Commonly, in a *one-to-many* type of relationship, you need more than one field to make a record unique. See Chapter 12 for a complete discussion of keys and relationships.

Table 6-6 shows a list of the original data items and the reworked items for the Visits and Visit Details tables. The identification fields are shown in bold to set them apart.

Table 6-6
A Final Design of Data Items

Customer	Pets	Visits	Visit Details
Customer Number	Pet ID	Visit Number	Visit Number
Customer Name	Pet Name	Visit Date	Line Number
Street	Type of Animal	Discount	Type of Visit
City	Breed	Tax Rate	Treatment
State	Date of Birth	Total Amount	Treatment Price
ZIP Code	Last Visit Date		Medication
Phone Number	Length		Medication Price
Type of Customer	Weight		
Last Visit Date	Colors		
Discount	Gender		
	Neutered/Spayed		
	Current Vaccinations		
	Deceased		
	Picture		
	Comments		

These are not the final fields that will be used in the Mountain Animal Hospital database. Actually, many more changes will be made as the design is examined and enhanced.

Step 4: Table design and relationships

After you complete the data design, the next step is the final organization of the data in tables. The final design for the four tables is shown in Figure 6-6. This is an actual database diagram found in Microsoft Access.

Creating the final set of tables is easy if you have lots of experience. If you don't, that's all right, too, because Access lets you change a table definition after you've created it without losing any data. In Chapter 7, you'll actually create a table in Access.

In Figure 6-6, you can see the relationships that join one table to another. Notice the relationship between customers and pets. This is created by adding the Customer Number field to the Pets table. In this way, a pet has a relationship to its owner — the customer. The same is true for establishing a relationship between pets and each visit. The Pet ID field can be added to the Visits table so that the visit itself involves a pet in the Pets table. The relationship between Visits and Visit Details is established by the Visit Number field.

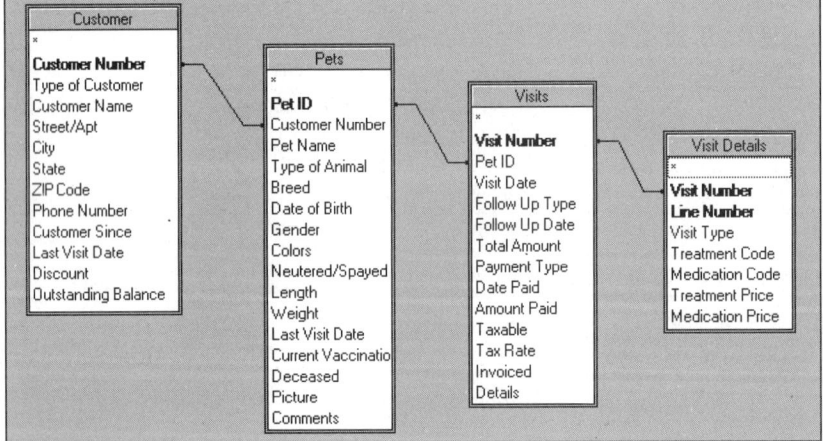

Figure 6-6: The final design: separating the data by function.

Setting relations

Later, in Chapter 12, you learn all about using multiple tables and how relations are set in Access. For now, this topic will be covered briefly so you can see how to design the relations between the various tables you've identified.

Tables are related to each other so that information in one table is accessible to another. In systems that are designed with Access, you usually have several tables all related to one another. Relations are established by having fields in both tables that share a common value. The field names in both tables need not be the same; only the values have to match. For example, in the Pets table, you have the customer number. By relating the customer number in the Pets table to the customer number in the Customer table, you can retrieve all there is to know about the customer. This setup saves you from having to store the data in two places.

That is the first reason to have a relation — for a table *lookup*. A field in one table can look up data in another table. There should also be a table lookup relation from the Visits table to the Pets table using the Pet ID field. Then, as you enter each item, data about the item, such as pet name, type of animal, breed, and date of birth, is passed from the Pets table to the Visits table.

There is a second reason to set a relation, however. As you decide how to relate the tables that you already designed, you must also decide how to handle multiple occurrences of data. In this system design, there can be multiple occurrences of visit details for each visit. When this happens, you should split the table into two tables. In this design, you need to place the visit number of the visit in a separate table from the single-occurrence visit. This new Visit Details table is related by the Visit Number field found in the Visits table.

The Visits and Visit Details tables are the central focus of the system. The Visits table needs to be related to the Pets table and also to the Customer table because it is important to be able to retrieve information from the Customer table. The reason is that the invoice report will need information from the Customer table. But you don't have to link the Visit table directly to the Customer table. You can go through the Pets table to get there. This is commonly referred to as a *chain link*. Figure 6-6 shows these relationships graphically. This figure shows an actual Access screen, which is the Query window, where you can set relations between tables.

The Pet ID field is entered as part of a visit and links the pet information to the Visits table. The Pets table uses the Customer Number field to retrieve the customer information from the Customer table, such as name and address. Although the name and address are not stored in the Visits tables, this information is needed to confirm that a pet in for a visit belongs to a particular customer.

Step 5: Field design — data-entry rules and validation

The next step is to define your fields and tables in much further detail. You also need to determine data-validation rules for each field and even define some new tables to help with data validation.

field names, types, and sizes

...name each field. The name should be easy to remember and yet descrip-...recognize the function of the field by its name. It should be just long ...scribe the field but not so short that it becomes cryptic. Access allows up to 64 c... ...ers for a field name, including spaces.

You must also decide what data type each of your fields will be. In Access, you have the option of several data types, as shown in Table 6-7.

Table 6-7
Data Types in Access

Data Type	Type of Data Stored
Text	Alphanumeric characters; up to 255 characters
Memo	Alphanumeric characters; long strings up to 64,000 characters
Number	Numeric values of many types and formats
Date/Time	Date and time data
Currency	Monetary data
Counter	Automatically incremented numeric counter
Yes/No	Logical values, Yes/No, True/False
OLE object	Pictures, graphs, sound, video, word processing, and spreadsheet files

These data types are explained in more detail in the next part of the book. One of these data types must be assigned to each of your fields. You also must specify the length of the text fields.

Designing data-entry rules

The last major decision to make concerns data validation. Data validation becomes important when data is input to make sure that only "good" data gets into a system. Good data can be defined as data that passes certain tests that you define. There are several types of data validation. You can test for known individual items, such as stipulating that the Gender field can accept only the values Male, Female, or Unknown. You can test for ranges such that the value of Weight must be between 0 and 1,500. Finally, you can test for compound conditions, such as finding whether the Type of Customer field indicates an individual, in which case the discount is 0 percent. Or, if the type of customer is a pet store, the discount field must show 20 percent, and, if the type of customer is a zoo, the discount is 50 percent. In the next chapter, you learn where you can enter conditions to perform data validation.

Designing lookup tables

Sometimes you need to design entire tables, known as *lookup tables*, to perform data validation or just to make it easier to create your system. For example, Mountain Animal Hospital needs a field to determine the customer's tax rate. So you decide to use a lookup table that contains the state code, state name, and state tax rate. This also allows you to enter no more than a two-digit state code in the Customer table and then look up the state name or tax rate when necessary. The state code then becomes the field that relates the tables. Because the tax rate can change, each time a visit record is created, the tax rate in force at that time is looked up, and the tax rate value is stored in the Visits table to capture the tax rate for each visit.

Although you can create a field on a data-entry form that limits the entry of valid genders to Male, Female, and Unknown, there are too many allowable animal types to create a field for this in a form. Rather, you can create a table with only one field, which is Type of Animal. The Type of Animal field in the Pets table is then used to link to this field in the Animals lookup table.

A lookup table is created in exactly the same way as any other table and then behaves as such. The only difference is in the way you use the table.

In Figure 6-7, notice that four lookup tables are added to the design. The States lookup table is necessary for determining an individual's tax rate. The Animal lookup table is added for ensuring that standard animal types are entered into the Pets table for the sake of consistency. The Animals lookup table is designed as an alphabetized listing of valid animal types.

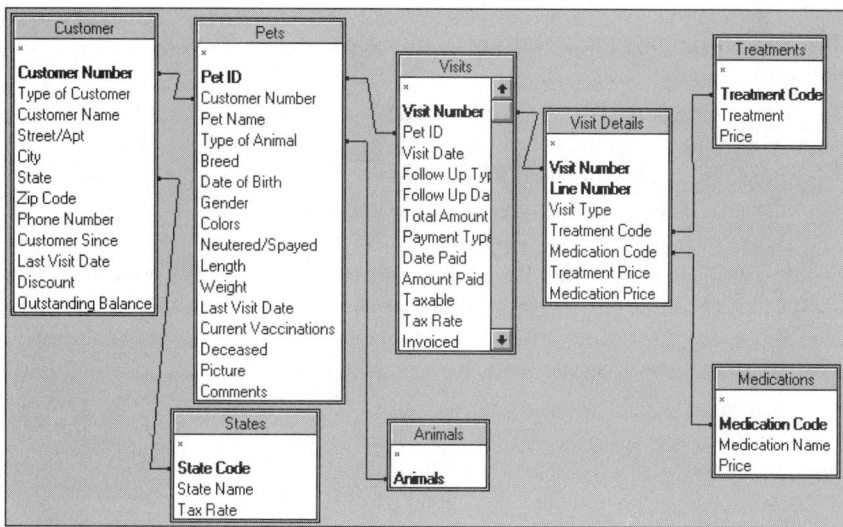

Figure 6-7: The final database diagram with lookup tables added.

The two tables on the far right, Treatments and Medications, are added for several reasons. The last thing you want is the doctor to be entering a long name to complete the Treatment or Medication fields after an animal's visit. The doctor should be able to either choose from a list or enter a simple code. The code can then be used for looking up and retrieving the treatment or medication name and the current price. In fact, the price that the doctor looks up must be stored in the Visit Details table, as prices can change between the time of the visit and the time the invoice is sent out. The Treatments lookup table is added for storing a listing of the treatments with their associated prices. Similarly, the Medications table is added for keeping a listing of the available medications with their associated prices.

Creating test data

After you define your data-entry rules and how the database should look, it's time to create test data. You need to prepare test data very scientifically in order to test many possible conditions. Test data should have many purposes. It should let you test the data entry. Do all the conditions you created generate the proper acceptance or error messages? You may find some conditions you should test for that you didn't think about. What happens when someone enters a blank into a field? How about numbers in a character field? Access automatically traps such things as bad dates or characters in Date and Numeric fields, but you must take care of the rest yourself.

You'll be creating two types of test data. The first is simply data that allows you to *populate,* or *fill,* the databases with meaningful data. This is the initial "good" data that should end up in the database and then be used to test output. Output will consist mainly of your reports. The second type of test data is used to test data entry. This includes designing data with errors that display every one of your error conditions, along with good data that can test some of your acceptable conditions.

Test data should let you test routine items of the type that you normally find in your data. You should also test for limits. Enter data that is only one character long for some fields and use every field. Create several records that use every position in the database (and thereby every position in the data-entry screen and in the reports).

Create some bad test data. Enter data that tests every condition. Try to enter a customer number that already exists. Try to change a customer number that's not in the file. These are just some of the things to consider when testing your system. Of course, testing your system begins with the test data.

Step 6: Form design — input

When the data and table relationships are established, it is time to design your forms. Forms are made up of the fields that can be input or viewed in the edit mode. If at all possible, your screens should look much like the forms that you'd use in a manual system. This setup makes for the most user-friendly system.

Designing data-entry screens

When you're performing form design, it is important to place three types of objects on the screen:

- Labels and text box data-entry fields
- Special controls (multiple-line text boxes, option buttons, list boxes, checkboxes, business graphs, and pictures)
- Graphic enhancements (color, lines, rectangles, and three-dimensional effects)

You should place your data fields on a form in the positions you want them. When you enter data, the cursor normally moves from top to bottom and left to right. But of course you can specify cursor movement from field to field. You can make the entry size any size you want. As you place the fields, you should make sure that you leave as much space around them as you will need. Calculated fields meant only for display can also be part of a data-entry form.

You can use labels to display messages, titles, or captions. Text boxes provide an area where you can type or display text or numbers that are in your database. Checkboxes indicate a condition and are either unchecked or checked (selected). Other types of controls available with Access include list boxes, combo boxes, option buttons, toggle buttons, and option groups.

Chapter 16 covers the various types of controls available in Access. Access provides a tool called Microsoft Graph that you can use to create a wide variety of graphs. You can display pictures using any OLE object that is stored in a database table.

In this book, you create several basic data-entry forms:

- The customer form
- The pets form
- The general visit information form
- The visit details form

The customer form

The Customer data-entry form shown in Figure 6-8 is the simplest of the data-entry forms you create in this book. It is very straightforward and simply lists the field descriptions on the left side, with the fields themselves on the right side. The unique key field is Customer Number. At the top of the form is the main header, which has the title of the type of data-entry form that it is: the Customer Data Entry Form. This simple form is created by use of a FormWizard (see Chapter 11 for details).

The pets form

The pets data entry form is more complicated. It contains several types of controls, including option buttons, a list box, several combo boxes, checkboxes, a picture, and a memo field. As shown in Figure 6-9, the form contains two sections. One section contains the pet information, and the other side of the form contains customer information. You learn how to create this form in Chapter 19.

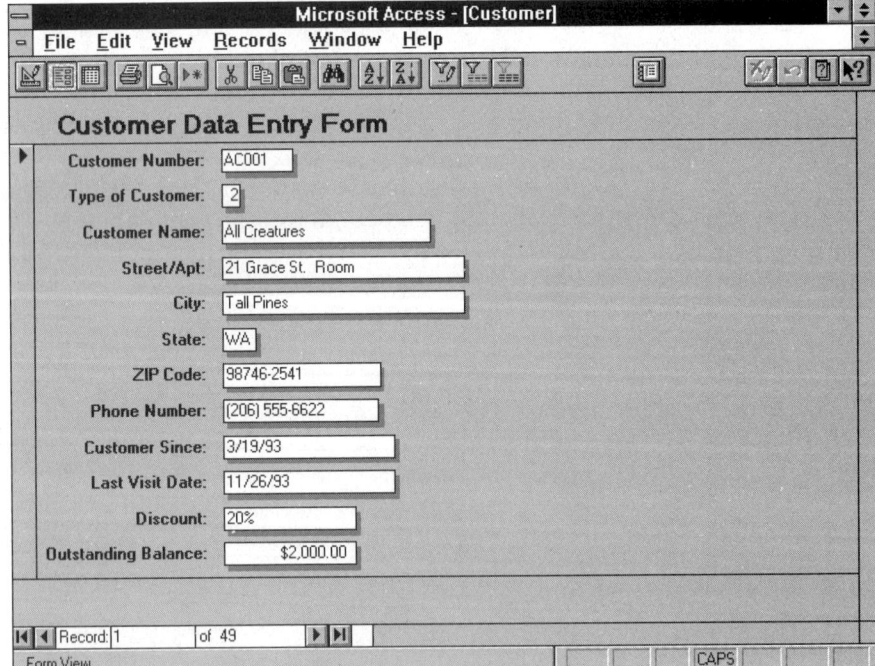

Figure 6-8: The Customer Data-Entry form.

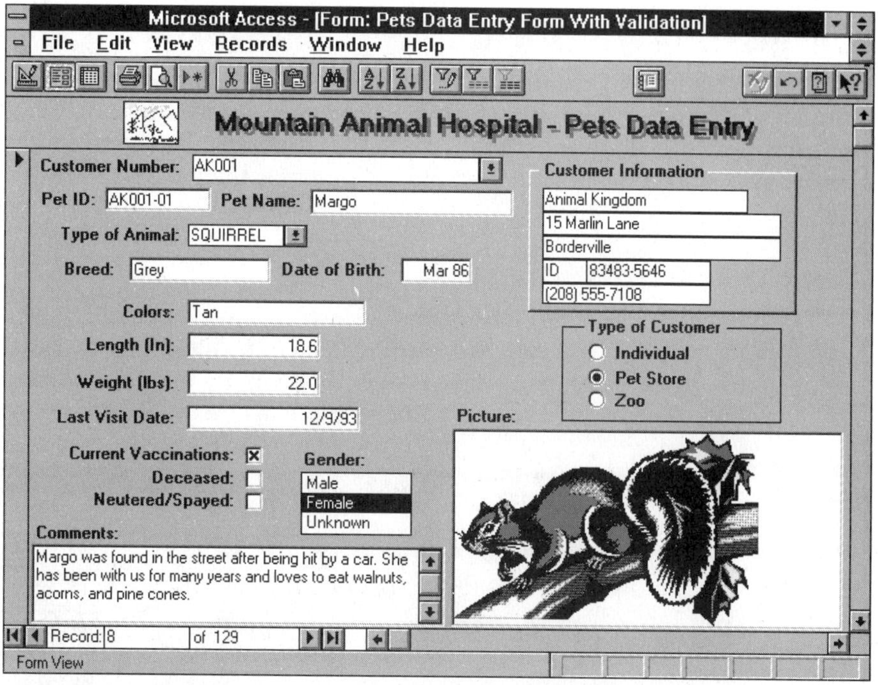

Chapter 6: A Case Study in Database Design

Figure 6-9:
The Pets Data-Entry form.

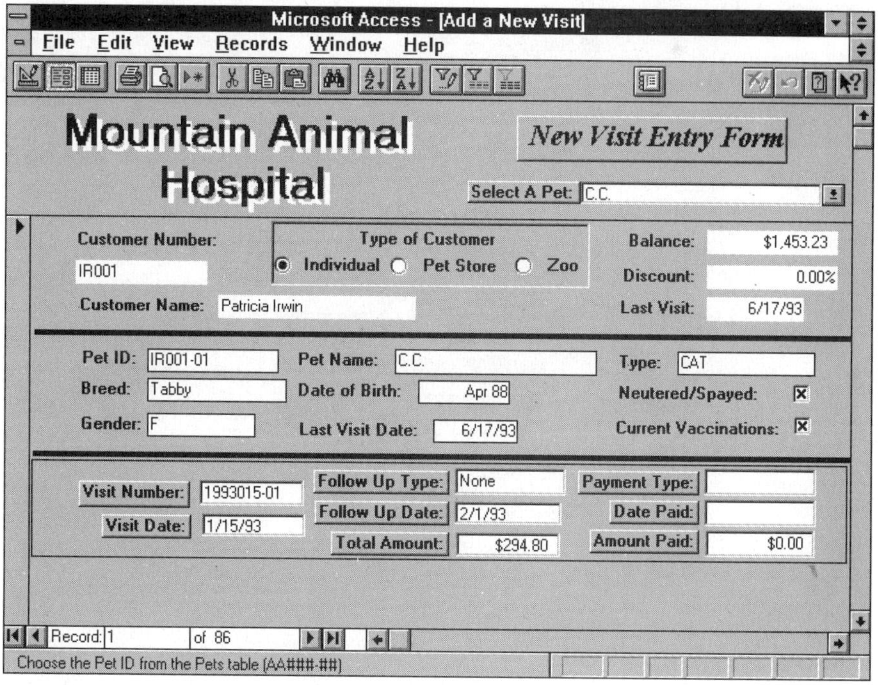

Figure 6-10:
The Visit Information Data-Entry form.

The general visit form

As shown in Figure 6-10, the next data-entry form is a general visit form. This form combines information from several tables. The key purpose of this form is to allow a user to enter information about the visits in the databases. This form contains information about customers, pets, and visits. Visit Number is the key field for this form.

The visit details form

The final form you see in this book is a form to add visit details, which is shown in Figure 6-11. You create this form in Chapter 28. This form contains a subform, so you can see many visit details at once. Many types of subforms can be linked to a form. You can even have a graph as a subform, as you discover in Chapter 20.

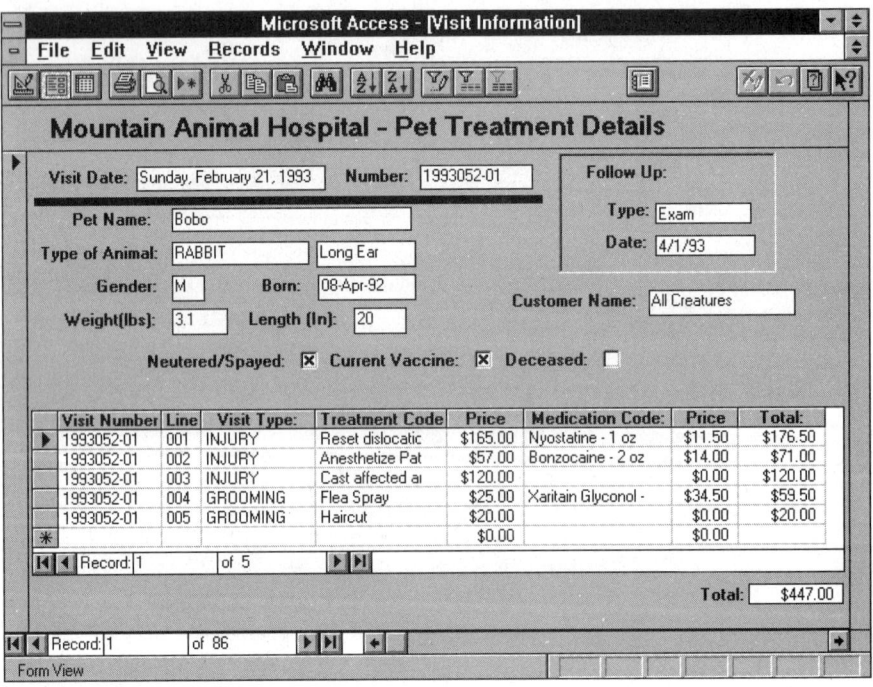

Figure 6-11:
A Visit Details Data-Entry form.

Step 7: Automation design — menus

After you create all your data, design your reports, and create your forms, it's time to tie them all together. You use switchboards and menus to tie a system together. Menus are the key to a good system. The user must be able to follow the system to understand how to move from place to place. Usually, each form or report is a menu choice. This means that in your design you must decide how to group the menus. From examining the overall design and looking at all your systems, you begin to see a distinct set of combinations. The data-entry and report forms and the reports designed so far are shown in Figure 6-12.

By use of Access macros, a menu is created at the top menu bar of the switchboard. The menu gives the user a choice of using pull-down menus or the switchboard buttons. You create this switchboard, along with the menus and a complicated dialog box, in Chapter 32.

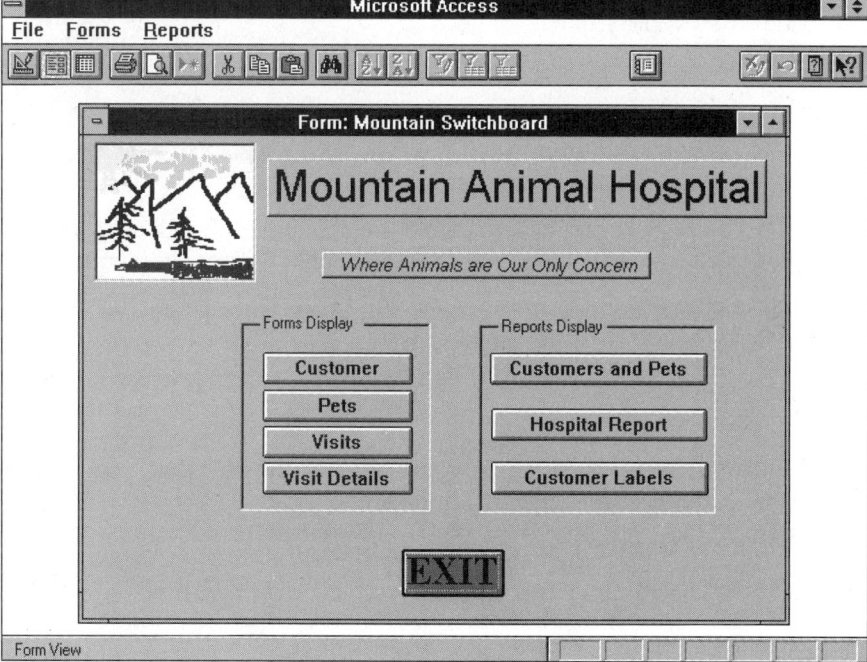

Figure 6-12: A switchboard and menu for the Mountain Animal Hospital.

Summary

In this chapter, you learned how to design reports properly and how to extract data items. You learned how to set relations and see the design of forms and menus that will be used in this book. You became acquainted with the Mountain Animal Hospital, which is a fictitious entity used to illustrate database processing. Mountain Animal Hospital is a medium-size veterinary hospital serving individuals, pet stores, and zoos in three states. The following points were explained:

- The seven-step method for design includes overall system design, report design, data design, table design, field design, form design, and menu design.

- The overall design phase helps you think through your system from concept to reality before you touch the keyboard. This makes implementation much more efficient.

- Report design lets you plan for the output necessary to provide information from your system.

- In data design, you extract fields from your report in order to group them logically.

- After you can group your fields logically, you can create tables in which to store your data. You can then define relationships between related tables.

- During field design, you define the data types of each field and their sizes. You also define data-entry rules to allow only valid data into your system.

- You can design forms by using the Access Form Design window, which gives you a WYSIWYG view of your data.

- In Access, you can create switchboards and menus to help you navigate through a system.

This chapter completes the first part of this book. In the next part, you learn how to create a table, enter and display data in datasheets, and create simple data-entry forms, queries, and reports. Finally, you learn how to use multiple files.

Part II

Basic Database Usage

- **101 Chapter 7:** Creating Database Tables
- **137 Chapter 8:** Entering, Changing, Deleting, and Displaying Data
- **175 Chapter 9:** Creating and Using Simple Data-Entry Forms
- **199 Chapter 10:** Understanding and Using Simple Queries
- **231 Chapter 11:** Creating and Printing Simple Reports
- **253 Chapter 12:** Setting Relationships between Multiple Tables

Creating Database Tables

CHAPTER 7

In This Chapter

- Creating a database
- Creating a table
- Navigating in the Table window
- Entering field names and descriptions
- Selecting a field data type
- Entering field properties
- Creating a primary key
- Changing a table design
- Saving and printing your table design
- Renaming, copying, and deleting tables

In this chapter, you learn how to start the process of database and table creation. You create a database container to hold the tables, queries, forms, reports, and macros that you create as you learn Access. You also create the Pets database table, which stores data about the pets serviced by the Mountain Animal Hospital.

Creating the Pets Table

The Pets table is one of the best examples in the Mountain Animal Hospital database because it illustrates the major field types used by Access. In most tables, you will find that the majority of fields are *text* fields. Most data in the world is either numbers or text. The Pets table contains many text fields to fully describe the animal but also contains several numeric fields to give the length and weight of each animal. Another common field type is *date and time*. The Pets table uses a date/time field to record the date of birth. The Pets table also contains several Yes/No fields used for making a single choice. Examples of this field are Neutered or Current Vaccination. Large amounts of text are stored in a *memo* field to record notes about the animal, such as special customer preferences or known allergies. Another field type is the *OLE* field. This field is used for storing sound, pictures, or even video. In the Pets example, this field will store a picture of the animal.

Before a table can be created, however, the overall database container must be created.

Creating a Database

The Database window displays all the various object files from your database that you may create while using Access. Actually, a database is a single file. As you create new object files, they are stored within the database file. The object files are not DOS files in themselves, as they are stored within the database file. The database file will start off at about 65,000 bytes and grow as new tables, queries, forms, reports, macros, and modules are created. As you add data to an Access database, the file size will also grow.

You can create a new database by selecting File⇨New Database... from the main Access menu, as shown in Figure 7-1, or by clicking the first icon in the toolbar.

Figure 7-1: Creating a new database by using File⇨New Database....

File	
New Database...	Ctrl+N
Open Database...	Ctrl+O
Compact Database...	
Convert Database...	
Encrypt/Decrypt Database...	
Repair Database...	
Toolbars...	
Unhide...	
Run Macro...	
Add-ins	▶
1 MTNSTART.MDB	
2 MTNANHSP.MDB	
3 D:\ACCESS20\FNLDISK\MTNANHSP.MDB	
4 D:\ACCESS20\FNLDISK\MTNANHS1.MDB	
Exit	

Create a new database now by clicking the first toolbar icon.

You can also create a new database by clicking the new database icon. This is the first icon in the toolbar.

Chapter 7: Creating Database Tables

After you start the creation process, you must create a name for the database. Figure 7-2 shows a standard Windows file box displayed. The file box has several areas. A default name of DB1.MDB is displayed in the File Name text box. You can simply type the name you want right over the default name. The MDB file extension is optional and will be added automatically when the file container is created. The filename for a database must conform to DOS naming conventions (eight characters or less). The database is a standard DOS file.

An Access 2.0 database cannot be used by Access 1.1 or 1.0.

Type **MTNANIML.MDB** in place of db1.MDB as the name for your database.

Only the database file conforms to DOS naming conventions. Virtually every other name for Access objects, such as tables, forms, and reports, can be up to 64 characters long.

If you enter a file extension other than MDB, Access saves the database file but does not display it when you later open the database. By default, Access searches and displays only those files with an MDB file extension.

The File Selector box displays a list of Access databases in the current subdirectory. The list is for reference only, so you use it only to see what databases already exist. All the database filenames appear *greyed out,* as they are not selectable. You can switch to a different subdirectory or drive to save the new database container by using the drive or directory selector boxes.

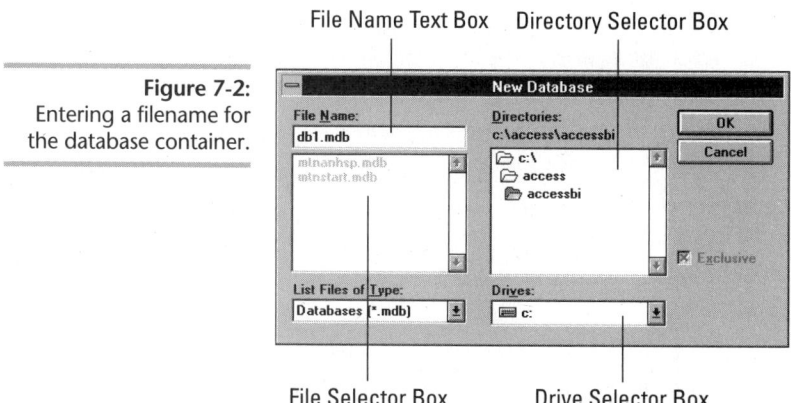

Figure 7-2: Entering a filename for the database container.

Access ignores the Caps Lock status when you enter a database filename. The name is always displayed and saved in lowercase.

Following Along in This Book

If you are following along with the examples in this book, note that we have chosen the name MTNANIML for the name of the database that you create as you complete the chapters. This database is for our hypothetical business, the Mountain Animal Hospital. After you enter the filename, Access creates the empty database. The files on the disk that comes with your book are MTNSTART, containing only the database tables, and MTNANHSP, containing the completed application, including tables, forms, queries, reports, and macros.

The Database Window

The Database window is shown in Figure 7-3. After you create or open a database, the look of the screen changes; additional menus are displayed that enable you to perform a variety of tasks. A toolbar is displayed so that you can quickly create a new query, form, or report, or get help.

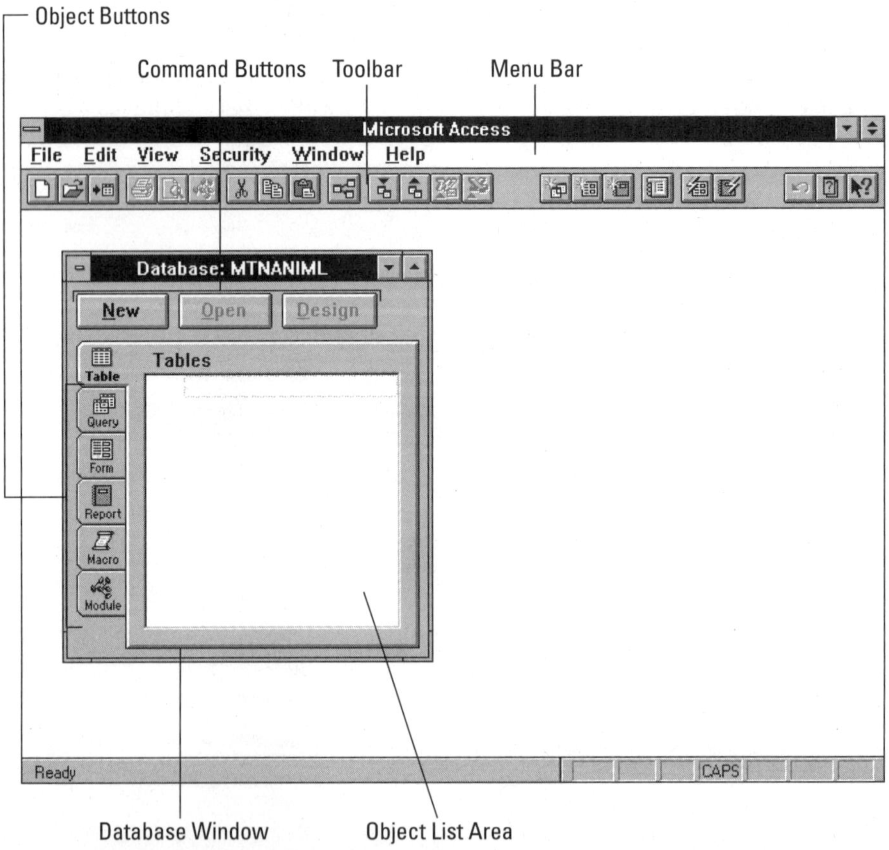

Figure 7-3: The Database window and the empty database.

Object buttons

The Database window contains picture buttons known as *object buttons* to let you quickly select any of these six objects available in Access:

- Tables
- Queries
- Forms
- Reports
- Macros
- Modules

As you create new object files, the names of the files appear in the Database window. You see only the files for the particular object type that is selected at that time. You can select an object type by clicking one of the object buttons.

The Database window toolbar

The toolbar shown in Figure 7-4 enables you to perform tasks quickly without using the menus and can be very productive. Tools that are not available are displayed in light gray.

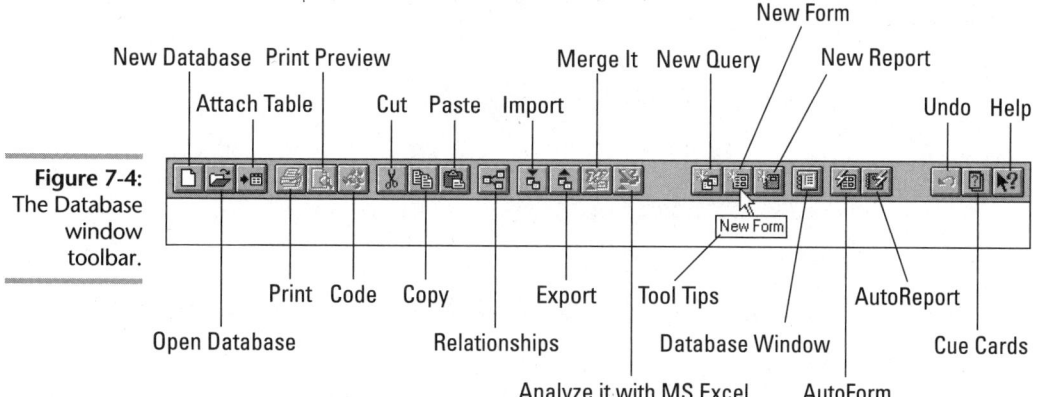

Figure 7-4: The Database window toolbar.

If you place the cursor on an icon without clicking, a help prompt will appear just below the icon, as shown in Figure 7-4.

Controlling Access 2.0 toolbars

In Access 2.0, you have complete control over your toolbars. You can move them, resize them, and even customize them. The toolbar is no longer anchored to the horizontal area just below the menu bar. You can place your cursor in any area of the toolbar between the icons and then drag the toolbar. As you drag the toolbar around the screen, it changes size and shape. In the middle of the screen, it can be sized to any shape you desire and can float anywhere on the screen. As it is dragged to the borders of the screen, it becomes horizontal on the top or bottom of the screen, vertical on the left or right, and anchors itself to the nearest border.

Normally, only the toolbar that belongs to a design screen is displayed. The menu View ⇨ Tool<u>b</u>ars... allows you to select from the various toolbars (one for each type of design screen) and determine which ones are to be simultaneously displayed on each screen. Sometimes, this makes no sense as every icon is *grayed out* as it is not appropriate for a specific screen.

Figure 7-5 shows the Toolbar customization screen. To add an icon to the toolbar, you would first press the Customize button to display it on the screen and then drag the new icon from the customization screen to the toolbar. To remove an icon, you would drag an icon from the toolbar and release the mouse button anywhere off the toolbar.

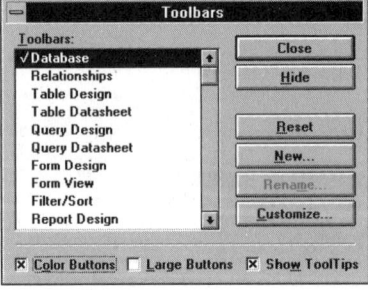

Figure 7-5: Customizing a toolbar.

The Database window command buttons

The command buttons in the Database window enable you to create a <u>N</u>ew object or <u>O</u>pen an existing object. You can also open an existing object for changes by selecting <u>D</u>esign mode. When the button is selected, the appropriate action is taken. Before selecting <u>O</u>pen or <u>D</u>esign, you should select a filename. When you select <u>N</u>ew, the type of the new object depends on the object button that you previously selected. If the Table button is selected, a new table is created. When some of the other object buttons are selected, the command buttons will change. For example, when you select Report, the three available command buttons are <u>N</u>ew, <u>P</u>review, and <u>D</u>esign. When you select a macro or module object, the button choices are <u>N</u>ew, <u>R</u>un, and <u>D</u>esign.

Creating a New Table

After you design your table on paper, you need to create the table design in Access. Although you can create the table interactively without any forethought, carefully planning out any database system is a good idea. You can make any type of changes later, but doing so wastes time and generally results in a system that is harder to maintain than one that is well planned from the beginning.

The table design process

Creating a table design is a multistep process. By following the steps in order, you can easily and quickly create your table design with a minimum of effort. You should create your table design by following these steps:

1. Create a new table.
2. Enter each field name, data type, and description.
3. Enter properties for each field you have defined.
4. Set a primary key.
5. Create indexes for necessary fields.
6. Save your design.

You can use two methods to create a new table. You can click the New command button in the Database window, or you can select File⇨New⇨Table from the menus.

If you create a new table by clicking the New command button in the Database window, make sure that the Table object button is selected first.

Select the first icon in the database toolbar to create a new table.

The New Table Dialog Box

The New Table dialog box is displayed as shown in Figure 7-6. This allows you to create a new table automatically with a wizard, or in a more traditional manner by entering each field name in the table.

Press the New Table button in the dialog box to create a new table.

Figure 7-6:
The New Table dialog box.

Using the Table Wizard

When you create a new table, you can type in every field name, data type, size, and other table property information or you can use the *Table Wizard* as shown in Figure 7-7 to select from a long list of predefined tables and fields.

Wizards can save you a lot of work. Wizards are meant to not only save you time but to make complex tasks much easier. Wizards work by taking you through a series of screens that *ask* you what you want. You answer these *questions* by clicking on buttons, selecting fields, entering text, and making yes/no decisions.

In the table wizard, you first choose between a list of either **Business** or **Personal** tables. Some of the Business tables include mailing list, contacts, employees, products, orders, suppliers, payments, invoices, fixed assets, students, and more. The Personal list includes guests, recipes, exercise log, plants, wine list, photographs, video collection, and more. You can even add more tables and field definitions if you want by using the Add-In Manager, found on the File menu.

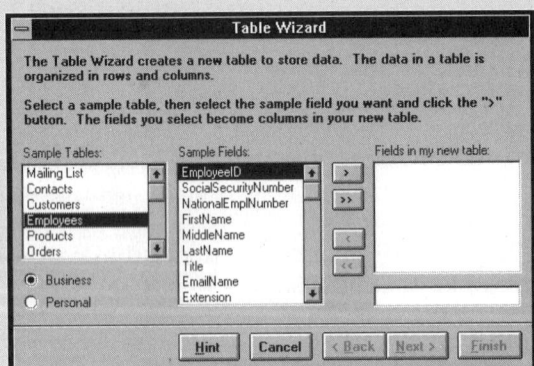

Figure 7-7: A table wizard screen.

When you select a table, a list of all the fields you might want in the table are displayed. You can then select only the fields you want in your table. They are all predefined for data type and size. You can select your fields and you can even rename a field once it's selected. Once you've chosen your fields, another screen is used to automatically create a primary key for you. Other screens will then help you automatically link the primary key to another table and establish relationships. Finally, the wizard can display the table, let you enter records into a datasheet, or even create an automatic form for you. The entire process of creating a simple table and form can take less than one minute! Whenever, you need to create a table for an application on the list, you can save a lot of time. Because you can customize the list of tables and fields using the Add-In manager, it becomes a tool that can grow with you too.

The Table window

The empty Table window is displayed in Figure 7-8. The Table window consists of two areas:

- The field entry area
- The property area or field property area

The *field entry area* is used for entering each field's name and data type and an optional description. The *property area* is used for entering more options for each field. Properties include field size, format, input mask, alternate caption for forms, default value, validation rules, required, zero length for null checking, and index specifications.

You can switch between areas (also referred to as *panes*) by clicking the mouse in the desired pane or by pressing F6.

You can also create an Access table by importing data from other databases, such as dBASE and Paradox. Or you can attach an external table to your database, leaving the data in its original form but giving it the appearance of an Access table. Importing and attaching external database files are described in Chapter 24.

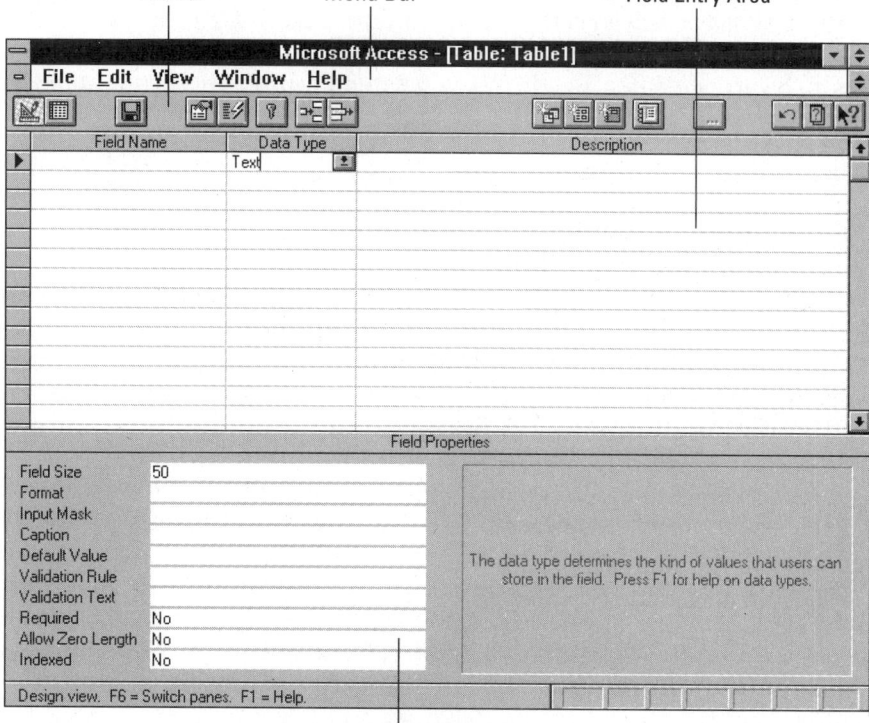

Figure 7-8: The empty Table Design window.

Using the Table window toolbar

The Table window toolbar, shown in Figure 7-9, contains many icons to assist you in creating a new table definition.

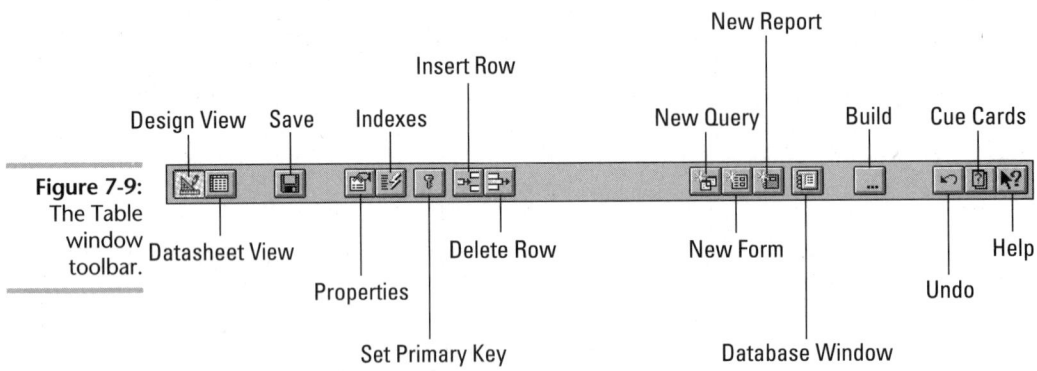

Figure 7-9: The Table window toolbar.

Creating Fields

You create fields by entering a field name and a field data type in each row of the field entry area of the Table window. The field description is an option to identify the field's purpose and is displayed in the status bar during data entry. After you enter each field's name and data type, you can further specify how each field is used by entering properties in the property area. But, before you enter any properties, you should enter all your field names and data types for this example.

Naming a field

A field name identifies the field both to you and to Access. Field names should be properly named to best suit your purpose. Names should be long enough to identify the purpose of the field but not overly long. Later, as you enter validation rules or use the field name in a calculation, you'll want to save yourself from unnecessary typing of long field names.

Enter a field name by positioning the pointer in the first row of the Table window under the Field Name column. Then enter a valid field name, observing the following rules for valid field names:

- Field names can be from 1 to 64 characters.
- Field names can include letters, numbers, and many special characters.

- Field names cannot include a period (.), exclamation point (!), or brackets ([ ]).
- You cannot use low-order ASCII characters (ASCII values 0–32).
- You cannot start with a blank space.

Field names can be entered in upper-, lower-, or mixed-case. If you make a mistake while entering the field name, you can simply position the pointer where you want to make the changes and change the name. If you spell a field name incorrectly, you can change it at any time. You can change a field name in a table even if it contains data.

Once you save your table, if you change a field name that is used in queries, forms, or reports, you will have to change it in those objects, too.

Specifying a data type

After you name a field, you must decide what type of data the field will hold. You should have a good grasp on the type of data that you'll enter into your system before you begin. Eight basic types of data are shown in Table 7-1. You'll note that some types have several options, such as numbers.

Table 7-1
Data Types Available in Microsoft Access

Data Type	Type of Data Stored	Storage Size
Text	Alphanumeric characters	0 – 255 bytes
Memo	Alphanumeric characters	0 – 32,000 bytes
Number	Numeric values	1, 2, 4, or 8 bytes
Date/Time	Date and time data	8 bytes
Currency	Monetary data	8 bytes
Counter	Automatic number increments	4 bytes
Yes/No	Logical values: Yes/No, True/False	1 bit (0 or –1)
OLE Object	Pictures, graphs, sound, video	Up to 128MB

The Data Type menu is shown in Figure 7-10. When you move the pointer into the Data Type column, a down arrow appears in the text entry box. To open this menu, move the cursor into the Data Type column and click on the down arrow.

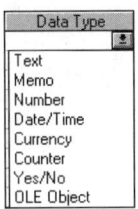

Figure 7-10:
The Data Type menu.

Text data is any type of data that is simply characters. Names, addresses, and descriptions are all text data. Numeric data that are not used in a calculation, such as phone numbers, social security numbers, and ZIP codes, are also text data. The maximum length of data that can be entered into a text field is 255 characters; you specify the size of each text field in the property area. Regardless of the number of characters you later enter into that field, you will automatically use the number of characters that you specify for each record because blanks will fill any remaining positions. You should probably limit text data to 50 characters, unless you plan to enter as many characters as you specify into each record. Assume, for example, that you specify a text field as 90 characters. Then, after you enter 100 records, only 10 of them have used more than 20 of the 90 characters allowed. You can see that you are wasting a great deal of storage space. You should then consider using a Memo data type.

The *Memo* data type holds a variable amount of data, from 0 to 32,000 characters for each record. Therefore, if one record uses 100 characters, another requires only 10, and yet another needs 3,000, you still use only as much space as each record requires. You therefore considerably cut down on the amount of space your database requires.

The *Number* data type enables you to enter numeric data. Numeric fields hold data that will be used in mathematical calculations. If you have data that will be used in monetary calculations, you should use the Currency data type, which enables you to specify many different currency types.

The *Date/Time* data type can store dates, times, or both types of data at once. Thus, you can enter a date, a time, or a date/time combination. Many types of formats can be specified in the property entry area, so you can display the date and time data according to your preference.

The *Counter* data type stores an integer that Access automatically increments as you add new records. The Counter data type is frequently used as a unique record identification for tables having no other unique value. For example, if you have no unique identification for a list of names, you can use a Counter field to identify one John Smith from another.

The *Yes/No* data type holds data that has one of two values and therefore can be expressed as a binary state. Data is actually stored as –1 for yes and 0 for no. However, you can adjust the format setting for a display of Yes/No, True/False, or On/Off. By using a Yes/No data type, you can use many of the form controls especially designed for this type of data.

The *OLE Object* data type provides access for data that is capable of being linked to an OLE server. This type of data includes bitmaps, such as Windows Paintbrush files; audio files, such as WAV files; business graphics, such as those found in Access and Excel; and even full-motion video files. Of course, you can play the video files only if you have the hardware and necessary OLE server software.

Entering a field description

The field description is completely optional; you use it only to help you remember a field's uses or to let another user know its purpose. Often, you don't use the description column at all, or you use it only for fields whose purpose is not readily recognizable. If you enter a field description, it is displayed in the status bar whenever you use that field in Access. The field description can help to clarify a field whose purpose is ambiguous or can give the user more explanation about valid values for the field during data entry.

Completing the Pets Table

The completed Pets table field entries are shown in Figure 7-11. If you are following along with the examples, you should create this table now. Enter the field names and data types exactly as shown:

Steps:	Entering a Field
Step 1.	Place the pointer in the Field Name column in the row where you want to enter the field.
Step 2.	Enter the field name and press Enter (you can also press Tab).
Step 3.	In the Data Type column, click the down arrow and select the data type.
Step 4.	Place the pointer in the Description column and type a description (optional).

Repeat each of these steps to complete the Pets data entry for all fields. You can press the down-arrow key to move between rows or simply use the mouse and click any row.

Figure 7-11: The completed Pets table design.

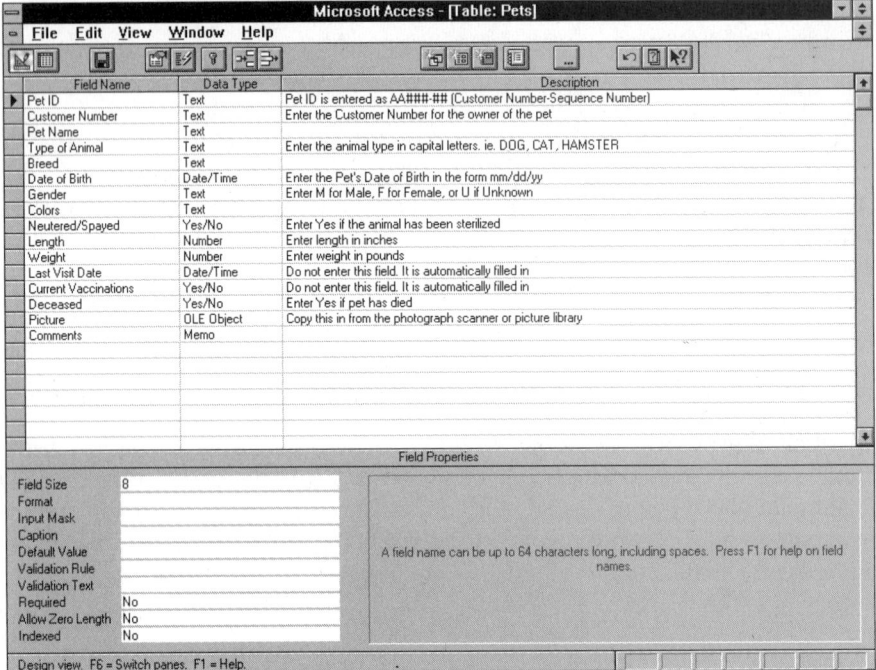

You can also type in the name of the data type or the first unique letters. The type will be automatically validated to make sure that it is on the drop-down list. A warning message is displayed for an invalid type.

Understanding Field Properties

After the field names, data types, and field descriptions are entered, you may want to go back and further define each field. Each field has *properties,* and the properties are different for each data type. In the Pets table, you must enter properties for several data types. Figure 7-12 shows the property area for the field Pet ID. Ten options are shown for the Pet ID field.

You can switch between the field entry area and the property area by pressing F6. You can also move between panes by simply clicking the desired pane. Some of the properties will display a list of the possible values. Properties with these lists display a downward-pointing arrow when the pointer is moved into the field. When you click the arrow, the values are displayed in a drop-down list.

Here is a list of all the properties (note that they may not all be displayed, depending on which data type was chosen):

Field Size	Text: limits size of the field to the specified number of characters (1–255)
	Numeric: allows specification of numeric type
Format	Changes the way data is displayed after it is entered (upper-case, dates, and so on)
Input Mask	Used for data entry into a predefined and validated format (Phone Numbers, ZIP Codes, Social Security Numbers, Dates, Custom IDs)
Decimal Places	Specifies number of decimal places (Numeric/Currency only)
Caption	Optional label for form and report fields (replacing the field name)
Default Value	The value automatically filled in for new data entry into the field
Validation Rule	Validates data based on rules created through expressions or macros
Validation Text	Message display when data fails validation
Required	Specifies whether or not a value must be entered into a field
Allow Zero Length	Determines if the value " " can be entered into a text field type to distinguish it from a null value
Indexed	Speeds up data access and, if desired, limits data to unique values

Entering field size properties

Field Size has two purposes. For Text fields, it simply specifies the storage and display size. For example, the field size for the Pet ID field is 8 bytes. You should enter the size for each field with a text data type. If you don't change the default field size, 50 bytes will be used for each record for the text field. You should limit the size to the value equal to the largest number of characters.

For Numeric data types, the field size enables you to further define the type of number, which determines the storage size. Figure 7-12 shows the property area for the Length Numeric field. There are five options in the Numeric Field Size property, as described in Table 7-2.

Figure 7-12:
Property area for the Length Numeric field.

Field Size	Single
Format	Standard
Decimal Places	1
Input Mask	
Caption	Length (In)
Default Value	0
Validation Rule	<120
Validation Text	Length must be less than 120"
Required	No
Indexed	No

Table 7-2
Numeric Field Settings

Field Size Setting	Range	Decimal Places	Storage Size
Byte	0 to 255	None	1 byte
Integer	– 32,768 to 32,767	None	2 bytes
Long Integer	– 2,147,483,648 to 2,147,483,647	None	4 bytes
Double	– 1.797 x 10^{308} to 1.797 x 10^{308}	15	8 bytes
Single	– 3.4 x 10^{38} to 3.4 x 10^{38}	7	4 bytes

You should make the field size the smallest one possible because Access will run faster with smaller field sizes. Note that the first three settings don't use decimal points but allow increasingly larger positive or negative numbers. The last two choices permit even larger numbers: Single gives you 7 decimal places, and Double allows 15. Use the Double setting when you need many decimal places or very large numbers.

Remember, data that stores monetary amounts should be defined with the Currency data type.

Using formats

Formats allow your data to be displayed differently from the actual keystrokes used to originally enter the data. Formats vary, depending on the data type you use. Some data types have predefined formats, whereas others only have user-defined formats, and some types have both. Formats affect only the way your data appears and not how it is actually stored in the table or how it is entered.

Text and Memo data type formats

Access uses four user-defined format symbols in text and memo data types:

@   Required text character (character or space)

&   Text character not required

| < | Forces all characters to lowercase |
| > | Forces all characters to uppercase |

The symbols @ and & work with individual characters that are input, but the < and > characters affect the whole entry. If you want to make sure that a name is always displayed as uppercase, you enter > in the Format property. If you want to enter a phone number and allow entry of only the numbers, yet display the data with parentheses and a dash, you enter the following into the Format property: **(@@@)@@@-@@@@**. You can then enter **2035551234** and have the data displayed as (203)555-1234.

In Access 2.0, the Input Mask property should be used to more precisely control data input.

Number and Currency data type formats

You can choose from six predefined formats for Numeric or Currency formats and many symbols for creating your own custom formats. The predefined formats are as shown in Table 7-3, along with a column showing how to define custom formats.

Table 7-3
Numeric Format Examples

Format Type	Number as Entered	Number as Displayed	Format Defined
General	987654.321	987654.321	######.###
Currency	987654.321	$987,654.32	$###,##0.00
Fixed	987654.321	987654.321	######.###
Standard	987654.321	987,654.321	###,###.###
Percent	.987	98.7%	###.##%
Scientific	987654.321	9.87654321E+05	#.####E+00

Date/Time data type formats

The Date/Time data formats are the most extensive of all the formats, giving you these seven predefined formats:

General Date   (Default) Display depends on the value entered; if only a date is entered, that is all that is displayed; if only time is entered, no date is displayed; standard format for date and time is 2/10/93 10:32 PM

Long Date   Taken from Windows International Control Panel Long Date setting; example: Wednesday, February 10, 1993

Medium Date	Example: 10-Feb-93
Short Date	Taken from Windows International Control Panel Short Date setting; example: 2/10/93
Long Time	Taken from Windows International Control Panel Time setting; example: 10:32:15 PM
Medium Time	Example: 10:32 PM
Short Time	Example: 22:32

You can also use a multitude of user-defined date and time defined settings, including the following:

: (colon)	Time separator; taken from Windows International Control Panel Separator setting
/	Date separator
c	Same as General Date format
d, dd	Day of the month — 1 or 2 numerical digits (1 – 31)
ddd	First three letters of the weekday (Sun – Sat)
dddd	Full name of the weekday (Sunday – Saturday)
ddddd	Same as Short Date format
dddddd	Same as Long Date format
w	Day of the week (1 – 7)
ww	Week of the year (1 – 53)
m, mm	Month of the year — 1 or 2 digits (1 – 12)
mmm	First three letters of the month (Jan – Dec)
mmmm	Full name of the month (January – December)
q	Date displayed as quarter of the year (1 – 4)
y	Number of the day of the year (1 – 366)
yy	Last two digits of the year (01 – 99)
yyyy	Full year (0100 – 9999)
h, hh	Hour — 1 or 2 digits (0 – 23)
n, nn	Minute — 1 or 2 digits (0 – 59)
s, ss	Seconds — 1 or 2 digits (0 – 59)

ttttt	Same as Long Time format
AM/PM or A/P	Twelve-hour clock with AM/PM in uppercase as appropriate
am/pm or a/p	Twelve-hour clock with am/pm in lowercase as appropriate
AMPM	Twelve-hour clock with forenoon/afternoon designator, as defined in the Windows International Control Panel forenoon/afternoon setting

Yes/No data type formats

Yes/No data is stored differently in Access from what you might expect. The Yes data is stored as a –1, whereas No data is stored as a 0. You'd expect it to be stored as a 0 for No, with a 1 for Yes. This simply isn't the case. Without a format setting, you must enter –1 or 0, and it will be stored and displayed that way. With formats, you can store Yes/No data types in a more recognizable manner. The three predefined format settings for Yes/No data types are as follows:

Yes/No	(Default) Displays –1 as Yes, 0 as No
True/False	Stores –1 as True, 0 as False
On/Off	Stores –1 as On, 0 as Off

You can also enter user-defined formats. User-defined Yes/No formats have two to three sections. The first section is always a semicolon (;). The second section is used for the –1 (Yes) values, and the last section is used for the 0 (No) values. For example, if you want to use the values Neutered for Yes and Fertile for No, you enter **";Neutered;Fertile"**. You can also specify a color to display different values. To display the Neutered value in red and the Fertile value in green, you enter **";Neutered[Red];Fertile[Green]"**.

Entering formats

The Pets table uses several formats. Several of the Text fields have a > in the Format property to display the data entry in uppercase. The Date of Birth field has an mmm yy display of the date of birth as the short month name, a space, and a two-digit year (Feb 90).

Numeric custom formats can vary, based on the value. You can enter a four-part format into the Format property. The first part is for positive numbers, the second for negatives, the third if the value is 0, and the last if the value is null — for example, **#,##0;(#,##0);"-0-";"None"**.

Table 7-4, for example, shows several formats.

Table 7-4
Format Examples

Format Specified	Data as Entered	Formatted Data as Displayed
>	Adam Smith	ADAM SMITH
#,##0;(#,##0);"-0-";"None"	15 -15 0 No Data	15 (15) -0- None
Currency	12345.67	$12,345.67
"Acct No. "0000	3271	Acct No. 3271
mmm yy	9/11/93	Sep 93
Long Date	9/11/93	Friday, September 11, 1993

Entering input masks

Input masks allow you to have more control over data entry by defining data validation placeholders for each character that is entered into a field. For example, if you set the property to (999)000-0000, parentheses and hyphens are displayed as shown, and an underscore (_) is displayed in place of each 9 or 0 of this phone number template. You would see (___)___-____ in your data entry field. Access will automatically add a \ character before each literal. For example, \(999\)000\-0000. You can also enter a multipart input mask. Another example of this would be **(999)000-0000!;0;" "**. The input mask can contain up to three parts separated by semicolons.

The first part specifies the input mask itself (for example, (999) 000-0000!). The ! is used to fill the Input Mask from right to left when optional characters are on the left side. The second part specifies whether Microsoft Access stores the literal display characters in the table when you enter data. If you use 0 for this part, all literal display characters (for example, the parentheses and hyphen) are stored with the value; if you enter 1 or leave this part blank, only characters typed into the text box are stored. The third part specifies the character that Microsoft Access displays for spaces in the input mask. You can use any character. The default is an underscore. If you want to display a space, use a space enclosed in quotation marks (" ").

When you have defined an input mask and set the Format property for the same data, the Format property takes precedence when the data is displayed. This means that even if you've saved an input mask with data, the input mask is ignored when data is formatted.

Some of the characters that can be used are shown in Table 7-5.

Table 7-5
Input Mask Characters

Character	Description
0	Digit (0-9, entry required, plus [+] and minus [-] signs not allowed).
9	Digit or space (entry not required, [+]/[-] not allowed).
#	Digit or space (entry not required, blanks converted to spaces, [+]/[-] allowed).
L	Letter (A-Z, entry required).
?	Letter (A-Z, entry optional).
A	Letter or digit (entry required).
a	Letter or digit (entry optional).
&	Any character or a space (entry required).
C	Any character or a space (entry optional).
<	Causes all characters that follow to be converted to lowercase.
>	Causes all characters that follow to be converted to uppercase.
!	Causes input mask to fill from right to left, rather than from left to right, when characters on the left side of the input mask are optional. You can include the exclamation point anywhere in the input mask.
\	Causes the character that follows to be displayed as the literal character (for example, \A is displayed as just A).

Setting the Input Mask property to the word **Password** creates a password entry text box. Any character typed in the text box is stored as the character but is displayed as an asterisk (*).

The input mask wizard

Instead of setting the property to create an input mask, you should create your input mask using the Input Mask Wizard for common masks. When you click the Input Mask property, the builder button (three periods) appears. You can click the Build button to start the wizard.

The first Input Mask wizard screen is shown in Figure 7-13. The name of each predefined input mask and an example of it are shown in the wizard. You can choose from the list of predefined masks. If you click the *Try It* text box, you can see how data entry will look. Once you choose the input mask, the next wizard screen lets you customize it and determine the placeholder symbol. Another wizard screen lets you decide if any special characters are stored with the data. When you complete the wizard, the actual Input Mask characters are placed in the property sheet.

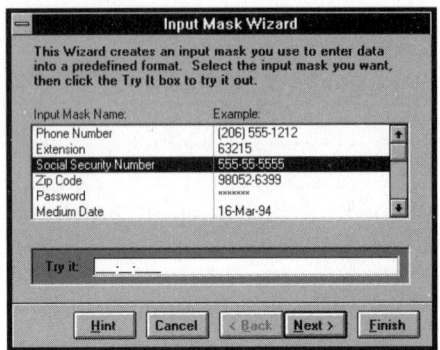

Figure 7-13:
An Input Mask Wizard screen.

You can enter as many custom masks as you want using the Add-In manager found in the File menu. Input Masks are entered and displayed based on the international settings chosen.

Entering decimal places

Decimal places are valid only for numeric or currency data. The number of decimal places can be from 0 to 15, depending on the field size of the numeric or currency field. If the field size is Byte, Integer, or Long Integer, you can have 0 decimal places. If the field size is Single, you can enter from 0 to 7 for the Decimal Places property. If the field size is Double, you can enter from 0 to 15 for the Decimal Places property. If you define a field as Currency or use one of the predefined formats, such as General, Fixed, or Standard, the number of decimal places is automatically set to 2. You can override this setting by entering a different value into the Decimal Places property.

Creating a caption

Captions are used when you want to display an alternative to the field name on forms and reports. Normally, the label used to describe a field in a form or a report is the field name. Sometimes you want to call the field name one thing while displaying a more (or less) descriptive label. You should keep field names as short as possible, which makes it easier to use them in calculations. You may then want a longer name to be used for a label in forms or reports. For example, you may use the field name *Length* but want the label *Length (in)* on all forms.

Setting a default value

A default value is the one automatically displayed for the field when a new record is added to the table. This value can be any value that matches the data type of the field. A default is no more than an initial value and can be changed during data entry. To enter a default value, simply enter the desired value into the Default Value property setting. A default value can be an expression, as well as a number or a text string. See Chapter 13 to learn how to create expressions.

Numeric and Currency data types are automatically set to 0 when a new record is added.

Understanding data validation

Data validation enables you to limit the values that will be accepted into a field. Validation may be automatic, such as the checking of a numeric field for text or a valid date. Validation can also be user-defined. User-defined validation can be as simple as a range of values, such as those found in the Length or Weight fields, or validation can be an expression like the one found in the Gender field.

Figure 7-12 (shown earlier) displays the property area for the Length field. Notice the validation options for the Length field. The Validation Rule <120 specifies that the number entered must be less than 120. The Validation Text Length must be less than 120" is displayed in a warning dialog box (see Figure 7-14) if a user tries to enter a length greater than 120.

Figure 7-14: Warning dialog box for the Length Numeric field.

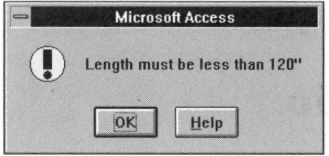

You can also use Date values with Date/Time data types in range validation. Dates are surrounded, or *delimited,* by pound signs when used in data validation expressions. If you want to limit the Date of Birth data entry to dates between January 1, 1980, and December 31, 1995, you enter **Between #1/1/80# and #12/31/95#.**

If you want to limit the upper end to the current date, you can enter a different set of dates, such as **Between #1/1/80# and Date().**

The Gender field contains a validation rule based on an expression. The Gender field validation rule is to limit the data entry to three values: M for Male, F for Female, and U for Unknown. The validation rule for this is InStr("MFU",[Gender])>0. The expression InStr means to validate that the entry is in the string specified.

Following Along in This Book

Following the design displayed in Figure 7-15, you should now be able to complete all the property areas in the Pets database. This database and others you see throughout this book are also found in the MTNSTART and MTNANHSP files on the disk that accompanies this book.

Figure 7-15: Properties for the Pets Table.

Pets Table Properties

Field Name	Field Size	Format	Input Mask	Caption	Default Value	Validation Rule	Validation Text	Required	Allow Zero Length	Index
Pet ID	8		LL000-00;0					Yes		Yes
Customer Number	10							Yes		No
Pet Name	35									No
Type of Animal	20									No
Breed	20									No
Date of Birth		mmm yy			#1/1/70 - DATE()		Date of Birth is Invalid	Yes		No
Gender	7	>@				M, F, U	Value must be M, F, or U			No
Colors	50									No
Neutered Spayed					No					No
Length	Single	Standard 1 decimal		Length(In)	0	< 120	Length must be less than 120"			No
Weight	Single	Standard 1 decimal		Weigth(lbs)	0	0 - 1500	Weight must be less than 1500lbs			No
Last Visit Date										No
Current Vaccinations										No
Deceased										No
Picture										No
Comments										No

Determining the Primary Key

Every table should have a *primary key*. The primary key is one or more fields that make a record unique. This is called *entity integrity* in the world of database management. In the Pets table, the Pet ID field is the primary key. Each pet has a different Pet ID field so that you can tell one pet from another. If you don't specify a unique value, Access creates one for you.

Creating a unique key

Without the Pet ID field, you'd have to rely on another field for uniqueness. You can't use the Pet Name because two customers could have pets with the same name. You could use the Customer Number and Pet Name fields as a multiple-field key, but theoretically, it's possible that a customer could have two pets each with the exact same name and even some of the same characteristics, such as Type of Animal and Breed. You will see a multiple-field primary key in Chapter 12.

If you don't designate a field as a primary key, Access creates a Counter field and adds it to the beginning of the table. This field will contain a unique number for each record in the table and will be maintained by Access. But for several reasons, you may want to create and maintain your own primary key:

- A primary key is an index that greatly speeds up queries, searches, and sort requests.
- When you add new records to your table, Access checks for duplicate data and doesn't allow any duplicates for the Primary Key field.
- Access will display your data in the order of the primary key.

By designating a field such as Pet ID as the unique primary key, you can see your data in an order you'll understand. In our example, the Pet ID field is made up of the owner's customer number followed by a dash and a two-digit sequence number. If the Adams family is the first customer on our list of those whose last name begins with AD, their customer number is AD001. If they have three pets, their Pet IDs will be designated AD001-01, AD001-02, and AD001-03. This way, the Pet ID field shows our data in the alphabetical order of customers by using the first two letters of their last name as a customer number.

Creating the primary key

You can create the primary key in four ways:

- Select the field to be used as the primary key and choose Edit⇨Set Primary Key.
- Select the field to be used as the primary key and select the Set Primary key button (the key) in the toolbar.
- Right-click the mouse to display the shortcut menu and select set primary key.
- Save the table without creating a primary key, and Access will create a Counter field for you.

Before you click on the key icon or select the menu choice, you must click the grey area in the far left side of the field you want as the primary key. A right-pointing triangle appears. After you select the primary key, a key appears in the grey area to indicate that the primary key has been created.

The Indexes window

A primary key is really an index. Notice the key icon in the Pet ID column, indicating that this is the primary key for the table. You can also see the primary key by looking at the Indexes window. Figure 7-16 shows a primary key entered into the Indexes window. You can display or remove this sheet from sight by toggling the Indexes button on the toolbar.

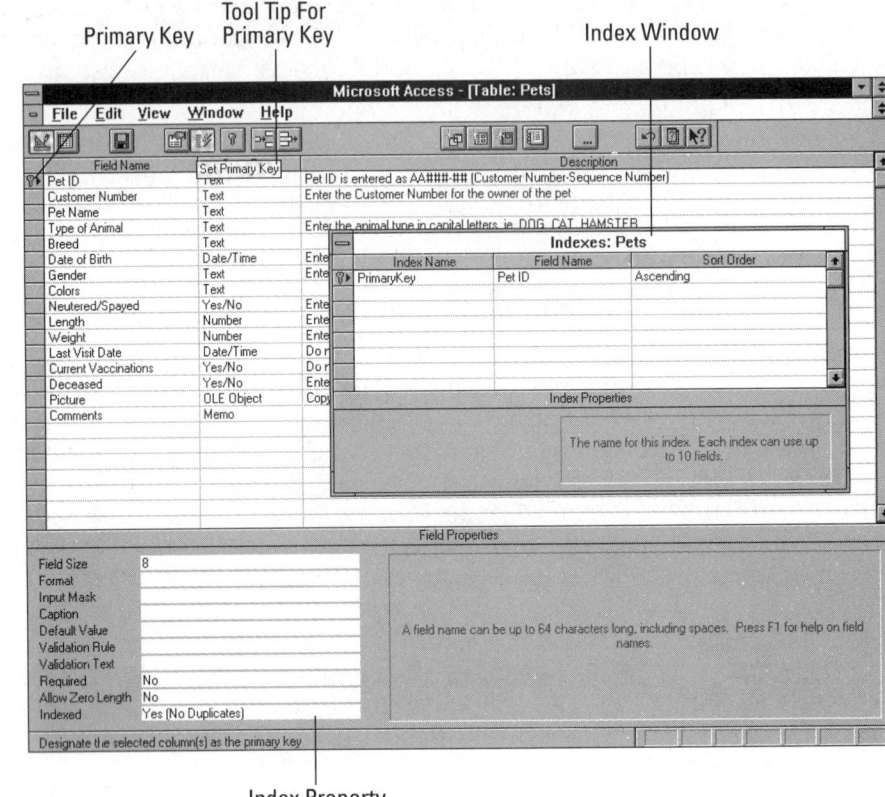

Figure 7-16: The Indexes window.

You can determine if an index is a primary key, whether or not it is unique, and if null values should be ignored.

The Table Properties window

Just as each field has a property area, the overall table has one too. Figure 7-17 shows the Table Properties window. Here you can enter a validation rule and message that are applied when a record is saved.

Figure 7-17: The Table Properties window.

Changing a Table Structure

As you create your table, you should be following a well-planned design. Yet sometimes, even with a plan, changes are necessary. Often, you find that you want to add another field, remove a field, change a field name or data type, or simply rearrange the order of the field names. You can make these changes to your table at any time. After you enter data into your table, however, things get a little more complicated. Now you have to make sure that any changes you make don't affect the data that has already been entered. Also, if you add, insert, or rename a field, you must change other existing database objects, such as forms, queries, and reports, to reflect the changes in your table.

Changing a field's location

One of the easiest changes to make is to move a field's location. The order of your fields, as entered, determines the initial display sequence in the datasheet that displays your data. If you decide that your fields should be rearranged, you can simply click a field selector twice and drag the field to a new location, as you see happening in Figure 7-18.

Inserting a new field

To insert a new field, place your cursor on an existing field and select Edit➪Insert Row or click the Insert Row icon in the toolbar. A new row is added to the table, and any existing fields are *pushed down*. You can then enter a new field definition. Inserting a field does not disturb other fields or existing data. If you have queries, forms, or reports that use the table, you may need to add the field to those objects as well.

Deleting a field

Deleting a field can be done in three ways:

- Select the field by clicking the row selector and press Delete.
- Select the field and then choose Edit➪Delete Row.
- Select the field and then click the Delete Row icon in the toolbar.

Figure 7-18: Changing a field's location.

Click on the field selector to select the field

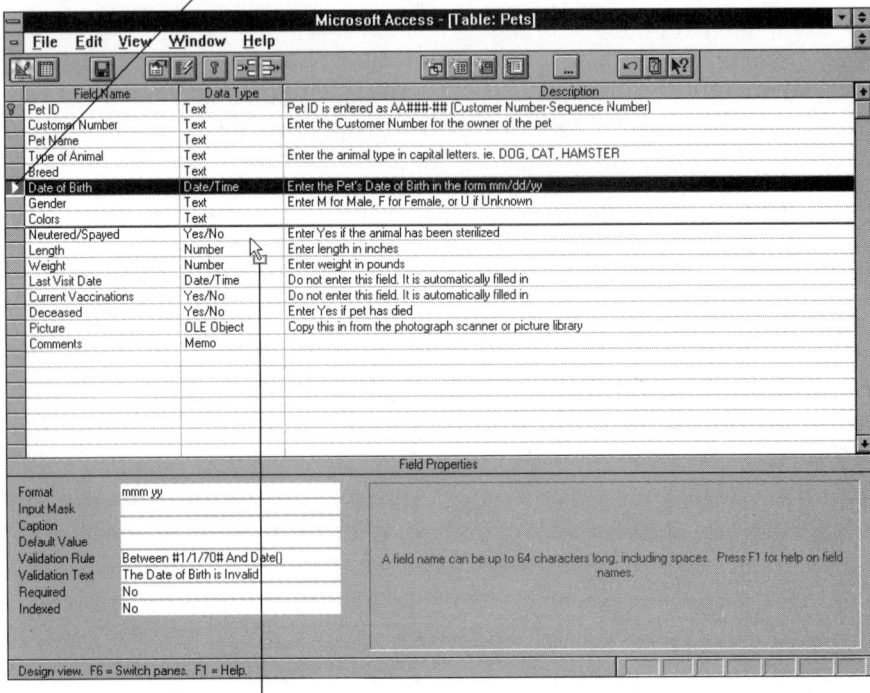

Click on the selector again and drag the field to the new location

When you delete a field containing data, you'll see a message warning that you will lose any data in the table for this field. If the table is empty, you won't care. However, if your table contains data, make sure that you want to eliminate the data for that field (column). You will also have to delete the field from queries, forms, and reports that use the field name.

When you delete a field, you can immediately select the Undo button and return the field to the table. But you must do this step before saving the changed table's definition.

If you delete a field, you must also delete all references to that field throughout Access. Because you can use a field name in forms, queries, reports, and even table data validation, you must carefully examine your system to find any instances where you may have used the specific field name.

Changing a field name

You can change a field name by simply placing your cursor over an existing field name in the Table design screen and entering a new name. The table design is automatically updated. As long as you are creating a new table, this process is easy. But if you used the field name in any forms, queries, or reports, you must also change it in them. Remember that you can also use a field name in validation rules, in calculated fields in queries, or in macro and module expressions — all of which must be changed. As you can see, it is a good idea not to change a field name because it creates additional work.

Changing a field size

Making a field size larger is simple in a table design. Only Text and Number field sizes can be increased. You simply increase the Field Size property for Text fields or specify a different field size for Number fields. You must pay attention to the decimal point property in Number fields to make sure that you don't select a new size that supports fewer decimal points than you currently have.

When you want to make a field size smaller, make sure that none of the data in the table is larger than the new field width or the existing data will be truncated. Text data types should be made as small as possible to take up less storage space.

Remember that each text field uses the maximum size of the field, regardless of the value of the data in the field. If your largest data value is 20 bytes long, set the Field Size to 20.

Changing a field data type

You must be very careful when changing a field's data type if you want to preserve your existing data. This is rarely done because most data types by definition limit the type of data that can be input. For example, you cannot normally input a letter into a Numeric field or a Date/Time field.

Some data types do convert readily to others. For example, a Numeric field can be converted to a Text data type, but you lose the understanding of mathematics in the value because you can no longer perform mathematical calculations with the values. Sometimes you accidentally create a phone number or ZIP code as Numeric and want to correctly redefine the data type as Text. Of course, you also have to remember the other places where you've used the field name, as it may appear in queries, forms, or reports.

 The OLE data type cannot be converted to any other format.

You'll need to understand four basic conversion types as you change from one data type to another. In the paragraphs that follow, each of these types is described.

To Text from other data types

Converting to Text is the easiest type of conversion. Practically any other data type can be easily converted to Text with no problems. Number or Currency data can be converted with no special formatting (dollar signs or commas) using the General Number format, although the decimal point remains intact. Yes/No data is converted as is, and Date/Time data is converted as is, using the General date format (mm/dd/yy hh:mm:ss AM/PM).

From Text to Number, Currency, Date/Time, or Yes/No

Only data stored as numeric characters (0,1,2,3,4,5,6,7,8,9) and periods, commas, and dollar signs can be converted to number or currency data from the Text data type. You must also make sure that the maximum length of the text string is not larger than the field size for the type of number or currency field you use in the conversion.

Text data being converted to Date data types must be in a correct date or time format. You can use any legal date or time format, such as, for example, 10/12/93, 12-Oct-93, or October 93, or any of the other date/time formats.

Text fields are converted to either a Yes or No value, depending on the specification in the field. Access recognizes Yes, True, or On as a Yes value and No, False, or Off as a No value.

 Access can also convert Number data types to Yes/No values. Null values or 0 are interpreted as No, and any nonzero value is interpreted as Yes.

From Currency to Number

Data can be converted between Currency and Number data types, as long as the receiving field is capable of handling the size and number of decimal places. Remember that the Field Size property in Numeric fields determines the size in bytes of the storage space and the maximum number of decimal places. Anything can be converted to Double, which holds 8 bytes and 15 decimals, whereas Single holds only 4 bytes and 7 decimal positions. (For more information, refer to the section "Entering field size properties" earlier in this chapter and Table 7-2.)

From Text to Memo

You can always convert from Text to Memo data types because the maximum length of a Text field is 255 characters, whereas a Memo field can hold 32,000 characters. However, you can convert from a Memo data type to Text only if each value in the Memo fields is less than the Text field size, with a maximum of 255 characters. Values longer than the field size are truncated.

Printing a Table Design

The menu item File⇨Print Definition... displays a dialog box as shown in Figure 7-19 that lets you select what information from the Table Design you want to print. You can print the various field names, all their properties, the indexes, and even network permissions.

Once you select which data you want to view, a report is generated and you can view it in a Print Preview window or send the output to a printer.

Access comes with a utility called the Database Documenter, which is used for documenting such database objects as tables, forms, queries, and reports. This utility creates a table of all objects and object properties that you specify.

Figure 7-19: The Print Definition dialog box.

Saving the Completed Table

You can save the completed table design by choosing File⇨Save or by clicking the save icon in the toolbar. You will be asked the name of the table, if it is the first time the table is being saved. Enter the name of the table and click on OK. Table names can be up to 64 characters in length and follow standard Access field-naming conventions. If you have saved this table before and want to save it with a different name, choose

File➪Save As... and enter a different table name. You will create a new table design and still leave the original table with its original name untouched. If you want to delete the old table, simply select it in the database window and press Delete.

Manipulating Tables in a Database Window

As you create many tables in your database, you may want to use those tables in other databases. Or you may need to make a copy of the table for use as a history file. You may want to copy only the table structure. You can perform many operations on tables in the Database window, including the following:

- Renaming tables
- Deleting tables
- Copying tables in a database
- Copying a table from another database

You can perform these tasks both by direct manipulation and by using menu items.

Renaming tables

You can rename a table with the following steps:

Steps:	Renaming a Table
Step 1.	Select the table name in the Database window.
Step 2.	Select File➪Rename....
Step 3.	Type the name of the new table and click the OK button.

A Rename table dialog box is displayed where you can type the name of the new table. After you type the new table name, it is displayed in the Tables list, which re-sorts the tables in alphabetical order.

If you rename a table, you must change the table name in any objects where it was previously referenced, including queries, forms, and reports.

Deleting tables

You can delete a table by simply selecting the table name and then pressing the Delete key. You can also delete a table by selecting the table name and then selecting Edit⇨Delete. Like most delete operations, you have to confirm the delete by selecting OK in a Delete Table dialog box.

Copying tables in a database

By using the Copy and Paste options from the Edit menu, you can copy any table in the database. When you paste the table back into the database, you can choose from three option buttons:

- Structure Only
- Structure and Data
- Append Data to Existing Table

Selecting the Structure Only button creates a new table design with no data. This allows you to create an empty table with all the same field names and properties as the original table. You typically use this option to create a temporary table or a history structure to which you can copy old records.

When you select Structure and Data, you create a complete copy of the table design and all its data.

Selecting the button Append Data to Existing Table adds the data of one table to the bottom of another. This option is useful for combining tables, as when you want to add data from a monthly transaction table to a yearly history table.

The following steps show how to copy a table:

Steps:	Copying a Table
Step 1.	Select the table name in the Database window.
Step 2.	Select Edit⇨Copy.
Step 3.	Select Edit⇨Paste.
Step 4.	Type the name of the new table.
Step 5.	Choose one of the Paste Options.
Step 6.	Click on OK to complete the operation.

Figure 7-20 shows the Paste Table As dialog box, where you make these decisions. To paste the data, you have to select the type of paste operation and type the name of the new table. When you are appending data to an existing table, you must type the name of an existing table.

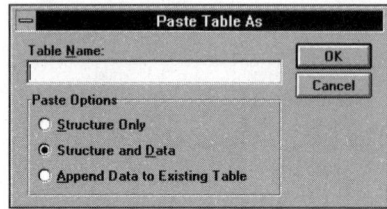

Figure 7-20: Pasting a table.

Copying a table to another database

Just as you can copy a table within a database, you can copy a table to another database. There are many reasons why you may want to do this. Possibly you share a common table among multiple systems. Or you may need to create a backup copy of your important tables within the system.

When you copy tables to another database, the relationships between tables are not copied; only the table design and the data are copied or appended. The method for copying a table to another database is essentially the same as for copying a table within a database. To copy a table to another database, follow these steps:

Steps:	Copying a Table to Another Database
Step 1.	Select the table name in the Database window.
Step 2.	Select Edit⇨Copy.
Step 3.	Open another database.
Step 4.	Select Edit⇨Paste.
Step 5.	Type the name of the new table.
Step 6.	Choose one of the Paste Options.
Step 7.	Click OK to complete the operation.

Summary

In this chapter, you learned about creating database tables by creating a database window and then examining the types of fields and properties you will typically use in a table. The following points were covered:

- Databases contain *objects,* such as tables, queries, forms, reports, macros, and modules.
- Table designs consist of field names, data types, and descriptions.
- You can choose from seven basic data types: Text, Number, Currency, Date/Time, Yes/No, Memo, and OLE.
- Each field has *properties,* which are Field Size, Format, Caption, Default Value, Validation Rule, Validation Text, and Indexed.
- Each table has a primary key field, which is an index and must contain a unique value for each record.
- When a table design is completed, you can still rearrange, insert, delete, and rename fields.
- You can rename, delete, or copy and paste tables in the Database window.

The next step is to input data into your table, which you can do in variety of ways. In the next chapter, you learn how to input your data using a datasheet.

Entering, Changing, Deleting, and Displaying Data

CHAPTER 8

In This Chapter

- Displaying a datasheet
- Navigating within a Datasheet window
- Opening a new datasheet
- Adding, changing, and deleting records
- Using special data-entry techniques
- Finding and replacing specific values
- Hiding, freezing, and rearranging datasheet columns
- Sorting or filtering records in a database
- Saving and printing datasheets

In this chapter, you learn how to input data into a Microsoft Access table by using a *datasheet*. Using a datasheet, you can see many records at once, as well as many of your fields. Using the Pets table created in the preceding chapter, you learn how to add, change, and delete data, and you learn about features for displaying data in a datasheet.

Understanding Datasheets

Using a datasheet is one of the many ways you can view data in Access. Datasheets display a list of records in a format commonly known as a *browse screen* in dBASE or a *table view* in Paradox. A datasheet is like a table or spreadsheet in that data is displayed as a series of rows and columns. Figure 8-1 shows a typical datasheet view of data. A datasheet displays your records across the screen in rows and also displays your fields vertically in columns. By scrolling the datasheet up or down, you can see records that don't fit on-screen at that moment, and by scrolling left or right, you can see more columns.

Datasheets are completely customizable, so you can look at your data in many ways. By changing the font size, you can see more or less of your table on-screen. You can rearrange the order of the records or the fields. You can hide columns, change the displayed column width or row height, and even lock several columns in position so that they continue to be displayed as you scroll around other parts of your datasheet.

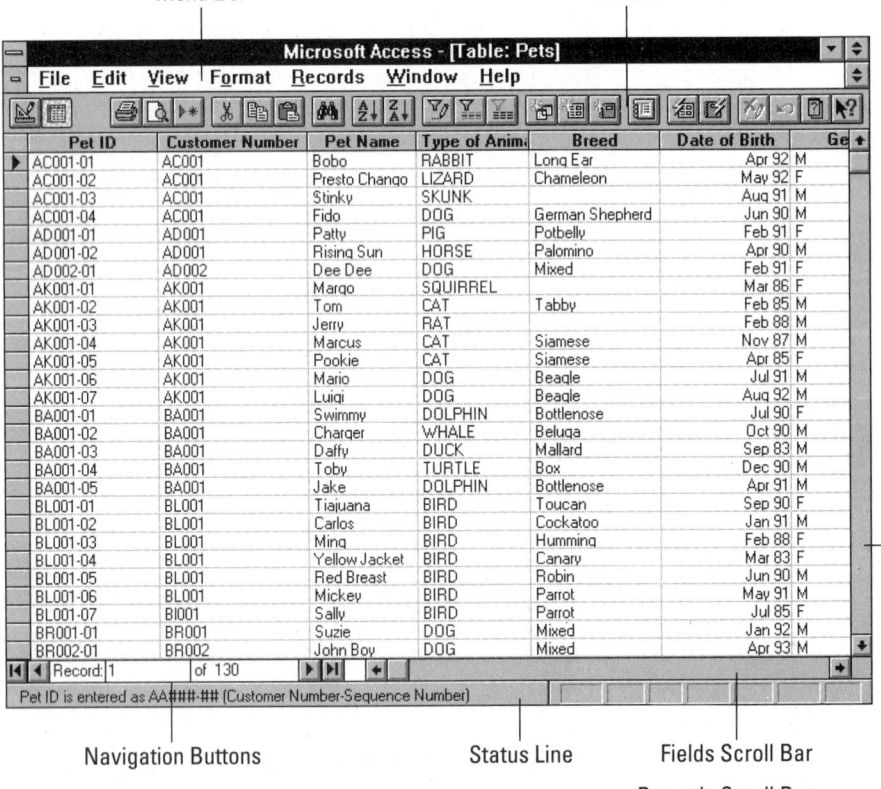

Figure 8-1: A typical datasheet.

 You can quickly sort the datasheet into any order you desire with one toolbar button. You can filter the datasheet for specific records making other records invisible. You can also import records directly to the datasheet or export formatted records from the datasheet directly to Word, Excel, or other OLE 2.0-enabled applications.

The Datasheet Window

The Datasheet window is similar to other object windows in Access. At the top of the screen, you see the title bar, menu bar, and toolbar. The center of the screen displays your data in rows and columns. Each record occupies one row; each column contains the same field's values and is headed by the field name. The records are initially displayed in order of the primary key, whereas the fields are displayed in the same order as they were created in the table design.

The right side of the window contains a scroll bar for quickly moving between records. There is also a scroll bar at the bottom of the screen for moving between fields.

The last line at the bottom of the screen contains a status bar. The status bar displays the Field Description that you entered into the table design for each field. If there is no Field Description for a specific field, the words `Datasheet View` are displayed. Generally, error messages and warnings appear in dialog boxes in the center of the screen rather than in the status bar. If you need help understanding the meaning of a button in the toolbar, the status line displays an explanation of the button that you click.

Navigation inside a datasheet

You can easily move around the Datasheet window by using the mouse pointer to click the desired field and record location to make changes or additions to your data. In addition, the menus, toolbar, scroll bars, and navigation buttons make it easy to move between fields and records. You can think of a datasheet as a spreadsheet without the row numbers and column letters. Instead, your columns have field names, and your rows are unique records that have identifiable values in each cell.

Table 8-1 lists the various navigational keys used for moving around within a datasheet.

Table 8-1
Navigating in a Datasheet

Navigational Direction	Keystrokes
Next field	Tab
Previous field	Shift+Tab
First field of current record	Home
Last field of current record	End
Next record	Down arrow
Previous record	Up arrow
First field of first record	Ctrl+Home
Last field of last record	Ctrl+End
Scroll up one page	PgUp
Scroll down one page	PgDn
Go to record number box	F5

The navigation buttons

The navigation buttons, shown in Figure 8-2, contain five controls that are used to move between records. You can simply click these buttons to move to the desired record. The two leftmost controls move you to the first record or the previous record in the datasheet (table). The two rightmost controls position you on the next record or last record in the datasheet (table). If you know the record number (row number of a specific record), you can click the record number box, enter a record number, and press Enter.

If you enter a record number greater than the number of records in the table, an error message appears. The message states that you can't go to the specified record.

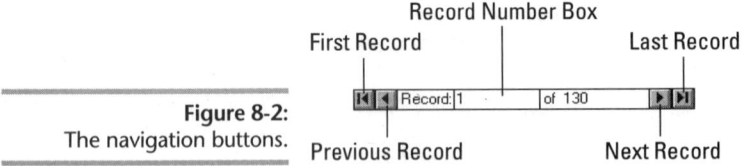

Figure 8-2: The navigation buttons.

Chapter 8: Entering, Changing, Deleting, and Displaying Data   **141**

The datasheet toolbar

The datasheet toolbar shown in Figure 8-3 provides another way for navigating around the datasheet. The toolbar has many familiar objects on it and some new ones you have not yet seen.

The first two icons let you switch between the Table Design and the Datasheet. By clicking the table design icon, you can make changes to the design of your table. You can then click the Datasheet icon to return to the datasheet.

The next two icons include Print, which looks like a printer and lets you send the datasheet values to your printer, and the Print Preview icon, which looks like a printed page with a magnifying glass. Print Preview is a tool you can use to view on-screen what your datasheet would look like if it were printed. The next button lets you display a blank record to enter new data. This is always one record past the end of the datasaheet.

The next three icons let you cut, copy, and paste selected objects within the datasheet or between other Access or OLE objects. This can include a single value, datasheet row, column, or range of values. You can copy and paste to other objects such as Microsoft Word or Excel.

The Find Specified Text icon is a pair of binoculars that, when pressed, displays a dialog box to let you search for a specific value in a specific field. The next two icons are the QuickSort icons. You can select one or more columns and press one of these buttons to instantly sort the data in ascending or descending order, using the selected columns as the sorting criteria.

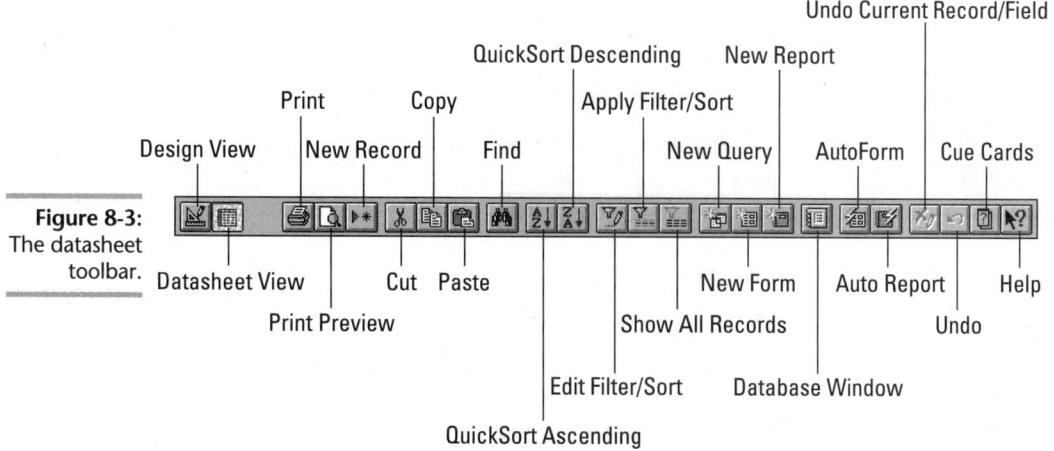

Figure 8-3: The datasheet toolbar.

The next three icons in this toolbar look like funnels. These let you determine and display only selected records. The first icon lets you determine which records are to be displayed. The second applies this selection, and the third redisplays all records.

The next group lets you create a new query, form, or report. The icon to the right of those displays the database container. Next is the AutoForm and AutoReport icons to create instant forms and reports using all the data fields and a default look for the form or report.

The next two icons let you Undo a change to a record or a more global undo for formatting. The last two icons display global help, which displays the Cue Card menu, or a help cursor that can be placed on the desired selection and clicked to get more specific help.

Opening a Datasheet

You can view your data in a datasheet in many ways. From the Database window, you should follow these steps:

Steps:	Opening a Datasheet
Step 1.	Click the table object.
Step 2.	Click the table name you want to open. (In this example, it will be Pets.)
Step 3.	Click Open.

An alternative method for opening the datasheet is to double-click the Pets table name.

If you are in any of the design windows, you can click the Datasheet button and view your data in a datasheet.

Entering New Data

When you open a datasheet, you see all the records in your table. If you just created your table design, you won't see any data in the new datasheet. Figure 8-4 shows an empty datasheet. When the datasheet is empty, the record pointer on the first record is displayed as a right-pointing triangle.

Chapter 8: Entering, Changing, Deleting, and Displaying Data 143

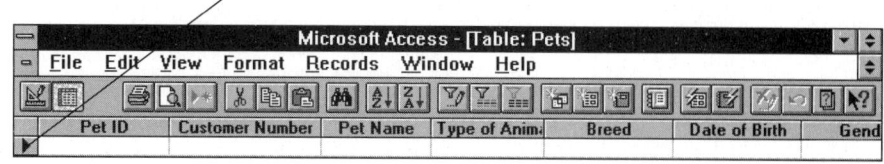

Figure 8-4:
An empty datasheet.

You can enter a record into a datasheet field by simply moving the cursor to the field and typing the value. As you begin to edit the record, the record pointer turns into a pencil, indicating that the record is being edited. A second row also appears as you begin to enter the record; this row contains an asterisk in the record-pointer position. The asterisk is the *new record pointer*. After you enter a record, all new records are entered in the last line of the datasheet, where the new-record pointer is always found.

The cursor generally starts in the first field of the table for data entry.

To enter the first record into the Pets table, follow these steps. A portion of the record is shown in Figure 8-5.

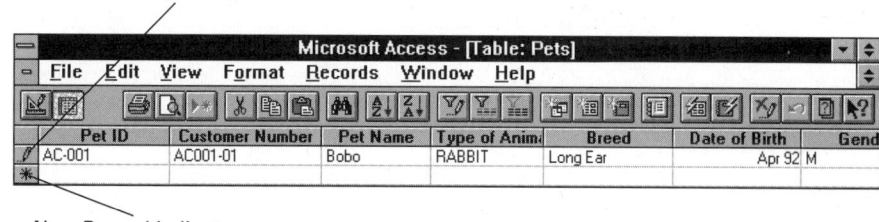

Figure 8-5:
A record entered into the datasheet.

Steps:	**Creating the First Record in the Pets Table**
Step 1.	Position the cursor in the Pet ID field.
Step 2.	Type **AC-001** and press Tab to move to the Customer Number field.
Step 3.	Type **AC001-01** and press Tab to move to the Pet Name field.
Step 4.	Type **Bobo** and press Tab to move to the Type of Animal field.
Step 5.	Type **RABBIT** and press Tab to move to the Breed field.
Step 6.	Type **Long Ear** and press Tab to move to the Date of Birth field.
Step 7.	Type **4/8/92** and press Tab to move to the Gender field.

Step 8.	Press **M** and press Tab to move to the Colors field.	
Step 9.	Type **Brown/Black/White** and press Tab to move to the Neutered/Spayed field.	
Step 10.	Press Tab to move to the Length field (because the default No is acceptable).	
Step 11.	Type **20.0** and press Tab to move to the Weight field.	
Step 12.	Type **3.1** and press Tab twice to move to the Current Vaccination field.	
Step 13.	Type **Yes** (over the default No) and press Tab three times to move to the Comments field.	
Step 14.	Type **Bobo is a great looking rabbit. He was originally owned by a nature center and was given to the pet store for sale to a loving family. Bobo was in good health when he arrived and was returned to the pet store for sale.**	
Step 15.	Press Enter to move to the Pet ID field of the second record.	

While adding or editing records, you may see four different record pointers:

- ▦ Current record pointer
- ✎ Record being edited
- ⊘ Record is locked (multiuser systems)
- * New-record indicator

Saving the record

After you enter all the values in the record, you normally move to the next record. This action saves the record. Any time you move to a different record or close the table, the last record you worked with is written to the database. You'll see the record pointer change from a pencil to a right-pointing triangle.

In order to save a record, you must enter a valid value into the primary key field. The primary key is validated for data type, uniqueness, and any validation rules that you entered into the Validation Rule property.

The Undo Current Field/Record icon in the toolbar will undo changes only to the current record. After you move to the next record, you must use the regular undo icon. After you change a second record, you cannot undo the first record.

Chapter 8: Entering, Changing, Deleting, and Displaying Data

 You can save the record to disk without leaving the record by selecting File⇨Save Record.

Now that you've seen how to enter a record, you should understand what happened as you entered the first record. Next, you learn about how Access validates your data as you make entries into the fields.

Understanding automatic data type validation

Certain data types automatically validate your data without any intervention. You don't have to enter any data validation rules in the table properties. The data types that automatically validate your data include:

- Number/Currency
- Date/Time
- Yes/No

Number or Currency fields allow only valid numerics to be entered into the field. Initially, Access will let you enter a letter into a Number field; however, when you move off the field, a dialog box appears with the message `The value you entered isn't appropriate for this field`. The same is true of any other inappropriate characters. If you try to enter more than one decimal point, you get the same message. If you enter a number too large for a certain Number data type, you will also get this message.

Date and Time fields are validated for valid date or time values. If you try to enter a date such as 14/45/90, a time such as 37:39:12, or a single letter in a Date/Time field, you'll also get the message `The value you entered isn't appropriate for this field` displayed in a dialog box.

Yes/No fields require the entry of one of the defined values: Yes, True, One, or a number other than 0 for Yes; or No, False, Off, or 0 for No. Of course, you can also define your own acceptable values in the Format property for the field, but, generally, these are the only acceptable values. If you try to enter an invalid value, the dialog box appears with the usual message indicating an inappropriate value.

Using various data-entry techniques

Because of the varying nature of field types, you use different types of data-entry techniques. You already learned that some data type validation is automatic. When the Pets table was designed, certain user-defined format and data validation rules were entered. The following sections examine types of data entry.

Standard text data entry

The first five fields that you entered in the Pets table were Text fields. You simply entered each value and moved on. The Pet-ID field used an input mask for data entry. There wasn't any special formatting for the other fields. Note that if you entered a value in lowercase, it is displayed in uppercase. Text can be validated for specific values, and it can be displayed with format properties.

Sometimes you want to enter a Text field on multiple lines. You can press Ctrl+Enter to add a new line. This is useful in large text strings for formatting a multiple-line address field, for example. It is also useful in Memo fields for formatting multiple-line entries.

Date/Time data entry

The Date of Birth field is a Date/Time data type that has been formatted using the *mmm yy* format. Even though you type **4/8/92,** the value `Apr 92` is displayed when you leave the field. The value 4/8/92 is really stored in the table and is displayed whenever the cursor is in the Date of Birth field. As an alternative choice, you can enter the value in the format specified. You can enter **Apr 92** in the field, and the value `Apr 92` will be stored in the table.

Date of Birth also has the validation rule `Between #1/1/70# And Date()`, which limits the data entry of Date of Birth values to between January 1, 1970, and the current date.

The Last Visit Date value is not entered for the Pets table. This is to be filled in when an animal is brought in for a visit and the record is entered in the Visits table. You learn how to do this procedure later in Chapter 32.

Only the display of the data is affected by formats. The storage of data in the table is not changed.

Text data entry with data validation

The Gender field of the Pets table has a data validation rule entered for it in the Validation Rule property. This rule limits valid entries to M, F, or U. If you try to enter a value other than M, F, or U into the Gender field, a dialog box appears with the message `Value must be M, F, or U`, as shown in Figure 8-6. The message comes from the Validation Text property that was entered into the Pets table Gender field.

Numeric data entry with data validation

The Length and Weight fields both have validation rules. The Length field has a Validation Rule property to limit the size of the animal to a realistic length below 10 feet. The Weight field has a Validation Rule property to limit the weight of the animal to below

Figure 8-6:
A data validation message dialog box in a datasheet.

1,500 lbs. If either of the rules is violated, a dialog box appears with the validation text entered for the field. If an animal arrives that weighs more than 1,500 lbs. or is more than 10 feet in length, the validation rule can simply be changed in the table design.

OLE object data entry

The OLE data type field named Picture can be entered into a datasheet, even though you don't see the picture of the animal. An OLE field can be many different items, including the following:

- Bitmap pictures
- Sound files
- Business graphs

Any object that is supported by an OLE server can be stored in an Access OLE field. OLE objects are generally entered into a form so that you can see, hear, or use the value. When OLE objects are displayed in datasheets, you see text that tells what the object is. For example, you might see `Paintbrush Picture` in the OLE field. You can enter OLE fields into a field in two ways:

- Pasting in from the Clipboard
- Inserting into the field from the Edit⇨Insert Object menu dialog box

You can paste an object from the Clipboard by using any of these methods:

Edit⇨Paste	Paste contents of Clipboard
Edit⇨Paste Append	Append contents of Clipboard
Edit⇨Paste Special	Paste Data in a specific format and optionally link to source

You can choose the type of OLE object to insert into the field by using the Edit⇨Insert Object... dialog box, as shown in Figure 8-7.

Using and displaying OLE objects is thoroughly covered in Chapter 20.

Figure 8-7:
Inserting OLE object into a field.

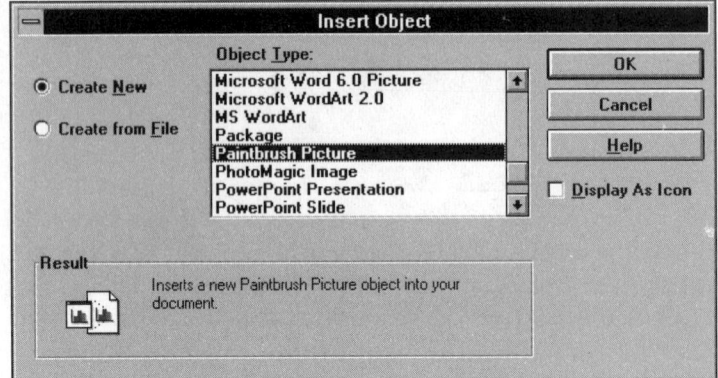

Memo field data entry

The last field in the table is Comments, and it is a Memo data type. This type of field allows up to 64,000 bytes of text for each field. Recall that you were instructed to enter a long string (about 160 bytes) into the Memo field. However, as you entered the string, you saw only a few characters at a time. The rest of the string scrolled out of sight. By pressing Shift+F2, you can display a Zoom box with a scroll bar (see Figure 8-8), which lets you see about 1,000 bytes at a time.

Figure 8-8:
The Zoom box for a Memo field.

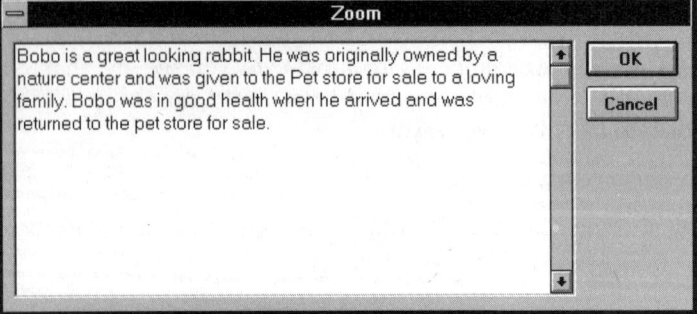

Navigating Records in a Datasheet

Following Along in This Book

If you are following along with the examples, you may want to use the MTNSTART database file now. For the remainder of this section, you'll work with all the data in the Pets table.

Chapter 8: Entering, Changing, Deleting, and Displaying Data 149

After you enter records, you generally want to make changes to them. You may want to change records for several reasons:

- You receive new information that changes existing values.
- You discover errors that change existing values.
- You need to add new records.

When you decide to edit data in a table, the first step is to open the table, if it is not open. From the Database window, open the Pets datasheet by double-clicking Pets in the list of tables.

If you are in any of the Design windows, you can click the Datasheet button to make changes to your data in a datasheet.

Moving between records

You can move to any record you want by simply scrolling through your records and positioning your cursor on the desired record. However, when your table is large, you probably want to get to a specific record as quickly as possible.

You can use the vertical scroll bar to move between records. The scroll bar arrows move the record pointer only one record at a time. You must use the scroll bar elevator to move many records at a time. You can also click on the area between the scroll bar elevator and the scroll bar arrows to move many records at once.

The Records⇨GoTo menu, shown open in Figure 8-9, contains several choices to help you quickly move around the worksheet.

The navigation buttons, also shown in Figure 8-9, provide five controls that are used for moving between records. You can simply click these buttons to move to the desired record. If you know the record number (row number of a specific record), you can click the record number box, enter a record number, and press Enter. You can also press F5 to move to the record number box.

Don't watch the record number box in the navigation buttons if you use scroll bars to move to another area of the datasheet. The record number box is not updated until you click a field.

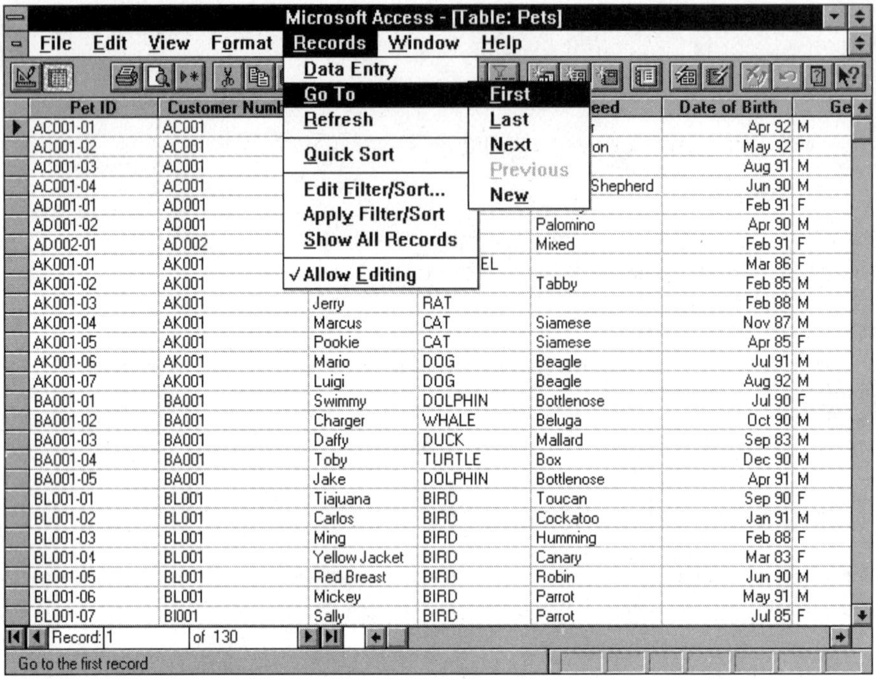

Figure 8-9: Moving between records.

Finding a specific value

Although you can move to a specific record (if you know the record number) or to a specific field in the current record, most of the time you really want to find a certain value in a record. You can use three ways to locate a value in a field:

- Select Edit⇨Find....
- Select the Find Specified Text button in the toolbar (a pair of binoculars).
- Press F7.

When you choose any of these methods, a dialog box is displayed, as shown in Figure 8-10. To limit the search to a specific field, your cursor must be on the field you want to use in the search before you open the dialog box. Access finds a value in only one specific field at a time unless you select the All Fields option in the dialog box.

The Edit⇨Find dialog box lets you control many aspects of the search. In the Find What text box, you enter the value to be searched for. You can enter the value just as it appears in the field, or you can use three types of wildcards:

*   Any number of characters

?   Any one character

\#   Any one number

Chapter 8: Entering, Changing, Deleting, and Displaying Data   **151**

Figure 8-10:
The Edit⇨Find...
dialog box.

To look at how these wildcards work, first suppose that you want to find any value beginning with *AB*; for this, you can enter **AB***. Then suppose that you want to search for values ending with *001,* so you search for ***001**. To search for any value that begins with *AB,* ends with *001,* and contains any two characters in between, you enter **AB??001**. If you want to search for any street number that ends in *th,* you can enter **#th** to find 5th or 8th. To find 5th or 125th, you can use ***th**.

The Where drop-down list contains three choices:

- Any Part of Field
- Match Whole Field
- Start of Field

The default is Match Whole Field. This option finds only the whole value that you enter. For example, the value SMITH is found only if the value in the field being searched is exactly SMITH. If you select Any Part of Field, Access searches to see whether the value is contained anywhere in the field; this search finds the value SMITH in the field values SMITHSON, HAVERSMITH, and ASMITHE. A search for SMITH using the Start of Field option searches from the beginning of the field and returns only values like SMITHSON.

You can click on one of two option buttons in the Search In group box. The choice Current Field searches only a single field. The choice All Fields searches all fields of the datasheet.

Two checkboxes appear at the bottom of the dialog box:

Match Case determines whether the search is case sensitive. The default is *not* case sensitive. A search for SMITH finds smith, SMITH, or Smith. If you check the Match Case checkbox, you must then enter the search string in the exact case of the field value. Obviously, Number, Currency, and Date/Time data types do not have any case attributes.

The default value of Search Fields as Formatted is unchecked. This default limits the search to the actual values as displayed in the table. If you format a field for display in the datasheet, you should check the box. In the Date of Birth field, for example, you can accomplish a search for an animal born in April 1992 by checking the box and entering **Apr 92**. Without this entry, you must search for the exact date of birth, which may be 4/8/92.

 Using Search Fields as Formatted may slow the search process.

When you press Enter in the Find What text box, the search begins. If the value is found, the cursor highlights the value in the datasheet. To find the next occurrence of the value, you must click on the Find Next command button on the right side of the dialog box. You can also select Find First to find the first occurrence.

The dialog box remains open so that you can find multiple occurrences. When you find the value you want, select the Close command button to close the dialog box.

Changing Values in a Datasheet

Usually, you change values by simply moving to the value you want to change or edit. You edit a value for several reasons:

- Adding a new value
- Replacing an existing value
- Changing an existing value

If the field you are in has no value, you can simply type a new value into the field. For new values entered into a field, follow the same rules as for a new-record entry.

Replacing an existing value

You generally enter a field with either no characters selected or the entire value selected. If you enter a field by using the keyboard, you usually select the entire value. You know that the entire value is selected when it is displayed in reverse video. When the entire value is selected, you can erase it by pressing any key and replacing it with the value of the pressed key. Pressing Delete simply deletes the value without replacing it. Pressing the spacebar erases the value and replaces it with a space.

To select the entire value with the mouse, you can use any of these methods:

- Click just to the left of the value when the cursor is shown as a diagonal arrow.
- Select any part of the value and double-click the mouse.
- Select any part of the value and press F2.

 You may want to replace an existing value with the default from the Default Value table property. To do so, select the value and press Ctrl+Alt+spacebar.

If you want to replace an existing value with that of the same field from the preceding record, you can press Ctrl+" [quotation mark].

 Be sure not to press Ctrl+- [hyphen], because the current record will be deleted.

Changing an existing value

If you want to change the existing value instead of replacing the entire value, you can use the mouse and click in front of any individual character in the field. When you position the mouse pointer in front of an individual character, you are placed in insert mode by default; the existing value is moved to the right as you type the new value. If you press Insert, your entry changes to overstrike mode and you replace one character at a time as you type. You can use the arrow keys to move between characters without disturbing them. Erase characters to the left by pressing Backspace or to the right of the cursor by pressing Delete.

Table 8-2 lists various editing techniques.

**Table 8-2
Editing Techniques**

Editing Operation	Keystrokes
Move the insertion point within a field	Press the right- and left-arrow keys
Insert a value within a field	Select the insertion point and type new data
Select the entire field	Press F2 or double-click the mouse
Replace an existing value with a new value	Select the entire field and type a new value
Replace a value with the value of the previous field	Press Ctrl+"
Replace the current value with the default value	Press Ctrl+Alt+spacebar
Insert a line break in a Text or Memo field	Press Ctrl+Enter
Save the current record	Press Shift+Enter or move to another record
Undo a change to the current record	Press Esc or click the Undo button

Fields that you can't edit

Some fields cannot be edited. If you find that your entire datasheet is uneditable, check the Records⇨✔Allow Editing menu item. If this menu item has no check in front of it, you won't be able to edit any of the fields in the datasheet.

These are the individual field types that you cannot edit:

Counter fields	Counter fields are automatically maintained by Access, and the values are calculated as each new record is created. Counter fields can be used as the primary key.
Calculated fields	Calculated fields are created in forms or queries; the values are not actually stored in your table.
Locked or disabled fields	You can set certain properties in a form to disallow entry for a specific field. You can lock or disable a field when you designate Form properties.
Fields in multiuser locked records	If another user locks the record, you won't be able to edit any fields in that record.

Using the Undo Features

The Undo and Undo Current/Field/Record buttons are often dimmed in Access so that they can't be used. As soon as you begin editing a record, you can use these buttons to undo the typing in the current field.

You can also undo a change with the Esc key. Pressing Esc cancels either a changed value or the previously changed field. Pressing Esc twice will undo changes to the entire current record.

Several Undo menu commands and variations are available to undo your work. The following list shows how you can undo your work at various stages of completion:

Edit⇒Undo Typing	Cancels the most recent change to your data
Edit⇒Undo Current Field	Cancels the most recent change to the current field
Edit⇒Undo Current Record	Cancels all changes to the current record
Edit⇒Undo Saved Record	Cancels all changes to last saved record

As you are typing a value into a field, you can select Edit⇒Undo or use the toolbar undo buttons to undo changes to that value. After you move to another field, you can undo the change to the preceding field's value by selecting Edit⇒Undo Current Field or by using the buttons. You can also undo all the changes to a current record that has not been saved by selecting Edit⇒Undo Current Record. After a record is saved, you can still undo the changes by selecting Edit⇒Undo Saved Record or by using the second undo button. However, after the next record is edited, changes are permanent.

Copying and Pasting Values

You can cut or copy a value by selecting Edit⇨Cut or Edit⇨Copy or by using the toolbar buttons. After a value is cut or copied, you can paste it into another field or record by using Edit⇨Paste or the Paste button in the toolbar. Data can be cut, copied, or pasted from any Windows application or between any task in Access. Copying or cutting data to the Clipboard is a Microsoft Windows task and is not actually a function of Access. You can copy entire records between tables or even databases, and you can copy datasheet values to and from Microsoft Word and Excel.

Replacing Values without Typing

Just as you can find a specific value, you can replace an existing value with another. The Edit⇨Replace... menu choice lets you display a dialog box to replace values, as shown in Figure 8-11.

The Replace dialog box is very similar to the Find dialog box. Instead of the Where text box, you see a Replace With text box, which lets you enter not only the search string but its replacement value. When you press Enter, the search begins. When the Find What value is found, the cursor highlights the value. You then have to select Replace to change the value. If you want to change multiple occurrences, you can select Replace All. Access locates all remaining occurrences and replaces them.

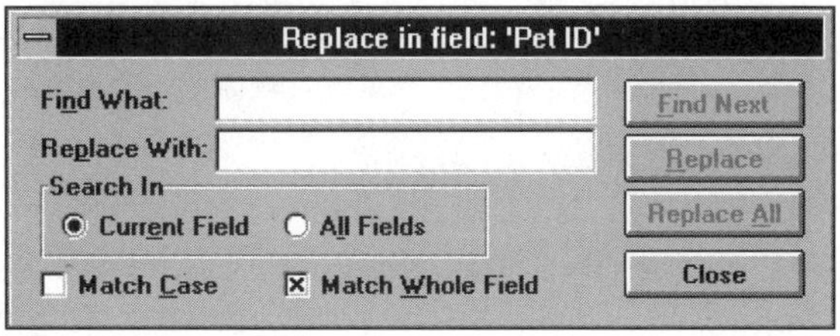

Figure 8-11:
The Edit⇨Replace... dialog box.

Adding New Records

You add records to the datasheet by positioning the cursor on the last line of the datasheet, where the record pointer is an asterisk; then enter the new record. You can also go directly to a new record by using the new-record button in the toolbar or by selecting Records⇨GoTo⇨New. Another way to quickly move to the new record is to go to the last record and press the down arrow.

Sometimes you want to add several new records and want to make all the existing records temporarily invisible. The menu item Records⇨Data Entry will temporarily clear the screen of all records while you are editing new records. When you want to restore all records, select Records⇨Show All Records.

Deleting Records

You can delete any number of records by selecting the records and pressing Delete. You can also select the records and choose Edit⇨Delete. When you press Delete or choose the menu selection, you'll see a dialog box asking you to confirm the deletion (see Figure 8-12). The dialog box forces you to confirm the delete. If you select OK, the records are deleted. If you select Cancel, no changes are made.

You can select multiple contiguous records. To do so, click the record selector of the first record you want to select and then drag the record pointer icon (right-pointing arrow) to the last record you want to select.

Figure 8-12:
The Delete Record dialog box.

Displaying Records

A number of mouse techniques and menu items can greatly increase productivity when you're adding or changing records. Either by selecting from the Format menu or by using the mouse, you can change the field order, hide and freeze columns, change row height or column width, change display fonts, and even display or remove gridlines.

Changing the field order

By default, the fields in a datasheet are displayed in the same order as they appear in a table or query. But sometimes you need to see certain fields next to each other to analyze your data better. To rearrange your fields, select a column, as you see in Figure 8-13. Next, drag the column to its new location.

Chapter 8: Entering, Changing, Deleting, and Displaying Data

You can select and drag columns just one at a time, or you can select multiple columns to drag. Say that you want the fields Pet Name and Type of Animal to appear first in the datasheet. The following steps take you through making this type of change:

Steps: Changing the Field Order

Step 1. Position the cursor on the Pet Name field (column) name. The cursor changes to a down arrow.

Step 2. Click to select the column and hold down the mouse button. The entire Pet Name column is now highlighted.

Step 3. Drag the mouse to the right to highlight the Type of Animal column.

Step 4. Release the mouse button; the two columns should now be highlighted.

Step 5. Click the mouse button again, and the pointer changes to an arrow with a box under it.

Step 6. Drag the two columns to the left edge of the datasheet.

Step 7. Release the mouse button; the two columns now move to the beginning of the datasheet.

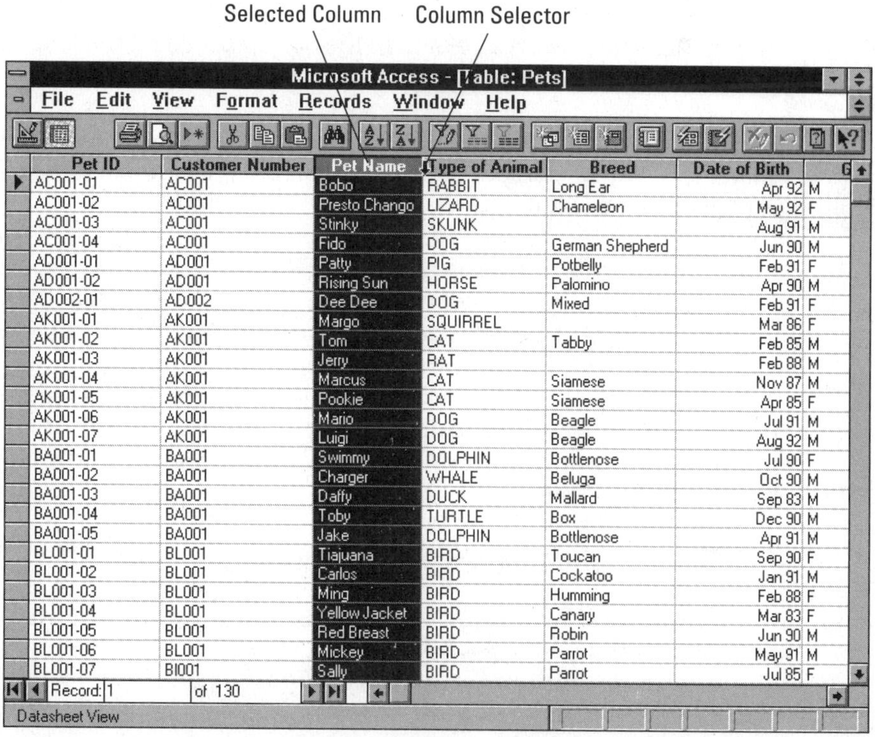

Figure 8-13: Selecting a column to change the field order.

With this method, you can move any individual field or contiguous field selection. You can move the fields left or right or even past the right or left boundary of the window.

 Moving fields in a datasheet does not affect the field order in the table design.

Changing the field display width

You can change the field display width (column width) either by specifying the width in number of characters in a dialog box or by dragging the column gridline. When you drag a column gridline, the cursor changes to the double-arrow symbol.

To widen a column or to make it narrower, follow these two simple steps:

Steps:	Changing a Column Width
Step 1.	Place the cursor between two column names on the field separator line.
Step 2.	Drag the column border to the left to make the column smaller or right to make it bigger.

 You can instantly resize a column to the best fit based on the longest data value by double-clicking the right column border.

 Resizing the column does not change the table field size in number of allowable characters. You are simply changing the amount of viewing space for the data contained in the column.

Alternatively, you can resize a column by choosing Format⇨Column Width.... Figure 8-24 shows the dialog box where you enter column width in number of characters. You can also return the column to its default size by checking the Standard Width checkbox.

 If you drag a column gridline to the gridline of the next column to the left, you'll hide the column. This also happens if you set the column width to 0 in the Column Width dialog box. If you do this, you must use Format⇨Show Columns to redisplay the columns.

Figure 8-14:
The Column Width dialog box.

Chapter 8: Entering, Changing, Deleting, and Displaying Data **159**

Changing the record display height

You can change the record (row) height of all rows. Either drag a row gridline to make the row height larger or smaller or select Format⇨Row Height.... Sometimes, you may need to raise the row height to accommodate larger fonts or text data displays of multiple lines.

When you drag a record gridline, the cursor changes to the vertical two-headed arrow that you see at the left edge of Figure 8-15. To raise or lower a row height, follow these steps:

Steps: Changing Row Height

Step 1. Place the cursor between two rows on the record separator line.

Step 2. Drag the row border upward to shrink all row heights. Drag the border downward to increase all row heights.

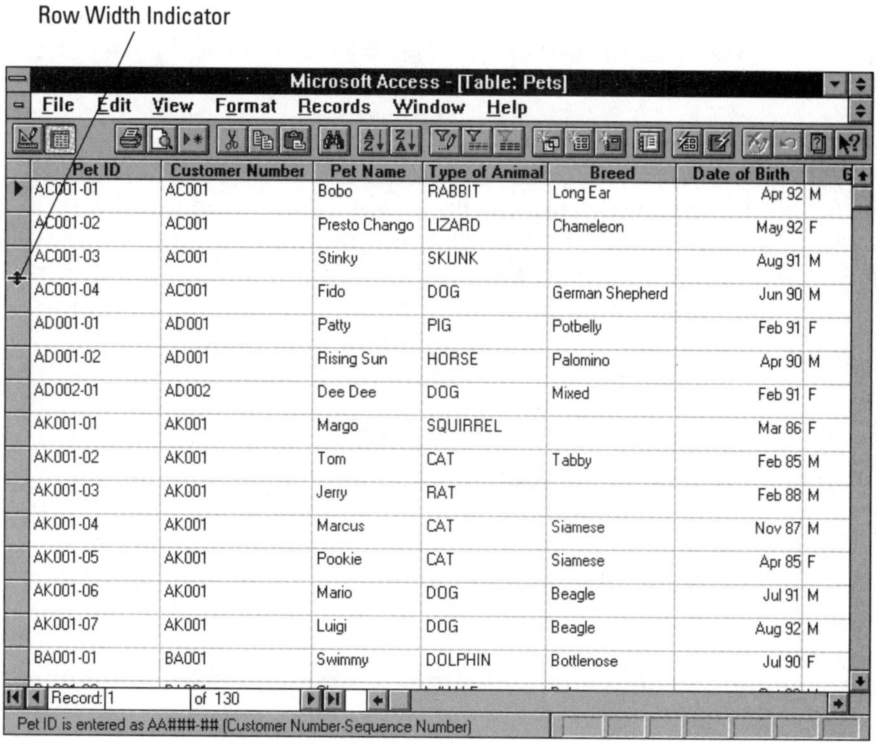

Figure 8-15: Changing a row heigth.

Pet ID	Customer Number	Pet Name	Type of Animal	Breed	Date of Birth	G
AC001-01	AC001	Bobo	RABBIT	Long Ear	Apr 92	M
AC001-02	AC001	Presto Chango	LIZARD	Chameleon	May 92	F
AC001-03	AC001	Stinky	SKUNK		Aug 91	M
AC001-04	AC001	Fido	DOG	German Shepherd	Jun 90	M
AD001-01	AD001	Patty	PIG	Potbelly	Feb 91	F
AD001-02	AD001	Rising Sun	HORSE	Palomino	Apr 90	M
AD002-01	AD002	Dee Dee	DOG	Mixed	Feb 91	F
AK001-01	AK001	Margo	SQUIRREL		Mar 86	F
AK001-02	AK001	Tom	CAT	Tabby	Feb 85	M
AK001-03	AK001	Jerry	RAT		Feb 88	M
AK001-04	AK001	Marcus	CAT	Siamese	Nov 87	M
AK001-05	AK001	Pookie	CAT	Siamese	Apr 85	F
AK001-06	AK001	Mario	DOG	Beagle	Jul 91	M
AK001-07	AK001	Luigi	DOG	Beagle	Aug 92	M
BA001-01	BA001	Swimmy	DOLPHIN	Bottlenose	Jul 90	F

Pet ID is entered as AA###-## (Customer Number-Sequence Number)

The procedure for changing row height changes the row size for all rows in the datasheet.

You can also resize all rows by choosing Format⇨Row Height.... A dialog box is displayed that lets you enter the row height in point size. You can also return the rows to their default point size by checking the Standard Height checkbox.

If you drag a record's gridline up to meet the gridline immediately above it in the previous record, you will hide all rows. This also occurs if you set the row height close to 0 (for example, a height of .1) in the Row Height dialog box. If you do this, you must select Format⇨Row Height... and reset the row height to a larger number to redisplay the rows.

Changing display fonts

You can automatically resize the row height and column width by changing the display font. By default, Access displays all data in the datasheet in the MS Sans Serif 8 pt. Regular font. You may find that this won't print correctly because MS Sans Serif is only a screen font. Arial 8 pt. Regular is a good match. If you are using Windows 3.1 with True Type fonts, you should switch to Arial 8 pt. Select Format⇨Font... to change the font type style, size, and style.

Setting the font display affects the entire datasheet. If you want to see more data on the screen, you can use a very small font, as shown in Figure 8-16. You can also switch to a higher-resolution display size if you have the necessary hardware. If you want to see larger characters, you can increase the font size. To change the font to Arial 6 pt. bold, follow these steps:

Steps:	Changing the Display Font
Step 1.	Select Format⇨Font.... A dialog box appears.
Step 2.	Select Arial from the Font combo box.
Step 3.	Select Bold from the Font Style combo box.
Step 4.	Select 6 from the Size combo box.
Step 5.	Click OK.

As you change font attributes, a sample is displayed in the Sample area. This way you can see what changes you are making before you make them. Figure 8-16 shows the screen after changes in the preceding steps were made and the dialog box was redisplayed.

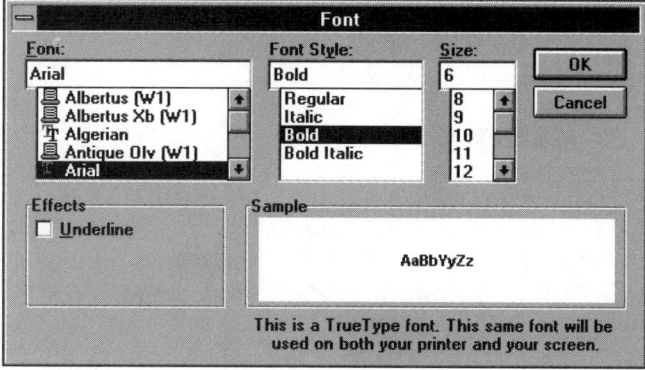

Figure 8-16: Changing to a smaller font size in the datasheet.

Hiding and showing columns

You can hide columns by dragging the column gridline to the preceding field or by setting the column size to 0. You can also use the Hide Columns dialog box to hide one or more columns. Hide a single column by following these steps:

Steps:	Hiding a Column
Step 1.	Position the cursor anywhere within the column that you want to hide.
Step 2.	Select Format⇨Hide Columns. The column disappears. Actually, the column width is simply set to 0. You can hide multiple columns by first selecting them and selecting Format⇨Hide Columns.

After a column is hidden, you can redisplay it by selecting Format⇨Show Columns.... This action displays a dialog box that lets you selectively hide or show columns by checking off the desired status of each field, as shown in Figure 8-17. Notice that the fields are shown in alphabetical order instead of table field name order.

To redisplay a column, click the field name in the dialog box and then click Show. You can also hide columns by clicking the column name in the dialog box and then clicking Hide. When you are finished, click Close and the datasheet is displayed with the desired fields.

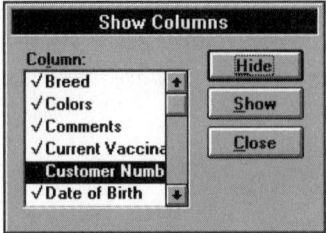

Figure 8-17:
The Show Columns dialog box.

Freezing columns

When you want to scroll among many fields but want to keep certain fields from scrolling out of view, you can use Format➪Freeze Columns. For example, with this selection, you can keep the Pet ID and Pet Name fields visible while you scroll through the datasheet to find the animals' lengths and weights. The columns you want to keep remain frozen on the far left side of the datasheet, and other fields scroll out of sight horizontally. The fields must be contiguous if you want to select more than one at a time to freeze. Of course, you can first move your fields to place them next to each other.

When you're ready to unfreeze the datasheet columns, simply select Format➪Unfreeze All Columns.

Displaying gridlines

Normally, gridlines are displayed between each field (column) and between each record (row). By selecting Format➪✔Gridlines, you can uncheck the default value, and the gridlines disappear.

To redisplay gridlines, simply select Format➪Gridlines again and the check reappears, indicating that gridlines will be displayed.

Saving the changed layout

When you close the datasheet, you save all your data changes, but you lose all your layout changes. As you make all these display changes to your datasheet, you probably won't want to make them again the next time you open the same datasheet. By default, the datasheet layout changes are not saved. But, if you want your datasheet to look the same way the next time you open it, you can select File➪Save Table to save the layout changes with the datasheet.

Chapter 8: Entering, Changing, Deleting, and Displaying Data **163**

Following Along in This Book
If you are following along with the example, do not save the changes to the Pets table.

Saving a record

As you move off a record, the record is saved. You can save a record without moving off of it by pressing Shift+Enter. The final way to save a record is to close the table.

Sorting and filtering records in a datasheet

Finding a value lets you display a specific record and work with that record. However, if you have multiple records that meet a find criteria, you may want to display just that specific set of records. Using the Filter/Sort: toolbar icons or the Records menu options, you can display just the set of records you want to work with. You can also use the QuickSort buttons to instantly sort the entire table or selected records into any order you want.

Using the QuickSort feature

There may be times when you simply want to sort your records into a desired order. The QuickSort buttons on the toolbar let you sort selected columns into either ascending or descending order. There is a different button on the toolbar for each order. Before you can press either the Ascending (A–Z) or Descending (Z–A) QuickSort buttons, you must select the fields you want to use for the sort.

You select a field to use in the sort by placing your cursor on the field in any record. After the cursor is in the desired column to use in the sort, the QuickSort button is pressed. The data is instantly redisplayed in the sorted order.

If you wanted to sort your data based on the values in multiple fields, you can highlight more than one column by highlighting a column as previously discussed, holding the Shift key down, and dragging the cursor to the right. These steps select multiple contiguous fields. When you select one of the QuickSort buttons, the records are then sorted into major order by the first highlighted field and into orders within orders based on subsequent fields. If you need to select multiple columns that aren't contiguous (next to each other), you can move them next to each other as discussed earlier in this chapter.

If you want to redisplay your records in their original order, use Records⇨Show All Records.

You can learn more about sorting in Chapter 10, "Understanding and Using Simple Queries."

Displaying the Filter/Sort window

The Filter/Sort toolbar icons let you have even more control over the display of your records. In addition to displaying just the set of records you want to work with, you can more precisely control the sorted order of your records.

To specify sort or filter criteria, you must first display the Filter/Sort window. To do this, select the first Filter/Sort button (a funnel with a pencil icon) or select Records⇨Edit Filter/Sort.... When you select the button, the Filter/Sort window is displayed, as shown in Figure 8-18. This window is actually a Query by Example (QBE) window with limitations. Unlike the full QBE window, you can specify only sort and filter criteria. You cannot perform field selection or any of the QBE tasks.

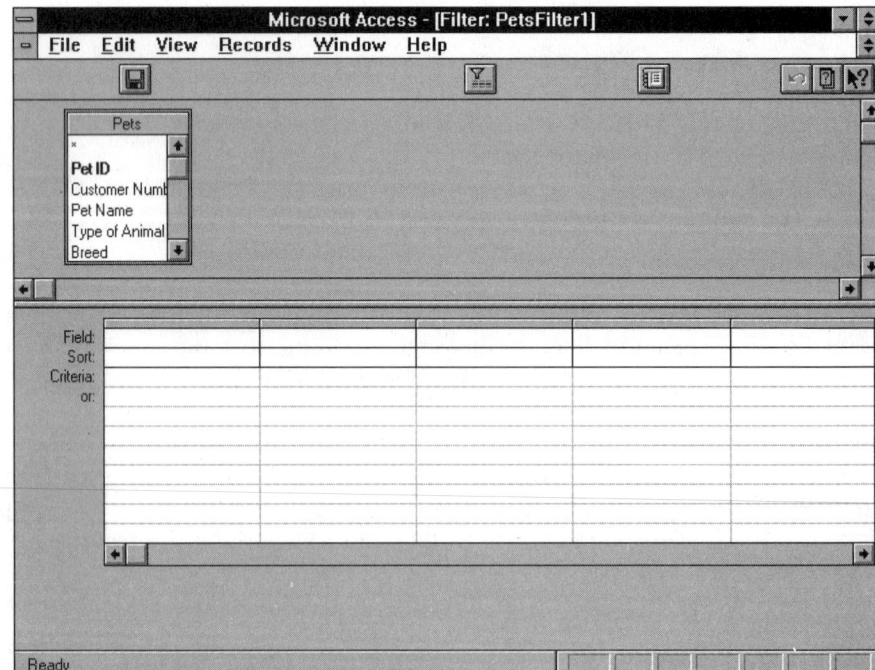
Figure 8-18:
The Filter/Sort window.

Chapter 8: Entering, Changing, Deleting, and Displaying Data   165

 QBE is covered in detail in several chapters of this book, including Chapter 10. QBE is discussed here only in sufficient detail so that you can create some simple filters and sorts.

The Filter/Sort window is divided into two panes. The top pane, called the *table pane*, displays the table or tables that are active. In this example, you can see in the table pane that the Pets table is being used. The bottom pane, called the *QBE pane*, is where you specify fields for sorting or filters, the type of sort, and any criteria.

To specify a sort or criteria, you must add fields to the QBE pane and then specify sorting types or criteria expressions. You can add a field to the QBE pane in several ways. One way is to double-click the field name in the table pane. The field name appears in the next available column in the query design pane. You can also add a field graphically to the query design pane by dragging one or more fields from the table pane to the QBE pane.

Adding a field to the QBE pane

Suppose that you want to sort the table into ascending order by type of animal. You'll need to add the Type of Animal field to the QBE pane. Follow these steps:

Steps:	Adding a Field to the QBE Pane by Double-Clicking
Step 1.	Click the Type of Animal field name in the table pane to select it.
Step 2.	Double-click the field name.

The field name appears in the first empty column in the QBE pane. Suppose that you are also going to filter the animals to display only male animals. For this, you also need to select the Gender field. You can also select fields by dragging the field name from the table pane to the QBE pane, as shown in the following steps:

Steps:	Adding a Field to the QBE Pane by Dragging
Step 1.	Highlight the Gender field by clicking the down arrow twice on the Pets table elevator.
Step 2.	Drag the Field icon, which appears as you move the mouse.
Step 3.	Drop the Field icon in the second column of the QBE design pane.

You notice from working with the Pets table that the Field icon takes the shape of a small rectangle while it's inside a table. When you drag the mouse outside of the table, the icon changes to the ⊘ symbol, warning that you can't drop the Field icon in that location. When the Field icon enters any column in the QBE pane, it reverts to its rectangular shape. When the field is dropped into the second QBE column, the field name appears in the Field row of the QBE pane.

Figure 8-19 illustrates the process of dragging a field to the QBE pane. In the figure, you see the QBE pane as it should look now with the Type of Animal and Gender fields in the QBE pane.

After you add the fields you need to the QBE pane, you can specify how each field is to be used.

 To select a field name, you can also simply click any cell in the Field row of the QBE pane. An arrow appears, and when you select the arrow, you see a drop-down list of all field names to choose from. In Chapter 10, you learn other ways of selecting fields, including a way to add several or all fields at once.

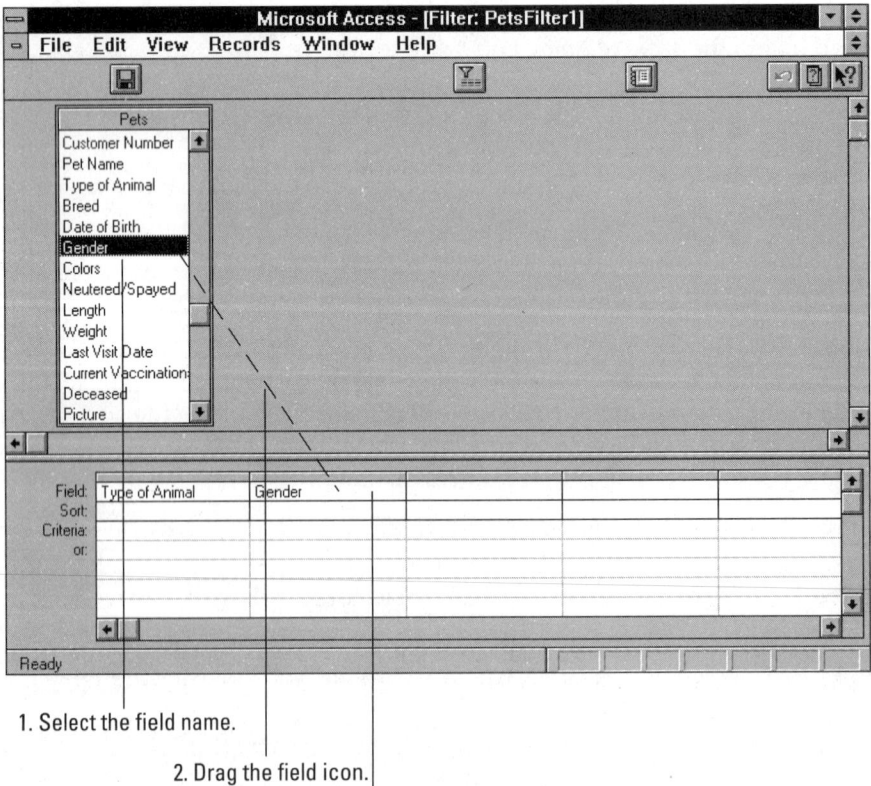

Figure 8-19: Dragging a field to the QBE pane.

Specifying a sort order

To sort the data in order, follow these steps, where you'll sort by Type of Animal:

Steps:	Sorting by Type of Animal
Step 1.	Click the Sort cell for the Type of Animal field. An arrow appears in the cell.
Step 2.	Click the down arrow at the right of the cell.
Step 3.	Select Ascending from the list of options in the pop-up list that appears.

When you select the type of sort, a drop-down list box presents you with three choices: Ascending, Descending, and (not sorted). In the preceding steps, the choice Ascending was placed in the Sort cell of the field because you chose Ascending from the drop-down list. You can also type **Ascending** into the Sort text box, but selecting from a list is easier. When you display the form or datasheet, your records are presented in order by type of animal.

Before displaying your data, you may also want to limit the selection of records to male animals. To do this, you must enter a criteria expression in the Gender column.

Specifying filter criteria

You can enter filter criteria into the Criteria row of the QBE pane by simply typing a valid Access expression. (Expressions are discussed in detail in Chapter 13.) In the following steps, you limit the display to males:

Steps:	Entering Filter Criteria
Step 1.	Position the cursor in the Gender column and click the Criteria row.
Step 2.	Press M and press Enter.

The M is displayed with double quotes around it. This is how Access displays Text data type expressions. As you learn more about expressions, you'll see that Text and Date/Time data types have certain special delimiters that are automatically placed around them. Figure 8-20 shows the QBE pane as it should currently look.

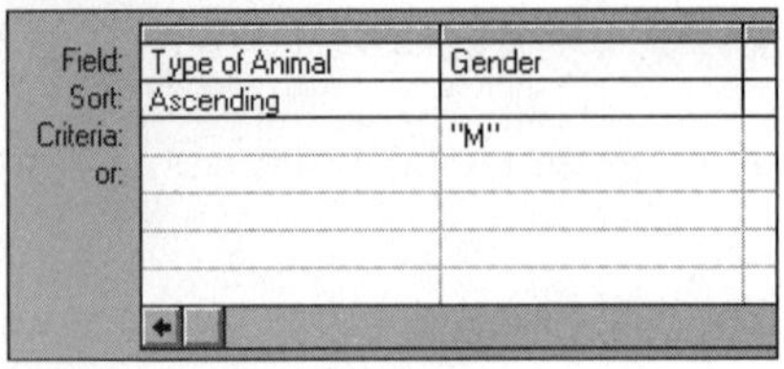

Figure 8-20:
The QBE pane with criteria entered in the Gender field.

Field:	Type of Animal	Gender
Sort:	Ascending	
Criteria:		"M"
or:		

Displaying the sorted or filtered data

Now that you specified the sorting and filter criteria, you can view your form or datasheet with these display options completed. Remember that you are changing only what is displayed and that the data in the underlying table is not affected.

To apply the filter or sorting criteria that you specified and then return to your form or datasheet, you can press the middle Filter/Sort button in the toolbar. Alternatively, you can select Records⇨Apply Filter/Sort. If you want to return to your form or datasheet without applying the filter and sort, choose the Window menu option and select the desired window.

You return to the first record in the table that meets the criteria specified for the sorted order that you asked for. You can switch to a datasheet by simply selecting the Datasheet button. The sorted and filtered datasheet is shown in Figure 8-21. The columns have been resized to display the type of animal and the gender. Notice the Type of Animal column. The data has been sorted alphabetically in this field. Also notice the Gender column. Only those animals with a Gender value of M are displayed.

Redisplaying all records

When you are ready to redisplay all your records in their original order, you can simply turn off the query filter by selecting the third Filter/Sort button on the toolbar or by selecting Records⇨Show All Records. The form or datasheet display instantly redisplays all records with the cursor placed in the first record of the table. You should redisplay all of your records before continuing.

Changing the Filter/Sort window

If you decide to make further changes in the Filter/Sort window, you can return to this window by simply reselecting the first Filter/Sort button in the toolbar. The Filter/Sort window still contains any changes you made. You can make further changes or additions and then redisplay your data with new sorts or filters. This can become quite an

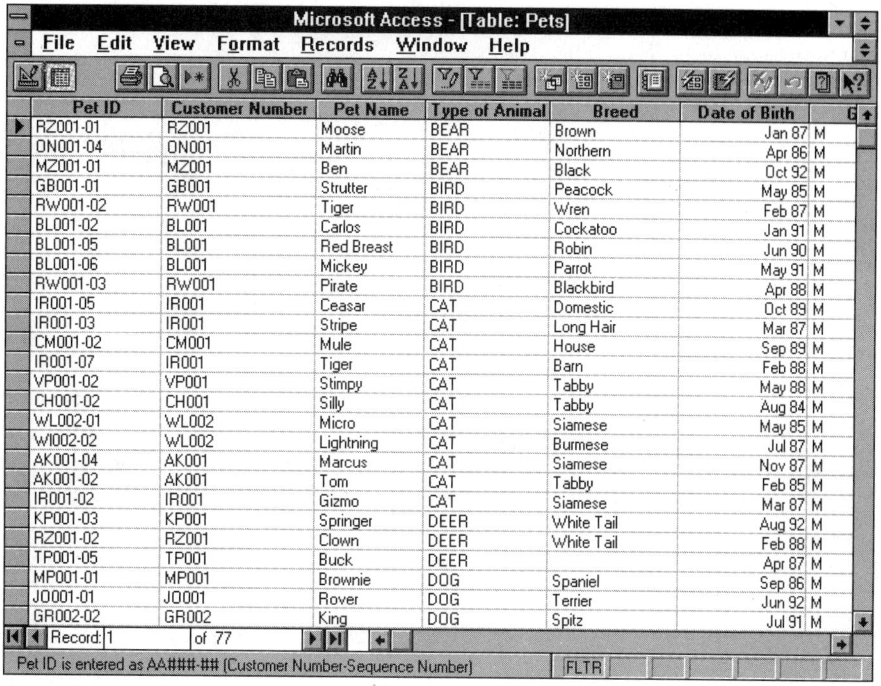

Chapter 8: Entering, Changing, Deleting, and Displaying Data 169

Figure 8-21: Datasheet displayed in order by type of animal and limited to males only.

Pet ID	Customer Number	Pet Name	Type of Animal	Breed	Date of Birth	G
RZ001-01	RZ001	Moose	BEAR	Brown	Jan 87	M
ON001-04	ON001	Martin	BEAR	Northern	Apr 86	M
MZ001-01	MZ001	Ben	BEAR	Black	Oct 92	M
GB001-01	GB001	Strutter	BIRD	Peacock	May 85	M
RW001-02	RW001	Tiger	BIRD	Wren	Feb 87	M
BL001-02	BL001	Carlos	BIRD	Cockatoo	Jan 91	M
BL001-05	BL001	Red Breast	BIRD	Robin	Jun 90	M
BL001-06	BL001	Mickey	BIRD	Parrot	May 91	M
RW001-03	RW001	Pirate	BIRD	Blackbird	Apr 88	M
IR001-05	IR001	Ceasar	CAT	Domestic	Oct 89	M
IR001-03	IR001	Stripe	CAT	Long Hair	Mar 87	M
CM001-02	CM001	Mule	CAT	House	Sep 89	M
IR001-07	IR001	Tiger	CAT	Barn	Feb 88	M
VP001-02	VP001	Stimpy	CAT	Tabby	May 88	M
CH001-02	CH001	Silly	CAT	Tabby	Aug 84	M
WL002-01	WL002	Micro	CAT	Siamese	May 85	M
Wl002-02	WL002	Lightning	CAT	Burmese	Jul 87	M
AK001-04	AK001	Marcus	CAT	Siamese	Nov 87	M
AK001-02	AK001	Tom	CAT	Tabby	Feb 85	M
IR001-02	IR001	Gizmo	CAT	Siamese	Mar 87	M
KP001-03	KP001	Springer	DEER	White Tail	Aug 92	M
RZ001-02	RZ001	Clown	DEER	White Tail	Feb 88	M
TP001-05	TP001	Buck	DEER		Apr 87	M
MP001-01	MP001	Brownie	DOG	Spaniel	Sep 86	M
JO001-01	JO001	Rover	DOG	Terrier	Jun 92	M
GR002-02	GR002	King	DOG	Spitz	Jul 91	M

iterative process, as you use this tool to switch back and forth to filter, sort, and then analyze your data. Although this method is not as powerful as the Query tool, you can perform many analyses using only sorts and filters.

Printing Records

You can print all the records in your datasheet in a simple row and column layout. Further on, you learn how to produce formatted reports. For now, the simplest way to print is to select File⇨Print... or use the print icon in the toolbar. This selection displays the dialog box shown in Figure 8-22.

Assuming that you set up a printer in Microsoft Windows, you can select OK to print your datasheet. Your datasheet is printed in the font you selected for display or the nearest printer equivalent. The printout also reflects all layout options in effect when the datasheet is printed. Hidden columns do not print. Gridlines print only if the Gridlines option is on. The printout reflects the specified row height and column width as well.

Figure 8-22:
The Print dialog box.

The printout will take up as many pages as required to print all the data. Only so many columns and rows can fit on a page. Access breaks up the printout as necessary to fit on each page. As an example, the Pets table printout is four pages long. Two pages across are needed to print all the fields, and the records take two pages in length.

When you display the datasheet in a font that has no printer equivalent, you may get unintelligible characters in your printout.

Printing the datasheet

You can also control printing from the Print dialog box, selecting from several options:

- **Print Range**   Prints the entire datasheet or only selected pages.
- **Print Quality**   Determines the print quality (important for dot-matrix printers).
- **Copies**   Determines the number of copies to be printed.
- **Collate Copies** Determines whether multiple copies are collated.
- **Print to File**   Prints to a file rather than to a printer.

Using the Print Preview window

Many times, you have all the information in the datasheet, but you aren't sure whether the columns or rows need to be changed for width or height, or whether the fonts need adjustment to print your output better. Perhaps you think that you only need printed records from pages 3 and 4. You'll probably want to view the report on-screen before making these adjustments to the datasheet properties.

To preview your print, you can either click the Print Preview button on the toolbar (a sheet of paper with a magnifying glass) or select File⇨Print Preview. The Print Preview window is shown in Figure 8-23.

Chapter 8: Entering, Changing, Deleting, and Displaying Data   **171**

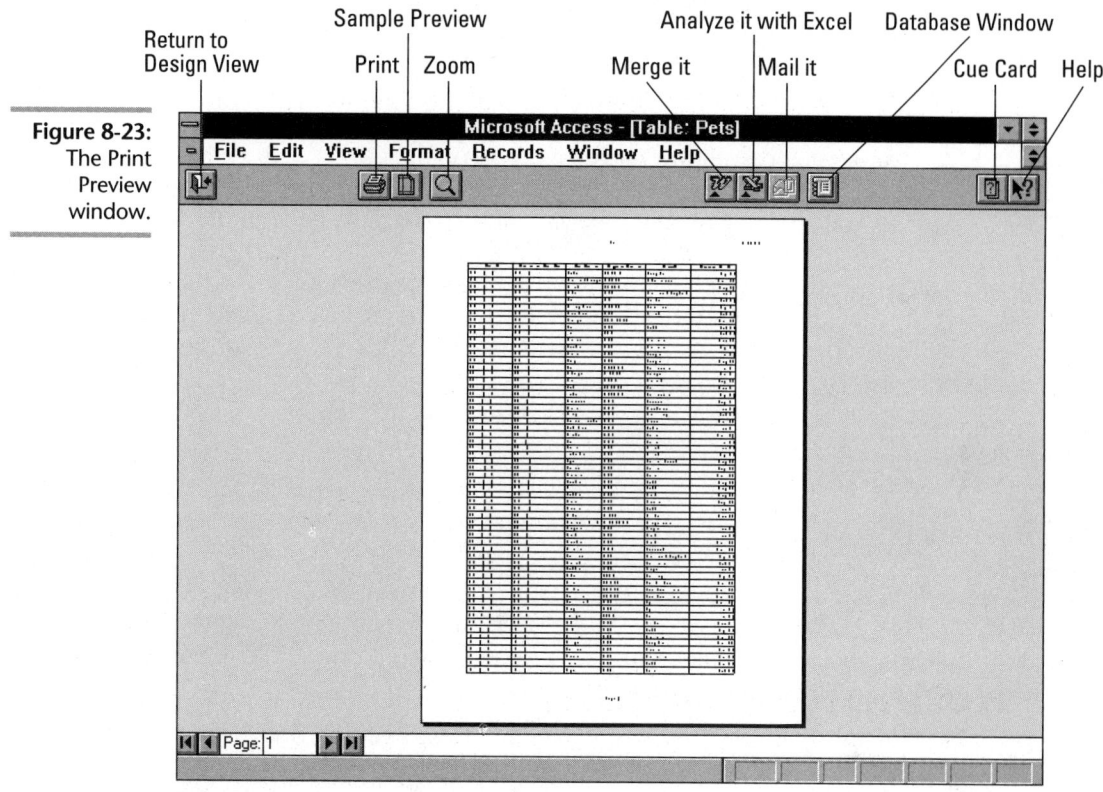

Figure 8-23: The Print Preview window.

After you select the Print Preview button, the screen changes to a print preview mode. You see a representation of your first printed page, and a set of icons are displayed on the toolbar.

You can use the navigation buttons, located in the lower left section of the Print Preview window, to move between pages just as you use them to move between records in a datasheet.

The toolbar buttons provide quick access to printing tasks:

Close Window   Returns to Datasheet view

Print...   Displays the Print dialog box, accessible when you select File⇨Print from the menu bar

Setup...   Displays the Printer setup dialog box, accessible when you select File⇨Print Setup...

Zoom   Toggles in and out to make the print preview page five times larger

Word   Copy the datasheet data to Microsoft Word

Excel   Copy the datasheet data to Microsoft Excel

You can zoom the datasheet in or out by selecting the Zoom button on the toolbar. Or you can simply click anywhere on the page. As you move over the page, the pointer changes to a magnifying glass. Simply click the left mouse button while the magnifying glass is visible to toggle in and out of zoom.

If you are satisfied with the datasheet after examining the preview, select the Print button on the toolbar to print the datasheet. If you are not satisfied, select the Close window button and you'll be returned to the datasheet mode to make further changes to your data or layout.

Summary

In this chapter, you learned about entering data into a datasheet. You learned how to navigate within the datasheet, to change the data, and to reposition and resize rows and columns. Then you learned how to preview and print the datasheet. The following points were covered:

- A datasheet displays data from a table in rows (records) and columns (fields).
- Using scroll bars, cursor keys, menu options, and the navigation buttons, you can quickly move around the datasheet and position the cursor on any record or field.
- You can open a datasheet from any Design window by clicking the Datasheet button or from the Database window by choosing Open with a table selected.
- Data is entered into a datasheet at the new-record indicator.
- Access performs automatic data validation for various data types, which are Number, Currency, Date/Time, and Yes/No fields. You can add your own custom data validation at the table or form level.
- OLE objects, such as sound, pictures, graphs, Word documents, and even video, can be pasted or inserted into OLE fields with Edit⇨Insert Object.
- The navigation buttons enable you to move quickly between records.
- You can find or replace specific values by using Edit⇨Find or Edit⇨Replace.

Chapter 8: Entering, Changing, Deleting, and Displaying Data — 173

- You can press Ctrl+Alt+spacebar to insert the default value into a field or press Ctrl+" to insert the preceding record's value into a field.

- Some types of fields can't be edited, which include counter, calculated, locked, disabled, record locked, and fields from certain types of queries.

- The Undo feature can undo typing, a field value, the current record, or a saved record.

- You can delete a record by selecting it and pressing Delete or by selecting Edit⇨Delete.

- You can change the display of your datasheet by rearranging fields, changing the field display's width or row height, or changing display fonts.

- You can hide or reshow columns, freeze columns, and remove the gridlines.

- You can save any layout changes by using File⇨Save Layout.

- Using the QuickSort buttons, you can instantly change the order the records are displayed in.

- Using the filter/sort buttons, you can specify sort orders or filters to limit the record display of a datasheet. This is a limited version of QBE (Query By Example).

- File⇨Print prints your datasheet, whereas File⇨Print Preview previews the pages on the screen.

In the next chapter, you learn how to create a form and how to use a form for data entry.

Creating and Using Simple Data-Entry Forms

CHAPTER 9

In This Chapter

- The types of forms you can create
- The difference between a form and a datasheet
- How to create a form with a Form Wizard
- How to use the Form window
- How to display data with a form
- How to enter pictures and data into OLE fields and Memo fields
- How to switch into a datasheet from a form
- How to find and replace data in a form
- How to make simple form design changes
- How to save a form
- How to print a form

Forms provide the most flexible way for viewing, adding, editing, and deleting your data. In this chapter, you see how to use Form Wizards as the starting point for your form. You learn about how forms work and the types of forms that you can create with Access.

Understanding Data-Entry Forms

Although you can view your data in many ways, a form provides the most flexibility for viewing and entering data. A form lets you view one or more records at a time while viewing all of the fields. A datasheet also lets you view several records at once, but you can see only a limited number of fields. When you use a form, you can see all your fields at once, or at least as many as you can fit on a screen. By rearranging your fields in a form, you can easily get 20, 50, or even 100 fields on one screen. You can also use forms to create multipage screens for each record. Forms can be used for simply viewing data in a formatted display, as well as for entering, changing, or deleting data. You can also print forms with all of the visual effects you have created.

What types of forms can you create?

You can create four basic types of forms:

- Full-screen forms (also called single-column forms)
- Tabular forms
- Main/Subforms
- Graphs

Figure 9-1 shows a full-screen form. The term *full-screen form* simply means that the fields are arranged on the screen, normally in a columnar format. The form can occupy one or more screen pages. Generally, this type of form is used to simulate the hard-copy entry of data, because the fields can be arranged any way you want. With Access forms, most of the standard Windows controls are available so that data entry is more productive and understandable. Lines, boxes, colors, and even special effects, such as shadows or three-dimensional looks, enable you to make forms great looking and easy to use.

A tabular form is displayed in Figure 9-2. In tabular forms, you can see several records at one time. Unlike datasheets, tabular forms can be formatted into multiple lines per record, and you can add special effects, such as shadows or three-dimensional effects, to the fields.

A main/subform, shown in Figure 9-3, is a type of form that is commonly used to display one-to-many relationships. Whereas the main form displays the main table, the subform is frequently a datasheet that displays the *many* portion of the relationship. For example, each pet's visit information shows up once, while the subform shows many visit detail records. This type of form combines all the benefits of a form and a datasheet. A subform can also show just one record or several records each on multiple lines.

Chapter 9: Creating and Using Simple Data-Entry Forms

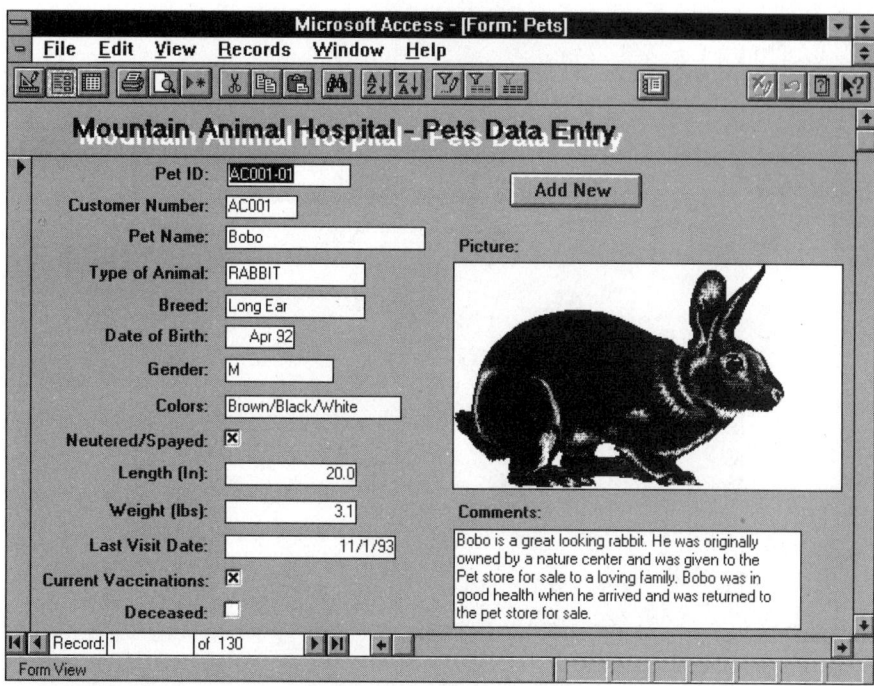

Figure 9-1: A full-screen form.

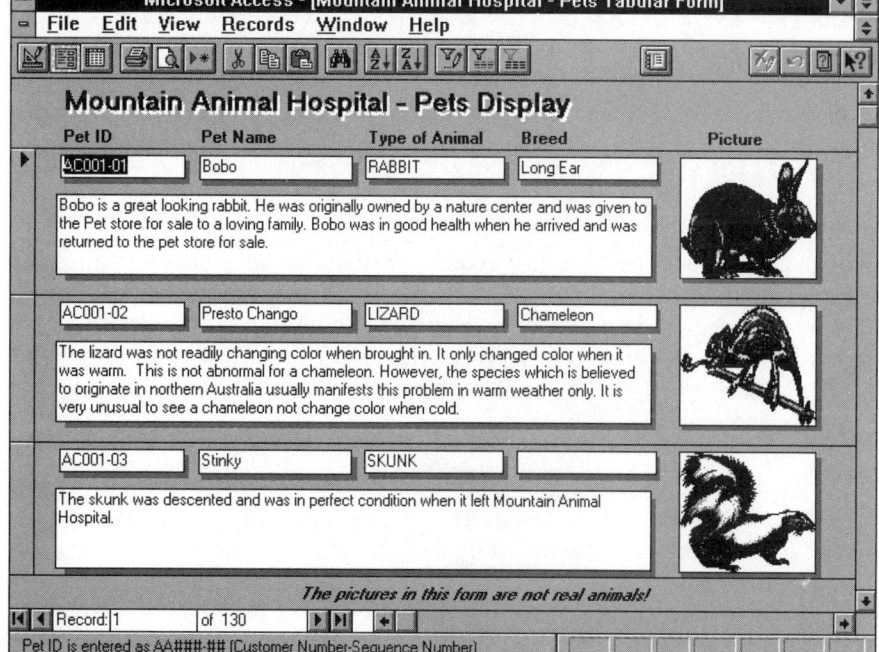

Figure 9-2: A tabular form.

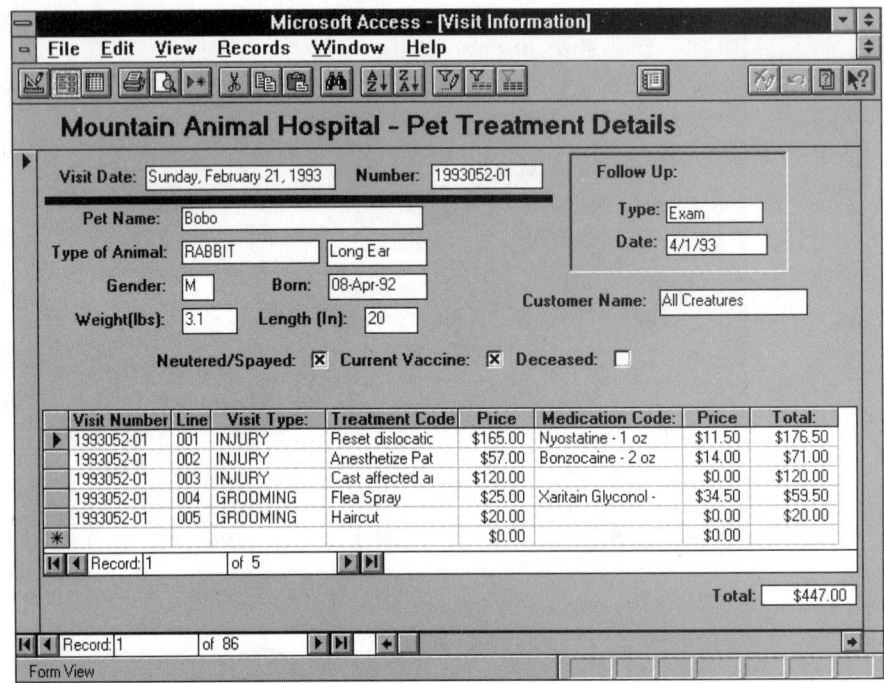

Figure 9-3: A main/subform.

How do forms differ from datasheets?

With a datasheet, you have very little control over the display of data. Although you can change the type and size of the display font, and rearrange, resize, and hide columns, you cannot significantly alter the appearance of the data. By using forms, you can place each field in an exact specified location, add color or shading to each field, and add text controls to make data entry more productive.

A form gives you more flexibility in data entry than a datasheet, because you can add to a form enhanced data validation and editing controls, such as option buttons, checkboxes, and pop-up list boxes. You can add lines, boxes, colors, and static bitmaps to enhance the look of your data. By using a form, you can greatly improve the productivity of working with data by making it easier for your form to be used. You can also add calculated fields to a form.

OLE objects, such as pictures or graphs, are visible only in a form. And although you can increase the row size to see more of a Memo field in a datasheet, using a form makes it easier to display large amounts of text in a scrollable text box.

 Once you create a form with editing controls or enhanced data validation, you can switch into datasheet mode and use data validation rules and controls, such as pop-up lists.

Creating a form With AutoForm

From a datasheet or nearly any design screen in Access, you can create a form instantly by clicking on the AutoForm button in the toolbar (form with a lightning bolt through it) or by using File➪New➪Form and selecting AutoForm from the dialog box that appears. When you use the AutoForm button, the form instantly appears with no additional work. To create an AutoForm using the Pets table, follow these steps:

Steps: Creating a Form With Autoform

Step 1. From the MTNANHSP Database Container, click the Table Object.

Step 2. Select Pets.

Step 3. Click the AutoForm Button in the Toolbar.

The form instantly appears as shown in Figure 9-4.

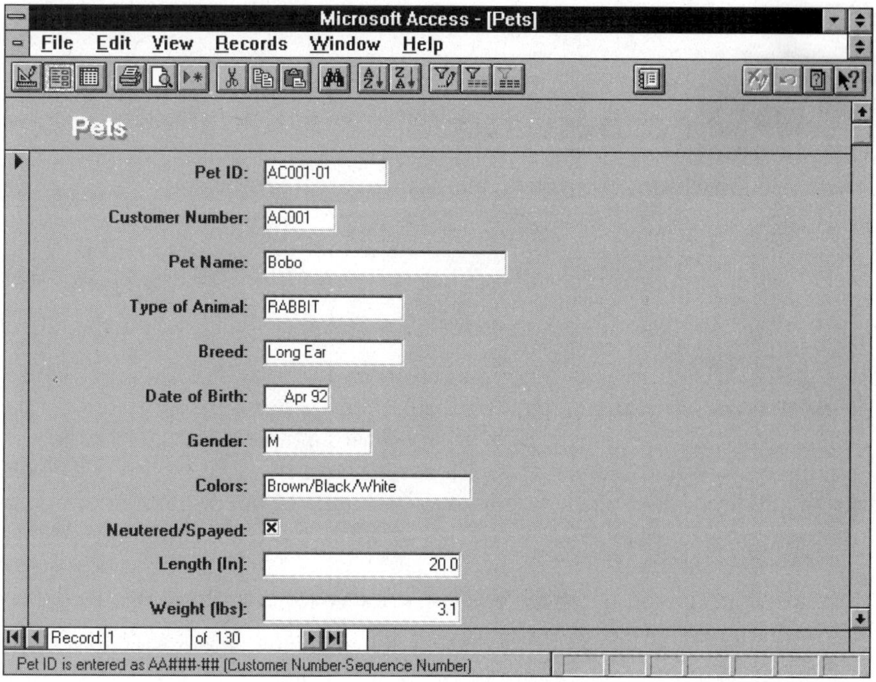

Figure 9-4: The AutoForm form.

If you look at different areas of the form, you can see that some values are not properly displayed. For example, if you scroll down and look at the picture of the rabbit in the first record, you see a portion of the rabbit. Later, you learn how to fix this as well how to customize the form exactly as you want.

AutoForm is the quickest way to create a form. However, generally you want more control over your form creation. There are other form wizards to help you create a more customized form to start with.

Creating a Form with Form Wizards

Form Wizards simplify the layout process for your fields. The Form Wizard visually steps you through a series of questions about the type of form you want to create and then automatically creates it for you. In this chapter, you learn how to create single-column forms with a Form Wizard. The single-column form is used as a starting point for creating a full-screen form.

Creating a new form

You can choose from these three methods to create a new form:

- Select File⇨New⇨Form from the Database window menu.
- Select the form object and then select New from the Database window dialog box.
- Select the New Form button from the Database window, the datasheet, or the Query toolbar.

Regardless of how you create a new form, the New Form dialog box is displayed, as you see in Figure 9-5. If you begin form creation with a table highlighted or from a datasheet or a query, the table or query you are using is displayed in the Select a Table/Query text box. If not, you can enter the name of a valid table or query before continuing. You can choose from a list of tables and queries by clicking on the combo box selection arrow.

The New Form dialog box gives you two choices for creating a form:

Form Wizards   Creates a form with one of five default layouts, using data fields that you specify

Blank Form   Displays a completely blank form for you to start with

Chapter 9: Creating and Using Simple Data-Entry Forms

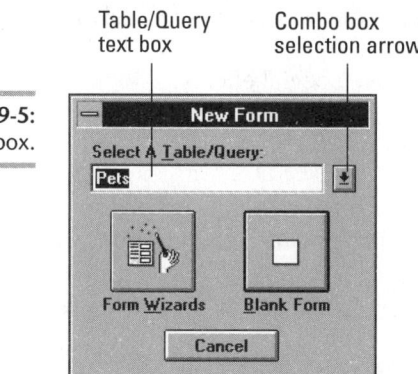

Figure 9-5: The New Form dialog box.

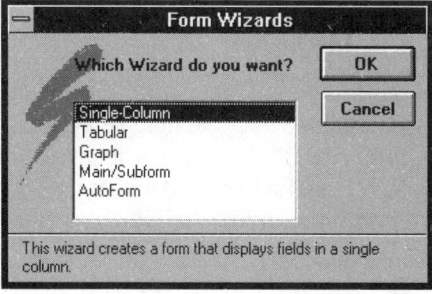

Figure 9-6: Selecting the form type.

 When you start with a blank form, you don't need to specify a table or query before you begin. Creating a form from a blank form is covered in Chapter 18.

Selecting the form type

Once you select a table or query and select the Form Wizards picture button, another dialog box is displayed. The Access Wizard dialog box, shown in Figure 9-6, offers five types of forms:

- Single-Column
- Tabular
- Graph
- Main/Subform
- AutoForm

The Single-Column and Tabular Wizards display essentially the same three screens:

Field Selection   Choose one, any combination of, or all of your fields for the form.

Type of Look   Choose from five special effects.

Form Title   Choose the title of the form.

The Graph Wizard steps you through selecting graph types, axis fields, labels, and titles. The Main/Subform Wizard assists you in creating a form with a subform.

 Graph forms are discussed in Chapter 20; main/subforms are discussed in Chapter 28.

Choosing the fields

After you select the single-column type of form and then select the OK button, you see the field-selection box shown in Figure 9-7. The field-selection dialog box contains two areas where you work. The first area is where you select fields for the form. At the bottom, you find a series of buttons to be used when field selection is completed. The types of buttons available here are common to most Wizard dialog boxes.

Following is a list of the buttons for navigating within the Wizard and an explanation of what they do:

Hint	Help for the current wizard function
Cancel	Cancel form creation and return to the starting point
< Back	Return to the preceding dialog box
Next >	Go to the next dialog box
Finish	Go to the last dialog box (usually the form title)

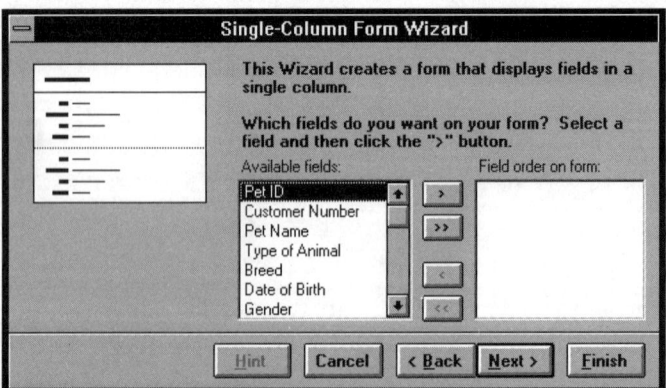

Figure 9-7: Choosing the fields for the form.

Chapter 9: Creating and Using Simple Data-Entry Forms

The field-selection area consists of two list boxes and four buttons. The `Available fields:` list box on the left displays all fields from the selected table/query used to create the form. The `Field order on form:` list box on the right displays the fields you have selected for this form. You can select one field, all the fields, or any combination of fields. The order in which you add the fields to the list box on the right is the order in which the fields will appear in the form. You can use the buttons to place or remove fields in the `Field order on form:` box. Following is a description of these buttons:

>   Add selected field.

\>\>   Add all fields.

<   Remove selected field.

<<   Remove all fields.

When you highlight a field in the `Available fields:` list box and select >, the field name is displayed in the `Field order on form:` list box. You can add each field you want to the list box. If you add a field by mistake, you can select the field in the `Field order on form:` list box and select < to remove it from the selection. If you decide to change the order in which your fields will appear in the form, you must remove any fields that are out of order and reselect them in the proper order. When you are finished, you select the <u>N</u>ext > button to display the Look of form dialog box.

You can double-click on any field in the `Available fields:` list box to add it to the `Field order on form:` list box.

If you select <u>N</u>ext > or <u>F</u>inish without selecting any fields, all fields are automatically selected when the form is created.

Click on the >> button to select all the fields.

Choosing the look of the form

After you select all of the fields, you can choose the look of your form from the dialog box shown in Figure 9-8.

You can choose from five selections by clicking on the desired option button. As you select one of the five looks, the display under the magnifying glass changes to illustrate the special effect used to create the look. Figure 9-9 is a composite that shows the five different looks available.

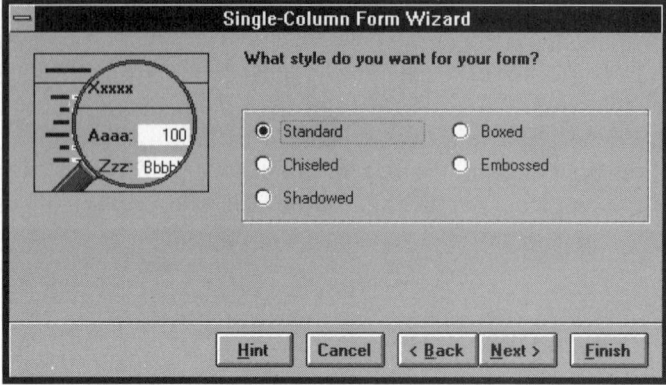

Figure 9-8: Choosing the look of your form.

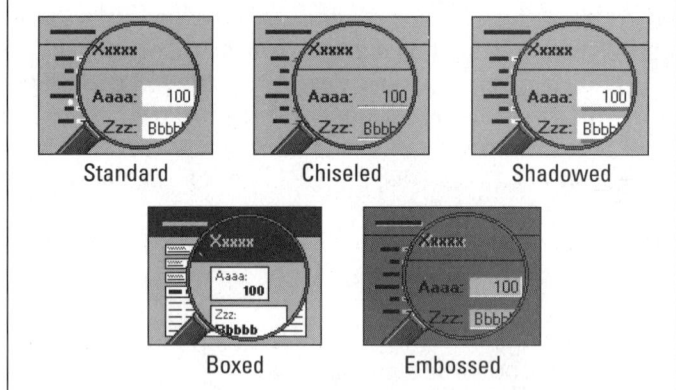

Figure 9-9: The five different looks for a form.

As you can see in Figure 9-8, the standard look is a simple one that displays in black ink on a grey background. The fields are placed in a white borderless box. For the first form you create in this chapter, you should select the Standard button. Once you select the look of your form, you are ready to create a title and view the form.

Creating a form title

The Form Title dialog box is usually the last dialog box in a Form Wizard. By default, the Form title text box contains the name of the table or query used for the form's data. You can accept the entry for the form title, enter your own, or erase it and have no title. As you can see, the title in Figure 9-10 has been erased. By not creating a title here, you can have more space on the form for data.

Figure 9-10: Choosing a form title.

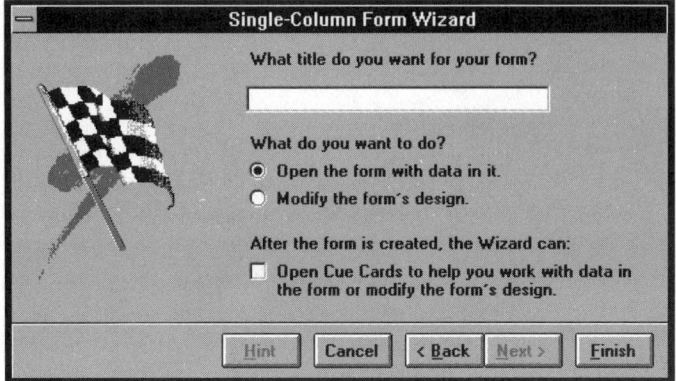

Opening the form

After you complete all the steps to design your form, you can open the form in one of two ways:

- Open the form in Form View
- Form design view

In this example, you view the form in the Form window by selecting the first option button and then selecting Finish.

Once you select the Finish button, the form is displayed in a window with the first record displayed, as shown in Figure 9-11. Note that you can maximize the window by selecting the maximize button on the top right corner of the window.

 You can customize the type and look of form wizards by using the File⇨Add-ins ⇨Add-In-Manager. After you select these menus, the Form and Report Wizards dialog box appears. Press the Customize... button and select the type of form you want to customize.

Customize Form Wizard Styles let you change the font and color of the label and field control for each of the looks in the wizard. Customize AutoForm lets you select the look of the form and the type (Single-Column or Tabular) to use when an Auto-Form is used. Figure 9-12 shows the customization screen for customizing a form wizard.

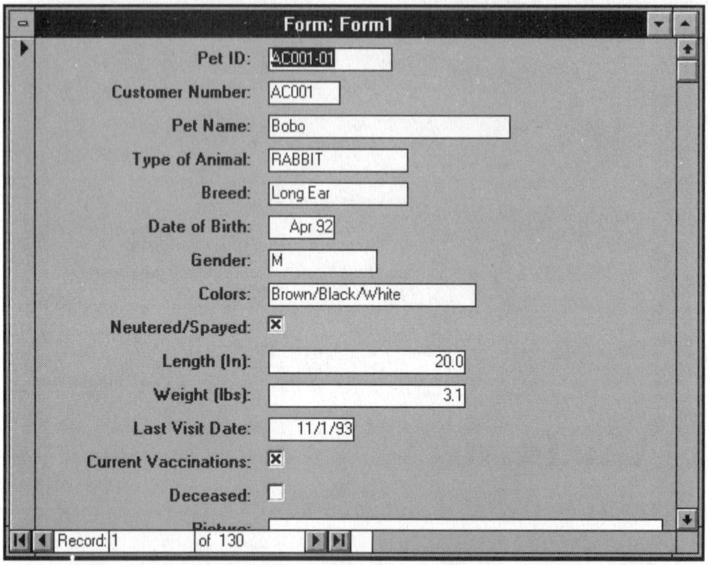

Figure 9-11:
A form created with a Form Wizard.

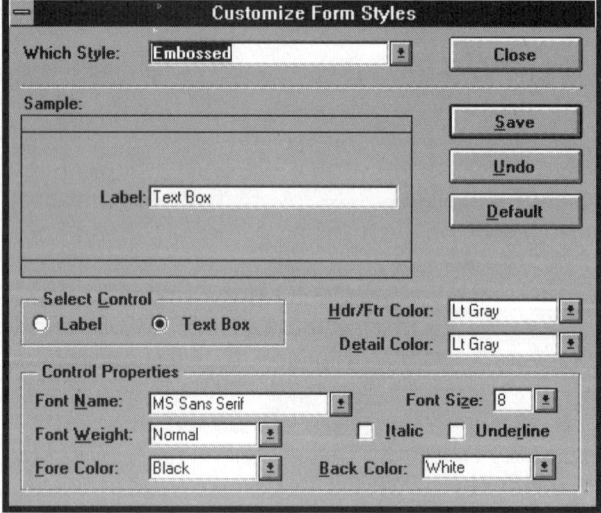

Figure 9-12: Customizing the Form Wizard.

Using the Form Window

If you look at the Form window, as shown in Figure 9-11, you see that this window is very similar to the Datasheet window. At the top of the screen is the title bar, menu bar, and toolbar. The center of the screen displays your data one record at a time. In this single-column layout, each field occupies one line. If the form contains more fields than will fit on-screen at one time, you can use the vertical scroll bar or press PgDn to see the rest of the record.

Chapter 9: Creating and Using Simple Data-Entry Forms

The last line at the bottom of the screen contains a status bar. The status bar displays the Field Description that you entered into the table design for each field. If there is no Field Description for a specific field, the words Form View are displayed. Generally, error messages and warnings appear in dialog boxes in the center of the screen rather than in the status bar. The navigation buttons are also displayed at the bottom of the screen. This feature lets you move quickly from record to record.

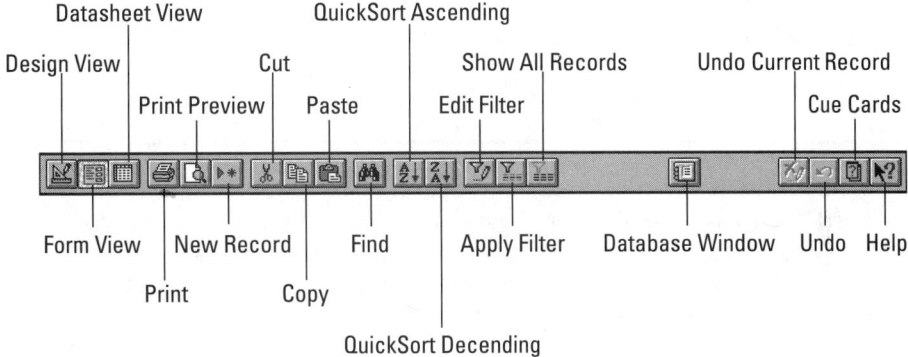

Figure 9-13: The Form window toolbar.

The Form toolbar

The Form toolbar, shown in Figure 9-13, is virtually identical to the datasheet icons with the New buttons missing. The first three icons also contain a form button not used in the datasheet toolbar.

Navigating between fields

Navigating a form is nearly identical to using a datasheet. You can easily move around the Form window by using the mouse pointer to click the desired field and make changes or additions to your data. Because the Form window displays only as many fields as fit on-screen, you find yourself using various navigational aids to move to different locations in your form or between records.

Table 9-1 displays the various navigational keys used to move between fields within a form.

Table 9-1
Navigating in a Form

Navigational Direction	Keystrokes
Next field	Tab, right- or down-arrow key, or Enter
Previous field	Shift+Tab, left-arrow, or up-arrow
First field of current record	Home or Ctrl+Home
Last field of current record	End or Ctrl+End
Next page	PgDn
Previous page	PgUp

If you have a form with more than one page, you see a vertical scroll bar. You can use the scroll bar to move to different pages on the form. You can also use the PgUp and PgDn keys to move between form pages. You can move up or down one field at a time by clicking the scroll bar arrows. With the elevator, you can move between many fields at once.

If your form is larger than the width of the screen, you also see a horizontal scroll bar. The horizontal scroll bar lets you move between areas of the screen horizontally.

Moving between records in a form

Although you generally use a form to display one record at a time, you still want to move between records. The easiest way to do this is to use the navigation buttons.

The navigation buttons offer the same five controls at the bottom of the screen that you saw in the datasheet. You can click on these buttons to move to the desired record.

Pressing F5 moves you instantly to the record number box.

You can also press Ctrl+PgDn to move to the current field in the next record or Ctrl+PgUp to move to the current field in the preceding record.

When you're in the first page of a multiple-page form, pressing PgUp takes you to the current field of the preceding record. When you're in the last page of the multiple-page form, pressing PgDn takes you to the current field in the next record.

Displaying Your Data with a Form

In Chapter 8, you learned techniques to add, change, and delete data within a datasheet. The techniques you learned there are the same ones that you use within a form. These techniques are summarized in Table 9-2.

Table 9-2 Editing Techniques	
Editing Technique	**Keystrokes**
Move insertion point within a field	Press the right- and left-arrow keys
Insert a value within a field	Select the insertion point and type the new data
Select the entire field	Press F2 or double-click the mouse
Replace an existing value with a new value	Select the entire field and type a new value
Replace value with value of preceding field	Press Ctrl+"
Replace current value with default value	Press Ctrl+Alt+spacebar
Insert current date into a field	Press Ctrl+;
Insert current time into a field	Press Ctrl+:
Insert a line break in a Text or Memo field	Press Ctrl+Enter
Insert new record	Press Ctrl++
Delete current record	Press Ctrl+–
Save current record	Press Shift+Enter or move to another record
Undo a change to the current record	Press Esc or click on the Undo button

Working with pictures and OLE objects

In a datasheet, you cannot view a picture or any OLE object without accessing the OLE server. But in a form, you can size the OLE control area large enough to display a picture, business graph, or visual OLE object so that you can see it. Memo controls on forms also can be sized so that you can see the data within the field — you don't have to zoom in on the value, as you do with a datasheet field. Figure 9-14 displays the bottom of the Form window. You can see both the picture and the Memo data displayed in the form. Each of these controls can be resized in the Form Design screen, and the picture can be correctly displayed.

Recall from Chapter 8 that any object supported by an OLE server can be stored in an Access OLE field. You generally enter OLE objects into a form so that you can see, hear, or use the value. Just as with a datasheet, you can enter OLE fields into a form field in two ways:

- Pasted in from the Clipboard
- Inserted into the field from the Edit⇨Insert Object menu

Chapter 20 covers using and displaying OLE objects in forms in more detail.

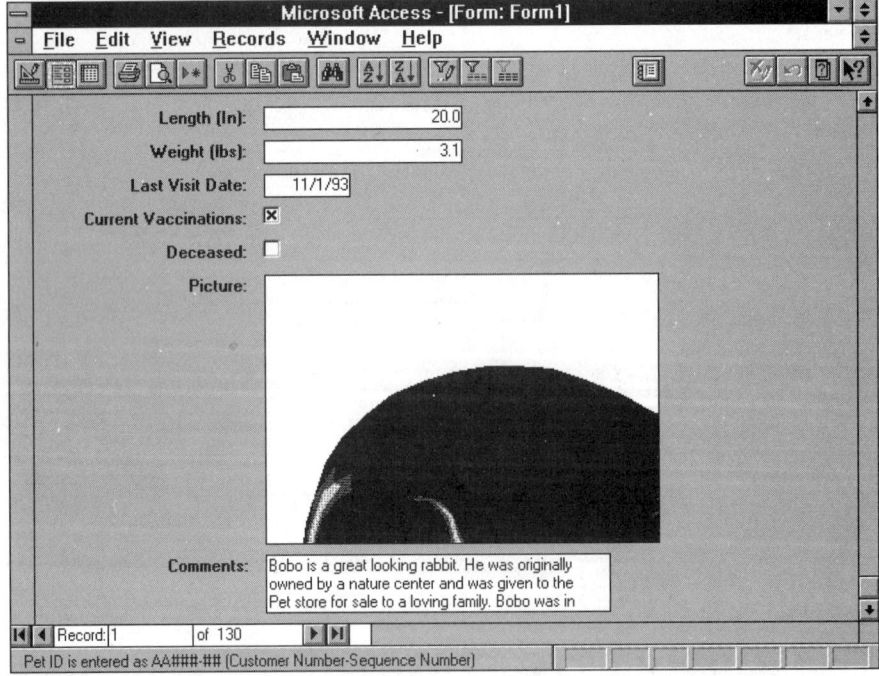

Figure 9-14: Displaying a picture and a Memo field in a form.

Memo field data entry

The last field in the table, Comments, is a Memo data type. This type of field allows for up to 64,000 bytes of text for each field. You can see the first two sentences of data in the Memo field. When the cursor is moved into the Memo field, a vertical scroll bar appears. Using the scroll bar, you can view the rest of the data in the field. You can resize the Memo control in the Form Design window to make it larger if you want. You can also press Shift+F2, as shown in Figure 9-15, and display a Zoom dialog box in the center of the screen, which lets you view about 12 lines at a time.

Switching to a datasheet

You can display a datasheet view of your data by one of two methods:

- Click on the Datasheet button in the toolbar.
- Select View⇨Datasheet.

The datasheet is displayed with the cursor on the same field and record that it was on in the form. If you move to another record and field and then redisplay the form, the form is now displayed with the cursor at the field and record that you were last on in the datasheet.

To return to the form from a datasheet, you can use either of two methods:

- Click on the Form button in the toolbar.
- Select View⇨Form.

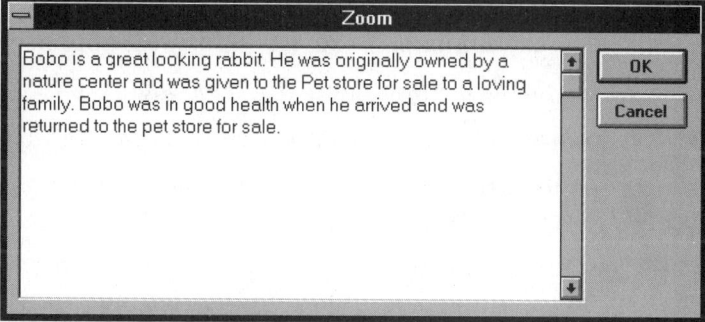

Figure 9-15: Pressing Shift+F2 for a Zoom box view in a Memo field.

Working with form records

You can use the same techniques to manipulate records in a form as you do in a datasheet (as you learned in the preceding chapter). The only difference is that instead of positioning on a specific record, you display a single record.

 If you need to review the techniques for finding and replacing data or filtering and sorting your records, see the appropriate sections in Chapter 8.

Changing the Design

You can change the design of the form at any time by selecting the Design button. The Form Design window is shown in Figure 9-16. As you can see, each field occupies a row in the Form Design window. A text label is shown for each field, which is separate from the field control. In this way, you can manipulate each field separately.

Note that a different toolbar is displayed, along with a toolbox. (If you don't see the toolbox, go to the View menu and choose Toolbox.) The toolbox, which you can move around the screen or resize, contains tools to make creating a custom form easy.

As an example of how easy it is to manipulate the field controls, you can move to the upper areas of the screen the Picture and Comments field controls, which are currently out of sight, just below the Current Vaccinations field. To do this, follow these steps:

Steps:	Moving the Picture and Comments Fields
Step 1.	Use the window elevator or press PgDn to display the bottom of the form.
Step 2.	Click anywhere on the Picture control (the large white box).
Step 3.	Hold Shift down and click the Comments control (a smaller white box).
Step 4.	With both controls selected, drag the controls until they are positioned as in Figure 9-17.
Step 5.	Double-click the Picture control. A property window is displayed.
Step 6.	Click the Size Mode property and change it from Clip to Stretch.

After you complete the move, press the Form button to redisplay the form, as shown in Figure 9-18. Notice that the animal's picture and comments are now displayed on one screen.

Figure 9-16:
The Form Design window.

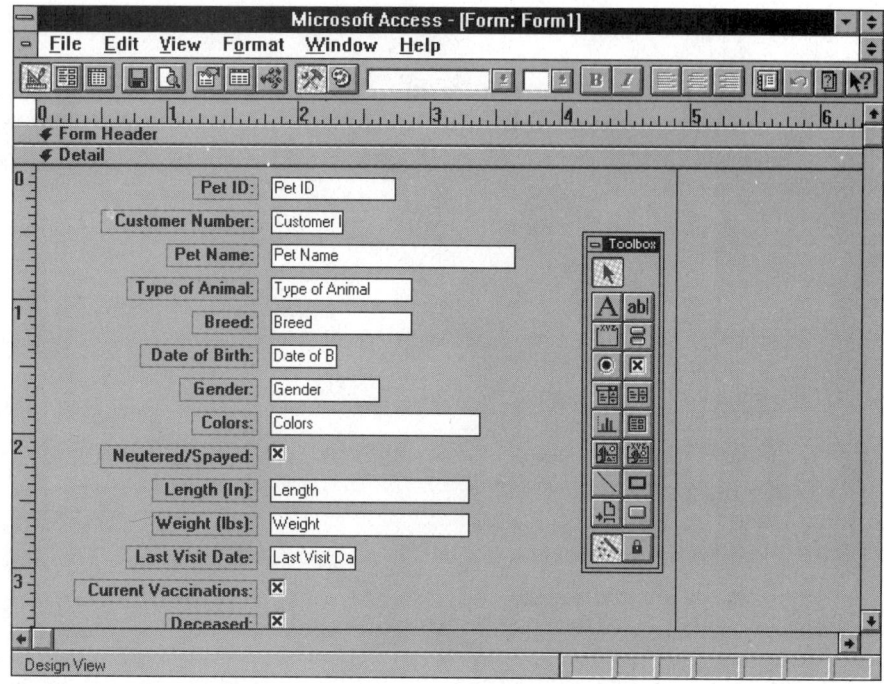

In Chapters 16-20, you learn how to completely customize a form. You learn how to use all the controls in the toolbox, add special effects to forms, create forms with graphs and calculated fields, and add complex data validation to your forms.

Saving a Record and the Form

As you move off each record, any changes to the record are saved. You can also save a record without moving off of it by pressing Shift+Enter. The final way to save a record is to save the form. You can save any changes to a form design by selecting File⇨Save Form. This saves any changes and keeps the form open. When you are ready to close a form and return to the Database window, query, or datasheet, you can select File⇨Close. If you made any changes to the form design, you are asked whether you want to save the design.

Figure 9-17: Moving field controls in a form.

Figure 9-18: The form redisplayed to show the picture and comments.

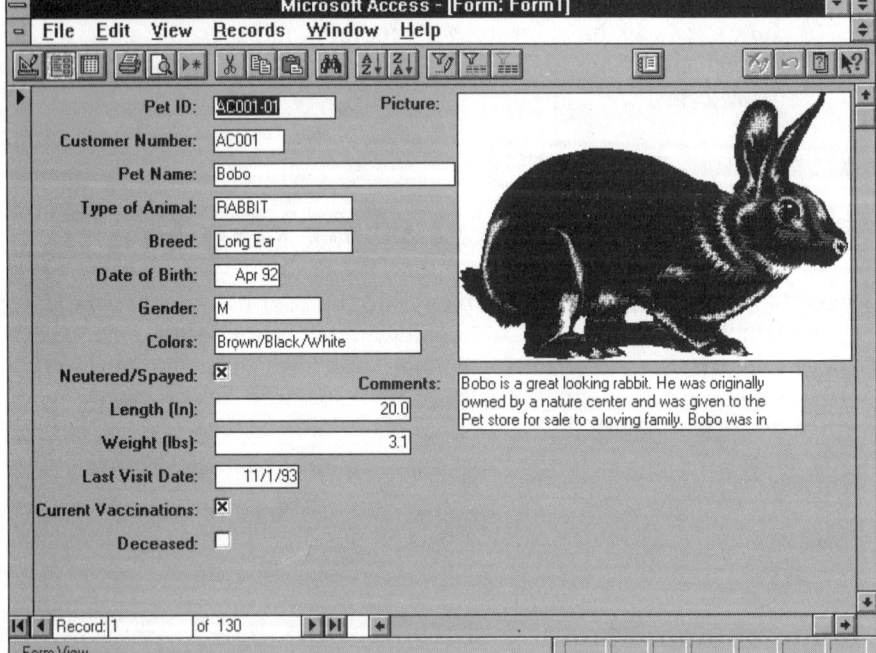

Printing a Form

You can print one or more records in your form exactly as they look on the screen. Later, you learn how to produce formatted reports. The simplest way to print is to use the File⇨Print... selection or the Print toolbar button. Selecting File⇨Print... displays the Print dialog box.

Assuming that you have set up a printer in Microsoft Windows, you can select OK to print your form. Your form is printed using the font you selected for display or using the nearest printer equivalent. The printout contains any formatting in the form, including lines, boxes, and shading. Colors are converted to various grey shades on a monochrome printer.

The printout prints as many pages as necessary to print all the data. If your form is wider than a printer page, you will need multiple pages to print your form. Access breaks up the printout as necessary to fit on each page.

Using the Print Preview Window

Many times, you have all the information in the form, but you aren't sure whether the form will print on multiple pages or will fit onto one printed page. Maybe you want to see whether the fonts need adjustment to print your output better. Perhaps you think you need only the printed records from pages 3 and 4. You probably want to view the report on-screen before printing to make these adjustments to the form design.

To preview your printout, you can either click the Print Preview button on the toolbar (a sheet of paper with a magnifying glass on top) or select File⇨Print Preview. The Print Preview window is shown in Figure 9-19. The Print Preview window works exactly like the datasheet Print Preview window you learned about in Chapter 8.

If, after examining the preview, you are satisfied with the form, simply select the Print button on the toolbar to print the form. If you are not satisfied, press the Close window button to return to the form to make further changes to your data or design.

Printing a Form Definition

The menu item File⇨Print Definition... displays a dialog box as shown in Figure 9-20 that lets you select what information from the Form Design you want to print. You can print the various field names, all their properties, code behind form controls, and even network permissions.

Once you select which data you want to view, a report is generated and you can view it in a Print Preview window or send the output to a printer.

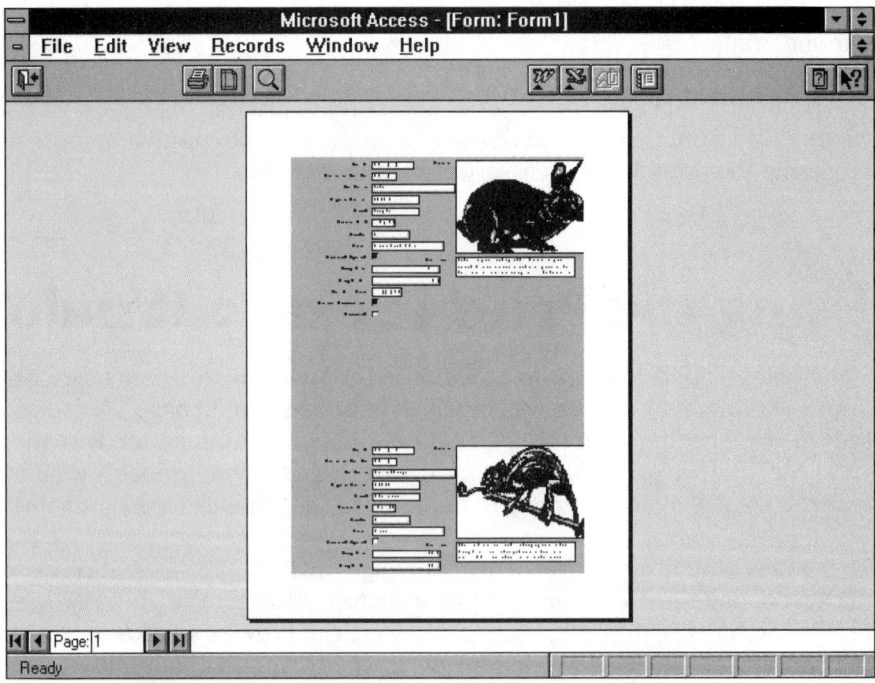

Figure 9-19: The Print Preview window.

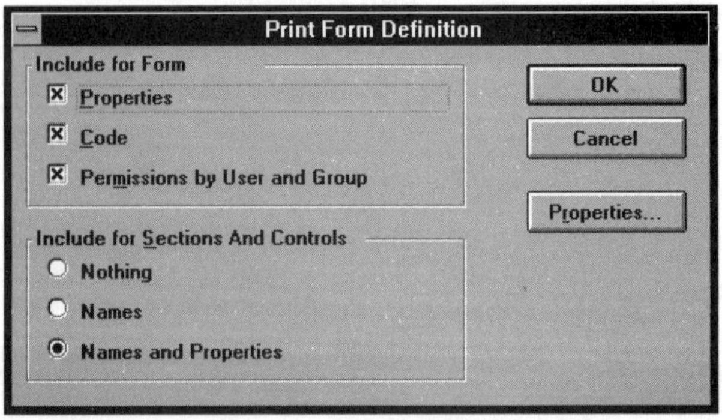

Figure 9-20: The Form Design Print Definition dialog box.

Summary

This chapter examined Form Wizards and how you can use them as the starting point for your form. You learned about how forms work and the types of forms you can create with Access. The following points were covered:

- Data-entry forms provide the most flexible format for viewing your data, as you can arrange your fields in any order you want.
- Whereas datasheets generally let you view many records at a time, a form is used to view one record at a time.
- AutoForm instantly creates a form for you with just one keystroke.
- Form Wizards simplify the process of form creation and give you a starting point for form design.
- There are four basic types of forms: full-screen forms, tabular, main/subforms, and graphs.
- A Form Wizard lets you specify the type of form, the fields to be used, the type of look you want, and a title.
- You can specify one or more fields in a Form Wizard.
- A Form Wizard lets you choose from several types of looks, including standard, chiseled, shadowed, boxed, and embossed.
- A form lets you enter data into Picture and Memo fields and displays the fields as well.
- You can switch to a datasheet from a form by selecting the Datasheet button.
- You can find or replace values in a form by using Edit⇨Find and Edit⇨Replace.
- You can print a form with all of its formatting, or you can preview it on the screen before printing.

In the following chapter, you learn about simple queries.

Understanding and Using Simple Queries

CHAPTER 10

In This Chapter

- Understanding the different types of queries
- Creating queries
- Selecting tables and fields for queries
- Displaying information in queries
- Sorting information in queries
- Selecting specific records in queries
- Printing the results of queries

In this chapter, you learn what a query is and about the process of creating queries. Using the Pets table, you create several types of queries for the Mountain Animal Hospital database.

Understanding Queries

The primary purpose of any database, manual or automated, is to store and extract information. Information can be obtained from a database immediately after you enter the data or years later. Of course, even with a manually assembled database, obtaining information requires knowledge of how the database is set up.

For example, reports may be manually filed in a cabinet, arranged by order of year and then by a sequence number that indicates the order of when the report was written. To obtain a specific report, you must know its year and sequence number. In a good manual system, you may have a cross-reference book to help you find a specific report. This book may have all reports categorized by type of report (rather than topic) in alphabetical order. Although this can be helpful, if you know only the topic of the report and its approximate date, you still may have to search through all sections of the book to find out where to obtain the report.

Finding information by a *nonstandardized method* in a manual database can be a very time-consuming if not an impossible task.

Unlike manual databases, computer-automated databases have a distinct advantage; with tools, you can easily obtain information by virtually any criteria that you specify.

This is the real power of a database — the capacity for you to examine the data any way that *you* want to look at it. Queries, by definition, ask questions about the data stored in the database. After you create a query, you can use its data for reports, forms, and even graphs.

What is a query?

The word *query* comes from the Latin word *quærere,* which simply means to ask or inquire. Over the years, the word query has become synonymous with quiz, challenge, inquire, or question. Therefore, you can think of a query as a question or inquiry posed to the database about information found in the tables of that database.

A Microsoft Access query is a question that you ask about the information stored in your Access tables. The way you ask questions about this information is through use of the query tools. Your query can be a simple question about information stored in a single table, or it can be a complex question about information stored in several tables. After you ask the question, Microsoft Access returns only the information you requested.

Using queries in this way, you can query the Pets database to show you only the dogs named within it. To see the dogs' names, you need to retrieve information from the Pets table. Figure 10-1 shows a typical Query screen, and Figure 10-2 shows the results of the query you create. Figure 10-2 contains only those records where the value of the Type of Animal field is DOG.

After you create and run a query, Microsoft Access can return and display the set of records that you asked for in a *datasheet.* This set of records is called a *dynaset,* which is simply the set of selected records from a query. As you've seen, a datasheet looks just like a spreadsheet, with its rows of records and columns of fields. The datasheet can display many records simultaneously.

As you saw demonstrated in Figures 10-1 and 10-2, information can be queried from a single table. But many database queries require information from several tables.

Chapter 10: Understanding and Using Simple Queries

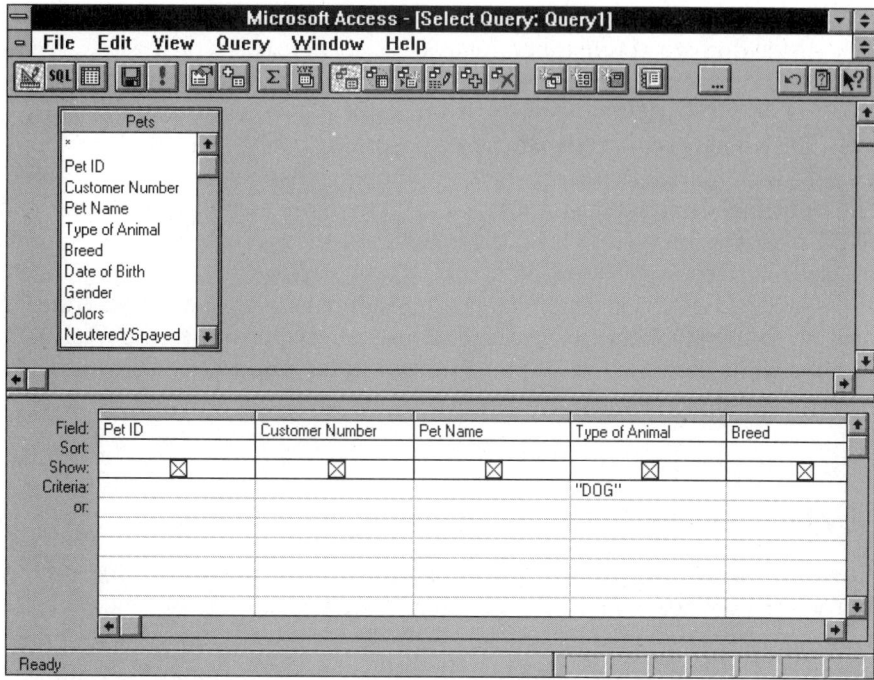

Figure 10-1: A typical select query.

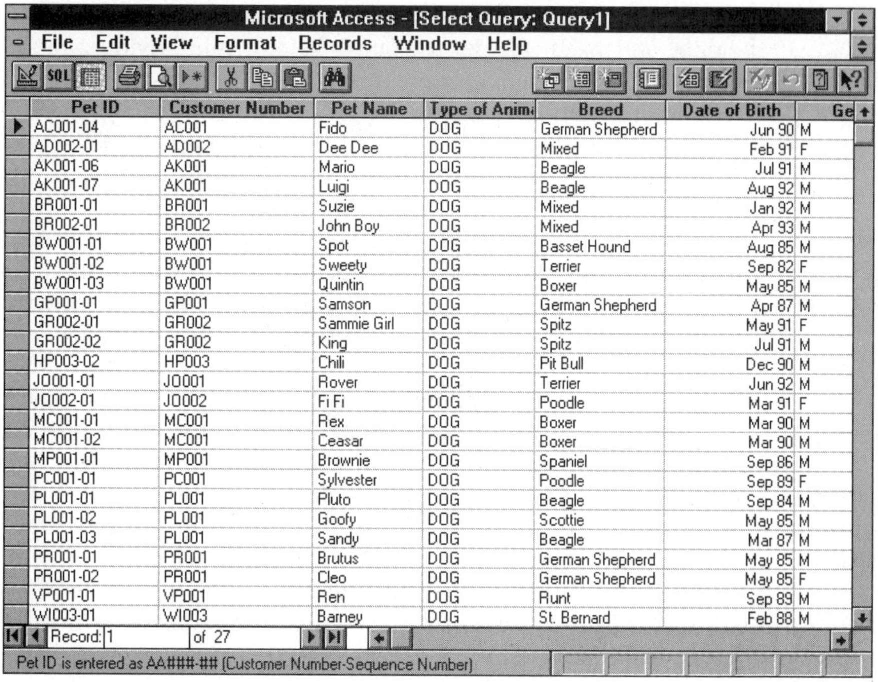

Figure 10-2: A datasheet displaying records for DOG only.

Suppose, for example, that you want to send a reminder to anyone living in a certain city whose dog or cat is due for an annual vaccination, based on the town license regulations. This type of query requires getting information from two tables: Customer and Pets.

 You may want Access to show you a single datasheet of all customers and their pets that meet your specified criteria. Access can retrieve customer names and cities from the Customer table, and then pet names, animal type, and current vaccination status from the Pets table. Access then takes the information common to your criteria, combines it, and displays all the information in a single datasheet. This datasheet is the result of a query that draws from both the Customer and Pets tables. The database query performed the work of assembling all the information for you. In this chapter, you work only with the Pets table. Multiple table queries are covered in Part III.

Types of queries

There are many different types of queries that Access supports. They can be grouped into six basic categories:

Select These are the most common. As its name implies, the select query selects information from one or more tables based on specific criteria and displays the information in a dynaset that you can use to view specific data, analyze the data, and make changes to your data in the underlying tables.

Total These are a special form of select queries. Total queries give you the ability to sum or produce totals (such as count) in a select query. When you select this type of query, access adds the Total row in the QBE pane.

Action These queries let you create new tables (Make Tables) or change data (delete, update, and append) in existing tables. When you make changes to records in a select query, the changes must be made one record at a time. In action queries, changes can be made to many records during a single operation.

Crosstab These queries can display summary data in *cross-tabular form* like a spreadsheet, with the row and column headings based on fields in the table. By definition, the individual cells of the resultant dynaset are tabular — that is, computed or calculated.

SQL There are three new query types in version 2.0 — *Union, Pass-Through, and Data Definition*. These queries can only be created by writing SQL specific commands. They are used for advanced SQL database manipulation (like working with Client/Server SQL databases).

Top(n) This is a query limiter that can be used in conjunction with the other five (5) types of queries. It lets you specify a number or percentage of the top records that you want to see in any type of query.

Query capabilities

Queries are flexible. They give you the versatile capability of looking at your data in virtually any way you can think of. Most database systems are continually evolving with more powerful and necessary tools. The original purpose they were designed for changes over time. You may decide that you want to look at the information stored in the database in a different way. Because information is stored in a database, you should be able to look at it in this new way. Looking at data in a way different from its intended manner is known as performing *ad-hoc* queries. You'll find that querying tools are one of the most powerful tools associated with your database, and Microsoft Access querying is indeed very powerful and flexible. Here is a sampling of what you can do:

Choose tables
: You can obtain information from a single table or from many tables that are related by some common data. Suppose that you're interested in seeing the customer name along with the type of animals each customer owns. This sample task takes information from the Customer and Pets tables. When using several tables, Access returns the data in a combined single datasheet.

Choose fields
: You can specify which fields from each table that you want to see in the resultant dynaset. For example, you can look at the customer name, customer ZIP code, animal name, and animal type separated from all the other fields in the Customer or Pets table.

Choose records
: You can select the records to display in the dynaset by specifying criteria. For example, you may want to see records for dogs only.

Sort records
: Many times, you'll want to look at the dynaset information sorted in a specific order. You may need to see customers in order by last name and first name.

Perform Calculations
: You can use queries to perform calculations on your data. You may be interested in performing such calculations as averaging, totaling, or simply counting the fields.

Create tables
: You may need another database table formed from the combined data resulting from a query. The query can create this new table based on the dynaset.

Create forms and reports based on a query	The dynaset that you create from a query may have just the right fields and data that you need for a report or form. By basing the form or report on a query, every time you print the report or open the form, your query will retrieve the most current information from your tables.
Create graphs based on queries	You can create graphs from the data in a query, which you can then use in a form or report.
Use a Query as a source of data for other queries (subquery)	You can create additional queries based on a set of records that you selected in a previous query. This is very useful for performing ad-hoc queries, where you may make a small change to the criteria over and over. The secondary query can be used for the criteria change, while the primary query and its data remain intact.
Make changes to data in non-Access tables	Access queries can obtain information from a wide range of sources. You can ask questions about data stored in dBASE, Paradox, Btrieve, and Microsoft SQL Server databases.

How dynasets work

Earlier, you learned that Access takes the resultant records from a query and displays them in a datasheet, in which the actual records are called a dynaset. Physically, a dynaset looks like a table, but in fact, it is not. The dynaset is a dynamic (or virtual) set of records. *This dynamic set of records is not stored in the database.*

 When you close a query, the query dynaset is gone; it will no longer exist. But even though the dynaset itself no longer exists, remember that the data that formed the dynaset remains stored in the underlying tables.

When a query is run, the resultant records are placed in the dynaset. When you save the query, the information is *not* saved; only the structure of the query is saved — the tables, fields, sort order, record limitations, query type, and so forth.

Consider these benefits of not saving the dynaset to a physical table:

- The storage device, usually a hard disk, uses less space.
- The query can use updated versions of any records changed since the query was last run.

Every time the query is executed, it goes out to the underlying tables and re-creates the dynaset. Because the dynaset records are not stored, a query automatically reflects any changes to the underlying tables whenever the query is executed, even in a real-time multiuser environment.

Creating a Query

After you create your tables and place data in them, you are ready to work with queries. To begin a query, follow these steps:

Steps:	Beginning a Query
Step 1.	From the Database window, click the Query Object button.
Step 2.	Select the New button. The New Query dialog box appears, as shown in Figure 10-3. The Query Wizards button is used to create special types of queries, such as crosstabs.
Step 3.	Select the New Query button in the New Query dialog box.

You can also begin a new query by selecting the New Query button on the toolbar or you can select File⇨New⇨Query from the main Access menu.

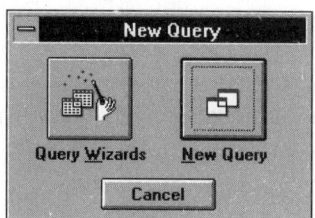

Figure 10-3:
The New Query dialog box.

After you choose the New Query button, Access opens two new windows. Figure 10-4 shows both windows. The underlying window is the Query window, and the surface window is the Add Table dialog box. This Add Table dialog box is *nonmodal,* which means simply that you must do something in the dialog box before continuing with the query. Before you continue, you should add tables for the query to work with.

Selecting a table

Following Along in This Book

The Add Table dialog box displays all tables and queries in your database. If you are following along with the examples, you should see one table named Pets. If you are using the MTNSTART or MTNANHSP databases, you should see all the tables in the Mountain Animal Hospital database. You can add the Pets table to the query design with these steps:

Steps:	Adding a Table
Step 1.	Click the Pets table.
Step 2.	Select the Add button to add the Pets table to the Query Design window.
Step 3.	Select the Close button.

Another method of adding the Pets table to the Design window is to simply double-click the Pets table.

You can activate the Add Table dialog box to add more tables at any time; select Query➪Add Table... from the Query menu.

In version 2.0 you can also add tables by moving the mouse to any empty place in the top half of the window (the table/query pane) and *right* mouse clicking. By right mouse clicking, you activate the shortcut menus and select Add Tables.

When you want to delete a table from the query pane, you can click on the table name in the query/table entry pane and either press Delete or select Query➪Remove Table.

You also can add a table to the query/table pane by selecting the Database window and dragging and dropping a table name from the table window into the Query window. To do this, follow these steps:

1. While in the Query Design window, press F11 or Alt+F1 or select the Database container button on the toolbar.

2. Select the table you want by clicking it. Then drag the table icon (holding the mouse button down) to the top pane of the Query window.

3. Drop the table icon anywhere in the top portion of the Query window.

In version 2.0, the Add Table dialog box in Figure 10-4 has three new radio buttons along the bottom of the box. There are three choices — Tables, Queries, and Both. In version 2.0, the dialog box only shows the tables by default. If you want to select from existing queries, you can select the Query button. Of course, if you want to select from Tables and Queries, you can select the Both button.

Using the Query window

The Query window has two modes, the *design mode* and the *datasheet mode*. The difference between the modes is self-explanatory: The design mode is where the query is created, and the datasheet is where the query dynaset is displayed.

Chapter 10: Understanding and Using Simple Queries 207

The Query window should now look like Figure 10-5, with the Pets table displayed in the top half of the Query window.

The Query window is currently in the design mode and is comprised of two panes:

- The table/query entry pane
- The query by example (QBE) design pane (also called the QBE grid)

The *table/query entry pane* is where tables and/or queries and their design structures are displayed. Each field is listed in the visual representation of the table. The *query by example (QBE) pane* is used for the fields and criteria that the query will display in the dynaset. Each column in the QBE design pane contains information about a single field from a table or query in the upper pane.

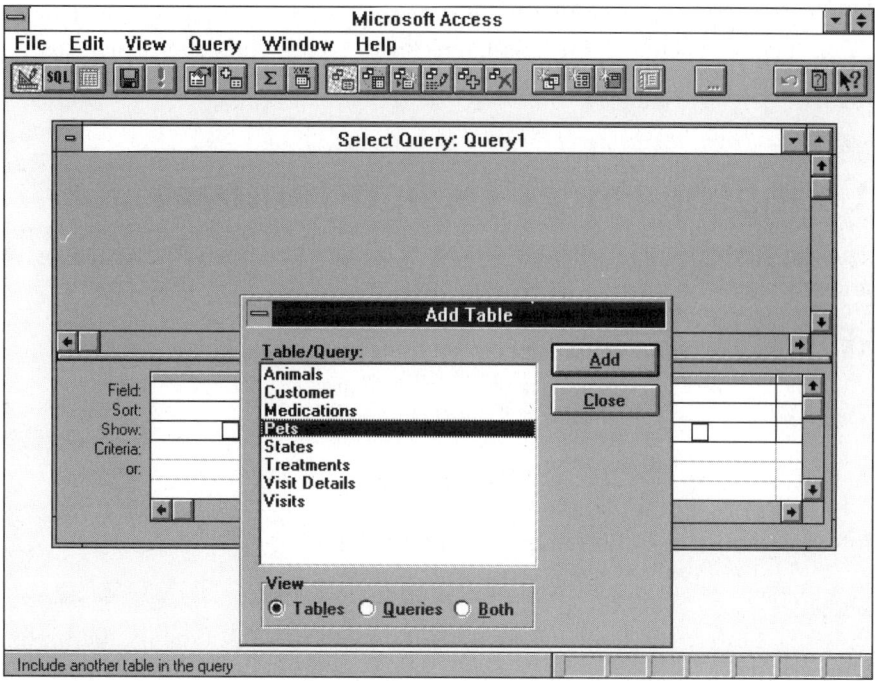

Figure 10-4: The Add Table dialog box in the Query window.

Navigating the Query Design window

The title bar, located at the top of the Query window, bears information about a particular window, the type of query, and the query name. A new query is named Query1. Note that the title bar in Figure 10-5 displays the query type and name as `Select Query:Query1`.

The two window panes are separated horizontally by a pane resizing bar (dividing bar). You'll use this bar to resize the windows: Click on the bar and then drag the bar down to enlarge the upper window — or drag the bar up to enlarge the lower window.

You can switch between the upper and lower panes either by clicking the desired pane or by pressing F6 to move to the other pane. Notice that each window pane has scroll bars to help you move around the pane.

If you vertically resize the Pets design structure, you can see more fields at one time. With horizontal resizing, you can see more of the field names. To see more fields, first resize the top pane to size the Pets structure vertically.

You can design a query with a feature known as *Graphical Query by Example (GQBE)*. As you'll see, graphical QBE lets you easily add fields to create queries. Using a graphical method, you drag fields from the upper pane to the lower pane of the Query window. After you place fields on the QBE pane (lower pane), you can set their display order by dragging a field from its current position to a new position in the pane.

Using the Query Design toolbar

The toolbar in the Query Design window contains several buttons specific to building and working with queries, as shown in Figure 10-6.

They are grouped into nine specific sections going from left to right:

View/Work	Design, SQL, and Datasheet
Action	Save and Run
Information	Properties and Add Table
Show	Totals and Table Names
Query Type	Select, Crosstab, Make Table, Update table, Append, and Delete
New Object	New Query, New Form, New Report
Database Container	Database window
Add-in	Build
General	Undo, Cue Cards, and Help

Chapter 10: Understanding and Using Simple Queries

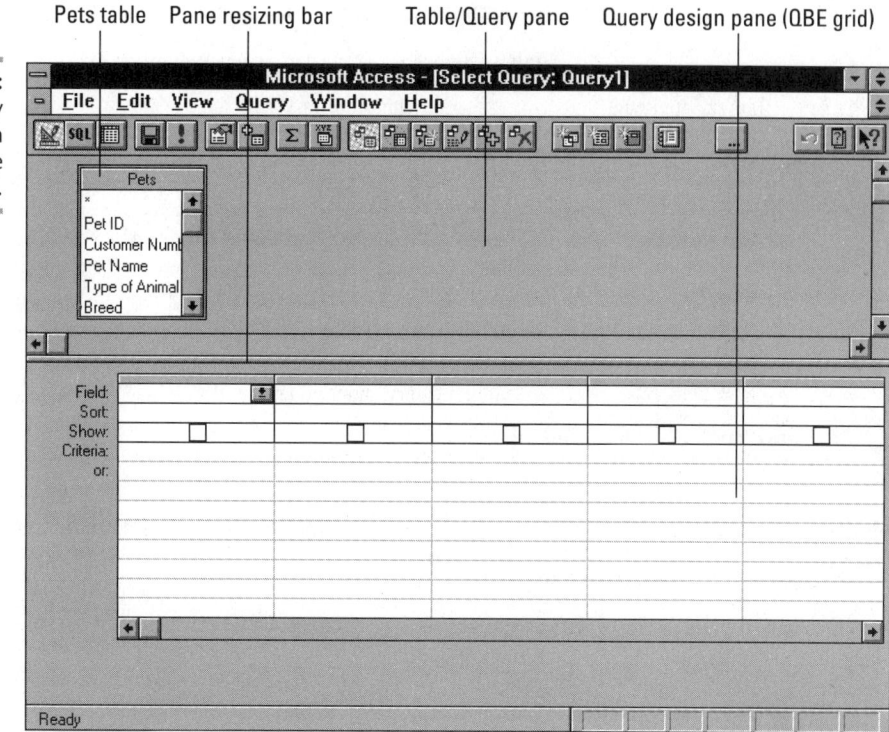

Figure 10-5: The Query window with the Pets table displayed.

All of these tool bar buttons are choices that can also be accessed using the Query Design menu. They offer a quick way for you to work with queries. As you create and use queries, this book will demonstrate which buttons to use to help you work smarter.

Using the Query Design menu

The Query Design menu is located on the second line of the screen, below the Microsoft Access title bar. As you saw in Figure 10-5, six menu prompts are offered in the Query Design window: File, Edit, View, Query, Window, and Help.

The View and Query menus contain choices specific to queries. The other menus contain options that are applicable to most Access functions.

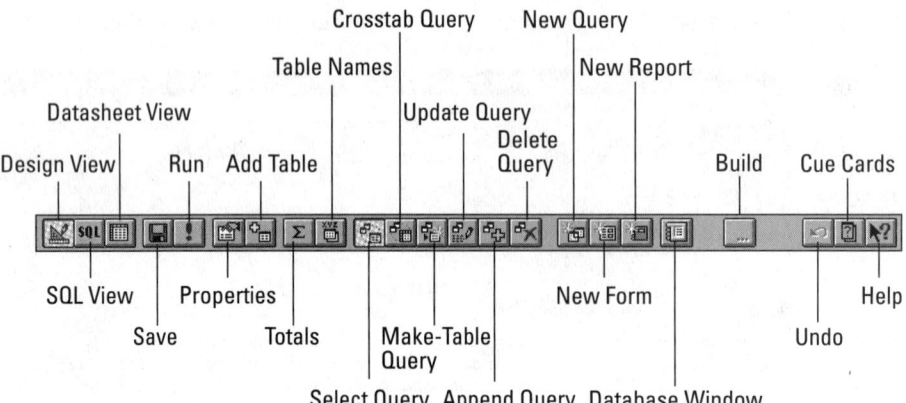

Figure 10-6: The Query Design toolbar.

Figure 10-7 shows the View menu in the query, which you use to perform these tasks:

- Viewing the query design
- Viewing the SQL commands that are generated when the query is run
- Viewing the query datasheet
- Displaying totals in the query design
- Displaying table names
- Displaying the properties dialog box
- Setting or using toolbars and global options

In Figure 10-8, you see the Query menu within the Query window. This menu gives you these options:

- Running a query
- Adding or removing tables from the query/table entry pane
- Determining the type of query with choices of Select, Crosstab, Make Table..., Update, Append, or Delete
- Creating SQL-specific queries
- Getting help on joining tables
- Entering parameters for creating a query

Chapter 10: Understanding and Using Simple Queries

Figure 10-7:
The Query window View menu.

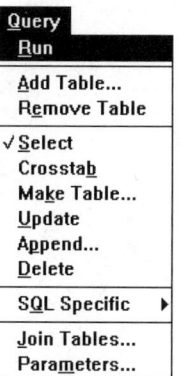

Figure 10-8:
The Query window Query menu.

Using the QBE pane of the query design window

Figure 10-9 shows you an empty query design pane (QBE grid). You'll see five named rows in this pane:

Field   This is where field names are entered or added.

Sort   This choice sorts directives for the query.

Show   This checkbox determines whether the field is displayed in the datasheet.

Criteria   This is where you enter the first line of criteria to limit the record selection.

Or   This is the first of a number of lines used to add multiple values to be used in criteria selection.

 The Access manual occasionally refers to the top and bottom portions of the Query Design window as *grids*. Here, both sections (top and bottom) are called *panes*. According to Microsoft's Windows Design Guide, a pane is a portion of a window (top or bottom) that has a distinct use in the window.

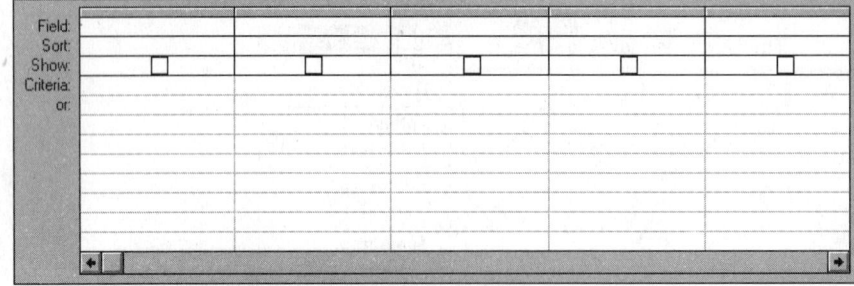

Figure 10-9: The Query window QBE design pane.

You learn more about these rows as you create several sample queries in this chapter.

Selecting Fields

You can use several ways to add fields to a query. You can add fields one at a time or select multiple fields or all fields. You can add the fields either by using the keyboard or the mouse.

Adding a single field

You can add a single field in several ways. One method is to double-click the field name; the field name then appears in the next available column in the query design pane. You can also add a field graphically to the query design pane by following these steps:

Steps:	Adding a Single Field to the Query
Step 1.	Highlight the field name in the table/query entry area.
Step 2.	Click the desired field and drag the Field icon, which appears as you move the mouse.
Step 3.	Drop the Field icon in the desired column of the QBE design pane.

The Field icon looks like a small rectangle when it is inside the Pets table. As the mouse is dragged outside the Pets table, the icon changes to a ⊘, meaning that you cannot drop the Field icon in that location. When this icon enters any column in the QBE column, the field name appears in the Field: row. If the field is dropped between two fields, it appears between the other fields and pushes all existing fields to the right.

Chapter 10: Understanding and Using Simple Queries   213

 If you accidentally select a field, you can deselect it by releasing the mouse button while the icon is the No symbol, ⊘.

To run the query, select the Datasheet button on the toolbar (the third one from the left). When you are finished, press the Design button on the toolbar (the first one on the left) to return to Design mode.

Another way to add fields to the QBE design pane is to click on the empty Field: cell in the QBE design pane and then type the field name in the field cell. Or select the field you want from the drop-down list that appears (see Figure 10-10).

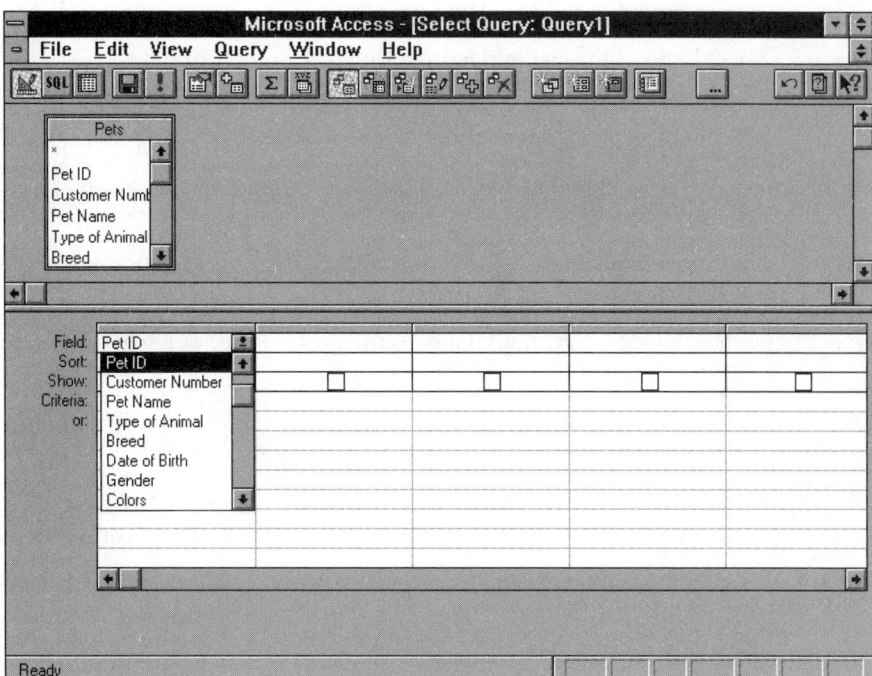

Figure 10-10: Adding a single field in the QBE design pane.

Adding multiple fields

You can add more than one field at a time by selecting the fields and then dragging the selection to the query pane. For you to add multiple fields from a table simultaneously, the selected fields do not have to be contiguous (one after the other). The process of adding multiple fields is illustrated in Figure 10-11.

Steps:	**Adding Multiple Contiguous Fields to the Query**
Step 0.	Remove any existing fields in the QBE pane by selecting Edit⇨Clear Grid from the menu.
Step 1.	Highlight the first field name in the table/query entry area that you want to add.
Step 2.	Hold the Shift key down and click the last field that you want to select. (All the fields in-between will be selected also.)
Step 3.	Click the selected fields and drag the Multiple Field icon, which appears as you move the mouse. The icon appears as a group of three field icons.
Step 4.	Drop the Multiple Field icon in the desired column of the QBE design pane.

Steps:	**Adding Multiple Noncontiguous Fields to the Query**
Step 0.	Remove any existing fields in the QBE pane by selecting Edit⇨Clear Grid from the menu.
Step 1.	Highlight the first field name in the table/query entry area that you want to add.
Step 2.	Hold the Control key down and click each field that you want to select. (Only the fields you select will be highlighted.)
Step 3.	Click the selected fields and drag the Multiple Field icon, which appears as you move the mouse. The icon appears as a group of three field icons.
Step 4.	Drop the Multiple Field icon in the desired column of the QBE design pane.

Adding all table fields

Besides adding fields just one at a time or multiple fields, you can move all the fields to the QBE pane at once. Access gives you two methods for choosing all fields: by dragging all fields as a group or by selecting the all-field reference tag — the asterisk (*).

Chapter 10: Understanding and Using Simple Queries 215

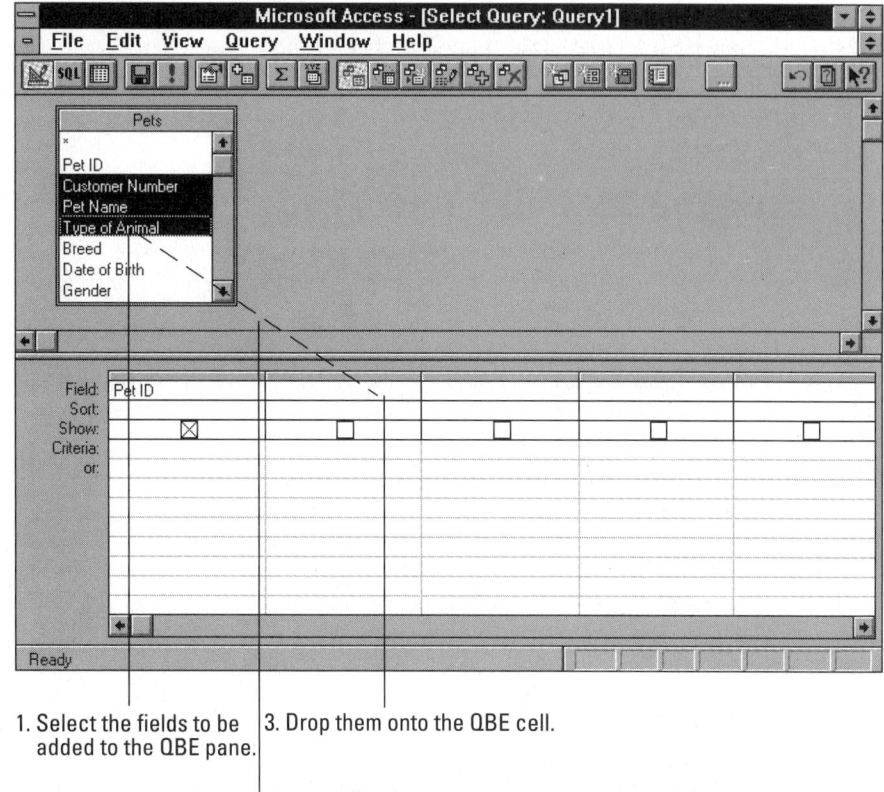

Figure 10-11: Selecting several fields grapically to move to the QBE pane.

1. Select the fields to be added to the QBE pane.
2. Drag them to the QBE pane.
3. Drop them onto the QBE cell.

Dragging all fields as a group

To select all the fields of a table, perform these three steps:

Steps:	Adding All Fields to a Query
Step 0.	Remove any existing fields in the QBE pane by selecting Edit⇨Clear Grid from the menu.
Step 1.	Double-click the title bar of the table to select all the fields.
Step 2.	Point to any of the selected fields with the mouse.
Step 3.	Drag the Multiple Field icon down to the QBE pane.

This method automatically fills in each column of the QBE pane. All the fields are added to the QBE pane from left to right, based on their field order in the Pets table. By default, only the first five fields are displayed. You can change the column width of each field to display more or fewer columns.

Selecting the all-field reference tag

The first object in the Pets table is an asterisk, which appears at the top of the field list. When you select all fields by using the asterisk, you don't see all the fields moved to the QBE design pane. You see only that `Pets.*` is displayed in the Field row to indicate that all fields from the table named Pets are now selected (see Figure 10-12). This example assumes that the QBE design pane is empty when you drag the asterisk from the Pets table to the QBE design pane.

The asterisk places the fields in a single Field: cell. When you dragged multiple fields with the first technique, you dragged actual table field names to the query design pane, thus placing each field in a separate Field: cell across the QBE pane. If you later change the design of the table, you also must change the design of the query. The advantage of using the asterisk for selecting all fields is that you won't have to change the query later if you add, delete, or rename fields in the underlying table or query. Changing fields in the underlying table or query will automatically be added or removed from the query.

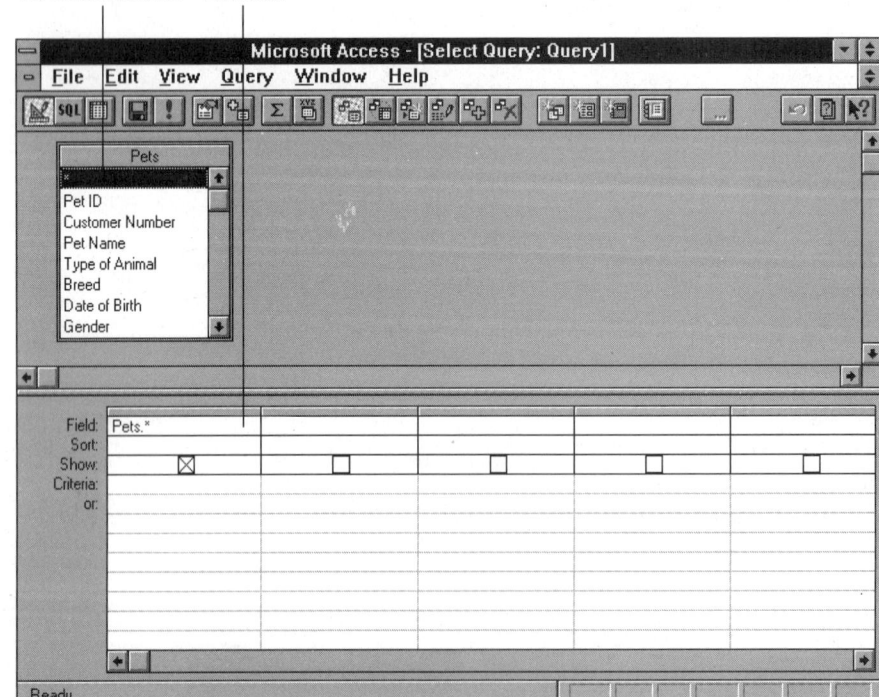

Figure 10-12: Selecting all fields in the Pets table with the asterisk.

Chapter 10: Understanding and Using Simple Queries   **217**

Following Along in This Book

If you are following along with the examples, you need to delete all fields from the query by selecting Edit⇨Delete All from the Query Design menu.

Now that you've cleared all the fields, you can select the first nine fields (Pet ID through Neutered/Spayed inclusively) in the Pets table and move them to the QBE design pane. Follow these steps:

Steps:	Adding the all-fields reference tag to the Query Design
Step 0.	Remove any existing fields in the QBE pane by selecting Edit⇨Clear Grid from the menu.
Step 1.	Click the asterisk (*) in the Pets table to select this field.
Step 2.	Click the selected field and drag the Field icon to the first cell in the QBE design pane.

You now have the all fields reference tag in the QBE pane. When you run this query all the fields from Pets will be displayed.

Displaying the Dynaset

With multiple fields selected, it is time to display the resultant dynaset. You can switch to the datasheet by either selecting View⇨Datasheet or selecting the Datasheet button on the toolbar. The datasheet should now look like Figure 10-13.

Working with the datasheet

The dynaset is displayed in a datasheet. The techniques for navigating, changing field order, and working with columns and rows of a query datasheet are exactly the same as for the other datasheets you worked with in Chapter 8.

Figure 10-13:
The datasheet with several fields.

Pet ID	Customer Number	Pet Name	Type of Anim.	Breed	Date of Birth	Ge
AC001-01	AC001	Bobo	RABBIT	Long Ear	Apr 92	M
AC001-02	AC001	Presto Chango	LIZARD	Chameleon	May 92	F
AC001-03	AC001	Stinky	SKUNK		Aug 91	M
AC001-04	AC001	Fido	DOG	German Shepherd	Jun 90	M
AD001-01	AD001	Patty	PIG	Potbelly	Feb 91	F
AD001-02	AD001	Rising Sun	HORSE	Palomino	Apr 90	M
AD002-01	AD002	Dee Dee	DOG	Mixed	Feb 91	F
AK001-01	AK001	Margo	SQUIRREL		Mar 86	F
AK001-02	AK001	Tom	CAT	Tabby	Feb 85	M
AK001-03	AK001	Jerry	RAT		Feb 88	M
AK001-04	AK001	Marcus	CAT	Siamese	Nov 87	M
AK001-05	AK001	Pookie	CAT	Siamese	Apr 85	F
AK001-06	AK001	Mario	DOG	Beagle	Jul 91	M
AK001-07	AK001	Luigi	DOG	Beagle	Aug 92	M
BA001-01	BA001	Swimmy	DOLPHIN	Bottlenose	Jul 90	F
BA001-02	BA001	Charger	WHALE	Beluga	Oct 90	M
BA001-03	BA001	Daffy	DUCK	Mallard	Sep 83	M
BA001-04	BA001	Toby	TURTLE	Box	Dec 90	M
BA001-05	BA001	Jake	DOLPHIN	Bottlenose	Apr 91	M
BL001-01	BL001	Tiajuana	BIRD	Toucan	Sep 90	F
BL001-02	BL001	Carlos	BIRD	Cockatoo	Jan 91	M
BL001-03	BL001	Ming	BIRD	Humming	Feb 88	F
BL001-04	BL001	Yellow Jacket	BIRD	Canary	Mar 83	F
BL001-05	BL001	Red Breast	BIRD	Robin	Jun 90	M
BL001-06	BL001	Mickey	BIRD	Parrot	May 91	M
BL001-07	BI001	Sally	BIRD	Parrot	Jul 85	F

Pet ID is entered as AA###-## (Customer Number-Sequence Number)

Changing data in the query datasheet

The query datasheet offers you an easy and convenient way to change data quickly. You can add and change data in the dynaset, and it will be saved to the underlying tables.

When you're adding or changing data in the datasheet, all the table properties defined at table level are in effect. For example, you cannot enter a length greater than 120 for any animal.

Returning to the query design

To return to the query design mode, select the Design button on the toolbar (the first one from the left).

You can also toggle between the design and datasheet mode by selecting View⇨Datasheet or View⇨Query Design from the Query menu.

Working with Fields

There are times when you'll want to work with the fields you've already selected — rearranging their order, inserting a new field, or deleting an existing field. You may even want to add a field to the QBE design but not show it in the datasheet. Access makes these tasks very simple by using its graphical QBE.

The field selector row is the narrow grey row above the Field: row. This row is approximately half the size of the others; it's important to identify this row because this is where you select columns, whether single or multiple. Recall that each column represents a field. To select the Pet Name field, move the mouse pointer until a small selection arrow, in this case an outlined downward arrow, is visible in the selector row; then click the column. Figure 10-14 shows the selection arrow in the next column and the column after it is selected.

 If extend mode (F8) is on, the cursor must be in the row whose column you want to select. If the cursor is in an adjacent column and you select a column, the column you selected and the adjacent one containing the cursor will also be selected. To deactivate extend mode (EXT), simply press the escape key.

Changing field order

Several methods are available for changing the order of the fields in the QBE design pane. One way is to simply add them in the order you want them to appear in the datasheet. This is not always the easiest method, however. You can move fields after they are placed on the QBE design by selecting columns and moving them, just as you learned to move columns in a datasheet. The following steps show you how to move a field:

Steps:	Moving a Field
Step 0.	Add several fields to the QBE pane.
Step 1.	Select the field you want to move by clicking on the field selector above the field name. The column is highlighted.
Step 2.	Click and hold the field selector again; the QBE Field icon, a small graphical box, appears under the arrow.
Step 3.	While holding down the left button, drag the column to its new position.

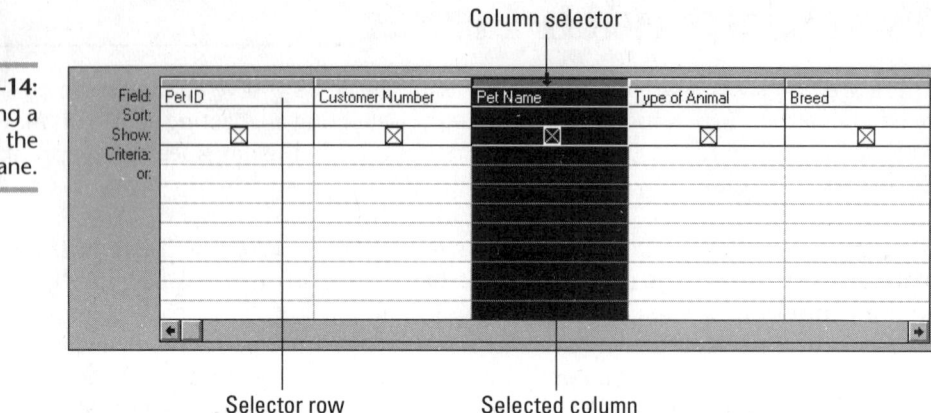

Figure 10-14: Selecting a column in the QBE pane.

Figure 10-15 shows the Breed field highlighted (selected). As you move the selector field to the left, the column separator between the fields Pet Name and Type of Animal changes (gets wider) to show you where Breed will go.

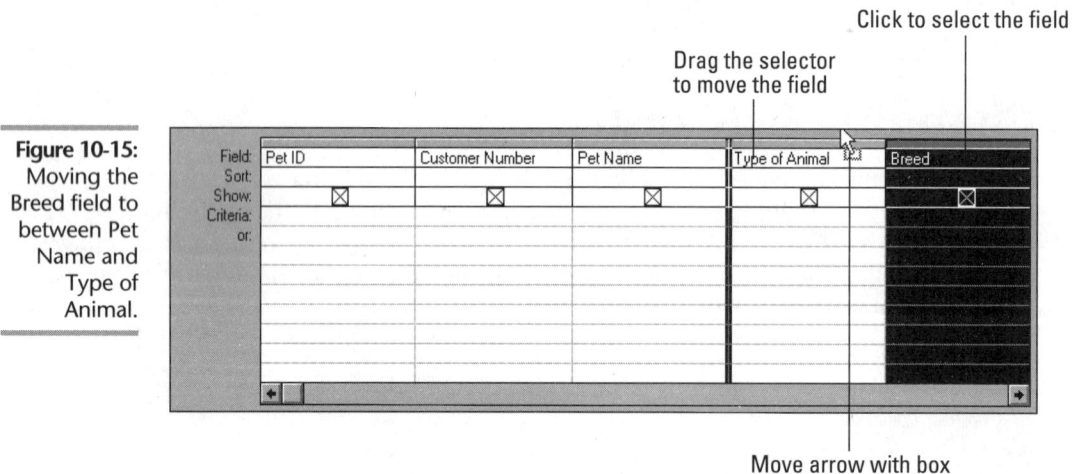

Figure 10-15: Moving the Breed field to between Pet Name and Type of Animal.

Removing a field

You can easily remove a field from the QBE design pane. Select the field or fields to be deleted in the QBE design pane and then press Delete or select Edit⇨Delete. To remove the Customer Number field from the QBE design pane, follow these steps:

Chapter 10: Understanding and Using Simple Queries

Steps:	Removing a Field
Step 1.	Select the Customer Number field (or any other field) by clicking the field selector above the field name.
Step 2.	Press Delete.

 You can delete all the fields in the QBE design pane in a single operation. Select Edit⇨Clear Grid from the Query Design menu.

Inserting a field

You insert a field from the table/query entry pane in the QBE design pane by first selecting the field or fields to be inserted from the table/query entry pane. Next, drag your field selection to the QBE design pane. The following steps show you how to insert the Customer Number field:

Steps:	Inserting a Field
Step 1.	Select the Customer Number field from the field list in the table/query entry pane.
Step 2.	Drag the field from the field list to the column where you want the field to go.
Step 3.	Drop the field by releasing the left mouse button.

When you drag a field to the QBE design pane, it will be inserted wherever you drop the field. If you drop the field on top of another field, it is inserted before that field. If you double-click the field name in the table/query entry pane, the field is added to the end of the Field: list in the QBE design pane.

Changing the field display name

To make the query datasheet easier to read, you may want to rename the fields in your query. The new names you choose will become the tag headings in the datasheet of the query. As an example, to rename the field Breed to Lineage, follow these steps:

Part II: Basic Database Usage

Steps:	**Renaming a Field Caption**
Step 1.	Click to the left of the *B* in Breed in the Field: row of the QBE design pane.
Step 2.	Type **Lineage** and then type a colon (:) between the new name and the old field name.

The heading now reads `Lineage:Breed`. When the datasheet is displayed, you'll see Lineage in place of Breed.

Renaming the field by changing the datasheet caption changes *only* the name of the heading for that field in the datasheet. It does *not* change the field name in the underlying table.

Showing a field

While performing queries, you may want temporarily to show only some of the fields. Suppose, for example, that you want to show only the fields Pet ID, Pet Name, and Breed. You can delete all other fields and restore them when you are done with the temporary dynaset. Or you can simply indicate which fields you want to see in the datasheet.

When you select fields, Access automatically makes every field a display field. Every Show: property is checked with an X in the box.

To deselect a field's Show: property, simply click the field's Show: box. The box clears, as you see in Figure 10-16. To reselect the field later, simply reclick the Show: box.

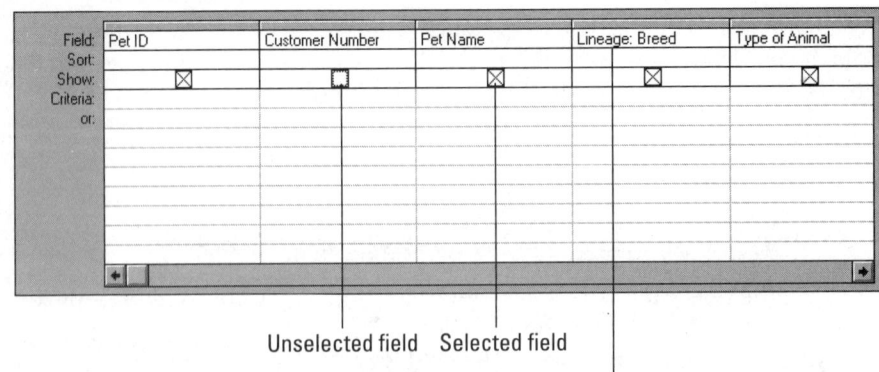

Figure 10-16: The Show: row is checked here only for the fields Pet ID, Pet Name, and Breed.

Chapter 10: Understanding and Using Simple Queries   223

Changing the Sort Order

When viewing a dynaset, you may want to display the data in some sorted order. You may want to sort the dynaset to make it easier to analyze the data, as, for example, to look at all the pets in order by Type of Animal.

Sorting places the records in alphabetical or numeric order. The sort order can be ascending (0 – 9 and A – Z) or descending (9 – 0 and Z – A).

Just as Access has a Show: property row for fields, there is a Sort: property row for fields in the QBE design pane. In the following section, you learn how to set this property.

Specifying a sort

To sort the records in the datasheet by Type of Animal in ascending order, perform the following steps:

Steps:	Sorting by Type of Animal
Step 1.	Click on the Sort: cell for the Type of Animal field. An arrow appears in the cell.
Step 2.	Click the down arrow at the right of the cell.
Step 3.	Select Ascending from the list.

Figure 10-17 shows the QBE pane with the Type of Animal field selected for sorting by ascending order. Notice that the word *Ascending* is placed in the Sort: cell of the field.

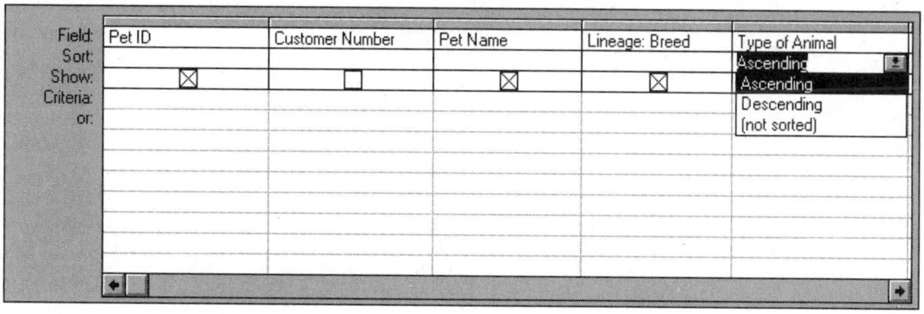

Figure 10-17: A field selected for sorting.

If you save a query that has a field specified for a sort order, Access automatically moves the field to the first field location (leftmost) in the QBE pane — even if you placed the field in a different location when you created the query. However, when you view the datasheet, the fields will appear in the order you specified before assigning the Sort: property to the field.

You *cannot* sort on a Memo or an OLE object field.

Sorting on more than one field

Access gives you the ability to sort on multiple fields. You may, for example, want a primary sort order of Type of Animal and a secondary sort order by Breed. To create this query, start with the query illustrated in Figure 10-17. Then add a sort to the Breed field by selecting Ascending in the Sort: cell.

The leftmost sort field is *always* sorted first. To make sure that Access understands how you want to sort your data, you must arrange the fields in order from left to right according to sort-order precedence. You can easily change the sort order by simply selecting a sort field and moving it relative to another sort field. Access automatically corrects the sort order.

That's all there is to it. Now the dynaset is arranged in order by two different fields. Figure 10-18 shows the multiple-field sort criteria. The sort order is controlled by the order of the fields in the QBE pane (from left to right); therefore, this dynaset is displayed in order first by Type of Animal and then by Breed, as you see in Figure 10-19.

Following Along in This Book
If you are following along with the examples, before continuing, start a new query and select all the fields.

Figure 10-18: A multiple-field sort in the QBE design pane.

Field:	Type of Animal	Lineage: Breed	Pet ID	Customer Number	Pet Name
Sort:	Ascending	Ascending			
Show:	☒	☒	☒	☒	☒
Criteria:					
or:					

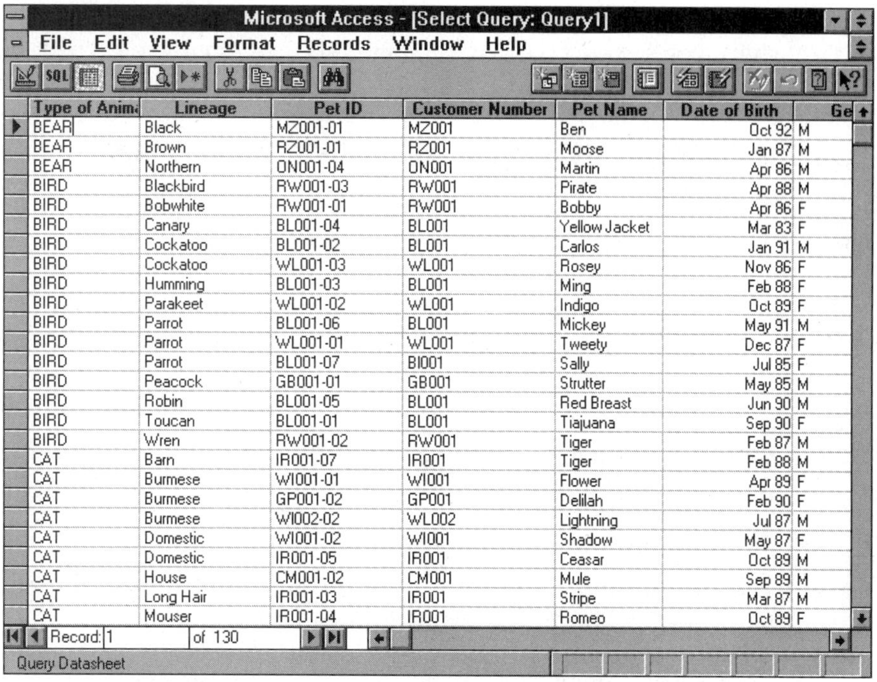

Type of Anim	Lineage	Pet ID	Customer Number	Pet Name	Date of Birth	Ge
BEAR	Black	MZ001-01	MZ001	Ben	Oct 92	M
BEAR	Brown	RZ001-01	RZ001	Moose	Jan 87	M
BEAR	Northern	ON001-04	ON001	Martin	Apr 86	M
BIRD	Blackbird	RW001-03	RW001	Pirate	Apr 88	M
BIRD	Bobwhite	RW001-01	RW001	Bobby	Apr 86	F
BIRD	Canary	BL001-04	BL001	Yellow Jacket	Mar 83	F
BIRD	Cockatoo	BL001-02	BL001	Carlos	Jan 91	M
BIRD	Cockatoo	WL001-03	WL001	Rosey	Nov 86	F
BIRD	Humming	BL001-03	BL001	Ming	Feb 88	F
BIRD	Parakeet	WL001-02	WL001	Indigo	Oct 89	F
BIRD	Parrot	BL001-06	BL001	Mickey	May 91	M
BIRD	Parrot	WL001-01	WL001	Tweety	Dec 87	F
BIRD	Parrot	BL001-07	BI001	Sally	Jul 85	F
BIRD	Peacock	GB001-01	GB001	Strutter	May 85	M
BIRD	Robin	BL001-05	BL001	Red Breast	Jun 90	M
BIRD	Toucan	BL001-01	BL001	Tiajuana	Sep 90	F
BIRD	Wren	RW001-02	RW001	Tiger	Feb 87	M
CAT	Barn	IR001-07	IR001	Tiger	Feb 88	M
CAT	Burmese	WI001-01	WI001	Flower	Apr 89	F
CAT	Burmese	GP001-02	GP001	Delilah	Feb 90	F
CAT	Burmese	WI002-02	WL002	Lightning	Jul 87	M
CAT	Domestic	WI001-02	WI001	Shadow	May 87	F
CAT	Domestic	IR001-05	IR001	Ceasar	Oct 89	M
CAT	House	CM001-02	CM001	Mule	Sep 89	M
CAT	Long Hair	IR001-03	IR001	Stripe	Mar 87	M
CAT	Mouser	IR001-04	IR001	Romeo	Oct 89	F

Figure 10-19: A multiple-field sort order displayed.

Displaying Only Selected Records

So far, you've been working with all the records of the Pets table. There are times when you may want to work only with selected records in the Pets table. For example, you may only want to look at records where the value of Type of Animal is DOG. Access makes it easy for you to specify a record's criteria.

Understanding record criteria

Record criteria is simply some rule or rules that you supply for Access. These criteria tell Access which records you want to look at in the dynaset. The criteria could be "all male animals" or "only those animals that are not currently vaccinated" or "all animals that were born before January 1990."

In other words, with record criteria, you create limiting filters to tell Microsoft Access which records to find and which to leave out of the dynaset.

You specify criteria starting in the Criteria: property row of the QBE pane. Here, you designate criteria with an expression. The expression can be simple example data or can take the form of complicated expressions using predefined functions.

As an example, you can type **DOG** in the Criteria: cell of Type of Animal. If you look at the datasheet, you see only records for dogs. This is an example of a simple data criteria.

Entering simple character criteria

Character type criteria is entered into Text data type fields. This type of criteria gives an example of the data contained within the field. To limit the record display to DOG, follow these steps:

Steps:	Creating the Character Query Type of Animals Equals DOG
Step 1.	Click the Criteria: cell in the Type of Animal column in the QBE design pane.
Step 2.	Type **DOG** in the cell.
Step 3.	Click the Datasheet button.

Only the dogs are displayed. Observe that you did *not* enter an equal sign or place quotes around the sample text, yet Access added double quotes around the value. Access, unlike many other applications, automatically understands what you want. This is an illustration of its powerful flexibility. You could enter the expression in any of these other ways:

>   Dog
>   = Dog
>   "Dog"
>   = "Dog"

In Figure 10-20, you see the expression entered under Type of Animal.

Figure 10-20 is an excellent example to demonstrate options for various types of simple character criteria. You can just as well type **Not Dog** in the criteria column, to say the opposite. In this instance, you are asking to see all records that are not dogs only by adding Not before the example text Dog.

Generally, when you deal with character data, you enter equalities, inequalities, or a list of values that are acceptable.

With both of these examples, Dog or Not Dog, you entered a simple expression in a Text type field. Access took your example and interpreted it to show you all records that equal the example data placed in the Criteria: cell.

This capability is a powerful tool. Consider that you have only to supply an example and Access interprets this example, using it to create the query dynaset. This is exactly what Query by Example means: You enter an example and let the database build the query based on this data.

Figure 10-20:
Specifying character criteria.

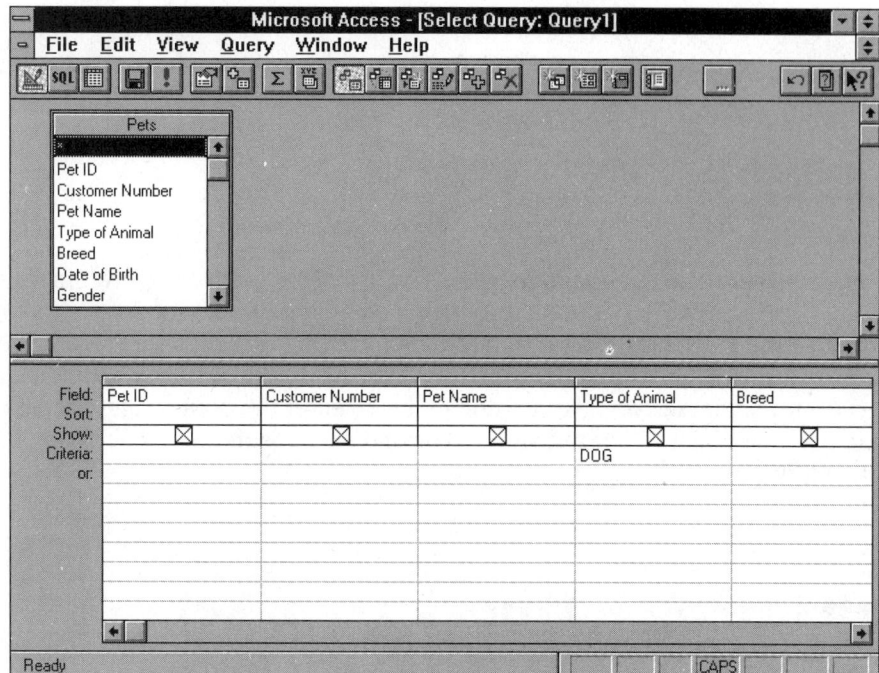

To erase the criteria cell, select the contents and press Delete, or select Edit⇨Delete from the Query Design menu.

Following Along in This Book

If you are following along with the examples, delete the criteria in the Type of Animal field before continuing.

Entering other simple criteria

Criteria can also be specified for numeric, date, and yes/no fields. For example, suppose that you want to look only at records for animals that were born after 1/1/91. To limit the display to records where the value of Date of Birth is greater than January 1, 1991, follow these steps:

Steps:	Creating a Date Query for Date of Birth > Jan 1, 1991
Step 0.	Remove any existing fields in the QBE pane by selecting Edit⇨Clear Grid from the menu.

Step 1.	Add the Date of Birth field to the QBE grid.
Step 2.	Click the Criteria: cell in the Date of Birth column in the QBE design pane.
Step 3.	Type > **1/1/91** in the cell.
Step 4.	Click the Datasheet button.

Date fields are also compared to a value by use of comparison operators such as less than (<), greater than (>), equal to (=), or a combination thereof. Notice that Access automatically adds the pound sign (#) delimiters around the date value. Access recognizes these delimiters as differentiating a Date field from Text fields. But just as with entering text data examples, you don't have to enter the pound signs; Access understands what you want, based on the type of data you enter in the field, and it converts the entry format for you.

Printing a Query Dynaset

After you create your query, you can quickly print all the records in the dynaset. Although you can't specify a type of report, you can print a simple matrix-type report (rows and columns) of the dynaset that your query created.

You do have some flexibility when printing a dynaset. If you know that the datasheet is set up just as you want it, you can specify some options as you follow these steps:

Steps:	**Printing a Dynaset**
Step 1.	Specify your record criteria in the query design mode.
Step 2.	Switch to the query datasheet mode by pressing the Datasheet button on the toolbar.
Step 3.	Select File⇒Print... from the Query Datasheet menu or press the Print button on the toolbar.
Step 4.	Specify the print options you want in the Print dialog box.
Step 5.	Choose the OK button in the Print dialog box.

Access now prints the dynaset for you. Assuming that you have set up a printer in Microsoft Windows, you can press OK to print your dataset. Your dataset is printed in the font selected for display or in the nearest equivalent that your printer offers. The printout also reflects all layout options that are in effect when the dataset is printed. Hidden columns do not print. Gridlines print only if the Gridlines option is on. The printout reflects the specified row height and column width as well.

When you display the datasheet, if you don't use a font that has a printer equivalent, you can get unintelligible characters in your printout.

Refer to Chapter 8 to review printing fundamentals; that chapter covers printing the datasheet and using the Print Preview functions.

Saving a Query

To save a query from the design mode, you can follow this procedure:

> Select File⇨Save from the Query Design menu or press the Save button on the toolbar. If this is the first time you're saving the query, enter a new query name in the Save As dialog box.

To save a query from the datasheet mode, follow this procedure:

> Select File⇨Save Query from the Datasheet File menu. If this is the first time you're saving the query, enter a new query name in the Save as dialog box.

The F12 key is the Save key in Access. You can press F12 to save your work and continue working on your query.

Both of these methods will save the query and return you to the mode you were working in. Occasionally, you'll simply want to save and exit the query in a single operation. To do this, select File⇨Close from the query or the datasheet and answer Yes to the question `Save changes to Query 'query name'?`. If this is your first time to save the query, you are prompted to supply a query name.

You can leave the Query window at any time by one of several ways:

- Selecting File⇨Close from the Query menu
- Selecting Close from the Query window
- Pressing Ctrl+F4 while inside the Query window

All three of these methods activate an Access dialog box asking, `Save changes to Query 'Query1'?`

Summary

In this chapter, you learned about the types of queries and how each is used. You had some practice in creating simple queries and found out about some of the query options Access provides. The following points were covered:

- Queries ask questions about your data and return the answers in the form of information.
- Types of queries include select, total, crosstab, action, SQL, definition, and TOP.
- Queries let you select tables, fields, sort order, and record criteria.
- Queries create a virtual view of the data, known as a dynaset. The data is displayed in a datasheet.
- A dynaset is the temporary answer set. Queries save only the instructions and not the data.
- The Query window has two panes. The top pane displays the design view of your tables; the bottom pane is used for entering QBE instructions.
- When you add fields with the asterisk button, the query automatically changes if the underlying table changes.
- You can display field names differently in the datasheet by adding a new caption with a colon in front of the existing field name.
- You can limit records being displayed with record criteria, specifying character, numeric, date/time, and yes/no.
- A queries dynaset datasheet can be used just like any table — in forms, reports, and other queries.

In the next chapter, you examine how to create and print simple reports.

Creating and Printing Simple Reports

CHAPTER 11

In This Chapter

- Understanding the types of reports you can create
- Knowing the differences between a report and a form
- Understanding the process of creating reports
- Creating reports with a Report Wizard
- Viewing reports on-screen
- Printing reports
- Saving reports

Reports provide the most flexible way for viewing and printing summarized information. Reports enable you to display information with a desired level of detail, while letting you view or print your information in almost any format. You can add multilevel totals, statistical comparisons, and even pictures and graphics to a report. In this chapter, you see how to use Report Wizards as a starting point for your report. You see how reports are created and the types of reports you can create with Access.

Understanding Reports

Reports are used for presenting a customized view of your data. Your report output can be viewed on-screen or printed to a hard-copy device. With reports, you have the ability to control summarization of the information. You can group your data and sort it in any order you want and then present the data in the order of the groupings. You can create totals that add numbers, calculate averages or other statistics, and even display your data graphically. You can print pictures and other graphics as well as Memo fields in a report. If you can think of a report you want, Access can probably create it.

What types of reports can you create?

Four basic types of reports are used in business today:

Groups/totals reports   Print data in rows and columns with groupings and totals. Variations include summary and tabular reports.

Column reports   Print data as a form; can include totals and graphs.

Mail-merge reports   Create form letters.

Mailing labels   Create multicolumn labels or snaked column reports.

Groups/totals reports

Groups/totals reports, also known as *tabular reports,* are similar to a table that displays data generally in neat rows and columns. Groups/totals reports, unlike forms or datasheets, usually have data grouped by one or more field values and have subtotals or statistical information calculated and displayed for numeric fields in each group. Some groups/totals reports also have page totals and grand totals. You can even have snaked columns so that you can create directories, such as telephone books. As shown in Figure 11-1, reports can have page numbers, report dates, and even lines and boxes to separate information. Reports can also have color and shading and can display pictures, business graphs, and Memo fields, just as forms can. A variation of groups/totals reports in Access, summary reports have no detail records and tabular reports have no groupings or subtotals.

Figure 11-1: A typical groups/totals report.

Daily Hospital Report - Saturday, January 16, 1993

Customer Name	Pet Name	Type of Animal	Total Amount
Johnathan Adams			
	Patty	PIG	$150.00
	Rising Sun	HORSE	$225.00
			$375.00
Stephen Brown			
	Suzie	DOG	$316.00
			$316.00
William Primen			
	Brutus	DOG	$381.00
	Little Bit	CAT	$332.50
			$713.50
		Grand Total :	$1,404.50

Column reports

Column reports, also known as *form reports,* generally display one or more records per page but do so in a vertical manner. Column reports display data very much as a data-entry form does, but the report is used strictly for viewing data and not for entering it. An invoice is a typical type of column report. This type of report can have sections that display one record and at the same time have sections that display many records from the *many* side of a one-to-many relationship — and even include totals. Figure 11-2 displays a typical column report from the Mountain Animal Hospital database system.

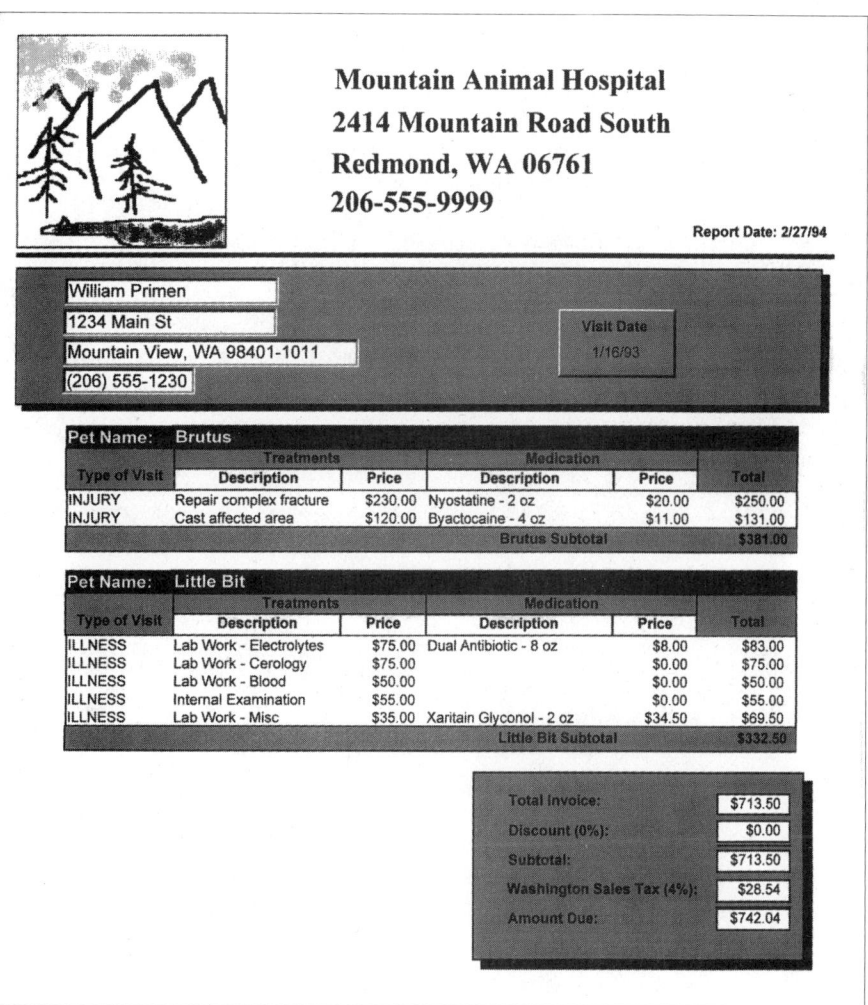

Figure 11-2: A typical column report.

Mailing labels

You can easily create mailing labels, shown in Figure 11-3, by using a report in Access. In fact, you'll want to use the Mailing Label Report Wizard to get you started. The Mailing Label Report Wizard lets you select from a long list of Avery label paper styles, after which Access correctly creates a report design, based on the data you specify to create your label. After the label is created, you can open the report in design mode and customize it as needed. Mailing labels are covered in detail in Chapter 29.

Figure 11-3: A typical mailing label report.

Village Pets 30 Murphy St. Russettown, ID 83019-8573 *Special Offer Enclosed!*	Mount Pilot Zoo 37 Mount Pilot St. Mount Pilot, ID 83124-1043 *Special Offer Enclosed!*	Rocky Nature Center 2234 Pine St. Russettown, ID 83124-5145 *Special Offer Enclosed!*
Pet City 91 Main St. Mount Pilot, ID 83187-5638 *Special Offer Enclosed!*	Stephen Brown 555 Sycamore Ave Three Corners, ID 83401-1023 *Special Offer Enclosed!*	We Love Birds 1434 Pauly St. Three Corners, ID 83412-1012 *Special Offer Enclosed!*
George Green 9133 Bookland Rd Russettown, ID 83412-1012 *Special Offer Enclosed!*	Tyrone Potter 9133 Bookland Rd Three Corners, ID 83412-1012 *Special Offer Enclosed!*	Bird Land 22 Eagle Blvd Russettown, ID 83412-1021 *Special Offer Enclosed!*
Karen Rhodes 3403 37th Ave Russettown, ID 83412-1021 *Special Offer Enclosed!*	Adam Johnson 55 Childs Ave Mount Pilot, ID 83124-1043 *Special Offer Enclosed!*	Animal Kingdom 15 Marlin Lane Borderville, ID 83483-5646 *Special Offer Enclosed!*
George Bird Sanctuary George St. Mount Pilot, ID 83908-1012 *Special Offer Enclosed!*	Three Corners Pets 990 Wise St. Three Corners, ID 83985-7123 *Special Offer Enclosed!*	Kiddie Petting Zoo 31 High Grove Rd. Lakeville, OR 97213-1011 *Special Offer Enclosed!*
House Of Pets 1256 Salmon Rd. Borderville, OR 97265-8128 *Special Offer Enclosed!*	William Adams 1122 10th St Lakeville, OR 97401-1011 *Special Offer Enclosed!*	James Brown 3454 Adams St Borderville, OR 97401-1019 *Special Offer Enclosed!*
Oregon Nature Center 12 Grassy Gutter St. Lakeville, OR 97401-1021 *Special Offer Enclosed!*	Patricia Irwin 456 Bishops Ln Lakeville, OR 97401-1021 *Special Offer Enclosed!*	Barbara Williamson 64 10th St Lakeville, OR 97401-2011 *Special Offer Enclosed!*
Margaret McKinley 5512 Green Acres Ct Borderville, OR 97412-1001 *Special Offer Enclosed!*	Borderville Aquarium 1 Whale Way Borderville, OR 97412-1001 *Special Offer Enclosed!*	Cat House Pets 76 Right Ln. Borderville, OR 97541-2856 *Special Offer Enclosed!*

The difference between reports and forms

The main difference between reports and forms is the purpose of the output. Whereas forms are used primarily for data entry, reports are used for viewing either on-screen or in hard-copy form. With forms, you can have calculated fields that generally calculate an amount based on fields in the record. With reports, you create calculations that are based on a common group of records, a page of records, or all the records processed during the report. With the exception of allowing data input, anything that can be done with a form can be duplicated on a report. In fact, you can save a form as a report and then customize the form controls in the Report Design window.

The process of creating a report

Planning a report begins long before the report design is actually created. The report process begins with your desire to view your data differently from the way a datasheet can display the data in a table. You begin with a design for this view, and Access begins with raw data. The purpose of the report is to transform the raw data into a meaningful set of information. The process of creating a report involves several steps:

- Defining the report layout
- Assembling the data
- Creating the report design using the Access Report Design window
- Printing or viewing the report

Defining the report layout

You should begin by having a general idea of the layout of your report. You can define the layout in your mind, on paper, or interactively, using the Access Report Design window. Figure 11-4 shows a report layout that is created in this chapter using the Access Report Designer. This report is laid out on paper, showing the fields needed and the placement of the fields.

Assembling the data

After you have a general idea of your report layout, you should assemble the data needed for the report. A report uses data from a single database table or from the results of a query dynaset. You can link many tables together with a query. Then you can use the result of the query, known as a dynaset, as the record source of a report. A dynaset appears in Access as if it were a single table. As you've learned, you can select the fields, records, and sort order of the records in a query. This dynaset data is then treated as a single table for processing purposes in datasheets, forms, and reports. The dynaset becomes the source of data for the report, and each record is processed in order to create the report. The data for the report and the report design are entirely separate. In the report design, you specify the field names that will be used in the report. Then, when the report is run, data from the dynaset or table is matched against the fields used in the report, and the actual report is produced using the data available at that moment.

Consider the layout shown in Figure 11-4. Here, you want to create a report that shows a daily total of all the pets you treated during a specific day. You call this the Daily Hospital Report. Looking at the layout, you can see that you'll need to assemble the following fields:

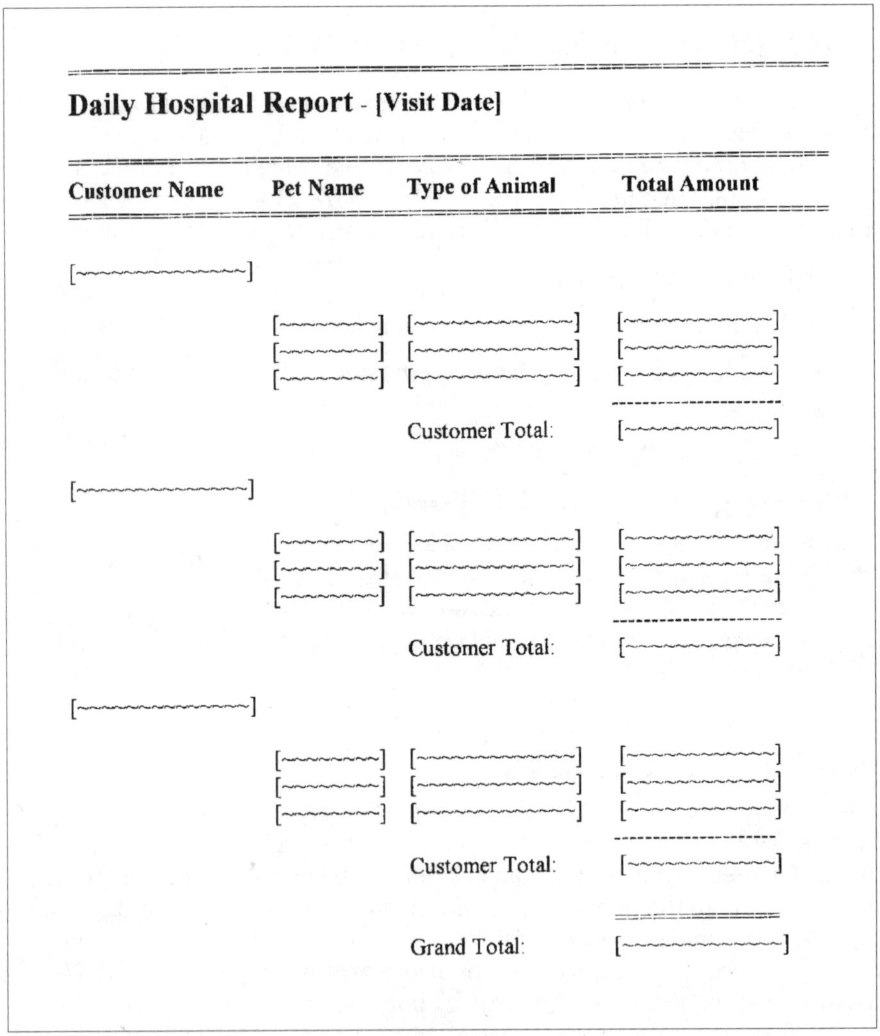

Figure 11-4: A sample report layout.

Daily Hospital Report - [Visit Date]

Customer Name	Pet Name	Type of Animal	Total Amount
[~~~~~]			
	[~~~~~]	[~~~~~]	[~~~~~]
	[~~~~~]	[~~~~~]	[~~~~~]
	[~~~~~]	[~~~~~]	[~~~~~]
		Customer Total:	[~~~~~]
[~~~~~]			
	[~~~~~]	[~~~~~]	[~~~~~]
	[~~~~~]	[~~~~~]	[~~~~~]
	[~~~~~]	[~~~~~]	[~~~~~]
		Customer Total:	[~~~~~]
[~~~~~]			
	[~~~~~]	[~~~~~]	[~~~~~]
	[~~~~~]	[~~~~~]	[~~~~~]
	[~~~~~]	[~~~~~]	[~~~~~]
		Customer Total:	[~~~~~]
		Grand Total:	[~~~~~]

Visit Date from the Visits table — Used to select the visit date as a query criteria

Customer Name from the Customer table — Displays and groups customers on the report

Pet Name from the Customer table — Displays the pet name on the report table

Type of Animal from the Customer table — Displays the type of animal on the report

Total Amount from the Visits table — Displays and calculates totals for amounts charged

You begin the report by creating a query, as shown in Figure 11-5. Figure 11-5 shows three tables linked together and the appropriate fields chosen for the report. Notice that the Visit Date field is limited to values of 1/16/93, indicating that this specific view of your data will be limited to customers who visited on January 16, 1993. The Customer Name field is being sorted in ascending sequence, as the report will be grouped by customer name.

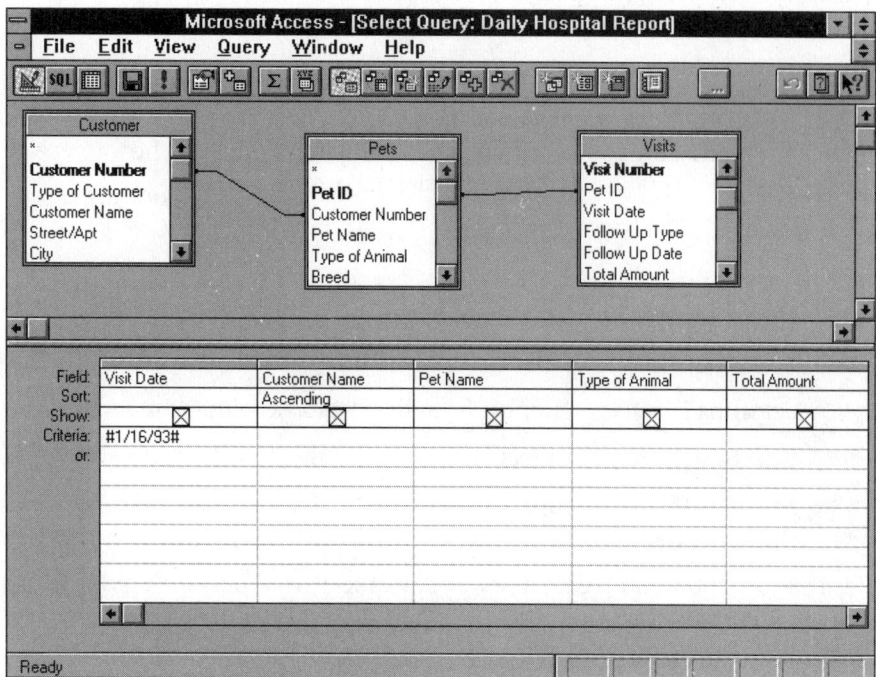

Figure 11-5: Creating a query for a report.

Figure 11-6:
The Daily Hospital Report dynaset datasheet.

Visit Date	Customer Name	Pet Name	Type of Animal	Total Amount
1/16/93	Johnathan Adams	Rising Sun	HORSE	$225.00
1/16/93	Johnathan Adams	Patty	PIG	$150.00
1/16/93	Stephen Brown	Suzie	DOG	$316.00
1/16/93	William Primen	Little Bit	CAT	$332.50
1/16/93	William Primen	Brutus	DOG	$381.00

After you assemble the data, you can create the report design. Figure 11-6 shows the results of this query. The datasheet shown in this figure is the dynaset created when the Daily Hospital Report query is run for 1/16/93.

Creating a Report with Report Wizards

With Access, you can create virtually any type of report. However, some reports are more easily created than others by using Report Wizards as a starting point. Like Form Wizards, Report Wizards give you a basic layout for your report, which you can then customize.

Report Wizards simplify the layout process of your fields by visually stepping you through a series of questions about the type of report you want to create and then automatically creating the report for you. In this chapter, you learn how to create both groups/totals and column reports by using a Form Wizard.

Creating a new report

You can choose from many ways to create a new report, including the following:

- Selecting File⇨New⇨Report from the Database window menu
- Selecting the report object and then selecting New from the Database dialog box
- Selecting the New Report button from the Database window, the datasheet, or the query toolbar

Regardless of how you create a new report, the New Report dialog box is displayed, as you see it in Figure 11-7.

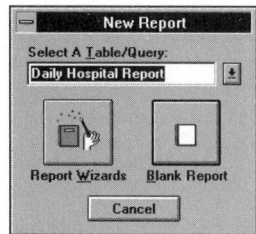

Figure 11-7:
The New Report dialog box.

The New Report dialog box lets you choose one of two ways to create a report:

Report Wizards   Creates one of three default layouts, using the data fields specified

Blank Report   Displays a completely blank report design window for you to start with

Choosing the data source

If you begin creating the report with a table highlighted or from a datasheet or a query, the table or query you are using is shown in the Select a Table/Query text box. Otherwise, you can enter the name of a valid table or query before continuing. You can also choose from a list of tables and queries by clicking on the list box selection arrow. In this example, you'll use the Daily Hospital Report query you saw in Figure 11-5, which creates data for customer visits on the date 1/16/93.

In order to create a new report, follow these steps:

Steps:	Creating a New Report with a Report Wizard
Step 1.	Create a new report by selecting a menu, an icon, or a button.
Step 2.	Select the table/query Daily Hospital Report in the New Report dialog box.
Step 3.	Select Report Wizards.

If you begin with a blank report, you don't need to specify a table or query before you start.

Creating a report from a blank report design is covered in Chapter 21.

Selecting the Wizard

After you select a table or query and select the Report Wizards picture button, another dialog box is displayed. The Report Wizards dialog box allows you to select one of the seven types of reports. The dialog box is shown in Figure 11-8. As you can see in the figure, these seven types are available:

Single-Column	Creates a report with each field on a separate line, much like a form
Groups/Totals	Creates a report with fields on one line and groupings and totals
Mailing Label	Creates mailing labels using standard Avery stock labels
Summary	Same as Groups/Totals but only displays the summary lines and ignores the detail lines
Tabular	Records displayed across rows with no groupings and only a grand total
AutoReport	An instant single-column report
MS Word MailMerge	An interface to the PrintMerge facility in Word 6.0

To specify a Groups/Totals report, follow this one step: Select Groups/Totals and press the OK button.

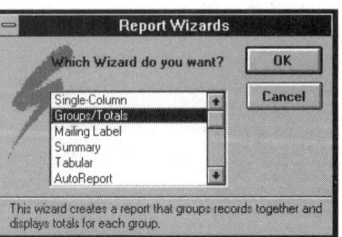

Figure 11-8: Selecting the report type.

In this example, you create a groups/totals report from the Daily Hospital Report query with all fields except Visit Date. The fields are grouped by Customer Name with a Normal grouping and sorted by Pet Name with an Executive look. The title is Daily Hospital Report.

Choosing the fields

After you select the type of report and select the OK button, a field selection box is displayed. This box is virtually identical to the field selection box used in Form Wizards (see Chapter 9 for detailed information). In this example, you select all the fields except Visit Date, as shown in Figure 11-9.

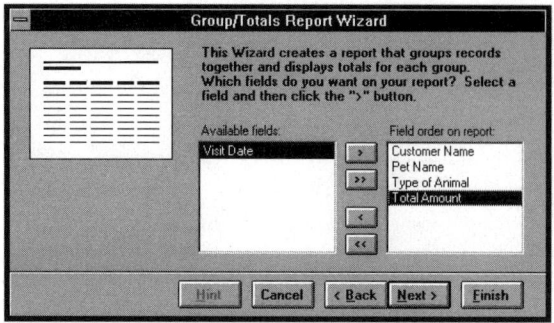

Figure 11-9:
Selecting report fields.

Steps: Selecting Fields in the Report Wizard Fields Dialog Box

Step 1. Select the All Fields button (>>) to place all the fields in the `Field order on report:` area.

Step 2. Select the Visit Date field and select the Remove Field button (<) to remove the field.

You can double-click any field in the Table/Query list box to add it to the `Field order on report:` list box. You can also double-click any field in the `Field order on report:` list box to remove it from the box. The field is then redisplayed in the `Available fields:` box.

Selecting the group by: field

The next dialog box lets you choose which field or fields you want to use for a grouping. In this example, the Customer Name field is chosen as the only group field, as you see in Figure 11-10. The Group records by: field designates the field or fields to be used to create group headers and footers. The field(s) you want to use in a grouping must be selected in the preceding dialog box. You can always return to the preceding dialog box and add a field if you need to. You can select up to four different Group records by: fields for the report using the Report Wizard. The order you select for the group fields is the order of the grouping hierarchy. Select the Customer Name field as the grouping field.

After you select the group field(s), you can select the Next > button to display the next dialog box, which lets you further define how the group field is used in the report.

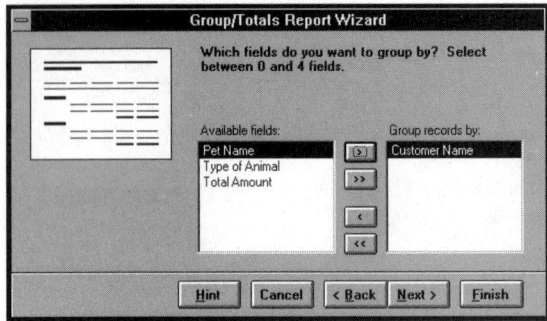

Figure 11-10: Selecting report group fields.

Defining the group data

The next Wizard screen lets you further define the grouping. Depending on the data type, this selection can be more or less important.

You will see different values in the list box for the various data types:

Text   Normal, 1st Character, 1st 2 Characters, 1st 3 Characters, 1st 4 Characters, 1st 5 Characters

Numeric Normal, 10s, 50s, 100s, 500s, 1000s, 5000s, 10000s, 50000s, 100000s, 500000s

Date   Normal, Year, Quarter, Month, Week, Day, Hour, Minute

Normal means that the grouping will be on the entire field. In this example, you want to use the entire Customer Name field. By selecting different values of the grouping, you can limit the group values. For example, suppose that you are grouping on the Pet ID field. A typical Pet ID value is AP001-01. The first five characters represent the owner, whereas the two after the hyphen represent the pet number for that owner. By choosing the Pet ID field for the grouping and then selecting 1st 5 Characters as the grouping data, you can group the pets by customer instead of by pet.

Selecting sort order

The Group records by: fields are automatically sorted in an order that helps the grouping make sense. The sort by: fields specify fields to be sorted in the detail section. In this example, the data is already being sorted by Customer Name in the group section. As you can see in Figure 11-11, the data is also going to be sorted by Pet Name so that the pets appear in alphabetical order in the detail section.

The sort fields are selected by the same method used for grouping fields in the report. The fields that are not already selected as group by: fields are selectable for sorting fields. The fields chosen in this dialog box do not affect grouping. Only the sorting order in the detail section fields are affected.

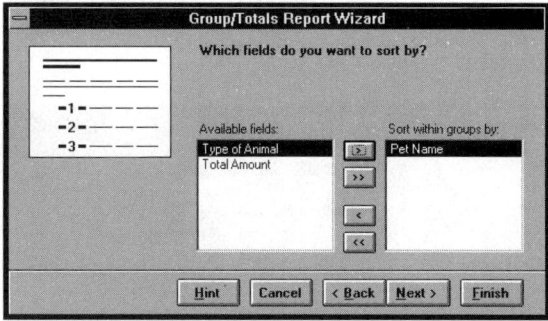

Figure 11-11: Selecting the field sorting order.

Choosing the print effect

After you choose the fields, you can choose the look of your report from the dialog box shown in Figure 11-12. You can also choose the orientation of the report (Portrait or Landscape) and the line spacing (0 – ½ inch). The default is Landscape and a ½-inch line spacing. For this example, change the orientation to Portrait because this report does not have a lot of fields.

You can choose any of look selections by clicking on the desired option button. As you select one of the three looks, the display under the magnifying glass changes to illustrate the special effect to be used. Figure 11-13 is a composite figure of the three different looks.

As you can see in Figure 11-12, the Executive look is simple. Double lines appear around headers, and lines are placed before totals. The Executive look is used in this example. After you choose the look of your form, you are ready to create a title and then view the form.

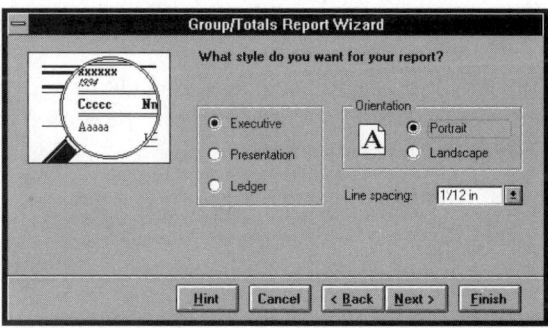

Figure 11-12: Choosing the look of your report.

Figure 11-13:
Three different report looks.

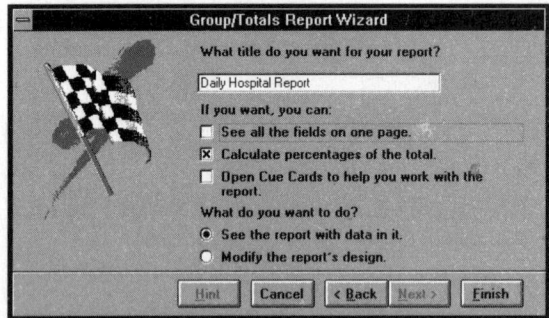

Figure 11-14:
The final Report Wizard dialog box.

Opening the report design

Figure 11-14 shows the final Report Wizard dialog box displayed. The checkered flag lets you know that you're at the finish line. The first part of the dialog box lets you enter a title for the report. This title will appear once at the beginning of the report — not at the top of each page. The default is the name of the table or query that was initially used. The next part of the dialog box lets you select one or all of three options:

See all the fields on one page	Fits all the fields by narrowing the column widths and truncating headers and fields. May not look very good.
Calculate percentages of the total	Adds a percentage of the total field under the subtotal value.
Open cue cards	Displays help for customizing the report design.

In this example, you can leave the default selection — Calculate percentages of the total — checked. When you are through, choose one of the option buttons at the bottom of the dialog box. You have two choices:

- See the report with data in it.
- Modify the report design.

Chapter 11: Creating and Printing Simple Reports **245**

For this example, leave the default selection to see the report design. When you select the Finish button, you will view your report in the Print Preview window.

Using the Print Preview window

Figure 11-15 displays the Print Preview window in a zoomed view. This view lets you see your report with the actual fonts, shading, lines, boxes, and data that will be on the printed report. When the print preview mode is in a zoomed view, pressing the mouse button changes the view to a page preview, where you can see the entire page.

You can move around the page by using both the horizontal and vertical elevators. You can also move from page to page by using the Page controls at the bottom left corner of the window.

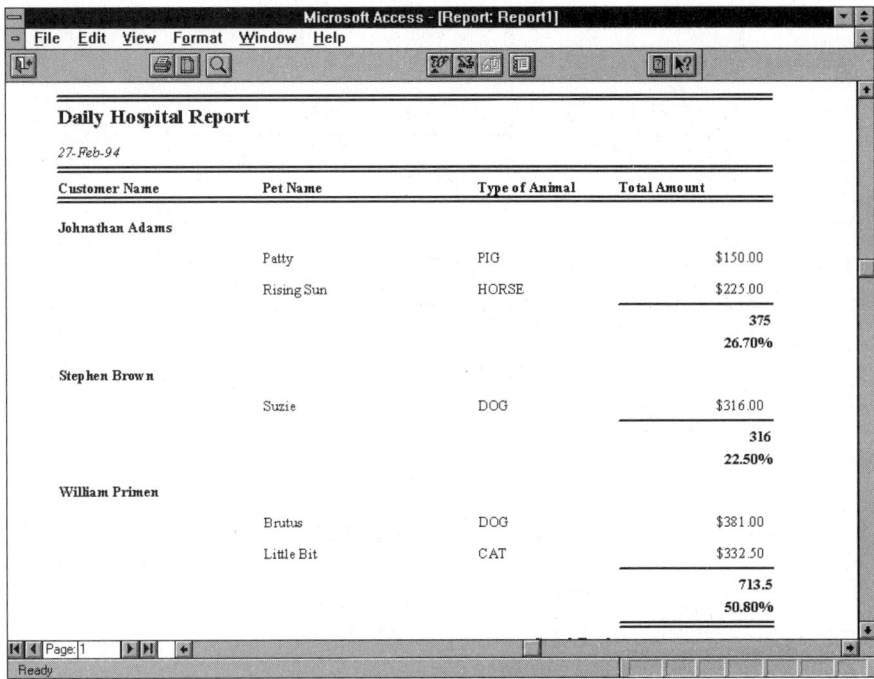

Figure 11-15: Displaying a report in the zoomed preview mode.

Figure 11-16: Displaying a report in a Page Preview print preview mode.

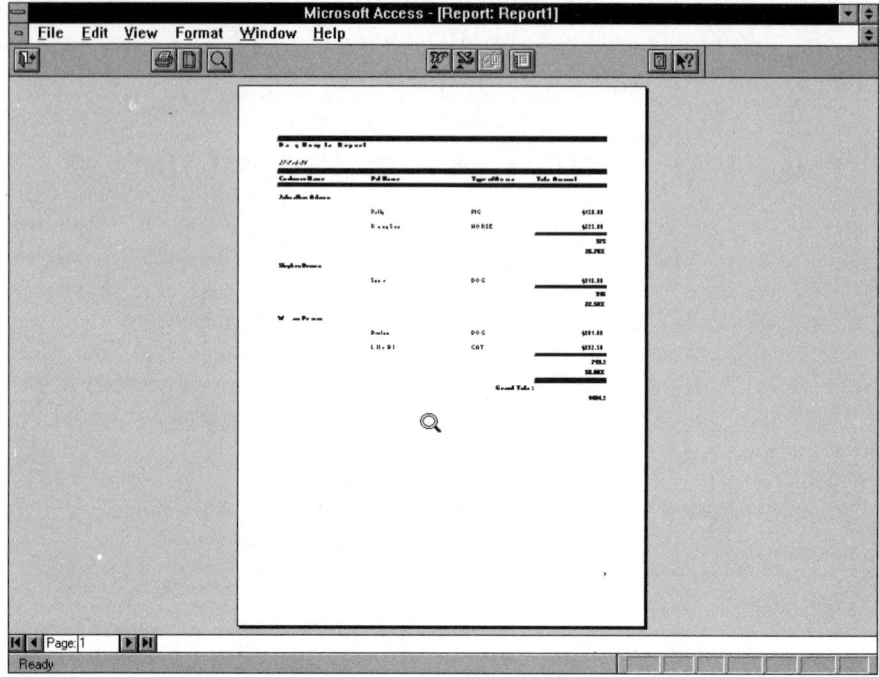

The page preview mode of Print Preview shows an entire page of the report, as you see it in Figure 11-16. By using the magnifying glass cursor here, you can select a portion of the page and then zoom in to that portion for a zoomed view.

In Figure 11-16, you can see a representation of the printed page. You can use the navigation buttons, located in the lower left-hand section of the Print Preview window, to move between pages, just as you use them to move between records in a datasheet. A set of icons is displayed on the toolbar.

If, after examining the preview, you are satisfied with the report, simply select the printer icon on the toolbar to print the report. If you are dissatisfied, select the return to design button (the first icon with a door), and you will be placed in the Report Design window to make further changes to your report.

Viewing the Report Design window

When you select the first icon from the toolbar, you are placed in the Report Design window. This window is similar to the Form Design window. The major difference is in the sections that make up the report design. As you can see in Figure 11-17, the report design reflects the choices that you made using the Report Wizard.

Chapter 11: Creating and Printing Simple Reports

Figure 11-17: The Report Design window.

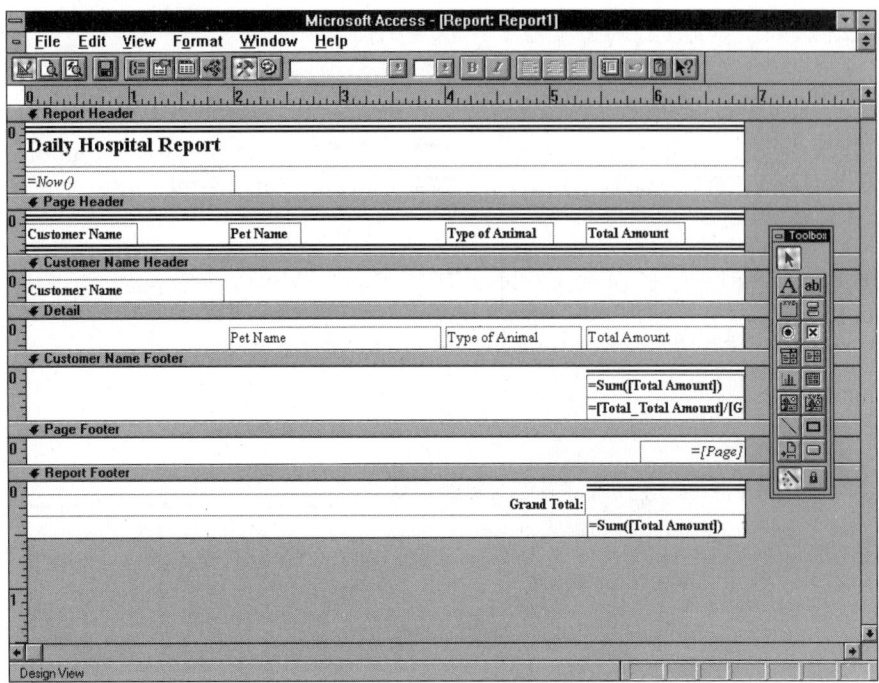

You may also see the toolbox, Sorting and Grouping dialog box, property sheet, Field List window, and palette, depending on whether you have pressed the toolbar buttons to see these tools. You learn how to change the design of a report in Chapters 21 and 22.

You can switch back to the print preview mode by either selecting the second icon button on the Report Design toolbar or by selecting the Print Preview option on the File menu. You can also select Print... or Print Setup... from the File menu, as shown in Figure 11-18. This menu also provides options for saving your report.

Figure 11-18: The File menu in the Report Design window.

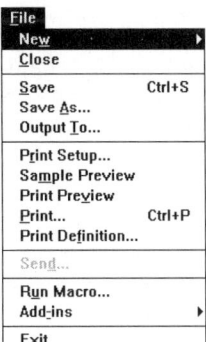

Using sample previews

A sample preview is different from a print preview. Whereas a print preview uses a query's dynaset, the sample preview ignores any criteria or joins in a query and displays the data. This type of preview limits the number of records but ignores limits based on criteria. The preview also ignores any sorting, thereby making the groupings fairly meaningless.

The purpose of a sample preview is strictly to show your field placement and formatting. The preview lets you create a report design without having to assemble your data properly. In a large query, this can save considerable time.

Printing a Report

You can print one or more records in your report exactly as they look on-screen by selecting from several places:

- File⇨Print in the Report Design window
- Print button in the Preview window
- File⇨Print in the Database window (with a report highlighted)

A standard Windows print dialog box is displayed. You can select the print range, copies, and quality. Figure 11-19 shows the printed report.

A complete discussion of printing is provided in Chapter 22.

Saving the Report

You can save the report design at any time by selecting File⇨Save or File⇨Save As from the Report Design window or by selecting the Save button on the toolbar. The first time you save a report, or any time you select Save As, a dialog box lets you select a name. The default name from the Report Wizard, Report1, is initially displayed in the text box.

Remember that only the report design is saved, not the data or the actual report. You must save your query design separately if you created a query to produce your report. You can re-create the dynaset at any time by running the query and then the report.

Figure 11-19:
The printed report from the Report Wizard.

Daily Hospital Report

27-Feb-94

Customer Name	Pet Name	Type of Animal	Total Amount
Johnathan Adams			
	Patty	PIG	$150.00
	Rising Sun	HORSE	$225.00
			375
			26.70%
Stephen Brown			
	Suzie	DOG	$316.00
			316
			22.50%
William Primen			
	Brutus	DOG	$381.00
	Little Bit	CAT	$332.50
			713.5
			50.80%
		Grand Total:	
			1404.5

Creating a Report with AutoReport

From a table, datasheet, form, or nearly any design screen in Access, you can create a report instantly by clicking on the AutoReport button in the toolbar (Report with a lightning bolt through it) or by using File⇨New⇨Report and selecting AutoReport from the dialog box that appears. When you use the AutoReport button, the report instantly appears with no additional work from you. To create an AutoReport by using the Pets table, follow these steps:

Steps:	Creating a Report with AutoReport
Step 1.	From the MTNANHSP Database Container, click the Table object.
Step 2.	Select Pets.
Step 3.	Click the AutoReport button in the toolbar.

The report instantly appears, as shown in Figure 11-20.

Figure 11-20:
The AutoReport report.

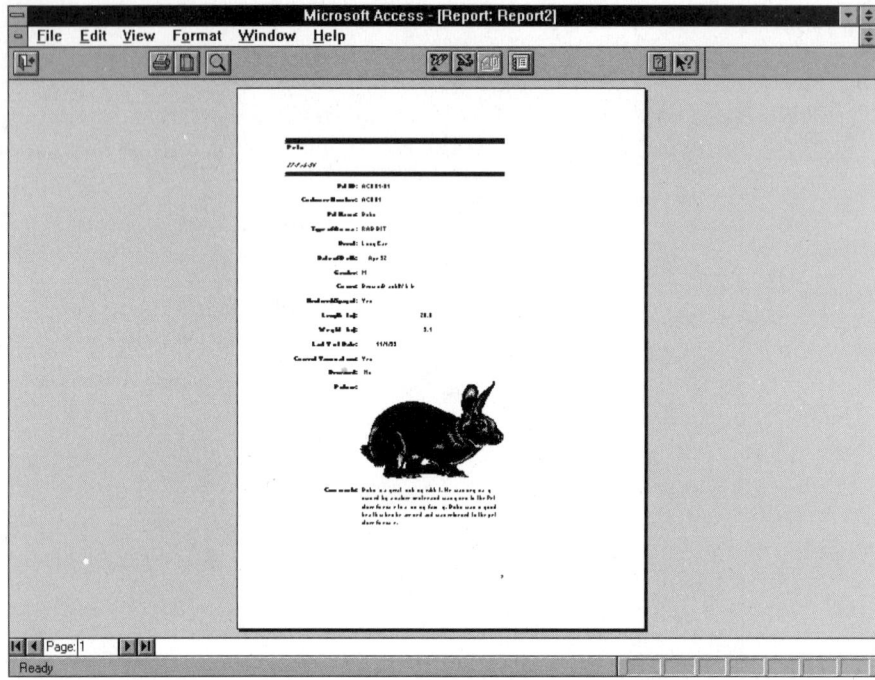

Using AutoReport is the quickest way to create a report. Generally, however, you will want more control over your report creation. Other Report Wizards are available to help you create more customized reports.

Summary

In this chapter, you learned how easily you can create reports in Access. You saw the basic types of reports and how the Report Wizards simplify the process. The following points were covered:

- The Access report writer lets you create groups/totals reports, column reports, and mailing labels.
- The process of creating a report consists of defining the layout, assembling the data, creating the report design, and printing or viewing the report.
- Report Wizards let you create the three types of reports by filling in dialog boxes.
- There are three types of looks: Executive, Presentation, and Ledger.
- Reports can be printed or viewed on-screen.
- You can view reports on-screen in a print preview or sample preview mode.
- Sample previews use a small portion of the data to let you quickly view the report without running the underlying query.

In the next chapter, you learn how to manipulate multiple tables with Access objects. You'll see how to relate tables to take full advantage of relational database capabilities.

Setting Relationships between Multiple Tables

CHAPTER 12

In This Chapter

- The tables that comprise the Mountain Animal Hospital database
- What a key is
- The benefits of using primary keys
- How to create a multiple-field primary key
- What a foreign key is
- The types of relations
- How referential integrity works
- How to create relationships
- How to delete relationships

So far, you learned how to create a simple table and to enter its data and display it in either a datasheet or a form. Then you learned how to use simple queries and reports. However, all these techniques were demonstrated with only a single table. The Pets table has been an excellent sample of a single table because it contains many different data types that lend themselves to productive examples.

It's time now to move into the real world of relational database management.

Tables Used in the Mountain Animal Hospital Database

Figure 12-1 diagrams the database of the Mountain Animal Hospital system. You see eight tables in the figure, each of which requires its own table design, complete with field names, data types, descriptions, and properties.

Following Along in This Book
If you're following along with the examples, you need to use either the MTNSTART or MTNANHSP files on the disk that accompanies this book, or you must create these tables yourself. If you want to create each of these tables, you can use Appendix B as a reference for each table's description; then follow the steps you learned in Chapter 7 to create each table.

In the diagram in Figure 12-1, you can see lines joining the tables. These are the *relationship lines* between the tables. Each line indicates a separate relationship, between two tables, that is established either at the relationships builder (table) level or by a query. You learn how to establish relationships in a query in Chapter 14. In this chapter, you see how to establish a relationship at the table level using the relationships builder.

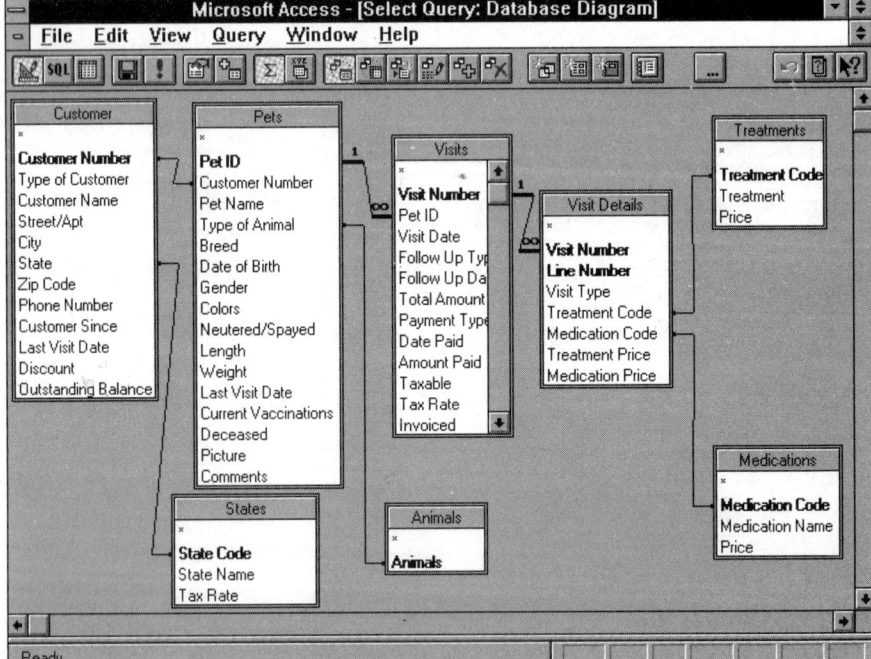

Figure 12-1: The database diagram for the Mountain Animal Hospital system.

Chapter 12: Setting Relationships between Multiple Tables

Of the eight tables in the database diagram, four actually hold data about Mountain Animal Hospital, and four tables are used for lookups. You can eliminate the lookup tables and still use the system if you want to. These are the four main tables:

Customer	Contains information about each customer
Pets	Contains information about each animal
Visits	Contains information about each visit
Visit Details	Contains multiple records about the details of each visit

Following are the four lookup tables:

States	Used by the Customer table to retrieve state name and tax rate
Animals	Used by the Pets table to retrieve a list of valid animal types
Treatments	Used by the Visit Details table to retrieve treatment name and price
Medications	Used by the Visit Details table to retrieve medication name and price

In order to set relations between tables, you must establish a link between fields that contain common information. The fields themselves do not need to have the same name. However, the field's data type and length must be the same, and, even more importantly, the information contained within both fields for a specific record must be the same in both tables for the link to work. When establishing a relation, you generally relate a field's primary key to a field in another table. This field in the second table is called a *foreign key*.

In Figure 12-1, each table has one or more fields in bold. These are the fields that define the primary key for each table.

Understanding Keys

Every table should have a *primary key*. A primary key is made up of one or more fields. The contents of the primary key are unique to each record. For example, the Customer Number field is the primary key in the Customer table — each record in the table has a different Customer Number (no two records have the same number). This is called *entity integrity* in the world of database management. By having a different primary key in each record, like the Customer Number in the Customer table, you can tell two customers apart. This is important because you can easily have two customers named Fred Smith or Animal Kingdom in your table.

Theoretically, you could use the customer name plus the customer's address, but two people named Fred Smith could live in the same town and state. And a father and son, Fred David Smith and Fred Daniel Smith, could live at the same address. The goal of setting primary keys is to create individual records in a table that will guarantee uniqueness.

Remember that when creating Access tables, if you don't specify a primary key, Access asks whether you want one. If you say yes, Access will create a primary key for you. The primary key that Access creates is a Counter data type. It will automatically place a new sequential number in the primary key field for each record. Table 12-1 shows a list of tables and their primary keys.

In Access, a Counter type data field cannot be used to enforce referential integrity between tables. Therefore, it is important to specify another data type for the primary key — like text or numeric. This information will be covered later in this chapter.

Table 12-1
Tables and Primary Keys

Table	Primary Key
Customer	Customer Number
Pets	Pet ID
Visits	Visit Number
Visit Details	Visit Number; Line Number
States	State Code
Animals	Animals
Treatments	Treatment Code
Medications	Medication Code

Deciding on a primary key

Most tables have a unique field or a combination of fields that makes each record unique. The field or fields that make the record unique are known as the primary key for that table. Often, the primary key field is some sort of ID field. The ID field is usually a Text type field. The contents of this ID field are usually determined by some simple method that you specify to create the value in the field. Your method can be as simple as using the first letter of the real value you are tracking along with a sequence number (like A001, A002, B001, B002, and so on). Sometimes the method may rely on a random set of letters and numbers for the field content (as long as each field has a unique value). Or your method can be a complicated calculation based on information in several fields in the table.

Table 12-2 shows a list of tables and explains how the primary key is defined in each table.

As you can see in Table 12-2, it doesn't take a great deal of work or even much imagination to create a key. Any rudimentary scheme and a good sequence number always seem to work. Because Access automatically tells you when you try to enter a duplicate key value, you can simply add one to the sequence number. You may think that all these sequence numbers make it hard to look up information in your tables. Just remember that *normally* you never look up information by an ID field. You generally look up information by the *purpose* of the table. In the Customer table, you can look up information by Customer Name. In some cases, the Customer Name is the same, so you can look at other fields in the table to find the correct customer (ZIP code or phone number). Unless you just happen to know the Customer Number, you'll probably never use it in a search for information.

Table 12-2
Deriving the Primary Key

Table	Derivation of Primary Key
Customer	Individuals: first two letters of last name, three-digit sequence number Pet Stores: first letter of first two major words, three-digit sequence number Zoos: first letter of first two major words, three-digit sequence number
Pets	Customer Number, a hyphen (-), and then a sequential number
Visits	Four-digit year and then the Julian day (sequential number)
Visit Details	Visit Number and then another field that holds a three-digit sequence number (Line Number field)
States	Common two-letter state abbreviation
Animals	Type of animal
Treatments	Four-digit unique number (arbitrarily selected)
Medications	Four-digit unique number (arbitrarily selected)

Benefits of a primary key

Have you ever placed an order with a company for the first time and then decided the next day to increase your order? You call the people at the order desk. Sometimes they ask you for your customer number. You tell them you don't know your customer number. This type of thing happens all the time. So they then ask you for some other information — generally, your ZIP code or telephone area code. Then, as they narrow down the list of customers, they ask your name. Then they tell you your customer number (like you care). Some businesses use phone numbers as a unique starting point. When I call for pizza delivery, I give them my phone number, and they proceed to tell me my name, address, and the last ten types of pizza I ordered!

Database systems usually have more than one table. The tables tend to be related in some manner. For example, the Customer table and Pets table are related to each other via a Customer Number. The Customer table will always have one record for each customer, and the Pets table will have a record for each pet the customer owns. Because each customer is *one* physical person, you only have one record about the customer in the Customer table. However, each customer can own several pets, which means that you set up another table to hold information about each pet. Again, each pet is *one* physical animal (a dog, a cat, a bird, and so on). So each animal has one record in the Pets table. Of course you relate the customers' pets in the Pets table to the right customer in the Customer table by using a common field between both tables. In this case, the field is the Customer Number. It is in both tables.

When linking tables, you should link the primary key field from one table (the Customer Number in the Customer table) to a field in the second table that has the same structure and type of data in it (the Customer Number in the Pets table). If the link field in the second table is *not* the primary key field, which is usually the case, it is known as a *foreign key* field (this topic is discussed later in the chapter).

Besides being a common link field between tables, a primary key field in Access has other advantages:

- A primary key field is an index that greatly speeds up queries, searches, and sort requests.

- When you add new records, you must enter a value in primary key field(s). Access will not allow you to enter NULL values, which guarantees that you only have valid records in your table.

- When you add new records to your table that has a primary key, Access checks for duplicate data and doesn't let you enter duplicates for the primary key field.

- By default, Access displays your data in the order of the primary key.

If you define a primary key based on part of the data in the record, you can have Access automatically place your data in an understandable order. In the example, the Pet ID field is made up of the owner's Customer Number, followed by a hyphen and a two-digit sequence number. If the All Creatures Pet Store is the first customer on the list whose last name begins with AC, the store's customer number is AC001. If someone from this store brings in three pets, the Pet IDs are designated AC001-01, AC001-02, and AC001-03. This way, the Pet ID field provides you with data in the order of customers displayed alphabetically.

 Primary key fields should be made as short as possible because they can affect the speed of operations in a database.

Creating a primary key

As discussed in Chapter 7, you create a primary key by selecting the field you want to specify as a primary key and clicking on the Primary Key button on the toolbar (the key). If you are specifying more than one field, you specify the fields you want for the primary key and again click on the Primary Key button. You specify the fields by selecting each field while holding down the Ctrl key.

When specifying multifield primary keys, the order of the selection is important. Therefore, you should check your selection by clicking the Indexes button on the toolbar and looking at the field order. Figure 12-2 shows the two-field index for the Visit Details table. Notice that the Visit Number is before the Line Number field in the index box.

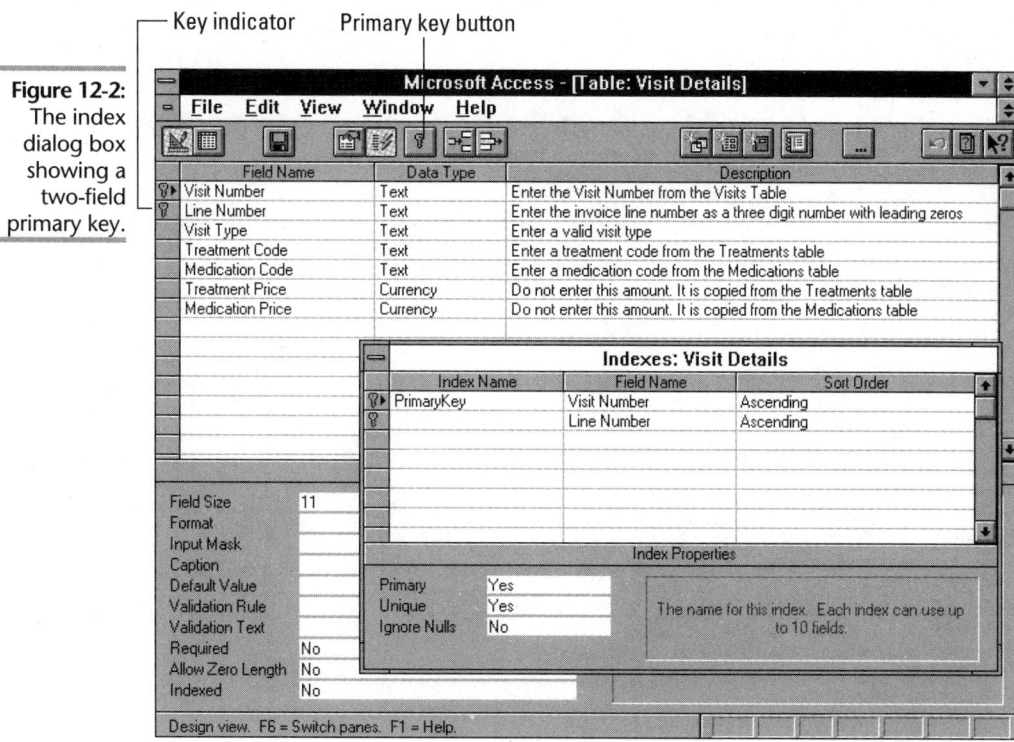

Figure 12-2: The index dialog box showing a two-field primary key.

Understanding foreign keys

Primary keys guarantee uniqueness in a table, and you use the primary key field in one table to link to another. The common link field in the other table may not be (and usually isn't) the primary key in the other table. The common link field is a field or fields that hold the same type of data as in the primary key of the link table. The field or fields used to link to a primary key field in another table are known as *foreign keys*. Unlike a primary key, which must be created in a special way, a foreign key is any field(s) used in a relation. By matching the values (from the primary key to the foreign key) in both tables, two records can be related.

In Figure 12-1, you saw a relation between the Customer and Pets tables. The primary key of Customer, Customer Number, is related to the Customer Number field in Pets. In Pets, Customer Number is the foreign key because it is the key of a related "foreign" table.

A relation also exists between the States and Customer tables. The primary key of States, State Code, is related to the State field in the Customer table. In the Customer table, State is the foreign key because it is the key of a related foreign table.

Understanding Relations between Tables

At the beginning of this chapter, you saw eight tables in the Mountain Animal Hospital database and seven relations. Before you learn how to create these relationships, it is important that you understand relations.

A review of relationships

Relationships established at the table level take precedence over those established at the query level. If you can set a relationship at the table level, the relationship will automatically be recognized when a multiple-table query is created that uses fields from more than one table. Relationships between tables can be grouped into four types:

- One to one
- One to many
- Many to one
- Many to many

Understanding the four types of table relationships

When you physically join two tables, by connecting fields with like information, you create a relationship that Access recognizes. Figure 12-3 shows the relationships between all the tables in the Mountain Animal Hospital system.

The relationship that you specify between tables is important. It tells Access how to find and display information from fields in two or more tables. The program needs to know whether it will only look for one record in a table or several records based on the relationship. For example, the relationship between the Customer table and the Pets table is known as a one-to-many relationship. There will *always* be one record in the Customer table for at *least* one record in the Pets table; however, there could be *many* related records in the Pets table. So Access knows to find only one record in the Customer table and look for any in the Pets table (one or more) that have the same Customer Number.

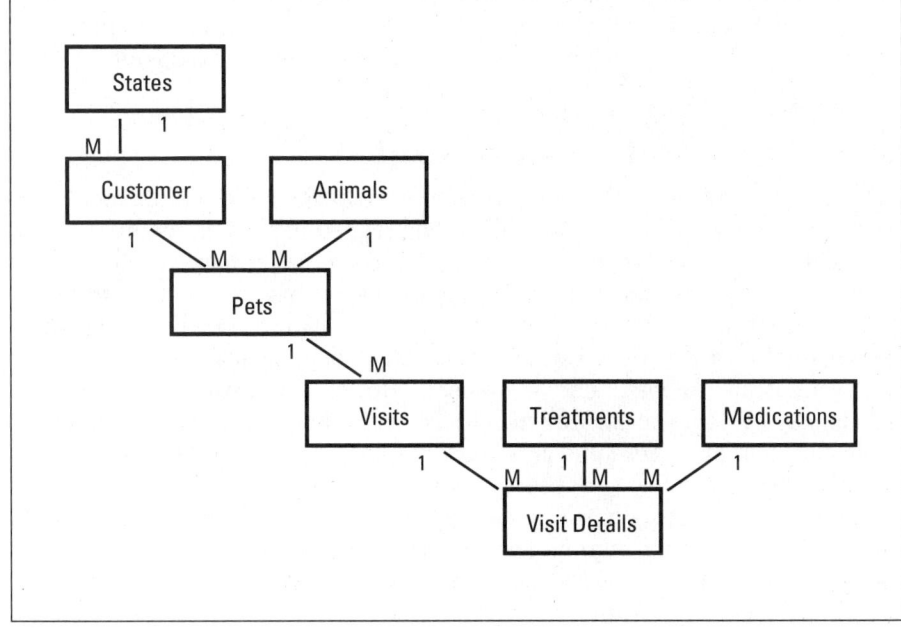

Figure 12-3: The Mountain Animal Hospital relations.

The one-to-one relationship

The one-to-one relation is rarely used in database systems although it can be a very useful way to relate or link two tables together. A good example of a one-to-one relation that occurs in most billing systems is a billing file that is created to allow additional information necessary to invoice customers at a location other than their listed addresses. This file usually contains the customer number and another set of address fields. Only a few customers would have a separate billing address, so you wouldn't want to add this information to the main customer table. A one-to-one relationship between a customer table and billing table may be established to retrieve the billing address for those customers who want to have a separate address. Although all the information on one table could be added to the other, the tables are maintained separately for efficient use of space.

The one-to-many relationship

The one-to-many relationship is used to relate one record in a table with many records in another. Examples are one customer to many pets or one pet to many visits. Both of these examples are one-to-many relationships. The Customer-Pets relationship links the customer number, which is the primary key of the Customer table, to the customer number in the Pets table, which becomes the foreign key of the Customer table.

The many-to-one relationship

The many-to-one relationship is often referred to as the lookup table relationship. It tells Access that many records in the table will be related to a single record in another table. Normally, many-to-one relationships are *not* based on a primary key field in either table. Mountain Animal Hospital has four lookup tables, each having a many-to-one relationship with the primary table. The States table has a many-to-one relation with the Customer table because each state record can be used by many customers. In theory, this relationship is a one-to-one relationship. However, because it does not use a primary key field for the link and many records from the primary table are linked to a single record in the other table, it is known as a many-to-one relationship.

Some one-to-many relationships can be reversed and made into many-to-one relationships. For example, if you set a relationship from Pets to Customers, the relationship becomes many-to-one. Many pets can have the same owner. So relationships depend on how you use and interpret the information in your tables. Thus, one-to-many and many-to-one relationships can be considered the same — just viewed from opposite perspectives.

The many-to-many relationship

The many-to-many relationship is the hardest for people to understand. Simply think of a many-to-many relationship as a relationship that generally involves a pair of one-to-many relations between two tables, as happens in the tables Pets and Visits in the

Mountain Animal Hospital database. A pet can be serviced at the hospital on many dates, so you see a one-to-many relation between Pets and Visits. On the other hand, on each date, many pets can be brought into the hospital. This is also a one-to-many relation. With a pair of two-way, one-to-many relations, you have a many-to-many relation. An individual pet may visit the hospital on many dates, and on a given date, many pets visit the hospital.

Thus, a many-to-many relationship can be thought of as two, separate, one-to-many relationships.

Understanding Referential Integrity

In addition to specifying relationships between tables in an Access database, you can also set up some rules that will help in maintaining a degree of accuracy between the tables. For example, you would not want to delete a customer record in your Customer table if there are related pets records in the Pets table. If you did delete a customer record without first deleting the customer's pets, you would have a system that has pets without an owner. This type of problem could be catastrophic.

Imagine being in charge of a bank that tracks loans in a database system. Now this system has *no* rules that say, "Before deleting a customer's record, make sure that there is no outstanding loan." It would be disastrous! So a database system needs to have rules that specify certain conditions between tables — rules to enforce the integrity of information between the tables. These rules are known as *referential integrity*. These rules keep relationships between tables intact in a relational database management system. Referential integrity is a set of rules based on your relationships that prohibits you from changing your data in ways that invalidate the links between tables.

Referential integrity operates strictly on the keys of a table, checking each time a key field, whether primary or foreign, is added, changed, or deleted. If the change to a key creates an invalid relation, it is said to violate referential integrity. You can set up your tables so that referential integrity is enforced automatically.

When tables are linked together, one table is usually called the *parent,* whereas the table it is linked to is usually called the *child.* This is known as a *parent-child* relationship. Referential integrity guarantees that there will never be an *orphan,* a child record without a parent record.

Creating Relationships

Unless you have a reason for not wanting your relationships to always be active, you should create your table relationships at the table level using the relationships builder. If you need to break the table relationships later, you can. However, for normal data entry and reporting purposes, having your relationships defined at the table level makes it much easier to use a system.

Access 2.0 has added a very powerful relationships builder. You can add tables, use drag-and-drop methods to link tables, easily specify the type of link, and set any referential integrity between tables.

Using the relationships builder tool

You create relationships in the Database window. From this window, you can select the menu item Edit⇨Relationships... or click the Relationships button on the toolbar. The main Relationships window appears, which lets you add tables and create links between them.

The main Relationships window is shown in Figure 12-4. Notice the new toolbar associated with it. When first opened, the Relationships window is a blank surface. You can add tables to the window by using one of several methods :

- Add the tables before entering the relationships builder from the dialog box that's first displayed.
- Click the Add tables button on the toolbar.
- Select Relationships⇨Add Table... from the main menu.
- While in the Relationships window, click the right mouse button, which calls up the shortcut menu, and select Add Table... from the menu.

To start the relationships builder and add tables to the Relationships window, follow these steps:

Steps:	Starting the Relationships Builder and Adding Tables
Step 1.	Click the Relationships button on the toolbar. Access opens an Add Table dialog box.
Step 2.	Select all the tables by double-clicking them — Customer, Pets, Visits, Visit Details, States, Animals, Medications, and Treatments.

Chapter 12: Setting Relationships between Multiple Tables 265

Step 3. Press the Close button on the Add table dialog box. Your screen should look like the one in Figure 12-4. Notice that Access has placed each table in the Relationships window. Each table is in its own box; the title of the box is the name of the table. Inside the table box are the names of the fields for each table. Currently, there are no links between the tables. Now you are ready to set relationships between them.

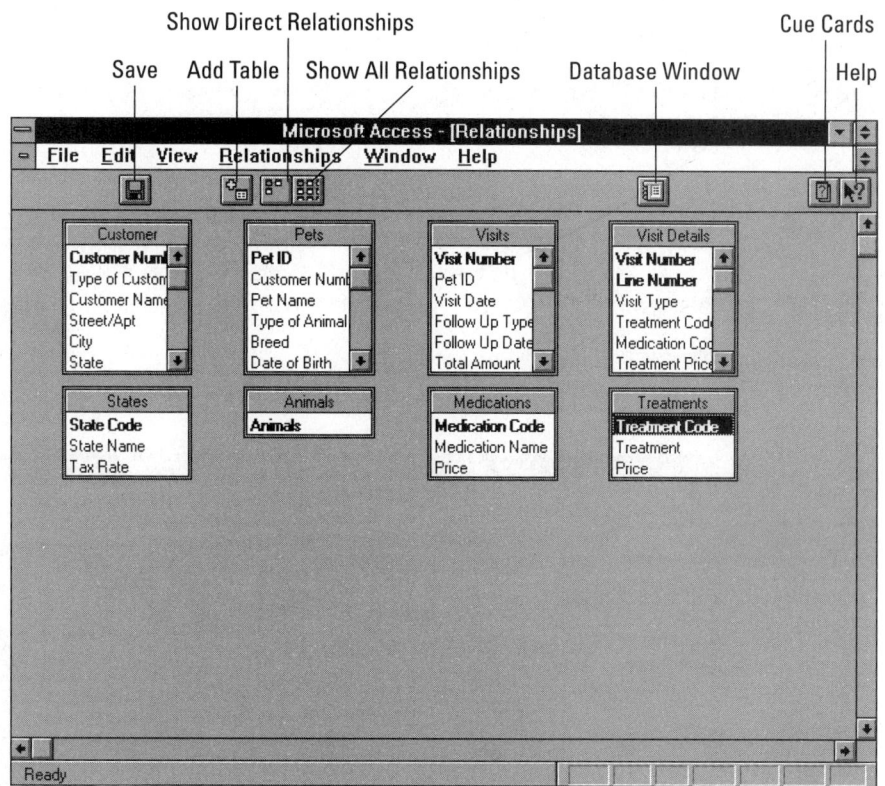

Figure 12-4: The Relationships window with all eight tables added.

If you select a table by mistake, you can remove it from the window by clicking in it and pressing the Delete key.

You can resize each table window to see all the fields as shown in Figure 12-5.

Creating a link between tables

With the tables in the Relationships window, you are ready to create links between the tables. To create a link between two tables, simply select the common field in one table and drag it over to the field in the table you want to link to, then drop it on the common field.

Follow these steps to create a link between the tables:

> **Steps: Setting Up Relations (Links) between the Tables in the Relationships Window**

Step 1. Click the Customer Number field of the Customer table.

If you select a field for linking in error, simply move the field icon to the window surface and it turns into the international no symbol. While it is displayed as this symbol, release the mouse button and the field linking will stop.

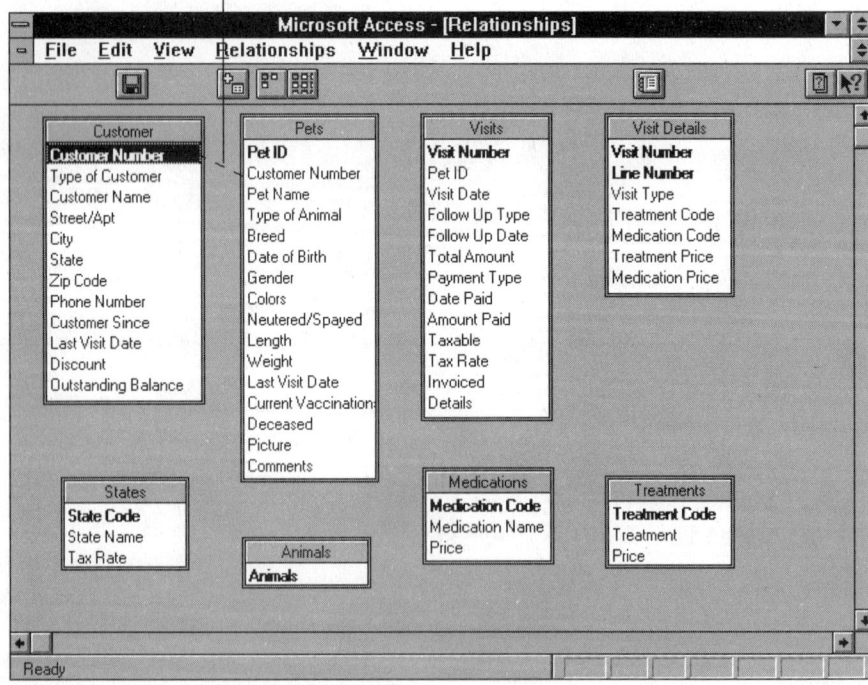

Figure 12-5: Creating relationships (links) between tables.

Chapter 12: Setting Relationships between Multiple Tables

Step 2. While holding down the mouse button, move the cursor to the Pets table. Notice that Access displays a field select icon.

Step 3. Drag the field select icon to the Customer Number field of the Pets table. Access activates the Relationships dialog box (see Figure 12-6).

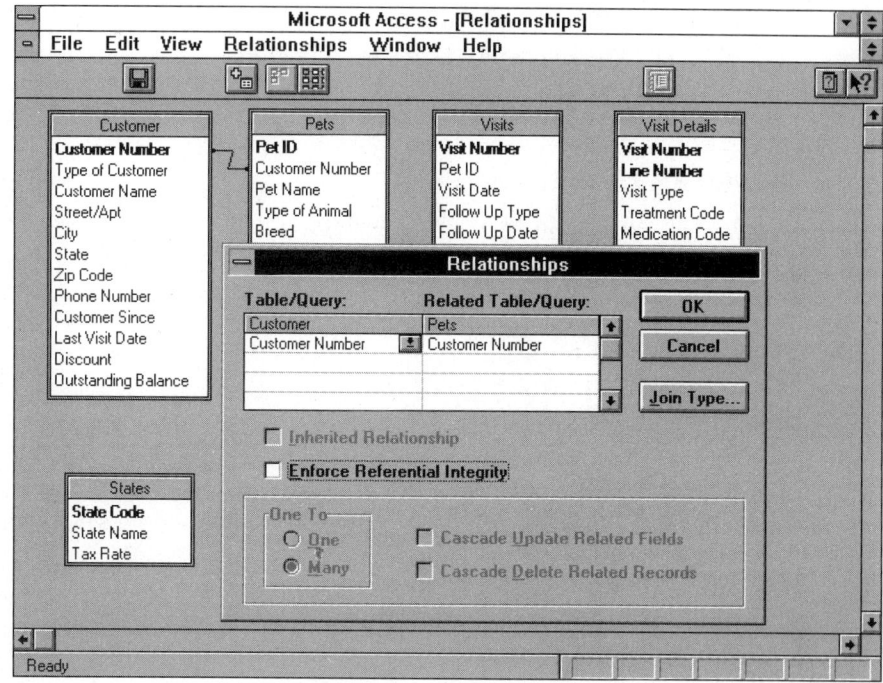

Figure 12-6: The Relationships dialog box.

Step 4. Select any options that you want for the relationship and then press the Create button. Access closes the dialog box and places a join line between the Customer and Pets table.

 You can reactivate the relationship dialog box for any join (link) by double-clicking the join line between the two tables. For example, double-clicking the join line between the Customer and Pets table will reactivate the relationship dialog box for that link.

Specifying relationship options in the relationship dialog box

The relationship dialog box has several options that you can specify for your relationship between the Customer and Pets tables. Figure 12-6 shows the dialog box and all the options. The dialog box tells you which table is the Primary table for the link and whether referential integrity is enforced. If referential integrity is enforced, the dialog box tells you the type of relationship (one-to-one or one-to-many) and lets you specify whether you want to allow cascading updates and deletes between linked tables.

Following Along in this Book

For the following sections, you will want to activate the Relationships dialog box for the link between the Customer and Pets tables. To do so, double-click the join line between the tables.

Specifying the primary table

The top of the dialog box has two table names — Customer on the left and Pets on the right. The Customer table is considered the primary table for this relationship. The dialog box shows the link fields for each table immediately below the table names. Make sure that the correct table name is in both boxes (Customer and Pets) and that the correct link field is specified.

If you link two tables in the wrong order, simply press the Cancel button in the dialog box. Access will close the dialog box and erase the join line. Then you can begin again.

If you link two tables by the wrong field, simply select the correct field for each table by using the combo box under each table name.

Enforcing referential integrity

After you specify the link and verify the table and link fields, you can set referential integrity between the tables by clicking on the Enforce Referential Integrity checkbox below the table information. If you choose not to enforce referential integrity, you can add new records, change key fields, or even delete related records without worrying about referential integrity. You can create orphans or parents without children. With normal operations, such as data entry or changing information, referential integrity rules should be in force. By setting this option, you can specify several additional options.

Simply click the checkbox in front of the option Enforce Referential Integrity. After you do so, Access activates several other choices in the dialog box — the type of relationship and cascade options.

Choosing the relationship type

If you specify that you want to enforce referential integrity, Access lets you choose the type of relationship between the tables. Access defaults the relationship to one-to-many. You can create only one of two types of relationships:

- One to one
- One to many

Remember that a one-to-many and a many-to-one relationship are the same relationship viewed from opposite perspectives. Make sure that you specify as the Primary table the side that gives you a one-to-many view.

For this example, Customer to Pets is a one-to-many relationship, so you should leave the choice one-to-many.

Also remember that the many-to-many relationship is really just a pair of one-to-many relationships between two tables. As such, you can use either side of the relationship as the primary table, and a many-to-many relationship is automatically created.

Access won't let you set referential integrity

You may specify Enforce Referential Integrity and press the Create button to create a relationship between two tables and find that Access will not allow you to. The reason is that you are asking Access to create a relationship supporting referential integrity between two tables that have records that violate referential integrity (the child table has orphans in it). When this situation happens, Access warns you by displaying a dialog box like the one shown in Figure 12-7. This warning happens because there is a Pet record in the database with no Customer record. There is also a Customer record with no Pet record. You will learn about these instances later in the book.

Access returns you to the Relationships window after you press the OK button, and you will need to re-create the relationship. If you are editing an existing join, Access also returns you to the Relationships window by removing the referential integrity option.

To solve any conflicts between existing tables, you can create a *Find Unmatched Query* using the new Query Wizards to find the records in the *many* side table that violates referential integrity. Then you can convert the unmatched query to a delete query to delete the offending records.

With the offending records gone, you can go back in and set up referential integrity between the two tables.

Choosing the Cascade update related fields option

If you specify Enforce Referential Integrity in the relationship dialog box, Access lets you select a checkbox option labeled Cascade update related fields. This option tells

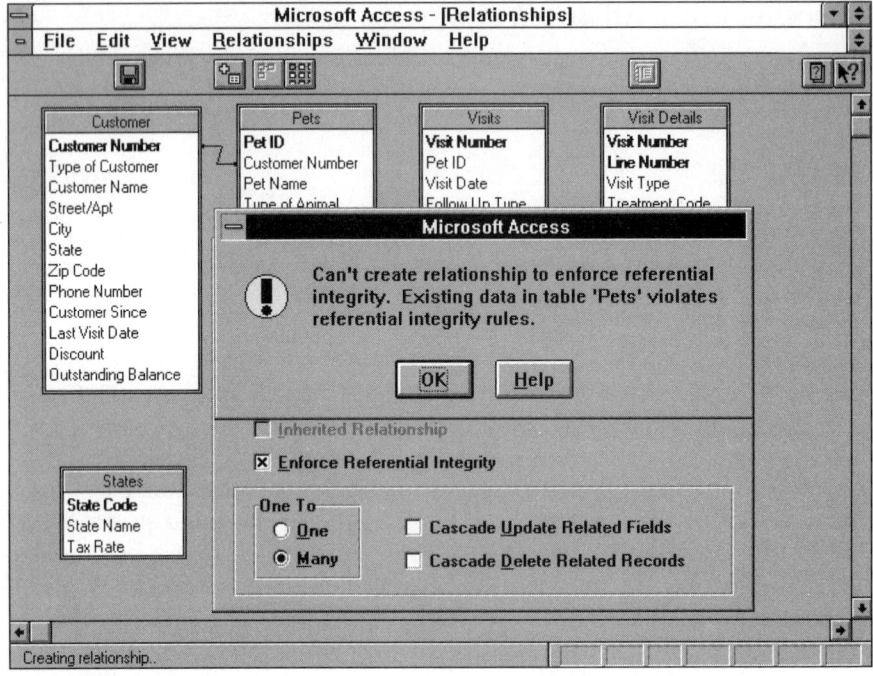

Figure 12-7:
A dialog box warning that referential integrity cannot be set between two existing tables.

Access that a user can change the contents of a link field (the primary key field in the primary table — like the Customer table).

If the user changes the contents of the primary key field in the primary table, Access will verify that the change is a new number (there cannot be duplicate records in the primary table) and then go through the related records in the other table and change the link field value from the old value to the new one.

If this option is not checked, you cannot change the primary key field in the primary table that is used in a link with another table.

If the primary key field in the primary table is a link field between several tables, this option must be checked for all related tables or it will not work.

Choosing the Cascade delete related records option

If you specify Enforce Referential Integrity in the relationship dialog box, Access activates the Cascade delete related records checkbox. If you select this option, you are telling Access that if a user attempts to delete a record in a primary table that has child records, first delete all the related child records and then delete the primary record. This can be a very useful option for deleting a series of related records. For example, if cascade delete is checked and you try to delete a particular customer (who moved away from the area) by deleting the Customer record, Access goes out to the related tables — Pets, Visits, and Visit Details — and also deletes all related records for the

Chapter 12: Setting Relationships between Multiple Tables   271

customer. Access deletes all the records in the Visits Details for each visit for each pet owned by the customer, the visit records, the associated pet records, and the customer record, with one step.

If you do not specify this option, Access will not allow you to delete a record that has related records in another table. In cases like this, you must delete all related records in the Visit Details table first, then related records in the Visits table, then related records in the Pets table, and finally the customer record in the Customer table.

To use this option, you *must* specify Cascade delete related records for the all table's relationships in the database. If you do not specify this option for all the tables down the chain of related tables, Access will not allow cascade deleting.

Access does not warn you that it is going to do a cascade delete when you press the Delete key. The program simply does it.

Saving the relationships between tables

The easiest way to save the relationships you created between the tables is to click the Save button on the toolbar and then close the window. However, you can also close the window and answer yes to the Save Relationships dialog box that appears.

Adding another relationship

After you specify all the tables, the fields, and their referential integrity status, you can add additional tables to the Relationships window by clicking on the Relationships button on the toolbar and adding new tables.

Again, if data that violates referential integrity exists in the tables being linked, you must fix the offending table by removing the records before you can set referential integrity between the tables.

Deleting an existing relationship

To delete an existing relationship, simply go into the Relationships window, click on the join line you want to delete, press the Delete key, and answer yes to the question
`Delete selected relationship?`.

Join lines in the Relationships window

When you create a relationship between two tables, Access automatically creates a thin join line from one table to another. The join line between States and Customer is shown in Figure 12-8.

However, if you specify that you want to enforce referential integrity, Access changes the appearance of the join line. It becomes thicker at each end of the line (alongside the table). It also has either a 1 or the infinity symbol (∞) over the thick bar of the line (on each side of the join line).

After referential integrity is specified, Access will add the thick lines to the join in any queries that use the tables. This gives you a visual way to know that referential integrity is active between the tables.

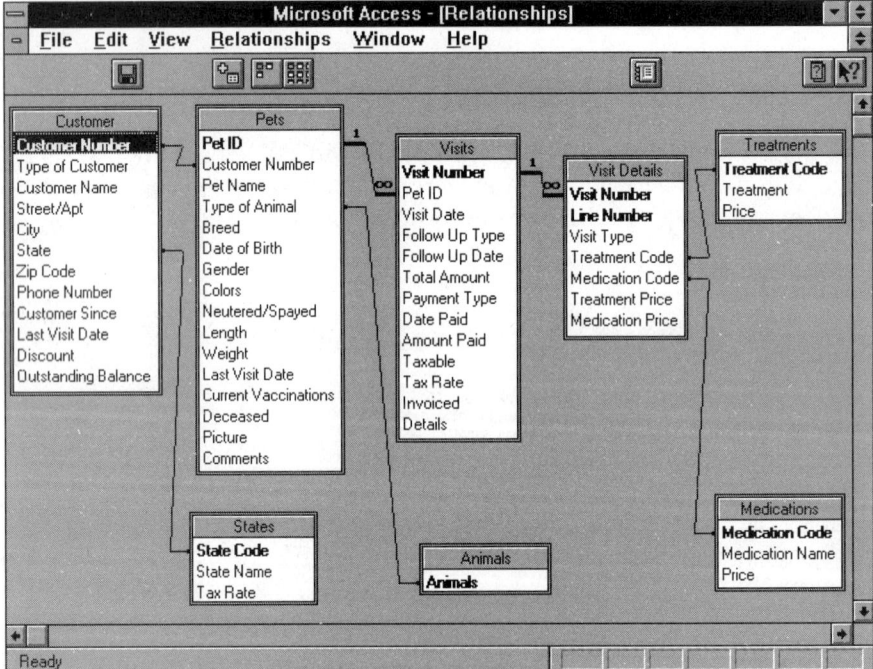

Figure 12-8: The relationships in the Mountain Animal Hospital system.

Creating the relationships for the Mountain Animal Hospital system

Table 12-3 shows how the relationships should be set between all the tables in the system. Notice that referential integrity is set between three of the four primary tables. In addition to having referential integrity, each of the four main tables has the Cascade delete related records option checked.

Table 12-3
Relationships in the Mountain Animal Hospital System

Primary Table / Field	Related Table / Field	Referential Integrity	Cascade Delete
Customer Customer Number	Pets Customer Number	No*	No*
Pets Pet ID	Visits Pet ID	Yes	Yes
Visits Visit Number	Visit Details Visit Number	Yes	Yes
State State Code	Customer State	No	No
Animals Animals	Pets Type of Animal	No	No
Medications Medication Code	Visit Details Medication Code	No	No
Treatments Treatment Code	Visit Details Treatment Code	No	No

*These will be changed in Chapter 14 after you delete orphan records.

Creating relationships using queries

Access 2.0 also lets you set relationships using queries. You set a query relationship just like a table relationship. However, a new option is available if a query is used — Inherited Relationship. You check this option if you want the query to inherit the relationship properties (referential integrity, for example) from the underlying tables.

Summary

Using multiple tables adds far more complexity to a system than working with a single table. Throughout the rest of this book, you learn how to create more-advanced forms, reports, and queries using multiple tables. A relational database management system can get quite involved. By paying attention to details and applying the concepts you learned in this chapter, you should be able to create a system of unlimited complexity with Access. In this chapter, the following points were covered:

- Eight tables make up the Mountain Animal Hospital example. The four main tables are Customer, Pets, Visits, and Visit Details; the four lookup tables are States, Animals, Treatments, and Medications.
- A primary key designates one or more fields that make a record unique. This uniqueness is called the entity integrity of a record.
- A primary key is an index that greatly speeds up searches and query requests.
- You create primary keys in the Table Design window by clicking the Key icon after selecting the primary key field.
- A multiple-field primary key is used when one field is not sufficient to guarantee uniqueness.
- A foreign key is a field that contains a value matching another table's primary key.
- A primary key field and a foreign key field are linked to form a relation.
- The four types of relations are one to one, one to many, many to one, and many to many.
- Referential integrity is a set of rules to prevent data entry that results in invalid relationships.
- When data violates referential integrity, you see an error message.
- In a multiple-table system, you cannot simply delete records without regard to referential integrity.
- Whenever you make changes to key field data in a multiple-table system, you potentially violate referential integrity. You must follow special steps to change or delete key field data.
- You create relationships by using the Relationships window from the Database window Edit menu.

In the next chapter, you learn to use operators, functions, and expressions that are used throughout Access in forms, reports, and queries.

Part III

Using Access in Your Work

277 Chapter 13: Using Operators, Functions, and Expressions

305 Chapter 14: Creating Relations and Joins in Queries

335 Chapter 15: Creating Select Queries

365 Chapter 16: Understanding Controls and Properties

401 Chapter 17: Creating and Customizing Data-Entry Forms

441 Chapter 18: Creating Great-Looking Forms

463 Chapter 19: Adding Data-Validation Controls to Forms

493 Chapter 20: Using OLE Objects, Pictures, and Graphs

529 Chapter 21: Creating and Customizing Reports

583 Chapter 22: Database Publishing and Printing

619 Chapter 23: Creating Calculations and Summaries in Reports

CHAPTER 13

Using Operators, Functions, and Expressions

In This Chapter

- What operators, functions, and expressions are and how they are used
- Types of operators
- Types of functions
- How to create an expression
- Special identifier operators and expressions

Operators, functions, and expressions are the fundamental building blocks for Access operations. These operations include entering criteria in queries, creating calculated fields in forms, and creating summary controls in reports.

Operators

Operators let you add numbers, compare values, put text strings together, and create complicated relational expressions. You use operators to inform Access that a specific operation is to be performed against one or more items. Access also uses several special operators for identifying an object.

Types of operators

Following are the types of operators that you learn about in this chapter:

- Mathematical (arithmetic) operators
- Relational operators
- String operators

- Boolean (logical) operators
- Miscellaneous operators

When are operators used?

You use operators all the time. In fact, you use them every time you create an equation. In Access, you use operators to specify data validation rules for table properties, to create calculated fields in forms, or to specify criteria in queries.

Operators indicate that an operation needs to be performed on one or more items. Following are some common examples of operators:

=

&

And

Like

+

Mathematical operators

There are seven basic mathematical operators. These are also known as *arithmetic operators* because they are usually used for performing arithmetic calculations:

*	Multiply
+	Add
–	Subtract
/	Divide
\	Integer Divide
^	Exponentiation
Mod	Modulo

By definition, mathematical operators work with numbers. When you work with mathematical operators, numbers can be any numeric data type. The number can be the actual number or one that is represented by a memory variable or a field's contents. Further, the numbers can be used individually or combined to create complex expressions. Some of the examples in this section are quite complex, but don't worry if you don't usually work with sophisticated mathematics.

The * (multiplication) operator

A simple example of when you use the multiplication operator is on an invoice entry form. A clerk enters the number of items and the per-item price; a calculated field calculates and displays the total price for that number of items. In this case, the control source property of the text box contains the formula [Price] * [Quantity]. Notice that the field names are enclosed in brackets, which is standard notation for dealing with field names in an expression.

The + (addition) operator

If you want to create a calculated field in the same form, adding fields such as Gross Amount and Tax, you enter the expression [Gross Amount] + [Tax]. This simple formula uses the addition operator to add the contents of both fields and place the result in the object that contains the formula.

Besides adding two numbers, the addition operator can be used for concatenating two character strings. For example, you may want to combine the fields First Name and Last Name and display them as a single field. This expression is [First Name] + [Last Name].

Although you can concatenate text strings by using the addition operator, you should use the ampersand (&). The reason for this is discussed in the section "String operators."

The – (subtraction) operator

An example of when you use the subtraction operator is on a form to calculate an invoice amount. For good repeat customers, you may offer a discount off their bill. To determine the Net Amount, you have a formula that uses the subtraction operator, such as [Gross Amount] - ([Gross Amount]*[Discount]).

Although not mathematical operators, parentheses play an integral part in working with operators. These are discussed later in the section "Operator precedence."

The / (division) operator

You can use the division operator to divide two numbers and, like the previous operators, place the result wherever you need it. Suppose, for example, that 212 people win the one-million-dollar lottery this week. The formula to determine each individual's payoff is 1,000,000 / 212, resulting in $4,716.98 per person.

The \ (integer division) operator

Should you ever need to take two numbers, round them both to integers, divide the two rounded integers, and receive a nonrounded integer, this operator will do it for you in one step. Here is an example:

Normal Division	Integer Conversion Division
100 / 6 = 16.667	100 \ 6 = 16
100.9 / 6.6 = 15.277	100.9 \ 6.6 = 14

Access has no specific function for rounding fractional numbers to whole numbers. You can use this operator to round any number. Simply take the number you want to round and integer divide (\) it by 1, as in 125.6 \ 1 = 126.

Access rounds numbers based on the greater than .5 rule, which is to say that any number with a decimal value of *x*.5 or less will round down; greater than .5 will round up to the next whole number. This means that 6.5 becomes 6 and 6.6 becomes 7.

What Are Integer Values?

Integers are whole numbers (numbers that contain no decimal places), which in Access are between –32768 and +32767. Examples are 1, 722, 33, –5460, 0, and 22. To determine the integer part of any number, simply drop any decimal values. For example, the integer of 45.123 is 45; for 2.987, the integer is 2; and so forth.

This can be a confusing operator until you understand just what it does. If you enter the following, it should become clear:

? 101 / 6 results in 16.833.

? 101.9 / 6.6 results in 15.439.

? 102 / 7 results in 14.571.

? INT(102 / 7) results in 14.

? 101.9 \ 6.6 results in 14.

The last entry is equivalent to rounding both numbers in the division operation — 101.9 = 102 and 6.6 = 7 — and then dividing 102 by 7 and converting the answer to an integer. In other words, it is equivalent to

INT((101.9 \ 1) / (6.6 \ 1))

The ^ (exponentiation) operator

The exponentiation operator (^) raises a number to the power of an exponent. Raising a number simply means indicating the number of times you want to multiply a number by itself. For example, to multiply the value 4 × 4 × 4 (4 cubed) is the same as entering the formula 4 ^ 3.

Relational operators

There are six basic relational operators, also known as *comparison operators*. They compare two values or expressions via an equation. The relational operators include the following:

=	Equal
<>	Not equal
<	Less than
<=	Less than *or* equal
>	Greater than
>=	Greater than *or* equal

The operators always return either a logical value or Null that says Yes it is True or No it is not True (False); or it is a Null (unknown/no value).

Access actually returns a numeric value for relational operator equations. It returns a –1 (negative 1) for True and a 0 (zero) for False.

If either side of an equation is a Null value, the resultant will always be a Null.

The = (equal) operator

The equal operator will return a logical True if the two expressions being compared are the same. Here are two examples of the equal operator in practice:

[Type of Animal] = "Cat" will be True if the animal is a cat; False is returned for any other animal.

[Date of Birth] = Date() will be True if the date in the Date of Birth field is today.

The <> (not equal) operator

The not equal operator is exactly the opposite of the equal operator. Here you see the cat example changed to not equal:

[Type of Animal] <> "Cat" will be True if Type of Animal is *anything but* a cat.

The < (less than) operator

The less-than operator returns a logical True if the left side of the equation is less than the right side, as in this example:

[Weight] < 10 will be True if the Weight field contains a value of less than 10.

The <= (less than or equal to) operator

The less than or equal to operator will return a True if the left side of the equation is either less than or equal to the right side, as in this example:

[Weight] <= 10 will be True if the value of Weight equals 10 or is less than 10.

Access is *not* sensitive to the order of the operators. Access accepts either of these forms as the same:

(<=) or (=<)

The > (greater than) operator

The greater-than operator is the exact opposite of the less-than operator. This operator returns a True whenever the left side of the equation is greater than the right side. Here is an example:

[Length (In)] > 22 will return True if the value of Length (In) is greater than 22.

The >= (greater than or equal to) operator

The greater than or equal to operator returns a True if the left side of the equation is either equal to or greater than the right side. Here is an example:

[Weight (lbs)] >= 100 will return True if the field Weight (lbs) contains a value equal to or greater than 100.

Access is *not* sensitive to the order of the operator. Access lets you enter either the form (>=) or (=>).

String operators

Access has two string operators. Unlike the other operators you've worked with, these string operators work specifically with text type data:

    &   Concatenation

    Like   Similar to ...

The & (concatenation) operator

The concatenation operator connects or links (concatenates) two or more objects into a resultant string. This operator works similarly to the addition operator; however, unlike the addition operator, the & operator always forces a string concatenation, as in this example:

    `[First Name] & [Last Name]` produces a single string.

However, in the resultant string, no spaces are automatically added. If `[First Name]` equals "Fred", and `[Last Name]` = "Smith", concatenating the field contents yields `FredSmith`. To add a space between the strings, you must concatenate a space string between the two fields. To concatenate a space string between first and last name fields, you enter a formula like

    `[First Name] & " " & [Last Name]`

This operator can easily concatenate a string object with a number or date type object. Using the & eliminates the need for special functions to convert a number or date to a string.

Suppose, for example, that you have a Number field, which is House Number, and a Text field, which is Street Name, and that you want to build an expression for a report of both fields. For this, you can enter the following:

    `[House Number] & " " & [Street Name]`

If House Number has a value of 1600 and Street Name is "Pennsylvania Avenue N.W.", the resultant concatenation of the number and string is

    `"1600 Pennsylvania Avenue N.W."`

Perhaps you have a calculated field in a report that prints the operator's name and the date and time the report was run. You can accomplish this by using syntax similar to the following:

    `"This report was printed " & Now() & "by " & [operator name]`

If the date is March 21, 1993, and the time is 4:45 PM, this concatenated line will print something like this:

This report was printed 3/21/93 4:45:40 PM by Michael R. Irwin

Notice the spaces at the end or the beginning of the strings. Knowing how this operator works will make maintenance of your database expressions easier. If you always use the concatenation operator for creating concatenated text strings, you won't have to be concerned with what data type the concatenated objects are. Any formula that uses the & operator converts all the objects being concatenated to a string type for you.

Using the & with Nulls: If both objects are Null, the resultant will also be a Null. If only one of the two objects is Null, Access converts the object that is Null to a string type with a length of 0 and builds the concatenation.

The Like (similar to ...) operator

This Like operator compares two string objects by using wildcards. This operator determines whether one object *matches* the pattern of another object. The resultant of the comparison will be a True, False, or Null.

The Like operator uses the following basic syntax:

expression object Like *pattern object*

Like looks for the *expression object* in the *pattern object,* and if it is present, it returns a True.

If either object in the Like formula is a Null, the resultant will be a Null.

This operator provides a powerful and flexible tool for string comparisons. The pattern object can use wildcard characters to increase the flexibility (see the sidebar "Using Wildcards").

If you want to match one of the wildcard characters in the Like operation, the wildcard character must be enclosed by brackets in the pattern object. In the example

```
"AB*Co" Like "AB[*]C*
```

the [*] in the third position of the pattern object will look for the asterisk as the third character of the string.

> **Using Wildcards**
>
> Access lets you use these five wildcards with the Like operator:
>
> Character Matches
>
>   ?   A single character (A to Z, 0 to 9)
>
>   *   Any number of characters (0 to *n*)
>
>   #   Any single digit (0 to 9)
>
>   [*list*]   Any single character in the list
>
> [!*list*]   Any single character *not* in the list
>
> Note that [*list*] and [!*list*] can use the hyphen between two characters to signify a range.

Following are some further examples using the Like operator:

`[Last Name] Like "M[Cc]*"` will be True for any last name that begins with "Mc" or "MC", "McDonald", "McJamison", "MCWilliams" will all be True; "Irwin" and "Prague" will be False.

`[Answer] Like "[!e-zE-Z]"` will be True if the `Answer` is A, B, C, D, a, b, c, d. Any other letter will be False.

`"AB1989" Like "AB####"` will result in True. This string looks for the letters AB and any four numbers after the letters.

`"#10 Circle Drive" Like "[#]*Drive"` will result in True. The first character must be the pound sign, and the last part must be the word *Drive*.

Boolean (logical) operators

Access uses six Boolean operators. Also referred to as *logical operators*, these operators are used for setting conditions in expressions. Many times you'll use Boolean operators to create complex multiple-condition expressions. Like relational operators, these operators always return either a logical value or a Null. Boolean operators include the following:

And	Logical and
Or	Logical inclusive or
Eqv	Logical equivalence
Imp	Logical implication
Xor	Logical exclusive or
Not	Logical not

The And operator

You use the And operator to perform a logical conjunction of two objects. Following is the general syntax of an And operation:

object expression 1 And *object expression 2*

Here is an example:

`[State] = "MN" And [Zip Code] = "12345"` will be True only if *both* conditions are True.

If the conditions on both sides of the And operator are True, the result is a True value. Table 13-1 demonstrates the results.

Table 13-1 And Operator Resultants

Expression 1	Expression 2	Return Resultant
True	True	True
True	False	False
True	Null	Null
False	True	False
False	False	False
False	Null	False
Null	True	Null
Null	False	False
Null	Null	Null

The Or operator

You use the Or operator to perform a logical disjunction of two objects. This is the general syntax of an Or operation:

object expression 1 Or *object expression 2*

The following two examples show how the Or operator works:

[Last Name] = "Williams" Or [Last Name] = "Johnson" will be True if Last Name is either Williams or Johnson.

[Animal Type] = "Frog" Or [Animal Color] = "Green" will be True if the animal is a frog or any animal that is green (a snake, bird, and so forth).

If the condition of either side of the Or operator is True, a True value is returned. Table 13-2 demonstrates the results.

Table 13-2
Or Expression Results

Expression 1	Expression 2	Return Resultant
True	True	True
True	False	True
True	Null	True
False	True	True
False	False	False
False	Null	Null
Null	True	True
Null	False	Null
Null	Null	Null

The Eqv operator

The Eqv operator performs a logical equivalence on two objects. The general syntax of an Eqv operation is as follows:

object expression 1 Eqv *object expression 2*

Here is an example:

[Last Name] = "Williams" Eqv [Animal] = "Cat" will be True if the last name is Williams and Animal is a cat.

[Animal Type] = "Frog" Eqv [Animal Color] = "Green" will be True if Animal Type is a frog and if the frog is green.

If neither condition is Null, and if the condition on both sides of the Eqv operator is the same, a True value is returned. Table 13-3 demonstrates the results.

Table 13-3
Eqv Operator Results

Expression 1	Expression 2	Return Resultant
True	True	True
True	False	False
True	Null	Null
False	True	False
False	False	True
False	Null	Null
Null	True	Null
Null	False	Null
Null	Null	Null

The Not operator

The Not operator is used for negating a numeric object. This operator reverses the logical result of the expression.

Following is the general syntax of a Not operation:

Not *numeric object expression*

The following example shows how to use the Not operator:

Not [Final Sales Amount] >= 1000 will be true if Final Sales Amount is less than 1000.

If the numeric object is Null, the resulting condition will be Null. Table 13-4 demonstrates the results.

Table 13-4
Not Operator Results

Expression	Return Resultant
True	False
False	True
Null	Null

Miscellaneous operators

Access has these three miscellaneous operators that can be very useful to you:

Between ... And	Range
In	List comparison
Is	Reserved word

The Between ... And operator

You can use Between ... And to determine whether an object is within a specific range of values. This is the general syntax:

object expression Between *value 1* And *value 2*

If the value of the object expression is between value 1 and value 2, the result is True; otherwise, it is False.

Following is an example of the Between ... And operator that uses the IIF function for a calculated control:

```
IIF([Amount Owed] Between 0 And 250, "Due 30 Days", "Due NOW")
```

This displays a 30-day-due notice for values of $250 or less and due-now notices for values over $250.

The In operator

You use the In operator to determine whether an object is equal to any value in a specific list. This is the general syntax:

object expression In (*value1*, *value2*, *value3*, ...)

If the object expression is found in the list, the result is True; otherwise, the result is False.

The IIF function is used again in this example. Here, the In operator is used for a control value in a form:

    IIF([Animal Type] In ("Cat", "Dog"), "Common Pet", "Unusual Pet")

This displays the message `Common Pet` if Animal Type is a cat or dog.

The Is *(reserved word)* operator

The Is operator is used only with the key word Null to determine whether an object has nothing in it. This is the general syntax:

   Is Null

This example is a validation check message in a data-entry form to force entry of a field:

    IIF([Customer Name] Is Null, "Name Must be Entered","")

Operator precedence

When you work with complex expressions that have many operators, Access must determine which operator to evaluate first, and then which is next, and so forth. To accomplish this task, Access has a built-in predetermined order, known as *operator precedence*. Access always follows this order unless you tell Access otherwise using parentheses.

You use parentheses to group parts of an expression and override the default order of precedence. Operations within parentheses are performed before any operations outside of them. Inside parentheses, predetermined operator precedence will be followed.

Precedence is determined first according to category of the operator. The following list ranks operators by order of precedence:

1. Mathematical
2. Comparison
3. Boolean

Each of these categories has within it its own order of precedence, which is explained next.

The mathematical precedence

Within the general category of mathematical operators, this order of precedence is in effect:

1. Exponentiation
2. Negation
3. Multiplication and/or division (left to right)
4. Integer division
5. Modulo
6. Addition and/or subtraction (left to right)
7. String concatenation

The comparison precedence

Within the category of comparison operators, the following order of precedence is observed:

1. Equal
2. Not equal
3. Less than
4. Greater than
5. Less than or equal to
6. Greater than or equal to
7. Like

The Boolean precedence

The third general category, Boolean, has within it this order of precedence:

1. Not
2. And
3. Or
4. Xor
5. Eqv
6. Imp

> ### Precedence Order
>
> An example of order of precedence can be found in simple mathematics. Bear in mind that operations within parentheses are performed before operations not in parentheses. Also, remember that multiplication and division come before addition or subtraction.
>
> What is the answer to this simple equation?
>
> > X=10+3*4
>
> If your answer is 52, you need a better understanding of precedence. If your answer is 22, you're right. If your answer is anything else, you need a calculator!
>
> Multiplication is performed before addition by the rules of mathematical precedence. Therefore, the equation 10+3*4 is evaluated in this order:
>
> 3*4 is performed first, yielding an answer of 12. Then 12 is added to 10, yielding 22.
>
> Look what happens when you add parentheses to the equation. What is the answer to this simple equation?
>
> > X=(10+3)*4
>
> Now the answer is 52. With parentheses, the values 10 and 3 are added first; then the result of 13 is multiplied by 4, yielding 52.

What Are Functions?

Functions are small programs that return a value. By definition, functions must always return a value. The value returned can be string, logic, or numeric, depending on the type of function. The resulting value is always based on some calculation, comparison, or evaluation that the function performs. Access provides hundreds of common functions that are used in tables, queries, forms, and reports. You can also create your own user-defined functions (UDFs), using the Access Basic language.

Using functions in Access

Functions perform specialized operations that enhance the use of Access. Many times, you find yourself using functions as an integral part of Access. The following gives you a feel for the types of tasks you'll use functions to accomplish:

- Determine a default value in a table
- Place the current date and time on a report
- Convert data from one type to another
- Perform financial operations
- Display a field in a specific format
- Look up and return a value based on another
- Perform an action upon the triggering of an event

Access functions can perform financial, mathematical, comparative, and other operations. Therefore, you'll find yourself using functions just about everywhere — in queries, forms, reports, validation rules, and so forth.

Many Access functions evaluate or convert data from one type to another; others perform an action. Some Access functions require use of *parameters,* whereas others operate with no parameters.

A parameter is some value that you supply to the function when you execute the function. The value can be an object name, a constant, or a quantity.

Access functions can be quickly identified because they always end with parentheses. If a function uses parameters, the parameters are placed inside the parentheses immediately after the function name.

Following are examples of Access functions:

Now( ) returns the current date and time.

Rnd( ) returns a random number.

Ucase( ) returns the uppercase of an object.

Format( ) returns a user-specified formatted expression.

> ### What Is a Program?
> A program is a series of defined steps that specify one or more actions that the computer should perform. A program can be created by the user or can already exist in Access; all Access functions are programs that are already created for you. For example, a Ucase() function is a small program. If you employ Ucase() on a string such as "Michael J. Irwin", Access creates a new string from the existing string, converting each letter to uppercase. The program starts at the leftmost letter, first converting *M* to *M* and then *i* to *I*, and so forth, until the entire string is converted. As it converts each letter, the program concatenates it to a new string.

Types of functions

Access offers several types of functions for you to use. They can be placed in the following general categories:

- Conversion
- Date/Time
- Financial (SQL)
- Financial (monetary)
- Mathematical
- String manipulation
- Domain

Conversion

Conversion functions change the data type from one type to another. A few common functions are listed here:

Str( ) returns a numeric as a string:

```
Str(921.234) returns "921.234".
```

Val( ) returns a numeric value from a string:

```
Val("1234.56") returns 1234.56.
Val("10 Farmview Ct") returns 10.
```

Format() returns an expression by the user-specified format:

```
Format("Next",">") returns NEXT.
Format("123456789","@@@-@@-@@@@") returns 123-45-6789.
Format(#12/25/93#,"d-mmmm-yyyy") returns 25-December-1993.
```

Date/Time

Date/Time functions work with date and time expressions. Following are a couple of common Date/Time functions:

Now() returns the current date and time:

```
3/4/93 12:22:34 PM.
```

Time() returns the current time in 12-hour format:

```
12:22:34 PM.
```

Financial (SQL)

Financial (SQL) functions perform aggregate financial operations on a set of values. The set of values is contained in a field. The field can be in a form, report, or query. Following are two common SQL functions:

Avg()	An example is `Avg([Scores])`.
Sum()	An example is `Sum([Gross Amount] + [Tax] + [Shipping])`.

Financial (monetary)

Financial (monetary) functions perform financial operations. Following are two monetary functions:

NPV() is the net present value, based on a series of payments and a discount rate. The syntax follows:

```
NPV(discount rate, cash flow array( ))
```

DDB() is the double-declining balance method of depreciation return. The syntax follows:

```
DDB(initial cost, salvage value, life of product, period of asset depreciation)
```

Mathematical

Mathematical functions perform specific calculations. Following are some mathematical functions, with examples of how to use them:

Int() determines the integer of a specific value:

`Int(1234.55)` results in 1234.

`Int(-55.1)` results in -56.

Fix() determines the correct integer for a negative number:

`Fix(-1234.55)` results in -1234.

Sqr determines the square root of a number:

`Sqr(9)` returns a 3.

`Sqr(14)` returns 3.742.

String manipulation

String functions manipulate text-based expressions. Here are several common uses of these functions:

Right() returns the rightmost characters of a string:

`Right("abcdefg",4)` returns `"defg"`.

Len() returns the length of a string:

`Len("abcdefgh")` results in 8.

Lcase() returns the lowercase of the string:

`Lcase("Michael R. Irwin")` returns `michael r. irwin`.

Domain

A *domain* is a set of records contained in a table, a query, or an SQL expression. A query dynaset is an example of a domain. Domain aggregate functions determine specific statistics about a specific domain.

Following are two examples of domain functions:

DAvg() returns the arithmetic mean (average) of a set of values:

`DAvg("[Total Amount]","Visits")` determines the average billing for patients.

`DCount()` returns the number of records specified.

What Are Expressions?

In general, an expression is the means used to explain, or model, something to someone or something.

An *expression* in computer terminology is generally defined as a symbol, a sign, a figure, or a set of symbols that present or represent an algebraic fact as a quantity or operation. The expression is a representative object that Access can use to interpret something and, based on that interpretation, to obtain specific information. Or more simply put, an expression is a *term* or *series of terms* controlled by operators. Expressions are a fundamental part of Access operations.

You can use expressions in Access to accomplish a variety of tasks. You can use an expression in SQL statements, as a property setting, or in queries and filters, or even in macros and actions. Expressions can set criteria for a query or filter, or control macros, or perform as arguments in user-defined functions.

Access evaluates an expression each time it is used. If an expression is in a form or report, Access calculates the value every time the form refreshes (as with changing records and so forth). This ensures accuracy of the results. If an expression is used as criteria in a query, the expression is evaluated every time the query is executed, thereby ensuring that the criteria reflects any changes, additions, or deletions to records since the last execution of the query. If an expression is used in the table design as a validation rule, Access executes the evaluation every time the field is trespassed to determine whether the value is allowed in the field; this expression may be based on another field's value!

 To give you a better understanding of expressions, consider the various examples that follow — all are examples of expressions:

```
=[Customer First Name] & " " & [Customer Last Name]
=[Total Amount] - ([Total Amount] * [Discount])
<25
[Deceased]=Yes
[Animal Type] = "Cat" And [Gender] = "M"
[Date of Birth] Between 1/88 And 12/91
```

All of these are valid expressions and are used by Access in a variety of ways: as validation rules, query criteria, calculated controls, control sources, and control-source properties.

The parts of an expression

As the many examples in the preceding section demonstrated, expressions can be very simple or quite complex. They can include a combination of operators, object names, functions, literal values, and constants.

Keeping in mind that expressions don't need to contain all these parts, you should have an understanding of each of the following uniquely identifiable portions of an expression:

Operators   `>, =, *, And, Or, Not, Like,` etc.

Operators indicate what type of action (operation) will be performed on one or more elements of an expression.

Object names   `Forms![Add a Customer & Pets], [Customer Address], [Pet Name]`

Object names, also known as *identifiers,* are the actual objects: tables, forms, reports, controls, or fields.

Functions   `Date(), DLookUp(), DateDiff()`

Functions always return a value. The resultant value can be created by a calculation, a conversion of data, or an evaluation. You can use a built-in Access function or a user-defined function (UDF) that you create.

Literal values   `100, Jan. 1, 1988, "Cat", "[A-D]*"`

These are actual, literal values that you supply to the expression. Literal values can be numbers, strings, or dates. Access uses the values exactly as they are entered.

Constants   `Yes, No, Null, True, False`

Constants represent values that do not change.

The following illustration demonstrates the parts of an expression:

`[Follow Up Date] = Date() + 30`

`[Follow Up Date]` is an object name, or identifier.
= is an operator.
`Date()` is a function.
+ is an operator.
30 is a literal.

Creating an expression

Expressions are commonly entered in very small property sheets, action arguments, and criteria grids. As you create expressions, the area is scrolled so that you can continue to enter the expression. Although you can enter an expression in this manner, it is often desirable to see the entire expression as you enter it. This is especially true when working with long, complex expressions. Access has a Zoom box that you can use for entering expressions. Open this box by clicking on where you want to enter your expression and then pressing Shift+F2.

As you enter expressions, Access may insert certain characters for you when you *change focus*. Access will check your syntax and will automatically insert these characters:

- Brackets ([]) around control names that have no spaces or punctuation in the name
- Pound Signs (#) around dates that it recognizes
- Quotation marks (" ") around text that contains no spaces or punctuation in the body

The term *changing focus* refers to the movement of the cursor out of the location where you are entering the expression. You accomplish this by pressing Tab, or by moving the mouse and clicking another area of the screen, etc.

Access reports an error when it changes focus under these conditions: Access doesn't understand the date form you enter, the name of the control contains spaces, or when a control is not placed in brackets.

Entering object names

You identify object names by placing brackets ([]) around the element. Use of brackets is required when the object contains a space or punctuation in its name. If these conditions are not present, you can ignore the brackets — Access inserts them automatically. Therefore, the following expressions are syntactically identical:

```
Breed + [Type of Animal]
[Breed] + [Type of Animal]
```

Notice that in both cases the brackets are placed around `Type of Animal` because this object name contains spaces.

Although it isn't necessary to enter brackets around objects like Breed in the second example, it is good programming practice always to surround object names with brackets for consistency in entry.

Entering text

You identify text by placing quotation marks around the text element of an expression. Access automatically places the quotation marks for you if you forget to add them.

As an example, you can type **Cat, Dog, Frog, ...** into separate criteria cells of a query, and Access automatically adds the quotation marks around each of these three entries. Access recognizes these as objects and helps you.

Entering date/time values

You identify date/time data by placing the pound signs (#) around the date/time element. Access will automatically evaluate any valid date/time format and automatically place the pound signs around the element for you.

Expression Builder

Access 2.0 has added an *Expression Builder* tool that helps you build complex expressions. You can use it anyplace you can build an expression (like when specifying criteria for a query or creating a calculated field on a form or report). You can activate the builder in two ways:

- Pressing the Build button on the toolbar (the ellipses [three dots]).
- Clicking the *Right* mouse button and selecting Build from the shortcut menu.

Special identifier operators and expressions

Access has two special *identifier operators:* the dot (.) and the exclamation point (!). When you work with Access tables, you have a diverse range of ways to display and access objects. You can use fields and their contents; any field object can be used over and over. You can display the field object in numerous forms and reports by using the same reference, the field object name, in every form and report.

For example, the field Pet Name in the Pets table can be used in six or seven different forms. When you want to use the Pet Name field in an expression for a comparison, how do you tell Access which copy of the field Pet Name it should use for the expression? In the Windows database, Access, it is possible to have several different forms in the same session on the same computer. In fact, it is possible to have multiple copies of Access running the same data and forms in different regions of the Windows operating system on the same computer.

With all this confusion, there must be a way to specify to Access which Pet Name field object you want the expression to use. That is the purpose of the dot and exclamation operator identifiers. These are key symbols that identify and maintain clarity in determining which field to use.

A Few Words about Controls and Properties

When you create a form or report, you place many different objects on the form — fields in text boxes, text labels, buttons, checkboxes, combo boxes, lines, rectangles, and so on.

As you select and place these objects on a form, each object is assigned a *control name*. The control name is supplied by Access using predefined rules. For example, control names for fields default to a control-source name of the field name. The field name is placed in the text box on the form. The label for the text box is assigned the control name Text, with a sequence number attached to it (for example, Text11 or Text12). The sequence number is added to make each control name unique.

After all objects are placed on the form, you can identify any object on the form (line, button, text box, etc.) by its unique control name. This control name is what you use to reference a specific table field (or field on a form). You can change the name of the control that Access assigned to the object if you want. The only requirement is that the new name must be a unique name for the form or report that it is on.

Every object on the form (and don't forget that the form itself is an object) has associated *properties*. Properties are the individual characteristics of each object and, as such, are accessible by a control name. Properties control the appearance of the object (color, size, sunken, alignment, and so forth). Properties also affect the structure, by specifying format, default value, validation rules, and control name. In addition, properties designate the *behavior* of a control — for instance, whether the field can grow or shrink and whether you can edit the field. Behaviors also affect actions specified for the event properties such as On Enter, On Push, etc.

The ! (exclamation) identifier operator

The exclamation mark (!) is a key symbol that is used in conjunction with several reserved words. One such reserve word is *Forms*. When this word is combined with !, you are telling Access that the next object name will be the *form object name* that you want to reference.

As an example, say that you have a Date of Birth field that is in two forms — [Customer & Pets] and [Pet Specifics]. (Note that these two form names are objects and will need to be referenced by use of brackets.) You want to refer to the Date of Birth field in the [Pet Specifics] form. The way to specify this form is by use of the ! and the Forms reserved word:

    Forms![Pet Specifics]

Now that the form is specified, you need to further refine the scope to add the field Date of Birth.

Although Chapter 16 covers controls and properties, you should have at this point a partial understanding of what properties and controls are (see the sidebar on form controls and properties).

Actually, what you are specifying is a control on the form. That control will be the one that uses the field you need, which is Date of Birth. The control has the same name as the field. Therefore, you access this specific object by using the following expression:

    Forms![Pet Specifics]![Date of Birth]

The second exclamation mark specifies a *control* on a form identified by the reserved word Forms.

Where did the control Date of Birth on the form named [Pet Specifics] come from? In this case, the control name for the *control source object* is Date of Birth, which is referenced against the field Date of Birth from the query Pets & Owners, which is built from the two tables Customers and Pets, which have the actual field Date of Birth.

By following the properties of each object, starting with the object Forms, you can trace the control source object back to a field in the original table.

In summary, the exclamation identifier is always followed by an object name. This object name is one that you define by using the name of a form, report, field, or other control name that you created in the database. If you don't use the existing name for the desired object, you can change the default value name of the source.

The . (dot) identifier operator

The . (dot) is also a key symbol that is used in conjunction with expression identification operators. Normally it is placed immediately after a user-defined object. Unlike the !, the . (dot) usually identifies a *property* of a specific object. Therefore, if you want to determine the value of the Visible property of the same control you worked with before, you specify it as follows:

```
Forms![Pet Specifics]![Date of Birth].Visible
```

This gives you the value for the visible property of the specific field on the specific form.

Normally the . (dot) identifier is used for obtaining a property value of an object. However, it can also be used in some circumstances between a table name and the field name for accessing a specific field value associated with a specific table, as it is here:

```
[Pets].[Pet Name]
```

A thorough analysis of the two special identifier operators is beyond the scope of this book. However, you'll find that with these identifiers, you can find any object and its associated property values.

Summary

In this chapter, you learned about the building blocks of Access operations, the operators, functions, and expressions. The following points were covered:

- Operators let you add numbers, compare values, put strings together, and create complicated relational expressions.
- The many types of operators include mathematical, relational, string, Boolean, and a group of miscellaneous operators.
- The relational operators =, <>, >, >=, <, and <= make comparisons.
- To concatenate two strings, use the & operator.
- You can use five pattern-matching wildcards with the Like operator: *, ?, #, [*list*], and [!*list*].
- The Boolean operators are And, Or, Eqv, Imp, Xor, and Not.
- Operator precedence determines the order in which various parts of an expression are evaluated.
- Functions are small programs that return a value. Access has hundreds of built-in functions.
- Functions are classified as conversion, date/time, financial, mathematical, string, or domain.
- Expressions are used for creating a calculation or for modeling a process.
- Expressions use operators, object names, functions, literal values, and constants.
- The Expression builder can be used to create an expression.
- Object names are entered in brackets ([]) to identify them. Common objects include field names.
- The two special identifiers, the exclamation and the dot, help identify Access objects, such as forms, reports, queries, and tables. These identifiers also are used for identifying properties.

In the next chapter, you examine how to create relations and joins in queries.

Creating Relations and Joins in Queries

CHAPTER 14

In This Chapter

- Adding more than one table to a query
- Manipulating the table/query pane
- Determining which table a field is from in a query
- Moving and resizing Table Design windows
- Creating a database diagram
- Adding single fields to a query
- Adding multiple fields to a query
- Working around query limitations
- Understanding types of joins
- Changing the type of join
- Creating an inner join, an outer join, and a self-join

In previous chapters, you worked with simple queries by using the single table Pets. Using a query to obtain information from a single table is common; however, many times you need to obtain information from several related tables. For example, you may want to obtain a customer's name and the type of pets the customer owns. In this chapter, you learn how to use more than one table to obtain information.

Adding More Than One Table to the Query Window

In Chapter 12, you learned about the different tables in the Mountain Animal Hospital database system. This system is comprised of four primary tables and four lookup tables. You learned about table keys, primary and foreign, and their importance for linking two tables together. You learned how to create relationships between two tables at the table level by using the Edit⇨Relationships... menu choice in the Database window. Finally, you learned how referential integrity rules affect data in tables.

After you create the tables for your database and decide how the tables are related to one another, you are ready to begin creating multiple-table queries to obtain information from several tables at the same time.

By adding more than one table to a query and selecting fields from the tables in the query, you can view information from your database just as though the information from the several tables were in one table. As an example, suppose that you need to send a letter to all owners of snakes who brought their pets in for visits in the last two months. For this data, you'd need to get the information from three separate tables: Pets, Customer, and Visits. You can do this by using the Pets and Visits tables and creating a query for all animals where the Type of Animal field equals *snake* and where Visit Date falls between today's date and today's date minus two months. Because of the relationship between Pets and Customer, you then have access to the customer information for each snake. You can then create a report form using the related information from the tables Pets, Visits, and Customer.

The first step in creating a multiple-table query is to open each table in the Query window. The following steps show how to open the Pets, Customer, and Visits tables in a single query:

Steps: Opening Multiple Tables in a Query

Step 1.	Click the Query Object button in the Database window.
Step 2.	Click the New button to create a new query.
Step 3.	Click the New Query button in the New query dialog box.
Step 4.	Select the Pets table by double-clicking the table name.
Step 5.	Select the Customer table by double-clicking the table name.
Step 6.	Select the Visits table by double-clicking the table name.
Step 7.	Click the Close button in the Add Table dialog box.

You can also add each table by highlighting the table in the list separately and clicking Add.

The top pane of the Query Design window is shown in Figure 14-1 with three tables: Pets, Customer, and Visits.

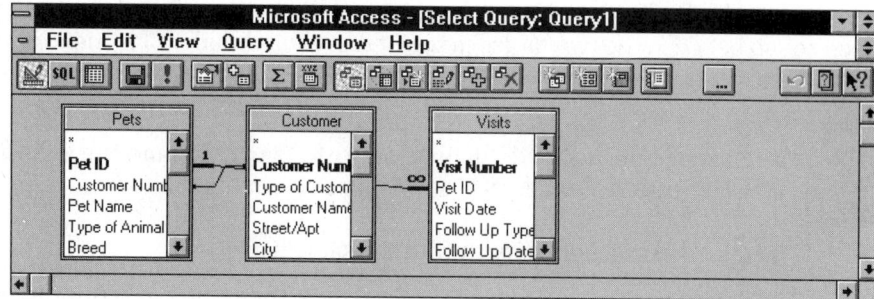

Figure 14-1: The Query Design window with three files added.

You can add more tables by selecting Query⇨Add Table... from the Query Design menu.

Working with the Table/Query Pane

As you can see in Figure 14-1, each table is connected by a single line from the primary key field to the foreign key field. Actually, on your screen it probably looks as if two lines connect Pets to Customer and a single line runs from Customer to Visits. You'll see how to move the table designs so that the lines appear correctly.

The join line

When Access displays each set of related tables, it places a line between the two tables. This line is known as a *join line*. A join line is a graphical line that represents the link between two tables. In this example, the join line goes from the Pets table to the Customer table to connect the two Customer Number fields. A join line also runs from Pets to Visits, connecting the Pet ID fields in these two tables.

This link is created automatically because a relationship was set in the Database window. If Access already knows what the relationship is, it automatically creates the link for you when the tables are added to a query. The relationship is displayed as a join line between two tables.

If Referential Integrity is checked in the relationship between two tables in Access 2.0, Access will display a thick portion of the line right at the table window like the line in Figure 14-2. Notice that the line starts heavy and then becomes thin between Pets and Visits (heavy on both sides). This line variation tells you that Referential Integrity has been set up between the two tables in the Relationship builder. If a one-to-many relationship exists, the many relationship is denoted by an infinity sign (∞).

If you have not specified relations between two tables and the following conditions are true, Access 2.0 will automatically join the tables:

1. The tables have a field in both with the same name.
2. The field with the same name in both tables is the same type (text, numeric, etc.).
3. The field is a *Primary Key* field in one of the tables.

Manipulating the Table Design window

Each Table Design window begins at a fixed size, which shows approximately 6 fields and 12 characters for each field. Each Table Design window is a true window and, as such, behaves like one; it can be resized and moved. If you have more fields than will fit in the Table Design window, an elevator is attached to the table design. The elevator lets you scroll through the fields in the Table Design window.

After a relationship is created between tables, the join line remains between the two fields. As you move through a table selecting fields, you'll notice that the graphical line will move, relative to the linked fields. For example, if you move the elevator down (toward the bottom of the structure) in the Customer table, you'll notice that the join line moves up with the customer number and eventually stops at the top of the table window.

When you're working with many tables, these join lines can become visually confusing as they cross or overlap. If you move through the table, the line eventually becomes visible, and the field it is linked to will be obvious.

Resizing the table/query pane

When you place table designs on the table/query pane, they appear in a fixed size with little spacing between tables. When you add a table to the top pane, it initially shows you five fields. If more fields are in the table, an elevator bar will be added to the box (right side). The table box may only show part of the long field names (the rest are truncated by the box size). You can move the tables around the pane and even resize them to show more field names and more of the field name. The first step, however, is to

Chapter 14: Creating Relations and Joins in Queries

resize the pane itself. The Query Design window is made up of two panes. The top pane displays your table designs, whereas the QBE pane below lets you enter fields, sort orders, and criteria. Often, the top pane can be larger than the bottom pane, as you may want more space for the design and less space for the QBE pane.

You can resize the table/query pane by placing your cursor on the thick line below the elevator. This is the window *split bar*. The cursor changes to a double vertical arrow, as shown in Figure 14-2. You can then drag the split bar up or down. The following steps show how to resize the panes:

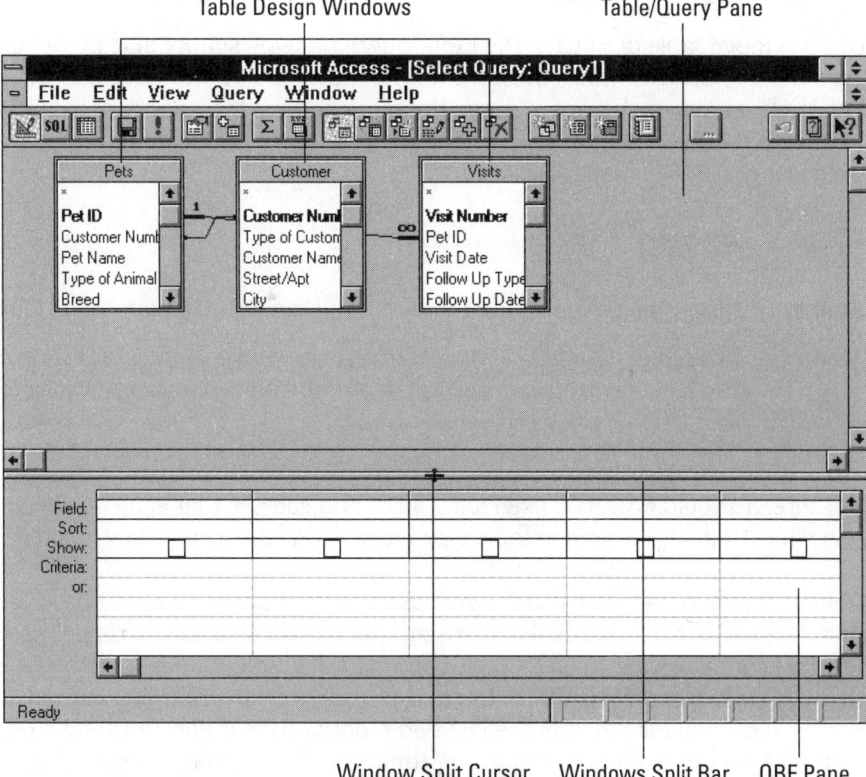

Figure 14-2: Resizing the query design panes.

Steps:	**Resizing the Query Design Pane**
Step 1.	Place the cursor on the window split bar.
Step 2.	Hold down the mouse button and drag the split bar down.
Step 3.	Release the bar when it is two lines below the QBE row marked or:.

The top pane is now much larger; the bottom pane is smaller but still displays the entire QBE design area. You now have space to move the table designs around and properly view the table/query pane.

 You can build a database diagram so that you view only the table designs by moving the split bar to the bottom of the screen and then positioning the table designs as you want within the full-screen area.

Moving a table

You can move table designs in the table/query pane by simply placing the cursor on the top of a table design (where the name of the table is) and then dragging the table to a new location. You may want to move the table designs for a better working view or to clean up a database diagram that is confusing, as the one shown in Figure 14-2. To move table designs, follow these steps:

Steps:	Moving a Table Design
Step 1.	Place the cursor on the top of the Customer table on the text Customer.
Step 2.	Drag the Customer table design straight down to the point where the top of the table design now appears where the bottom was when you started.

The screen should now look like Figure 14-3. You can see that each line is now an individual line that goes from one table's primary key to the foreign key in another table.

You can move the table designs anywhere in the top pane. You can spread out the diagram by moving the table designs farther apart. You can also rearrange the table designs. You may want to place the Customer table first, followed by the Pets table and then the Visits table. Remember that in this example you are trying to view the snakes that have been in for a visit in the last two months so that you can send a letter to the customer. So the sequence of Pets, Customer, and Visits makes sense. You generally want to view your diagram with a particular business purpose in mind. Pets is the main table in this business example and needs to retrieve information from both the Visits and Customer tables.

Figure 14-3:
A database diagram for the Pets, Customer, and Visits tables.

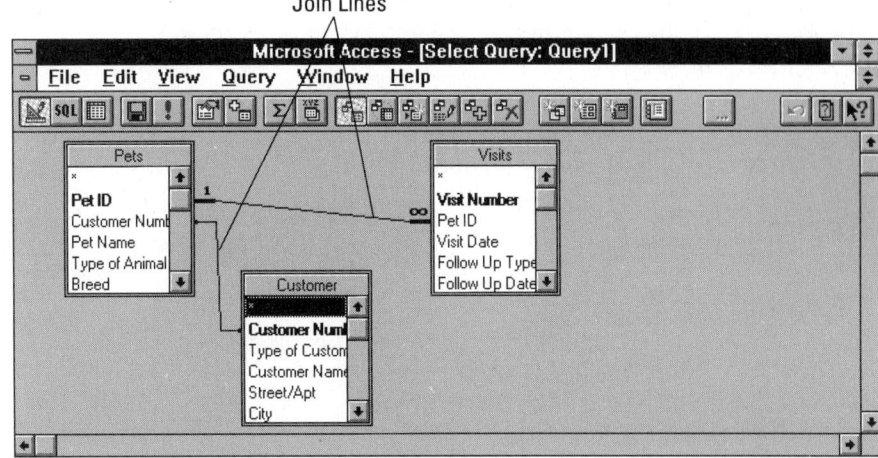

Removing a table

There are times when you need to remove tables from a query. Any table can be removed from the Query window. Follow these steps to delete the Visits table, bearing in mind that you can restore it later:

Steps:	Deleting a Table
Step 1.	Select the Visits table in the top pane of the Query window by clicking either the table or a field in the table.
Step 2.	Press the Delete key or select Edit➪Delete from the Edit menu.

Only one table can be removed from the Query window at a time. The menu choice Edit➪Clear Grid does *not* remove all tables; this selection is used for removing all fields from the QBE pane.

When you delete a table, any join lines to that table are deleted as well. When you delete a table, there is no warning or confirmation dialog box. The table is simply removed from the screen.

Adding more tables

You may decide to add more tables to a query, or you may accidentally delete a table and need to add it back. You can accomplish this task by either selecting Query➪Add Table.... from the menu or clicking the *right* mouse button and selecting Add Table...

from the menu. When you use one of these methods, the Add Table dialog box that appeared when you created the query is redisplayed. To restore the Visits table to the screen, follow these steps:

Steps:	Adding a Table to an Existing Query
Step 1.	Move the mouse pointer to the top pane (outside of any existing tables) and press the *right* mouse button. Select Add Table... from the menu.
Step 2.	Select the Visits table by double-clicking the table name.
Step 3.	Click the Close button in the Add Table dialog box.

The Visits table is returned to the table/query pane, and the join line is redisplayed.

Resizing a table design

You can also resize each of the table designs by placing the cursor on one of the table design borders. The table design is nothing but a window, and thus you can enlarge or reduce it vertically, horizontally, or diagonally by placing the cursor on the appropriate border. When you enlarge the table design vertically, you can see more fields than the default number of five. By making the table design larger horizontally, you can see the complete list of field names. Then, when you resize the table/query pane to take up the entire window, you can create a database diagram.

Creating a database diagram

Figure 14-4 shows a database diagram for these three tables in which you can see all the fields. The more tables and relationships you have, the more important a database diagram becomes in helping you view your data graphically with the proper relationships visible. In upcoming chapters, you'll see many different database diagrams as you use queries to assemble the data for various forms and reports.

In Figure 14-4, the table/query pane is expanded to its full size, so you can't see any of the QBE pane below. You can get to the QBE pane by resizing with the split bar. When you're working with fields in the QBE pane, you should keep the screen split so that you can see both panes.

Although you can switch panes by pressing F6, you can't see where the cursor is in the QBE pane while the table/query pane is displayed in full-screen size.

Figure 14-4:
A database diagram.

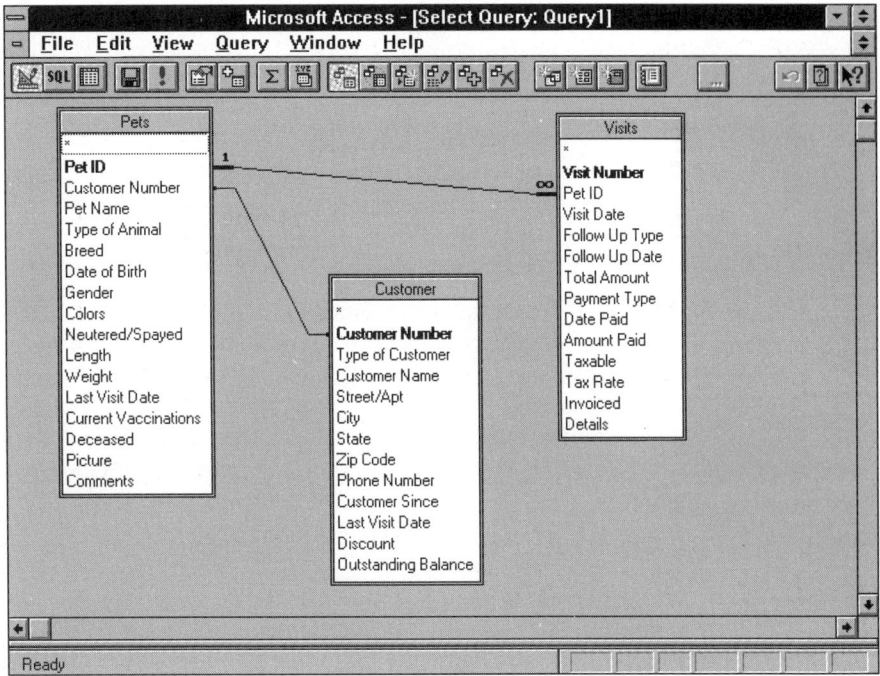

Following Along in This Book

If you are following along on your computer with the examples in this chapter, resize the panes so that you can see both the Table Design pane and the QBE pane.

Adding Fields from More Than One Table

You can add fields from more than one table to the query in exactly the same way as when you're working with a single table. You can add fields one at a time, many fields grouped together, or all the fields from one or all tables.

Adding fields from a single table is covered in detail in Chapter 10; this topic is covered here in less detail but focuses on the differences between single- and multiple-table field selection.

Adding a single field

You can select a single field from any table by using several methods:

- Double-click a field name in the table/query pane.
- Click a field name in the table/query pane and drag it to the QBE pane.
- Click an empty Field: cell in the QBE pane and type a field name.
- Click an empty Field: cell and select the field from the drop-down list.

 If you type a field name in an empty Field: cell that is in both tables, Access enters the field name from the first table it finds with that field. Access will search the tables starting from the left side in the top pane.

If you select the field from the drop-down list in the Field: cell, you see the name of the table first, followed by a period and the field name. For example, the field Pet ID in the Pets table is displayed as Pets.Pet ID. This helps you to select the right field name. Using this method, you can select a common field name from a specific table.

The easiest way to select fields is still to double-click the query/table designs. To do so, you may have to resize the table designs to see the fields you want to select. To select Customer Name, Pet Name, Type of Animal, and Visit Date, follow these steps:

Steps:	Selecting Fields from the Customer, Pets, and Visits Tables
Step 1.	Double-click Customer Name in the Customer table.
Step 2.	Double-click Pet Name in the Pets table.
Step 3.	Double-click Type of Animal in the Pets table.
Step 4.	Double-click Visit Date in the Visits table.

Viewing the table names

When you're working with two or more tables, the field names in the QBE pane can become confusing. You may find yourself asking, for example, just which table the field Customer Number is from.

Access automatically maintains the table name that is associated with each field displayed in the QBE pane. But sometimes you want to know the table name, so you'll need to display it. To show the table name in the QBE pane, select View⇨Table Names from the View menu or click the Table Names button on the toolbar. The Table Names button is the ninth button from the left (it looks like several tables with the name **XYZ** across the top of them).

This selection controls the display of table names immediately below the corresponding field name in the QBE pane. Figure 14-5 shows the QBE pane with the new row Table: added below the Field: row. Notice that it contains the name of the table for each field.

Figure 14-5: The QBE pane with the Table: row displayed.

Field:	Customer Name	Pet Name	Type of Animal	Visit Date	
Table:	Customer	Pets	Pets	Visits	
Sort:					
Show:	☒	☒	☒	☒	☐
Criteria:					
or:					

The display of the table name is only for your information. Access always maintains the table name associated with the field names.

To hide the table names, either click the Table Names again or choose View⇨Table Names again. (When the table names are displayed, a check mark appears next to the choice in the View menu).

After you add fields to a query, you can view your data at any time. Although you'll eventually limit the display of data to snakes that have visited you in the last two months, you can view all the data at any time by selecting the Datasheet icon. Figure 14-6 displays the data as currently selected.

Adding multiple fields

The process of adding multiple fields is identical to adding multiple fields in a single table query. When you're adding multiple fields from several tables, you must add them from one table at a time. The easiest way to do this task is to select multiple fields and drag them together down to the QBE pane.

You can select multiple fields contiguously by selecting the first field of the list, holding down the Shift key and going to the last field (using the mouse). You can also select random fields in the list by holding down the Control key (Ctrl) while selecting fields with a mouse click.

Adding all table fields

As with adding multiple fields, when you're adding all table fields, you do it by selecting which table you want to add first and then selecting the next table. You can select all the fields in two ways: by double-clicking on the title bar of the table name or by selecting the Asterisk (*) field. Remember that these two methods produce very different results.

Figure 14-6: Viewing data from multiple tables.

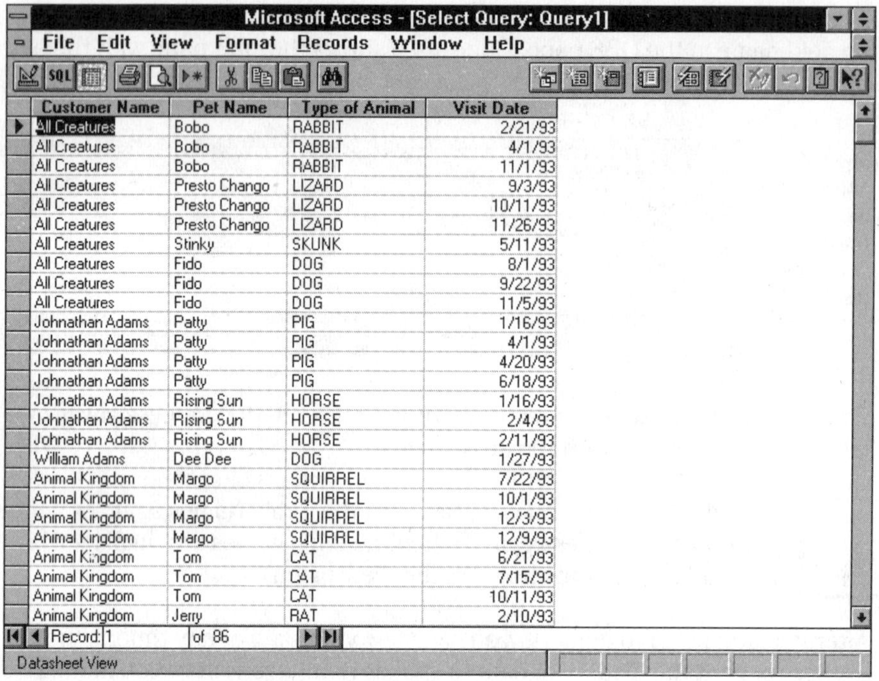

Customer Name	Pet Name	Type of Animal	Visit Date
All Creatures	Bobo	RABBIT	2/21/93
All Creatures	Bobo	RABBIT	4/1/93
All Creatures	Bobo	RABBIT	11/1/93
All Creatures	Presto Chango	LIZARD	9/3/93
All Creatures	Presto Chango	LIZARD	10/11/93
All Creatures	Presto Chango	LIZARD	11/26/93
All Creatures	Stinky	SKUNK	5/11/93
All Creatures	Fido	DOG	8/1/93
All Creatures	Fido	DOG	9/22/93
All Creatures	Fido	DOG	11/5/93
Johnathan Adams	Patty	PIG	1/16/93
Johnathan Adams	Patty	PIG	4/1/93
Johnathan Adams	Patty	PIG	4/20/93
Johnathan Adams	Patty	PIG	6/18/93
Johnathan Adams	Rising Sun	HORSE	1/16/93
Johnathan Adams	Rising Sun	HORSE	2/4/93
Johnathan Adams	Rising Sun	HORSE	2/11/93
William Adams	Dee Dee	DOG	1/27/93
Animal Kingdom	Margo	SQUIRREL	7/22/93
Animal Kingdom	Margo	SQUIRREL	10/1/93
Animal Kingdom	Margo	SQUIRREL	12/3/93
Animal Kingdom	Margo	SQUIRREL	12/9/93
Animal Kingdom	Tom	CAT	6/21/93
Animal Kingdom	Tom	CAT	7/15/93
Animal Kingdom	Tom	CAT	10/11/93
Animal Kingdom	Jerry	RAT	2/10/93

This method automatically fills in each column of the QBE pane. The fields are added in order of their selection in the table, from left to right based on their field order in the table. By default, only the first five fields are displayed. You can change the column width of each field to display more or fewer columns.

Selecting all fields with the double-clicking method

One method of selecting all the fields is to double-click on the title bar of the table whose fields you want to select.

Selecting all fields with the Asterisk (*) method

The first object in each table is an asterisk (at the top of the field list), which is known as the *all-field reference tag.* When you select and drag the asterisk, all fields in the table are added to the QBE pane. But there is a distinct difference between this method and the double-clicking method. When you add all-field with the all-field reference tag (*), the QBE pane shows only one cell with the name of the table and an asterisk. For example, if you select the * in the Pets table, you see Pets.* displayed in one field row cell.

Unlike selecting all the fields, the asterisk places reference to all the fields in a single column. When you drag multiple columns, as in the preceding example, you drag actual table field names to the query. If you later change the design of the table, you also have to change the design of the query. The advantage of using the asterisk for selecting all fields is that you won't have to change the query later if you add, delete, or rename fields in the underlying table or query. Changing fields in the underlying table or query will automatically add fields to or remove fields from the query.

Selecting the * has one drawback: You cannot perform criteria conditions on the asterisk column itself. You have to add an individual field from the table and enter the criteria. If you add a field for a criteria (when using the *), the query displays the field twice — once for the * field and a second time for the criteria field. Therefore, you may want to uncheck the "show field" choice of the criteria field.

Understanding the Limitations of Multiple-Table Queries

When you create a query with multiple files, there are limitations as to what fields can be edited. Generally, you can change data in a query dynaset, and your changes will be saved to the underlying tables. A primary key field normally cannot be edited if referential integrity is in effect and if the field is part of a relationship.

In order for you to update a table from a query, a value in a specific record in the query must represent a single record in the underlying table. This means that you cannot update fields in a Crosstab or Totals query because they both group records together to display grouped information. Instead of displaying the actual underlying table data, they display records of data that are calculated and stored in a virtual (nonreal) table called a *snapshot*.

Updating limitations

In version 1.x, only the records on the *many* side of a one-to-many relationship were updatable. That has changed in version 2.0. Table 14-1 shows when a field in a table is updatable. As you can see in Table 14-1, queries based on one-to-many relationships are updatable in both tables (based on how the query was designed). However, any query that creates a *snapshot* is not updatable.

Table 14-1
Updatability Rules for Queries

Type of Query or Field	Updatable	Comments
One Table	Yes	
One-to-One relationship	Yes	
One-to-Many relationship	Mostly	Restrictions based on design methodology (see text)
Crosstab	No	Creates a *snapshot* of the data
Totals Query (Sum, Avg, etc.)	No	Works with Grouped data creating a *snapshot*
Unique Value property is Yes	No	Shows unique records only in a *snapshot*
SQL-specific queries	No	Union & Pass-through work with ODBC data
Calculated field	No	Will recalculate automatically
Read-only fields	No	If opened read-only or on read-only drive (CD-ROM)
Permissions denied	No	Insert, Replace, or Delete are not granted
ODBC Tables with no Primary Key	No	A primary key (unique index) must exist
Paradox Table with no Primary Key	No	A primary key file must exist
Locked by another user	No	Cannot be updated while a field is locked by another

Overcoming query limitations

Table 14-1 shows that there are times that queries and fields in tables are not updatable. As a general rule, any query that does aggregate calculations or is an ODBC-based SQL query is not updatable. All others can be updatable. When your query has more than one table and some of the tables have a one-to-many relationship, there may be fields that are not updatable, based on the design of the query.

A unique index (primary key) and updatability

If a query uses two tables that have a one-to-many relationship, the "one" side of the join must have a unique (primary key) index on the field that is used for the join. If not, the fields from the one side of the query cannot be updated.

Replacing existing data in a query with a one-to-many relationship

Normally, all the fields in the many-side table are updatable in a one-to-many query; the one side table can update all the fields *except* the primary key (join) field. Normally, this is sufficient for most database application purposes. Normally, you would never change the primary key field in the one-side table because it is the link to the records in the joined tables.

However, there are times that you may need to change the link field contents in both tables (make a new primary key in the one table and have the database program change the link field in all the related records from the many table). Access 2.0 will let you do this by defining a relationship between the two tables and using referential integrity. If you define a relationship and enforce referential integrity in the Relationship builder, two checkboxes are activated. If you want to allow changes (updates) to the primary key field, check the Cascade Updated Related Fields box on, as in Figure 14-7. By checking this option, you can change the primary key field in a relationship, and Access will automatically go out to the related records in other tables and update the link field in them to the new value.

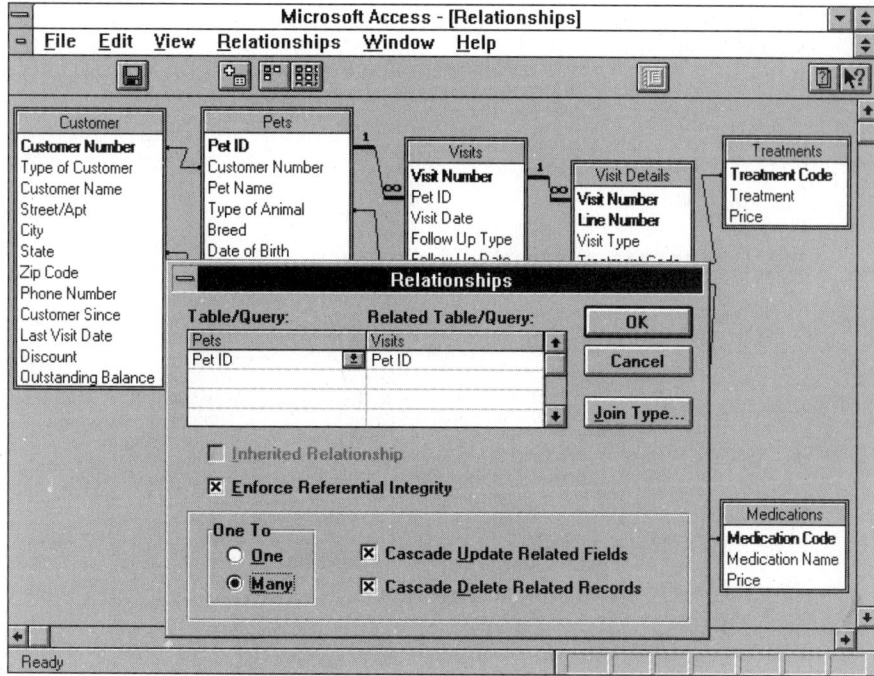

Figure 14-7: The relationship builder dialog box with referential integrity set on.

Design tips for updating fields in queries

- If you want to use AutoLookup between forms, be sure to include the join field from the "many" table in your form (instead of the "one" table). Also use a combo or list box to display this field.

- If you want to add records to both tables of a one to many relationship, be sure to include the join field from the "many" side table and show the field in the datasheet. By doing this, you can add records starting with either table. The one side "join" field will automatically be copied to the many-side join field.

- If you do not want any fields updatable, set the Default Editing property of the form to Read Only and the Allow Editing property of the form to Unavailable.

- If you do not want to update some fields on a form, set the Tab Stop property for the control (field) to No for these fields.

- If you want to add records to multiple tables in a form, remember to include all (or most) of the fields from both tables. Otherwise you will not have a complete record of data in your form.

Temporary non-updatability in a one-to-many relationship

When updating records on the one side of a one-to-many query, you will *not* be able to change the many side *join* field until you save changes to the one side. You can quickly save changes to the one side by pressing Shift+Enter or selecting File⇨Save Record from the menu. Once the one side changes are saved, the join field in the many side record can be changed.

Creating Query Joins

You can create joins between tables in the following three ways:

- By creating relationships between the tables when you design the database (selecting Edit⇨Relationships... from the Database window menu or the Relationship button on the toolbar).

- By selecting two tables for the query that have a field that is the same type and name in both, *and* that field is a primary key field in one of the tables.

- By creating joins in the Query window at the time you create a query.

The first two methods are automatic. If you create relationships when designing the tables of your database, Access automatically displays join lines based on those relationships when you add the related tables to a query. It also automatically joins two tables that have a common field, and that field is a primary key in one of the tables.

There may be times when you add tables to a query that are *not* already related to a specific file, as in these examples:

- The two tables have a common field, but it is not the same name.
- A table is not related — and cannot be related to the other table (for example, the Customer table cannot be directly joined to the Treatments table).

If you have two tables that are not automatically joined and you need to relate them, you join them in the Query Design window. Joining tables in the Query Design window does *not* create a permanent join between the tables. Rather, the join (relationship) will apply only to the table for the query that you are working on.

This is unlike relationships that are set at the database level, which are automatically joined whenever you work with the two tables in a query.

All tables in a query must be joined to at least one other table. For example, if you place two tables into a query and do *not* join them, Access will create a query based on a *Cartesian product,* also known as a cross product, of the two tables. This subject will be discussed later in this chapter. For now, note that a Cartesian product means that if you have five records in table one and six records in table two, the resulting query will have thirty records (5 * 6) that will probably be useless to you.

Joining tables

Figure 14-8 shows two fictitious tables that are not currently joined. This situation occurs if they are not joined at the table level or they do not have a common named field that is primary.

The following steps show how to join tables in a query, using the fictitious Owner table and the Pets table as an example:

Steps:	Joining Tables in a Query
Step 1.	Select the Owner Number field in the Owners table in the query/table pane.
Step 2.	Drag the highlighted field to the Pets table (as you drag the field, the Field icon is displayed).
Step 3.	Drop the Field icon on the Customer Number field in the Pets table.

Figure 14-9 illustrates the process of joining tables. The Field icon first appears in the Owner Number field of the Owner table; it then moves to the Pets table. As it moves between tables, the Field icon changes to the symbol indicating that the icon cannot be dropped in the area between the tables. When the icon is over the Customer Number field, it changes back to the Field icon, indicating that it can be dropped in that location. When you release the mouse button, the join line appears.

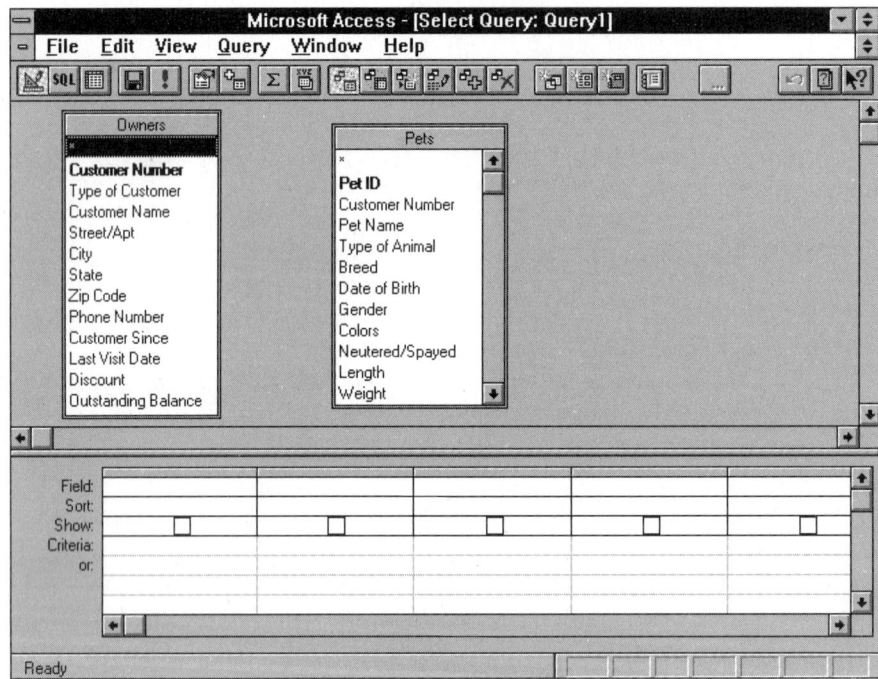

Figure 14-8: Unrelated tables in the table/query pane.

You can also create joins that make no sense. However, when you view the data, you will get less-than-desirable results. If two joined fields have no values in common, you have a datasheet in which no records are selected.

You can select either table first when you create a join.

You would never want to create a meaningless join. For example, you would not want to join the City field from the Customer table to the Date of Birth field in the Pets table. Although Access will let you create this join, the resulting dynaset will have no records in it.

Figure 14-9: Joining the Owner and Pets tables.

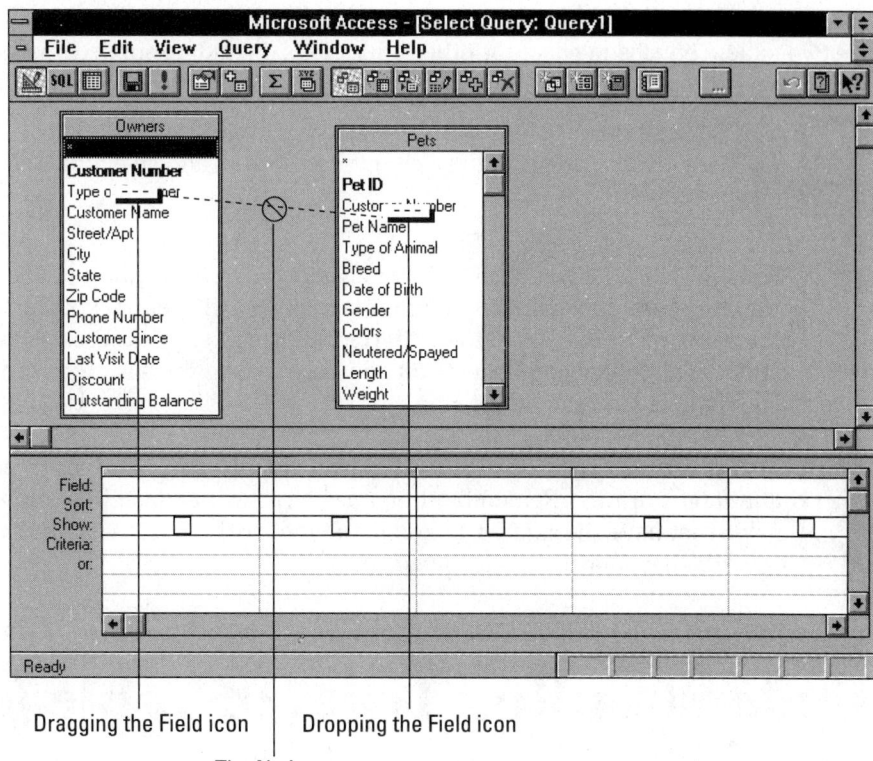

Dragging the Field icon   Dropping the Field icon
The No icon

Deleting joins

To delete a join line between two tables, you select the join line and press the Delete key. You can select the join line by placing the cursor on any part of the line and clicking once. For example, create a new query by adding the Customer and Pets table to a query, and then following these steps, you can delete the join line between the Pets and Customer tables:

Steps:	Deleting Join Lines
Step 1.	Select the join line between the Customer Number field in the Pets table and the Customer table by placing the cursor on the line and clicking the mouse.
Step 2.	With the join line highlighted, press the Delete key.

After Step 2, the line should disappear. If you delete a join line between two tables that have a relationship set at the database level, the broken join is effective only for the query in which you broke the join. When you exit the query, the relationship between the two tables remains in effect for other operations, including subsequent queries.

You can also delete a join by selecting it and choosing Edit⇨Delete, or by clicking the join line, pressing the right mouse button, and selecting Delete from the shortcut menu.

Remember that if you delete a join between two tables and the tables remain in the Query window unjoined to other tables, you will get unexpected results in the datasheet. This is due to the Cartesian product Access creates from the two tables. The Cartesian product will only be effective for this query. The underlying relationship remains intact.

Access enables you to create multiple-field joins between tables (more than one line can be drawn). Remember that normally the join must be between two fields that have the same data and data type, or the query will not find any records to display from the datasheet.

Understanding Types of Table Joins

In Chapter 12, you learned about table relationships. Access understands all types of table and query relations, which include the following:

- One to one
- One to many
- Many to one
- Many to many

When you specify a relationship between two tables, you establish rules for the type of relationship, not for viewing the data based on the relationship.

To view data in two tables, you must join them through a link. The link is established via a common field (or group of fields) between the two tables. The method of linking the tables is known as *joining*. In a query, tables with established relationships are shown already joined. Yet within a query, you can create new joins or change an existing join line. But just as there are different types of relationships, there are different types of joins. In the following sections, you'll learn about these types of joins:

- Equi-joins (inner joins)
- Outer joins

- Self-joins
- Cross-product joins (Cartesian joins)

Inner joins (equi-joins)

The default join in Access is known as an equi-join, or inner join. With this type of join, you tell Access to select all records from both tables that have the same value in the fields that are joined together.

The Access manuals refer to a default join as an equi-join. This join is also commonly referred to as an inner join in database relational theory. The terms are interchangeable and will be used as such throughout this chapter.

For an example of an equi-join, recall the Customer and Pets tables. Bear in mind that you are looking for all records from these two tables with matching fields. The fields Customer Number are common to both, so the equi-join does not show any records for customers that have no pets or any pets that do not relate to a valid customer number. The rules of referential integrity prevent pet records that are not tied to a customer number. Of course, it's possible to delete all pets from a customer or to create a new customer record with no pet records, but a pet should always be related to a valid customer. Referential integrity should keep a customer number from being deleted or changed if a pet is related to it.

Regardless of how it happens, it's possible to have a customer in the Customer table who has no pets. It's less likely, but still theoretically possible, to have a pet with no owner. If you create a query to show customers and their pets, any record of a customer without pets or a pet record without a matching customer record will not be shown in the resulting dynaset.

It can be important for you to find these "lost" records. One of the features of a query is to perform several types of joins.

Access 2.0 can help you find "lost" records between tables by building a "Find Unmatched Query" using the new Query Wizards.

Changing join properties

With the Customer and Pets tables joined, certain join behaviors, or properties, exist between the tables. The join property is a rule that says to display all records (for the fields you specify) that correspond to the characters found in the *Customer Number* field of the *Customer* table and in a corresponding *Customer Number* field of the *Pets* table.

Part III: Using Access in Your Work

To translate this rule into a practical example, this is what happens in the Customer and Pets tables:

- If a record in the Customer table has a number for a customer not found in the Pets table, that Customer record will not be shown.

- If a record in the Pets table has a number for a customer number not in the Customer table, that Pets record will not be shown.

This makes sense, at least most of the time. You don't want to see records for customers without pets — *or do you?*

A join property is a rule that is operated by Access. This rule tells Access how to interpret any exceptions (possibly errors) between two tables. Should the noncorresponding records be shown or not?

Access has several types of joins, each with its own characteristics, or behaviors. Access lets you quickly change the type of join by changing its properties. You can change join properties by selecting the join line between tables and double-clicking the line. When you do so, a Join Properties dialog box appears. The dialog box in Figure 14-10 is the result of selecting the join line between the Customer and Pets tables.

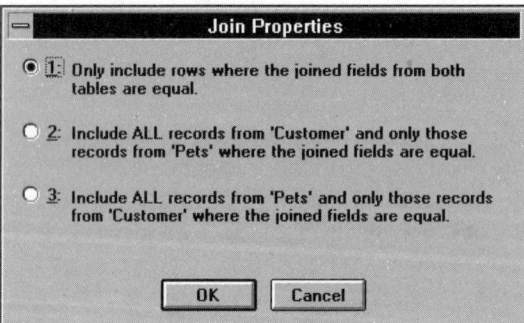

Figure 14-10: The Join Properties dialog box.

The Join Properties dialog box has three option buttons, which are displayed in this manner for the Pets and Customer tables:

1. Only include rows where the joined fields from both tables are equal. *(This is the default.)*

2. Include ALL records from 'Customer' and only those records from 'Pets' where the joined fields are equal.

3. Include ALL records from 'Pets' and only those records from 'Customers' where the joined fields are equal.

The first choice is commonly known as an *inner join,* and the other two are known as *outer joins.* These joins control the behavior of Access as it builds the dynaset from the query.

Inner and outer joins

Your Query Design window should presently display two tables in the top pane of the Query window — Pets and Customers. In the following sections, these tables are used as examples in the explanation of how inner and outer joins operate.

Displaying an inner join

To display an inner join, follow this procedure: In the QBE pane, select the fields Customer Number and Customer Name from the Customer table and the fields Pet Name and Type of Animal from the Pets table. Then display the dynaset by selecting the Datasheet button on the toolbar. The datasheet should now look like Figure 14-11, displaying each customer, all the customers' pets, and the type of animal for each pet. Scroll through the records until you reach the bottom of the datasheet.

Figure 14-11: The data sheet for an inner join.

Customer Number	Customer Name	Pet Name	Type of Animal
AC001	All Creatures	Bobo	RABBIT
AC001	All Creatures	Presto Chango	LIZARD
AC001	All Creatures	Stinky	SKUNK
AC001	All Creatures	Fido	DOG
AD001	Johnathan Adams	Patty	PIG
AD001	Johnathan Adams	Rising Sun	HORSE
AD002	William Adams	Dee Dee	DOG
AK001	Animal Kingdom	Margo	SQUIRREL
AK001	Animal Kingdom	Tom	CAT
AK001	Animal Kingdom	Jerry	RAT
AK001	Animal Kingdom	Marcus	CAT
AK001	Animal Kingdom	Pookie	CAT
AK001	Animal Kingdom	Mario	DOG
AK001	Animal Kingdom	Luigi	DOG
BA001	Borderville Aquarium	Swimmy	DOLPHIN
BA001	Borderville Aquarium	Charger	WHALE
BA001	Borderville Aquarium	Daffy	DUCK
BA001	Borderville Aquarium	Toby	TURTLE
BA001	Borderville Aquarium	Jake	DOLPHIN
BL001	Bird Land	Tiajuana	BIRD
BL001	Bird Land	Carlos	BIRD
BL001	Bird Land	Ming	BIRD
BL001	Bird Land	Yellow Jacket	BIRD
BL001	Bird Land	Red Breast	BIRD
BL001	Bird Land	Mickey	BIRD
BL001	Bird Land	Sally	BIRD

Record: 1 of 129

Enter Customer Number as AA###. For example: AB001

Notice that each of the 129 records has entries in all four fields. This means that for every record displayed from the Customer table, there is a corresponding record, or records, in the Pets table.

Return to query design mode by pressing the Design icon on the toolbar. When you double-click the join line between the tables Customer and Pets, you see that the join property for these two tables becomes the first selection shown in the Join Properties dialog box (see Figure 14-10). This type of join is commonly known as an inner join, or an equi-join. Equi-joins are the most common type of joins between tables. These joins show only the records having a correspondence between tables.

Creating an outer join

Unlike equi-joins (inner joins), outer joins are used for showing all records in one table while showing common records in the other. An outer join will graphically point to one of the tables. When you look at the join line, it says, "Show all records from the main table (the one missing the arrow) while only showing matching records in the table being pointed to." For further explanation, follow these instructions:

Return to the query design and again double-click on the join line between Customer and Pets.

Select the second choice from the Join Properties dialog box, which includes all records from the Customer table and only those records from Pets where the joined fields are equal. Then select the OK button. Notice that the join line now has an arrow at one end pointing rightward to the Pets table. This is known as a *right outer join* in database terminology.

Select the Datasheet button to display this dynaset. Everything looks the same as before. Now page down until you can see record number 63. You should see a record for Customer Number JO003, which is Carla Jones, who has no corresponding entry in the field Pet Name or Type of Animal (see Figure 14-12). This record results from selecting the join property that specifies "include all records from Customer. . . ."

Unlike equi-joins, outer joins show all corresponding records between two tables *and* records that do *not* have a corresponding record in the other table. In the preceding example, you see a record for Carla Jones but no corresponding record for any pets she owns.

If you've changed the display order of the tables since adding them to the Query window, Access does not follow the table order that you set up; rather, it uses the original order in which you selected the tables. As the information is normally the same in either table, it won't make a difference which field is selected first.

Select the Design button on the toolbar to return to the Query Design window. When you created the outer join for the Customer table with the Pets table, Access changed the appearance of the graphical join line to show an arrow at one end. As shown in Figure 14-13, the arrow is pointing toward the Pets table. This tells you that Access has created an outer join and therefore will show you *all* records in the Customer table and *only* those that match in the Pets table.

Chapter 14: Creating Relations and Joins in Queries

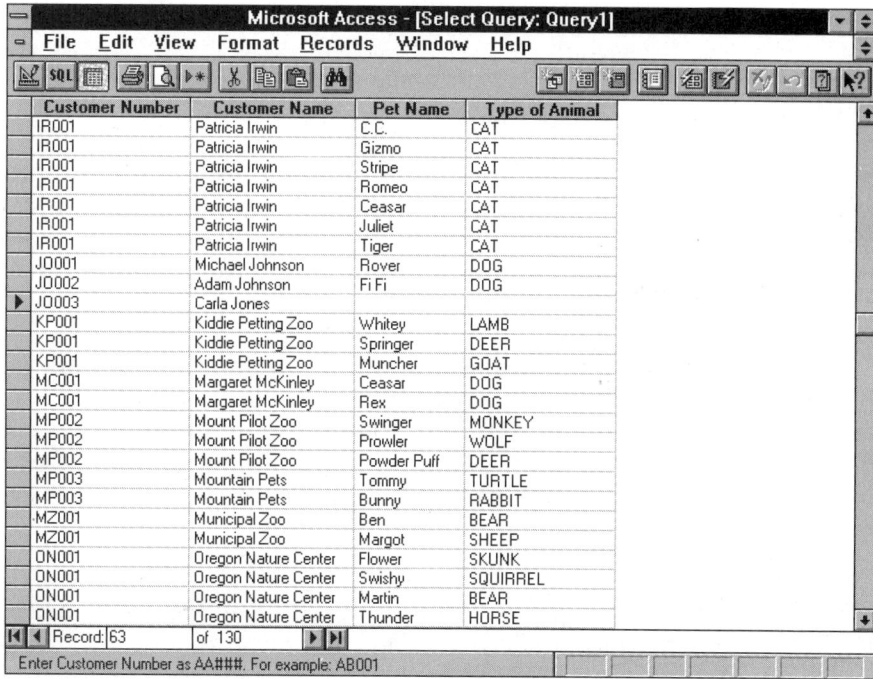

Figure 14-12: A datasheet with a right outer join.

Right outer join line

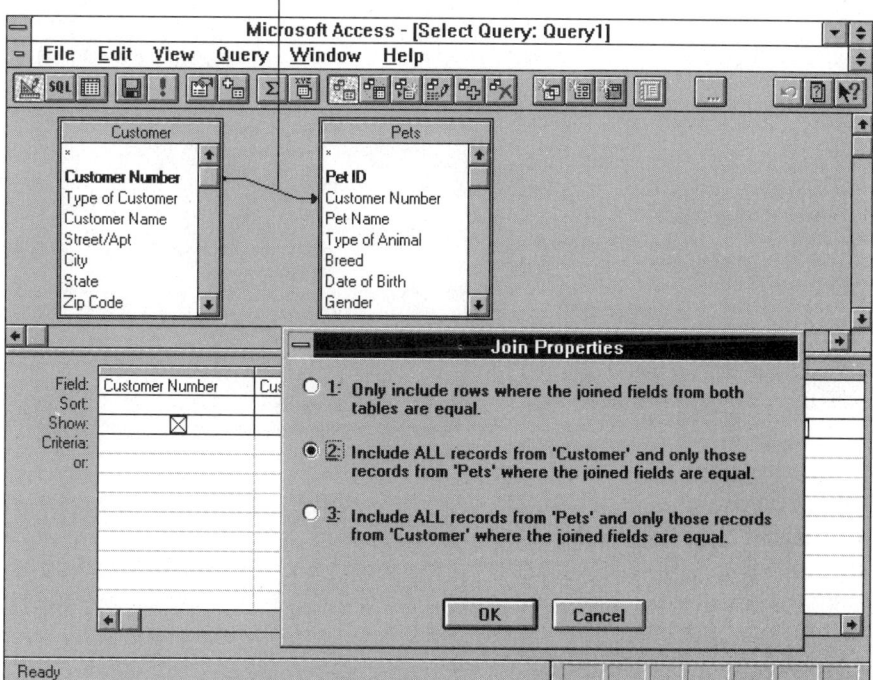

Figure 14-13: The table/query pane showing a right outer join.

Creating another outer join

Return to the query design and again double-click the join line between the Customer and Pets tables.

Select the third choice from the Join Properties dialog box, which asks to "include all records from Pets. . ." Then select the OK button. Notice that the join line now has an arrow pointing to the Customer table, as shown in Figure 14-14. This in known as a *left outer join*. If the arrow is pointing to the right in the top pane, the join is known as a right outer join; when the arrow points to the left outer join.

Select the Datasheet button to display this dynaset. Now page down until you can see record number 68, as shown in Figure 14-15. You should see a record with nothing in the field Customer Number or Customer Name. All you see is Animal Name, which is Brownie, and the fact that it's a dog. This record results from selecting the join property to include all records from Pets. This is known as a *left outer join* in database terminology.

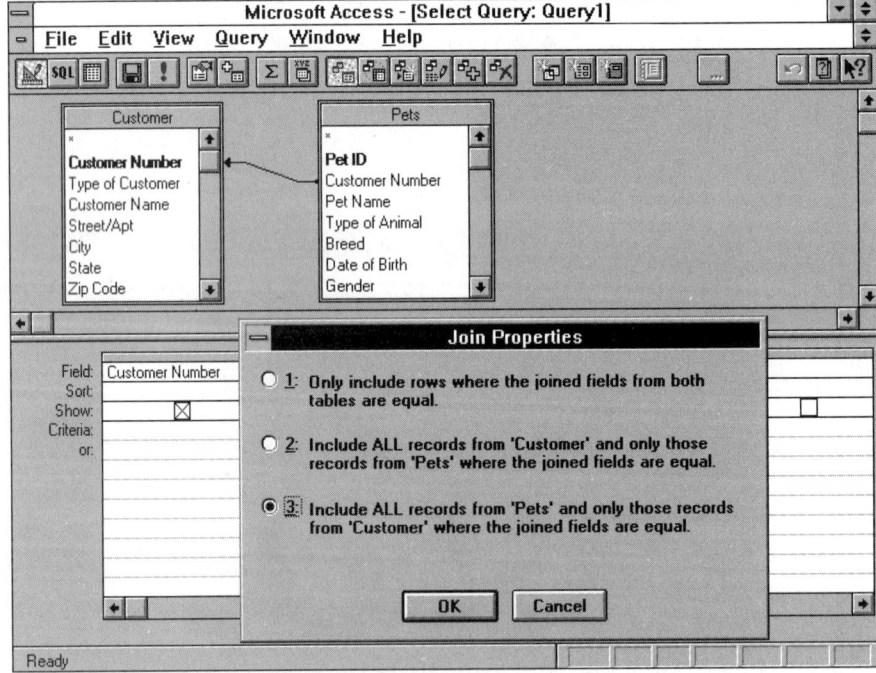

Figure 14-14: The table / query pane showing a left outer join.

Besides the equi-(inner) and outer joins, one further type of join needs to be examined — self-joins.

Chapter 14: Creating Relations and Joins in Queries

Creating a self-join

There is a special-case join, known as a *self-join*. A self-join can be either an inner or an outer join. As the name suggests, a self-join occurs when a table is brought into a query twice and is linked to itself. Access automatically assigns a different name to the duplicated table. For example, if you bring the Pets table in twice, the first copy is called Pets and the second is named Pets_1.

For an explanation of a self-join, suppose that in the Pets table you have one field for male parentage and another for female parentage. These fields indicate the Pet ID number of the father and mother of each pet (if known). The table will resemble Figure 14-16. Notice the two fields Male Parentage and Female Parentage at the bottom of the Pets table.

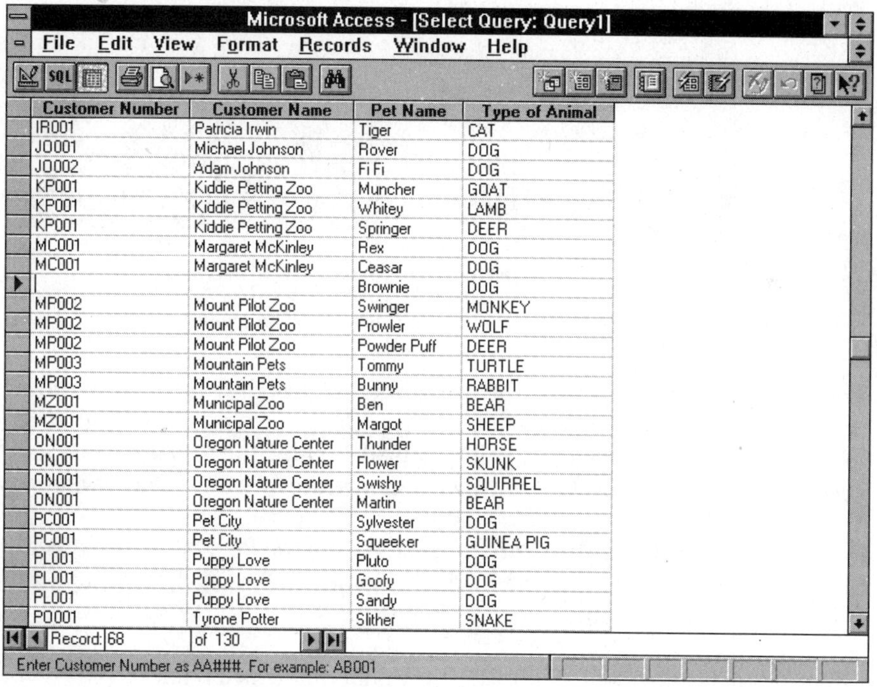

Figure 14-15: A datasheet with a left outer join.

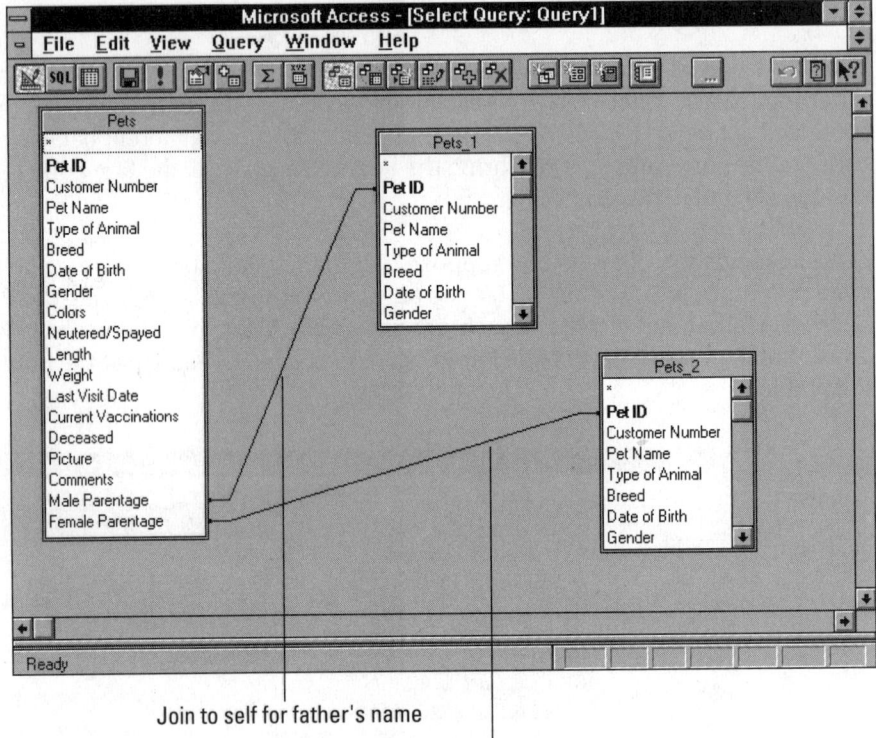

Figure 14-16:
Three copies of the same table are displayed to perform a self-join.

Join to self for father's name

Join to self for mother's name

This table can be brought into the query three times; the first copy of the table is brought in to list the individual animals, and the second and third copies to list their fathers and mothers. One table will be linked to show the father's name and the other to show the mother's name. Figure 14-16 demonstrates what the Query window will look like.

Notice that you link the Male Parentage field from the Pets table to the Pet ID field in the table Pets_1. The Female Parentage field is joined to Pets_2. The father's name comes from Pets_1 and the mother's name from Pets_2.

This self-join is an equi-join and will show only the records that have both parentage fields filled out. The table Pets uses the contents (Pet ID of father and mother) of parentage to look back into itself and find the names of the father and mother.

Creating a Cartesian product

If you add both the Customer and Pets tables to a query and don't specify a join between the tables, Access takes the first Customer record and combines it with all the Pets records and then takes the second record and also combines it with all the Pets

Chapter 14: Creating Relations and Joins in Queries

records. This combining of records between tables produces a total of 6,321 records in the resultant dynaset. The combining of each record in one table with each record in the other is called a Cartesian product, or a cross product of both tables.

Summary

In this chapter, you learned about creating relationships between tables and how to use joins in queries. The following points were covered:

- You can add multiple tables to a query, including multiple copies of the same table.
- Access automatically creates join lines for any tables that have their relations set at table level.
- By selecting View⇨Table Names, you can view table names in the QBE pane.
- You can add fields from multiple-table queries in any order. Multiple-table fields are moved and changed in the same way as fields from single tables.
- To view data from two or more tables, you must join them.
- You can create joins between two tables by dragging and dropping a field from one table to another. A graphic join line is drawn between the fields by Access.
- There are two types of joins — inner joins (equi-joins) and outer joins.
- An inner join is also known as an equi-join and displays records that have a common field in both tables with corresponding data in those fields.
- An outer join displays all records having corresponding data in both fields and also displays records from one table that does not have corresponding records in the other table.
- The two types of outer joins are left and right. Access displays a pointer in the table/query pane to show the type of outer join that you create.
- A self-join can be either an inner or outer join. This type of join is called a self-join because a table is brought into the query two or more times and joined to itself.

In the next chapter, you examine how to create select queries.

Creating Select Queries

CHAPTER 15

In This Chapter

- Creating and using Text expressions as criteria
- Using the Like operator and wildcards
- Using the Not operator for nonmatching values
- Creating and using Memo expressions as criteria
- Creating and using Date expressions as criteria
- Creating and using Numeric expressions as criteria
- Using the And/Or operators in single-field criteria
- Using the In operator for selecting from a list of values
- Using the Between ... And operator
- Searching for Null data
- Using the And/Or operators across several fields
- Building complex expressions for queries
- Using functions as expressions for criteria
- Creating and using a calculated field

Up to this point, you worked with queries based on criteria against a single field. You also learned how to add multiple tables to a query and how to join tables together. This chapter focuses on extracting information from multiple tables in select queries.

Moving Beyond Simple Queries

Select queries are the most common type of query you will use. With these queries, you have the ability to ask questions and receive answers about information stored in your database tables. Select queries *select* information from one or more related tables, based on a specific criteria. So far, you worked with queries that pose simple criteria for a single field in a table. You worked with math operators, such as equal (=) and greater than (>).

Knowing how to specify criteria is critical to designing effective queries. Although queries can be created against a single table for a single criteria, most queries extract information from several tables and more complex criteria. Because of this complexity, your queries can retrieve only the data that you need and in the order you need it. You may, for example, want to select and display data from the Mountain Animal Hospital database with these limitations:

- All owners of horses or cows or pigs
- All animals that were given a specific medication during a specific week last year
- All owners whose dogs or cats had bloodwork performed over the past four months
- Only the first animal of each type that you have treated
- Any animal that has the word "color" in the Memo field Comments

As a database system evolves, you find yourself asking questions such as these about the information stored in the system. Although the system was not originally developed specifically for these questions, the information needed to answer them is stored in the tables. Because the information is there, you find yourself performing *ad-hoc* queries against the database. The ad-hoc queries that you perform by using select queries can be very simple or quite complex.

Select queries are the easiest way to obtain information from several tables without resorting to writing programs.

Using query comparison operators

When you're working with select queries, you may need to specify one or more criteria to limit the scope of information you want to see. You accomplish this by use of *comparison operators,* which are used in equations and calculations. The categories of operators include mathematical, relational, logical, and string operators. In select queries, operators are normally used in either the Field: or Criteria: cell of the QBE pane.

Chapter 15: Creating Select Queries   337

A good rule of thumb to observe is the following:

> You use mathematical and string operators for creating calculated fields; you use relational and logical operators for specifying scoping criteria.

Calculated fields will be discussed later in this chapter. An in-depth explanation of operators is found in Chapter 13.

Table 15-1 shows most of the common operators that are used with select queries.

Table 15-1
Common Operators Used in Select Queries

Mathematical	Relational	Logical	String	Miscellaneous
* (multiply)	= (equal)	And	& (concatenate)	Between ... And
/ (divide)	<> (not equal)	Or	Like	In
+ (add)	> (greater than)	Not		Is Null
– (subtract)	< (less than)			

Using these operators, you can ferret out such types of records as the following:

- Pet records that have a picture associated with them
- A range of records, such as all patients seen between November and January
- Records that meet And and Or criteria, such as all pets that are dogs *and* are not either neutered *or* have a current vaccine
- All records that do *not* match a value, such as any animal that is not a cat

When you supply a criteria to a query, you use the operator with an *example* that you supply. In Figure 15-1, the example entered is PIG. The operator is equal (=). Notice that the equal sign is *not* shown in the figure. The equal sign is the default operator for criteria selection.

When working with criteria for select queries, you supply an example of what type of information Access needs to find in the Criteria: cell of the Query By Example (QBE) pane.

Chapter 10 gives an in-depth explanation of working with queries.

Understanding complex criteria selection

As Table 15-1 shows, you can use several operators to build complex criteria. To most people, complex criteria consists of a series of Ands and Ors, as in these examples:

- State must be Idaho *or* Oregon
- City must be Borderville *and* state must be Washington
- State must be Idaho *or* Washington *and* city must be Borderville

These examples demonstrate use of both the logical operators And/Or. Many times, you can create complex criteria by entering example data in different cells of the QBE pane. Figure 15-2 demonstrates how you can create complex And/Or criteria without having to enter the operator key words And/Or at all. This example displays all customers and their pets who satisfy these criteria:

> Live in the city of Borderville and live in either the state of Washington or live in the state of Idaho and whose pet is not a dog

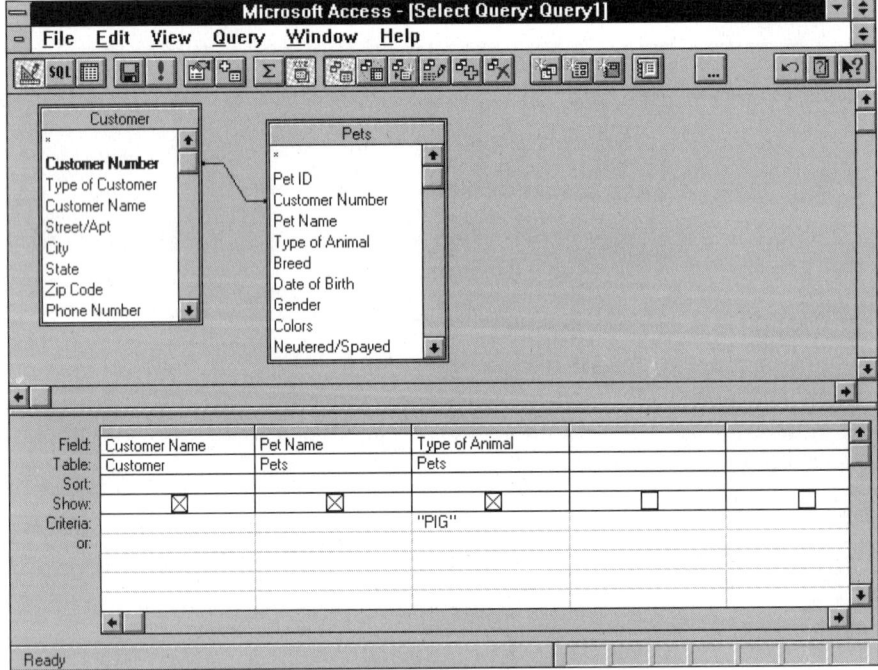

Figure 15-1: The QBE pane with a simple criteria.

Revisiting Record/Field Criteria

Record or field criteria is simply the rule or sample data that you supply to Access in the Criteria: cell of the QBE pane. This criteria is used by Access to return a dynaset of only the records you are interested in. The criteria may be = "Bird" in the field Type of Animal or > #12/31/92# in the Visit Date field.

A criteria can be thought of as the limiting filter, or rule, that you create for limiting the records that you want to see in your database tables.

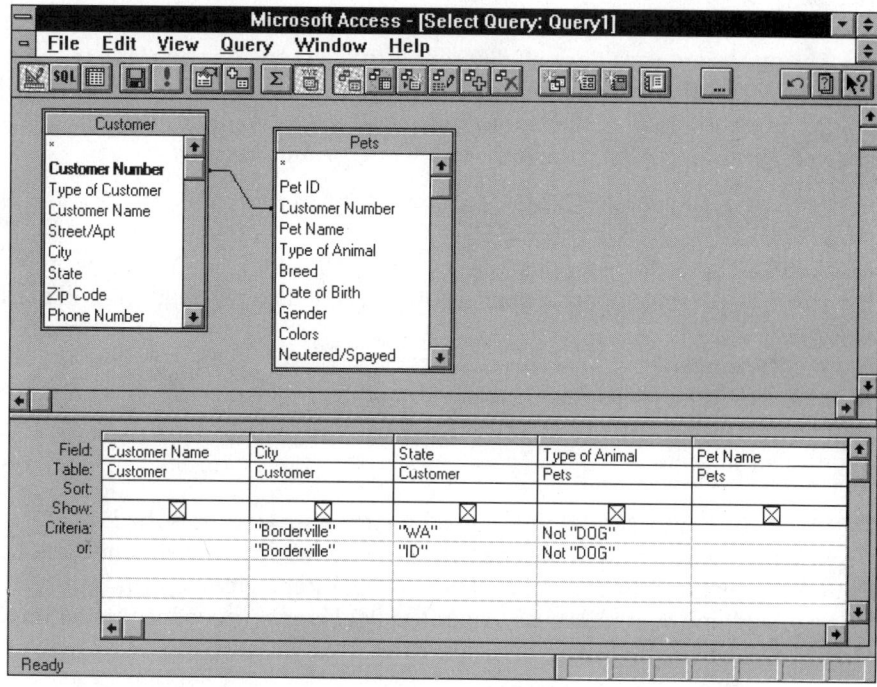

Figure 15-2: Creating a complex And/Or criteria by example without using the And/Or operators.

You sometimes see a field name referenced by the table name first and then the field name, with a dot (period) in between the two names. This way, you understand which table a field belongs to. This is especially critical when you're describing two fields having the same name but coming from different tables. In a multiple-table query, you see this format in the field list when you add a field to the QBE pane by clicking an empty column. You can also see this format when you create a multiple-table form and use the field list. The general format is *Table Name.Field Name*. Examples are `Pets.Type of Animal` or `Customer.Customer Name`.

If you build a formula for this query, it will look something like this:

```
((Customer.City="Borderville") AND (Customer.State="WA") AND (Not
Pets.[Type of Animal]="DOG")) OR ((Customer.City="Borderville") AND
(Customer.State="ID") AND (Not Pets.[Type of Animal]="DOG"))
```

Notice that you must enter the city and pet example for each state line in the QBE pane of Figure 15-2. Later, you use the And/Or operators in a Criteria: cell of the query, eliminating the need for redundant entry of these fields.

To find records that do *not* match a value, use the Not operator with the value. For example, enter the expression *Not Dog* to find all animals except dogs.

The And/Or operators are the most common when you're working with complex criteria. The operators consider two different formulas (one on each side of the And/Or operators) and then determine whether they are True or False, individually. Then they compare the resultant of the two formulas against each other for a logical True/False answer. For example, take the first And in the formula just given:

```
(Customer.City="Borderville") AND (Customer.State="WA")
```

The first half of the formula, `Customer.City = "Borderville"`, is converted to a True if the city is Borderville (False if a different city; Null if no city was entered in the field).

Then the second half of the formula, `Customer.State = "WA"`, is converted to a True if the state is Washington (False if a different state; Null if no state was entered). Then the And compares the logical True/False from each side against the other to give a resulting True/False answer.

A field has a Null value when it has no value at all; it is the lack of entry of information in a field. Null is neither True nor False; nor is it equivalent to all spaces or zero — it has no value. If you never enter a city name in the City field, simply skipping over it, Access leaves the field empty (no value was entered). This state of emptiness is known as Null.

When the resultant of an And/Or is True, the overall condition is True, and the query displays those records meeting the True condition. A quick review of True conditions for each operator is given in Table 15-2.

Table 15-2
Results of Logical Operators And/Or

Left Side Is	Operator Is	Right Side Is	Resultant Answer Is
True	AND	True	True
True	OR	True	True

Left Side Is	Operator Is	Right Side Is	Resultant Answer Is
True	OR	False	True
True	OR	Null	True
False	OR	True	True
Null	OR	True	True

Notice that the And operator is True only when *both* sides of the formula are True, whereas the Or operator is True whenever *either* side of the formula is True. In fact, one side can be a Null value, and the Or operator is still True if the other side is True. This is the distinct difference between And/Or operators.

Refer to Chapter 13 for further details about logical operators.

Using functions in select queries

When you work with queries, you may want to use built-in Access functions to display information. For example, you may want to display such items as the following:

- The day of week (Sunday, Monday, and so forth) for visit dates
- All customer names in uppercase
- The difference between two date fields

You can display all this information by creating calculated fields for the query. This will be discussed in depth later in this chapter.

Referencing fields in select queries

When you work with a field name in queries, as you do with calculated fields or criteria values, you should enclose the field name in brackets ([ ]). Access requires brackets around field names whenever the field name is in a criteria or if the name contains a space or punctuation. An example of a field name in brackets is the criteria [Visit Date] + 30. Further examples of using fields will be shown later in this chapter.

If you omit the brackets ([ ]) around a field name in the criteria, Access automatically places quotes around the field name.

Entering Single-Value Field Criteria

Many times, you want to limit query records based on a single field criteria, as in these queries:

- Customer information for customers living in the state of Washington
- Animals you have treated from the local zoos in the area
- Customers and animals you treated during the month of January

All three of these queries require a single-value criteria. Simply put, *single-value criteria* is the entry of only one expression in a field. That expression can be example data or a function: `"WA"` or `DatePart("m",[Visit Date])=1` are both examples of single-value criteria.

You can specify criteria expressions for any type of data, whether Text, Numeric, Date/Time, and so forth. Even OLE Object and Counter field types can have criteria specified.

Expressions, operators, identifiers, literals, and functions are fully explained in Chapter 13.

Following Along in This Book

All the examples in this chapter rely on several tables: Customer, Pets, and Visits. The majority of these examples use only the Customer and Pets tables. You should create a new query and add the Customer and Pets tables.

As you read each series of steps in this chapter, we tell you which tables and fields make up the query. In most examples, you should clear all previous criteria before going to the next example. Each of the examples focuses on the criteria lines of the QBE pane. You can also view each figure to make sure that you understand the correct placement of the criteria in each example. Only a few dynasets are shown, so you can follow along and view the data if you want. The MTNSTART database contains only the tables used in this chapter.

Entering character (Text or Memo) criteria

Character type criteria is used for Text or Memo data type fields. This is example data of or about the contents of the field. For example, to create a text criteria to display customers who own birds, follow these steps:

Steps:	Setting Criteria for Type of Animal
Step 1.	Select Customer Name from the Customer table, Pet Name and Type of Animal in the Pets table.

Step 2. Click the Criteria: cell of Type of Animal.
Step 3. Type **BIRD** in the cell.

Your query should look similar to Figure 15-3. Notice that only two tables are open and only three fields are selected. You can click the Datasheet button to see the results of this query.

Figure 15-3: The Query Design window with two files open (and automatically linked).

When you specify example type criteria, it is not necessary to match capitalization. Access defaults to case insensitive when working with queries. You can enter any of the following and receive the same results: BIRD, bird, BiRd.

Notice that you didn't have to enter an equal sign before the literal word *bird*. This is because Access uses the equal operator as the default. If you want to see all animals except birds, you use either the <> (not equal) or the Not operator before the word *bird*.

You also didn't have to place quotes around the word *bird*. Access does this for you automatically. Access understands that you are talking about the example literal *BIRD* and places the quotes for you.

In Version 1.x, Access places quotation marks (") only around example literals that contain no spaces. If the literal has spaces, you must provide the quotes or Access reports an error on execution. However, in Version 2.0, Access automatically places quotation marks around any example data that you provide as long as it is not enclosed in brackets ([]).

You should use the double quotation marks to surround literals. Access normally uses the single quotation, in its programming language, as a remark character; however, when you use this in the Criteria: cell, Access interprets it as a double quotation mark.

The Like operator and wildcards

Up to this point, you've been working with *literal* criteria. You specified the exact field contents for Access to find, which in the example was "Bird." Access used the literal to find the specific records. Sometimes, however, you know only a part of the field contents, or you may want to see a wider range of records based on a pattern. For example, you may want to see all pet visits for pets that begin with the letter *G*, for gerbils, goats, and so forth. Perhaps another, more practical example is where you have a customer who owns a pig that was born Siamese. You remember making a note of it in the Comments field; you don't, however, remember which pig it was. This requires using a wildcard search against the Memo field to find any records that contain the word Siamese.

Access uses the string operator Like in the Criteria: cell of a field to perform wildcard searches against the field's contents. Access searches for a pattern in the field; you use the question mark (?) to represent a single character or the asterisk (*) for several characters. (This is just like DOS level when you work with filenames.) Besides the two characters, the ? and *, Access uses three additional characters for performing wildcard searches. Table 15-3 lists the wildcards that the Like operator can use.

The question mark (?) stands for any single character located in the same position as the question mark in the example expression. An asterisk (*) stands for any number of characters in the same position in which the asterisk is placed. Unlike the asterisk at DOS level, Access can use the asterisk any number of times in an example expression. The pound sign (#) stands for any single digit found in the same position as the pound sign. The brackets ([ ]) and the list they enclose stand for any single character that matches any one character of the list located within the brackets. Finally, the exclamation point (!) inside the brackets represents the Not word for the list — that is, any single character that does *not* match any character of the list within the brackets.

Table 15-3
Wildcards Used by the Like Operator

Wildcard	Purpose
?	A single character (0-9, Aa-Zz)
*	Any number of characters (0 to *n*)
#	Any single digit (0-9)
[*list*]	Any single character in the list
[!*list*]	Any single character not in the list

These wildcards can be used alone or in conjunction with each other. They can even be used several times within the same expression. The examples in Table 15-4 demonstrate how the wildcards can be used.

To create an example using the Like operator, say that you want to find that record of the Siamese pig. You know that this fact is referenced in one of the records in the Comments field. To create the query, follow these steps:

Steps:	Finding a Record Using the Like Operator
Step 1.	Remove the criteria field for Type of Animal.
Step 2.	Double-click the Comments field in the Pets table.
Step 3.	Click the Criteria: cell of the Comments field.
Step 4.	Type *Siamese* in the cell.

Table 15-4
Using Wildcards with the Like Operator

Expression	Field Used In	Results of Criteria
Like "Re?"	Pets.Pet Name	Finds all records of pets whose names are three letters long and begin with "Re"; examples: Red, Rex, Ren
Like "*Siamese*"	Pets.Comments	Finds all records with the word "Siamese" somewhere within the Comments field
Like "G*"	Pets.Type of Animal	Finds all records for animals of a type that begins with the letter G
Like "1/*/93"	Visits.Visit Date	Finds all records for the month of January 1993
Like "## Main St."	Customer.Street/Apt	Finds all records for houses with house numbers between 10 and 99 inclusively; examples: 10, 22, 33, 51
Like "[RST]*"	Customer.City	Finds all records for customers who live in any city with a name beginning with R, S, or T
Like "[!EFG]*"	Pets.Type of Animal	Finds all records for animals of a type that does not begin with the letters E, F, or G; all other animals are displayed

When you move the cursor, leaving the Criteria: cell, Access automatically adds the operator Like and the quotation marks around the expression. Your query should appear similar to Figure 15-4.

Figure 15-4: Using the Like operator with a select query.

Access adds the Like operator and quotation marks for you if you meet the following conditions:

- There are no spaces in your expression.
- You use only the wildcards ?, *, #.
- You use brackets [ ] inside quotation marks " ".

If you use the brackets without quotation marks, you must supply the operator Like and the quotation marks.

Using the Like operator with wildcards is the best way to perform pattern searches through Memo fields.

The Like operator and its wildcards can be used only against three types of fields: Text, Memo, and Date. Using these with any other type can result in an error.

Specifying nonmatching values

To specify a nonmatching value, you simply use either the Not or the <> operator in front of the expression that you don't want to match. For example, you may want to see all customers and their pets for all states, but you want to exclude Washington. You see how to specify this nonmatching value in the following steps:

Steps:	Specifying a Nonmatching Value
Step 1.	Start with an empty query, using the Customer and Pets tables.
Step 2.	Select the Customer Name and State fields from Customer and Pet Name from Pets.
Step 3.	Click the Criteria: cell of State.
Step 4.	Type **Not "WA"** in the cell.

The query should now look similar to Figure 15-5. The query will select all records *except* those for customers who live in the state of Washington.

You can use the <> operator instead of Not. In Step 4 of the steps for excluding Washington from the criteria, the resulting dynaset is the same with either operator. These two operators are interchangeable. The exception is with the use of the keyword Is. You cannot say Is <> Null. Rather, you must say Is Not Null.

Figure 15-5: Using the Not operator in criteria.

Entering numeric (Number, Currency, or Counter) criteria

Numeric type criteria is used for Number, Currency, or Counter data type fields. You simly enter the digits and the decimal symbol, if required. For example, you may want to see all animals that weigh over 100 pounds. To create a query like this, follow these steps:

Steps:	Specifying Numeric Criteria
Step 1.	Start with a new query, using the Customer and Pets tables.
Step 2.	Select the Customer Name in the Customer table, Pet Name, Type of Animal, and Weight in the Pets table.
Step 3.	Click the Criteria: cell of Weight.
Step 4.	Type **>100** in the cell.

When you follow these steps, your query looks similar to Figure 15-6. When working with numeric data, Access does not enclose the expression, as it does with string or date criteria.

Numeric fields are generally compared to a value string that uses comparison operators, such as less than (<), greater than (>), or equal to (=). If you want to specify a comparison other than equal, you must enter the operator as well. Remember that Access defaults to equal for all criteria. That is why you needed to specify greater than, or >100, in the query for animals over 100 pounds.

Working with Currency and counter data in a query is exactly the same as working with numeric data; you specify an operator and a numeric value.

Figure 15-6: Criteria set for weight of animals.

Field:	Customer Name	Pet Name	Type of Animal	Weight	
Table:	Customer	Pets	Pets	Pets	
Sort:					
Show:	☒	☒	☒	☒	☐
Criteria:				>100	
or:					

Entering Yes/No (logic) criteria

Yes/No criteria is used for Yes/No type fields. The example data that you supply in the criteria can be only for Yes or No states. You can use the Not and the <> operators to signify the opposite, but unlike the other field types, the Yes/No data has only these two states. When entering criteria in a Yes/No field, you are not limited to entering a Yes or No expression. Access recognizes several forms of Yes and No. Table 15-5 lists all the positive and negative values that you can use.

Thus, instead of typing Yes, you can enter any of the following in the Criteria: cell: On, True, Not No, <> No, <No, or –1.

As stated earlier, a Yes/No field can have only two criteria states, Yes or No. Unlike other types of fields, a Yes/No field can *never* be Null. Therefore, checking for Is Null will always display no records, and checking for Is Not Null will always display all records.

Table 15-5
Positive and Negative Values Used in Yes/No Fields

Yes	True	On	Not No	<> No	<No	–1
No	False	Off	Not Yes	<>Yes	>Yes	0

Entering OLE object criteria

You can even specify criteria for OLE objects. The criteria that you can specify is the Is Not Null. As an example, suppose that you don't have pictures for all the animals, and you want to view only those records where you have a picture of the animal — or where picture is not Null. You specify the Is Not Null criteria for the Picture field of the Pets table. By doing this, Access limits the records to only those that have a picture in them.

Although the correct syntax is Is Not Null, you can also type **Not Null** and Access will supply the Is operator for you.

Entering Multiple Criteria in One Field

So far, you've worked with single-condition criteria on a single field at a time. As you learned, single-condition criteria can be specified for any field type. Now, you'll work with multiple criteria based on a single field. As an example, you may be interested in seeing all records where the type of animal is either a cat or a dog. Or perhaps you want to view records of all animals that you saw between January 15, 1993, and February 20, 1993.

The QBE pane provides the flexibility for solving these types of problems. You can specify several criteria for one field or for several fields in a select query. Using multiple criteria, for example, you can determine which customers and pets are from Idaho or Washington, or which animals you saw for general examinations in the past 30 days.

To specify several criteria for one field, you use the And and the Or operators.

Understanding an Or operation

You use an Or operation in queries when you want a field to meet either of two conditions. For example, you may want to see the customer and pet names of all rabbits and squirrels. In other words, you want to see all records where a customer owns a rabbit *or* a squirrel, *or* both. Following is the general formula for this:

```
[Type of Animal] = "Rabbit" Or [Type of Animal] = "Squirrel"
```

If either side of this formula is True, the resulting answer is also True. To clarify this point, consider the following conditions:

- Customer One owns a rabbit but does not own a squirrel — the formula is True.
- Customer Two owns a squirrel but does not own a rabbit — the formula is True.
- Customer Three owns a squirrel and a rabbit — the formula is True.
- Customer Four does not own a rabbit and does not own a squirrel — the formula is False.

Specifying multiple values for a field using the Or operator

You use the Or operator to specify multiple values for a field. For example, you use the Or operator if you want to see all records of owners of fish or frogs or ducks. To accomplish this task, follow these steps:

Steps:	Entering Multiple Values Using the Or Operator
Step 1.	Create a new query, using the Customer and Pets tables.
Step 2.	Select the Customer Name field in the Customer table, Pet Name and Type of Animal in the Pets table.
Step 3.	Click the Criteria: cell of Type of Animal.
Step 4.	Type **Fish Or Frog Or Duck** in the cell.

Your QBE pane should resemble Figure 15-7. Notice that Access automatically placed quotation marks around your example data, Fish, Frog, and Duck.

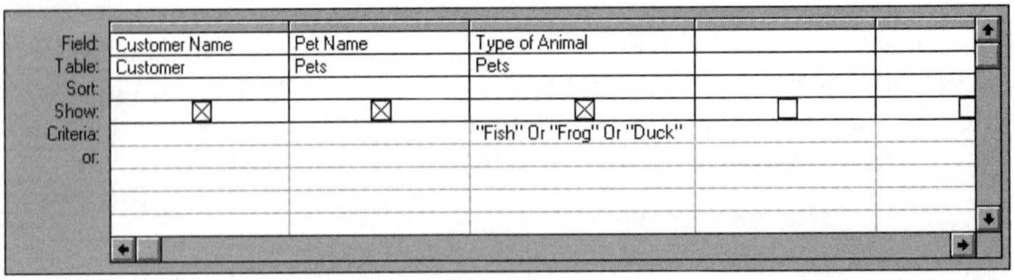

Figure 15-7: Using the Or operator.

Field:	Customer Name	Pet Name	Type of Animal		
Table:	Customer	Pets	Pets		
Sort:					
Show:	☒	☒	☒	☐	
Criteria:			"Fish" Or "Frog" Or "Duck"		
or:					

This dynaset can be seen in Figure 15-8. Notice that the only records selected contain FISH, FROG, or DUCK in the Type of Animal column.

Figure 15-8: Selecting records with the Or operator.

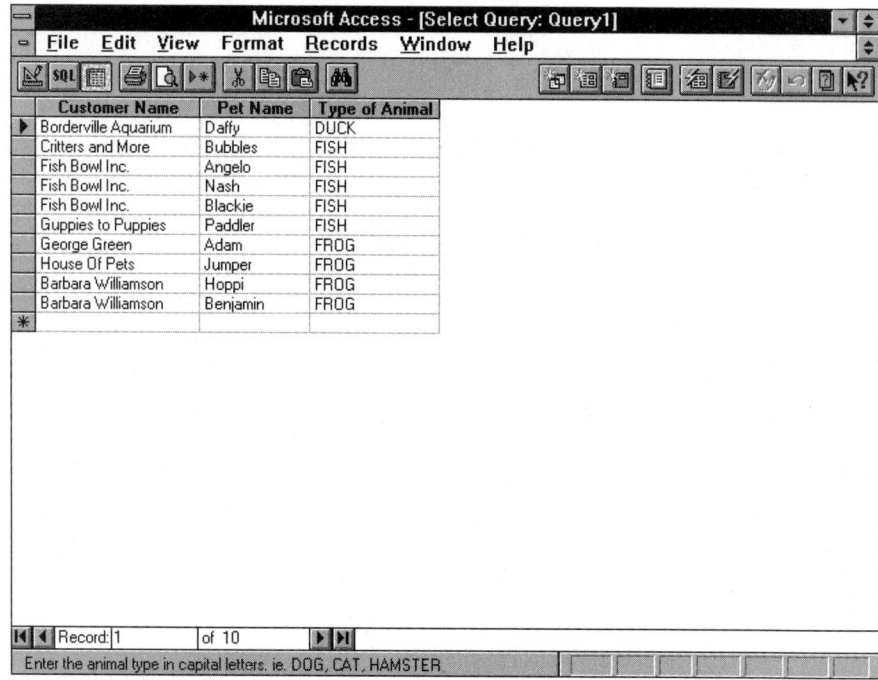

Using the or: cell of the QBE pane

Besides using the literal Or operator, you can supply individual criteria for the field on separate lines of the QBE pane. To do this, you enter the first criteria example in the Criteria: cell of the field, just as you have been. Then you enter the criteria example in the or: cell of the field. Enter the next criteria in the cell directly beneath the first example; then continue entering further examples vertically down the column. This is exactly equivalent to typing the Or operator between each example. Using the example where you queried for fish, frogs, or ducks, change your QBE pane to look like the one in Figure 15-9. Notice that each type of animal is on a separate line in the query.

Access gives you five Or cells for each field. If you need to specify more Or conditions, use the Or between conditions (Cat Or Dog Or Pig).

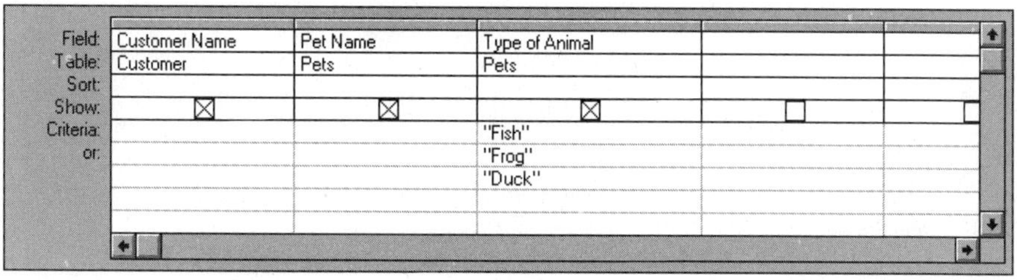

Figure 15-9: Using the or: cell of the QBE pane.

Using a list of values with the In operator

You can use another method for expressing the multiple values of a single field. This method uses the operator named *In*. The In operator finds a value that is one of a *list of values*. For example, enter the expression **IN(FISH, FROG, DUCK)** under the Type of Animal field. This action creates a list of values, where any item in the list becomes an example criteria. After you create the query, it should resemble Figure 15-10.

In this example, you can see that quotation marks are automatically entered around Fish, Frog, and Duck.

When you work with the In operator, each value (example data) must be separated from the others by a comma.

Figure 15-10: Using the In operator.

Understanding an And query

You use And operations in queries when you want a field to meet both of two conditions that you specify. For example, you may want to see records of pets that had a visit date >= Jan 1, 1993 And <= Mar 31, 1993. In other words, the animal had to be a patient during the first quarter of the year 1993. The general formula for this is as follows:

```
[Visit Date] >= 1/1/93 And [Visit Date] <= 3/31/93
```

Unlike the Or operator, which has several conditions under which it is True, the And is True only when both sides of the formula are True. When both sides are True, the resulting answer will also be True. To clarify use of the And operator, consider the following conditions:

- Visit date (9/22/92) is not greater than 1/1/93, but it is less than 3/31/93 — the formula is False.
- Visit date (4/11/93) is greater than 1/1/93, but it is not less than 3/31/93 — the formula is False.
- Visit date (2/1/93) is greater than 1/1/93, and it is less than 3/31/93 — the formula is True.

Both sides of the operation must be True for the And operation to be True.

An And operation can be performed in several ways against a single field in Access.

Specifying a range using the And operator

And operators are frequently used in fields that are numeric or of the Date/Time type. They are seldom used in Text type, although they can be. For instance, you may be interested in viewing all animals whose names start with *D*, *E*, or *F*. You can do this by using the And operator, although the like operator would be better (Like"[DEF]*"). When you use an And operator with a single field, you are using it to set a *range* of acceptable values in the field. Therefore, the key purpose of an And operator in a single field is to define a range of records to be viewed. An example of using the And operator to create a range criteria is to display all animals that weigh between 100 and 300 lbs., inclusively. To create this query, follow these steps:

Steps:	Using the And Operator for a Number Field
Step 1.	Create a new query, using the Customer and Pets tables.
Step 2.	Select the Customer Name field in the Customer table, Pet Name, Type of Animal and Weight in the Pets table.
Step 3.	Click the Criteria: cell of Weight.
Step 4.	Type **>=100 And <=300** in the cell.

The query should resemble Figure 15-11. Note that you can change the formula to >99 And <301 with identical results.

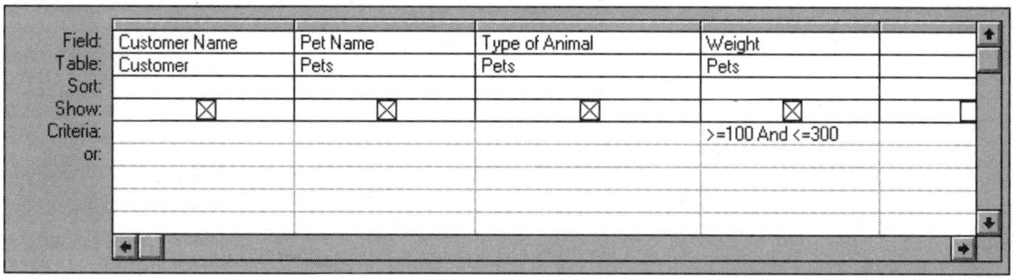

Figure 15-11: Using the And operator with numeric fields.

Field:	Customer Name	Pet Name	Type of Animal	Weight	
Table:	Customer	Pets	Pets	Pets	
Sort:					
Show:	☒	☒	☒	☒	
Criteria:				>=100 And <=300	
or:					

Using the Between ... And operator

You can use another method for expressing a range of records from a single field. This method uses the operator called *Between ... And*. With the Between ... And operator, you can find records meeting a range of values — for example, all pets *Between* Dog *And* Pig. Using the example of animals weighing between 100 and 300 pounds, create the query using the Between ... And operator, as shown in Figure 15-12.

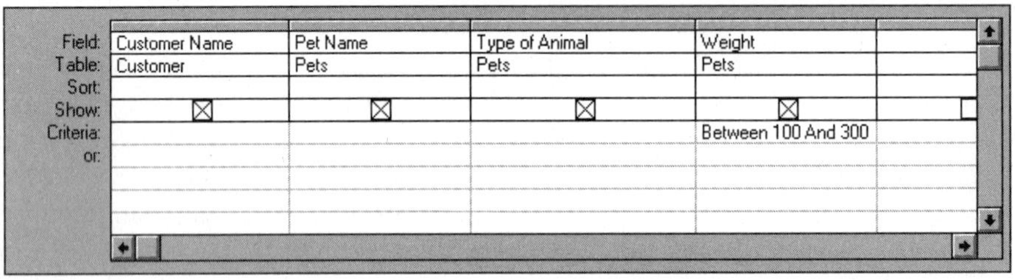

Figure 15-12: Using the Between ... And operator.

Field:	Customer Name	Pet Name	Type of Animal	Weight
Table:	Customer	Pets	Pets	Pets
Sort:				
Show:	☒	☒	☒	☒
Criteria:				Between 100 And 300
or:				

When you use the Between ... And operator, each value (example data) is included in the resulting dynaset.

Searching for Null data

A field may have no contents; possibly the value wasn't known at the time of data entry, or the data-entry person simply forgot to enter the information, or the field's information has been removed. Access does nothing with this field; it simply remains an empty field. A field is said to be *Null* when it is empty.

Logically, a Null is neither True nor False. A Null is not equivalent to all spaces or zero. A Null simply has no value.

Access lets you work with Null value fields by means of two special operators:

    Is Null

    Is Not Null

These operators are used to limit criteria based on Null values of a field. You already worked with a Null value when you queried for animals having a picture on file. In the next example, you look for animal records that don't specify gender. To create this query, follow these steps:

Steps:	Using the Is Null Operator
Step 1:	Create a new query using the Customer and pets tables.
Step 2:	Select the Customer Name field in the Customer table, Pet Name, Type of Animal and Gender field in the Pets table.
Step 3:	Click the Criteria: cell of Gender.
Step 4:	Type **Is Null** in the cell.

Your query should now look like Figure 15-13. If you select the Datasheet button, you'll see that there are no records without a gender.

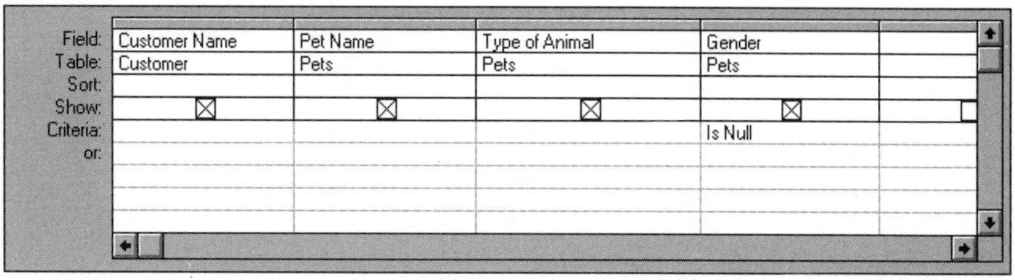

Figure 15-13: Using the Is Null operator.

Field:	Customer Name	Pet Name	Type of Animal	Gender
Table:	Customer	Pets	Pets	Pets
Sort:				
Show:	☒	☒	☒	☒
Criteria:				Is Null
or:				

Entering Criteria in Multiple Fields

You've worked with criteria specified in single fields up to this point. Now you'll work with criteria across several fields. When you want to limit the records based on several field conditions, you do so by setting criteria in each field that will be used for the scope. Say, for example, that you want to search for all dogs or for all animals in Idaho. Or you may want to search for dogs in Idaho or Washington. Again you may search for all dogs in Washington or all cats in Oregon. Each of these queries requires placing criteria in multiple fields and on multiple lines.

Using *And* and *Or* across fields in a query

To *And* and *Or* across fields, place your example or pattern data in the Criteria: and the or: cells of one field relative to the placement in another field. When you want to And between two fields, you place the example or pattern data across the same line. When you want to Or between two fields, you place the example or pattern data on different lines in the QBE pane. Figure 15-14 shows the QBE pane and a conceptual representation of this placement.

Figure 15-14:
The QBE pane with And/Or criteria between fields.

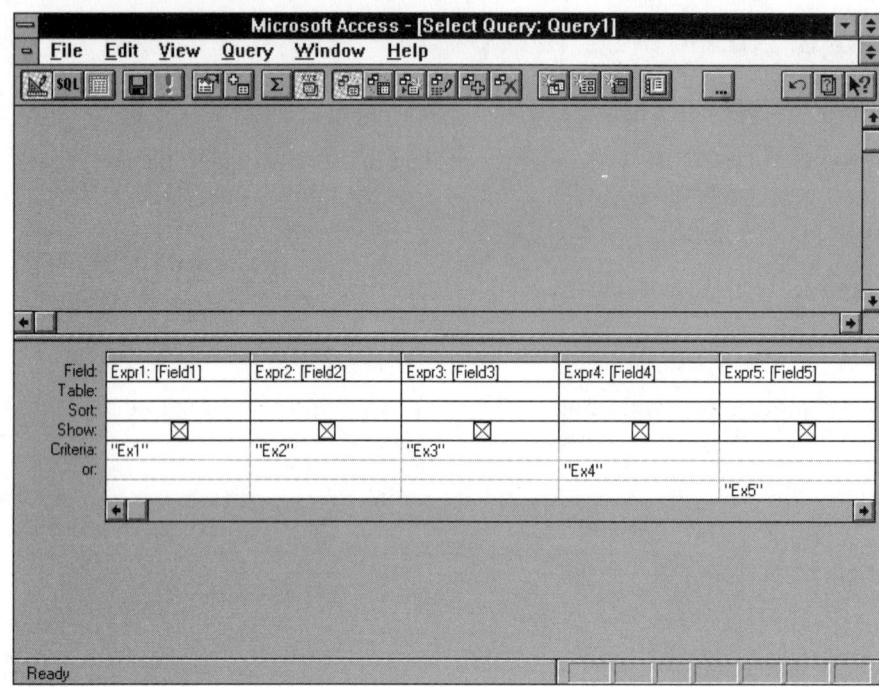

Looking at Figure 15-14, you see that if the only criteria fields present were Ex1, Ex2, and Ex3 (with Ex4 and Ex5 removed), all three would be Anding between the fields. If only the criteria fields Ex4 and Ex5 were present (with Ex1, Ex2, and Ex3 removed), the two would be Oring between fields. As it is, the selection for this example is (EX1 AND EX2 AND EX3) OR EX4 OR EX5. This means that this query is True if a value matches any of these criteria:

EX1 AND EX2 AND EX3   OR

EX4   OR

EX5

As long as one of these three criteria is True, the record will be selected.

Specifying And criteria across fields of a query

The most common type of condition operator between fields is the And operator. Most of the time, you are interested in limiting records based on several field conditions. For example, you may want to view only records of customers who live in Washington State and own rabbits. To create this query, follow these steps:

Chapter 15: Creating Select Queries

Steps:	**Creating an And Criteria between Two Fields**
Step 1.	Create a new query, using the Customer and Pets tables.
Step 2.	Select the Customer Name and State fields in the Customer table, Pet Name and Type of Animal fields in the Pets table.
Step 3.	Click the Criteria: cell of State.
Step 4.	Type **WA** in the cell.
Step 5.	Click the Criteria: cell of Type of Animal.
Step 6.	Type **Rabbit** in the cell.

Your query should look like Figure 15-15. Notice that both example data are in the same row.

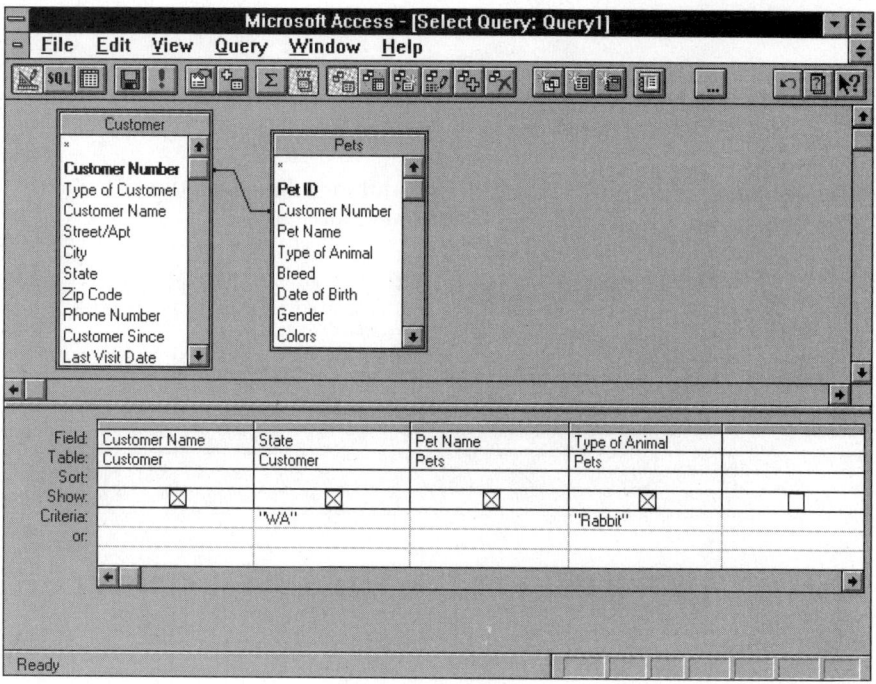

Figure 15-15: An And operation across two fields.

Because you placed data for both criteria on the same row, Access interprets this as an And operation.

Specifying Or criteria across fields of a query

Although the Or operator across fields is not as common as the And, occasionally Or is very useful. For example, you may want to see records of any animals in Washington, or you may want all rabbits, regardless of the state they live in. To create this query, follow these steps:

Steps:	Using the Or Operator across Fields
Step 1.	Use the query from the previous example, emptying the two criteria cells.
Step 2.	Click the Criteria: cell of State.
Step 3.	Type **WA** in the cell.
Step 4.	Click the or: cell of Type of Animal.
Step 5.	Type RABBIT in the cell.

Your query should resemble Figure 15-16. Notice that the criteria entered this time is not in the same row for both fields.

When you place criteria for one field on a different line from the criteria for another field, Access interprets this as an Or between the fields.

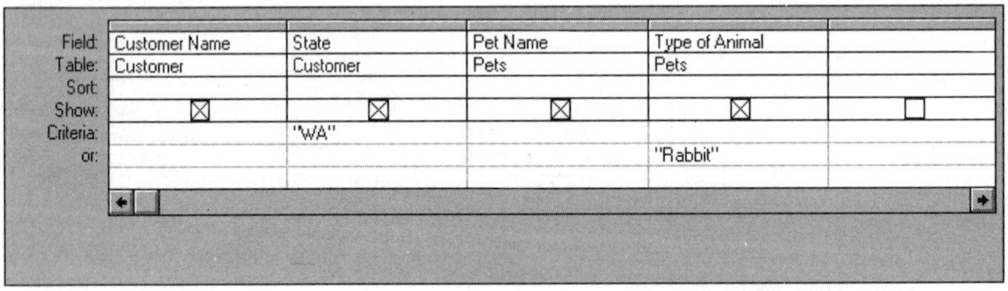

Figure 15-16: Using the Or operator between fields.

Using And and Or together in different fields

Now that you've worked with Anding and Oring separately, you're ready to create a query using And and Or in different fields. In the next example, you want to display information for all skunks in Washington and all rabbits in Idaho. Perform the following steps to create this query:

Chapter 15: Creating Select Queries **361**

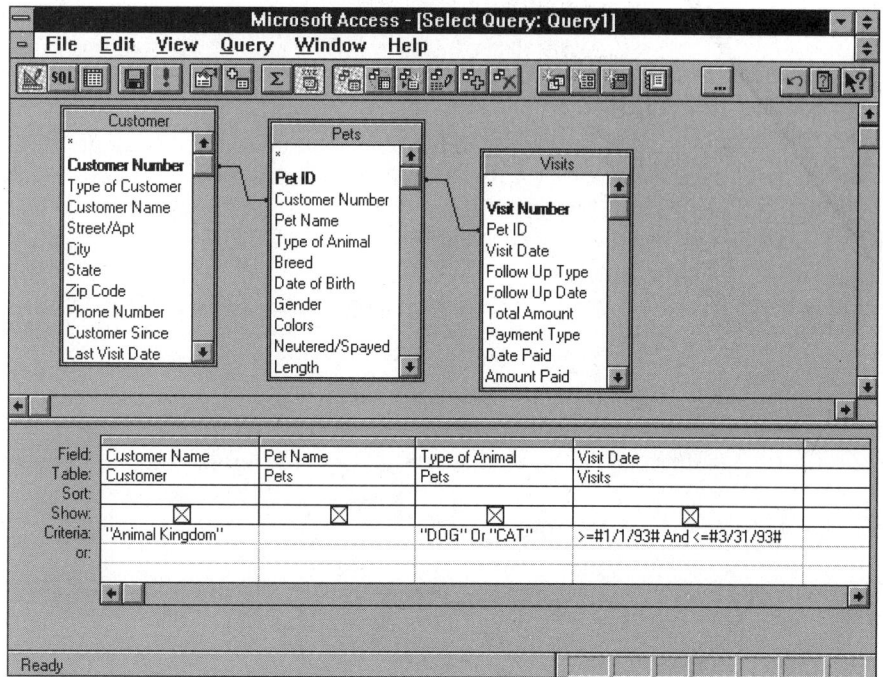

Figure 15-19: Using multiple Ands and Ors across fields on one line.

Creating a New Calculated Field in a Query

When you work with fields in a query, you are not limited to the fields from the tables you use in the query. You can also create calculated fields to use in a query. For example, you may want to create a calculated field named Discount Amount that will display an amount by multiplying the value of Discount times Outstanding Balance in the Customer table.

To create this calculated field, follow these steps:

Steps:	Creating a Calculated Field
Step 1.	Create a new query, using the Customer table.
Step 2.	Select the Customer Name, Discount, and Outstanding Balance fields in the Customer table.
Step 3.	Click the empty Field: cell.
Step 4.	Type **[Discount]*[Outstanding Balance]** and move the cursor off of the cell.

If you did this correctly, the cell looks like Figure 15-20. The expression is changed to `Expr1:[Discount]*[Outstanding Balance]`. The `Expr1:` is the name of the field that is displayed in the dynaset and the name by which the field is known.

For two reasons, a calculated field has a name (either user-supplied or by default by Access). First, a name is needed to supply a label for the datasheet column. Second, the name is necessary for referencing to the field in a form, a report, or another query.

Notice that the general format for creating a calculated field is as follows:

Calculated Field Name: Expression to build calculated field

You can change the expression to

`Discount Amount: [Discount]*[Outstanding Balance]`

to change the name to Discount Amount.

To do this, erase the word Expr1 and replace it with **Discount Amount**. Make sure that the colon (:) is between the name and the expression.

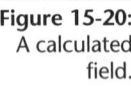

Figure 15-20:
A calculated field.

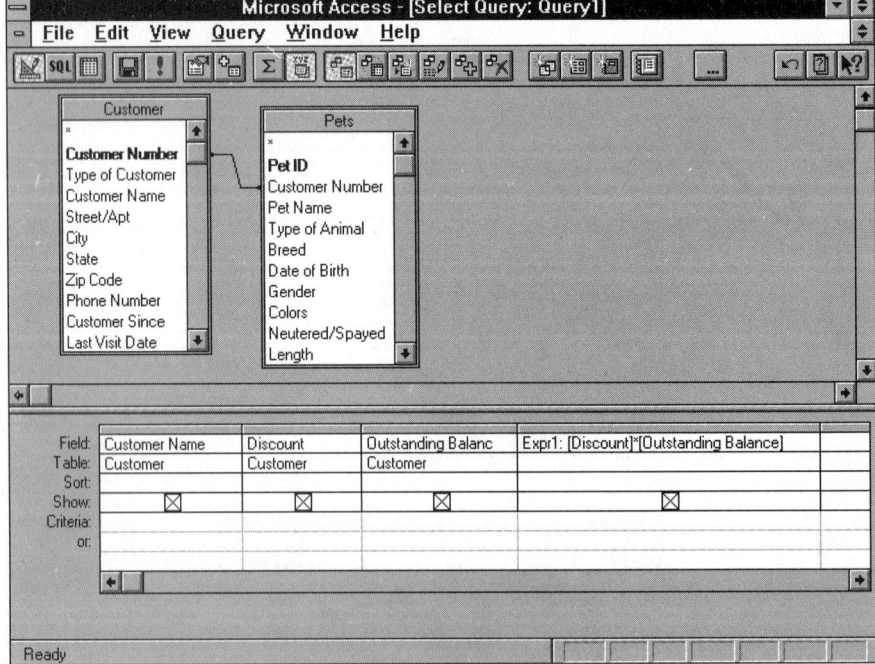

Summary

In this chapter, you learned how to specify criteria to design select queries. You learned about the operators that help you query against fields for the exact information that you want. The following points were covered:

- With select queries, you select information from tables that you can use for datasheets, forms, reports, and other queries.

- You can specify record criteria for any type of field.

- You can build expressions in the Criteria: cell of a field, based on literal data (examples) or with functions that build the example data.

- Access has five distinct wildcards that it uses with the Like operator: ?, *, #, [], and [!]. You can use these operators independently or in conjunction with each other.

- The Not operator, similar to the <> operator, specifies nonmatching values as criteria.

- The And operator forms a True expression only when both sides of a formula are True. An Or operator is True when either side of the formula is True.

- With the Or operator, you can specify a list of values for a field. The And operator lets you specify a range of values in a field.

- Many times, the In operator can be used in lieu of an Or operator; the Between ... And operator can be used in place of the And operator.

- You can search fields for empty conditions through use of the Is Null operator. A Null is the absence of any value in a field.

- Calculated fields are created from an expression. The expression can use one or more fields, functions, or other objects.

In the next chapter, you examine controls and properties.

Understanding Controls and Properties

CHAPTER 16

In This Chapter

- What a control is
- How to create a new blank form
- The three types of controls: bound, unbound, and calculated
- Standards for using controls
- How to create a new control
- How to use the Field List window
- How to use the toolbox
- How to select controls
- How to manipulate controls
- What properties are
- How to view the property sheet
- How to create templates

This is the first of eight chapters in Part III that examine forms and reports in detail. Controls and properties form the basis of forms and reports. It is critical to understand the fundamental concepts of controls and properties before you begin to apply them to forms and reports.

Following Along in This Book

In this chapter, you use the Pets table in the MTNANHSP database. Each control is explained by examining one or more fields in the Pets table. To create the first form that you need for this chapter, follow these steps:

Steps:	Creating a New Form
Step 1.	Open the MTNANHSP database.
Step 2.	Select File⇨New⇨Form.
Step 3.	Select the Pets table from the drop-down list in the New Form dialog box.
Step 4.	Select the Blank Form picture button.
Step 5.	Maximize the form by clicking the maximize button in the top right corner of the window.
Step 6.	Expand the white area of the form to the full-window size by dragging the bottom right corner of the white area to the bottom right corner of the window.

After you create the form and then maximize and resize it, the form should look like Figure 16-1.

If the toolbox is not displayed, select View⇨Toolbox to display the toolbox.

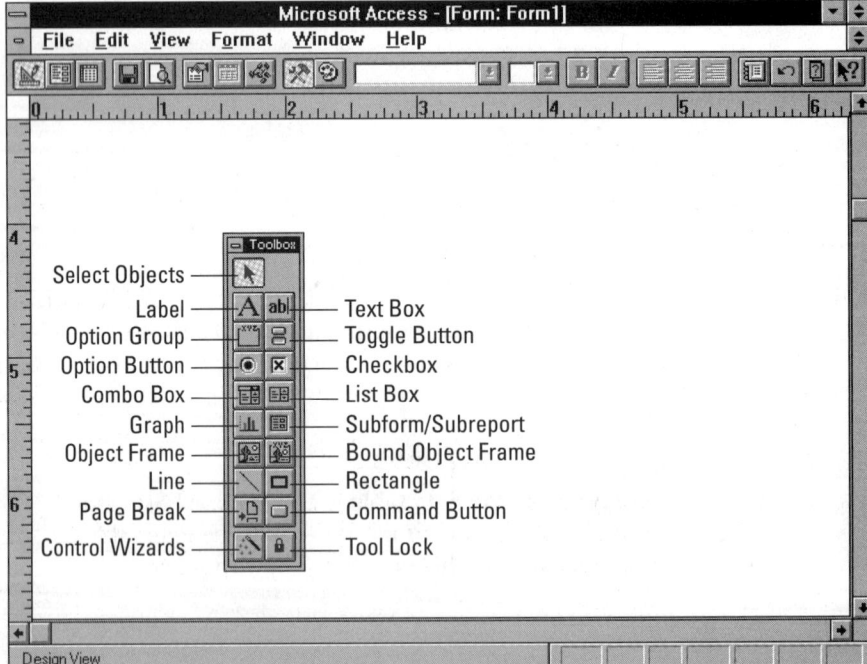

Figure 16-1: A new blank form and the toolbox.

 The toolbox can be moved, resized, and anchored on the window. You can anchor it to any border, grab it, and resize it in the middle of the window.

What Is a Control?

A *control* has many definitions in Access. Generally, a control is any object on a form or report, such as a label or text box. Values are entered into controls and displayed by the use of a control. A control can be bound to a table field, but it can also be an object, such as a line or rectangle. Calculated fields are also controls, as are pictures, graphs, option buttons, checkboxes, and objects.

Whether you're working with forms or reports, creating and using controls is done with essentially the same process. In this chapter, you see controls explained from the perspective of a form.

The different control types

You find many different control types on a form or report. These include the controls that you can create by using the toolbox shown in Figure 16-1. In this book, you learn how to create and use the most often used controls listed in Table 16-1. In this chapter, you learn when to use each control table and how these controls work.

Table 16-1
Controls You Can Create in Access Forms and Reports

Basic Controls	
Label	Literal text is displayed in a label control
Text box	Data is typed into a text box
Enhanced Data-Entry and Data-Validation Controls	
Option group	This group holds multiple option buttons, checkboxes, or toggle buttons
Toggle button	This is a two-state button, up or down, which usually uses pictures or icons
Option button	Also called *radio buttons,* these buttons are displayed as a circle with a dot when the option is on
Checkbox	This is another two-state control, shown as a square that contains an X if it's on, an empty square if it's off
Combo box	This box is a pop-up list of values that allows entries not on the list
List box	This is a list of values that is always displayed on the form or report

(continued)

Table 16-1 (continued)

Graphic and Miscellaneous Controls	
Graph	This control displays a graph of values from a table or query
Subform/Subreport	This control displays another form or report within the original form or report
Unbound object frame	This frame holds an OLE object or embedded picture that is not tied to a table field
Bound object frame	This frame holds an OLE object or embedded picture that is tied to a table field
Line	This is a single line of variable thickness and color, which is used for separation
Rectangle	A rectangle can be any color or size, or can be filled in or blank; the rectangle is used for emphasis
Page break	This is usually used for reports and denotes a physical page break
Command button	Also called a *push button,* this button is used to call a macro to initiate an action

The Control Wizard icon does not create a control but rather determines if a wizard is automatically activated when creating some of the controls. The option group, combo box, list box, graph, object frame, and command button controls all have wizards that are started when a new control is created.

Understanding bound, unbound, and calculated controls

There are three basic types of controls:

- Bound controls
- Unbound controls
- Calculated controls

Bound controls are those that are bound to a table field. When you enter a value into a bound control, Access automatically updates the table field in the current record. Most of the controls that let you enter information can be bound, including OLE fields. Bound controls can be most data types, including text, dates, numbers, Yes/No, pictures, and memo fields.

Chapter 16: Understanding Controls and Properties

Unbound controls are controls that retain the value entered but do not update any table fields. You can use these controls for text display, for values to be passed to macros, lines, and rectangles, or for holding OLE objects, such as a bitmap picture, that are not stored in a table but on the form itself. Unbound controls are sometimes called *variables,* or *memory variables.*

Calculated controls are based on expressions, such as functions or calculations. Calculated controls are also unbound, as they do not update table fields. An example of a calculated control is =[Medication Price] + [Treatment Price]. This control calculates the total of two table fields for display on a form.

Examples of these three control types are shown in Figure 16-2. The picture of the mountain, which is the company's logo, and the text *Mountain Animal Hospital* are unbound controls. The controls below the text and logo that contain field names, including the picture, are bound controls. You also see one calculated control, which is the animal's age. You can see that the function DateDiff is used to calculate the number of years from the Date of Birth bound control to the function Now( ), which returns the current date.

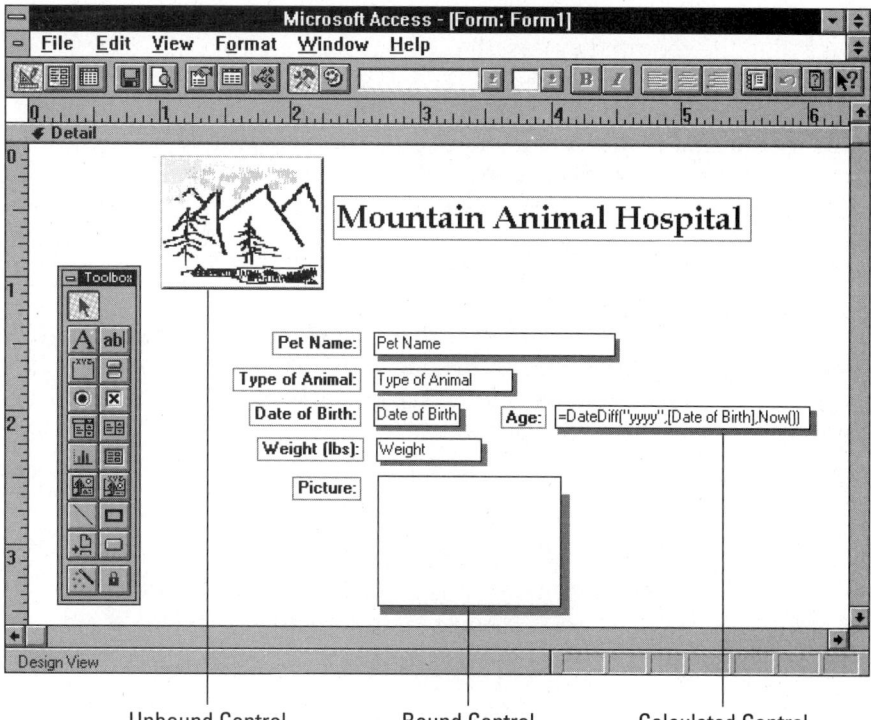

Figure 16-2: The three control types.

Standards for Using Controls

Most of you who are reading this book have used Microsoft Windows, and you've probably used other applications in Windows, such as word processing applications (Word for Windows, WordPerfect for Windows, or AmiPro) or spreadsheet applications (Excel, 1-2-3 for Windows, or Quattro Pro for Windows). However, using a Windows application and designing one are very different.

The controls in Microsoft Access have specific purposes. Their use is not decided by whim or intuition. Rather, there is a scientific method that determines which control should be used for each specific situation. Experience will show you that correct screen and report designs lead to more usable applications.

Label controls

A *label control* displays descriptive text, such as a title, a caption, or instructions on a form or report. Labels can be separate controls. This is common when they are used for titles or data-entry instructions. When labels are used for field captions, they are often attached to the control they describe.

Labels can be displayed on a single line, or they can occupy multiple lines. Labels are unbound controls that accept no input. You use them strictly for one-way communication. They are read and that's all. You can use labels on many types of controls. Figure 16-3 shows many uses of labels, including titles, captions, button text, and button and box captions. You can use different font styles and sizes for your labels, and you can boldface, italicize, and underline them.

You should capitalize each word in a label, except for articles and conjunctions, such as *the, an, and, or,* etc. There are several guidelines to follow for label controls when you use them in other controls, as you can see in Figure 16-3. The following list explains some of these guidelines for placement:

Command buttons	Inside the button
Checkboxes	To the right of the checkbox
Option buttons	To the right of the option button
Text box	Above or to the left of the text box
List or combo box	Above or to the left of the box
Group box	On top of and replacing part of the top frame line

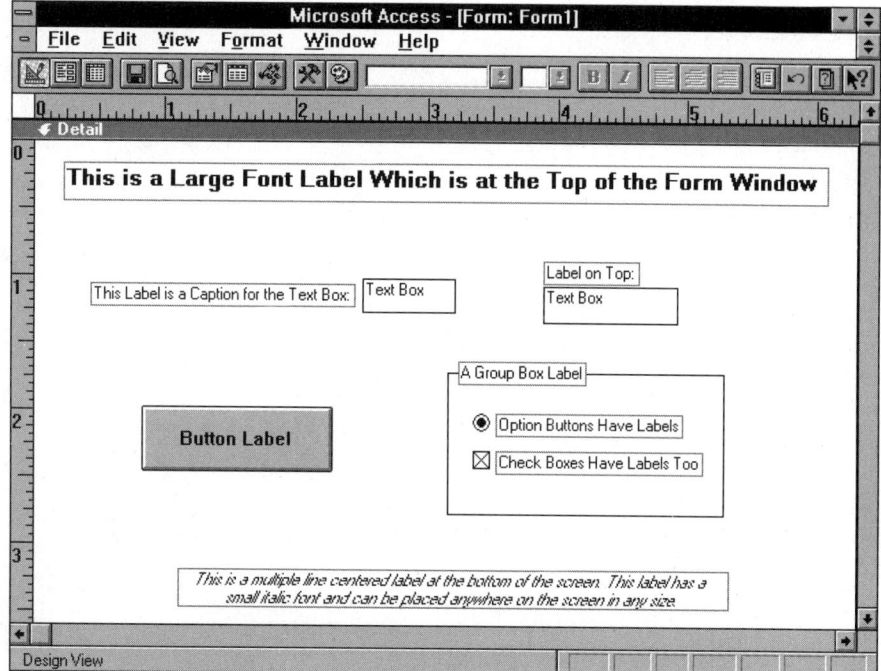

Figure 16-3: Sample label controls.

Text box controls

Text boxes are controls in which the user types information or data is displayed. In a text box, you can accept the current text, edit it, delete it, or replace it. Text boxes can accept any type of data, including Text, Number, Date/Time, Yes/No, and Memo data types. Text boxes can be bound or unbound. You can use text box fields from tables or queries, and the text box can also contain calculated expressions. A text box is the most used control because editing and displaying data are the main purposes of any database system.

Text boxes should have an associated label to identify the purpose of the text box. Text boxes can contain multiple lines of data. When you use a text box to display Memo field data, you normally use a multiple-line text box. Data that is too long for the text field width automatically wraps within the field boundaries. Figure 16-4 shows several different text boxes in the Form view. Notice how the different data types vary in their alignment within the text boxes. The Comments text box displays multiple lines in the resized text box, which also has a scroll bar added.

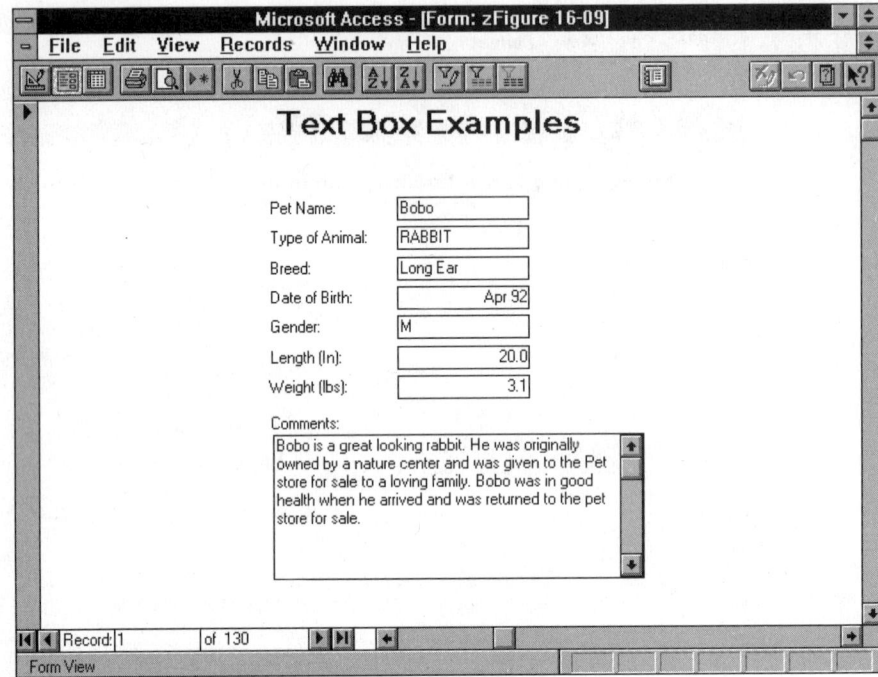

Figure 16-4: Sample text box controls.

Toggle buttons, option buttons, and checkboxes

There are three types of buttons that act in the same way, and yet their visual display is very different:

- Toggle buttons
- Option buttons (also known as radio buttons)
- Checkboxes

These controls are used with Yes/No data types. Each of these buttons can be used individually to represent one of two states, whether Yes or No, On or Off, or True or False. Table 16-2 describes the visual representation of these controls.

Toggle buttons, option buttons, and checkboxes return a value of –1 to the bound table field if the button value is Yes, On, or True, and a value of 0 if the button is No, Off, or False. You can enter a default value to display a specific state. The control is initially displayed in a Null state if no default is entered and no state is selected. The Null state's visual appearance is the same as in the No state.

Chapter 16: Understanding Controls and Properties

Although you can place Yes/No data types in a text box, it is better to use one of these controls. The values that are returned to a text box (–1 and 0) are very confusing, especially because Yes is represented by –1 and No is 0.

The checkbox is the commonly accepted control for two-state selection. Toggle and option buttons are nice but not always appropriate. Each of these controls can also use pictures instead of a text caption to represent the two states. Figure 16-5 shows these buttons, including text box values and toggle buttons.

Table 16-2
Button Control Visual Displays

Button Type	State	Visual Description
Toggle button	True	Button is sunken
Toggle button	False	Button is raised
Option button	True	Circle with a large solid dot inside
Option button	False	Hollow circle
Checkbox	True	Square with an X in the middle
Checkbox	False	Empty square

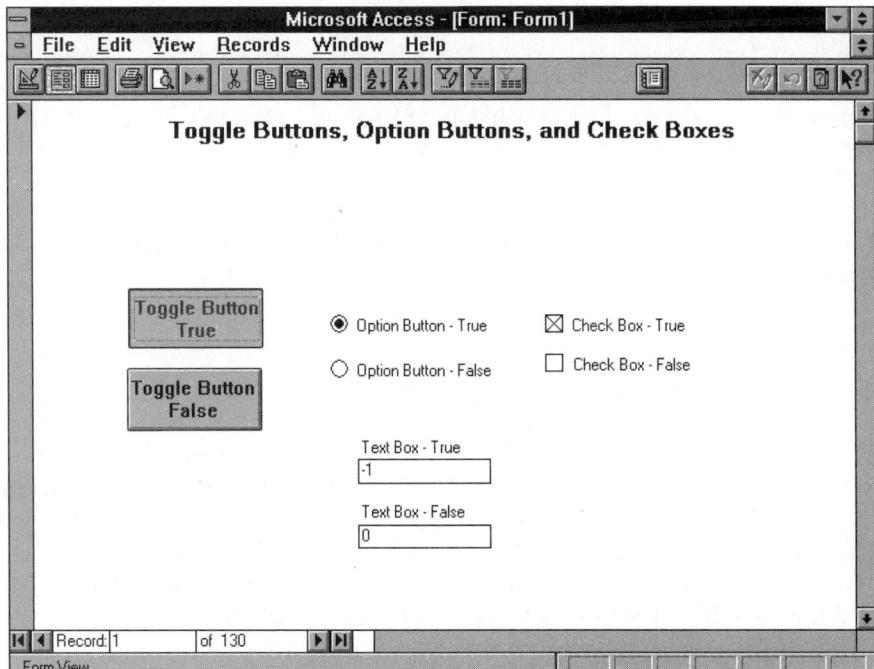

Figure 16-5: Sample toggle buttons, option buttons, and checkboxes.

 You can format the display of the Yes/No values in the Datasheet or Form view by setting the Format property of the text box control to Yes/No, On/Off, or True/False. If you don't use the Format property, the datasheet will display –1 or 0. Using a default value also speeds up data entry by setting as the default the value that is selected most often.

Option groups

An option group can contain multiple toggle buttons, option buttons, or checkboxes. When these controls are placed inside an option group box, they work together instead of individually. Rather then representing a two-state Yes/No data type, controls within an option group return a number based on the position in the group. Only one control within an option group can be selected at one time. The maximum number of buttons in an option group should be four. When you exceed that number, unless you have plenty of room on your screen, you should switch to a drop-down list box.

An option group is generally bound to a single field or expression. Each button inside passes a different value back to the option group, which in turn passes the single choice to the bound field or expression. The buttons themselves are not bound to any field but to the option group box.

Figure 16-6 shows three types of buttons in an option group box. Each option group has the second choice selected. When you make a new selection, the current selection is deselected. For example, in the middle option group box in Figure 16-6, if you click on Option Button 3, the solid dot will appear to move to the third circle, and the second circle will become hollow.

The option button is the generally accepted control to be used within an option group. Checkboxes should be used only in two-state or multiple-state selections when more than one selection is allowed in a group.

Buttons in rectangles

The three types of buttons act very differently, depending on whether they are used individually or in an option group. You can create buttons that look like a group but do not function as a single entity. Figure 16-7 shows a multiple-selection group. Notice that checkboxes 2 and 3 are simultaneously selected. This is not an option group; rather this is a group of controls that are enclosed in a box. They act totally independently, so they don't need to be enclosed in a box together. Each control passes either a –1 (True) or a 0 (False) to the field, expression, or control it is bound to. A common use for this type of grouping is to let a user select from a list of nonexclusive options, such as a list of reports or a list of days on which a process should occur.

Chapter 16: Understanding Controls and Properties 375

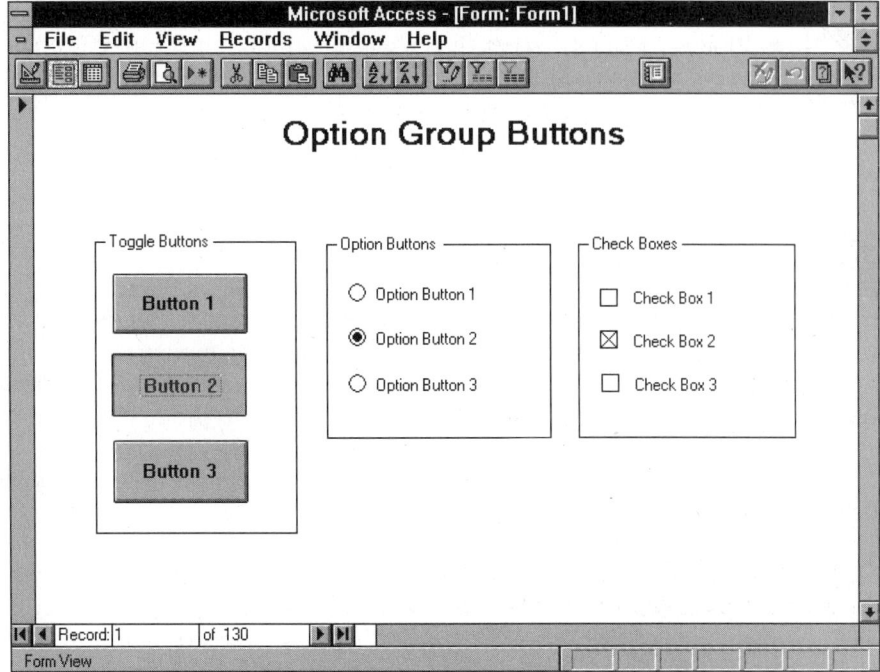

Figure 16-6:
Three types of option groups.

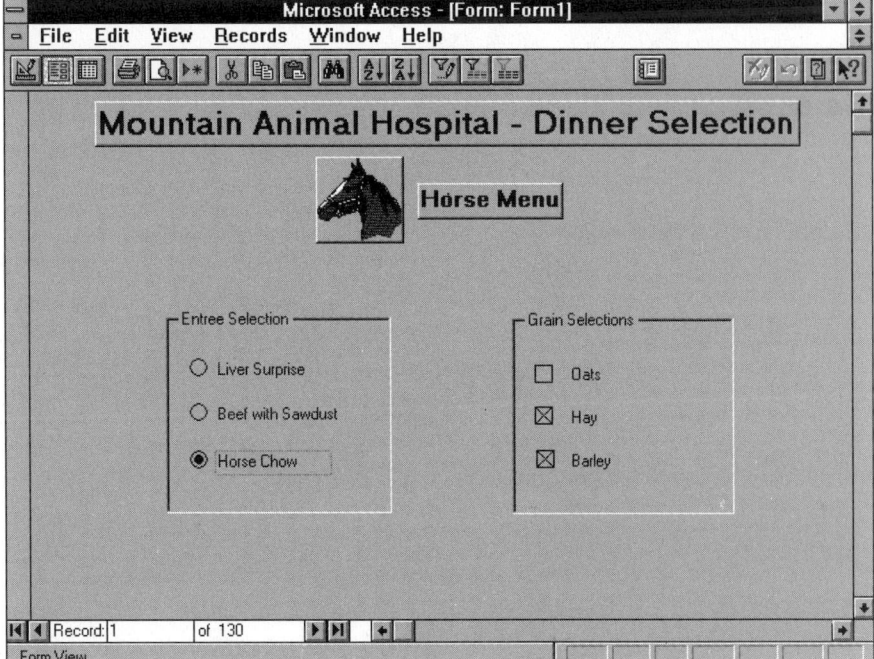

Figure 16-7:
Selecting a meal.

You may want to create groups of buttons that look like option groups but have multiple selections. Rather than using an option button, simply enclose the group of buttons with a rectangle. Each button remains an individual entity instead of becoming part of a group.

List boxes

A list box control displays a list of data on-screen just as a pull-down menu does, but the list box is always open. You can highlight an item in the list by moving the cursor to the desired choice and then pressing Enter or clicking the mouse to complete the selection. You can also type the first letter of the selection to highlight the desired entry. After you select an item, the item's value is passed back to the bound field.

List boxes can display any number of fields and any number of records. By sizing the list box, you can make it display more or fewer records.

List boxes are generally used when there is plenty of room on-screen and you want the operator to see the choices without having to click a drop-down arrow. A vertical — and even horizontal — scroll bar is used for displaying records and fields that are not visible when the list box is in its default size. The highlighted entry will be the one currently selected. If no entries are highlighted, either a selection has not been made or the selected item is not currently in view. Only items in the list can be selected.

You also have a choice of whether to display the column headings on list boxes. Figure 16-8 displays list boxes with three layout schemes.

Combo boxes

In Access, combo boxes differ from list boxes in two ways:

- The combo box is initially displayed as a single row with an arrow that lets you open the box to the normal size.
- As an option, the combo box lets you enter a value that is not on the list.

In Figure 16-9, you see a list box and the combo box both open and closed.

Chapter 16: Understanding Controls and Properties

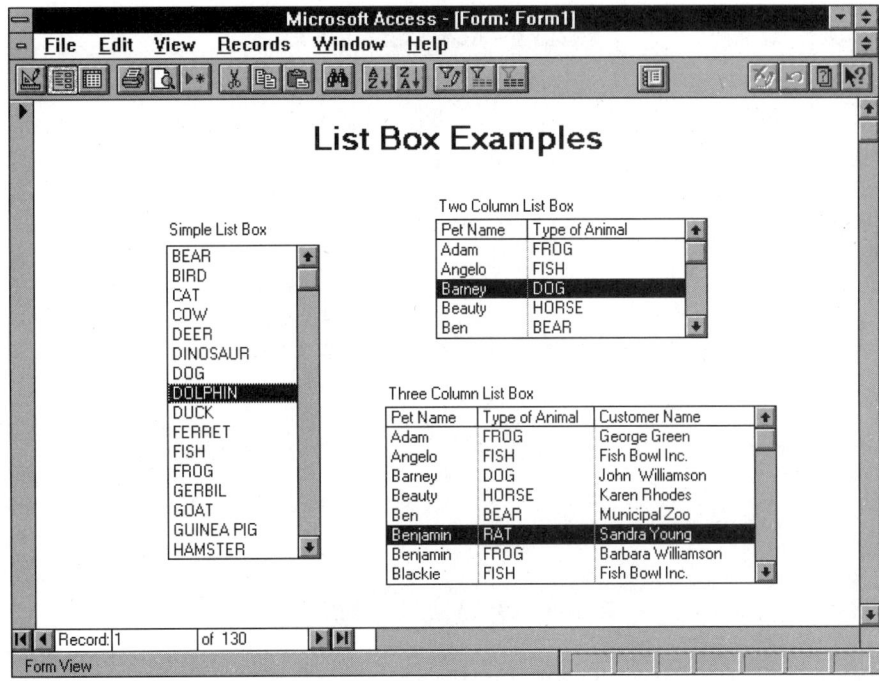

Figure 16-8: Sample list boxes.

Button to open combo box

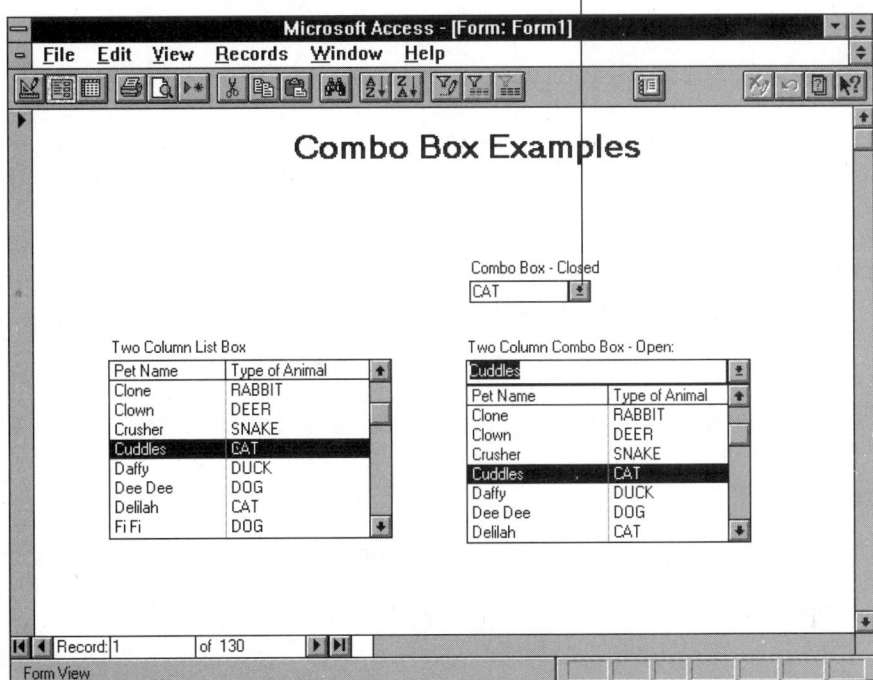

Figure 16-9: Sample combo boxes.

Creating New Controls

Now that you learned about the controls that can be used on a form or report, you should learn how to add controls to a form and how to manipulate them in the Form Design window. Although the Form Wizard can quickly place your fields in the Design window, you still may need to add more fields to a form. There are also many times when you simply want to create a report from a completely blank form.

The two ways to create a control

You can create a control in either of two ways:

- Dragging a field from the Field List window to add a bound control
- Clicking a button in the toolbox and then adding a new unbound control to the screen

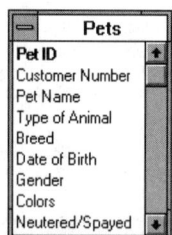

Figure 16-10: The resized Field List window.

Using the Field List window

The Field List window shown in Figure 16-10 displays all the fields in the open table/query that was used to create a form. This window is movable and resizable and also displays a vertical scroll bar if there are more fields than will fit in the window.

You can use two ways to display the Field List window:

- Click on the Field List button in the toolbar. (This button looks like a table).
- Select View⇨Field List... from the Form menu bar.

After you resize or move the Field List window, it remains that size for all forms even if it is toggled off or if the form is closed. Only if you exit Access is the window set to its default size.

When a field is dragged from the Field List window, it generally creates a bound text box on the Form Design screen. If an OLE field is dragged from the Field List window, a bound object frame is created. You can optionally select the type of control by first selecting a control from the toolbox and then dragging the field to the Form Design window.

When you drag fields from the Field List window, the first control is placed where you release the mouse button. Make sure that there is enough space to the left of the control for the labels. If there is insufficient space, the labels will slide under the controls.

There are several distinct advantages to dragging a field from the Field List window:

- The control is automatically bound to the field that you dragged.
- Field properties inherit table-level formats, status-bar text, and data-validation rules and messages.
- The label text is created with the field name as the caption.

Using the toolbox

By using the toolbox buttons to create a control, you can decide what type of control is to be used for each field. If you don't create the control by dragging it from the Field List window, the field will be unbound with a default label name such as Field3 or Button11. After you create the control, you can decide what field to bind the control to, and you can also enter any text you want for the label and set any properties you want.

The basic deciding factor for using the field list or the toolbox is simply whether the field exists in the table/query or whether you want to create an unbound or calculated expression. By using the Field List window and the toolbox together, you can create bound controls of nearly any type. You will find, however, that some data types do not allow all the control types found in the toolbox. For example, if you attempt to create a graph from a single field, you simply get a text box.

If you want to create multiple controls with the toolbox, you can select a control button and then click on the Lock button. This action locks the last control button and lets you create multiple controls. To unlock the button, simply click again on Lock or click on the Pointer button at the top of the toolbox.

You cannot change the type of control! For example, suppose that you create a field as a text box control and you want to change it to an option button. You must delete the text box control and then create a new option button control.

Dragging a field name from the Field List window

The easiest way to create a text box control is to drag a field from the Field List window. When the Field List window is open, you can click on an individual field and drag it to the Form Design window. This window works exactly in the same way as a Table/Query window in QBE. You can also select multiple fields and then drag them to the screen together. The techniques include the following:

- Selecting multiple contiguous fields by holding down the Shift key and clicking the first and last field you want
- Selecting multiple noncontiguous fields by holding down the Ctrl key and clicking each field you want
- Double-clicking the table/query name in the window's top border to select all the fields

After you select one or more fields, you can drag the selection to the screen.

To drag the Pet Name, Type of Animal, Date of Birth, and Neutered/Spayed fields from the Field List window, follow the next set of steps. If you haven't created a new form, create one first and resize the form as instructed at the beginning of this chapter.

Steps:	Dragging Fields from the Field List Window
Step 1.	Click the Field List button to display the Field List window.
Step 2.	Resize the Field List window so you can see the Neutered/Spayed field.
Step 3.	Click the Pet Name field.
Step 4.	Hold the Ctrl key down and click Type of Animal.
Step 5.	Hold the Ctrl key down and click Date of Birth.
Step 6.	Hold the Ctrl key down and click Neutered/Spayed.
Step 7.	Release the Ctrl key and click any highlighted field while holding down the mouse button.
Step 8.	Drag the fields (a Multiple Field icon appears) to the Form Design window and release.

When you complete these steps successfully, your screen should look like Figure 16-11.

Four controls are displayed in the Form Design window. Each of the controls is made up of a label control and a text box control. Access automatically attaches the label control to the text box. You can work with these controls as a group or independently, and you can select, move, or delete them. To resize them, you must work with them separately. Notice that each control is a text box control. Each control has a label with a caption matching the field name, and the text box control displays the bound field name used in the text box control.

Chapter 16: Understanding Controls and Properties   381

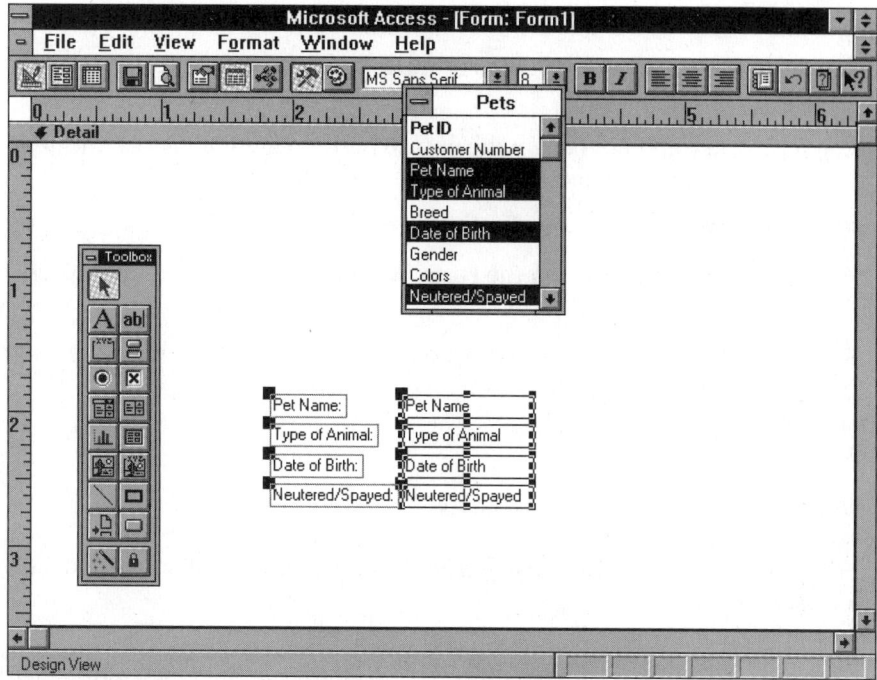

Figure 16-11: Fields dragged from the Field List window.

 You can close the Field List window by clicking the Field List button in the toolbar.

Creating unbound controls with the toolbox

You can create one control at a time by using the toolbox. You can create any of the controls listed in the toolbox. Each control becomes an unbound control that has a default label and a name.

To create three different unbound controls, perform the following steps:

Steps:	Creating Unbound Controls with the Toolbox
Step 1.	Click the Text Box button in the toolbox (the button appears sunken).
Step 2.	Place the cursor in the Form Design window (the cursor has changed to the Text Box button).
Step 3.	Click and hold down the mouse button where you want the control to begin and drag the mouse to size the control.

Part III: Using Access in Your Work

Step 4. Click the Option Button button in the toolbar (the button appears sunken).

Step 5. Place the cursor in the Form Design window (the cursor has changed to an Option button).

Step 6. Click and hold down the mouse button where you want the control to begin and drag the mouse to size the control.

Step 7. Click the Checkbox button in the toolbar (the button appears sunken).

Step 8. Place the cursor in the Form Design window (the cursor has changed to a checkbox).

Step 9. Click and hold down the mouse button where you want the control to begin and drag the mouse to size the control.

When you are done, your screen should resemble Figure 16-12.

 If you just click the Form Design window, Access will create a default-sized control.

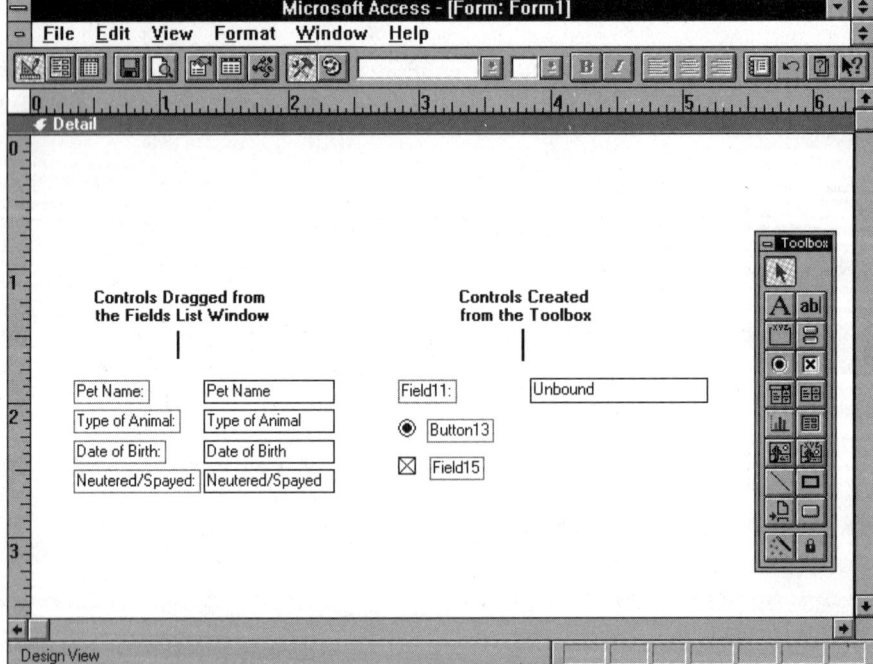

Figure 16-12: Adding three new controls.

Notice in Figure 16-12 the difference between the controls that were dragged from the Field List window and the controls that were created from the toolbox. The Field List window controls are bound to a field in the Pets table and are appropriately labeled and named. The controls created from the toolbox are unbound and have default names. Notice that control names are automatically assigned based on the type of control and a number.

Later, you learn how to change the control names, captions, and properties. By using properties, you will quickly be able to name the controls and bind the controls to specific fields.

Selecting Controls

After you have a control on the Form Design window, you can begin to work with it. The first step in working with the control is to select one or more controls. A selected control appears with *handles* around the control box area. A selected control generally has from four to eight handles. A handle appears as a small square and is generally located on the corners of a control box and also at the midpoint of the sides, depending on the size of the control. The handle in the upper left corner is larger than the other handles and is used to move the control. The other handles are used to size the control. Figure 16-13 displays these controls.

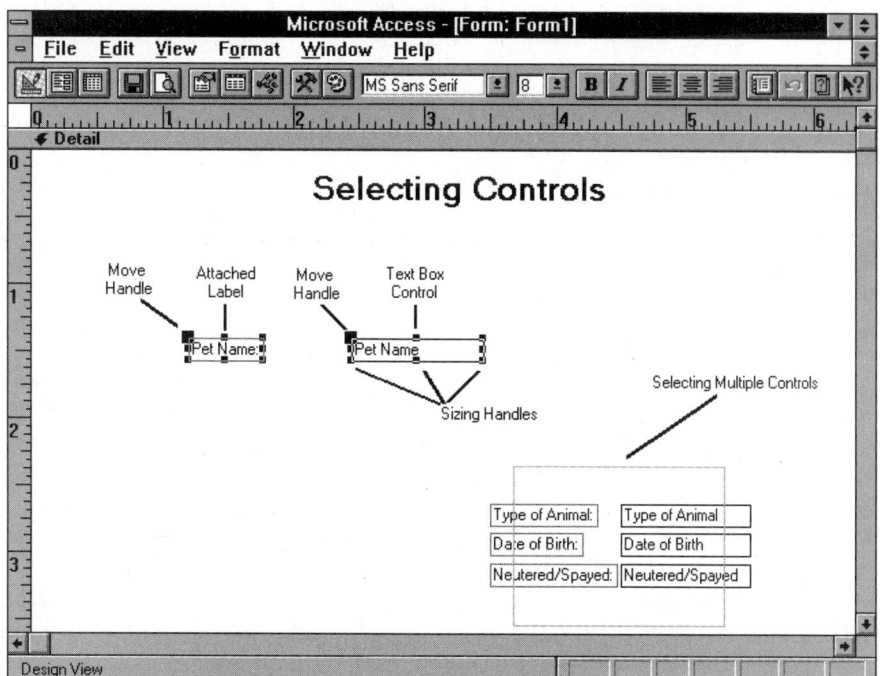

Figure 16-13: A conceptual view of selecting controls.

The pointer tool in the toolbox must be on for you to select a control. The pointer always appears as an arrow pointing diagonally to the upper left corner. If you selected another button in the toolbox and then selected the Lock button in the toolbox, you must click on the pointer again to change the cursor to a selection pointer. If you use the toolbox to create a single control, Access automatically reselects the pointer as the default cursor.

Deselecting selected controls

It is good practice to deselect any selected controls before you select another control. You can deselect a control by simply clicking on an unselected area of the screen that does not contain a control. When you do so, the handles disappear from any selected control.

Selecting a single control

You can select any single control by simply clicking anywhere on the control. When you click on a control, all the handles appear. If the control has an attached label, the handle for moving the label appears as well. If you select a single label control that is part of an attached control, all the handles in the label control are displayed, and only the move handle is displayed in the attached control.

Selecting multiple controls

You can select multiple controls in these ways:

- Click each desired control while holding down the Shift key.
- Drag the pointer through the controls you want to select.
- Click either ruler and drag to the desired area

The screen in Figure 16-13 shows some of these concepts graphically. When you select multiple controls by dragging the mouse, a light grey rectangle appears as you drag the mouse. When you select multiple controls by dragging the pointer through the controls, be careful to select only the controls you want to select. Any control that is touched by the line or enclosed within it is selected. If you want to select labels only, you must make sure that the selection rectangle encloses only your passes through the labels.

When you click on a ruler, an arrow appears and a line is displayed across the screen. You can drag the cursor to widen the line. Each control that the line touches is selected.

Chapter 16: Understanding Controls and Properties

If you find that controls are not selected when the rectangle passes through the control, you may have the Selection Behavior global property set to Fully Enclosed. This means that a control will be selected only if the selection rectangle completely encloses the entire control. The normal default for this option is Partially Enclosed. You can change this option by first selecting View⇨Options... and then selecting Form & Report Design Category in the Options dialog box. The option Selection Behavior should be set to Partially Enclosed.

By holding down the Shift key, you can select several noncontiguous controls. This lets you select controls on totally different parts of the screen, cut them, and then paste them together somewhere else on-screen.

Manipulating Controls

Creating a form is generally a multistep process. The next step is to make sure that they are properly sized and moved into the correct position.

Resizing a control

You can resize controls by using any of the smaller handles on the control. The handles in the control corners let you make the field larger or smaller both in width and height and at the same time. You use the handles in the middle of the control sides to size the control larger or smaller in one direction only. The top and bottom handles control the height of the control, whereas the handles in the middle change the control width.

When a corner handle is touched by the cursor in a selected control, the cursor becomes a diagonal double arrow. You can then hold down the mouse button and drag the control size handles to the desired size. If the cursor touches a side handle in a selected control, the cursor changes to a horizontal or vertical double-headed arrow. Figure 16-14 shows the Pet Name control after resizing. Notice the double-headed arrow in the corner of the Pet Name control.

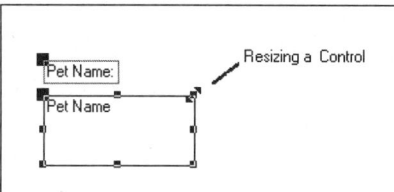

Figure 16-14: Resizing a control.

You can resize a control in very small increments by using the Shift + arrow keys.

You can resize only one control at a time. If a control is attached to a label, each must be resized separately.

Moving a control

After you select a control, you can move it. Use either of these methods to move an unselected control:

- Click the control and drag the control to a new location.
- Select the control and then place your cursor *between* any two move handles on the control's border.

As soon as you enter an area of a selected control that can be clicked and moved, your cursor changes to a hand button, as shown in Figure 16-15.

If the control has an attached label, you can move both the label and the control by this method. It doesn't matter whether you click on the control or the label; they are moved together.

You can move a control separately from an attached label by simply grabbing the move handle of the control and moving it. You can also move the label control separately from the other control by selecting the move handle of the label control and moving it separately.

Figure 16-15 shows a label control that has been separately moved to the top of the text box control. The Hand button indicates that the controls are ready to be moved together.

You can move a control in small increments with the keyboard by using Ctrl + the arrow keys after a control or group of controls is selected.

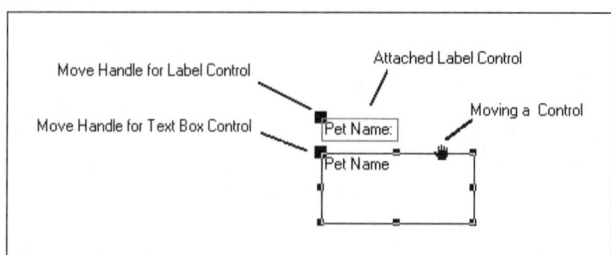

Figure 16-15: Moving a control.

You can restrict the direction in which a control is moved so that it maintains alignment within a specific row or column. To do this procedure, hold down the Shift key as you press the mouse button to select and move the control. The control will move only in the direction you first move it, whether horizontally or vertically.

You can cancel a move or a resizing operation by pressing Esc before you release the mouse button. After a move or resizing operation is completed, you can select the Undo button or select Edit⇨Undo Move or Edit⇨Undo Sizing to undo the changes.

Aligning controls

You may want to move several controls so that they are all aligned (lined up). The Format⇨Align menu has several options, as shown in Figure 16-16 and described in the following list:

Left   Aligns the left edge of the selected controls with that of the leftmost selected control.

Right   Aligns the right edge of the selected controls with that of the rightmost selected control.

Top   Aligns the top edge of the selected controls with that of the topmost selected control.

Bottom   Aligns the bottom edge of the selected controls with that of the bottommost selected control.

To Grid   Aligns the top left corners of the selected controls to the nearest grid point.

By selecting from this menu, you can align any number of controls. When you choose one of the options, the control that is the closest to the desired selection is used as the model for the alignment. For example, suppose you have three controls and you want to left align them. They will be aligned based on the control farthest to the left in the group of the three controls.

Figure 16-16 shows several groups of controls. The first group is not aligned. The label controls in the second group of controls has been left aligned. The text box controls in the second group have been right aligned. Each label and its attached text box have been bottom aligned.

Each type of alignment must be done separately. In this example, you can left align all of the labels or right align all of the text boxes at once. However, you would have to align each of the label and text control's bottoms separately. That would take three separate alignments.

You might notice a series of dots in the background of Figure 16-16. This is the *grid*. The grid is used to assist you in aligning controls. The grid is displayed by selecting View⇨Grid.

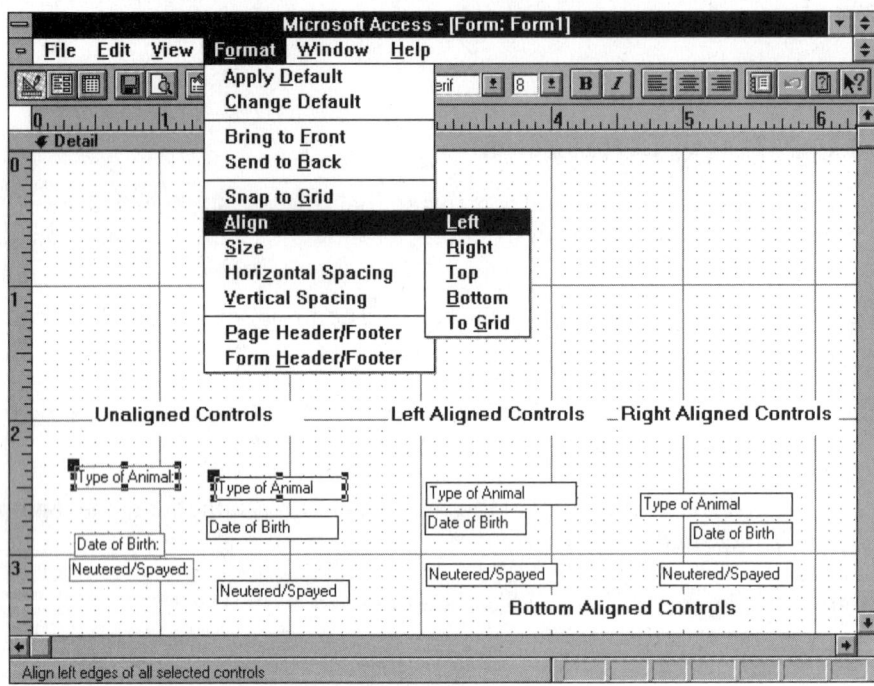

Figure 16-16: Aligning controls and the grid.

In Figure 16-16, you can see the Snap to Grid option above the Align menu option. This aligns new controls to the grid as you draw or place them on a form. It also aligns existing controls when you move or resize them.

When Snap to Grid is on and you draw a new control by clicking and dragging the form, Access aligns all four corners of the control to points on the grid. When you place a new control just by clicking the form or report, only the upper left corner is aligned.

As you move or resize existing controls, Microsoft Access lets you move only from grid point to grid point. When Snap to Grid is off, Microsoft Access ignores the grid and lets you place a control anywhere on the form or report.

You can temporarily turn off Snap to Grid by holding down the Ctrl key before or while you're creating or moving a control.

The Size option on the Format menu has several options that assist you in sizing controls based on the value of the data, the grid, or other controls. The options of the size menu are the following:

to Fit	Adjusts the height and width of controls to fit the font of the text they contain.
to Grid	Moves all sides of selected controls in or out to meet the nearest points on the grid.
to Tallest	Sizes selected controls so that they have the same height as the tallest selected control.
to Shortest	Sizes selected controls so that they have the same height as the shortest selected control.
to Widest	Sizes selected controls so that they have the same width as the widest selected control.
to Narrowest	Sizes selected controls so that they have the same width as the narrowest selected control.

The grid's fineness (number of dots) can be changed from form to form by using the GridX and GridY Form properties. The grid is invisible if its fineness is greater than 16 units per inch horizontally or vertically. (Higher numbers indicate greater fineness.)

In Access 2.0, there is another pair of alignment options that can make a big difference when aligning the space between multiple controls. The options Horizontal Spacing and Vertical Spacing change the space between controls based on the space between the first two selected controls. If the controls are across a screen, use the horizontal spacing. If they are down a screen, use the vertical spacing. This may be one of the most useful new features of Access 2.0.

Deleting a control

If you find that you no longer want a specific control on the Form Design window, you can delete it by selecting the control and pressing Delete. You can also select Edit⇨Delete to delete a selected control or Edit⇨Cut to cut the control to the Clipboard.

You can delete more than one control at a time by selecting multiple controls and pressing one of the Delete key sequences. If you have a control with an attached label, you can delete the label only by clicking on the label itself and then selecting a delete method. If you select the control, both the control and the label will be deleted. To delete the label only of the Pet Name control, follow the next steps. This example assumes that you have the Pet Name text box control in your Form Design window:

Steps:	Deleting the Pet Name Label Control
Step 1.	Select the Pet Name label control only.
Step 2.	Press Delete.

The label control should be removed from the window.

Attaching a label to a control

If you accidentally delete a label from a control, you can reattach it. To create and then reattach a label to a control, follow these steps:

Steps:	Attaching a Label to a Control
Step 1.	Click the Label button in the toolbox.
Step 2.	Place the cursor in the Form Design window (the cursor has changed to the Text Box button).
Step 3.	Click and hold down the mouse button where you want the control to begin and drag the mouse to size the control.
Step 4.	Type **Pet Name:** and click outside the control.
Step 5.	Select the Pet Name label control.
Step 6.	Select Edit⇨Cut to cut the label control to the Clipboard.
Step 7.	Select the Pet Name text box control.
Step 8.	Select Edit⇨Paste to attach the label control to the text box control.

Copying a control

You can create copies of any control by duplicating them or by copying them to the Clipboard and then pasting them where you want them. If you have a control for which you entered many properties or if you formatted the control a certain way, you can copy it and revise only the properties, such as the control name and bound field name, to make it a different control. This is also useful when you have a multiple-page form and you want to display the same values on different pages and in different locations.

Changing the control type

If, after creating a control and customizing it, you decide to change the control, you have to do some work. Unfortunately, there is no way to simply change a control. Suppose, for example, that you created a text box control for the Neutered/Spayed field and you decide to change it to a checkbox. You have to delete the text box control and create the checkbox control by using the toolbox. This is true for all controls.

You may have noticed that the Form Wizard automatically creates Yes/No fields as checkboxes. It does this by creating a checkbox control and then binding the control to the Yes/No field.

What Are Properties?

Properties are named attributes of controls, fields, or database objects that you can use to modify the characteristics of the control, field, or object. These attributes can be the size, color, appearance, or name. Or a property can modify the behavior of a control, such as by determining whether the control is editable or visible.

Properties are used extensively in forms and reports for changing the characteristics of controls. Each control has properties. In a form, the form itself also has properties, as does each section of a form. The same is true for reports. The report itself has properties, as does each report section and each individual control. The label control also has its own properties even if it is attached to another control. In the last example, you actually changed the Caption property of the label control from Pet Name to Name of Pet.

Properties are displayed in a property sheet. The property sheet is also commonly called a property window because it is an actual window. The first column contains the property names, whereas you enter properties in the second column. Figure 16-17 shows a property sheet for the Date of Birth text box.

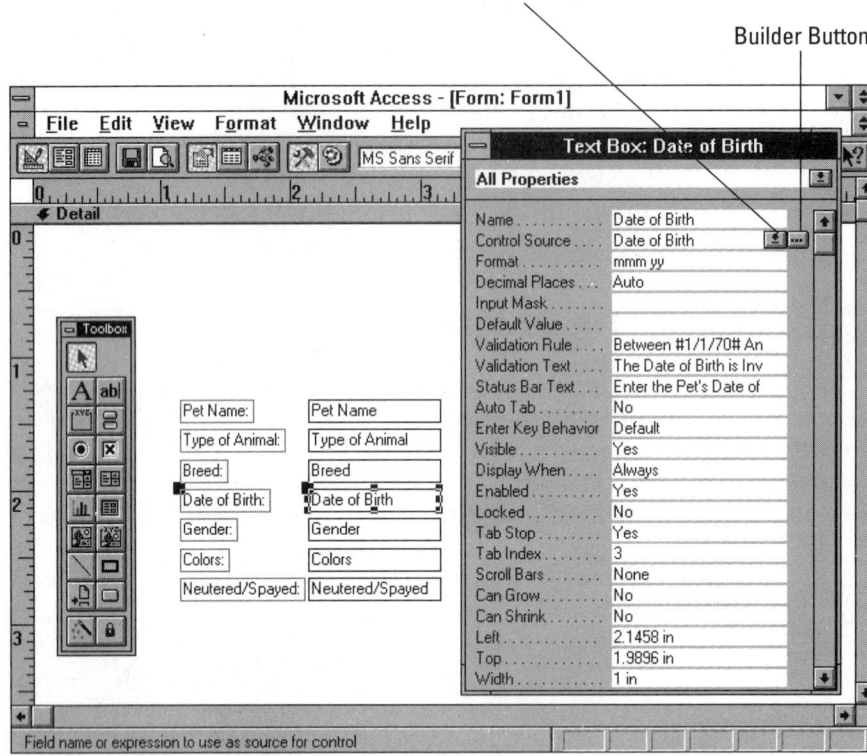

Figure 16-17: The property sheet for the Date of Birth text box.

Viewing a control's properties

There are several ways to view a control's properties:

- Select View➪Properties... from the menu bar.
- Click the control and then click the Properties button in the toolbar.
- Double-click any control.
- Right-click and choose Properties from the shortcut menu.

To display the property sheet for the Date of Birth text box control, follow these steps:

Steps:	Displaying the Property Sheet
Step 1.	Create a new blank form, using the Pets table.
Step 2.	Drag the fields Pet Name through Neutered/Spayed from the Field List window to the Form Design window.

Step 3. Click the Date of Birth text box control to select it.

Step 4. Click the Properties button in the toolbar.

As you can see in Figure 16-17, a partial property sheet is displayed. It has also been resized larger. By widening the property sheet, you can see more of the property values, and, by increasing the vertical size, you can see more controls at one time. The vertical scroll bar lets you move between various properties. Only the text box control has more properties than can fit on-screen at one time. Because the property sheet is a true window, it can be moved anywhere on-screen and resized to any size. It does not, however, have Maximize or Minimize buttons.

The property window lets you see all the properties for a control or you can limit the view to specific properties. The specific groups of properties include:

Data — Properties that effect how a value is displayed and the control it is bound to: Control source, formats, input masks, validation, default value, and other table level properties

Layout — How a label or value looks: font, size, color, special effects, borders, scroll bars

Event — Event properties are the named events, such as a mouse click, adding a record, pressing a key for which you can define a response (in the form of a call to a macro or an Access Basic procedure), and so on

Other — Other Properties shows additional characteristics of the control, such as the name of the control or the description that appears on the status bar

The number of properties available in Access 2.0 are nearly double those in Access 1.1. The most important new properties are described in various chapters of this book. New event properties and event procedures are discussed specifically in Chapters 30, 31, and 32.

The properties displayed in Figure 16-17 are the specific properties for Date of Birth. The first two properties, Name and Control Source, reflect the field name Date of Birth.

The Name is simply the name of the control itself. You can give the control any name you want. Unbound controls have names such as Field11 or Button13. When a control is bound to a field, it automatically is named to match the bound field name.

The Control Source is the name of the table field that the control is bound to. In this example, the Date of Birth field is the name of the field in the Pets table. An unbound control has no control source, whereas a calculated control's control source is the calculated expression, as in the example =[Weight] * .65.

The following properties are always inherited from the table definition of a field for a text box or other type of control. Figure 16-17 shows these properties inherited from the Pets table:

- Format
- Decimal Places
- Status Bar Text
- Input Mask
- Default Value
- Validation Rule
- Validation Text

 Changes made to a control's properties don't affect the field properties in the source table.

Each type of control has a different set of properties, as do objects such as forms, reports, and sections within forms or reports. In the next few chapters, you learn about many of these properties as you use each of the control types to create complex forms and reports.

Changing a control property

You can display properties in a property sheet, and you can change the properties by using many methods. Following is a list of methods you can use to change properties:

- Entering the desired property in a property sheet
- Directly changing a property by changing the control itself
- Using inherited properties from the bound field
- Using inherited properties from the control's default selections
- Entering control color selections using the palette
- Changing text style, size, color, and alignment by using the toolbar buttons

Chapter 16: Understanding Controls and Properties

You can change a control's properties by simply clicking on a property and typing the desired value.

In Figure 16-17, an arrow and a button with three dots are displayed to the right of the Control Source property entry area. Some properties display the arrow in the property entry area when you click into the area. This tells you that a pop-up list of values is provided to choose from. If you click on the down arrow in the Control Source property, you find that the choices are a list of all fields in the open table.

The three dots on a button is the builder button. This is used to open one of the many builders in Access 2.0. This includes the macro builder, the expression builder, and the module builder.

Some properties have a list of standard values such as Yes or No, whereas others display varying lists of fields, forms, reports, or macros. The properties of each object are determined by the object itself and what the object is used for.

Default properties

The properties you see in a specific control's property sheet are for that specific control. You can see a control's properties by clicking the control. You can also create a set of default properties for the type of control by clicking the toolbar button for that control type. For example, to view or change the default properties for a text box in the current form, follow these steps:

Steps:	Displaying Default Properties
Step 1.	Make sure that the property sheet is displayed.
Step 2.	Click the Text Box button in the toolbox.

As you can see in Figure 16-18, these are some of the default properties for a text box. You can set these properties, and from then on, each new text box that you create will have these properties as a starting point. This set of default properties can determine the color and size for new controls, the font used, the distance between the attached label and the control, and most other characteristics.

By changing the default property settings, you can create customized forms much more quickly than by changing every control.

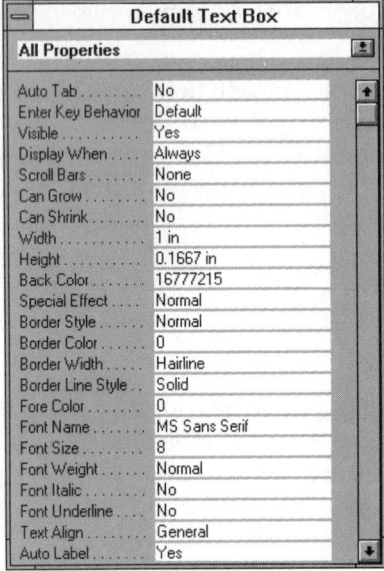

Figure 16-18: Displaying default properties.

Access provides many tools for customizing your data entry and display forms, as well as reports. You can also apply the default properties to existing controls and even save a set of default controls as a template. You can then use the template as the basis for a new form. By learning these techniques, you can save even more time when creating new forms and reports.

Applying default properties to existing controls

You can apply a set of default properties to selected controls by using the Format➪Apply Default menu option. When you choose this option, each selected control will reflect the current default properties for its specific control type — text box defaults applied to text boxes, option button defaults applied to option button controls, and so on.

Changing default properties

You've learned that you can change individual default properties by changing them one at a time in the default property sheet for each control. You also learned that you can apply the default properties to new or existing controls. You can also change a set of default properties by applying the properties of an existing control. In this way, the property settings of selected controls become the default settings for new controls of the same type when placed on the current form or report. To do this, select the control whose properties you want as the default and select Format⇨Change Default.

 These types of changes apply to the current form or report only. You can also change the defaults for all forms and reports by creating new templates.

Creating a new template for forms and reports

When you create a form or report without using a Form Wizard or Report Wizard, Access uses a template to define the default characteristics of the form or report. The template determines which sections a form or report will have and defines each section's dimensions. The template also contains all the default property settings for the form or report and its sections and controls. The default templates for forms and reports are called *Normal*. However, you can use any existing form or report as a template. You can also create a special form or report to use as a template. To set the Form Template or Report Template option, you must set the options in the global Options window, as shown in Figure 16-19. To change the template, follow these steps:

Steps:	Changing the Default Template
Step 1.	From the View menu, choose Options.
Step 2.	In the Category drop-down list, select Form & Report Design.
Step 3.	In the Items box, select Form Template or Report Template and then type the name of the form or report you want to use as a template.

Form and report templates define the following:

- Whether to include a form or report header and footer
- Whether to include a page header and footer
- What the dimensions (height and width) of the sections will be
- Which control default properties to use

A template doesn't create controls on a new form or report. You must still do that. But each new control you create has the properties of the default controls.

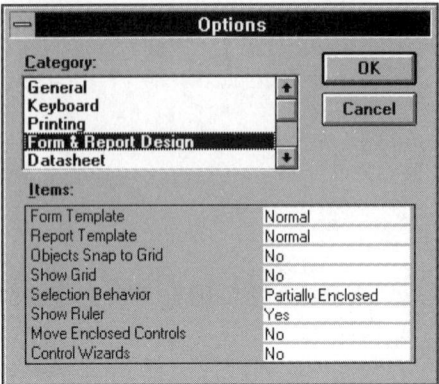

Figure 16-19:
The global Options menu.

To use your templates in other databases, copy or export the templates to them. If your templates are not in a database, Access uses the Normal template for any new forms and reports you create. However, the names of your templates appear in the Form Template and Report Template options in every database in your database system even if the templates are not in every database.

Summary

In this chapter, you learned the basic usage of controls and properties for forms and reports. The following points were examined:

- You can create a new blank form by selecting File⇨New⇨Form⇨Blank Form.

- A control is an object on a form or report, such as a label or a text box.

- There are three types of controls: bound, unbound, and calculated.

- Text boxes are the most common type of control and let you enter and display data.

- Controls often have attached label controls to identify the purpose of the control.

- You can create a new control by dragging a field from the Field List window or by using the toolbox.

- The Field List window displays a list of all fields from the current table or query.

- You can drag a field from the Field List window to create a bound control.

- You can select a control by clicking on it. You can select multiple controls by either clicking on them while holding down the Shift key or by dragging a rectangle to enclose the controls.

Chapter 16: Understanding Controls and Properties

- You can resize controls by using the small resizing handles found in a selected control.

- You can move controls by dragging them. An attached control can be moved separately from its attached label by use of the larger move handles in the upper left corner of a selected control.

- You can align controls by using the Align options of the Format menu. Controls can also be copied, duplicated, and deleted.

- Using the Size options of the Format menu, you can change the size of controls consistently.

- You can space controls evenly by using the Horizontal and Vertical Spacing options in the Format menu.

- Properties are named attributes of controls, fields, or database objects. You can set properties that modify the characteristics of the control, such as size, color, or appearance.

- Properties are displayed in a property sheet. Each type of control has different properties.

- Although an individual control has its own properties, each form maintains a set of default properties for each type of control on the form.

- You can create a template based on the current value of all default controls to be used in other forms.

In the next chapter, you learn how to use controls to create a new form without using a Form Wizard.

Creating and Customizing Data-Entry Forms

CHAPTER 17

In This Chapter

- Creating a multiple-file query to be used for the form
- Creating a blank form bound to the query
- Learning about form-level properties
- Reviewing placement of fields on a form
- Modifying controls on a form
- Setting the tab order of a form
- Creating controls for Memo and OLE fields
- Creating a form using two tables
- Creating a multiple-page form
- Learning how to use form and page headers and footers
- Printing a form
- Converting a form to a report

In Chapter 16, you learned about all the tools necessary to create and display a form. In this chapter, you use all the skills you learned to create several types of data-entry and display forms.

Following Along in This Book

In this chapter, you use the Customer and Pets tables in the MTNSTART database to create several types of simple forms. Each control will be explained by the use of one or more fields in these tables.

Creating a Standard Data-Entry Form

The first form that you create in this chapter is a simple data-entry form that uses two tables. In Chapter 9, you created a simple pets data-entry form by using a Form Wizard. In this section of the chapter, you create the more complicated form that you see in Figure 17-1. This form demonstrates the use of label and text box controls from multiple tables, as well as embedded pictures. You'll continue to modify this form in the next several chapters, adding more complicated controls and emphasis.

Assembling the data

With this design in mind, you need to assemble the data. To create this form, you need fields from two tables, Customer and Pets. Table 17-1 lists the necessary fields and their table location.

To assemble this data, you first need to create a query called Pets and Owners, which includes all fields from both tables even though you aren't going to use all the fields. This gives you the flexibility to add a field later without redoing the query. This can happen, for example, when you see that you'll need another field from which to derive a calculated control.

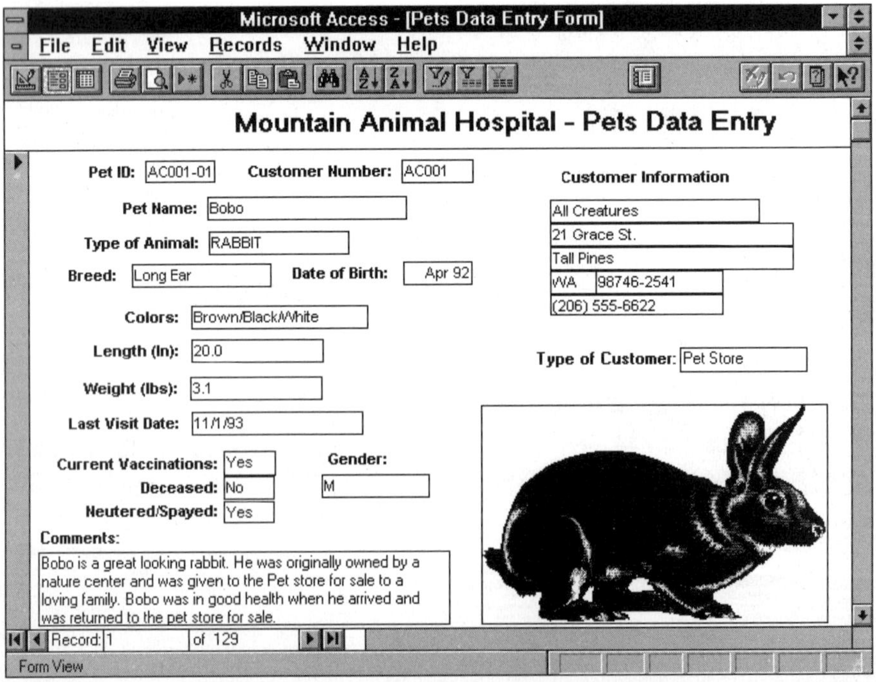

Figure 17-1:
A complicated data-entry form.

Table 17-1
The Fields Needed for the Pets Data-Entry Form

Fields from Pets Table	Fields from Customer Table
Pet ID	Customer Name
Customer ID	Street/Apt
Pet Name	City
Type of Animal	State
Breed	ZIP Code
Date of Birth	Phone Number
Colors	Type of Customer
Length	
Weight	
Last Visit Date	
Current Vaccinations	
Deceased	
Neutered/Spayed	
Gender	
Comments	
Picture	

In this example, you also create a sort by Pet ID. It's always a good idea to arrange your data into some known order. When you display a form, you see the data in its *physical* order unless you sort the data.

To create the Pets and Owners query, follow these steps:

Steps: Creating the Pets and Owners Query

Step 1. Click the query object to create a new query.

Step 2. Click New Query in the New Query dialog box. The Add Table dialog box appears.

Step 3. Add the Customer table.

Step 4. Add the Pets table.

Step 5. Close the Add Table dialog box.

Step 6. Drag the asterisk (*) from the Customer field list to the first column in the QBE design pane.

Step 7. Drag the asterisk (*) from the Pets field list to the second column in the QBE design pane.

Step 8. Drag the Pet ID field from the Pets field list to the third column in the QBE pane.

Step 9. Click the Pet ID Show: box to turn it off.

Step 10. Change the Sort to Ascending in the Pet ID field, as shown in Figure 17-2.

Step 11. Select File⇒Close, then select Yes, and name the query **Pets and Owners**.

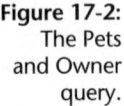

You use the asterisk (*) to select all fields from each table.

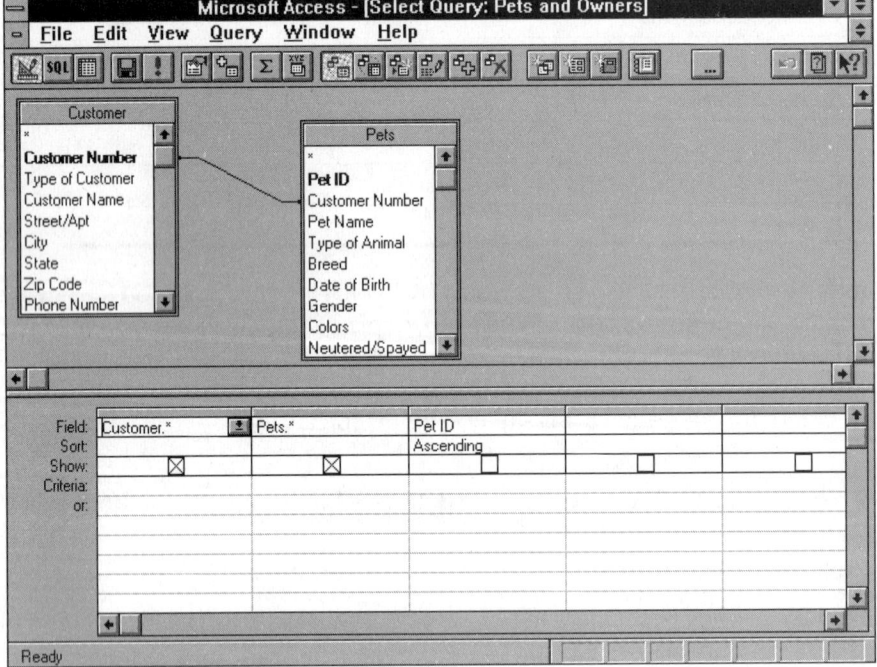

Figure 17-2: The Pets and Owner query.

Creating a new form and binding it to a query

Now that you've created the Pets and Owners query, you can create a new form and bind it to the query. Follow these steps to complete this process:

Steps:	Creating a New Form and Binding It to a Query
Step 1.	Press the database icon to display the Database window if it is not already displayed.
Step 2.	Click the Form object button.
Step 3.	Click the New command button. The New Form dialog box appears.
Step 4.	Click the Select A Table/Query edit box. A drop-down list of all tables and queries in the current database appears.
Step 5.	Select the Pets and Owners query.
Step 6.	Click the Blank Form button.
Step 7.	Maximize the Form window.

You now see a blank Form Design window, as shown in Figure 17-3. The form is bound to the query Pets and Owners, as you can see in the property sheet on the screen. This means that the data from that query will be used when the form is viewed or printed. The fields from the query are available for use in the form design and will appear in the Field List window.

If you need to create a form that contains no field controls, you may want to create a blank form that is not bound to a query. You can do this simply by not selecting a table/query before you select the Blank Form button.

Defining the form display size

When you are creating your form, you must resize the workspace of the form. The white area in the form shown in Figure 17-3 is your *workspace*. However, if you place controls in the grey area, the workspace automatically expands larger than the area where the control is placed. The size of the workspace depends on the size of your form. If you want the form to fill the screen, you should size it to the size of your screen. This depends on your screen resolution. You can fit more on-screen if you are using a Super

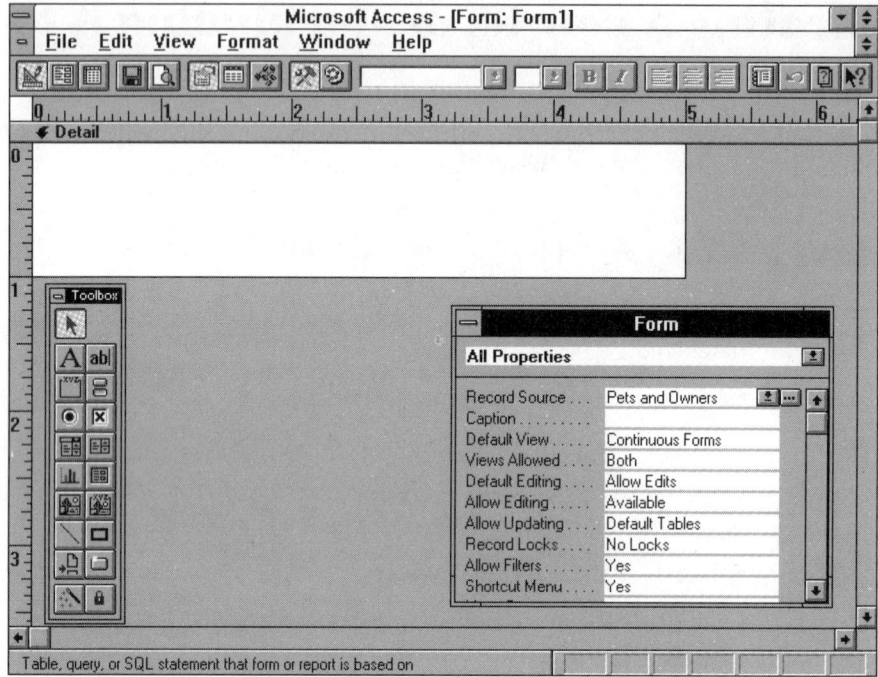

Figure 17-3:
The blank Form Design window.

VGA screen size of 800 × 600 or 1024 × 1024 than you can if you are using the standard VGA size of 640 × 480. However, because you never know who may use a form you create, you should stay with the smallest size that any anticipated user may have.

A maximized standard VGA screen set to 640 × 480 can display a full-screen size of slightly less than 6⅜ inches by 4 inches. This includes the space for the title bar, menu bar, and toolbar at the top, the record-pointer column down the left side, the vertical scroll bar areas down the right side, and the navigation buttons/scroll bar and status line at the bottom. Of course, you can control most of these elements by setting the form properties.

The easiest way to set the form size is simply to use your mouse to grab the borders of the white area and resize it as you want. If you can grab either the top or bottom borders, your cursor turns into a double arrow. If you grab the corner, the cursor becomes a four-headed arrow, and you can size both sides at the same time. You can see this four-headed arrow cursor in Figure 17-4. For this example, you should set the form size to 6 5/16 inches by 3 15/16 inches by following the next steps and using Figure 17-4 as a guide. At this size, no form scroll bars appear.

Chapter 17: Creating and Customizing Data-Entry Forms

Steps: Changing the Form Size

Step 1. Place the cursor at the bottom right corner of the vertical and horizontal borders, where the white space meets the grey area. The cursor should appear as a four-headed arrow.

Step 2. Grab the corner and drag the borders by pressing the left mouse button until the size is exactly 6 5/16 inches by 3 15/16 inches.

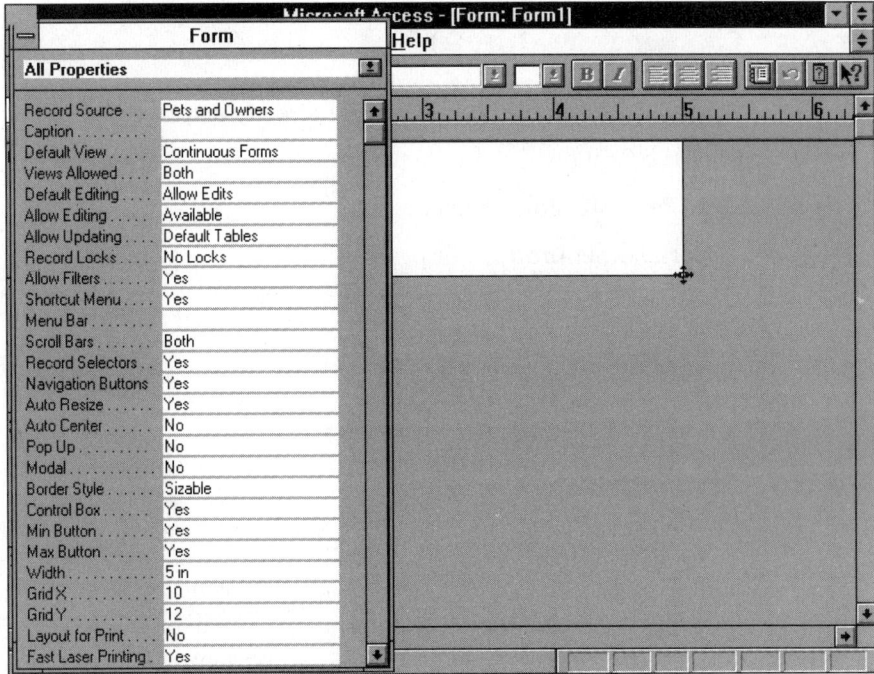

Figure 17-4: Form Properties.

If you add controls beyond the right border, you have to scroll the form to see these controls. This is generally not acceptable in a form. If you add controls beyond the bottom border, you have to scroll the form to see these controls as well. This is acceptable, as the form becomes a multiple-page form. Later in this chapter, you learn how to control multiple-page forms.

Changing form properties

You can set many form properties to change the way the entire form is displayed. Some of the most important properties shown in Figure 17-4 are described in Table 17-2.

Some of these properties work together to create certain behaviors in the form that are worth noting in more detail here. Other property characteristics are noted later in this chapter.

Changing the title bar text with the Caption property

Normally, the title bar displays the name of the form after it is saved. By changing the Caption property, you can display a different title in the title bar when the form is run. To change the title bar text, follow these steps:

Steps:	Changing the Title Bar Text
Step 1.	Display the property sheet if it is not already displayed.
Step 2.	Click the Caption property in the property sheet.
Step 3.	Type **Pets Data Entry Form.**
Step 4.	Click any other property or press Enter.

You can display the blank form by selecting the Form button on the toolbar to check the result. The caption you enter here overrides the name of the saved form.

Setting the various views

Two properties determine how your form displays records: Default View and Views Allowed. The Views Allowed property has three settings: Form, Datasheet, and Both. The default setting is Both. This setting lets the user switch between form and datasheet view. If the Views Allowed property is set to Datasheet, the Form button and the View⇨Form menu selections are not selectable, and the data can be viewed only as a datasheet. If the Views Allowed property is set to Form, the Datasheet button and the View⇨Datasheet menu selections are not selectable, and the data can be viewed only as a form.

Table 17-2
Form Properties

Property	Description	
Caption	Displayed in the title bar of the displayed form	
Default View	Determine the type of view when the form is run	
	Single Form	One record per page
	Continuous Forms	As many records per page as will fit (Default)
	Datasheet	Standard row and column datasheet view

Chapter 17: Creating and Customizing Data-Entry Forms

Property	Description	
Views Allowed	Determines whether the user can switch between the two views	
	Form	Form view only is allowed
	Datasheet	Datasheet view only is allowed
	Both	Form or Datasheet view are allowed
Default Editing	Determines the type of input and editing allowed when the form is run	
	Allow Edits	Allows both new input and edits
	Read Only	For display only, no changes or new entries allowed
	Data Entry	Displays a new blank form for new record entry only
	Can't Add Records	New records cannot be added
Allow Editing	Allows access to the Records⇨Allow Editing menu to change a Default Editing property of Read Only to Allow Edits temporarily	
	Available	Menu is available to the user
	Unavailable	Menu is not available to the user
Allow Updating	Used to override the standard updatability rules	
	Default Tables	Only the default tables are updateable
	Any Tables	Controls from all tables are editable
	No Tables	All controls are display only
Record Locks	Used to determine multiuser record locking	
	No Locks	Record is only locked as it is saved
	All Records	Locks entire form records while using the form
	Edited Records	Locks only the current record being edited
Allow Filters	Determines if new filters can be created and applied (Yes/No)	
Shortcut Menus	Determines if Shortcut menus are active	
Menu Bar	Used to specify an alternate menu bar; Builder button lets you create a new menu bar if you want	
Scroll Bars	Determines if any scroll bars are displayed	
	Neither	No scroll bars are displayed
	Horizontal Only	Display only the horizontal scroll bar
	Vertical Only	Displays only the vertical scroll bar
	Both	Displays both the horizontal and vertical scroll bars
Record Selectors	Determines if vertical record selector bar is displayed (Yes/No)	
Navigation Buttons	Determines if navigation buttons are visible (Yes/No)	
Auto Resize	Form is opened to display a complete record (Yes/No)	
Auto Center	Centers form on the screen when opened (Yes/No)	
Pop Up	Form is a pop-up form which floats above all other objects (Yes/No)	

(continued)

Table 17-2 *(continued)*

Property	Description	
Modal	A modal form is used when you must close the form before anything else can be done. Disables other windows. When Pop up is set to Yes, it also disables menus and the toolbar, creating a dialog box (Yes/No).	
Border Style	Determines form's border style	
	None	No border or border elements (scroll bars, navigation buttons)
	Thin	Thin border, not resizeable
	Sizeable	Normal form settings
	Dialog	Thick border, Title bar only, not sizeable, Use for dialog boxes
Control Box	Determines if control menu (Restore, Move Size...) is available (Yes/No)	
Min Button	Minimize Button is displayed (Yes/No)	
Max Button	Maximize Button is displayed (Yes/No)	
Width	Displays the value of the width of the form	
Grid X	Determines the number of points per inch when the X grid is displayed	
Grid Y	Determines the number of points per inch when the Y grid is displayed	
Layout for Print	Determines whether the form uses screen fonts or printer fonts	
	Yes	Printer Fonts
	No	Screen Fonts
Fast Laser Printing	Prints rules instead of lines and rectangles (Yes/No)	
Help File	Name of the compiled help file to assign custom help to the form	
Help Context ID	ID of the context-sensitive entry point in the help file to display	

The Default View property is very different. This property determines how the data is displayed when the form is first run. Three settings are possible: Single Form, Continuous Forms, and Datasheet. The first setting, Single Form, displays one record per form page regardless of the size of the form. The next setting, Continuous Forms, is the default. This tells Access to display as many detail records as will fit on-screen. Normally, you use this setting when you define a very small form in height, and many records can be displayed at one time. Figure 17-5 shows such a form. The records are small enough in height that a number of these records can be seen at once. The final Default View setting, Datasheet, simply displays the form as a standard datasheet when run. You should now change this property to single form.

Chapter 17: Creating and Customizing Data-Entry Forms

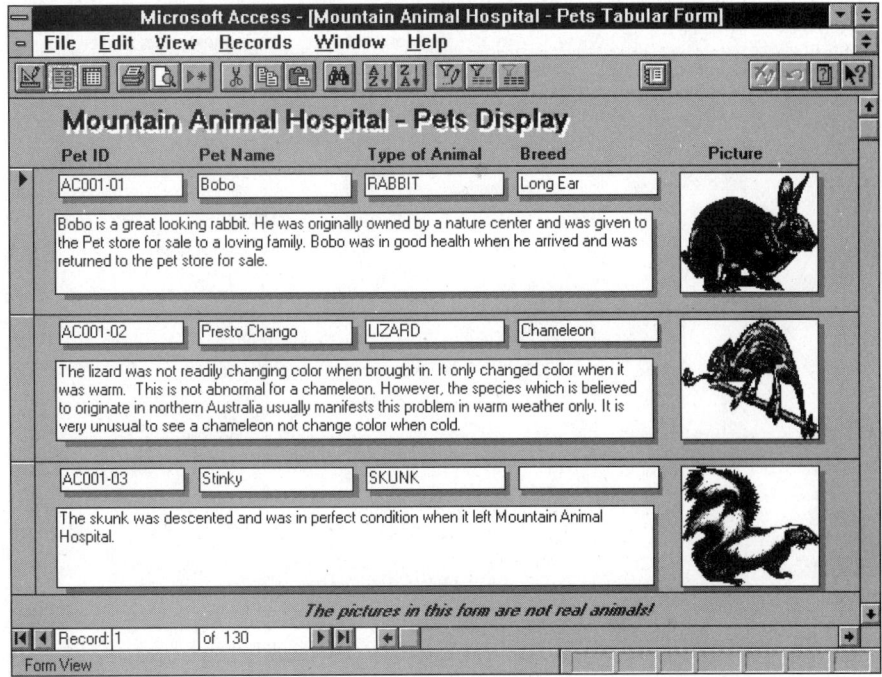

Figure 17-5: Using the Continuous Forms Default View property.

Placing fields on the form

The next step is to place the necessary fields onto the form. When you place a field on a form, it is no longer called a field; it is called a *control*. A control has a *control source*, which is a field that the control is bound to. Therefore, you see the terms *control* and *field* used interchangeably in this chapter.

As you've learned, the process of placing controls on your form consists of three basic tasks:

- Displaying the Field List window by clicking the Field List button in the toolbar
- Clicking the desired toolbox control to determine the type of control that is created
- Selecting each of the fields that you want on your form and dragging the fields to the Form Design window

Displaying the field list

To display the Field List window, click on the Field List button on the toolbar. You can resize the Field List window and move it around. The enlarged window is illustrated in Figure 17-6 and shows all the fields in the Pets and Owners query dynaset.

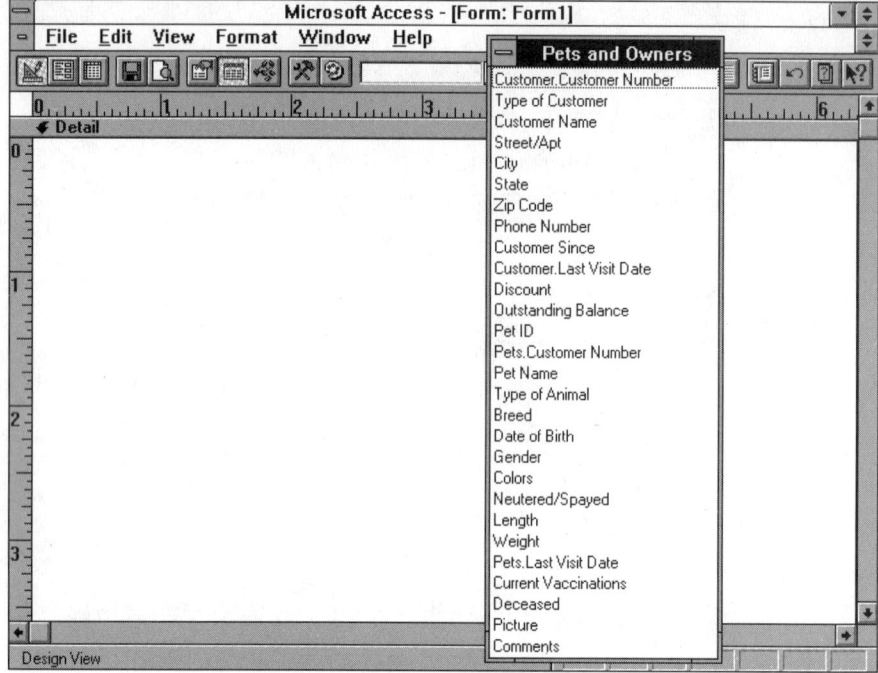

Figure 17-6:
The Field List window.

Notice, in Figure 17-6, that the fields Customer.Customer Number and Pets.Customer Number, as well as Customer.Last Visit Date and Pets.Last Visit Date, have the table name as a prefix. This prefix distinguishes fields of the same name that come from different tables within a query.

You can move the Field List window simply by clicking the title bar and dragging it to a new location. You can also select the Move command from the window's Control menu.

Selecting the fields for your form

Selecting a field in the Field List window is the same as selecting that field from a query field list. The easiest way to select a field is simply to click it. As you click a field, it is highlighted. Once a field is highlighted, you can drag it to the Form window.

You can highlight *contiguous* (adjacent) fields in the list. To do this, click the first field you want in the field list and then move the cursor to the last field you want; hold down the Shift key as you click the last field. The block of fields between the first and last field are displayed in reverse video as you select them. You can then drag the block of fields to the Form window.

Chapter 17: Creating and Customizing Data-Entry Forms

You can highlight noncontiguous fields in the list by clicking each field while holding down the Ctrl key. Each field is then displayed in reverse video and can be dragged as part of the group to the Form design window.

 Unlike the query field list, you *cannot* also double-click a field to add it to the Form window.

You can begin by selecting the Pets table fields for the detail section. To select the fields you need for the Pets Data Entry form, follow these steps:

Steps:	Selecting the Pets Table Fields
Step 1.	Click the Pet ID field.
Step 2.	Scroll down the field list until the Comments field is visible.
Step 3.	Hold down the Shift key and click the Deceased field.

The block of fields from Pet ID to Deceased should be highlighted in the Field List window.

Dragging fields onto your form

After you select the proper fields from the Pets table, all you need to do is drag the fields onto the form. Depending on whether you choose one or several fields, the cursor changes to reflect your selection. If you select one field, you see a Field icon, a box containing text. If you select multiple fields, you see a Multiple Field icon instead. These are the cursor icons you've seen in the Query Design screens.

To drag the Pets table fields onto the form, follow these steps:

Steps:	Dragging Selected Fields to the Form Design Window
Step 1.	Click within the highlighted block of fields in the Field List window.
Step 2.	Without releasing the mouse button, drag the cursor onto the form, placing it under the 1 ½-inch mark on the horizontal ruler at the top of the screen and the ⅜-inch mark of the vertical ruler along the left edge.
Step 3.	Release the mouse button. The fields now appear in the form, as shown in Figure 17-7.
Step 4.	Close the Field List window by clicking the Field List button on the toolbar.

Notice that there are two controls for each field you dragged onto the form. When you use the drag-and-drop method for placing fields, Access automatically creates a label control that uses the name of the field and is attached to the text control that the field is bound to.

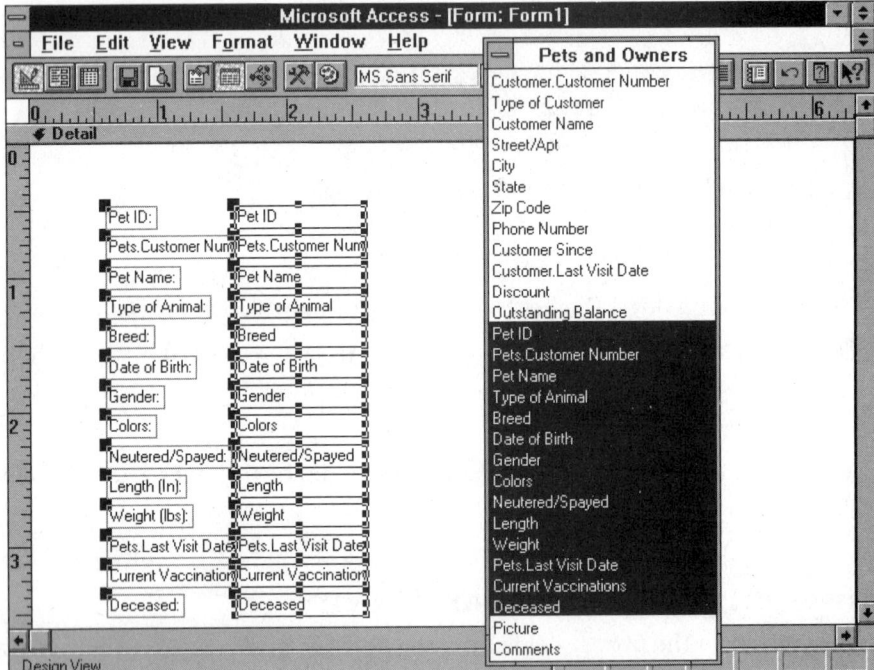

Figure 17-7: Dragging fields to the form.

Working with Label Controls and Text Box Controls

You've already seen how attached label controls are automatically created. You drag a field from the Field List window to a form with the Text Box button selected in the toolbox; this creates a text box control and also a label control *attached* to the text box control. But sometimes you want to add text label controls by themselves to create headings or titles for the form.

Creating unattached labels

To create a new, unattached label control, you must use the toolbox unless you copy an existing label. The next task in the example is to add the text header Mountain Animal Hospital Pets Data Entry to your form. This task is divided in segments to demonstrate adding and editing text. To begin this task, follow these steps:

Steps:	Creating an Unattached Label Control
Step 1.	Display the toolbox.
Step 2.	Click the Label button in the toolbox.
Step 3.	Click near the top left edge of the form at about the 1 ½-inch mark on the horizontal ruler; next, drag the cursor to make a small rectangle about 3 inches long and ¼ inch wide.
Step 4.	Type **Pets Data.**
Step 5.	Press Enter.

To create a multiple-line label entry, press Ctrl+Enter to force a line break where you want it in the control.

Modifying the text in a label or text control

To modify the text in a control, you need to click the inside of the label. When you do this, the cursor changes to the standard Windows text cursor, an I-beam. Also notice that the toolbar changes, and if you have the property sheet open, the properties are no longer displayed. The toolbar does not include any of the character-formatting buttons such as Bold, Italics, Font Size, and so forth. This is because within a label control — or any control — you cannot apply specific formatting to individual characters.

You can now make any edits you want to the text. If you drag across the entire selection so that it is highlighted, whatever is in this area is replaced by anything new that you type. Another way to modify the text is to edit it from the control's property sheet. The second item in the property sheet is Caption. In the Caption property, you can also edit the contents of a text (for a text control the property is called *Control Source*) or label control by clicking on the edit box and typing. To edit the label so that it contains the proper text, follow these steps:

Steps:	Editing Text in a Label Control
Step 1.	Click in front of the *P* in Pets Data in the label control.
Step 2.	Type **Mountain Animal Hospital** - before Pets Data.
Step 3.	Type **Entry** after Pets Data.
Step 4.	Press Enter.

If you want to edit or enter a caption that is longer than the space in the property sheet, the contents will scroll as you type. Or you can press Shift+F2 to open up a zoom box that gives you more space to type.

Modifying the appearance of text in a control

To modify the appearance of text within a control, select the control by clicking its border (not in it). You can then select a formatting style that you want to apply to the label. Just click on the appropriate button in the toolbar. To add visual emphasis to the title, follow these steps:

Steps:	Modifying the Appearance of Label Text
Step 1.	Click the form heading label.
Step 2.	Click the Bold button in the toolbar.
Step 3.	Click the drop-down arrow of the Font-Size list box.
Step 4.	Select 14 from the Font-Size drop-down list.

The label control still needs to be resized to display all the text.

Sizing a text box control or label control

You can select a control by simply clicking on it. Depending on the size of the control, from three to seven sizing handles appear. One appears on each corner except the upper left, and one appears on each side. When you move the cursor over one of the sizing handles, the cursor changes into a double-headed arrow. When this happens, click and drag the control to the size that you want. Notice that, as you drag, an outline of the new size appears. This outline indicates the new size of the label when you release the mouse button.

When you double-click any of the sizing handles, Access usually resizes a control to a "best fit" for the text in the control. This is especially handy if you increase the font size and then notice that the text is cut off, either at the bottom or to the right. For label controls, note that best-fit sizing adjusts the size vertically and horizontally, although text controls are resized only in the

Chapter 17: Creating and Customizing Data-Entry Forms

vertical dimension. This is because in form design mode, Access cannot predict how much of a field you want to display — the field name and field contents can be radically different. Sometimes, however, label controls are not resized correctly and must be manually adjusted.

You see that the text no longer fits within the label control. You can resize the text control to fit the enhanced font size. To do this, follow these steps:

Steps:	Resizing the Label Control
Step 1.	Click the Mountain Animal Hospital - Pets Data Entry label control.
Step 2.	Move the cursor over the control. Notice that the cursor changes as it moves over the sizing handles.
Step 3.	Double-click one of the sizing handles.

The label control size may still need readjustment. If so, you can place the cursor on the bottom right corner of the control so that the diagonal arrow appears; then drag the control until it is the correct size.

You can also select Format⇨Size⇨to Fit to change the size of the label control text automatically.

As you create your form, you should constantly test it by selecting the Form button in the toolbar. Figure 17-8 shows the form in its current state of completion.

Now that you dragged the Pets fields to the form design and added a form title, you can move the text box controls into the correct position. You then want to size each control to properly display the information within each field.

Moving label and text controls

Before you move the label and text controls, it is important to remind you of a few differences between attached and unattached controls. When an attached label is automatically created with a text control, it is called a *compound control*. In a compound control, whenever one control in the set is moved, the other control in the set is also moved.

To move both controls in a compound control, select one of the pair by clicking anywhere on it. Move the cursor over either of the objects. When the cursor turns into a hand, you can click and drag the controls to their new location.

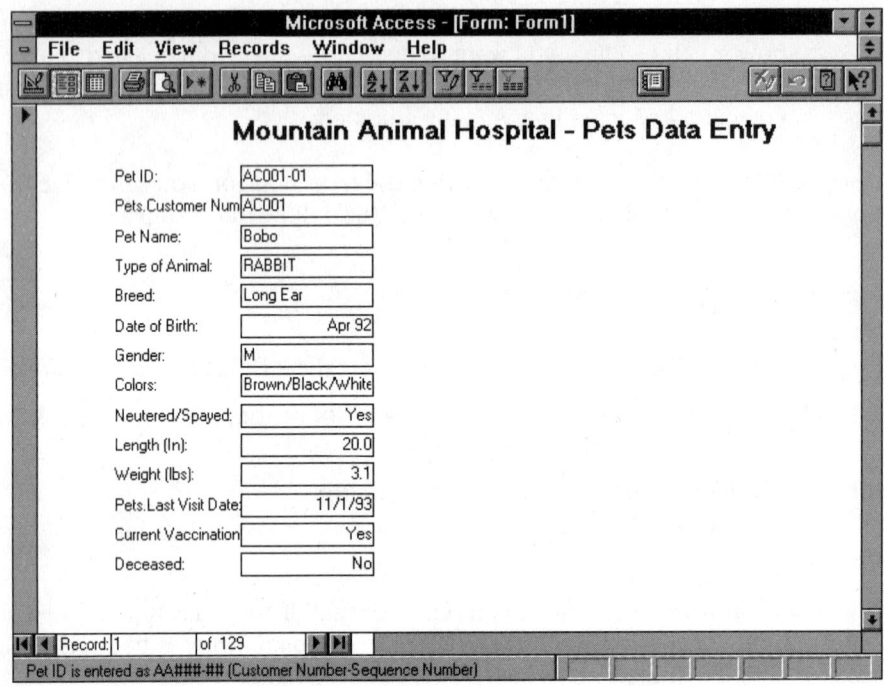

Figure 17-8: A form in progress.

Place the controls in their proper position to complete the form design and layout, as shown in Figure 17-9. Notice that the Gender control has its label moved to a position above the text box control. Also notice that some of the text labels are updated. Remember that you can do this by selecting the attached label control and then using the move handle to move only the label. Also notice that some formatting is added, as you'll do in the next section.

Modifying the appearance of multiple controls

The next step is to make all the label controls in the form bold. This helps you differentiate between label controls and text controls because some of them currently have the same text. The following steps guide you through modifying the appearance of multiple controls:

Chapter 17: Creating and Customizing Data-Entry Forms 419

Steps: Modifying the Appearance of Text in Multiple Label Controls

Step 1. Select all the attached label controls in the form by clicking them individually while holding down the Shift key. There are 14 label controls to select, as shown in Figure 17-9.

Step 2. Click the Bold button on the toolbar.

Step 3. Select Format⇨Size⇨to Fit to resize all the labels.

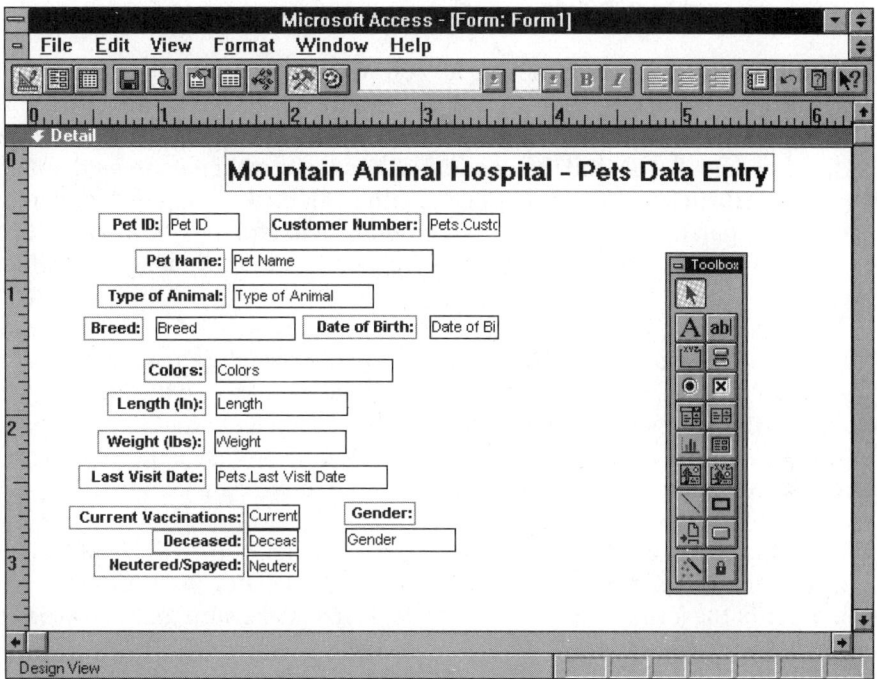

Figure 17-9: Selected and resized label controls in the detail section.

You cannot select all the label controls in the preceding steps by using the drag-and-surround method. This method also selects all the text boxes, but you want to only bold and resize the labels.

If you run the form now, you notice that the Length, Width, and Last Visit Date data items are all right-aligned within the text controls. You want to left-align these controls so that values appear left-aligned next to the label. To do this, follow these steps:

Steps:	**Modifying the Appearance of Multiple Text Box Controls**
Step 1.	Select the Length, Weight, and Pets. Last Visit Date text box controls only by drawing a box with the cursor around the three text box controls.
Step 2.	Click the Left Align button on the toolbar.

Setting the tab order

Now that you've completed moving all your controls into position, you should again test the form. If you run the form and use Tab to move from field to field, you notice that the cursor does not move from field to field in the order you expect. The cursor begins in the first field, Pet ID, and then continues vertically from field to field until it reaches the Date of Birth field. After the Date of Birth field, the cursor jumps down to the Gender field. After that, it moves back up to the Colors field and then down again to the Neutered/Spayed field. This may seem strange, but it's the original order in which the fields were added to the form.

This is called the *tab order* of the form. The form's default tab order is always the order in which the fields were added to the form. If you don't move the fields around, this is all right. However, if you move the fields around, you may want to change the order. Although you may make heavy use of the mouse when designing your forms, the average data-entry person uses the keyboard to move from field to field.

When you need to change the tab order of a form, select the Edit⇨Tab Order... menu option in the Design window to change the order to match your layout. To change the tab order of the form, follow the next set of steps. Make sure that you are in the Design window before continuing.

Steps:	**Changing the Tab Order**
Step 1.	Select Edit⇨Tab Order....
Step 2.	Click the Gender row in the Tab Order dialog box.
Step 3.	Click the Gender row again and drag the row to the bottom of the dialog box below the Deceased row, as shown in Figure 17-10.
Step 4.	Click the Neutered/Spayed row in the dialog box.

Chapter 17: Creating and Customizing Data-Entry Forms

Step 5. Click the Neutered/Spayed row again and drag the row to the bottom of the dialog box between the Deceased and Gender rows.

Step 6. Click the OK button to complete the task.

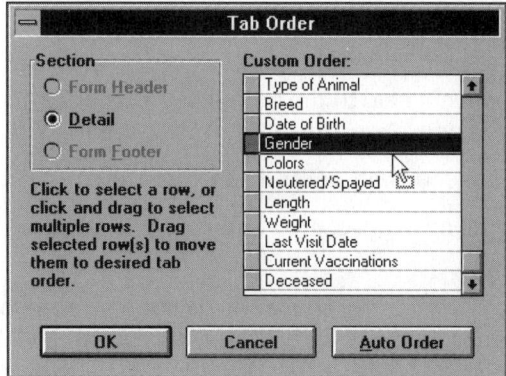

Figure 17-10: The Tab Order dialog box

The Tab Order dialog box lets you select either one row or multiple rows at a time. You can select multiple contiguous rows by clicking on the first row and then dragging down to select multiple rows. Once the rows are highlighted, you can drag the selected rows to their new position.

The Tab Order dialog box has several buttons at the bottom of the box. The Auto Order button places the fields in order from left to right and top to bottom, based on their position in the form. This button is a good place to start when you have significantly rearranged the fields.

Adding multiple-line text box controls for Memo fields

Multiple-line text box controls are used for Memo data types. The Comments field in the Pets table is a Memo field. When you add a Memo field to a form, make sure that there is plenty of room in the text box control to enter large amounts of text. You can use several ways to make certain you allow enough space.

The first way is to resize the text box control large enough to accommodate any text you may enter into the Memo field. However, this is rarely possible. Usually, the reason you create a Memo field is to hold very large amounts of text. The text can easily be larger than the entire form can display.

One of the options in a text box control is a vertical scroll bar. By adding scroll bars to your Memo field text box control, you can allow for any size of data entry. To create a Memo field text box control, follow these steps:

Steps:	Creating a Memo Field Text Box Control
Step 1.	Display the Field List window.
Step 2.	Drag the Comments field to the bottom left corner of the form below the Neutered/Spayed field just above the 3⅜-inch mark on the left ruler.
Step 3.	Move the Comments label control just above the text box control.
Step 4.	With the Comments label control selected, click the Bold button in the toolbar.
Step 5.	Resize the text box control so that the bottom of the control touches the bottom of the form border at the 3⅞-inch mark on the left ruler. The right side of the control should be just past the right side of the Gender text box control at 3¼ inches on the upper ruler.
Step 6.	Close the Field List window.

The next step is to add a vertical scroll bar to make it easier to scroll through large amounts of text. It is not mandatory to add a vertical scroll bar. When you display the Memo field in the text box control on the form, you can move through the data one line at a time. By adding the scroll bar, you greatly speed up your navigation abilities. To add a vertical scroll bar to the text box control, follow these steps:

Steps:	Adding a Vertical Scroll Bar to a Text Box Control
Step 1.	Select the Comments text box control.
Step 2.	Display the property sheet.
Step 3.	Click the Scroll Bars property and click the arrow.
Step 4.	Select Vertical.

The added control is shown in Figure 17-11.

When you run the form, the scroll bar appears only once when you move into the Comments Memo field.

Figure 17-11:
Adding a multiple-line text box control.

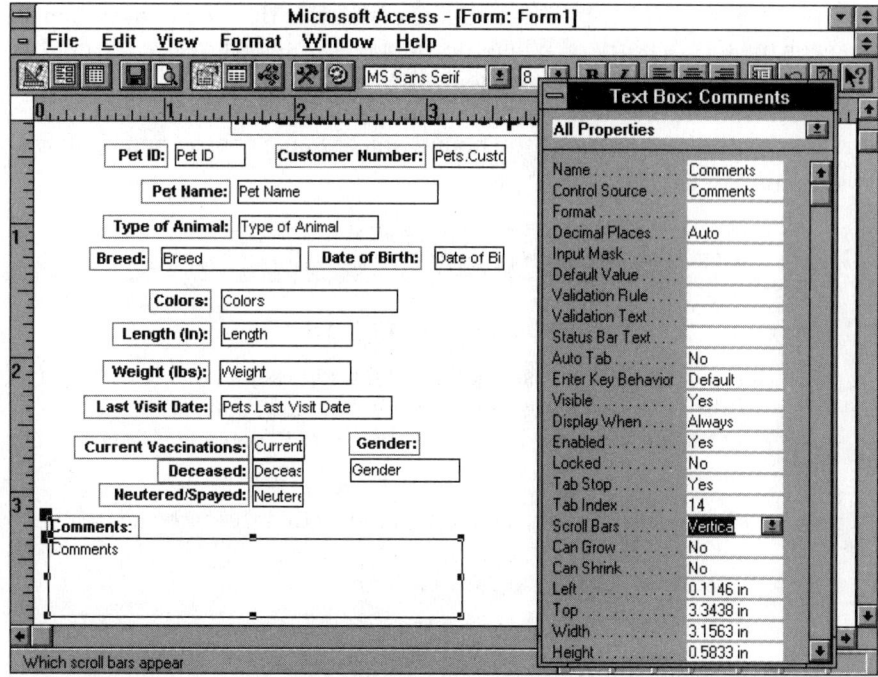

Adding a bound object frame to the form

When you drag an OLE data type field to a form, a bound object frame is automatically created. You can resize and move this control, just as you can move any control. To add the Picture OLE field to the form, follow these steps:

Steps:	Adding an OLE Field to a Form
Step 1.	Display the Field List window.
Step 2.	Drag the Picture field to the center right area of the form.
Step 3.	Select the Picture attached label control.
Step 4.	Press Delete to delete the attached label control.
Step 5.	Move the left edge of the bound object frame just to the right of the Comments text box at approximately 2 ¼ inches on the left ruler and 3 ½ inches on the top ruler.

One problem you may have when adding controls is that sometimes their default size exceeds the form's borders. When this happens, you must resize the control and also resize the border. If you don't resize the border, you find that the form becomes scrollable outside the normal screen boundaries. This may work, but it doesn't create a well-displayed form. To resize the bound object frame control and the form border, follow these steps:

Steps:	Resizing a Control and the Form's Border
Step 1.	Select the Picture bound object frame.
Step 2.	Resize the control so that the right edge is just inside the original form border at 6 1/8 inches on the top border and the bottom edge is at 3 7/8 inches at the left ruler. As you resize the control, you can follow the illustration in Figure 17-12.
Step 3.	Resize the form borders to make sure that they are at 6 5/16 inches and 3 15/16 inches.

When you are done, the design should look like Figure 17-12. Before you complete the OLE field, there is one more task to perform. The default value for the Size Mode property of a bound object frame is Clip. This means that a picture displayed within the frame is shown in its original size and truncated to fit within the frame. In this example, you need to display the picture so that it fits completely within the frame. Two property settings let you do this:

Zoom   Keeps picture in its original proportion; may result in extra white space

Stretch   Sizes picture to fit exactly into the frame borders

Although the Zoom setting more correctly displays the picture, the Stretch setting looks better, unless the picture's proportions are important to viewing the data. To set the Size Mode property, follow these steps:

Steps:	Setting the Scaling Property of a Bound Object Frame
Step 1.	Select the Picture bound object frame.
Step 2.	Display the property sheet.
Step 3.	Select the Size Mode property.
Step 4.	Select Stretch.

Chapter 17: Creating and Customizing Data-Entry Forms 425

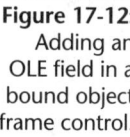

Figure 17-12:
Adding an OLE field in a bound object frame control.

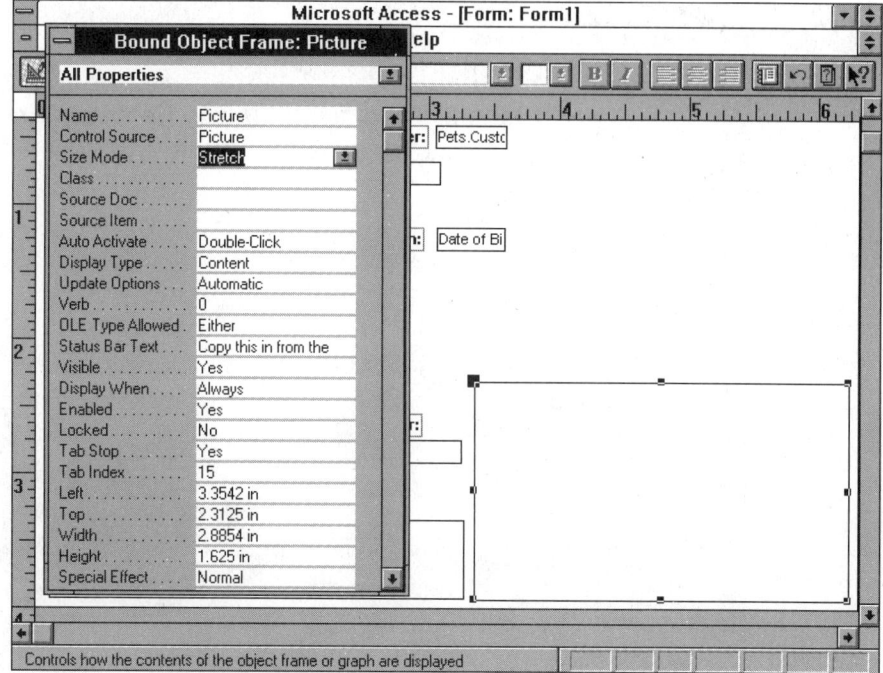

Figure 17-12 shows the form design as it currently is completed. Notice the property sheet for the bound object frame control. The Size Mode property is set to Stretch.

When you complete this part of the design, you should save the form and then display it. You can now name this form Pets Data Entry if you want. The form is shown in Figure 17-13.

So far, you created a blank form and added several types of controls to the form. However, only fields from the Pets table are on the form. You originally created a query that linked the Pets and Customer tables. The Customer table can serve as a lookup table for each Pet record. This allows you to display customer information for each pet.

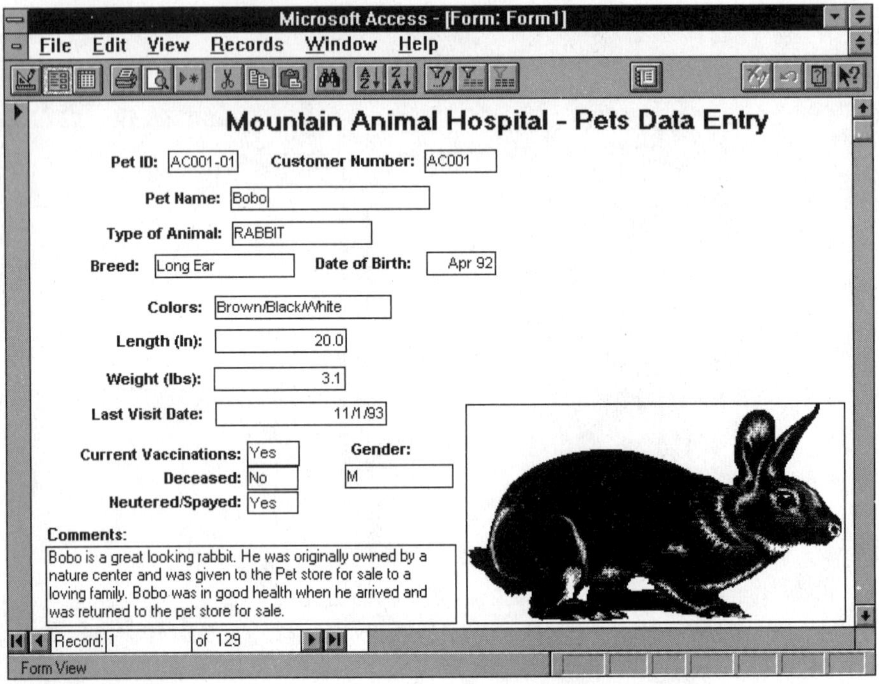

Figure 17-13:
The form with a Memo and OLE field.

Creating a Form Using Multiple Tables

When you create a form from a single table, you simply use fields from the one table. When you create a form from multiple tables, you usually use fields from a second table as lookup fields to let you display additional information. In this section, you learn how to display the customer information.

Adding fields from a second table

You now add the fields from a second table. You want to add the fields to be displayed in the Pets form from the Customer table. These fields will display the customer name and address, along with the Type of Customer field. You place these fields in the upper right portion of the form. Follow these steps to add the customer fields to the form:

Chapter 17: Creating and Customizing Data-Entry Forms   427

Steps:	**Selecting and Placing the Fields from the Customer Table**
Step 1.	Display the Field List window.
Step 2.	Click the Type of Customer field.
Step 3.	Hold down the Shift key and click the Phone Number field.
Step 4.	Click within the highlighted block of fields in the Field List window.
Step 5.	Without releasing the mouse button, drag the cursor onto the form under the 5-inch mark on the ruler at the top of the screen and the ½-inch mark of the ruler along the left edge.

At this point, your form should look like Figure 17-14. You've now placed all the fields needed for the Pets Data Entry form.

As you can see in Figure 17-14, the form begins with the Type of Customer field. Actually, you want that field separated from the others. Follow the next steps to move the Type of Customer control below the other customer controls. Use Figure 17-15 as a guide for the final placement of the field. Later, you'll change the field to a calculated field, as shown in Figure 17-15.

Figure 17-14: Adding the customer fields.

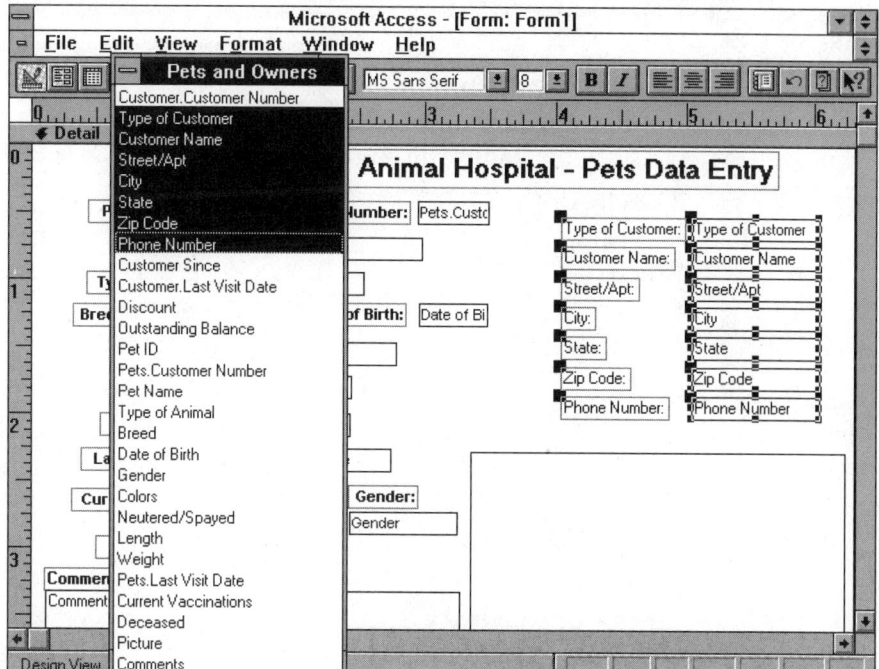

Steps:	**Moving a Single Control**
Step 1.	Deselect all the selected controls by clicking any empty area of the form.
Step 2.	Select just the Type of Customer text box control and its attached label.
Step 3.	Move the control just below the Phone Number control so that it is just above the Picture bound object frame control.

Working with attached label and text controls

As you can see in Figure 17-15, the remaining customer fields are to be displayed in a very small area of the screen. The fields will be displayed with no labels other than the label control Customer Information. It is very easy to delete one or more attached label controls in a form. You simply select the desired label control (or controls) and press Delete. When you delete attached controls, you have two choices:

- Delete only the label control
- Delete both the label control and the field control

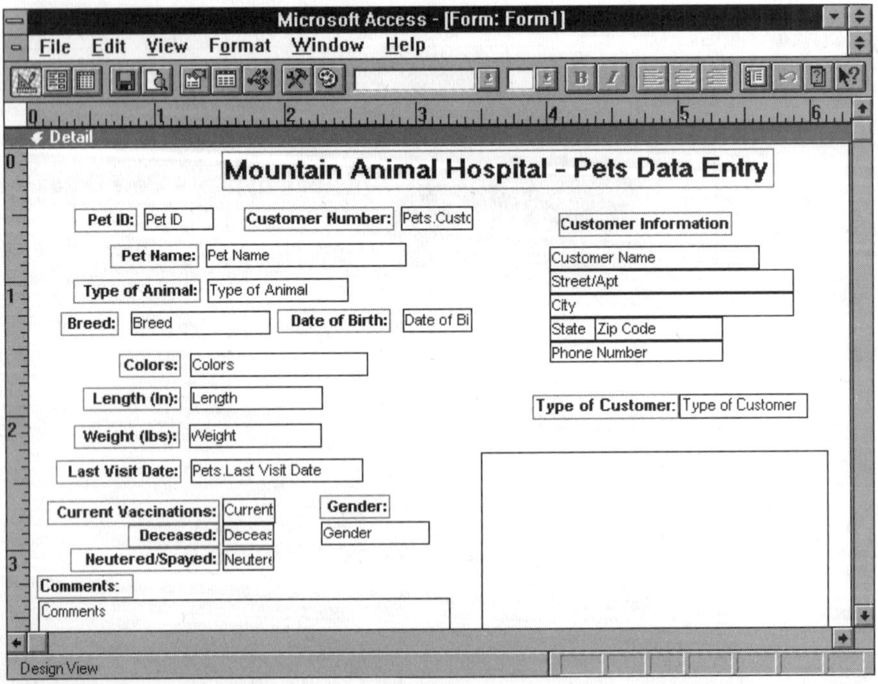

Figure 17-15: Customer fields in the Pets form.

Chapter 17: Creating and Customizing Data-Entry Forms 429

If you select the label control and press Delete, only the label control is deleted. If you select the field control and press Delete, both the label control and the field control are deleted. To delete only the Customer label controls, follow these steps:

Steps: Deleting an Attached Label Control

Step 1. Draw a box that surrounds only the six label controls from Customer Name through Phone Number.

Step 2. Verify that only the label controls are selected (sizing handles are displayed in all the label controls; only the move handle is displayed in the text box controls).

Step 3. Press Delete.

If you want to delete the field control yet keep the attached label control, you can do this by first selecting the label control and choosing Edit⇨Copy. Then select the field control and press Delete to delete both the field control and the label control. Finally, choose Edit⇨Paste to paste the copied label control to the form.

As you learned in Chapter 16, you can attach a label to an unlabeled control by cutting the unattached label control and then pasting it onto another control.

The final task is to move the customer controls to their final positions and add a label control, as shown in Figure 17-15. Follow these steps to complete this part of the form:

Steps: Completing Fields from a Second Table

Step 1. Rearrange the controls in the page header to resemble a typical mailing label address format, with State and ZIP Code on the same line.

Step 2. Move the Phone Number text box control under the City text box control.

Step 3. Move the block of name, address, and phone number controls into position so that it resembles Figure 17-15. Notice that all the control lines need to touch one another.

You can use the new Format⇨Vertical Spacing⇨Make Equal option to line up all the controls above each other. If there is still space between, then use the Decrease option as well.

Step 4. Create a label control with the text **Customer Information**, as shown in Figure 17-15.

Creating a calculated field

The field Type of Customer is a numeric field that displays a 1 if the customer is an individual, 2 if the customer is a pet store, and 3 if the customer is a municipal zoo, a bird sanctuary, or an aquarium. Rather than having the number displayed, you can transform the value into a more recognizable text expression.

The easiest way to do this is to delete the original Type of Customer control and replace it with a calculated expression. In Chapter 13, you learned about the function called the Immediate IF function (IIf) that lets you transform one value to another. In this example, the expression uses two IIf functions together.

The expression must transform the value of 1 to "Individual," the value of 2 to "Pet Store," and the value of 3 to "Zoo." This is the complete expression:

```
=IIf([Type of Customer]=1,"Individual",IIf([Type of Customer]=2,"Pet Store","Zoo"))
```

The first IIf function checks the value of the Type of Customer field; if the value is 1, the value of the calculated control is set to Individual. If the value is not 1, another IIf checks to see whether the value of Type of Customer is 2. If the value is 2, the value of the calculated control is set to Pet Store. If not 2, the value of the calculated control is set to the only other possibility, which is Zoo. To create this calculated control, follow these steps:

Steps:	Creating a New Calculated Control
Step 1.	Select the Type of Customer text box control.
Step 2.	Display the property sheet.
Step 3.	Change the Name to **Calculated Type of Customer.**
Step 4.	Click the Control Source property and press Shift+F2 to display the zoom box.
Step 5.	In the Control Source property, type the following: **=IIf([Type of Customer]=1,"Individual",IIf([Type of Customer]=2,"Pet Store","Zoo")).**
Step 6.	Select OK.
Step 7.	Close the property sheet.

Now that the form is complete, you can test it. Run the form and observe that the customer information is now displayed as you see it in Figure 17-16.

Chapter 17: Creating and Customizing Data-Entry Forms 431

Figure 17-16:
The form Pets Data Entry shown with customer information.

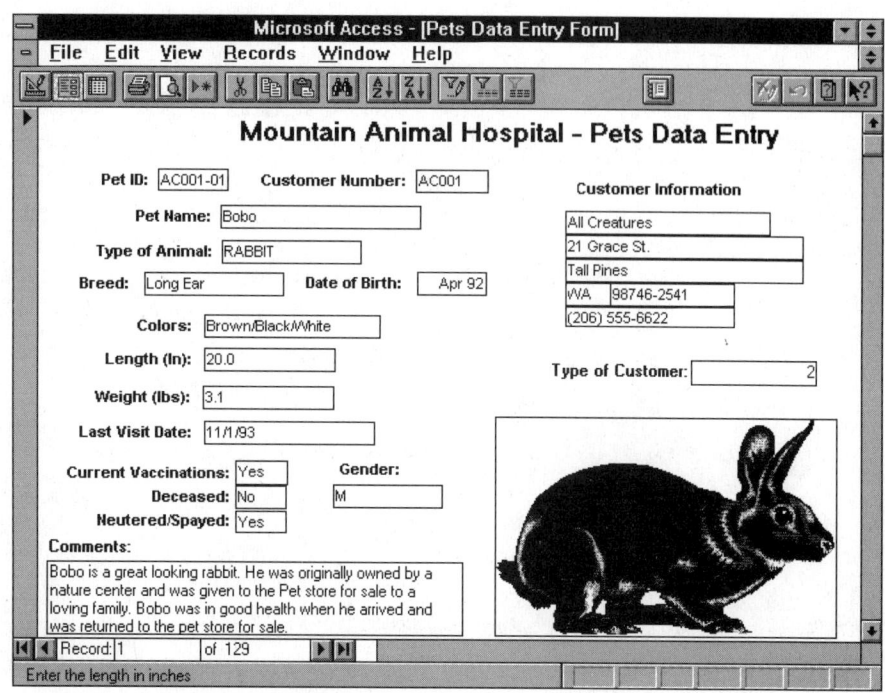

Following Along in This Book

You should save this form with all the changes currently made. Name the form Pets Data Entry Form - Without Formatting. You use this form later in the chapter and again in the next few chapters, starting with the form in its current state.

Changing the updatability of a multiple-table form

If you run the form you just created, you may notice that you can edit the existing pet data or even add new pet records. As you enter a new pet's valid customer number, the customer information is automatically filled in. However, you can change the customer information. This information is being looked up in the customer table. Since it can affect all records for this customer, you don't want to allow changes to the information fields.

To prevent changes to the customer information fields, use the Locked property. Select all of the fields under Customer information. Change the Locked property to Yes.

The Customer Number field is automatically locked because it is a primary key on one side of the relationship.

Changing Defaults for Attached Label Positioning

Attached label controls are called compound controls because the two controls are *attached*. Sometimes you want to disable this feature, which you can do by changing a default property named AutoLabel. When AutoLabel is set to Yes, a label control is automatically created that bears the name of the field that the text control is bound to. And with AutoLabel in effect, a label is automatically created every time you drag a field onto a form. Follow these steps to change the AutoLabel default:

1. Display the toolbox if it is not already displayed.
2. Display the property sheet if it is not already displayed.
3. Click on the Text Box button in the toolbar. The title of the property sheet should be Default Text Box.
4. Scroll down until you see the AutoLabel property.
5. Click the AutoLabel text box.
6. Change the contents in the text box to **No**.

The next property, AutoColon, automatically places a colon following any text in a new label if the value of the property is set to Yes.

Two properties control where the label appears relative to the control itself. These are the Label X and Label Y properties. Label X controls the horizontal position of the label control relative to the text box control. The default is –1 (to the left of the text box control). As you make the value a smaller negative number, as with .5, you decrease the space from the attached label to the control. If you want the label after the control (as you may for an option button), you use a positive number, such as 1.5, to move the label to the right of the control.

Label Y controls the vertical position of the label control relative to the text box control. The default is 0, which places the label on the same line as the text box control. If you want to place the label above the control, change Label Y to –1 or a larger negative number. The last option, Label Align, lets you control the alignment of the text within the label.

If you changed the AutoLabel default to No, and you now drag fields from the Field List window to the form, you see no label controls attached. The AutoLabel property is in effect only for this form. Because you don't need to add further labeled fields to this form, you can leave the setting of AutoLabel as No.

Chapter 17: Creating and Customizing Data-Entry Forms

 You must remember that by updating a field such as Customer Name, which is on the *one* side of a one-to-many relationship, you change the one data field in the Customer table that changes a value for all records of pets owned by that customer.

Figure 17-17 shows this property being changed for the Pets Data Entry form.

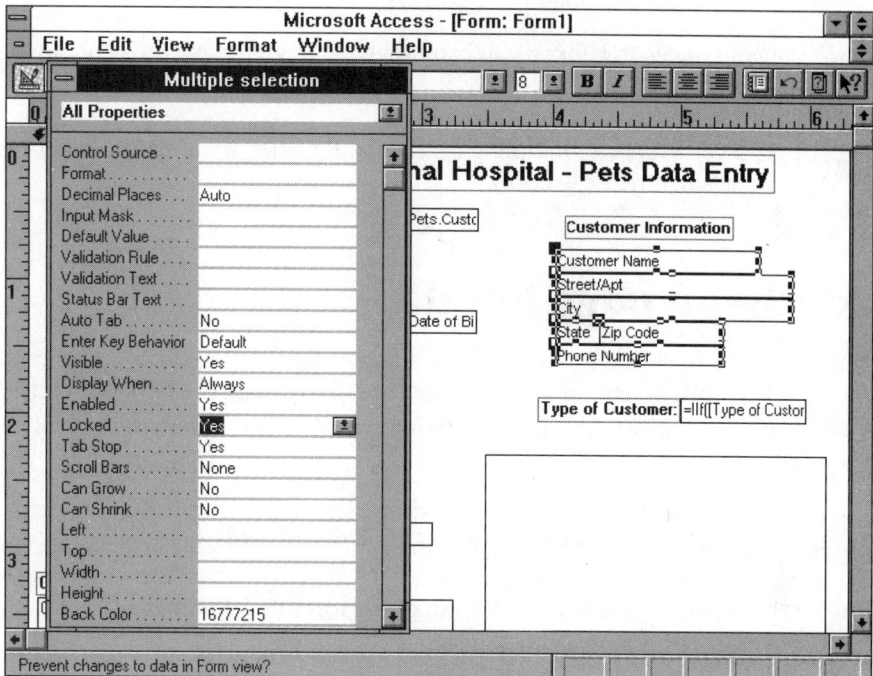

Figure 17-17: Locking the customer data from changes.

Creating a Multiple-Page Form

Suppose that you want to add more information to the form. There is little room left on the form to add more fields or labels. But you may want to see a larger picture of the animal and to see all comments at one time in the multiple-line text box. Without getting a larger form, you can't do that. You can't just make the screen bigger unless you change to a higher screen resolution, which means getting the necessary hardware. One solution is to create a multiple-page form.

Why use multiple-page forms?

You use multiple-page forms when all your information won't fit on one page or when you want to segregate specific information on separate pages. By using multiple-page forms, you can display less information on a page, making a complicated form look less cluttered. You can also place data items that are not always necessary on the second or even the third page, which makes data entry easier on the first page for the user.

You can have as many pages as you need on a form, but the general rule is no more than five pages or the form becomes very tedious. There is also a 22-inch size limitaiton in the form. By using a macro, you can attach other forms to buttons on the form; then you can call up the other pages as you need them by selecting a button.

Once you add pages to a form, you can move between the pages by using the PgUp and PgDn keys.

 You can create a multiple-page form only when the Default View property of the form is set to Single Form.

Adding a page break

You can add page breaks to a form by adding a page break control. This control is found in the bottom left corner of the toolbox. To change the Pets Data Entry form to add a separate page for resized picture and comments controls, follow the next steps. Use Figure 17-18 as a guide.

Steps:	Adding a New Page and a Page Break
Step 1.	Increase the bottom margin of the form to 7¾ inches.
Step 2.	Move and resize the Comments text box control, as shown in Figure 17-18.
Step 3.	Move and resize the Picture text box control.
Step 4.	Select the Pet Name text box control in the upper area of the control and select Edit⇒Copy.
Step 5.	Select Edit⇒Paste and move the copy to the second page of the form.
Step 6.	Display the toolbox.
Step 7.	Click on the Page Break button in the toolbox.
Step 8.	Move the cursor to the left corner of the intersection of the two pages.
Step 9.	Click the mouse to add the page break.

The completed design is shown in Figure 17-18.

Chapter 17: Creating and Customizing Data-Entry Forms 435

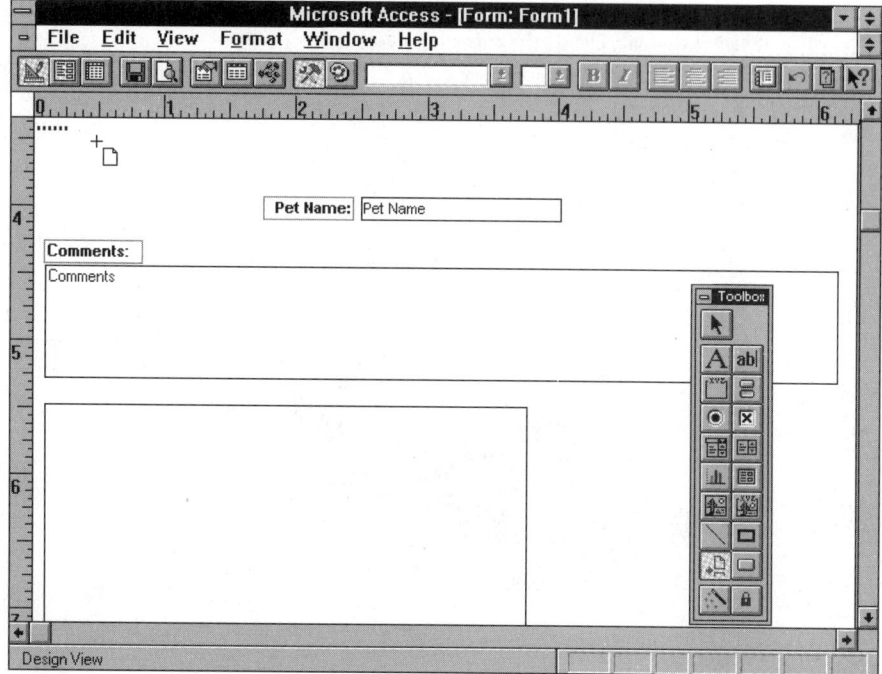

Figure 17-18: Adding a new page and a page break.

Notice that you copied Pet Name into the second page. This was for display-only purposes. Unless you change the properties of the second Pet Name control, you can also edit its value. When working with forms that require multiple pages, you may want to place controls that are used as headers in a form header section. If you are working with numeric data, you may want to also add a form footer section to display totals.

Figure 17-19 shows the second page of the form for the first record in the table.

Using Form and Page Headers and Footers

The most common use of a page or form header is to repeat identification information. For example, in the Pets Data Entry form, the text header is part of the form itself. When you have a second page, you don't see the text header. In Access forms, you can add both form and page sections. Sections include headers, which come before the detail controls, and footers, which come after the detail controls.

Figure 17-19: The second page of the form.

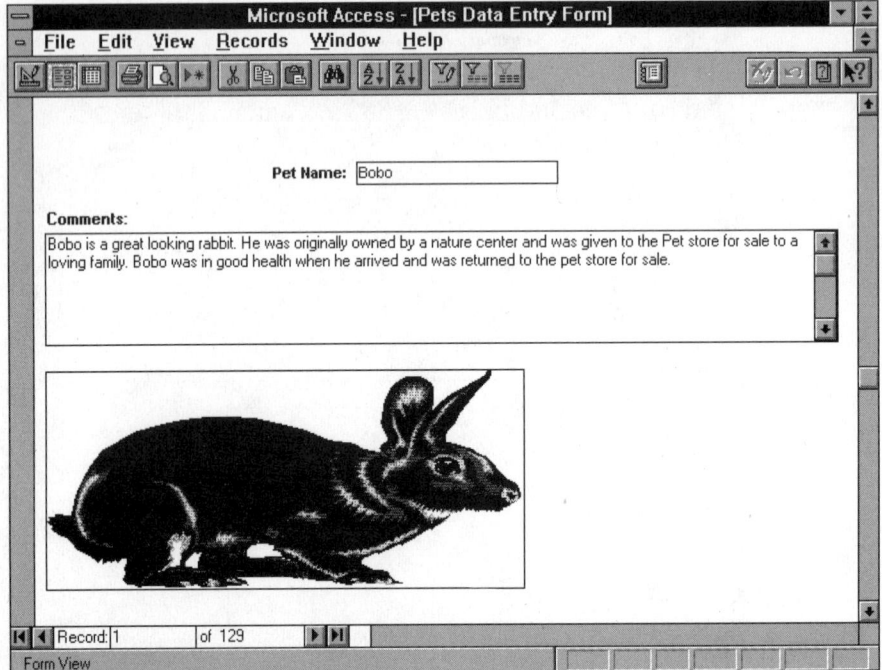

The different types of headers and footers

Several types of headers and footers can appear in a form:

Form header	Displayed at the top of each page when viewed and at the top when the form is printed
Page header	Displayed only when the form is printed; prints after the form header
Page footer	Appears only when the form is printed; prints before the form footer
Form footer	Displayed at the bottom of each page when viewed and at the bottom of the form when the form is printed

Form headers and footers are used in the displayed form and optionally can be used in a printed form. Page headers and footers are displayed only when a form is printed. Generally, unless you are printing the form as a report, you won't use the page headers or footers. Because you can easily create reports in Access and even save a form as a report, you won't find much use for page headers and footers.

Creating a form header and footer

You create form headers and footers by selecting Format➪Form Header/Footer. When you select this menu option, both the form header and form footer sections are added to the form.

 You can add page headers and footers by selecting Format➪ Page Header/Footer.

You can create a form header and move the text header label control into it by following the next steps:

Steps:	Creating a Form Header
Step 1.	Open the original Pets Data Entry Form - Without Formatting form in design view.
Step 2.	Select Format➪Form Header/Footer to display the form header and footer.
Step 3.	Select the label control Mountain Animal Hospital - Pets Data Entry.
Step 4.	Move the label control straight up from the detail section to the form header section.
Step 5.	Resize the form header to fit the label control properly.
Step 6.	Select all the controls in the detail section and move them up slightly.

If you display the form now, you see that the picture and comments controls are truncated at the bottom of the screen and a small white area is left at the bottom of the screen. When you add form header and footer sections, you lose that much space from the detail section. You must adjust the size of your detail section to compensate for this space.

In this example, you would need to make the height of the detail section smaller because you moved the text label control to the form header section and moved the other controls up in the detail section. You also have to close the form footer section, as you are not using it.

You change the size of a section by placing the cursor on the bottom border of the section, where it turns into a two-headed arrow. You can then drag the section border up or down.

Part III: Using Access in Your Work

When you display a form with a header or footer section, you see the sections separated from the detail section by a line. The form headers and footers are literally anchored in place. If you create a scrollable or a multiple-page form, the headers and footers remain where they are while the data in the detail section moves.

Printing a Form

You can print a form by simply selecting the File⇒Print option and entering the desired information in the Print dialog box. Printing a form is like printing anything. You are in a WYSIWYG environment, so what you see on the form is essentially what you get in the printed hard copy. If you added page headers or page footers, you see them at the top or bottom of the printout.

You can also preview the printout by selecting the File⇒Print Preview menu option. This displays a preview of the printed page, as shown in Figure 17-20.

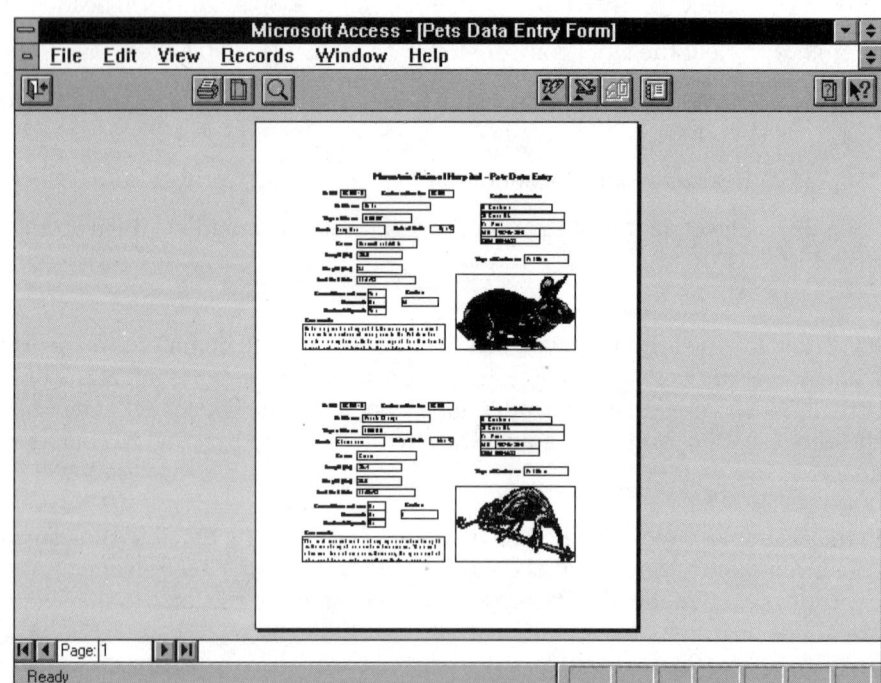

Figure 17-20: A print preview of a form.

Converting a Form to a Report

By selecting the File⇨Save As Report... option, you can save the form design as a report. The entire form is placed in the report form. If the form has form headers or footers, these are placed in the report header and report footer sections. If the form has page headers or footers, these are placed in the page header and footer sections in the report. Once the design is in the Report Design window, you can enhance it using the report design features. This allows you to add group sections and additional totaling in a report without having to re-create a great layout!

Summary

In this chapter, you learned how to create several types of forms without Form Wizards.

- When you create a form, you can adjust the form size by grabbing the borders and moving them.
- The Caption form property changes the text on the title bar.
- The Views Allowed form property lets you determine whether the user can switch to the datasheet view.
- The Default View form property determines whether the form can display more than one record at a time.
- The Default Editing form property determines whether the form is read-only or allows only new records.
- You can place fields on a form by using the Field List window and the toolbox.
- The tab order determines the direction in which the cursor moves within a data-entry form. You can change this order by selecting Edit⇨Tab Order....
- Memo fields are generally displayed by use of multiple-line text box control with a scroll bar.
- Picture fields (OLE) are generally displayed in a bound object frame. The best way to display a picture is to set the Scaling control property to either Stretch or Zoom.
- The AutoLabel and AutoColon global properties let you determine where the labels, if any, appear when you create an attached label control.
- You can create a multiple-page form with the Page Break control.
- Page headers and footers appear only on the printed form.
- Form headers and footers appear at the top and bottom of each page in the form.
- You can print or print preview a form by using the options in the File menu.
- You can save a form as a report design and later modify it by selecting File⇨Save As Report....

In the next chapter, you learn how to add special effects to your forms. These effects include colors, background shading, and other enhancements, such as lines, rectangles, and three-dimensional appearance.

Creating Great-Looking Forms

CHAPTER 18

In This Chapter

- Enhancing text controls by controlling font size and style
- Learning how to apply special display effects to forms
- Adding lines and rectangles to a form
- Adding color or shading to a form
- Adding three-dimensional effects to a form
- Adding a background bitmap to a form

In Chapter 17, you built a form that started with a blank Form Design screen. That form had no special formatting other than some label and text box controls. The most exciting object on the form was the rabbit. By using the form palette, the line and rectangle controls, and your own imagination, you can create great-looking forms with a small amount of work.

In this chapter, you learn how to format the data-entry form. Starting with the form you created in the preceding chapter, you now enhance the form to make it more readable and more presentable.

Making a Good Form Look Great

The Access form designer has the capability to do with a form what any good desktop publishing package can do with words. Just as a desktop publishing package can enhance a word-processed document to make it more readable, the form designer can enhance a database form to make it more usable.

442 Part III: Using Access in Your Work

By making a database form more usable, you can draw attention to areas of the form that you want the reader to notice. Just as a headline in a newspaper calls your attention to the news, an enhanced section of the form calls attention to the information it contains.

The Access form designer gives you a number of tools to make the form controls and sections visually stand out:

- Lines and rectangles
- Color and background shading
- Three-dimensional effects (raised or sunken appearance and shadows)

In this chapter, you enhance your previously created form by adding special text features to create shading, shadows, lines, rectangles, and three-dimensional effects. Figure 18-1 shows you the form after some special effects have been added.

Understanding WYSIWYG

Access has a WYSIWYG (what you see is what you get) form designer. As you create your controls on-screen, you instantly see what they look like in your form. If you want to see what the data will look like during your form design, the on-screen preview mode lets you see the actual data in your form design without using a hard-copy device.

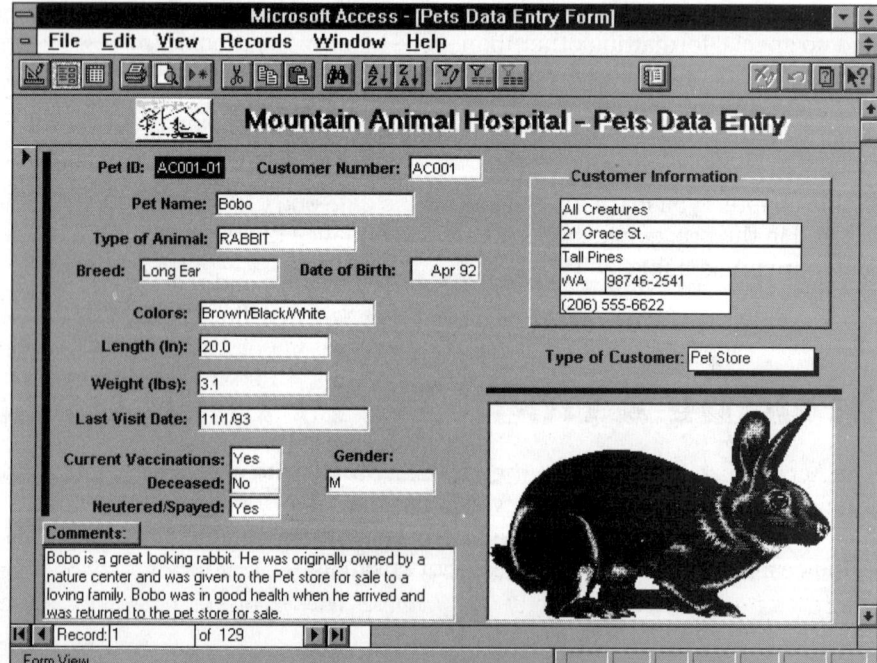

Figure 18-1: An enhanced form.

Chapter 18: Creating Great-Looking Forms 443

The Access form designer lets you add color and shading to your form text and controls. You can also display them in reverse video, which shows white letters on a black background. You can even color or shade the background of form sections. As you specify these effects, you see the change instantly on the Design screen.

Using the palette

One of the most important controls for enhancing a form is the palette. The palette has three basic uses:

- Controlling text foreground color, background color, border color, and shading
- Controlling line thickness for lines, types of lines, rectangles, and control borders
- Controlling three-dimensional effects, such as a raised or sunken appearance

You modify the appearance of a control by using the palette. To modify the appearance of a control, select the control by clicking on it and then click on the palette options you want to apply to the control.

You can display the palette by selecting the Palette button (the icon showing a painter's palette) in the toolbar or by selecting View⇨Palette.... This action displays the Palette window (known simply as the palette), which is shown in Figure 18-2. The palette is a window, just like the toolbox or the field list. You can move the palette around the screen, change its size, and even anchor it like a toolbar to a window border. The palette can remain on-screen all the time, and you can use it to change the options for one or more controls.

The palette has several distinct option areas.

The first three buttons of the palette determine whether a control appears flat or has a three-dimensional appearance. You can select the second button to give the control an illusion of being above the screen or the third button to make the control look as if it's below the screen surface. The first option removes the three-dimensional effect. To select one of the options, just click the appropriate button.

The next set of buttons controls the thickness for lines and rectangles. A line can be the border of a control or a stand-alone line control. You define the thickness of the line by using the thickness buttons. Available thicknesses in points, from left to right on the palette, are hairline, 1 point, 2 points, and 3 points. The last three buttons are the line type. The choices are solid line, dashed line and dotted line.

 A point is approximately ½₂ inch and is a unit of measurement that denotes character height.

You see three rows of colored squares on the palette, which let you choose one of 16 colors for the various objects you can change. These objects include foreground color for text, background fill color, and border color.

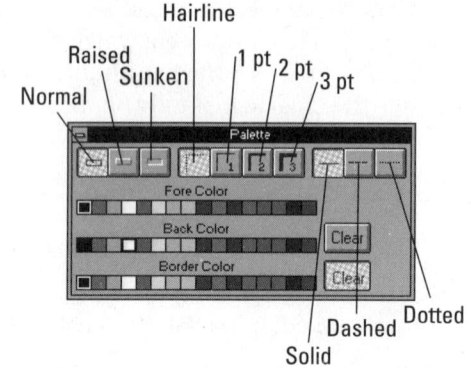

Figure 18-2: The palette window.

Until you select a control, the palette appears without colors.

The Fore Color choice determines the color of the text itself within a control. To select a color, click the color you want to use. To change the background color of a control or section, use the Back Color choice, clicking the color to select it. Clicking the Clear button creates a transparent control that lets you see whatever is underneath it. The Clear setting can be useful for placing text over OLE objects, such as bitmaps, or for creating shadowed text.

You use the Border Color option on the palette to define a control's border color. Again, choose the color you want by clicking it. Clicking the Clear button creates a transparent border that lets you see anything underneath, just as with the Back Color option. You can also create the illusion of having no border at all by selecting the same border color that you choose for Back Color.

When you are finished with the palette, you can close it in several ways:

- Click on the Palette button on the toolbar.
- Select View⇨Palette....
- Double-click the palette's Control menu.
- Select Close from the palette's Control menu.

Creating special looks

Figure 18-3 shows some of the special effects that can be easily created for controls with the palette. In the figure, you see that controls with a grey back color show off special effects much better than those with white. In fact, a form background in grey or a dark color is almost mandatory for seeing various special effects. The effects shown in the figure are the same types that are available from the various Form Wizard looks. Each of these special effects is described in the next sections. Later, you'll apply some of these effects to modify the Pets Data Entry form.

The special looks can be applied to rectangles, label controls, text box controls, checkboxes, option buttons, and option group boxes. Anything that has a box or circle around it can be raised or sunken. Actually, checkboxes and option buttons look the same whether raised or sunken.

By simply selecting the control and adding the special effect, you can make your forms look much better and draw attention to the important areas of the form.

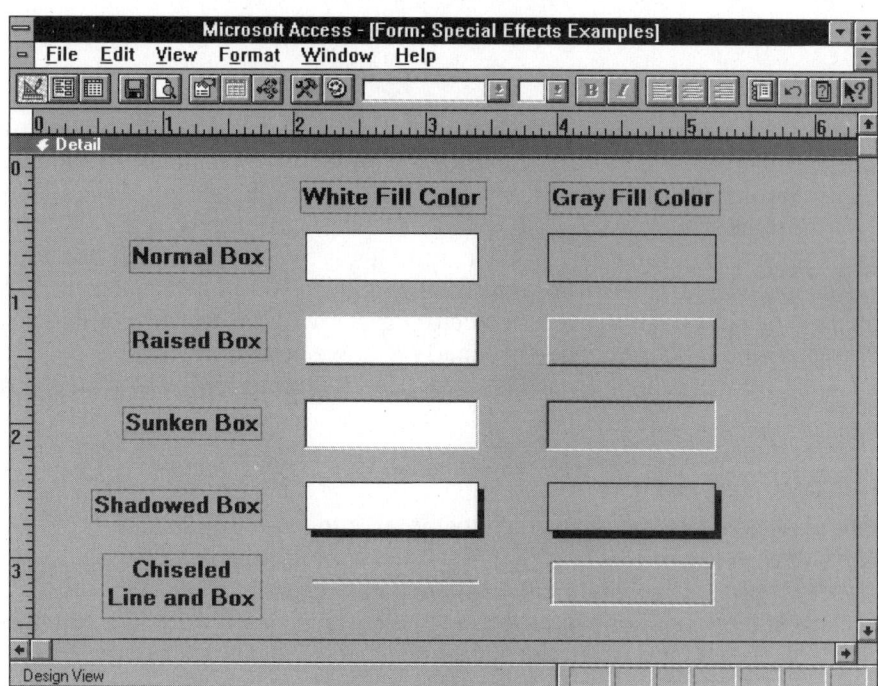

Figure 18-3: Special effects.

Standard

In Figure 18-3, you see a pair of boxes that are both created with no special 3-D effect. As you can see in Figure 18-3, the normal box stands out better when set against the grey background. You can also increase the width of the border lines to make the box more prominent. The Border Color setting lets you change the color of the box. A thick white box also stands out.

Raised

This box is best when used for a rectangle that surrounds other controls or for label controls. The raised box gives the best effect in a dark color against a dark background. As you can see in Figure 18-3, the raised box is difficult to see with a white fill color. By increasing the width of the box, you can give the appearance that the control is higher than it really is. You achieve the raised three-dimensional effect by contrasting the white left and top borders with the black right and bottom borders.

Sunken

The sunken special effect is the most dramatic and most often used. This is known as the *embossed* look in the Form Wizard. As you can see in Figure 18-3, either the white or the grey fill color looks very good on a grey form background as well. You can also increase the width of the border to give the effect of a deeper impression. The sunken three-dimensional effect is achieved with black left and top borders and white right and bottom borders. The sunken effect also works well with checkboxes and option buttons.

Shadowed

You don't create the shadowed special effect by selecting a palette option button. Instead, you create this look by hiding a solid dark-colored rectangle behind the original control, which is slightly offset to give the shadowed effect. As you can see in Figure 18-3, the black shadow works well behind the white or grey filled box. To create this effect, the first step is to duplicate the original control if it is a rectangle or text box control, or create a new control if you are creating a shadow behind a text box control. Next, change the back color to black or a color darker than the original control. Finally, select Format⇨Send to Back to move the solid rectangle behind the original control so as to show only the bottom and right areas slightly. This procedure creates the shadowed effect.

Chiseled

The chiseled effect is perhaps the most interesting of all the special looks. The chiseled line shown in Figure 18-3 is not a line at all, but a very thin rectangle that is sunken. The chiseled box is actually formed by four separate chiseled lines (rectangles). Two are vertical and two are horizontal. Although it requires much work to create this chiseled box look, the result is worth the effort if you need a great-looking box border.

Following Along in This Book

In this chapter, you modify the form that you created in Chapter 17 to look like Figure 18-1. If you are following along with this book using Microsoft Access, you should have the form named Pets Data Entry Form - Without Formatting open in the Form Design window.

Changing the form's background color

If you are usually going to view your form on-screen instead of printing it, it may be beneficial to color the background. A light grey background seems to be the best neutral color in all types of lighting and visual conditions. To change the background for the form header and detail sections, follow these steps:

Chapter 18: Creating Great-Looking Forms 447

Steps:	Changing the Background Color of a Form
Step 1.	Display the palette.
Step 2.	Select the form header line (click the text Form Header so that the header line becomes darker).
Step 3.	Select the light grey color that is third from left in the Back Color row.
Step 4.	Select the detail section (click the text Detail so that the detail section line becomes darker).
Step 5.	Select the light grey color that is third from the left in the Back Color row.

This should give both sections of the form a light grey background. Later, you change the background of individual label and text box controls for a more natural look. The white background of these controls does not look good on the grey background of the form.

When you select a section, the section line becomes dark grey, and the unselected sections remain light grey. When a section is highlighted, only the Back Color row is active. When the form is selected, both section headers are light grey and the palette is not active.

Enhancing Text-Based Controls

Generally, before you start enhancing display items with shading or three-dimensional effects, it is important to first get the label text and data right. When your enhancements include label and text box control changes, you should begin with them.

Enhancing label and text box controls

You can enhance label and text box controls in several ways:

- Changing the text font type style (Arial, Times New Roman, Wingding)
- Changing the text font size (4-200)
- Changing the text font style (bold, italic, underline)
- Changing the text color (using the palette)
- Adding a shadow

 In Chapter 17, you changed the title in the form header. You then changed the text font size and font style. Now, you see how to add a text shadow to the label control.

Creating a text shadow

Text shadows give text a three-dimensional look by making the text appear to float above the page while its shadow stays on the page. This effect uses the same basic principle as a shadowed box. Text shadows are created by this process:

1. Duplicating the text
2. Offsetting the duplicate text from the original text
3. Changing the duplicate text to a different color (usually a lighter shade)
4. Placing the duplicate text behind the original text
5. Changing the original text back color to clear

To create a shadow for the title's text, follow these steps:

Steps:	Creating a Text Shadow
Step 1.	Select the Palette button in the toolbar to display the palette.
Step 2.	Select the label control with the text Mountain Animal Hospital - Pets Data Entry.
Step 3.	Select the light grey Back Color in the palette. Make sure that the Clear button is not depressed.
Step 4.	Select Edit⇨Duplicate.
Step 5.	Select the white Fore color fourth from the left to change the duplicate text color.
Step 6.	Drag the duplicate text up and to the right to create the offset from the text below.
Step 7.	Select Format⇨Send to Back.
Step 8.	Select the original copy of the text, which is now in front. You may have to click on an empty area before you can select the original copy of the text.
Step 9.	Select the Clear button in the Back Color row of the palette. You may have to drag the text a little to make the offset look better.

Chapter 18: Creating Great-Looking Forms

After you complete the shadow, you may have to move the text and its shadow to accommodate the changes you made when you moved the controls. You also may have to move the section border. The text now appears to have a shadow, as shown in Figure 18-4.

The box around the label control is not visible when the form is printed because the Clear button in the Border Color row in the palette is depressed.

When the original text was duplicated, the duplicate copy was automatically offset below the original text. When you place the duplicate text behind the original, it is hidden. You redisplayed it by placing the original text in front and then made it transparent by changing the Back Color Clear botton. If the offset, or distance from the other copy, is too great, the effect will not look like a shadow. By moving one of the label controls slightly, you can perfect the shadowed appearance.

Although the shadow appears correctly on-screen and looks great, it won't print correctly on most monochrome printers. What you normally see is two lines of black text, which looks horrible. If you plan to print your forms and do not have a printer that prints text in color or prints many shades of grey using graphics rather than text fonts, you should avoid the use of shadowed text on a form.

Changing text to a reverse video display

Text really stands out when you create white text on a black background. This setup is called *reverse video* because the text is white against a black background rather than the usual black letters on white. You can convert text in a label control or text box to reverse video by changing the Back Color to black and the Fore Color color to white. To change the Pet Name text control to reverse video, follow these steps:

Steps:	Creating a Reverse Video Effect
Step 1.	Select the Pet ID text box control (not the label control).
Step 2.	Display the palette if it is not already displayed.
Step 3.	Click the black Back Color button.
Step 4.	Click the white Fore Color button.

If you are using a laser printer, such as the HP Laserjet, you may not see reverse video if you print your form. This is because of a limitation of the Windows 3.1 printer driver for the HP Laserjet series.

Figure 18-4: Creating text with a shadow and reverse video.

Displaying label or text box control properties

As you change values in a label control or text box control by using the palette, you are actually changing their properties. Figure 18-5 displays the property window for the label control in the form header you just modified. As you see in Figure 18-5, many properties can be affected by the palette. Table 18-1 shows the various properties and their possible values for both label and text box controls.

Figure 18-5: Label control properties.

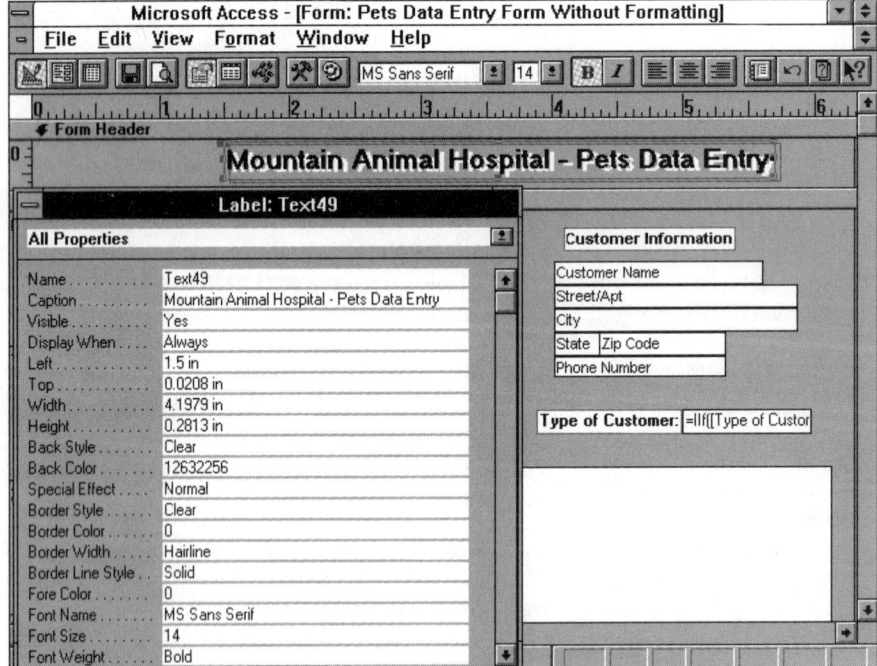

Table 18-1
Label or Text Box Layout Properties

Property	Options	Description
Left	Position of the left corner of the control in the current measure (include an indicator, such as cm or in, if you use a different unit of measurement)	Specifies the position of an object on the horizontal axis
Top	Position of the top corner of the control in the current measure	Specifies the position of an object on the vertical axis
Width	The width of the control in the current unit of measure	Specifies the width of an object
Height	The height of the control in the current unit of measure	Specifies the height of an object
Back Style	Clear or Normal	Determines whether a control's background is opaque or transparent
Back Color	Any available palette color	Specifies the color for the interior of the control or section
Special Effect	Normal, Raised, or Sunken	Determines whether a section or control appears flat, raised, or sunken
Border Style	Clear or Normal	Determines whether a control's border is opaque or transparent
Border Color	Any available palette color	Specifies the width of a control's border
Border Width	Hairline, 1pt, 2pt, 3pt, 4pt, 5pt, or 6pt	Specifies the width of a control's border
Border Line Style	Solid, Dashes, Short Dashes, Dots, Sparse Dots, Dash Dot, Dash Dot Dot	Specifies the line style of a line, rectangle, or control border
Fore Color	Any selection from the palette	Specifies the color for text in a control or the printing and drawing color
Font Name	Any system font name that appears on the toolbar; depends on the fonts installed	Specifies the name of the font used for text or a control
Font Size	Any size that is available for a given font	Specifies the size of the font used for text or a control
Font Weight	Extra Light, Light, Normal, Medium, Semi-bold, Bold, Extra Bold, and Heavy	Specifies the width of the line that Windows uses to display and print characters
Font Italic	No or Yes	Italicizes text in a control
Font Underline	No or Yes	Underlines text in a control
Text Align	General (default), Left, Center, and Right	Sets the alignment for text in a control

Although you can set many of these controls from the property sheet, you find that it's much easier to initially drag the control to set the Top, Left, Width, and Height properties or to use the palette to set the other properties of the control.

 Access 2.0 lets you press Ctrl + arrow key to move the selected control a very small amount in the direction of the arrow key used.

Displaying Unbound OLE Objects in Forms

You can display pictures in forms by using object frames. The two types of object frames are *bound,* which are attached to a data field in the record, and *unbound,* which are embedded in the form itself.

You can add an unbound OLE object to your form by either pasting a bitmap from the Clipboard or embedding or linking a bitmap file that contains a picture. Suppose that you have a logo for Mountain Animal Hospital. On the disk that accompanies this book is a bitmap called MTN.BMP. In this section, you add this bitmap to the page header section of the form.

An OLE object that is a picture can be displayed in one of three ways:

Clip	Displays picture in its original size
Stretch	Fits picture into the control regardless of size; often displayed out of proportion
Zoom	Fits picture into the control either vertically or horizontally and maintains proportions; often results in white space on top or right side

To add the logo to the form, follow these steps:

Steps:	Adding an Unbound Object Frame
Step 1.	Display the toolbox by selecting View⇒Toolbox.
Step 2.	Click the Object Frame button in the standard toolbox.
Step 3.	Click the left corner below the title and drag the box so that it is sized as shown in Figure 18-5. The Insert Object dialog box appears as shown in Figure 18-6.

Chapter 18: Creating Great-Looking Forms

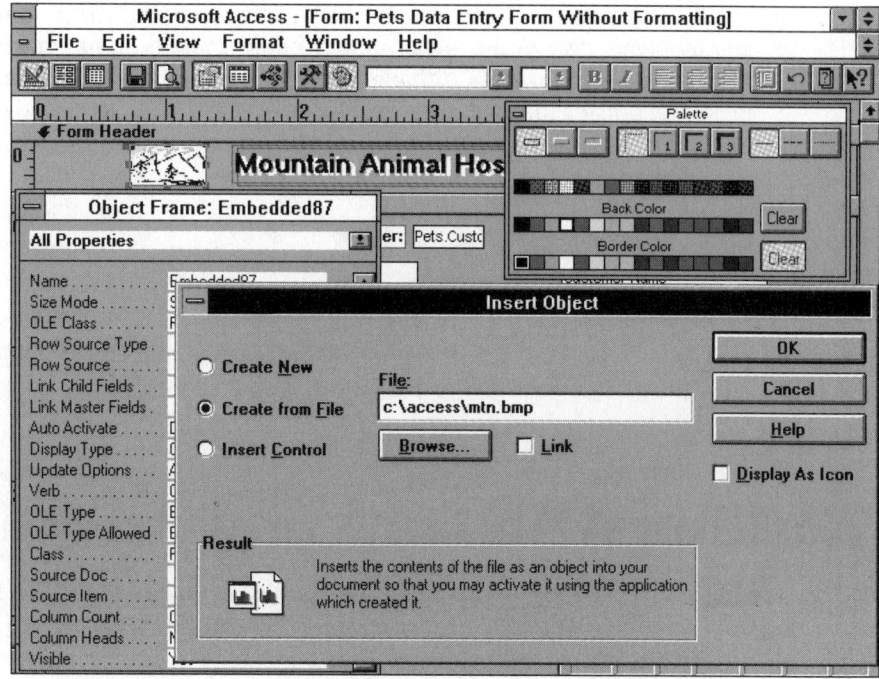

Figure 18-6: Creating an unbound object frame.

From this dialog box, you can select the type of object you want to insert into your form. Any object installed on your system that supports OLE is displayed, including such software packages as Paintbrush, Excel, Word, Draw, Powerpoint, or Word Art.

Step 4. Select the Create from File option button.

Step 5. Enter MTN.BMP and the path of Access directory and click OK.

If the file does not already exist and you want to create a new object, such as a Paintbrush Picture, you click the Create New Option button in Step 4 and select the type of object from the list box. You can then create the new object and return to Access. After completing Step 5, you are returned to the Access Form Design window, where the picture is displayed. But you must still change the Size Mode property to Stretch.

You must have the source application on your PC to create a new object and return to Access.

Step 6. Display the property sheet.

Step 7. Change the Size Mode property to Stretch.

Finally, you have to change the Border property so that the picture does not simply blend in with the background because there is so much white in the picture. You can do this by changing the border color to black. Or you can make the border three-dimensional by selecting the Raised option button in the palette.

Step 8.   Display the palette.

Step 9.   Click the Raised option button.

The unbound object frame is complete. Figure 18-6 shows the main Insert Object dialog box, palette, and property sheet. The picture is also shown completed.

Working with Lines and Rectangles

You can use lines or rectangles, commonly called boxes, to make certain areas of the form stand out and bring attention to these areas. In Figure 18-1, you saw several groups of lines and rectangles that were used for emphasis. In the present example, you still need to add the lines and the rectangle.

To create the rectangle for the customer information block, follow these steps, using Figure 18-7 as a guide:

Steps: Creating a Rectangle

Step 1.   Select the Rectangle button in the toolbox.

Step 2.   Click to the left of the text Customer Information so that the rectangle encompasses the customer fields and cuts through the middle of the text, Customer Information.

Step 3.   Drag the rectangle around the entire set of customer text box controls and release the mouse.

Step 4.   Select Format⇔Send to Back to redisplay the text boxes.

You may notice that when you create the rectangle, it blocks out the controls beneath it. By sending the rectangle to the background, you make the controls reappear.

Step 5.   Select the grey Back Color in the palette.

Chapter 18: Creating Great-Looking Forms

Step 6. Select the Raised appearance button in the palette.

You now have to change the background color of the label control Customer Information, which stands out because of the white background color.

Step 7. Select the Customer Information label control.

Step 8. Select the grey Back Color in the palette.

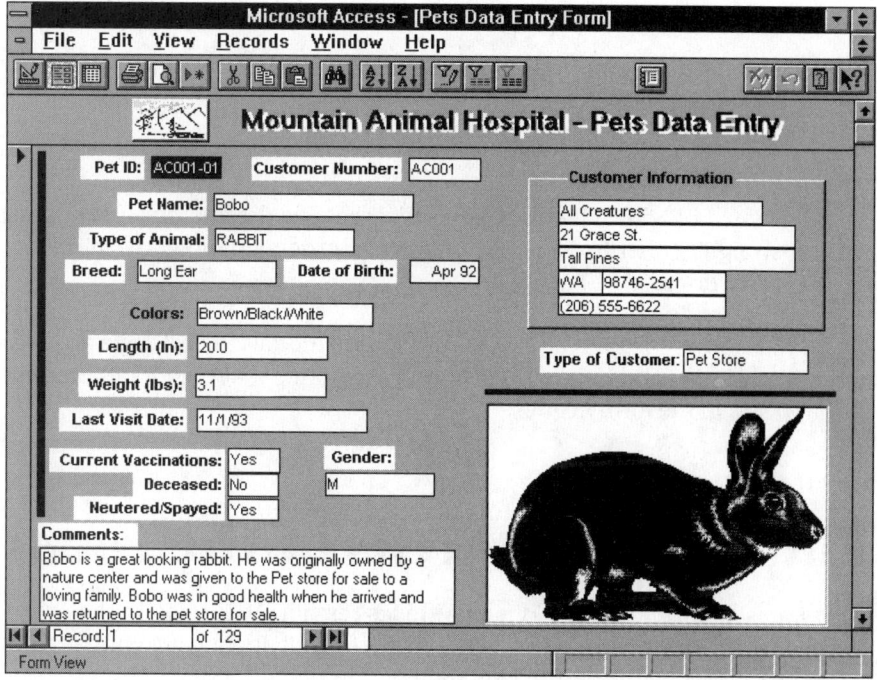

Figure 18-7: Completing the rectangles and lines.

You can also redisplay the controls behind the rectangle by checking the Clear button of the Back Color option in the palette. This method, however, does not allow you to add other shading effects. For a rectangle, you should always select Format⇨Send to Back.

You still need to create several lines for the form. A single horizontal line needs to be added just below the Type of Customer control, and a thick vertical line needs to be added down the left side of the form beginning with Pet ID and ending with Neutered/Spayed. To add these lines, complete these steps, using Figure 18-7 as a guide:

Steps:	Creating Lines
Step 1.	Click the Line button in the toolbox and then click the Lock button.
Step 2.	Create a new horizontal line just above the Picture bound object control.
Step 3.	Select the 2 button in the line thickness section of the palette to make the line thicker.
Step 4.	Create a new vertical line starting just to the left of the Pet ID field. Hold down the Shift key as you drag the line to just left of the Neutered/Spayed field, as shown in Figure 18-7, to keep the line vertical.
Step 5.	Select the 3 button in the line thickness section of the palette to make the line thicker.

 If you hold down the Shift key while creating the line, the line remains perfectly straight, either horizontally or vertically, depending on the initial movement when drawing the line.

Figure 18-7 shows the form after it is run. Notice the raised rectangle around the customer information and the two new lines. Also notice that the Mountain Animal Hospital logo appears in the form header.

Emphasizing Areas of the Form

The form is almost complete. But a few tasks remain. According to the original form shown in Figure 18-1, you still need to shade the individual label controls and sink the active text box controls for the Pets data.

Adding background color to a control

You already added background color to the form. You can also add a background color to any control. As you've seen, adding background shading to a form section does not necessarily add background color to any controls contained within the section. You can, however, add background coloring to all controls that are selected at one time. To add background color to all the label controls in the detail section, follow these steps:

Chapter 18: Creating Great-Looking Forms **457**

Steps:	Adding Background Color to a Control
Step 1.	Select each of the label controls in the detail section by holding down the Shift key and selecting each one individually.
Step 2.	Display the palette if it is not already displayed.
Step 3.	Select the light grey Back Color in the palette.

You can also simply push the Clear button. However, doing so does not let you make further changes to any of the label controls, such as raising the Comments label control.

Sinking controls

Generally, in a form, you cannot sink controls because they don't look sunken on a white background. But against a grey background, the depth of a control is enhanced. Both sunken and raised controls stand out on a grey background. In this form, only the Pets data fields are editable. To make them stand out more, you want to sink all the Pets data controls. To give the Pets text box controls a sunken look, follow these steps:

Steps:	Sinking Text Box Controls
Step 1.	Select each of the Pets text box controls in the detail section of the form.
Step 2.	Click the Sunken appearance button in the palette.

Raising controls

Just as you can sink a control, you can raise one as well. Raised controls, like sunken controls, look much better on a grey or dark background. To raise the Comments label control, follow these steps:

Steps:	Raising a Control
Step 1.	Select the Comments label control.
Step 2.	Click the Raised appearance button in the palette.

Creating a shadow on a rectangle

If you really want to emphasize an area of the form, you can add a shadow to any control. The most common types of controls to add a shadow to are rectangles and text boxes. You can create shadows by adding a solid-color rectangle slightly offset from and behind the original control. If the background is light or white, a dark-colored rectangle is needed. If the background is dark or black, use a light-colored or white rectangle. To create a shadow for the Type of Customer text box, follow these steps:

Steps:	Creating a Shadow
Step 1.	Select the Rectangle button in the toolbox.
Step 2.	Create a rectangle the same size as the Type of Customer text box control.
Step 3.	Offset the rectangle so that it is slightly to the right of and below the original text box control.
Step 4.	Click the black Back Color in the palette.
Step 5.	Select F_ormat⇨Send to Bac_k.

If you want to create a form in which all controls have shadows, you can use the Form Wizard and create a form using the Shadow type of look. You can then copy the shadowed text controls to the Clipboard and paste them into a form.

Figure 18-8 shows the final form in the Form Design window. You can look at Figure 18-1 to see this final form after it is run.

You'll use this final form in the next chapter, so you should save it now. Select F_ile⇨Save _As and name the form **Pets Data Entry - With Formatting.**

Chapter 18: Creating Great-Looking Forms **459**

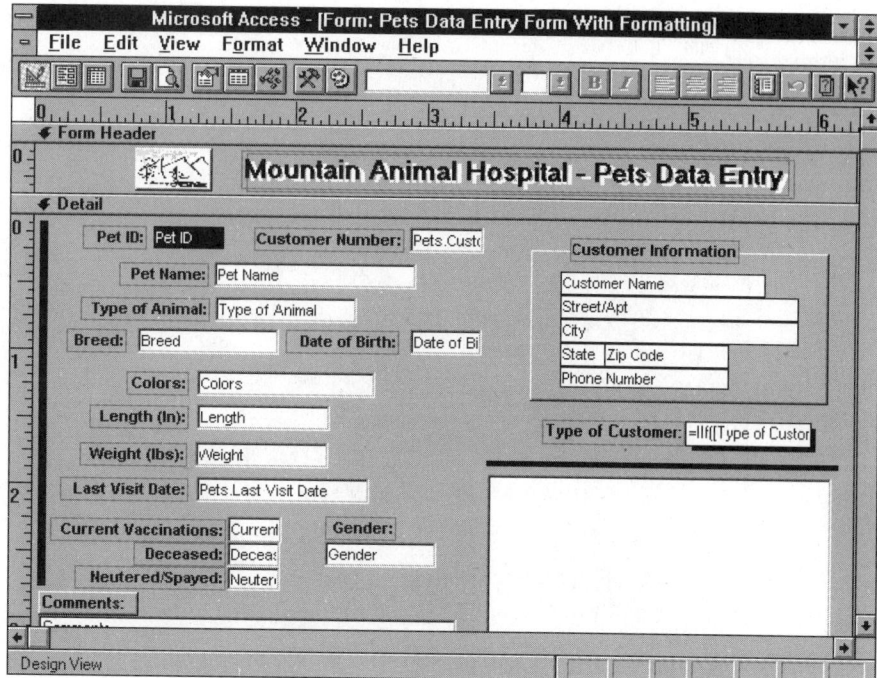

Figure 18-8: The final form.

Adding a Background Bitmap

If you want to emphasize a form even further, you can add a background bitmap to any form, just as you added one control behind another. By checking the Clear button of any control, you can add it to the background of the form and have other controls appear to sit on top of it. Figure 18-9 demonstrates this concept.

In Figure 18-9, you can see a map of the United States placed behind the simple Pets Data Entry form. You can also place a giant Mountain Animal Hospital logo here — or perhaps just a representation of the three states that Mountain Animal Hospital serves. In fact, anything can go behind the form.

This map is copied to the Clipboard from a standard Windows drawing package, such as Microsoft Draw, Micrografx Windows Draw, Lotus Smartpics, or any other software you may have with clip art. It is then placed on the form and resized to fit the entire form. The Size Mode property is changed to Stretch, and the Clear button of the Back Color row in the palette is checked. That's all it takes to add powerful bitmaps to your form.

Figure 18-9:
A bitmap picture behind a form.

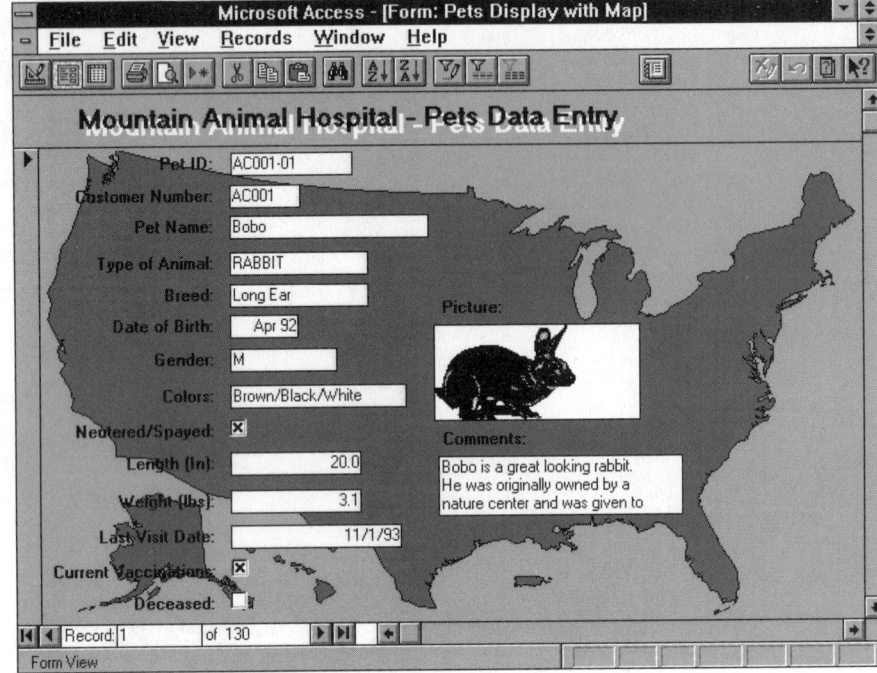

You can go even further if you want by incorporating the bitmap into your application. A bitmap can have buttons tied to macros placed in the right locations. For example, to help the office staff look up a patient, you can create a form that has three states behind it. By adding a large button over each state, the operator can then click on the state to select the state to look in for the patient records.

You can scan in a form and then place fields on top of the form itself without having to spend a lot of time re-creating the form, which gives the phrase *filling out a form* a whole new meaning.

Summary

No matter what type of form you are creating with the tools in Access, you can get the job done quickly and easily. In this chapter, the following points were covered:

- The Access form designer is a WYSIWYG (what you see is what you get) form tool. What you see in the Design window is what you get when you run the form.

- The palette is a tool in the Form window that lets you set foreground and background colors, control line widths and line types, and add three-dimensional effects to controls, such as a raised or sunken appearance.

- You can enhance label and text box control text by changing the font type style and size and by changing the font style to bold or italic. You can specify font color and even add a shadow by duplicating the text.

- To display pictures in forms, you can use *bound object frames,* which are attached to a data field in the record, or *unbound object frames,* which are embedded in the form itself.

- Lines and rectangles let you separate areas of the form to add emphasis.

- You can further emphasize areas of the form by adding color, background shading, and three-dimensional effects. You can also use shadows and reverse video for emphasis.

In the next chapter, you learn how to add data-validation controls to your form, including list boxes, option buttons, checkboxes, combo boxes, and other items.

Adding Data-Validation Controls to Forms
CHAPTER 19

In This Chapter

- Creating data-validation expressions
- Using the Option Group Wizard
- Working with option buttons
- Creating Yes/No checkboxes
- Making visual selections with toggle buttons
- Using the List Box Wizard
- Working with list boxes
- Using the Combo Box Wizard
- Working with combo boxes

In the last three chapters, you learned how to create a basic form and how to enhance it by using visual effects to make data entry and display easier. In this chapter, you learn various techniques that assist you in making sure that the data being entered and edited in your forms is as correct as possible. You learn to create several data-validation controls that will aid in validating input data and thereby make the form more productive.

Following Along in This Book

In this chapter, you modify your form from Chapter 18 to look like Figure 19-1. If you are following along with the examples in this book, you should open either the form you created in the Chapter 18 (Pets Data Entry - With Formatting) or the form on the disk that comes with this book (Pets Data Entry Form - Without Validation).

Figure 19-1:
The Pets Data Entry form after adding validation controls.

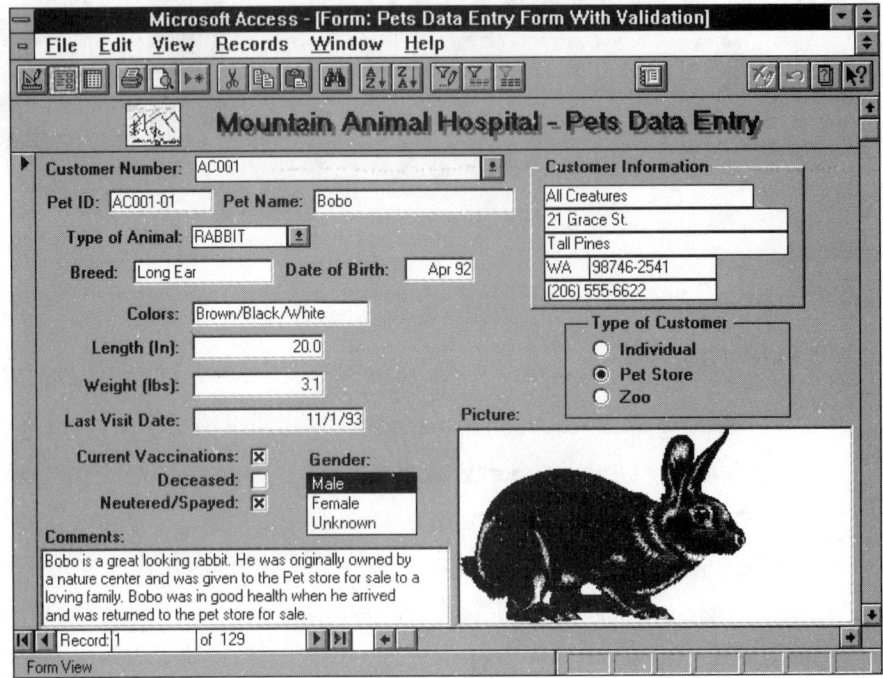

Creating Data-Validation Expressions

You can enter expressions into table design properties or a form control's property sheet that will limit input to specific values or ranges of values when a specific control or form is used. In addition, you can display a status line message that advises users how to properly enter the data into the table or form when they move the cursor into a particular field. You can also have an error message that advises users of the error after they enter an invalid entry. You can enter these expressions in a table design or in a form.

Table-level validation

You can enter several types of validation text into a table design, as shown in Table 19-1.

Status line messages appear when the user of a form or datasheet moves the cursor into the field. These messages appear in the status line of the form or datasheet in the lower left corner of the form. They are entered into the Description column of the table design, as shown in Figure 19-2. In this example, the status line message displays `Enter M for Male, F for Female, or U if Unknown` when the cursor moves into the Gender field.

Chapter 19: Adding Data-Validation Controls to Forms

Table 19-1
Types of Validation Entered into a Table Design

Type of Validation	Stored In	Displayed In Form
Status line message	Description/Status Bar Text	Status bar
Validation expression	Validation rule	
Error message	Validation text	Dialog box
Input mask	Input mask	Control text box

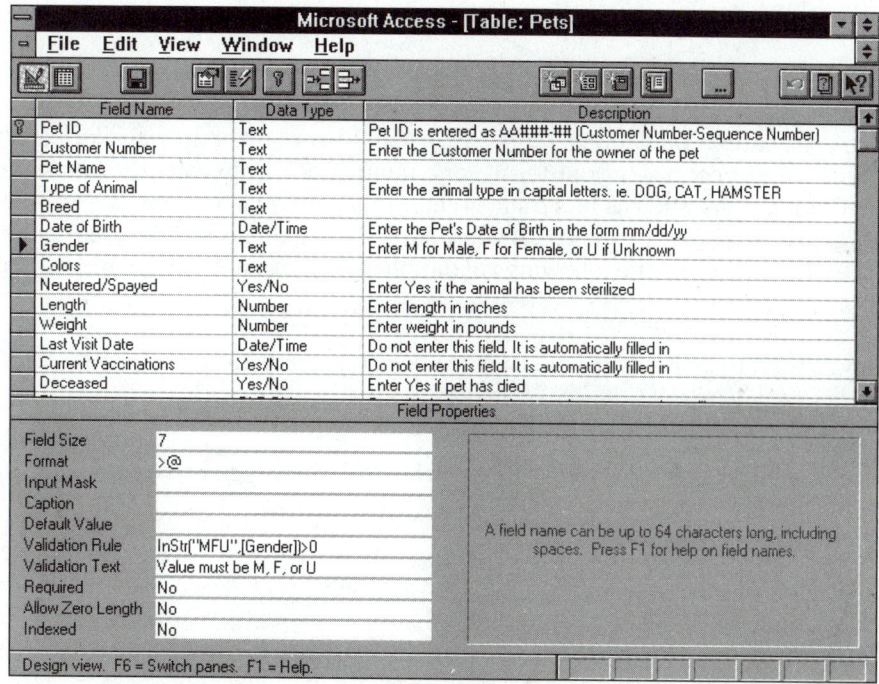

Figure 19-2: The validation properties for the Gender field in the table design.

Validation expressions are the rules that data must follow. Any type of expression can be entered into the Validation Rule property found in the field properties area of the table design. In Figure 19-2, the expression `InStr("MFU",[Gender])>0` limits the valid entry to the three letters M, F, or U.

You can also display an error message in a dialog box when data entry does not pass the validation rule. This text is entered into the Validation Text property found in the field properties area of the table design. In this example, the dialog box will tell you `Value must be M, F, or U`. Figure 19-2 shows a table design with the Gender field selected in the Pets table. Notice that only the properties are displayed for the highlighted field, although you can see all the descriptions in the upper part of the Table Design window.

Form-level validation

You can enter the same types of validation text into a form's property sheet. When you create a form, the table validation properties are copied into each bound field on the form. This way, you don't have to enter them for each form if you entered them at the table level. If you want to override them for a particular form, you can do so here by simply entering a new value for any of the properties.

Although status bar instructions are entered into a table designs Description column, they appear in the form design's status bar text property.

Entering a validation expression

You can enter a validation expression in a number of different ways for each field in your table or control in your form. For a number field, you can use standard mathematical expressions, such as less than, greater than, or equal to, using the appropriate symbols (<, >, =). For example, if you want to limit a numerical field to numbers greater than 100, you enter the following validation expression in the appropriate property box:

> **> 100**

If you want to limit a date field to dates before January 1993, you enter

> **< #1/1/93#**

If you want to limit a numeric or date value to a range, you can enter

> **Between 0 And 1500**

or

> **Between #1/1/70# And Date()**

You can use a series of functions that are included within Access to validate your data. In Figure 19-2, the validation expression that is used to limit the input into the Gender field is interpreted by Access as "allow only the letters M, F, or U." The Access function InStr means *in string*. Access will search the Gender input field and allow only those entries. Chapter 13 details the various functions that are available to you for validation purposes.

Creating Choices with Option Buttons

Sometimes, you don't want to allow the user to enter anything at all — only to pick a valid entry from a list. An *option button* is a form of input limitation that can be used on a form. This is a control that indicates whether a situation is True or False. The control consists of a string of text and a button that can be clicked either on or off. When you click the button, a black dot appears in its center to indicate that the situation is True; otherwise, the situation is False. This type of button is also known as a *radio button*.

Option buttons are generally used when you want to limit data entry but more than two choices are available. However, you should limit the number of choices to four when using option buttons. If you have more than four choices, you should use a list or combo box. These items are described later in this chapter.

By using option buttons, you can increase flexibility in validating data input. For example, the current control for Type of Customer displays a number: 1 means individual, 2 means pet store, and 3 means zoo. It is much more meaningful to a user if the choices are displayed on-screen, showing all choices. In Figure 19-1, you can see that the numerical field input has been changed into an option group box that shows the three choices available to the user.

Only one of the option buttons can be made True for any given record. This approach also ensures that no other possible choices can be entered on the form. In an option group, the option group box itself is bound to a field or expression. Each button inside passes a different value back to the option group box, which in turn passes a single value to the field or expression. Each option button is bound to the option group box rather than a field or expression.

Only fields with a numeric data type can be used for an option group in a form. In a report, you can transform nonnumeric data into numeric data types for display-only option buttons (see Chapter 22).

To create an option group with option buttons, you must do two things:

- Create the option group box and bind it to a field.
- Create each option button and bind each one to the option group box.

Creating option groups

In Access 1.x, creating option groups was a long multi-step manual process. First, you had to create an option group box to hold the option group controls. Next, you had to manually create each option button, toggle button, or checkbox that was going to be used inside the option group box. After creating these, there were many complicated control properties to set. A simple option group could easily take a half hour to create.

In Access 2.0, the easiest and most efficient way to create option groups is with the new Option Group Control wizard. This wizard allows you to easily create Option Groups, with multiple option buttons, toggle buttons, or check boxes. When you are through, all of your control's property settings are correctly filled out. Though this wizard greatly simplifies the process and allows you to more quickly create an option group, you still need to understand a little about the process.

Creating an option group box

The Option Group Wizard is automatically triggered by creating a new option group. You can create a new option group by depressing the Option Group icon on the toolbox and then drawing the control box rectangle. You can also depress the Option Group button and then drag the appropriate field from the field list window.

 The Control Wizard icon on the toolbox must be depressed for any of the control wizards to be triggered.

Before creating an option group for the *Type of Customer* field, you must first delete the current display of the field by highlighting it with your mouse, and pressing the Delete key. You may also want to delete the shadow, the thick line below the control and also narrow the height of the picture so the option group box will fit. Use the completed option group in Figure 19-1 as a guide.

Once you've deleted the existing Type of Customer text box control, you can create the Type of Customer option group box by following these steps:

Steps:	Creating an Option Group Using the Option Group Wizard
Step 1.	Select the Option Group button from the toolbox.
Step 2.	Drag the Type of Customer field from the Field List window to the space under the Customer Information box.
	The first screen of the Option Group Wizard should be displayed as shown completed in Figure 19-3. In this screen you can enter the text label for each

Chapter 19: Adding Data-Validation Controls to Forms

of the option buttons, checkboxes, or toggle buttons that will be in your option group. Each entry is entered just like in a datasheet. You can use the down-arrow key to move to the next choice.

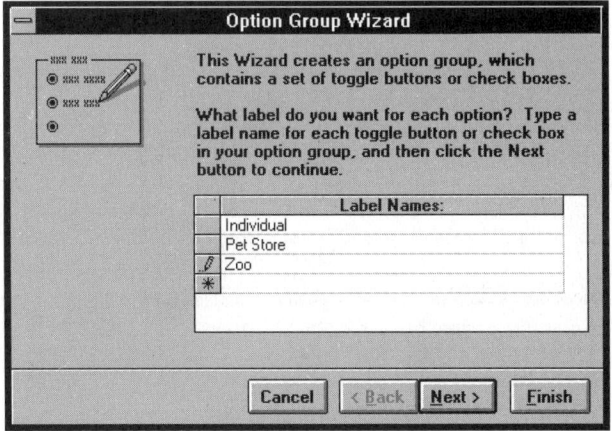

Figure 19-3: Entering the option group choices.

Step 3.   Enter **Individual**, **Pet Store**, and **Zoo,** pressing the down-arrow key between choices.

Step 4.   Press the Next > button to move to the default option wizard screen.

The next screen lets you select the default control for when the option group is selected. Normally, the first option is the default. If you want to make a different button the default, you would first select the **Yes, the default is** option button and then select the default value from the combo box that contains all of your choices. In this example, the first value will automatically be the default.

Step 5.   Press the Next > button to move to the assigning values wizard screen.

This wizard screen, shown in Figure 19-4, displays the actual values you entered along with a default set of numbers that will be used to store the selected value into the bound option group field. The screen looks like a datasheet with two columns. In this example, this is the Type of Customer field. Your first choice, Individual, is automatically assigned a 1, Pet Store a 2, and Zoo a 3. When Pet Store is selected, a 2 will be stored in the Type of Customer field.

In this example, the default values are acceptable. Sometimes, you may want to assign values other than 1,2,3 ... You might want to use 100, 200, and 500 for some reason. As long as you use unique numbers, you can assign any values you want.

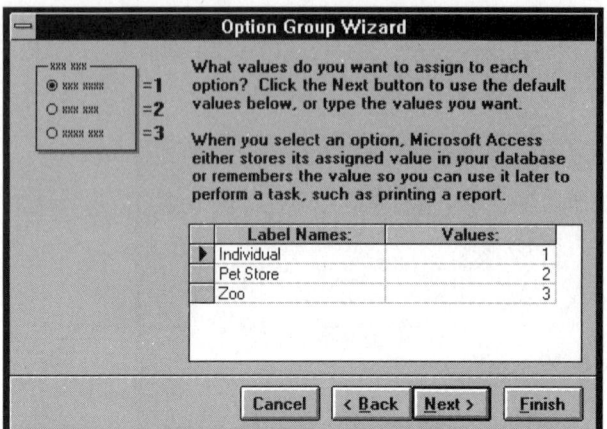

Figure 19-4: Assigning the value of each option button.

Step 6. Press the Next > button to move to the next wizard screen.

In the wizard screen, you then have to decide whether the option group itself is bound to a form field or unbound. The first choice in the wizard — *Remember the value for later use* — creates an unbound field. When you are using the option group in a dialog box that uses the selected value to make a decision, you don't want to store the value in a table field. In this example, the second value — *Store that value in this field* — is automatically selected, since you started with the Type of Customer field. If you want to bind the option group value to a different table field, you can select from a list of all form fields. Again, in this example, the default is acceptable.

Step 7. Press the Next > button to move to the option group style wizard screen.

Again, as shown in Figure 19-5, for this example, the defaults are acceptable. Notice, your actual values are used as a sample. In this wizard screen, the lower half of the wizard screen lets you choose what type of buttons you want. The upper half lets you can choose the style for the option group box and the type of group control. The style affects the option group rectangle. If you choose Raised or Sunken, that value is applied to the Special Effect property of the option group. Additionally, for Option Buttons and Check Boxes, if you choose Raised or Sunken, the Special Effects property for each option button or checkbox is set to Sunken.

As you change your selections, the Sample changes as well.

Step 8. Press the Next > button to move to the final option group wizard screen.

The final screen lets you give the option group control a label that will appear in the option group border. You can then add the control to your design and optionally display Cue Cards to further customize the control.

Chapter 19: Adding Data-Validation Controls to Forms

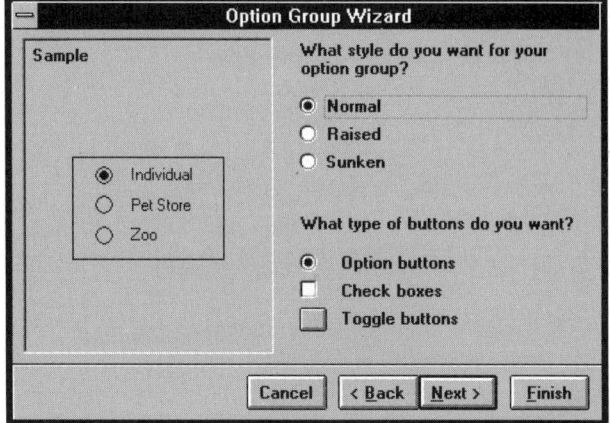

Figure 19-5: Selecting the type and look of your buttons.

Step 9. Enter Type of Customer as your label for the Option Group.

Step 10. Press the Finish button to complete the wizard.

> Your wizard work is now complete and the controls appear on the design screen. Eight controls have been created: the option group, its label, and three option buttons and their labels. You still may have some work to do. If you refer back to Figure 19-1, you might want to bold the text labels of the option group control and each individual option button. You might want to move the option buttons closer together and change the shape of the option group box. You might want to change the Special Effect property of each button to Sunken. As you have learned, you can do this by changing palette options or control properties.

Figure 19-6 shows the option group controls and the property sheet for the first option button as automatically created. Notice the Option Value property. This is only found in controls that are part of an option group. You should make all the suggested modifications to make the control look like Figure 19-1.

If you manually want to create an option group, our best advice is not to. The steps to do this are the same as creating any control. But, first you must create the option group box and then manually create each button inside the box. You have to set all data properties, palette properties, and specific option group or button controls manually.

 If you create the option buttons outside of the option group box and then drag or copy them into the option group box, they will not work. The automatic setting of the Option Value for buttons is not done, nor is the option button control bound to the option group box control.

Once this is complete, you can turn your attention to Yes/No controls.

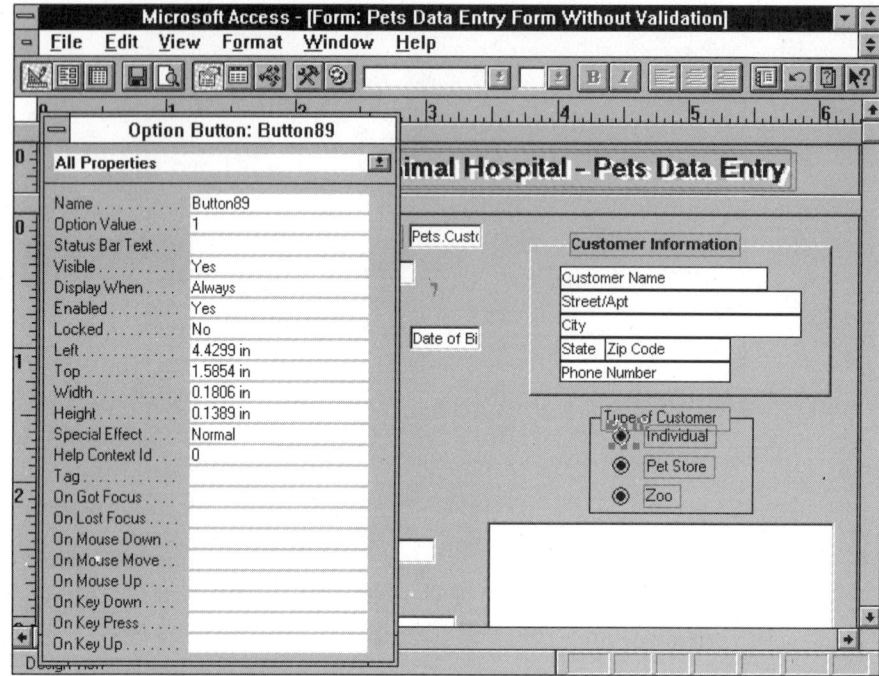

Figure 19-6: The Option Group controls and property sheet.

Creating Yes/No Options

There are three ways to properly show data from Yes/No data types:

- Display the values Yes or No in a text box control, using the Yes/No Format property.
- Use a checkbox.
- Use a toggle button.

Although you can place values from Yes/No data types in a text box control and then format the control by using the Yes/No property, it is better to use one of the other controls. Yes/No data types require the values –1 or 0 to be entered into them. The values that are returned to an unformatted text box control (–1 and 0) are very confusing, especially because Yes is represented by –1 and No by a 0. Setting the Format property to Yes/No or True/False to display those values will help, but it still requires reading the text Yes/No or True/False. A visual display is much better.

Toggle buttons and checkboxes return a value of –1 behind the scenes to the field if the button value is on and a value of 0 if the button is off. But these values are displayed as a box or button, which is faster to read. You can even enter a default value in the Default property of the form control to display a specific state. The control is initially displayed in a Null state if no default is entered and no state is selected. The Null state appears visually the same as the No state.

The checkbox is the commonly accepted control for two-state selection. Toggle buttons are nice but not always appropriate. Option buttons can also be used but would never be proper as a single Yes/No control. Toggle buttons can also use pictures instead of a text caption to represent the two states.

Creating checkboxes

A checkbox is a Yes/No control that acts the same as an option button but is displayed differently. A checkbox contains two entities — a string of text that describes the option and a small square that indicates the answer. If the answer is True, an X is displayed in the box. If the answer is False, the box is empty. The user can toggle between the two allowable answers by clicking the mouse within the box.

The Pets Data Entry form contains three fields that have Yes/No data types. These fields are Current Vaccinations, Deceased, and Neutered/Spayed. It is easier to understand if these fields are shown as a checkbox as opposed to a simple text box control. To change these fields into a checkbox, you must first delete the original text box controls. The following steps detail how to create a checkbox for each of the Yes/No fields once you've deleted the original controls.

Steps:	Creating a Checkbox
Step 1.	Depress the Checkbox icon from the toolbox.
Step 2.	While holding down the Ctrl key, select Current Vaccinations, Deceased, and Neutered/Spayed from the Field List window.
Step 3.	Using Figure 19-7 as a guide, drag these fields just below the Last Visit Date control.
	This creates each of the checkboxes and automatically fills in the Control Source property.
Step 4.	Rearrange the fields so that they look like Figure 19-7. Notice that this example calls for the checkboxes to be on the right of the labels.
Step 5.	Select each label control and add a colon to the end of the labels. Size the controls to fit and align the controls as necessary. Also change the Back Color to light gray.
Step 6.	Use the Palette to set the Special Effect property of each checkbox control to Sunken.

 Before creating the checkbox controls, you could change the Default Checkbox Label X property to a negative value to automatically place the checkboxes to the right of the labels when they are created. The value depends on the length of the labels. You can change the Add Colon property to Yes to automatically add a colon and also change the Special Effect property to Sunken. This would save you several steps when creating a group of similarly looking controls.

The completed checkboxes are complete as shown in Figure 19-7.

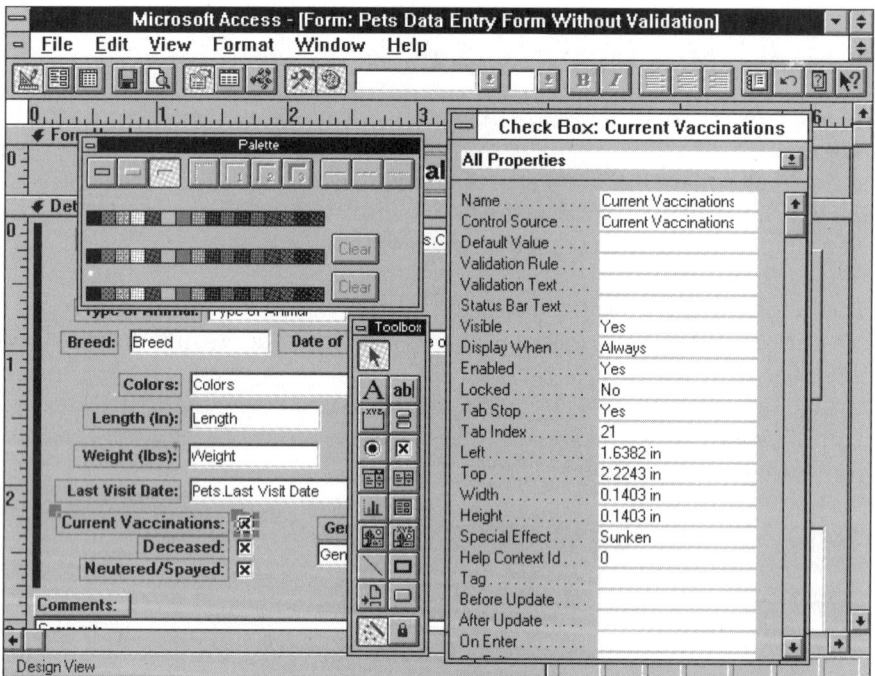

Figure 19-7: Creating checkboxes.

Creating visual selections with toggle buttons

A toggle button is another type of True/False control. Toggle buttons act in the same manner as option buttons and checkboxes but are displayed differently. When a toggle button is set to True (in the *pushed* mode), the button appears on-screen as sunken. When it is set to False, the button appears raised.

Toggle buttons provide a capability additional to what other button controls offer. You can set the size and shape of a toggle button, and you can display text or pictures on the face of the button to illustrate the choice that a user can make. This additional capability provides great flexibility in making your form user-friendly.

As an example of how to create a toggle button, you can follow the next steps, using the Deceased Yes/No field (this example is not part of the final form):

Steps:	Creating a Toggle Button
Step 1.	Delete the original checkbox control.
Step 2.	Select the Toggle Button option of the toolbox.
Step 3.	Move the cursor to the upper left corner.
Step 4.	Drag the square to the desired size.
Step 5.	Double-click the lower half of the toggle button.
Step 6.	Type the text **Deceased** to be displayed on the face of the button and press Enter.
Step 7.	Using the arrows keys on the keyboard, correct the size of the button to fit the text or select Format⇨Size⇨to Fit.
Step 8.	Type **Deceased** in the Control Source.

Adding a bitmapped image to the toggle button

As previously mentioned, you can display a picture on a toggle button instead of displaying text. Using the button that you just created in the preceding steps, you can modify the button to display a picture that is included in the sample files. Perform the following steps to modify the toggle button for the entry field called Deceased. This example assumes that you completed the steps to create the toggle button.

Steps:	Adding a Bitmap to a Toggle Button
Step 1.	Select the toggle button.
Step 2.	Open the property sheet and select the Picture property.
Step 3.	Press the Builder button.

The Picture Builder dialog is displayed. In this dialog box, you can select from over 100 predefined pictures. In this example, you want to select a bitmap named COFFIN.BMP that came with your Access Bible disk. It should be on the same directory as your Access book files were copied to. For this example, it is assumed that it is C:\ACCESS.

Step 4. Press the Browse button in the Picture Builder dialog box.

Step 5. Select COFFIN.BMP from the C:\ACCESS directory and press the OK button.

A sample of the picture appears in the Picture Builder dialog box, as shown in Figure 19-8.

Step 6. Press the OK Button to add the picture to the Toggle Button. The coffin appears on the toggle button in the design screen. You may need to move it on the screen to make it fit between other controls.

Although option buttons, checkboxes, and toggle buttons are great to handle a few choices, they are not a good idea where many choices are possible. Access has other controls that make it easy to pick from a list of values.

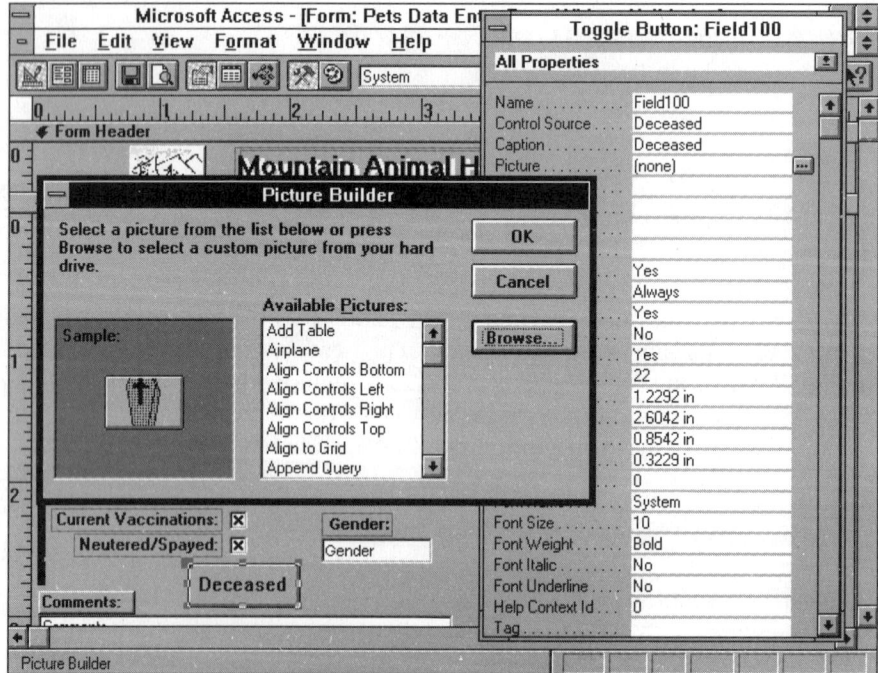

Figure 19-8:
The Picture Builder dialog box.

Working with List Boxes and Combo Boxes

Access has two types of controls that let you show lists of data that a user can select from. These controls are *list boxes* and *combo boxes*.

Understanding the differences between list boxes and combo boxes

The basic difference between a list box and a combo box is that the list box is always open, whereas you have to click on the combo box to open the list for selection. In addition, the combo box lets you enter a value that is not on the list.

Chapter 16 contains details on this subject. Review Figures 16-8 and 16-9 if you are not familar with list and combo boxes.

A closed combo box appears as a single text box field with a downward-pointing arrow on the far right side of the text box. A list box, which is always open, can have one or more columns and anywhere from one to as many rows as will fit on-screen. When open, a combo box displays a single-column text box above the first row, followed by one or more columns and as many rows as you specify in the property sheet. Optionally, a list box or combo box can display column headers in the first row.

Settling real-estate issues

You need to consider the amount of space on the form required for displaying either a list box or a combo box. If only a few choices are allowed in a given field, a list box is sufficient. If there is insufficient room on the form to display the choices, it is advisable to use a combo box. Remember that a list box is always open, whereas a combo box is initially closed. When you use a list box, the user cannot type any new values but must choose from the selection list.

When you design a list box, decide exactly what choices will be allowed for the given field. You should select an area of your form that has sufficient room for the open list box to display all selections.

Creating a single-column list box

List Boxes and Combo Boxes can be even more difficult to create than option groups, especially when a combo box uses a query as its source and contains multiple columns. The new list box and combo box wizards make the process much easier. In this first example, you will use the List Box Wizard to create a simple list box for the Gender field.

To create the List Box, follow these steps:

Steps: Creating a Single-Column List Box with a Wizard

Step 1.   Delete the existing Gender text box field control and its label.

Step 2.   Depress the List Box icon in the toolbox.

Step 3.   Display the field list and drag the Gender field to the right of the recently created checkboxes.

The List Box Wizard is automatically started, as shown in Figure 19-9. The first screen lets you decide whether you want to type in a list of values or if the values will come from a table/query. Depending on your answer, you can either select the number of columns and type in the values or select the fields you want to use from the selected table/query.

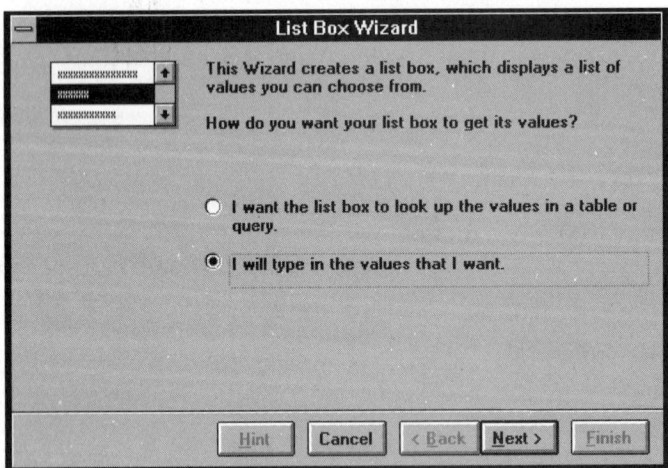

Figure 19-9: Selecting the data source for the list box.

Step 4.   Select the second option, *I will type in the values that I want,* and press the Next > button.

Chapter 19: Adding Data-Validation Controls to Forms 479

In the next screen, you can choose the number of columns and enter the values you want to use in the List Box. You can also resize the column widths, just like any datasheet. In this example, you will just enter three values in a single column: M, F, and U as shown completed in Figure 19-10.

Step 5. Enter 1 in the Number of columns field and then click into the first row under the Col1: header.

Step 6. Enter M, press the down arrow, enter F, press the down arrow, then enter U.

Step 7. Resize the width of the column to match the single character entry.

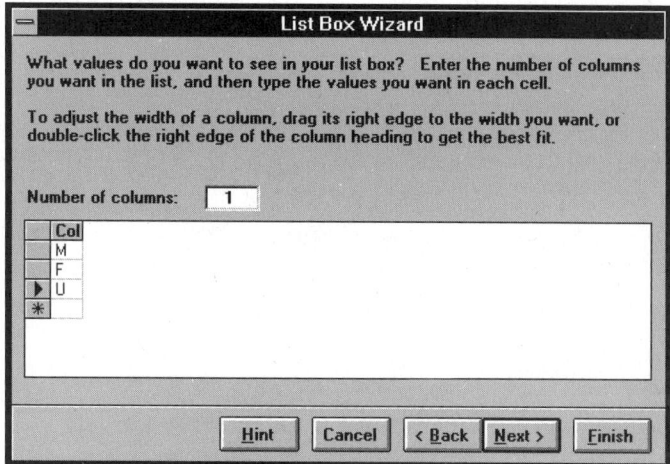

Figure 19-10: Entering the choices for the list box.

Step 8. Press Next > to move to the next screen.

In the next wizard screen, you then have to decide whether the list box is bound to a form field or unbound. This is exactly the same screen as you used in the Option Group Wizard. The first choice in the wizard, *Remember the value for later use,* creates an unbound field. In this example, the second value, *Store that value in this field.* is automatically selected, since you started with the Gender field. If you want to bind the option group value to a different table field, you can select from a list of all form fields. Again, in this example, the default is acceptable.

Step 9. Press the Next > button to move to the final wizard screen.

The final screen lets you give the list box control a label that will appear with your list box. When you press the Finish button, your control is added to your design and you can optionally display Cue Cards to further help you customize the control.

Step 10. Enter Gender: as your label for the Option Group.

Step 11. Press the Finish button to complete the wizard.

Your work with the wizard is now complete, and the control appears on the design screen. You will have to move to label control above the list box control rather than to its left. You will also have to resize the list box rectangle. The wizard does not do a good job of sizing the box to the number of entries.

Figure 19-11 shows the list box control and the property sheet for the list box.

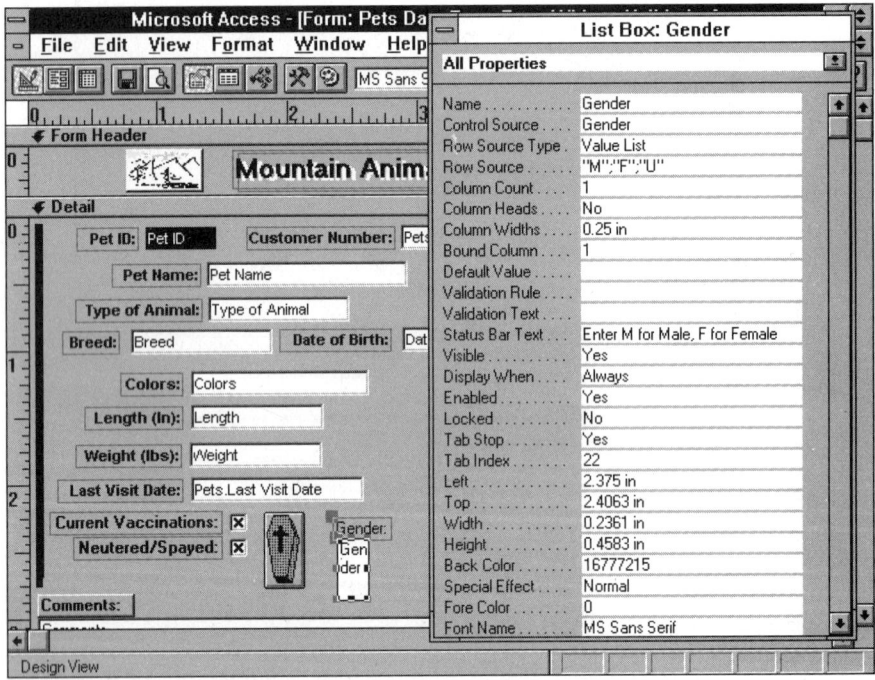

Figure 19-11: The List Box Control and property sheet.

Understanding list box properties

You can see in Figure 19-11, that there are several properties that define a list box. The wizard takes care of all of these excluding the Column Heads property, which adds the name of the column at the top of the list box.

Chapter 19: Adding Data-Validation Controls to Forms

The Row Source properties are the first two properties you have to set. These are the following:

Row Source Type   The source of the data type (See below)

Row Source   Either the Table/Query name or a List of values

The valid Row Source Type property settings are the following:

Table/Query   (Default setting) Data is from a table or is the result of a query or SQL statement.

Value List   List of items specified by the Row Source setting.

Field List   List of field names from the Table/Query named by the Row Source setting.

The Row Source property settings depend on the source type specified by Row Source Type.

Row Source Type	Setting
Table/Query	Enter the name of a table, a query, or an SQL statement.
Value List	Enter a list of items separated by semicolons.
Field List	Enter the name of a table or query.

In this example, you entered the values in the wizard screen. So the Row Source Type is set to Value List, and the Row Source is set to "M";"F";"U". As you can see, the values are entered separated by semicolons.

When you specify Table/Query or Field List as the Row Source Type, you can then pick from a list of tables and queries for the Row Source. The table or query must already exist. The list box will display fields from the table or query in the order they appear in the table or query. The number of columns, their size, whether or not there are column headers, and the column that is bound to the fields control source are all specified by settings in the property sheet.

 If you want to use non-contiguous table/query fields in the list box, you should use an SQL statement rather than a list of field names. The wizard can do this for you automatically. The following is an example of an SQL statement for a two-column list drawn from the Pets table in the Mountain Animal Hospital sample database:

SELECT [Pet Name], [Type of Animal] FROM [Pets] ORDER BY [Pet ID];

These settings include:

Column Count   The number of columns to be displayed.

Column Heads   Yes or No. Yes displays the first set of values or the field names.

Column Width   The width of each column. Each value is separated by semicolons.

Bound Column   The column that passes the value back to the control source field.

For example, suppose you want to list the Pet Name, Type of Animal, and Breed and return the Pet Name to the field control. You could enter *Table/Query* in the Row Source Type, and Pets in the Row Source. You would then enter 3 for the Column Count and 1.5;1;1 in the Column Width, and 1 for the Bound Column.

The following are valid entries for the Row Source property for a Value List list box:

M;F;U

One-column list with three rows (Column Count = 1).

M;Male;F;Female;U;Unknown

Two-column list with three rows (Column Count = 2).

Pet Name;Type of Animal;Bobo;Rabbit;Fido;Dog;Daffy;Duck;Patty;Pig;Adam;Frog

Two-column list with five rows of data and a column header (Column Count = 2, Column Heads = Yes).

Creating a multiple-column list box

List boxes are not limited to a single column of data. It is easy to create a list box with multiple columns of data. You could easily go back and run the wizard again to create a two-column list box. However, it is just as easy now to modify the list box you have on the design screen. Follow these next steps to modify the List Box control to change it to a two-column list.

Chapter 19: Adding Data-Validation Controls to Forms

Steps: To Create a Multiple-Column List Box Using a Value List

Step 1. Change the *Row Source* property to **M;Male;F;Female;U;Unknown**.

Step 2. Set the *Column Count* property to **2**.

Step 3. Enter the *Column Widths* property as **.25;.75**.

Step 4. Set the *Bound Column* property to **1**.

Step 5. Resize the List box control to fit the new column widths.

By changing the Number of Columns property to 2 and setting the Column Widths to the size of the data, you can display multiple columns. As you can see in Figure 19-12, there are multiple columns. The first column's value (specified by the Bound Column property) is passed back to the Gender field.

Though you enter the column widths as decimal numbers, Access will automatically add the inches (in) abbreviation. You can also change it to *cm* or any other unit of measurement.

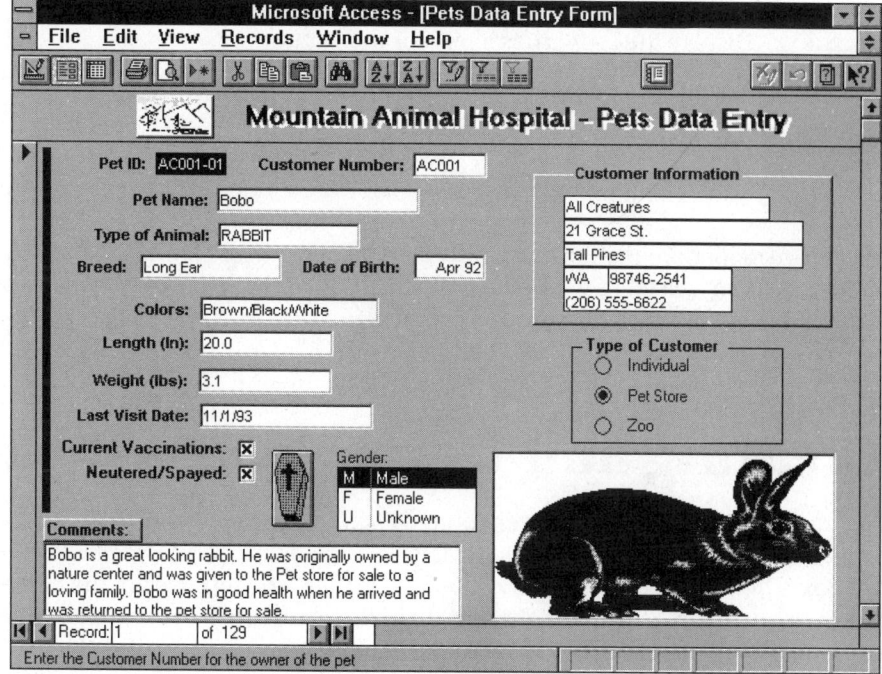

Figure 19-12: Creating a two-column list box.

 If you don't size the list box wide enough to match the sum of the column widths, a horizontal scroll bar will appear at the bottom of the control. If you don't size the list box deep enough to display all the items in the list (including the horizontal scroll bar), a vertical scroll bar will appear.

When you look at this list box, you may wonder Why display the single letter code at all. Your first reaction may be that you need it to pass the single letter code back to the Gender field. In fact, that is the reason for the first column, but there is no need to display it. Data in hidden columns can be used as a bound column just as a column that is displayed.

Hiding a column in a list box

When creating a multiple-column list box, you have the ability to *hide* any column that you do not want to be displayed. This is especially useful when you have a list box that is bound to a field that you do not necessarily want to be displayed. You can *hide* the first column in the list box you just created by following these steps:

Steps:	To Hide a List Box Column
Step 1.	Display the Properties sheet for the list box.
Step 2.	Change the **Column Widths** property to **0;.75**.
Step 3.	Resize the List Box Control to the new width.

When you display the list box, you only see the one column in the list box while the hidden column is used as the bound column. In this way, you can bind a list box on a field that is not even displayed on the screen.

Creating and Using Combo Boxes

As previously mentioned in this chapter, a *combo box* is very similar to a list box. It is named combo box because this control is a combination of a normal entry field and a list box. The operator can directly enter a value into the text area of the combo box, or the directional arrow (at the right portion of the combo box) can be clicked for the list to be displayed. In addition, the list remains hidden from view unless the arrow is activated. In this way, valuable form space is conserved. A combo box is often used when there are many rows to display and a vertical scroll bar will be displayed to show the records that are out of sight.

Chapter 19: Adding Data-Validation Controls to Forms   **485**

In this next example, you are going to change the Type of Animal control from a text box to a combo box, using the Combo Box Wizard.

To create a combo box using the wizard follow these steps:

Steps: Creating a Single-Column Combo Box With a Wizard

Step 1. Delete the existing Type of Animal text box field control and its label.

Step 2. Depress the Combo Box icon in the toolbox.

Step 3. Display the field list and drag the Type of Animal field to the area below Pet Name.

The Combo Box Wizard is automatically started. The first screen is exactly the same as the first list box screen. You decide whether you want to type in a list of values or if the values will come from a table/query. In this example, you will get the values from a Table.

Step 4. Select the first option, *I want the combo box to look up the values in a table or query,* and press the Next > button.

As shown in Figure 19-13, this wizard screen lets you select the table you want to select the values from. By using the row of option buttons under the list of tables, you can view all the Tables, Queries, or both all tables and queries.

Step 5. Select the Animals table and press the Next > button.

The next screen lets you pick the fields you want to use to populate the combo box. This lets you pick any of the fields in the table or query. You can select the fields in any order as a SQL statement is created for you. In this screen, only one field is shown. The Animals table only has one field: Animals, which is a list of valid animals.

Step 6. Select the Animals field and press the > button to add it to the Columns list.

Step 7. Press the Next > button to move to the next wizard screen.

In the next wizard screen, a list of the actual values in your selected field is displayed, as shown in Figure 19-14. Here, you can adjust the width of any columns for their actual display.

The rest of the wizard screens are the same as with the list box. First you accept or change the name of the bound field. Then, the last screen lets you enter a label name, and the wizard creates the combo box.

Step 8. Press Finish to complete the entries with the default choices.

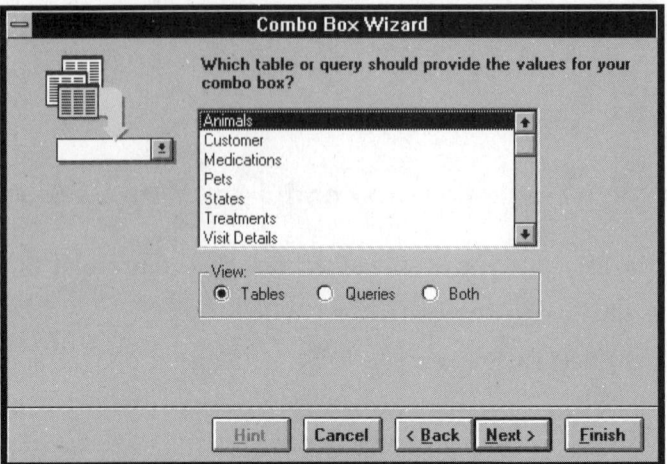

Figure 19-13: Selecting the table for the Row Source of the Combo Box.

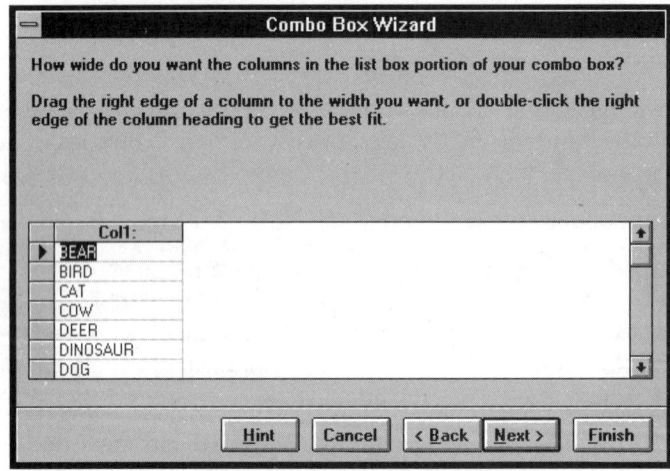

Figure 19-14: Adjusting the column width of the selection.

The control appears on the design screen. Figure 19-15 shows the combo box control and the property sheet for the list box.

The *Row Source Type property* is set to Table/Query. *The Row Source* property is set to the SQL statement **Select [Animals] From [Animals]**. This selects the Animal field from the Animals table. If you wanted to display the animals in a sorted order, you could either enter the data into the Animals table in a sorted order or create a simple query sorting the data into the desired order and then use the query as the basis for the combo box. You can also add sorting directives to the SQL statement.

Figure 19-15:
The Combo Box Control and property sheet.

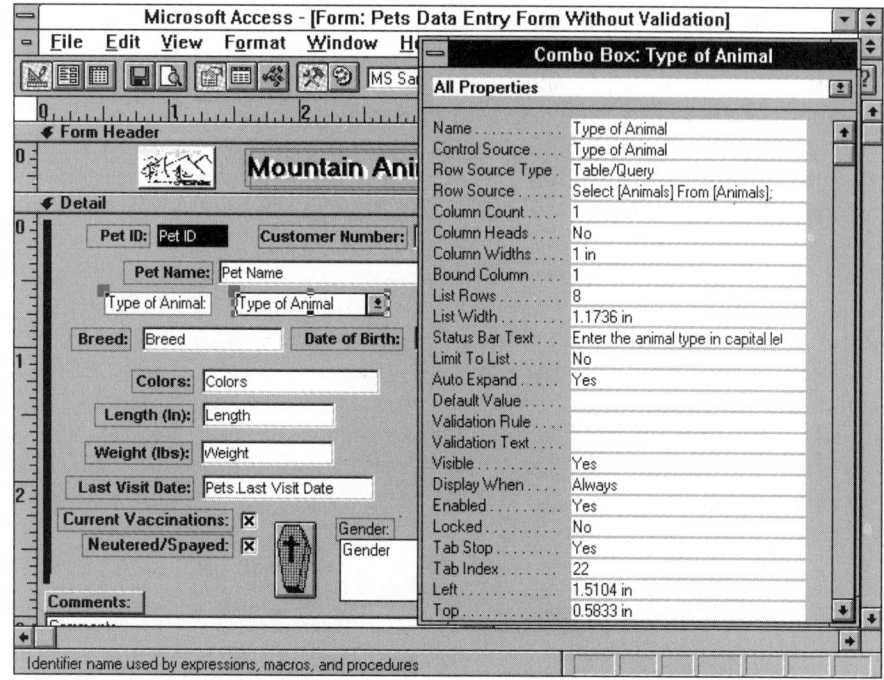

The *List Rows* property sets the number of rows to 8 when the combo box is opened. The wizard does not allow you to select this. The last property, *Limit to List,* determines whether you can enter a value into the Pets table that is not in the list. The wizard also does not allow you to specify this property. You must set directly from the property sheet. The default *No* value says you can enter new values as you are not limiting the entry to the list.

Setting the AutoExpand property to Yes enables the user to select the combo box value by entering text into the combo box that matches a value in the list. As soon as a unique match is found, Access displays the value without having to display the list.

Creating a multiple-column combo box from a query

Just as with list boxes, combo boxes may have multiple columns of information. The columns are displayed when the operator activates the field list. Unless you are extracting fields from a single table in the order of the fields in the table, you probably want to use a query.

Figure 19-16 displays the combo box you will create next. Notice that this combo box displays the Customer Number and Customer Name in the order of the Customer Name. This is accomplished by creating a query. Also notice in Figure 19-16, that the Customer Number and Customer Name heads are displayed.

To understand the selection criteria of a multiple column combo box, you should first establish the query that will select the proper fields.

The query that is called *Customer Number Lookup* is shown in Figure 19-17. Note that the Customer table is related to the Pet table and that the Customer Name field is selected to be used as the sorting field of the query. When used for the combo box, this query will select the Customer Name from the Customer table, match it with the Customer Number within the Customer table, and pass it to the Customer Number within the Pet table. When a Customer is selected, the Customer Number in the Pets table is updated and the correct customer is displayed in the Customer area of the form. This lets you reassign the ownership of a Pet or, more usefully, add a new pet to the system and correctly choose the pet's owner.

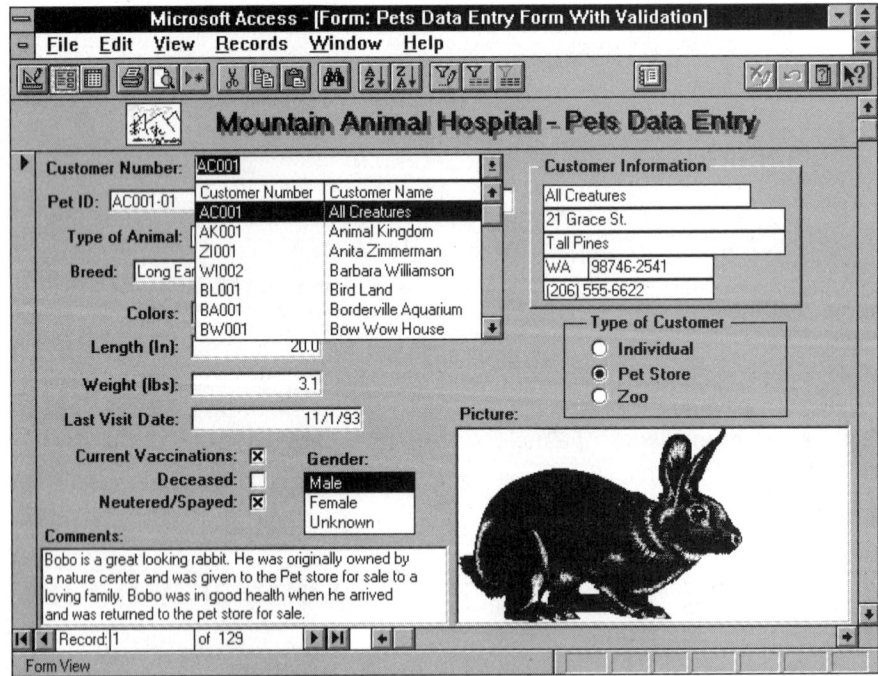

Figure 19-16: Displaying a Multicolumn Combo Box

The query shown in Figure 19-17 will be the basis for a multiple-column combo box for the field *Pets.Customer Number* on the form. The following steps describe how to create this new combo box without using the wizard:

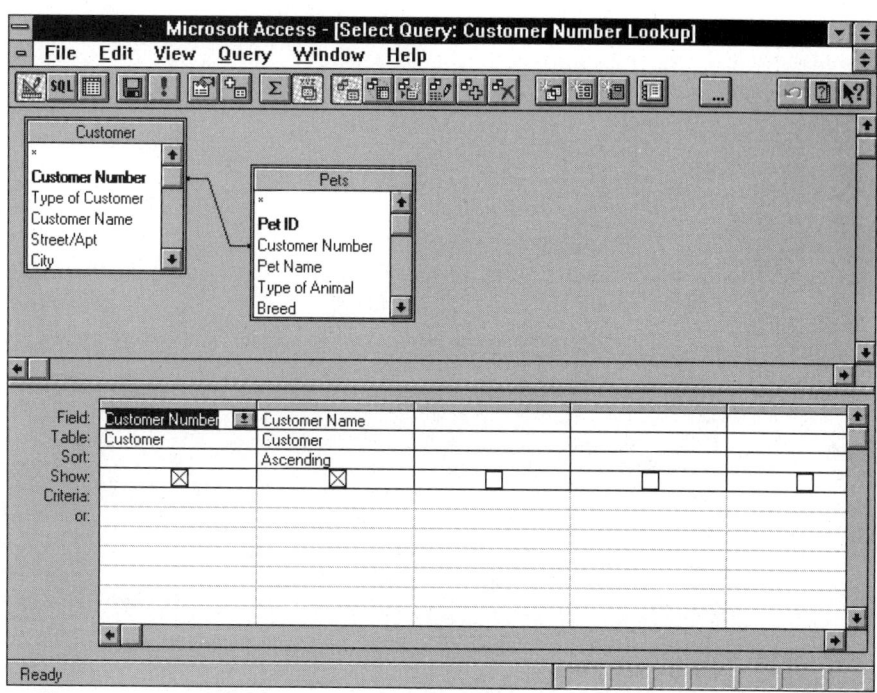

Figure 19-17:
Customer Number Lookup query.

Steps: To Create a Multiple-Column Combo Box

Step 1. Delete the original Pets.Customer Number text box control.

Step 2. Move the original Pet ID and Pet Name controls, as shown in Figure 19-18.

Step 3. Create a new combo box manually and size it, as shown in Figure 19-18.

Step 4. Double-click the label portion of the combo box control.

Step 5. Enter **Customer Number** in the Caption property.

Step 6. Click the data-entry portion of the new combo box.

Step 7. Enter **Pets.Customer Number** in the Control Source property.

Step 8. Select Table/Query in the Row Source Type property.

Step 9. Set the Row Source property to the query Customer Number Lookup.

Step 10. Enter **2** in the Column Count property.

Step 11. Set the Column Heads property to Yes.

Step 12. Set the Column Widths property to 1;1.25.

Step 13. Set the Bound Column property to **1**.
Step 14. Set the List Rows property to **8**.
Step 15. Set the List Width property to **Auto**.

If you have followed the preceding steps properly, your screen form design should resemble the form shown in Figure 19-18, while the form view looks like Figure 19-16.

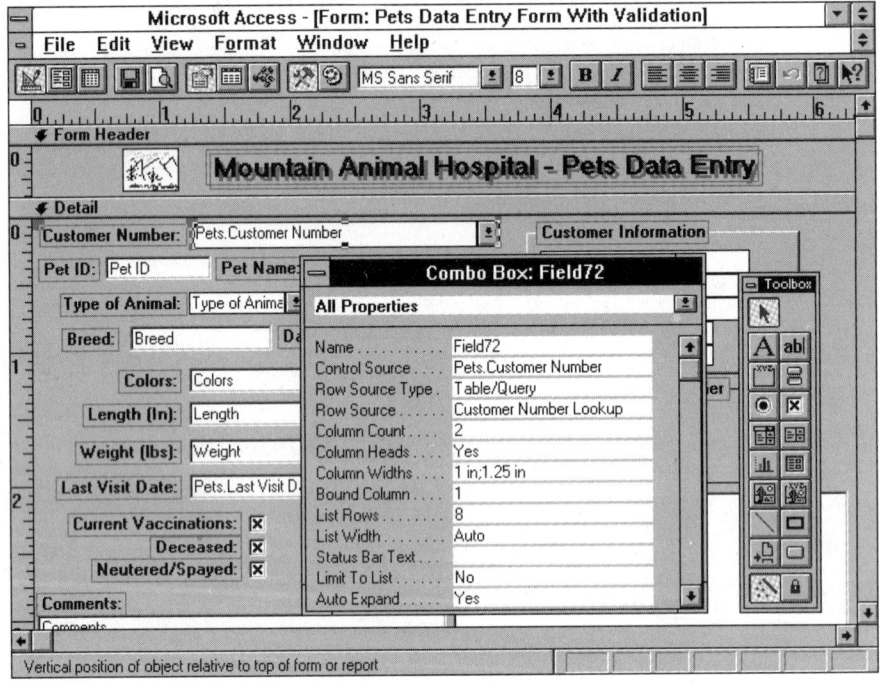

Figure 19-18: A multiple-column combo box.

Summary

In this chapter, you learned many ways to create forms that accept only good data. Validation rules, option buttons, checkboxes, list boxes, and combo boxes make it easy. The new Access 2.0 control wizards make it simple. In this chapter, the following points were explained:

- Data-validation expressions are entered in either tables or forms.
- The Description column in a table becomes the status bar text in a form.
- The Validation Rule and Validation Text properties let you trap for errors and display error messages.
- You can use option buttons, checkboxes, and toggle buttons individually to display a two-state choice or as part of an option group to display one of several possible choices.
- An option button (also called a radio button) is the preferred choice for showing three to four choices.
- Yes/No data is best shown with checkboxes.
- You can also use toggle buttons to display Yes/No data, and you can attach pictures to the face of the button.
- List boxes display choices in an open box.
- Combo boxes display choices in a closed box that the user must select to view the choices.
- List boxes and combo boxes can have one column or many.

In the next chapter, you learn how to link and embed pictures and graphs in your forms and reports.

Using OLE Objects, Pictures, and Graphs

CHAPTER 20

In This Chapter

- The types of objects that you can create
- The differences between bound and unbound objects
- The differences between linking and embedding
- The different ways of storing these objects
- How to modify an existing OLE object from your form design
- How to create and link a graph to a form
- How to create a new graph using a Form Wizard
- How to customize a graph

Access provides many powerful tools for enhancing your forms and reports. These tools let you add pictures, graphs, sound, and even video to your database application. Graph Wizards make it easy to build business graphs and add them to your forms and reports. In this chapter, you learn the different types of graphical and OLE objects that you can add to your system and how to manipulate them to create professional and productive screen displays and reports.

Understanding Objects

Access gives you the ability to embed pictures, graphs, spreadsheets, and word-processed documents, as well as to link any OLE object (Object Linking and Embedding) within both your forms and reports. In addition to being able to add these objects to your forms, Access lets you directly edit them from within your form.

Types of objects

As a general rule, Access can add any type of picture or graphic object to a form or report. Access can also interact with any application through DDE (Dynamic Data Exchange) or OLE. These objects can be complete spreadsheets, ranges of cells, or even an individual cell. They also include pictures from Windows Paintbrush or Microsoft Draw and documents from Word for Windows or other word processors.

Access can embed and store any binary file within an object frame control. This even includes sound and full-motion video. As long as you have the driver for the embedded object, you can play or view the contents of the frame.

These objects can be bound to a field in each record *(bound)* or to the form or report itself *(unbound)*. Depending on how you want to process the OLE object, you may either place the copy right in the Access database *(embed)* or tell Access where to find the object *(link)* and place it in the bound or unbound object frame in your form or report. The following sections describe the different ways to process and store both bound and unbound objects by using embedding and linking.

Using bound and unbound objects

A *bound object* is an object that is displayed and potentially stored within a field of a record in a table. Access can display the object in a form or print it on a report. A bound object is bound to an OLE object data type field in the table. If you use a bound object in a form, you can add and edit pictures or documents record by record in the same way that you can with values. In Figure 20-1, the picture of the squirrel is a bound object. Each record stores a photograph of the animal in the Pets table field named Picture. You can enter a different picture for each record.

An *unbound object* is an object that is not stored in a table but is placed on the form or report itself. An unbound object control is the graphic equivalent of a label control. These are generally used for logos or pictures in the form or report itself rather than belonging to a field of a record. Unbound objects don't change from record to record. In Figure 20-1, the picture of the mountain is an unbound object. Both bound and unbound objects can either be linked or embedded within a form or report.

Linking and embedding

The basic difference between linking and embedding objects within a form or report is that *embedding* the object causes a copy of the object to be stored within your database. *Linking* an object from another application does not cause the object to be stored in your database; rather, the external location of the object is stored.

Chapter 20: Using OLE Objects, Pictures, and Graphs   **495**

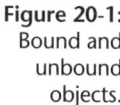

Figure 20-1:
Bound and
unbound
objects.

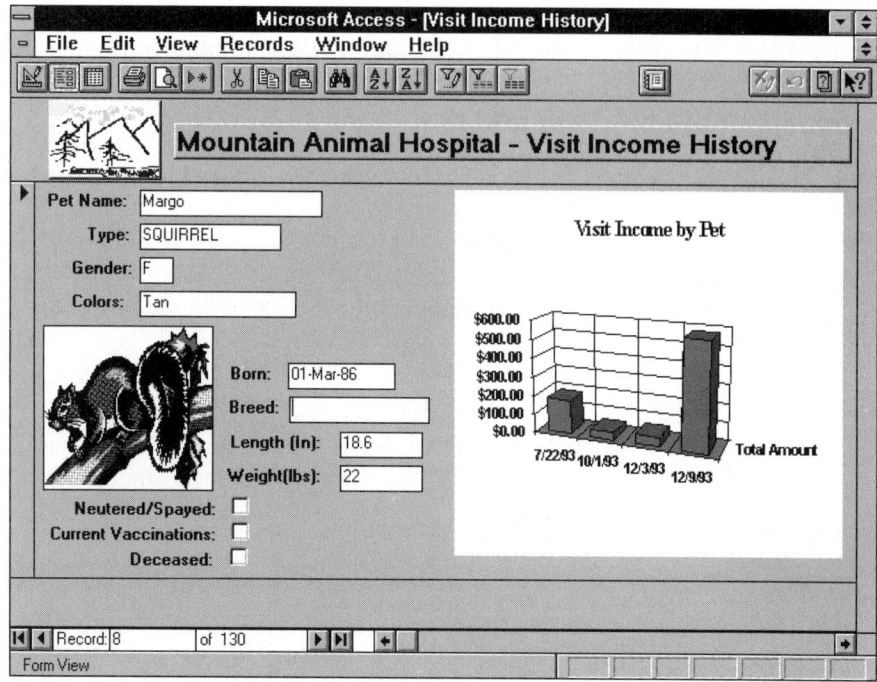

Linking an object gives you two benefits:

- You can make changes using the external application even without opening Access.

- The external file does not use any space in the Access MDB database file.

 If the external file is moved to another directory, or if the file is renamed, the link to Access is broken.

One of the benefits of embedding is that you don't have to worry about someone changing the location or the name of the linked file. Because it is embedded, it is part of the Access MDB database file. Embedding does have its costs, however. The first is that it takes space in your database and sometimes a great deal of it. Some pictures can take 500,000 bytes of space. In fact, if you embed a full-motion video clip of just 30 seconds in your database for one record, this can use several megabytes of space. Imagine the space that 100 records with full-motion video could use.

After the object is embedded or linked, you can use the source application (such as Excel or Paintbrush) to make changes to the object directly from the form. To make changes to these objects, all you need to do is display the object in Access and double-click it. This automatically launches the source application and lets you make changes to the object. When you save the object, it is saved within Access.

Suppose, for example, that you have embedded a Windows Draw picture in Access. When you double-click the picture, Windows Draw is automatically launched and you can edit the picture.

When the external application is started and changes are made to the object, the changes are made to the external file, as opposed to within your database.

To edit an OLE object, you must have the associated OLE application installed in Windows. If you have an Excel XLS file but don't own Excel, you can view the spreadsheet or use its values, but you won't be able to edit or make changes to the spreadsheet.

Following Along in This Book

In the next section of the chapter, you use the form shown in Figure 20-2. You can find the form in the MTNANHSP.MDB database file, named Pets Picture Creation - Empty.

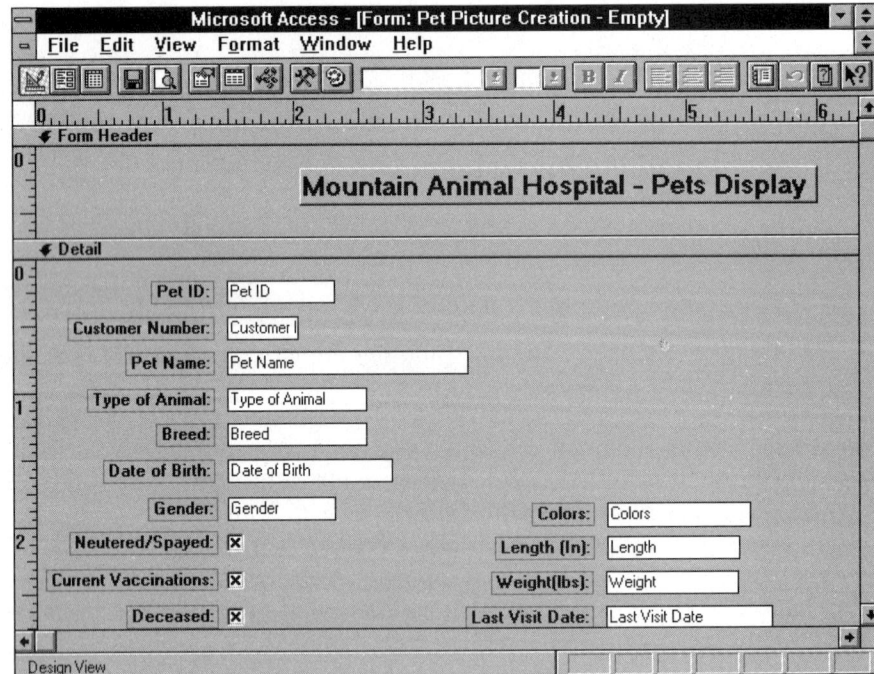

Figure 20-2: The Pets Picture Creation - Empty form.

… Chapter 20: Using OLE Objects, Pictures, and Graphs

Embedding Objects

You can embed objects both in unbound and bound object frames. Embedding places the object right into the Access database, and it is stored either in the form or report or in a record of a table.

Embedding an unbound object

You can use two ways to embed an unbound object in a form or report:

- You can simply paste an object onto the form or report, and an unbound object frame is created that contains the object.
- You can embed an unbound object onto a form or report by creating an unbound object frame and then inserting the object into the frame.

Pasting an unbound object

If the object you want to insert is not an OLE object, you *must* paste the object onto the form. As an example, to cut or copy an object and then paste the object into an unbound object frame, follow these steps:

Steps:	Pasting an Object into an Unbound Object Frame
Step 1.	Create or display the object using the external application.
Step 2.	Select the object and choose Edit➪Cut or Edit➪Copy.
Step 3.	Display the Access form or report and select Edit➪Paste.

This automatically creates an unbound object frame and embeds the pasted object in it.

If the object you paste into a form is an OLE object and you have the OLE application loaded, you can still double-click the object to edit it. For example, you can highlight a range of cells in an Excel worksheet and paste the highlighted selection into an Access form or report. You can highlight a paragraph of text in Word for Windows and paste it onto the Access form or report. You can paste both OLE and non-OLE objects onto a form or report with this method, but you'll see that there are other ways to add an OLE object.

Inserting an unbound OLE object

You can also use another method to embed OLE objects into an unbound object frame. Suppose that you want to embed a file containing a Paintbrush picture. In Figure 20-1, the picture of the mountain is displayed on the form in the form header. This is an unbound object frame. You can embed the picture by either pasting it into the unbound object frame or by inserting the object into the unbound object frame. Follow these steps to create an unbound object frame:

Steps:	Creating an Unbound Object Frame
Step 1.	Open the form Pets Picture Creation - Empty in Design view.
Step 2.	Select the Object Frame button in the toolbar.
Step 3.	Create the unbound object frame, using the Object Frame button from the toolbox to draw a rectangle, as shown in Figure 20-3.

When you create an unbound object frame, the Insert Object dialog box is displayed. This dialog box, shown in Figure 20-4, displays the OLE objects that you have installed on your system. From this dialog box, you can create a new object, and save it as an unbound object within Access. Alternatively, you can select Create from File... to display a file selector dialog box, select an existing object, and embed it in the unbound object frame.

To embed the existing file MTN.BMP in the unbound object frame, follow these steps:

Steps:	Embedding a Paintbrush File
Step 1.	Select Create from File... from the Insert Object dialog box.
Step 2.	Select the Browse button.
Step 3.	Select the file MTN.BMP from your Access directory.
Step 4.	Select OK after the filename appears in the Insert Object dialog.

Chapter 20: Using OLE Objects, Pictures, and Graphs

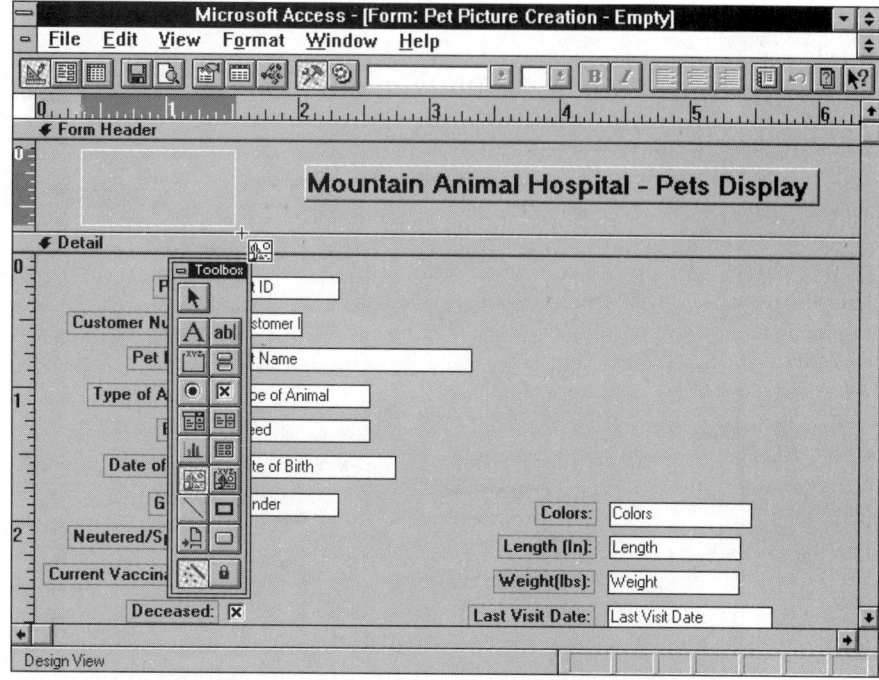

Figure 20-3: Creating an unbound object frame.

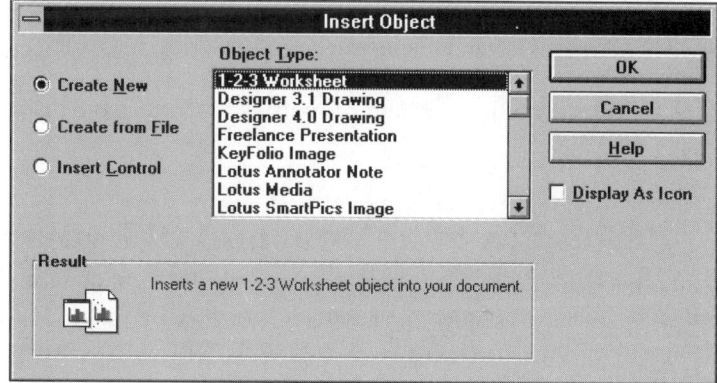

Figure 20-4: The Insert Object dialog box.

Access embeds and displays the picture in the unbound object frame, as you can see in Figure 20-5. Notice in this figure that the picture of the mountain does not appear to be displayed correctly.

The property sheet shows the OLE Class as Paintbrush Picture. One of the features of OLE is that when you originally install the OLE application, it registers itself with Microsoft Windows. The concept of registering is that when you install an OLE application, Windows learns how the application behaves when being displayed and edited.

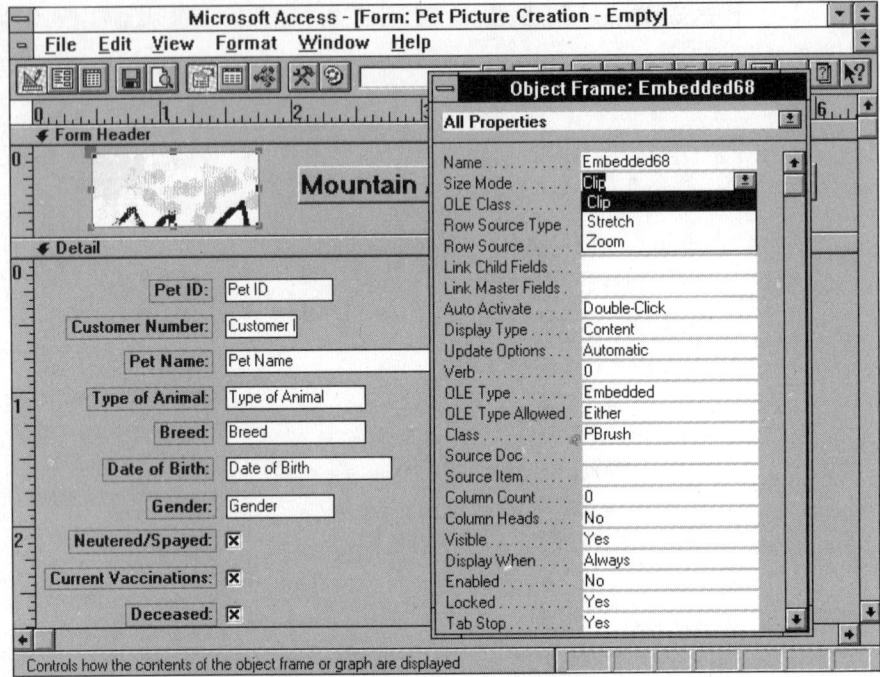

Figure 20-5:
The unbound object fame property sheet.

This information is also available to Access. For example, a group of cells from an Excel worksheet behaves differently than a Paintbrush Picture does.

OLE objects that are displayed have certain properties that affect the display of the object.

Changing the display of an unbound OLE object

After you add an object to a form or a report, you may want to change the size of the object or the object frame. If you embed a small picture, you may want to adjust the size of the object frame to fit the picture. Similarly, you may want to reduce the size of the picture to fit a specific area on your form or report.

You can change the appearance and proportions of the object you embed by changing the size of the unbound object frame and by setting the Size Mode property. In Figure 20-5, you see three choices for the Size Mode property:

Clip   Shows the picture using the actual size and truncating both right and bottom

Stretch Fits the picture within the frame; distorts proportions of the picture

Zoom   Fits the picture proportionally within the frame; may result in extra white space

Clip should be used only when the frame is the exact size of the picture or when you want to crop the picture. Stretch is useful when you have pictures where you can accept a slight amount of distortion. Although using Zoom fits the picture to the frame and maintains the original proportions, it may cause empty space within the frame. Figure 20-6 shows the MTN.BMP file using each of the property selections, as well as the correct view of the picture.

To change the Size Mode options for the MTN.BMP file on the Pets form, follow these steps:

Steps: Changing the Size Mode Property

Step 1. Select the unbound object frame in the Design view.

Step 2. Display the property sheet.

Step 3. Change the Size Mode setting to **Stretch**.

 If you want to return the selected object to its original size, select that object and choose the Size⇨To Fit option from the Format view.

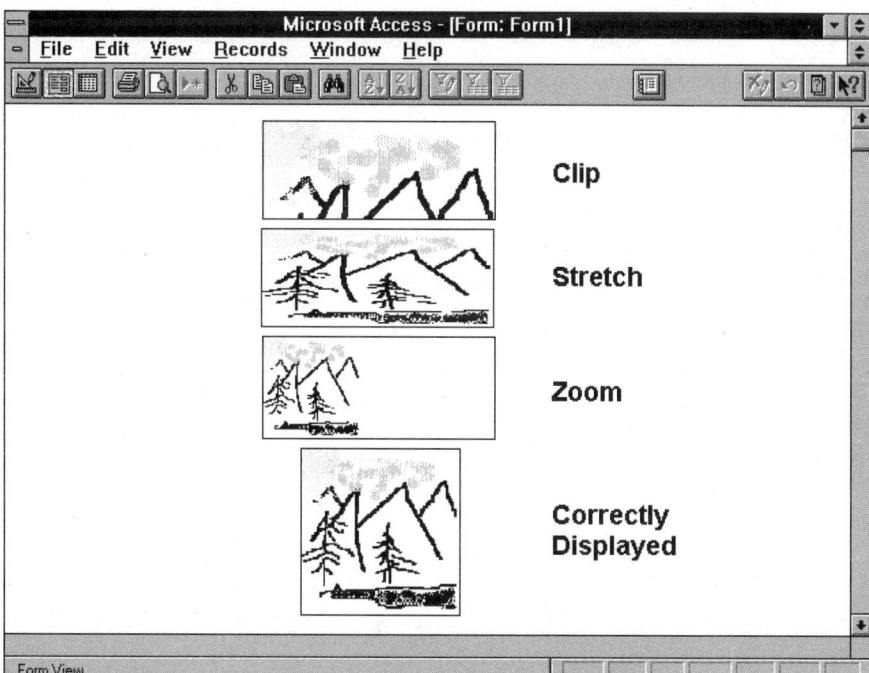

Figure 20-6: Results of using the various scaling options.

Embedding bound objects

You can store pictures, spreadsheets, word-processed documents, or other objects as data in a table. For example, you can store a Paintbrush picture, an Excel worksheet, or an object created in any other OLE application.

You store objects in a table by creating a field with a data type of OLE object. Once you create a bound object frame, its Control Source can be bound to the OLE object field in the table. You can then embed an object into each record of the table by using the bound object frame.

You can also insert objects into a table from the Datasheet view of a form, table, or query, although the objects cannot be displayed other than in the Form view. When you switch to a Datasheet view, you'll see text describing the OLE class of the embedded object. For example, if you insert a BMP picture into an OLE object field in a table, the text "Paintbrush Picture" appears in the Datasheet view.

Creating a bound OLE object

As an example of how to create and bind a bound object frame, follow these steps:

Steps:	Creating an Embedded OLE Object in a New Bound Object Frame
Step 1.	Select the Bound Object Frame button from the toolbox.
Step 2.	Drag and size the frame as shown in Figure 20-7.
Step 3.	Display the properties sheet.
Step 4.	Type **Picture** in the Control Source property.
Step 5.	Set the Size Mode property to **Zoom** so that the picture will be zoomed within the area you defined.
Step 6.	Select and delete the bound object frame label (only).
Step 7:	Close and save the changes to this form.

Adding a picture to a bound object frame

After you define the bound object frame control and place it on a form, you can add pictures to it in several ways. You can paste a picture into a record, or you can insert a

Chapter 20: Using OLE Objects, Pictures, and Graphs   503

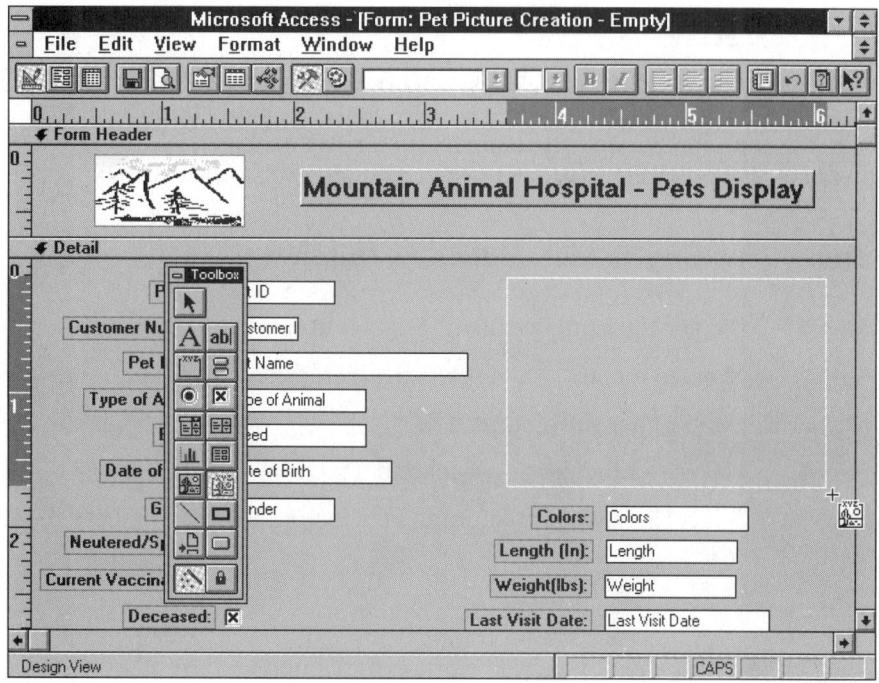

Figure 20-7: Creating a bound object frame.

file object into the frame. You insert the file object for a bound frame in nearly the same way as for an unbound object frame. The only difference is that where an unbound object frame has a picture inserted in the design screen, a bound object frame has a picture inserted in Form view.

To insert a picture or other object into a bound object frame, display the form in form view, move to the correct record (each record can have a different picture or object), select the bound object frame, and then follow the same steps as for an unbound object frame, which you have previously learned. When you are through, the picture or object appears in the space used for the bound object frame in the form.

 If you create the object rather than embedding an existing file, some applications display a dialog box asking whether you want to close the connection and update the open object. Choose Yes, and then Access embeds the object in the bound object frame (or embeds the object in the datasheet field along with text that describes the object such as "Paintbrush Picture").

After you embed an object, you can start its source application and edit the object from your form or report by selecting the object in the Form view and double-clicking it.

Editing an embedded object

Once you have an embedded object, you may want to modify the object itself. You can edit an OLE object in several ways. Usually, you can simply double-click the object. This launches the source application and lets you edit the object. As an example, follow these steps to edit the picture of the cat in Windows Paintbrush:

Steps:	Editing an Embedded OLE Object
Step 1.	Display the form Pets Picture Creation - Empty in Form view.
Step 2.	Move to record 12 and select the Picture bound object frame of the cat.
Step 3.	Double-click the picture.
Step 4.	Make any changes you want to the picture.
Step 5.	Select File⇨Exit and return to Pets Picture Creation - Empty to return to Access.

If you make any changes, you will be prompted to update the embedded object before continuing.

In this example, Windows Paintbrush is launched with the picture of the cat in the editing area, as shown in Figure 20-8. You can make changes to the embedded image and store it back into the table.

When you finish editing the picture, you can select File⇨Exit in Paintbrush, and the modified image replaces the embedded image in the table.

In most cases, you can modify an OLE object by double-clicking it. But when you attempt to modify either a sound or video object, double-clicking the object causes it to "play" as opposed to allowing you to modify it. For these objects, you must follow the preceding steps to modify the object properly.

Linking Objects

Besides embedding objects, you can also link them. You can link to external application files in much the same way as you embed them. The difference is that the object itself is not stored in the form or report or the database table. Rather, information about the link is stored in the table, form, or report. This saves valuable space in the MDB file and also allows the object to be edited in the source application without having to go through Access.

Chapter 20: Using OLE Objects, Pictures, and Graphs

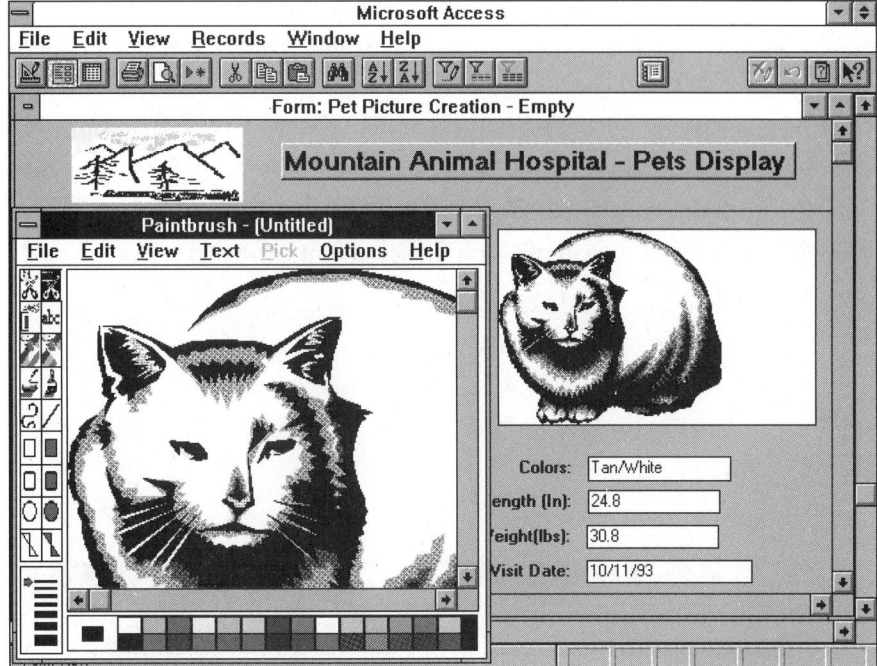

Figure 20-8: Editing the embedded object.

Linking a bound object

When you create a link from information in another application (for example, a Microsoft Excel file) to a field in a table, the information is still stored in its original file.

Suppose that you decide to use the OLE object field to store an Excel file containing additional information about the animal. If the Excel file contains history about the animal, you may want to link the information from the Pet record to this file.

Before linking information in a file to a field, you must first create and save the file in the source application. The following steps show how to use the Picture bound object frame to link a Pets table record to an Excel worksheet:

Steps:	Linking Information to a Bound Object
Step 1.	In the source application (Microsoft Excel), open the document that contains the information you want to link to.
Step 2.	Select the information that you want to link, as shown in Figure 20-9.
Step 3.	Select Edit⇨Copy.

Once you copy the range to the Clipboard, you can paste it into the bound object frame in the Access form by using the Paste Special option of the Edit menu.

Step 4. Switch to Access and open the Pets Picture Creation - Empty form in Form view.

Step 5. Go to record number 32 in the Access form.

Step 6. Select the bound object frame containing the picture of the cat.

Step 7. Select Edit⇨Paste Special.

The Paste Special dialog box appears. When you link a data range to a bound object frame, the link is always manual.

Step 8: Select Paste Link and choose Excel worksheet.

Step 9. Choose OK.

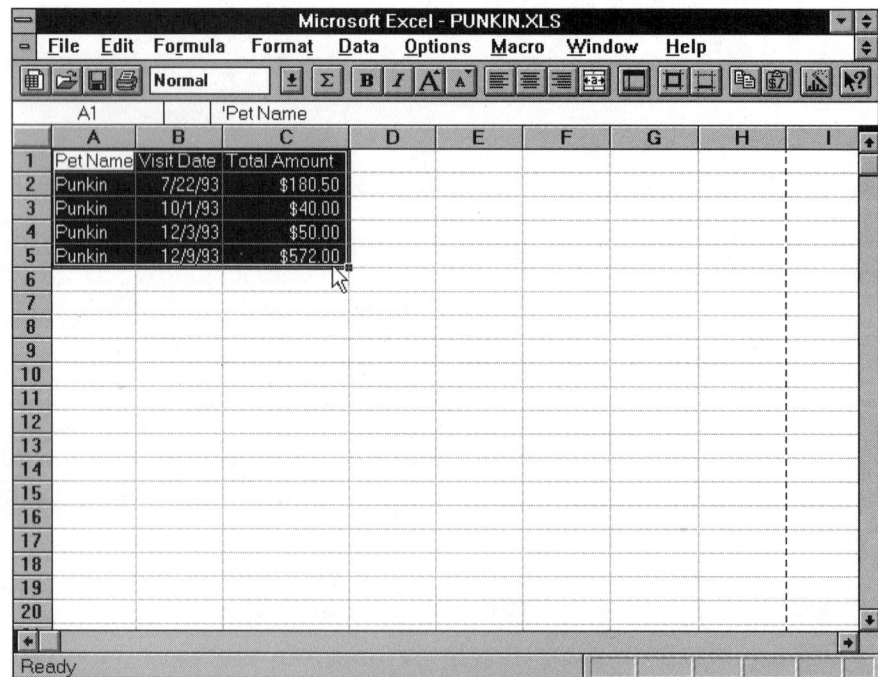

Figure 20-9: Copying a range from Microsoft Excel.

Figure 20-10:
A linked worksheet in a bound object frame.

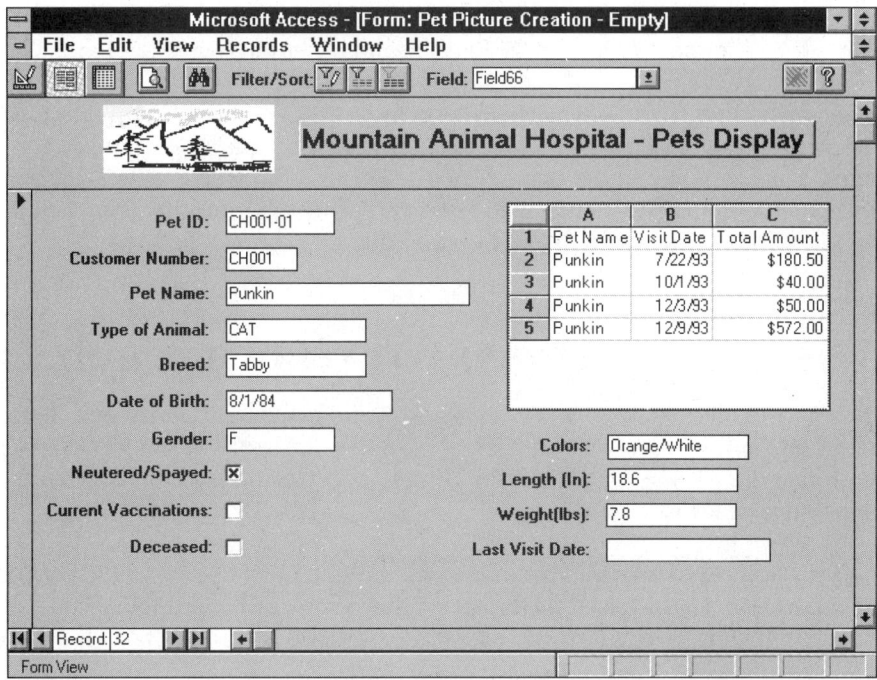

The linked Excel worksheet appears in the bound object frame, as shown in Figure 20-10.

Access creates the link and displays the object in the bound object frame (or it links the object to the datasheet field and displays text that describes the object, such as "Microsoft Excel").

Creating a Graph

Access has the capability to incorporate graphs within a form or report. You can create graphs with the Microsoft Graph applet that is included in your Access package. (An applet is a mini-application.) Or you can create a graph by using any of the other OLE applications. As a general rule, a graph is merely a specialized type of unbound object frame.

You can graph data from any of your database tables, or you can graph data that is stored within other applications, such as Microsoft Excel. With Graph, you can create a wide variety of styles of graphs, such as bar graphs, pie charts, line charts, and others. Because Graph is an embedded OLE application, it does not work as a stand-alone application. It must be run from within your Access program.

 The Graph applet found within Access is essentially the same graphic application found within Word 6, Excel 5, and other Microsoft software.

After you embed a graph, you can treat it as any other OLE object. You can modify the graph from the Design view of your form or report by double-clicking on the graph itself. You can also edit the graph from the Form or Datasheet view of a form. The following sections describe how to build and process graphs that use data from within an Access table, as well as from tables of other OLE applications.

The different ways to create a graph

Access provides two ways to create a graph and place it on a form or a report. You can use the Graph Wizard to create a graph as a new form, or you can click the Graph button in the toolbox from the Form Design mode to add a graph to a existing form and link it to a table data source.

As a general rule, for both types of graph creation, before you enter a graph into a form or report that will be based on data from one or more of your tables, you must first specify which table or query will supply the data for the graph. You should keep in mind several rules when setting up your query:

- Make sure that the fields containing the data to be graphed are selected.
- Be sure that the fields containing the labels that identify the data are included.
- Include any linking fields if you want the data to change from record to record.

Embedding a Graph in a Form

As you learned earlier in this chapter, you can both link and embed objects in your Access tables, and you can create and display objects on your Access forms. In the final section of this chapter about OLE objects and their relationships with Access, you create and display a graph based on the Mountain Animal Hospital data and then display it on a form.

This graph will represent the visits of a pet, showing the visit dates and the dollars received for each visit. When you move through the Pets table, the form recalculates each pet's visits and displays the graph in a graph format. Figure 20-11 shows the completed form in the Form view that you create. You'll use a form that already exists but doesn't contain the graph. The name of the form is Visit Income History - Without Graph.

Chapter 20: Using OLE Objects, Pictures, and Graphs **509**

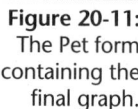

Figure 20-11:
The Pet form containing the final graph.

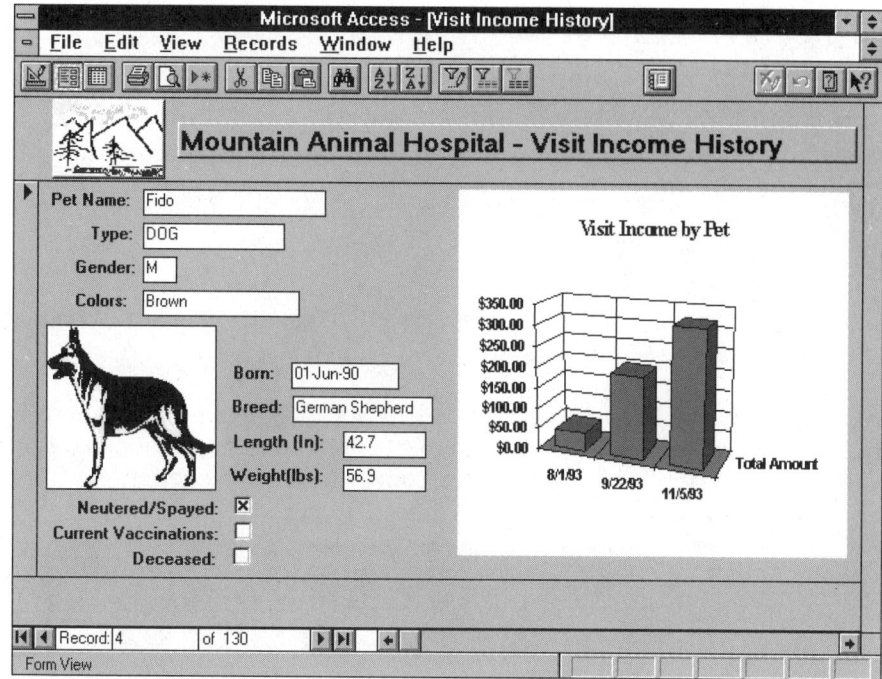

Following Along In This Chapter
The form Visit Income History - Without Graph is in the MTNANHSP.MDB database, along with the final version called Visit Income History that contains the completed graph.

Assembling the data

As a first step in embedding a graph, it is important to make sure that the information you need for the graph is provided for in the query associated with the form. In this example, you need both the Visit Date and the Total Amount fields from the Visits table as the basis of the graph. You also need the Pet ID field from the Visits table to use as a link to the data on the form. This link allows the data in the graph to change from record to record.

Sometimes, you'll need to create a query when you need data items from more than one table.

Adding the graph to the form

The following steps detail how to create and place the new graph on the existing form. You should be in the Design view of the form named Visit Income History - Without Graph.

Steps: Creating the New Graph on the Form

Step 1. Select the Graph button in the toolbox.

Step 2. Position the new cursor at the upper left position for the new graph.

Step 3. Click the mouse and hold it while dragging the box to the desired size on the right portion of the form.

Once you size the blank area for the graph and release the mouse button, Access activates the Graph Wizard used to embed a graph in a form.

As shown in Figure 20-12, this wizard screen lets you select the table or query you want to select the values from. By using the row of option buttons under the list of tables, you can view all the Tables, Queries, or both all tables and queries.

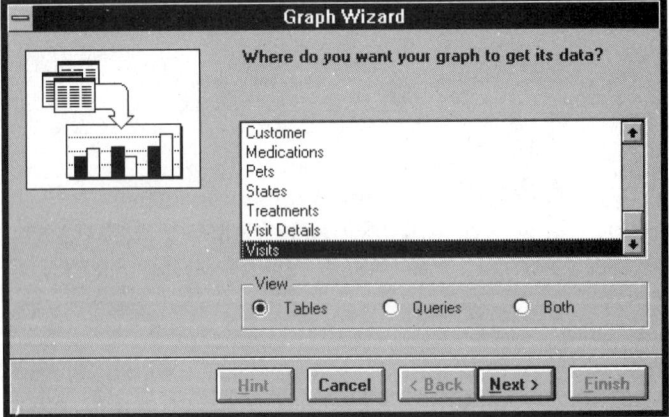

Figure 20-12: Selecting the table for the source of data for the graph.

The following steps take you through the Wizard in order to create the desired graph and link it to your form:

Steps: Creating the Graph Using the Graph Wizard

Step 1. Choose the Visits table as the source for the graph.

Step 2. Click Next > to go to the next wizard screen.

The Graph Wizard lets you select the fields you want to include in your graph.

Step 3. Select the Visit Date and Total Amount Fields by double-clicking them to move them to the Fields for graph box.

Step 4. Click Next > to go to the next wizard screen.

Because you are working with a date field for the x-axis, you have to answer some additional questions in order to properly summarize the date data. This is true for any graph wizard. There are two choices in the dialog box shown in Figure 20-13:

Only along the graph's axis	Displays the data as is
Along the graph's axis and the graph's legend	Groups months within years, days within in months, and so on.

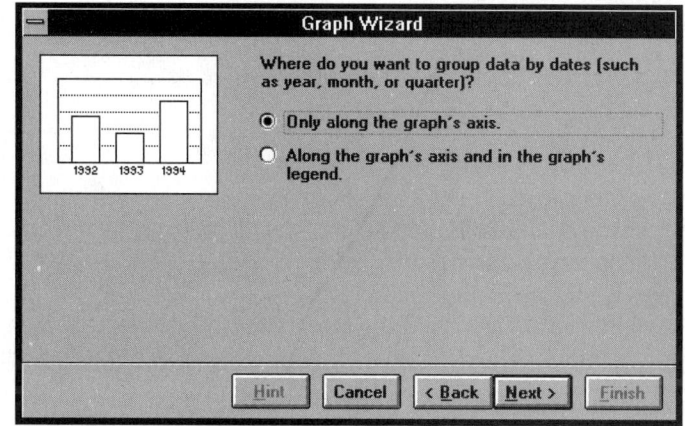

Figure 20-13: Selecting the date grouping.

For example, suppose you had 24 data points — one for each month for the years 1994 and 1995. The first choice, Only along the graph's axis, would create 24 data values in the x-axis. The second choice, Along the graph's axis and in the graph's legend, would create only 12 data values, one for each month, but would create two different lines or groups of bars — one for 1994 and one for 1995. This option lets you separate like values for different time periods for comparison purposes. As you choose between the two different selections in the wizard screen, the picture changes to show this same concept. In this example, you want to display each individual Visit date regardless of the month or year.

Step 5. Select Only along the graph's axis.

Step 6. Select Next > to go to the next Wizard screen.

After you select the date grouping setting, you can select whether you want to summarize or rollup the data within a date hierarchy and whether you want to limit the data used to a certain date range. Figure 20-14 displays the dialog box for this.

Part III: Using Access in Your Work

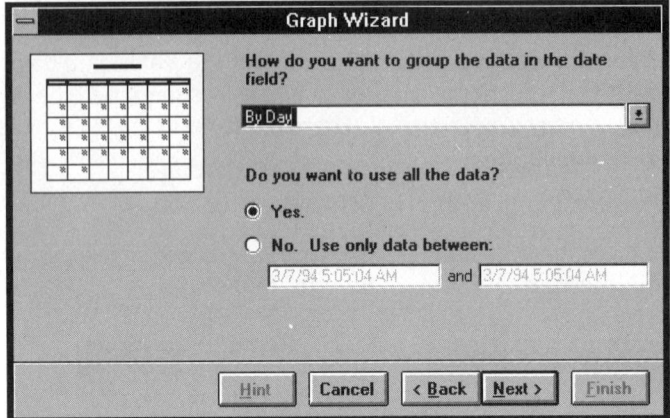

Figure 20-14: Grouping Selections for Date Data

The dialog box shown in Figure 20-14 lets you choose the date hierarchy from larger to smaller rollups. The choices range from Year, Quarter, Month, Week, Day, Hour, Minute. If you have data for many dates within a month and want to roll it up by month, you would choose month. In this example, you want to see all of the detail data. Since the data is in Visits by date (mm/dd/yy), you would select Day to view all of the detail records.

Step 7. Open the combo box and select *Day* for this example.

You also have the option of limiting the data used to a specific range of dates. In this example, you select Yes to use all of the data. This could let you only see the current year if you had several years of data.

Step 8. Select Yes to use all of the data in the Table.

Step 9. Select *Next* to display the linking dialog box.

As can be seen, you have a lot of flexibility when determining the criteria of data selection for date fields. This should be kept in mind when designing other graphs for display. You may use the same graph and the same data, but then select a different date criteria in order to analyze your data in various ways.

The next wizard screen is shown in Figure 20-15. This lets you determine how the numeric data (in this example, the Total Amount field) is summarized for each catagory. You can sum, average, or count the records. In this example, you want a sum of the visit amounts by day.

Step 10. Select Add (sum) the numbers.

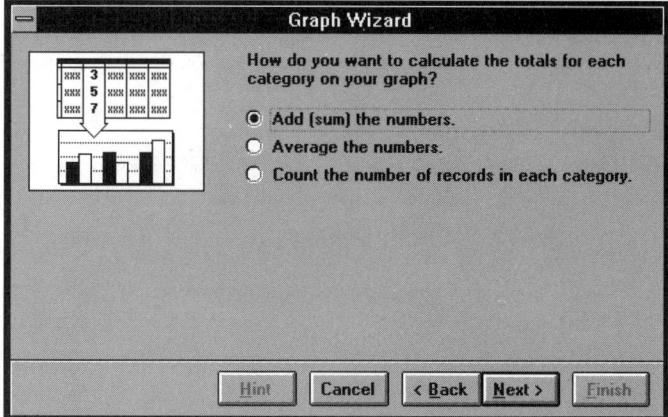

Figure 20-15: Deciding how to calculate numeric totals for each graph category.

Step 11.   Select Next > to display the field linking dialog box.

After you select the summarization choice for the new graph, the Graph Wizard gives you the option as to whether you would like to link the new graph to the form you are working with. This is a simple dialog box with two choices, Yes or No.

Step 12.   Select the Yes option.

When you answer Yes, another dialog box is displayed letting you choose fields on the original form to link to a field you also have to choose in the table/query used for the graph. As you can see in Figure 20-16, you will link the Pet ID field from the Pets table used in the form, to the Pets ID field from the Visits table used in the graph.

Step 13.   Select Pet ID in the Fields on the form: list box.

Step 14.   Select Pet ID in the Fields in the graph: list box.

Step 15.   Press the <=> button that is between the two list boxes.

This copies the link to the Links: box below. This step links the new graph to your form using the Pet ID fields. If you need a multifield link, you can select more than one link. If you make a mistake, you can select the button next to the right of the Links box to remove the selected link.

Step 16.   Select Next>to display a sample graph and choose the type of graph to create.

The next screen shows you a picture of your graph as presently designed and lets you choose the type of graph you want to create and whether the data series are in rows or columns.

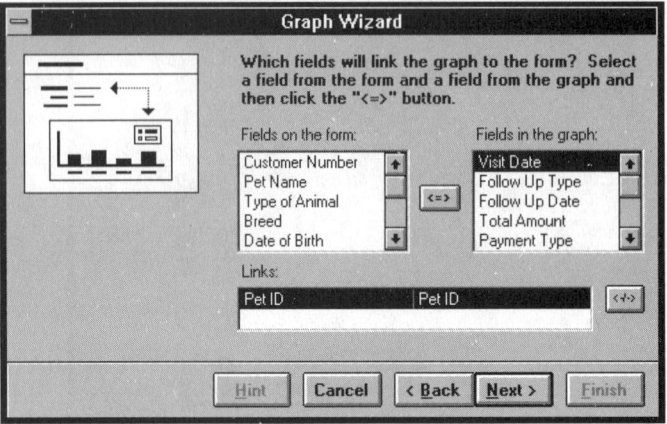

Figure 20-16: Linking the graph to your form.

In this example, you are going to select a 3-D column chart and later customize it using many of the graph options. This screen appears in Figure 20-17.

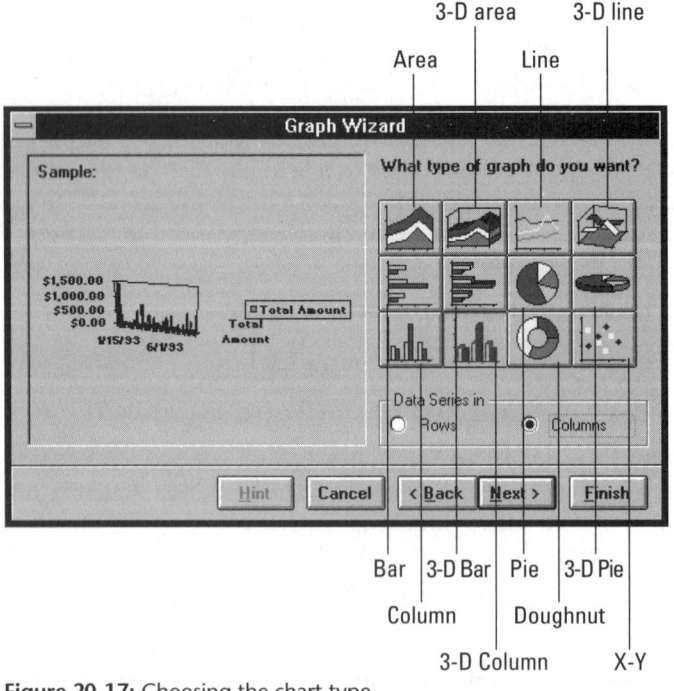

Figure 20-17: Choosing the chart type.

Chapter 20: Using OLE Objects, Pictures, and Graphs

Step 17. Select the 3-D Column chart type by clicking the picture of the 3-D column chart.

This screen, shown in Figure 20-17, lets you visually pick very important choices that determine how your chart is constructed. Each time you make a selection, the graphic in the chart changes, using your actual data.

Step 18. Because the data series (actual values) are in the Total Amount column, you would select the Column option button of the Data Series In option group.

All of the data for all Pets is shown in the Sample Chart. Until you complete your chart, the link to each individual pet is not included in the sample chart information. As a result, all records are included in the sample.

Step 19. Select Next > to move to the last Wizard screen.

The last Chart Wizard screen, shown in Figure 20-18, lets you enter a title and determine whether a legend is needed. In this example, you won't need a legend because you only have one data series.

Step 20. Enter Visit Income History for the graph title.

Step 21. Select No for the *Do you want the chart to display a legend?* question.

Notice as you enter each value, the graph shown in the Sample Chart screen changes to reflect the changes.

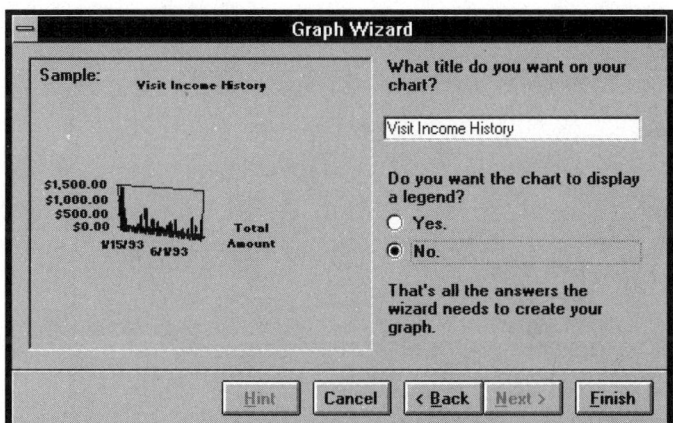

Figure 20-18: Specifying a chart title and legend.

Step 22. Press Finish to complete the wizard.

After you complete all the entries, the sample chart appears in the graph object frame in the design screen. Until you display the form in form view, the link to the individual pet is not established and the graph is not recalculated to show only the visits for the specific pet's record.

Step 23. Click the Form view button in the toolbar to recalculate the graph.

Figure 20-19 shows the final graph in form view.

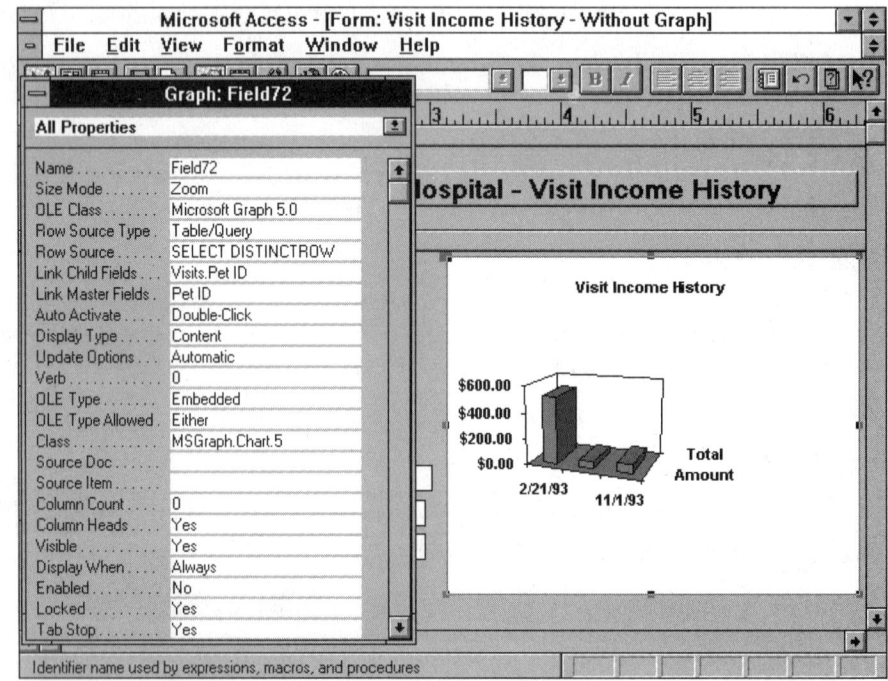

Figure 20-19: Recalculating the graph in form view.

In the Design view, you have the ability to customize your new graph using the Microsoft Graph application. To customize the graph, select the graph in Design view and double-click the graph.

In Figure 20-19, you see the graph and the property sheet.

A graph is displayed by using a graph frame. A graph frame displays its data either in the Form view or the Design view. Take note of some of the properties in the property sheet. The Size Mode property is initially set to Zoom. You can change this to Clip or Stretch, although the graph should always be displayed proportionally. You can size and move the graph to fit onto your form. When you work with the graph in the Graph applet, the size of the graph you create is the size that the graph will be in the Design window.

The OLE Class is Microsoft Graph 5.0. This is automatically linked by the Graph Wizard. The data source comes from the query you created but is displayed as an SQL statement, which is passed to the Graph.

The next two properties, Link Child Fields and Link Master Fields, control linking of the data to the form data itself. By using the link properties, you can link the graph's data to each record in the form. In this example, the Pet ID from the current Pets record is linked to Visit Details records with the same Pet ID.

To change the appearance of the graph, you can double-click the graph in Design view to open Microsoft Graph. After you make the changes you want, you can select File⇒Exit and return to Microsoft Access to go back to the Design view.

Customizing a Graph

Once you create a graph within Access, you have the ability to make enhancements to it by using the tools within Microsoft Graph. As demonstrated in the preceding section, just a few mouse clicks will create a basic graph. This section describes a number of ways to enhance your graph and make it a powerful presentation and reporting tool.

In many cases, the basic chart that you create presents the idea you want to get across. However, in other cases, it may be necessary to create a more illustrative presentation to fulfill your needs. You can accomplish a better presentation with any of these enhancements:

- Entering free-form text to the graph to highlight specific areas of the graph
- Changing attached text for a better display of the data being presented
- Annotating the graph with lines and arrows
- Changing certain graphic objects with colors and patterns
- Moving and modifying the legend
- Adding gridlines to reflect the data better
- Manipulating the 3-D view to more accurately show your presentation
- Adding a bitmap to the graph for a more professional presentation
- Changing the graph type to show the data in a different graphic format, such as Bar, Line, or Pie.
- Adding or modifying the data in the graph

Once the graph is displayed in the Graph applet, you can begin to make changes to it.

Understanding the Graph window

The Graph window, shown in Figure 20-20, lets you work with and customize the graph. As you can see, there are actually two windows within the Graph window:

Datasheet   A spreadsheet of the data used in the graph

Chart   The displayed chart of the selected data

 You can change the look of the graph by resizing the chart window. Figure 20-20 shows a wider graph window, which enables you to see labels better.

In the datasheet, you can add, change, or delete data. Any data that you add, change, or delete in the datasheet is immediately reflected in the graph. After you change the datasheet in the Graph window, you can even tell Access whether to include each row or column when the graph is drawn.

In the chart portion of the Graph window, you can change the way the graph is displayed. By clicking on such objects as attached text or on areas of the graph such as the columns, you can make changes to these objects. You can double-click an object to display a customization dialog box or you can make selections from the menus at the top of the window.

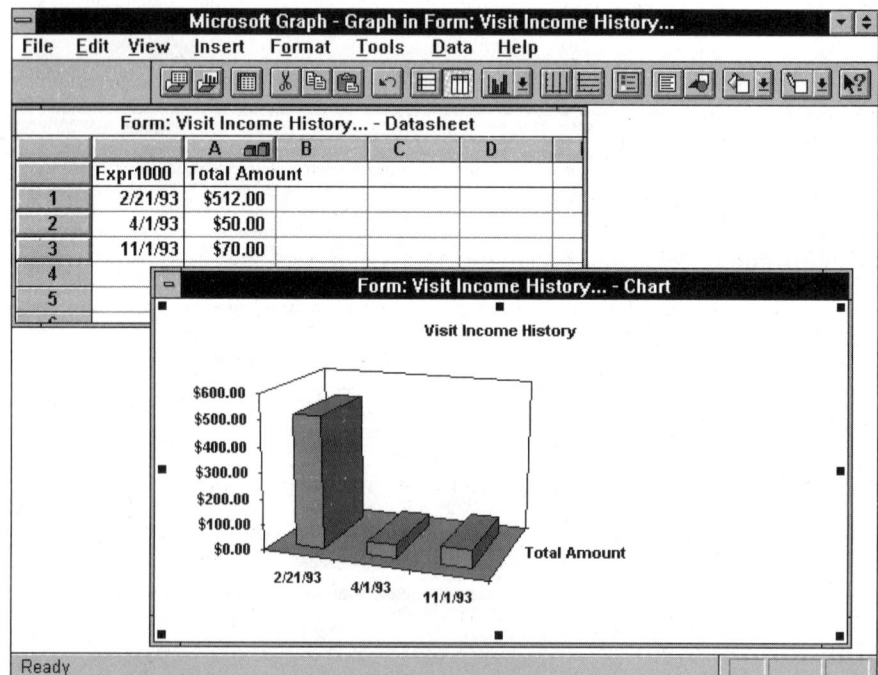

Figure 20-20: The Graph window.

Working with attached text

Text that is generated by the program is called *attached* text. These graph items are attached text:

- Graph title
- Value of y-axis
- Category of x-axis
- Data series and points
- Overlay value of y-axis
- Overlay value of x-axis

Once the initial graph is displayed, you have the ability to change this text. You can click a text object to change the text itself. You can double-click on any of the text items in the preceding list and then modify their properties.

You can choose from three categories of settings to modify an attached text object:

Patterns   Background and foreground colors, borders, and shading

Fonts   Text font, size, style, and color

Alignment   Alignment and orientation

 You can change attributes from the Format menu, too.

The Font options let you change the font assignment for the text within the text object, as shown in Figure 20-21. The Chart Fonts dialog box is a standard Windows font-selector box. Here, you can select Font, Size, Style, Color, and Background effects. To change the text, follow these steps:

Steps:	Changing the Default Fonts
Step 1.	Double-click the chart title — Visit Income History.
Step 2.	Select the Font tab from the Format dialog box.
Step 3.	Select Times New Roman in the Font list box.
Step 4.	Select Italic in the Font Style list box.

Step 5. Select 12 in the Size list box.

Step 6. Select OK to complete the changes.

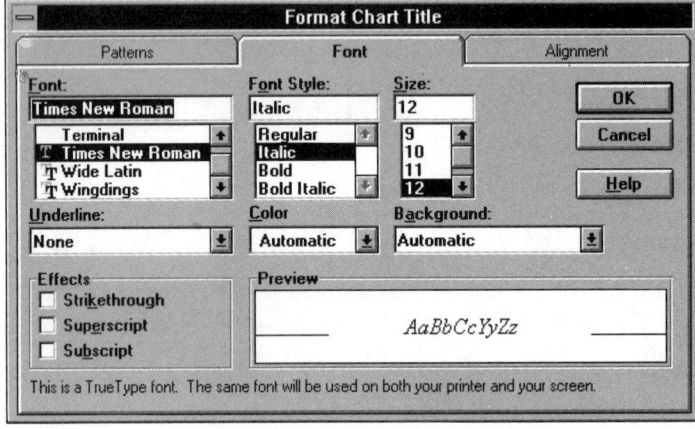

Figure 20-21: The Chart Fonts dialog box.

As you make the font changes, a sample of the change appears in the Sample box.

The Alignment tab in the dialog box lets you set the horizontal alignment (left, center, or right), the vertical alignment (top, center, or bottom), and the orientation, with four options available for displaying the text in either horizontal or vertical format. Figure 20-22 shows the Alignment dialog box and the options available.

The most important part of this dialog box is the Orientation setting. Although for some titles it is not important to change any of these settings, it becomes very necessary to changes these for titles that normally run vertically, such as axis titles.

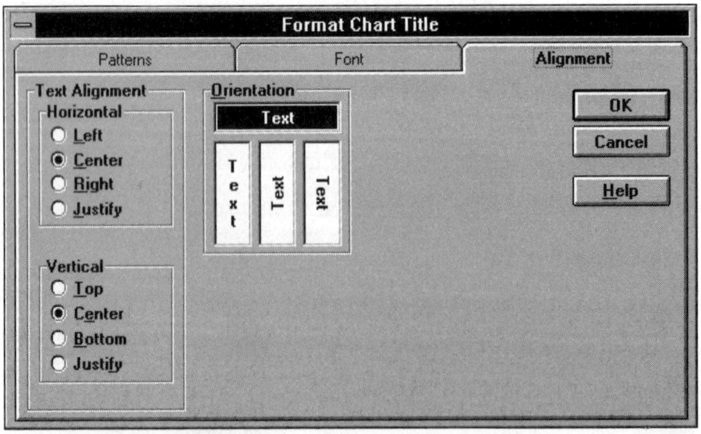

Figure 20-22: The Alignment dialog box.

Chapter 20: Using OLE Objects, Pictures, and Graphs — 521

Sometimes, you may need to add text to your graph to present your data better. This text is called *free-form,* or *unattached, text.* You can place this text anywhere on your graph and combine it with other objects to illustrate your data as you want. Figure 20-23 shows free-form text being entered on the graph, as well as the changes you previously made to the graph title.

In the next steps, you see how to add free-form text to the graph:

Steps: Adding Free-Form Text to Your Graph

Step 1.   Type **For the Period May 1-15, 1993** anywhere on the graph, as shown in Figure 20-23.

Microsoft Graph positions the text near the middle of the graph. The text is surrounded by handles so that you can size and position the text.

Step 2.   Drag the text to the bottom left corner of the graph.

Step 3.   Right-click the text, select Format Object, and change the font to Times New Roman, 12 point, regular.

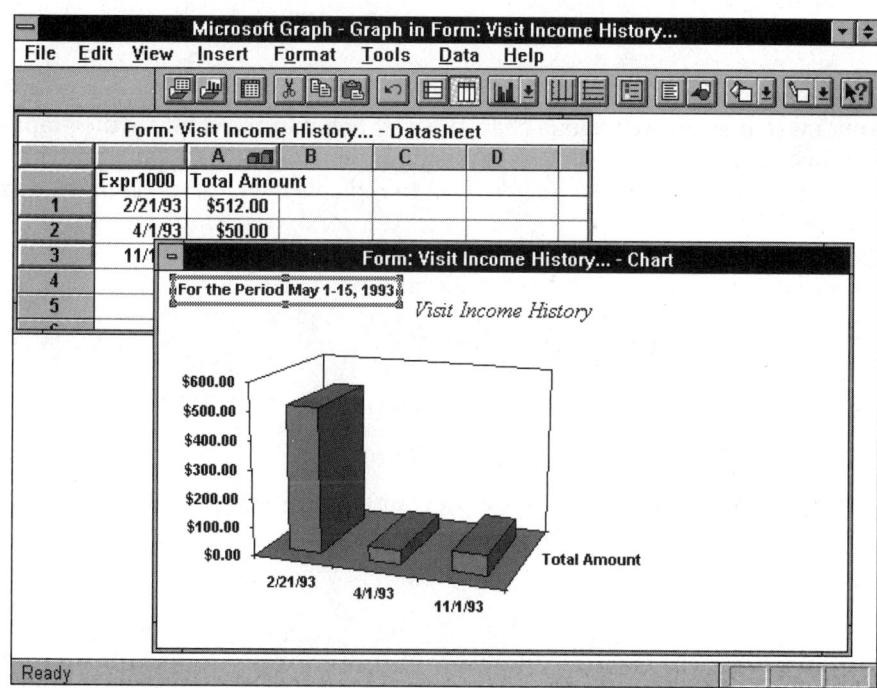

Figure 20-23: Free-form text on a graph.

Changing the graph type

After you create your initial graph, you can experiment with changing the graph type to make sure that you selected the type that most properly reflects your data. Microsoft Graph provides a wide range of graphs to select from, and merely a few clicks of the mouse can change the type of graph presentation.

The following are the different types of graphs that you can select from:

Two-Dimensional Charts	*Three-Dimensional Charts*
Area	3-D Area
Bar	3-D Bar
Column	3-D Column
Line	3-D Line
Pie	3-D Pie
Doughnut	3-D Surface
Radar	
Xy (Scatter)	

To select a different type of graph, select the Format⇨Chart Type... menu of the Chart window to display the various chart types. When you select any of the graph options, a window opens to display all the different graphing options available within the selected graph type. Click the selection you want to redisplay your graph in the new type.

To see some of the different graph types, follow these steps:

Steps:	**Displaying the Graph Type**
Step 1.	Select Format⇨Chart Type... as shown in Figure 20-24.
Step 2.	Click OK to return to the graph window.

You can change the look of your chart by resizing the chart itself. The graph in Figure 20-25 has been selected and resized.

Chapter 20: Using OLE Objects, Pictures, and Graphs

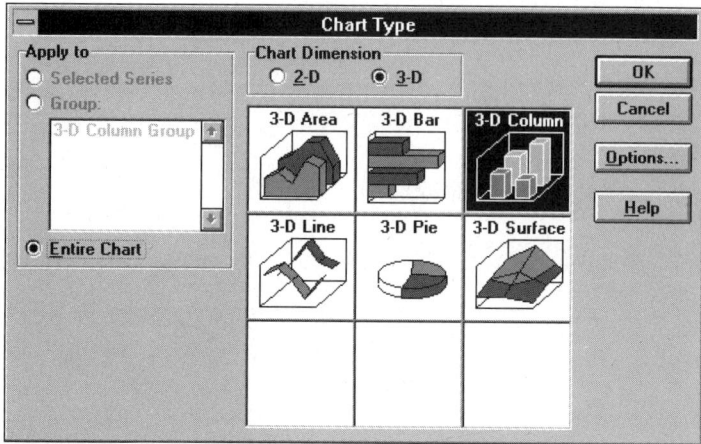

Figure 20-24: The chart types.

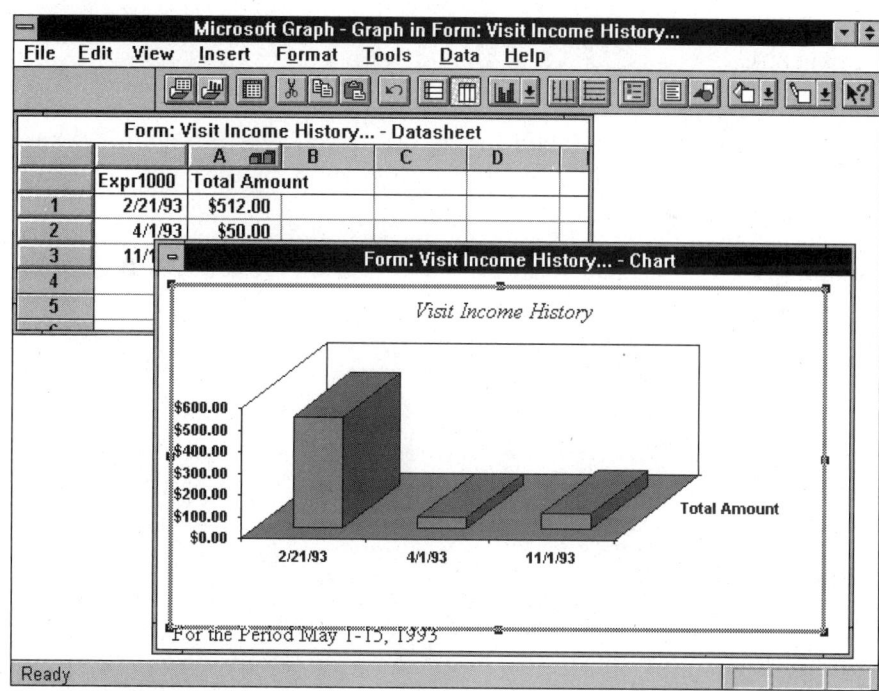

Figure 20-25: Resizing the graph.

Changing axis labels

You may want to change the text font of the x-axis so you can see all the labels. Follow these steps to change labels:

Steps:	Changing Axis Labels
Step 1.	Double-click the x-axis. The x-axis is the bottom axis with the dates on it.
Step 2.	Select the Font... rom the Format Axis dialog box.
Step 3.	Change the Size setting to 6 points by entering 6 into the font size box.
Step 4.	Select OK to return to the chart.

Changing a bar color and pattern

If you are going to print the graph in monochrome, you should always adjust the patterns so they are not all solid colors. You can change the color or pattern of each bar by double-clicking any bar in the category you want to select.

The Format Data Series dialog box appears as shown in Figure 20-26. Here you can make your desired changes. In this example, a striped bar is appropriate.

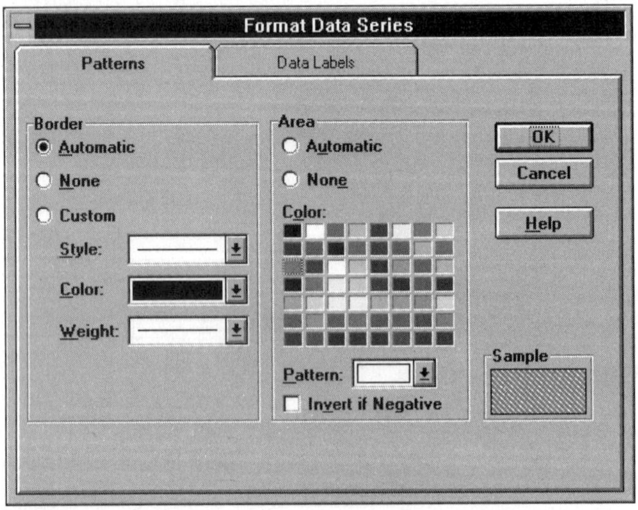

Figure 20-26: Data Series Patterns.

Modifying gridlines

Gridlines are lines that extend from the axis across the plotting area of the graph to help you read the graph properly. You can add two types of gridlines to a graph — x-axis gridlines and y-axis gridlines. If the graph is three-dimensional, there is an additional gridline for the z-axis. You can add gridlines for any axis on the graph. The z-axis gridlines are displayed along the back and side walls of the plotting area. The x- and y-axis gridlines are displayed across the base and up the walls of the graph.

You can work with gridlines on your graph by selecting Insert⇨Gridlines. On the left wall are the y-axis gridlines, and on the back wall are the z-axis gridlines. On the floor are the x-axis gridlines. When you double-click on one of these areas, you can change the line type.

Manipulating three-dimensional graphs

In any of the three-dimensional chart options, you can modify the following graph display characteristics:

- Elevation
- Perspective (if Right Angle Axes is turned off)
- Rotation
- Scaling
- Angle and height of the axes

By adjusting these options, you can modify your graph to best display the information you are working with. Figure 20-27 shows the dialog box that lets you make these modifications to your three-dimensional graph.

The Elevation button controls the height at which you view the data. The elevation is measured in degrees and can range from –90 to 90 degrees.

 An elevation of zero displays the graph as if you were level with the center of the graph. An elevation of 90 degrees shows the graph as you would view it from above the center of the graph. A –90 degree elevation shows the graph as you would view it from below the center of the graph.

The Perspective button controls the amount of perspective that will be in your graph. Adding more perspective makes data markers at the back of the graph smaller than those at the front of the graph. This option provides a sense of distance to the data markers that are farther away. If your graph contains a great amount of data, you may want to use a greater perspective so that data markers in the back of the graph appear smaller relative to those near the front.

The perspective value is the ratio of the front of the graph to the back of the graph. The value can range from 0 to 100. A perspective of 0 makes the back edge of the graph equal in width to the front edge. You can experiment with these settings until you get the effect you need.

The Rotation buttons control the rotation of the entire plotting area. The rotation is measured in degrees and can range from 0 to 360. A rotation of 0 displays your graph as you view it from directly in front. A rotation of 180 degrees displays the graph as if you were viewing it from the back. This setting visually reverses the plotting order of your data series. A rotation of 90 degrees displays your graph as if you were viewing it from the center of the side wall.

The Auto Scaling checkbox lets you scale a three-dimensional graph so that it is closer in size to the two-dimensional graph using the same data. To activate this option, click the Auto Scaling checkbox so that the X appears in the box. By having this option activated, whenever you switch from a two-dimensional type graph to a three-dimensional graph, the scaling is done automatically.

Two options within the Format 3-D View dialog box pertain specifically to display of the axes. The Right Angle Axes checkbox lets you control the orientation of the axes. If the checkbox is on, all axes are displayed at right angles to each other.

If the Right Angle Axes checkbox is selected, you cannot specify the perspective for the three-dimensional view.

The Height entry box contains the height of the z-axis and the walls relative to the width of the base of the graph. The height is measured as a percentage of the x-axis length. A height of 100 percent makes the height equal to the x-axis. Similarly, a height of 50 percent makes the height half the x-axis length. You can set this height percentage over the 100 percent setting. By doing this, you can make the height of the z-axis greater than the length of the x-axis.

If you change the Height setting, your change will not be displayed in the sample graph shown in the 3-D View dialog box.

You can change the 3-D view by selecting Format⇨3-D View. The dialog box shown in Figure 20-27 appears. You can then either enter the values for the various settings or use the six buttons to rotate the icon of the graph in real time. When you like the view of the graph, select OK and your chart will change to that perspective.

Chapter 20: Using OLE Objects, Pictures, and Graphs 527

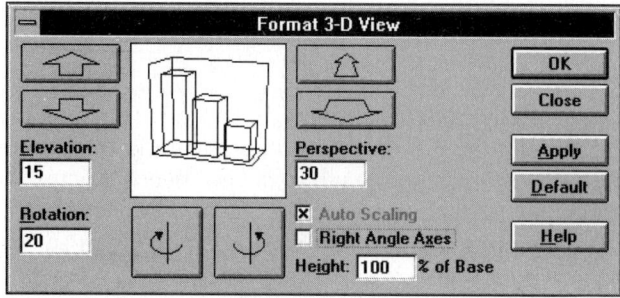

Figure 20-27:
The Format 3-D View dialog box.

Summary

In this chapter, you learned the differences between linking and embedding graphs and other OLE objects to your forms. You created a graph by using the Graph Wizard, and you used Microsoft Graph to customize the graph to fit your needs. Microsoft Access, because of its Windows compatibility, has the power to share data, pictures, and other objects with any other OLE-compatible products. You also learned that you can embed or link a full range of graphs to your forms with just a few keystrokes. In this chapter, the following points were explained:

- Access adds any type of picture or graphic object to an Access table, including sound and video, a worksheet, or a document.
- A bound object is attached to a specific record, whereas an unbound object is attached only to a form or report.
- Embedded objects are stored in a table, form, or report, but linked objects merely link to an external file.
- You can embed an object by either pasting it into an object frame or inserting the object.
- If the embedded object supports OLE, you can double-click the object to launch the source application and edit the object.
- The easiest way to create graphs is to use the Graph Wizard in a form.
- Once you create a graph, you can customize the graph by using the Microsoft Graph applet.
- To customize a graph, double-click it; then you can change the graph type, text, axis labels, legend, gridlines, colors, patterns, and even the view of the graph.
- You can embed a graph in a form and link it to the data in the form by using the Graph button in the toolbox of the Form or Report Design window and then following the steps in the Wizard.

In the next chapter, you learn how to create reports.

CHAPTER 21

Creating and Customizing Reports

In This Chapter

- Learning the eleven tasks necessary to create a great report
- Learning how to create a report from a blank form
- Learning how to sort and group data
- Learning how to add label and text controls to your report
- Learning how to modify the appearance of text and label controls
- Learning how to add page breaks
- Learning how to copy an existing report

In previous chapters, you learned how to create a report from a single table by using a wizard. You also learned how to create multiple-table queries, as well as to work with controls. In this chapter, you combine and build on these concepts. You learn how to create from scratch a report that lets you view data from multiple tables and to group and sort the data in meaningful ways.

Starting with a Blank Form

In Chapter 11, you learned how to create a report using an Access Report Wizard and a single table as the data source. Wizards are great for creating quick and simple reports, but they are fairly limited and give you little control over field type or placement. Although there are advantages to creating a report with a wizard and then modifying the report, this chapter focuses on creating a report from a blank form without the help of the wizards. If you didn't read Chapter 11 yet, now is a good time to read or review it. Chapter 11 covers the basic report concepts that the present chapter assumes you are already familiar with. This chapter also assumes that you have read Chapter 16 so that you are familiar with basic form and report controls and properties.

In previous chapters on forms, you were exposed to all the tools that are available in the Report window. You use some of the tools in the Report window in a slightly different manner when you create reports than when you use them in forms. It is important to review some of the unique menus and toolbar buttons.

You can view a report in three different views: Design, Sample Preview, and Print Preview. You can also print a report to the defined Windows hard-copy device. You've already seen the preview windows in previous chapters. This chapter will focus on the Design window.

The Design window is where you create and modify reports. The empty Design window, shown in Figure 21-1, contains various tools, including the toolbox.

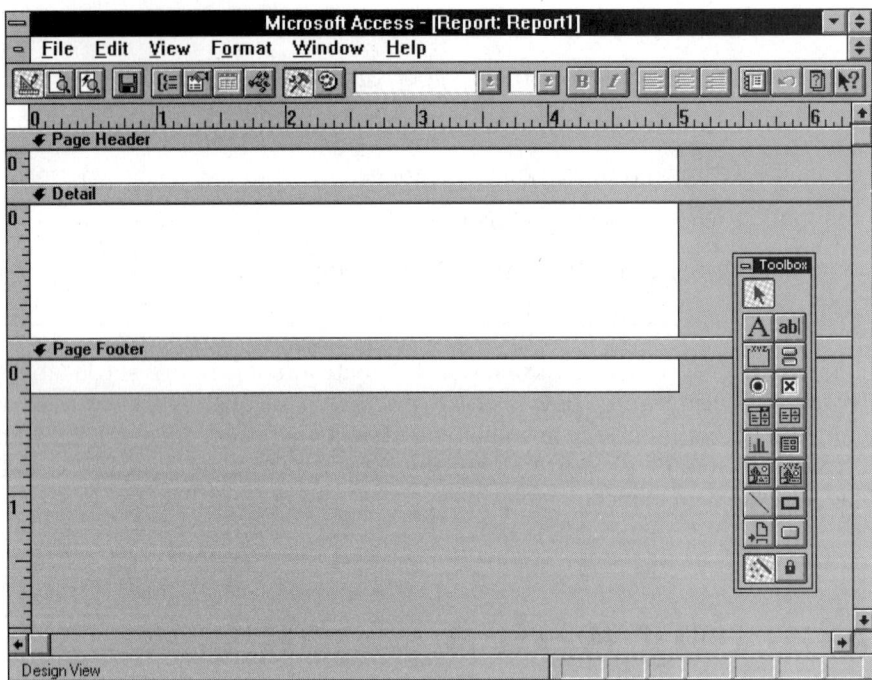

Figure 21-1: The Report Design window showing the toolbox.

The Design window toolbar

The Report Design View toolbar is shown in Figure 21-2. You can click the desired button for quick access to such design tasks as displaying different windows and applying various formatting styles. Table 21-1 summarizes what each item on the toolbar does. (The table defines each tool from left to right on the toolbar.)

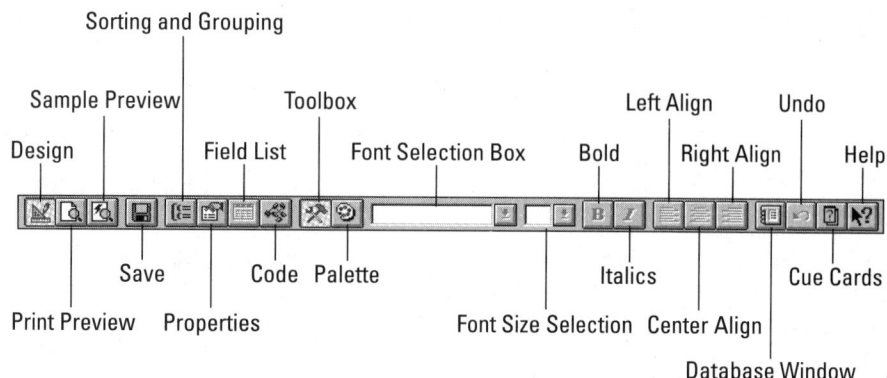

Figure 21-2: The Report Design toolbar.

Table 21-1: The Design View Toolbar

Toolbar Item	Description
Design view button	Toggles to design view
Print Preview button	Toggles to print preview mode
Sample Preview button	Toggles to sample preview mode
Save button	Saves the current report design
Sorting and Grouping button	Displays or hides the Sorting and Grouping box
Properties button	Displays or hides the property sheet
Field List button	Displays or hides the Field List window
Code button	Displays or hides the module window
Toolbox button	Displays or hides the toolbox
Palette button	Displays or hides the Palette window
Font box	Selects the font for a control
Font-size box	Selects the font-size control
Bold button	Bolds the text in a control
Italics button	Italicizes the text in a control
Left-Align button	Aligns the text in a control to the left side of the control
Center button	Aligns the text in a control to the center of the control
Right-Align button	Aligns the text in a control to the right side of the control
Database Window	Displays the database window
Undo button	Undoes the last command
Cue Cards button	Displays cue cards
Help button	Displays Access Help

 The tools in the reports design screen are virtually identical to the form design tools.

Banded Report Writer Concepts

In a report, your data is processed one record at a time. Depending on how you create your report design, each data item is processed differently. Reports are divided into sections, known as *bands* in most report writing software packages. In Access, these are simply called *sections*. As each data record is processed from a table or dynaset, each section is processed in order. For each record, a decision is made whether or not to process fields or text in the section. For example, the report footer section is processed only after the last record is processed in the dynaset.

A report is made up of groups of *details* — all animals Johnathan Adams brought in on a certain day and how much Mr. Adams paid. Each group must have an identifying *group header,* which in this case is customer Johnathan Adams. Each group has a footer that calculates the total amount for each customer. For Johnathan Adams, this amount is $375. The page header contains column descriptions, and the report header contains the report title. Finally, the report footer contains grand totals for the report, and the page footer prints the page number.

The Access sections are as follows:

Report header	Prints only at the beginning of the report; used for title page
Page header	Prints at the top of each page
Group header	Prints before the first record of a group is processed
Detail	Prints each record in the table or dynaset
Group footer	Prints after the last record of a group is processed
Page footer	Prints at the bottom of each page
Report footer	Prints only at the end of a report after all records are processed

Figure 21-3 shows these sections superimposed on a report.

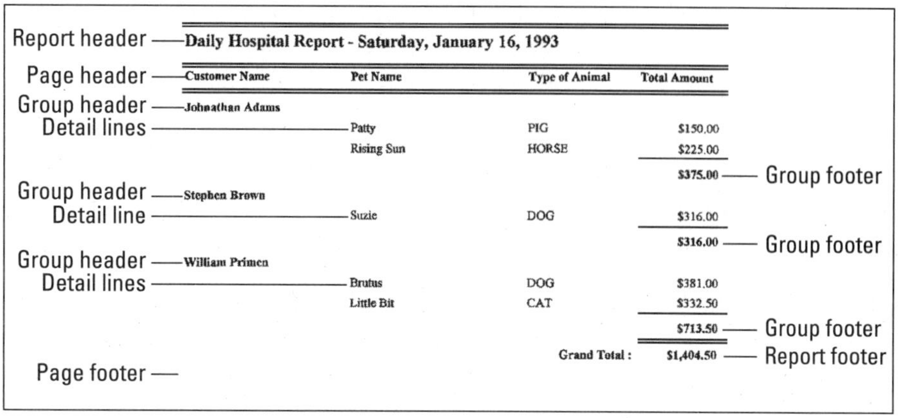

Figure 21-3: Typical report writer sections.

```
Report header ——— Daily Hospital Report - Saturday, January 16, 1993
Page header ——— Customer Name        Pet Name          Type of Animal    Total Amount
Group header ——— Johnathan Adams
    Detail lines ———————————————— Patty             PIG               $150.00
                                     Rising Sun         HORSE             $225.00
                                                                          $375.00  ——— Group footer
Group header ——— Stephen Brown
    Detail line ————————————————— Suzie             DOG               $316.00
                                                                          $316.00  ——— Group footer
Group header ——— William Primen
    Detail lines ———————————————— Brutus            DOG               $381.00
                                     Little Bit         CAT               $332.50
                                                                          $713.50  ——— Group footer
                                                     Grand Total :    $1,404.50  ——— Report footer
Page footer ———
```

How sections process data

Most sections are triggered by the values of the data. Table 21-2 shows the five records that comprise the dynaset for the Daily Hospital Report. Yes indicates that a section is triggered by the data.

Table 21-2
Processing Report Sections

Customer Name	Pet Name	Report Header	Page Header	Group Header	Detail	Group Footer	Page Footer	Report Footer
Johnathan Adams	Rising Sun	Yes	Yes	Yes	Yes	No	No	No
Johnathan Adams	Patty	No	No	No	Yes	Yes	No	No
Stephen Brown	Suzie	No	No	Yes	Yes	Yes	No	No
William Primen	Little Bit	No	No	Yes	Yes	No	No	No
William Primen	Brutus	No	No	No	Yes	Yes	Yes	Yes

As you can see, Table 21-2 contains five records. Three groups of records are grouped by the customer name. Johnathan Adams has two records, Stephen Brown has one, and William Primen has two records. For each record in the table, there are corresponding columns for each section in the report. Yes means that the record triggers processing in that section. No means that the section is not processed for that record. This report has only one page, so it is very simplistic.

The report header section is triggered only by the first record in the dynaset. This section is always processed first, regardless of the data. The report footer section is triggered only after the last record is processed, regardless of the data.

The page header section is processed after the report header section for the first record only and then every time a new page of information is started. The page footer section is processed at the bottom of each page and after the report footer section.

Group headers are triggered only by the first record of a group. Group footers are triggered only by the last record in a group. Notice that the Stephen Brown record triggers both a group header and a group footer because it is the only record in a group. If three or more records are in a group, only the first or the last record triggers a group header or footer; the middle records trigger only the detail section.

Each and every record is always processed in the detail section. The detail section is always triggered, regardless of the value of the data. Most reports with a great amount of data have many detail records and significantly fewer group header or footer records. In this small report, there are as many group header and footer records as there are detail records.

The report writer sections

To get an idea of what a report design looks like in Access, look at Figure 21-4. In this figure, you see the Report Design window that produced the Daily Hospital Report. As you can see, the report is divided into sections. One group section displays data grouped by Customer Name, so you see the sections Customer Name Header and Customer Name Footer. Each of the other sections is also named for the type of processing it performs.

You can place any type of text or field controls in any section, but data is processed one record at a time. And, based on the values of the group fields, the location of the page, or placement in the report, certain actions are taken to make the bands or sections active. The example in Figure 21-4 is typical of a report with multiple sections. As you've learned, each section in the report has a different purpose and different triggers.

Figure 21-4: The Report Design window.

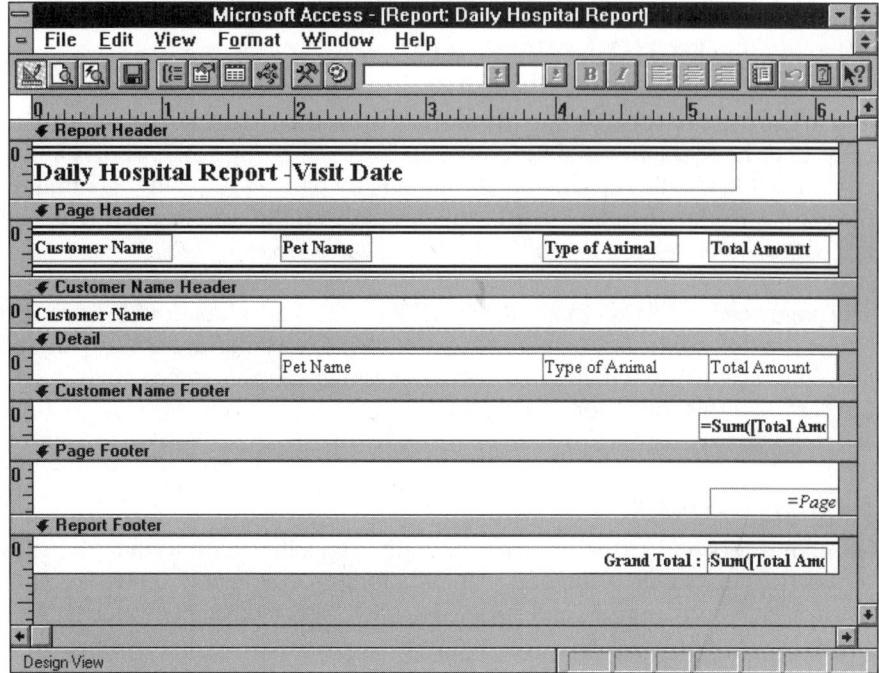

Report header section

Anything in the report header is printed once only at the beginning of the report. In the report header section is a text control that places the words Daily Hospital Report in a large font size at the top of the report. Only the first page of the report has this text. You can also see the field control Visit Date. This control places the value of the visit date from the first record in the report header. In Figure 21-3, you saw that this date is Saturday, January 16, 1993. This was the value of the Visit Date field for the first record in the dynaset. It has been formatted using the long date format.

The report header section also has a double line placed before the text and field controls. You can place lines, boxes, shading, color, and special effects in any band. You'll learn more about formatting and special effects in later chapters.

You can also have anything in the report header section on a separate page. This way, you can create an entire page and include a graphic or picture in the section. A common use of a report header section is as a cover page — or even as a cover letter. Because the header appears only once and doesn't necessarily have to contain any data, a separate page with the report header is a perfect place for a cover page or letter.

 Only data from the first record can be placed in a report header.

Page header section

Text or field controls in the page header section normally print at the top of every page. If there is a report header on the first page that is not on a page of its own, the information in the page header section prints just below the report header information. Typically, page headers are used for column headers in group/total reports and also can contain a title for the report. In this example, by placing the Daily Hospital Report title in the report header section, the title appears only on the first page. You can move it into the page header section if you want it to appear on every page.

The page header section that you see in Figure 21-4 also has double lines above and below the text controls. Each of the text controls is a separate control and can be moved or sized individually. You can also control special effects, such as color, shading, borders, line thickness, font type, and font size for each text control.

Group header

Group headers are normally used to identify a specific value so that you know that all the records displayed in a detail section belong to that group. In this example, the detail records are about animals and the cost of their treatments. The group header field control Customer Name tells you that these animals are owned by the customer who appears in the group header band. Group header sections immediately precede detail sections.

You may have multiple levels of group headers and footers. In this report, for example, the data is only for January 16, 1993. The detail data is grouped by the one field, Customer Name. If you want to see one report for the entire month of January 1993, you can change the query and then add a second group section. In this second group section, you can group the data by date and then, within each date, by customer. You can have many levels of groupings. You should limit the number to between three and six, as it becomes impossible to read reports with too many levels. You don't want to defeat the purpose of the report, which is to show information clearly in a summarized format.

Detail section

The detail section processes *every* record. This is where each value is printed. The detail section frequently contains calculated fields, such as a price extension that multiplies a quantity times a price. In this example, the detail section simply displays the Pet Name, Type of Animal, and Total Amount, which is the cost of the treatments. Each of the records in the detail section *belongs* to the value in the group header — Customer Name.

You can tell Access whether you want to display a section in the report by changing the section's Visible property in the Report Design window. By turning off the display of the detail section, or by excluding selected group sections, you can display a summary report with no detail or with only certain groups displayed.

Group footer

The group footer is used to summarize the detail records for that group. In the Daily Hospital Report, the expression =Sum(Total Amount) adds the Total Amount fields for a specific customer. In the group for customer Johnathan Adams, this value sums the two Total Amount records $225.00 and $150.00 and produces the value $375.00. This type of field is automatically reset to 0 each time the group changes. You learn more about expressions and summary fields in later chapters.

You can change the way summaries are calculated by changing the Running Sum property of the field box in the Report Design window.

Page footer

The page footer section usually contains page numbers or control totals. In very large reports, you sometimes want page totals, as well as group totals, when you have multiple pages of detail records with no summaries. For the Daily Hospital Report, you print the page number by combining a text control Page: with the expression =Page, which keeps track of the page number in the report.

Report footer

The report footer section is printed once at the end of the report after all the detail records and group footer sections are printed. Report footers typically display grand totals or other statistics for the entire report, such as averages or percentages. The report footer for the Daily Hospital Report uses the expression =Sum(Total Amount) to add the Total Amount fields for all treatments. This expression, when used in the report footer, is not reset to 0, as it is in the group footer. The expression is used only for a grand total.

When there is a report footer, the page footer band is printed after the report footer.

The report writer in Access is a *two-pass* report writer. The report writer is capable of preprocessing all records in order to calculate the totals needed for statistical reporting, such as percentages. This lets you create expressions that calculate percentages as records are processed that require foreknowledge of the grand total.

 Calculating percentages is covered in Chapter 23.

Creating a New Report

Fundamental to all reports is the concept that a report is another way to view the records of one or more tables. It is important to understand that a report is bound either to a single table or query that accesses one table or multiple tables. When you create a report, you must select which fields from a query or table are to be placed in your report. Unless you want to view all the records from a single table in your report, you probably want to bind your report to a query. If you are accessing data from a single table, using a query lets you create your report based on a particular search criteria and sorting order. If you want to access data from multiple tables, you have no choice but to bind your report to a query. In the examples in this chapter, you'll see all reports bound to a query, even though it is possible to bind a report to a table.

 Access lets you create a report without first binding it to a table or object, but you will have no fields on the report. This capability can be used to work out page templates, which can serve as models for other reports. You can later add fields by changing the underlying control source of the report.

Throughout this chapter and the next chapter, you learn the tasks needed to create the Mountain Animal Hospital Pets and Owners Directory, of which the first hard-copy page is shown in Figure 21-5. In this chapter, you will design the basic report, assemble the data, and place the data in the proper positions. In Chapter 22, you will enhance the report by adding lines, boxes, and shading to make certain areas stand out. You will also add enhanced controls, such as option buttons and checkboxes, to make the data more readable.

As with almost every task in Access, there are many ways to create a report without wizards. It is important, however, to follow some type of methodology. Creating a good report involves a fairly scientific methodology. You can follow a set of tasks to create a good report every time. You can arrange these tasks to create a checklist. As you complete each of these tasks, you can check it off your list. When you are done, you will have a great-looking report.

Chapter 21: Creating and Customizing Reports

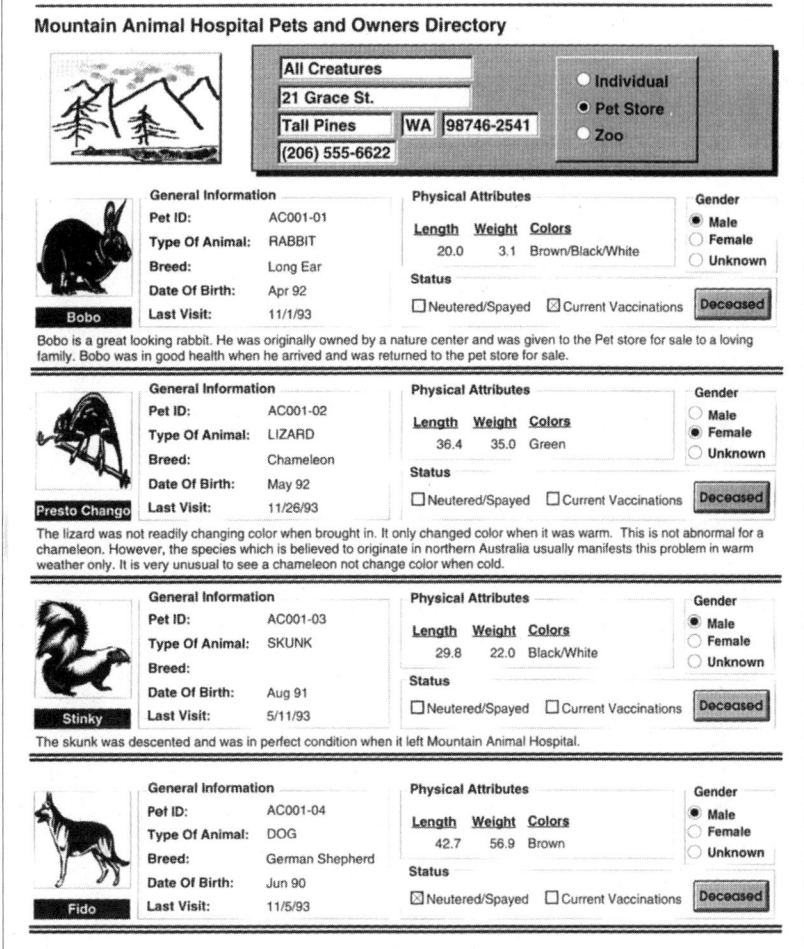

Figure 21-5: The Mountain Animal Hospital Pets and Owners Directory - first page.

Eleven tasks to creating a great report

To create a good report, you need to perform these eleven tasks:

1. Design your report.
2. Assemble the data.
3. Create a new report and bind it to a query.
4. Define your page layout properties.

5. Place the fields on the report, using text controls.
6. Add other label and text controls as necessary.
7. Modify the appearance, size, and location of text and the text and label controls.
8. Define your sorting and grouping options.
9. Save your report.
10. Enhance your report by using graphics and other control types.
11. Print your report.

 This chapter covers tasks 1 through 9. Chapter 22 discusses using other controls, such as group boxes, option buttons, and Memo fields, as well as methods to enhance your report visually.

Designing the report

The first step in this process is to design the report. By the nature of the report name — Mountain Animal Hospital Pets and Owners Directory — you know that you want to create a report that contains detailed information about both the customer and the customer's pets. You want to create a report that first lists important customer information at the top of a page and then lists detailed information about each pet a customer owns, including a picture. You want no more than one customer on a page, and, if a customer has more than one pet, you want to see as many as possible on the same page. If a customer has more pets than will fit on one page, you want to duplicate the customer details on the top of each page. This task will be discussed in the grouping section of this chapter.

A design of the data is shown in Figure 21-6. This is not the complete design for the report that you saw in Figure 21-5 but a plan of only the major data items roughly placed where they will appear in this report. You can sketch this by hand on a piece of paper, or you can use any good word processor or drawing tool, such as Micrografx Draw or Word for Windows Draw, to lay out the basic design. Because Access has a WYSIWYG report writer, you can also use that to lay out your report. We personally like the pencil-and-paper approach to good design.

The data design is created only to lay out the basic data elements with no special formatting. Although this may seem like a rudimentary design for the report, it is nevertheless a good starting point. This layout represents the report you will create in this chapter.

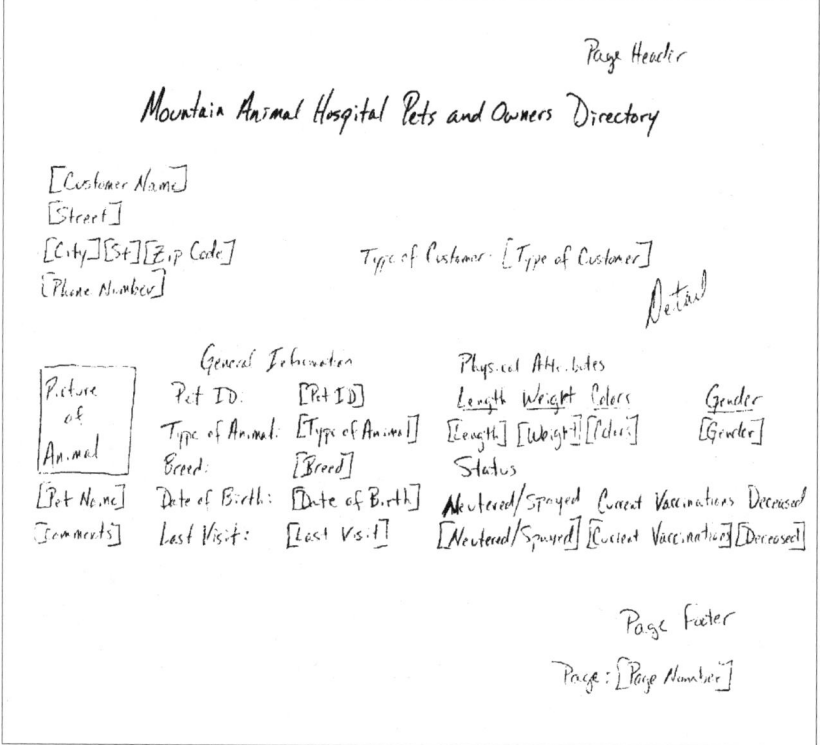

Figure 21-6: The data design for the Mountain Animal Hospital Pets and Owners Directory.

Assembling the data

With this design in mind, you now need to assemble the data. To create this report, fields are needed from two tables, Customer and Pets. Table 21-3 lists the necessary fields and identifies the table that contains the fields.

Table 21-3
Tables and Fields Needed for the Pets and Owners Directory

Fields from Pets Table	Fields from Customer Table
Pet ID	Customer Number
Picture	Customer Name
Pet Name	Type of Customer
Type of Animal	Street/Apt
Breed	City
Date of Birth	State

(continued)

Table 21-3 *(continued)*

Fields from Pets Table	Fields from Customer Table
Last Visit Date	ZIP Code
Length	Phone Number
Weight	
Colors	
Gender	
Neutered/Spayed	
Current Vaccinations	
Deceased	
Comments	

To assemble this data, you first need to create a query, which you can call Pets and Owners. This query includes *all* fields from both tables, even though you aren't going to use all of them. Some of the fields that don't appear on the report itself are used to derive other fields. Some fields are used merely to sort the data, although the fields themselves are not displayed on the report. In this example, you also create a sort by Pet ID. It is always a good idea to arrange your data into some known order. When reports are run, the data is used in its *physical* order unless you sort the data.

To create the Pets and Owners query, follow Figure 21-7

You use the asterisk (*) to select all fields from each table.

Creating a new report and binding it to a query

Now that you have created the Pets and Owners query, you need to create a new report and bind it to the query. Follow these steps to complete this process:

Steps:	Creating a New Report and Binding It to a Query
Step 1.	Press F11 to display the Database window if it is not already displayed.
Step 2.	Click the Report task object button.
Step 3.	Click the New command button. The New Report dialog box appears.

Chapter 21: Creating and Customizing Reports **543**

Step 4. Click the Select A Table/Query box. A drop-down list of all tables and queries in the current database appears.

Step 5. Select the Pets and Owners query.

Step 6. Click the Blank Report button.

Step 7. Maximize the Report window.

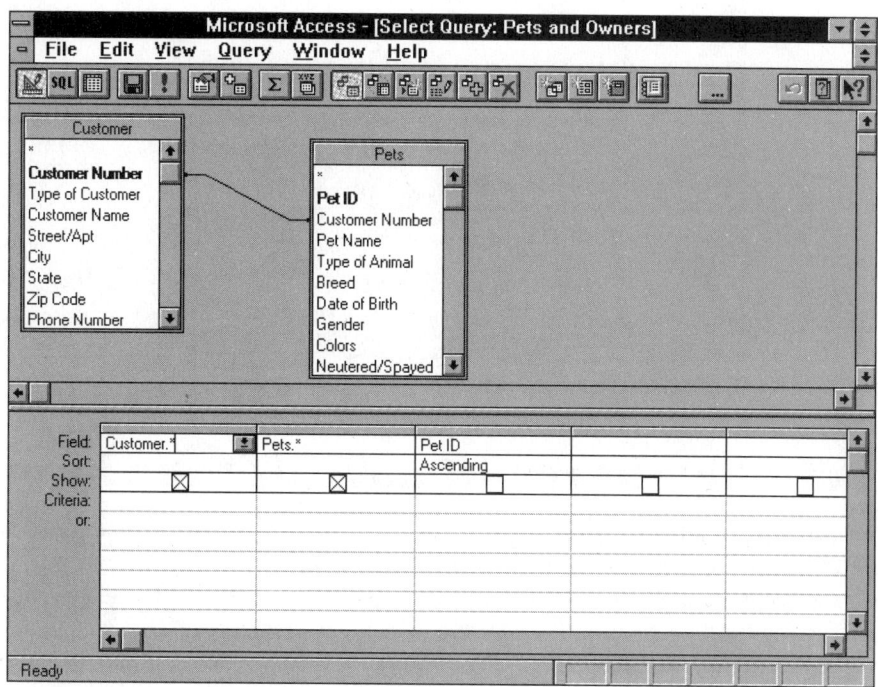

Figure 21-7: The Pets and Owners query.

A blank Report Design window appears (see Figure 21-8). Notice the three sections in the screen display: Page Header, Detail, and Page Footer. The report is bound to the query Pets and Owners. This means that the data from that query will be used when the report is viewed or printed. The fields from the query are available for use in the report design and will appear in the Field List window.

 You can also create a new report by using any of these methods:

- Clicking on the New Report toolbar button
- Selecting File⇨New⇨Report from any module
- Copying and renaming an existing report

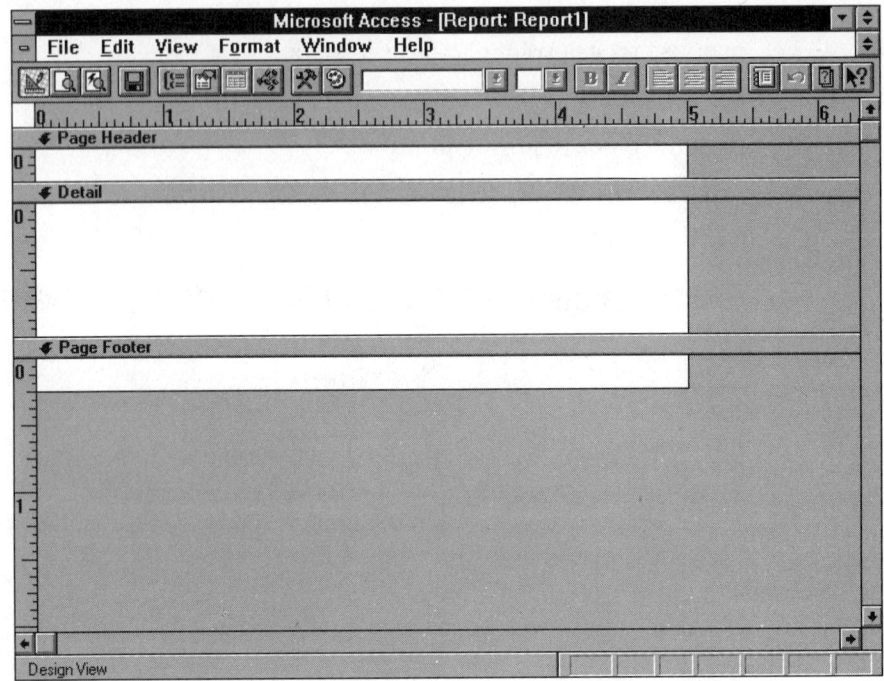

Figure 21-8:
A blank Report Design window.

Defining the report page size and layout

As you are planning your report, you consider the page layout characteristics and what kind of paper and printer you want to use for the output. If you are going to use an Epson dot-matrix printer with a wide-carriage feed, you'll want to design your report differently than for printing on a Hewlett-Packard LaserJet with 8½ x 11-inch paper. After you make these decisions, there are several dialog boxes and properties that you can use to make adjustments. All of these work together to create the output you want. You learn how to use these tools in the next several chapters.

First, you need to select the correct printer and page layout characteristics by selecting File⇨Print Setup.... The Print Setup dialog box, which is shown in Figure 21-9, lets you select your printer, set printer options, and define page layout characteristics. Print Setup options are discussed in detail in Chapter 22.

The Print Setup dialog box is divided into several sections:

Printer	Selects the printer that you want
Orientation	Selects the page orientation that you want
Paper	Selects the paper size and paper source that you want

Figure 21-9:
The Print Setup dialog box.

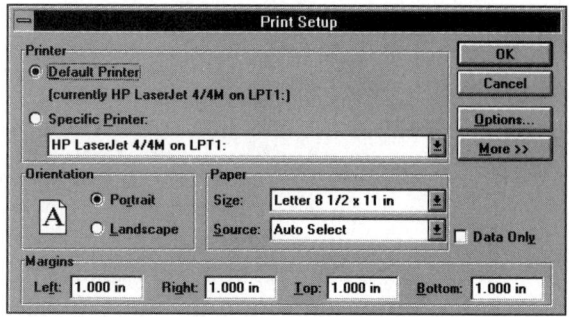

Data Only   Prints data only; does not print graphics

Margins   Sets the page margins

Options   Sets printer-specific options

More>>   Sets report-specific options used for snaking columns and mailing labels

For the Pets and Owners report, you'll create a *portrait* report, which is taller than it is wide. The paper you'll use is 8½ x 11 inches, and the left, right, top, and bottom margins are all set to 0.250.

Follow these steps to create the proper report setup:

Steps: Setting the Printer Setup for the Pets and Owners Report

Step 1. Click the Portrait option button.

Next to the Orientation buttons is the letter *A* pictured on a sheet of paper with a corner turned down. When you choose the portrait style, the sheet appears in the vertical position; if you choose landscape, the sheet changes to a horizontal position.

Step 2. Click the Left margin setting and change the setting to **.250**.

Step 3. Click the Right margin setting and change the setting to **.250**.

Step 4. Click the Top margin setting and change the setting to **.250**.

Step 5. Click the Bottom margin setting and change the setting to **.250**.

Step 6. Click OK to close the Print Setup dialog box.

The default unit of measurement in Access is *in (inches)*. If you want to use centimeters or another unit of measurement, place the symbol after the numeric designation, as in a length expressed as 1.5cm.

Access displays your reports in the Print Preview view, using the driver of the currently active printer. If you don't have a good quality laser available for printing, install the driver for a Postscript printer so that you'll be able to view any graphics that you create and see the report in a high-resolution display. Later, you can print to your dot-matrix or other available printer and get the actual hard copy in the best resolution your printer offers.

After you define your page layout in the Print Setup dialog box, you need to define the size of your report, which is not necessarily the same as the page definition, as you'd expect.

To define the report size, place the cursor on the rightmost edge of the report (where the white page meets the grey background). The cursor changes to the two-headed arrow like the cursor for changing column width in queries or datasheets. Drag the cursor to change the width of the report. As you drag the edge, a vertical line appears in the ruler to let you know the exact width if you release the mouse at that point. Be careful not to exceed the width of the page that you defined in the Print Setup dialog box.

When you position the cursor at the bottom of the report, the cursor looks similar to the one for determining width. This cursor determines the height, not of the page length but of the page footer section or other specified bottom section. Predefining a page length directly in the report section doesn't really make sense because the detail section will vary in length, based on your groupings. Keep in mind that the Report Design view is only a representation of the various report sections, not the actual report.

To set the right border for the Pets and Owners report to eight inches, follow these steps:

Steps:	Setting the Report Width
Step 1.	Click the rightmost edge of the report body (where the white page representation meets the grey background). The cursor changes to a two-headed arrow.
Step 2.	Drag the edge to the 8-inch mark.
Step 3.	Release the mouse button.

 Alternatively, you can select the Width property in the report property sheet.

Because the report design screen is set to a width of eight inches, you see most of the screen printouts in this chapter taken with an 800 x 600-resolution Super VGA Windows screen driver rather than the standard 640 x 480 VGA Windows driver. This resolution lets you see almost the entire screen in the screen figures.

Placing fields on the report

As you've seen, Access takes full advantage of the drag-and-drop capabilities of the Windows environment. The method for placing fields on a report is no exception. When you place a field on a report, it is no longer called a field; it is called a *control*. A control has a *control source* (a field) that it is bound to, so the terms *control* and *field* are used interchangeably in this chapter.

The process of placing controls on your report consists of three basic tasks:

- Displaying the Field List window by clicking the Field List toolbar button
- Clicking the desired toolbox control to determine the type of control that will be created
- Selecting each of the fields that you want on your report and dragging them to the Report Design window

Displaying the field list

To display the Field List window, click on the Field List button on the toolbar. A small window with a list of all the fields from the underlying query appears. This window is called a modeless dialog box because it remains on-screen even while you continue with other work in Access. The Field List window can be resized and moved around the screen. This enlarged window is illustrated in Figure 21-10, showing all the fields in the Pets and Owners query dynaset.

Notice that in Figure 21-10 the fields Customer.Customer Number and Pets.Customer Number, as well as Customer.Last Visit Date and Pets.Last Visit Date, use the table name as a prefix. This setup is necessary to distinguish fields of the same name that come from different tables used in the query.

 You can move the Field List window simply by clicking on the title bar and dragging it to a new location. You can also use the <u>M</u>ove command from the Report window Control menu.

Figure 21-10: Dragging fields to the Design window.

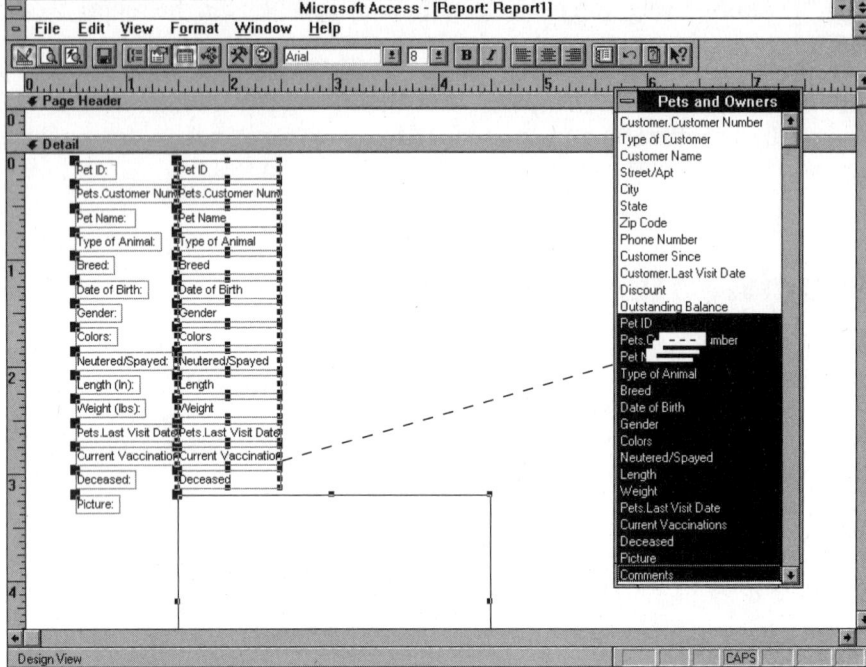

Selecting the fields for your report

Selecting a field in the Report field list is the same as selecting a field in the Query field list. The easiest way to select a field is to simply click it. As you click a field, it becomes highlighted. After a field is highlighted, you can drag it to the Report window.

You can highlight *contiguous* (adjacent) fields in the list by following these steps:

1. Clicking the first field you want in the field list
2. Moving the cursor to the last field that you want from the list
3. Holding down the Shift key and clicking the last field you want

The block of fields between the first and last field you selected is displayed in reverse video as it is selected. You can then drag the block of fields to the Report window.

You can highlight noncontiguous fields in the list by clicking on each field while holding down the Ctrl key. Each field will be displayed in inverse video, and the fields can then be dragged as a group to the Report Design window.

 Unlike the query field list, you *cannot* also double-click a field to add it to the Report window.

You can begin by selecting the Pets table fields for the detail section. To select the fields needed for the Pets and Owners report detail section, follow these steps:

Steps:	Selecting the Pets Table Fields
Step 1.	Click the Pet ID field.
Step 2.	Scroll down the field list until the Comments field is visible.
Step 3.	Hold down the Shift key and click the Comments field.

The block of fields from Pet ID to Comments should be highlighted in the Field List window.

Dragging fields onto your report

After you select the proper fields from the Pets table, all you need to do is drag them onto the detail section of your report. Depending on whether you choose one or several fields, the cursor changes to represent your selection. If you select one field, you see a Field icon, which shows a single box with some unreadable text inside. If you select multiple fields, you see a set of three boxes. These are the same icons you saw in the query design screens.

To drag the Pet table fields into the detail section, follow these steps:

Steps:	Dragging Selected Fields to the Report Design Window
Step 1.	Click within the highlighted block of fields in the Field List window. You may need to move the horizontal elevator bar back to the left before starting this process.
Step 2.	Without releasing the mouse button, drag the cursor into the detail section and place the icon under the 1 ½-inch mark on the horizontal ruler at the top of the screen and the 0-inch mark of the vertical ruler along the left edge of the screen.
Step 3.	Release the mouse button.

The fields appear in the detail section of the report, as shown in Figure 21-10. Notice that for each field you dragged onto the report, there are two controls. When you use the drag-and-drop method for placing fields, Access automatically creates a label control that uses the name of the field and is attached to the text control that the field is bound to.

Notice the OLE (Object Linking and Embedding) control for the field named Picture. An OLE control is always created for a picture or the OLE-type object. Also notice that the detail section automatically resizes itself to fit all the controls. Below the OLE control is the control for the Memo field Comments.

You also need to place the desired field controls on the report for the customer information you need in the page header section. But, before you do this, you need to resize the page header frame to leave room for a title you will later add.

Resizing a section

To make room on the report for both the title and the Customer table fields that are placed in the page header, you must resize the page header. You can resize a section by placing the cursor at the bottom of the section you want to resize. The cursor turns into a vertical double-headed arrow. You can then drag the section border up or down to make the section smaller or larger.

To make the page header section larger, follow these steps:

Steps:	Resizing a Section
Step 1.	Move the cursor between the bottom of the page header section and the top of the detail section.
Step 2.	When the cursor is displayed as a double-sided arrow, hold the left mouse button down.
Step 3.	Drag the page header section border down until it intersects the detail section ruler at ½ inch.
Step 4.	Release the button to enlarge the page header section.

You can now place the Customer table fields in the page header section:

Chapter 21: Creating and Customizing Reports **551**

Steps:	Selecting and Placing the Fields for the Customer Table
Step 1.	Click the Customer.Customer Number field.
Step 2.	Scroll down the field list until the Phone Number field is visible.
Step 3.	Hold down the Shift key and click the Phone Number field.
Step 4.	Click within the highlighted block of fields in the Field List window.
Step 5.	Without releasing the mouse button, drag the cursor into the page header section and place the icon under the 1 ½-inch mark on the horizontal ruler at the top of the screen and the ⅝-inch mark of the vertical ruler along the left edge of the screen.
Step 6.	Release the mouse button; the fields now appear in the page header section of the report, as shown in Figure 21-11.
Step 7.	Close the Field List window by clicking the Field List toolbar button.

Notice that the page header section also expanded to fit the fields that were dragged into the section. At this point, your report should look like Figure 21-11. You have now placed all the fields you need for the Pets and Owners report.

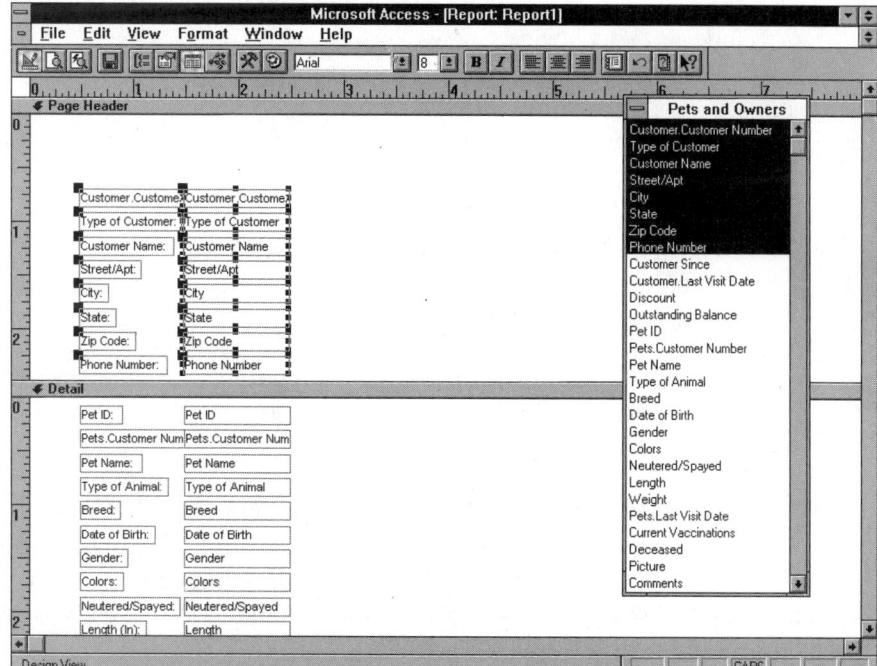

Figure 21-11: The Report Design window for Pets and Owners with all fields shown.

Working with label controls and text

As you've learned, when you drag a field from the Field List window to a report while the Text Box button is selected in the toolbox, not only is a text box control created, but a label control that is attached to the text box control is created as well. There are times when you want to add text label controls by themselves to create headings or titles for the report.

Creating unattached labels

To create a new, unattached label control, you must use the toolbox (unless you copy an existing label). The next task in the present example is to add the text header *Mountain Animal Hospital Pets and Owners Directory* to your report. You will do this task in segments for a demonstration of adding and editing text. To begin this task, follow these steps:

Steps:	Creating an Unattached Label Control
Step 1.	Display the toolbox.
Step 2.	Click the Label tool in the toolbox.
Step 3.	Click near the top left edge of the page header at about the 1-inch mark on the ruler and drag the cursor to make a small rectangle about 2¾ inches long and ¼ inch wide.
Step 4.	Type **Mountain Animal Hospital Pets and Owners Directory.**
Step 5.	Press Enter.

To create a multiple-line label entry, press Ctrl+Enter to force a line break where you want it in the control.

If you want to edit or enter a caption that is longer than the space in the property sheet, the contents will scroll as you type. Or you can press Shift+F2 to open up a Zoom box that gives you more space to type.

Modifying the appearance of text in a control

To modify the appearance of the text in a control, select the control by clicking on its border (not in the control). You can then select a formatting style that you want to apply to the label by clicking the appropriate button in the toolbar. To make the title stand out, follow these steps:

Steps:	Modifying the Appearance of Label Text
Step 1.	Click the report heading label.
Step 2.	Click the Bold button on the toolbar.
Step 3.	Click the arrow beside the Font-Size drop-down box.
Step 4.	Select 18 from the Font-Size drop-down list box.

The label control appears. The label control needs to be resized to display all the text. You will do this later in the chapter.

Working with text boxes and attached label controls

After you enter label controls to define text on the report, you will want to place additive fields on the report.

Adding text box controls

Text box controls serve two purposes in reports. First, they let you display stored data from a particular field in a query or table. The second purpose these controls serve is to display the result of an expression. Expressions can be calculations that use other controls as their operands or calculations that use Access functions (either built-in or user-defined) or a combination of the two. You've learned how to use a text box control to display data from a field and how to create that control. Next, you learn about text controls that use expressions.

Entering an expression in a text control

Expressions let you create a value that is not already in a table or query. Expressions can range from simple functions, such as a page number, to complex mathematical computations. Expressions are covered in greater detail in Chapter 23, but for this example you'll use an expression that is necessary for the report.

A function is a process that returns a single value. The function can be one of many built-in Access functions, or it can be user-defined. To facilitate page numbering in reports, Access has a function called Page, which returns the value of the current page in a report.

Steps:	Adding a Page Number to the Report
Step 1.	Select the Text Box tool from the toolbox.
Step 2.	Scroll down to the page footer section by using the vertical elevator to see this section.
Step 3.	Select the Properties button in the toolbar.
Step 4.	Click in the middle of the page footer section and create a text box approximately three quarters of the height of the section and about ¾-inch wide.
Step 5.	Click the label control to select it.
Step 6.	Click the beginning of the label control text, drag over the default text in the label control, and type **Page:**.
Step 7.	Click the text box control (unbound) twice, type **=Page,** and press Enter. Notice that the Control Source property changes on the property sheet to =Page, as shown in Figure 21-12.
Step 8.	Click the Page label control move handle (upper left corner) and move the label closer to the =Page text box control until the right edge of the label control touches the left edge of the text box control. You will move the entire control to the right side of the page later.

You can always check your result by clicking on the Print Preview button on the toolbar. You may want to zoom in on the page footer section to check the page number.

Sizing a text box control or label control

You can select a control by simply clicking on it. Depending on the size of the control, from three to seven sizing handles will appear — one on each corner except the upper left and one on each side. When you move the cursor over one of the sizing handles, the cursor changes into a double-headed arrow. When the cursor changes, click on and drag the control to the size that you want. Notice that, as you drag, an outline of the new size appears. This outline indicates what the new size of the label control will be when you release the mouse button.

If you double-click any of the sizing handles, Access will usually resize a control to a best fit for the text in the control. This feature is especially handy if you increase the font size and then notice that the text is cut off, either on the bottom or to the right. Note that for label controls, best-fit sizing resizes both vertically and horizontally,

Chapter 21: Creating and Customizing Reports

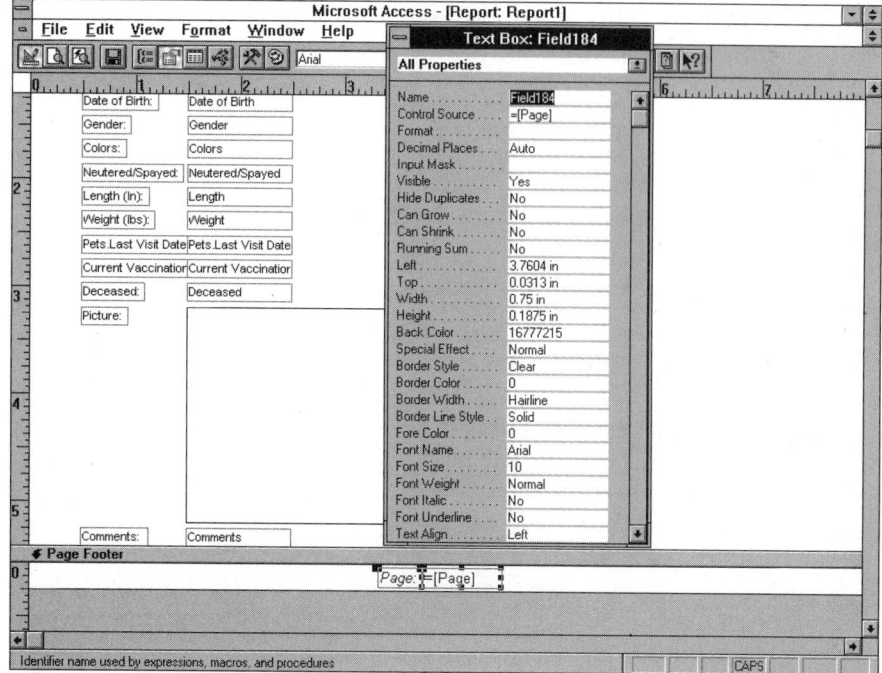

Figure 21-12: Adding a page number expression in a text box control.

although text controls only resize vertically. The reason is that in the report design mode, Access doesn't know how much of a field you want to display; the field name and field contents can be radically different. However, sometimes label controls are not resized correctly and have to be manually adjusted.

Changing the size of a label control

Earlier in this chapter (in the steps "Modifying the Appearance of Label Text"), when you changed the characteristics of the Pets and Owners label, the text changed but the label itself did not adjust. The text no longer fits within the label control. You can resize the text control to fit the enhanced font size. To correct the size of the label control, follow these steps:

Steps:	Resizing the Label Control
Step 1.	Click the Mountain Animal Hospital Pets and Owners Directory label control.
Step 2.	Move your cursor over the control. Notice how the cursor changes over the sizing handles.

556 Part III: Using Acess in Your Work

Step 3.	Double-click one of the sizing handles. The label control size may still need to be readjusted.
Step 4.	Place the cursor on the bottom right corner of the label control so that the diagonal arrow appears.
Step 5.	Hold the left mouse button down and drag the handle to resize the label control box until it correctly displays all the text if it doesn't already.

 You can also select Format⇨Size⇨to Fit to change the size of the label control text automatically.

Before continuing, you should see how the report is progressing. You should do this frequently as you design a report. You can send a single page to the printer, or you can view the report in a print preview. Figure 21-13 shows a zoomed print preview of how the report currently looks. The customer information is at the top of the page, and the Pet information is below that and offset to the left. Notice the title at the top of the page. You can see the page number at the bottom if you click the magnifying glass button to zoom out and see the whole page. Only one record is shown on the report per page because of the vertical layout. In the next section of this chapter, you move the fields around and create a more horizontal layout.

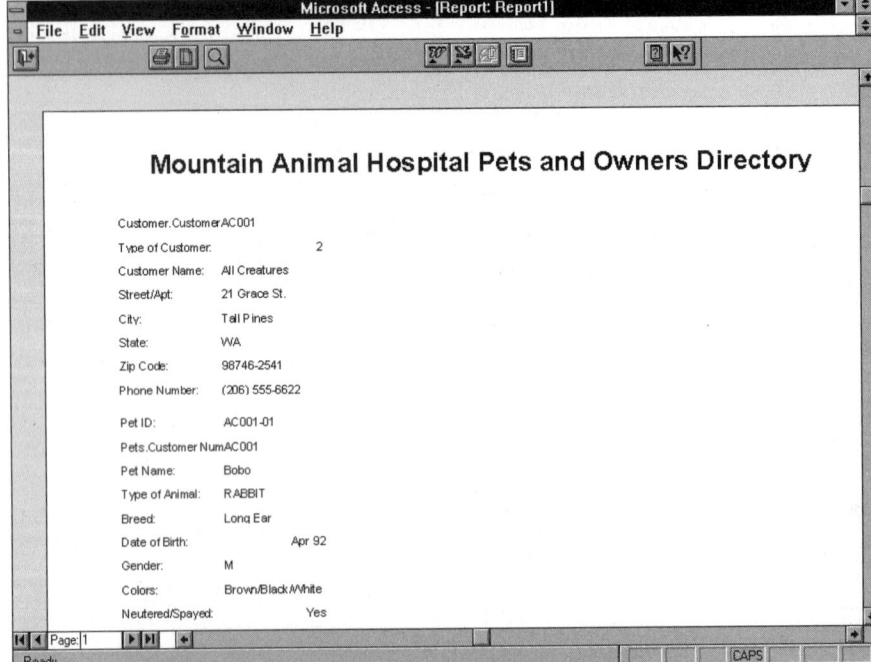

Figure 21-13: A print preview of the report.

Deleting attached label and text controls

As you can see in Figure 21-13, the report begins with the Customer Number field. The original design in Figure 21-6 did not have the Customer Number field on the report. After talking to the report design architect (who is usually yourself), you find that the Customer Number field is not wanted on the report in either the page header section or the detail section. It is very easy to delete one or more attached controls in a report. You simply select the desired controls and press Delete. When deleting attached controls, you have two choices:

- Delete the label control only.
- Delete both the label control and the field control.

If you select the label control and press Delete, only the label control is deleted. If you select the field control and press Delete, both the label control and the field control are deleted. To delete the Customer Number controls and their attached label, follow these steps:

Steps:	Deleting an Attached Control
Step 1.	Select the first icon in the toolbar to exit Print Preview mode. Select the text box control Customer.Customer (Customer Number) in the page header.
Step 2.	Press Delete.
Step 3.	Select the text box control Pets.Customer Num in the detail section.
Step 4.	Press Delete.

If you accidentally selected the label control that precedes the text box control, the text box control is still visible. You can then simply click the control and press Delete.

 If you want to delete only the field control and keep the attached label control, you can do so by first selecting the label control and selecting Edit⇨Copy. Next, select the field control and press Delete to delete both the field control and the label control. Finally, select Edit⇨Paste to paste only the copied label control to the report.

Moving label and text controls

Before discussing how to move label and text controls, it is important to review a few differences between attached and unattached controls. When an attached label is automatically created with a text control, it is called a *compound control*. In a compound control, whenever one control in the set is moved, the other control in the set is also moved. With a text control and a label control, whenever the text control is moved, the attached label is also moved. Likewise, whenever the label control is moved, the text control is also moved.

To move both controls in a compound control, select one of the pair by clicking anywhere on the control. Move the cursor over either of the objects. When the cursor turns into a hand, you can click on and drag the controls to their new location. Notice that as you drag, an outline for the compound control moves with your cursor.

The concepts of moving controls are covered visually and in more detail in Chapter 16.

To move only one of the controls in a compound control, you must drag the desired control by its move handle. The large square in the upper left-hand corner of a control is the control's *move handle*. When you click on a compound control, it appears that both controls are selected. If you look closely, you'll see that only one of the two controls is actually selected, as indicated by both moving and sizing handles being displayed. The deselected control displays only a moving handle. To move either control individually, select the control's move handle and drag it to its new location.

To move a label that is not attached, simply click on any border (except where there is a handle) and drag it. You can also move groups of controls with the selection techniques you learned in Chapter 16.

To make a group selection, click on the cursor anywhere outside a starting point and drag the cursor through (or around) the controls you want to select. A grey, outlined rectangle is displayed to show the extent of the selection. When you release the mouse button, all the controls that the rectangle surrounds are selected. You can then drag the group of controls to a new location.

The global option View⇨Options - Form & Report Design category - Selection Behavior property controls whether the selections are fully enclosed (rectangle must completely surround) or are the default, which is partially enclosed (rectangle needs only to touch the control).

In the next steps, you begin to place the controls in their proper position to complete the report design and layout as created (see Figure 21-6). You want this first pass at rearranging the controls to look like Figure 21-14. The steps to move all the controls will be broken up into logical groups. This is the way that most reports are created. By making a series of block moves (where many controls are selected) and then refining the positioning, a report design is completed. Follow these steps to begin placing the controls where they should be:

Steps: Roughly Positioning the Page Header Controls

Step 1. Move the Type of Customer control to the right and downward so that the top of the control intersects 1 inch in the vertical ruler and the left edge is under the *P* in Pets in the title.

Step 2. In the page header, delete the attached labels (only) from all the text controls except Type of Customer.

Step 3. Rearrange the controls in the page header to resemble a typical mailing-label address format with City, State, and ZIP Code on the same line.

Step 4. Move the Phone Number text box control under the City text box control.

Step 5. Move the block of name, address, and phone number controls into position so that the top of the block intersects ½ inch in both the vertical and horizontal rulers.

Step 6. Resize the page header section so that it intersects 1 ¾ inches on the left vertical ruler.

Steps: Roughly Positioning the Detail Controls

Step 1. Select the Pet ID, Type of Animal, Breed, Date of Birth, and Last Visit Date controls and their attached labels by clicking each text control while holding down the Shift key.

Step 2. Drag the block of controls to the right so that the left edge intersects 3 inches on the top ruler.

Step 3. Select the Last Visit Date (only) control and its attached label.

Step 4. Drag the Last Visit Date control up so that it is just under the Date of Birth control.

Step 5. Select the Gender control and its attached label.

Step 6. Drag the control to the right so that the left edge intersects 5 ¼ inches on the top ruler and ¼ inch on the left-side ruler.

Step 7. Select the Colors, Length, and Weight controls and their attached labels by clicking on each text control while holding down the Shift key.

Step 8. Drag the block of controls to the right so that the left edge intersects 5 ¼ inches on the top ruler and ¾ inch on the left-side ruler.

Step 9.	Select the Neutered/Spayed, Current Vaccinations, and Deceased controls and their attached labels by clicking each text control while holding down the Shift key.
Step 10.	Drag the block of controls to the right so that they are just under the most recently moved block.
Step 11.	Select the Current Vaccinations and Deceased controls and their attached labels by clicking each text control while holding down the Shift key.
Step 12.	Drag the block of controls upward so that they are just under the Neutered/Spayed control.
Step 13.	Delete the Pet Name label control (only).
Step 14.	Delete the Picture label control (only).
Step 15.	Delete the Comments label control (only).
Step 16.	Select the bottom right handle to resize the Picture control to 1 inch by 1 inch.
Step 17.	Move the Picture control to ⅛ inch by ⅛ inch on the rulers (top-left corner) of the detail section.
Step 18.	Move the Pet Name text box control under the picture so that it intersects the left ruler at 1½ inches.
Step 19.	Move the Comments text box control under the picture so that it intersects the left ruler at 1¾ inches.
Step 20.	Resize the Detail section so that it intersects 2½ inches on the left ruler.

At this point, you are about half done. The screen should look like Figure 21-14. (If it doesn't, adjust your controls until the screen matches the figure.) Remember that these screen pictures are taken with the Windows screen driver set at 800 x 600. If you are using normal VGA, you'll have to scroll the screen to see the entire report.

The next step is refining the design to get as close as possible to the design created in Figure 21-6. The page header band is complete for now. Later in this chapter, you'll reformat the controls to change the font size and style. In the next set of steps, you complete the layout of the detail section.

Figure 21-14:
Rearranging the controls on the report.

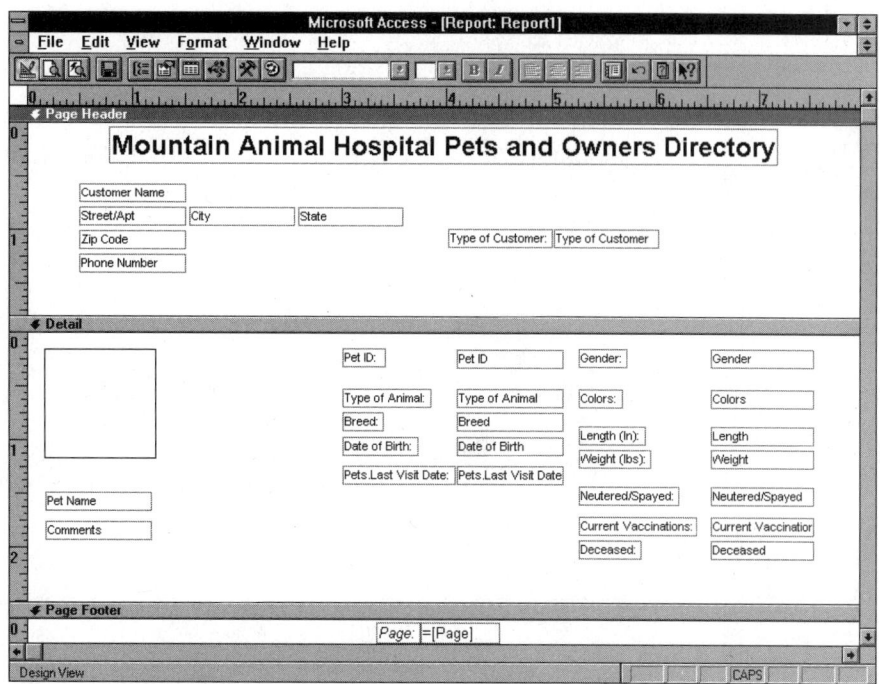

Steps: Completing the Detail Section Layout

Step 1. Drag the Pet ID attached control to the top of the block of controls containing Type of Animal.

Step 2. Select and drag that block to the right of the Picture OLE control, as shown in Figure 21-15.

Step 3. Drag the controls Neutered/Spayed, Current Vaccinations, and Deceased away from other controls to allow space to move the label controls above the text box controls, as shown in Figure 21-15.

Step 4. Drag each of the label controls above the text box controls by grabbing each move handle individually and then moving the controls above the text box controls.

Step 5. Select all three label controls and align the three label controls by selecting Format⇨Align⇨Bottom.

Step 6. Repeat Steps 3 and 4 for the Length, Weight, Colors, and Gender controls, moving them into position as shown in Figure 21-15.

Step 7. Move the Comments text box control so that it appears below all other controls.

Figure 21-15:
The selected and resized label controls in the detail section.

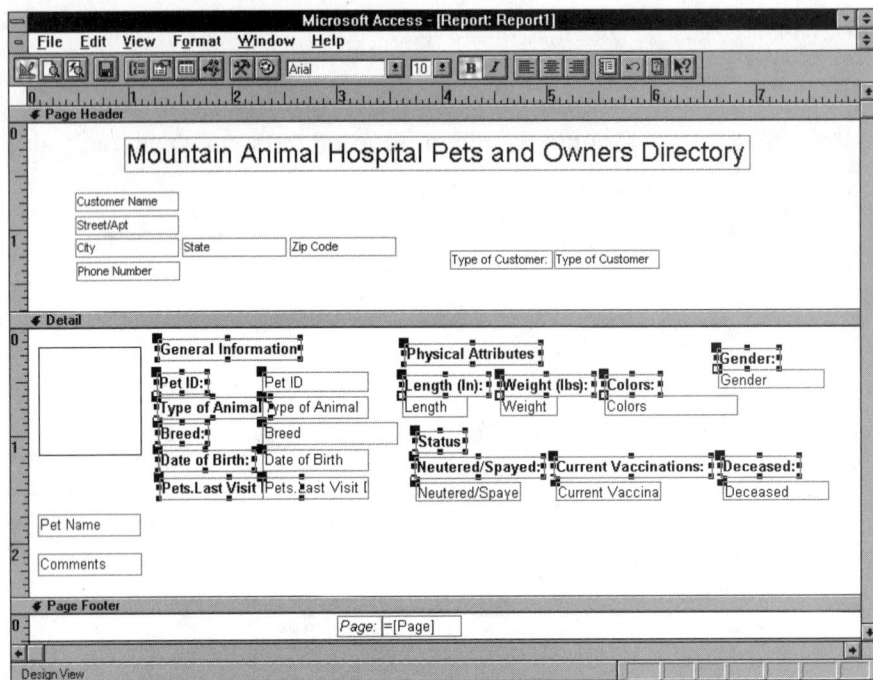

There is still some text to add as label controls. If you compare the design shown in Figure 21-6 to your screen, you can see that you still need to add some label controls to define the groups. To add the label controls, follow these steps:

Steps: Adding Label Controls

Step 1. Click the label control button in the toolbox.

Step 2. Click the Lock button at the bottom of the toolbox so that you can add more than one label control.

Step 3. Create a new label control above the Pet ID field and enter **General Information.** Make sure that you press Enter after entering the text of each label control so the control is automatically sized to fit the text.

Step 4. Create a new label control above the Length field and enter **Physical Attributes.**

Step 5. Create a new label control above the Neutered/Spayed field and enter **Status.**

Step 6. Click the Pointer button in the toolbox to unlock the toolbox.

Chapter 21: Creating and Customizing Reports

This completes the rough design for this report. There are still properties, fonts, and sizes to change. When you make these changes, you'll have to move fields around again. The design in Figure 21-6 is to be used only as a guideline. How it looks to you as you refine the look of the report in the Report window is the real design.

Modifying the appearance of multiple controls

The next step is to change all the label controls in the detail section to 10-point size and bold. This will help to differentiate between label controls and text controls, which currently have the same text formatting. The following steps guide you through modifying the appearance of multiple controls:

Steps:	Modifying the Appearance of Text in Multiple Label Controls
Step 1.	Select all label controls in the detail section by individually clicking them while holding down the Shift key. There are 15 label controls to select, as shown in Figure 21-15.
Step 2.	Click the Bold button on the toolbar.
Step 3.	Click the arrow in the Font-Size drop-down box.
Step 4.	Select 10 from the Font-Size drop-down list.
Step 5.	Select Format⇨Size⇨to Fit to resize all the labels.

You cannot select all the label controls in the preceding steps using the drag-and-surround method. This method would also select all the text boxes, and you want only to bold and resize the labels.

You also need to make all the text box controls bold and increase their font size to 12 points in the page header section. To do so, follow these steps:

Steps:	Modifying the Appearance of Text Box Controls
Step 1.	Select all the controls except the title in the page header section by clicking the cursor on the top left corner of the section and then dragging the cursor to surround all the controls. Include the Type of Customer label control as well.
Step 2.	Click the Bold button on the toolbar.
Step 3.	Click the Font-Size box drop-down arrow.

Step 4.	Select 12 from the Font-Size drop-down list.
Step 5.	Select Format⇨Size⇨to Fit to resize all the text box controls.

Notice that the text box controls do not display the entire field name. Remember sizing to fit works only on the vertical height of a control. It is impossible to know how wide a field's value will be — you need to adjust these values manually. You can use the Print Preview window to check on your progress. Figure 21-16 shows the Print Preview window.

Looking at the print preview reveals many problems. These problems include the following:

Page header section:

- The Customer Name text box is not wide enough.
- There is too much space after the State text box before the ZIP Code.
- The Phone Number text box is not wide enough.
- The Type of Customer text box is under the label and must be moved to the right.
- The Type of Customer text box value needs to be left-aligned.

Detail section:

- None of the text boxes in the detail section is 10 point; all are 8 point.
- The Pet Name needs to be bolded, centered, and moved closer to the picture.
- The data under General Information is not lined up properly.
- The Pets.Last Visit Date label needs to have the prefix Pets deleted.
- Pet ID, Type of Animal, and Breed are left-aligned, whereas the other two values are right-aligned.
- The Length and Weight values under Physical Attributes are right-aligned and don't line up with the labels above them.
- The Gender control doesn't quite fit.
- The Current Vaccinations and Deceased labels are running into each other.
- The Picture OLE control is not correctly displayed.
- The Comments memo field displays only the first few words.

Page footer section:

- The Page Number control needs to be moved to the right edge of the page.
- The page number needs to be left-aligned, and both controls need to be italicized.

Figure 21-16:
Previewing the report.

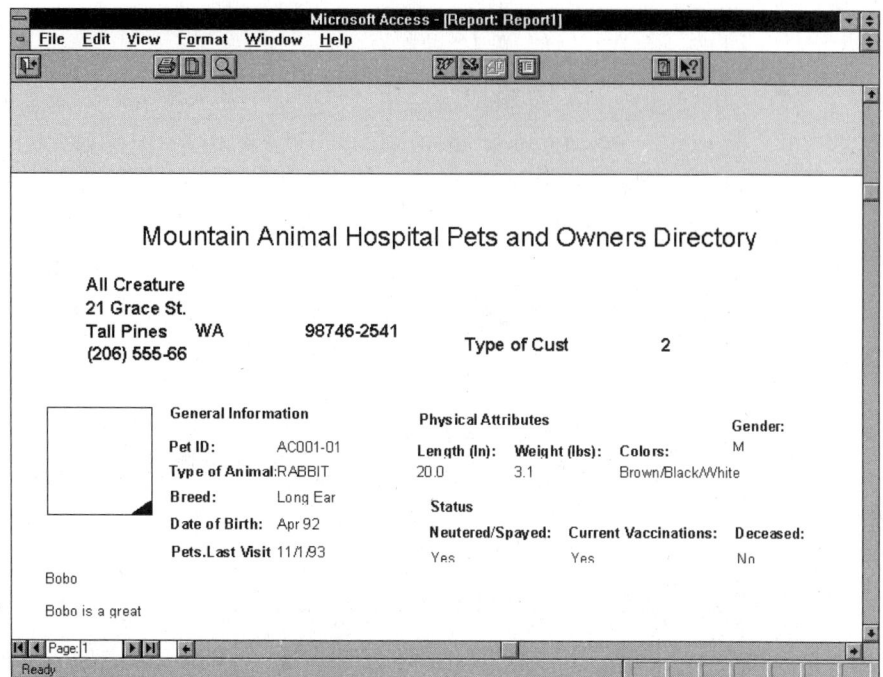

Remember that you may have only looked at the data for one record. Make sure that you look at data for many records before completing the report design. You need to watch the maximum sizes of your data. Another suggestion is to create a dummy record that you use only for testing. The dummy record should contain values that use each position of the field. For example, Fred Rumpelstiltskin III is a great name to test a 24-character field. Of course, with proportional fonts, you really can't count characters because an *i* uses less space than an *m*.

The problems just noted will have to be fixed before this report is considered complete. Many of the problems can easily be fixed with the techniques you've already performed. Complete the changes as outlined in the list on the previous pages. When you are through, your screen should look like Figure 21-17.

Once you make the final modifications, you are finished, except for fixing the picture. To do this, you'll need to change properties, which you do in the next section. This may seem to be an enormous number of steps because every step was designed to show you how laying out a report design can be a slow process. However, remember that when you are clicking away with the mouse, you don't realize how many steps you are doing as you visually design the report layout. With a WYSIWYG layout, such as the Access report designer, you may need to perform many tasks, but it's still easier and faster than programming. Figure 21-17 shows the final version of the design layout as you'll see it in this chapter. In the next chapter, you will continue to improve this report layout.

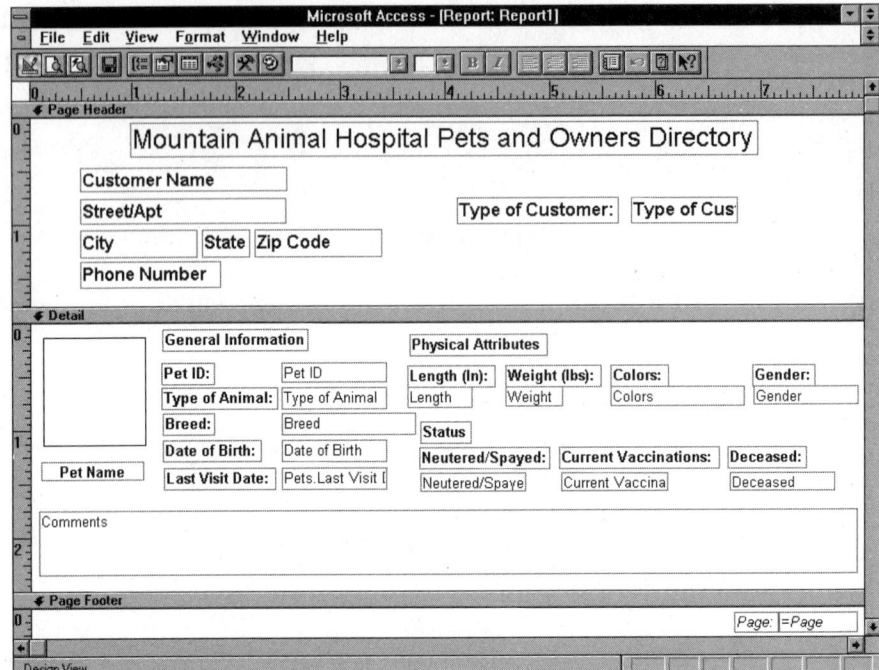

Figure 21-17: The final design layout.

Changing label and text box control properties

To change the properties of a text or label control, you need to display the control's property sheet. If it is not already displayed, perform one of these actions:

- Double-click the border of the control (anywhere but a sizing or moving handle).
- Click on the Properties button on the toolbar.
- Select View⇨Properties....
- Right-click the mouse and select Properties....

The property sheet lets you look at a control's property settings and gives you an easy way to edit the settings. When you use such tools as the palette and text-formatting buttons on the toolbar, you are changing the property settings of a control. For example, when you click the Bold button, you are really setting the Font Weight property to Bold. It is usually much more intuitive to use the toolbar or even the menus, but some properties are not accessible this way. And objects sometimes have more options available through the property sheet.

The Size Mode property of an OLE object (bound object frame) with the options of Clip, Stretch, and Zoom is a good example of a property available only through the property sheet.

The Picture control, which is a bound object frame, presently has its Size Mode property set to Clip, which is the default. With Clip, the picture is displayed in its original size. For this example, you need to change the setting to Stretch so that the picture is automatically sized to fit the picture frame.

 Use of pictures, OLE objects, and graphs is covered in Chapter 20.

To change the property for the picture bound object frame control, follow these steps:

Steps:	Changing a Bound Object Control Property
Step 1.	Click the picture bound object frame control.
Step 2.	Click the Size Mode property.
Step 3.	Click the arrow to display the drop-down list box.
Step 4.	Select Stretch.

This completes the changes to your form. A print preview of a single record is shown in Figure 21-18. Notice how the picture is now properly displayed and the Comments field is now displayed across the bottom of the detail section.

Formatting the display of text controls

With the palette and toolbar, you can change the appearance of a control and its text. For example, you can make a control's value bold or change its font size. You can make further changes by using the property sheet. Depending on the type of field a text box is bound to, or whether it contains an expression, you can use various types of format masks. You can type the character > to capitalize all letters, or you can create an input mask to add parentheses and hyphens to a phone number. For numeric and date formatting properties, you can select from a drop-down list box, which lets you add dollar signs to a number or format a date in a more readable way.

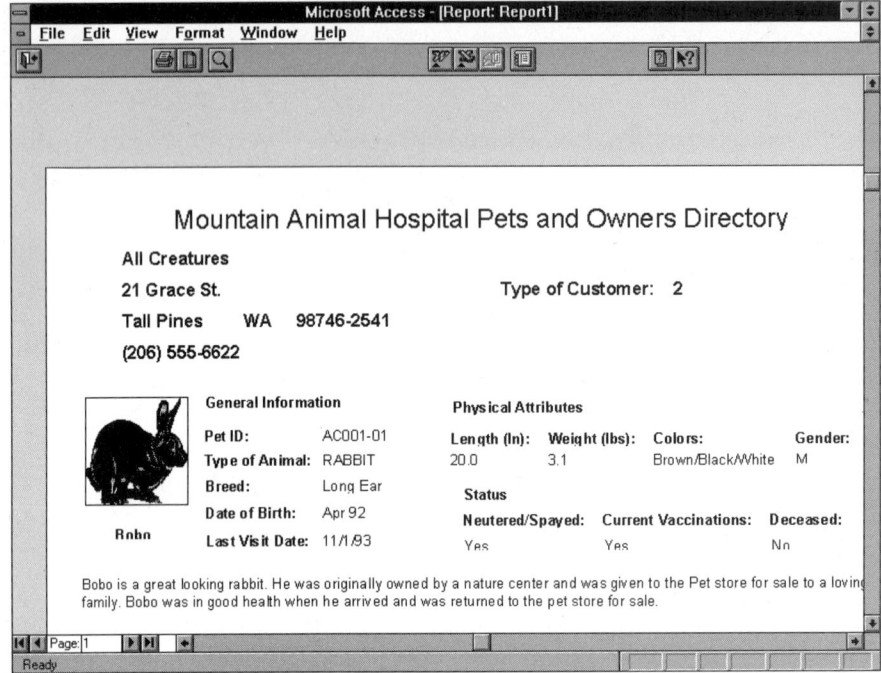

Figure 21-18: The final report print preview.

Growing and shrinking text box controls

When you print or print preview fields that can have variable text lengths, Access provides options for enabling a control to grow or shrink vertically, depending on the exact contents of a record. The option Can Grow determines whether a text control will add lines to fit additional text if the record contains more lines of text than the control is defined to display. The option Can Shrink determines whether a control will delete blank lines if the record's contents use fewer lines than the control is defined to display. Although you can use this property for any text field, it is especially helpful for Memo field controls.

An explanation of the acceptable values for these two properties is given in Table 21-4.

Table 21-4
Text Control Values for Can Grow and Can Shrink

Property	Value	Description
Can Grow	Yes	If the data in a record uses more lines than the control is defined to display, the control resizes to accommodate additional lines.
Can Grow	No	If the data in a record uses more lines than the control is defined to display, the control does not resize and truncates the data display.

Property	Value	Description
Can Shrink	Yes	If the data in a record uses fewer lines than the control is defined to display, the control resizes to eliminate blank lines.
Can Shrink	No	If the data in a record uses fewer lines than the control is defined to display, the control does not resize to eliminate blank lines.

To change the settings for Can Grow, follow these steps:

Steps: Changing Can Grow Properties for a Text Control

Step 1. Select the Comments text control.

Step 2. Display the property sheet.

Step 3. Click the Can Grow property; then click on the arrow and select Yes.

The Can Grow and Can Shrink properties are also available for report sections. Use a section's property sheet to modify these values.

As you near completion of testing of your report design, you should also test the printing of your report. Figure 21-19 shows a hard copy of the first page of the Customer and Pets report. As you can see, three pet records are displayed for the Customer All Creatures.

You should, however, print several pages of the report. When you get to page 2, you may see a problem; the animals owned by Johnathan Adams are listed on the page that is for the Pet Store All Creatures. What is wrong? The problem is that you haven't told Access how to group your data. Figure 21-19 displays three records on a page, but All Creatures brought in four pets. The next page begins again with All Creatures in the page header. Then the first record is Fido, the dog belonging to All Creatures. But the next record is Patty the Pig, belonging to Johnathan Adams. This record needs to trigger a page break because the Customer record has changed. Later in this chapter, you learn how to do this. You may also notice on page 2 that the Breed field is not fully displayed. You should expand the text box so that the entire text German Shepherd is displayed.

If your page 2 and every even page is blank, you accidentally widened the report past the 8-inch mark. If you move a control to brush up against the right page-margin border or exceed it, the right page margin automatically increases. Once it is past the 8-inch mark, it can't display the entire page on one physical piece of paper. The blank page you get is actually the right side of the preceding page. To correct this, make sure that all your controls are within the 8-inch right margin and then drag the right page margin back to 8 inches.

Figure 21-19:
The final report hard-copy printout.

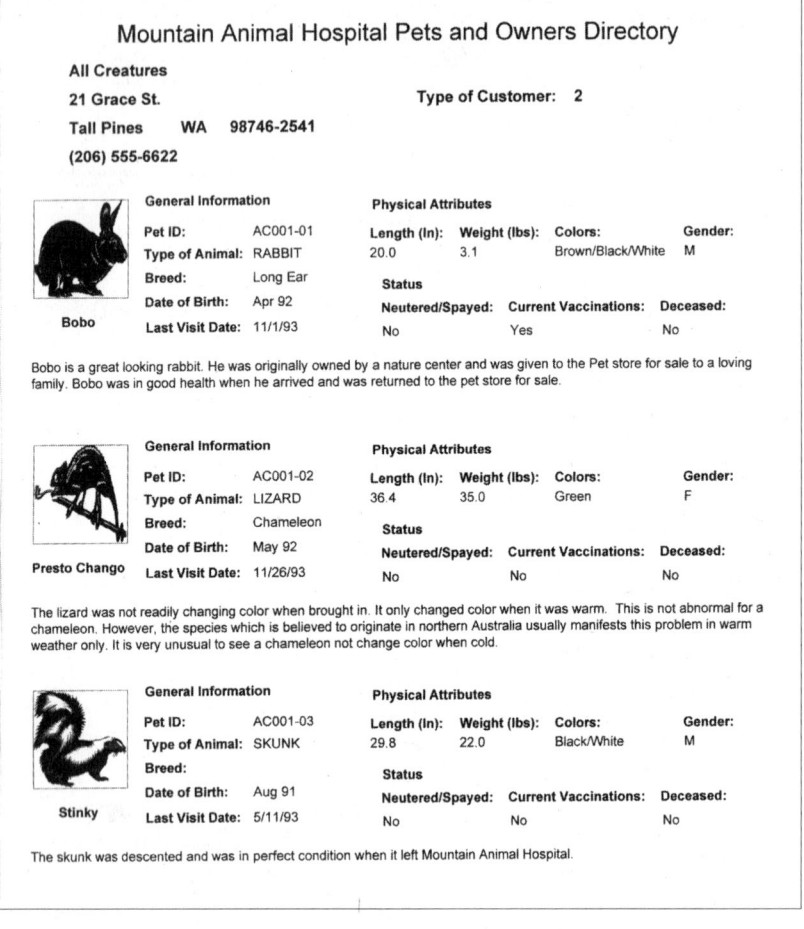

Sorting and grouping data

So far in this report, you've completely designed the layout of your report. You may think you are done, but some tasks still remain.

Sorting lets you determine the order in which you view the records in a datasheet, form, or report, based on the values in one or more fields. This is important when you want to view the data in your tables in a sequence other than your input. For example, new customers are added to the Customer table as they become clients of the hospital. As such, the physical order of the database reflects the date and time a customer is added. Yet when you think of the customer list, you probably expect it to be in alphabetical order, and you want to sort it by Customer Number or Customer Name. By sorting in the report itself, you don't have to worry about what order the data is in. Although you can sort the data in the query, it is more advantageous to do it in the report. This way if you change the query, the report is still in the correct order.

The Customer Name and Customer Number Fields

You may have noticed that the Customer Name field is not in last name/first name order, but the Customer Number is generally in a sorted order by the customer's last name. The Customer Number field begins with the first two characters of a customer's last name if the customer is an individual (Type of Customer = 1). If the customer is a pet store (Type of Customer = 2) or zoo (Type of Customer = 3), the Customer Number field begins with the first two logical characters of the pet store or zoo name.

For an illustration, examine the following list, which shows Type of Customer, Customer Name, and Customer Number for the first five records in the Customer table:

Type of Customer	Customer Name	Customer Number
2 - Pet Store	All Creatures	AC001
1 - Individual	Johnathan Adams	AD001
1 - Individual	William Adams	AD002
2 - Pet Store	Animal Kingdom	AK001
3 - Zoo	Borderville Aquarium	BA001

With grouping, you can take this report concept even further by breaking related records into groups. As an example, you want to list your customers first by Customer Name and within each Customer Name group by Pet Name. To do this, you must use the Customer Number field to sort the data. Groupings that can create group headers and footers are sometimes called *control breaks* because the report groups are triggered by changes in data.

Before you can add a grouping, you must first define a sort order for at least one field in the report. You do this by using the Sorting and Grouping box, which is shown completed in Figure 21-20. In this example, you will use the Customer.Customer Number field to sort on first and then the Pet ID field, which you will use as the secondary sort. To define a sort order based on Customer Number and Pet ID, follow these steps:

Steps:	Defining a Sort Order for Fields
Step 1.	Click the Sorting and Grouping button on the toolbar to display the Sorting and Grouping box.
Step 2.	Click the cursor in the first row of the Field/Expression column of the Sorting and Grouping box. A downward-pointing arrow appears.

572   Part III: Using Acess in Your Work

Step 3.	Click the arrow to display a list of fields in the Pets and Owners query.
Step 4.	Click the Customer.Customer Number field in the field list. Notice that Sort Order defaults to Ascending.
Step 5.	Click the cursor in the second row of the Field/Expression column.
Step 6.	Click the arrow to display a list of fields in the Pets and Owners query.
Step 7.	Scroll down to find the Pet ID field in the field list and then select Pet ID. The Sort Order defaults to Ascending.

To see more of the Field/Expression column, you can drag the border between the Field/Expression and Sort order columns to the right. This has been done in Figure 21-20.

You can drag a field from the Field List into the Sorting and Grouping box Field/Expression column instead of entering a field or choosing one from the field list in the Sorting and Grouping box Field/Expression column.

Although in this example you used a field, you can alternatively sort (and group) by using an expression. To enter an expression, click in the desired row of the Field/Expression column and enter any valid Access expression, making sure you start it with an equal sign, as in =[Length]*[Weight].

To change the sort order for fields that you placed in the Field/Expression column, simply click the Sort Order column and click the down arrow to display the Sort Order list; then select Descending.

Figure 21-20:
The Sorting and Grouping box.

Creating a group header or footer

In this example, you'll need to sort by the Customer Number and Pet ID. You will also need to create a group header for Customer Number in order to force a new page break before each new customer page. This way, a customer page will display pet records only for that customer, and customers who have more pets than will fit on one page will continue to generate new pages with only the customer information and pets for that customer. You don't need a group footer in this example, as there are no totals by customer number or other reason to use a group footer.

To create a group header that lets you sort and group by customer number, follow these steps:

Steps:	Creating a Group Header
Step 1.	Click the Sorting and Grouping button on the toolbar if the Sorting and Grouping box is not displayed. The field Customer.Customer Number should be displayed in the first row of the Sorting and Grouping box, and it should indicate that it is being used as a sort in Ascending order.
Step 2.	Click Customer.Customer Number in the Field/Expression column.
Step 3.	Click the Group Header property in the bottom pane. Notice that an arrow appears.
Step 4.	Click the arrow in the right-hand side of the edit box. A drop-down list appears.
Step 5.	Select Yes from the list.
Step 6.	Press Enter.

After you define a header or footer, the row pointer changes to the grouping symbol shown in Figure 21-21. This is the same symbol you see in the Grouping button in the toolbar. In Figure 21-21, not only can you see the grouping row pointer, but a new section has been created. The Customer.Customer Number header section is displayed between the page header and detail sections. If you define a group footer, it appears below the detail section. If there are multiple groupings in a report, each subsequent group becomes the one closest to the detail section. The groups that are defined first will be farthest from the detail section.

Figure 21-21:
The group header definition.

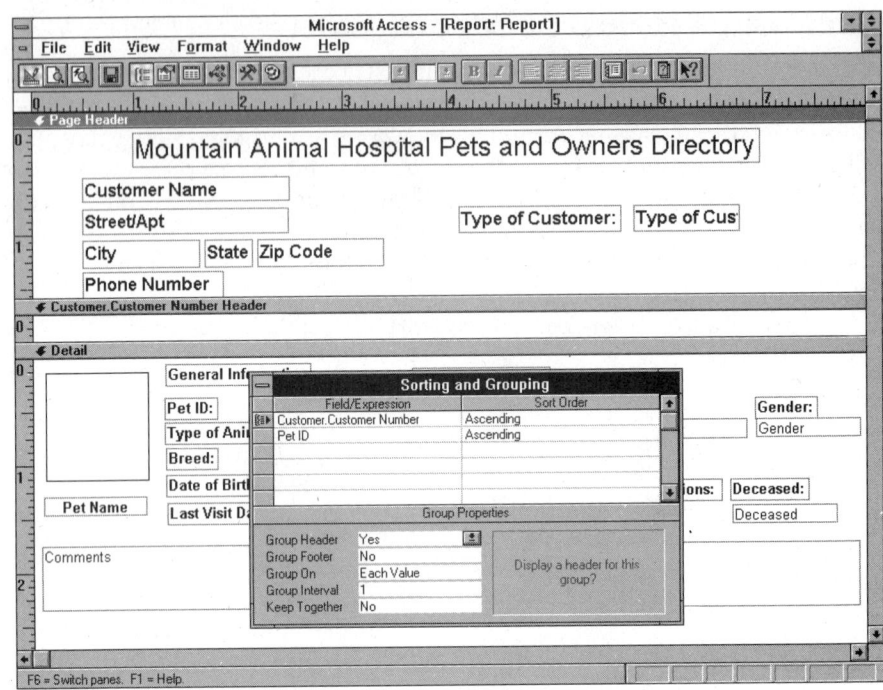

The Group Properties pane displayed at the bottom of the Sorting and Grouping box contains five properties:

Group Header   Yes creates a group header. No removes the group header.

Group Footer   Yes creates a group footer. No removes the group footer.

Group On   Specifies how you want the values grouped. The options you see in the drop-down list box depend on the data type of the field on which you're grouping. If you group on an expression, you see all the options.

       For Text data types, you have two choices:

           Each Value   The same value in the field or expression

           Prefix Characters   The same first *n* number of characters in the field

       For Date/Time data types, you have further options:

           Each Value   The same value in the field or expression

           Year   Dates in the same calendar year

Chapter 21: Creating and Customizing Reports

Qtr	Dates in the same calendar quarter
Month	Dates in the same month
Week	Dates in the same week
Day	Dates on the same date
Hour	Times in the same hour
Minute	Times in the same minute

With Counter, Currency, or Number data types, you have two options:

Each Value	The same value in the field or expression
Interval	Values falling within the interval you specify

Group Interval — Specifies any interval that is valid for the values in the field or expression you're grouping on.

Keep Together — Whole group prints header detail and group footer on one page. First detail prevents the contents of the group header from printing without any following data or records on a page.

Following Along in This Book

After you create the Customer Number group header, you are done with the Sorting and Grouping box for this report. Sometimes you need to make further changes to groupings as you change the way a report looks. The following three topics detail how to make these changes. You should not make any of these changes if you are following along with the examples. If you want to practice these skills, you can save the report before practicing and then retrieve the original copy of the report that you saved. After the next three sections, you will have to size the group header section and change its properties.

Changing the group order

Access lets you easily change the Sorting and Grouping order, without having to move all the individual controls in the associated headers and footers. The steps to change the sorting/grouping order are detailed next.

Steps:	Changing the Sorting/Grouping Order
Step 1.	Click the selector of the field or expression you want to move in the Sorting and Grouping window.
Step 2.	Click the Selector again and hold down the left mouse button.
Step 3.	Drag the row to a new location.
Step 4.	Release the mouse button.

Removing a group header or footer

To remove a page or report header/footer section, use the Format⇨Page Hdr/Ftr and Format⇨Report Hdr/Ftr toggles as detailed earlier in this chapter. To remove a group header or footer but leave the sorting intact, follow these steps:

Steps:	Removing a Group Header
Step 1.	Click the selector of the field or expression you want to remove from the grouping in the Sorting and Grouping window.
Step 2.	Click the Group Header edit box.
Step 3.	Change the value to **No**.
Step 4.	Press Enter.

To remove a group footer, follow the same steps; but in Step 2, click Group Footer.

To permanently remove both the sorting and grouping for a particular field (and thereby remove the group header and footer sections), follow these steps:

Steps:	Removing the Sorting and Grouping for a Field
Step 1.	Click the selector of the field or expression you want to delete.
Step 2.	Press Delete. A dialog box appears, asking you to confirm the deletion.
Step 3.	Click OK.

Hiding a section

Access also lets you hide headers and footers so that you can break data into groups without having to view information about the group itself. You can also hide the detail section so that you get only a summary report. To hide a section, follow these steps:

Steps:	Hiding a Section
Step 1.	Click the section that you want to hide.
Step 2.	Display the section property sheet.
Step 3.	Click the Visible property's edit box.
Step 4.	Click the drop-down list arrow on the right side of the edit box.
Step 5.	Select No from the drop-down list box.

Sections are not the only objects in a report that can be hidden. Controls also have a Visible property. This property can be useful for expressions that trigger other expressions.

Following Along in This Book

If you are following along in the examples, you should complete the next steps.

Sizing a section

Now that you've created the group header, you must decide what to do with it. In this example, its only purpose is to trigger a page break before a new customer record is displayed. You learn how to do this later in this chapter. In this example, you don't need to place any controls within the section. Unless you want to see the empty space on the report from the height of the group header section, you need to close the section. You can do this by resizing the section height to 0.

To modify the height of a section, you must drag the border of the section below it. For example, if you have a report with a page header, detail section, and page footer, change the height of the detail section by dragging the top of the page footer section's border. You can make a section larger or smaller by dragging the bottom border of the section. To change the height of the group header section to zero in this example, follow these steps:

Steps:	Sizing a Section
Step 1.	Move your cursor over the section borders. Notice that the cursor changes to a horizontal line split by two vertical arrows.
Step 2.	Select the top of the detail section border.
Step 3.	Drag the selected border until it meets the bottom of the Customer.Customer Number header. Notice the grey line that indicates where the top of the border will be when you release the mouse button.
Step 4.	Release the mouse button.

Adding page breaks

Access lets you add page breaks based on group breaks, as well as insert forced breaks within sections except in page header/footer sections.

In some report designs, it is advantageous to have each new group start on a different page. In the Pets and Owners report you created in this chapter, one of the design criteria is that no more than one customer will appear on a page (although a customer can appear on more than one page). This effect is easily achieved by using the Force New Page property of a group section, which lets you force a page break every time the group value changes.

The four Force New Page settings are as follows:

None	No forced page break (the default)
Before Section	Starts printing the current section at the top of a new page every time there is a new group
After Section	Starts printing the next section at the top of a new page every time there is a new group
Before & After	Combines the effects of Before Section and After Section

To create the report you want, you must force a page break before the Customer Number group by using the Force New Page property in the Customer Number header. To change the Force New Page property, follow these steps:

Steps:	Forcing Page Breaks Based on Groupings
Step 1.	Click anywhere in the Customer.Customer Number header.
Step 2.	Display the property sheet.
Step 3.	Select the Force New Page property.
Step 4.	Click the drop-down list arrow on the right side of the edit box.
Step 5.	Select Before Section from the drop-down list box.

This property sheet is shown in Figure 21-22.

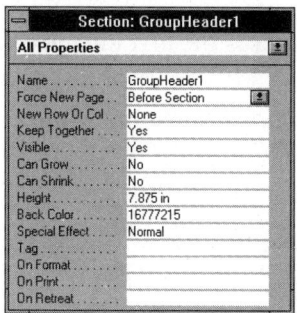

Figure 21-22: Forcing a page break in a group header.

If you run the report now, you'll see that page 2 has correctly printed only the last record from All Creatures. Page 3 now contains the two pets owned by Johnathan Adams.

 Alternatively, you can create a Customer Number footer and set its Force New Page property to After Section.

Sometimes you don't want to force a page break based on a grouping but still want to force a page break. The solution is to use the Page Break tool from the toolbox. An example of when you may want to do this is to split a report title across several pages. The steps to add a page break are detailed next.

Steps:	Adding a Page Break to a Section
Step 1.	Display the toolbox.
Step 2.	Click the Page Break tool.
Step 3.	Click in the section where you want the page break to occur.
Step 4.	Test the results by using Print Preview.

 Be careful not to split the data in a control. Place page breaks above or below controls and not overlapping them.

Saving your report

After all the time you spent creating your report, you want to save it. As a matter of fact, even though it is covered toward the end of this chapter, it is good practice to save your reports frequently, starting as soon as you create them. This prevents the frustration of losing your work due to a power failure or human error. The steps to save your report are detailed next.

Steps:	Saving Your Report
Step 1.	Select File⇨Save. If this is the first time you've saved the report, the Save As dialog box appears.
Step 2.	Type in a valid Access name. For this example, type **Pets and Owners - Unformatted.**
Step 3.	Select OK.

If you already saved your report, Access silently (or not so silently, depending on your disk drive) saves your file, with no message about what it is up to.

Summary

In this chapter, you learned the basic operations involved in creating a report. Concepts covered include the following:

- A report gives you a different way of viewing data in one or more tables.
- Because of the advanced capabilities of Access, you are limited only by your imagination and your printer in the types of reports you can create.
- In the Report Design window, Access provides you with powerful but easy-to-use tools. These tools are the toolbar, the palette, the Properties window, the Sorting and Grouping box, and the field list.
- The Report Design View toolbar gives you quick access to such design tasks as displaying various windows and applying formatting styles.
- With the toolbox, you can create, place, or select the controls on a report.
- The Field List window displays all fields available to a report from the query or table the report is bound to.
- Properties for a control can be viewed and edited from the control's property sheet.
- The Sorting and Grouping box lets you create group or summary sections on the report, as well as to define sort orders.
- You can place fields on a report by displaying the field list, selecting your fields, and then dragging the fields onto your report.
- Control properties can be edited by direct manipulation through the various tools of the Report Design window. Or you can edit these properties from the property sheet.
- Summary reports can be created by hiding the detail section.
- Sorting lets you organize your data in a different order from the order you used during input.
- Grouping lets you organize your data in related groups that make the data easier to understand.

In the next chapter, you learn how to publish your reports using Access database publishing features.

Database Publishing and Printing

CHAPTER 22

■ ■

In This Chapter

- Understanding the terms *database publishing* and *WYSIWYG*
- Enhancing text controls by controlling font size and style
- Working with multiline text controls
- Applying special display effects to reports
- Using a set of option buttons instead of a text box control
- Using checkboxes and toggle buttons to display Yes/No fields
- Adding lines and rectangles to a report
- Adding color or shading to a report
- Adding three-dimensional effects to a report
- Reviewing the Print and Print Setup dialog boxes

■ ■

In Chapter 21, you built a report from a blank form. That report was fairly simple. You worked only with label and text box controls, and the report had no special formatting. There were no lines or boxes, and there was no shading to emphasize any areas of the report. Although the report displays all the necessary data, you can make the data more readable by using checkboxes, option buttons, and toggle buttons to display certain fields.

In this chapter, you see how to complete the formatting of the report. You enhance the report you created in the preceding chapter, making it more readable and more presentable.

Because the Report Design window is set to a width of eight inches, most of the screen printouts in this chapter appear as if an 800 × 600-resolution Super VGA Windows screen driver is used rather than the standard 640 × 480-VGA Windows driver. This lets you see almost the entire screen in the figures.

Database Publishing with Access

The term *database publishing* generally refers to the process of enhancing a report from a database by using special effects that desktop publishing packages provide. The Access report writer can accomplish with data, reports, and forms what any good desktop publishing package can do with words. Just as a desktop publishing application can enhance a word-processed document to make it more readable, a database publisher can enhance a database report to make it more usable.

You can, for example, draw attention to areas of the report that you want the reader to notice. Just as a headline in a newspaper screams out the news, an enhanced section of the report screams out the information.

You accomplish database publishing in reports with a variety of controls and by enhancing the controls with color, shading, or other means of emphasis. In Chapters 18, 19, and 20, you learned how to add to a form many of the controls you work with in this chapter. You use a somewhat different process to add and enhance these controls in a report. One major difference is the ultimate viewing medium. Because the output of these controls is usually viewed on paper, you have different design concerns than you do when creating a design to be viewed on-screen. Another difference is the way each data control is used. In a form, you must input or edit the data. In a report, you merely view the data.

Figure 22-1 shows the hard copy of the final report you create in this chapter. Notice that it has been significantly enhanced by adding special effects and more control types than mere labels or text boxes. Important information, such as the type of customer, gender, and current vaccinations, is easily understood at a glance. This is because readers only need to look at an option button (⦿/○) or a checkbox (☒/☐) rather than at a numeric code or text.

The Access report writer offers you a number of tools to make the report controls and sections stand out visually. These tools enable you to create such special effects as

- Lines and rectangles
- Color and background shading
- Three-dimensional effects (raised, sunken, and shadowed)

In this chapter, you use all of these features as you change many of the text box controls into option buttons, toggle buttons, and checkboxes. You also enhance the report with special text options: shading, shadows, lines, rectangles, and three-dimensional effects.

When you add shading to a report, you can increase printing time dramatically. Also, avoid adding colors unless you plan to print to a color printer.

Figure 22-1: An enhanced report.

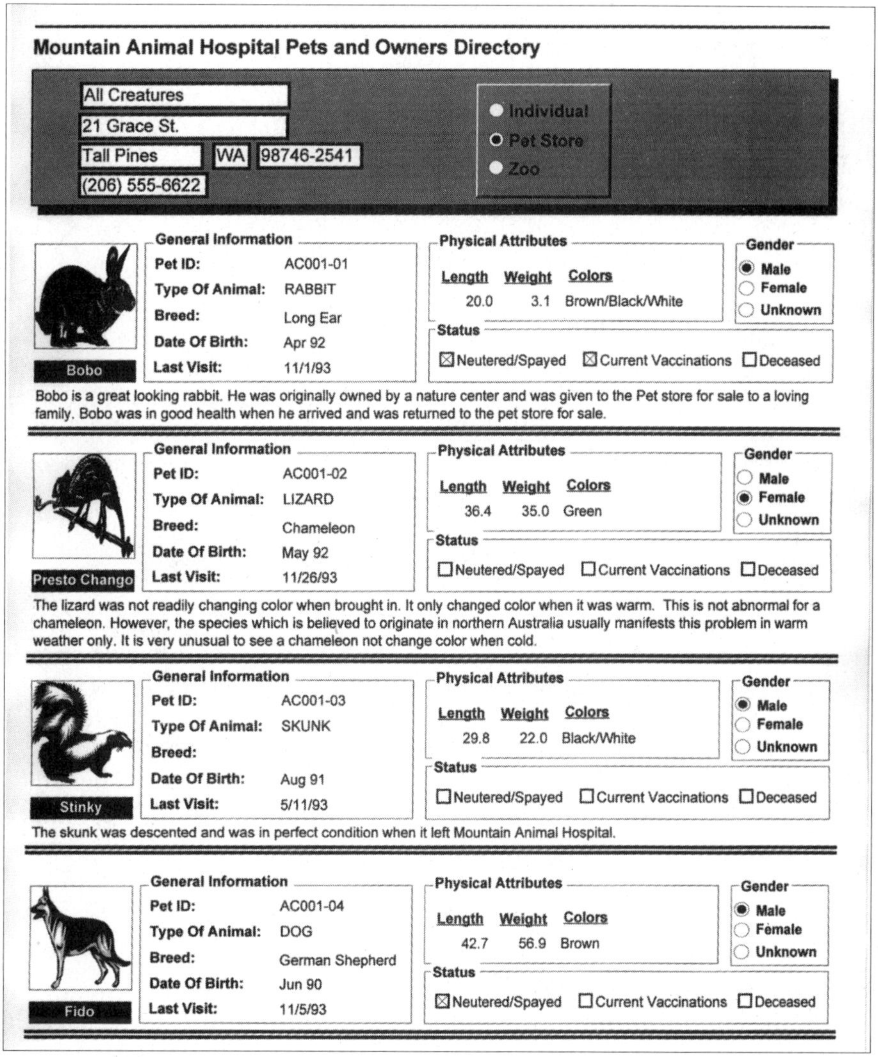
Mountain Animal Hospital Pets and Owners Directory

All Creatures
21 Grace St.
Tall Pines WA 98746-2541
(206) 555-6622

Individual
Pet Store
Zoo

Bobo
General Information
Pet ID: AC001-01
Type Of Animal: RABBIT
Breed: Long Ear
Date Of Birth: Apr 92
Last Visit: 11/1/93
Physical Attributes
Length Weight Colors
20.0 3.1 Brown/Black/White
Gender
Male
Female
Unknown
Status
Neutered/Spayed Current Vaccinations Deceased
Bobo is a great looking rabbit. He was originally owned by a nature center and was given to the Pet store for sale to a loving family. Bobo was in good health when he arrived and was returned to the pet store for sale.

Presto Chango
General Information
Pet ID: AC001-02
Type Of Animal: LIZARD
Breed: Chameleon
Date Of Birth: May 92
Last Visit: 11/26/93
Physical Attributes
Length Weight Colors
36.4 35.0 Green
Gender
Male
Female
Unknown
Status
Neutered/Spayed Current Vaccinations Deceased
The lizard was not readily changing color when brought in. It only changed color when it was warm. This is not abnormal for a chameleon. However, the species which is believed to originate in northern Australia usually manifests this problem in warm weather only. It is very unusual to see a chameleon not change color when cold.

Stinky
General Information
Pet ID: AC001-03
Type Of Animal: SKUNK
Breed:
Date Of Birth: Aug 91
Last Visit: 5/11/93
Physical Attributes
Length Weight Colors
29.8 22.0 Black/White
Gender
Male
Female
Unknown
Status
Neutered/Spayed Current Vaccinations Deceased
The skunk was descented and was in perfect condition when it left Mountain Animal Hospital.

Fido
General Information
Pet ID: AC001-04
Type Of Animal: DOG
Breed: German Shepherd
Date Of Birth: Jun 90
Last Visit: 11/5/93
Physical Attributes
Length Weight Colors
42.7 56.9 Brown
Gender
Male
Female
Unknown
Status
Neutered/Spayed Current Vaccinations Deceased

Understanding WYSIWYG printing

Access has a WYSIWYG (what you see is what you get) report writer. As you create controls on-screen, you instantly see how they will look in your report. If you want to see how the data will look, you can take advantage of several types of on-screen preview modes. These modes enable you to see the actual data without involving a hard-copy device.

The Access report writer lets you add color, shading, or even reverse video (white letters on a black background) to your report text and controls. You can even color or shade the background of report sections. As you do this, you see the effect immediately. Although it appears that what you see on the Report Design screen is exactly what you'll get when you print, you should be aware of some things that affect just how close what you see is to what you really get.

The first problem is with fonts. If you use Windows 3.1 and TrueType fonts, generally about 95 percent of your fonts appear perfectly, both on the Report Design window on-screen and in the hard-copy report. If you use Windows 3.0 or some other font manager, you can find a much higher variation between the Report Design window and the print previews or hard-copy output (Adobe Type Manager and Bitstream FaceLift usually approach or exceed TrueType in WYSIWYG quality). A common problem is that letters don't all fit on the report even though they appear to fit in the Report Design window. Another problem is that controls shift very slightly from perfect alignment. For example, although the Report Design window shows that the word *Deceased* fits perfectly in the report, when you view the report in print preview mode or print it to a printer, only the letters *Decease* print out. The final *d* simply vanishes.

Other problems occur when you place controls very tightly within a rectangle or group box. In fact, most of the time, the print preview modes are perfect for determining what the hard copy will look like, whereas the Report Design window view may differ slightly. The print preview should be your only method (or hard copy) of determining when your report is complete. Make sure that you are using the right Windows screen driver when previewing a report, as you can get vastly different results depending on the driver. For example, a dot-matrix driver is probably only 100–150 dpi (dots per inch), whereas an HP LaserJet 4 can be 600 dpi.

Using the palette

One of the most important controls for enhancing a report is the palette. The palette, which was described in detail in Chapter 18, has four basic uses:

- Controlling foreground color, border color, and background color and shading
- Controlling line thickness in lines, rectangles, and control borders
- Controlling like type in lines, rectangles, and control borders
- Controlling three-dimensional effects, such as a raised or sunken appearance

Figure 22-2 shows the Access palette and its options. You can modify the appearance of a control with the palette. To do this, first select the control by clicking it. Then click the palette options that you want to apply to the control.

Chapter 22: Database Publishing and Printing   587

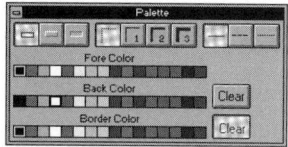

Figure 22-2: The palette.

Following Along in This Book

In this chapter, you modify your report from Chapter 21 to look like the one shown in Figure 22-1. Before you begin, you should start with a design. Figure 22-3 shows a sample design for enhancing the report. Lines and rectangles are drawn in the design. Changes to controls and their appearance are noted with instructions and arrows that point to the area to be changed.

If you are following along with this book using Access, you should have the Pets and Owners report that you created in Chapter 21 open in the Report Design window or the Pets and Owners-Unformatted report design that came in your MTNANHSP database.

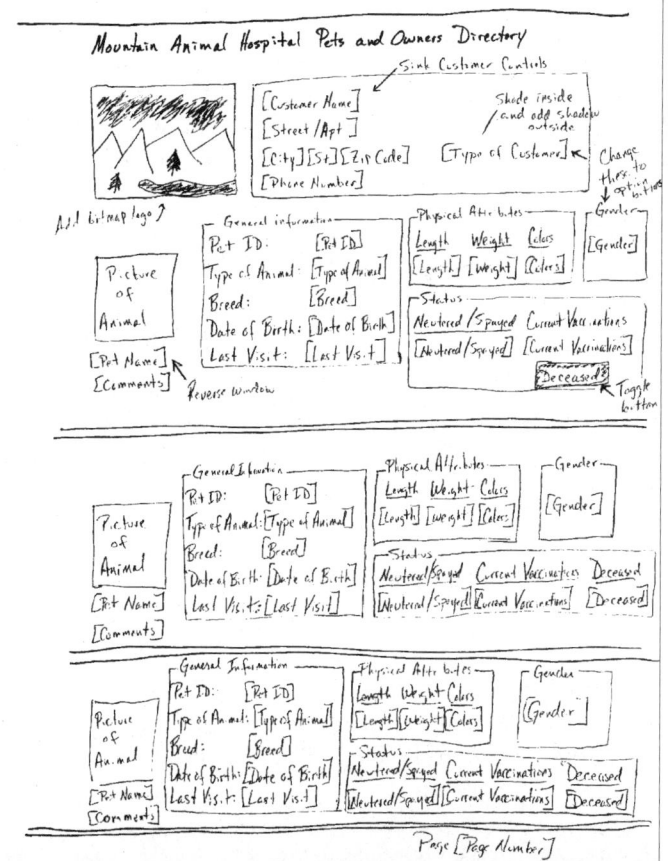

Figure 22-3: A design for report enhancements.

Enhancing Text-Based Controls

Before you start using such display items as shading or three-dimensional effects, it generally is important to get the data right. If your enhancements include control changes, start with these changes.

Enhancing label controls

You can enhance label controls in several ways, including the following:

- Changing the type style of the text font (Arial, Times New Roman, Wingding)
- Changing the text font size (4-200)
- Changing the text font style (bold, italic, underline)
- Changing the text color (using the palette)
- Adding a shadow

Changing text fonts and size

In Chapter 21, you learned how to change the text font type, size, and style. Now you learn how to make further changes as you change the title to match the design in Figures 22-1 and 22-3. These figures show that the text needs to be left-justified on the page and made one size smaller. To change the font placement and size, follow these steps:

Steps:	Changing the Font Placement and Size
Step 1.	Select the label control with the text Mountain Animal Hospital Pets and Owners Directory.
Step 2.	Drag the label control to the left side of the Report window.
Step 3.	Change the font size to **16**.

You will need to adjust the Label frame so that all the text is displayed.

Creating a text shadow

Text shadows create a three-dimensional look. They make the text appear to float above the page while its shadow stays on the page. You can create text shadows using these techniques:

- Duplicating the text
- Offsetting the duplicate text from the original text
- Changing the duplicate text to a different color (usually a lighter shade)
- Placing the duplicate text behind the original text
- Changing the original text Back Color Clear button

To create a shadow for the title's text, follow these steps:

Steps:	Creating a Text Shadow
Step 1.	Select the Palette button in the toolbar to display the palette.
Step 2.	Select the label control with the text Mountain Animal Hospital Pets and Owners Directory.
Step 3.	Select Edit⇨Duplicate.
Step 4.	Select the light grey Fore color (third from left) to change the duplicate text color.
Step 5.	Drag the duplicate text slightly to the right and upward to lessen the offset from the text below.
Step 6.	Select Format⇨Send to Back.
Step 7.	Select the original copy of the text (the one now in front).
Step 8.	Press the Clear button in the Back Color row of the palette.

The text now appears to have a shadow, as you see in Figure 22-4. The box around the label control will not be visible when the report is printed.

Although the on-screen shadow looks great, it does not print correctly on most monochrome printers. What you normally get are two lines of black text that look horrible. Unless you have a printer that prints text in shades of grey, using graphics rather than text fonts, or a color printer that prints grey, avoid using shadowed text on a report.

Displaying label or text box control properties

As you use the palette to change values in a label or text box control, you actually change their properties. Figure 22-4 displays the property sheet for the label control you just created. As you can see in the figure, many properties can be affected by the palette. These properties were described in detail in Chapter 15.

Although you can set many of these controls from the property sheet, it is much easier to drag the control to set the Top, Left, Width, and Height and to use the palette to set the other properties of the control.

Working with multiple-line text box controls

There are two reasons to use a multiple-line text box:

- To display a Text data type on multiple lines
- To display large amounts of text in a Memo data type

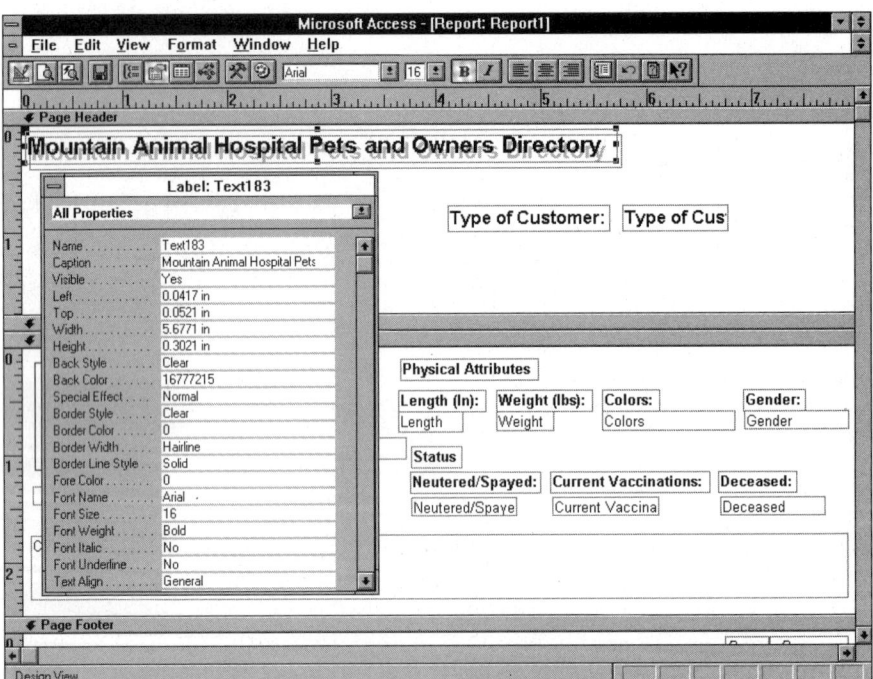

Figure 22-4: Label control properties.

Displaying multiple lines of text using a text box

In the sample report, the Street/Apt text box control in the page header sometimes contains data that takes up more than one line. The way the text box control is sized, you can only see the first line of data. There are generally two ways to see multiple lines of text in a text box control.

- Resize the control vertically to allow more lines to be displayed.
- Change the Can Grow or Can Shrink properties.

When you resize a control by making it larger vertically, it uses as much space as you allow for it. However, this can take up more space than necessary if the value of the data does not occupy the entire space allotted. For example, most of the values of the Street/Apt text box control use one line. Some, however, use two. If you resize the Street/Apt text box control to display two lines, the control displays two lines for every customer. This leaves a blank line between the Street/Apt control and the City control whenever the Street/Apt value uses only one line.

One solution to this problem is to use the Can Grow or Can Shrink properties of the text box control rather than resizing the control. If you change the value of the Can Grow property to Yes, the control grows vertically if there are more lines than can be displayed in the default control. Another solution is to resize the control so that it is larger and then use the Can Shrink property to remove any blank lines if the value of the data does not use the full size of the control.

When you set the Can Grow property in a text box control to Yes, this also sets the property for the detail, group header, and group footer, or report header or footer sections.

Displaying Memo fields in multiple-line text box controls

The Memo data type fields generally use large amounts of text. You can display these fields on a report by simply placing the text box in the desired section (usually the detail section) and resizing the text box to the desired width and height.

In a form, you can add scroll bars to display any text that doesn't fit the space allotted. But in a report, you don't have that option. To display text properly, you need to use the Can Grow and Can Shrink properties. In Chapter 21, you created a large text box control to accommodate several lines of memo text. However, you never set the Can Grow and Can Shrink properties. If you have a record with more than four lines of text, you won't see the other lines. Similarly, any records without Memo field data display only four empty lines. You should set the Can Grow and Can Shrink properties to Yes for the Comments Memo data type text box control. To change these properties, perform the following steps:

Steps:	Setting Can Grow and Can Shrink Properties for a Text Box Control
Step 1.	Select the Properties button in the toolbar to display the property sheet.
Step 2.	Select the Comments text box control.
Step 3.	Change the height of the control to one line to fit the Comments caption.

> **Step 4.** Change the Can Grow property to **Yes.**
>
> **Step 5.** Change the Can Shrink property to **Yes.**
>
> **Step 6.** Shrink the detail section height by dragging the page footer border upward until it is just below the Comments control.

To see the effect of the Can Grow and Can Shrink properties, display the report in the Print Preview window. Notice the Comment line and the shadowed line in Figure 22-5, which shows the Print Preview window. If you look at the print preview in zoom mode, you'll see that the spaces between the records are the same, regardless of the size of the Comments field. If no comment text is present, the next record begins immediately below the preceding record's information.

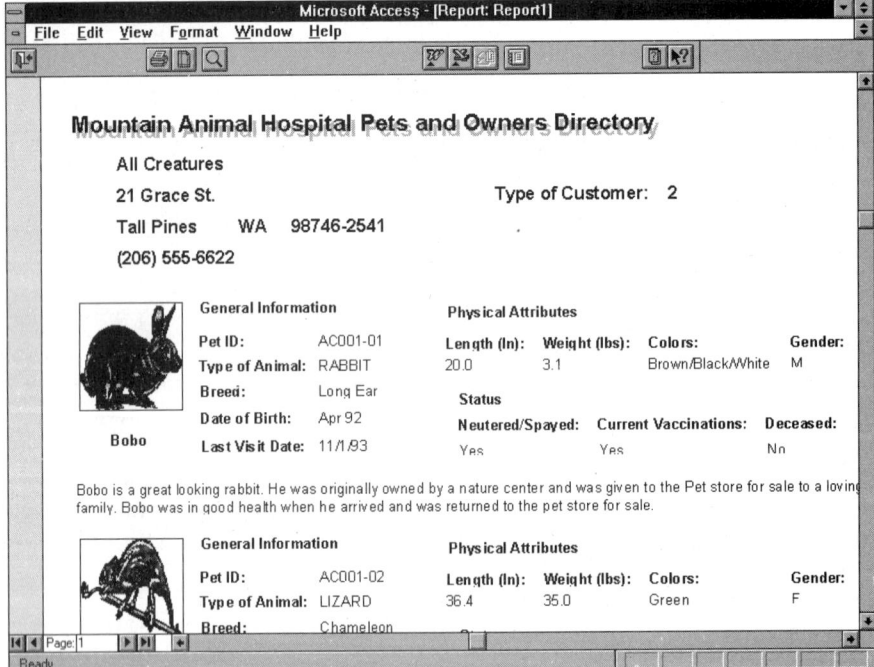

Figure 22-5: Displaying the Print Preview window.

Adding New Controls

You can change many data types to control types other than text box controls. These types include Text, Number, and Yes/No data types. By using these types of controls, you can create the following items:

Chapter 22: Database Publishing and Printing

- Option buttons
- Checkboxes
- Toggle buttons

Microsoft Access doesn't let you simply change the type of control. To change the way a control is displayed, you must create a new control and then delete the original text box control.

Displaying values with option groups and option buttons

In your design, as shown in Figure 22-3, you see two text box controls that should be changed to option buttons within an option group. These text box controls are the Type of Customer field in the page header section and the Gender field in the detail section.

An option group is generally bound to a single field or expression. Each button in the group passes a different value to the option group, which in turn passes the single choice to the bound field or expression. The buttons themselves are not bound to a field, only to the option group box.

If you haven't used an option button or option group yet, you should read Chapter 16 before continuing.

You can use only numeric data values to create an option button within an option group. The Type of Customer field is the easier control of the two to change into an option group because its values are already numeric, expressed as customer types 1, 2, or 3.

Creating the option group

To create the option group for the Type of Customer control, you must first delete the existing Type of Customer control. Once you do this, you can create a new option group and use the Option Group Wizard to create the option buttons.

A more complete example of creating an option group and option buttons with the Option Group Wizard can be found in Chapter 19.

Steps:	Creating an Option Group Using the Option Group Wizard
Step 1.	Delete the existing Type of Customer control.
Step 2.	Select the option group button from the toolbox.

Part III: Using Access in Your Work

Step 3. Drag the Type of Customer field to the space in the Page Header setion.

The first screen of the Option Group Wizard should be displayed, as shown completed in Figure 22-6. In this screen, you can enter the text label for each of the option buttons that will be in your option group. Each entry is entered just like in a datasheet. You can use the down-arrow key to move to the next choice.

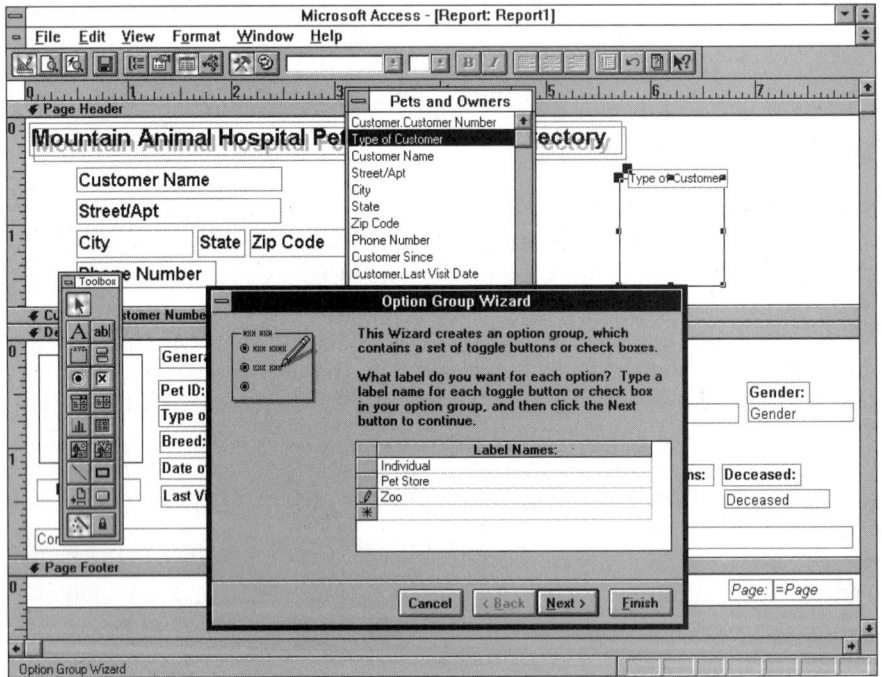

Figure 22-6: Entering the option group choices.

Step 4. Enter **Individual**, **Pet Store**, and **Zoo**, pressing the down-arrow key between choices.

Step 5. Press the Next > button to move to the default option wizard screen.

The next screen lets you select the default control for when the option group is selected. Normally, the first option is the default. If you want to make a different button the default, you would first select the Yes, the default is option button and then select the default value from the combo box that contains all of your choices. In this example, the first value will automatically be the default.

Chapter 22: Database Publishing and Printing

Step 6. Press the <u>N</u>ext > button to move to the assigning values wizard screen.

The next wizard screen displays the actual values you entered along with a default set of numbers that will be used to store the selected value into the bound option group field. The screen looks like a datasheet with two columns. In this example, this is the Type of Customer field. Your first choice, Individual, is automatically assigned a 1, Pet Store a 2, and Zoo a 3. When Pet Store is selected, a 2 will be stored in the Type of Customer field.

In this example, the default values are acceptable. Sometimes, you may want to assign values other than 1,2,3 ... You might want to use 100, 200, and 500 for some reason. As long as you use unique numbers, you can assign any values you want.

Step 7. Press the <u>N</u>ext > button to move to the next wizard screen.

In the wizard screen, you then have to decide whether the option group itself is bound to a form field or unbound. The first choice in the wizard, *Remember the value for later use,* creates an unbound field. When you are using the option group in a dialog box that uses the selected value to make a decision, you don't want to store the value in a table field. In this example, the second value, *Store that value in this field,* is automatically selected, since you started with the Type of Customer field. If you want to bind the option group value to a different table field, you can select from a list of all form fields. Again, in this example, the default is acceptable.

Step 8. Press the <u>N</u>ext > button to move to the option group style wizard screen.

Again, as shown in Figure 22-7, for this example, the defaults are acceptable. Notice that your actual values are used as a sample. In this wizard screen, the lower half of the wizard screen lets choose what type of buttons you want. The upper half lets you choose the style for the option group box and the type of group control. The style affects the option group rectangle. If you choose Raised or Sunken, that value is applied to the Special Effect property of the option group. Additionally, for Option Buttons and Check Boxes, if you choose Raised or Sunken, the Special Effects property for each option button or checkbox is set to Sunken.

As you change your selections, the Sample changes as well.

Part III: Using Access in Your Work

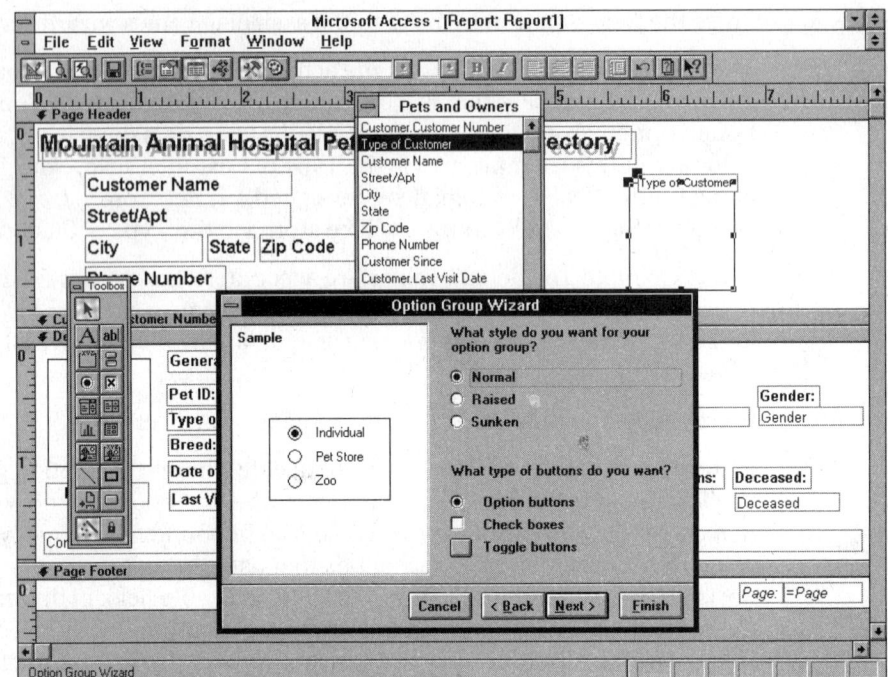

Figure 22-7: Selecting the type and look of your buttons.

Step 9. Press the Next > button to move to the final option group wizard screen.

The final screen lets you give the option group control a label that will appear in the option group border. You can then add the control to your design and optionally display Cue Cards to further customize the control.

Step 10. Enter Type of Customer as your label for the Option Group.

Step 11. Press the Finish button to complete the wizard.

Your wizard work is now complete, and the controls appear on the design screen. Eight controls have been created: the option group, its label, and three option buttons and their labels. In this example, you don't want the option group label.

Step 12. Select the option group label, Type of Customer, and press the Delete key.

Creating an option group with a calculated control

You also want to display the Gender field as a set of option buttons. There is one problem, however. The Gender field is a Text field with the values of M, F, and U. You can create option buttons only with a Numeric field. You can do this easily with the Type of Customer field, which is numeric. How can you solve this problem with the Gender field? The solution is to create a new calculated control that contains an expression. The expression must transform the values M to 1, F to 2, and U to 3. You create this calculation by using the Immediate IF function (IIf), with this expression:

```
=IIf([Gender]="M","1",IIf([Gender]="F","2","3"))
```

The first IIf function checks the value of Gender; if the value is "M", the value of the calculated control is set to 1. If the value is not "M", another IIf checks for a Gender value of "F". If the value is "F", the calculated control value is set to 2. If the value is not "F", the value of the calculated control is set to 3. To create this calculated control, follow these steps:

Steps: Creating a New Calculated Control

Step 1. Create a new text box control under the Pet Name control, as shown in Figure 22-8.

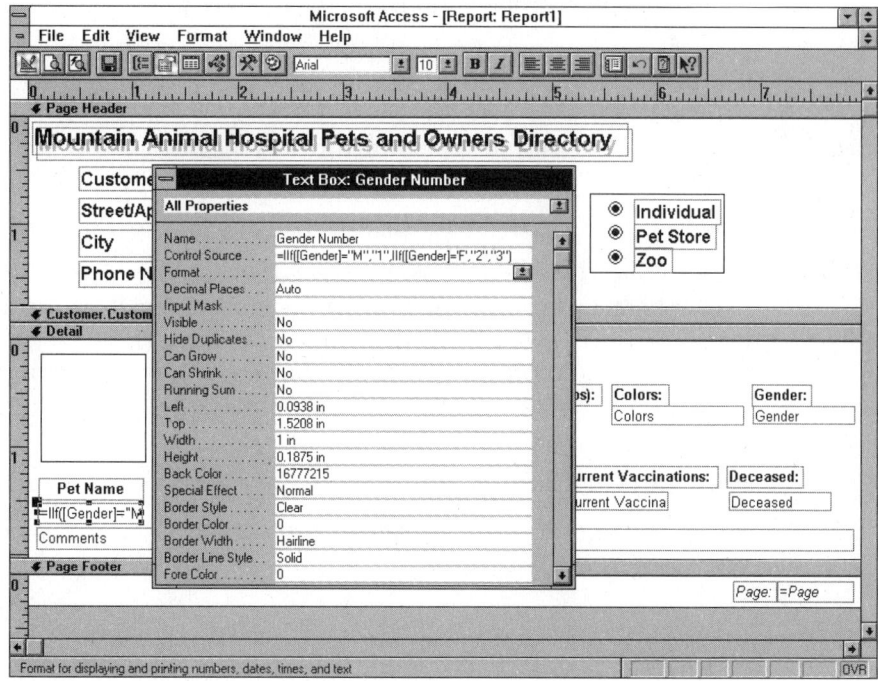

Figure 22-8: Creating a calculated control.

Part III: Using Access in Your Work

Step 2.	Delete the attached label control.
Step 3.	Display the property sheet for the text box control.
Step 4.	Change the Control Name property to **Gender Number.**
Step 5.	Type =IIf([Gender]="M","1",IIf([Gender]="F","2","3")) in the Control Source property.
Step 6.	Change the Visible property to **No.**

Because you change the Visible property of the calculated control to No, the control is not displayed when you produce the report. Once you create the calculated control, you can use it as the control source for an option group. Figure 22-8 shows this new calculated control.

To create the option group for Gender, follow these steps:

Steps:	**Creating an Option Group Based on a Calculated Control**
Step 1.	Delete the existing Gender text box and label control in the Detail section.
Step 2.	Select the option group button from the toolbox.
Step 3.	Drag the option group rectangle to the space in the Detail section.
	The first screen of the Option Group Wizard should be displayed.
Step 4.	Enter Male, Female, and Unknown, pressing the down-arrow key between choices.
Step 5.	Press the <u>N</u>ext > button three times to move to the control source screen.
	In this wizard screen, you then have to decide whether the option group itself is bound to a form field or unbound. In this example, you will use the first choice in the wizard, *Remember the value for later use*, which creates an unbound field. You cannot select a calculated field in the wizard. After completing the wizard, you will change the control source of the option group.
Step 6.	Press the <u>N</u>ext > button to move to the option group style wizard screen.
	Again, for this example, the defaults are acceptable. Notice that your actual values are used as a sample.

Step 7. Press the <u>N</u>ext > button to move to the final option group wizard screen.

Step 8. Enter Gender.

Step 9. Press the <u>F</u>inish button to complete the wizard.

Your wizard work is now complete, and the controls appear on the design screen. Currently, as an unbound control, the Control Source property is blank. You must set this to the calculated control Gender Number.

Step 10. Select the option group control and change the Control Source property to =[Gender Number], as shown in Figure 22-9.

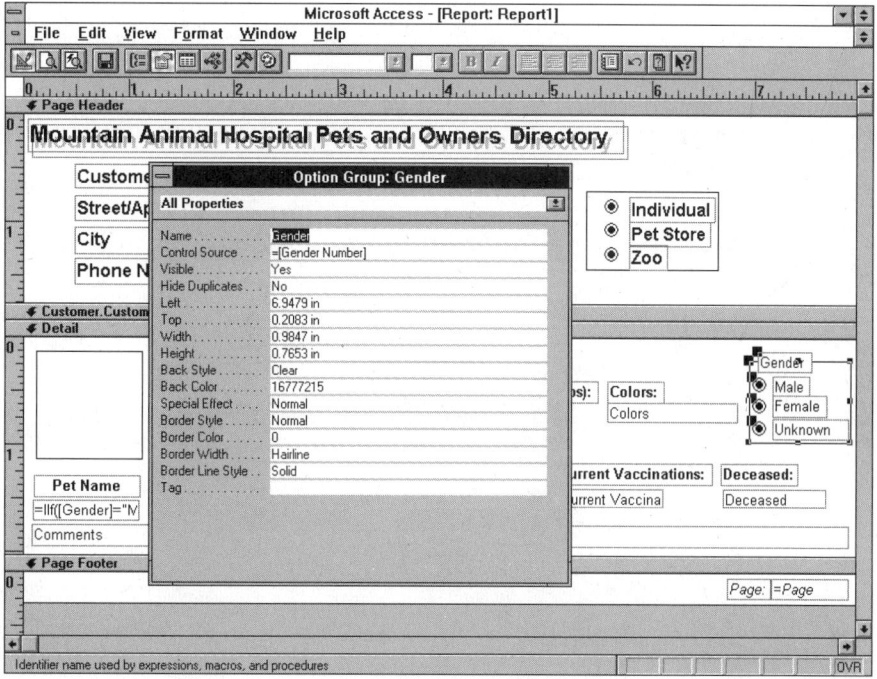

Figure 22-9: Completing an option group for a calculated control.

You may need to change the size of the rectangle to fit within the 8-inch margin. If you have to make it smaller, remember to change the margin which may be larger than 8 inches now.

Step 11. Resize the option group rectangle and reset the right margin to 8 inches.

Part III: Using Access in Your Work

The last task is to enhance all of the control text to 12 point bold. To accomplish this, follow these steps:

Steps:	**Enhancing the Option Buttons**
Step 1.	Select the entire Gender option group box and all the buttons and their attached labels.
Step 2.	Click the Bold button in the toolbar.
Step 3.	Select Format⇨Size⇨to Fit to resize the label control boxes.

You may still need to align the labels before your task is complete. The final design for the option buttons is shown in Figure 22-9, including the option button properties.

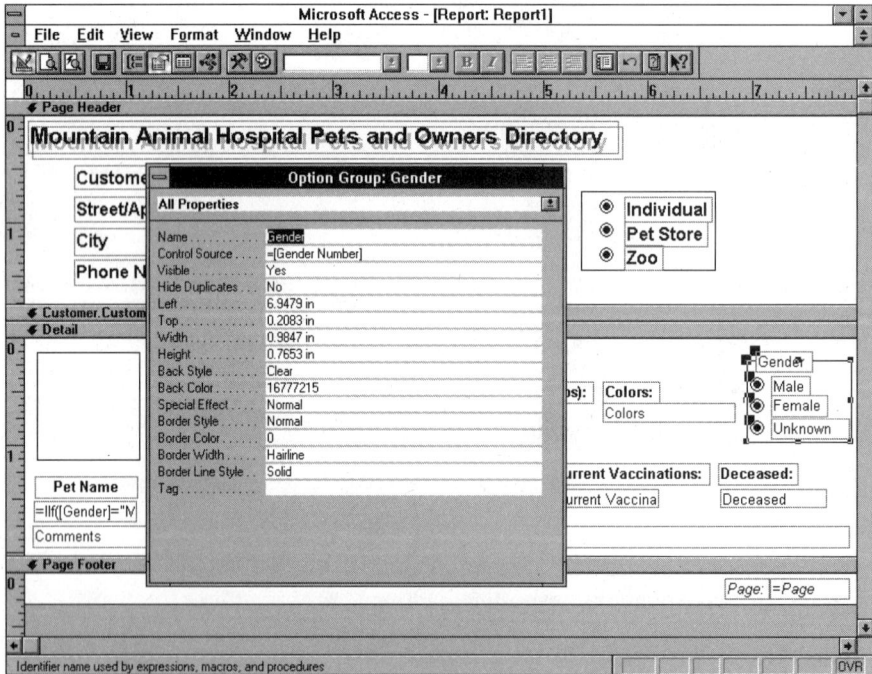

Figure 22-9: Completing an option group for a calculated control.

Displaying Yes/No values with checkboxes

You can make Yes/No values more readable on a report by using checkboxes. Although checkboxes can also be used in an option group, their primary purpose is to display one of two states for a single value. Checkboxes are more easily created than option

Chapter 22: Database Publishing and Printing

groups. You will now change the Neutered/Spayed and Current Vaccination fields into checkboxes. As with option button controls, you must first delete the existing text box controls to create a checkbox that uses the fields. To create the checkboxes, follow these steps, using Figure 22-10 as a guide:

Steps: Creating Checkboxes

Step 1. Select the Neutered/Spayed and Current Vaccination text box controls and their associated labels in the detail section.

Step 2. Press Delete to delete both the text box controls and the attached label controls.

Step 3. Select the Check Box button from the toolbox.

Step 4. Using Figure 22-10 as a guide, drag the Neutered/Spayed and Current Vaccination fields from the field list to create two new checkboxes.

Figure 22-10: The completed checkboxes.

Step 5. Select both checkbox controls and change the font size to **10**.

Step 6. Size the controls to fit and move the controls as necessary.

The completed checkboxes are shown in Figure 22-10.

Displaying values as toggle buttons

You can use toggle buttons as another way to make Yes/No data type easier to read. A toggle button appears to sit above the screen if the value of the Yes/No data type is No. If the value is Yes, the button appears to be pressed in the screen. To create a toggle button for the Deceased field, follow these steps:

Steps:	Creating a Toggle Button
Step 1.	Select the Deceased text box control and its associated label in the detail section.
Step 2.	Press Delete to delete both the text box control and the attached label control.
Step 3.	Select the button for Toggle Button from the toolbox.
Step 4.	Using Figure 22-11 as a guide, create a new toggle button by dragging the Deceased field from the field list.
Step 5.	Double-click on the toggle button and type **Decreased**.
Step 6.	Select Format⇨Size⇨to Fit to fit the button around the caption text.

The toggle button is displayed with the caption centered within the control.

You can also display a picture on the face of the toggle button instead of text by entering the filename of a bitmap image in the Picture property of the toggle button.

Displaying bound OLE objects in reports

In the report you are creating in this chapter, a picture of each animal is shown in the detail section. Some of the animals are displayed as they look, but others appear stretched out of proportion. Presto Chango, who is not really a hunchbacked lizard, illustrates this distortion.

Pictures are stored in OLE controls. The two types of OLE controls are as follows:

Bound object frames   Pictures are stored in a record.

Unbound object frames   Pictures are embedded or linked to a report section itself.

In this report, there is already on bound object frame. The picture field is an OLE data type that has bitmaps embedded in each record. The Picture bound object control gets its values from the Picture field in the Pets table.

Displaying unbound OLE objects in reports

You can also add an unbound OLE object to your report. Do this by either pasting a bitmap from the Clipboard or by embedding or linking a bitmap file containing a picture. Suppose that you have a logo for the Mountain Animal Hospital. On the disk that accompanies this book is a bitmap called MTN.BMP. In this section, you can add this bitmap to the page header section if you copied it to your Access directory.

Using Figure 22-11 as a guide, you will move the customer information to the right side of the page header section and then add the bitmap to the left side after creating the unbound object frame. To accomplish this task, follow the next set of steps.

Steps: **Adding an Unbound Object Frame**

Step 1.   Select the customer information in the Page Header section and move it to the right, as shown in Figure 22-11.

Figure 22-11: Creating an unbound object frame.

Step 2.	Click the Object Frame button in the toolbox.
Step 3.	Click the left corner below the title and drag the box so that it is sized as shown in Figure 22-11. The Insert Object dialog box appears.

From this dialog box, you can select the type of object you want to insert into your report.

Step 4.	Select Create from File.
Step 5.	Enter MTN.BMP from your Access directory (or wherever you copied the files for the book) and click OK.

If the file does not already exist and you want to create a new object, such as a new Paintbrush Picture, you don't click on the Create from File in Step 4; click the OK button instead. You can then create a new object and then return to Access. After completing Step 5, you are returned to the Access Report Design window, where the picture is displayed. You must still change the Size Mode property to Stretch.

Step 6.	Display the property sheet.
Step 7.	Change the Size Mode property to **Stretch.**

Finally, you have to change the Border property so that the picture does not simply blend into the background, as there is too much white in the picture. You can do this by changing the border color to black. Or you can make the border three-dimensional by selecting the Raised option button in the Palette window.

Step 8.	Display the palette.
Step 9.	Click the Raised special effect button.

The unbound object frame is now complete. This is a good time to view the report in the Print Preview window. Figure 22-12 shows the report in print preview mode.

You can see that the toggle button does not correctly display the text in the button. At this size, there is no text font that can correctly display text in the previewed size in a button. When the report is printed, however, the text will appear correctly.

Figure 22-12:
Previewing the report.

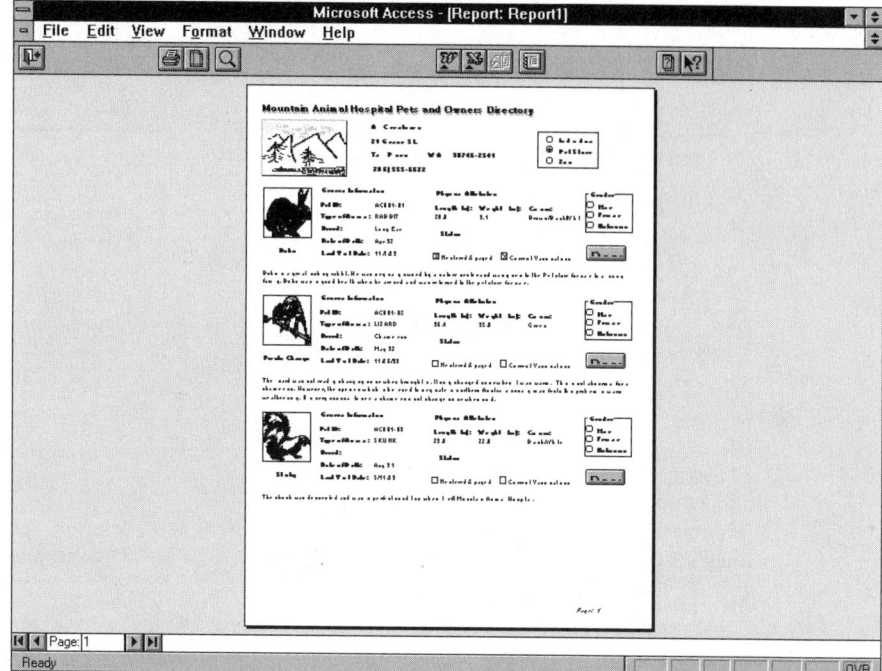

Working with Lines and Rectangles

You can use lines and rectangles (commonly called boxes) to make certain areas of the report stand out or to bring attention to desired areas of the report. In Figure 22-1, you saw several groups of lines and rectangles that were used to emphasize data in the report. You need four rectangles and two different lines to complete the lines and boxes in this report.

To create the rectangle for the page header, follow these steps, using Figure 22-13 as a guide:

Steps:	Creating Rectangles
Step 1.	Select the Rectangle button in the toolbox.
Step 2.	Select the Lock button in the toolbox, as you will create several rectangles.
Step 3.	Click the upper-left part of the page header section to the right of the picture and just below the title.
Step 4.	Drag the rectangle around the entire set of customer text boxes and option buttons.
Step 5.	Select Format⇨Send to Back to redisplay the text boxes and option buttons.

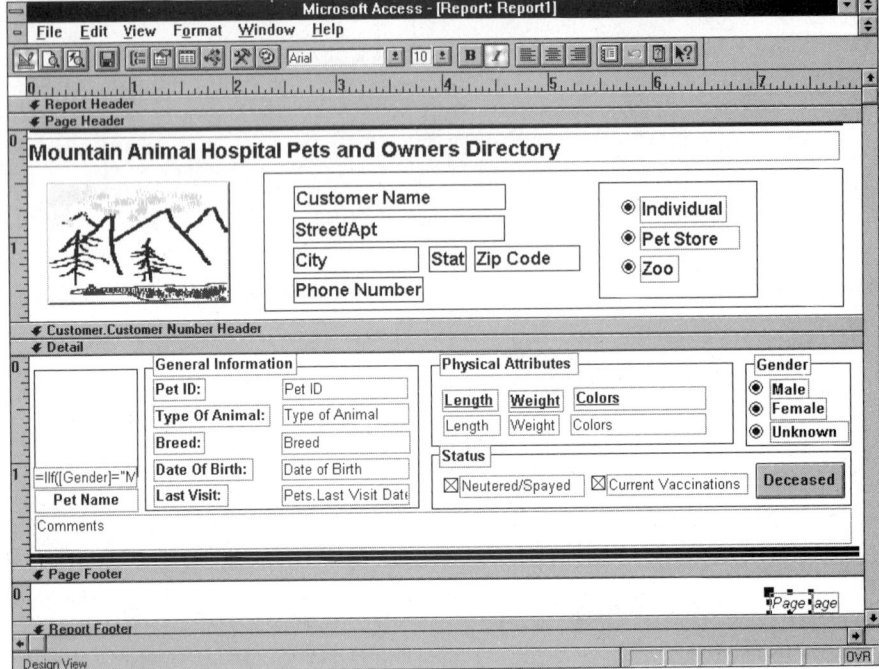

Figure 22-13: Completing the rectangles and lines.

You may notice that when you create the rectangle, it blocks out the controls beneath it. By sending the rectangle to the background, you make the controls reappear.

You can also redisplay the controls by changing the Clear button of the Back Color row in the palette. This option, however, does not let you add other shading effects. For a rectangle, you should always select Send to Back.

The next three rectangles are in the detail section. You can create the rectangles by following the same steps that you used to create the rectangle in the page header section. As you create them, you may find yourself rearranging some of the controls to fit better within the rectangles. You'll also want to change the label controls for Length, Weight, and Colors, as shown in Figure 22-13.

You also need several lines for the report. A single line needs to be added to the top of the report above the title, and two lines need to be added below the Comments text box. To add these lines, complete the next set of steps, using Figure 22-13 as a guide. You can also take this opportunity to remove the shadow on the title.

Steps:	Creating Lines
Step 1.	Select the grey title line of text (Mountain Animal Hospital Pets and Owners Directory) used to create the shadow.
Step 2.	Delete the label control of the shadow only.
Step 3.	Move the title line down so that the bottom border of the label control touches the top border of its enclosing rectangle.
Step 4.	Click the Line button in the toolbox and then click the Lock button.
Step 5.	Create a new line above the title in the page header across the entire width of the report.
Step 6.	Display the palette. Select the third button in the Width buttons of the palette to make the line thicker.
Step 7.	Create a new line below the Comments text box in the detail section.
Step 8.	Select the third width button of the palette to make the line thicker.
Step 9.	Duplicate the line below the comments and align it with the line above.

If you hold down the Shift key while creating a line, the line remains perfectly straight, either horizontally or vertically, depending on the initial movement of drawing the line.

Emphasizing Areas of the Report

The report is now almost completed. But several tasks still remain. According to the original printout and design shown in Figures 22-1 and 22-3, you still need to shade the rectangle in the page header, add a shadow to the rectangle, sink the Customer text box controls, raise the Type of Customer option group box, and change Pet Name to reverse video.

Adding background shade

You can add a background shade to any control. Adding background shading to a rectangle shades any controls contained within the rectangle. You can, however, add background shading to all controls that are selected at one time. To add background shading to the rectangle in the page header section, follow these steps:

Steps:	**Shading a Rectangle**
Step 1.	Display the palette if it is not already displayed.
Step 2.	Select the Rectangle control in the page header section.
Step 3.	Select the light grey Back Color in the palette.

Sinking controls

Generally, in a report, you cannot sink controls because on a white background, the controls don't look sunken. However, you can use a grey back ground to enhance the depth of a control. Both sunken and raised controls stand out on a grey background. Because you just added a grey background to the rectangle in the page header, you can sink or raise controls within the rectangle. To give the Customer text box controls a sunken appearance, follow these steps:

Steps:	**Sinking Text Box Controls**
Step 1.	Select each of the Customer text box controls in the page header section.
Step 2.	Click the Sunken special effect button in the palette.

Raising controls

Just as you can sink a control, you can raise one as well. Raised controls, like sunken controls, look much better on a grey or dark background. To raise the Type of Customer option group control, follow these steps:

Steps:	**Raising a Control**
Step 1.	Select the Type of Customer option group control.
Step 2.	Click the Raised special effect button in the palette.

If you sink or raise a checkbox, a different, smaller check that has the appearance of depth is used.

Creating a shadow on a rectangle

If you want to truly emphasize an area of the report, you can add a shadow to any control. The most common types of controls to be given this effect are rectangles and text boxes. You create the shadows by adding a solid-color rectangle that is slightly offset and behind the original control. If the background is light or white, you need a dark-colored rectangle. If the background is dark or black, you need a light-colored or white rectangle. To create a shadow for the page header rectangle, follow these steps:

Steps:	Creating a Shadow
Step 1.	Select the rectangle in the page header.
Step 2.	Select Edit⇨Duplicate.
Step 3.	Select Format⇨Send to Back.
Step 4.	Click on the black Back Color in the palette.
Step 5.	Drag the black rectangle up and slightly to the right to form the shadow.
Step 6.	Resize the Page Header section.

If you want a report in which all controls have shadows, you can use the Form Wizard and create a form using the Shadow type of look. You can then copy the controls to the Clipboard and paste them into a report, text controls and shadows all!

Changing text to a reverse video display

Text really stands out when you create white text on a black background. This is called reverse video because text is white on black rather than the usual black on white. You can convert text in a label control or text box to reverse video by changing the fill color to black and the text color to white. To change the Pet Name text control to reverse video, follow these steps:

Steps:	Creating a Reverse Video Effect
Step 1.	Select the Pet Name text control (not the label control).
Step 2.	Display the palette if it is not already displayed.
Step 3.	Click the black Back Color button.
Step 4.	Click the white Fore Color button.

 If you use one of the laser printers, such as the HP LaserJet, you may not see reverse video on your printout. This is because of a limitation of the Windows 3.1 printer driver for the HP LaserJet series.

Figure 22-14 shows the final report in the Report Design window.

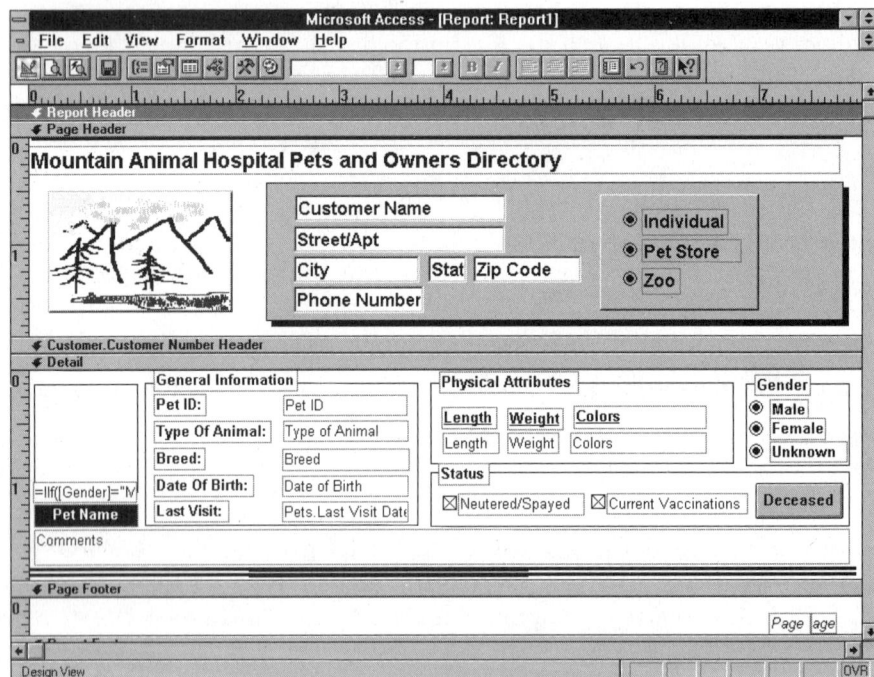

Figure 22-14: The final report.

Seeing Your Output in Different Ways

You can see your output from a report in several ways:

- Print previewing
- Printing to hard copy
- Printing to a file
- Printing the report definition

Chapter 22: Database Publishing and Printing **611**

Using the Print Preview window

Throughout this chapter, you used the Print Preview window to view your report. Figure 22-5 displayed your report in the Print Preview window in a zoomed view. This lets you see your report with the actual fonts, shading, lines, boxes, and data that will be on the printed report. When the print preview mode is in a zoomed view, you can press the mouse button to change the view to a page preview, where you can see the entire page.

You can move around the page by using both the horizontal and vertical elevators. You can also move from page to page by using the page controls at the bottom left corner of the window.

The page preview mode of the Print Preview window displays an entire page of the report, as shown in Figure 22-15. You may have noticed that the cursor is shaped like a magnifying glass in the Print Preview windows. Using the magnifying glass cursor during page preview lets you select a portion of the page and then zoom in to that portion for a zoomed view.

In Figure 22-15, you see a representation of the printed page. You can use the navigation buttons, located in the lower left hand section of the Print Preview window, to move between pages just as you use them to move between records in a datasheet.

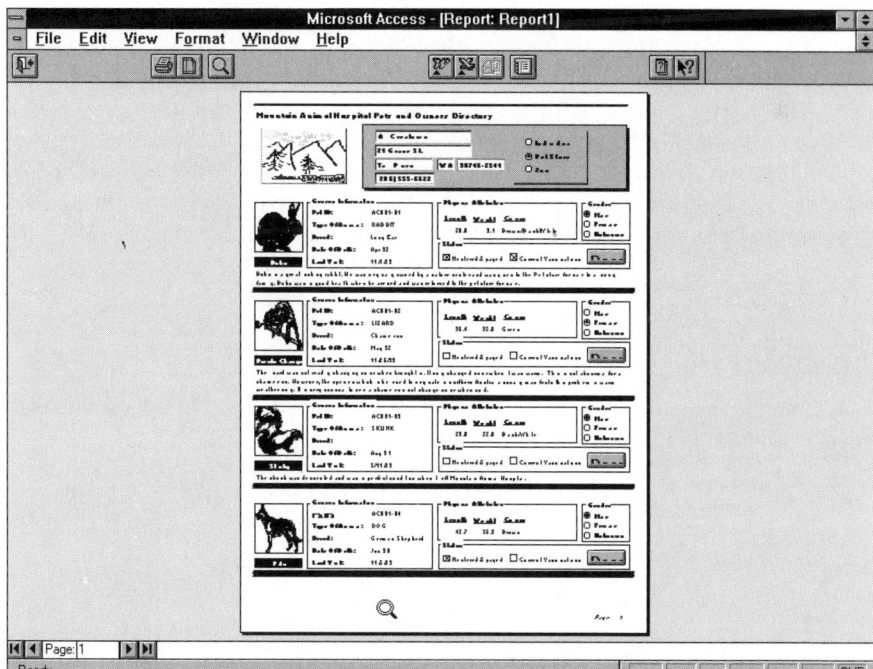

Figure 22-15: Displaying a report in a page preview print preview mode.

The first four buttons are displayed on the toolbar. The toolbar buttons provide quick access to printing tasks:

Close Window	Returns to design view
Print	Displays the Print dialog box
Print Setup	Displays the Print Setup dialog box
Zoom	Toggles in and out of Page Preview and Zoomed view

If, after examining the preview, you are satisfied with the report, simply select the Print button on the toolbar to print the report. If you are not satisfied, select the Close Window button to return to the Report Design window and make further changes to your report.

Using sample previews

Another type of preview is the *sample preview*. This is different from a print preview in that a print preview uses a query's dynaset, but the sample preview displays the first set of data it finds. The sample preview limits the number of records but ignores limits based on criteria. It also ignores any sorting, making groupings fairly meaningless.

The purpose of a sample preview is strictly to show you the field placement and formatting. This lets you create a report design without having to assemble your data properly. In a large query, this can save considerable time. The only way to see a sample preview is to select File➪Sample Preview or click the Sample Preview icon (third from left) in the Report Design toolbar. You can switch back to the Report Design window by selecting the Close Window button. You can also zoom in to a sample page preview on the sample data or print the sample report from the Sample Preview window.

Printing a report

You can print one or more records in your form exactly as they look on-screen from several places:

- Select File➪Print in the Report Design window.
- Select the Print button in the Preview window.
- Select File➪Print in the Database window with a report highlighted.

If you are in the Print Preview window, your actual data prints. If you are in the Sample Preview window, only sample data prints.

Chapter 22: Database Publishing and Printing

The Print dialog box

Once you decide to print your report, the Print dialog box is displayed, as shown in Figure 22-16. The Print dialog box lets you control several items by giving you the following choices:

- Print Range (prints the entire report or selected pages)
- Print Quality (important for dot-matrix printers)
- Copies (selects the number of copies)
- Collate Copies (selects whether or not to collate copies)
- Print to File (prints to a file rather than the printer)

The Print dialog box that is displayed is specific to your printer, based on the setup in Microsoft Windows. Although each printer is different, the dialog box is essentially the same. Generally, dot-matrix or impact printers have a few more options for controlling quality than do laser printers.

Assuming that you set up a printer in Microsoft Windows, you can select OK to print your form. Your form is printed using the font that you selected for display or the nearest printer equivalent. The printout contains any formatting in the form, including lines, boxes, and shading. Colors are converted to shades on a monochrome printer.

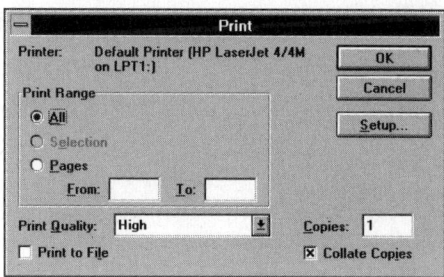

Figure 22-16: The Print dialog box.

If you need to further set up your Windows printer options, you can choose the Setup... button in the Print dialog box. This dialog box sets up your printer, not your report. If you want to further set up your report, you must use the Print Setup dialog box, which provides more options for controlling your report.

You can display print setup options in several other ways, including the following:

- Selecting the Print Setup icon in the Print Preview or Sample Preview window
- Selecting File⇨Print Setup... from the Report Design window
- Selecting File⇨Print Setup... from the Database window

The Print Setup dialog box

The Print Setup dialog box, shown in Figure 22-17, is divided into several sections:

Printer	Selects the printer
Orientation	Selects the page orientation
Paper	Selects the paper size and paper source
Data On<u>l</u>y	Prints only the data; does not print any graphics
Margins	Sets the page margins
<u>O</u>ptions	Sets printer-specific options
<u>M</u>ore>>	Sets report-specific options used for snaking columns and mailing labels

The Printer section determines which printer you are going to use. The <u>D</u>efault Printer option button displays your default Windows printer and connection. If this is the printer you want to use, click on this button (it is the default). If you want to choose an alternate printer (or device such as a fax driver), click the Specific <u>P</u>rinter option button. After you select this option, you can click the arrow on the drop-down list for a list of all printers installed on your system. Select one by clicking it.

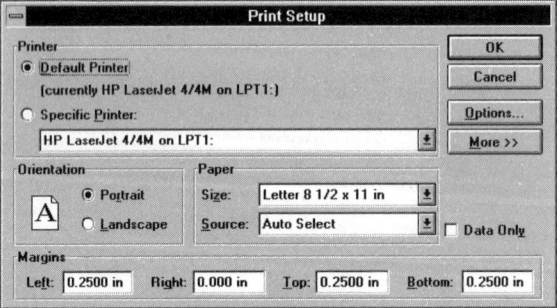

Figure 22-17: The Print Setup dialog box.

If you want to use a printer that is not installed, you can add it by clicking the Printers button in the Windows Control Panel.

The Orientation section determines the page orientation. Clicking the P<u>o</u>rtrait button changes the report orientation to portrait, which means that the page is taller than it is wide. Clicking the <u>L</u>andscape button changes the report orientation to landscape, which means that the page is wider than it is tall.

A good way to remember the difference between landscape and portrait is to think of paintings. Portraits of people are usually taller than wide, and landscapes of the outdoors are usually wider than tall. When you click either button, the page icon (letter A) changes to show your choice graphically.

Chapter 22: Database Publishing and Printing   **615**

The Paper section indicates the size of the paper that you want to use, as well as the paper source (for printers that have more than one source available). Clicking Source displays a drop-down list of paper sources available for the printer you selected. Depending on the printer selected, you may have one or more paper trays or manual feed available. Click the source you want to use.

Clicking Size displays a drop-down box of all of the paper sizes available for the printer (and paper source) you selected. Click the size you want to use.

If you click the Data Only checkbox, Access prints only the data from your report and does not print any graphics. This feature is handy if you use preprinted forms. This is also helpful if you want to save time by not printing complex graphics, which slows down all but the most capable printers.

The Margins section displays and allows you to edit the left, right, top, and bottom margins. To edit one or more of these settings, click the appropriate text box and type in a new number.

You can click the Options button to open a settings dialog box that is specific to the printer you have installed. Because this dialog box is specific to the printer installed, it is beyond the scope of this book to describe all the possible variations. Note that if you change any settings in this dialog box, you are changing the default Windows settings, which carry through to any other Windows applications you are using.

You can click the More>> button to expand the Print Setup dialog box. This displays the more advanced options used for snaking columns and mailing labels, which are available only for forms and reports. These options are discussed in Chapter 23.

Print Setup settings are stored with each report. It is therefore possible to use several different printers for various reports, as long as you don't use the default Windows printer. This can also be a problem, though, because if you exchange files with another user who doesn't have the same printer installed, the other user must modify the Print Setup settings.

Someone may send you a report that you can't view or print because a Windows printer driver that you don't have was used. In this case, follow these steps to print or view your report:

Steps:	**Printing or Viewing a Report Created with a Driver Not Installed on Your System**
Step 1.	Open the report in the Design window. You will see an error informing you that Access cannot locate the printer driver that created this report.
Step 2.	Select File⇨Print Setup....
Step 3.	Choose *your* printer driver.
Step 4.	Close the Print Setup dialog box.

You can now view or print the report.

The first page of your report is shown printed out in Figure 22-18.

Printing the report definition

Access 2.0 has a documentation facility to print each of the form objects. Each object, control property, and user permission is printed in a standard Access report. To use this feature, simply select File⇨Print Definition..., select the options you want, and the object appears in a print preview window. You can even print module code.

Figure 22-18:
The Pets and Owners Report shown in hardcopy printout.

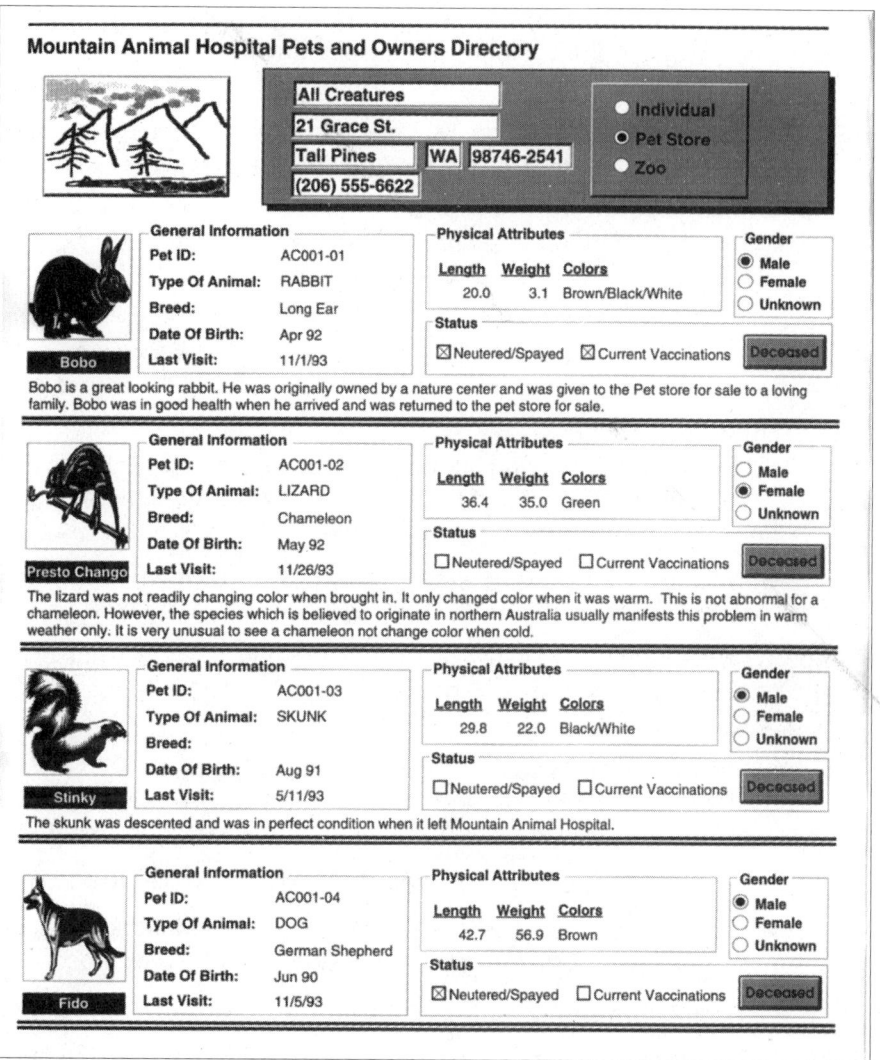

Summary

In this chapter, you learned how to enhance your reports and how to print them. The following topics were discussed:

* *Database publishing* is a term that generally describes report formatting from a database application that offers lines, boxes, shading, and other types of desktop publishing enhancements.

- The Access report writer is a WYSIWYG (what you see is what you get) report writer. What you see in the Design window is generally what you get on the hard-copy report.

- The palette is a tool in the Report window that lets you set text and fill colors, control line widths, and add three-dimensional effects to controls, such as a raised or sunken appearance.

- You can enhance the text of label and text box controls by changing the font type style, font size, and such font style attributes as bold or italic or font color. You can even add a shadow by duplicating the text.

- Multiple-line text box controls can display large amounts of text. You can set the Can Grow and Can Shrink properties to control the precise amount of space needed and avoid leaving blank lines.

- Controls such as option buttons, checkboxes, and toggle buttons make it easier to view your data. You must delete an existing control before you can create one of these controls using the same data field.

- When any of these controls are placed inside an option group, they act together instead of separately, and only one is active at a time.

- Option buttons are generally used to let a user select only one of a group, whereas checkboxes and toggle buttons are used to represent a two-state selection from Yes/No data types.

- You can display pictures in reports by using object frames. The two types of object frames are *bound,* which are objects attached to a data field in each record, and *unbound,* which are objects embedded in the report itself.

- Lines and rectangles let you separate areas of the report to add emphasis.

- You can further emphasize areas of the report by adding color, background shading, three-dimensional effects, shadows, and reverse video.

- You can view your report by previewing it or by printing it to a hard copy device.

- Two types of print previews are available: print preview and sample preview. With print preview, you see your actual data in the preview. A sample preview uses only portions of your table data but is very fast.

- You can set printing selections from the Print Setup dialog box.

- The Print Definition option documents your report objects.

In the next chapter, you learn how to create reports with totals and summaries.

Creating Calculations and Summaries in Reports

CHAPTER 23

In This Chapter

- Designing a report with multiple group totals
- Creating several levels of sorting and grouping totals
- Entering and using expressions and functions in text boxes
- Using concatenation in text expressions
- Calculating sums for each group
- Calculating running sums
- Calculating percentages based on group totals
- Creating a report cover page

In the last two chapters, you learned how to design and build reports from a blank form and how to use many of the advanced features in Access to create striking and effective output. In this chapter, you learn how to use expressions to calculate results.

Following Along in This Book

If you don't want to build the reports created in this chapter, they are included on your sample disk in the Reports objects. The reports are named Monthly Invoice Report - No Cover, Monthly Invoice Report, Monthly Invoice Report - Percentages, and Monthly Invoice Report - Running Sum.

Because the Report Design window is set to a width of eight inches, you see most of the screen printouts in this chapter taken with an 800 x 600-resolution Super VGA Windows screen driver rather than the standard 640 x 480 VGA Windows driver, which lets you see almost the entire screen in the figures.

Creating a Multilevel Grouping Report with Totals

You now create a report that displays information about visits to the hospital for each customer's pets on specific days. This report displays data in an invoice format that lists the type of visit, treatments given, medication dispensed, and the cost of each of these items. The data is totaled for each line item and summarized for each visit. The report can display multiple pets for the same customer on the same day. Finally, totals are shown for each visit by a customer, including the total amount spent, any discounts, and tax. A sample hard-copy page of the report is shown in Figure 23-1. Later in this chapter, you see how to enhance this report to display individual line-item percentages and cumulative running totals.

Designing the Invoice Report

This report is an excellent example for showing the types of tasks necessary to create common types of reports. The report uses many of the advanced report writing features of Access, such as sorting and grouping, group summaries, text expressions, and graphical objects. Following is a summary of what the Invoice Report's design includes:

- The Mountain Animal Hospital name, address, phone number, and logo on the top of every page
- Owner detail information (customer name, street/apt., city, state, ZIP code, and telephone)
- Visit date
- Pet name
- Visit detail information for each pet (including type of visit, treatment, treatment price, medication, medication price, and total cost)
- A subtotal that summarizes each pet's visit details (total cost subtotal for the pet)
- A subtotal that summarizes the total cost for each pet on a visit date for a particular owner and calculates a total that lists and incorporates the owner's discount and proper state sales tax

The report design also must be shaped according to the following considerations:

- The report must be sorted by the fields Visit Date, then Customer Number, and then Pet ID.
- No more than one visit date per printed page should appear.
- No more than one customer per printed page should appear.
- One or more pets belonging to the same owner can appear on each printed page.
- If there is more than one pet per invoice, the pets should be listed in Pet ID order.

Figure 23-1:
The sample Invoice Report page.

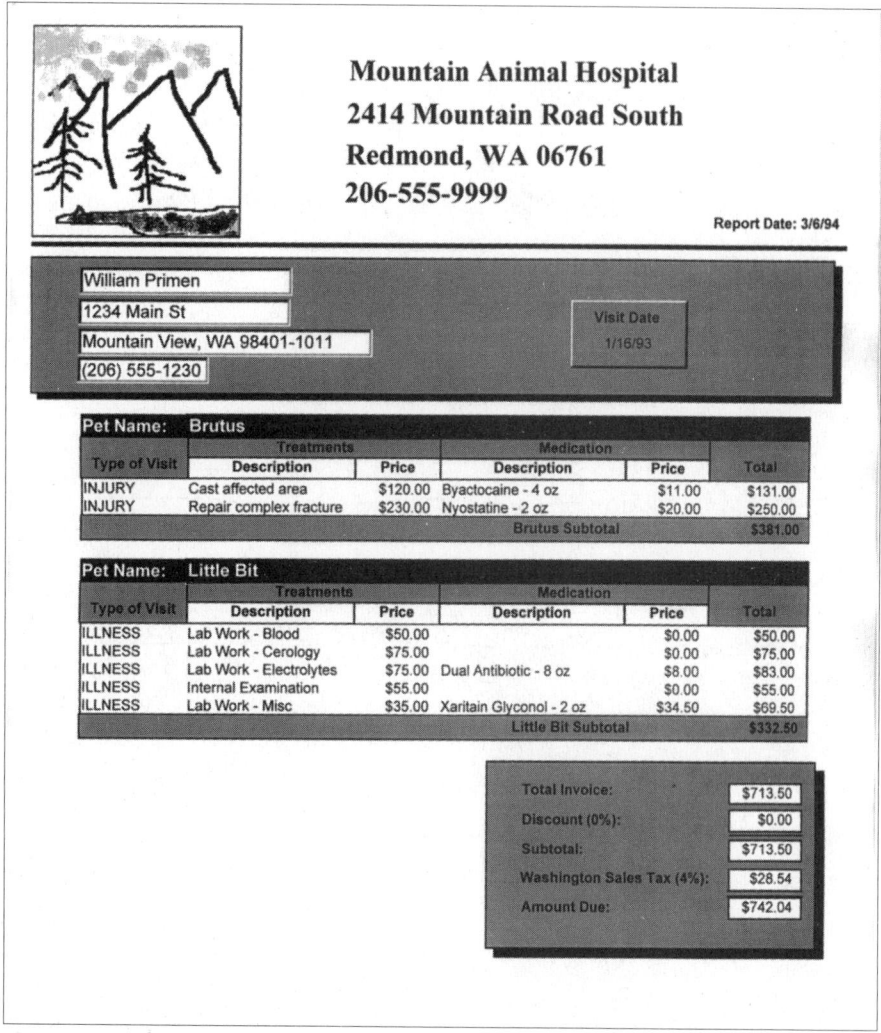

The design for this report is shown in Figure 23-2. As you can see, each section is labeled, and each control displays either the field name control or the calculated control contents. With the exception of the Mountain Animal Hospital logo (an unbound object frame) and several lines and rectangles, the report consists primarily of text box controls.

Designing and creating the query for the report

The Invoice Report uses fields in practically every table you've seen in the Mountain Animal Hospital database. Although the design in Figure 23-2 shows the approximate position and use of each control, it is equally important to perform a data design that lists each table field or calculated control. This data design should include the purpose

Figure 23-2:
A design for the Invoice Report.

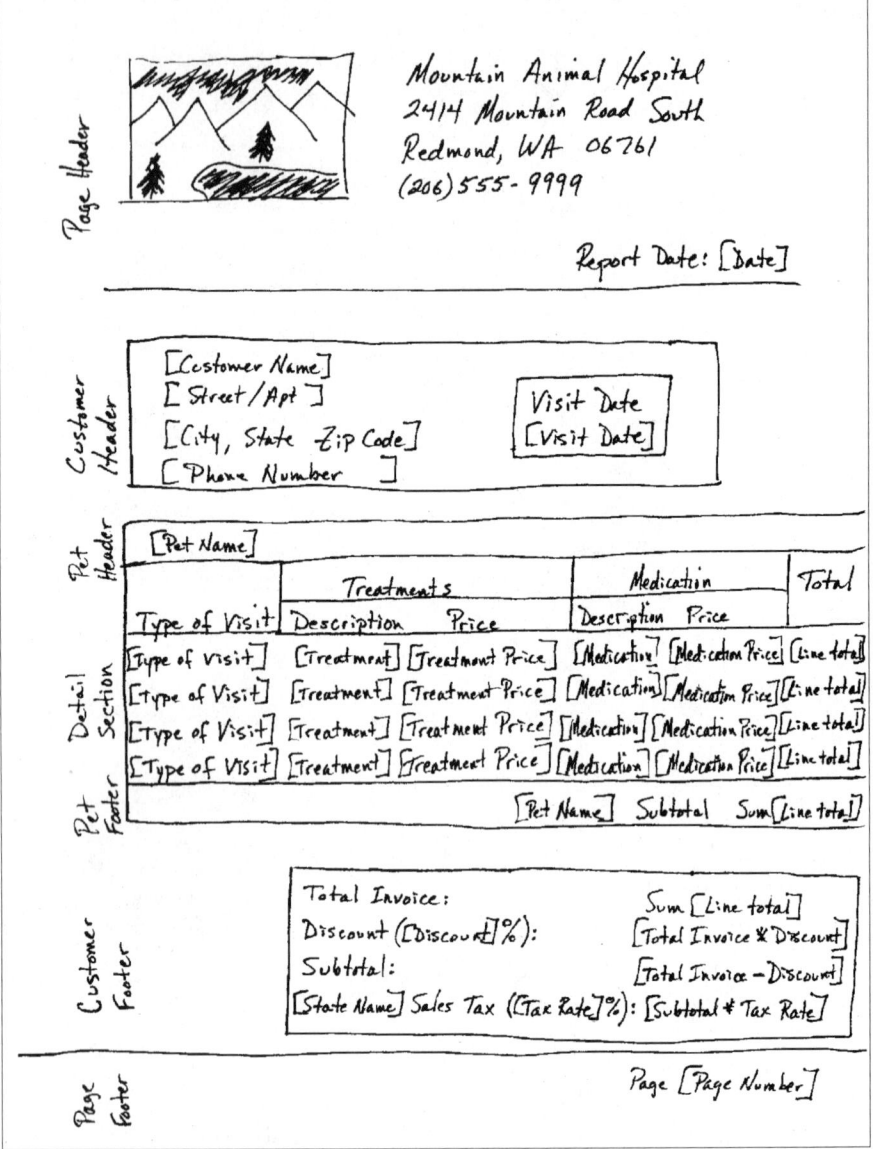

of the field or control and the table in which the field originates. With this type of design plan, you can be sure to build a query that contains all the fields that you may need. Table 23-1 lists these controls, the section in the report where they are used, and the originating table. It is very important to do this type of data design *before* creating the query to build your report from.

Table 23-1
The Data Design for the Invoice Report

Report Section	Control Purpose	Type of Control	Table Field/Calculation	Table
Page header	Logo	Unbound object frame		
Page header	Name and address	Label controls (4)		
Page header	Report date	Calculated text box	Date function	
Customer header	Customer name	Bound text box	Customer Name	Customer
Customer header	Street/Apt.	Bound text box	Street/Apt	Customer
Customer header	City	Bound text box	City	Customer
Customer header	State	Bound text box	State	Customer
Customer header	ZIP code	Bound text box	ZIP Code	Customer
Customer header	Visit date	Bound text box	Visit Date	Visits
Pet header	Pet name	Bound text box	Pet Name	Pets
Pet header	Text labels	Label controls (8)		
Detail	Type of visit	Bound text box	Type of Visit	Visit Details
Detail	Treatment	Bound text box	Treatment	Treatments
Detail	Treatment price	Bound text box	Treatment Price	Visit Details
Detail	Medication	Bound text box	Medication Name	Medications
Detail	Medication price	Bound text box	Medication Price	Visit Details
Detail	Line total	Calculated text box	Treatment Price + Medication Price	
Pet footer	Pet name	Calculated text box	Pet Name + Text	Pets
Pet footer	Line total sum	Calculated text box	Sum(Line Total)	
Customer footer	Text labels	Label controls (3)	Lines 1, 3, 5	
Customer footer	Discount label	Calculated text box	Text + Discount	Customer
Customer footer	State sales tax	Calculated text box	State Name + Tax Rate	States/Visits
Customer footer	Total invoice	Calculated text box	Sum(Line Total)	
Customer footer	Discount amount	Calculated text box	Total Invoice * Discount	
Customer footer	Subtotal	Calculated text box	Total Invoice - Discount	
Customer footer	Sales tax	Calculated text box	Subtotal * Tax Rate	Visits
Customer footer	Amount due	Calculated text box	Subtotal - Sales Tax	
Page footer	Page number	Calculated text box	Text + Page Number	

After you complete the data design for a report, you can scan the Table column to determine the tables necessary for the report. When you create the query, you may not want to select each field individually but to use the asterisk (*) field to select all the fields in each table. This way, if a field changes in the table, the query can still work with your report.

Remember that if a table field name changes in your query, you'll also need to change your report design. If you see a parameter dialog box when running your report or the text #Error in place of one of your values after running your report, chances are that a table field has changed.

After examining Table 23-1, you may notice that every table in the Mountain Animal Hospital database is needed for the report — with the exception of the Animals lookup table. You may wonder why you need any of the four lookup tables. Although the States, Animals, Treatments, and Medications tables are mainly to be used as lookup tables for data validation when adding data to forms, you may want to use them to look up data when printing in reports, too.

In the Invoice Report, the State Name field from the States table is used for looking up the full state name for the sales tax label in the Customer footer. The Tax Rate field can also be found in the States table, but at the time of the visit, the current tax rate is copied to the Visits table for that record. The Treatment and Medication Name fields are looked up from their respective tables because only the codes are stored in the Visit Details table.

These seven tables are all joined together using the Monthly Invoice Report query, which is illustrated in Figure 23-3.

After your query is completed, you can create your report.

Chapter 21 contains a detailed explanation of creating a new report from a blank form. That chapter also shows you how to properly set the page size and layout. If you are unfamiliar with these topics, read Chapter 21 before continuing. The present chapter's main focus is multiple-level groupings, calculated and summarized fields, and expressions.

Chapter 23: Creating Calculations and Summaries in Reports

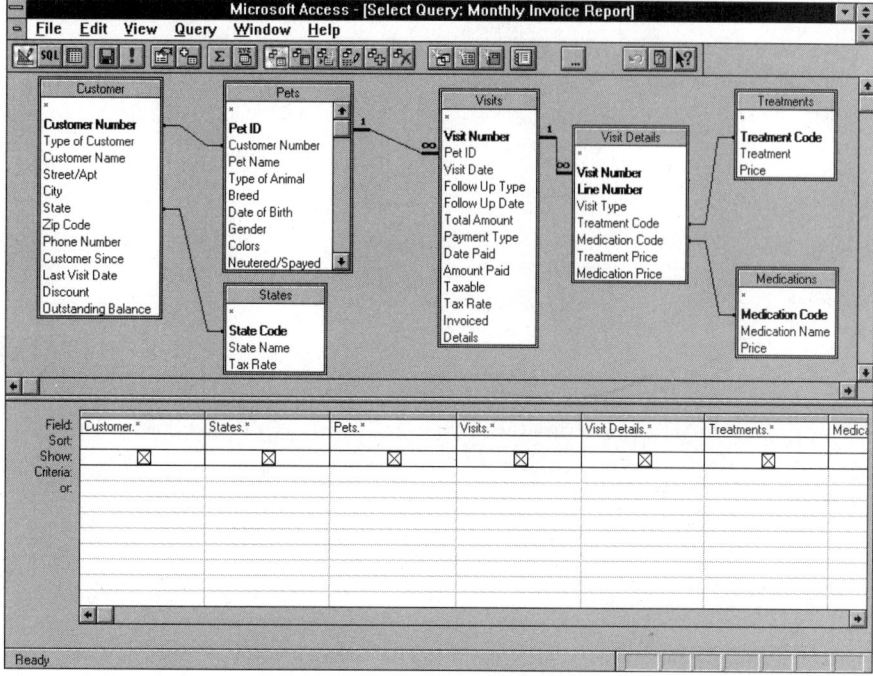

Figure 23-3:
The Query Design window for the Monthly Invoice Report query.

Designing test data

One of the biggest mistakes you can make when designing and creating complex reports is not checking the results that your report displays. Before you create your complete report, you should have a good understanding of your data. One way is to create a query using the same sorting order that the report will use and create any detail line calculations. You can then check the query's datasheet results and use these results to check the report results. When you are sure that the report is using the correct data, you can be sure that it will always produce great results. Figure 23-4 shows a simple query that you can use for checking the report you create in this chapter. This query is called the Monthly Invoice Report.

Generally, you can make a copy of the report query, adding the sorting orders and using only the detail fields you need to check totals. You can then manually add the numbers or convert the query to a Total query to check group totals. The datasheet produced by this query is shown in Figure 23-5. You can compare the results of each task in the report design to this datasheet.

Figure 23-4: A query for checking data results.

Figure 23-5: The datasheet for checking data results.

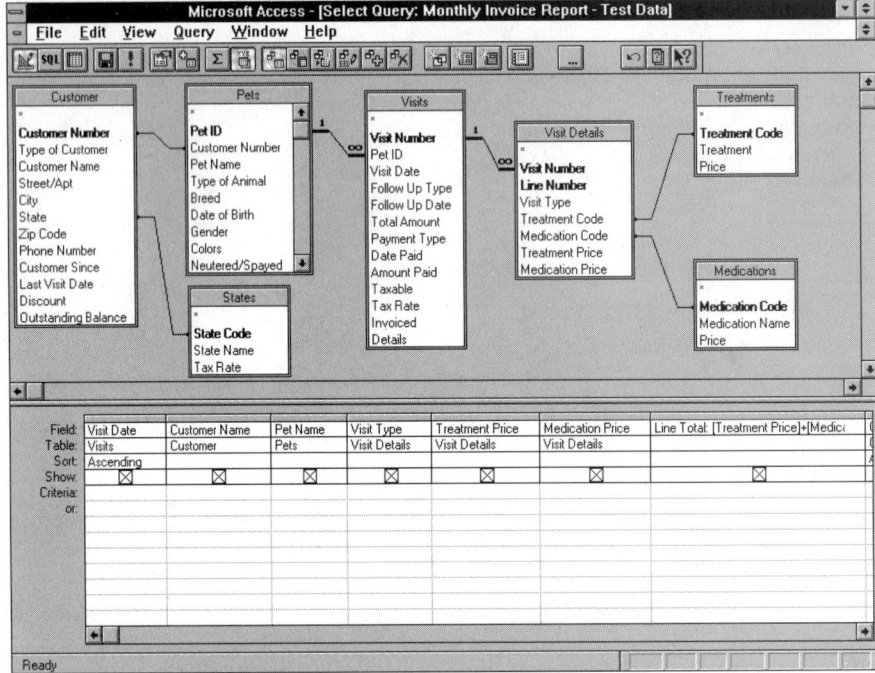

Creating a new report

With the report planning and data testing completed, it's time to create the new report. In Chapter 21, you learned how to create a report from a blank form. The steps to create a new report are repeated for you here:

Steps:	Creating a New Report and Binding It to a Query
Step 1.	Press F11 to display the Database window if it is not already displayed.
Step 2.	Click the Report task object button.
Step 3.	Click the New command button. The New Report dialog box appears.
Step 4.	Click the Select A Table/Query edit box. A drop-down list of all tables and queries in the current database appears.
Step 5.	Select the Monthly Invoice Report query.
Step 6.	Click the Blank Report button.
Step 7.	Maximize the Report window.

A blank Report Design window appears with three sections (Page Header, Detail, and Page Footer). The report is bound to the query Monthly Invoice Report. This means that the data from that query will be used when the report is viewed or printed. The fields from the query are available for use in the report design and will appear in the field list window.

You must also change the Printer Setup settings and resize the Report Design window area for the report. These procedures are also discussed in detail in Chapter 21. The steps are again shown here:

Steps:	Setting the Printer Setup Settings for the Monthly Invoice Report
Step 1.	Select File⇒Print Setup.
Step 2.	Click the Left Margin setting and change the setting to **.250**.
Step 3.	Click the Right Margin setting and change the setting to **.250**.
Step 4.	Click the Top Margin setting and change the setting to **.250**.
Step 5.	Click the Bottom Margin setting and change the setting to **.250**.
Step 6.	Click OK to close the Print Setup window.

Steps:	Setting the Report Width
Step 1.	Click the rightmost edge of the report body (where the white area meets the grey).
Step 2.	Drag the edge to the 8-inch mark on the ruler.
Step 3.	Release the mouse button.

These steps should complete the initial setup for the report. The next task is to create the sorting order for the report.

Creating the sorting orders

In a query, you can specify sorting fields. In the query you created to display test data, you created three sorting fields. However, in a report, you must also specify the sorting order when you create groups because the underlying query sorting is ignored. In the underlying query for this report, there is no sorting specified because it must be entered here as well.

In this report design, there are three sorting levels: Visit Date, Customer Number, and Pet ID. You'll need to use all these levels to define group headers, and you need the latter two for group footers. If you look back at the original design in Figure 23-2, you see that Visit Date is not shown as a group. Later, as you create your report, you'll see why a grouping to use the Visit Date header section is necessary.

Before you can add a grouping, you must first define the sort order for the report. As you've learned, this task is done with the Sorting and Grouping box, which is shown completed in Figure 23-6 on the blank Report Design window. To complete the sorting orders, as shown in Figure 23-6, follow the next set of steps:

Steps:	Defining a Sort Order for Fields
Step 1.	Click the Sorting and Grouping button on the toolbar to display the Sorting and Grouping box.
Step 2.	Click the cursor on the first row of the Field/Expression column of the Sorting and Grouping box. A downward-pointing arrow appears.
Step 3.	Click the arrow to display a list of fields in the Monthly Invoice Report query.

Step 4. Click the Visit Date field in the field list. Notice that Sort Order defaults to Ascending.

Step 5. Click the cursor on the second row of the Field/Expression column.

Step 6. Click the arrow to display a list of fields in the Mountain Invoice Report query.

Step 7. Click the Customer.Customer Number field in the field list. Notice that Sort Order defaults to Ascending.

Step 8. Click the cursor on the third row of the Field/Expression column.

Step 9. Click the arrow to display a list of fields in the Mountain Invoice Report query.

Step 10. Click the Pets.Pet ID field in the field list. Notice that Sort Order defaults to Ascending.

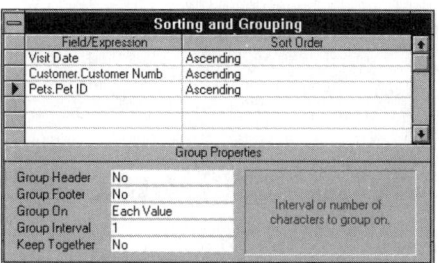

Figure 23-6: Creating the sorting orders.

 To see more of the Field/Expression column, you can drag the border between the Field/Expression and Sort Order columns to the right, which has been done in Figure 23-6.

You next see how the detail section is created for this report. Because this chapter's intent is to focus on expressions and summaries, it is assumed that you've read Chapters 21 and 22 and that you understand how to create and enhance labels and text boxes in a report.

Creating the detail section

The detail section is shown completed in its entirety in Figure 23-7. The section has been completed and resized. Notice that there is no space above or below any of the controls, which allows multiple detail records to be displayed as one comprehensive section on a report. This section must fit snugly between the Pet header and Pet footer, as shown in Figures 23-1 and 23-2, and so it has been resized to the exact size of the controls.

Figure 23-7: The detail section.

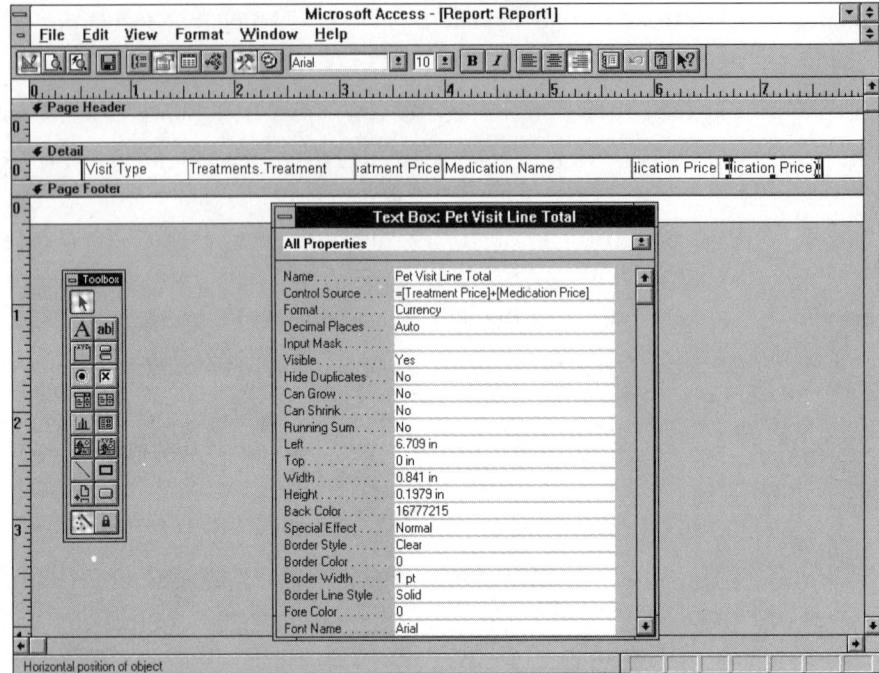

Creating the detail section controls

The detail section has five unlabeled bound text box controls, two line controls, and one calculated control. The bound text box controls are as follows:

- Visits.Type of Visit
- Treatments.Treatment
- Visit Details.Treatment Price
- Medications.Medication Name
- Visit Details.Medication Price

You need to drag each of these bound text box controls from the Report window field list onto the detail section and then properly size the controls. The default text box property Auto Label should be set to No.

The two line controls are vertical lines. One is on the left side of the detail section under the left edge of the Type of Visit text box control. The other is on the right side of the detail section under the right edge of the calculated control.

Chapter 23: Creating Calculations and Summaries in Reports

The last control is a calculated text box control. This control calculates the total of the Treatment Price and the Medication Price for each detail line. You need to enter the formula into a new unlabeled text box: **=[Treatment Price]+[Medication Price]**. A calculated control always starts with an equal sign (=), and each field name must be placed in brackets. Figure 23-7 also shows the property sheet for this calculated text box control, which is named Pet Line Visit Total. The Pet Line Visit Total control is also formatted with the Currency format property so that the dollar signs appear. If any of the totals is over $1,000.00, the comma also appears. The Decimal Place property is set to Auto, which is automatically set to 2 for the Currency format.

Creating calculated controls

You can use any valid Access expression in any text control. Expressions can contain operators, constants, functions, field names, and literal values. Some examples of expressions are shown next:

=Date()	Date function
=[Customer Subtotal]*[Tax Rate]	A control name multiplied by a field name
=Now()+30	A literal value added to the result of a function

The control (Control Source property) shown in Figure 23-7 calculates the total for each individual line in the detail section. To create this control, follow these steps:

Steps:	Creating a Calculated Control
Step 1.	Create a new text control in the detail section, as shown in Figure 23-7.
Step 2.	Display the property sheet for the new text box control.
Step 3.	Enter =[Treatment Price]+[Medication Price] in the Control Source property cell.
Step 4.	Set the Format property to Currency.

Naming controls used in calculations

Every time you create a control, Access automatically inserts a name for it in the Control Name property of the control's property sheet. The name is really a description that defines what kind of control it is; for example, text controls show the name Field, and label controls show the name Text. The names are followed by a sequential number. An example of a complete name is Field13. If the next control you create is a label, it is named Text15. These names can be replaced with user-defined names, such as Report Date, Sales Tax, or any other valid Access name, which lets you easily reference other controls (especially other controls that contain an expression).

For example, if you have the fields Tax Rate and Subtotal and want to calculate Amount of Tax Due, you enter the expression =**[Tax Rate]*[Subtotal]** and call it Amount of Tax Due. You can then calculate Total Amount Due by entering the expression =**[Subtotal]+[Amount of Tax Due]**. This lets you change an expression in a calculated field without having to change all other references to that expression. To change the name of the control for Treatment Price + Medication Price Total, follow these steps:

Steps:	**Changing the Name of a Control**
Step 1.	Select the calculated control (=[Treatment Price]+[Medication Price]).
Step 2.	Display the property sheet.
Step 3.	Select the Name property.
Step 4.	Replace the default with **Pet Visit Line Total**.

Later, you learn that you cannot use a calculated control name in a *summary* calculation. You'll learn that you must summarize the original calculation. For example, instead of creating an expression such as =Sum(Pet Visit Line Total), you must enter the summary expression =**Sum([Treatment Price]+[Medication Price])**.

Testing the detail section

As you complete each section, you should compare the results against the test datasheet you created, as displayed in Figure 23-5. The easiest way to view your results is to either select the Print Preview button on the toolbar and view the report on-screen or to actually print the first few pages. Figure 23-8 displays the Print Preview screen. If you compare the results to the test data in Figure 23-5, you'll see that all the records are correctly displayed. You may notice that the records are not exactly in the right order, however. This is acceptable as long as groups of the same visit date for the same customer and pet are together. In Figure 23-5, the first five total amounts are $57.00, $52.00, $20.00, $82.80, and $83.00. In Figure 23-8, the first five totals are $52.00, $83.00, $82.80, $20.00, and $57.00. Because the data is not also sorted by the line number in the Visit Details table, the final sort is not precise.

Notice that the calculated control correctly calculates the sum of the two numeric price text box controls and displays them in the Currency format.

Chapter 23: Creating Calculations and Summaries in Reports   **633**

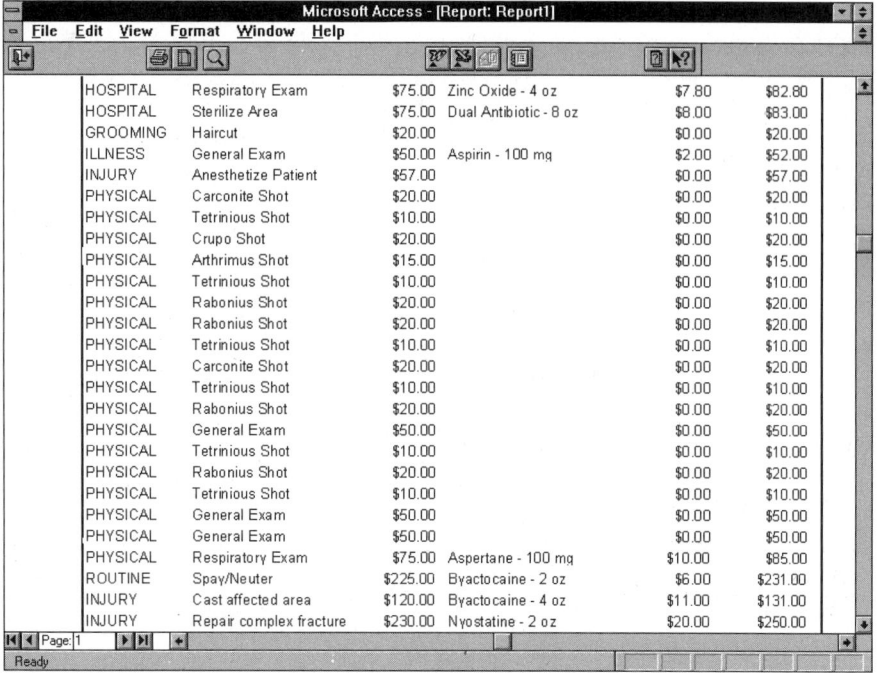

Figure 23-8: A print preview of the detail section.

Creating the Pet ID header and footer sections

When the detail section is complete, you can move *outward* to create the inner group headers and footers. The innermost group is the Pet ID group. You need to create both a header and a footer for this section.

As you've learned, to create group headers and footers for the Pet ID sort you already created, you only have to change the Group Header and Group Footer properties of the Pets.Pet ID Field/Expression to Yes, as shown in Figure 23-9. To make this change, follow these steps:

Steps:	**Displaying Group Headers and Footers**
Step 1.	Display the Sorting and Grouping box if it is not displayed.
Step 2.	Click the Pets.Pet ID row in the window.
Step 3.	Click the Group Header property and change it to **Yes**.
Step 4.	Click the Group Footer property and change it to **Yes**.

 After a group header or footer is defined, the first column of the Sorting and Grouping box displays a grouping icon, which is the same icon you see when you select the Sorting and Grouping button on the toolbar.

The Pet ID header and footer sections should now be displayed.

Creating the Pet ID header controls

The Pets.Pet ID group header, shown in Figure 23-9 along with the Sorting and Grouping box, creates a group break on Pet ID, which causes each pet's individual visit details to be grouped together. This is the section where the pet's name is displayed, as well as labels that describe the controls that appear in the detail section.

There are no calculated controls in this header. There are no lines or rectangles. In fact, with the exception of the pet name itself, all the controls are label controls. Each label control is stretched so that the borders make perfect rectangles on the desired areas and the text is centered where appropriate. The palette is then used for coloring the background and the text.

Notice the use of reverse video in the Pet Name label and text control. Also notice that the Type of Visit, Treatments, Medication, and Total label controls display black text on

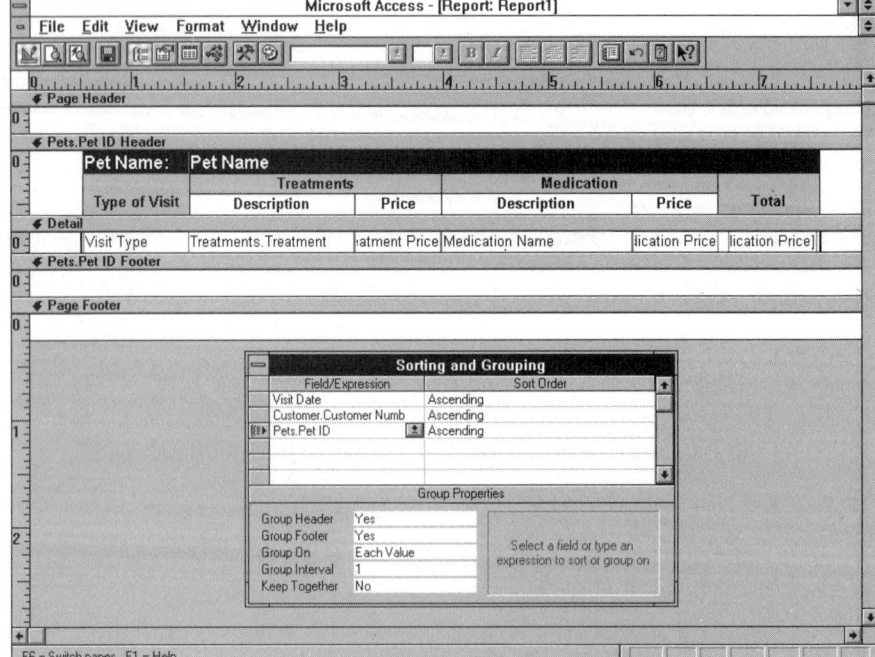

Figure 23-9: The Report Design window for the Pets.Pet ID group header.

a light grey background. This setup, along with the borders, creates a visually appealing section. Notice that there is no room between the bottom of the controls and the bottom of the section. This and the lack of space in the detail section gives the illusion that several sections are really one. You create the label controls Type of Visit and Total by pressing Ctrl+Enter before you enter the text, which makes it use two lines.

Creating the Pet ID footer controls

The Pets.Pet ID group footer, shown in Figure 23-10, is where you subtotal all the visit detail information for each pet. Thus, if a pet has more than one treatment or medication per visit, this is the section in which the report summarizes the visit detail line items. In fact, even if there is only one detail record for a pet, a summary is displayed.

The Pets.Pet ID footer section contains three controls:

Rectangle	Displays the boundaries of the section and is shaded in light grey
Label control	Displays Pet Name and the text Subtotal
Summary text box control	Displays the total of all Pet Visit line totals for each pet

The rectangle completes the area displayed under the detail section and serves as a *bottom cap* on the previous two sections. Notice again that there is no space between the top of the controls and the top of the section. Notice also how the edges line up. This setup sets apart the entire section (Pet ID header, detail section, Pet ID footer) from other areas of the report.

The first control combines the Pet Name field with the text Subtotal. You use a process known as *concatenation*.

Using concatenation to join text and fields

You can use the concatenation operators to combine two strings. A string is either a field or an expression. Several different operators can be used for concatenation, including the following:

+	Joins two Text data type strings
&	Joins two strings; also converts non-Text data types to text data

The + operator is standard in many languages. However, this operator can easily be confused with the arithmetic operator used to add two numbers together. The + operator requires that both strings being joined are Text data types.

The & operator also converts nonstring data types to string data types and is therefore used more than the + operator. If, for example, you enter the expression =**"Today's Date Is:" & Date()**, Access converts the result of the date function into a string and adds it to the text Today's Date Is:. If the date is December 25, 1993, the result returned is a string with the value `Today's Date Is:12/25/93`. The fact that there is no space between the colon and the 12 is no error. If you want to add a space between two joined strings, you must physically add one.

Access can join any data type to any data type using this method. If you want to create the control for the Pet Name and the text Subtotal using this method, you enter the expression =**[Pet Name] & " Subtotal"**, which appends the contents of the Pet Name field to the text Subtotal. No conversion occurs because the contents of both Pet Name and the literal value Subtotal are already text. Notice that there is a space between the first double quotation mark and the text Subtotal.

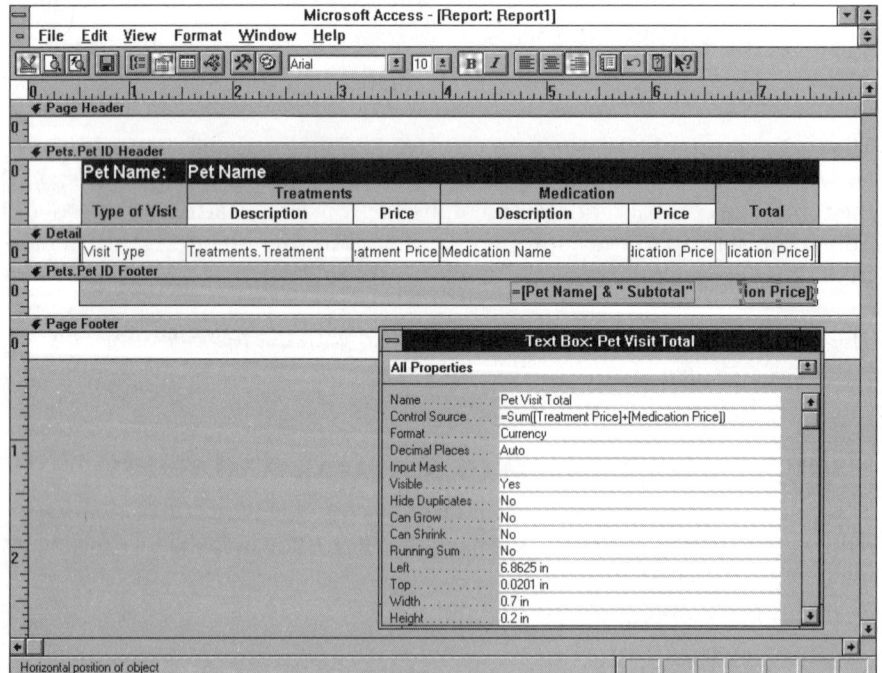

Figure 23-10: Creating a group summary control.

Chapter 23: Creating Calculations and Summaries in Reports

 If you use the + operator for concatenation, you must convert any nonstring data types (such as a date returned with the Date( ) function) to a string data type by using the CStr( ) function. If you want to display the system date with some text, you have to create a text control with the following contents:

="Today's Date Is:" +cstr(Date())

You can directly insert the contents of a field into a text expression by using the ampersand (&) character. The syntax is

="Text String "&[Field or Control Name]&" additional text string"

Or

[Field or Control Name]&" Text String"

To use this method to create the control for the Pet Name text box control, follow these steps:

Steps:	Using the Ampersand Character to Insert a Field or Control into a Text Expression
Step 1.	Create a new text control in the Pets.Pet ID Footer section.
Step 2.	Enter the expression = **[Pet Name]&" Subtotal"** (as shown in Figure 23-10).

Calculating group summaries

Creating a sum of numeric data within a group is very simple. Following is the general procedure for summarizing group totals for bound text controls:

- Create a new text control in the group footer (or header).
- Enter the expression **=Sum([Control Name])** where *Control Name* is a valid field name in the underlying query or a control name in the report.

If, however, the control name is for a calculated control, the control expression must be repeated. Suppose, for example, that in the Pets.Pet ID footer you want to enter the following expression into the text box control to display the total of the detail line:

=Sum([Pets Line Visit Total])

This, however, does not work. This is simply a limitation of Microsoft Access. To create a sum for the totals in the detail section, you have to enter

=Sum([Treatment Price]+[Medication Price])

This is how the summary shown in Figure 23-10 is created.

 Access knows to sum the detail lines for the Pet ID summary because you put the summary control in the Pets.Pet ID section. Access automatically resets the summary control each time the value of the Pet ID changes. Later, when you create this same summary control in the Customer ID footer section, Access will reset the total only when the value of Customer ID changes.

You can use expressions in a report in two ways. The first is to enter the expression directly in a text control. For example, enter

[Treatment Price]+[Medication Price]

The second way is to create the expression in the underlying query, as you saw in Figure 23-4, where you created a field named Line Total in the query itself. You can then use the calculated field of the query in a text control on the report. The advantage of the former method is that you have the flexibility to create your expressions *on the fly,* as well as being able to reference other report objects, such as text controls with expressions. The disadvantage is that you cannot use summary expressions on calculated controls.

If you add a calculated field to your underlying query, you can then reference this calculated field in both the detail section as well as any group section. The syntax for this is

=Sum([Calculated Field Name])

If you want to create the detail section Line Total and Pet ID Subtotal using the calculation from the query method, you create the calculated field in the query as

Line Total: [Treatment Price]+[Medication Price]

Then you create the summary control in the report as

=Sum([Line Total])

Either method works and is acceptable.

By using the Print Preview window, you can check the progress of your report. Figure 23-11 displays the report created so far. Notice how the three sections come together to form one area.

Figure 23-11:
The Print Preview window of a report's group header and the detail and group footer sections.

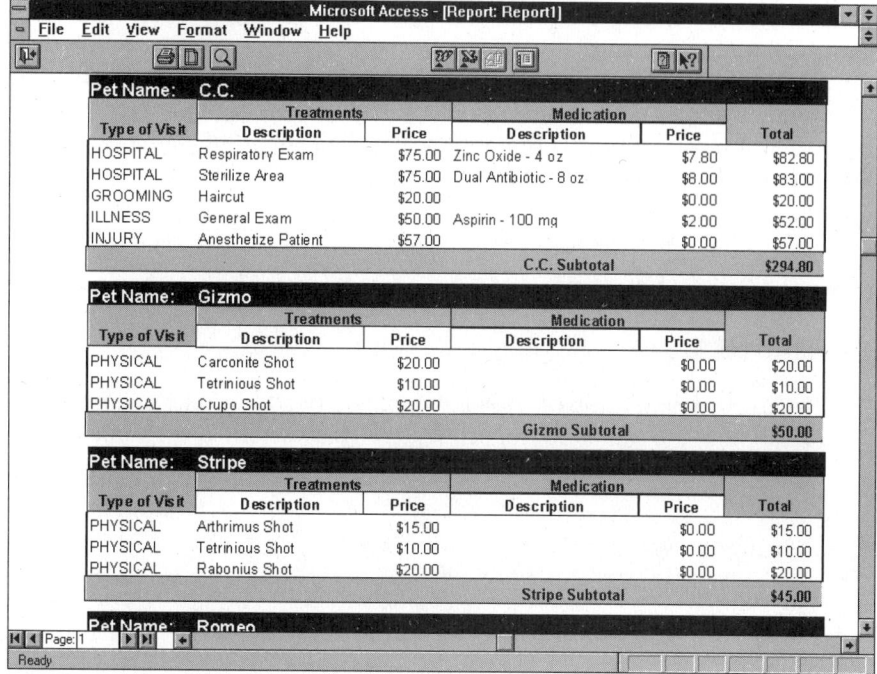

Creating the Customer Number header and footer sections

When the Pet ID sections are complete, you can move *outward* again to create the next outer group header and footer. The next group as you move outward is the Customer Number group. You need to create both a header and a footer for this section. To create the Customer Number sections, follow these steps:

Steps:	Creating Group Headers and Footers
Step 1.	Display the Sorting and Grouping box if it is not already displayed.
Step 2.	Click the Customer.Customer Number row in the window.
Step 3.	Click the Group Header property and change it to **Yes**.
Step 4.	Click the Group Footer property and change it to **Yes**.

There is one task left to do. You want each new customer for a specific date to be displayed on a separate page. If you view the report as it currently exists, you notice that there are no specific page breaks. You can create a page break every time the customer number changes by setting the Force New Page property of the Customer.Customer Number header to Before Section. Doing so will ensure that each customer's information is printed on a separate page.

Creating the Customer Number header controls

The Customer.Customer Number group header is shown completed in Figure 23-12 at the top of the report design. This section is very similar to the Customer section created in Chapters 21 and 22. There are seven fields used in this section:

- Customer Name
- Street/Apt
- City
- State
- ZIP Code
- Phone Number
- Visit Date

The first six controls are from the Customer table, and the Visit Date control is from the Visits table. The entire section is surrounded by a grey shaded rectangle and a shadow box. Refer to Chapter 22 on how to create this effect. The Visit Date control has an attached label and is surrounded by a transparent rectangle, which you create by setting the palette's Back Color clear button. The control also uses the Raised appearance option. Each of the Customer controls is sunken to give it a three-dimensional effect. You do this task by selecting the Sunken special effect button in the palette.

One change that you can make is to rearrange the display of the City, State, and ZIP Code fields. Instead of displaying these fields as three separate controls, you can concatenate them to appear together. You can save space by compressing any trailing spaces in the city name, adding a comma after city, and also by compressing the space between State and ZIP Code. You can make the changes by following these steps:

Chapter 23: Creating Calculations and Summaries in Reports

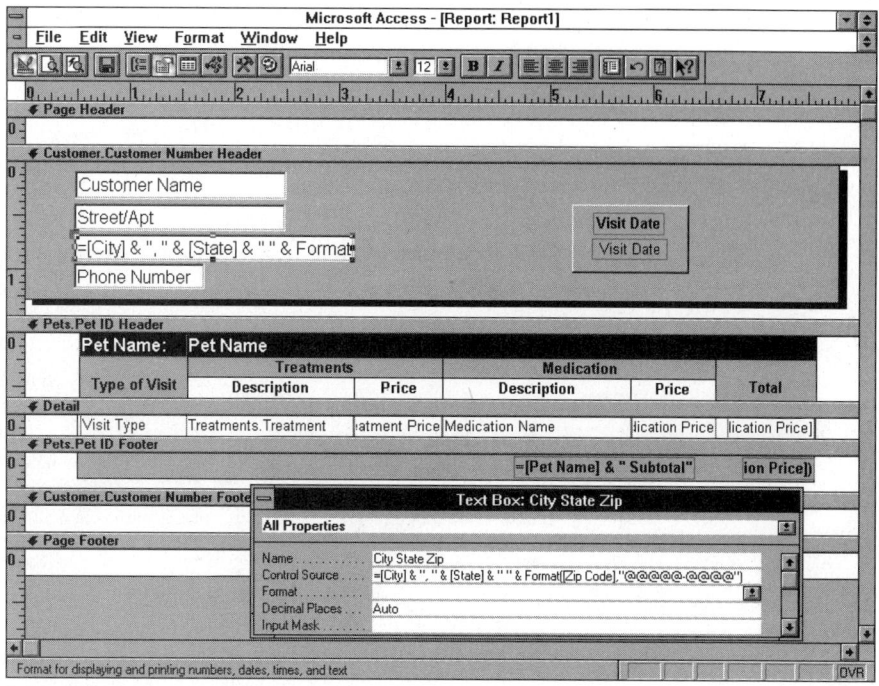

Figure 23-12: The Report Design window for the Customer.Customer Number group Header.

Steps: Creating a Concatenated Text Box Control

Step 1. Delete the City, State, and ZIP Code controls in the Customer Number header.

Step 2. Create a new unlabeled text box control.

Step 3. Enter =[City]&", "&[State]&" "&[Zip Code] in the Control Source property of the text box control.

The only problem with this expression is that the ZIP code is formatted in the ZIP Code table field using the @@@@@-@@@@ format to add a hyphen between the first five and last four characters. As currently entered, the control may display the following value when run: Lakeville, OR 974011021.

You still need to format the ZIP Code field. Normally, the function Format( ) is used for formatting an expression. In this example, the function should be written as

Format([Zip Code],"@@@@@-@@@@")

You can add this to the concatenation expression substituting the Format expression in place of the ZIP Code field. To complete this example, change the control to

=[City]&", "&[State]&" "&Format([Zip Code],"@@@@@-@@@@")

To check the Customer Number group heading, you can view the report in the Print Preview window, as shown in Figure 23-13.

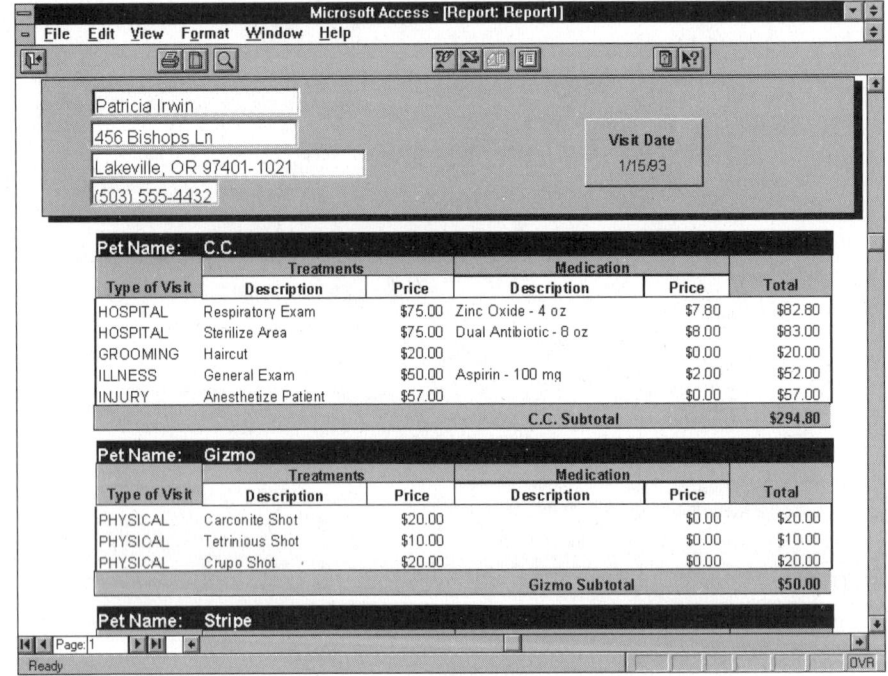

Figure 23-13: Viewing the report in the Print Preview window.

Creating the Customer Number footer controls

The Customer.Customer Number footer section contains ten different controls. There are five label controls and five text box controls. The text box control expressions and their associated labels are listed in Table 23-2.

Each of the concatenated label controls uses the same standard notation that you learned in this chapter. Each of the text box controls is a simple expression. Notice that Customer Total uses exactly the same expression as the Pet ID total, except that it now resets the total by Customer Number.

Chapter 23: Creating Calculations and Summaries in Reports

Table 23-2
Expressions in the Customer Number Footer

Expression Name	Label Control	Text Box Control
Customer Total	Total Invoice:	=Sum([Treatment Price]+[Medication Price])
Discount Amount	="Discount ("&[Discount]*100&"%):"	=[Customer Total] *[Discount]
Customer Subtotal	Subtotal:	=[Customer Total]-[Discount Amount]
State Sales Tax	=[State Name]&" Sales Tax ("&[Visits.Tax Rate]*100&"%):"	=[Customer Subtotal] *[Visits.Tax Rate]
Amount Due	Amount Due:	=[Customer Subtotal]+[State Sales Tax]

The Customer.Customer Number footer, as shown in Figure 23-14, is where you create and summarize the line-item totals for each pet for a particular owner for a particular visit. You also want to display a customer's discount rate, the amount of the discount in dollars, the customer's state, the state sales tax as a percentage, the state sales tax in dollars, and, finally, a total for the amount due. All this information will appear in a separate box with a shadow that you create by duplicating the original box and changing the placement and color of the duplicate. If you are following along with this example, the steps for each of the controls are displayed next.

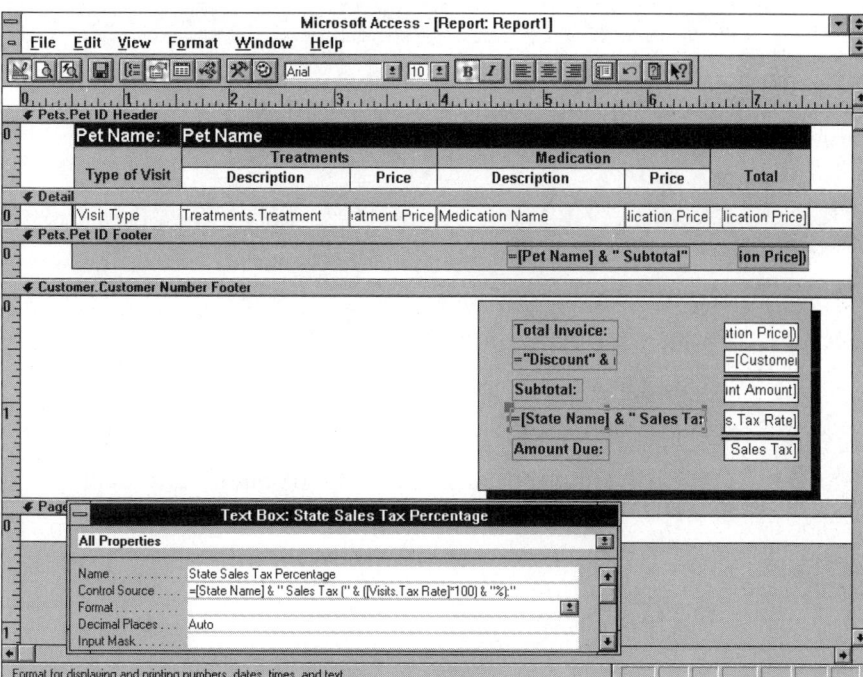

Figure 23-14: The Report Design window for the Customer.Customer Number group footer.

To check the Customer Number group heading, you can view the report in the Print Preview window, as shown in Figure 23-15.

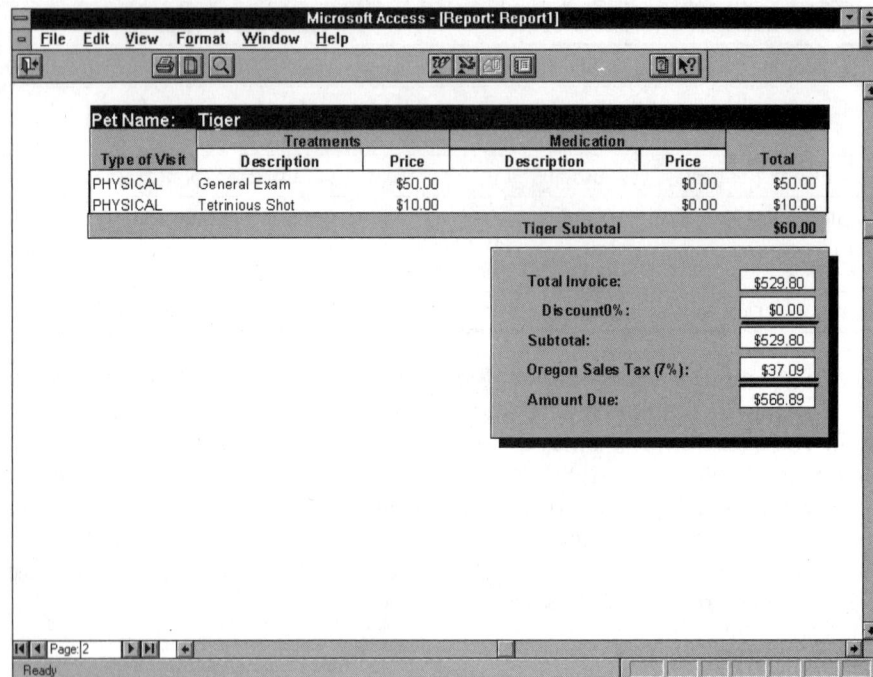

Figure 23-15: Viewing the report in the Print Preview window.

Because the first group has many pets and visit detail lines, you need to look at page 3 to see the first customer number footer.

Steps:	Creating the Total Invoice Label and Text Box Controls
Step 1.	Create a new label control.
Step 2.	Change the Caption property to **Total Invoice:**.
Step 3.	Create a new text box control.
Step 4.	Change the Name property to **Customer Total**.
Step 5.	Change the Control Source property to **=Sum([Treatment Price]+[Medication Price])**.

Steps: Creating the Discount Amount Label and Text Box Controls

Step 1. Create a new label control.

Step 2. Change the Control Source property to ="Discount ("&[Discount]*100&"%):" which concatenates the word Discount with the customer's discount rate and multiplies by 100 to give a percentage.

Step 3. Create a new text box control.

Step 4. Change the Name to **Discount Amount.**

Step 5. Change the Control Source to =**[Customer Total]*[Discount]**, which multiplies the customer's discount rate by the amount calculated in the Customer Total control.

Steps: Creating the Customer Subtotal Label and Text Box Controls

Step 1. Create a new label control.

Step 2. Change the caption to **Subtotal:.**

Step 3. Create a new text box control.

Step 4. Change the Name to **Customer Subtotal.**

Step 5. Change the Control Source to =**[Customer Total]-[Discount Amount]**, which subtracts the amount calculated in the Discount Amount control from the sum calculated in the Customer Total control.

Steps: Creating the State Sales Tax Label and Text Box Controls

Step 1. Create a new label control.

Step 2. Change the Control Source to =[State Name]&" Sales Tax ("&[Visits.Tax Rate]*100&"%):"

This concatenates the customer's state name (full spelling), the words Tax Rate, and the customer's tax rate, and multiplies by 100 to give a percentage.

Step 3. Create a new text box control.

Steps:	Creating the Amount Due Label and Text Box Controls (cont.)
Step 4.	Change the Name to **State Sales Tax.**
Step 5.	Change the Control Source to **=[Customer Subtotal]*[Tax Rate]**, which multiplies the customer's state tax rate by the amount calculated in the Customer Subtotal control.

Steps:	Creating the Amount Due Label and Text Box Controls
Step 1.	Create a new label control.
Step 2.	Change the Caption to **Amount Due:**.
Step 3.	Create a new text box control.
Step 4.	Change the Name to **Amount Due.**
Step 5.	Change the Control Source to **=[Customer Subtotal]+[State Sales Tax]**, which adds the customer's calculated state sales tax to the amount calculated in the Customer Subtotal control.

Creating the Visit Date header

You have one more group header to create. You still need to create a group header for Visit Date. But the Visit Date header won't display anything in the section. In fact, the section has a height of 0. Essentially, the section is *closed.* The purpose of the Visit Date header is to force a page break whenever the Visit Date changes. Without this section, if you have two customer records for the same customer on different dates that appear consecutively in the report's dynaset, the records will appear on the same page. The only forced page break you created so far was for Customer Number. By adding one for Visit Date, you complete the report groupings. To create the Visit Date grouping and add the page break, follow these steps:

Steps:	Creating the Visit Date Header
Step 1.	Display the Sorting and Grouping box if it is not already displayed.
Step 2.	Click the Visit Date row Field/Expression column.
Step 3.	Click the Group Header property.
Step 4.	Click the arrow and select Yes from the drop-down list.
Step 5.	Double-click the section to display its property sheet.

> Change the Height property to **0**.
>
> Change the Visible property to **No**.
>
> Change the Force New Page property to **Before Section**.

Creating the page header controls

The page header appears at the top of every page in the Invoice Report. The page header and footer controls are not controlled by the Sorting and Grouping box but by the selection F_ormat⇨_Page Header/Footer. In this report, the page header has been open all the time. This section contains a small version of the Mountain Animal Hospital logo in the upper left-hand corner, as well as the name, address, and phone number for the hospital. The section also contains the report date and a horizontal line at the bottom to visually separate it from the rest of the page. By default, the page header and footer are automatically created and displayed when a new report is created. All you have to do is change the height and add the proper controls.

 In Chapter 22, you learned how to add the unbound bitmap MTN.BMP to the report. The label controls that display the Mountain Animal Hospital page header are four separate controls. The only control that needs explanation is the Report Date control.

Access offers several built-in functions that let you display and manipulate date and time information. The easiest to start with is the Date() function, which returns the current system date when the report is printed or previewed. To add a text control to the report header that displays the date when the report is printed, follow these steps:

Steps:	Adding the Current System Date
Step 1.	Create a new text control in the page header, as shown in Figure 23-16.
Step 2.	Display the control's property sheet.
Step 3.	In the Control Source property cell, type **="Report Date: "&Date()**.

This concatenates the text Report Date with the current system date.

Another date function that Access offers is DatePart( ). The function DatePart( ) returns a numeric value for the specified portion of a date. The syntax for the function is

DatePart(*interval,date*)

where *interval* is a string expression for the interval of time you want returned and *date* is the date you want to apply the function to.

Figure 23-16:
The page header.

Table 23-3 provides a listing of valid intervals and the time periods they represent.

Table 23-3
DatePart( ) Intervals

Interval	Time Period
yyyy	Year
q	Quarter
m	Month
y	Day of year
d	Day
w	Weekday
ww	Week
h	Hour
n	Minute
s	Second

Chapter 23: Creating Calculations and Summaries in Reports

The date can be a literal date, such as 1-Jan-1993, or a field name that references a field containing a valid date.

Expression	Result
`=DatePart("yyyy",25-Dec-1992)`	1992 (the year)
`=DatePart("m",25-Dec-1992)`	12 (the month)
`=DatePart("d",25-Dec-1992)`	25 (the day of the month)
`=DatePart("w",25-Dec-1992)`	6 (the weekday; Sunday=1, Monday=2 ...)
`=DatePart("q",25-Dec-1992)`	4 (the quarter)

Creating the page footer controls

Normally, you use the page footer for the placement of the page number or for page totals. For this report, the footer's only purpose is to display a thick horizontal line at the bottom of every page, followed by the page number in the right bottom corner.

To number the pages in your report, Access provides the Page function. You access the Page function by using it in an expression in a text control that returns the current page of the report. Like all expressions, an expression with the Page property in it must be preceded by an equal sign (=). To create a page number in the footer of your report, follow these steps:

Steps:	**Displaying Page Numbers**
Step 1.	Create a new text control in the lower right-hand section of the page footer.
Step 2.	Display the control's property sheet.
Step 3.	In the Control Source property cell, type `="Page: "&Page`.
Step 4.	Select the Italics button in the toolbar.

Although it makes the most sense to put the page number in the page header or page footer, you can place a control with the Page property in any section of your report. It is also possible to use the Page property as part of an expression. For example, the expression =Page*10 will display the result of multiplying the actual page number by ten.

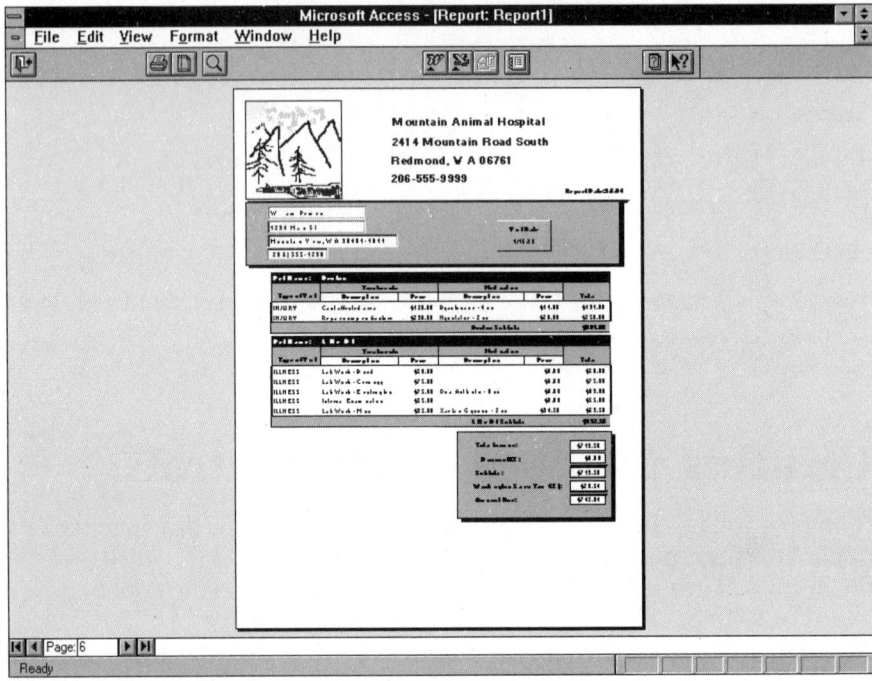

Figure 23-17:
The report design output on-screen.

You have now completed the Monthly Invoice Report. Compare your report design with the design originally shown in Figure 23-2 and then with the final output in Figure 23-17. Figure 23-17 shows page 6 of the report, which is a good example of all the sections displayed on one page. A hard copy of the report page is found in Figure 23-1.

Before moving on, you need to create a few more controls. The Access report writer is a two-pass report writer, which means that it lets you create controls based on knowledge of the final report. For example, you can create a control that displays the percentage of one total to a grand total. You can also display a cumulative total.

Calculating percentages using totals

You can calculate a line percentage to determine what percent of the total cost for a pet's visit each line is. By comparing the line item to the total, you can calculate the percentage of a particular item to a whole. To do so, you need to move all the controls to the far left side of the report for the Pet ID header and footer and the detail section. To create a new control that displays what percentage of the whole (Mountain Animal Hospital Charges) each pet accounts for, follow these steps:

Chapter 23: Creating Calculations and Summaries in Reports

Steps: Calculating an Individual Record's Percentage of a Total

Step 1. Duplicate the Pet Visit Line Total control.

Step 2. Position the duplicate to the right of the original.

Step 3. Change the Control Source to =**[Pet Visit Line Total]/[Pet Visit Total]**.

Step 4. Change the Format property to **Percent.**

Step 5. Create a new label control with the caption Percent above it, as shown in Figure 23-18.

The calculation takes the individual line total control [Pet Visit Line Total] in the detail section and divides it by the summary control [Pet Visit Total] in the page header section. The Percent format automatically handles the conversion and displays a percentage.

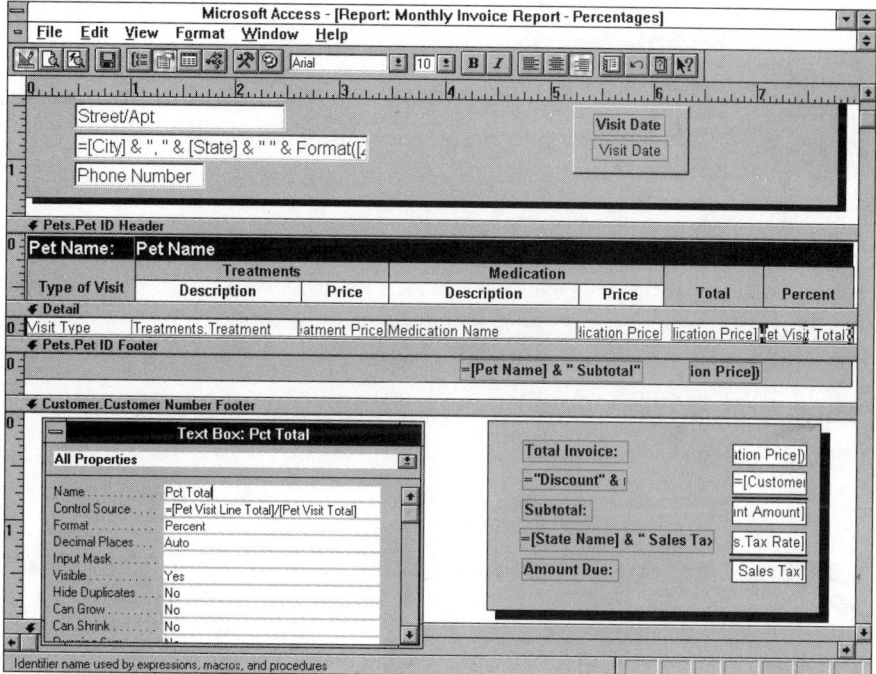

Figure 23-18: Creating a percentage control.

Calculating running sums

Access also lets you easily calculate running sums, also known as *cumulative totals,* simply by changing the Running Sum property for a control. If you want to create a running total of how much is spent as each pet's charges are totaled, follow these steps:

Steps:	Creating a Running Sum over a Group
Step 1.	Duplicate the rectangle and its controls in the Pets.Pet ID footer section.
Step 2.	Display the new rectangle just below the existing one, as shown in Figure 23-19.
Step 3.	Select the label control and change the caption to =**[Pet Name]&" Running Total"**.
Step 4.	Select the new control with the expression =**Sum([Treatment Price]+[Medication Price])**.
Step 5.	Display the control's property sheet.
Step 6.	Change the Name to **Running Total.**
Step 7.	Click the Running Sum property.
Step 8.	Select Over Group from the drop-down list, as shown in Figure 23-19.

Access will now add the current subtotal to all previous subtotals for each owner. You can alternatively create a running sum across all values in a report. This is useful in a report footer section where you want to present an overall summary.

You can display the percentages and the running total by performing a print preview, as shown in Figure 23-20.

Creating a title page in a report header

The main purpose of the report header, which is illustrated in Figure 23-21, is to provide a separate title page. From the report description given earlier, you know that the report header must contain Mountain Animal Hospital's logo, name, address, and phone, as well as a report title. In the sample file Monthly Invoice Report, all these controls are created for you. If you created the report from scratch, you can follow these steps:

Chapter 23: Creating Calculations and Summaries in Reports

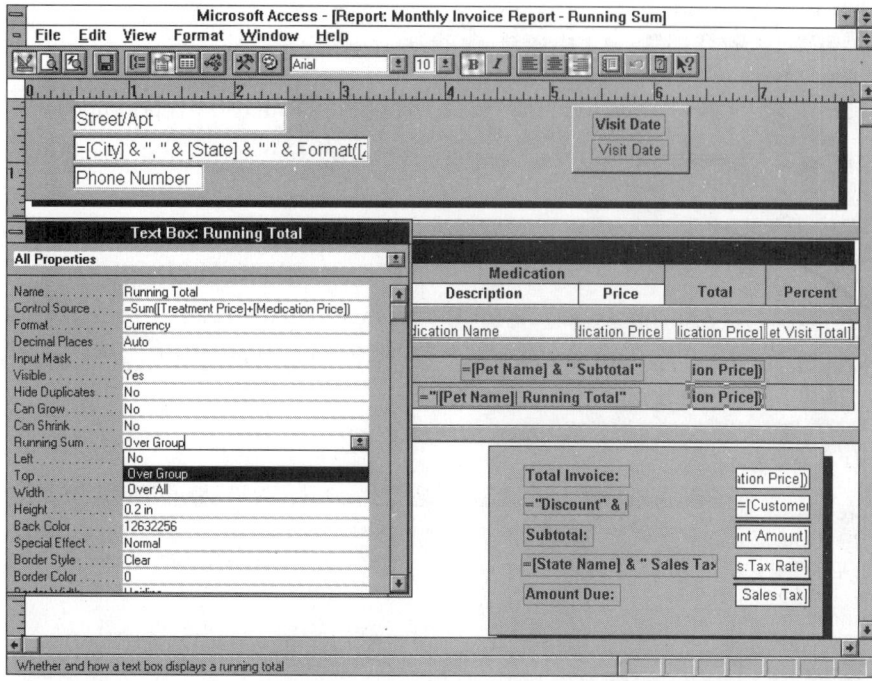

Figure 23-19: Creating a running sum control.

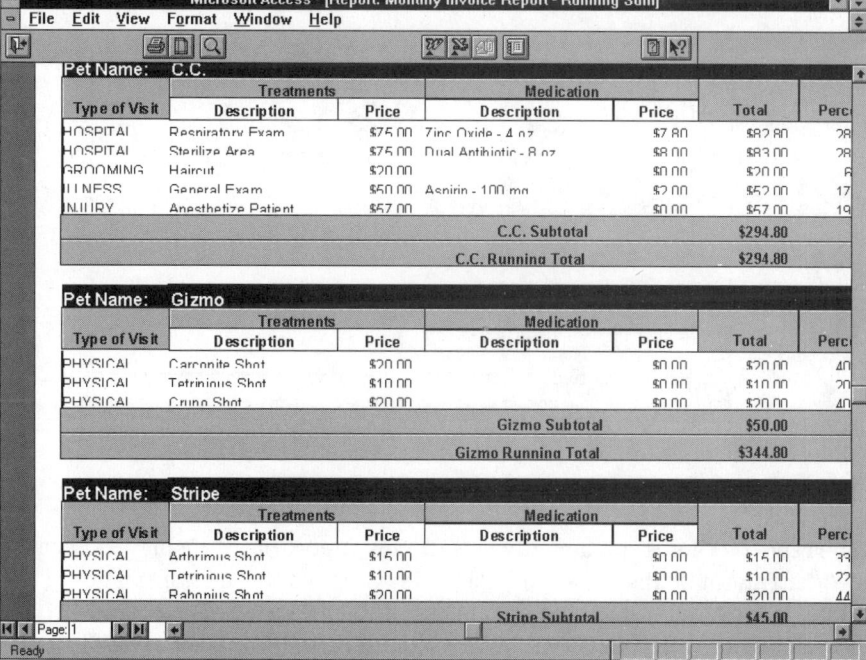

Figure 23-20: A print preview displaying percentages and running totals.

Steps: Creating a Report Header

Step 1. Select Format⇨Report Header/Footer to display the report header and footer.

Step 2. Resize the height of the report header section so that it is approximately 9 ½ inches high.

Step 3. Set the Force New Page property of the report header section to After Section so that a page break occurs after the report header.

Step 4. Create label controls for the report title, name, address, and phone.

Step 5. Create an unbound picture control using MTN.BMP and change the Size Mode property to Stretch.

Figure 23-21: The Report Design Print Preview window for the report header.

Using the report footer

The report footer is not actually used in this report but is displayed because the report header cannot be displayed in Design view without it. The normal use of the report footer is for grand totals that occur once in the report. This footer is also used for an accounting type of report or a letter concerning the totals for an audit trail.

Chapter 23: Creating Calculations and Summaries in Reports

Summary

In this chapter you learned how to create multilevel reports as well as subreports. The following points were covered:

- Access lets you easily create multilevel grouping reports.
- A calculated control contains mathematical expressions.
- Text box controls can contain field names or expressions.
- Text expressions use the concatenation operators +, &, or | to combine text strings and/or text strings and other data types.
- The Date( ) function returns the current system date.
- The DatePart( ) function returns a numeric value for the specified portion of a date.
- Controls can, and should be, named. You can then reference them in other controls.
- When the =SUM( ) function is used in a group header or footer (or page or report header or footer), it summarizes all the values of a field within that group.
- Access can use summary totals to calculate line-item or group total percentages.
- Access can perform running sums within a group, as well as across groups.

In the next chapter, you learn how to link to external data by attaching, importing, and exporting.

Part IV

Advanced Database Features

659 Chapter 24: Working with External Data

707 Chapter 25: Advanced Select Queries

741 Chapter 26: Creating Action Queries

769 Chapter 27: Advanced Query Topics

797 Chapter 28: Creating and Using Subforms

829 Chapter 29: Creating Mailing Labels and Mail Merge Reports

Working with External Data

CHAPTER 24

In This Chapter

- Attaching to external data
- Working with attached tables
- Importing from external data
- Creating import/export specifications
- Exporting to external tables and files
- Moving data between Windows applications

So far, you have worked with data in Access tables only. In this chapter, you explore using data from other types of files. You work with data from dBASE and Paradox files and learn how to work with data in text, FoxPro, Lotus 1-2-3, Microsoft Excel, Btrieve, and SQL server formats.

Access and External Data

The ability to exchange information between Access and other programs is essential in today's database world. Information is usually stored in a wide variety of application programs and data formats. Access, like many other products, has its own native file format. Its format is created to support referential integrity and to provide support for such rich data types as OLE objects. Most of the time, this format is sufficient; however, occasionally you need to move data from one Access database file to another or even to a different software program format.

Types of external data

Access has the capability to use and exchange data among a wide range of applications. For example, you may need to get data from an existing dBASE or Paradox file or to obtain information that is in an SQL server or a network Btrieve file. Access can move data among several categories of applications:

- Windows applications
- Spreadsheets
- PC database management systems
- Server-based database systems (ODBC)
- Btrieve data files
- Text files

Methods of working with external data

Many times, you need to move data from one application or file into your Access database. You may need to obtain information that you already have in a spreadsheet file. You can reenter all the information by hand, or you can have the information *imported* into your database. Perhaps you need to put information into a Paradox system that you already have in your Access tables. Again, you can reenter all the information into Paradox by hand, or you can have the information *exported* to the Paradox table. Access has tools that allow you to move data from one database table to another table or file. That new table may be another Access table, a dBASE table, a Paradox table, or a Lotus 1-2-3 file. In fact, Access can exchange data with over 14 different file types, including the following:

- Access database objects (all six types)
- dBASE (III+, IV – 1.x/2.x)
- FoxPro (2.0 and 2.5)
- Paradox 3.0 and 3.5
- Text files (ANSI and ASCII; DOS or OS/2; delimited and fixed-length)
- Lotus 1-2-3, 2.x and 3.x
- Lotus 1-2-3/W (Windows)
- Excel 2.x and greater
- Btrieve (5.x and 6.x)
- ODBC (Microsoft SQL server, Sybase server, and Oracle server)

Access can work with these external data sources in several ways; Table 24-1 shows how Access can work with external data and to what purpose.

Table 24-1
Methods of Working with External Data

Method	Purpose
Attach	Create a link to a table in another Access database or using the data in a different database format.
Import	Copy data from a text file, another Access database, or another applications format into an Access table.
Export	Copy data from an Access table to a text file, another Access database, or another applications format.

Should you import or attach data?

As Table 24-1 shows, you can work with data from other sources in two ways: attaching or importing. Both methods allow you to work with the external data.

There is a distinct difference between the two methods:

- Importing makes a copy of the external data and brings the copy into the Access table.
- Attaching uses the data in its current file format (such as dBASE or Paradox file).

There are clear advantages and disadvantages to each method.

When to import external data

Access cannot attach to several file formats. Obviously, if you need to work with data from these file formats, you must import the information. These file formats include text files and spreadsheet files.

Of course, importing data means that you have doubled the storage space for that particular data because it now resides in two different files on the storage device (hard drive, floppy, and so forth).

> ## Working with Other Access Databases
>
> Access can open only one database at a time; therefore, you cannot directly work with a table in a different database. If you need to work with tables or other Access objects (forms, queries, and so on) from another Access database, you don't have to close the current one. Instead of closing the current database, simply import or attach the object in the other database to your current database. By doing this, you can view or edit data in another database table directly.

Because importing makes another copy of the data, you may want to erase the old file once you import the copy into Access. However, sometimes you won't want to erase it. For example, the data may be sales figures from a spreadsheet still being used. In cases like this, you simply have to maintain the duplicate data and accept the increased amount of space necessary for storing the data.

One of the principal reasons to import data is to have the ability to customize the data to meet your needs. You can specify a primary key, change field names (up to 64 characters), and set other field properties. On the other hand, with attached tables, you are restricted to setting very limited field properties. For example, you cannot specify a primary key, thus eliminating the ability to enforce integrity against the attached table.

Imported tables also tend to perform better than attached tables. Therefore, if you know that you will use your data only in Access, you should always import it.

When to attach external data

If you leave data in another database format, Access can actually make changes to the table while it is still being used by the original application. This is very useful when you want to work with data in Access that other programs also need to work with. For example, you may need to obtain updated personnel data from a dBASE file that is maintained in an existing networked dBASE application so that you can print out a monthly report in Access. Another example is when you use Access as a front end to your SQL database. You can attach to an SQL table and update the data directly to the SQL server without having to batch upload it later.

The biggest disadvantage to working with attached tables is the loss of Access's internal capability to enforce referential integrity between tables.

Attaching External Data

Access can directly attach to several Database Management System (DBMS) tables individually or simultaneously. Once an external file is attached, a link is built to the table and stored in Access.

Database connectivity

As the database market continues to grow, the need to obtain information from many different sources will escalate. If you have information being captured in an SQL server table or a Paradox table, you don't want to reenter the information from these tables into Access. Ideally, you want to open the table and use the information in its native format without having to copy it or write a translation program to access it. This capability to access information from one database format while in another is the primary goal of many companies today.

Copying or translating data from one application format to another is both time-consuming and costly. The time it takes can be the difference between success and failure. Therefore, you want an environment that is *heterogeneous* between your DBMSs and the data stored in them. By attaching tables, Access gives you this ability.

Types of Database Management Systems (DBMSs)

Access lets you connect, or *attach,* to several different DBMSs, directly accessing information stored in them. Following are the database systems that Access supports:

- Other Access database tables
- dBASE (versions III and IV)
- FoxPro (versions 2.0 and 2.5)
- Paradox (version 3.*x* and 4.*x*)
- Btrieve (versions 5.*x* and 6.*x*, with Xtrieve dictionary file)
- Microsoft SQL server

You can attach to any of these table types, individually or mixed together. If you attach to an external file, Access displays the filename in the Database Table window just as it does other Access tables. However, the icon attached with the table will be different. It starts with an arrow pointing from the left to the right and points to an icon. A table icon tells you that it is an Access table, a dB icon tells you it is a dBASE table, and so on. Figure 24-1 shows several attached tables at the top of the list, which are all external tables. These tables are attached to the current database. Notice that all the attached tables have an icon with an arrow (The icon clues you in to the type of file attached).

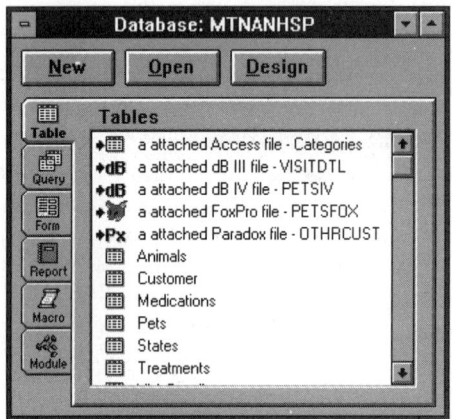

Figure 24-1:
Five attached tables in the database.

In Figure 24-1, OTHRCUST is a Paradox table, and PETSIV is a dBASE table (composed of a database [DBF] and memo [DBT] file). Notice the arrow on the left side of the icon pointing to the table icon.

When attaching to external tables, you are limited to available Windows memory. If you run out of memory, Access reports an error and does not perform the link to the attached table.

Once you attach a table to your Access database, you can use it just like any other table. You can query against it, link another table to it, and so forth. For example, Figure 24-2 shows a query design and dynaset using the linked tables Customer, from Access, and PETSIV, from dBASE. You can just as easily link the Paradox and dBASE tables; an Access table does not have to be used.

After you attach an external table to an Access database, you *cannot* move the table to another drive or directory. Because Access does not physically bring the file into the MDB file, it maintains the link via the filename *and* the drive:path.

Following Along In This Chapter

The examples in this chapter use the database ATCIMPEX.MDB. This database is included on your disk, along with several different types of DBMS files: Paradox, dBASE IV, dBASE III+, and FoxPro 2.*x* with indexes.

Figure 24-2:
A query design and dynaset of an Access table and an attached dBASE IV table.

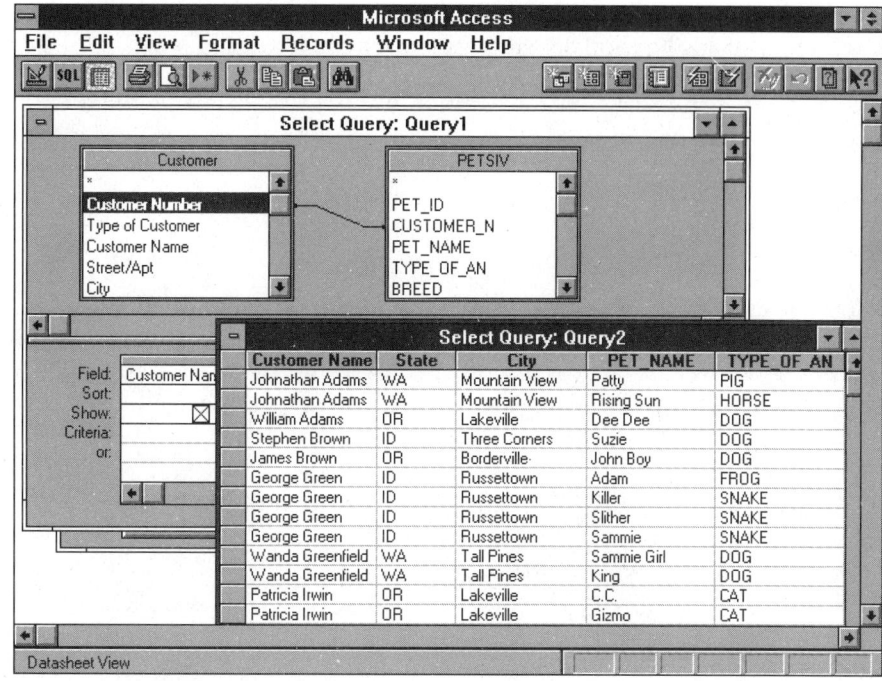

Attaching to other Access database tables

When you work with an Access database, you normally create every table you want to use in the database. However, if the table exists in another Access database, you can attach to this other Access database and use the table rather than re-creating the table and duplicating the data.

You may, for example, want to attach to another Access table that is on a network. Once you attach to another Access table, you use it just like another table in the open database. To attach to the table Visits in the MTNANHSP Access database, follow these steps:

Steps:	Attaching to Another Access Database Table
Step 1.	Open the ATCIMPEX database and select File⇨Attach Table.... Access opens the Attach dialog box, showing a list box underneath Data Source.
Step 2.	In the list box (see Figure 24-3), select Data Source: Microsoft Access. Access closes the dialog box and displays the Select Microsoft Access Database dialog box.

Part IV: Advanced Database Features

Step 3.	Double-click MTNANHSP.MDB in the File Name list box. Access closes the dialog box and displays the Attach Tables dialog box.
Step 4.	Double-click the Visits table name. Access displays a message box.
Step 5.	Click the OK button. Access redisplays the Attach Tables dialog box.
Step 6.	Click the Close button.

After you attach the Visits table from the MTNANHSP database, Access returns to the Database window and shows you that the Visits table is now attached to your database. Figure 24-4 shows the table Visits attached to the current database. Notice the arrow on the Visits table icon. This arrow shows that the table has been attached from another source.

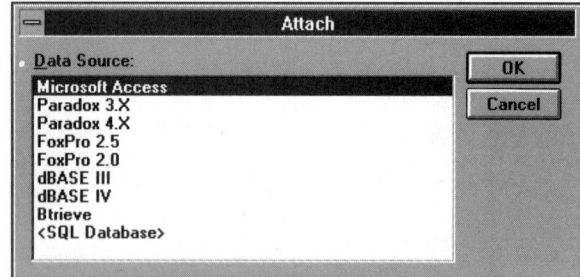

Figure 24-3: A dialog box showing data sources for attaching tables.

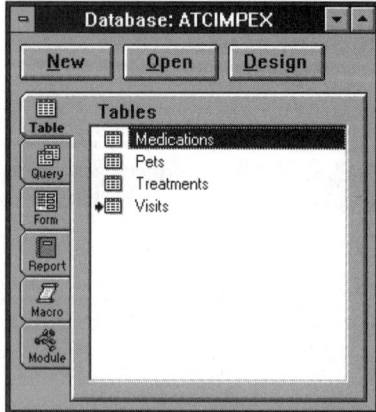

Figure 24-4: The Database windows with the Visits table added.

When you attach tables from other Access databases, you will not be able to set up permanent relationships between the attached Access tables and actual tables in the database by using the Edit⇨Relationships... choice from the Database menu. You can set up a relationship in a query, if you want. Any relationships that the attached Access table has with other tables in the database in which they are actually stored remain effective.

Attaching to dBASE and FoxPro databases (tables)

You can attach DBF files in either dBASE or FoxPro format. Like with other Access database tables, once an *x*BASE (dBASE or FoxPro) file is attached, you can view and edit data in the DBF format.

dBASE and FoxPro save tables individually in a file with the extension DBF. In *x*BASE, DBF files are usually referred to as databases. In Access, the equivalent to an *x*BASE database is a table. The database in Access is the complete collection of all tables and other related objects. To maintain consistency in terminology, *x*BASE databases will be referred to as dBASE or FoxPro tables.

Access and dBASE/FoxPro indexes

When you attach a dBASE or FoxPro file, you can also tell Access to use one or more index files (NDX and MDX for dBASE, and IDX and CDX for FoxPro). Use of these indexes will improve performance of the link between *x*BASE and Access.

If you inform Access of the associated index files, Access will update the indexes every time it changes the DBF file. By attaching a DBF file and its associated indexes, Access can link to DBFs in real time in a network environment. Access recognizes and enforces the automatic record locking of dBASE and FoxPro, as well as the file and record locks placed with *x*BASE commands and functions.

You should always tell Access about any indexes associated with the database. If you don't let Access know about the indexes, it will not update them. By not updating the associated index files, dBASE or FoxPro will have unexpected problems.

When you tell Access to use one or more associated indexes (NDX, MDX, IDX, or CDX) of a dBASE or FoxPro file, Access maintains information about the fields used in the index tags in a special information file. This file has the same name as the dBASE or FoxPro file with an extension of INF.

If you attach to a dBASE or FoxPro table on a read-only drive (like a CD-ROM), you must set a parameter in the MSACC20.INI file to tell Access where it can write the INF file. For example, if you want Access to write the INF file to the Access directory — ACCESS20 — on drive C, you add the following entry to the [dBASE ISAM] section of the MSACC20.INI file:

INFPath=C:\ACCESS20

If you attach a dBASE or FoxPro file and associated indexes, Access must have access to the index files in order to attach the table. If you delete or move the index files or the Access INF file, you will not be able to open the attached DBF file.

Attaching to dBASE IV tables

To attach the dBASE IV table PETSIV.DBF and its associated memo file (DBT), follow these steps:

Steps:	Attaching to a dBASE IV Table with No Index
Step 1.	Open the ATCIMPEX database and select either File⇨Attach Table... or press the Attach Database button on the toolbar.
Step 2.	In the Attach dialog box, select Data Source: dBASE IV. Access activates the Select File dialog box and displays all DBF files.
Step 3.	Double-click PETSIV.DBF in the File Name list box. (The memo file PETSIV.DBT is automatically attached with the DBF extension.) Access activates the Select Index Files box and displays all NDX and MDX files.
Step 4.	Click the Close button (there are no related indexes for this table). Access closes the Select Index Files box and displays a dialog box similar to Figure 24-5. **Note:** If there were any indexes to associate with this table, you would select them here.
Step 5.	Click the OK button. Access redisplays the Select File dialog box.
Step 6.	Click the Close button to end attaching dBASE files. Access displays the Database window with the file PETSIV attached.

You can cancel attaching at any time by clicking the Close button in the Select File dialog box before selecting a table.

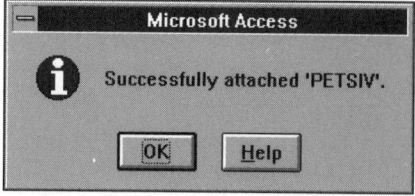

Figure 24-5:
The message box showing that the attached DBF database is completed.

Attaching to dBASE III table with an index

You attach to dBASE III or FoxPro tables exactly the same way you attached to the PETSIV.DBF. For example, there is a dBASE III table named VISITDTL.DBF and an associated index VISITDTL.NDX that you can attach to. When you attach this table, you need to specify the index file. In Step 4 of *Attachng to a dBASE Table with No Index,* you would select the File Name — VISITDTL.NDX — in the dialog box and Access will inform you that it added the index file.

When you add index files, Access automatically creates and updates an Access information file with information about the index and associated dBASE or FoxPro file. This information file has the same name as the dBASE or FoxPro file and ends in the extension INF.

Attaching to Paradox tables

You can attach DB files in either Paradox 3.x or Paradox 4.x format. Like with other Access database tables, once a Paradox file is attached, you can view and edit data in the DB format.

Access and Paradox index files

If a Paradox table has a primary key defined, it maintains the index information in a file that ends in the extension PX. When you attach a Paradox table that has a primary key defined, Access automatically attaches the associated PX file.

 If you attach a Paradox table that has a primary key, Access needs the PX file to open the table. If you move or delete the PX file, you will not be able to open the attached table.

Part IV: Advanced Database Features

If you attach a Paradox table to Access that does not have a primary key defined, you will not be able to update data in the table using Access. The table can be used only for viewing.

Access can link to DBs in real time in a network environment. Access recognizes and enforces the file and record locking of Paradox.

If you attach a Paradox table to an Access database that is on a server (such as an SQL server) with multiple users, you will have to set the ParadoxNetPath option in the [Paradox ISAMs] section of the MSACCESS.INI file. For example, if the database resides in directory \GRPDOX on drive M, you use the following setting:

ParadoxNetPath = M:\GRPDOX\

Attaching to Paradox tables

To attach the Paradox 3.5 table OTHRCUST.DB and its associated index file (PX), follow these steps:

Steps:	Attaching to a Paradox Table with Index
Step 1.	Open the ATCIMPEX database and select File⇨Attach Table....
Step 2.	In the Attach list box, select Data Source: Paradox. Access activates the Select File dialog box and displays all DB files.
Step 3.	Double-click OTHRCUST.DB in the File Name list box. Access displays a dialog box informing you that it has attached the table.
Step 4.	Click the OK button. Access redisplays the Select File dialog box.
Step 5.	Click the Close button to end attaching Paradox files. Access displays the Database window with the file OTHRCUST attached.

If the Paradox table you select is encrypted, Access activates a dialog box and prompts you for the password. Type the password for the table and select the OK button.

Attaching to Btrieve tables

With Access, you can attach to Btrieve tables (5.*x* and 6.*x* format). You do not specify the actual table name (DAT file). Rather, you specify where to find the Xtrieve dictionary files (FILE.DDF and FIELD.DDF). These files contain information about your Btrieve database. Access uses them to determine the tables you can attach to.

You must have the Xtrieve files FILE.DDF and FIELD.DDF to attach Btrieve files.

To use Btrieve data, you must have the Btrieve for Windows dynamic-link library (WBTRCALL.DLL), which is not included with Access. It is available with Windows-based products that use Btrieve, such as Novell Btrieve for Windows and Novell NetWare SQL.

The following steps demonstrate how to attach to a Btrieve file:

Steps:	Attaching to a Btrieve File
Step 1.	Open an Access database and select File⇨Attach Table....
Step 2.	In the Attach list box, select Data Source: Btrieve. Access activates the Select File dialog box and displays the filename FILE.DDF.
Step 3.	Double-click the Xtrieve dictionary file, FILE.DDF, in the File Name list box. Access displays a Tables box showing you all tables you can attach to.
Step 4.	Double-click the table you want.
Step 5.	Click the Attach button. If the table requires a password, Access prompts you for it. Access presents a dialog box informing you that it has attached the table.
Step 6.	Click the OK button. Access redisplays the Tables box.
Step 7.	Click the Close button to end attaching Btrieve files. Access displays the Database window with the Btrieve files attached.

If you move or delete the Xtrieve dictionary files, FILE.DDF, or your DAT files, Access will not be able to open the attached Btrieve tables.

Attaching to SQL database tables

Using Access, you can attach to tables in SQL databases (for example, a Microsoft SQL server, a Sybase server, or an Oracle server database). Unlike when attaching to other tables, you are required to use Microsoft's Open Database Connectivity (ODBC) drivers.

Before attaching to SQL server tables, you must install the appropriate ODBC drivers. The drivers may not be included with Access. If the drivers are not included, contact the ODBC database vendor for the specific driver (such as Oracle, and so on). When installing ODBC, be sure to install the ODBC*.DLLs to the *Windows*/System subdirectory.

Once attached to an SQL server, you can work with tables or views. Tables can be viewed and edited. In contrast, views are read-only and can only be viewed.

Attached SQL server tables can be edited only when the table contains a unique index. If the SQL server table does not have a unique key index, the table can be used for viewing only.

When you want to attach SQL server tables, Access prompts you for the name of the ODBC data source you want to connect to. When installing ODBC, you can specify several different data sources available on your network. The following steps explain how to attach SQL server tables:

Steps:	Attaching to an SQL Table
Step 1.	Open an Access database or switch to the Database window and select File⇒Attach Table....
Step 2.	In the Attach list box, select Data Source: <SQL Database>. Access activates the SQL Data Sources dialog box.
Step 3.	Double-click the ODBC data source you want to attach to. Access displays the Login dialog box for the ODBC data source selected.
Step 4.	Enter your login ID and password on the SQL server.
Step 5.	Click the OK button. Access connects to the SQL database and displays the SQL Tables dialog box.
Step 6.	Select the table you want to attach to in the Import Objects dialog box.
	When you attach an SQL table, you choose whether you want Access to prompt for a login ID and password each time you connect to the SQL server. You can have Access prompt you one time and store the connection information in your database. By storing connection information in Access, you won't have to type it each time you attach to the table. To do this, select the Save Login ID and Password Locally checkbox when you attach the table.
Step 7.	Click the Attach button. Access returns to the SQL Tables dialog box. Access informs you that it attached the SQL table.
Step 8.	Click the Close button.

 Once an SQL server table is attached, Access maintains information about the table's name and field structure. If these are changed after you attach to the table, or if your password changes on the SQL server, you must delete the link to the table and reattach to it.

Working with Attached Tables

After you attach to an external table from another database, you can use it just as you do another Access table.

Once attached, external tables can be used with forms, reports, and queries. When working with external tables, you can modify certain features of the external tables. For example, you can rename the table, set view properties, and set links between tables in queries.

Setting view properties

Although an external table can be used like another Access table, you cannot change the structure (delete, add, or rearrange fields) of an external table. However, several table properties can be set for the fields in an attached table. The following field properties can be set for attached tables:

- Format
- Decimal Places
- Caption
- Input Mask

Setting relationships

Access does not let you set permanent relations at the table level between external tables and Access tables. If you need to set a relation between an external table and another Access table, you must do it in a query. The query can then be used in a form, another query, or a report.

Setting links between external tables

To set a link between an external table and another Access table, simply create a query and use the drag-and-drop method of setting links. Once a link is set, you can change the join properties from an equi-join (inner join) to an external join by double-clicking the link.

Using external tables in queries

When using a query, you can join the external table with another table, internal or external. This gives you powerful flexibility when working with queries. Figure 24-6 shows a query using several different database sources:

- Several internal Access tables
- An external Access table
- A Paradox 3.5 table
- A dBASE III table
- A dBASE IV table

Notice that the query in Figure 24-6 has joins between all tables. It contains both equi-joins (default) and outer joins (between the VISITDTL table and the two lookup tables). This query will obtain information from all the tables and display a datasheet similar to the one in Figure 24-7.

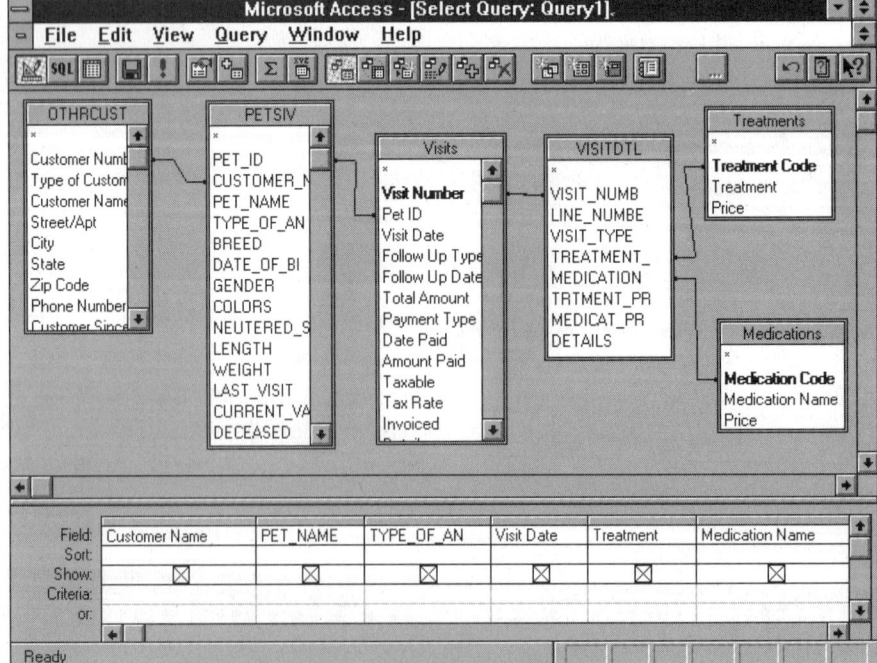

Figure 24-6: A query using several external database tables.

Figure 24-7: A datasheet display of the dynaset created by the query in Figure 24-6.

Customer Name	PET_NAME	TYPE_OF_AN	Visit Date	Treatment	Medica
Johnathan Adams	Patty	PIG	4/20/93	Repiratory Examination	Aspirin - 10
Johnathan Adams	Patty	PIG	4/20/93	Spay/Neuter	Dual Antibi
Johnathan Adams	Patty	PIG	4/20/93	Sterilize Area	Lariephogy
Johnathan Adams	Rising Sun	HORSE	2/11/93	General Examination	Aspertane
William Adams	Dee Dee	DOG	1/27/93	Repiratory Examination	Aspirin - 10
Stephen Brown	Suzie	DOG	1/16/93	Spay/Neuter	Byactocain
Stephen Brown	Suzie	DOG	1/16/93	Repiratory Examination	Aspertane
George Green	Adam	FROG	3/22/93	Anestizie Patient	Dual Antibi
George Green	Adam	FROG	1/26/93	Amputation of limb	Byactocain
George Green	Adam	FROG	5/17/93	Rectal Examination	Byactocain
George Green	Adam	FROG	1/26/93	Reset dislocation	Hydrocortir
George Green	Adam	FROG	3/22/93	Removal of external growth	Tylinol - 40
George Green	Adam	FROG	6/17/93	Repiratory Examination	Nyostatine
Patricia Irwin	C.C.	CAT	1/15/93	Haircut	
Patricia Irwin	C.C.	CAT	1/15/93	General Examination	Aspirin - 10
Patricia Irwin	C.C.	CAT	1/15/93	Sterilize Area	Biopurple F
Patricia Irwin	C.C.	CAT	6/17/93	Eye/Ear Examination	Byactocain
Patricia Irwin	C.C.	CAT	1/15/93	Spay/Neuter	Dual Antibi

Renaming tables

You can rename an attached external table. Because Access lets you name a table with up to 64 characters (including spaces), you may want to rename an attached table to be more descriptive. For example, you may want to rename the dBASE III table called VISITDTL to Visit details file for pets from dBASE III file VISITDTL.

To rename a file you can select File⇨Rename... from the Database menu. Another, quicker method is to right-click the filename and select Rename... from the shortcut menu.

In renaming an external file, Access does not rename the actual DOS filename or SQL server table name. It only renames it in the Table object list of the Access database.

Optimizing attached tables

When working with attached tables, Access has to retrieve records from another file. This process takes time, especially when the table resides on a network or in an SQL database. When working with external data, you can optimize performance by observing these points:

- Avoid using functions in query criteria.

    This is especially true for aggregate functions like DTotal or DCount. These functions automatically retrieve all records from the attached table and then perform the query.

- Limit the number of external records to view.

    Create a query specifying a criteria limiting the number of records from an external table. This query can then be used by other queries, forms, or reports.

- Avoid excessive movement in datasheets.

    View only the data you need to in a datasheet. Avoid paging up and down and jumping to the last or first record in very large tables. The exception to this is when adding records to the external table.

- When you add records to external tables, use a form.

    If you add records to external attached tables, create a form to add records and set the Default Editing property to Data Entry. This makes the form an entry form and starts with a blank record every time it is executed.

- Minimize locks against records.

    When working with tables in a multiuser environment, minimize locking records. This will free up records for other users.

Deleting a linked table reference

To delete a linked table from the Database window, follow these steps:

Steps:	Deleting a Linked Table from the Database
Step 1.	In the Database window, select the attached table you want to delete.
Step 2.	Either press the Delete key or select Edit⇨Delete from the Database menu.
Step 3.	Select OK in the Access dialog box to delete the file.

 Deleting an external table will delete only its name from the database object list. The actual file will not be deleted at the DOS level.

Viewing or changing information for attached tables

Once a table is attached, it or its associated indexes cannot be moved. If they are, Access will not be able to find the table. In version 1.x, this meant that you had to delete the attached table from the database container and reattach it. In version 2.0, you can use one of the new Add-In tools — the Attachment Manager.

Chapter 24: Working with External Data

If you move, rename, or modify indexes associated with an attached table, you can use the Attachment Manager tool to change the information. To use the tool, select File⇨ Add-Ins⇨Attachment Manager. Access will activate a Zoom dialog box similar to the one in Figure 24-8. Select the attached table that needs the information changed, and Access will verify that the file cannot be found and prompt you for the new information.

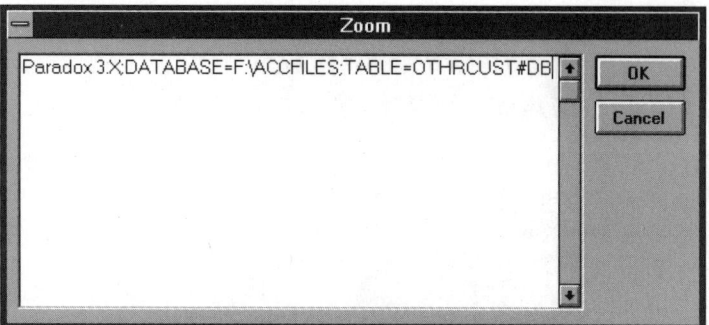

Figure 24-8: The Attachment Manager.

Importing External Data

Unlike when attaching tables, when you import a file, you copy the contents from an external file into an Access table. You can import external file information from several different sources:

- Microsoft Access (other unopened databases)
- Paradox 3.*x* and 4.*x*
- FoxPro (2.0 and 2.5)
- dBASE (III and IV)
- Btrieve (5.*x* and 6.*x*, with Xtrieve dictionary file)
- SQL databases (Microsoft SQL server, Sybase server, and Oracle server)
- Delimited text files (fields separated by a delimiter)
- Fixed-width text files (specific widths for each field)
- Microsoft Excel (versions 2.*x*, 3.*x*, and 4.*x*)
- Lotus 1-2-3 and 1-2-3/W (versions WKS, WK1, and WK3)

You can import information either to new tables or existing tables, depending on the type of data being imported. All data types can be imported to new tables. However, only spreadsheet and text files can be imported to existing tables.

When Access imports data from an external file, it does not erase or destroy the external file. Therefore, you will have two copies of the data — the original file in the original format and the new Access table.

 If the filename of the importing file is already an Access table, Access adds a chronological number (1, 2, 3, and so on) to the file until it has a unique table name. For example, if an importing spreadsheet name is Customer.XLS and if there is an Access table named Customer, the imported table name becomes Customer1. If Customer and Customer1 tables already exist, Access creates a table named Customer2.

Importing other Access objects

You can import other Access database tables or any other object in another database. This means that you can import an existing table, query, form, report, macro, or module from another Access database. As an example, you can import the States table from the MTNANHSP Access database by following these steps:

Steps:	Importing Another Access Database Table
Step 1.	Open the ATCIMPEX database and select File⇒Import...from the menu or press the Input Table button on the toolbar.
Step 2.	In the Import box, select Data Source: Microsoft Access. Access closes the Import box and displays the Select Microsoft Access Database box.
Step 3.	Double-click MTNANHSP.MDB in the File Name list box. Access closes the selection box and opens the Import Objects dialog box.
Step 4.	Double-click States in the objects in the MTNANHSP.MDB list box. Access displays a dialog box that says Successfully Imported 'States'.
Step 5.	Click the OK button in the dialog box. Access returns you to the Import Objects dialog box.
Step 6.	Click the Close button.

Figure 24-9 shows the Database window display with the new table States added to the database. The table does not have an attach symbol in the icon. Unlike attaching the table, you have physically copied the States table and added it to the current database.

Besides adding tables from other Access databases, you can add other objects as shown in Figure 24-10. For example, you may want to add the query Database Diagram from the database MTNANHSP or some of the forms. To import other Access database objects, you use the same procedure you did for the Access table. You would change the Object Type: from databases to the object type you want to import (forms, queries, etc).

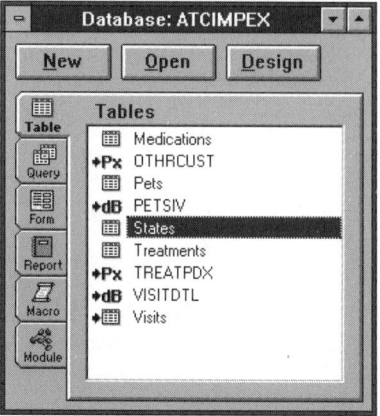

Figure 24-9:
The imported States table added to the Database window.

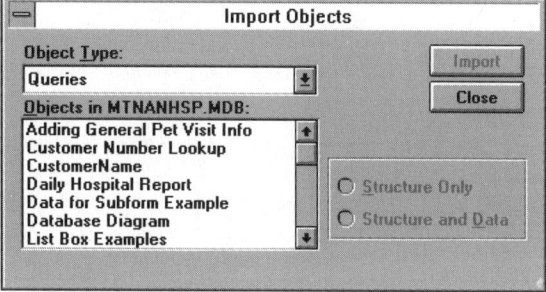

Figure 24-10:
Selecting a different Access database object to import.

 When importing Access objects, you may have to make changes to objects other than tables after you import them. For example, the database diagram you just imported includes several files that are not in the current table, so the diagram needs to be revised to reflect the new changes.

Importing PC-based database tables

When importing data from personal computer-based databases, you have two basic categories of database file types that you can import from:

- xBASE (dBASE, FoxPro)
- Paradox

Each type of database can be directly imported into an Access table. The native data types are converted to Access data types during the conversion.

Importing a PC-based database

You can import any Paradox, dBASE III, dBASE IV, or FoxPro 2.*x* database table into Access. To import a Paradox, dBASE III, dBASE IV, or FoxPro 2.*x* database, simply select the correct database type in the Import Data Source box of the import process.

After selecting the type of PC based database, you select which file you want to import, and Access imports the file for you automatically.

If you try to import a Paradox table that is encrypted, Access prompts you for the password after you select the table in the Select File dialog box. Enter the password and select the OK button to import an encrypted Paradox table.

When Access imports *x*BASE fields, it converts them from their current data type into an Access data type. Table 24-2 lists how the data types are converted.

When importing any *x*BASE database in a multiuser environment, you must have exclusive use of the file. If other people are using the file, you will not be able to import it.

Table 24-2
Conversion of Data Types from *x*BASE to Access

xBASE Data Type	Access Data Type
Character	Text
Numeric	Number (property of Double)
Float	Number (property of Double)
Logical	Yes/No
Date	Date/Time
Memo	Memo

Like with xBASE tables, when Access imports Paradox fields, it converts them from their current data type into an Access data type. Table 24-3 lists how the data types are converted.

Table 24-3
Conversion of Data Types from Paradox to Access

Paradox Data Type	Access Data Type
Alphanumeric	Text
Number	Number (property of Double)
Short Number	Number (property of Integer)

Paradox Data Type	Access Data Type
Currency	Number (property of Double)
Date	Date/Time
Memo	Memo
Blob (Binary)	OLE

Importing Btrieve tables

You can import a Btrieve table by following these steps:

Steps:	Importing Btrieve Tables
Step 1.	Open a database that you want to import into and select File⇨Import....
Step 2.	In the Import box, select Data Source: Btrieve. Access closes the Import box and displays the Select File dialog box.
Step 3.	Double-click the Xtrieve dictionary file, FILE.DDF, in the File Name list box. Access displays a Tables box of tables that can be imported.
Step 4.	Click the Btrieve table you want to import.
Step 5.	Click the Import button. Access displays a message box informing you that it has imported the table.
Step 6.	Click the OK button in the message box. Access returns you to the Tables dialog box.
Step 7.	Click the Cancel button. Access returns you to the Select File dialog box.
Step 8.	Click the Close button.

Access automatically imports the Btrieve table, naming the new Access table the same as the Btrieve table.

If you try to import a Btrieve table that is encrypted, Access prompts you for the password after you select it in the Tables dialog box (Step 4 of the preceding steps). Enter the password and select the OK button to import an encrypted Btrieve table.

When Access imports Btrieve fields, it converts them from their current data type into an Access data type. Table 24-4 lists how the data types are converted.

Table 24-4
Conversion of Data Types from Btrieve to Access

Btrieve Data Type	Access Data Type
String	Text
Istring	Text
zstring	Text
Integer 1 byte	Number (property of Byte)
Integer 2 byte	Number (property of Integer)
Integer 4 byte	Number (property of Long Integer)
Float - 4 byte	Number (property of Single)
bfloat - 4 byte	Number (property of Single)
Float - 8 byte	Number (property of Double)
bfloat - 8 byte	Number (property of Double)
Decimal	Number (property of Double)
Numeric	Number (property of Double)
Money	Currency
Logical	Yes/No
Date	Date/Time
Time	Date/Time
Note	Memo
Lvar	OLE object

Importing from an ODBC server database

When you want to import SQL server tables, Access will prompt you for the name of the ODBC data source you want to connect to. When you install ODBC, you specify the data source available on your network. The following steps explain how to import SQL server tables:

Steps:	Importing an SQL Table
Step 1.	Open an Access database or switch to the Database window and select File⇨Import....
Step 2.	In the Import box, select Data Source: <SQL Database>. Access activates the SQL Data Sources dialog box.

Chapter 24: Working with External Data

Step 3. Double-click the ODBC data source you want to attach to. Access displays the Login dialog box for the ODBC data source selected.

Step 4. Enter your login ID and password on the SQL server.

Step 5. Click the OK button. Access connects to the SQL database and displays the SQL Tables dialog box.

Step 6. Select the table you want to import in the Objects box.

Step 7. Click the Import button. Access returns to the SQL Tables dialog box. Access informs you that it attached the SQL table.

Step 8. Click the Close button. Access imports the SQL server file and gives it the same name in the Access database.

If you have problems while importing an SQL server table, the problem may be with your account on the SQL database server or the database itself. If you cannot access an SQL table, contact the SQL server administrator.

Importing spreadsheet data

You can import data from Excel or Lotus 1-2-3 spreadsheets. When you import data from a spreadsheet, you can import it to a new table or an existing table. The key to importing spreadsheet data is that the data must be arranged in tabular (columnar) format. In other words, each cell of data in a spreadsheet column must contain the same type of data. Table 24-5 demonstrates correct and incorrect columnar type data.

Table 24-5
Spreadsheet Cells with Contents

	A	B	C	D	E	F
1	TYPE	WEIGHT	BDATE		JUNK	GARBAGE
2	DOG	122	12/02/92		123	YES
3	CAT	56	02/04/89		22	134.2
4	BIRD	55	05/30/90		01/01/91	DR SMITH
5	FROG	12	02/22/88		TEST	$345.35
6	FISH	21	01/04/93		======	
7	RAT	3	02/28/93		$555.00	<== TOTAL

Table 24-5 is representative of several cells in a spreadsheet, with cells in the range A1 through F7. Notice that the data in columns A, B, and C and rows 2 through 7 is the same type. Row 1 contains field names. These columns can be imported into an Access table. On the other hand, columns E and F do *not* have the same type of data in each cell; therefore, these columns may cause problems when you try to import into an Access table.

To import an Excel spreadsheet named MORECUST.XLS, follow these steps:

Steps:	Importing an Excel Spreadsheet Database
Step 1.	Open the ATCIMPEX database and select File⇨Import....
Step 2.	In the Import box, select Data Source: Microsoft Excel. Access closes the Import box and displays the Select File dialog box.
Step 3.	Double-click MORECUST.XLS in the File Name list box. Access opens an Import Spreadsheet Objects dialog box for the table MORECUST.XLS; the dialog box resembles the one in Figure 24-11.
Step 4.	Click First Row Contains Field Names in the dialog box.
Step 5.	Click the Spreadsheet Range text box and enter **A1:C7**.
Step 6.	Click the OK button in the dialog box. Access displays a message box informing you that it has imported the records.
Step 7.	Click the OK button in the message box. Access returns you to the Select File dialog box.
Step 8.	Click the Close button.

Access added the table MORECUST to the Database window. Access creates a new table using the same name as the spreadsheet filename.

As Figure 24-11 shows, you have several options available to use when importing spreadsheet data. With the Import Spreadsheet Options dialog box, you can choose from the following options:

- Specify to use the first row for field names
- Create a new table (Table Options)
- Append to existing table (Table Options)
- Define a spreadsheet range to import from

You can set each option independently, so that you have flexibility in importing spreadsheet data.

Figure 24-11:
The Import Spreadsheet Options dialog box.

The First Row Contains Field Names option

The option First Row Contains Field Names is a checkbox you use to specify that the field names for the table are found in the first row of the spreadsheet. When you check this box, Access takes the first row and uses the contents of each column cell for the field names of the Access table.

If the spreadsheet's first row does not contain field names, Access automatically names the fields in numeric order from 1 to n. Therefore, the first field name is 1, the second is 2, and so on.

Table Options

Under Table Options, you have two choices: Create New Table or Append to Existing Table. If you append to an existing table, you specify the filename to append to by using the drop-down list box alongside the Append button.

The Spreadsheet Range option

The Spreadsheet Range option is used to specify a spreadsheet range to import from. For example, you can specify the range A1:C7 to import seven rows from columns A, B, and C.

If you specify a range and want to have the first row contain field names, you must include the first row in the range.

You can also specify a range name in the spreadsheet to import from a cell address range.

Importing from word processing files

Access does not offer a specific way to import data from word processing files. If you need to import data from a word processing file into Access, create a text file first and import the text file.

Importing text file data

You can import from two different types of text files, *delimited* and *fixed width*. These types of files use an *import/export specification* file. The file is optional for delimited text files, but it is mandatory for fixed-width text files. Unformatted mainframe data is generally transferred from the mainframe to a personal computer as a text file.

Delimited text files

Delimited text files (sometimes known as *CSV*, or *Comma Separated Values* files) are files in which each record is on a separate line in the text file. The fields on the line contain no trailing spaces, are separated by field separators (usually a comma), and require certain fields to be enclosed in a delimiter, such as single or double quotation marks. Usually, text fields are also enclosed in quotation marks or some other delimiter. The following material demonstrates this:

"Irwin","Michael","Metropolitan Police Dept",05/12/72
"Prague","Cary","Travelers Insurance",02/22/86
"Zimmerman-Schneider","Audrie","IBM",01/01/59
.
.
.

Notice that the file has three records (rows of text) and four fields. Each field is separated by a comma, and the text fields are delimited with double quotation marks. The starting position of each field, after the first one, is different. Each record has a different length because the field lengths are different.

You can import records from a delimited text file that has fields with no values. To specify a field with no value, place delimiters where the field value would be with no value in between, as in the example "Irwin","Michael",,05/12/72. Notice that there are two commas after the field content Michael and before the field content 05/12/72. The field between these two has no value and will be imported with no value into an Access file.

Fixed-width text files

Fixed-width text files also place each record on a separate line. However, the fields in each record are of a fixed length. If the field contents are not long enough, trailing spaces are added to the field. The following material demonstrates this:

Irwin	Michael	Metropolitan Police Dept	05/12/82
Prague	Cary	Travelers Insurance	02/22/86
Zimmerman-Schneider	Audrie	IBM	01/01/59

Notice that the fields are not separated by delimiters. Rather, they start at exactly the same position in each record. Each record has exactly the same length. If a field is not long enough, trailing spaces are added to fill the field.

You can import a text file to a new table or an existing Access table. If you decide to append to an existing table, the structure of the text file must match the Access table you want to import to.

If the Access table being imported into has a key field, the text file cannot have any duplicate key values or the import will report an error.

Importing delimited text files

To import a delimited text file named MEDLIMIT.TXT, follow these steps:

Steps:	Importing a Delimited Text File
Step 1.	Open the ATCIMPEX database and select File⇨Import....
Step 2.	In the Import box, select Data Source: Text (Delimited). Access closes the Import box and displays the Select File dialog box.
Step 3.	Double-click MEDLIMIT.TXT in the File Name list box. Access opens an Import Text Options dialog box for the table MEDLIMIT.TXT. The dialog box resembles the one in Figure 24-12.
Step 4.	Click the option First Row Contains Field Names in the dialog box.
Step 5.	Click the OK button in the dialog box. Access displays a message box informing you that it has imported the records.
Step 6.	Click the OK button in the message box. Access returns you to the Select File dialog box.
Step 7.	Click the Close button.

Figure 24-12:
The Import Text Options dialog box.

Access added the table MEDLIMIT to the Database window. Access creates a new table using the same name as the text filename.

As Figure 24-12 shows, you have several options available when you import delimited text file data. Three options are available in the Import Text Options dialog box:

- First Row Contains Field Names, where you specify use of the first row for field names
- Create New Table (under Table Options)
- Append to Existing Table (under Table Options), where you enter the existing Access table

If you select the Options>> button, the initial dialog box expands to one like you see in Figure 24-13. The additional options are the same as several setup options in the Import/Export Setup, which you'll learn about later in this chapter.

Using this dialog box, you can import delimited text files with a wide range of options.

If the delimited text file's first row does not contain field names, Access automatically names the fields in numeric order from 1 to *n*. Thus, the first field name is 1, the second 2, and so on.

Importing fixed-width text files

In fixed-width text files, each field has a specific width and position in the text file. The most common type of fixed-width text files are mainframe download files.

Before importing or exporting a fixed-width text file, you must specify an import/export setup specification. You create this setup file by selecting File⇒Imp/Exp Setup... in the Database menu.

Creating an Import/Export Setup

Access offers several options for importing and exporting text files. These options differ based on the operation and type of file being worked with. The different text file formats that Access can work with are as follows:

- Delimited text (separated by commas, tabs, none, or user-specified)
- Fixed-width text (each field has the same length with filler of blanks)

Each type of text file has records and fields. The records are specified by rows or lines of text. The fields are contained from left to right in a row of text.

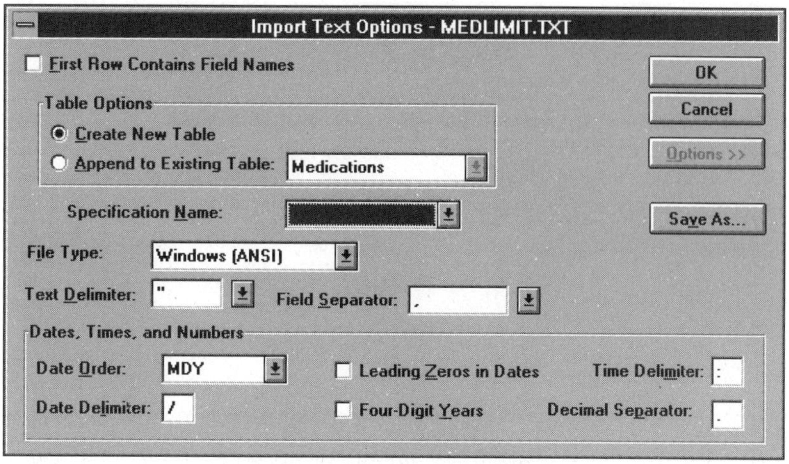

Figure 24-13:
The expanded Import Text Options dialog box for delimited text files.

Creating or editing text file setup specifications

An import/export specification stores information needed by Access to import/export a text file, such as the format you want Access to use for date fields. You can create an import/export specification and save it in a setup specification file. Once you save specific setup options, you can use the setup file every time you import or export similar data to or from your database.

If you import or export delimited text files, a setup file is optional. If your delimited text files are comma delimited, with dates in the format MM/DD/YY, you do not need a setup file. However, if you want to specify a different delimiter or date format, you may want to create a setup file.

On the other hand, when you work with fixed-width text, you must create an import/export setup file. This setup file must, at the minimum, specify the field names, field positions (order), and field lengths for each record of the file.

For example, you may need to import a fixed-width data file that you downloaded from your company's mainframe computer. The file you download may have a structure similar to that of Table 24-6.

Because this data has fixed lengths and specific formats, you will have to import it as a fixed-width text file. You must set up an import/export specification to assign field information and compensate for the date format.

Table 24-6
File Structure of Table

Field Name	Access Type	Format Information	Width
Pet Name	Text	Mixed case	22
Pet Date of Birth	Date	YYYY/MM/DD	10
Neutered or Spayed	Yes/No	1=yes, 0=no	1
Gender	Text	M or F, uppercase	1
Length	Number - Double	left justified 2 decimal	8
Type of Animal	Text	Uppercase	15

Note that Yes/No fields must have a 1 for Yes and a 0 for No in the text file. This is different from the way Access actually stores the Yes (−1 in Access).

To create an import/export specification for this table, follow these steps:

Steps: Creating an Import/Export Specification for a Fixed-Width Text File

Step 1. Open the ATCIMPEX database and select File⇒Imp/Exp Setup... from the main menu. Access opens the Import/Export Setup dialog box.

Step 2. Select DOS or OS/2 (PC-8) as the File Type option.

Step 3. Select YMD as the Date Order option.

Step 4. Click the Leading Zeros in Dates checkbox.

Step 5. Click the Four Digit Years checkbox.

Step 6. In the Field Information: (fixed width only) drop-down box, enter the contents found in Figure 24-14.

Step 7. Click the Save As... button.

Step 8. Type **Pet Fixed Length Text File** in the Specification Name box and press Enter or click the OK button.

Understanding setup options

Each setting (attribute or option) in the Import/Export Setup dialog box can be independently set. These settings, such as date formats, give you flexibility to fine-tune the type

Chapter 24: Working with External Data

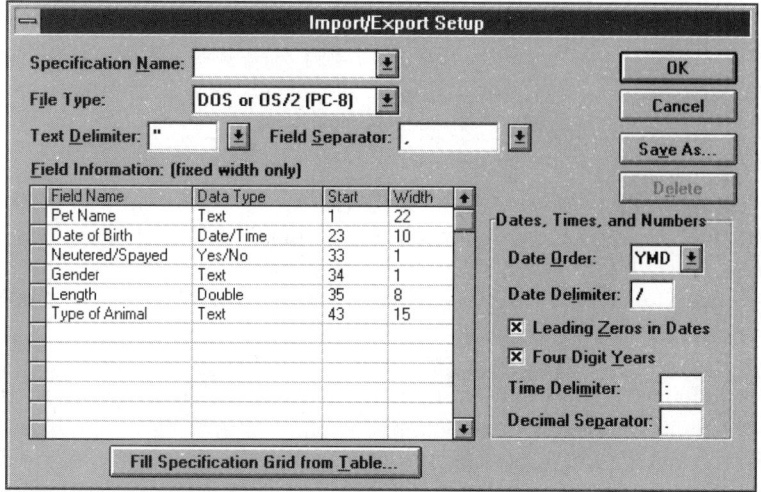

Figure 24-14: The Import/Export Setup dialog box.

of text file you can export or import. This eliminates the need to receive a restrictively formatted type of text file from another source. Once you create the settings, you must save them in a specification file.

The Specification Name option

After you create a setup specification file, you can use the Name option to select and edit an existing import/export specification. To edit an existing specification file, select the name of the specification you want to change.

The File Type option

You use the File Type option to specify a Windows text file or a DOS or an OS/2 text file. Two pull-down choices are offered:

- Windows (ANSI)
- DOS or OS/2 (PC-8)

The default value is the Windows text file. If the type of file you are importing is an MS/PC DOS or OS/2 text file, you select the DOS or OS/2 (PC-8) choice.

The Text Delimiter option

You use the Text Delimiter option for delimited text files only. This option specifies the type of delimiter to be used when you're working with Text type fields. Normally, in delimited text files, the text fields are enclosed by a specified delimiter, such as the quotation mark. This is useful for specifying Number type data (like Social Security numbers) as Text type rather than Number type. There are three list box choices:

{none} No delimiter

"   Double quotation mark

'   Single quotation mark

The default value is a double quotation mark. The list box is actually a combo box, where you can enter your own delimiter. If the delimiter you want is not one of these three choices, you can specify a different delimiter by entering a new text delimiter directly into the combo box. For example, the delimiter can be the caret symbol (^).

 If you specify your own delimiter, the specified delimiter must be the same on both sides of the text. For example, the curly braces ({}) cannot be used as a user-specified delimiter, as you can only specify one character. If you specify the left curly brace, Access looks only for the left curly brace as the delimiter on both sides of the text. The following illustrates how Access will look for the delimiters if you specify a brace:

{This is Text data enclosed in braces}

Notice that the left brace is used as the text delimiter on both sides of the text.

The Field Separator option

The Field Separator option is also used for delimited text files only. Delimited text files separate the fields by use of a special character, such as a comma or semicolon. Three field separator choices are available in this combo box:

{tab}   Tabulation mark

{space} Single space

,   Comma

As with the text delimiter, you can specify your own field separator directly in this combo box. For example, many delimited text files use the semicolon as a separator between fields.

 If you use CSV files, you should set the text delimiter to the double quotation mark (") and the field separator to a comma (,).

The Date Order option

When importing or exporting, Access converts dates to a specific format, such as MMDDYY, as it imports or exports the data. In the example MMDDYY, Access converts all dates to two digits for each portion of the date — the month, day, and year — separating each by a specified delimiter. For example, January 19, 1993, is converted to 1/19/93. Six choices are available in the pull-down box:

- DMY
- DYM
- MDY
- MYD
- YDM
- YMD

These choices specify the order for each portion of a date. The *D* is the day of month (1-31), *M* is the calendar month (1-12), and *Y* is the year. The default date order is set to the American format of month, day, and year. When you work with European dates, the order must changed to day, month, and year.

The Date Delimiter option

You use the Date Delimiter option to specify the date delimiter. This option tells Access what type of delimiter to use between the parts of date fields. The default is a forward slash (/), but this can be changed to any user-specified delimiter. For example, in Europe, date parts are separated by periods, as in 22.10.93.

When you import text files with date type data, you must have a separator between the month, day, and year, or Access reports an error if the field is specified as a Date/Time type. When you're exporting date fields, the separator is not needed.

The Leading Zeros in Dates option

The Leading Zeros in Dates option is a checkbox where you specify that date values include leading zeros. For example, you can specify that date formats include leading zeros, as in 02/04/93. To specify leading zeros, check this box. The default is without leading zeros, as in 2/4/93.

The Four Digit Years option

You use the Four Digit Years checkbox when you want to specify that the year value in date fields will be formatted with four digits. By checking this box, you can export dates that include the century, as in 1881 or 1993. The default is to exclude the century, as in a date expressed as 93.

The Time Delimiter option

With the Time Delimiter option, you can specify a separator between the segments of time values in a text file. The default value is the colon (:). In the example 12:55, the colon separates the hours from the minutes. To change the separator, simply enter another in the Time Delimiter box.

The Decimal Separator option

You use the Decimal Separator option to specify the character that separates the whole number from the fractional portion of a number. The default value is a period, as in the number 1234.56.

The Field Information: (fixed width only) option

As the option name specifies, the Field Information option is used only with fixed-width text files. You must create a specification file for importing or exporting fixed-width text files. At a minimum, you must enter information about each field that you want to import or export. Following is a list of the type of information you need to specify:

Field Name   The Access field name in the Access table

Data Type   The data type of the field, such as Text, Date/Time, Yes/No, and so on

Start   The field's starting position (column) in the text file

Width   The width of the individual field

Each of these columns must be specified for each field that you import or export.

When you export data to a fixed-width text file, you only have to specify field information for Access fields that you want to export to the text file. You are not required to specify all the fields in an Access table.

If you are importing fixed-width text files into an existing table, you must supply field information for each field in the correct order of the fields for the Access table. If you don't specify each field, Access may report an error.

Setup command buttons

In addition to all the options in the Import/Export Setup dialog box, there are four command buttons. Table 24-7 shows each button and explains its purpose.

Table 24-7
Setup Buttons and Purpose

Button Name	Purpose
OK	Leave and save changes in dialog box
Cancel	Abandon changes and leave dialog box
Save As...	Prompt for specification filename to save options to
Delete	Delete a specification name for import/export

Importing a text file (fixed width)

After you create the import/export specification, you can import a fixed-width text file. To import a file using the Pet Fixed Length Text File specification, follow these steps:

Steps: Importing a Fixed-Width Text File

Step 1. Open the ATCIMPEX database and select File⇒Import....

Step 2. In the Import box, select Data Source: Text (Fixed Width). Access closes the Import box and displays the Select File dialog box.

Step 3. Double-click PETFIXED.TXT in the File Name list box. Access opens the Import Text Options dialog box for the table PETFIXED.TXT. The dialog box resembles the one in Figure 24-15.

Step 4. Select Specification Name: Pet Fixed Length Text File.

Step 5. Click the OK button in the dialog box. Access displays a message box informing you that it has imported the file.

Step 6. Click the OK button in the message box. Access returns you to the Select File dialog box.

Step 7. Click the Close button.

Notice that Access has added the table PETFIXED to the Database window. Access creates a new table using the same name as the text filename.

As Figure 24-15 shows, there are only three import options available for fixed-width text files:

- Create New Table (Table Option)
- Append to Existing Table (Table Option)
- Specification Name

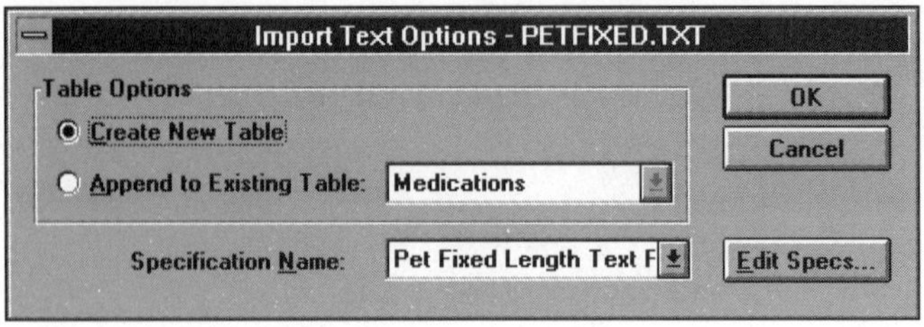

Figure 24-15: The Import Text Options dialog box.

You can append fixed-width text files to existing Access tables or create a new table by clicking the appropriate button.

Because fixed-width text files require an import/export specification setup file, the only other option is to specify a name in the Specification Name box. All the table options for this file are specified in the Import/Export Setup choice of the main menu. That is where you specified the field names, lengths, type of data, and special options (such as date format).

Modifying imported table elements

Once you import a file, you can refine the table in the Design view. The following list itemizes and discusses some of the primary changes you may want to make to improve your table:

- Add field names or descriptions

    You may want to change the names of the fields you specified when you imported the file. For example, *xBASE* databases allow only up to ten characters in names.

- Change data types

    Access may have guessed the wrong data type when it imported several of the fields. You can change these fields to reflect a more descriptive data type, such as Currency instead of Number or Text instead of Number.

- Set field properties

    You can set field properties to enhance the way your tables work. For example, you may want to specify a format or default value for the table.

- Define a primary key

    Access works best with tables that have a primary key. You may want to set a primary key for the imported table.

Figure 24-16:
The Import Results error message box.

Troubleshooting import errors

When you import an external file, Access may not be able to import one or more records and will report an error when importing the records. The error message will be similar to the one shown in Figure 24-16, which reports that errors were found. When Access encounters errors, it creates an Access table named Import Errors (with the user's name attached to the table name). The Import Errors table contains one record for each record that causes an error.

When errors are encountered and the Import Errors table is created, you can open the table to view the error descriptions.

Import errors for new tables

Access may not be able to import records into a new table for the following reasons:

- A row in a text file or spreadsheet may contain more fields than are present in the first row.
- Data in the field cannot be stored in the data type Access chose for the field.
- Access automatically chose the incorrect data type for a field, based on the first row's contents. The first row is OK, but the remaining rows are blank.

Import errors for existing tables

Access may not be able to append records into an existing table for the following reasons:

- The data is not consistent between the text file and the existing Access table.
- Numeric data being entered is too large for the field size of the Access table.
- A row in a text file or spreadsheet may contain more fields than the Access table.
- The records being imported have duplicate primary key values.

The Import Errors table

When errors occur, Access creates an Import Errors table that you can use to determine which data caused the errors.

Open the Import Errors table and try to determine why Access couldn't import all the records. If the problem is with the external data, edit it. If you are appending records to an existing table, the problem may be with the existing table, which requires modification, such as changing data types, rearranging field locations, and so forth. After you solve the problem, erase the Import Errors file and import the data again.

Access attempts to import all records that do not cause an error. If you reimport the data, you may need to clean up the external table or the Access table before reimporting. If you don't, you may have duplicate data in your table.

If importing a text file seems to take an unexpectedly long time, it may be because of too many errors. You can cancel importing by pressing Ctrl+Break.

Exporting to External Formats

You can copy data from an Access table or query into a new external file. This process of copying Access tables to an external file is called *exporting*. You can export tables to several different sources:

- Microsoft Access (other unopened databases)
- Delimited text files (fields separated by a delimiter)
- Fixed-width text files (specific widths for each field)
- Microsoft Excel (versions 2.*x*, 3.*x*, and 4.*x*)
- Lotus 1-2-3 and 1-2-3/W (versions WKS, WK1, and WK3)
- Paradox 3.*x* and 4.*x*
- FoxPro 2.*x*
- dBASE III and dBASE IV
- Btrieve (5.*x* and 6.*x*, with Xtrieve dictionary file)
- SQL databases (Microsoft SQL server, Sybase server, and Oracle server)

When Access exports data from an Access table to an external file, it does not erase or destroy the Access table. This means that you will have two copies of the data — the original Access file and the external data file.

Exporting objects to other Access databases

You can export objects from the current database to another, unopened Access database. The objects you export can be tables, queries, forms, reports, macros, or modules. To export an object to another Access database, follow these steps:

Steps:	Exporting to Another Access Database
Step 1.	Open the database that has the object you want to export and select File⇨Export... from the Database menu or select the Export button on the toolbar.
Step 2.	In the Export dialog box, select Data Destination: Microsoft Access. Access opens the Select Microsoft Access Object box.
Step 3.	In the Object Type list box, select the type of object (table, query, etc.) you want to export.
Step 4.	In the Objects list box, select the table or object you want to export. Access closes the dialog box and opens the Export to File dialog box.
Step 5.	In the Export to File dialog box, select the Access database you want to export to. Access closes the Export to File dialog box and opens the Export dialog box.
Step 6.	In the Export dialog box, enter a new object name or select OK.

Access copies the object you specified to the other database and immediately returns you to the Database window.

If you attempt to export an object to another Access database that has an object of the same type and name, Access warns you before copying. You then have the option to cancel or overwrite.

Exporting to spreadsheets

You can export data from a table or query to Microsoft Excel or Lotus 1-2-3 files. To export Access data to a spreadsheet, you would select the Data Destination as any spreadsheet type you want, pick the table or query to export, and enter the name of the file to export to.

Access copies the object to the specified spreadsheet file and immediately returns you to the Database window.

When exporting to a spreadsheet, Access places the current field names in the first row of the spreadsheet.

If you attempt to export an object to a spreadsheet that already exists, Access warns you before copying. You then have the option to replace the existing spreadsheet file or to cancel.

Exporting to PC-based databases

You can export Access tables or queries to several PC-based databases: dBASE III/IV, FoxPro 2.*x*, and Paradox 3.*x* and 4.*x*. When exporting tables to external databases, Access follows the field-naming convention of the destination file. For example, dBASE files can have field names only up to ten characters. Access uses the first ten characters for the name and truncates the remainder.

To export a table to a PC-based database, remember to specify the type of database to export to and the destination name of the new table to export to.

If field names are truncated, as can happen in a dBASE file export, the shortened names may now become duplicates. This causes Access to report an error. The error message specifies that Access cannot define a field more than one time. For example, if you try to export the OTHRCUST table to a dBASE file, Access converts the field name Customer Number to Customer_ and the field name Customer Name also to Customer_. Because the fields now have the same name, Access cannot export the data to the new dBASE file. Although Access cannot copy the data to the new file, it will create the dBASE file with header information.

Exporting to text files

You can export data from Access tables and queries to two different types of text files — delimited or fixed length. If you export to a fixed-length text file, you must specify an import/export specification file that you already created.

You export to text files the same way you export to any other external database — simply specify the type of text file to export to and any options if needed.

Exporting to word processor files

If you are working with a Windows word processing program, you can use the Clipboard to copy records from the datasheet into the document. If you are using a non-Windows (DOS) word processing program, you need to export the data to a text file first. Then you can import the text file into the word processing document.

Exporting to a Microsoft Word for Windows mail merge data file

You can create a *data file* (data source) for mail merging with Word for Windows. This data file can be used with the main document in Word for Windows for any merge document — mailing labels, form letters, and so on.

When Access creates a *data source file* (merge file), it places the field names from the table in the *header record,* the first row of the data file. Word for Windows uses this record to match the fields in the mail merge main document with the field names in the merge file. The order of the fields in the data source file is not critical. However, the field names to be merged must be spelled the same as the field names in the main document.

Access creates a data source file with the extension TXT. Word for Windows will look for a file with the extension DOC. Therefore, you should look in your directories for the extension TXT when you work with the data source file.

To create a Word for Windows merge text file, follow these steps:

Steps:	Exporting to a Word for Windows Merge Text File
Step 1.	Open the database that has the object you want to export and select File⇨Export... from the Database menu.
Step 2.	In the Export dialog box, select Data Destination: Word for Windows Merge. Access opens the Select Microsoft Access Object box.
Step 3.	In the Objects list box, select the table you want to export. Access closes the dialog box and opens the Export to File dialog box.
Step 4.	In the Export to File dialog box, enter the merge data filename you want to export to (the default is a TXT file).

Step 5.	Click the OK button or press Enter after entering a filename. Access opens the Export Word Merge Options dialog box.
Step 6.	If necessary, specify any merge text options.
Step 7.	Click the OK button. Access copies the object to the specified text file and immediately returns you to the Database window.

Access field names can have spaces and characters that are not allowed in a Word for Windows merge file. In addition, the field names in Access can be longer than ones allowed in a mail merge data file. Therefore, Access will create the data file automatically converting any field names to those allowed by Word for Windows. To do so, Access uses the following rules:

- Truncate all characters after the 20th character.
- Convert all spaces and illegal characters to underscores.
- Add the prefix "m_" to any field name that begins with a number or underscore.

Because of these potential conflicts, Access may create duplicate field names in the data file. If this happens, you can open the data file and change duplicate field names in Word for Windows. You may also need to open the file to correct field names to match any names in the main document.

Access will export all fields and all the data from the table to the mail merge data file. Word for Windows will ignore any fields that are not referenced by the main document. However, if you just want to export some of the data — for example, a range of data and/or a limited number of fields — create a make-table query first. You can then export only the data created from the query.

Exporting to Btrieve tables

You can export data to Btrieve tables by following these steps:

Steps:	Exporting to a Btrieve Table
Step 1.	Open the database that has the object you want to export and select File⇨Export... from the Database menu.
Step 2.	In the Export dialog box, select Data Destination: Btrieve. Access opens the Select Microsoft Access Object dialog box.

Chapter 24: Working with External Data

Step 3.	In the Tables in ATCIMPEX list box, select the table you want to export. Access closes the dialog box and opens the Export to File dialog box.
Step 4.	In the Export to File dialog box, select the Xtrieve dictionaryfile, FILE.DDF. Access displays the Export dialog box.
Step 5.	Enter a filename for the new table.
Step 6.	Click the OK button or press Enter after entering a filename.

Access copies the object to the specified Btrieve table and immediately returns you to the Database window.

 If you don't have a dictionary file, you can create one by exporting a table with a macro using the TransferDatabase action.

Exporting to an SQL database

You can export a table to an SQL database. However, before you can export to an SQL server, you must install the SQL server ODBC driver included with Access.

To export a table to an SQL server, follow these steps:

Steps:	Exporting to an SQL Server Table
Step 1.	Open the database that has the object you want to export and select File⇨Export... from the Database menu.
Step 2.	In the Export dialog box, select Data Destination: <SQL Database>. Access opens the Select Microsoft Access Object box.
Step 3.	In the Tables in ATCIMPEX list box, select the table you want to export. Access closes the dialog box and opens the Export dialog box.
Step 4.	In the Export dialog box, enter the table name to export to.
Step 5.	Click the OK button or press Enter after entering a filename. Access displays the SQL Data Sources dialog box.
Step 6.	Select the ODBC data source you want to export to and select the OK button. Access displays the Login dialog box for the ODBC data source.
Step 7.	Enter your login/user ID and password and then click the OK button.

Access copies the object to the specified SQL server table and immediately returns you to the Database window.

Moving Data between Windows Applications

Access supports Windows Dynamic Data Exchange as both a destination (client) and a source (server). Access also supports the Windows copy and paste capabilities for exchanging data between Windows applications.

To move data between Access and other Windows programs, you can use the Clipboard for copying. To copy Access data, select it and press Ctrl+C (or choose Edit⇨Copy). To paste the data, go to the other Windows application and press Ctrl+V (or choose Edit⇨Paste) where you want to paste the data.

Summary

- Access can work with various types of external data, including spreadsheets, PC-based databases, Btrieve tables, SQL server tables, and text files.

- Access can attach to other Access tables, *x*BASE (dBASE and FoxPro) databases, Paradox tables, and Btrieve and SQL server tables. When you attach to these tables through Access, you can view and edit the files in their native formats.

- You can use attached tables for queries, forms, and reports. You can set relations between attached tables and Access tables. You can even rename an attached table for better clarity.

- When you're working with text files (delimited and fixed length), you have extensive flexibility for importing and exporting them by using the import/export specifications setup file.

- When you create an import/export setup file, you can set several options, such as a specific delimiter, the format of date fields, and so forth.

- You can import data from other Access objects, dBASE databases, FoxPro databases, Paradox tables, Btrieve tables, SQL server tables, Excel spreadsheets, Lotus 1-2-3 spreadsheets, and text files. All these file types can be imported to new tables.

- Spreadsheets and text files can also be appended to existing Access tables.

- You can export Access table data to several different external files: dBASE databases, FoxPro databases, Paradox tables, Btrieve tables, SQL server tables, Excel spreadsheets, Lotus 1-2-3 spreadsheets, and text files.

- You can transfer data between Access and other Windows applications by using the Clipboard and the copy and paste operations.

In the next chapter, you examine advanced select queries.

Advanced Select Queries

CHAPTER 25

In This Chapter

- Creating queries that calculate totals
- Performing totals on groups of records
- Using different types of queries that total
- Specifying criteria for queries that total
- Creating crosstab queries
- Specifying criteria for crosstab queries
- Specifying fixed column headings for crosstab queries
- Creating a parameter query
- Running a parameter query
- Using the Parameter Query dialog box

In this chapter, you work with advanced select queries. So far, you've worked with relatively simple select queries, where you selected specific records from one or more tables based on some criteria. This chapter shows you queries that display totals, create cross tabulations, and obtain criteria from the user at run time.

So far, your queries specified criteria for single or multiple fields (including calculated fields) using multiple tables. You also worked with wildcard characters and fields not having a value (Is Null). You are already accustomed to using functions in queries to specify record criteria or to create calculated fields. Finally, you've realized that Access queries are a great tool for performing ad-hoc "what ifs."

This chapter focuses on three specialized types of advanced select queries:

- Total
- Crosstab
- Parameter

Using these queries, you can calculate totals for records, summarize data in row-and-column format, and run a query that obtains criteria by prompting the operator of the query.

Creating Queries That Calculate Totals

Many times, you want to find information in your tables based on total-type data. For example, you may want to find the total number of animals you've treated or the total amount of money each customer spent on animals last year. Access supplies the tools to accomplish these queries without the need for programming.

Access performs calculation totals by using nine aggregate functions that let you determine a specific value based on the contents of a field. For example, you can determine the average weight of all cats, the maximum and minimum length of all animals you have treated, or the total count of all records where the type of animal is either a duck or fish. Performing each of these examples as a query results in a dynaset of answer fields based on the mathematical calculations you requested.

To create a total query, you use a new row in the QBE pane — the Total: row.

Displaying the Total: row in the QBE pane

To create a query that performs a total calculation, you create a select query and then activate the Total: row of the QBE pane. You can activate the Total: row by either of these two selections:

- Select View⇨Totals from the Design menu.
- Select the Totals button (the Greek Sigma symbol button, which is third from the left) on the toolbar.

What Is an Aggregate Function?

The word *aggregate* implies gathering together a mass (group or series) of things and working on this mass as a whole — a total. Therefore, an aggregate function is a function that takes a group of records and performs some mathematical function against the entire group. The function can be a simple *count* or a complex *expression* that you specify, based on a series of mathematical functions.

Figure 25-1 shows the Total: row after it is added in the QBE pane. Notice that the Totals button is selected on the toolbar and the Total: row is placed in the QBE pane between the Table: and Sort: rows.

If the toolbar is not visible, select View⇨Options... from the Query menu. Then select Category: General and select the Items: Show Tool Bar and change its parameter to Yes.

If the Table: row is not present on your screen, the Total: row will be between the Field: and Show: rows. You can activate the Table: row by selecting View⇨Table Names from the Design menu.

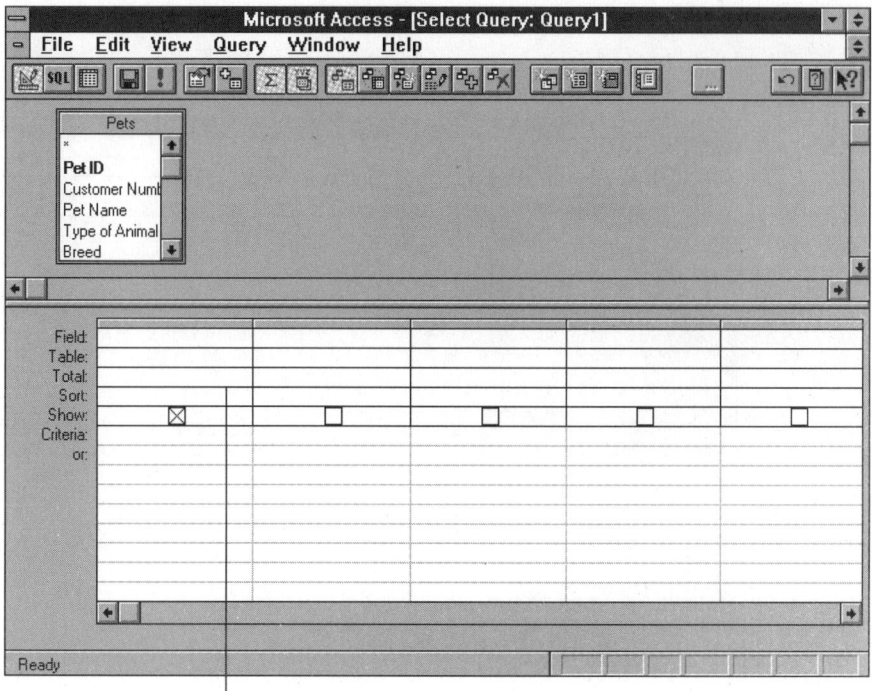

Figure 25-1: Activating the Total: row of the QBE pane.

Removing the Total: row from the QBE pane

To deactivate the Total: row in the QBE pane, simply reselect either activation method (with the Totals button or the menu choice). The Total activation is a toggle that alternately turns the Total: row on and off.

The Total: row options

You can perform total calculations against all records or groups of records in one or more tables. To perform a calculation, you must select one of the options from the drop-down list box in the Total: row for every field you include in the query, including any hidden fields (Show: option turned off). Figure 25-2 shows the drop-down list box active in the Total: row of the field Pet ID.

Although you see only eight options in Figure 25-2, there are actually twelve to choose from. You can view the remaining options by using the elevator on the right side of the box. The twelve options can be broken into four distinct categories:

- Group By
- Aggregate
- Expression
- Total field record limit

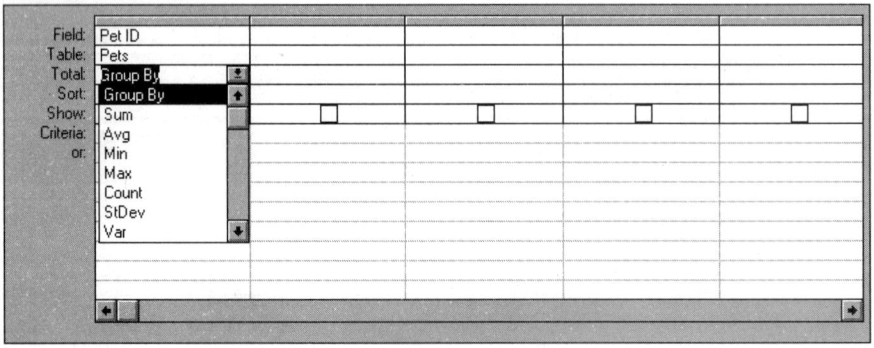

Figure 25-2: The dropdown list box of the Total: row.

Table 25-1 lists each category, its number of Total: options, and its purpose.

Table 25-1
Four Categories of Total Options

Category	Number of Options	Purpose of Operator
Group By	1	Groups common records together to perform aggregate calculations against
Aggregate	9	Specifies a mathematical or selection operation to perform against a field
Expression	1	Groups several total operators together and performs the group totals
Total field	1	Limits records before record limit performing a total calculation against a field

Notice that the aggregate category has nine options. Its options are used by the other three categories.

Group By category

This category has one option, the Group By option. You use this option to specify that a certain field in the QBE pane is to be used as a grouping field. For example, if you select the field Type of Animal, the Group By option tells Access to group all cat records together, all dog records together, and so on. This is the default option for all Total: cells; when you drag a field to the QBE pane, Access automatically selects this option. Figure 25-2 shows that this is also the first choice in the drop-down list box. These groups of records will be used for performing some aggregate calculation against another field in the query. This will be discussed later in further detail.

Expression category

Like the Group By category, the Expression category has only one option — Expression. This is the second-from-last choice in the drop-down list box. You use this option to tell Access that you will create a calculated field using one or more aggregate calculations in the Field: cell of the QBE pane. For example, you may want to create a query that shows each customer and how much money the customer saved, based on the individual's discount rate. This requires creating a calculated field that uses a sum aggregate against the Total Amount field in the Visits table, which is then multiplied by the Discount field in the Customer table. This type of calculation is be discussed in detail later.

Total Field Record Limit category

The Total Field Record Limit category is the third category that has a single option — the Where option. This option is the last choice in the drop-down list box. When you select this option, you tell Access that you want to specify a limiting criteria against an aggregate type field, as opposed to a Group By or an Expression field. The limiting criteria will be performed *before* the aggregate options are executed. For example, you may want to create a query that will count all pets by type of animal that weigh less than 100 pounds. Because the Weight field is not to be used for a grouping, as is Type of Animal, and won't be used to perform an aggregate calculation, you specify the Where option. By specifying the Where option, you are telling Access to use this field as a limiting criteria field only — before it performs the aggregate calculation (counting types of animals). This type of operation is also discussed in detail later in this chapter.

Aggregate category

The aggregate category, unlike the others, has nine options: Sum, Avg, Min, Max, Count, StDev, Var, First, and Last. These options appear as the second through tenth options of the drop-down list box. Each of these options performs some operation. Seven of the options perform mathematical operations, whereas two perform simple selection operations. When each option is executed, it finds — calculates or determines — some answer or value and supplies it to a cell in the resulting dynaset. For example, you may want to determine the maximum (Max) and minimum (Min) weight of each animal in the Type of Animal field in the Pets table. On the other hand, you may want the total number (Count) of animals in the Pets table. You use these aggregate options to solve such types of queries.

Options like these are what most people think about when they hear the words *total query*. Each of the options performs a calculation against a field in the QBE pane of the query and returns a single answer in the dynaset. As an example, there can only be one maximum weight for all the animals. Several animals may have the same maximum weight, but only one weight is the heaviest of all.

The other three categories of options can be used against any type of Access field (Text, Memo, Yes/No, etc.). However, some of the aggregate options can be performed only against specific field types. For example, you cannot perform a Sum option against Text type data, and you cannot use a Max option against an OLE object.

Table 25-2 lists each option, what it does, and what field types you can use with the option.

Performing totals on all records

You can use total queries to perform calculations against all records in a table or query. For example, you can find the total number of animals in the Pets table, their average weight, and the maximum weight of the animals. To create this query, follow these steps:

Steps: Creating a Totals Query against All Records of a Table

- **Step 1.** Select the Pets table.
- **Step 2.** Click the Totals button in the toolbar to turn it on.
- **Step 3.** Double-click the Pet ID field in the Pets table.
- **Step 4.** Double-click the Weight field in the Pets table.
- **Step 5.** Double-click the Weight field in the Pets table again.
- **Step 6.** In the Total: cell of Pet ID, select Count.
- **Step 7.** In the Total: cell of Weight, select Avg.
- **Step 8.** In the second Total: cell of Weight, select Max.

Table 25-2
Aggregate Options of the Total: Row

Option	Finds	Field Type Support
Count	The number of non-Null values in a field	Counter, Number, Currency, Date/Time, Yes/No, Text, Memo, OLE object
Sum	The total of the values in a field	Counter, Number, Currency, Date/Time, Yes/No
Avg	The average of values in a field	Counter, Number, Currency, Date/Time, Yes/No
Max	The highest value in a field	Counter, Number, Currency, Date/Time, Yes/No, Text
Min	The lowest value in a field	Counter, Number, Currency, Date/Time, Yes/No, Text
StDev	The standard deviation of values in a field	Counter, Number, Currency, Date/Time, Yes/No
Var	The population variance of values in a field	Counter, Number, Currency, Date/Time, Yes/No
First	The field value from the *first* record in a table or query	Counter, Number, Currency, Date/Time, Yes/No, Text, Memo, OLE object
Last	The field value from the *last* record in a table or query	Counter, Number, Currency, Date/Time, Yes/No, Text, Memo, OLE object

Your query should look similar to Figure 25-3.

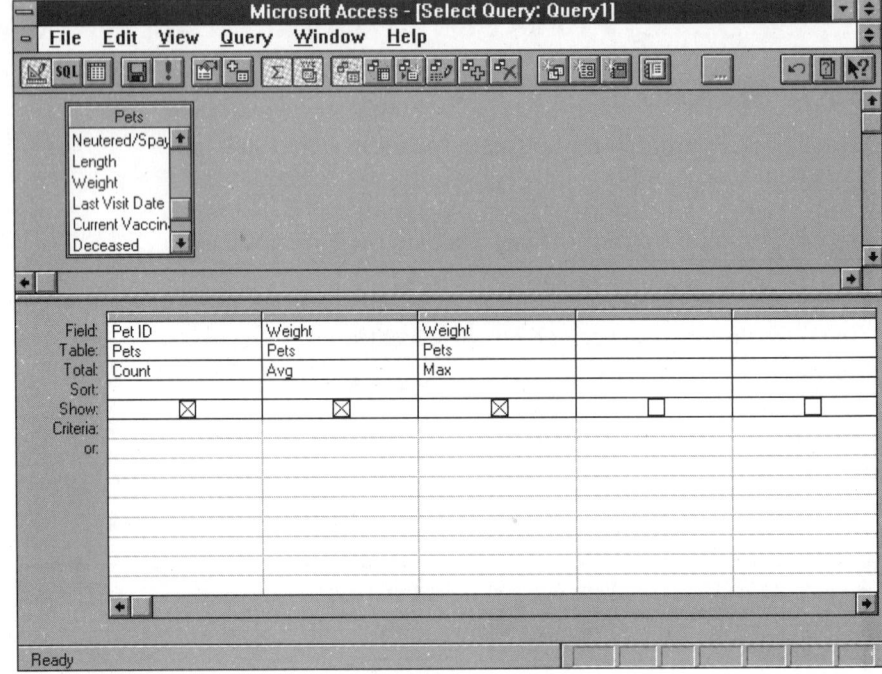

Figure 25-3:
A query against all records in the Pets table.

This query calculates the total number of pet records in the Pets table, as well as the average weight of all animals and the heaviest weight of all the animals.

The Count option of the Total: cell can be performed against any field in the table (or query). However, Count will eliminate any records that have a Null value in the field you select. Therefore, you may want to select the primary key field on which to perform the Count total, because this field cannot have any Null values, thus assuring an accurate record count.

If you select the Datasheet button on the toolbar, you should now see a query similar to Figure 25-4. Notice that the dynaset has only one record. When performing calculations against *all records* of a table or query, the resulting dynaset will have only *one* record.

Access creates a default column heading for all total fields in a totals datasheet, like the one you see in Figure 25-4. The heading name is a product of the name of the total option and the field name. Thus, you see in the figure that the heading names are CountOfPet ID, AvgOfWeight, and MaxOfWeight. You can change the column heading name to something more appropriate by renaming the field in the QBE pane of the Design window. As you do with any other field you want to rename, simply place the cursor at the beginning of the field cell you want to rename (to the left of the field name). After you place the cursor at the beginning, type the name you want to display, followed by a colon.

Chapter 25: Advanced Select Queries

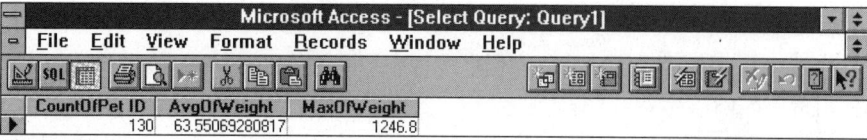

Figure 25-4:
This datasheet of a dynaset was created from a total query against all records in a table.

Performing totals on groups of records

Most of the time, you need to perform totals on a group of records rather than on all records. For example, you may need to calculate the total number of animals that you've treated for each type of animal. In other words, you want to create a group for each type of animal — bear, cat, dog, and so on — and then perform the total calculation against each of these groups. In database parlance, this is known as *control break* totaling.

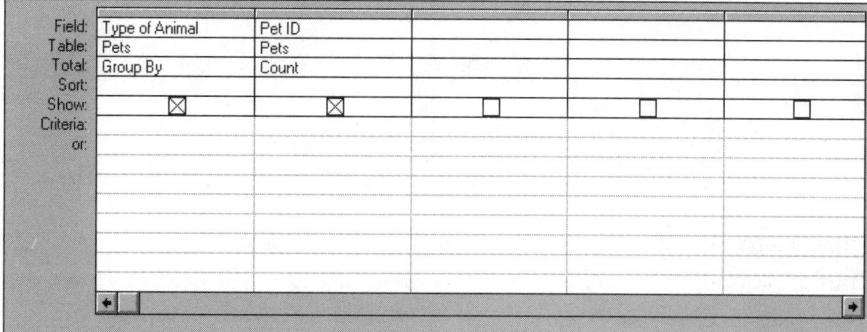

Figure 25-5:
Totals against a group of records.

Calculating totals for a single group

When you create your query, you specify which field or fields to use for grouping the totals and which fields to perform the totals against. Using the preceding example, to group the Type of Animal field, you select the Group By option of the Total: cell. Follow these steps to create the query:

Steps:	Creating a Totals Query Based on a Group
Step 1.	Select the Pets table.
Step 2.	Click the Totals button on the toolbar to turn it on.
Step 3.	Double-click the Type of Animal field in the Pets table.
Step 4.	Double-click the Pet ID field in the Pets table.
Step 5.	In the Total: cell of Type of Animal, select Group By.
Step 6.	In the Total: cell of Pet ID, select Count.

Figure 25-6: Datasheet of totals against the group Type of Animal field.

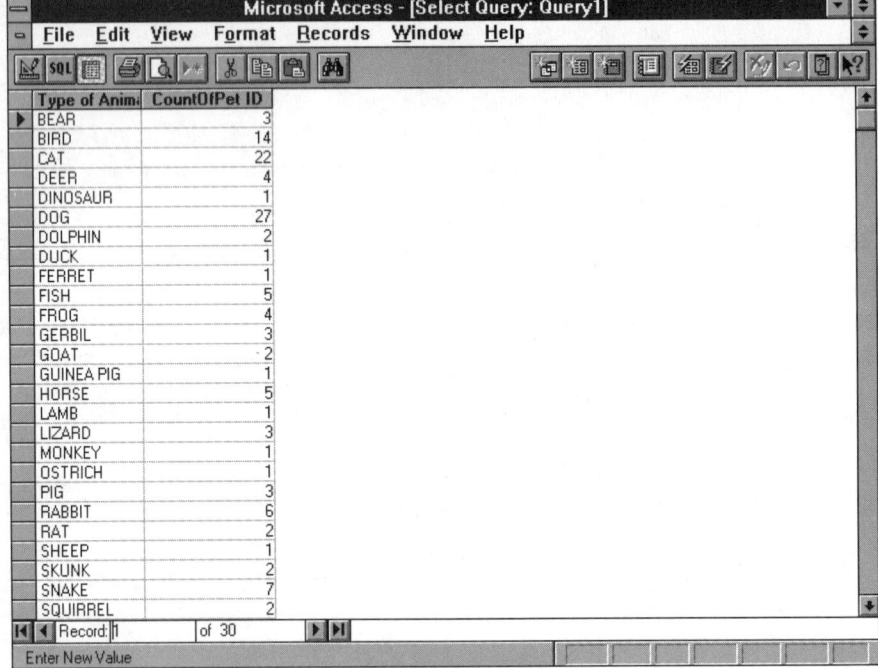

The query in Figure 25-5 groups all like animals together and then performs the count total for each type of animal. Unlike performing totals against all records, this query produces a dynaset of many records — one record for each type of animal. Figure 25-6 demonstrates how the datasheet looks if you select the Datasheet button on the toolbar.

The dynaset in Figure 25-6 has a single record for each type of animal. Notice that the count was performed against each type of animal; there are three bears, fourteen birds, and so on. Also notice that the Group By field displays one record for each unique value in that field. The Type of Animal field is specified as the Group By field and displays a single record for each type of animal, showing Bear, Bird, Cat, Dog, etc. Each of these records is shown as a row heading for the datasheet, indicating a unique record for each type of animal specified that begins with the Group By field content (bear, bird, etc.). In this case, each unique record is easy to identify by the single-field row heading under Type of Animal.

Calculating totals for several groups

You can perform group totals against multiple fields and multiple tables as easily as with a single field in a single table. For example, you may want to group by both customer and type of animal to determine the number of animals each customer owns by animal type. To create a total query for this example, you specify **Group By** in both Total fields (Customer Name and Type of Animal).

Chapter 25: Advanced Select Queries 717

This query, shown in Figure 25-7, uses two tables and also groups by two fields to perform the count total. First, the query groups by Customer Name and then by Type of Animal. When you select the Datasheet button on the toolbar, you see a datasheet similar to the one in Figure 25-8.

The datasheet in Figure 25-8 shows several records for the customer Animal Kingdom. This customer has three cats, two dogs, one rat, and one squirrel. This datasheet has a unique record based on two Group By fields — Customer Name and Type of Animal. Therefore, the unique row headings for this datasheet are created by combining both fields — first the Customer Name and then the Type of Animal.

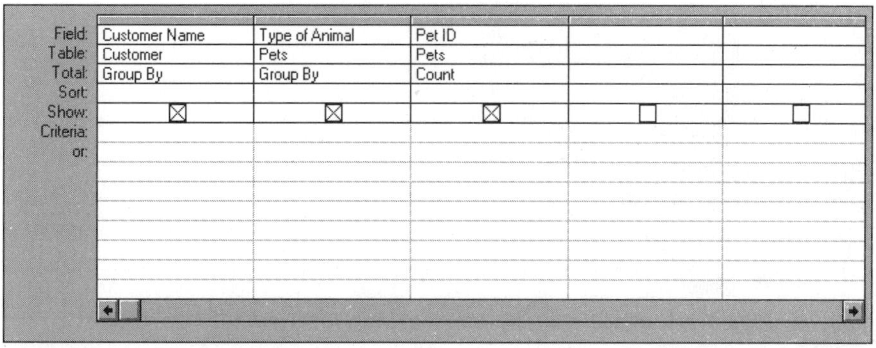

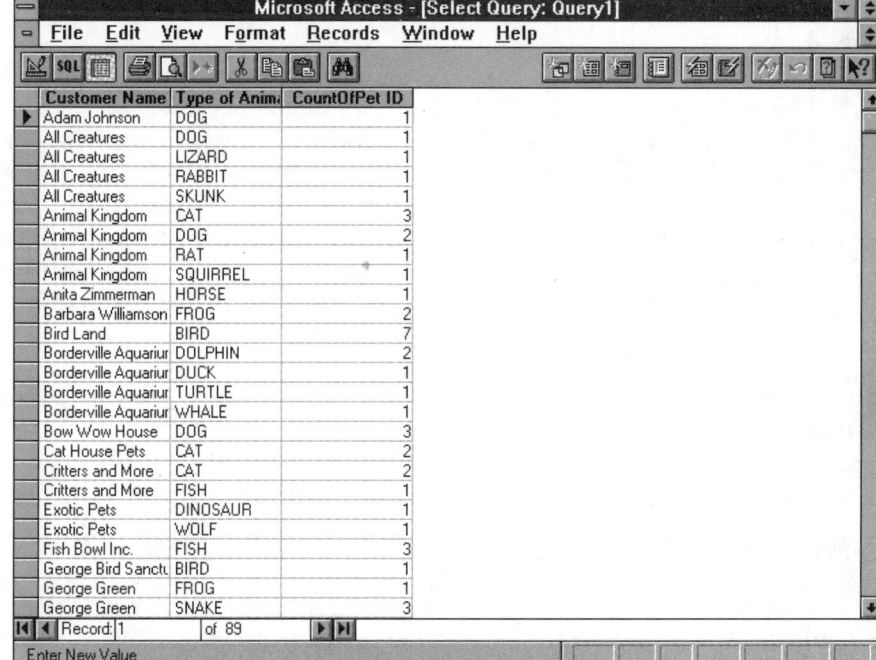

Figure 25-7: A multiple-table, multiple-field Group By total query.

Figure 25-8: Datasheet of a multiple-field Group By query.

Figure 25-9: Changing the order of Group By fields.

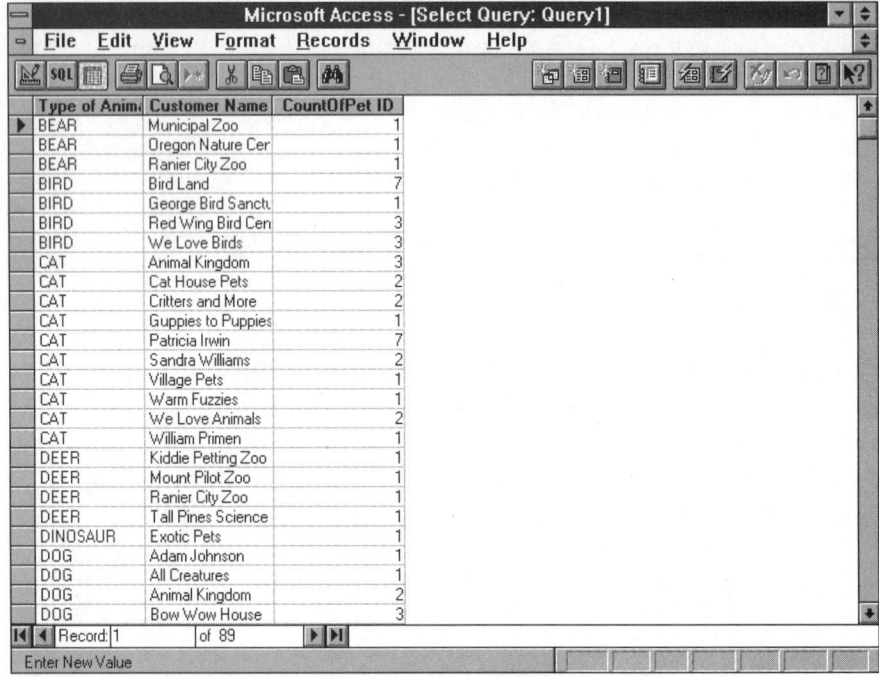

You can think of the Group By field(s) in a total query as fields that specify the row headings of the datasheet.

Access groups records based on the order of the Group By fields in the QBE pane (from left to right). Therefore, you should pay attention to the order of Group By fields. Although the order doesn't change the aggregate totals of the fields, the order of Group By fields does determine how you see the results in the datasheet. If you place the Type of Animal field before the Customer Name field, the resulting datasheet shows the records in order by animal first and then customer. Figure 25-9 demonstrates this setup, showing the bear records and their owners (with the total number) and then the bird records and their owners, and so on.

By changing the order of the Group By fields in a totals query, you can look at your data in new and creative ways.

Specifying criteria for a total query

Besides grouping records for total queries, you can also specify criteria to limit the records that will be processed or displayed in a total calculation. When you're specifying record criteria in total queries, you have several options available to you. You can create a criteria against these three fields:

- A Group By field
- An Aggregate Total field
- A Non-Aggregate Total field

Using any one or all three of these criteria types, you can easily limit the scope of your total query to a finite criteria.

Specifying criteria for a Group By field

To limit the scope of records that will be used in a grouping, you specify a criteria in the Group By fields. For example, you may want to calculate the average length and weight of only three animals — bears, deer, and wolves. Doing so requires specifying a criteria on the Group By field Type of Animal. Such a query looks like Figure 25-10.

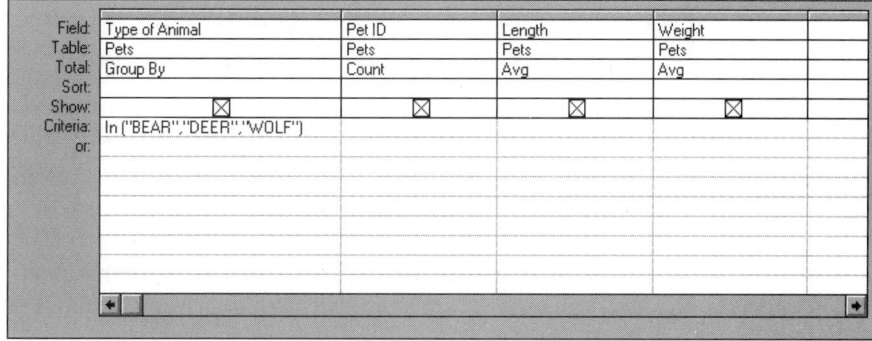

Figure 25-10: Specifying a criteria in a Group By field.

By specifying a criteria in the Group By field, only those records that meet the Group By criteria will have the aggregate calculations performed. In this example, the count, average length, and average weight will be performed only for animals that are bears, deer, and wolves. This results in a three-record dynaset, with one for each animal.

Specifying criteria for an Aggregate Total field

There are times when you want a query to calculate aggregate totals first and then display only those totals from the aggregate calculations that meet a specified criteria. In other words, you want Access to determine all totals for each Group By field and then take the totals field and perform the criteria against the totals before creating the resulting dynaset.

For example, you may want a query to find the average length of all animals, grouped by type of animal, where the average length of any animal is greater than 20 inches. This query should look like Figure 25-11. Notice that the criteria >20 is placed in the aggregate total field, Length. This query calculates the average length of all animals grouped by type of animal. Then the query determines whether the calculated totals for each record are greater than 20. Records greater than 20 are added to the resulting dynaset, and records less than or equal to 20 are discarded. Note that the criteria is performed *after* the aggregate calculations are performed.

Figure 25-11: A query with a criteria set against an Aggregate Total field.

Specifying criteria for a Non-Aggregate Total field

The preceding example limited the records *after* performing the calculations against total fields. You also can specify that you want Access to limit the records based on a total field *before* performing total calculations. In other words, limit the range of records against which the calculation is performed. Doing so creates a criteria similar to the first type of criteria; the field you want to set a criteria against is not a Group By field.

For example, you may want to display the total amount of money charged for each animal during the first quarter of 1993. You want to use the Visit Date field to specify a criteria, but you don't want to perform any calculations against this field or to use it to group by. In fact, you don't even want to show the field in the resulting datasheet.

Figure 25-12 shows how the query should look. Notice that Access automatically turned the Show: cell off in the Visit Date field.

 Access automatically turns off the Show: cell whenever it encounters a Where option in the Total: cell of a field. Access understands that you are using the field only to specify criteria so you don't want to see it.

In the query that you just completed, Access displays only those records for pets that have visited the hospital in the first quarter of 1993. All other records are discarded.

Figure 25-12: Specifying a criteria for a Non-Aggregate field.

When you specify a Where option in a Total: cell, you cannot show the field. The reason is that Access uses the field to evaluate the Where criteria before performing the calculation. Therefore, the contents are useful only for the limiting criteria. If you try to turn on the Show: cell, Access will display an error message.

Creating expressions for totals

Besides choosing one of the Access totals from the drop-down list box, you can create your own total expression. You can base your total expression on several types of totals in an expression, such as when you use Avg and Sum or multiple Sums together. Or you can base your expression on a calculated field comprised of several functions — or a calculated field based on several fields from different tables. Suppose, for example, that you want a query that shows the total amount of money each customer owed before discount. Then you want to see the amount of money these customers saved based on their discount. You want the information to be grouped by customer. Follow these steps to create this query:

Steps: Creating an Expression Total

Step 1. Select the Customer, Pets, and Visits tables.

Step 2. Click the Totals button on the toolbar to turn it on.

Step 3. Double-click the Customer Name field in the Customer table.

Step 4. Double-click the Total Amount field in the Visits table.

Step 5. In the Total: cell of Customer Name, select Group By.

Step 6.	In the Total: cell of Total Amount, select Sum.
Step 7.	Click an empty Field: cell of the QBE pane.
Step 8.	Type **Total Saved:Sum([Visits]![Total Amount]*[Customer]![Discount])** in the cell.

Access generally places the total option Expression in the Total: cell of the calculated field Total Saved: (if it doesn't, place the total option Expression in the Total: cell).

Your query should be similar to Figure 25-13. Notice that the query uses two fields from different tables to create the Total Saved: calculated field. You had to specify both the table and the field name for each field that the Sum function used.

If you click the Datasheet button on the toolbar, your dynaset should be similar to Figure 25-14.

Notice in the datasheet in Figure 25-14 that the calculated field Total Saved shows up to 12 decimal places. You can limit the decimal places by using the Format( ) function around the Sum( ) function. To do so, add the following to the existing criteria formula in the calculated Field: cell:

Total Saved:**Format**(Sum([Visits]![Total Amount]*[Customer]![Discount]),**"Standard"**)

Creating Crosstab Queries

With Access, you can use a specialized type of total query, the crosstab, to display summarized data in a compact and readable format. A crosstab query summarizes the data in the fields from your tables and presents the resulting dynaset in a row-and-column format.

Understanding the crosstab query

Simply put, a crosstab query is a two-dimensional summary matrix that is created from your tables. This query presents summary data in a spreadsheet-like format that you create from fields you specify. This is a specialized type of total query in which the Total: row in the QBE pane is always active. The Total: row cannot be toggled off in a crosstab query!

Figure 25-13:
A query using an Expression total.

Field:	Customer Name	Total Amount	Total Saved: Sum([Visits]![Total Amount]*[Customer]![Discount])
Table:	Customer	Visits	
Total:	Group By	Sum	Expression
Sort:			
Show:	☒	☒	☒
Criteria:			
or:			

Figure 25-14:
A datasheet created by an Expression total.

Customer Name	SumOfTotal Amt	Total Saved
Adam Johnson	$167.80	0
All Creatures	$1,810.00	362.00000539422
Animal Kingdom	$1,273.00	254.60000379384
Anita Zimmerman	$50.00	
Barbara Williamson	$100.00	0
George Green	$1,389.50	0
James Brown	$100.00	10.000000149012
Johnathan Adams	$936.00	46.800000697374
Karen Rhodes	$281.00	0
Margaret McKinley	$60.00	0
Michael Johnson	$70.00	0
Patricia Irwin	$1,340.80	0
Sandra Williams	$643.00	0
Sandra Young	$234.00	0
Stephen Brown	$316.00	0
Tyrone Potter	$106.00	0
Wanda Greenfield	$30.00	0
William Adams	$77.00	3.8500000573695
William Price	$385.00	0
William Primen	$843.50	0

In addition, the Total: row of the QBE pane is used for specifying a Group By total option for both the row and the column headings. Like other total queries, the Group By option specifies the row headings for the query datasheet and comes from the actual contents of the field. However, unlike other total queries, the crosstab query also obtains its column headings from the value in a field (table or calculated) instead of from the field names themselves.

The fields used as rows and columns must always have Group By in the Total row. Otherwise, Access reports an error when you attempt to display or run the query.

For example, you may want to create a query that will display the Type of Animal field as the row heading and the owner's state as the column heading, with each cell containing a total for each type of animal in each state. Table 25-3 demonstrates how you want the query to look.

In Table 25-3, the row headings are specified by Type of Animal: Bear, Bird, and so on. The column headings are specified by the state: ID, OR, and WA. The cell content in the intersection of any row and column is a summary of records that meet both conditions. For example, the Bear row that intersects the OR column shows that there are two bears in the state of Oregon. The Dog row that intersects with the WA column shows that there are 13 dogs in the state of Washington.

Table 25-3
A Typical Crosstab Query Format

Type of Animal	ID	OR	WA
Bear	0	2	1
Bird	11	0	3
Cat	4	12	6
Dog	6	7	13
Pig	0	0	3

This table shows a very simple crosstab query that is created from the fields Type of Animal and State, with the intersecting cell contents determined by a Count total on any field in the Pets table.

Creating the crosstab query

Now that you have a conceptual understanding of a crosstab query, it is time to create one. To create a crosstab query like the one described in Table 25-3, follow these steps:

Steps:	Creating a Crosstab Query
Step 1.	Select the Customer and Pets tables.
Step 2.	Double-click the Type of Animal field in the Pets table.
Step 3.	Double-click the State field in the Customer table.
Step 4.	Double-click the Pet ID field in the Pets table.
Step 5.	Select Query⇨Crosstab in the Query menu or press the Crosstab button on the toolbar.
Step 6.	In the Crosstab: cell of Type of Animal, select Row Heading.

Step 7. In the Crosstab: cell of State, select Column Heading.

Step 8. In the Crosstab: cell of Pet ID, select Value.

Step 9. In the Total: cell of Pet ID, select Count.

Your query should look similar to Figure 25-15. Notice that Access inserted a new row named Crosstab: between the Total: and Sort: rows in the QBE pane.

As Figure 25-15 demonstrates, you *must* specify a minimum of three items for crosstab queries:

- The Row Heading field
- The Column Heading field
- The summary Value field

These three items are specified in the appropriate Crosstab: cells of the fields. After you specify the contents for the three Crosstab: cells, you specify Group By in the Total: cell of both the Row Heading and the Column Heading fields and an aggregate Total: cell operator (such as Count) for the Value field.

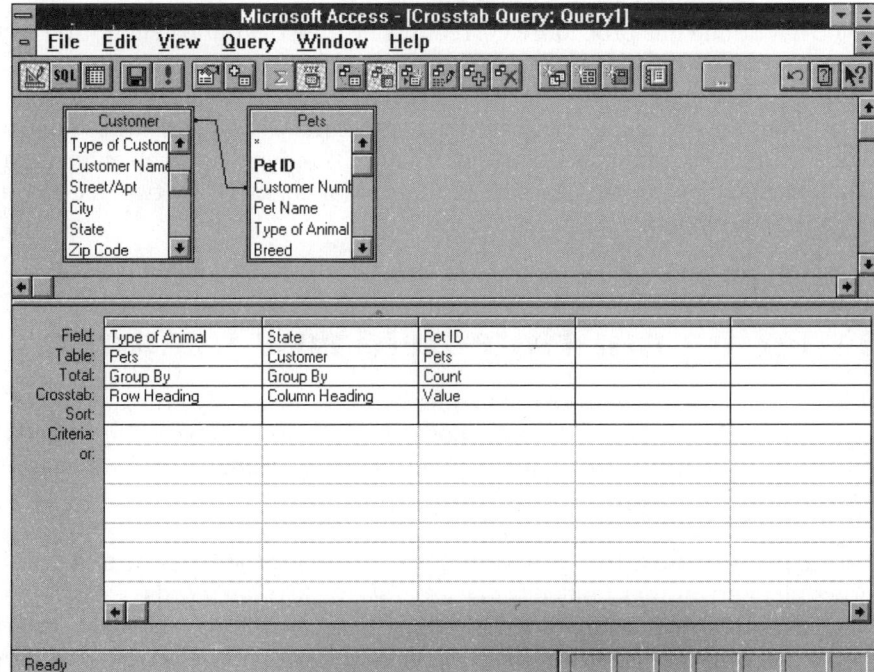

Figure 25-15: Creating a crosstab query.

Figure 25-16:
Datasheet of a crosstab query.

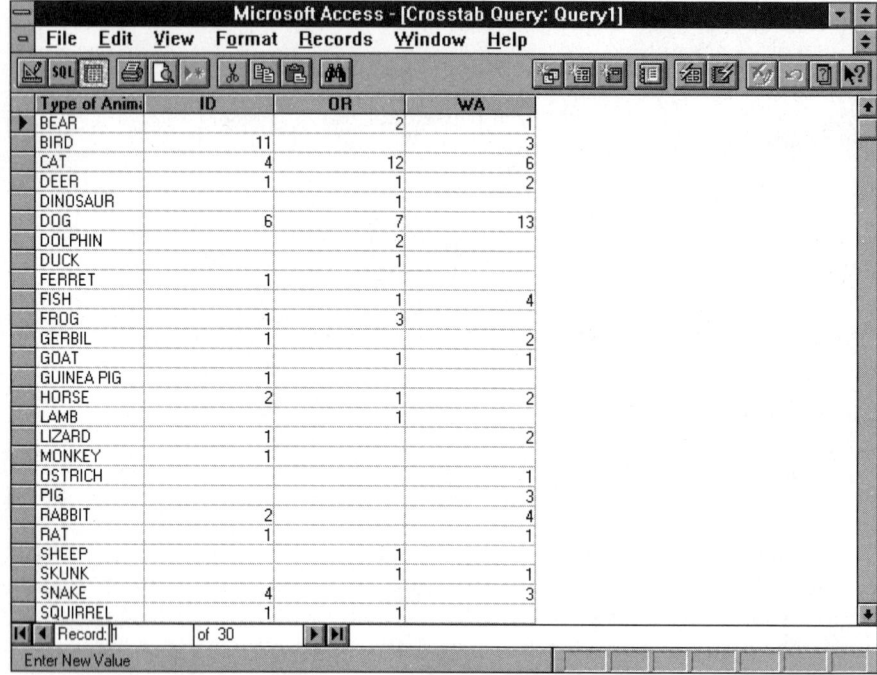

If you have done this procedure correctly, selecting the Datasheet button on the toolbar reveals a datasheet similar to the one in Figure 25-16.

Notice that the dynaset is comprised of distinct (nonrepeating) rows of animals, three columns (one for each state), and summary cell contents for each animal against each state; that is, there are no bears in the state of Idaho, there are two in Oregon, and there is one in Washington.

Entering multiple-field row headings

When you're working with crosstab queries, you can specify only one Value field and one Column Heading field. You can, however, add more than one Row Heading field. By adding multiple Row Heading fields, you can further refine the type of data you want presented in the crosstab query.

For example, suppose that you're interested in seeing the types of animals from the last crosstab query further refined to the level of city. In other words, you want to see how many of each type of animal you have from each city within each state. Such a query is shown in Figure 25-17. Notice that there are two Crosstab: cells that show Row Heading for the fields State and City. Access groups the crosstab rows first by the State and then by the City. Access specifies the group order from left to right.

Figure 25-17:
Crosstab query using two fields for the row heading.

Field:	State	City	Type of Animal	Pet ID
Table:	Customer	Customer	Pets	Pets
Total:	Group By	Group By	Group By	Count
Crosstab:	Row Heading	Row Heading	Column Heading	Value
Sort:				
Criteria:				
or:				

If you select the Datasheet button on the toolbar, Access presents a datasheet similar to the one in Figure 25-18. Notice that the row heading depends on both the State and City fields. The dynaset is displayed in order first by the state (ID, OR, WA) and then by the city within the state (Borderville, Mount Pilot, Russettown, etc.).

A crosstab query can have several row headings but only one column heading. If you want to display a several-field column heading and a single-field row heading, simply reverse your heading types. Change the multiple-field column headings to multiple-field row headings and change the single-row heading to a single-column heading.

Figure 25-18:
Datasheet with multiple-field row headings of a crosstab query.

State	City	BEAR	BIRD	CAT	DEER	DINOSAUR
ID	Borderville			3		
ID	Mount Pilot		1		1	
ID	Russettown		7	1		
ID	Three Corners		3			
OR	Borderville			2		
OR	Lakeville	1		10	1	
OR	Small Tree	1				
WA	Borderville			2		
WA	Mountain View			3	1	
WA	Ranier City	1		1	1	
WA	Tall Pines		3			

Specifying criteria for a crosstab query

When you work with crosstab queries, you may want to specify a record criteria for the crosstab. Criteria can be specified in a crosstab query against any of these fields:

- A new field
- A Row Heading field
- A Column Heading field

Specifying criteria in a new field

You can add criteria based on a new field that will not be displayed in the crosstab query itself. For example, you may want to create the crosstab query that you see in Figure 25-17, where the two fields State and City are used as the row heading. However, you only want to see records where the type of customer is an individual (or the contents equal the number 1). To specify a criteria, simply follow these additional steps:

Steps:	Adding a Criteria to a Crosstab Query
Step 1.	Start with the crosstab query in Figure 25-17.
Step 2.	Double-click the Type of Customer field in the Customer table.
Step 3.	Select the Criteria: cell of Type of Customer.
Step 4.	Type 1 in the cell.

The Crosstab: cell of the Type of Customer field should be blank. If it is not, select (not shown) to blank the cell.

Your query should now resemble the one in Figure 25-19. Notice that you added a criteria in a field that will not be displayed in the crosstab query.

Now that the new criteria is specified, you can click on the Datasheet button of the toolbar to see a datasheet similar to the one portrayed in Figure 25-20.

Notice that the datasheet in Figure 25-20 shows only columns where at least one of the intersecting row cells has a value. For example, only two gerbils appear in the Gerbil column. Several types of animal columns are gone. Bears, birds, deer, and others are missing because none of these types is owned by an individual.

Specifying criteria in a Row Heading field

Besides specifying criteria for a new field, you can specify criteria for a field that is being used for a Row Heading. When you specify a criteria for a Row Heading, Access excludes any rows that do not meet the criteria specified.

For example, you may want to view a crosstab query for all animals where the state is Idaho (ID). To create this query, start with the crosstab query shown in Figure 25-17. If you created the last query, simply remove the Type of Customer column from the QBE pane. To create this query, make the GQBE pane look like Figure 25-21. When you view this query, you see only records from Idaho.

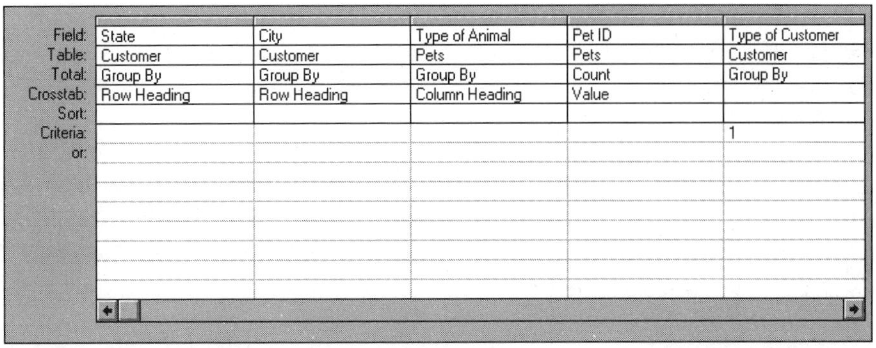

Chapter 25: Advanced Select Queries **729**

Figure 25-19: Specifying a criteria in a crosstab query on a new field.

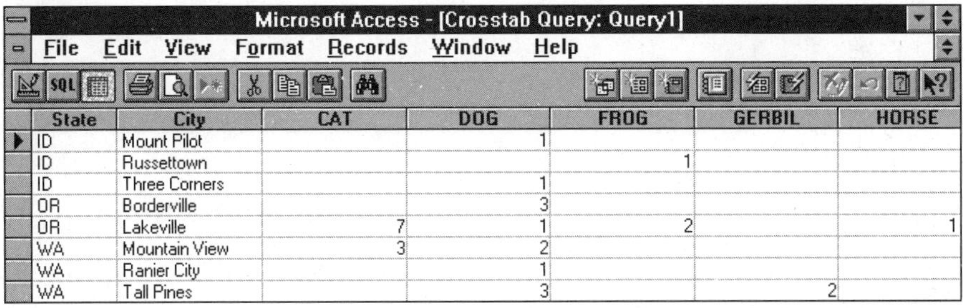

Field:	State	City	Type of Animal	Pet ID	Type of Customer
Table:	Customer	Customer	Pets	Pets	Customer
Total:	Group By	Group By	Group By	Count	Group By
Crosstab:	Row Heading	Row Heading	Column Heading	Value	
Sort:					
Criteria:					1
or:					

Figure 25-20: The datasheet after specifiying a criteria on a new field.

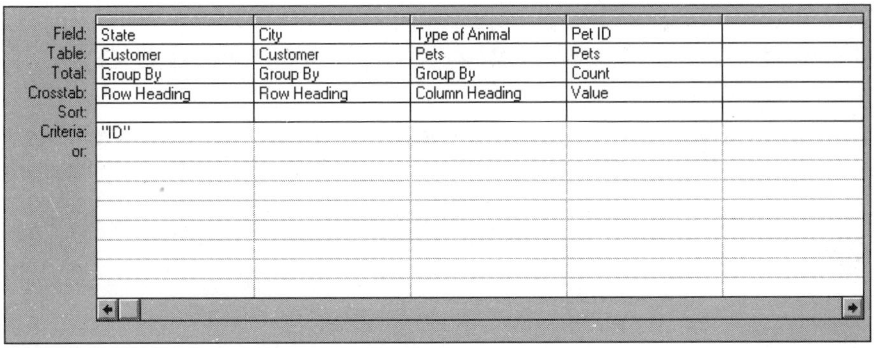

State	City	CAT	DOG	FROG	GERBIL	HORSE
ID	Mount Pilot		1			
ID	Russettown			1		
ID	Three Corners		1			
OR	Borderville		3			
OR	Lakeville	7	1		2	1
WA	Mountain View	3	2			
WA	Ranier City		1			
WA	Tall Pines		3		2	

Figure 25-21: Criteria set against a Row Heading field.

Field:	State	City	Type of Animal	Pet ID	
Table:	Customer	Customer	Pets	Pets	
Total:	Group By	Group By	Group By	Count	
Crosstab:	Row Heading	Row Heading	Column Heading	Value	
Sort:					
Criteria:	"ID"				
or:					

You can specify criteria against any field that is used as a Row Heading field. You can even specify criteria for multiple Row Heading fields to create a finely focused crosstab query.

Specifying criteria in a Column Heading field

You also can specify criteria for the field being used as the column heading. When you specify the criteria for a column heading, Access excludes any columns that don't meet the specified criteria. In the next example, you want a crosstab query for any animal that is either a cat or a dog. To create this query, again start with the crosstab query shown in Figure 25-17. If you created the last query, simply remove the criteria for the State field from the QBE pane. The GQBE pane should look similar to the one in Figure 25-22.

Notice that the criteria specified is placed in the Criteria: cell of the Column Heading field Type of Animal. If you now select the Datasheet button on the toolbar, you should see a datasheet that has only two column headings, Cat and Dog. The other headings have been eliminated.

Figure 25-22:
A criteria specified against the Column Heading field.

Field:	State	City	Type of Animal	Pet ID	
Table:	Customer	Customer	Pets	Pets	
Total:	Group By	Group By	Group By	Count	
Crosstab:	Row Heading	Row Heading	Column Heading	Value	
Sort:					
Criteria:			"CAT" Or "DOG"		
or:					

You cannot specify a criteria in a field used as the Value field for the crosstab query. However, if you need to specify a criteria based on this field, simply drag the field again to the QBE pane and set a criteria against this second copy of the field, while keeping the Crosstab: cell empty.

Specifying criteria in multiple fields of a crosstab query

Now that you've worked with each type of criteria separately, you may want to specify criteria based on several fields. In the next example, you see how to create a crosstab query with complex criteria. You want a row heading based on the Type of Animal field and a column heading based on the Month value of the Visit Date field. The Value cells are based on the Sum of Total Amount.

Finally, you want to limit the months to the first quarter of 1993. To create this complex crosstab query, make the GQBE pane look like Figure 25-23. This is clearly the most complex crosstab query you have created. Notice that you specified a column heading based on a calculated field.

This query should display a datasheet in which the columns are Jan, Feb, Mar, and Apr for the year 1993. When you select the Datasheet button on the toolbar, you should see a datasheet similar to the one in Figure 25-24. Notice that the datasheet has only four columns; the order of the columns is alphabetical, not the chronological by-month order that you entered in the Criteria: cell of the field. The next section of this chapter shows you how to fix the column order.

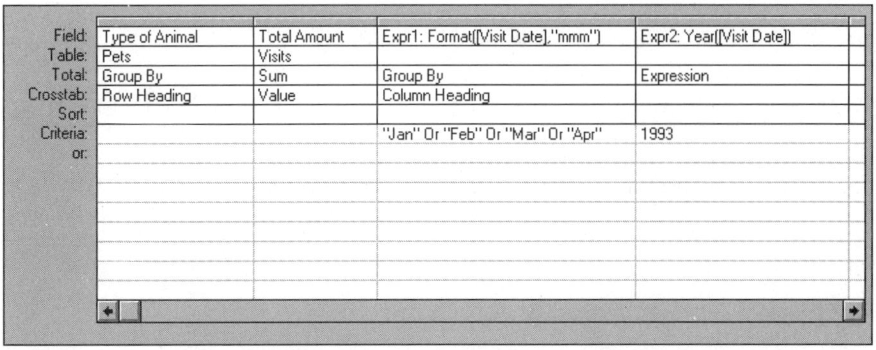

Figure 25-23:
A complex crosstab query.

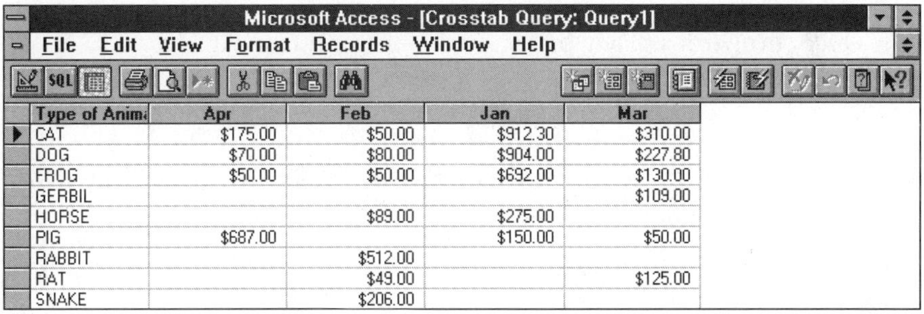

Figure 25-24:
The datasheet of very complex crosstab criteria.

As the preceding crosstab query shows, you can have criteria set for a number of fields, including calculated fields, in the QBE pane. Because you have the ability to set complex, or focused, criteria, you can create very specific crosstab queries.

Specifying fixed column headings

There are times when you want more control over the appearance of the column headings. By default, Access sorts column headings in alphabetical or numeric order. This can be a problem, as you saw in the preceding example and illustrated in Figure 25-24. Your columns will be more readable if the columns are in chronological order instead of alphabetical. You can use the option Fixed Column Headings in the Query Properties box to solve this problem. This option lets you make these choices:

- Specify an exact order for the appearance of the column headings.
- Specify fixed column headings for reports and forms that use crosstab queries.

To specify fixed column headings, follow these steps:

Steps:	**Setting Fixed Column Headings**
Step 1.	Begin with the crosstab query shown in Figure 25-23. Move the pointer to the top half of the query screen and click once.
Step 2.	Click the Properties button (a hand holding a piece of paper) on the toolbar or select View⇨Query Properties... from the Query Design menu.
Step 3.	Select the Fixed Column Headings text box entry area.
Step 4.	Type **Jan, Feb, Mar, Apr** in the box.

The Query Properties dialog box should look like the one in Figure 25-25. When you move to another entry area, Access converts your text into "Jan", "Feb", "Mar", "Apr" in the Query Properties dialog box.

If you look at the datasheet, you see that it now looks like Figure 25-26. The order for the column headings is now chronological.

The column names that you enter *must* match the query headings exactly. If you enter January instead of Jan, Access will accept the heading without reporting an error. But when you display the query, no records for that column will appear.

You can enter column names without separating them by semicolons. To do so, enter each name on a new line (press Ctrl+Enter to move to a new line).

Figure 25-25:
The Query Properties dialog box.

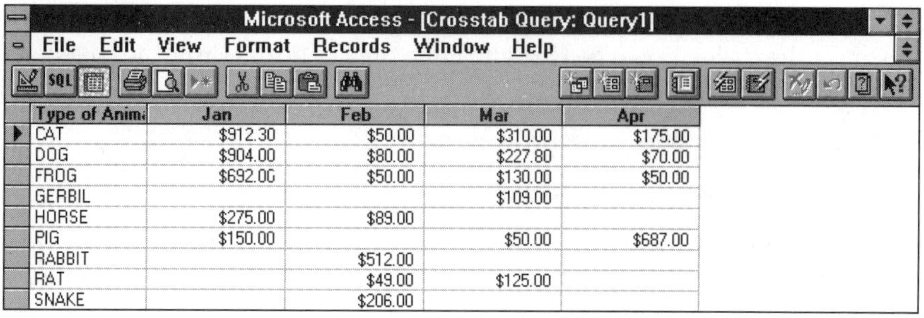

Figure 25-26:
The datasheet with the specified column order.

Type of Animal	Jan	Feb	Mar	Apr
CAT	$912.30	$50.00	$310.00	$175.00
DOG	$904.00	$80.00	$227.80	$70.00
FROG	$692.00	$50.00	$130.00	$50.00
GERBIL			$109.00	
HORSE	$275.00	$89.00		
PIG	$150.00		$50.00	$687.00
RABBIT		$512.00		
RAT		$49.00	$125.00	
SNAKE		$206.00		

Crosstab Query Wizard

Access 2.0 employs several query wizards, helpful additions to the query design surface. One such wizard, the Crosstab Query Wizard (Figure 25-27), is an excellent tool to help you quickly create a crosstab query.

Figure 25-27:
The Access Query Wizard.

There are some limitations, however:

- If you need to use more than one table for the crosstab query, you need to create a separate query that has the tables you need for the crosstab query. For example, you may have a Group By Row Heading from the Pets Table (Type of Animal) and a Group By Column Heading from the Customer Table (State). The Crosstab Query Wizard allows you to select only one table or query for the Row and Column heading.

    The workaround: Create a query of the Customer and Pets tables, selecting the all fields reference for each, and then save this intermediate query. Then use this intermediate query as the record source for the wizard.

- You cannot specify a limiting criteria for the wizard's query.

    The workaround: Make the wizard do the query and then go in and set the limiting criteria.

- You cannot specify column headings or column orders.

    The workaround: Again, have the wizard create the query and then modify it.

To use the crosstab query, simply click the New button and then click the Query Wizard button in the dialog box. The first choice in the list box is Crosstab; select it and then follow the prompts. Access asks for

- The table or query name for the source
- The fields for the column headings
- The field for the body
- The title

After you specify these things, Access creates your crosstab query and then runs it for you.

Creating a Parameter Query

You can automate the process of changing criteria for queries that you run on a regular basis by creating *parameter queries*.

Understanding the parameter query

As the name *parameter* suggests, a parameter query is one that you create that prompts the user for a quantity or a constant value every time the query is executed. Specifically, a parameter query prompts the user for criteria every time it is run, thereby eliminating the need to open the query in design mode to change the criteria manually.

Parameter queries are also very useful with forms or reports because you can have Access prompt the user for the criteria when the form or report is opened.

Creating a single-parameter query

You may have queries that require minor modifications to the criteria of a field every time they are run. Suppose that you have a query that displays all pets for a specific customer. If you run the query often, you can design a parameter query to prompt the user for a customer number whenever the query runs. To create the query, follow these steps:

Steps: Creating a Single-Parameter Query

Step 1. Starting with a select query, select the Customer and Pets tables.

Step 2. Double-click the Customer Number field in the Customer table.

Step 3. Double-click the Customer Name in the Customer table.

Step 4. Double-click the Pet Name field in the Pets table.

Step 5. Click the Criteria: cell for Customer Number.

Step 6. Type **[Enter a Customer Number]** in the cell.

Step 7. Deselect the Show: cell of Customer Number if you don't want this field to show in the datasheet.

That's all there is to creating a single-parameter query. Your query should resemble Figure 25-28.

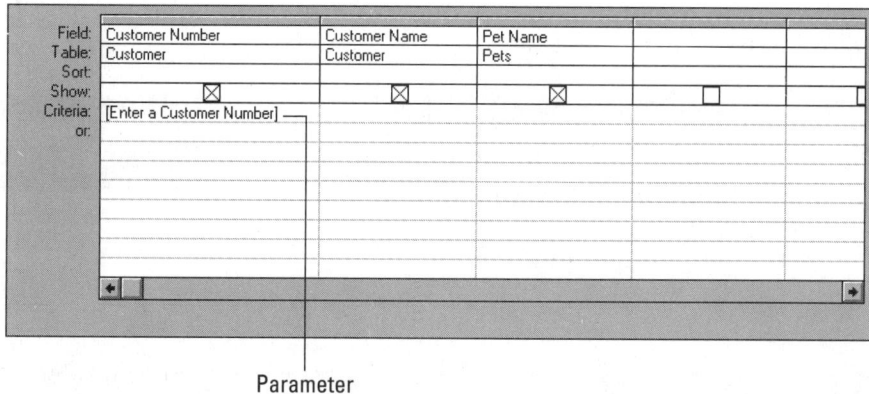

Figure 25-28: A single-parameter query.

Parameter

In the preceding example, you created a parameter query that prompts the user for a customer number by displaying the message `Enter a Customer Number` every time the query is run. Access will convert the user's entry to an equals criteria for the field Customer Number. If a valid number is entered, Access will find the correct records.

 When you specify a prompt message for the parameter, you should make the message meaningful yet brief. When the parameter query is run, Access will display up to approximately 50 characters of any prompt message. If the message is longer than this, it will be truncated to approximately the first 50 characters.

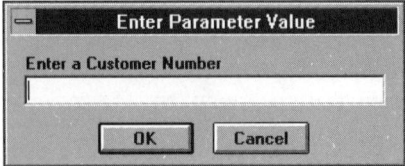

Figure 25-29:
The Enter Parameter Value dialog box.

Running a parameter query

To run a parameter query, select either the Run button or the Datasheet button on the toolbar. A parameter dialog box appears on-screen, like the one in Figure 25-29, prompting the user for a value.

After the user enters a value or presses Enter, Access runs the query, based on the criteria entered. If the criteria is valid, the datasheet will show records matching the criteria; otherwise, the datasheet displays no records.

If the user types **GR001** in the parameter dialog box, Access will display a datasheet similar to the one in Figure 25-30.

Notice that the records displayed in Figure 25-30 are only those for George Green, whose customer number is GR001.

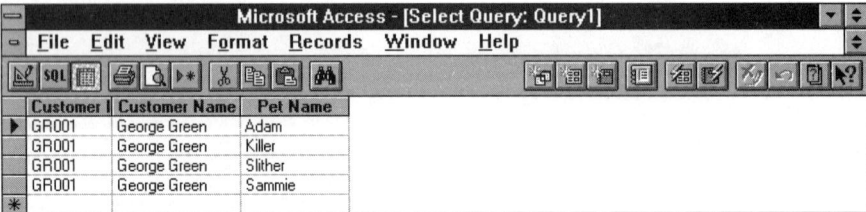

Figure 25-30: Datasheet of records specified by a parameter query.

Creating a multiple-parameter query

You are not limited to creating a query with a single parameter. You can create a query that asks for multiple criteria. For example, you may want a query that displays all pet and visit information based on a type of animal and a range of visit dates. You can design this multiple-parameter query as simply as you did the single-parameter query. To create this query, follow these steps:

Steps:	Creating a Multiple-Parameter Query
Step 1.	Select the Pets and Visits tables.
Step 2.	Double-click the Pet Name field in the Pets table.

Step 3.	Double-click the Type of Animal field in the Pets table.
Step 4.	Double-click the Visit Date field in the Visits table.
Step 5.	Click the Criteria: cell for Type of Animal.
Step 6.	Type **[Enter an Animal Type]** in the cell.
Step 7.	Click the Criteria: cell for Visit Date.
Step 8.	Type **Between [Start Date] And [End Date]** in the cell.

Steps 6 and 8 contain the prompt messages that you specify for the prompt criteria. This query will display three parameter query prompts. Your query should resemble the one in Figure 25-31.

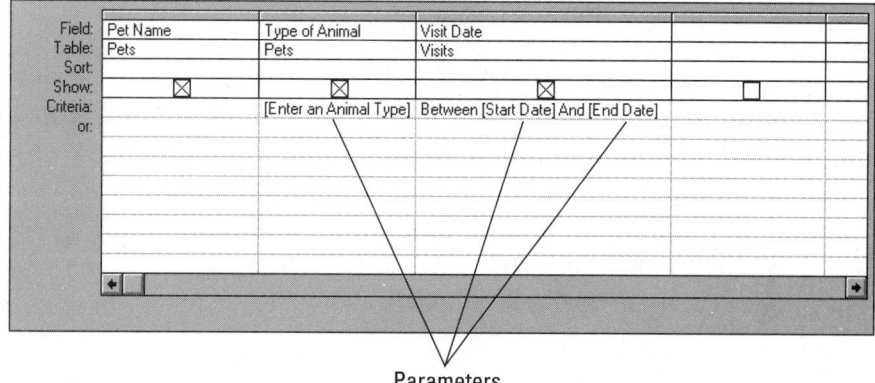

Figure 25-31: A parameter query with three criteria specified.

When you run this query, Access prompts the user for the three criteria in this order:

- Enter an Animal Type
- Start Date
- End Date

Like the single-parameter example, the user must enter valid criteria. If the user enters valid criteria in all three dialog boxes, Access displays all records meeting the specified criteria. Otherwise, it will display no records.

 You can create parameter queries using any valid operator, including the Like operator with wildcards. An example is the query with the parameter Like [Enter a State Abbr. or Enter for all States] & *. This parameter lets the user run the query for a single state or for all states.

Viewing the parameter dialog box

Access defaults the prompt order to left to right, based on the position of the fields and their parameters. However, you can override the prompt order by selecting the Query⇨Parameters ... Query menu choice and specifying an order.

To specify a specific prompt order, enter the criteria on the QBE pane just as you have until now. For example, to specify a prompt order of Start Date, End Date, and Animal Type, follow these steps:

Steps:	Specifying a Prompt Order
Step 1.	Start with the query in Figure 25-31.
Step 2.	Select Query⇨Parameters ... from the Query menu.
Step 3.	Type **[Start Date]** in the first cell under the Parameter column.
Step 4.	Press Tab to move to the Data Type column.
Step 5.	Type **Date/Time** or select the Date/Time type from the drop-down list box.
Step 6.	Press Tab to move to the Parameter column.
Step 7.	Type **[End Date]** in the first cell under the Parameter column.
Step 8.	Press Tab to move to the Data Type column.
Step 9.	Type **Date/Time** or select the Date/Time type from the drop-down list box.
Step 10.	Press Tab to move to the Parameter column.
Step 11.	Type **[Enter an Animal type]** in the first cell under the Parameter column.
Step 12.	Press Tab to move to the Data Type column.
Step 13.	Enter **Text** or select the Text type from the drop-down list box.
Step 14.	Press Enter or select the OK button to leave the dialog box.

Your Query Parameters dialog box should look like the one in Figure 25-32.

Notice that the message prompt in the Parameter column must exactly match the message prompt in each of the Criteria: cells of the QBE pane. If the prompt message does not match, the query will not work correctly.

When you specify a parameter order, you must specify the correct data type for each parameter in the Query Parameters dialog box, or Access will report a data type mismatch error.

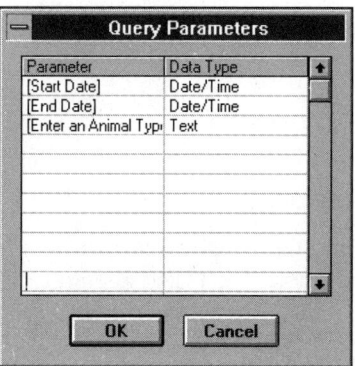

Figure 25-32:
The Query Parameters dialog box.

Summary

In this chapter, you learned how to work with complex select queries. You learned how to use totals, crosstab, and parameter queries. The following points were discussed:

- The three specialized select query types are totals, crosstab, and parameter.

- The Total: row of the QBE pane can be broken into four distinct total categories: Group By, Expression, Total Field Record Limit, and Aggregate.

- Access has nine Aggregate Total options. These operators perform mathematical or selection operations.

- Total queries can perform calculations against all records of a table or against groups of records in a table.

- Total queries can be used to specify criteria that limits the records that can be processed. The criteria can be against a Group By field, an Aggregate Total field after totaling is performed, or a Non-Aggregate Total field before totaling is performed.

- You can create a total query based on an expression that uses one or more of the Aggregate Total options and/or a series of Access functions.

- A crosstab query is a two-dimensional summary matrix that has field contents specified for both the row and column headings. Each intersecting cell between the row and column heading has a Value content (usually an Aggregate Total option).

- Crosstab queries can have multiple fields for specifying row headings but can have only one field for specifying column headings and one for specifying the total operation against the Value cell.

- You can specify the order of the column headings in a crosstab query in the Query Properties box by specifying the order in the Fixed Column Headings box.

- The new Crosstab Query Wizard simplifies creating a crosstab query.

- A parameter query is used for obtaining user-specified criteria when the query is run. This eliminates the need to redesign the query every time the user runs it.

- A parameter query can prompt the user for more than one parameter. If the user wants the order of prompting to be different from the default, it must be specified in the parameter dialog box.

In the next chapter, you work with action queries. You make tables, perform global updates, and delete records using queries.

Creating Action Queries

CHAPTER 26

In This Chapter

- What action queries are
- How action queries work
- How to create an action query
- How to create an update action query
- How to create new tables with a make-table query
- How to create an append query
- How to create a delete query
- How to run action queries
- How to troubleshoot action queries

As you've seen, queries are tools that let you question or request information from your database. In this chapter, you learn about a special type of query, called the *action query*, that lets you *change* the field values in your records. For example, you can change a medications field to increase all prices by 10 percent. Or you can delete all information for records of a deceased animal.

What Is an Action Query?

The name *action query,* as you can guess, defines a query that does something more than simply select a specific group of records and present them to you in a dynaset. The word action suggests performing some operation. By definition, action means doing something or influencing or affecting something. The word action is synonymous with operation, performance, and work. This is exactly what an action query does: It performs some specific operation or work.

An action query can be considered a select query that is given the duty to perform some operation or work against a specified group of records in the dynaset.

When you create any query, Access automatically creates a select query. You can specify a different type, such as an action query, from the Query design menu. From this menu, you can choose from several types of action queries. (The menu's selections are Ma<u>k</u>e Table..., <u>U</u>pdate, A<u>p</u>pend..., and <u>D</u>elete.)

Like select queries, action queries create a dynaset that you can view in a datasheet. To see the dynaset, you simply press the Datasheet button on the toolbar. Unlike select queries, action queries perform some action when you press the Run button (the button with the exclamation point) on the toolbar. The action performed is the action specified in the QBE pane of the query design.

You can quickly identify an action query in the Database window by the special exclamation point icons that sit beside the action query name. There are four different types of action queries (see Figure 26-1) — each has a different icon.

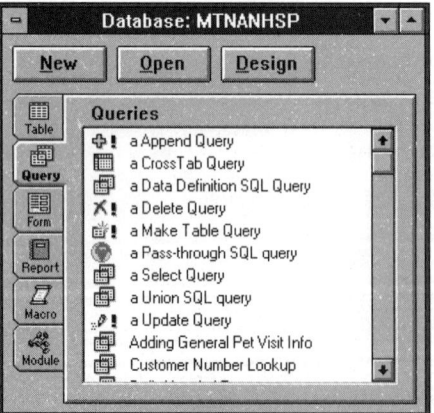

Figure 26-1: The query container of the Database window showing select and action queries.

Uses of Action Queries

You can use action queries to accomplish the following tasks:

- Delete specified records from a table or group of tables
- Append records from one table to another
- Update information in a group of records
- Create a new table from specified records in a query

Chapter 26: Creating Action Queries 743

The following examples describe some practical uses for action queries:

- You want to create history tables and then copy all inactive records to these tables. (You consider a record inactive if the customer hasn't brought a pet to the office in over three years.) And you decide to remove the inactive records from your active database tables.

   What to do? Use a make-table query to create the history tables and a delete query to remove the unwanted records.

- One of your old patients, whom you haven't seen in over four years, comes in with a new puppy, and you need to bring the old information back into the active file from the backup files.

   What to do? Use an append query to add records from your backup tables to your active tables.

Action queries change, add, or delete data. As a result, it is a good idea to observe the following rules:

- Always back up your table *before* performing the query.
- Always create and view the action query (use the Datasheet button on the toolbar) before performing an action query.

The Process of Action Queries

Because action queries are irreversible, you should consider following this four-step process when working with them:

1. Create the action query specifying the fields and the criteria.
2. View the records selected in the action query by clicking the Datasheet button of the toolbar.
3. Run the action query by clicking the Run button of the toolbar.
4. Check the changes in the tables by clicking the datasheet button of the toolbar.

If you follow the preceding steps, you should be able to use action queries in relative safety.

Viewing the Results of an Action Query

Action queries perform a specific task — many times a destructive task. As a result, be very careful when using them. It is important to view the changes that they will make before you run the action query and to verify afterward that they made the changes that you anticipated. Before you learn how to create and run an action query, it is important to review the process for seeing what your changes will look like before you change a table permanently.

Viewing the query before using update and delete queries

While working with action queries in Access 1.x, the Datasheet button is unavailable to you. And when you're working with update and delete queries, the Epsilon button (Totals toggle display button) is also dimmed and unavailable. In version 1.x, to see what an action query will do, you must create a select query with Query⇨Select because the Datasheet button is unavailable. In version 2.0, however, you can click the Datasheet View button to see with which set of data the action query will work. Meanwhile, when you're updating or deleting records with an action query, the actions take place on the underlying tables of the query currently in use. Therefore, to view the results of an update or a delete query, you can press the Datasheet button to see whether the records were updated or deleted.

If your update query made changes to the fields you used to select the records, you may have to look at the underlying table or change the selection query to see the changes. For example, if you deleted a set of records with an action button, the resulting select dynaset of the same record criteria will show that no records exist. By removing the delete criteria, you can view the table and verify that all the records specified have been deleted.

Switching to the result table of a make-table or append query

Unlike the update or delete queries, make-table and append queries copy resultant records to another table. After specifying the fields and the criteria in the QBE pane of the Query Design window, the make-table and the append queries copy the specified fields and records to *another* table. When you run the queries, the results take place in another table, not the current table.

Pressing the Datasheet button shows you a dynaset of only the criteria and fields that were specified, not the actual table that contains the new or added records. To view the results of a make-table or append query, you need to open the new table and view the contents to verify that the make-table or append query worked correctly. If you won't be using the action query again, do not save the query. Delete it.

Reversing action queries

Action queries copy or change data in underlying tables. After an action query is executed, it cannot be reversed. Therefore, when you're working with action queries, you should consider creating a select query first to make sure of the record criteria and selection for the action query.

Because of the destructive nature of action queries, you should always make a backup of the underlying tables before you perform an action query.

Creating an Action Query

Creating an action query is very similar to creating a select query. You specify the fields for the query and any *scoping criteria*.

Besides specifying the fields and criteria, you specify an action-specific property — Append to, Make new table, Update to, or Delete where.

Scoping Criteria

Action queries can use any expression comprised of fields, functions, and operators to specify any limiting condition you need to place on the query. *Scoping criteria* is a form of record criteria. Record criteria is normally thought of as a filter to tell Access which records to find and/or leave out of the dynaset. Because action queries do not create a dynaset, you use scoping criteria to specify a set of records that are to be operated on by Access.

Creating an Update Action Query to Change Values

In this section, we describe how to handle an event that requires you to change many records.

Suppose that the city of Mountain View has passed an ordinance that requires horses residing in its borders to receive a new type of vaccination, starting this year. To create this query, you work with the Customer and Pets tables. First, change the existing status of the Current Vaccinations field in the Pets table from Yes to No wherever the field shows a current vaccination status. Then enter horse in the Criteria: row for Type of Animal and Mountain View in the Criteria: row for the City field.

It's possible to update each record in the table individually by using a form or a datasheet. To make these changes by using a select query dynaset, though, takes a very long time. The method is not only time-consuming, but it is also inefficient — especially if you have many records to change. In addition, this method also lends itself to typing errors as you enter new text into fields.

The best way to handle this type of event is to use an update action query because the query makes many changes in just one operation. By using action queries, you save time and eliminate many of those typos that crop up in manually edited records.

To create an update query that performs these tasks, follow a two-phase process:

1. Create a select query. View the data you want to update by pressing the Datasheet button.
2. Convert the select query to an update query. Then run the update query after you are satisfied that it will affect only the records you want.

Creating a select query before an update action

The first step in making an update query is to create a select query. In this particular case, the query is for all customers who live in Mountain View and own horses. Perform the following steps to create this query:

Chapter 26: Creating Action Queries

Steps: Creating the Select Query

Step 1. Create a new query using the Customer and Pets tables.

Step 2. Select the City field from the Customer table and Type of Animal and Current Vaccination from the Pets table.

Step 3. Specify a criteria of **"Mountain View"** in the City field and **"HORSE"** in the Type of Animal field.

The Select Query Design window should now resemble the one in Figure 26-2. Notice that the QBE pane shows all three fields but shows criteria only in the fields City and Type of Animal.

Step 4. Examine the datasheet to make sure that it only has the records that you want to change. Return to the design surface when you are finished.

The select query datasheet should resemble the one shown in Figure 26-3. Notice that only the records for horses whose owners reside in Mountain View are shown in the dynaset.

Figure 26-2: Entering a select query.

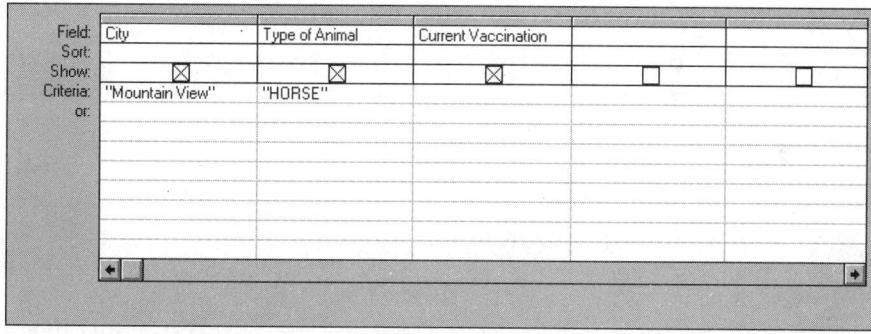

Figure 26-3: Dynaset showing only the records for horses whose owners live in Mountain View.

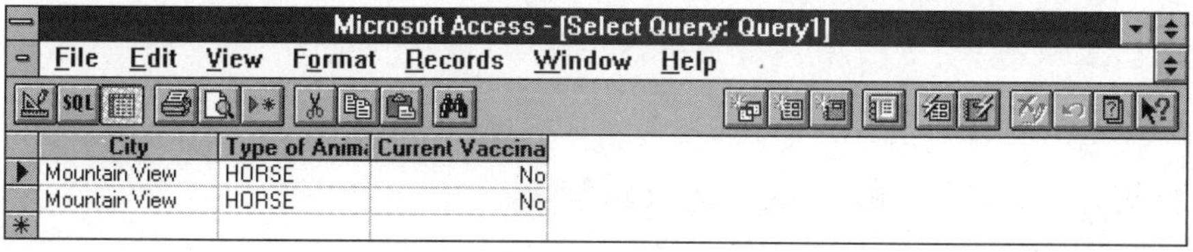

You are now ready to convert the select query to an update query.

Converting a select query to an update query

After you create a select query and verify the selection of records, it's time to create the update query. To convert the select query to an update query, follow these steps:

Steps:	Converting a Select Query to an Update Query
Step 1.	Press the Update Query button on the toolbar or select Query⇨Update from the menu. Access changes the title of the Query window from Select Query: Query1 to Update Query: Query1. Access also adds the Update To: property row to the QBE pane, as shown in Figure 26-4.
Step 2.	In the Update to: cell of Current Vaccination, enter No.
Step 3.	Click the Run button on the toolbar (or select Query⇨Run from the menu). Access displays the dialog box shown in Figure 26-5. This dialog box displays the message `x row[s] will be updated`. Three buttons — OK, Cancel, and Help — also appear.
Step 4.	Click the OK button to complete the query and update the records. Selecting Cancel stops the procedure (no records are updated), and selecting Help displays Help about this dialog box.

If you are changing tables that are attached to another database, you *cannot* cancel the query.

You can change more than one field at a time by filling in the Update To: section of any field you want to change. You can even change field contents of fields that you used for limiting the records (criteria).

Checking your results

After completing the update query, you should check your results. You can do so by changing the update query back to a select query (click the Select Query button on the toolbar). After changing the query back to a select query, you can review the changes in the datasheet.

Chapter 26: Creating Action Queries

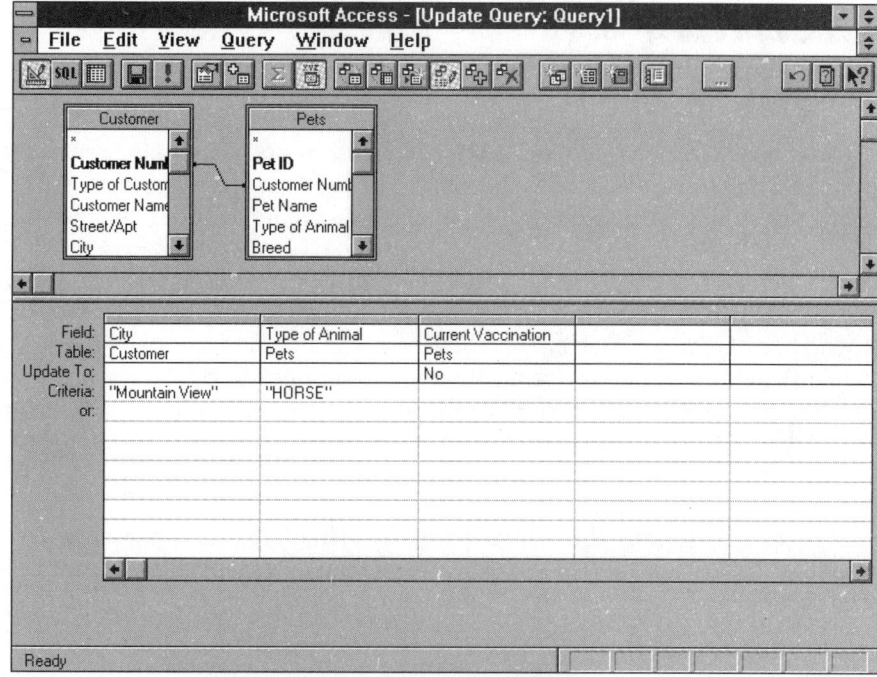

Figure 26-4: The update query design pane.

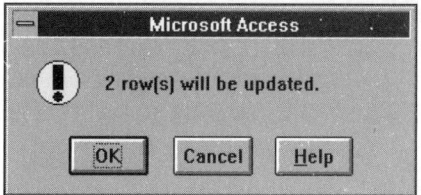

Figure 26-5: The dialog box for updating records.

The update made *permanent* changes to the field Current Vaccination for all horses whose owners live in Mountain View. If you did not back up the Pets table before running the update query, you cannot easily return the contents back to their original Yes or No settings. Hope you have a good memory.

 If you update a field that was used for a limiting criteria, you must change the criteria in the select query to the new value to verify the changes.

Creating a New Table Using a Make-Table Query

You can use an action query to create new tables based on scoping criteria. To make a new table, you create a make-table query. The following paragraph describes a situation giving rise to this particular task for which you'll create a make-table query.

A local pet food company has approached you for a mailing list of customers who own a dog or cat. This company wants to send these customers a coupon for a free four-pound bag of food for each animal they own. The pet food company plans to create the mailing labels and send the form letters if you supply a table of customer information, pet names, and type of animal. The pet food company also stipulates that because this is a trial mailing, only those customers you've seen in the past six months should receive letters.

You've decided to send the company the requested table of information. So now you need to create a new table from the Customer and Pets tables. To accomplish this task, you create a make-table query that will perform these actions.

Creating the select query

You decide to create a make-table query for all customers who own a dog or cat and who have visited you in the past six months. For this example, assume that six months ago was February 1, 1993. Perform the following steps to create this query:

Steps:	Creating the Select Query
Step 1.	Create a new query using the Customer and Pets tables.
Step 2.	Click the Make table button of the toolbar. Access displays the Query Properties dialog box, shown in Figure 26-6.
Step 3.	Type **Mailing List for Coupons** in the Table Name: field and either press Enter or click the OK button. Notice that after you select OK, the name of the window changes from Select Query:Query1 to Make Table Query:Query1.
Step 4.	Select the mailing information fields (customer name through ZIP code) from the Customer table and the fields Pet Name, Type of Animal, and Last Visit Date from the Pets table.

Step 5. Specify the criteria **In("CAT","DOG")** in the Type of Animal field and **>#2/1/93#** in the Last Visit Date field.

The Query Design window should resemble the one in Figure 26-7. Notice that the fields are resized so that all appear in the QBE pane. Two fields (Type of Animal and Last Visit Date) contain criteria.

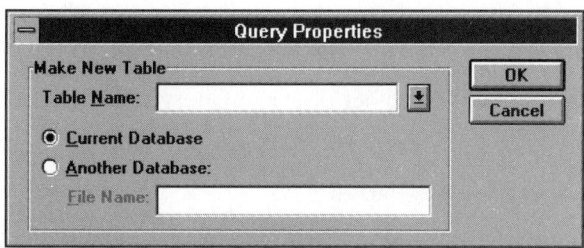

Figure 26-6: The Query Properties dialog box.

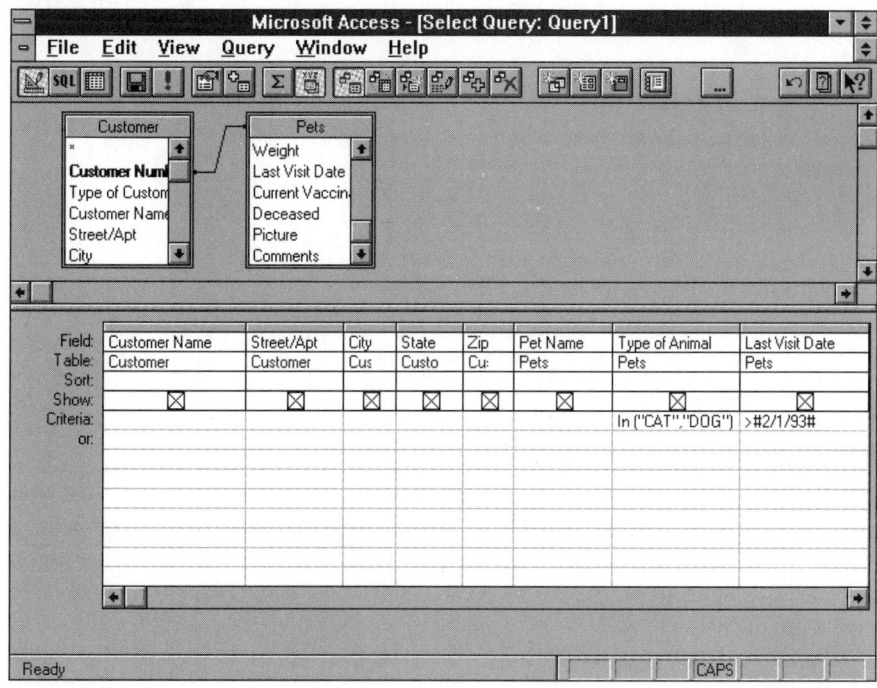

Figure 26-7: The Customer and Pets tables are in the top pane; the fields Customer Name, Street/Apt, City, State, ZIP Code, Pet Name, Type of Animal, and Last Visit Date are in the bottom pane.

Step 6. Click the Datasheet View button on the toolbar to view the dynaset (see Figure 26-8).

Part IV: Advanced Database Features

Step 7. Make sure that the dynaset has only the records that you specified.

Step 8. Click the Design button to switch back to the Query Design view.

Step 9. Deselect the Show: property of the field Last Visit Date.

You do not want to copy this field to the new table Mailing List for Coupons. Only those fields selected with an X in the checkbox of the Show: row are copied to the new table. By deselecting a field with a criteria set, you can base the scoping criteria on fields that will *not* be copied to the new table.

Step 10. Click the Run button on the toolbar or select Query⇒Run from the menu.

Access indicates how many records it will copy to the new table (see Figure 26-9).

Customer Name	Street/Apt	City	State	Zip Code	Pet Name	Type of Anim	Last
All Creatures	21 Grace St.	Tall Pines	WA	98746-2541	Fido	DOG	
Animal Kingdom	15 Marlin Lane	Borderville	ID	83483-5646	Tom	CAT	
Animal Kingdom	15 Marlin Lane	Borderville	ID	83483-5646	Marcus	CAT	
Animal Kingdom	15 Marlin Lane	Borderville	ID	83483-5646	Pookie	CAT	
Animal Kingdom	15 Marlin Lane	Borderville	ID	83483-5646	Mario	DOG	
Animal Kingdom	15 Marlin Lane	Borderville	ID	83483-5646	Luigi	DOG	
James Brown	3454 Adams St	Borderville	OR	97401-1019	John Boy	DOG	
Bow Wow House	76 Canine Ln.	Ranier City	WA	98756-2175	Sweety	DOG	
Bow Wow House	76 Canine Ln.	Ranier City	WA	98756-2175	Quintin	DOG	
Cat House Pets	76 Right Ln.	Borderville	OR	97541-2856	Silly	CAT	
Critters and More	200 Feline Rd	Borderville	WA	98453-8567	Mule	CAT	
Wanda Greenfield	66 Farmaccess Rd	Tall Pines	WA	98401-2201	Sammie Girl	DOG	
Patricia Irwin	456 Bishops Ln	Lakeville	OR	97401-1021	C.C.	CAT	
Patricia Irwin	456 Bishops Ln	Lakeville	OR	97401-1021	Gizmo	CAT	
Patricia Irwin	456 Bishops Ln	Lakeville	OR	97401-1021	Stripe	CAT	
Patricia Irwin	456 Bishops Ln	Lakeville	OR	97401-1021	Romeo	CAT	
Patricia Irwin	456 Bishops Ln	Lakeville	OR	97401-1021	Ceasar	CAT	
Patricia Irwin	456 Bishops Ln	Lakeville	OR	97401-1021	Juliet	CAT	
Patricia Irwin	456 Bishops Ln	Lakeville	OR	97401-1021	Tiger	CAT	
Michael Johnson	77 Farmaccess Rd	Ranier City	WA	98401-2201	Rover	DOG	
Adam Johnson	55 Childs Ave	Mount Pilot	ID	83412-1043	Fi Fi	DOG	
Margaret McKinley	5512 Green Acres	Borderville	OR	97412-1001	Rex	DOG	
Margaret McKinley	5512 Green Acres	Borderville	OR	97412-1001	Ceasar	DOG	
Pet City	91 Main St.	Mount Pilot	ID	83187-5638	Sylvester	DOG	
William Primen	1234 Main St	Mountain View	WA	98401-1011	Brutus	DOG	
Village Pets	30 Murphy St.	Russettown	ID	83019-8573	Ren	DOG	

Figure 26-8: The dynaset of cats and dogs seen since February 1, 1993.

Step 11. Click the OK button to complete the query and make the new table. Selecting Cancel stops the procedure (no records are copied), and selecting Help displays Help about this dialog box.

Chapter 26: Creating Action Queries

When you're creating numerous make-table queries, you need to click the Make table button on the toolbar or select Query⇨Make Table... from the menu to rename the make-table query each time. Access assumes that you want to overwrite the existing table if you don't reselect the make-table option. Access warns you about overwriting before performing the new make-table query.

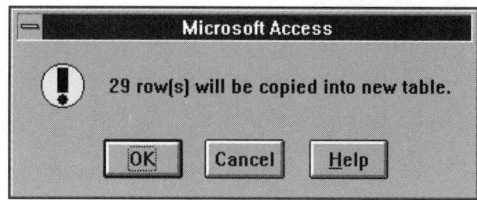

Figure 26-9: The dialog box for copying records.

Checking your results

After you complete the make-table query, you should check your results. You can do so by opening the new table Mailing List for Coupons, which has been added to the database container (see Figure 26-10).

When you create a table from a make-table query, the fields in the new table inherit the data type and field size from the fields in the query's underlying tables; however, no other field or table properties are transferred. If you want to define a primary key or other properties, you need to edit the design of the new table.

You can also use a make-table action query to create a backup of your tables before you create action queries that change the contents of the tables. Backing up with this method does *not* copy the table's properties or primary key to the new table.

To copy any database object (table, query, form, or other object) while you're in the Database window, follow these steps:

Steps:	Copying a Database Object
Step 1.	Highlight the object that you need to copy.
Step 2.	Press Ctrl+C (or select Edit⇨Copy) to copy the object to the Clipboard.
Step 3.	Press Ctrl+V (or select Edit⇨Paste) to paste the object from the Clipboard.
Step 4.	Enter the new object name (table, form, and so forth) and select the OK button in the dialog box. If the object is a table, you also can specify Structure with/without the data and append it to an existing table.

Figure 26-10:
The new table MAILING LIST FOR COUPON.

Customer Name	Street/Apt	City	State	Zip Code	Pet Name	Type
All Creatures	21 Grace St.	Tall Pines	WA	987462541	Fido	DOG
Animal Kingdom	15 Marlin Lane	Borderville	ID	834835646	Tom	CAT
Animal Kingdom	15 Marlin Lane	Borderville	ID	834835646	Marcus	CAT
Animal Kingdom	15 Marlin Lane	Borderville	ID	834835646	Pookie	CAT
Animal Kingdom	15 Marlin Lane	Borderville	ID	834835646	Mario	DOG
Animal Kingdom	15 Marlin Lane	Borderville	ID	834835646	Luigi	DOG
James Brown	3454 Adams St	Borderville	OR	974011019	John Boy	DOG
Bow Wow House	76 Canine Ln.	Ranier City	WA	987562175	Sweety	DOG
Bow Wow House	76 Canine Ln.	Ranier City	WA	987562175	Quintin	DOG
Cat House Pets	76 Right Ln.	Borderville	OR	975412856	Silly	CAT
Critters and More	200 Feline Rd	Borderville	WA	984538567	Mule	CAT
Wanda Greenfield	66 Farmaccess Rd	Tall Pines	WA	984012201	Sammie Girl	DOG
Patricia Irwin	456 Bishops Ln	Lakeville	OR	974011021	C.C.	CAT
Patricia Irwin	456 Bishops Ln	Lakeville	OR	974011021	Gizmo	CAT
Patricia Irwin	456 Bishops Ln	Lakeville	OR	974011021	Stripe	CAT
Patricia Irwin	456 Bishops Ln	Lakeville	OR	974011021	Romeo	CAT
Patricia Irwin	456 Bishops Ln	Lakeville	OR	974011021	Ceasar	CAT
Patricia Irwin	456 Bishops Ln	Lakeville	OR	974011021	Juliet	CAT
Patricia Irwin	456 Bishops Ln	Lakeville	OR	974011021	Tiger	CAT
Michael Johnson	77 Farmaccess Rd	Ranier City	WA	984012201	Rover	DOG
Adam Johnson	55 Childs Ave	Mount Pilot	ID	834121043	Fi Fi	DOG
Margaret McKinley	5512 Green Acres	Borderville	OR	974121001	Rex	DOG
Margaret McKinley	5512 Green Acres	Borderville	OR	974121001	Ceasar	DOG
Pet City	91 Main St.	Mount Pilot	ID	831875638	Sylvester	DOG
William Primen	1234 Main St	Mountain View	WA	984011011	Brutus	DOG
Village Pets	30 Murphy St.	Russettown	ID	830198573	Ren	DOG

Creating a Query to Append Records

As the word *append* suggests, an append query attaches or adds records to a specified table. An append query adds records from the table you are using to another table. The table that you want to add records to must already exist. You can append records to a table in the same database or in another Access database.

Append queries are very useful for adding information to another table based on some scoping criteria. However, append queries are not always the fastest way of adding records to another database. For example, if you need to append all fields and all records from one table to a new table, the append query is *not* the best way to do it. Instead, use the Copy and Paste options of the Edit menu when you're with working the table in a datasheet or form.

Chapter 26: Creating Action Queries

 You can add records to an open table. You don't have to close the table before adding records. However, Access does not automatically refresh the view of the table that has records added to it. To refresh the table, press Shift+F9. This action requeries the table so that you can see the appended records.

When you're working with append queries, you need to be aware of the following rules:

1. If the table you are appending records to has a primary key field, the records that you add cannot have Null values or duplicate primary key values. If so, Access will not append the records.

2. If you add records to another database table, you must know the location and name of the database.

3. If you use the asterisk (*) field in a QBE row, you cannot also use individual fields from the same table. Access will not append the records, thinking that you're trying to add field contents twice to the same record.

4. If you append records with a Counter field (an Access-specified primary key), do not include the Counter field if the table you are appending to also has the field and record contents (this causes the problem specified in rule 1). Also, do not use the Counter field if you are adding to an empty table and you want the new table to have a new Counter number (order number) based on the criteria.

If you follow these simple rules, your append queries will perform as expected, becoming a very useful tool.

Here's an example that will help illustrate the use of append queries: Every February, you archive all records of animals that died in the preceding year. To archive the records, you perform two steps. First, you append them to existing backup files. Second, you delete the records from the active database.

In this case, you want to add records to the backup tables for deceased animals in your active tables. In other words, you will copy records to three tables — Pets, Visits, and Visits Detail. You need three backup files to perform this exercise. To create the backup files, perform the following steps:

Steps: Creating Backup File Structures

Step 1. Press F11 or Alt+F1 to display the Database window.

Step 2. Click the Table button to display the list of tables.

Step 3. Click the table Pets to highlight it.

Part IV: Advanced Database Features

Step 4.	Press Ctrl+C (or select Edit⇨Copy) to copy the object Pets table to the Clipboard.
Step 5.	Press Ctrl+V (or select Edit⇨Paste) to display the Paste Table As dialog box.
Step 6.	Click Structure Only in the Paste Options section of the dialog box (or tab to the Paste Options section and press S).
Step 7.	Click the Table Name: box and type **Pets Backup**.
Step 8.	Click the OK button (or press Enter after typing the filename).
Step 9.	Open the Pets Backup table (it should be empty); then close the table.

Repeat this process for both the Visits and Visit Details tables, naming them Visits Backup and Visit Details Backup, respectively.

To create an append query that copies the deceased animals' records, follow a two-step process:

1. Create a select query to verify that only the records that you want to append are copied.
2. Convert the select query to an append query and run it.

When you're using the append query, only fields with names that match in the two tables are copied. For example, you may have a small table with six fields and another with nine. The table with nine fields has only five of the six field names that match fields in the smaller table. If you append records from the smaller table to the larger table, only the five matching fields are appended. The other four fields will remain blank.

Creating the select query for an append query

To create a select query for all pets that died last year, along with their visit histories, follow these steps:

Steps: Creating the Select Query

Step 1. Create a new query using the Pets, Visits, and Visit Detail tables.

Step 2. Select the Deceased field from the Pets table.

Step 3. Specify a criteria of **Yes** in the Deceased field.

You may want to select some additional fields from each table, such as Pet Name, Visit Date, Visit Type, Treatment Code, and so forth. The Select Query Design window should resemble the one in Figure 26-11. Notice that all the fields are resized to appear in the QBE pane. The only field and criteria that must be in this select query is the first field, Deceased. If you add additional fields, make sure that you remove them before converting this query to an append query.

Step 4. Go to the datasheet and make sure that all the Deceased field contents say YES. (See Figure 26-12.)

Step 5. Return to Design mode. With the select query created correctly, you are ready to convert the select query to an append query.

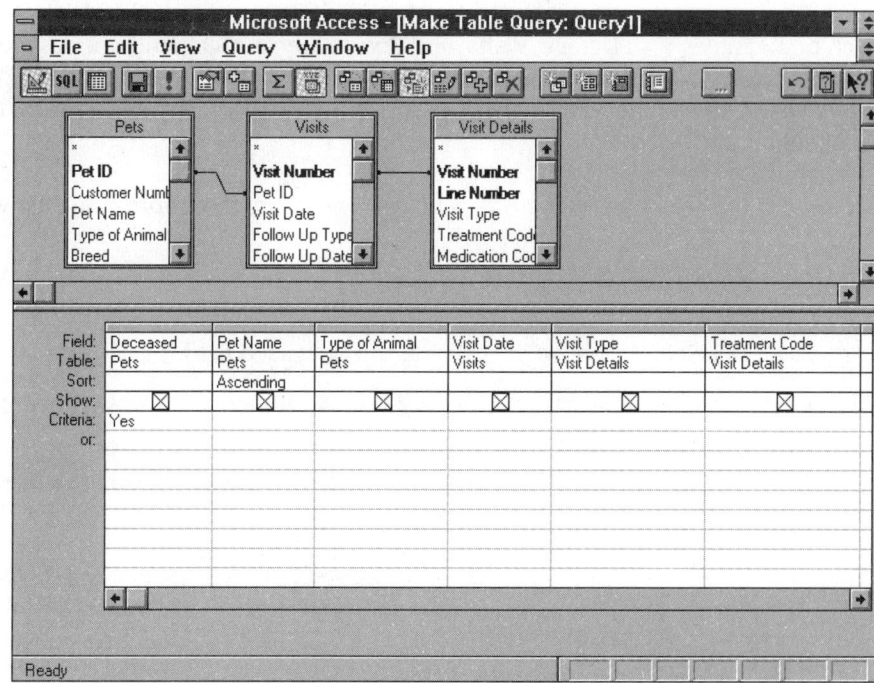

Figure 26-11: The tables Pets, Visits, and Visit Details are in the top pane, and selected fields are in the QBE pane.

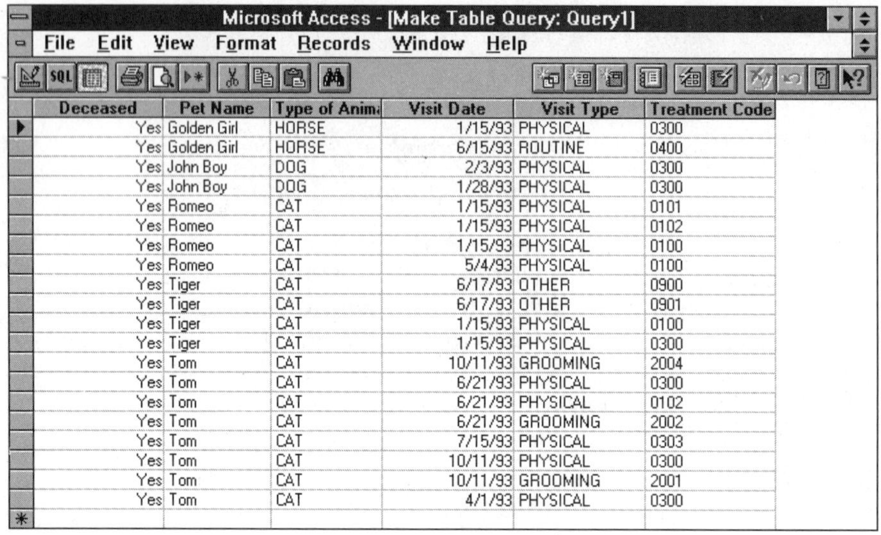

Figure 26-12: A dynaset of records for all deceased animals.

Deceased	Pet Name	Type of Animal	Visit Date	Visit Type	Treatment Code
Yes	Golden Girl	HORSE	1/15/93	PHYSICAL	0300
Yes	Golden Girl	HORSE	6/15/93	ROUTINE	0400
Yes	John Boy	DOG	2/3/93	PHYSICAL	0300
Yes	John Boy	DOG	1/28/93	PHYSICAL	0300
Yes	Romeo	CAT	1/15/93	PHYSICAL	0101
Yes	Romeo	CAT	1/15/93	PHYSICAL	0102
Yes	Romeo	CAT	1/15/93	PHYSICAL	0100
Yes	Romeo	CAT	5/4/93	PHYSICAL	0100
Yes	Tiger	CAT	6/17/93	OTHER	0900
Yes	Tiger	CAT	6/17/93	OTHER	0901
Yes	Tiger	CAT	1/15/93	PHYSICAL	0100
Yes	Tiger	CAT	1/15/93	PHYSICAL	0300
Yes	Tom	CAT	10/11/93	GROOMING	2004
Yes	Tom	CAT	6/21/93	PHYSICAL	0300
Yes	Tom	CAT	6/21/93	PHYSICAL	0102
Yes	Tom	CAT	6/21/93	GROOMING	2002
Yes	Tom	CAT	7/15/93	PHYSICAL	0303
Yes	Tom	CAT	10/11/93	PHYSICAL	0300
Yes	Tom	CAT	10/11/93	GROOMING	2001
Yes	Tom	CAT	4/1/93	PHYSICAL	0300

Converting to an append query

After you create the select query and verify that it is correct, you need to create the append query. Actually, you need to create three different append queries — one for each of the tables Visit Details, Visits, and Pets — because append queries work with only one table at a time. For this example, first copy all fields from the Visits Detail table. Then copy all the fields from the Visits table. Finally, copy all the fields from the Pets table.

To convert the select query to an append query and run it, perform the following steps:

Steps: Converting to an Append Query

Step 1. Deselect the Show: property of the Deceased field.

Step 2. Click the Append Query button on the toolbar or select Query⇨Append... from the Design menu.

Access displays the Query Properties dialog box, shown in Figure 26-13.

Chapter 26: Creating Action Queries

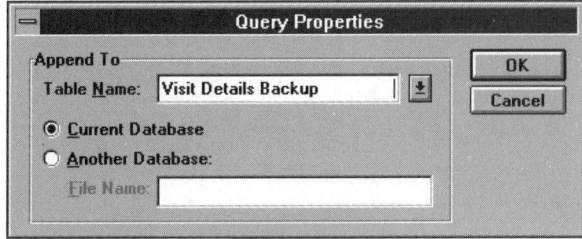

Figure 26-13: The Query Properties dialog box.

Step 3. Type **Visit Details Backup** in the Table Name: field and either press Enter in the field or click on the OK button in the dialog box.

Step 4. Drag the asterisk (*) field from the Visit Details table to the QBE pane to select all fields.

The QBE pane should look like Figure 26-14. Access automatically fills in the Append To: field under the All fields selector column.

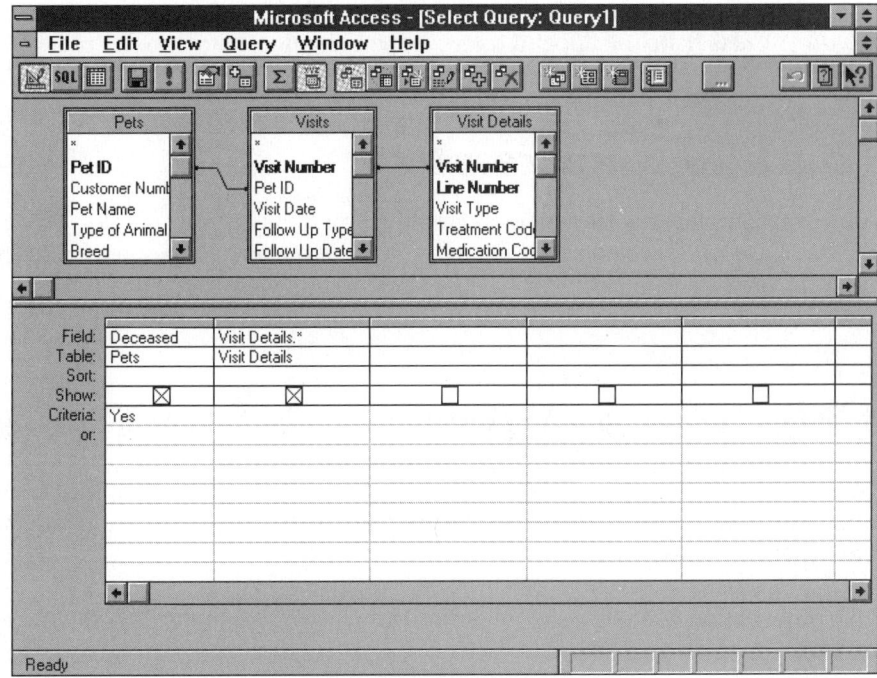

Figure 26-14: The QBE pane for an append query.

> **Step 5.** Click the Run button on the toolbar (or select Query⇨Run from the menu).
>
> Access displays a dialog box that displays the message `x row[s] will be appended`. Access also displays three buttons — OK, Cancel, and Help.
>
> **Step 6.** Click the OK button to complete the query and copy (append) the records to the backup table. Selecting Cancel stops the procedure (no records are copied), and selecting Help displays Help about this dialog box.

With the deceased Visits Detail records backed up, go back and repeat Steps 2 through 5 for the Visits and the Pets tables. When you go to append fields from these other tables, however, you must remove the previous all selector field [Visits Detail.*] field from the QBE pane.

If you create an append query by using the asterisk (*) field and you also use a field from the same table as the asterisk to specify a criteria, you must take the criteria field out of the Append To: row. If you don't, Access reports an error. Remember, the field for the criteria is already included in the asterisk field. If you leave the Show on, it tries to append the field twice, repeating an error. Access halts the append query, appending no records to the table.

Checking your results

After you complete the three append table queries, check your results. To do so, go to the database window and select each of the three tables to be appended to (Pets backup, Visits backup, and Visits Detail backup) and view the new records.

Creating a Query to Delete Records

Of all the action queries, the delete query is the most dangerous. Unlike the other types of queries that you've worked with, delete queries delete records from tables permanently and *irreversibly*.

Like other action queries, delete queries act on a group of records based on a scoping criteria.

In version 2.0, a delete action query can work with multiple tables to delete records. However, to delete related records from multiple tables you must do the following:

- Define relationships between the tables in the Relationships builder.
- Check the Enforce Referential Integrity option for the join between tables.
- Check the Cascade Delete option for the join between tables.

Figure 26-15 shows the Relationships dialog box for the join line between tables. Notice that the Referential Integrity and Cascade Delete options are selected.

In version 1.x, Access allows multi-table deletes with one-to-one relations only. When working with one-to-many relations in version 1.x or 2.0 without defining relationships and putting Cascade Delete on, Access deletes records from one table at a time only. Specifically, Access deletes the *many side* of the relation first. Then you must remove the *many side* table from the query and delete the records from the *one side* of the query.

This method is time-consuming and awkward. So when deleting related records from one-to-many relation tables, make sure that you define relations between the tables and check the Cascade Delete box in the Relationships builder.

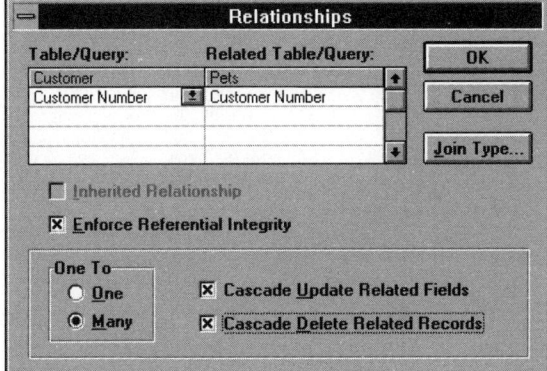

Figure 26-15: The Relationships dialog box.

Because of the permanently destructive action of a delete query, you should always make backup copies of your tables before working with them.

The following example will help illustrate the use of Access action queries. In this case, you have a large number of records to delete.

In this situation, you are going to delete all records of deceased animals. Recall that you already copied all deceased pet records to backup tables in the append query section. The tables you are dealing with have these relations:

One pet has many visits.

One visit has many visit details.

The relations are a pair of one-to-many relationships. As a result, if you don't define permanent relations between the tables and set Cascade Delete on, you need to create three separate delete queries. (You would need to delete from the Visit Details, Visits, and Pets tables — in that order.)

With relations set and Cascade Delete On, however, you simply have to delete the records from the Pets table; Access automatically deletes all related records. Assume for this example that you have already appended the records to another table — or that you made a new table of the records you are about to delete and you have set up permanent relations between the three tables and set Cascade Deletes on for both relationships (that is, between Pets and Visits and between Visits and Visit Details).

Creating a Cascading Delete query

To create a cascading delete query for all pets that died last year, along with their visit histories, perform the following steps:

Steps:	Creating the Delete Query
Step 1.	Create a new query using the Pets, Visits, and Visits Details tables.
Step 2.	Click the Delete query button on the toolbar or select Query⇨Delete from the Design menu.
	Notice that the name of the window changes from Select Query:Query1 to Delete Query:Query1.
Step 3.	Select the Deceased field from the Pets table.
Step 4.	Specify the criteria **Yes** in the Deceased field.
	The Delete Query Design window is shown in Figure 26-16. The only field and criteria that must appear in this delete query is the first field, Deceased.
Step 5.	Go to the datasheet and verify that only records that say Yes are there.
Step 6.	Return to the design window.
Step 7.	Click the Run button on the toolbar (or select Query⇨Run from the menu).
	Access displays a dialog box with the message `x row[s] will be deleted from the primary table (Pets)`. Access does not specify how many rows will be deleted from the other tables.
Step 8.	Click the OK button to complete the query. The records are removed from all three tables. When you click the OK button, Access deletes the records in the Pets table and then automatically deletes the related records in the Visits and Visits Detail tables. Selecting Cancel stops the procedure (no records are copied) and selecting Help displays Help about this dialog box.

Remember that a delete query permanently and irreversibly removes the records from the table(s). Therefore, it is important to back up the records you want to delete *before* you delete them.

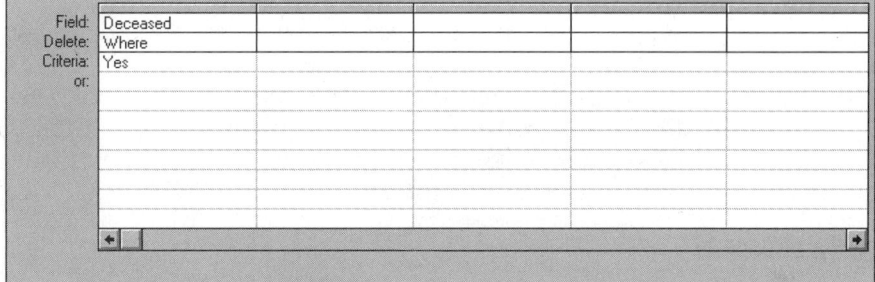

Figure 26-16: The delete query QBE pane.

Checking your results

After completing the delete query, you can check your results by simply pressing the Datasheet button on the toolbar. If the delete query worked correctly, you will see no records in the datasheet.

You have now deleted all records of deceased animals from the database tables Pets, Visits, and Visit Details.

Delete queries remove entire records, not just the data in specific fields. If you need only to delete values in specific fields, use an update query to change the values to empty values.

Creating Other Queries Using the Query Wizards

In the preceding chapter, we described how to use a Query Wizard to create a crosstab query. Access 2.0 has three other wizards that can help you maintain your databases:

- Find Duplicate Records Wizard: Show any duplicate records in a single table based on a field in the table
- Find Unmatched Records Wizard: Show all records that do not have a corresponding record in another table (for example, a customer with no pets or a pet with no owner)
- Archive Wizard: Lets you back up records in a single table and then delete records just backed up

Both the Duplicate Records Query and Archive Query work on a single table. The Unmatched Records Query compares records from one table to another.

Find Duplicate Records Wizard

This wizard helps you quickly create a query that reports which records in a table are duplicated based on some field(s) in the table. Access asks which field(s) you want to use for checking duplication and then prompts you to enter another field(s) you may want to see in the query. Finally, Access asks for a title and then creates and displays the query.

This type of query can help you find duplicate key violations, a valuable trick when you want to take an existing table and make a unique key field with the existing data. If you try to create a unique key field and Access reports an error, you know that you have either nulls in the field or duplicate records. This query helps you find duplicate records.

Find Unmatched Records Wizard

This wizard helps you quickly create a query that reports any orphan or widow records between two tables.

An *orphan* is a record in a many-side table that has no corresponding record in the one-side table. For example, say you have a pet in the Pets table that does not have an owner in the Customers table (the pet is an orphan).

A *widow* is a record in the one side of a one-to-many or one-to-one that does not have a corresponding record in the other table. For example, say you have a Customer that has no animals in the Pets table.

Access asks for the names of the two tables that you want to compare and the link field name between the tables. Then Access prompts you for the fields that you want to see in the first table and a title. Then it creates the query.

This type of query can help you find records that have no corresponding records in other tables. If you create a relationship between tables and try to set Referential Integrity but Access reports that it cannot activate Referential Integrity, this query lets you quickly find the records that are violating integrity.

Archive Records Wizard

This wizard helps you quickly create a query that will back up records for a specific criteria and then delete the records from the current table (if the user so requests). The query actually comprises two queries — a make-table query and a delete query. However, this query works with one table at a time only and is based on a single field criteria (based on a field in the table).

Access prompts you for the table you want to archive and then for a single field criteria that you want to archive for. Then Access reports the number of records to be archived and shows them to you for verification. It also asks you whether you want to delete the records after archiving. Finally Access prompts you for a title and runs the query. When the query runs, Access again prompts you to verify that you want to archive the records. If you answer yes, Access copies the records to a table by the same name with Arc added to the back of the name.

This type of query can help you back up any table that is not related to other tables, such as lookup tables.

Saving an Action Query

Saving an action query is just like saving any other query. From the design mode, you can save the query and continue working by clicking the Save button of the toolbar or selecting File⇨Save from the Query menu. If this is the first time you're saving the query, Access prompts you for a name in the Save As dialog box.

You can also save the query and exit either by selecting File⇨Close from the menu or by double-clicking the window menu button (top left corner of the Query window) and answering Yes to the dialog box question `Save changes to Query '<query name>'?`. You also can save the query by pressing F12.

Running an Action Query

After you save an action query, you can run it by simply double-clicking the name. Access will warn you that an action query is about to be executed and ask you to confirm before it continues with the query.

Troubleshooting Action Queries

When you're working with action queries, you need to be aware of several potential problems. While you're running the query, any of several messages may appear, including messages that several records were lost due to *key violations* or that records were *locked* during the execution of the query. This section discusses some of these problems and how to avoid them.

Data-type errors in appending and updating

If you attempt to enter a value that is not appropriate for the specified field, Access doesn't enter the value, simply ignoring the incorrect values and converting the fields to Null values. When you're working with append queries, this means that Access will append the records, but the fields may be blank!

Key violations in action queries

When you attempt to append records to another database that has a primary key, Access will not append records that contain the same primary key value.

Access does not let you update a record and change a primary key value to an existing value. You can change a primary key value to another value under these conditions:

- The new primary key value does not already exist.
- The field value you are attempting to change is not related to fields in other tables.

Access does not let you delete a field on the one side of a one-to-many relation without first deleting the records from the many side.

Access does not let you append or update a field value that will duplicate a value in a unique index field. (A unique index field is one that has the index property set to `Yes (No Duplicates)`.)

Record-locked fields in multiuser environments

Access will not perform an action query on records locked by another user. When you're performing an update or append query, you can choose to continue and change all other values. But remember that by allowing Access to continue with an action query, you won't be able to determine which records were left unchanged!

Text fields

When appending or updating to a Text field that is smaller than the current field, Access will truncate any text data that doesn't fit in the new field. Access will *not* warn you that it truncated the information.

Summary

In this chapter, you learned how to create and use a special type of query called the action query. This type of query goes beyond performing searches; the query can make changes to the data. The following points were covered:

- Action queries perform some operation on the tables you are using. The operation can be deleting records, changing the contents of records, adding records to another table, or making new tables.

- The various types of action queries include make-table, append, update, and delete.

- Action queries do not create a dynaset. To view the results of an action query, you must convert it to a select query (if a delete or an update query) or view the affected table.

- Always back up your tables first when you work with action queries.

- When you create an action query, it's best to create a select query first to make sure that the action is going to affect the correct records.

- Append action queries can work with only one table at a time.

- Append action queries must already have an existing table to append to. The query does not create a table for you if one doesn't already exist.

- The append query is not the best method for appending all records from one table to another. It's better to copy the table to the Clipboard and paste it to the other table.

- Make-table action queries can take fields from one or many tables and combine them into a single table.

- Delete action queries can delete records from multiple tables that have a one-to-one relation.

- Delete action queries for tables with one-to-many relations require deleting the many side records first; then the one side can be deleted.

- Unless an action query is going to be executed over and over, do not save it.

- Access enforces all referential rules when performing action queries. If an action query attempts to perform an operation that violates referential integrity, Access halts the operation.

In the next chapter, you examine advanced query topics.

Advanced Query Topics

CHAPTER 27

In This Chapter

- Using calculated fields
- Hiding fields and columns
- Understanding what happens when queries are saved
- Sorting fields and using existing indexes
- Setting query design options
- Setting query properties
- Viewing and using SQL statements

In this chapter, you work with queries in more detail and complexity than in earlier chapters. So far, you have worked with all types of queries: select, action, crosstab, and parameter. You have not, however, worked with all the options that you can use with these types of queries.

This chapter focuses on a wide range of advanced query topics. You will read about several topics that were explained in other chapters, but this chapter will address the topics in more detail. A firm understanding of advanced query issues can solve unexpected problems for you later.

Using Lookup Tables and Joins

A *lookup table* is a database table that you can use to validate entry of information. Or you can use the table to find additional information based on a key value. It is by definition a many-to-one relationship, which means that many records in the primary table can reference information from one record in the lookup table. By definition, a lookup table can be permanent or transient:

Permanent   A table that is created solely for lookup purposes

Transient   A table used as a lookup table or a primary table

In the Mountain Animal Hospital database, there are four permanent lookup tables: States, Animals, Treatments, and Medications.

An example of a transient lookup table is the Customer table. When you're working with a form to add pet personal information (name, type, etc.), the Customer table becomes a lookup table based on the customer number. Although the Customer table is a primary table of the database, in this form it may become a lookup table for the Pets table.

Working with lookup tables in queries does require an understanding of joins and how they work. For example, you may be interested in displaying visit details and the specific treatment and medication given for each of the visits. Treatment and medication information will come from the lookup tables — Treatments and Medications. To create this query, follow these steps:

Steps: Creating a Query Using Two Lookup Tables

Step 1.   Select the Visit Details, Treatments, and Medications tables and join them if they are not already joined.

Step 2.   Double-click the Visit Type field in the Visit Details table.

Step 3.   Double-click the Treatment field of the Treatments table.

Step 4.   Double-click the Medication Name field of the Medications table.

Your query should look like Figure 27-1. Notice that Visit Details uses both Treatments and Medications as lookup tables.

After you create the query, you can select the Datasheet button on the toolbar to display a dynaset similar to the one in Figure 27-2. Notice that all records displayed have both a treatment and a medication listed.

Most, if not all, visit detail records have a treatment. However, many visit detail records do not have a medication issued. You wouldn't normally administer a medication for an animal that is in for a general examination or grooming.

Therefore, the dynaset produced in Figure 27-2 is not correct! It does not show you records where there is a treatment with no medication — or a medication with no treatment. Has Access made a mistake? No. When you created the query, Access automatically made the join between the tables an equi-join (inner join).

Chapter 27: Advanced Query Topics

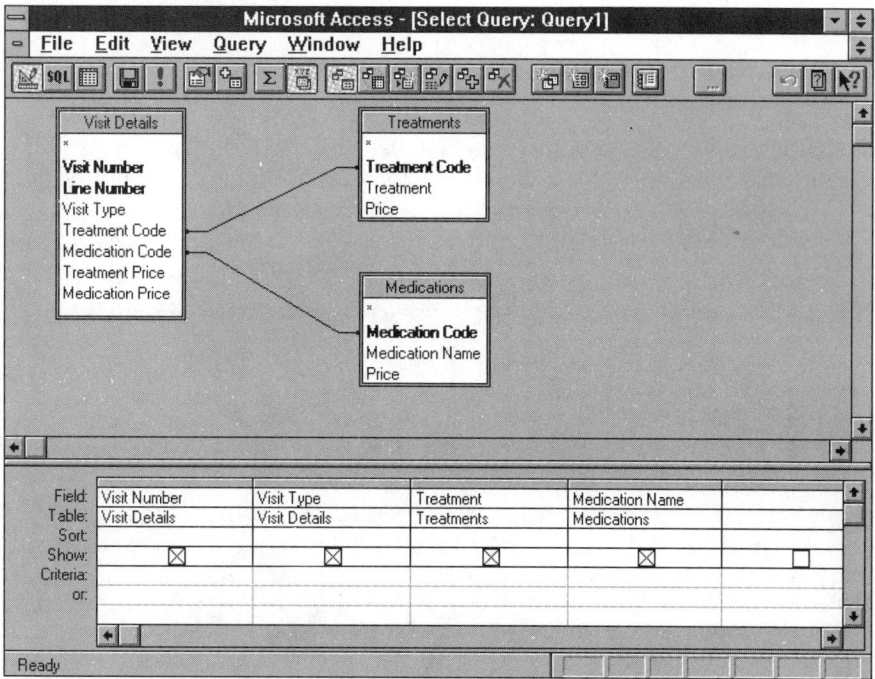

Figure 27-1: Creating a two lookup table query.

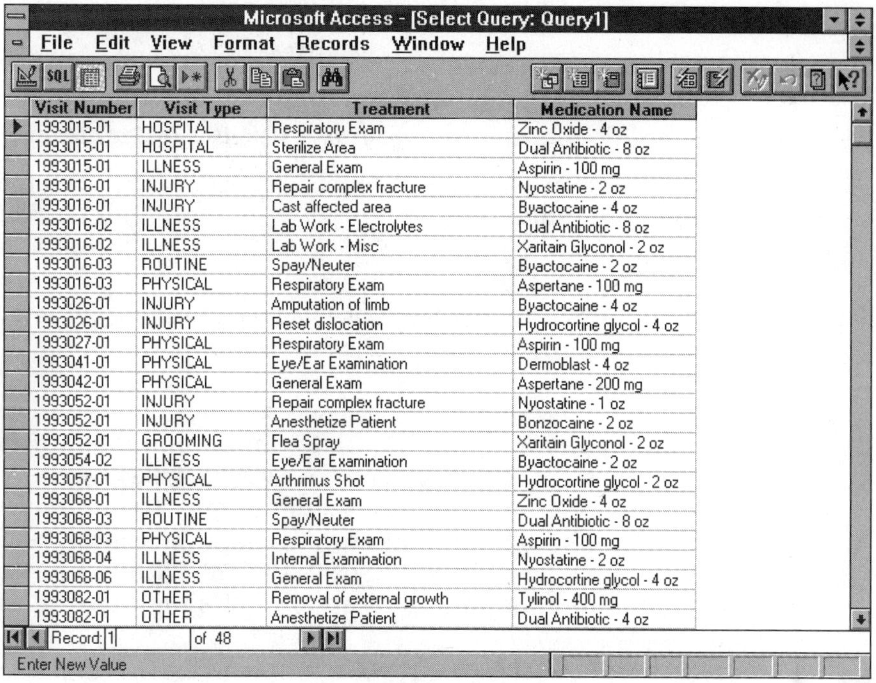

Figure 27-2: Datasheet of two lookup table query.

An *equi-join (inner join)*, which is the default join type in Access, is governed by this rule:

> All records from both tables must have the same value in the fields that are joined together.

This rule means that a treatment value must be in both the Visit Details table and the Treatments table. If a value is Null in the Visit Details table, it will not be found in the Treatments table. This is also true for the Medications table.

To correct this problem, you need to make an outer join between the primary table, Visit Details, and both of its lookup tables. An *outer join* specifies that you want to see

> All records from one table and only those records from the other table where the joined fields are equal.

This means that you want to see a value from the Treatments table only if there is a corresponding record value in the join field of the Visit Details table. In addition to this, you *always* want to see the Visit Details records even if there is no corresponding record in the lookup table. To accomplish this task, follow these additional steps:

Steps: Creating an Outer Join for Lookup Tables

Step 1. Double-click the join line between the Visit Details and Treatments tables. Access displays a Join Properties dialog box.

Step 2. Select the "Include ALL records from 'Visit Details' and ..." button, or press 2 and then press Enter.

Step 3. Double-click the join line between Visit Details and Medications.

Step 4. Select the "Include ALL records from 'Visit Details' and ..." button, or press 2 and then press Enter.

Your query should resemble Figure 27-3. Notice that the join lines now have arrowheads pointing to the Treatments and Medications tables.

When you're working with outer joins, Access always displays an arrow on the side where only records that are equal are displayed. In other words, the arrow should point toward the lookup table, not away from the table.

Select the Datasheet button on the toolbar, and you should see a datasheet that looks like Figure 27-4. Notice that the datasheet displays all Visit Details records and information from the lookups only if it is present; otherwise, it displays a Null (or blank) field.

Joins are discussed in detail in Chapter 14.

Chapter 27: Advanced Query Topics 773

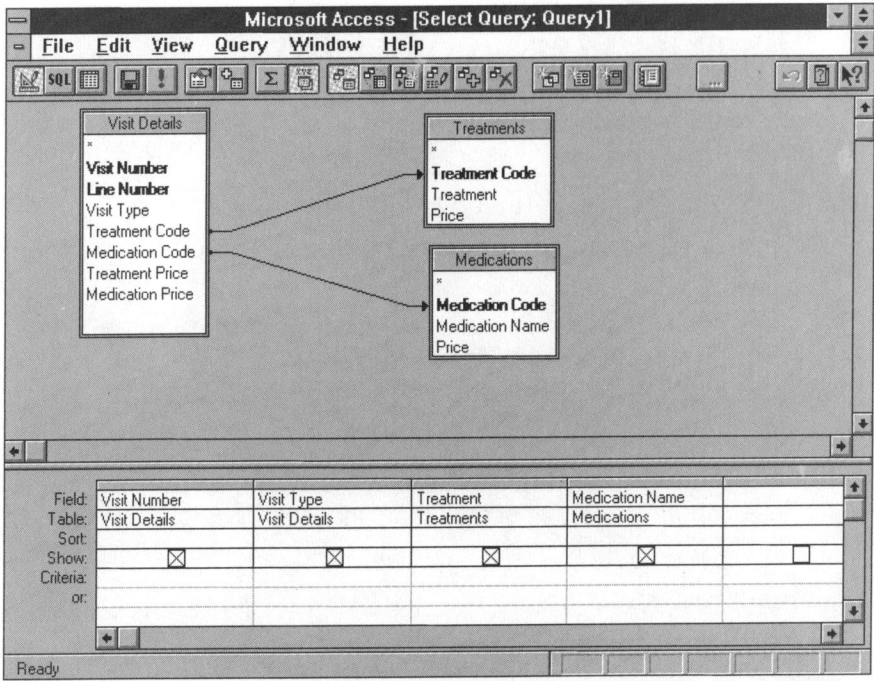

Figure 27-3: A query with an outer join specified for lookup tables.

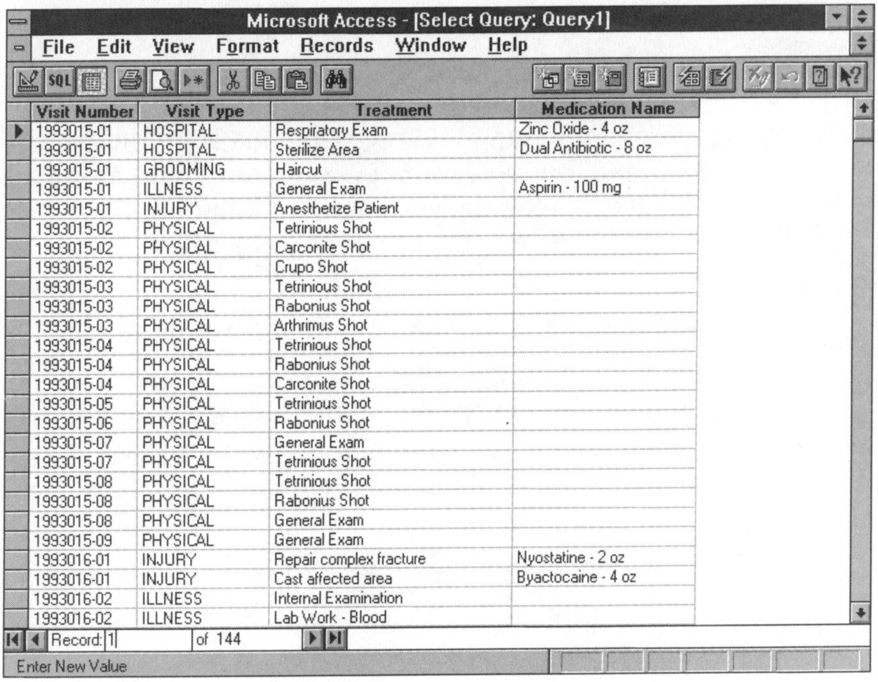

Figure 27-4: A datasheet with a corrected lookup table reference.

Using the DLookUp() Function for Lookup Tables

Another way to find specific lookup information based on a field is to create a calculated field using the DLookUp() function. You use DLookUp() to find information in a table that is not currently open. The general syntax for DLookUp() is as follows:

DLookUp("[*Field to display*]", "[*Lookup Table*]", "<*Criteria for Search*>")

[*Field to display*] in quotation marks is the field in the lookup table that you want to find.

[*Lookup Table*] in quotation marks is the table where the field you want to display is located.

<*Criteria for Search*> in quotation marks is the criteria used by the lookup function.

Although Access suggests that *Criteria for Search* is not necessary, if you want to use a different criteria for each record, it is essential. When you use DLookUp(), the criteria format is critical. The format of the *Criteria for Search* is as follows:

"[*Field in Lookup Table*] = '<*Example Data*>' "

The equal operator can be substituted with any valid Access operator.

'<*Example Data*>' in single quotation marks is usually a literal, such as 'DOG', 'AC001', etc. If the data is a field in the current table, you must use the following syntax:

" & [*Field in This Table*] & "

Notice that the field is surrounded with double quotation marks (") and ampersands (&).

Although this seems complex, building a calculated field using the DLookUp() function can be a very simple way to create a query for use by a form or report. To create a query that finds the medication name and treatment in the Treatments and Medications tables, follow these steps:

1. Select the Visit Details table.

2. Double-click on the Visit Type field in the Visit Details table.

3. Type **TreatmentType:DLookUp ("[Treatment] ","[Treatments]","[Treatment Code] = "'&[Treatment Code]&"'")** in an empty field in the QBE pane.

4. Type **MedicationType:DLookUp ("[Medication Name]","[Medications]", "[Medication Code] = "'&[Medication Code]&"'")** in an empty field in the QBE pane.

When you enter the field name of the current table in the criteria for the DLookUp function, you must not use spaces. After the equal sign, you type the entry in this format:

Chapter 27: Advanced Query Topics 775

single quote — double quote — ampersand — [*field name*] — ampersand — double quote —single quote — double quote

No spaces can be entered between the quotation marks (single or double).

Figure 27-5 shows how the query looks after you enter the calculated fields Treatment Type and Medication Type. Notice that you do not see the entire formula that you entered.

If you are having problems typing in Steps 3 or 4, press Shift+F2 to activate the Zoom window. After you activate the window, the entire contents will be highlighted; press F2 again to deselect it and move to the end of the contents. Figure 27-6 demonstrates use of the Zoom dialog box for entering complex calculated field formulas.

If you now select the Datasheet button on the toolbar, you see a datasheet similar to Figure 27-7. Notice that several records have no medication type.

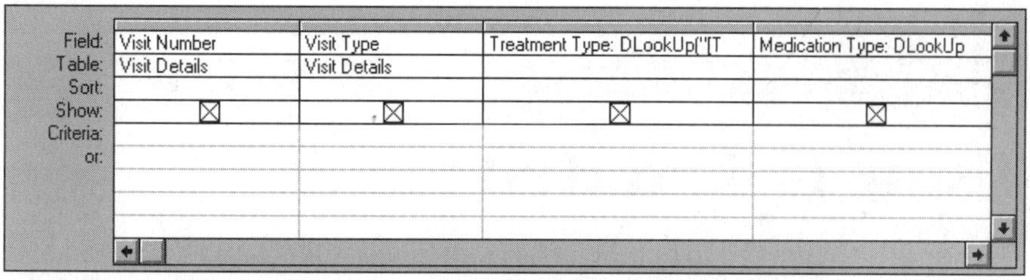

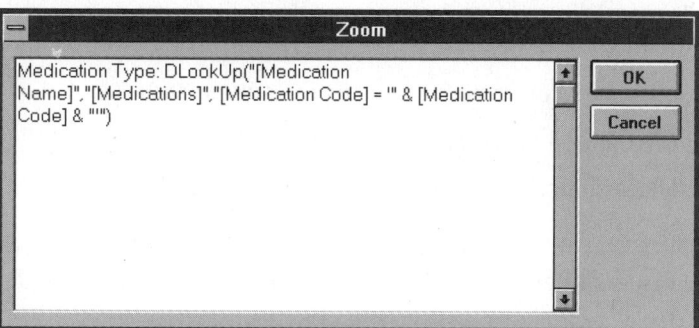

Figure 27-5: The QBE pane showing two calculated fields using the DLookUp() function.

Figure 27-6: Using the Zoom dialog box for entry of complex or long formulas.

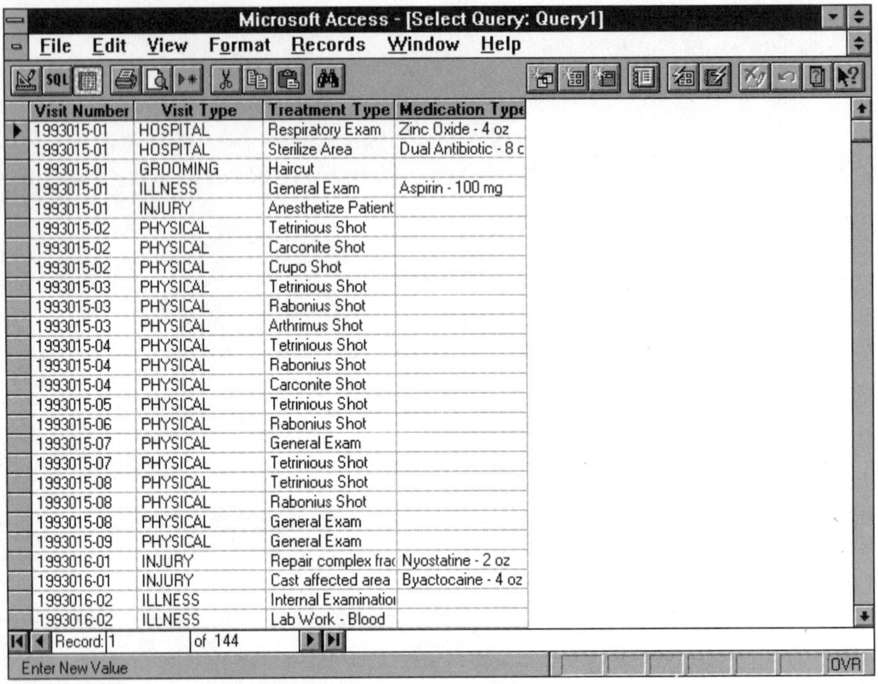

Visit Number	Visit Type	Treatment Type	Medication Type
1993015-01	HOSPITAL	Respiratory Exam	Zinc Oxide - 4 oz
1993015-01	HOSPITAL	Sterilize Area	Dual Antibiotic - 8 c
1993015-01	GROOMING	Haircut	
1993015-01	ILLNESS	General Exam	Aspirin - 100 mg
1993015-01	INJURY	Anesthetize Patient	
1993015-02	PHYSICAL	Tetrinious Shot	
1993015-02	PHYSICAL	Carconite Shot	
1993015-02	PHYSICAL	Crupo Shot	
1993015-03	PHYSICAL	Tetrinious Shot	
1993015-03	PHYSICAL	Rabonius Shot	
1993015-03	PHYSICAL	Arthrimus Shot	
1993015-04	PHYSICAL	Tetrinious Shot	
1993015-04	PHYSICAL	Rabonius Shot	
1993015-04	PHYSICAL	Carconite Shot	
1993015-05	PHYSICAL	Tetrinious Shot	
1993015-06	PHYSICAL	Rabonius Shot	
1993015-07	PHYSICAL	General Exam	
1993015-07	PHYSICAL	Tetrinious Shot	
1993015-08	PHYSICAL	Tetrinious Shot	
1993015-08	PHYSICAL	Rabonius Shot	
1993015-08	PHYSICAL	General Exam	
1993015-09	PHYSICAL	General Exam	
1993016-01	INJURY	Repair complex frac	Nyostatine - 2 oz
1993016-01	INJURY	Cast affected area	Byactocaine - 4 oz
1993016-02	ILLNESS	Internal Examinatio	
1993016-02	ILLNESS	Lab Work - Blood	

Figure 27-7: A datasheet with some of the records for the Medication Type field left blank.

Using Calculated Fields

Queries are not limited to actual fields from tables. Calculated fields can also be used. A *calculated field* is one that is created by performing some calculation. A calculated field can be created in many different ways. For example, you can create a calculated field by using these methods:

- Concatenating two Text type fields using the ampersand (&)
- Performing a mathematical calculation on two Number type fields
- Using an Access function to create a field based on the function

In the next example, you create a simple calculated field, Total Due, from the Outstanding Balance and Discount fields in the Customer table. To create the calculated field, follow these steps:

Steps: Creating Calculated Field

Step 1. Create a new query by using the Customer table.

Step 2. Select the Outstanding Balance and Discount fields from the Customer table.

Step 3.	Double-click the Discount field of the Customer table.
Step 4.	Click an empty Field: cell of the QBE pane.
Step 5.	Press Shift+F2 to activate the Zoom box.
Step 6.	Type **Total Due: [Outstanding Balance]-([Outstanding Balance]*[Discount])**.
Step 7.	Select the OK button in the Zoom box or press Enter.

After completing these steps, your query should look like Figure 27-8. Total Due is the calculated field name for the expression [Outstanding Balance] - ([Outstanding Balance] * [Discount]). The field name and expression are separated by a colon.

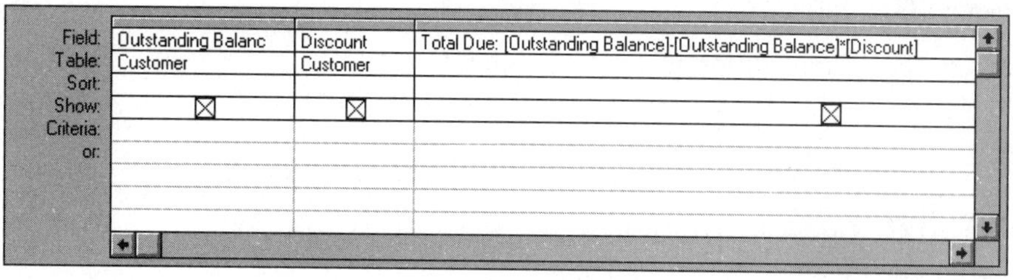

Figure 27-8: Creating a simple calculated field.

Access 2.0 has an Expression Builder that you can use to help you create any expression — like a complex calculated field for a query. In the following example, you create a calculated field named Next Visit Date that displays a date six months later. You can use this date for a letter report that you plan to send to all customers. The date is based on the Last Visit Date field of the Pets table. To create this calculated field, follow these steps:

Steps:	**Creating a Calculated Field with an Access Function**
Step 1.	Create a new query by using the Pets table.
Step 2.	Select the Pet Name, Type of Animal, and Last Visit Date fields from the Pets table.
Step 3.	Click an empty Field: cell in the QBE pane.
Step 4.	Activate the Expression Builder by clicking the Builder button on the toolbar (the ellipsis) or *right*-mouse click for the Menu on Demand and select Build. Access displays the Expression Builder dialog box, as shown in Figure 27-9. Now build the expression **DateAdd("m",6,[Pets]![Last Visit Date])** for the calculated field.

Part IV: Advanced Database Features

Step 5.	Go to the bottom left window of the Expression Builder dialog box and expand the Functions tree (click it).
Step 6.	Select the Built-in Functions choice (double-click it).
	Access places information into the two windows to the right of the one you are in (see Figure 27-10).
Step 7.	Go to the third window (which lists all the functions).
Step 8.	Select the DateAdd function (double-click it).
	Access places the Function in the top left window with information about the necessary parameters.
Step 9.	Go to the top left window and click on the parameter **<interval>**.
Step 10.	Type "m".
Step 11.	Click **<number>** and replace it with 6.
Step 12.	Click **<date>** and highlight it.
	The function should look like the one in Figure 27-10.
Step 13.	Go back to the bottom left window; click Tables.
Step 14.	Select the Pets table (click it).
Step 15.	Select [Last Visit Date] from the middle window on the bottom (double-click it).
	Access places the table and field name in the last part of the DateAdd function.
Step 16.	Select the OK button in the Expression Builder.
	Access returns you to the QBE pane and places the expression in the cell for you.
Step 17.	Change the name of the expression from Expr1 to **Next Visit Date**.

If you perform these steps correctly, the cell looks like Figure 27-11. The DateAdd() function lets you add six months to Pets.Last Visit Date. The *m* signifies that you are working with months rather than days or years.

Of course, you can type the calculated field in directly, but the Expression Builder is a valuable tool when creating complex, hard-to-remember expressions.

Figure 27-9: The Expression Builder dialog box.

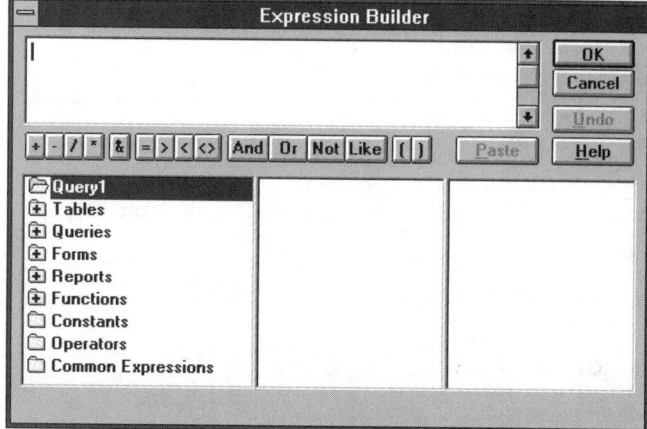

Figure 27-10: Creating a calculated field.

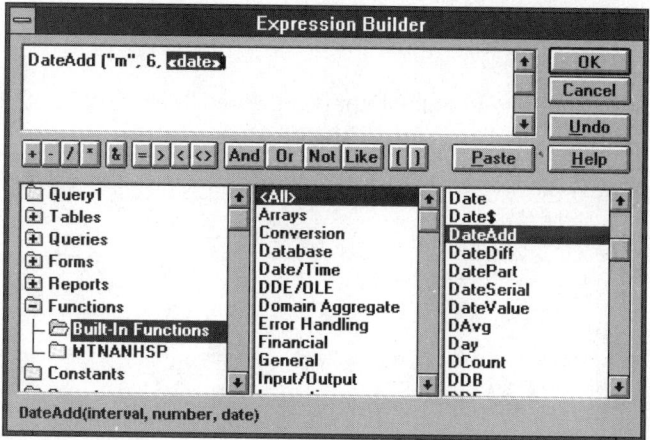

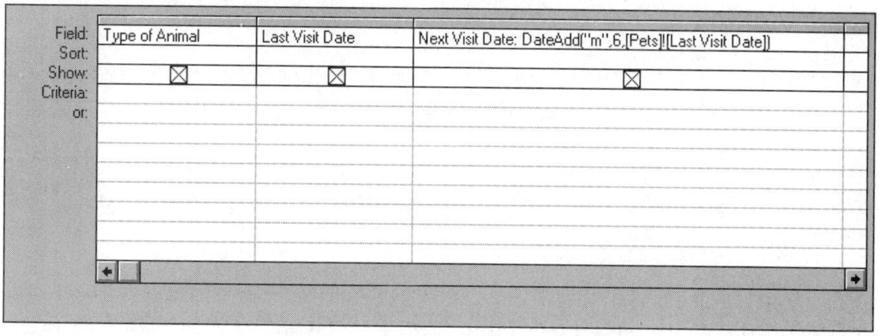

Figure 27-11: A calculated field named Next Visit Date.

Finding the Number of Records in a Table or Query

To determine quickly the total number of records in an existing table or query, use the Count(*) function. This is a special use of the Count( ) function. For example, to determine the total number of records in the Pets table, follow these steps:

Steps:	Finding the Number of Records in a Table
Step 1.	Select the Pets table.
Step 2.	Click the first empty Field: cell in the QBE pane.
Step 3.	Type **Count(*)** in the cell.

Access adds the calculated field name Expr1 to the cell in front of the Count( ) function. Your query should now look like Figure 27-12.

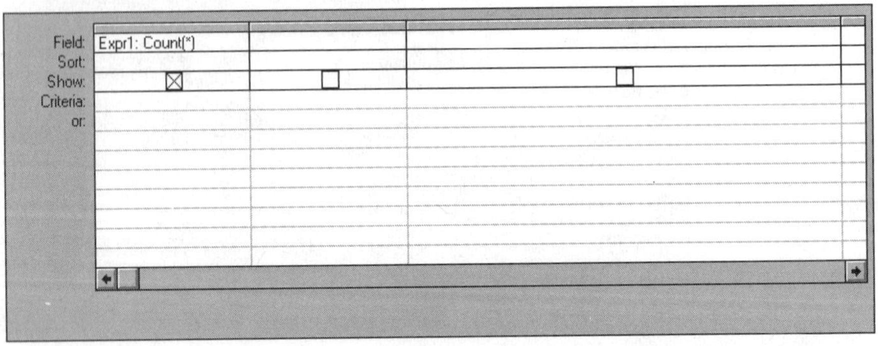

Figure 27-12: Using the Count(*) function.

When you look at the datasheet, you'll see a single cell, which shows the number of records for the Pets table. The datasheet should look like the one in Figure 27-13.

If you use this function with the asterisk wildcard (*), this is the only field that can be shown in the datasheet. That is why you entered the expression Count(*) in an empty QBE pane.

You can also use the Count(*) function to determine the total number of records that match a specific criteria. For example, you may want to know how many cats you have in the Pets table. Follow these steps to ascertain the number of cats in the table:

Chapter 27: Advanced Query Topics

Steps: Using Count(*) to Determine the Number of Records Matching a Criteria

Step	
Step 1.	Select the Pets table.
Step 2.	Click the first empty Field: cell in the QBE pane.
Step 3.	Type **Count(*)** in the cell.
Step 4.	Double-click the Type of Animal field of the Pets table.
Step 5.	Deselect the Show: cell of Type of Animal.
Step 6.	Type **CAT** in the Criteria: cell of Type of Animal.

Figure 27-14 shows how the query should look. If you select the Datasheet button on the toolbar, Access will again display only one cell in the datasheet, which contains the number of cats in the Pets table.

Remember that only the field that contains the Count(*) function can be shown in the datasheet. If you try to display any additional fields, Access reports an error.

Figure 27-13: The datasheet of a Count(*) function.

Figure 27-14: The query showing the number of cats.

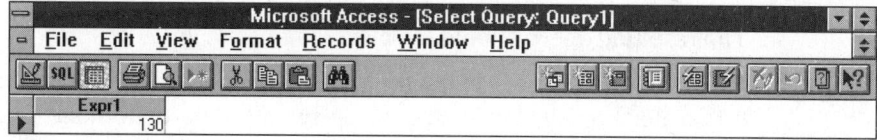

Finding the Top (n) Records in a Query

Access 2.0 not only enables you to find the number of records in an existing table or query, but it gives you the ability to find the first *(n)* records in a query. (The first *[n]* records can be a set number or a percentage of the records in the query).

Suppose you want to identify the top ten animals that you have treated — in other words, for which animal has which owner paid the most to your business. To determine the top ten animals and their owners, follow these steps:

Steps:	Finding the Number of Records in a Table
Step 1.	Create a new query using the Customer, Pets, and Visits tables.
Step 2.	Select Customer Name from the Customer Table, Type of Animal and Pet Name from the Pets table, and Total Amount from the Visits table.
Step 3.	Click the Totals button on the toolbar.
Step 4.	Change Group By under the Total Amount field to Sum.
Step 5.	Sort the Total Amount field in Descending order.
	The resulting query should look like the one in Figure 27-15.
Step 6.	Point to an empty area in the top pane of the query and activate the Property dialog box by clicking the Property button of the toolbar.
	Access displays the Query Property dialog box (see Figure 27-16).
Step 7.	In the Top Values property cell, type **10**.

You are ready to run your query. When you press the Datasheet button on the toolbar, you should see the top ten money-producing records in the dynaset, which should look like Figure 27-17.

Chapter 27: Advanced Query Topics **783**

Figure 27-15: A total query with three Group By fields.

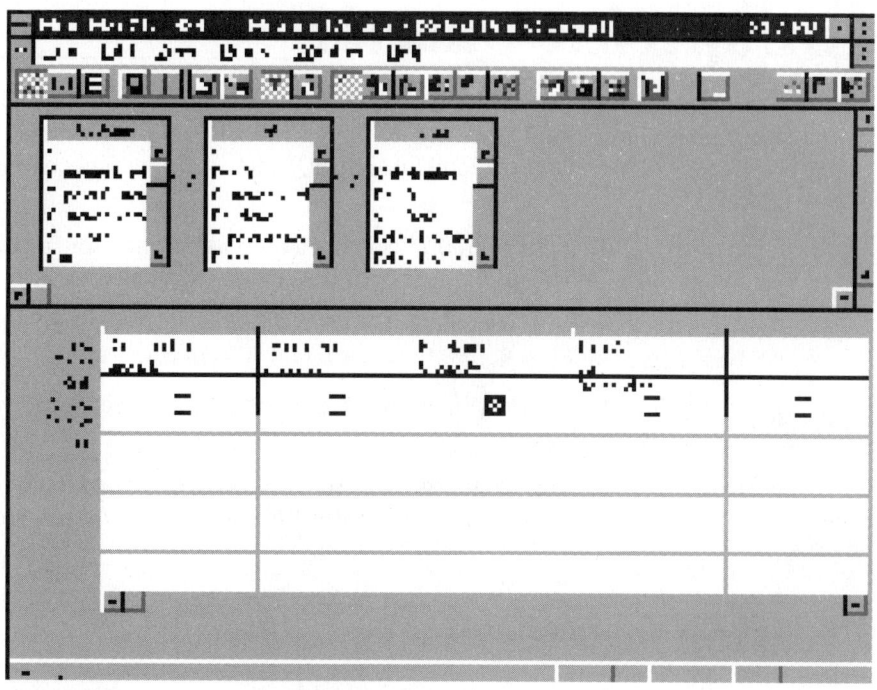

Figure 27-16: The Query Property dialog box.

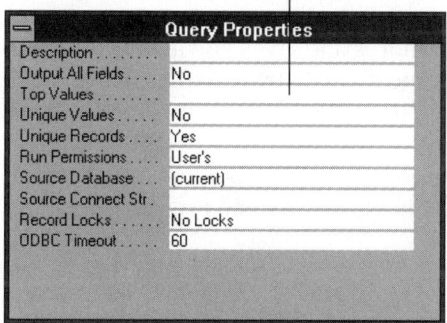

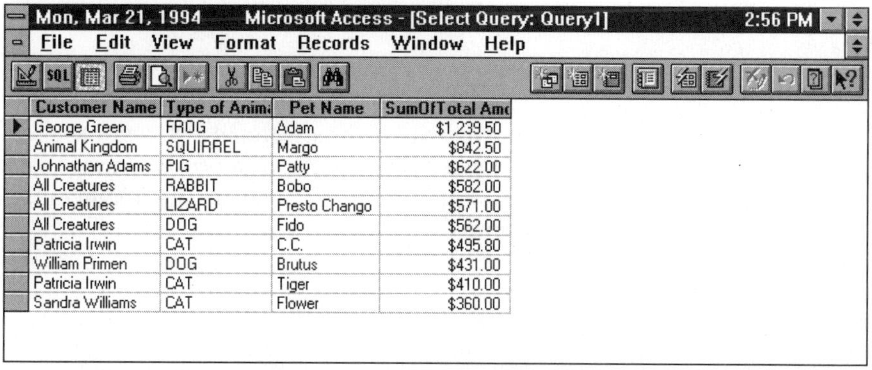

Top Values

Figure 27-17: Dynaset of the top ten records in a query.

Customer Name	Type of Animal	Pet Name	SumOfTotal Amo
George Green	FROG	Adam	$1,239.50
Animal Kingdom	SQUIRREL	Margo	$842.50
Johnathan Adams	PIG	Patty	$622.00
All Creatures	RABBIT	Bobo	$582.00
All Creatures	LIZARD	Presto Chango	$571.00
All Creatures	DOG	Fido	$562.00
Patricia Irwin	CAT	C.C.	$495.80
William Primen	DOG	Brutus	$431.00
Patricia Irwin	CAT	Tiger	$410.00
Sandra Williams	CAT	Flower	$360.00

SQL Specific Queries

Access 2.0 has added three new query types that are created by entering SQL statements only. These queries cannot be created by using the QBE pane; instead, you type the appropriate SQL statement directly into the SQL view window. These new SQL specific queries are

- Union query: Combines common fields from more than one table or query into one recordset.
- Pass-through query: Allows you to send SQL commands directly to any SQL database server in the SQL database servers SQL syntax.
- Data definition query: Lets you create or alter database objects in Access databases directly.

To create any of these queries, select the type that you want to create from the Query⇨SQL Specific menu. There is no applicable button available on the toolbar.

Creating union queries

Union queries let you quickly combine several tables that have common fields. The resultant snapshot (like a dynaset) is not updatable.

For example, a competing veterinarian retires and gives you all its clients' records. You decide to create a union query to combine the data from both practices. Figure 27-18 shows a union query that returns the Customer name and city in order by city.

Notice that a union query has two or more SQL SELECT statements. Each SELECT statement requires the same number of fields in the same order.

When you run a union query, it creates a *snapshot* rather than a dynaset. A snapshot is a type of recordset that is not updatable.

Creating pass-through queries

A pass-through query sends SQL commands directly to an SQL database server (such as Microsoft SQL Server, Oracle, and so on). You send the command by using the syntax required by the particular server. Be sure to consult the documentation for the appropriate SQL database server.

Figure 27-18:
A SQL union query.

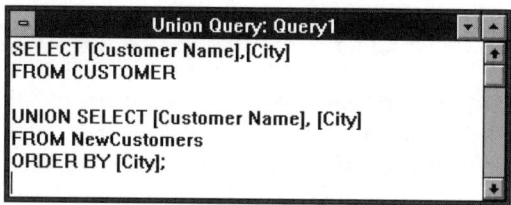

Figure 27-19 shows a pass-through query for SQL Server that creates a new table named Payroll and defines the fields in the table.

 Never attempt to convert a pass-through query to another type query. If you do, Access erases the entire SQL statement you typed in.

 When working with pass-through queries, you should not perform operations that change the state of the connection. For example, halting a transaction in the middle may cause unexpected results.

Figure 27-19:
A pass-through query for SQL Server.

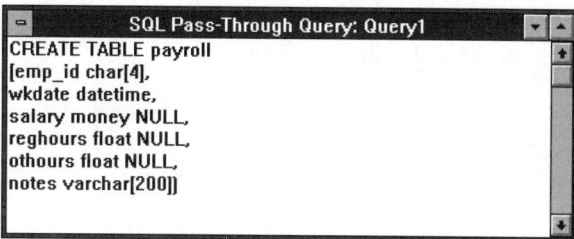

Creating data definition queries

Of these three new SQL specific queries, the data definition query is the least useful. Everything that you can do with it, you can also do using the design tools in Access. However, the data definition query is an efficient way to create or change database objects. With a data definition query, you can use any of the following SQL statements:

- CREATE TABLE
- ALTER TABLE
- DROP TABLE
- CREATE INDEX
- DROP INDEX

How Queries Save Field Selections

When you open a query design, you may notice that the design has changed since you last saved the query. When you save a query, Access rearranges fields and even eliminates fields based on several rules. The following list summarizes these rules:

- Fields not having the Show: box checked but having criteria specified are moved to the rightmost columns in the QBE pane.
- Fields not having the Show: box checked are eliminated from the QBE pane column.

Because of these rules, your query may look very different after you save and reopen it. In fact, it is possible to save a query that produces a datasheet with fields in the order A and then B and then after saving, closing, reopening, and rerunning the query, the fields are displayed in the order B and then A. In this section of the chapter, you learn how this happens and some ways to prevent it.

Hiding (not showing) fields

There are times when you won't want certain fields in the QBE pane to show in the actual dynaset of the datasheet. For example, you may want to specify a criteria or a sort by a field such as Customer Number, but you don't want to show the actual field.

To *hide*, or exclude, a field from the dynaset, you simply click the Show: box off under the field you want to hide. Figure 27-20 demonstrates this. Notice that the field Type of Customer is used to specify a criteria of displaying only individuals ("1"). You don't want the Type of Customer field in the actual datasheet, so you click the Show: cell off for the Type of Customer field.

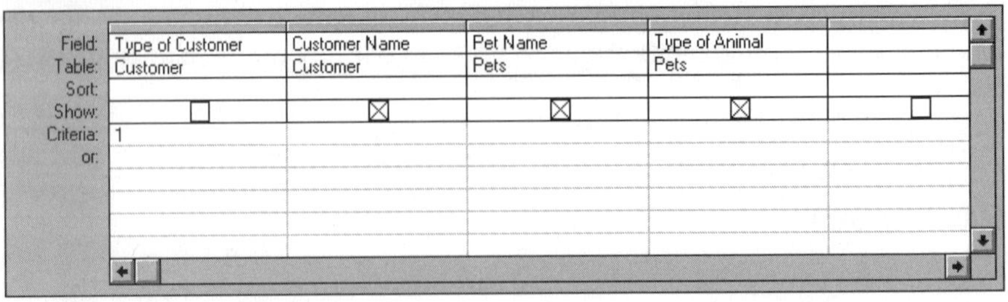

Figure 27-20: Hiding a field.

Any fields that have the Show: cell turned off and for which you entered criteria are placed at the end of the QBE pane when you save the query. Figure 27-21 shows the same query as Figure 27-20 after it is saved and brought back into the design screen. Notice that the field Type of Customer has been moved to the end (extreme right) of the QBE pane. The location of a hidden field will not change the dynaset. Because the field is not displayed, where it is located in the QBE pane is unimportant. You always get the same results wherever a hidden field is placed in the QBE pane.

Figure 27-21: A query that has been saved with hidden fields.

If you hide any fields in the QBE pane that are not used for sorts or criteria, Access automatically eliminates them from the query when you save it. If you want to use these fields and need to show them later, you'll have to add them back to the QBE pane.

If you are creating a query to be used by a form or report, you must show any fields to be used by the form or report. This includes showing any fields that you want to bind a control to in the form or report.

Renaming Fields in Queries

When working with queries, you can rename a field to describe the field's contents more clearly or accurately. For example, you may want to rename the Customer Name field to Owner Name. This is very useful when working with calculated fields or calculating totals; Access automatically assigns names such as Expr1 or AvgOfWeight. Renaming fields in Access queries is extremely simple. For example, to change the display name of the Customer Name, follow these steps:

Steps:	Changing a Field Name
Step 1.	Select the Customer table.
Step 2.	Double-click the Customer Name field of the Customer table.
Step 3.	Place the cursor in front of the first letter of Customer Name in the Field: cell.
Step 4.	Type **Owner Name:** (be sure to include a colon).

Figure 27-22:
Renaming a query field.

[Figure 27-22: QBE pane showing Field row with "Owner Name:Customer Name"]

Figure 27-22 shows the query field renamed. Notice that the field has both the display name, which is Owner Name, and the actual field name, which is Customer Name.

When naming a query field, you should delete any names assigned by Access (on the left of the colon). For example, the calculated field name Expr1 should be removed when you name the field.

If you rename a field, Access uses only the new name for the heading of the query datasheet or a control source in a form or report that uses the query. Access does not change the actual field name in the underlying table.

If you need a colon in the new name, enclose the entire name in brackets, as in [Month: 2].

When working with renamed fields, you can use an expression name (the new name you specified) in another expression within the same query. For example, you may have a calculated field called First Name that uses several Access functions to separate an individual's first name from the last name. For this calculated field, you can use the field called Owner Name that you created earlier.

When you work with referenced expression names, you cannot have any criteria specified against the field that you are referencing. For example, you cannot have a criteria specified for Owner Name if you reference Owner Name in the First Name calculation. Access will not display the contents for the expression field Owner Name in the datasheet.

Hiding and Unhiding Columns in the QBE Pane

Sometimes you may want to hide specific fields in the QBE pane. This is not the same as hiding a field by clicking on the Show box. Hiding a column in the QBE pane is similar to hiding a datasheet column. Hiding columns is extremely easy. You simply resize a column (from right to left) until it has no visible width. For example, Figure 27-23 shows several fields in the QBE pane.

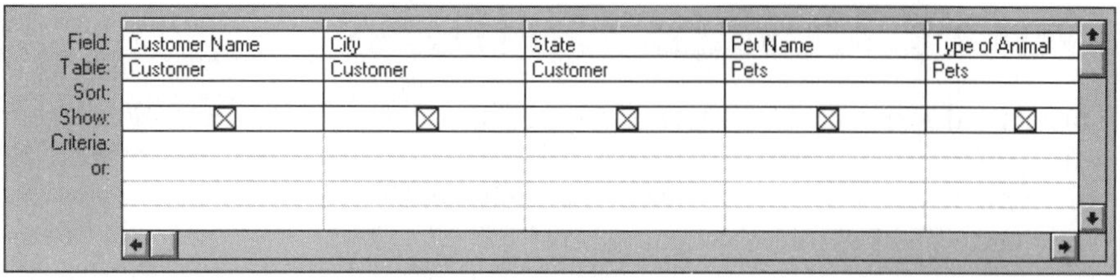

Chapter 27: Advanced Query Topics   789

Figure 27-23:
A typical QBE pane.

Field:	Customer Name	City	State	Pet Name	Type of Animal
Table:	Customer	Customer	Customer	Pets	Pets
Sort:					
Show:	☒	☒	☒	☒	☒
Criteria:					
or:					

In the next example, you hide a column. Follow these steps to hide the City column:

Steps: Hiding a Column

Step 1. Move the mouse to the right side of the City field on the field selector (a small, thick bar icon with arrows on both sides appears).

Step 2. Click and drag the right side (toward the Customer Name field) of the City field until it totally disappears.

Figure 27-24 shows the QBE pane with the City field hidden.

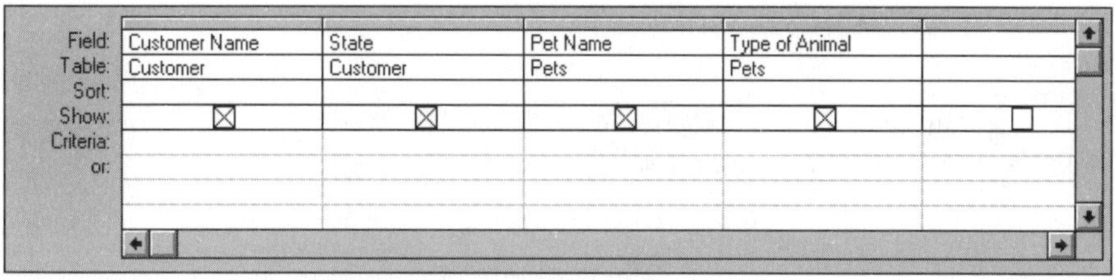

Figure 27-24:
The QBE pane with a column hidden.

Field:	Customer Name	State	Pet Name	Type of Animal	
Table:	Customer	Customer	Pets	Pets	
Sort:					
Show:	☒	☒	☒	☒	☐
Criteria:					
or:					

After you hide a field, you can unhide it by reversing the process. If you want to unhide the City column, follow these steps:

Steps: Unhiding a Column

Step 1. Move the mouse to the left side of the field State on the selector bar (the bar with arrows appears). Make sure that you are to the right of the divider between Customer Name and State.

Step 2. Click on and drag the left side of State (toward the Pet Name field) until you size the column to the correct length.

Step 3. Release the button, and the field name City will appear in the column you unhide.

Query Design Options

There are three default options that you can specify when you work with a query design. You can view and set these options by selecting View⇨Options from the main Query menu and then selecting Query Design in the Category: box of the Options dialog box. Figure 27-25 shows this dialog box.

Notice these three Items: that you can set for queries:

- Output all Fields
- Run Permissions
- Show Table Names

These are the default options that Access uses when you open a new query. The default for Show Table Names and Output All fields is No. Run Permissions offers you a choice of either owners or users (default). Table 27-1 briefly describes each option and its purpose.

When you set query design options, they do not take effect against the current query. These options are used to specify actions for new queries only. To show table names in the current query, select View⇨Table Names from the main Query menu. To specify the other two options for the current query, select View⇨Query Properties....

Figure 27-25: The Options dialog box.

Table 27-1
Table of Query Design Options

Option	Purpose
Output all Fields	Shows all fields in the underlying tables or only the fields displayed in the QBE pane.
Run Permissions	Restricts use in a multiuser environment. A user restricted from viewing the underlying tables can still view the data from the query.
Show Table Names	Shows the Table: row in the QBE pane when set to Yes. Hides the Table: row if set to No.

Setting Query Properties

To set query properties, either click the Properties button on the toolbar, *right* mouse click and choose Properties from the Menu on Demand, or select View⇨Query Properties... from the main Query menu. Access displays a Query Properties dialog box. Your options depend on the query type and the table or field with which you are working. Tables 27-2, 27-3, and 27-4 show the query properties that can be set.

The File- and Field-Level properties, which are new to version 2.0 (as are many of the Query-Level properties), can be used just like the properties in forms, reports, and tables. The Query-Level Properties depend upon the type of query being created.

Table 27-2
File-Level Properties

Property	Purpose
Alias	A custom name for the table
Source	Connecting string and database

Table 27-3
Field-Level Properties

Property	Purpose
Description	Text that describes the field
Format	Format to be used to specify the data
Decimal Place	Number of decimal places to display
Input Mask	An input guide — dashes, spaces, and so on
Caption	Column header name in the datasheet

Table 27-4
Query-Level Properties

Property	Description	Query					
		Select	Crosstab	Update	Delete	Make-Table	Add-Table
Description	Text describing the table or query	X	X	X	X	X	X
Output All Fields	Show all fields from the underlying tables in the query	X				X	X
Top Values	Number of highest or lowest values to be returned	X				X	X
Unique Values	Return only unique field values in the dynaset	X				X	X
Unique Records	Return only unique records for the dynaset	X		X	X	X	X
Column Headings	Names and order of columns to display		X				
Run Permissions	Establish permissions for the specifed user	X	X	X	X	X	X
Source Database	External database name for all table/queries in the query	X	X	X	X	X	X
Source Connect Str	Name of application used to connect to external database	X	X	X	X	X	X
Destination Table	Name of new table or external table to be appended to					X	X
Destination DB	Connection string necessary to connect to the new table					X	X
Dest Connect Str	Name of the product used to create the external database					X	
Record Locks	Records locked while query runs (usually action queries)	X	X	X	X	X	X
ODBC Timeout	Number of seconds before reporting error for opening DB	X	X	X	X	X	X

Viewing SQL Statements in Queries

When you use graphical Query By Example, Access converts what you create into a *Structured Query Language (SQL)* statement. This SQL statement is what Access actually executes when you run your query.

SQL is a standardized language that is used by many relational databases to query and update tables. It is relatively simple to learn and use. However, Access does not require that you know it or use it — Access does use it, but you won't ever have to know it's there.

If you are familiar with SQL, you can view and/or edit an SQL statement. If you make changes to an SQL statement, Access automatically reflects them in the QBE pane for you.

Table 27-5
Query Options and What They Do

Property	Purpose
Unique Values Only	Retrieves only unique data values in the fields displayed. Any dynaset record that shows duplicate information is ignored.
Restrict Available Fields	Restricts available fields to those in the QBE pane. If you plan to use this query for a form or report, deselect this option.
Run with Owner's Permissions	Restricts a user in a multiuser environment from viewing an underlying table. This option lets a user access a query that uses an underlying table that the user has no right to access.
Fixed Column Headings	Specifies the order of column headings and stabilizes the heading for use in a report or form. Enter the headings in the box in the order you need them for the datasheet, separated by semicolons.
Table Name	Lets you type the new table name or select a table from the box.
Another Database/File Name	Lets you select the database (if different from the current one) that you want to specify a table name for.

To view an SQL statement that Access creates, select <u>V</u>iew⇨SQL ... from the Query menu. Figure 27-26 shows a typical SQL statement that will display the fields Customer Name, Pet Name, and Type of Animal.

 If you want to modify an existing SQL statement or create your own, enter changes directly into the SQL dialog box. To add new lines in the dialog box, press Ctrl+Enter. This is also true for adding data to a Memo field.

You can use SQL statements directly in expressions, macros, forms, and reports. For example, an SQL statement can be used in the RowSource or RecordSource properties of a form or report. Using an SQL statement directly in a form or report does not require knowledge of SQL. Rather, you can simply create the SQL statement (selecting specific records, etc.) in the Query window. Activate the SQL dialog box and copy (Ctrl+C) the entire SQL statement that was created. Switch to the location where you want to use the statement and paste (Ctrl+V) the statement where you need it (RowSource property of the property sheet, and so on).

 You can create SQL statements in the SQL dialog box. If you write your own SQL statement or edit one, the Query window is updated when you leave the dialog box. Tables are added to the top portion; fields and criteria are added to the QBE pane.

Figure 27-26:
An SQL statement in Access.

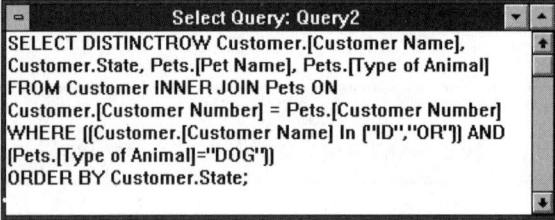

Summary

In this chapter, you worked with queries in great detail. The following points were covered:

- When you're working with lookup tables, always set an outer join that points to the lookup table. An alternative is to use the DLookUp( ) function.
- Dynamic queries — those that use the asterisk field of a table — automatically display any changes to the underlying tables.
- When using tables in queries, open (use) only the tables whose fields you will use. Because Access automatically creates equi-joins, you may not see all the records unless you set outer joins.
- You can create calculated fields for display, to set criteria against, and even to sort on in a query.
- Access 2.0 offers several new queries, including top record, union, pass-through, and data definition.
- If you hide a field and save the query, Access moves the hidden field to the end of the display. If you don't use a hidden field for a criteria or sort and you save the query, Access deletes the hidden field from the QBE pane.
- Columns in the QBE pane can be hidden and unhidden by clicking on and dragging the side of the field on the selector bar.
- Query properties are optional for all queries except make-table and append queries.
- SQL statements can be viewed and modified. If you modify an SQL statement, Access automatically updates the QBE pane to reflect the changes.
- You can use SQL statements in expressions, macros, forms, and reports by copying and pasting them where you need them.

In the following chapter, you learn how to create multiple-table forms.

Creating and Using Subforms

CHAPTER 28

In This Chapter

- What a subform is
- How to create a subform with a wizard
- How to create a subform by dragging a form from the Database window to a form
- How to add validation to a subform
- How to add totals to a subform

Subforms give you great flexibility in displaying and entering data with multiple tables. You can display data from multiple tables and be able to edit all the fields without worrying about integrity problems. With a subform, you can even enter data into a one-to-many form relationship.

What Is a Subform?

Simply put, a subform is a form within a form. A subform lets you use data from more than one table in a form, where data from one table can be displayed in one format while data from another is displayed in a different format. For example, you can display one customer record in a form while displaying several pet records in a datasheet subform.

Subforms give you the flexibility to display data from several tables or queries in one form. Although you can edit multiple tables on a form, using a subform gives you far greater flexibility.

You can display data on a form in several ways:

Form — Display one record on a form

Continuous — Display multiple records on a form

Datasheet — Display multiple records using one line per record

By including a subform on a form, you can display your data in multiple formats simultaneously. This lets you display data in formats like the form shown in Figure 28-1. This figure shows a form to enter visit details. Data from a query that lists information from the Customer, Pets, and Visits tables is shown on the top part of the form in a form view. In the bottom part of the form is a subform displaying information from the Visit Details table. Notice that both the form itself and the subform have record selectors. By using a subform, each portion of the form acts independently.

In fact, the subform actually contains data from three tables. The descriptions of each treatment come from the Treatments table, whereas the medication listings come from the Medications table. As you'll learn when you create this form later in the chapter, when you select either of these fields in the datasheet, a drop-down list box appears. Each of these fields is actually a combo box that lets you select a description from the Treatments or Medications table and then store the appropriate code in the Visit Details table.

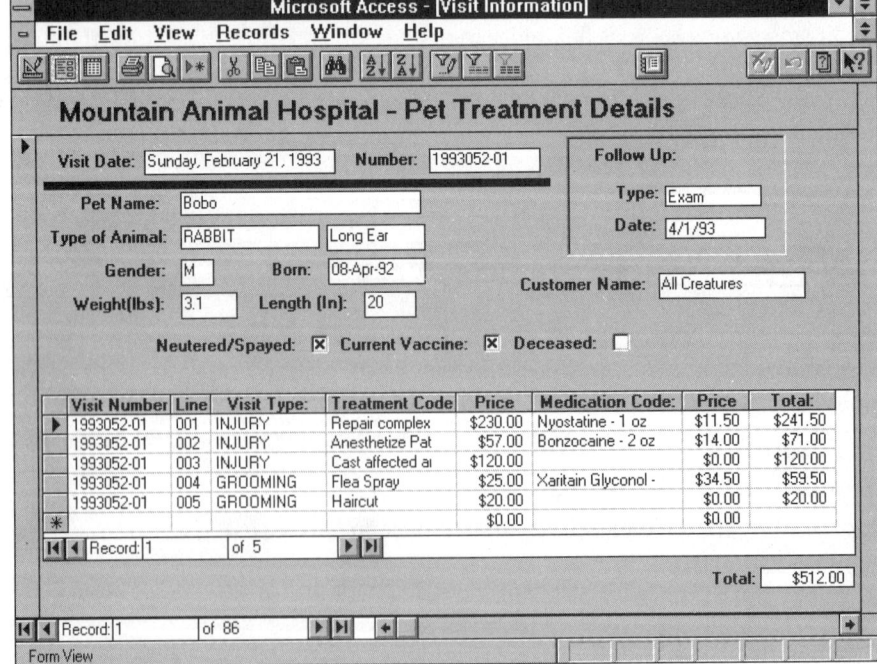

Figure 28-1: The form for adding visit details.

When you create a subform, you link the main form to the subform by a common field of expression. The subform will then display only records that are related to the main form. The greatest advantage of subforms is their ability to show the one-to-many relationship. The main form represents the *one* part of the relationship, and the subform represents the *many* side.

You can create a subform in several ways:

- Using the Subform Wizard
- Using the Subform button in the toolbox
- Dragging a form from the Database window to another form

Creating Subforms with the Form Wizard

One of the choices in the Access Form Wizard is Main/Subform. This choice lets you quickly create a form with an embedded subform. Without the wizard, you have to create both the form and the subform separately and then embed and link the subform to the main form.

Creating the form and selecting the Form Wizard

Both the form and the subform are automatically created by the Form Wizard. In this example, you create a form that displays information from the Customer table in the main form and information from the Pets table in the subform. To create the form, follow these steps:

Steps:	Creating a New Form and Selecting the Main/Subform Form Wizard
Step 1.	Create a new form.
Step 2.	Select the Customer table and select the Form Wizard button.
Step 3.	Select Main/Subform from the first Form Wizards dialog box, as shown in Figure 28-2.

After you select the Main/Subform Form Wizard, you need to select the table/query for the subform.

Part IV: Advanced Database Features

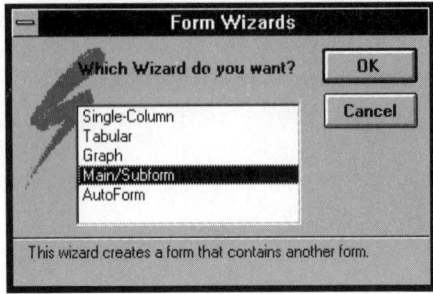

Figure 28-2: Selecting the Main/Subform Form Wizard.

When you build a form with an embedded subform, you must create the subform first.

Selecting the subform table or query

Because a subform uses a separate data source from the form, you have to select the table or query that is used for the subform. To select the subform table/query, follow these steps:

Steps:	Selecting the Subform Table/Query
Step 1.	Select the Pets table from the list box, as shown in Figure 28-3.
Step 2.	Select the Next > button to move to the next dialog box.

Notice in Figure 28-3 that the table/query you selected for the main form is displayed above the list box as you select the subform table/query. After you complete this selection, you can select the fields for the main form.

Figure 28-3: Selecting the subform table/query.

Choosing the fields for the main form

As with other wizards, you select each of the fields you want in the main form. Figure 28-4 shows the completed field selection. To select the fields for this example, follow these steps:

Steps:	Selecting Fields for the Main Form
Step 1.	Select Customer Name and select the > button.
Step 2.	Select Street/Apt and select the > button.
Step 3.	Select City and select the > button.
Step 4.	Select State and select the > button.
Step 5.	Select Zip Code and select the > button.
Step 6.	Select Phone Number and select the > button.
Step 7.	Select Last Visit Date and select the > button.
Step 8.	Select the Next > button to move to the next dialog box.

Notice the picture in the left side of the dialog boxes. The picture helps you understand what you are selecting. The fields you select for the main form are placed in the top part of the form. If you select enough fields, you won't see the subform on the first page of the form. However, you can always rearrange the fields and move the subform.

After you select all the fields for the main form, you have to select the fields for the subform. Remember that the fields in the subform are displayed horizontally in a datasheet. You should select only as many fields as you think will fit across the screen.

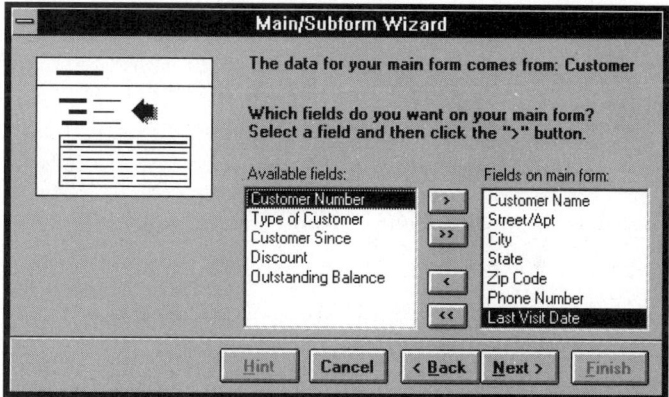

Figure 28-4: Selecting the fields for the main form.

You can always change the font size of the datasheet after the Form Wizard is completed, but there is a limit. Generally, you need to understand your data before you begin to use the wizard.

Choosing the fields for the subform

Fields for the subform are selected in exactly the same way as fields for the form. Figure 28-5 shows the Form Wizard dialog box for selecting fields from the subform. As you can see, the fields listed in the dialog box are from the Pets table, which you previously selected in the Form Wizard. You may also notice that the picture is different; this one shows the subform as the area you are selecting fields for.

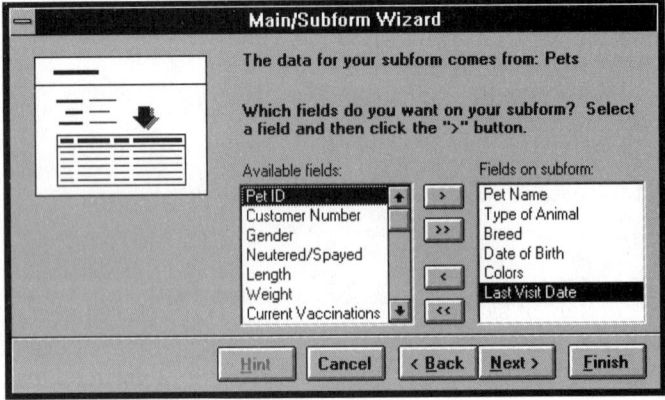

Figure 28-5: Selecting the fields for the subform.

To select the fields for the subform, follow these steps:

Steps:	Selecting Fields for the Subform
Step 1.	Select Pet Name and select the > button.
Step 2.	Select Type of Animal and select the > button.
Step 3.	Select Breed and select the > button.
Step 4.	Select Date of Birth and select the > button.
Step 5.	Select Colors and select the > button.
Step 6.	Select Last Visit Date and select the > button.
Step 7.	Select the Next > button to move to the next dialog box.

After you select the fields for the subform, you can then specify the look of the form.

Selecting the visual effect

As with other Form Wizards, you can select the look of the form. You can select from five choices. The look is only for the main form. The subform, which is displayed as a datasheet, has no specific look. To select the look of the main form, follow these steps:

Steps:	Selecting the Look for the Form
Step 1.	Select the Boxed look for the form.
Step 2.	Select the Next > button to move to the next dialog box.

A more detailed explanation of the look of the form and of Form Wizards in general is found in Chapter 9.

The next dialog box lets you select the title for the form.

Selecting the form title

You can accept the default title, which is the main form's table name, or you can enter a custom title. The text you enter is placed in the form's form header section. To enter the title, follow these steps:

Steps:	Selecting the Form Title
Step 1.	Type **Customer and Pets Form,** as shown in Figure 28-6.
Step 2.	Select Finish to move to the next dialog box.

After the title is entered and you select the continuation button, you may expect to see the form in Design view or Form view. Actually, another set of dialog boxes is displayed. You first have to save the subform as a separate form.

Saving and naming the subform

Figure 28-7 displays the dialog box that appears after the button is selected. The dialog box actually contains a statement rather than a question. The statement You must

Figure 28-6: Selecting the title for the form.

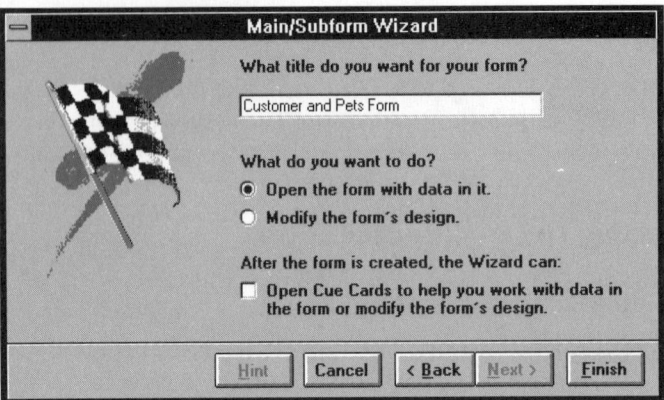

Figure 28-7: The dialog box for saving the subform.

`save the subform before the Main/Subform Form Wizard can proceed` is accompanied by a single OK button. You have no choice but to select OK, or you lose everything you just did.

Select OK to continue. A dialog box appears, letting you enter a name for the subform. The default is Form1. You should name the subform Pets Subform. When you accept this name or enter a name of your choice, the subform is saved as a form and will appear in the database window when you select Forms. You should try to name your forms and subforms something similar so you can tell that they go together. After you complete this step, you can view your form or its design.

Normally, when you provide Access with two tables/queries that have a common field name, Access can automatically establish the link between the two tables. If Access can't figure out which fields in the main form and the subform should be linked, you see the message `Main/Subform Form Wizard couldn't establish a link between main form and subform`. You then have to establish the link yourself by entering the field names in the main form property sheet. As described later in this chapter, you use the Link Child Fields and Link Master Fields properties to establish a manual link.

Displaying the form

After the subform is named, the screen displays either the form or its design. In this example, you see the form as shown in Figure 28-8.

The datasheet is the default view of a subform. Whether the subform is created through a wizard, dragged to the form, or created from the toolbox, a datasheet is always created. You can change this by changing the Default View property to either Single Form or Continuous Form.

You can change the look of the datasheet here in the Form view. You can adjust the column widths or row height. You can also rearrange the columns. When you make these changes, they will be changed the next time you view the subform. if you scroll down to the bottom of the datasheet, you'll notice that the asterisk (*) appears in the record selector column. Like any datasheet, you can add new records by using this row.

The main Form view is the only place you can define how a subform looks.

Both the main form and the subform have record selectors because they are actually separate forms. As you use the outer record selector in the main form, you move from customer record to customer record. As you move from one customer record to an-

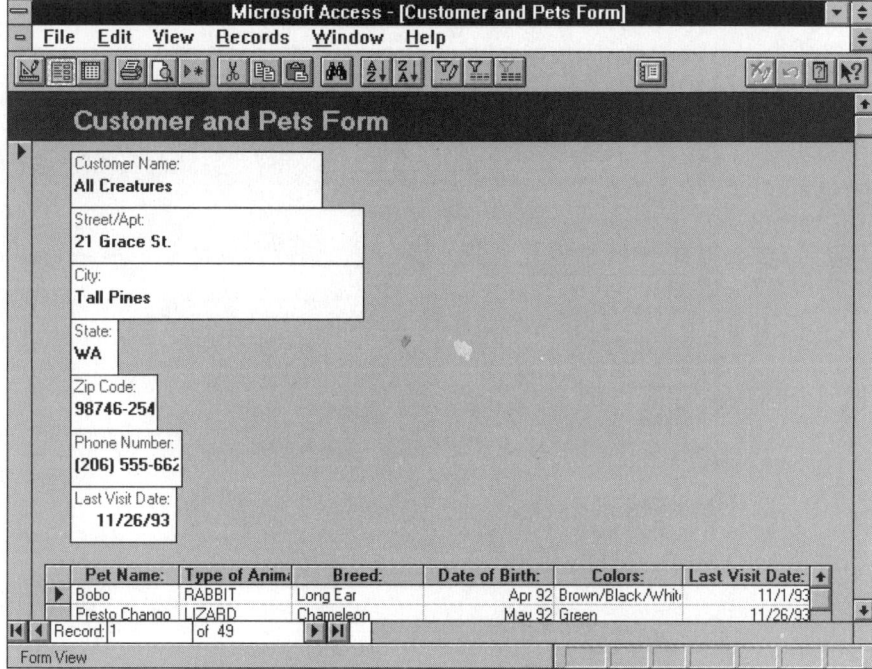

Figure 28-8: The Customer and Pets form.

other, the link automatically changes the pets that are displayed. This way, when you look at the record for All Creatures, you see pets for All Creatures. When you switch to Animal Kingdom, their pets are displayed.

When you use the inner record selector of the subform, you can scroll the records within the datasheet. This is especially important if there are more records in the subform than can be displayed in the open height of the data-sheet. You can use the scroll bar too. However, if you are viewing records in a continuous form or single form view, you may want to go directly to a known record.

Displaying the main form design

In order to understand how the forms are actually linked from the main form to the subform, you need to view the main form in Design view. Figure 28-9 shows this form in Design view.

The design for the main form shows the fields from the Customer table at the top of the form and the subform control at the bottom of the form. The subform control is similar to other controls, such as the unbound object control. Rather than storing the fields in the form, the name of the subform is stored. The subform is retrieved, and the fields in the subform are displayed when the form is run.

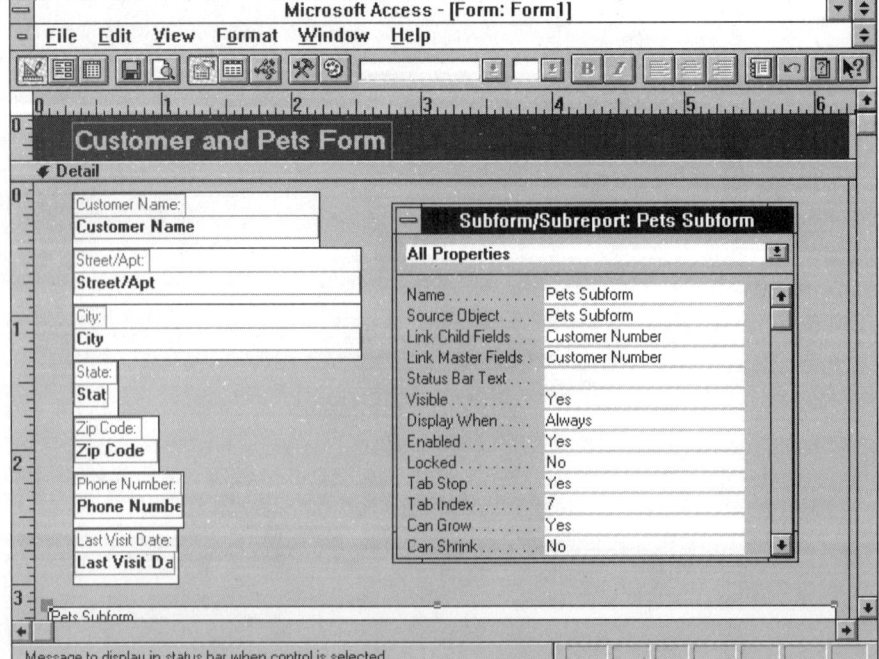

Figure 28-9: The Customer and Pets main form design.

 You must always first create the form used for the subform or the form will not be usable until the subform form is created.

The Subform control property sheet is also shown. Notice the two properties Link Child Fields and Link Master Fields. These two properties determine the link between the main form and the subform. The field name from the main table/query is entered in the Link Master Fields property. The field name from the subform table/query is entered in the Link Child Fields property. When the form is run, the link determines which records from the child form are displayed in the subform.

 This control is used for both subforms and subreports.

Displaying the subform design

To understand how the subform is actually built, you need to view the subform in Design view. Figure 28-10 shows this form in Design view. A subform is just another form. It can be run by itself without a main form. In fact, you should always test your subform by itself before running it as part of another form.

 A subform that will be viewed as a datasheet needs only to have its fields added in the order you want them to appear in the datasheet. Remember that you can rearrange the fields in the datasheet.

In Figure 28-10, you can see that all the fields are from the Pets table. You can also create a subform design with fields from multiple tables by using a query as the data source. If you do this, only the many side of any one-to-many relationships is editable in the subform.

Notice that in the Form property sheet for the Pets Subform, the Default View property is set to Datasheet. This means that the subform is displayed as a datasheet when run by itself or when used in a form.

 You can use the form footer of a subform to calculate totals or averages and then use the results on the main form. You learn how to do this later in the chapter.

The Main/Subform Form Wizard is a great place to start when creating a form with a subform. In the next section, you learn how to create a subform without using a Form Wizard. Then you customize the subform to add combo box selections for some of the fields, as well as calculating both row and column totals.

Figure 28-10:
The Pets subform design.

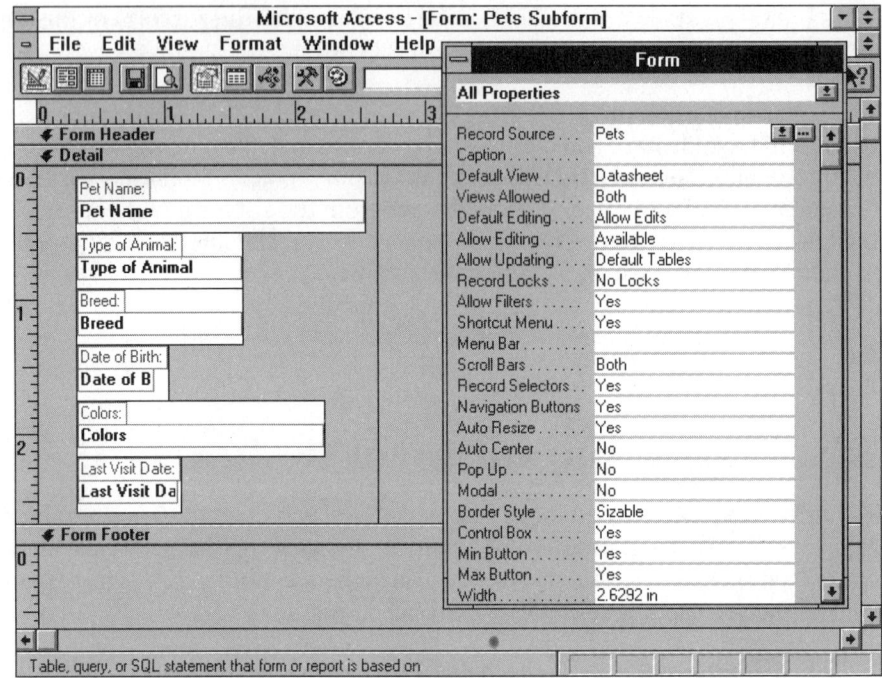

Creating a Simple Subform without Wizards

As mentioned earlier, there are several ways to create a subform without wizards. You can drag a form from the Database window to a form, or you can use the subform tool in the toolbox. The most desirable way is to drag the form from the Database window because it will allow Access to try to create the links for you.

Following Along in This Book

In this section, you create the form shown in Figure 28-11. The entire form is on your disk in the MTNANHSP database and is called Adding Visit Details. The completed subform is called Data for Subform Example.

In this chapter, you'll work only with the Adding Visit Details form as you create and embed the Data for Subform Example form as a subform. You may want to copy the Adding Visit Details form from the example disk and delete the subform and subform totals box. You can use that copy to create the main form for this section of the chapter and save yourself a great deal of work.

The Adding Visit Details form is divided into several sections. The top half of the form uses the query Pets, Owners, and Visits to display data from the Pets, Customer, and Visits tables. The Adding Visit Details form's only purpose is to let you add or review details about an existing visit. The middle of the form contains the subform that displays information about the visit details in a datasheet. Data in this subform comes from the query Data for Subform Example. Finally, there is a total for the data in the subform displayed in a text box control in the main form.

Creating a form for a subform

The first step in creating an embedded subform is to create the form to be used as the subform. Of course, this begins with a plan and a query. The plan is what you see in Figure 28-11. This datasheet, however, is not just a few fields displayed as a datasheet. The field Visit Type is a combo box that uses a Value List. You create that layer in this section. The fields Treatment Code and Medication Code do not display codes at all but display instead the treatment description and the medication description. The Price fields are really coming from the Treatments table and Medications table by way of a link to those tables. Finally, the total is a calculated field.

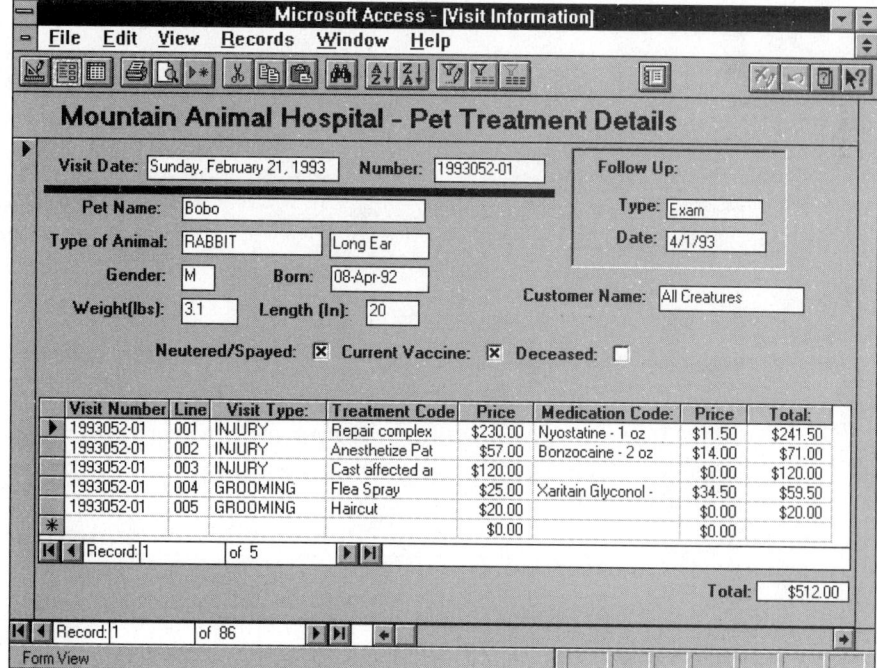

Figure 28-11: The Adding Visit Details Form.

To create this datasheet, you start at the beginning. Figure 28-12 shows the query that is used for the subform.

The figure is actually a composite made up of two screen shots in order to show all the fields selected in the query.

At the top of the query, you can see the three tables needed. Notice that the Visit Details table is joined to both the Treatments and Medications table using a *right outer join*. This is necessary so that if a Visit Detail record has either no treatment or no medication, it will not appear because of referential integrity.

Chapter 12 discusses the implications of referential integrity on a system using lookup tables.

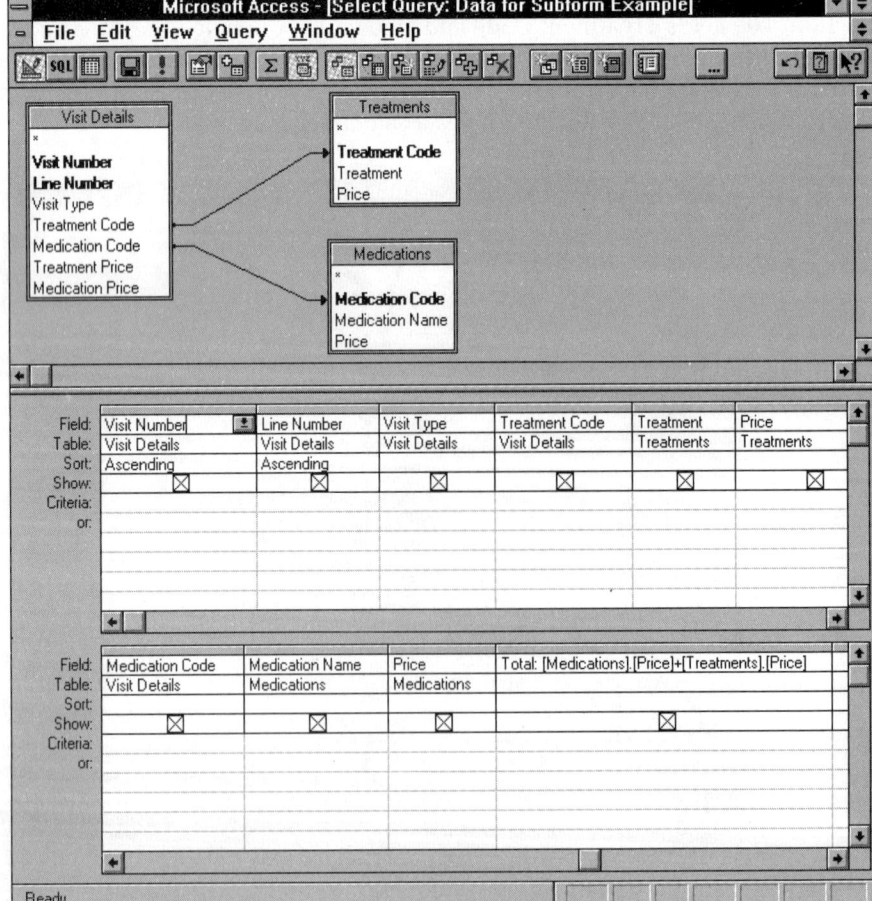

Figure 28-12: A composite figure showing the subform query.

The bottom pane of the query shows the fields that are potentially used for the datasheet. These include the Visit Number, Line Number, Visit Type, Treatment Code, and Medication Code fields from the Visit Details table. The fields Treatment and Price from the Treatments table and the fields Medication Name and Price from the Medication table can be used to display the description and price of the treatments and medication instead of the codes. This can be further enhanced by using the combo boxes, as you'll soon see.

The final field in the query, Total: [Medications].[Price]+[Treatments].[Price], names the field Total and sets the calculation to the total of the Price field in the Medications table and the Price field in the Treatments table. This is used to display the line totals for each record in the datasheet.

Creating a subform datasheet is an iterative process because you have to see how many fields can fit across the screen at once. If your goal is not to use a horizontal scroll bar, you have to use only as many fields as you can fit across the screen.

You can create the basic subform by either using a Form Wizard or by creating a new form and placing all the fields into the form.

To create the initial subform, follow these steps:

Steps: Creating the Initial Subform

Step 1. Create a new form by selecting the Data for Subform Example query and using a Blank Form.

Step 2. Open the field list window and drag all the fields to the form.

Step 3. Change the Default View property to Datasheet, as shown in Figure 28-13.

Step 4. Display the form as a datasheet to check the results.

When you display the datasheet, you see that the fields don't even come close to fitting. There simply isn't enough room to display all these fields. There are two solutions: Use a scroll bar or get creative. By now, you've learned enough to get creative!

First of all, what fields are absolutely necessary to the entry of data and which fields are strictly lookup fields? The first necessary field is Visit Number, which is used to link to the main form and needs to be included. Next is the second field that makes up the multiple-field key in Visit Details, Line Number. You must enter a Visit Type for each record, so that needs to be there too. Next come the details themselves. To enter a treatment, you must enter a treatment code and a medication code if any. The codes

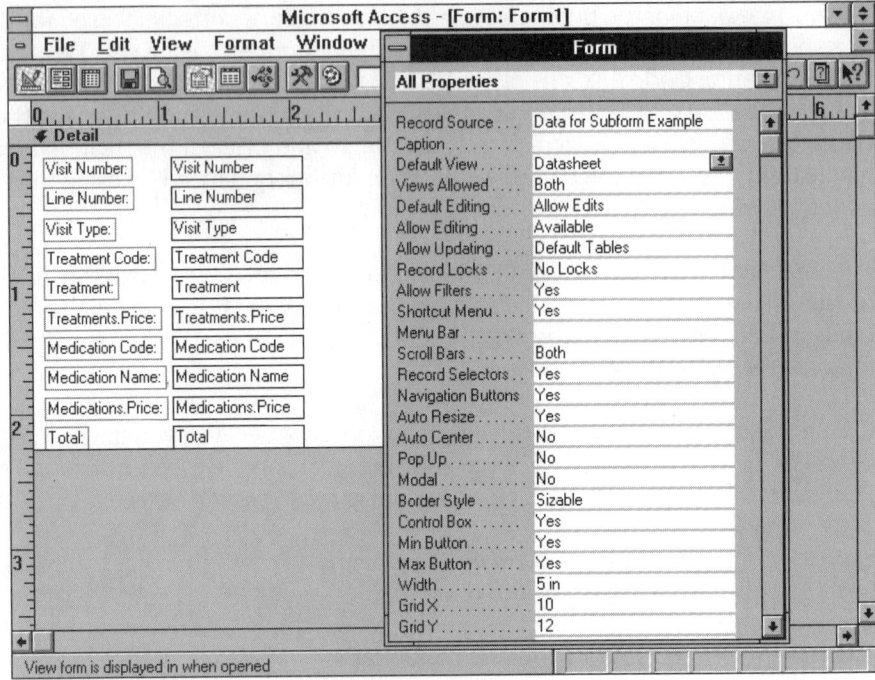

Figure 28-13: Creating the subform.

themselves are used to look up the description and price. Therefore, you only need Treatment Code and Medication Code. However, you also want to display the prices and the line total. So the only fields you can eliminate are Treatment and Medication Name. After you do that, you still find that the datasheet doesn't fit across the page. To make it all fit, follow these steps:

Steps: Creating a Datasheet for a Subform That Fits

Step 1. Switch to Form Design view.

Step 2. Delete the fields Treatment and Medication Name.

Step 3. Change the labels for Treatment.Price and Medication.Price to simply **Price**.

Step 4. Switch back to Datasheet view.

Step 5. The fields still don't fit. But by changing the column widths, you can fix that. Adjust the column widths, as shown in Figure 28-14.

Step 6. Save the form as **Data for Subform Example**.

This is usually a good starting point. Notice in Figure 28-14 that there is some extra space on the right side. Because this datasheet will be placed in the center of another form, you must take into consideration the space the record selector column and scroll bar of the main form will use. After you view the datasheet in the main form, you can make final adjustments. You may also wonder why so much space was left for the Treatment Code and Medication Code columns. Later, when you change these into combo boxes, you'll need this amount of space. Normally, you may not have realized this yet.

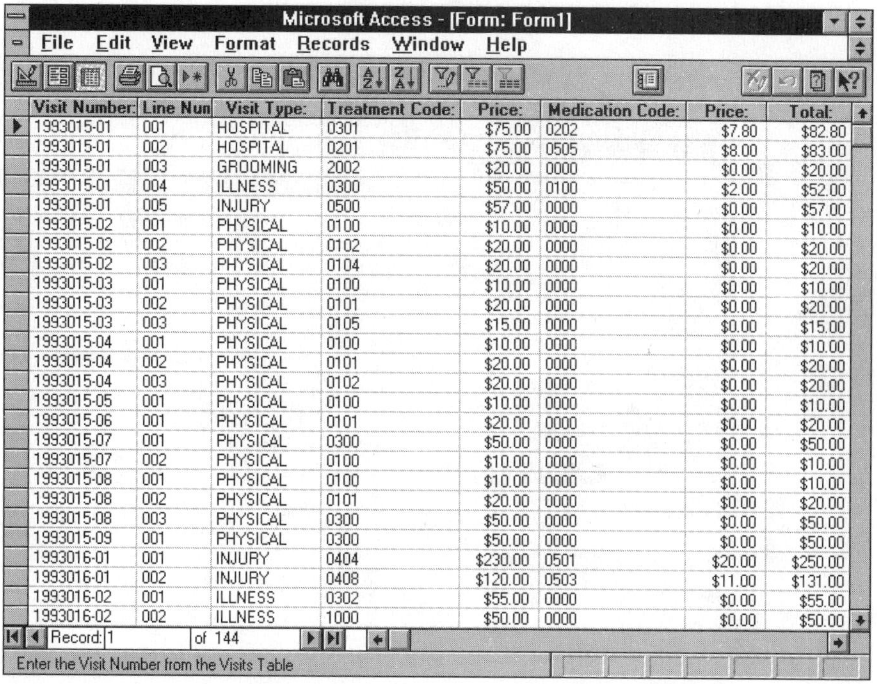

Figure 28-14:
Adjusting the subform datasheet.

Visit Number:	Line Num	Visit Type:	Treatment Code:	Price:	Medication Code:	Price:	Total:
1993015-01	001	HOSPITAL	0301	$75.00	0202	$7.80	$82.80
1993015-01	002	HOSPITAL	0201	$75.00	0505	$8.00	$83.00
1993015-01	003	GROOMING	2002	$20.00	0000	$0.00	$20.00
1993015-01	004	ILLNESS	0300	$50.00	0100	$2.00	$52.00
1993015-01	005	INJURY	0500	$57.00	0000	$0.00	$57.00
1993015-02	001	PHYSICAL	0100	$10.00	0000	$0.00	$10.00
1993015-02	002	PHYSICAL	0102	$20.00	0000	$0.00	$20.00
1993015-02	003	PHYSICAL	0104	$20.00	0000	$0.00	$20.00
1993015-03	001	PHYSICAL	0100	$10.00	0000	$0.00	$10.00
1993015-03	002	PHYSICAL	0101	$20.00	0000	$0.00	$20.00
1993015-03	003	PHYSICAL	0105	$15.00	0000	$0.00	$15.00
1993015-04	001	PHYSICAL	0100	$10.00	0000	$0.00	$10.00
1993015-04	002	PHYSICAL	0101	$20.00	0000	$0.00	$20.00
1993015-04	003	PHYSICAL	0102	$20.00	0000	$0.00	$20.00
1993015-05	001	PHYSICAL	0100	$10.00	0000	$0.00	$10.00
1993015-06	001	PHYSICAL	0101	$20.00	0000	$0.00	$20.00
1993015-07	001	PHYSICAL	0300	$50.00	0000	$0.00	$50.00
1993015-07	002	PHYSICAL	0100	$10.00	0000	$0.00	$10.00
1993015-08	001	PHYSICAL	0100	$10.00	0000	$0.00	$10.00
1993015-08	002	PHYSICAL	0101	$20.00	0000	$0.00	$20.00
1993015-08	003	PHYSICAL	0300	$50.00	0000	$0.00	$50.00
1993015-09	001	PHYSICAL	0300	$50.00	0000	$0.00	$50.00
1993016-01	001	INJURY	0404	$230.00	0501	$20.00	$250.00
1993016-01	002	INJURY	0408	$120.00	0503	$11.00	$131.00
1993016-02	001	ILLNESS	0302	$55.00	0000	$0.00	$55.00
1993016-02	002	ILLNESS	1000	$50.00	0000	$0.00	$50.00

Enter the Visit Number from the Visits Table

Adding the subform to the main form

After the subform is complete, you can add it to the main form. The easiest way to add a subform to a main form is to display the main form in a window and then drag the subform to the main form. This automatically creates the subform object control and potentially links the two forms.

To add the Data for Subform Example to the Adding Visit Details form that is used for the main form, follow the next steps:

Part IV: Advanced Database Features

Steps:	**Dragging a Subform to Another Form**
Step 1.	Display the Adding Visit Details form in a window in Design view so that you can also see the Database window.
Step 2.	Display the form objects in the Database window.
Step 3.	Click the form name Data for Subform Example and drag it to the Adding Visit Details form, as depicted in Figure 28-15.

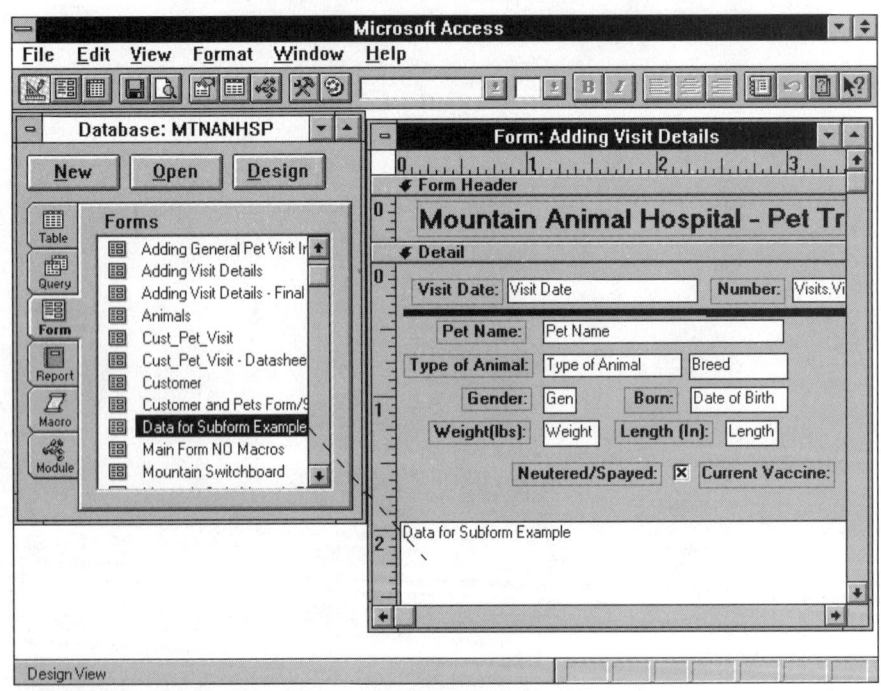

Figure 28-15: Dragging a subform to a main form.

Step 4.	Maximize the Form window.
Step 5.	Resize the subform so that it fits on-screen below the three checkboxes.
Step 6.	Delete the subform label control.
Step 7.	Display the property sheet for the subform control to verify the link.

The form should look like Figure 28-16.

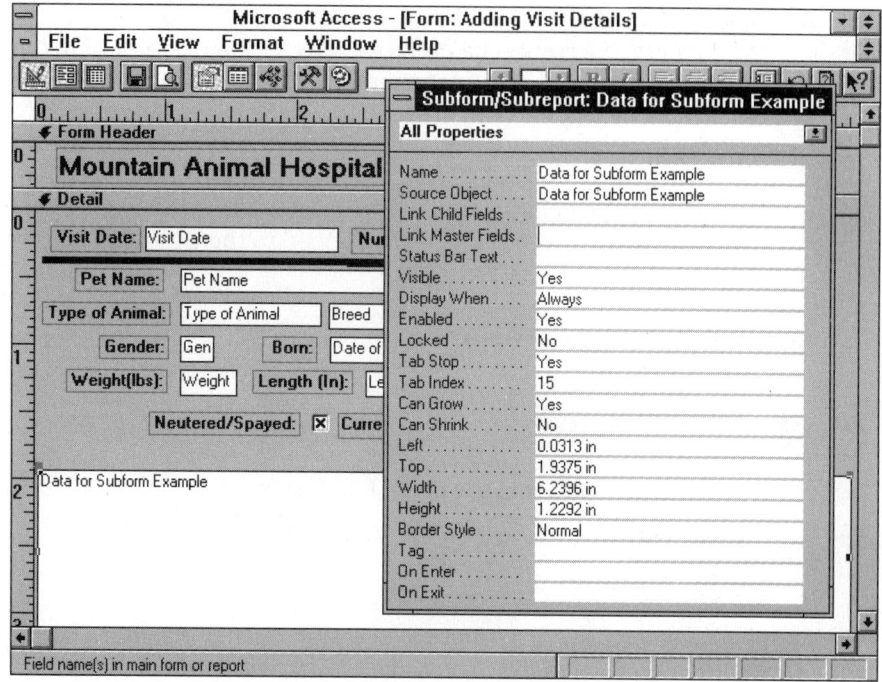

Figure 28-16: The subform in the main form.

As you can see, the main form and the subform are not linked. This is because the primary key for the Visit Details table is a multiple-field key. Access cannot automatically link this type of primary key.

Linking the form and subform

When you drag a form from the Database window onto another form to create a subform, Microsoft Access automatically tries to establish a link between the forms. This is also true when you drag a form or report onto a report.

Microsoft Access establishes a link under these conditions:

- Both the main form and subform are based on tables, and a relationship has been defined with the Relationships command.

- The main form and subform contain fields with the same name and data type, and the field on the main form is the primary key of the underlying table.

If Access finds a relationship or a match, these properties automatically show the field names that define the link. You should verify the validity of an automatic link. If the main form is based on a query, or if neither of the conditions just listed is true, Access cannot automatically match fields to create a link.

The Link Child Fields and Link Master Fields property settings must have the same number of fields and must represent data of the same type. For example, if the Customer table and the Pets table each has a Customer ID field that contains the same type of data, you enter Customer ID for both properties. The subform automatically displays all the pets found for that customer identified in the Customer ID field on the main form.

Although the data must match, the names of the fields can differ. For example, the Customer ID field from the Customer table can be linked to the Customer Number field from the Pets table.

To create the link, follow these steps:

Steps:	Creating a Link
Step 1.	Enter **Visit Number** in the Link Child Fields property.
Step 2.	Enter **Visit Number** in the Link Master Fields property.

Without the link, if you display the form, you see all the records in the Visit Details table in the subform. By linking the forms, you see only the visit details for the specific visit being displayed in the main form.

Display the form, as shown in Figure 28-17. Notice that the only visit numbers displayed in the datasheet are the same as the visit number in the main form. In Figure 28-17, you may notice that the user will have to enter the Treatment Code and Medication Code. In the type of systems that Access lets you create, you should never have to enter a code that can be looked up automatically. You can change some of the fields in the datasheet to use lookup tables by creating combo boxes in the subform form.

Adding lookup tables to the subform fields

You can change the way the data is displayed in a subform of a main form by changing the design of the subform itself. You now make three changes:

- Display the Visit Type field as a Value List combo box.
- Display the Treatment Code as a combo box showing the Treatment Name and letting Access automatically enter the Treatment Code.
- Display the Medication Code as a combo box showing the Medication Name and letting Access automatically enter the Medication Code.

Combo boxes are discussed in detail in Chapter 19.

Figure 28-17: Displaying the main form and the subform.

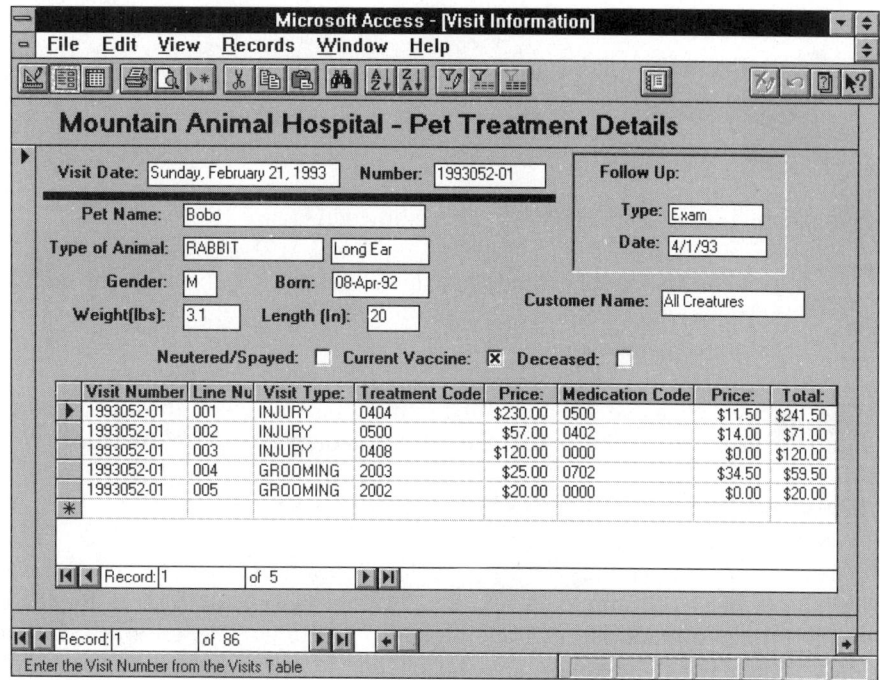

By changing a field in a subform to a combo box, when you click the field in the datasheet of the subform, the list will drop down and you can select from the list.

The first control to change is the Visit Type field. To create a value list combo box without using the wizard, follow these steps:

Steps:	Creating a Combo Box for the Visit Type Field
Step 1.	Display the subform in the Design view.
Step 2.	Delete the existing Visit Type text box control.
Step 3.	From the toolbox, select the Combo Box control. (Make sure the Control Wizard icon is toggled off.)
Step 4.	From the field list, drag the Visit Type field to the form.
Step 5.	With the Visit Type combo box selected, display the property sheet.
Step 6.	Select Value List for the Row Source Type property.
Step 7.	Enter **INJURY;PHYSICAL;GROOMING;HOSPITAL** in the Row Source property.
Step 8.	Set the Column Count property to **1** and the Column Heads property to **No**.

Step 9. Set the Bound Column property to **1** and the List Rows property to **8**.

Step 10. Set the Limit to List property to **No** to allow an alternative treatment type to be added.

This combo box and property sheet are shown in Figure 28-18.

 You can also display fields in a datasheet as checkboxes or as individual option buttons. You cannot display an option button group, a list box, or a toggle button in a datasheet.

When the user clicks on the Visit Type field in the datasheet, the combo box appears. When the user selects the arrow, the list box is displayed with the values INJURY, PHYSICAL, GROOMING, or HOSPITAL. Because the Limit to List property is set to No, the user can also add new values to the Visit Details table.

The next two combo boxes are very similar. You want to create two combo boxes. The first allows you to see the treatment descriptions instead of the treatment codes. When you select a treatment description, the code is automatically entered. The second combo box is the same except that it uses the Medications table instead of the Treatments table.

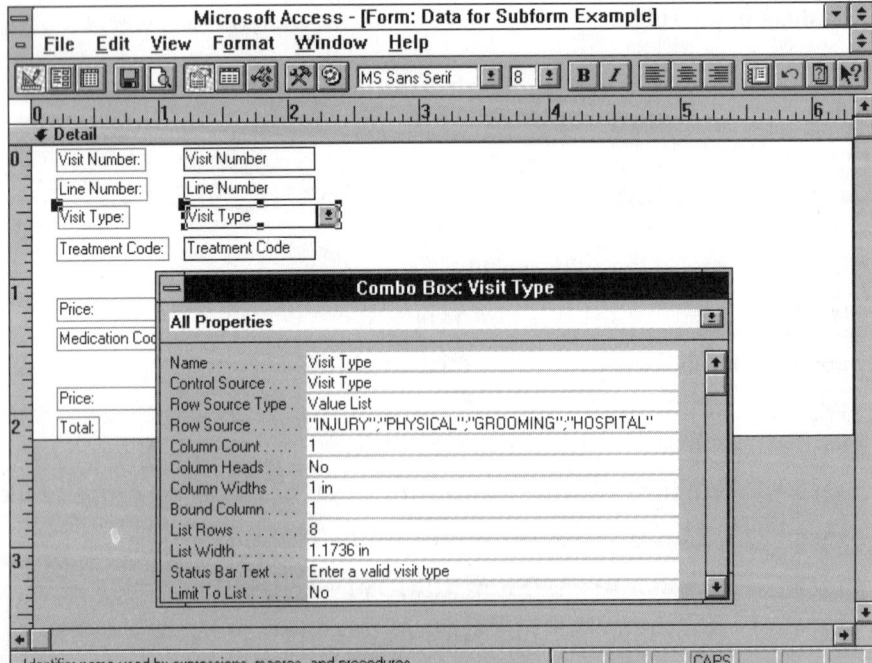

Figure 28-18: Creating a value list combo box for the Visit Type field.

Chapter 28: Creating and Using Subforms

In order to create these combo boxes, you need to create several queries. Figure 28-19 shows the query for the Treatment Code combo box.

As you can see, all fields come from the Treatments table. The fields appear in the combo box in order of the value of Treatment. This is the treatment name. This is an alphabetical listing because the field is a Text field data type. Notice that two fields are used in the query. The treatment code will actually be hidden so that only the treatment name is displayed.

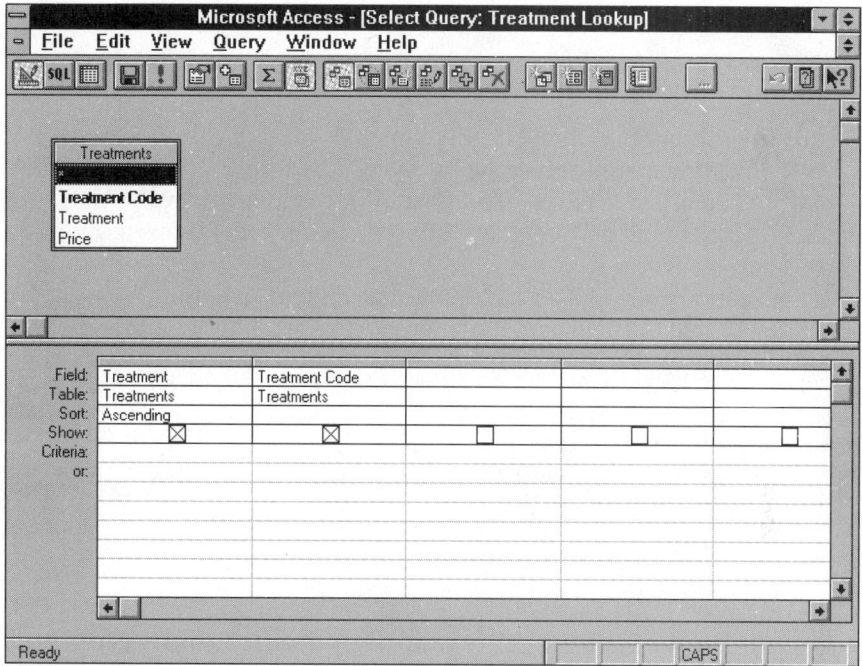

Figure 28-19: The query for the Treatment Code lookup table.

After you create the query, you can create the combo box. To create the combo box for the treatment code, follow these steps:

Steps:	Creating a Combo Box for the Treatment Code Field
Step 1.	Display the subform in the Design view.
Step 2.	Delete the existing Treatment Code text box control.
Step 3.	From the toolbox, select the Combo Box control. (Make sure the Control Wizard icon is toggled off.)
Step 4.	From the field list, drag the Treatment Code field to the form.

Step 5. With the Treatment Code combo box selected, display the property sheet.
Step 6. Select Table/Query for the Row Source Type property.
Step 7. Enter **Treatment Lookup** in the Row Source property.
Step 8. Set the Column Count property to **2** and the Column Heads property to **Yes**.
Step 9. Set the Column Widths property to **2,0**.
Step 10. Set the Bound Column property to **2** and the List Rows property to **4**.
Step 11. Set the Limit to List property to **Yes** so that the user must select from the list.

Figure 28-20 shows this combo box completed. When the form is run and the user selects the Treatment Code field, the list of valid treatment codes is shown. Because the bound column is 2, the hidden Treatment Code column, the value of the Treatment Code is placed into the Treatment Code field in the Visit Details table.

The Medication Code lookup table is virtually identical to the Treatment Code lookup table except that the field name is different. To create this combo box, you also need to create a query. Figure 28-21 shows the query for the Medication Code combo box.

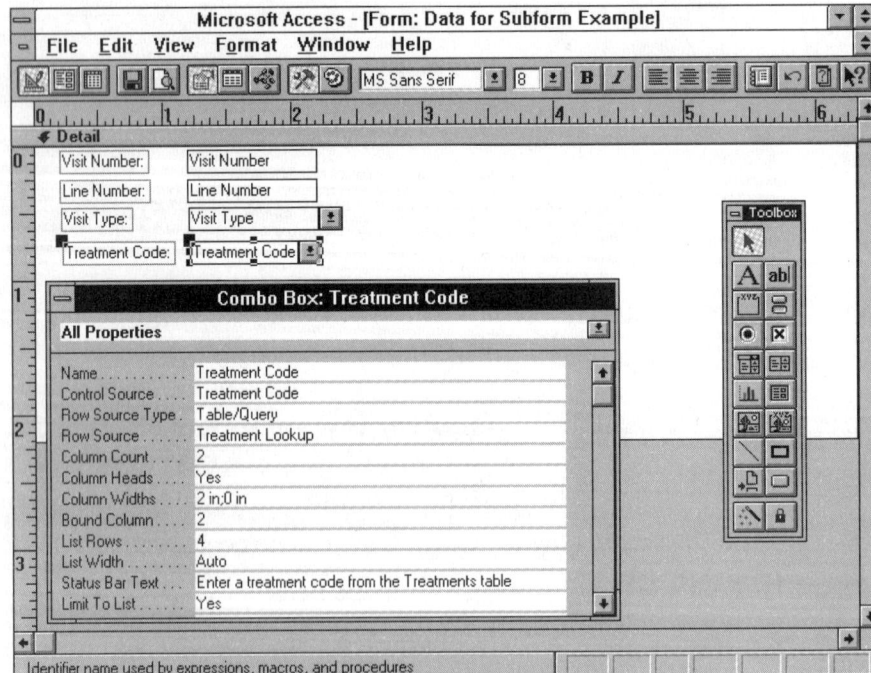

Figure 28-20: Creating a combo box for the Treatment Code.

Figure 28-21:
The query for the Medications Code lookup table.

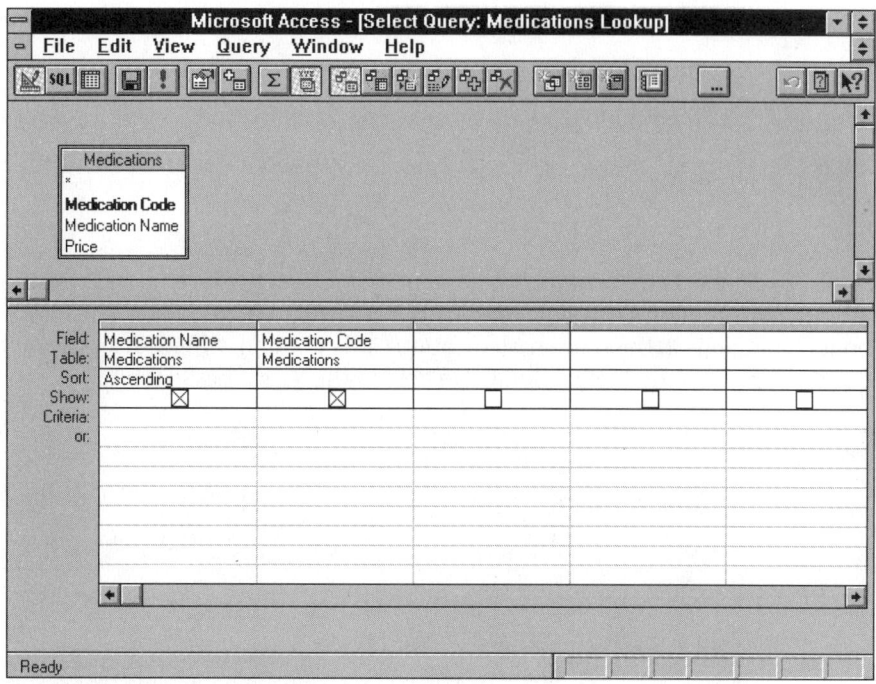

As you can see, all fields come from the Medications table. The fields appear in the combo box in order of the value of the Medication Name. This is an alphabetical listing because the field is a Text field data type. Notice that two fields are used in the query. The Medication Code is actually be hidden so that only the Medication name is displayed.

After you create the query, you can create the combo box. To create the combo box for the Medication Code, follow these steps:

Steps:	Creating a Combo Box for the Medication Code Field
Step 1.	Display the subform in the Design view.
Step 2.	Delete the existing Medication Code text box control.
Step 3.	From the toolbox, select the Combo Box control.
Step 4.	From the field list, drag the Medication Code field to the form.
Step 5.	With the Medication Code combo box selected, display the property sheet.
Step 6.	Select Table/Query for the Row Source Type property.
Step 7.	Enter **Medications Lookup** in the Row Source property.

Step 8. Set the Column Count property to **2** and the Column Heads property to **Yes**.

Step 9. Set the Column Widths property to **2,0**.

Step 10. Set the Bound Column property to **2** and the List Rows property to **4**.

Step 11. Set the Limit to List property to **Yes** so that the user must select from the list.

Figure 28-22 shows this combo box completed. When the form is run and the user selects the Medication Code field, the list of valid treatment codes is shown. Because the bound column is 2, the hidden Medication Code column, the value of the Medication Code is placed in the Medication Code field in the Visit Details table.

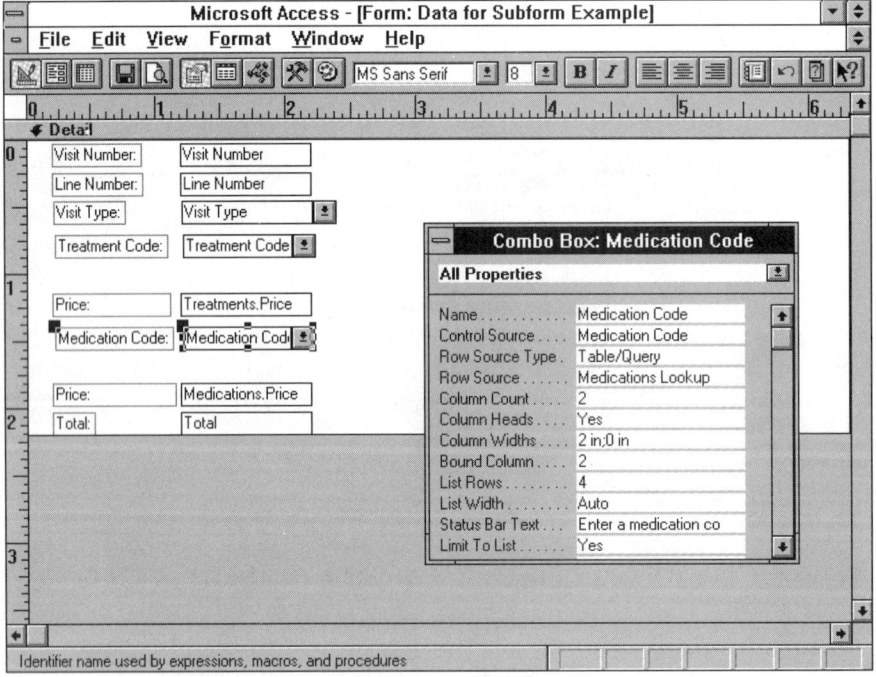

Figure 28-22: Creating a combo box for the Medication Code.

After you make these changes, you can test your changes. You may want to first display the form as a datasheet in the Form view of the subform. You can also close the form and display the subform in the main form. Close the subform and run the main form named Adding Visit Details.

Figure 28-23 shows the results. The Treatment Code and Medication Code fields are moved to the right of the datasheet. This is because the controls were deleted and re-created. In the datasheet of the subform, you can select the Visit Type, Treatment Code, and Medication Code fields and move them into their proper order.

Figure 28-23:
Displaying the subform.

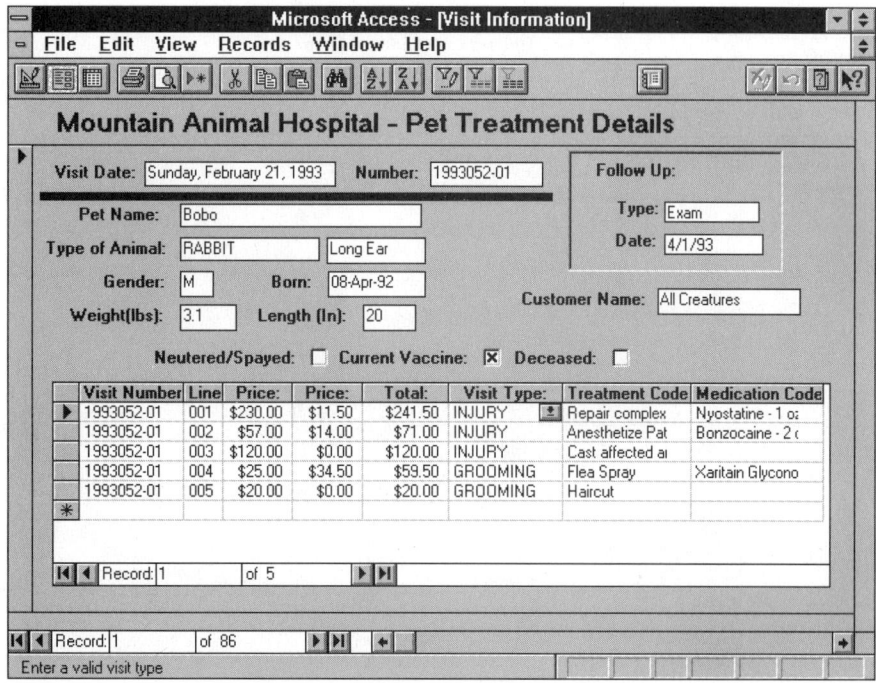

After you arrange the fields in their proper order and set the column widths so that the datasheet exactly fills the allotted space, you can test the combo boxes. Click the Visit Type field. An arrow should appear. When you click the arrow, the list of valid visit types is displayed. You can then select the desired visit type or enter a new one into the combo box. When the combo box is closed, the data is entered into the Visit Type field of the Visit Details table.

When you select the Treatment Code field and select the arrow, a combo box is also displayed, as shown in Figure 28-24. The combo box displays only three columns because the List Rows property is set to 4 and the Column Heads property is set to Yes.

The treatment description is shown in its entirety, even though the Treatment Code field entry area is smaller. This is controlled by setting the List Width property to Auto. If you don't set this property to Auto, you may find that your data is be truncated or displayed with too much white space after the values. When you select the desired treatment, the hidden value of treatment code in the Treatments table is entered automatically into the Treatment Code field in Visit Details.

The Medication Code field works in exactly the same way. Notice as you select various treatments that the price is automatically updated in each line to reflect the selection. The Total field is also updated as either the Treatment Price or Medication Price changes.

The last change to make to the form is to create a field to display totals of all the line items in the datasheet.

Figure 28-24: Displaying the subform correctly and testing the combo boxes.

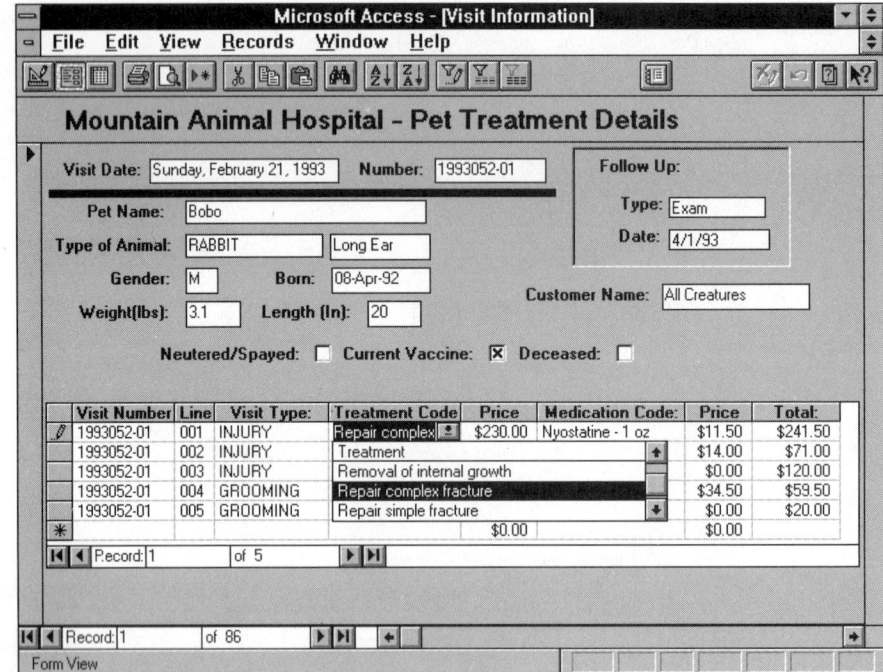

Creating totals in subforms

To create a total of the line items in the subform, you have to create an additional calculated field in the subform form. Figure 28-25 shows a new field being created in the form footer in the subform form.

Just as you can create summaries in reports, you can create them in forms. The form footer is used so that the calculation occurs after all the detail records are processed. When the form is displayed in single-form view, this total is always equal to the detail record. However, in continuous-form or datasheet view, this calculation is the sum of the processed record.

As shown in Figure 28-25, the text box Control Source property is the expression =Sum([Total]). This sums all the values of the field Total. The field Format property is set to Currency and the number of decimal places is set to 2. This displays the data as a dollar amount.

Although the text box control is created in the subform, it is actually displayed by a text box control placed in the main form that references the subform control. This control is shown in Figure 28-26.

Chapter 28: Creating and Using Subforms **825**

Figure 28-25: Creating a summary calculation.

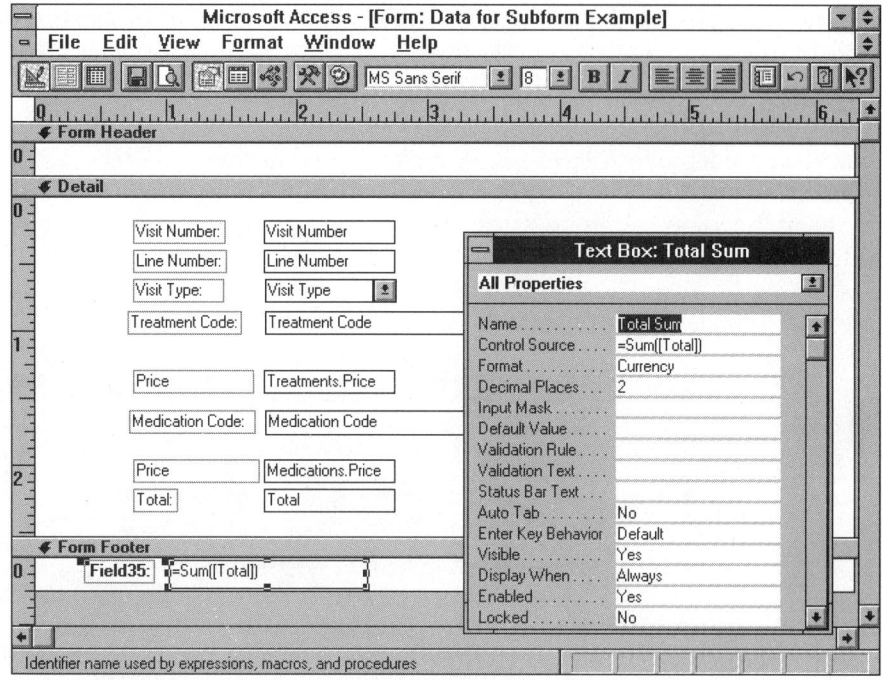

Figure 28-26: Referencing a control in another form.

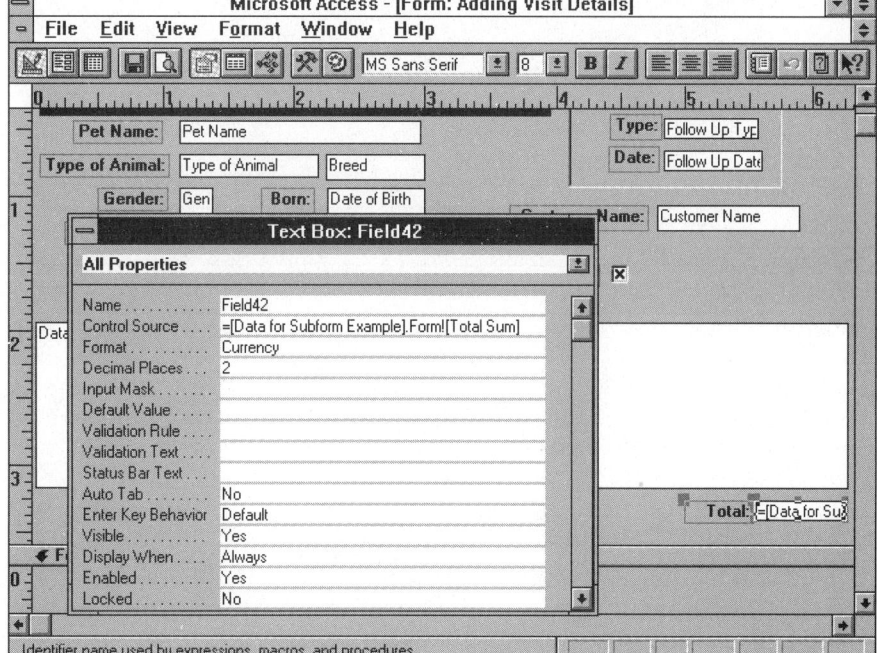

Because the field is in another form, it must be referenced with the fully qualified terminology. As you can see in the property sheet, the Control Source property is as follows:

    =[Data for Subform Example].Form![Total Sum]

The first part of the reference specifies the name of the form, whereas the .Form tells Access that it is the name of a form. By using the ! character, you tell Access that the next part is a lower hierarchy. The control name [Total Sum] actually contains the value to be displayed.

The final form, including the total for the subform, is shown in Figure 28-27.

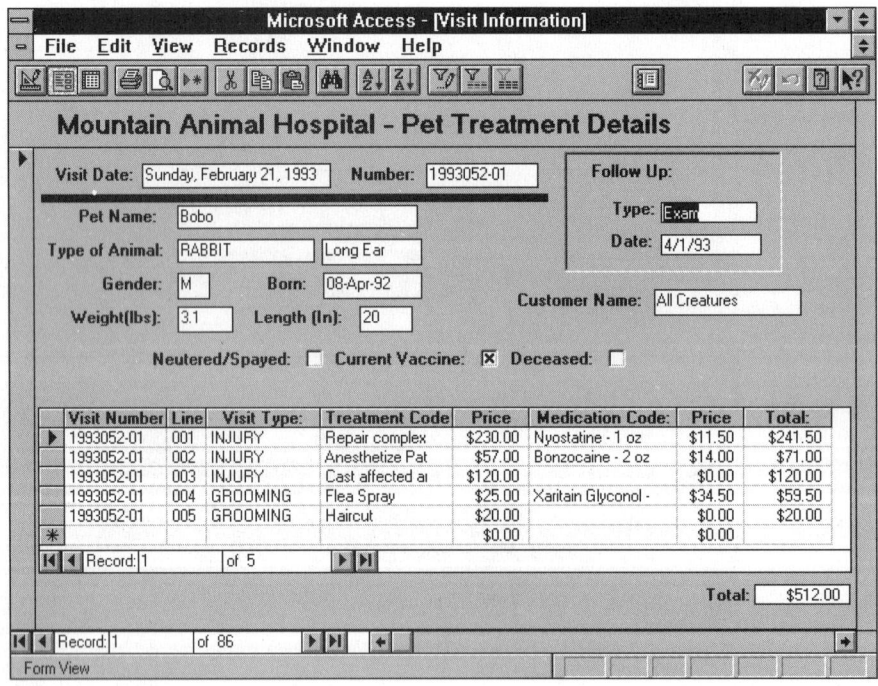

Figure 28-27: Displaying the totals.

Summary

In this chapter, you learned how you can use subforms to make displaying data from multiple tables easier. You learned how to create a subform with a wizard and how to create subforms by dragging the form from the Database window to another form. You also learned how to change the display of the subform. The following points were covered:

- A subform is simply a form within a form.
- There are three ways to create a subform:

    Use the subform wizard.

    Drag a form from the Database window to another form.

    Create a subform by using the toolbox.

- A subform can be displayed as a single form, a continuous form, or a datasheet.
- Before adding a subform to an existing form, you must create the subform.
- By using the Form Wizard, you can create a form with an embedded subform datasheet.
- When you create a subform by dragging a form from the Database window, you may have to manually link the form and subform.
- You link a form and subform by entering the field names for the link in the Link Master Fields and Link Child Fields properties.
- You can add lookup tables and even checkboxes to the datasheet used in a subform.

In the next chapter, you learn how to create mailing labels, snaked column reports, and mail merge reports.

Creating Mailing Labels and Mail Merge Reports

CHAPTER 29

In This Chapter

- Using the Mailing Label Report Wizard
- Modifying mailing label reports
- Using the expanded Print Setup dialog box
- Understanding snaked column reports
- Creating a snaked column report
- Creating a mail merge letter in Access
- Using the Access to Word for Windows 6.0 Mail Merge Wizard

For correspondence, you often need to create mailing labels and form letters, commonly known as *mail merges*. The Access report writer helps you create these types of reports, as well as the reports with multiple columns known as *snaked column* reports.

Creating Mailing Labels

You create mailing labels in Access by using a report. You can create the basic label by starting from a blank form, or you can use the Mailing Label Report Wizard. The Mailing Label Report Wizard is much easier and saves you a great deal of time and effort.

There is no special mailing label type of report. The report for a mailing label is like any other report and is made up of controls. The secret to the mailing label is using the margin settings and the Print Setup screen. In previous chapters, you learned how to use the Print Setup dialog box to change your margins. One of the command buttons in the dialog box is More >>. When you select this button, the dialog box expands to reveal additional choices that you use to control the number of labels across the report and how the data is placed on the report. You learn how to use this dialog box later in this chapter.

The best way to create mailing labels is to use the Mailing Label Report Wizard.

Creating the new report

You create a new report to be used for a mailing label just as you create any other report. To create a new report for a mailing label, follow these steps:

Steps:	Creating a New Report
Step 1.	From the Database window, select the Report object button.
Step 2.	Select New to create a new report.
Step 3.	Select Customer from the Select a Table/Query drop-down list.
Step 4.	Select Report Wizards.

The Microsoft Access Report Wizard dialog box is displayed.

Choosing the Report Wizard

The Report Wizard dialog box should now be displayed. Select Mailing Label, as shown in Figure 29-1.

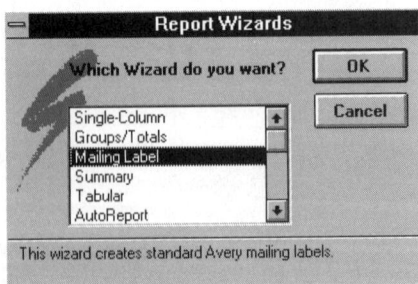

Figure 29-1: Choosing the Report Wizard.

Creating the mailing label text and fields

Once you select the Mailing Label Report Wizard, another dialog box is displayed, as shown in Figure 29-2. This dialog box lets you choose the fields from the table or query to appear in the label. You can also add spaces, unbound text, blank lines, and even punctuation.

The dialog box is divided into two areas. The left area, titled Available fields:, lists all the fields in the query or table. Figure 29-2, shown completed, displays the fields from the Customer table. The right area, titled Label appearance:, shows the fields that are used for the label and displays a rough idea of how the mailing label will look when it is completed.

The fields or text that you use in this dialog box serve only as a starting point for the label. You can make additional changes later in the Report Design window.

You can select a field either by double-clicking the field name in the Available fields: area or by selecting the field name and then clicking the > command button between the two areas. You can remove a field by clicking the < command button.

You can use the buttons under the Available fields: area to add punctuation to the label, including a colon (:), comma (,), hyphen (-), period (.), or slash (/). You can also click the Space button to add a blank space anywhere in the label or click the NewLine button to add a new line to the label.

If you add a new line to the label and leave it blank, it will appear only as a blank line in the label if you also manually change the Can Shrink property to No for the unbound text box control that you create to display the blank line. The default property for this control is Yes; the blank line is not displayed, and the lines above and below the blank line appear together.

You can add text to the label by clicking in the text box just below the Available fields: list and typing the text you want. You can then add it to the label by clicking the Text→ button.

To create the label, as shown completed in Figure 29-2, follow these steps:

Steps:	Creating a Customer Label
Step 1.	Double-click the Customer Name field in the Available fields: list.
Step 2.	Click the NewLine button to go to the next line.
Step 3.	Double-click the Street/Apt field in the Available fields: list.

Step 4.	Click the NewLine button to go to the next line.
Step 5.	Double-click the City field in the Available fields: list.
Step 6.	Click the Comma (,) punctuation button to add a comma to the label.
Step 7.	Click the Space button to add a blank space to the label.
Step 8.	Double-click the State field in the Available fields: list.
Step 9.	Click the Space button to add a blank space to the label.
Step 10.	Double-click the Zip Code field in the Available fields: list.
Step 11.	Click the NewLine button twice to add a blank line to the label.
Step 12.	Click the text area below the Available fields: list.
Step 13.	Type **Special Offer Enclosed**.
Step 14.	Click the Text→ button to add the text to the label.
Step 15.	Click the Next > button to go to the next dialog box.

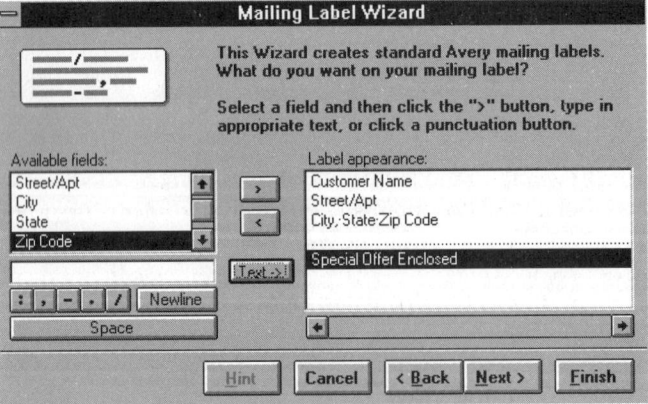

Figure 29-2: The completed label in the Report Wizard.

The completed label is displayed in Figure 29-2.

Selecting the label size

After you determine the sorting fields, you can select the type of label stock you want to print to. There are nearly one hundred Avery label stock forms listed. (Avery is the name of the world's largest producer of label paper.)

Chapter 29: Creating Mailing Labels and Mail Merge Reports

You can find nearly every type of paper Avery makes in these lists. You can select from lists of English or Metric labels. You can also select sheet feed for laser printers or continuous for tractor-fed printers. Select between the two from the option buttons below the label sizes.

The list box shown in Figure 29-3 contains three columns:

Avery number: The model number found on the Avery label box

Dimensions: The height and width of the label in either inches or millimeters

Number across: The number of labels that are physically across the page

When you select a label size, you are actually setting the print setup parameters, as you learn later in this chapter.

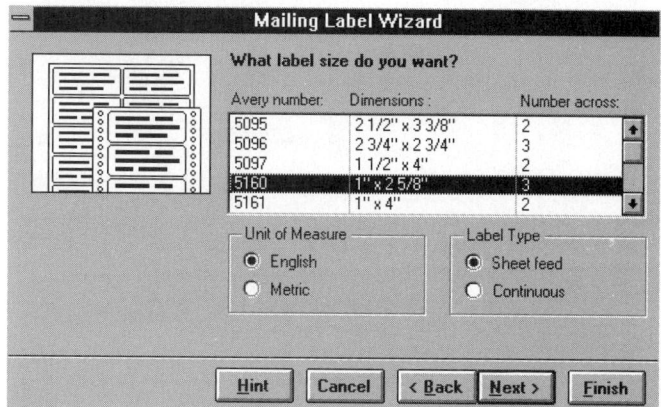

Figure 29-3: Selecting the label size.

Select Avery number: 5160, as shown in Figure 29-3. Notice that there are three labels across, and the size is shown as 1" x 2⅝". You'll see these values again when you examine the Print Setup dialog box. Once you select the label size, you can again select the Next > button to go to the next dialog box.

Selecting the font and color

The next dialog box shown in Figure 29-4 displays a set of combo boxes to let you select various attributes about the font and color of the text used in the mailing label. For this example, click the Italic checkbox (if it is checked) to turn off the italic effect. Notice the sample text changes to reflect the difference. Change the font size to 8 in order to fit all of the mailing label text in the label. The rest of the defaults, Arial, Bold, and black text, are acceptable. Press the Next > button to move to the next dialog box.

Part IV: Advanced Database Features

 If you select a font size that won't accomodate the line width or number of lines in the label, you will get a warning message when the report design is created and your lines will be truncated or skipped. In this example, the Special Offer Enclosed line is omitted if the font size is greater than 8.

The last dialog box in the Mailing Label Report Wizard sequence lets you decide whether to view the labels in the Print Preview window or to modify the report design in the Report Design window. This final dialog box is shown in Figure 29-5.

In this example, the next course of action is to display the labels in the Print Preview window as shown in Figure 29-6.

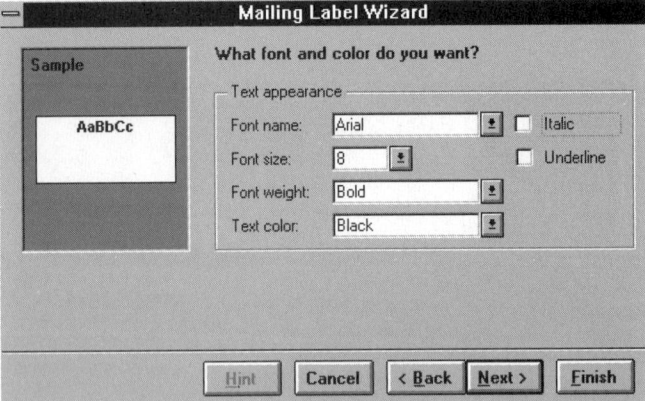

Figure 29-4: Selecting the font type, size, and color.

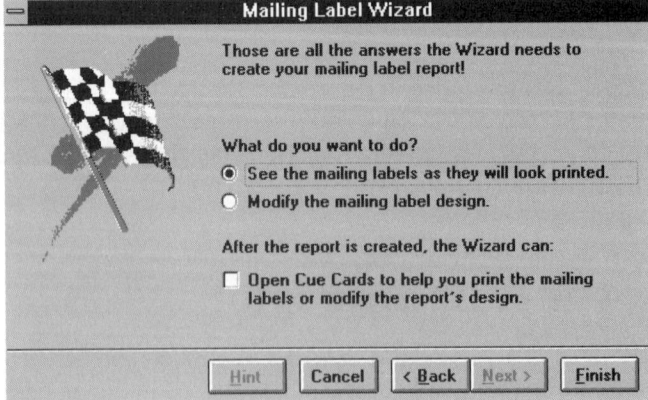

Figure 29-5: The final mailing label Report Wizard dialog box.

Displaying the labels in the Print Preview window

When you press the Finish button, you are taken directly to the Print Preview window as shown in Figure 29-6. This is the normal Print Preview window for a report. By using the magnifying glass cursor, you can switch to a page view to see an entire page of labels at once. Or you can zoom in to any quadrant of the report. By using the navigation buttons at the bottom left corner of the window, you can display other pages of your mailing label report.

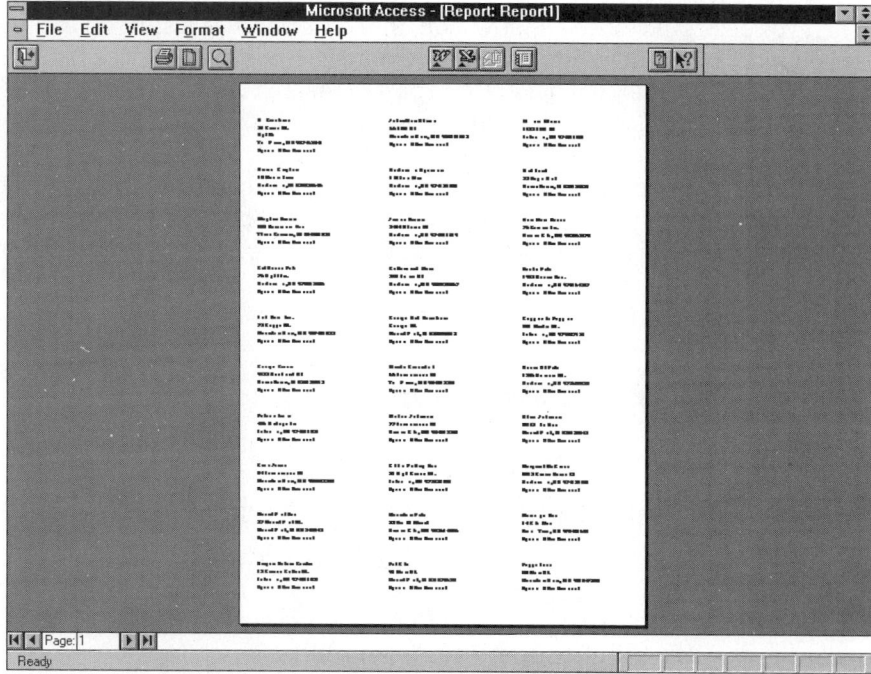

Figure 29-6: Viewing labels in the Print Preview window.

 Remember that mailing label is simply a report, which behaves as a report normally behaves.

You can print the labels directly from the Print Preview window, or you can select the first icon in the toolbar to display the Report Design window.

Modifying the label design in the Report Design window

When you select the Close Window icon, the label design is displayed in the Report Design window, as shown in Figure 29-7. Notice that the height of the Detail band is set at 1 inch, and the right margin of the report is set at 2⅝ inches. This gives you the measurement that you defined when you chose the label size of 1" x 2⅝".

If you looked closely in the Print Preview window, you could see that the blank line you placed between the address information and the text Special Offer Enclosed! is not there. You can fix this by changing the Can Shrink property of the unbound control to No.

To change the blank line property, follow these steps:

Steps:	Changing a Control Property
Step 1.	Display the property sheet.
Step 2.	Select the Unbound control (between city information and the last line).
Step 3.	Change the property Can Shrink to **No.**

Another problem is with the City, State, and Zip Code fields. If you look at the report print preview, you notice that the first record's ZIP code value is 830198573. As you learned in Chapter 23, the Zip Code field is normally formatted using the @@@@@-@@@@ format. This format displays the stored sequence of nine numbers with a hyphen placed where it properly goes.

The control source was originally =[City] & ", " & [State] & " " & [Zip Code]. The Mailing Label Report Wizard uses the & type of concatenation when concatenating text strings. However, any formatting is missing. In the property sheet, you can see that the control source is changed to =[City] & ", " & [State] & " " & Format([Zip Code],"@@@@@-@@@@").

Chapter 29: Creating Mailing Labels and Mail Merge Reports   837

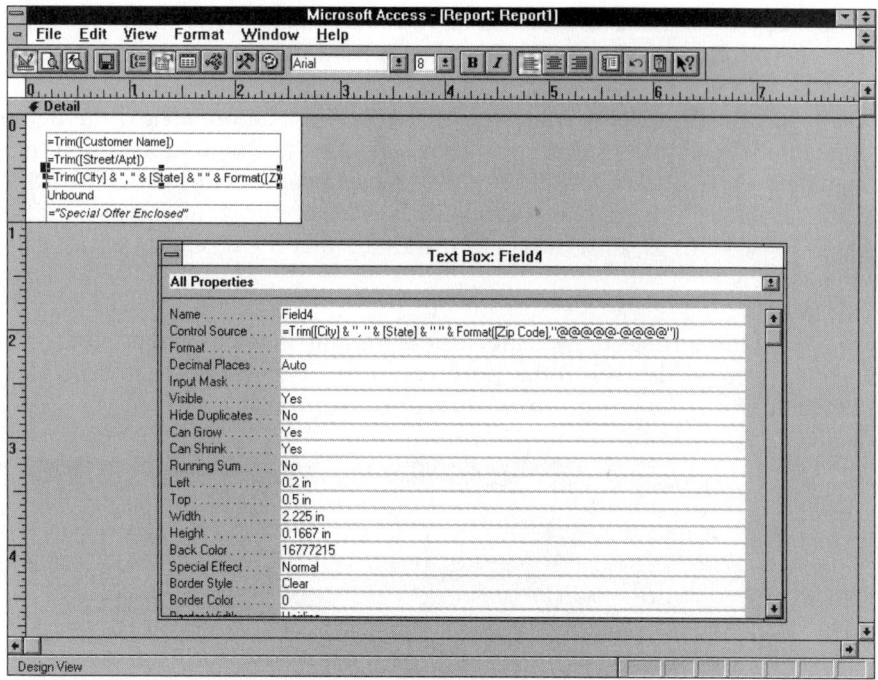

Figure 29-7: The Report Design window.

This control source correctly displays the ZIP code as 83019-8573 when it is printed or displayed. You can make this change by simply selecting the control and adding the Format( ) function.

Another change you could make is to the font size. In this example, Arial (the Helvetica TrueType font) with a point size of 8 is used. Suppose that you want to make the text 10 point. To do this, you select all the controls and then click the Font Size drop-down list box and change the font size to 10 points. The text inside the controls becomes larger, but the control itself does not change size. As long as the text is not truncated or cut off on the bottom, you can make the font size larger.

You can also change the font style of any text. For example, suppose that you want the text "Special Offer Enclosed" to appear in italics. You need only select the text box control and select the Italics button on the toolbar.

Now that you've changed your text as you want, it's time to print the labels. Before you do this, you should examine the Print Setup window.

To display the Print Setup window, select File⇒Print Setup…. The Print Setup window appears. Here, you can select the printer, change the Orientation option (have you ever seen landscape label paper?) to Portrait or Landscape, change the Paper Size or Source settings, and set the margins. The margin setting controls the margins for the entire page. These settings, as shown in Figure 29-8, affect the report itself, not just the individual labels.

To change the settings of each label and determine the size and number of labels across the page, you need to select the More >> button. The window then expands to display some additional options, as shown in Figure 29-8.

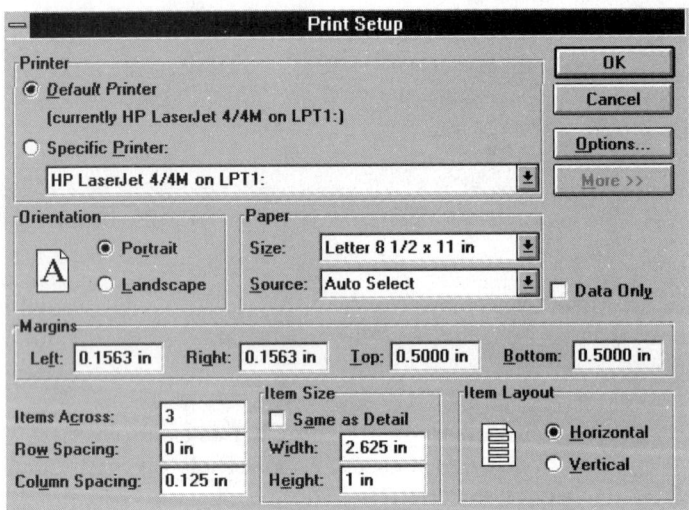

Figure 29-8: The Print Setup window with More >>.

Several new items appear in the expanded Print Setup dialog box. The first three items determine the spacing of the labels on the page:

> Items Across   Number of columns in the output
>
> Row Spacing   Space between the rows of output
>
> Column Spacing   Amount of space between each column (this property not available unless you enter a value of greater than one for the Items Across property)

Chapter 29: Creating Mailing Labels and Mail Merge Reports

The Item Size settings determine the size of the label itself:

S<u>a</u>me as Detail	Sets the Width and Height properties to the same width and height as the detail section of your report
W<u>i</u>dth	Sets the width of each label
H<u>e</u>ight	Sets the height of each label

The Item Layout section determines in which direction the records are printed:

<u>H</u>orizontal	Prints consecutive labels across the page and then moves down a row when there is no more room
<u>V</u>ertical	Prints consecutive labels in the first column and then starts in the second column when the first column is full

Once the settings are completed, you can print the labels.

Printing labels

After you create the labels, change any controls as you want, and check the Print Setup settings, you can print the labels. It's always a good idea to preview the labels one last time. Figure 29-9 shows the final labels in the Print Preview window. The ZIP code is correctly displayed. Also notice that there is a space between the address and the text *Special Offer Enclosed* This text is now displayed in italics.

You can print the labels by simply selecting the <u>P</u>rint button in the toolbar and then selecting OK in the Print dialog box. You can also print the labels directly from the Report Design window by selecting <u>F</u>ile⇨<u>P</u>rint.

Of course, you must insert your label paper first. If you don't have any #5160 label paper, you can use regular paper. The labels will simply be printed in consecutive format like a telephone directory. In fact, that's actually another feature of Access reports — the capability to create what is known as a snaked column report.

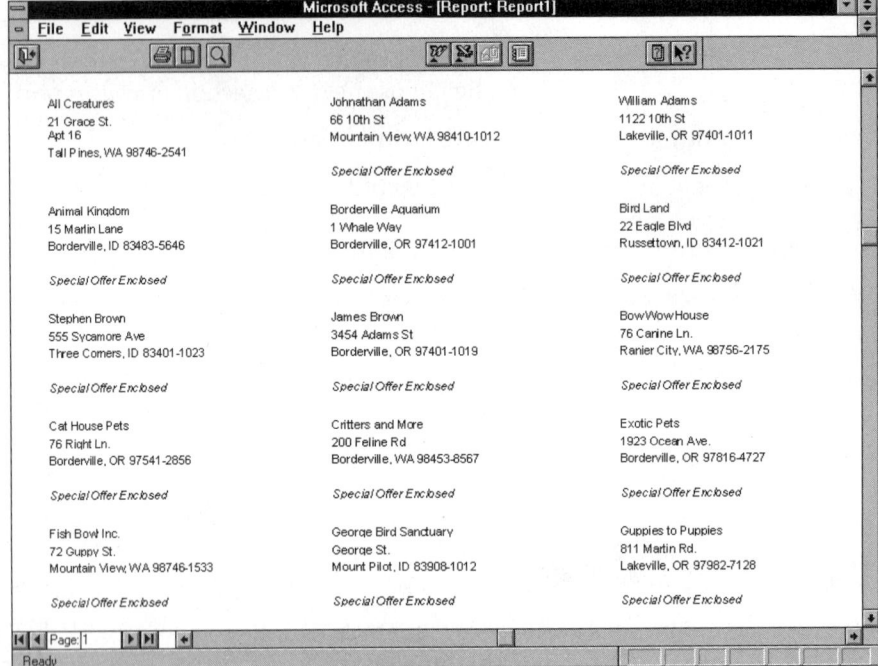

Figure 29-9:
The final report print preview.

Creating Snaked Column Reports

All the reports discussed in this book so far are either form-based (free-form) or single-column lists. (Single column means that each column for each field appears only once on each page.) Often, this is not the best way to present your data. Access gives you another option known as *snaking columns*. With snaking columns, you can define the sections of a report so that they fit in an area that is less than half the width of the printed page. When the data reaches the bottom of the page, instead of a page break naturally occurring, the data snakes up to the top of the same page to form a new column.

This technique is commonly used for text in telephone directories or newspapers and other periodicals. An example of a database use is a report that prints several addresses, side by side, for a page of adhesive mailing labels that you feed through your laser printer. You just learned how to create labels for mailing. Now, you learn how to apply these same techniques to a report. The major difference between mailing labels and snaked column reports is that the snaked column reports often have group sections and page headers and footers, whereas mailing labels have only data in the detail section.

The general process for creating a snaked column report is as follows:

- Decide how you want your data to be displayed — how many columns do you want and how wide should each column be?
- Create a report that has detail and group section controls no wider than the width of one column.
- Set the appropriate options in the expanded Print Setup dialog box.
- Verify your results by using a print preview.

Creating the report

You create a snaked column report in the same way you create any report. You start out with a blank Report Design window. Then you drag field controls to the report design and add label controls, lines, and rectangles. Next, you add any shading or special effects that you want. Then you're ready to print your report. The major difference is the placement of controls and the use of the expanded Print Setup window.

Figure 29-10 shows a completed design for the Customer Directory report. The report displays a label control and the date in the page header, along with some solid black lines to set the title apart from the directory details. The detail section contains information that lists the customer number, customer name, address, and phone number. Then, within this section, you see three information fields about the customer's history with Mountain Animal Hospital. The page footer section contains another solid black line and a page number control (not seen in the figure).

What's important here is to make sure that the controls in the detail section use no more space for their height or width than you want for each occurrence of the information. Because you are going to be printing or displaying multiple detail records per page in a snaked column fashion, you must note the size. In this example, you can see that the detail section data is about 1 ¾ inches in height and about 2 inches wide. This is the size of the item that you will define in the expanded Print Setup dialog box.

Figure 29-10:
Defining a snaked column report design.

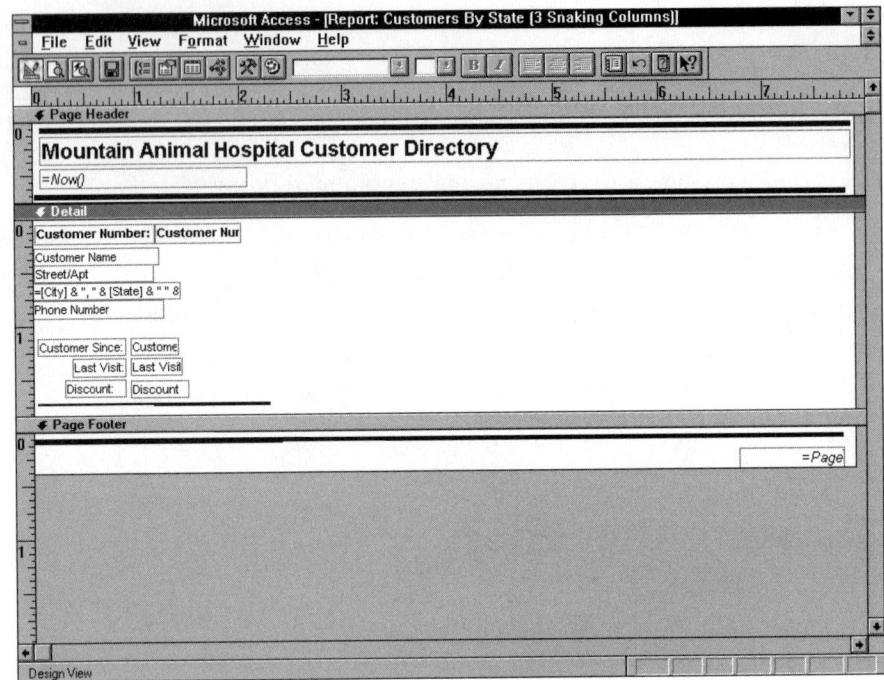

Defining the print setup

You learned in the Mailing Labels section of this chapter how to enter values for print setup settings. Next, you learn some other ways to enter these values. Figure 29-11 shows the expanded Print Setup dialog box and the settings that are used to produce the Customer Directory report. Notice that the Items Across setting is set to 3. This means that you want three customer listings across the page.

The next groups of settings to change are the Item Size and Row and Column spacing. These settings actually work together. As you learned in the Mailing label section, these controls set the size of each data group and the spacing between each group of data. You don't have to define the Item Size to exactly match the size of the data.

Figure 29-11: Defining the print setup for a snaked column report.

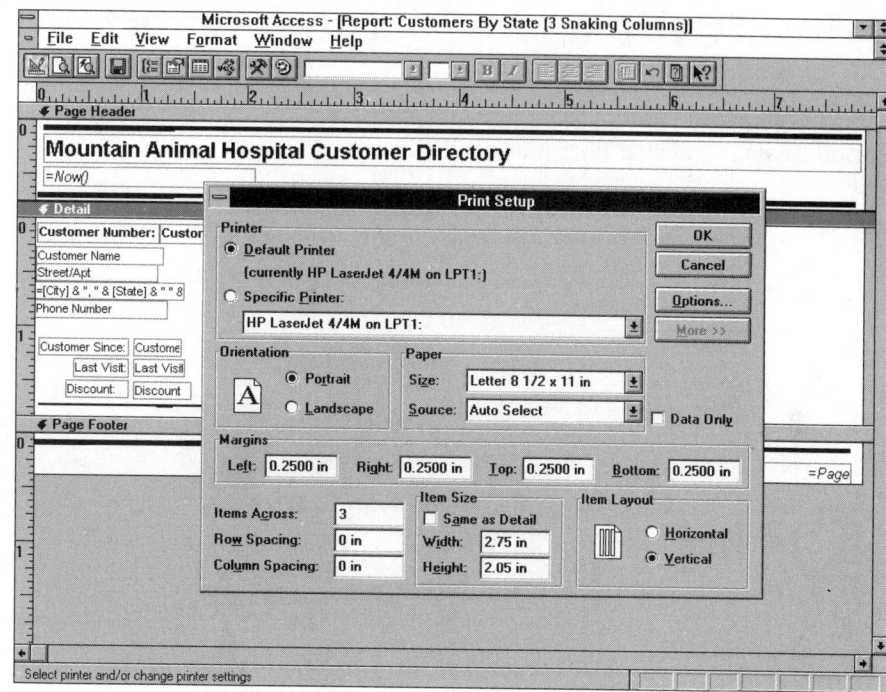

In this example, the data is 1 ¾ inches in height and about 2 inches wide in the detail section. You can define Width as 2 in and Height as 1.75 in. You can then define the Row Spacing to be .5 in and the Column Spacing to be .75 in. This is one way to set up the multiple columns and allow enough space between both the rows and the columns.

However, in this example, you set the Row Spacing and Column Spacing to 0 and increase the Width and Height settings to include the row and column spacing needs. Setting the Width for 2.75 inches is the same as having the Width set to 2 inches and the Column Spacing set to .75 inches. The same is true for the Height and Row Spacing. There is no difference whether the Height is set for 1.75 inches and the Row Spacing is set to .3 inches or the Height is set to 2.05 inches and the Row Spacing is set to 0 inches.

Notice that the Item Layout setting is Vertical. The icon under Item Layout shows the columns going up and down. You saw in Figure 29-8 that when the setting is Horizontal, the icon shows rows of labels going across. In this customer directory, you want to fill an entire column of names first before moving to the right to fill another column.

Printing the snaked column report

Once the expanded Print Setup dialog box settings are completed, you can print your report. Figure 29-12 shows the first page of the final snaked column report. The data is sorted by state and customer number. Notice that the data snakes down the page. The

Figure 29-12: A snaked column report.

Mountain Animal Hospital Customer Directory
Sunday, March 06, 1994

Customer Number: AK001
Animal Kingdom
15 Marlin Lane
Borderville, ID 83483-5646
(208) 555-7108

   Customer Since 5/22/90
       Last Visit: 12/9/93
       Discount: 20%

Customer Number: BL001
Bird Land
22 Eagle Blvd
Russettown, ID 83412-1021
(208) 555-4367

   Customer Since 8/9/92
       Last Visit:
       Discount: 20%

Customer Number: BR001
Stephen Brown
555 Sycamore Ave
Three Corners, ID 83401-1
(208) 555-1237

   Customer Since 9/1/92
       Last Visit: 1/16/93
       Discount: 0%

Customer Number: GB001
George Bird Sanctuary
George St.
Mount Pilot, ID 83908-1012
(208) 555-4852

   Customer Since 4/20/93
       Last Visit:
       Discount: 50%

Customer Number: GR001
George Green
9133 Bookland Rd
Russettown, ID 83412-1012
(208) 555-8898

   Customer Since 12/4/92
       Last Visit: 6/17/93
       Discount: 0%

Customer Number: JO002
Adam Johnson
55 Childs Ave
Mount Pilot, ID 83412-1043
(208) 555-2211

   Customer Since 4/1/93
       Last Visit: 3/7/93
       Discount: 0%

Customer Number: MP002
Mount Pilot Zoo
37 Mount Pilot St.
Mount Pilot, ID 83124-1043
(208) 555-9000

   Customer Since 3/15/92
       Last Visit:
       Discount: 50%

Customer Number: PC001
Pet City
91 Main St.
Mount Pilot, ID 83187-5638
(208) 555-1765

   Customer Since 12/24/9
       Last Visit: 6/18/93
       Discount: 20%

Customer Number: PO001
Tyrone Potter
9133 Bookland Rd
Three Corners, ID 83412-1
(208) 555-1199

   Customer Since 3/11/93
       Last Visit: 6/15/93
       Discount: 0%

Customer Number: RH001
Karen Rhodes
3403 37th Ave
Russettown, ID 83412-1021
(208) 555-9113

   Customer Since 11/11/9
       Last Visit: 6/15/93
       Discount: 0%

Customer Number: RN001
Rocky Nature Center
2234 Pine St.
Russettown, ID 83124-5145
(208) 555-0983

   Customer Since 2/10/93
       Last Visit:
       Discount: 50%

Customer Number: TC001
Three Corners Pets
990 Wise St.
Three Corners, ID 83985-7
(208) 555-4132

   Customer Since 6/27/92
       Last Visit:
       Discount: 20%

Customer Number: VP001
Village Pets
30 Murphy St.
Russettown, ID 83019-8573
(208) 555-1234

   Customer Since 7/5/92
       Last Visit: 6/28/93
       Discount: 20%

Customer Number: WL001
We Love Birds
1434 Pauly St.
Three Corners, ID 83412-1
(208) 555-7763

   Customer Since 9/6/93
       Last Visit:
       Discount: 20%

Customer Number: AD002
William Adams
1122 10th St
Lakeville, OR 97401-1011
(503) 555-6187

   Customer Since 10/22/9
       Last Visit: 1/27/93
       Discount: 5%

Chapter 29: Creating Mailing Labels and Mail Merge Reports

first record is for Customer Number AK001, which is in Idaho. Below that is customer BL001. There are five customers in the first column. After the fifth customer, Customer Number GR001, the next customer is found at the top of the middle column. Notice that the last record in the last column of the first page starts the Oregon customers.

Creating Mail Merge Reports

Now that you've learned how to create snaked column reports and mailing labels (actually, they are the same thing), there is one more type of report to create — the *mail merge report*. Mail merge reports are also known as *form letters*. A mail merge report is simply a report that contains large amounts of text that have embedded database fields. For example, a letter may contain the amount owed by a customer and the name of a pet within the body of the text.

The problem is to control the word wrap. This means that depending on the length of the text and the embedded field values, the text may take more than one line. Different records may have different length values in the embedded fields. One record may use two lines in the report, another may use three, and still another record may require only one line.

Access 2.0 contains a Report Wizard that exports your data to Word for Windows 6.0 and launches Word's Print Merge feature. Why would you want to use a word processor, however, when you're in a database? What happens if you don't own Word 6.0? Most word processors can perform mail merges using database data. Access itself does not have a specific capability to perform mail merging. However, as you see in this section, Access can indeed perform mail merge capabilities with nearly the same precision as any Windows word processor!

In the first section of this chapter, you created mailing labels that indicated a special offer. You can use these labels to address the envelopes for the mail merge letter you now create. Suppose that you need to send a letter to all your customers who have an outstanding balance. You need to let them know that you need payment now.

Figure 29-13 shows a letter created with Access. Many data fields are embedded in this letter that come from an Access query. The letter itself and the embedded fields are created entirely with the Access report writer.

Figure 29-13:
A letter created with the Access report writer.

Mountain Animal Hospital
2414 Mountain Road South
Redmond, WA 06761
(206) 555-9999

March 06, 1994

All Creatures
21 Grace St.
Tall Pines, WA 98746-2541

Dear All Creatures:

It has come to our attention that you have an outstanding balance of $2,000.00. We must have payment within 10 days or we will have to turn this account over to our lawyers. We give great service to your pets. In fact, according to our records, we have helped care for your animals since March 1993.

The entire staff is very fond of your animals. They especially like Bobo, and they would be very upset if your pet was no longer cared for by us. Since your last visit date on November 26, 1993, we have tried to contact you several times without success. Therefore, we are giving you 10 days to pay at least half of the outstanding balance, which comes to $1,000.00.

In advance, thank you, and we look forward to hearing from you and receiving your payment by March 16, 1994.

Sincerely,

Fred G. Rizzley

President
Mountain Animal Hospital

Assembling data for a mail merge report

You can use data from either a table or a query for a report. A mail merge report is no different from any other report. As long as you specify a table or query as the control source for the report, the report can be created. Figure 29-14 displays a typical query that will be used for the letter.

Table 29-1 shows the fields or functions that are embedded in the text blocks used to create the letter. Compare the values found in each line of the letter shown in Figure 29-13 to the fields shown in the table. You'll see how each of these fields or functions is embedded in the text later in this chapter.

Table 29-1
Fields Used in the Mail Merge Report

Field Name	Table	Usage in Report
Date()	Function	Page header; displays current date; formatted as mmmm dd, yyyy
Customer Name	Customer	Page header; displays customer name
Street/Apt	Customer	Page header; displays street in the address block
City	Customer	Page header; part of city, state, zip code block
State	Customer	Page header; part of city, state, zip code block
ZIP Code	Customer	Page header; part of city, state, zip code block; formatted as @@@@@-@@@@
Customer Name	Customer	Detail; part of salutation
Outstanding Balance	Customer	Detail; first line of first paragraph; formatted as $#,##0.00
Customer Since	Customer	Detail; fourth line of first paragraph; formatted as mmmm yyyy
Pet Name	Pets	Detail; first line of second paragraph
Last Visit Date	Customer	Detail; second/third line of second paragraph; formatted as mmmm dd, yyyy
Outstanding Balance *.5	Customer/ Calculation	Detail; fifth line of second paragraph; formatted as $#,##0.00
Date Add(); Now()	Function; Function	Detail; second line of third paragraph; Date Add adds ten days to system date Now(); formatted as mmmm dd, yyyy

Creating a mail merge report

Once you assemble the data, you can create your report. Creating a mail merge report is very much like creating other reports. A mail merge report frequently has only a page header and a detail section. You can, however, use sorting and grouping sections to enhance the mail merge report if you want, although form letters are usually fairly consistent in their content.

Usually, the best way to begin is with a blank report. The Report Wizards don't really help you create a mail merge report. Once you create the blank report, you can begin to add your controls to the report.

Figure 29-14:
A typical query for a mail merge report.

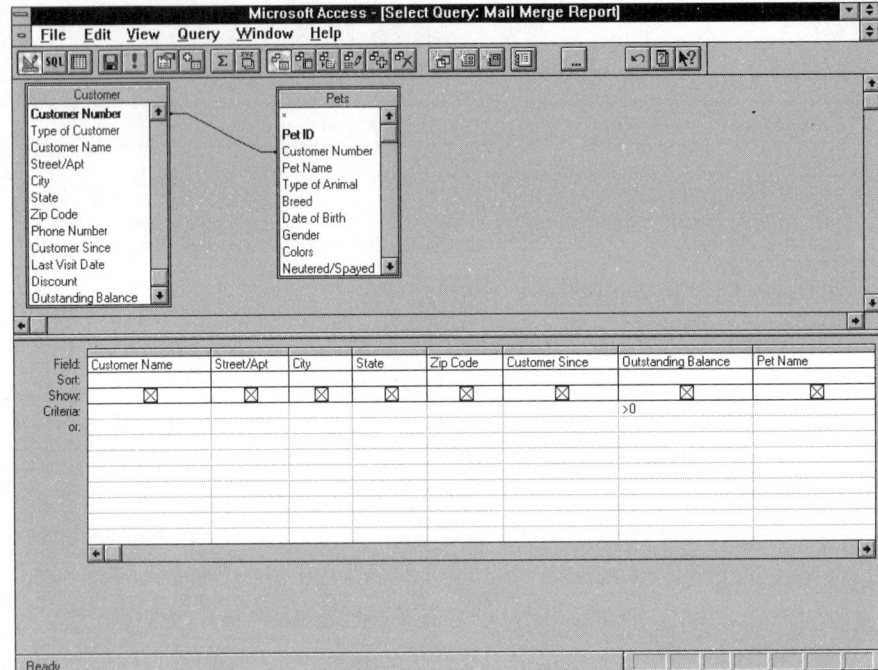

Creating the page header area

Generally, a form letter has a top part, which consists of your company's name, address, and possibly a logo. You can print on preprinted forms that contain this information, or you can scan in the header and embed it in an unbound object frame. The top part of a letter usually also contains the current date and the name and address of the person or company you are sending the letter to.

Figure 29-15 shows the page header section of the mail merge report. In this example, an unbound bitmap picture is inserted that contains Mountain Animal Hospital's logo. The text for the company information is created with individual label controls. As you can see in the top half of the page header section, the current date is also displayed along with a line to separate the top of the header from the body of the letter. You can see the

Chapter 29: Creating Mailing Labels and Mail Merge Reports

calculated text box control's properties at the bottom of Figure 29-15. The Format( ) and Date( ) functions are used to display the date with the full text for month, followed by the day, a comma, a space, and the four-digit year.

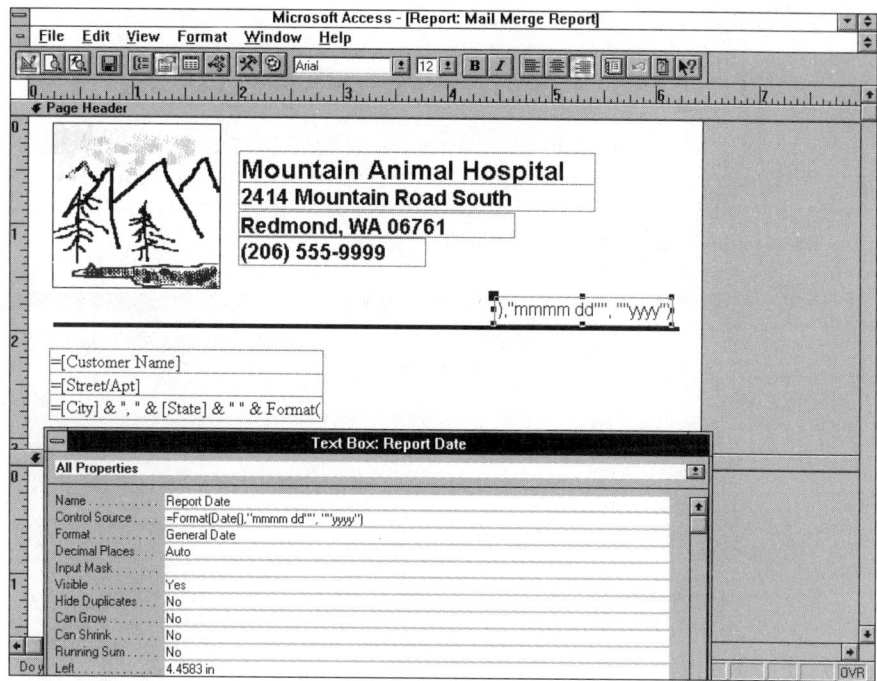

Figure 29-15: The page header section of a mail merge report.

The date expression is entered as

=Format(Date(),"mmmm dd, yyyy")

and then automatically changed to

```
=Format(Date(),"mmmm dd"","""yyyy")
```

This expression takes the system date of 12/10/93 and formats the date as December 10, 1993.

The customer name and address fields are also displayed in the page header. The standard concatenated expression is used to display the city, state, and ZIP code fields:

```
=[City] & ", " & [State] & " " & Format([Zip Code],"@@@@@-@@@@")
```

Working with embedded fields in text

The body of the letter is shown in Figure 29-16. Each paragraph is one large block of text. A standard text box control is used to display each paragraph. The text box control's Can Grow and Can Shrink properties are set to Yes. This allows the text to take up only as much space as needed.

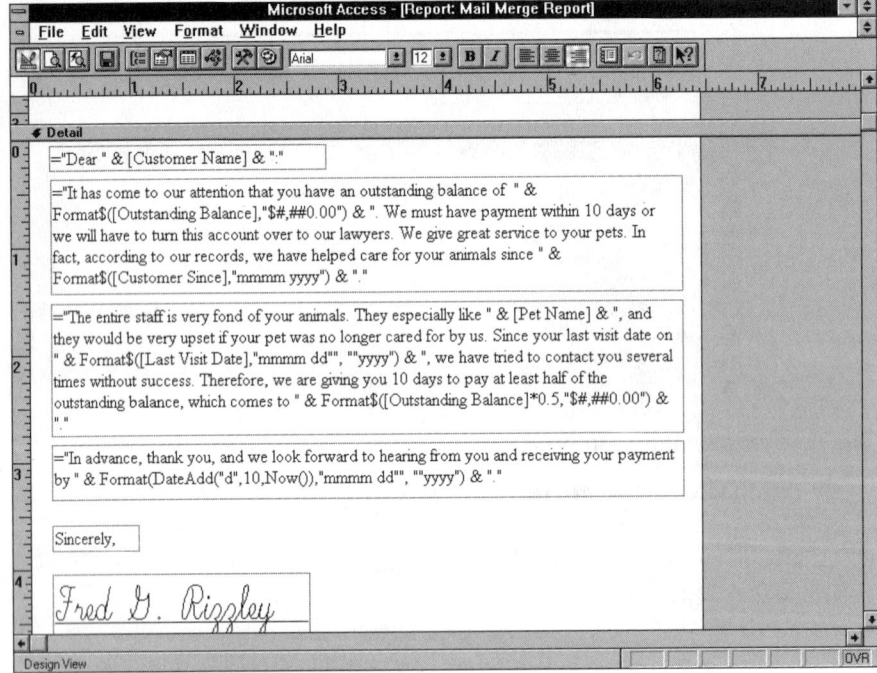

Figure 29-16: The body of the letter in the Report Design window.

Embedded in each text block are fields from the query or expressions that use the fields from the query. In the page header section, the & method of concatenation is used to concatenate the city, state, and ZIP code. Although this method works for single concatenated lines, it does not allow word wrapping, which is critical to creating a mail merge report. If you use this method in large blocks of text, you get only a single truncated line of text.

As you learned in Chapter 23, the & method of concatenation handles word wrap within the defined width of the text box. When the text reaches the right margin of a text box, it shifts down to the next line. Because the Can Grow property is set to on, the text box can have any number of lines. It is best when you concatenate with the & method to convert nontext data to text. Although this isn't mandatory, it more correctly displays the embedded fields when they are correctly converted and formatted.

If you don't understand the concepts of concatenation you should read the section about concatenation in Chapter 23 before reading the rest of this section.

The first text block is a single-line text box control that concatenates the text "Dear" with the field Customer Name. Notice that there are some special symbols within the first text box control. Remember that each text box is made up of smaller groups of text and expressions. By using the & character, you can concatenate them.

The expression **="Dear" & [Customer Name] & ":"** begins with an equal sign and a double quote. Because the first item is text, it is surrounded by " characters. The field [Customer Name] needs to be enclosed in brackets because it is a field name and also surrounded by & characters for concatenation. The colon at the end of the expression appears in the letter and must be surrounded by double quotes because it too is text.

The next control produces the first paragraph of the letter. Notice there are five lines in the text box control but there are only four lines in the first paragraph of the letter shown in Figure 29-13. However, if you compare the two figures carefully you will see that text *your animals since* is on the fifth line of the paragraph in the text control, whereas it is in the fourth line of the paragraph in the printed letter. This is a good example of word wrap. The lines shrunk to fit the data.

The first line of the text control simply displays a text string. Notice the text string is both enclosed in double quotes and is concatenated to the next expression by the & character. The second line begins with an expression.

The expression **Format$([Outstanding Balance],"$#,##0.00") & "."** converts the numeric expression to text and formats the field Outstanding Balance so it shows a dollar sign, a comma if the value is 1,000 or more, and displays two decimal places. Without the format, the field would have simply displayed 381 for the first record rather than $381.00.

The rest of the second line of the paragraph through the end of the fourth line of the paragraph is one long text string. It is simply enclosed in double quotes and concatenated by the & character. The last line of the first paragraph contains an expression that formats and converts a date field. The expression **Format$([Customer Since],"mmmm yyyy")** formats the date value to display only the full month name and the year. The date format in the Page Header demonstrated how to display the full month name, day, and year.

The maximum length of a single concatenated expression in Access is 254 characters between a single set of quotes. To get around this limitation, just end one expression, add an & character and start another. The limit of the length of an expression in a single text box is 2,048 characters (almost 40 lines)!

The last line of the second paragraph formats a numeric expression, but it also calculates a value within the format function. This is a good example of an expression within a function. The calculation **[Outstanding Balance] * .5** is then formatted to display dollar signs and a comma if the number is 1,000 or more.

The last paragraph contains one text string and one expression. The expression advances the current date Now() by 10 days by using the expression **DateAdd("d",10,Now())**.

The bottom of the letter is produced using the label controls as shown in Figure 29-17. This figure shows one of the body paragraphs at the top of the figure and three label controls below. These label controls display the closing, the signature, and the owners title. The signature of Fred G. Rizzley is created here by using the Script font. Normally, you would scan in the signature and then use an unbound frame object control to display the bitmap picture containing the signature.

Notice in Figure 29-17 that the *Force New Page* property of the Detail section is set to **After section** so there is always a page break after each letter.

Printing the mail merge report

The mail merge report is printed in exactly the same way as you do any report. From the Print Preview window, you can simply select the Print button. From the Report Design window, you can select File⇒Print. The report is printed out like any other report.

Figure 29-17:
The bottom of the letter in the Report Design window.

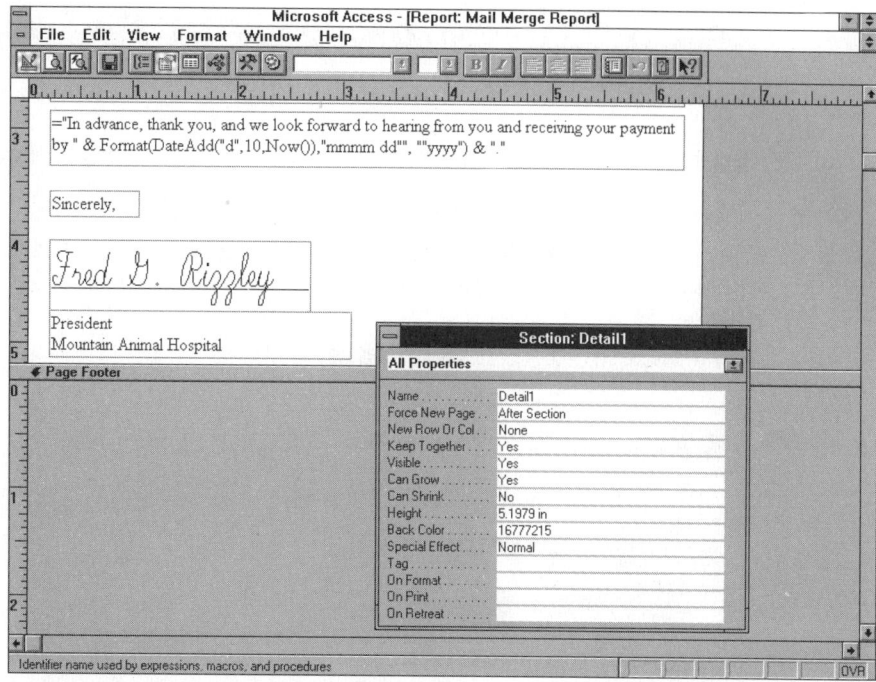

Using the Access Mail Merge Wizard for Word for Windows 6.0

A new feature in Access 2.0 is the addition of a wizard to automatically open Word for Windows 6.0 and start the Print Merge feature. The table or query you specify when you create the new report is used as the data source for the Word for Windows print merge.

You must have Word for Windows 6.0 to use the Mail Merge Wizard in Access 2.0.

Steps: Using the Access Mail Merge Wizard for Word for Windows 6.0

Step 1. Create a New Report.

Step 2. Select the Mail Merge Report query from the Select a Table/Query dialog box.

Step 3. Select the Report Wizards button.

Step 4. Select the MS Word Mail Merge Report Wizard as shown in Figure 29-18 and press OK.

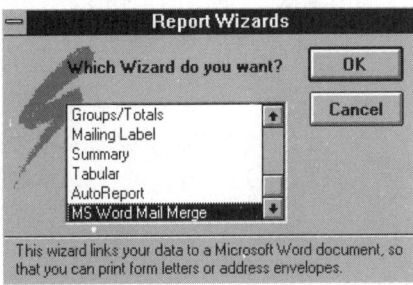

Figure 29-18: Selecting the MS Word Mail Merge Wizard.

After you select the MS Word Mail Merge Wizard, Access displays the Microsoft Word Mail Merge Wizard screen as shown in Figure 29-19.

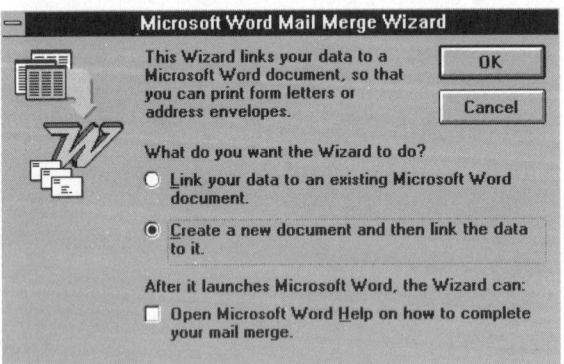

Figure 29-19: The Microsoft Word Mail Merge Wizard screen.

This screen lets you decide whether to start Word for Windows 6.0 with a new document or whether Word should open an existing document. If you select the option Link your data to an existing Microsoft Word document,

Chapter 29: Creating Mailing Labels and Mail Merge Reports

Access displays a standard Windows file selection box that lets you select an existing document. The document is retrieved, Word 6.0 is displayed, and the Print Merge feature is active. You can then modify your existing document.

In this example, you will start with a new document.

Step 5. Select Create a new document and then link the data to it.

Step 6. Press OK to launch Word and display the Print Merge toolbar.

You can now create your document, adding merge fields where you want them. As shown in Figure 29-20, you simply type your text and click the Insert Merge Field button whenever you want to display a field list from your Access table or query. The fields appear with a pair of carets around them.

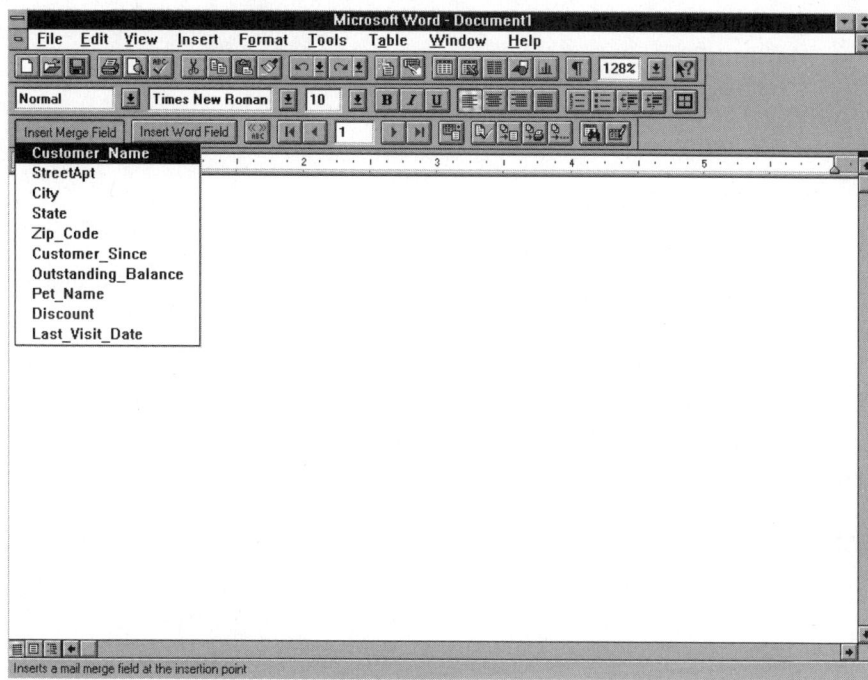

Figure 29-20: The Word for Windows Print Merge screen.

When you are through, you can use the standard Word for Windows 6.0 toolbar to merge the actual data and print your mail merge letters. There are some advantages to using the Microsoft Word print merge facility to create your letters. You have the availability of a spell checker, you can properly justify your paragraphs, and you can individually change the font type, size, or weight of individual words or characters. The negatives are that you have to use a word processor, you can't format numeric or date data, and you can't embed other Access objects such as datasheets or graphs.

Third party developers offer Mail Merge Report Wizard products that work totally within Access and don't require Microsoft Word 6.0. These products offer all the advantages of working within Access and automate the process of creating the type of mail merge reports taught earlier in this chapter. In fact, the authors of this book are the leading vendors of Access Add-On tools, including a Mail Merge Report Wizard and an Envelope Wizard for Access. These products are available from Cary Prague Books and Software, 60 Krawski Dr., South Windsor, CT 06074. You can reach us by calling (800) 277-3117 in the U.S. and Canada or (203) 644-5891 internationally or by fax anywhere.

When you are through editing and printing your letter, you can return to Access by selecting File⇨Close or File⇨Exit.

Summary

In this chapter, you learned how to create mailing labels, snaked column reports, and mail merge reports. The following concepts were discussed:

- Mailing labels are most easily created using the Access Mailing Label Report Wizard.
- The Report Wizard lets you select the fields for the mailing label and also select from over 100 Avery mailing label forms.
- Using the Report Design window, you can customize the mailing label further.
- The secret to mailing labels is changing the settings in the expanded Print Setup dialog box.
- Snaked column reports can be snaked vertically or horizontally.
- Snaked column reports are essentially large labels on paper and are used for such things as customer directories.
- You can create mail merge reports with the Access report writer.
- By using concatenated text boxes, you can create paragraphs of text with embedded fields that word wrap to create form letters.
- You can use the Format( ) function to reformat numeric and date fields in a mail merge report.
- The new Access Word for Windows 6.0 Mail Merge Wizard makes exported Access data easy to use with the Print Merge feature in Word 6.0.

This completes Part IV of the book, which deals with advanced Access query, form, and report topics. The next section covers the use of Access macros that you can use to automate tasks without programming.

Part V

Applications in Access

861 Chapter 30: An Introduction to Macros and Events

889 Chapter 31: Using Macros in Forms and Reports

937 Chapter 32: Creating Switchboards, Menus, and Dialogs

987 Chapter 33: Next Steps — Modules and Access Basic

An Introduction to Macros and Events

CHAPTER 30

In This Chapter

- How macros work
- The various components of the Macro window
- How to create and run a macro
- How to edit, delete, and rename macros
- How to create macro groups
- How to create a macro that starts automatically
- How to supply conditions to macros
- How to troubleshoot macros
- How events work
- How events are triggered

When you work with your database system, you may perform the same tasks over and over. Instead of doing the same steps every time, you can automate the process by using macros.

Database management systems continually grow as you add records in a form, perform *ad-hoc* queries, and print new reports. As the system grows, you save many of the objects for later use — for a weekly report, a monthly update query, and so on. You tend to create and perform many tasks repetitively. For example, every time you add customer records, you open the same form. Or you print the same form letter for customers whose pets are overdue for their annual shots.

Access *macros* can be created to perform these tasks. Once you create the macros, you may want certain macros to take effect whenever a user performs some action, such as pressing a button or opening a form. Access uses *events* to trigger a macro automatically.

Understanding Macros

In Access, many repetitive tasks can be automated without writing complex programs or subroutines. Rather, you create an Access macro to perform these tasks. In the example of the form letter for customers whose pets are overdue for annual shots, a macro can perform a query and print the results for all such customers.

What is a macro?

A *macro* is an object just like other Access objects such as tables, queries, forms, and reports. You create the macro to automate a particular task or series of tasks. Each task can be thought of as the result of one or more steps, with each step being an action not found in the Access menu but in the Access Basic language. You can also use Access macros to simulate menu choices or mouse movements.

Unlike macros in spreadsheets, Access macros usually are not used to duplicate individual keystrokes or mouse movements. Rather, Access macros perform specific user-specified tasks, such as opening a form or running a report.

Every task you want Access to perform is known as an *action*. Access provides more than 45 actions that you can select and perform in your macros. For example, you may have a macro that performs the four actions shown in Figure 30-1:

- Places the hourglass on the screen
- Automatically opens a form
- Maximizes the form after opening it
- Displays a message box saying that the macro is complete

Macro actions are created in a Macro Design window. The macros are run by entering the macro name in the event properties of a form or report.

When to use a macro

You can use macros for any repetitive task you find yourself doing in Access. By automating routine or repetitive tasks, you save time and energy. In addition, because the macro performs the actions in the same way every time, macros add accuracy and efficiency to your database. You can use macros to perform the following tasks:

Figure 30-1:
A macro designed with four actions (tasks).

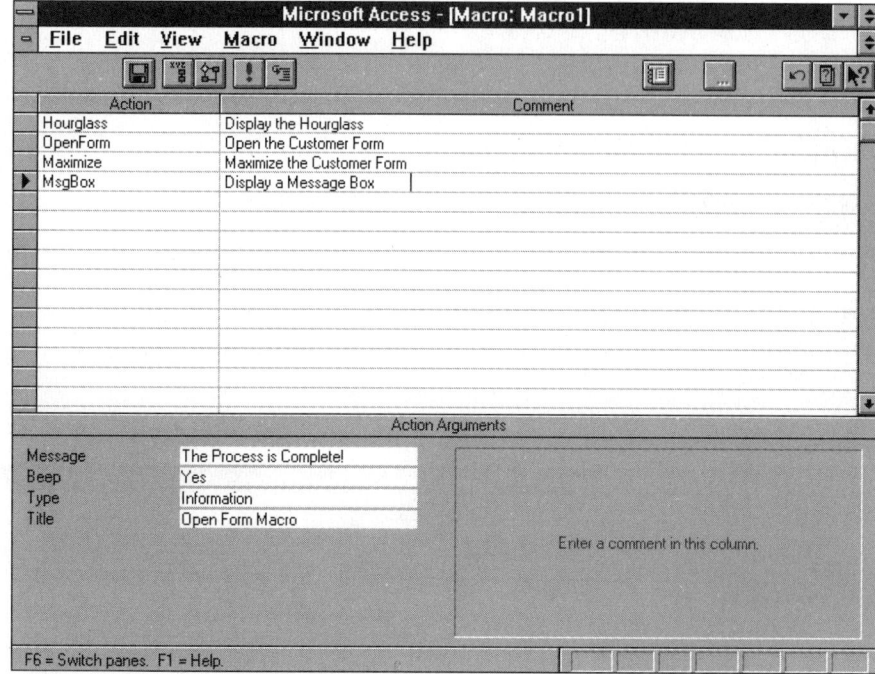

- Link and run queries and reports together
- Open multiple forms and/or reports together
- Check for data accuracy on validation forms
- Perform actions when a command button is selected

As an example, a macro can find and filter records for a report. Or by adding a button to a form, the macro can perform a user-specified search. In short, macros can be used throughout the Access database system.

The Macro Window

When you create a macro, as you do with other Access objects, you create it in a graphical design window. To open a new Macro window, follow these steps:

864 Part V: Applications in Access

Steps:	**Creating a New Macro**
Step 1.	In an open database, press F11 (or Alt+F1) to select the Database window.
Step 2.	Click the Macro object button.
Step 3.	Click the New command button in the Database window.

After you complete these steps, Access displays an empty Design window similar to the one in Figure 30-2. Notice the different parts of the window in this figure.

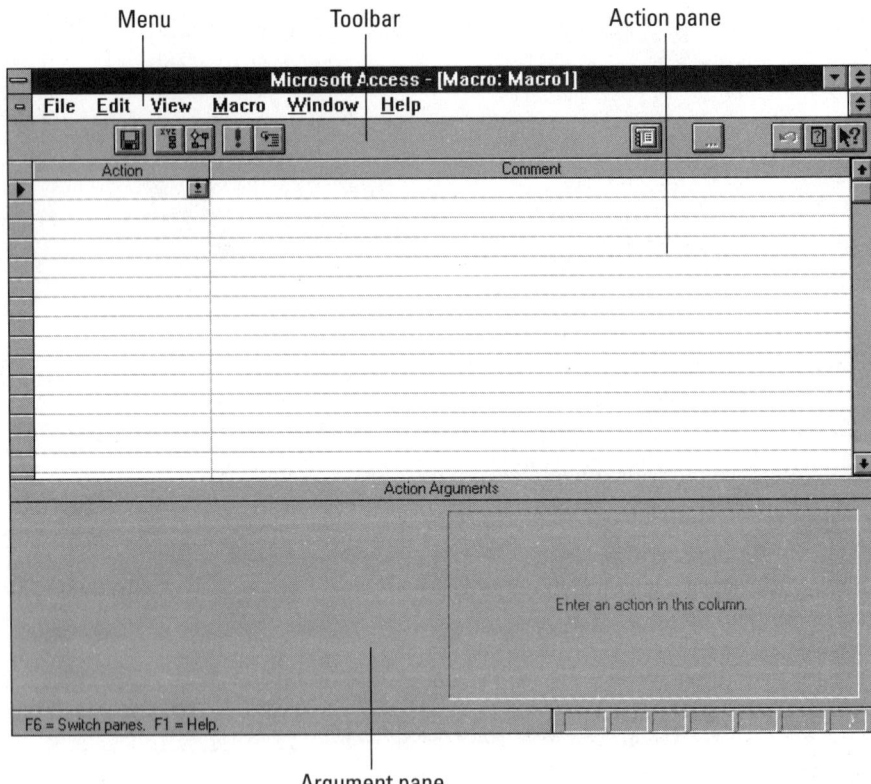

Figure 30-2: The empty Macro Design window.

As Figure 30-2 shows, the Macro Design window is comprised of four parts: a menu and a toolbar above the Design window and these two window panes:

- Action pane (top portion of window)
- Argument pane (bottom portion of window)

If the toolbar is not present in your window, select View➪Options... and then select Show Tool Bar in the General (Category); change the value to **Yes** to turn the toolbar on.

The Action pane

By default, when you open a new Macro Design window, as in Figure 30-2, Access displays two columns in the Action pane (top pane). These are the Action and Comment columns. Two more columns, Macro Name and Condition, can be displayed in the Action pane by selecting View➪Macro Names and View➪Conditions.

If you want to change the default to all four columns open, select View➪Options... and then select Macro Design (Category); change the values of both items to **Yes.**

Actions are the individual tasks you want Access to perform. Each macro can have one action or many. You add individual actions in the Action column. Besides adding individual actions, you can add a description of each action in the Comment column. The comments are ignored by Access when the macro is run.

For a complete listing and explanation of all actions, refer to Appendix B.

The Argument pane

The lower portion of the window is the Argument pane. This is where you supply the specific arguments (properties) needed for the selected action. Most actions need additional information to carry out the action, such as which object should be used. For example, Figure 30-3 shows the action arguments for a typical action named OpenForm. This action opens a specific form and has six different arguments that can be specified:

Form Name	Specifies the Access form to open
View	Specifies the view mode to activate — a form, datasheet, etc.
Filter Name	Applies the specified filter or query

Where Condition   Limits the records displayed
Data Mode   Specifies a data-entry mode — add, edit, or read only
Window Mode   Specifies a window mode — normal, hidden, icon, dialog

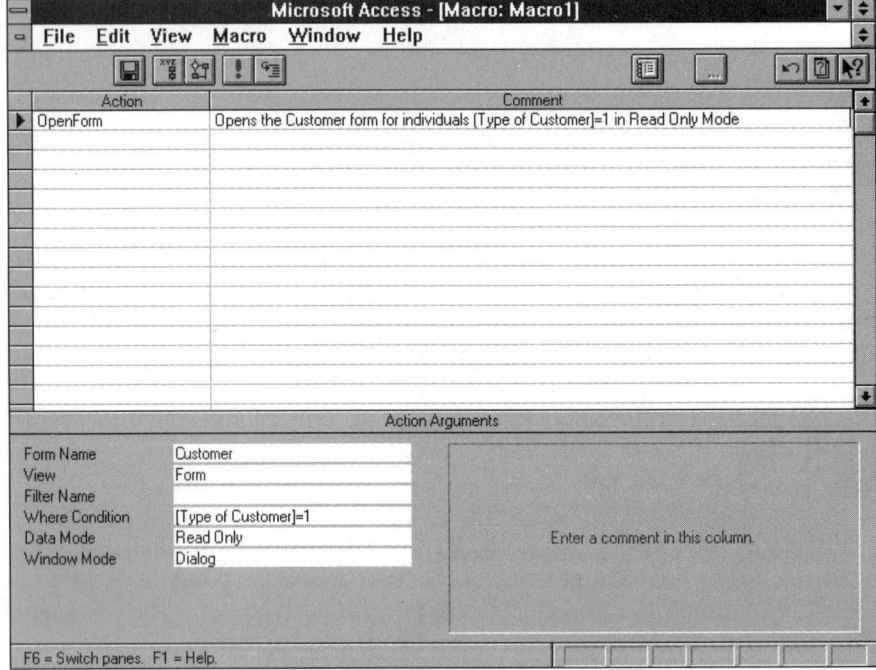

Figure 30-3: Arguments displayed for the OpenForm action.

Some actions, such as Beep and Maximize, have no arguments, but most require at least one argument.

The Macro window menu bar

The Macro window menu bar has one menu prompt that you haven't seen yet. This is the Macro menu, with two choices:

Run   Runs the macro
Single Step   Runs the macro one step at a time

Chapter 30: An Introduction to Macros and Events

The macro design toolbar

The toolbar in the Macro window has several buttons specifically used for macros (see Figure 30-3). These buttons, which perform the same functions as the menu options, are as follows (from left to right):

Save	Saves the macro
Macro Names	Displays the macro name column
Conditions	Displays the macro conditions column
Run	Runs a macro
Style Step	Runs the macro one step at a time

Creating a macro

To create a macro, you use both panes of the macro window — Action and Argument. Once you supply actions and associated arguments, you can save the macro for later use.

Entering actions and arguments

You can add actions to a macro in the following several ways:

- Enter the action name in the Action column of the Macro window.
- Select actions from the action pull-down list box (in the Action column).
- Drag and drop an object from the Database window into an action cell.

The last method, drag and drop, is useful for common actions associated with the database. For example, you can drag a specific form to an action cell in the macro Action column, and Access will automatically add the action OpenForm and the known arguments, such as the form name.

Selecting actions from the pull-down list

The easiest way to add an action is by using the pull-down list box, which can be accessed in any action cell. For example, if you want to open a form, you specify the action OpenForm. To create the OpenForm action, follow these steps:

Steps:	Creating an OpenForm Action by Using the Pull-Down List Box
Step 1.	Open a new Macro Design window.

Step 2.	Click the first empty cell in the Action column.
Step 3.	Click the arrow that appears in the action cell.
Step 4.	Select the OpenForm action from the pull-down list box.

You don't have to add comments to the macro, but it is a good idea to document the reason for each macro action as well as a description of the entire macro.

Specifying arguments for actions

After entering the OpenForm action, you can enter the arguments into the bottom pane. Figure 30-3, which displays the completed arguments, shows that the bottom pane has six action arguments associated with this specific action. The arguments View, Data Mode, and Window Mode have default values. Because Access does not know which form you want to open, you must at least enter a form name. To open the form named Customer as a dialog in read-only mode, you enter the three arguments Form Name, Data Mode, and Window Mode, as shown in Figure 30-3.

To add the arguments, follow these steps:

Steps:	Adding Arguments to an OpenForm Action
Step 1.	Click in the Form Name cell (or press F6 to switch to the Argument pane).
Step 2.	Select the Customer form from the pull-down list box (or type the name).
Step 3.	Click in the Data Mode cell.
Step 4.	Select the Read Only choice from the pull-down list (or type the choice).
Step 5.	Click in the Window Mode cell.
Step 6.	Select the Icon choice from the pull-down list (or type the choice).

Your macro should now resemble the one in Figure 30-3. Notice that the Form Name is now specified and the default values of the Data Mode and Window Mode cells are changed.

Selecting actions by dragging and dropping objects

You can also specify actions by dragging and dropping objects from the Database window. When you add actions in this manner, Access automatically adds the appropriate arguments. To add the same form, Customer, to an empty Macro window, follow these steps:

Chapter 30: An Introduction to Macros and Events

Steps: Adding a Form Using the Drag-and-Drop Method

Step 1. Start with an empty Macro Design window.

Step 2. Select Window⇨Tile from the Design menu. Access places the Macro and Database windows side by side.

Step 3. Click the Form button in the Database window. Access displays all the forms, as in Figure 30-4.

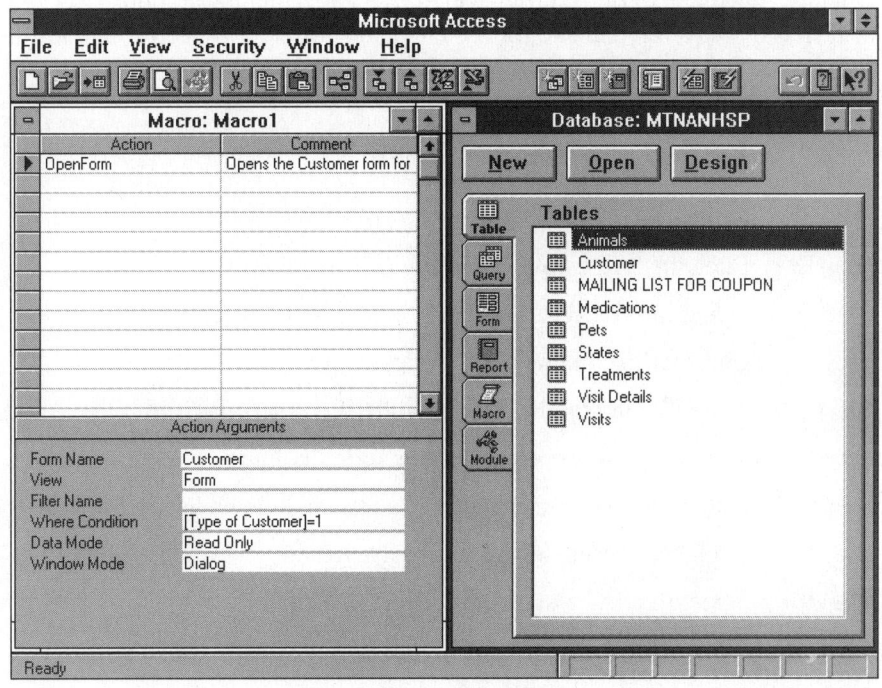

Figure 30-4: The Macro and Database windows are tiled side by side.

Step 4. Click on and drag the form Customer from the Database window. Access displays a Form icon as it moves into the Macro window.

Step 5. Continue to drag and drop the Form icon in any empty action cell of the Macro window.

Access automatically displays the correct action and arguments.

 After using the drag-and-drop method to select actions, you may need to modify the action arguments to further refine them from their default values. Recall that in the last example, you changed Data Mode and Window Mode for the form.

Adding multiple actions to a macro

You are not limited to adding a single action in a macro. You can have multiple actions assigned to a macro. For example, you may want to display an hourglass and then, while it is displayed, open two forms. Then you can have a beep sound for the user after completing the macro. To accomplish these multiple actions, follow these steps:

Steps:	Specifying Multiple Actions for a Macro
Step 1.	Open a new Macro Design window.
Step 2.	Click the first empty cell in the Action column.
Step 3.	Select the Hourglass action from the pull-down list box or type it.
Step 4.	Click in the comment cell alongside the Hourglass action.
Step 5.	Type **Display the hourglass while the macro is running.**
Step 6.	Click the next empty cell in the Action column.
Step 7.	Select the OpenForm action from the pull-down list box or type the action.
Step 8.	Click in the argument cell Form Name.
Step 9.	Select the Add a Customer and Pets form.
Step 10.	Click in the comment cell alongside the OpenForm action.
Step 11.	Type **Open the Add a Customer and Pets form.**
Step 12.	Click in the next empty cell in the Action column.
Step 13.	Select the OpenForm action from the pull-down list box or type the action.
Step 14.	Click in the argument cell Form Name.
Step 15.	Select the Adding Visit Details form.
Step 16.	Click in the comment cell alongside the OpenForm action.
Step 17.	Type **Open the Adding Visit Details form.**
Step 18.	Click in the next empty cell in the Action column.
Step 19.	Select the Beep action from the pull-down list box or type the action.

Your macro design should now look similar to Figure 30-5. Notice that this macro will open both forms as it displays the hourglass. After both forms are open, the macro beeps to signal that the macro is finished.

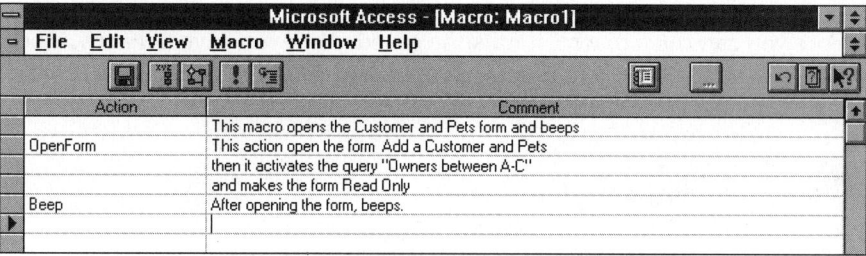

Figure 30-5: Adding multiple actions to a single macro.

When you're adding more than one action, you can specify each action, one after the other, with several rows of spaces in between. These blank rows can contain extended comments for each macro action. Figure 30-6 demonstrates how you can specify two actions with comments for each.

Figure 30-6: Actions with multiple-line comments in the Action pane.

The macro described in Figure 30-6 performs two actions — OpenForm and Beep. Notice that the first line has no action, but does have a comment; the action OpenForm has three comment lines associated with it.

Rearranging macro actions

When you work with multiple actions in a macro, you may change your mind about the order of the actions. For example, you may decide that the macro created in Figure 30-5 should have the Beep action come first in the macro. To move the action, follow these steps:

Steps:	**Moving an Action**
Step 1.	Select the action by clicking the row selector to the left of the action name.
Step 2.	Click the highlighted row again and drag it to the top row.

Deleting macro actions

If you placed an action in a macro that you no longer need, you can delete it. In the example of the macro shown in Figure 30-5, you may decide that you don't want to open the form Adding Visit Details. To delete the action, follow these steps:

Steps:	Deleting an Action
Step 1.	Select the action by clicking the row selector to the left of the action name.
Step 2.	Press Delete or select Edit⇨Delete from the menu.

You can also delete a row by using the shortcut menu — select Row and press the right mouse button.

Saving macros

Before you can run a macro, it must be saved. After you save a macro, it becomes another database object that you can open and run from the Database window. To save a macro, follow these steps:

Steps:	Saving a Macro
Step 1.	Select File⇨Save from the Macro Design menu or press the Save button on the toolbar.
Step 2.	If the macro has not been saved, you must enter a name in the Save As dialog box. Press Enter or choose OK when you are through.

 The fastest way to save a macro is to press F12 or Alt+F2 and give the macro a name. Another way is to double-click the Macro window's Control menu (top left corner) and answer the appropriate dialog box questions.

Editing existing macros

Once you create a macro, you can edit it by following these steps:

Steps:	Editing a Macro
Step 1.	In the Database window, select the Macro object button.

Step 2.	Highlight the macro you want to edit.
Step 3.	Click the Design button in the Database window.

 You can also edit a macro by highlighting the macro name and double-clicking the right mouse button.

Copying macros

To copy a macro, follow these steps:

Steps:	Copying a Macro
Step 1.	Click the Macro button in the Database window.
Step 2.	Select the macro you want to copy.
Step 3.	Press Ctrl+C or choose Edit⇨Copy to copy the macro to the Clipboard.
Step 4.	Press Ctrl+V or choose Edit⇨Paste to paste the macro from the Clipboard.
Step 5.	In the Paste As dialog box, type the new name.

Renaming macros

Sometimes you need to rename a macro because you changed the event call in the form or report property. To rename a macro, follow these steps:

Steps:	Renaming a Macro
Step 1.	Select the Database window by pressing F11 or Alt+F1.
Step 2.	Click the Macro button to display all the macro names.
Step 3.	Highlight the macro you want to change the name of.
Step 4.	Choose File⇨Rename... from the Database menu or *right* mouse click and choose Rename from the shortcut menu.
Step 5.	Enter the new name in the Rename dialog box.

Running Macros

Once a macro is created, you can run it yourself from several locations within Access:

- A Macro window
- A Database window
- Other object windows
- Another macro

Running a macro from the Macro window

You can run a macro directly from the Macro Design window by clicking the toolbar's Run button (the exclamation mark) or by choosing Macro⇨Run from the Design menu.

Running a macro from the Database window

You can run a macro from the Database window by following these steps:

Steps:	Running a Macro from the Database Window
Step 1.	Click the Macro button in the Database window.
Step 2.	Select the macro you want to run.
Step 3.	Either double-click the macro or choose the Run button.

Running a macro from any window in the database

To run a macro from any window in the database, follow these steps:

Steps:	Running a Macro from Any Window
Step 1.	Select File⇨Run Macro... from the window menu.

Chapter 30: An Introduction to Macros and Events

Step 2.	In the Macro dialog box, enter the name or select it from the pull-down list box.
Step 3.	Click the OK button or press Enter.

Running a macro from another macro

To run a macro from another macro, follow these steps:

Steps:	**Running a Macro from Another Macro**
Step 1.	Add the action RunMacro to your macro.
Step 2.	Enter the name of the macro you want to run in the Macro Name argument.

You can also run a macro based on an event in a form or report or by using an AutoExec macro.

Using the AutoExec macro

You can have Access automatically run a macro every time a database is opened. Access recognizes a special macro named *AutoExec*. If Access finds this macro in a database, it automatically executes it every time the database is opened. For example, you may want to open some forms and queries automatically, immediately upon opening the database.

To run a macro automatically when a database is opened, follow these steps:

Steps:	**Creating an AutoExec Macro**
Step 1.	Create a macro with the actions you want to run when the database is opened.
Step 2.	Save the macro and name it **AutoExec.**

If you now close that database and reopen it, Access automatically runs the AutoExec macro.

 If you have a macro named AutoExec but you don't want to run it when you open a database, hold down the Shift key as you select the database in the Open Database... dialog box. (Alternatively, you can select the database from any of the last four databases opened.)

Macro Groups

As you create macros, you may want to group a series of related macros into one large macro. To do this, you need some way of uniquely identifying the individual macros within the group. Access lets you group macros into a *macro group*. A macro group is a macro that contains one or more macros in a single macro file.

Creating macro groups

Like individual macros, macro groups are database objects. When you look in the macro object list of the Database window, you see only the macro group name. Inside the macro group, each macro has a unique name that you assign to it along with the actions for each macro.

You may, for example, want to create a macro group of all macros that will open forms. To create this type of macro, follow these steps:

Steps:	Creating a Macro Group of All Macros That Open Forms
Step 1.	In the Database window, select the Macro object button.
Step 2.	Click the New command button in the Database window. Access opens the Macro Design window.
Step 3.	Select View⇨Macro Names or select the Macro Names button on the toolbar. Access adds the Macro Name column to the Action pane.
Step 4.	In the Macro Name column, enter a name for the macro.
Step 5.	In the Action column, next to the macro name you just entered, enter an action for the macro.
Step 6.	Select the Action column under the action you just entered so that you can enter the next action.

Chapter 30: An Introduction to Macros and Events

Step 7. Enter the next action (if the macro has more than one) in the Action column. Continue to enter actions until all are specified for that specific macro. To add another macro to the group, repeat Steps 4 through 7.

Step 8. Save the macro group, giving it an appropriate name.

Figure 30-7 shows how a macro group named Open and Close Forms will look. Notice that there are five macros within the macro group.

Figure 30-7: A macro group.

Macro Name	Action	Comment
Customer	OpenForm	Opens the Customer form
Visits	OpenForm	Opens the Visits form
Details	OpenForm	Opens the Visits Details form
Close All Forms	Close	Close the Visits Details form
	Close	Close the Visits form
	Close	Close the Customer form
Exit	Quit	Quit Access

The macro group in Figure 30-7 shows five macros: Customer, Visits, Details, Close All Forms, and Exit.

Although not necessary, it's a good idea to leave a blank line between macros to improve readability and clarity.

Running a macro in a macro group

Once you create a macro group, you will want to run each macro inside the macro group. To run a macro contained within a macro group, you must specify both the group name and the macro name.

To specify both group and macro names, type the group name, a period, and then the macro name. For example, if you type **Open and Close Forms.Visits**, you specify the macro Visits in the group macro named Open and Close Forms.

If you run a group macro from the Macro Design window or from the Database window, you cannot specify a macro name inside the macro group. Therefore, Access will run only the first macro or set of actions specified in the group macro. Access stops executing actions when it reaches a new macro name in the Macro Name column.

To run a macro inside a group macro using the other windows in the database or another macro, you simply enter both the macro group name and macro name, placing a period between the two names.

You also can run a macro by selecting Run macro from the File menu and typing the group and macro name.

Supplying Conditions for Actions

In some cases, you may want to run some action or actions in a macro only when a certain condition is true. For example, you may want to display a message if there are no records available for a report and then stop execution of the macro. In a case like this, you can use a condition to control the flow of the macro.

What is a condition?

Simply put, a condition is a logical expression. That is, it can be True or False only. The macro will follow one of two paths, based on the condition of the expression. If the expression is True, the macro follows the True path; otherwise, it follows the False path. Table 30-1 shows several conditions and the True/False results.

Activating the Condition column in a macro

As Table 30-1 demonstrates, a condition is an expression that results in a logical answer of Yes or No. The answer must be either True or False. You can specify a condition in a macro by following these steps:

Steps:	Specifying a Condition in a Macro
Step 1.	Enter the Macro Design window by creating a new macro or editing an existing one.
Step 2.	Select View⇨Conditions or select the Conditions button on the toolbar. The Condition column is inserted to the left of the Action column. If the Macro Name column is visible, the Condition column is between the Macro Name and the Action columns (see Figure 30-7).

Chapter 30: An Introduction to Macros and Events

Referring to Control Names in Expressions

When working with macros, you may need to refer to the value of a control in a form or report. To refer to a control in a form or report, use the following syntax:

Forms!*form-name*!*control-name*

Reports!*report-name*!*control-name*

If a space occurs within the name of a form, report, or control, you must enclose the name in brackets. For example, Forms![Add a Customer and Pets]!State refers to the State control (field on form) on the currently open form called Add a Customer and Pets.

If you run a macro from the same form or report that contains the control, you can shorten this syntax to the control name:

control-name

To reference a control name on a form or report, the form or report must be open.

Table 30-1
Conditions and Their Results

Condition	True Result	False Result
Forms!Customer!State="WA"	If the state is Washington	Any state except Washington
IsNull(Gender)	If there is no gender specified (not Null)	Gender is male or female
Length <= 10	If length is less than or equal to 10 inches	If the length is greater than 10 inches
Reports![Pet Directory]![Type Animal] = "CAT" OR Reports![Pet Directory]![Type of Animal] = "DOG"	If type of animal is a cat or dog	Any animal other than cat of or dog

With the Condition column visible, you can specify conditions for one or many actions within a macro.

In Figure 30-8, you can see that the Condition and Comment columns are wider than the Action column. You can widen or shrink columns by positioning the cursor on the column border and dragging the column line.

Figure 30-8: The Condition column added to the Macro Design window.

Condition	Action	Comment
	OpenForm	Open the Pets form
Not IsNull([Forms]![Pets]![Pet ID])	OpenReport	If the Pets form has at least one record
		then run the Pet Directory report in
		Print Preview mode
		Using the Filter named Cats and Dogs

Specifying a condition for a single action

You may want to specify a condition for a single action. An example of this is activating the report Pet Directory only when there are records in the form Pets, based on a query named Only Cats and Dogs. If there are no records present, you want the macro to skip activation of the report. To have the macro specify this condition, as shown in Figure 30-8, follow these steps:

Steps: Adding a Condition to a Macro

Step 1. In the Macro window, click the Conditions button on the toolbar.

Step 2. In the first action cell of the Action pane, select OpenForm.

Step 3. In the Form Name cell of the Argument pane, select Pets.

Step 4. In the Filter Name cell, select Cats and Dogs.

Following Along In This Book

To create the macro, you need to create a sample query that displays cat and dog records. You must name this record *Cats and Dogs*.

Step 5. In the next action cell of the Action pane, select OpenReport.

Step 6. In the Report Name cell of the Argument pane, select Pet Directory.

Step 7. In the Filter Name cell, select Cats and Dogs.

Step 8. Click the condition cell next to the action OpenReport.

Step 9. Type **Not IsNull(Forms![Pets]![Pet ID])**.

At the completion of these steps, your macro should resemble the one in Figure 30-8.

In this example, the condition specified is True if there are no records (the first Pet ID is Null) in the open form Pets. If the condition is True, when the macro is run, the action OpenReport is not performed; otherwise, the report is opened in print preview mode.

 When you specify conditions in a macro and reference a control name (field name), the source (form or report) of the control name must already be open.

Specifying a condition for multiple actions

Besides specifying a condition for a single action, you can specify a condition that will be effective for multiple actions. That is, a single condition will cause several actions to occur. In this way, you can also create an If-Then-Else condition.

If you want Access to perform more than one action, add the other actions below the first one. In the Condition column, place an ellipsis (...) beside each action. Figure 30-9 shows a macro in which two actions are performed based on a single condition. Notice that the condition has been changed to `IsNull` from `Not IsNull`.

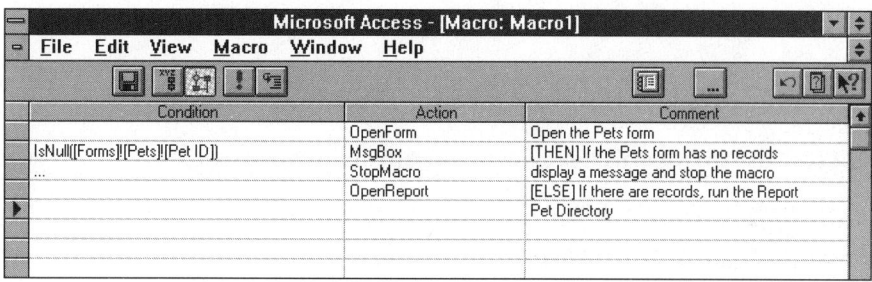

Figure 30-9: This macro shows two actions based on a single condition.

In Figure 30-9, the condition `IsNull(Forms![Pets]![Pet ID])` performs the two actions MsgBox and StopMacro if the condition is True. Notice the ellipsis (...) in the cell immediately under the specified condition, which is the condition cell for the action StopMacro.

When you run the macro, Access evaluates the expression in the condition cell. If the expression is True, Access performs the action beside the expression and all the following actions that have an ellipsis in the Condition column. Access continues the True actions until it comes to another condition (using the new condition from that point on).

If the expression is False, Access ignores the action or actions and moves to the next action row that does not have an ellipsis.

 If Access reaches a blank cell in the Condition column, it performs the action in that row regardless of the conditional expression. The only way to avoid this is to control the flow of actions by use of a redirection action, such as RunMacro or StopMacro. For example, if the second conditional action (StopMacro) is not

after the MsgBox action, the OpenReport action is executed regardless of whether the conditional expression is True or False. On the other hand, the MsgBox action takes effect only if the field Pet ID is Null (True).

Controlling the flow of actions

By using conditional expressions, you can control the flow of action in the macro. The macro in Figure 30-9 uses the action StopMacro to stop execution of the macro if the field is Null and thus avoids opening the report Pet Directory if the table is empty.

Several macro actions can be used to change or control the flow of actions based on a condition. The two most common are the actions StopMacro and RunMacro. By using these two actions, you can control the flow of actions within a macro.

Troubleshooting Macros

Access has two tools to help you find problems in your macros:

- The single-step mode
- The Action Failed dialog box

The single-step mode

If, while running a macro, you receive unexpected results, you can use the single-step mode to move through the macro one action at a time, pausing between actions. By single stepping, you can observe the result of each action and isolate the action or actions that caused the incorrect results.

To use single stepping, click the single-shoe button on the toolbar. For example, to single step through the macro in Figure 30-9, follow these steps:

Steps:	Single Stepping through a Macro
Step 1.	Edit the macro, bringing it into the Macro Design window.
Step 2.	Click the Single Step button on toolbar or select Macro⇨Single Step.
Step 3.	Run the macro as you normally would or by clicking the Run button on the toolbar.

Access displays the Macro Single Step dialog box, showing the macro name, the action name, and the arguments for the action. Figure 30-10 shows a typical Macro Single Step dialog box.

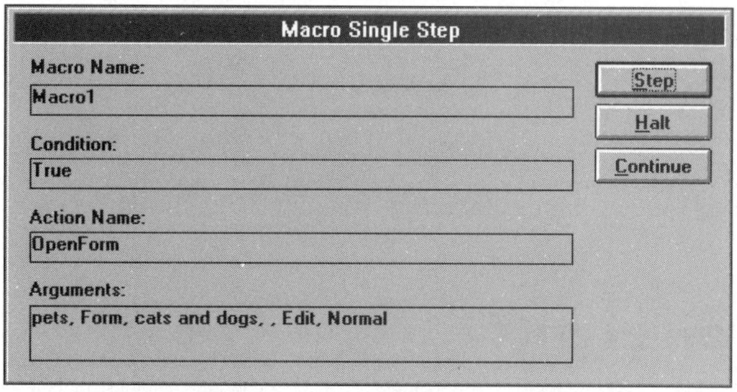

Figure 30-10:
The Macro Single Step dialog box.

If Action Name has a specified condition, the Arguments box displays the results of that condition (Yes or No). Notice that the dialog box in Figure 30-10 has three buttons: Step, Halt, and Continue. Table 30-2 summarizes each button's purpose.

The Action Failed dialog box

If a macro action causes an error, either during single-step mode or when running normally, Access opens a dialog box that looks exactly like the Macro Single Step dialog box except that the only available button is the Halt button.

This box, like the one in Figure 30-11, reports the action and its arguments that caused the error.

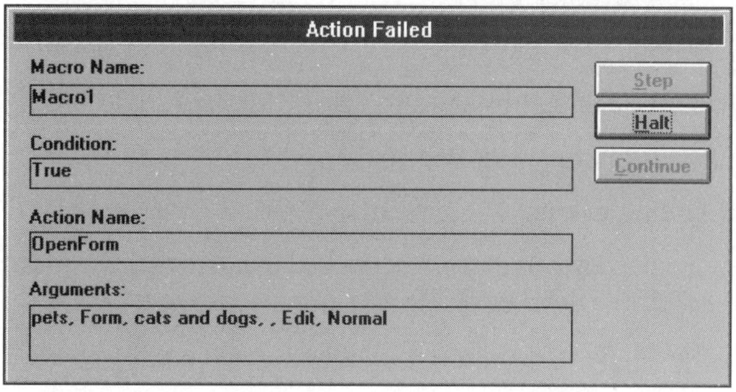

Figure 30-11:
The Action Failed dialog box.

To correct the problem, choose Halt, return to the Macro Design window, and correct the problem.

Understanding Events

With the actions stored in macros, you can run the macro either via a menu choice or by naming the macro AutoExec. The AutoExec macro automatically runs every time you open the database. However, Access offers another method to activate macros.

You can run a macro based on a user action. For example, the user can select a command button to activate a macro or by the action of opening a form.

To accomplish this, Access takes advantage of something known as an *event*.

What is an event?

An Access event is the result or consequence of some user action. An Access event can occur when a user moves from one record to another in a form, closes a report, or selects a command button on a form.

Your Access applications are *event-driven*. Objects in Access respond to many types of events. Access responds to events with behaviors that are built-in for each object. Access events can be recognized by specific object properties. For example, if a user presses the mouse key in a checkbox, the property OnMouseDown recognizes that the mouse was pressed. You can have this property run a macro when the user presses the mouse key.

Events in Access 2.0 can be categorized into seven groups:

Windows events: Opening, Closing, Resizing, and so on

Data events: Making Current, Deleting, After Updating, and so on

Focus events: Activating, Entering, Exiting, and so on

Keyboard events: Pressing a key, Releasing a key, and so on

Mouse events: Clicking, Pressing a mouse down, and so on

Print events: Formatting, Printing, and so on

Error and Timing events: After some time, On an error

In all, there are over 30 events that can be checked in Forms and Reports to specify some action upon their taking place.

Table 30-2
Macro Single Step Button Options

Button	Purpose
Step	Runs the action in the dialog box. If no error is reported, the next action appears in the dialog box.
Halt	Stops the execution of the macro and closes the dialog box.
Continue	Turns off the single-step mode and runs the remainder of the macro.

How do events trigger actions?

You can have Access run a macro when a user performs any one of the 35 events that Access 2.0 recognizes. Access can recognize an event through use of special properties for forms, controls (fields), and reports.

For example, Figure 30-12 shows the property sheet for a checkbox on a form. This checkbox has many properties, which may be used to respond to corresponding events. There are eight new properties — On Got Focus, On Key Down, On Key Press, On Key Up, On Lost Focus, On Mouse Down, On Mouse Move, and On Mouse Up — to Access 2.0.

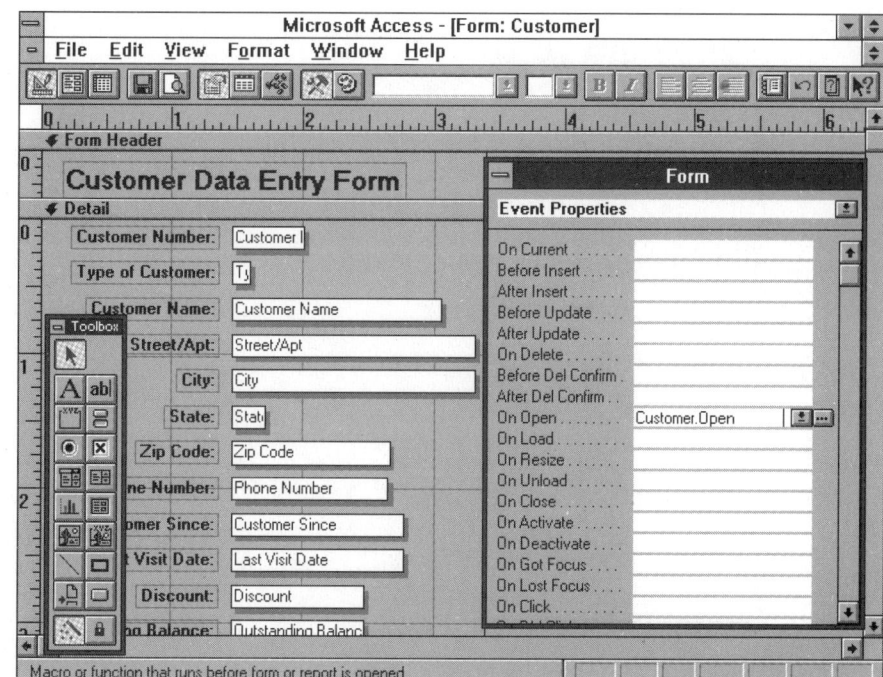

Figure 30-12: The property sheet for a form showing the On Open property entered.

Where to trigger macros

In Access, you can run event-driven macros by using properties in forms and reports. There are no event properties for tables or queries.

However, when you work with forms, you can run macros based on Access switchboards, command buttons, and pull-down menus. These features make the use of event-driven macros very powerful and easy to use.

Summary

In this chapter, you learned the basics of macros and events:

- An Access macro is a database object that lets you automate tasks without writing complex programs. Macros should be used to automate repetitive tasks. In Access, the tasks you perform are known as *actions.*

- The Macro Design window is comprised of two panes: Action and Argument. In the Action pane, you specify Access actions. You can add these actions by using a pull-down list box or by dragging and dropping common objects.

- Most actions require some argument. Arguments are the variables needed for Access to perform the action.

- Macros can be saved, renamed, edited, and copied just like any other Access object.

- Access has a special macro called AutoExec, which automatically runs when the database is opened. You can deactivate the AutoExec macro by holding down the Shift key when you open the database.

- When you create macros, you can group them into a group macro. Group macros use another column in the Action pane called the Macro Name column.

- When you work with macros, you can specify a condition for one or more actions. If the condition is True, the action is performed; if False, the action is skipped.

- Access offers two methods for troubleshooting macros: single stepping and using the Action Failed dialog box. With these tools, you can trace any errors in your macros.

- An event, which is a result or consequence of some action performed by the user, can be used to run a macro. In Access, events are recognized by use of special properties. The only objects in which Access recognizes events are forms and reports.

In Chapter 32, you learn how to create menu-based systems using events and macros. In the next chapter, you see many uses of macros and how they are generally run from triggered events.

Using Macros in Forms and Reports

CHAPTER 31

In This Chapter

- How to respond to events in forms and reports
- How to use macros in forms
- How to use macros in reports
- How to filter records with a macro
- How to validate data with a macro
- How to create hotkeys

At this point, you should know how to create and run macros, and you should know how to automatically start a macro when opening a database. In addition, you should be able to create and specify conditions for macros.

Now, you're going to learn how to use macros in real examples by using tables, forms, queries, and reports that you created in previous chapters.

Types of Macros

In Chapter 30, you learned how to create macros, and you learned how to associate a macro with a form or report property. *Macros* are Access objects consisting of one or more actions. Macros can open a dialog box, run a report, or even find a record.

Usually, you create macros to perform redundant tasks or to do a series of required actions after some initial action. For example, macros can synchronize two forms while a user moves from record to record, or macros can validate new data after it is entered by a user.

Before activating a macro, you need to decide where and how you will use it. For example, you may have a macro that opens the Customer form, and you want Access to run the macro every time a user opens the Pets form. In this case, you place the name of the macro in the On Open property of the Pets form. Then, every time the user opens the Pets form, the On Open property will trigger the macro opening the Customer form.

Or you may want to trigger another macro every time a user presses a hotkey. For example, if you want an Import dialog box to be activated when the user presses Ctrl+I, you should attach the macro to the key combination Ctrl+I in a hotkey macro file.

Although the second macro performs some tasks or actions, it is different from the first one. The second macro is activated based on a user action of pressing a hotkey; the first one is activated when a user performs some action that is recognized by a form property.

Macros can be grouped together based on their usage. The four basic groups follow:

- Form
- Report
- Import/Export
- Hotkey

Macros used in forms and reports are the most common. Using macros in these objects lets you build intelligence into each form and report. Macros are also used for importing or exporting data to and from other data sources. And, finally, macros can be activated by the use of hotkeys.

Review of Events and Properties

Simply put, an *event* is some user action. The event can be an action such as opening a form or report, changing data in a record, selecting a button, closing a form or report, and so forth. Access recognizes over 30 events in forms and reports.

To recognize one of these events, Access uses form or report *properties*. Each event has an associated form or report property. For example, the On Open property is associated with the event of opening a form or report.

You trigger a macro by specifying the macro name. The name is specified as a parameter for the event property you want to have the macro run against. For example, if you want to run a macro named OpenPets every time the user opens the Customer form, you place the macro name in the parameter field alongside of the property On Open in the form named Customer.

Macros for forms

You can create macros that respond to *form events*. These events are triggered by some user action, which may be opening a form or selecting a control button on a form. Access knows when the user triggers an event through its recognition of event-specific form properties. Forms let you set properties for field controls. These properties can be quite useful during the design phase of a form, as when you use a property to set a format or validation rule.

However, macros give you added power by letting you specify actions to be performed automatically based on a user-initiated event. The event is recognized by Access by use of event properties such as Before Update, On Delete, or On Enter. Unlike a simple format or field-level validation rule, a macro can perform multiple-step actions based on the user event. For example, after a user presses the Delete key to delete a record but before the deleted record is removed from the table, you can have a macro that automatically runs asking the user to verify that the record should be deleted. In this case, you use the On Delete property to trigger execution of the macro.

Macros for forms can respond both to *form events* and *control events*. Form events take effect at the form level; control events take effect at the individual control level. Form events include deleting a record, opening a form, or updating a record. These events work at the form and record level. Control events, on the other hand, work with the individual control level. These controls are the ones you specify when you create your form and include such items as a field (text box), a toggle button, an option button — even a command button. Each control has its own event properties that can trigger a macro. These events include selecting a command button, double-clicking a control, or selecting a control.

By specifying a macro at the control level, you can activate a customer form when the user double-clicks on a field object or its label object. For example, you may have a form that identifies the customer by name but gives no further customer information. When the user double-clicks the customer's name, your macro can activate a customer form that shows all the customer information. To accomplish this, you use the field object property On Dbl Click to specify a macro that opens the customer form. Then, every time the user double-clicks the customer field, the macro will run and open the customer form.

Figure 31-1 shows a form with a label named Customer Name and a field containing the name Patricia Irwin. When the user double-clicks either the label (Customer Name) or the name (Patricia Irwin), the Customer form opens.

Notice that the form in Figure 31-1 does not display any outward sign that the user can initiate a macro by double-clicking the label or field. However, the On Dbl Click property is set for the field to automatically execute the macro that opens the Customer form. In Figure 31-2, the user has double-clicked the label Customer Name and the Customer form is opened for that customer.

Figure 31-1:
A typical form with labels and control (fields).

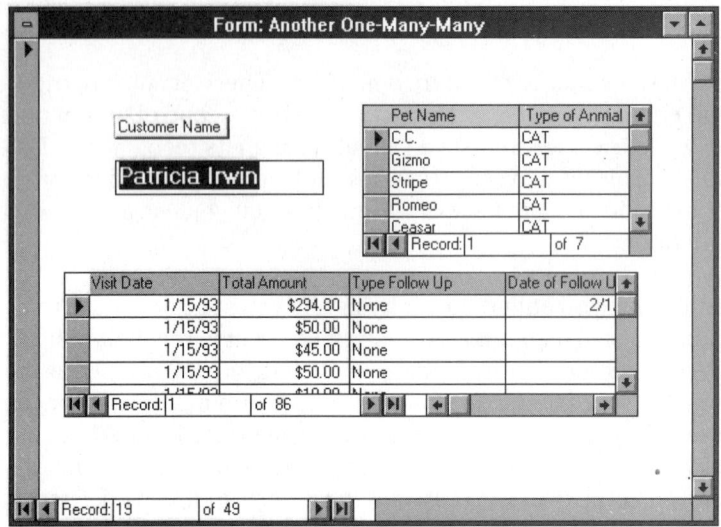

Figure 31-2:
A form opened by double-clicking a label.

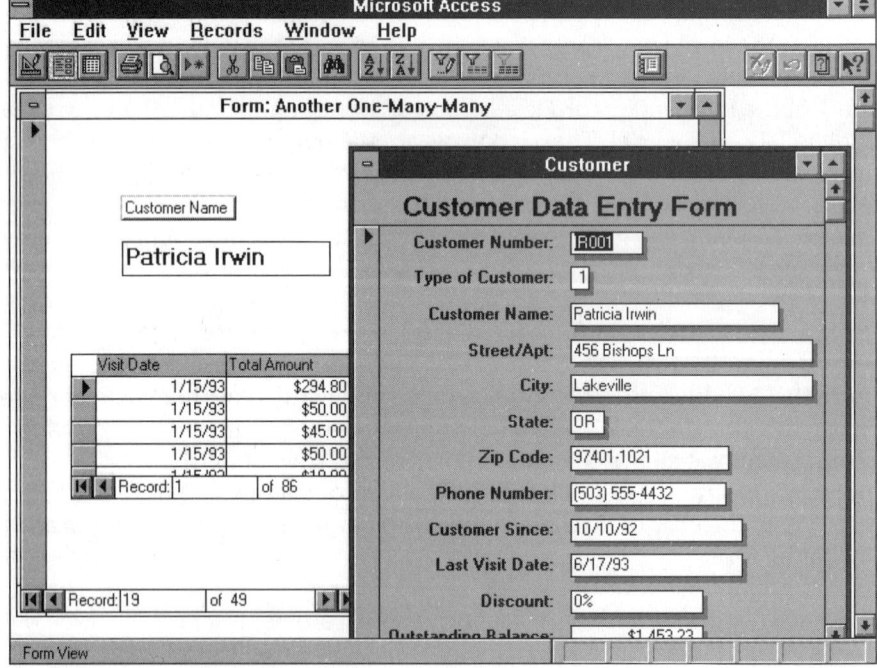

 By using the properties of text boxes, the event will be triggered when it occurs on the text box (field) or its associated label.

Notice that the Customer form shows detailed information about the customer, whereas the first form showed you only the customer's name. By using a control property in the first form, you trigger the macro that opens this form whenever the user performs the double-click event on the control.

Macros for reports

Just as with forms, macros can also enhance the use of the reports. You may, for example, want to prompt the user for a range of records to be printed before printing the report. Or you may want to display a message on the report whenever a certain condition is met. You may even want to underline or highlight a field based on its value, as when the value is too small or too great. Macros give you this type of refined control in reports.

Macros for reports can respond both to *report events* and *report section events*. Report events take effect at the report level; report section events take effect at the section level of the report.

Macros for hotkeys

You can also associate a macro with a specific key or combination of keys. By assigning a macro to a key combination, it can be activated by a user pressing the key or key combination. For example, you may assign the key combination Ctrl+P to print the current record displayed on-screen. Another example is assigning the key combination Ctrl+N to skip to the next record in the report or form. Creating hotkeys gives you additional capabilities in your forms and reports without your having to write complicated programs.

You use most hotkey macros when working with forms and reports, although hotkey macros can be used in queries or other Access objects.

Macros for importing and exporting

Normally, you import and export tables by using the File menu in the Database window. But you can also import or export data by using a macro. The macro can be executed by selection of a command button on a form or by triggering an event property, such as On Close of a form or report.

Import and export macros are specialized macros that can be triggered in either a form or report event or by use of a hotkey.

Following Along in This Book
In this chapter, you use the MTNANHSP database to work with macros in forms and reports.

Form-Level Event Macros

When you work with forms, you can specify macros based on events at the form level or at the control level. If you attach a macro to a form-level event, whenever the event occurs, the action takes effect against the form as a whole, such as when you change the record pointer or leave the form.

Attaching macros to forms

To have your form respond to an event, you write a macro and attach the macro to the event property in the form that recognizes the event. Many properties can be polled to trigger macros at the form level. Table 31-1 shows each property, the event it recognizes, and how the property works.

As Table 31-1 shows, there are many form-level events that can trigger a macro. Most of these are new to version 2.0 (in 1.x there were only seven events that worked at form level). These events work at form- or record-level only. They take effect when the pointer is changed from one record to another or when a form is being opened or closed. Control at a level of finer detail, such as at the field level, can be obtained by the control-level events covered later in this chapter.

Table 31-1
The Form-Level Events and Associated Properties

Event Property	Event	When the Macro is Triggered
On Current	Current	When the focus moves to the record, making it the current record
Before Insert	BeforeInsert	A new character is first entered into a record but before the record is created
After Insert	AfterInsert	After the new record is added
Before Update	BeforeUpdate	Before changed data is updated

Event Property	Event	When the Macro is Triggered
After Update	AfterUpdate	After changed data is updated
On Delete	Delete	When a record is deleted but *before* the deletion takes place
Before Del Confirm	BeforeDelConfirm	Just before Access displays the confirm delete dialog box
After Del Confirm	AfterDelConfirm	After the delete confirm dialog box closes
On Open	Open	A form is opened, but the first record is not displayed yet
On Load	Load	A form is opened and records displayed before the Current event
On Resize	Resize	When the size of a form changes
On Unload	Unload	A form is closed and the records unload, before the form is removed from the screen
On Close	Close	Form is closed and removed from the screen
On Activate	Activate	The form receives the focus, becoming the active window
On Deactivate	Deactivate	When a different window becomes the active window, but before it becomes the active one
On Got Focus	GotFocus	A form with no active or enabled controls receives the focus
On Lost Focus	LostFocus	A form loses the focus
On Click	Click	Press and release (click) the left mouse button on a control in a form
On Dbl Click	DblClick	Press and release (click) the left mouse button twice on a control/label in a form
On Mouse Down	MouseDown	Pressing the mouse button while the pointer is on a form
On Mouse Move	MouseMove	Moving the mouse pointer over a form
On Mouse Up	MouseUp	Releasing a pressed mouse button while the pointer is on a form
On Key Down	KeyDown	Pressing any key on the keyboard when a form has the focus or using the SendKeys macro
On Key Press	KeyPress	Press and release a key on a form that has the focus or use SendKeys macro
On Key Up	KeyUp	Releasing a pressed key or immediately after the SendKeys macro
On Error	OnError	When a run-time error is produced
On Timer	OnTimer	When a specified time interval passes
Timer Interval	Not an event	Property to specify the time for OnTimer

Opening a form with a macro

Sometimes, you may want to open a form with a macro. For example, every time you open the Pet Display form, you may also want to open the Customer form. This will enable a user to click either form to see information from both at once.

To accomplish this, you create a macro named OpenCust and attach it to the On Open property of the Pet Display form.

To create the macro, follow these steps:

Steps:	Creating an Open Form Macro
Step 1.	Select the Macro Object button in the database window to select the macro object list.
Step 2.	Click the New button to display the Macro Design window.
Step 3.	Click the first empty Action cell.
Step 4.	Select the OpenForm action from the pull-down menu of the action cell.
Step 5.	Click in the Form Name cell of the Action Arguments (bottom part of window).
Step 6.	Select or type **Customer**.
Step 7.	Save the macro by clicking the Save button of the toolbar and naming it **OpenCust**.

Notice in Figure 31-3 that the OpenCust macro only has one action – OpenForm with the action argument Form Name of Customer.

The macro in Figure 31-3 has only a single action associated with it, which is the OpenForm action. The OpenForm action has six possible arguments, although in this example you only entered the form name Customer. You accepted the default values of the other arguments. This action opens the specified form (Customer) for you automatically.

With the OpenCust macro created, you need to enter design mode for the Pet Display form and attach the macro OpenCust to the form property On Open.

Attaching a macro to a form

With the OpenForm macro saved, you are now ready to *associate,* or *attach,* it with the On Open property of the form Add a Customer and Pets. To attach the OpenCust macro to the form, follow these steps:

Steps:	Attaching a Macro to a Form
Step 1.	Select the Form Object button in the database window to select the form list.
Step 2.	Select the form named Pets and bring it into the design mode.
Step 3.	Display the property sheet by clicking the Properties button on the toolbar.
	The title of the Property sheet dialog box should be **Form**. If it isn't, select the form by clicking the white box in the top left corner of the form (or outside the form sections).
Step 4.	Select the **Event Properties** from the combo box at the top of the dialog box.
Step 5.	Move to the On Open property in the Form property sheet. Select or type the macro name **OpenCust** in the On Open property cell.
	The property sheet should look similar to the one in Figure 31-4. Notice that the macro name OpenCust is placed in the parameter box of the On Open property.
Step 6.	Save the form and return to the Database window.

With the OpenCust macro attached to the form Pets, you are ready to try it. Open the Pet Display Form. Notice that Access automatically opens the Customer form for you, placing it behind the Pet Display Form. Now you can use either form by clicking it to look at the individual records. Figure 31-5 shows both forms open.

The only problem with these two forms is that they are not related. Every time you change the pet, it would be nice if the Customer form showed you the correct owner of the pet.

Of all the form-level events, the most common are On Open and On Current. Although the others are available for use, these two events probably are used for 80 percent of all form-level macros.

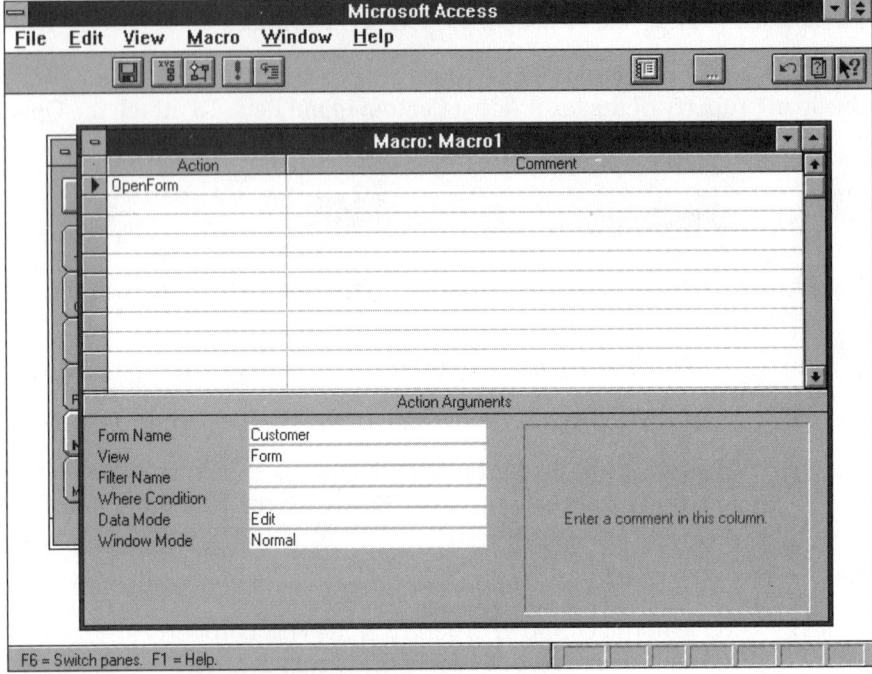

Figure 31-3: A macro to open a form.

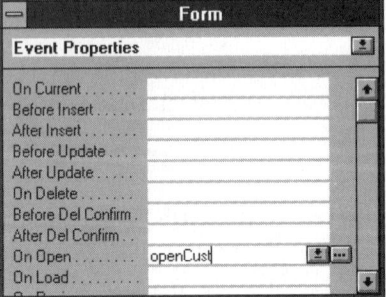

Figure 31-4: Relating a macro to the On Open property of a form.

Synchronizing two forms with On Current

Notice that the forms in Figure 31-5 are independent of each other. This means that when you skip through the Pet Display Form, the Customer form is not automatically updated to display the related owner information for the pet. To make these two forms work together, you can synchronize them by relating the data between the forms with the On Current property.

You can use the same macro you used before, which is OpenCust. However, now you must specify a Where Condition for the OpenForm action. The condition on which to

Chapter 31: Using Macros in Forms and Reports

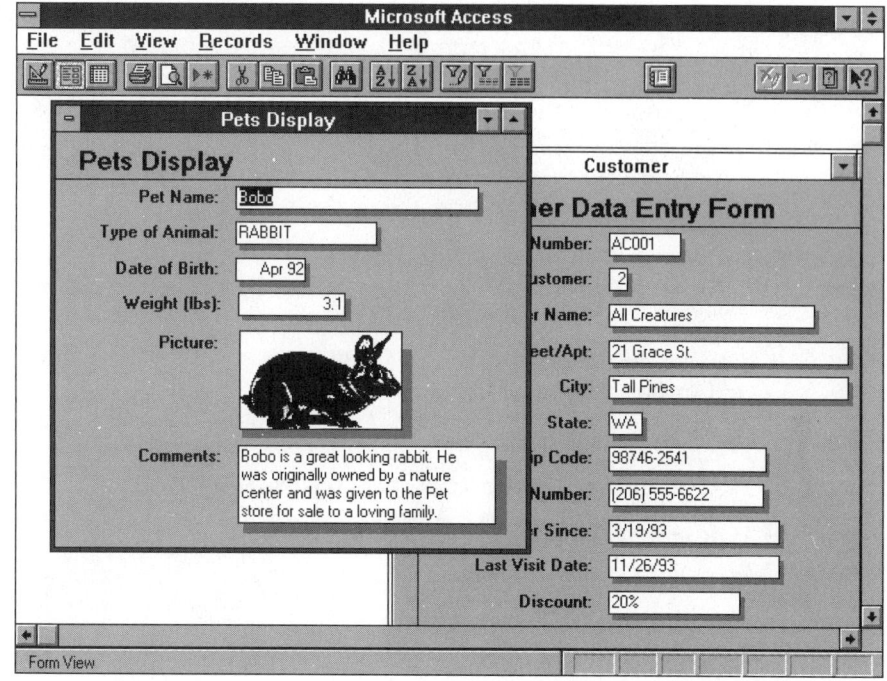

Figure 31-5: Two forms open; one form is opened automatically by a macro attached to the On Open property of the other form.

synchronize these two forms occurs when the Customer Number is the same in both forms. To specify the synchronizing condition between these two forms, follow these steps:

Steps:	Setting a Where Condition in a Macro
Step 1.	Open the macro OpenCust in design mode.
Step 2.	Click the Where Condition box of the Action Arguments.
Step 3.	Type **[Customer Number] = Forms![Pet Display Form]![Customer Number]**.
Step 4.	Resave the OpenCust macro.

Notice in Step 3 that you typed **[Customer Number]**, which is the control name for the Customer Number field in the Customer form. You typed this on the left side of the expression without reference to the form name. The left side of the Where expression in an OpenForm action uses the form specified in the Form Name action argument, three lines above. The right side of the expression requires the keyword *Forms*, the form name, and the control name.

If you specify an unopened form in the Where Condition box, you will get an error message at run time, but not as you create the macro.

Now that you have modified the macro, you need to set the On Current property of the Pet Display Form.

To add the OpenCust macro to the form, follow these steps:

Steps:	Adding a Macro to the On Current Property of a Form
Step 1.	Remove the macro from the On Open property of the form and add it to the On Current property.
Step 2.	Open the form in design mode.
Step 3.	Move to the On Current property of the property sheet.
Step 4.	Type **OpenCust** in the On Current parameter box.
Step 5.	Save the changes to the form.

Now, when you open the Pets form and a pet record is displayed, the Customer form also opens and displays the correct owner for that pet. As you change pets, the Customer form automatically displays the new owner information. These two forms are now synchronized.

Even though the two forms are synchronic, based on the On Current property, you must still close both forms separately. Closing one form does not automatically close the other. If you want to close both forms at the same time automatically, you need to specify another macro for the On Close property.

To see how these two forms work together, open the Pets form and then click on the Datasheet button on the toolbar. The Customer form becomes active and is moved to the front of the Pets form. If you click a different pet record in the Pets datasheet, the Customer form is automatically updated to reflect the new owner. Figure 31-6 demonstrates how this works.

As Figure 31-6 demonstrates, you are not limited to a single-record view when synchronizing forms. The Pets form has been set to datasheet so that as you click different records in the datasheet, the Customer form is automatically updated to reflect the new owner.

Figure 31-6:
Two forms synchronized.

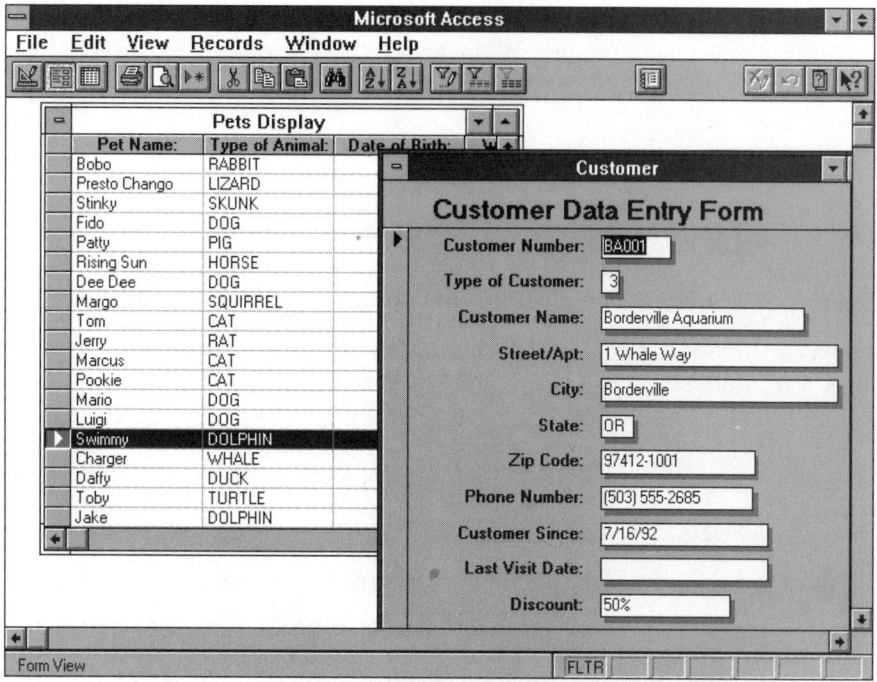

The On Current property of the Pets form triggers the OpenCust macro every time the record changes. If you click the next navigation button, you see that the Customer form shows only one record — the owner record that is related to the current individual pet record in the Pets form. If you know this, you can easily understand the use of the On Current property: the On Current property activates a macro that performs actions based on the specific record currently being pointed to by the form using the On Current property. In this case, the current pet record triggers the macro that finds the correct owner in the Customer form. Every time the pet record changes, the On Current property is activated and the next owner is found.

Running a macro when closing a form

There are times when you'll want to perform some action when you close or leave a form. For example, you may want to automatically log the name of everyone who uses the form. Using the two forms from the previous examples, you may want to automatically close the Customer form every time the user closes the Pets form.

To automatically close the Customer form every time the Pets form is closed, you need to create a new macro to perform the actions. Then you need to attach the macro to the On Close property of the Pet Display Form.

To create a macro that closes a form, follow these steps:

Steps: Creating a Macro That Closes a Form

Step 1. Select the OpenCust macro and enter the design mode.

Step 2. Activate the Macro Name column by clicking the Macro Name button on the toolbar. This lets you create a macro group.

Step 3. Select a blank Macro Name cell below the OpenForm action.

Step 4. In the empty Macro Name cell, type **ClosCust.**

Step 5. Select the empty Action cell alongside the ClosCust macro name.

Step 6. Select the Close action from the pull-down menu.

Step 7. Select the action argument Object Type.

Step 8. Type (or select) the type **Form.**

Step 9. Select the action argument Object Name.

Step 10. Type (or select) the form name **Customer.** The macro should now look similar to Figure 31-7.

Step 11. Resave the macro with the new changes.

Figure 31-7 shows the new macro ClosCust added to the macro OpenCust. Until now, the OpenCust macro has been a single-purpose macro. By adding another macro, it has become a group macro of two macros. The first macro is the default macro, which opens a form, and the second is a macro named ClosCust.

 Macro groups are covered in Chapter 30.

Notice that the ClosCust macro has only one action, which is Close. This action has two arguments, both of which you must enter. The first argument is the Object Type, which specifies the type of object you want to close (form or report, etc.). The second argument is the Object Name, which specifies by name the object you want to close, which in this case is the form named Customer.

Chapter 31: Using Macros in Forms and Reports

Figure 31-7:
Adding a close action macro to a macro group.

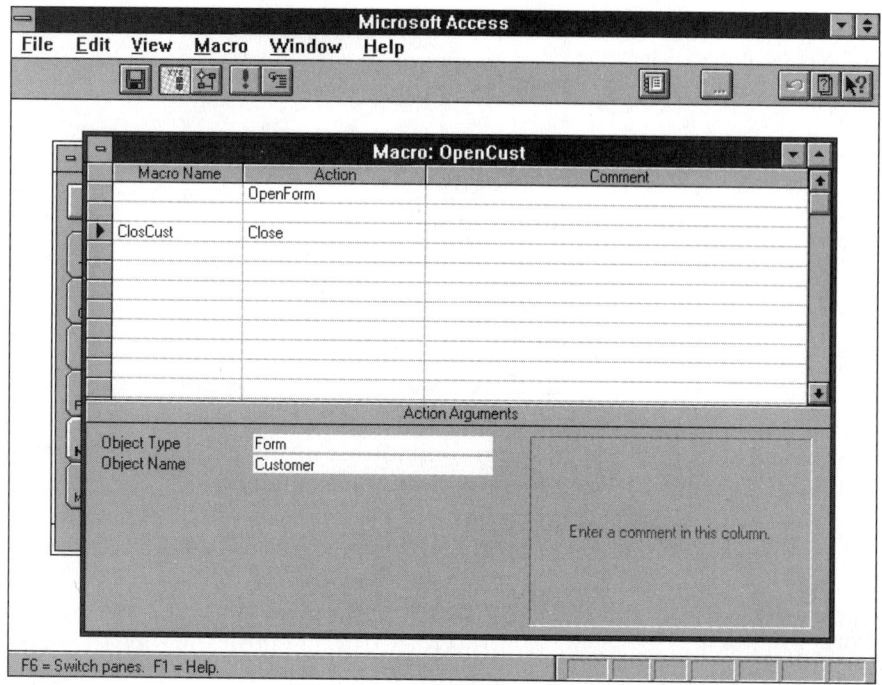

Now that you created the ClosCust macro, you can attach it to the form named Pet Display Form by following these steps:

Steps:	Attaching a Macro to the On Close Property of a Form
Step 1.	Select the Pet Display Form and click <u>D</u>esign.
Step 2.	Activate the property sheet for the form.
Step 3.	Select the On Close property in the property sheet.
Step 4.	Type **OpenCust.ClosCust** in the On Close property parameter box. The property sheet should look like Figure 31-8.
Step 5.	Save the form with the new changes.

Notice in Figure 31-8 that when you type the macro name in the On Close parameter box you specify the macro group name; then you type a period; and, finally, you type the name of the customer.

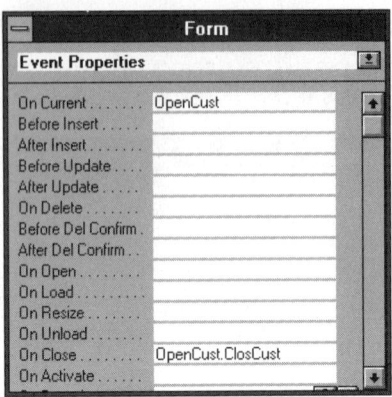

Figure 31-8:
The property sheet with the On Close property set.

Opening the form Pet Display Form continues to maintain the current owner information in the Customer form because you left the macro in the On Current property set. But now the On Close property is also set. Because you specified On Close with the Pets form, when you close the Pets form, the Customer form is automatically closed for you.

The macro attached to the On Close property simply closes the Customer form. If the user accidentally closes the Customer form and then the Pets form, Access does not report an error. Therefore, you don't have to specify an On Close for the Customer form to allow closing only via the Pets form. Using this principle, you can have one form that specifies closing of many forms. If the forms are open, Access will close them; otherwise, Access will issue the Close with no harm done.

Confirming a delete with On Delete

The On Delete property can be used to execute a macro that displays a message and confirms that the user wants to delete a record. For example, to create a macro named ConfirmDelete, follow these steps:

Steps:	Creating a Delete Record Macro
Step 1.	Enter the macro design mode and click the Condition column.
Step 2.	Select the first Condition cell.
Step 3.	Type **MsgBox("Do you Want to Delete this Record?", 273, "Delete")<>1**.
Step 4.	Select the Action cell next to the Condition box.
Step 5.	Select or type the **CancelEvent** action.

Chapter 31: Using Macros in Forms and Reports

Step 6.	Select the next Condition cell.
Step 7.	Type an ellipsis, which is three periods (...).
Step 8.	Select the Action cell next to the Condition box.
Step 9.	Select or type the **StopMacro** action.
Step 10.	Select the next Action cell.
Step 11.	Select or type the **SendKeys** action.
Step 12.	Select the Keystrokes action argument.
Step 13.	Type **{Enter}**.
Step 14.	Save the macro to the name **ConfirmDelete**.

The macro should look like the one in Figure 31-9. Notice that this macro also uses the CancelEvent action. The condition for this macro uses the MsgBox( ) function (see the sidebar "Using the MsgBox( ) Function" for a detailed explanation).

The macro in Figure 31-9 shows the use of another new action — SendKeys. This action lets you send preassigned keystrokes to Access or another active application. The passed keystrokes are processed just as if you press them in an application. In this case, Access displays a message box like the one in Figure 31-10. Notice that the message box has two buttons — OK and Cancel. Access displays the box and waits for a keystroke. When the user selects the Cancel button, the macro cancels the delete event and stops the macro.

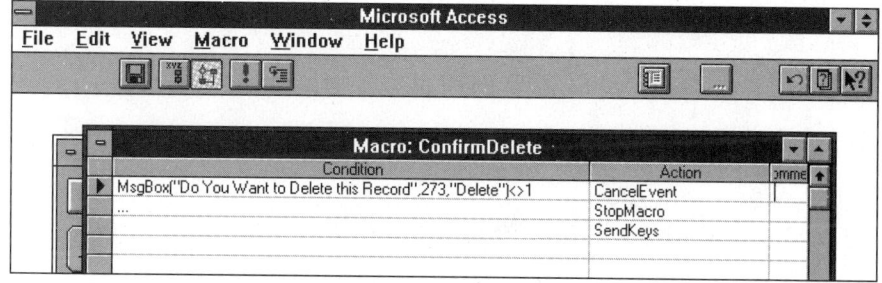

Figure 31-9: A macro to delete a record.

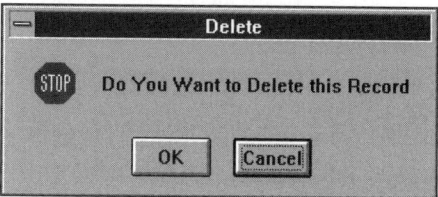

Figure 31-10: A message box for the delete macro.

Part V: Applications in Access

If the user selects the OK button in the message box, the macro performs the SendKeys action. In this case, the macro sends the Enter keystroke. If this action is not here, Access displays its Delete message dialog box, forcing the user to verify again that the record should be deleted. By using SendKeys, the Enter keystroke is sent to the Access Delete message box to accept the delete option.

This macro does not bypass referential integrity between tables. If you have referential integrity set between the Customer table and the Pets table and have not authorized Cacade Delete through the entire application, the macro fails. To override this, either setup cascade deletes through all the tables or you can expand the macro to perform a cascade delete by creating an SQL statement and running the SQL statement using the RunSQL action.

With the delete macro, ConfirmDelete, completed, you next attach it to the Customer form by placing the macro name in the parameter box of the On Delete property of the form. Figure 31-11 shows the property sheet for the Customer form with the On Delete property set.

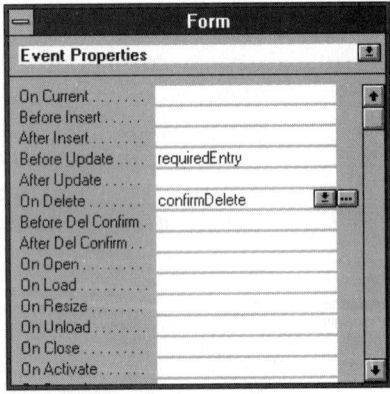

Figure 31-11: Setting an On Delete property.

To see how this macro and the On Delete property work, follow these steps:

Steps: Using the On Delete Property

Step 1. Use the form named Customer.

Step 2. Select Records⇒Data Entry from the main menu.

Step 3. Type **QA1111** in the Customer Number field.

Step 4. Type **1** in the Type of Customer field.

Step 5. Type **Your Name** in the Customer Name field.

Step 6. Press Ctrl+ − (minus sign) to delete the record.

Access responds with the message box that you see in Figure 31-12. In this message box, the Cancel button is the default.

Step 7. Select the OK button to delete this dummy record.

Access displays the message box that is created in the condition of the ConfirmDelete macro. Figure 31-12 shows the message box.

Notice that the message box in Figure 31-12 shows the stop sign, your message, and the two buttons OK and Cancel. The Cancel button is set as the default button.

Figure 31-12:
A message box for deleting a record.

Control Event Macros

So far, you've worked with event macros at the form level. You can also trigger macros at the control level based on an event. By attaching a macro at the control level, the macro takes effect against the control. For example, you can immediately verify complex data validation at the field level instead of when the record is exited by using the Before Update property of the field instead of the form.

Attaching macros to controls

To have a control respond to an event, you write a macro and attach the macro to the property in the control that recognizes the event. There are several properties that can be polled to trigger macros at the control level. Table 31-2 shows each property, the event it recognizes, and how it works.

As Table 31-2 demonstrates, you can use any of the control-level events to trigger a macro. One of these, On Click, works only with command buttons.

Using the MsgBox() Function

The MsgBox() function is a very powerful function that can be used to display a message in a dialog box, wait for a user response, and then return a value based on the user's choice. The function has three arguments:

MsgBox(*"message"* [, *type of msg* [, *box title*]])

The *message* here is the string displayed in the dialog box as a message.

The *type of msg* is the numeric expression controlling the buttons and icons in the dialog box.

The *box title* is the string displayed in the title bar of the dialog box.

Only the message is required. If you don't specify *type of msg* or *box title,* Access displays one button — OK. There is no icon and no title.

Access offers a wide range of type of message numbers. The type of message number specifies three message parts: (1) number and type of buttons, (2) icon style, and (3) default button. The following table describes each:

Number and Button Type

Value	Display Button
0	OK
1	OK, Cancel
2	Abort, Retry, Ignore
3	Yes, No, Cancel
4	Yes, No
5	Retry, Cancel

Icon Style

Value	Display Icon
0	None
16	Stop sign
32	? Question mark
48	! Exclamation
64	i Information

Default Button

Value	Button
0	First
256	Second
512	Third

Using the preceding table, you specify the second parameter of the MsgBox() function by summing the three option values. For example, to have a message box that shows three buttons —Yes, No, and Cancel [3] — and uses the Question mark (?) [32] and makes the Cancel button the default [512], add the three values (512+32+3) to get the second parameter number, which is 548.

If you omit *type of msg* in the function, MsgBox displays a single OK button and makes it the default button with no icon displayed.

Besides displaying the message box with all the options, the MsgBox() function also returns a value indicating which button the user selects. The number that it returns depends on the type of button selected. The following table shows each button and the value that MsgBox() returns:

Button Selected	Value Returned
OK	1
Cancel	2
Abort	3
Retry	4
Ignore	5
Yes	6
No	7

If the dialog box displays a Cancel button, pressing the Esc key is the same as selecting the Cancel button.

Table 31-2
The Control-Level Events and Associated Properties

Event Property	Event	When the Macro is Triggered
Before Update	BeforeUpdate	Before changed data is updated
After Update	AfterUpdate	After changed data is updated
On Change	Change	When contents of a text box or combo box's text changes
On Update	Updated	When an OLE object's data has been modified
OnNotInList	NotInList	When a value is entered into a combo box that isn't in the list
OnEnter	Enter	Before a control actually receives the focus from another control
OnExit	Exit	Just before the control loses focus to another control
On Got Focus	GotFocus	A nonactive or enabled control receives the focus
On Lost Focus	LostFocus	A control loses the focus
On Click	Click	Press and release (click) the left mouse button on a control
On Dbl Click	DblClick	Press and release (click) the left mouse button twice on a control/label
On Mouse Down	MouseDown	Pressing a mouse button while the pointer is on a control
On Mouse Move	MouseMove	Moving the mouse pointer over a control
On Mouse Up	MouseUp	Releasing a pressed mouse button while the pointer is on a control
On Key Down	KeyDown	Pressing any key on the keyboard when a control has the focus or using the SendKeys macro
On Key Press	KeyPress	Press and release a key on a control that has the focus or use SendKeys macro
On Key Up	KeyUp	Releasing a pressed key or immediately after the SendKeys macro

Forms have several different types of objects on them — Labels, Text boxes, OLE, Subforms, Command buttons, checkboxes, and so on. Each of these has several event properties associated with it. You can attach a macro, an expression, or Access basic code to any of them. To see any objects event properties, simply activate the properties dialog box and select event properties while working with the object.

> ### Creating a Quick Command Button
>
> Although command buttons are covered in depth in the next chapter, it is necessary to use them in this chapter. What you need to know here is that you can quickly create a command button by selecting it from the toolbox and placing it on the form. For example, to place a command button on the form named Cust_Pet_Visit, follow these steps:
>
> 1. Open Cust_Pet_Visit in design mode.
> 2. Turn off the Control Wizard by clicking the Control Wizard toggle button in the toolbox.
> 3. Select the Command Button on the toolbox by clicking it.
> 4. Bring the button icon over to the form (below the customer name) where you want the top right corner of the button to be.
> 5. Click on and drag the button to a size about the same as the Customer Name field.
> 6. Click inside the button to erase the current button name.
> 7. Type **Customer Info** in place of the original button name and press Enter.
> 8. Save the form with the new command button on it.
>
> You just created a command button. It should look similar to the one in Figure 31-13. The button can now be used to trigger a macro based on the On Click property of the button.

Clicking on a command button to open a form

When you're using a form to look at data and need to look at information more detailed than the form offers, you can use a command button to open another form. The form you open can show you only data that is related to the first form, or it can enable you to perform some other task, such as adding a new record. For example, using the form Cust_Pet_Visit, there is only one field on the form concerning the customer, which is Customer Name. You may need to look up additional information about the customer. To do this, you need a macro that opens the Customer form and shows you the related record in the Customer form. A command button can be used to trigger this action by use of the On Push property of the form.

Creating a macro to open another form

To create a macro that displays the detailed customer record, follow these steps:

Steps:	Creating a Macro to Open and Relate to Forms
Step 1.	Open the Update Form macro in design mode.
Step 2.	Create a new macro named **ShowCustomer**.
Step 3.	Give the macro an OpenForm action.
Step 4.	Type **Customer** for the Form Name argument.
Step 5.	Type **[Customer Number] = Forms![Cust_Pet_Visit]![Customer Number]** for the Where Condition argument.
Step 6.	Select Read Only for the Data Mode argument.
Step 7.	Save the macro.

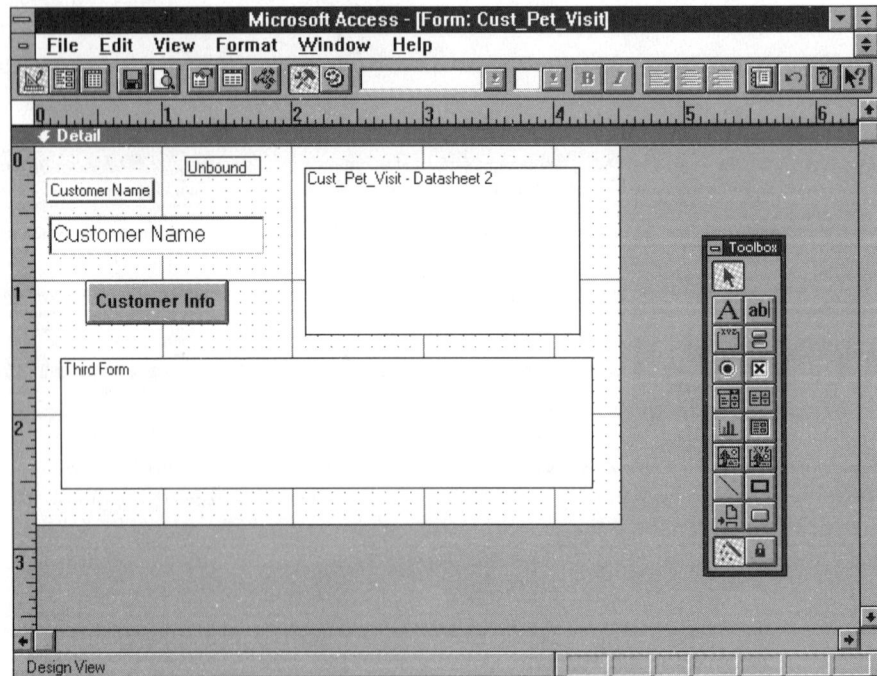

Figure 31-13: Creating a command button.

Your macro should look like the one in Figure 31-14. Notice that the macro only has one action, which is OpenForm.

Relating information from two forms using a macro

Relating information between two forms simply means supplying a way to show related records between the two forms. To link two forms, you need to decide which field (control) will be used to relate them. In the example from Figure 31-14, that field is the Customer Number; this field is in both forms and is the link between them.

When you work with the OpenForm action, you can relate two forms by using the Where Condition argument of OpenForm. The macro in Figure 31-14 uses the Where Condition argument to specify which record should be shown in the form. When you attach this macro to a command button and then select the button, only the record that meets the Where Condition is shown in the Customer form when it is opened. The two forms are said to be *synchronized*.

When you work with Where Condition arguments in the OpenForm action, remember that the left side of the expression is the control (field) from the form being opened. The right side is the control (field) in a form that is already opened. In this macro, the [Customer Number] on the left of the formula is for the form Customer.

Figure 31-14: A macro to open a form based on a condition.

Activating a related form using a command button

Earlier, you synchronized two forms by using the On Current property of a form. Because the forms were both open and constantly being updated, the On Current property was used to synchronize the two *open* forms. Now, however, you are interested in relating two forms by using the On Push property of a command button. In this case, you are interested only in viewing the Customer table when the user presses the Customer Info command button on your form. The following steps let you assign the macro to a command button:

Steps:	Assigning a Macro to the On Push Property of a Button
Step 1.	Open the form Cust_Pet_Visit in design mode.
Step 2.	Select the command button labeled Customer Info.
Step 3.	View the property window for the command button.
Step 4.	Type **Update Form.ShowCustomer** in the On Push property of the button's property sheet.
Step 5.	Save the form.

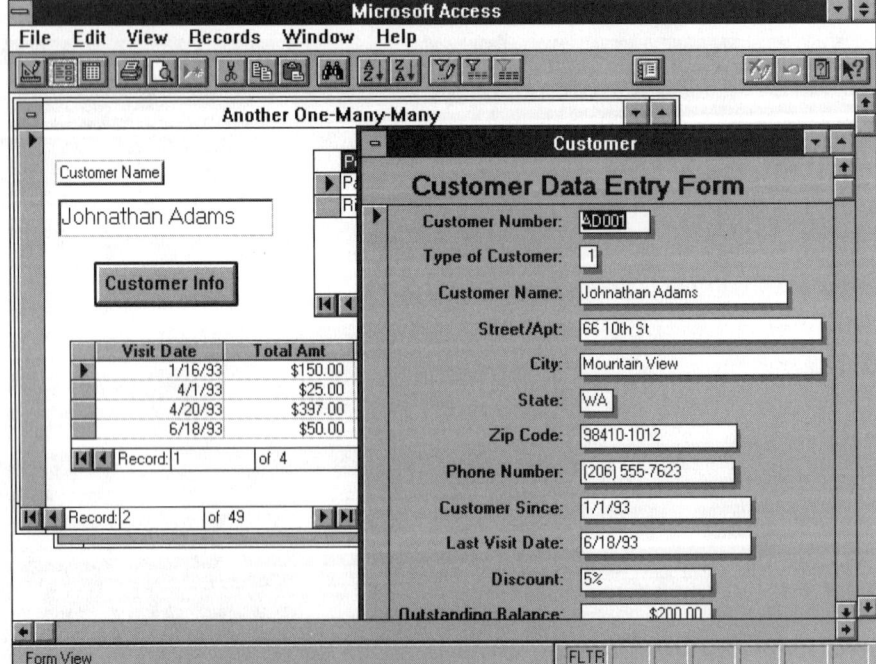

Figure 31-15: The Customer form opened by selecting a button in another form.

Chapter 31: Using Macros in Forms and Reports

With the macro attached to the On Push property of the Customer Info button, you can execute the form. If you select the button, the Customer table opens and displays the correct related customer record. It should look similar to Figure 31-15.

Notice that the customer is the same in both forms. When you are finished looking at the customer information in the Customer form, you can close it or simply click the Cust_Pet_Visit form.

Unlike the synchronized forms set with the On Current property at form level earlier in this chapter, these two forms are not synchronized. If you skip to the next record in the Cust_Pet_Visit form and then click the Customer form, you see that the two forms have different records. To see the new current customer information in the Customer form, you need to reselect the command button named Customer Info. The macro is reexecuted, and the Customer form is updated to reflect the new customer information.

Double-clicking on a field control or its label

In the preceding example, you used a command button to open the Customer table. Another way to open the same form is to use the On Dbl Click property of a control. For instance, you may want to open the related Customer form every time the user double-clicks the Customer Name field or its related label. To do this, you can use the same macro you created before and simply add the macro name to the On Dbl Click property of the control (field) named Customer Name. Figure 31-16 illustrates how your property sheet will look.

By attaching the macro to the On Dbl Click property of the Customer Name field, you can open the Customer form by double-clicking either the label or the field. For example, opening the form Cust_Pet_Visit and double-clicking the label marked Customer Name (top left of form, above the Customer Name field) will open the Customer form and display the current customer information. Besides clicking the label, you can also double-click the field itself!

Figure 31-16:
Attaching a macro to the On Dbl Click property.

Double-clicking on a command button

You can use the On Dbl Click property of a command button just as you use the On Push property. However, you cannot use On Push and On Dbl Click together. Access will interpret the first click as the On Push and execute the macro associated with it. The On Dbl Click will never be reached.

Working with Macros on Forms

You can group macros for forms in six categories according to their function:

- Validating data
- Setting values
- Navigating between forms and records
- Filtering records
- Finding records
- Printing records

Each category uses specific macro actions to perform its job.

Validating data

You already worked with macros to validate data at both the form level and control level. When validating data, you worked with several macro actions: MsgBox, CancelEvent, StopMacro, and GoToControl.

The most common event properties that trigger validation macros are the On Delete and Before Update properties, although any property can be used.

Displaying a message

To display a message, you use the MsgBox action. This action has four arguments:

Message	Specifies the user message in a dialog box
Beep	Sounds a computer beep when the dialog box is opened
Type	Specifies the type of icon displayed in the dialog box, such as the stop sign or a question mark, etc.
Title	Specifies a user-entered title for the box

Canceling events

To cancel an event, you use the CancelEvent action. This action has no arguments — it simply cancels the event that triggers the macro to run. For example, if the macro is attached to the Before Update property of a form, the update is canceled.

Stopping a macro

To stop execution of a macro, use the StopMacro action. This action stops execution of the macro immediately and returns the user to the calling form. This action is useful for stopping a macro based on a condition specified in the macro.

Going to a specific control

If you need to return to a specific control (field) in a form, use the GoToControl action. This action has one argument, the control name. If you supply a control name, this action takes you to that control. You normally use this action just before the StopMacro action.

Setting values

By setting control, field, and property values with macros, you can make data entry easier and more accurate. Besides these advantages, you can link several forms, databases, and reports to make them work together more intelligently.

Setting values with a macro can accomplish these tasks:

- Hide or display a control based on a value in the form (Visible property)
- Disable or lock a control based on a value in the form (Enable and Locked properties)
- Update a field in the form based on the value of another control
- Set the value of a control in a form based on the control of another form

The SetValue action is used to set values with a macro. This action has two arguments:

Item   The name of the control or property

Expression   The expression used to set the value

If you use the SetValue action to change the value of a control (field) being validated, do not attach it to the Before Update property. Access cannot change the value of a control while it is being validated; it can only change the value after it has been saved. Therefore, you should use the After Update property instead.

Converting a field to uppercase

If you allow entry of a field in either uppercase or lowercase, you may want to store it in uppercase. To accomplish this, create a macro that uses the SetValue action to set the value of the field for you. In the Item argument box, enter the name of the field you want to convert to uppercase. In the Expression argument box, enter the function UCase( ) with the name of the field to be converted. Figure 31-17 shows the arguments for converting the field Customer Name to uppercase.

After you create the macro, place the macro name in the After Update property sheet.

If the user enters a customer name in lowercase or mixed case, Access automatically runs the macro and converts the field to uppercase when the user completes the update.

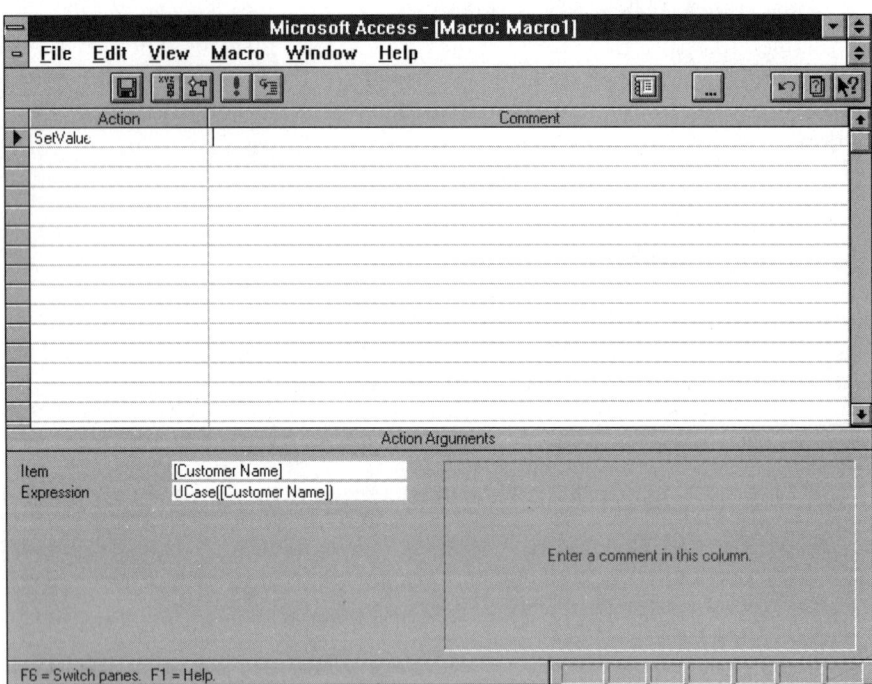

Figure 31-17: Converting a field to uppercase.

Assigning values to new records

When you add new records to a form, it is often convenient to have values automatically filled in for fields using values from another open form. SetValue is also used to do this.

For example, after adding a new customer in the Customer form, you may immediately want to add a pet record in another form and have the Customer Number automatically filled in.

Figure 31-18:
Macro arguments to set a field value in another form based on a value in the current form.

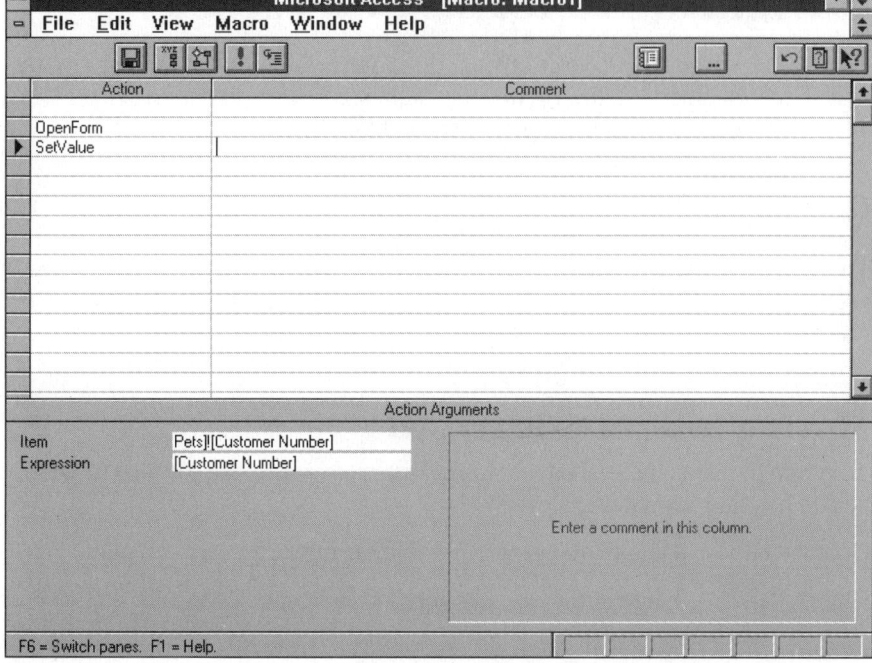

For example, the Customer form has a command button that when selected adds a pet record. When the user selects this button, a macro opens the Pet form in the Add Data Mode using the OpenForm action. The next macro action, SetValue, automatically sets the value of Customer Number in the Pet form to the Customer Number in the Customer form. Figure 31-18 shows the arguments for this macro.

 Notice that the Item argument specifies the new form that is being opened by its full syntax:

Forms![Pets]![Customer Number]

The Expression argument references the Customer Number in the currently open form, which is the Customer form. When working with the SetValue action in this way, you must specify the entire syntax for the name of the field being replaced in the Item box.

After you create the macro, you can attach it to the command button by using the On Push property.

Navigating in forms and records

You already used the GoToControl action in this chapter. Whenever you need to move to a specific control (field), record, or page in a form, you use the GoTo*XXXX* actions, where *XXXX* represents the control, record, or page.

Moving to a specific control

To move to a specific control, use the GoToControl action. This action has one argument, which is Control Name. To move to a specific field, simply supply the control name in this argument.

Moving to a specific record

To move to a specific record in a table, query, or form, use the GoToRecord action. This action has four arguments:

Object Type	Type of object (form, table, or query)
Object Name	Name of the object specified in Object Type
Record	Specifies which record to go to (previous, next, new, first, last, etc.)
Offset	The number of records to offset from (if 10, go back 10 records)

Using this action, you can move to any record in a form, query, or table.

Moving to a specific page

To move to a specific page and place focus in the first control of the page, use the GoToPage action. This action has three arguments:

Page Number	Specifies the page number you want to move to
Right	The upper left-hand corner of page (horizontal position)
Down	The upper left-hand corner of page (vertical position)

This action is useful for working with multiple-page forms.

Filtering records

You can create a macro or series of macros to filter records in a form. For example, you may want to have a Customer form with four buttons to limit the form's records to a single state or allow all states. The form will look similar to Figure 31-19. Notice that there are four buttons in the box named Filter Records.

Chapter 31: Using Macros in Forms and Reports

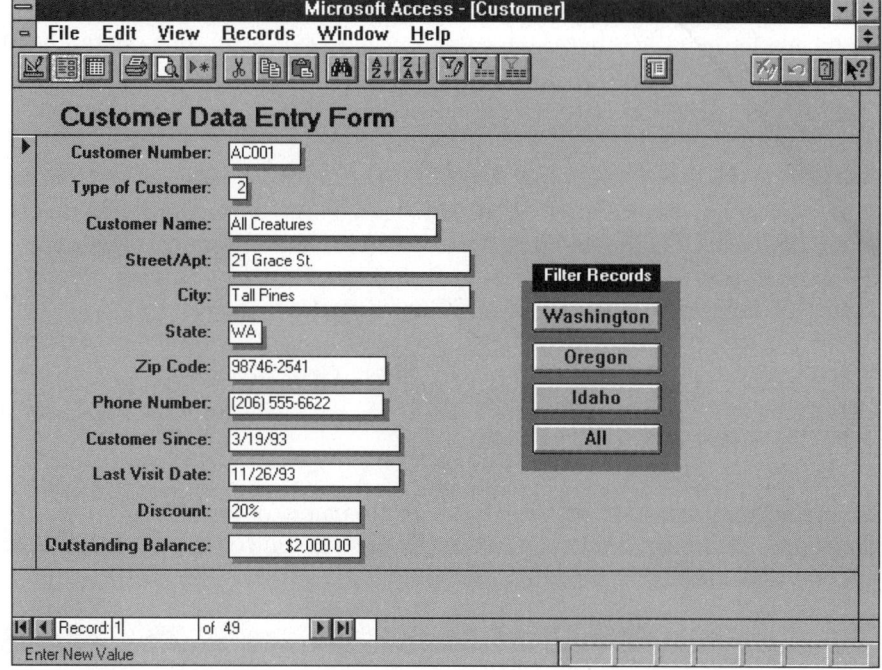

Figure 31-19: A form with buttons used to activate filter macros.

Each button in Figure 31-19 is attached to a different macro. Three of the macros use the ApplyFilter action, and one uses the ShowAllRecords action.

Using the ApplyFilter action

To set a filter condition in a macro, use the ApplyFilter action. This action has two arguments: Filter Name and the Where Condition. You can use either one, but use only one. For this example, you use the Where Condition argument. To create a macro named StateFilter.WA, follow these steps:

Steps:	Creating an ApplyFilter Macro
Step 1.	Enter the Macro Design window.
Step 2.	Enter the macro name **WA** into the group macro StateFilter.
Step 3.	Select or type **ApplyFilter** for the action.
Step 4.	Type **[State] = "WA"** in the Where Condition argument box.

After you create this macro, you next create two more. One macro is named StateFilter.ID, and the other is named StateFilter.OR. These set a condition equal to the individual state.

Using the ShowAllRecords action

When you create filter conditions with macros, you should always create another macro that uses the ShowAllRecords action. This action removes an existing filter set by another macro. This action has no arguments. For the next example, create a macro named StateFilter.All with the ShowAllRecords action.

When you complete this, all four macros should look like the ones in Figure 31-20.

Running filter macros

To run a filter macro, simply attach the macro name to the On Push property of the appropriate command button. Then every time the button is selected, the macro will execute and implement the filter condition.

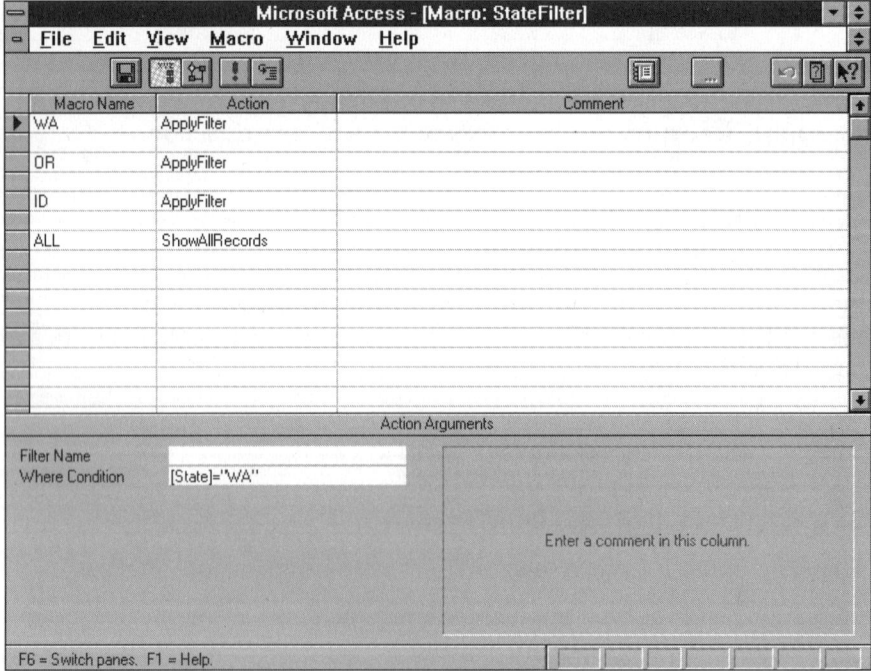

Figure 31-20: A macro group with four filter macros.

Finding Records

One of the most powerful ways of using macros is to locate user-specified records. This type of macro uses two macro actions: GoToControl and FindRecord.

For example, to add a search routine to the Customer form, as in Figure 31-21, you first create an unbound combo box and name it CustomerSelect [Control Name].

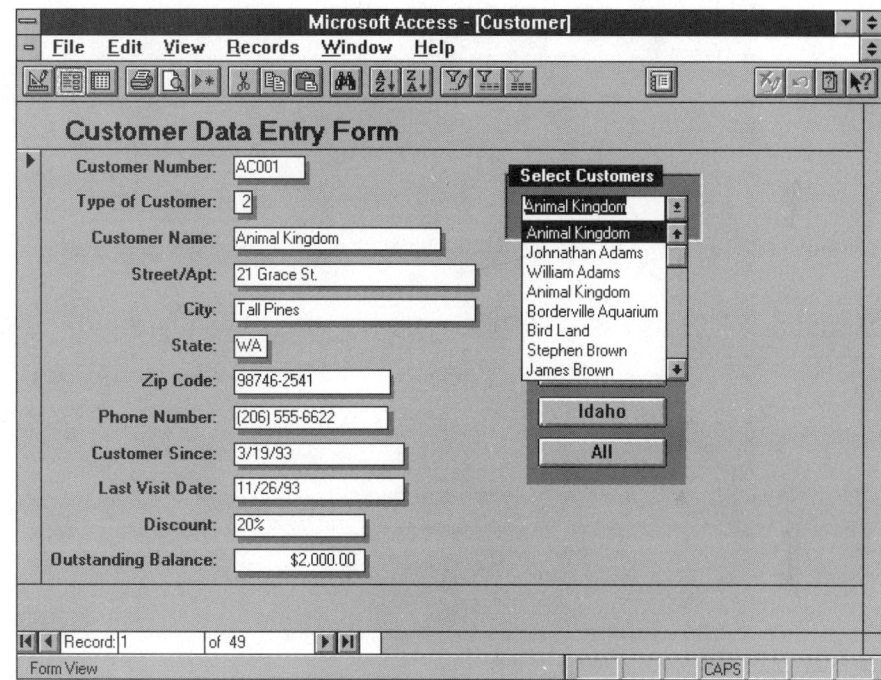

Figure 31-21: The Customer form with a combo box used to find records.

Your property sheet for the combo box should look similar to Figure 31-22.

Beyond completion of these steps, you can beautify the label and combo box area as Figure 31-21 shows. However, these enhancements aren't required.

After you create the unbound combo box, you are ready to create the FindRecord macro to find the customer record by the Customer Name field. To create the macro, follow these steps:

Steps: Creating a FindRecord Macro

Step 1.   Select or type **GoToControl** in the first empty action cell.

Step 2.   Type **[Customer Name]** in the Control Name argument cell.

Step 3. Select or type **FindRecord** in the next empty action cell.

Step 4. Type = **[CustomerSelect]** in the FindWhat argument box.

Step 5. Save the macro, naming it **FindRecord.**

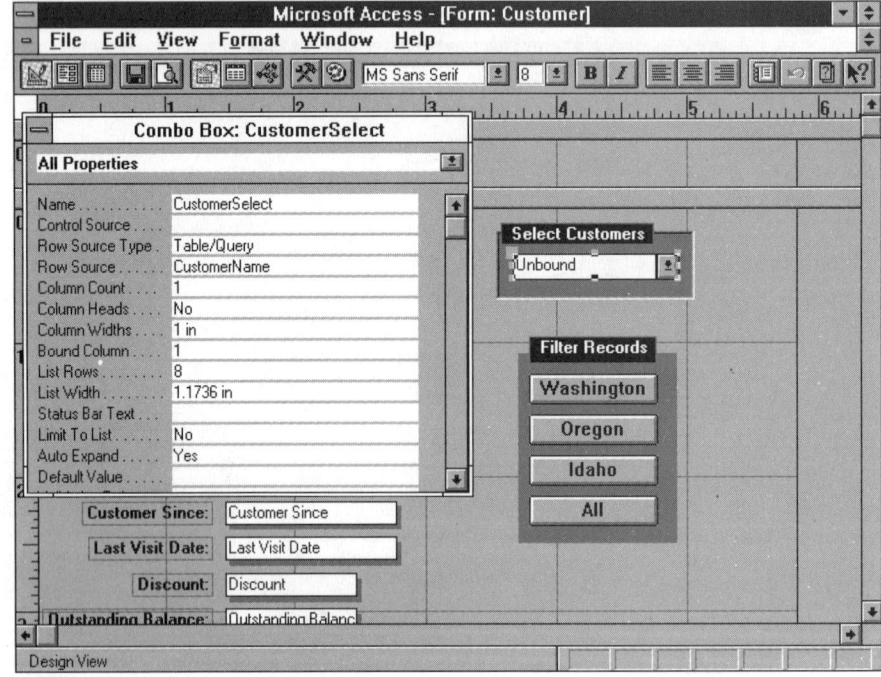

Figure 31-22: The property sheet for an unbound combo box.

That's it! Your macro should now resemble the one in Figure 31-23.

In the GoToControl argument, you placed the form control name [Customer Name], which is the same as the field name, to limit the scope of the search to the current field (Customer Name). Then in the FindRecord argument Find What, you placed the control name for the unbound combo box. By placing the unbound combo box in the Find What box, you specify that the macro will find the name via the combo box but update the record based on the Customer Name.

 Note that you entered an equal sign before the control name, CustomerSelect, in the Find What argument box. If you don't enter the equal sign, the macro will not work.

Now that you created the macro, you're ready to attach it to the After Update property for the unbound combo box. To attach the macro, follow these steps:

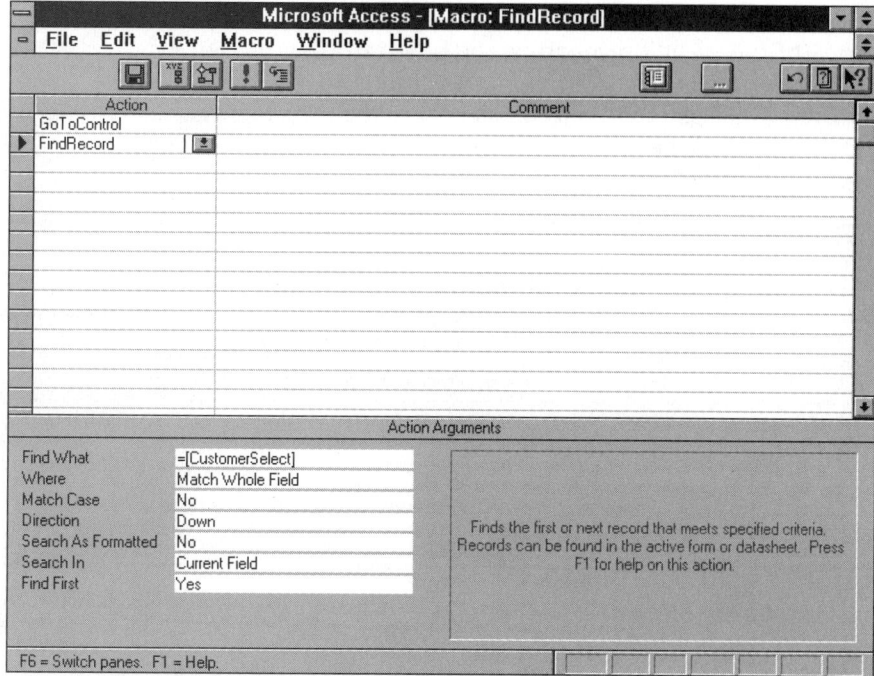

Figure 31-23:
A macro to find a record based on the customer's name.

Steps:	**Attaching the FindRecord Macro**
Step 1.	Move to the After Update property of the CustomerSelect control (unbound combo box).
Step 2.	Type **FindRecord** in the Action Arguments cell (the name of the macro).

The form now uses the combo box to find any Customer!

Report Event Macros

Just as with forms, reports can also use macros that perform actions based on events that you specify. You can work with macros at the report level or the section level. If you attach a macro at the report level, it takes effect when the event occurs against the report as a whole, such as when you open or close the report. If you attach the macro at the section level, it takes effect when the event occurs within a section, as when you format or print the section.

Several event properties can be used for report-level macros. Table 31-3 shows each property, the event it recognizes, and how it works.

As Table 31-3 illustrates, you can use any of the report-level events to trigger a macro. These events can be used just as you use their counterparts in forms.

Table 31-3
The Report-Level Events and Associated Properties

Event Property	Event	When the Macro is Triggered
On Open	Open	When a report is opened but before it prints
On Close	Close	When a report is closed and removed from the screen
On Activate	Activate	When a report receives the focus, becomes the active window
On Deactivate	Deactivate	When a different window becomes the active window
On Error	Error	When a run-time error is produced in Access

Opening a report with a macro

You may want to use the On Open property of a report to run a macro that prompts the user to identify the records to print. The macro can use a filter, or it can use the ApplyFilter action.

For example, you may want to activate a form or dialog box that prompts the user to identify a state or to print the report Customer Mailing Labels. To accomplish this task, you create a filter macro similar to the one in the section on forms and attach it to the On Open property of the report.

Report Section Macros

Besides the report-level properties, Access offers three event properties that you can use at the section level for a report macro. Table 31-4 shows each property, the event it recognizes, and how it works.

Table 31-4
The Report Section-Level Events and Associated Properties

Event Property	Event	When the Macro is Triggered
On Format	Format	When Access knows what data goes in a section, but prior to laying the data out for printing
On Print	Print	After Access lays out the data in a section for printing, but prior to actually printing the section
On Retreat	Retreat	After the Format event, but before the Print event. It occurs when Access has to "back up" past other sections on a page to perform multiple formatting passes

Using On Format

You use the On Format property when a user's response can affect page layout or when the macro contains calculations that use data from sections that you don't intend to print. The macro will run before Access lays out the section following your other property settings for the report, such as Keep Together, Visible, or Can Grow.

You can set the On Format and On Print properties for any section of the report. However, the On Retreat is not available for the Page Header or Page Footer sections.

For example, you may want to highlight some data on the form, based on a certain condition that the macro determines. If the condition is met, the macro uses the SetValue action to change a control's Visible property to Yes.

Using On Print

You use the On Print property when no user's response affects page layout or when the macro depends on what page it finds the records to be printed. For example, you may want to have a total calculation placed in either the header or footer of each page.

Report Properties

When working with macros that use the On Print and On Format properties of report sections, you may need to use two special conditional printer properties:

- Format Count
- Print Count

These two conditional printer properties are used in the Condition Expression column of a macro. These are both read-only properties, and Access sets the value of a read-only property. Therefore, you can check these properties, but you cannot change their values. These properties determine when an event occurs twice.

Using Format Count

The Format Count property is used as a macro condition to determine the number of times the On Format property setting is evaluated for the current line on the report.

It is possible for a line to be formatted more than once. For example, when printing labels, the last label may not fit on a page, where there is room only for one line of a two-line label. If the label won't fit on the page, Access prints it on the next page. The Format Count for any lines moved from the bottom of the page to the top of the next page is set to 2 because the lines are formatted twice.

If you are accumulating a count of the number of labels being printed, you use the Format Count property in the Condition box of the macro to disregard counting the label a second time.

Using Print Count

Like the Format Count property, the Print Count property is used as a macro condition. This property determines the number of times the On Print setting is evaluated for the current line of the report.

It is possible for part of a record to be printed on one page and the remainder to be printed on the next page. When that occurs, the On Print event occurs twice, so the Print Property is incremented to 2. When this occurs, you don't want to have the macro perform its action twice; therefore, you check to see whether the Format Count has changed and stop the macro action.

To understand how this works, suppose that you have a macro that counts the number of records being printed on a page. The record number is placed in the page footer section of each page of the report. If a record is printed across two pages, you want the records counted on only one of the pages.

Working with macros in reports

Like form macros, report macros can be triggered at two levels — report and section. A macro triggered at report level can prompt a user for a range of records to print before doing anything with the report.

On the other hand, a section-level macro can be used for printing messages on a report when a condition is met. For example, if a customer has not paid on his or her bill in 30 days, the report may print a reminder line that a partial payment is overdue.

Report-level macros can be executed before or after a report is printed or previewed. Section-level macros can be executed before or after a section of the report is printed or previewed. Thus, section-level macros tend to be used for more-refined actions, like including conditional lines of text in the report.

Underlining data in a report with a macro

You can use a macro to underline or highlight data dynamically in a report. This is accomplished by hiding or displaying controls and sections.

For example, suppose that you print the Monthly Invoice Report and you want to underline the Amount Due control if the total amount is over $500.00. You can do this by adding a control to the group footer named Customer.Customer Number Footer and creating a macro that toggles the Visible property for the control.

Figure 31-24 shows a line (actually a rectangle with a width of 0.02in.) added below the Amount Due control. This control is named AmtDueLine.

In Figure 31-24, notice that the Visible property is currently set to Yes in the property sheet for the control AmtDueLine.

With the control (line) placed on the report, create a macro that sets the Visible property for this control. This macro requires two conditions — one for [Amount Due]>500 and the other for not being greater than this amount. To create the macro, follow these steps:

Steps:	Creating a Macro to Toggle a Control's Visible Property
Step 1.	Create a macro named PrtLine.
Step 2.	Select an empty cell in the Condition column.
Step 3.	Type **[Amount Due]>500** in the Condition cell.
Step 4.	Select the associated action cell.

Part V: Applications in Access

Step 5.	Select or type **SetValue.**
Step 6.	Select the Item argument.
Step 7.	Type **[AmtDueLine].Visible.**
Step 8.	Select the Expression argument.
Step 9.	Type **Yes.**
Step 10.	Select another empty Condition cell.
Step 11.	Type **Not [Amount Due]>500.**
Step 12.	Select the associated action cell.
Step 13.	Select or type **SetValue.**
Step 14.	Select the Item argument.
Step 15.	Type **[AmtDueLine].Visible.**
Step 16.	Select the Expression argument.
Step 17.	Type **No.**
Step 18.	Save the macro.

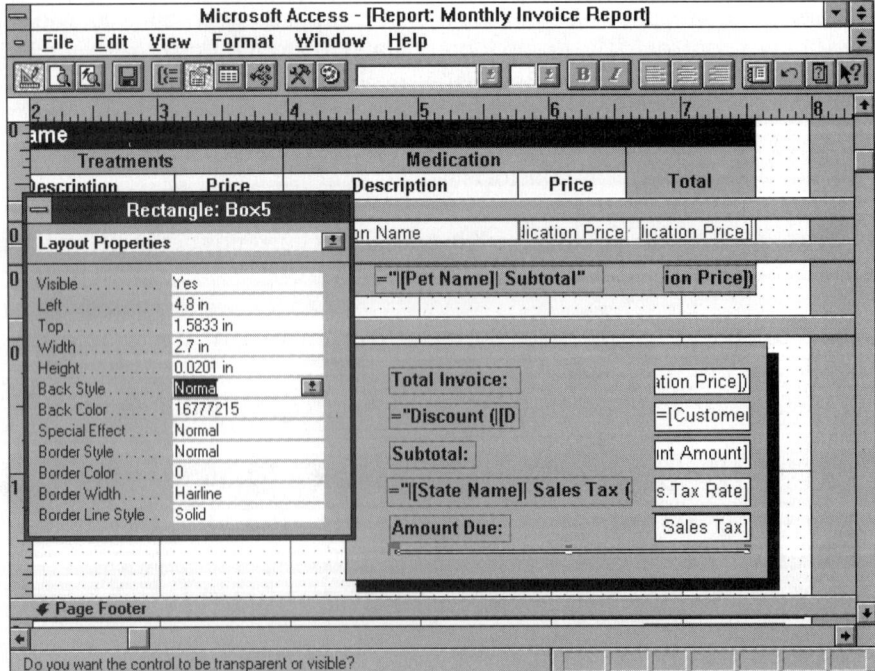

Figure 31-24: A report form with a line added.

Chapter 31: Using Macros in Forms and Reports

The macro should look similar to the one in Figure 31-25. Notice that the macro in this figure has a separate condition to turn the Visible property on (set to Yes) and off.

Now that the macro is created, you need to attach it to the group section named Customer.Customer Number Footer in the Monthly Invoice Report. The macro is attached to the On Format property of the section. Figure 31-26 shows the property sheet with the macro added to the On Format property.

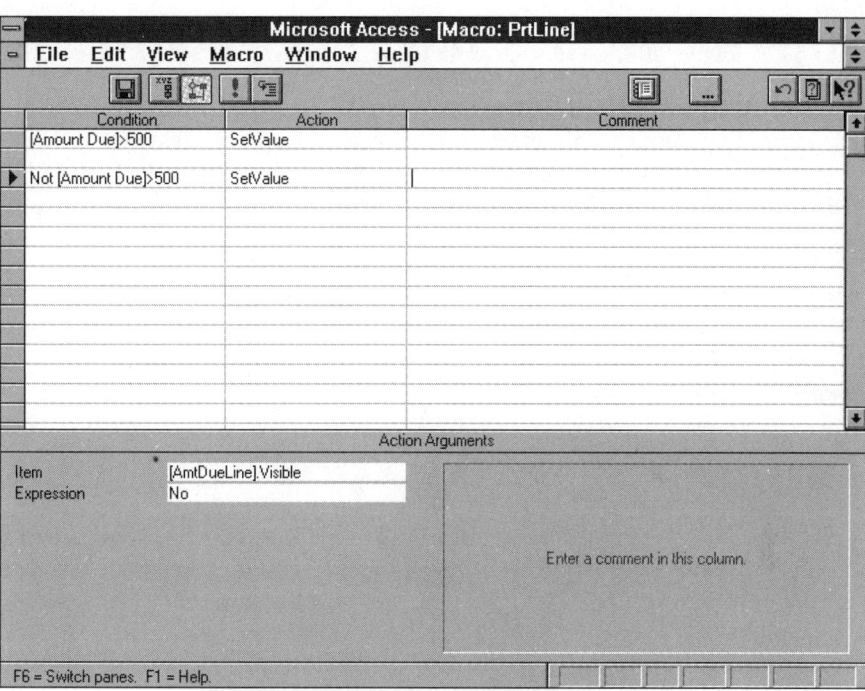

Figure 31-25: A macro to turn the Visible property of a control on or off.

Figure 31-26: A property sheet with a macro name in the On Format property.

Hiding data in a report with a macro

You can hide data in a report with the same method you just used to display or hide a line. You simply set the Visible property to Yes or No in a macro. After you set the property to Yes or No in a macro, attach the macro to the On Format property of the section where the data resides.

Filtering records for a report with a macro

You can filter records for a report by creating a macro and attaching it to the On Open property of the report. This gives you a consistent way of asking for criteria. The On Open property runs the macro no matter how the user opens the report. For example, the user can double-click the report name, choose a command from a custom menu, or select a command button on a form. If the On Open property is used to trigger the macro, you have only to run the dialog box against this single property.

 Chapter 32 shows a menu and dialog box that perform this type of filtering.

Importing and Exporting Macros

You can easily use data from other formats in Access. You can import, export, and attach tables via commands on the File menu in the Database window. However, if you consistently transfer the same data, you may want to automate the process in a macro.

Using command buttons to import or export

If you create a macro to transfer data, you can activate the macro by use of a command button and the On Push property of the button.

When you create the macro, Access provides three actions to help you transfer the data:

- TransferDatabase
- TransferSpreadsheet
- TransferText

By using these actions and their arguments, you can create very powerful and yet simple transfer-data macros.

Creating Hotkeys

You can assign a macro to a specific key or combination of keys, such as Ctrl+P. Once you assign a macro to a key, the key is known as a *hotkey*. By assigning hotkeys, you can create one macro to perform an action no matter what form, view, or table you're in. For example, the Ctrl+P key combination can be used to print the current record.

You can assign macros to any number of hotkeys. All hotkey macros are stored in a single group macro that is used by Access. That group macro is known as a key assignment macro. When you open a database, Access looks for a macro name that is specified in the Options dialog box of the View menu. If the macro exists, it runs automatically, assigning macros to hotkeys.

Changing the default key assignment macro

You specify the name of the macro for the hotkeys in the Options dialog box of the View menu choice in the Database window. The default name for this macro is AutoKeys. However, you can give it any name you want. To specify a different hotkey (default key assignment) macro name, follow these steps:

Steps:	Specifying a Key Assignment Macro
Step 1.	Select View⇨Options... from the Database window menu.
Step 2.	Select the Options Category — Keyboard.
Step 3.	Enter the new name of the hotkey macro in the Key Assignment Macro box of the Items.
Step 4.	Select the OK button.

Figure 31-27 shows the Options dialog box. In the Key Assignment Macro box, you see the default name AutoKeys. You could have placed a new macro name in here instead.

You can have several different key assignment macros, each under a different name. To change from one hotkey macro to another, simply enter the new name in the Options box. Then close and reopen the database to make the new key assignment macro active.

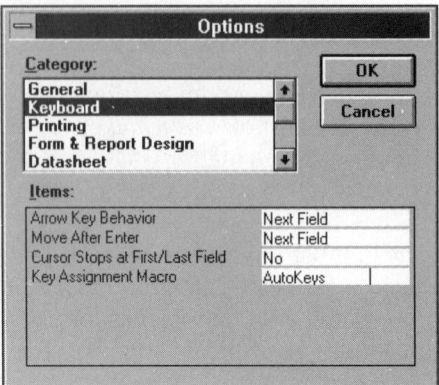

Figure 31-27: Specifying a key assignment macro.

Creating a hotkey combination

To create a hotkey combination and assign actions to it requires creating a macro named AutoKeys and using macro names based on the key combination you want to use to specify an action. The macro names are based on a specific Access syntax called SendKeys syntax.

Using SendKeys syntax for key assignments

When you enter a key combination in the Macro Name column, you specify the key combination by using a specific syntax known as SendKeys syntax. Table 31-5 shows several key combinations and their corresponding SendKeys syntax. When you assign actions to a key combination, you enter the SendKeys syntax in the Macro Name column.

Using Table 31-5 as a reference, you see that to assign some macro actions to the Tab key, you name a macro {TAB} in the group macro Autokeys.

Creating a hotkey

To create a hotkey, follow these steps:

Steps:	Creating a Hotkey
Step 1.	Create a macro named AutoKeys.
Step 2.	Type the key combination in the Macro Name column.
Step 3.	Type the set of actions you want to associate with the key combination.
Step 4.	Repeat Steps 2 and 3 for every hotkey you want to assign actions to.
Step 5.	Save the macro.

Table 31-6: SendKeys Syntax

Key Combo	SendKeys Syntax	Key Combo	SendKeys Syntax
Backspace	{BKSP} or {BS}	F2	{F2}
Caps Lock	{CAPSLOCK}	Ctrl+A	^A
Enter	{ENTER} or ~	Ctrl+F10	^{F10}
Insert	{INSERT}	Ctrl+2	^2
Left arrow	{LEFT}	Shift+F5	+{F5}
Home	{HOME}	Shift+Delete	+{DEL}
PgDn	{PGDN}	Shift+End	+{END}
Escape	{ESC}	Alt+F10	%{F10}
PrintScreen	{PRTSC}	Alt+Up arrow	%{UP}
Scroll Lock	{SCROLLLOCK}	Left arrow 10 times	{LEFT 10}
Tab	{TAB}	Shift+BA together	+(BA)

Access makes the key assignment immediate. When you press the key combination, Access runs the macro actions. In the preceding steps, you can also make several key assignments, creating a macro for each key combination. Just remember to name the macro group AutoKeys or whatever name you specified in the Options dialog box.

Summary

This chapter provided an in-depth explanation of macro usage. You learned how to use macros in forms and reports and how to create hotkeys. The following topics were covered:

- An event is some user action. The action may be opening a form, changing data in a record, or selecting a command button.
- Access recognizes user events by use of a corresponding form or report *property*. For example, the On Open property is associated with the event of opening a form.
- You can attach form macros to the form or to individual controls. Forms can use form-level events and control-level events.
- Form-level macros can display messages, open a form, synchronize two forms, and validate data entry.
- When validating data at the form level, the two most common form properties used are On Delete and Before Update.
- With the MsgBox( ) function, you can specify conditions in macros. It is a very powerful function that displays messages and command buttons to obtain user input.
- Control-event macros can be triggered when the user enters or exits a control, clicks a button, or double-clicks a control.
- You use the SetValue action in macros to hide a control, update a field based on another field value, or disable a control.
- Report macros can be triggered at report level or at the report section level. Only two event properties are used at the report level, and two are used at the report section level.
- By using macros in reports, you can apply a filter to a report, hide or print a line, or hide some other object on a report based on a condition.
- You can assign macro actions to combinations of keys by using a key assignment macro and macro names based on the SendKeys syntax of Access.

In the next chapter, you work with macros in menus, switchboards, and dialog boxes to further automate your database system.

Creating Switchboards, Menus, and Dialogs

CHAPTER 32

In This Chapter

- How to create a switchboard by using a form and command buttons
- How to use the Access 2.0 Command Button Wizard
- How to use the Access 2.0 Picture Builder
- How to add a custom menu to a form or report
- How to use the Access 2.0 Menu Builder
- How to create a print dialog box

Until this chapter, you created an assortment of Access objects: tables, queries, forms, reports, and macros. You worked with each of these objects interactively in Access, selecting the database window and using the individual objects.

In this chapter, you tie these objects together into a single database application without the need for writing or knowing how to use a complex database program. Rather, you automate the application through the use of switchboards, dialogs, and menus. These objects make your system easier to use and hide the Access interface from the final user.

What Is a Switchboard?

A switchboard is fundamentally a form. The switchboard form is a customized application menu that contains user-defined command buttons. With these command buttons, you can run macros that automatically select such actions as opening forms or printing reports. Using a switchboard button, you replace many interactive user steps with a single button selection, or "push." For example, if you want to open the form Add a Customer and Pets interactively, you must perform three steps: switch to the Database window, select the Form object button, and open the form. If you use a switchboard button to perform the same task, you simply select the button. Figure 32-1 shows a

Figure 32-1:
A switchboard with several command buttons for forms and reports.

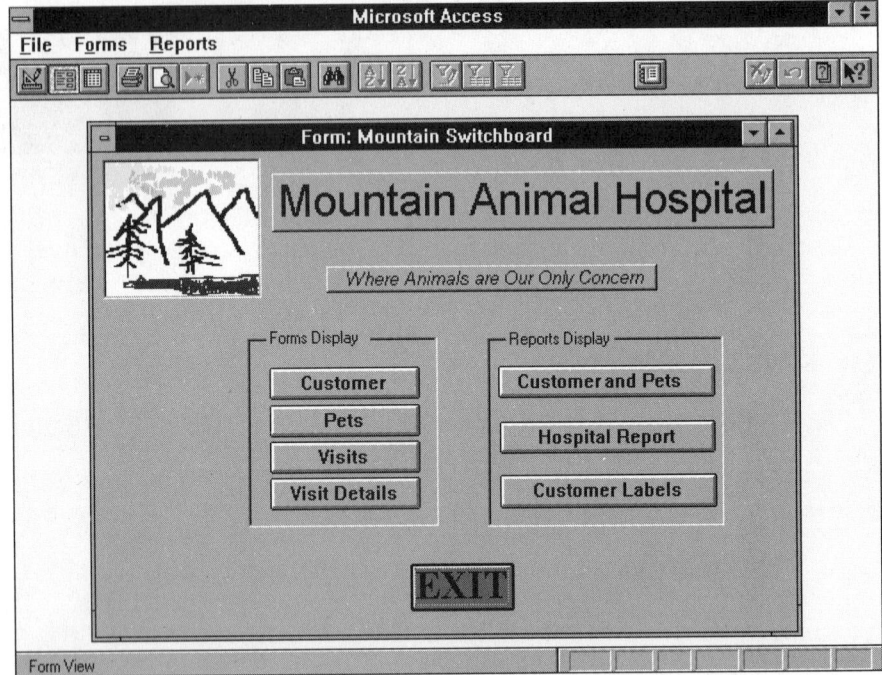

switchboard with several buttons. Each command button triggers a macro that performs a series of steps, such as opening the Customer form or running the Hospital Report. Notice that this figure shows the database MTNANHSP as an icon, because the database has been minimized.

By using a switchboard and other objects covered in this chapter, you can tie your database objects together in a single database application. The application will have a user interface that you create rather than the Access interactive interface. A primary component of that user-defined interface is the switchboard you create.

Using a switchboard

A switchboard's primary use is as an application interface menu. The switchboard in Figure 32-1 is the application interface menu for the Mountain Animal Hospital database. As you see in the figure, the switchboard contains several command buttons. When the user clicks on any switchboard button, a macro is triggered that performs some action or a series of actions.

Creating the basic form for a switchboard

You create a switchboard by adding command buttons to an existing Access form. The form in Figure 32-1 is a basic display form.

Because switchboard forms are used as application menus, they tend to use a limited number of form controls. Typically, you find command buttons, labels, object frames (OLE objects such as pictures), lines, and rectangles. Normally, switchboards lack the other types of form controls such as text boxes (bound to fields), list and combo boxes, graphs, subforms, and page breaks.

To create a basic switchboard form, you place labels like titles and group headings on the form. In addition to the labels, you may also want to place lines, rectangles, and pictures on the form to make it aesthetically appealing. You create the basic switchboard form by using the techniques you already learned in chapters covering form objects.

Consider, for example, the switchboard in Figure 32-1. Minus the command buttons, this is a typical Access application form. Its major components are a title and two group sections. The title is comprised of three parts:

- The main text title, Mountain Animal Hospital
- A picture logo showing mountains and trees
- A text logo: Where Animals are Our Only Concern

Below the title are two sunken rectangles. On the top border of each rectangle is a label; the rectangle to the left is labeled Forms Display, and the rectangle to the right is labeled Reports Display. Each rectangle, which now appears in a "sunken" state, will contain several command buttons when the switchboard form is completed.

Working with command buttons

Command buttons are the type of form control you use to run macros. Command buttons are the simplest type of form controls, with the single purpose of executing a macro.

Command buttons run macros that perform a multitude of tasks in Access:

- Opening and displaying other forms
- Opening a pop-up form, or dialog box, to collect additional information
- Opening and printing reports
- Activating a search or displaying a filter
- Exiting Access

In version 2.0, you can trigger a macro by assigning one of 12 event properties to a command button. Figure 32-2 shows a command button named Button01 and its property sheet. In this property sheet, you see the event properties available for a command button:

- On Enter
- On Exit
- On Got Focus
- On Lost Focus
- On Click
- On Dbl Click
- On Mouse Down
- On Mouse Move
- On Mouse Up
- On Key Down
- On Key Press
- On Key Up

Each event property can trigger a macro. For example, to trigger a macro named OpenCust when the user selects the button, place the macro name OpenCust in the parameter box for the On Click property. The keyword *On* identifies an event property. The property identifies the user event that must occur to trigger an action.

On Click and On Dbl Click are mutually compatible. If you activate both the On Click property (giving it a macro name) and the On Dbl Click property, Access follows this order of precedence for the mouse clicking and trapping:

1. On Click (single mouse click)
2. On Dbl Click (double click)
3. On Click (single click)

In other words, Access processes an On Click first and then an On Dbl Click and, finally, an On Click *again*. So Access *always* processes the On Click if it is defined. To prevent the second On Click macro from running, place a CancelEvent action in the On Dbl Click macro.

In addition, if the macro you call from an On Click opens a dialog box (message box, pop-up form, and so forth), the second click is lost and the On Dbl Click is never reached! If you use On Click and On Dbl Click, the On Click should not open a dialog box if you need to capture the On Dbl Click.

Chapter 32: Creating Switchboards, Menus, and Dialogs 941

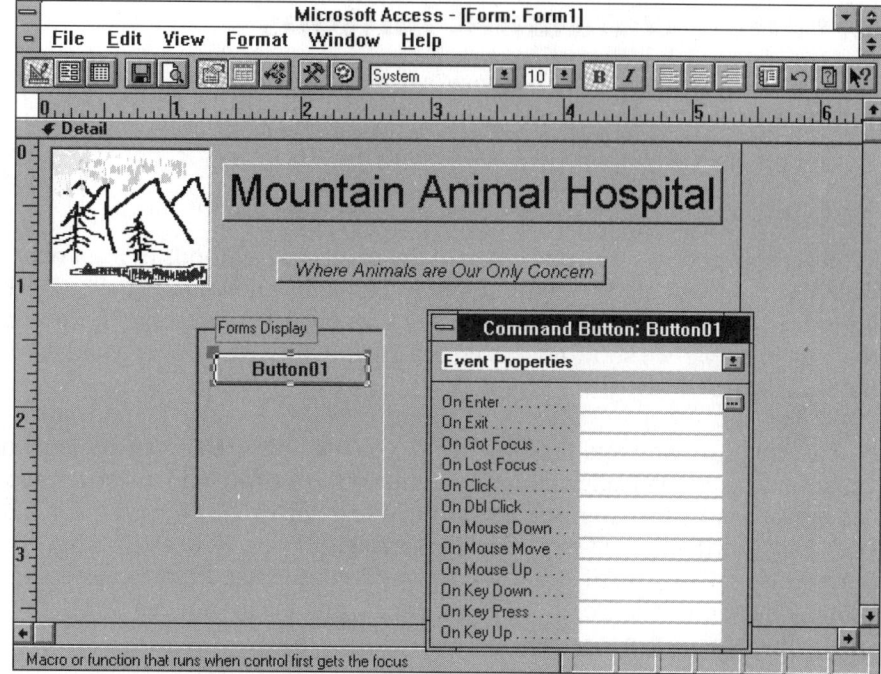

Figure 32-2: A single-button switchboard form with its open property sheet.

What Is Focus?

To understand the terminology associated with command buttons, you need to know the term *focus*. The two command button properties On Enter and On Exit gain or lose focus. In other words, the focus represents the next item of input from the user. For example, if you tab from one button to another, you lose the focus on the first button as you leave it, and you gain the focus on the second as you enter it. In a form with several command buttons, you can tell which button has focus by the dotted box around the label of the button. Focus does not denote the state of input, as when you press a button; rather, focus is the object that is currently active and awaiting some user action.

The focus for mouse input always coincides with the button down, or pointer, location. Because focus occurs at the moment of clicking a command button, the property On Enter is not triggered. The reason is that On Enter occurs just before the focus is gained and that state is not realized when selection of a command button is performed by the use of a mouse. The On Enter state never occurs. Rather, the focus and On Click occur simultaneously, bypassing the On Enter state.

Creating command buttons

A command button's primary purpose is to activate, or run, a macro. Access 2.0 gives you two ways to create a command button:

- Click the Command Button icon in the form toolbox
- Drag a macro name from the database container to the form

In this chapter, we demonstrate each of the preceding methods at least once as we describe how to create the eight command buttons shown in Figure 32-1 (four buttons to display a form, three to display a report, and one to exit the application). In this first example, we show how to create the first form button by using the Command Button Wizard.

When using the Command Button Wizard, you not only create a command button, but you also can automatically embed a picture on the button. And, more important, you can create a module to perform a task, including Record Navigation (Next, Previous, First, Last, Find), Record Operations (Save, Delete, Print, New, Duplicate), Form Operations (Open, Close, Print, Filter), Report Operations (Print, Preview, Mail), Applications (Run Application, Quit, Notepad, Word, Excel), and Miscellaneous (Print Table, Run Query, Run Macro, AutoDialer).

To create the Customer button by using the Command Button Wizard, follow these steps:

Steps: Creating a Command Button by Using the Command Button Wizard

Step 1. Open the Form Mountain Switchboard - No Buttons in design mode.

Step 2. Make sure that the Control Wizard icon is toggled on.

Step 3. Select the Command Button icon in the toolbox.

Step 4. Place the cursor on the form in the upper left corner of the Form Display rectangle and draw a small rectangle.

Command buttons have no control source. If you try to create a button by dragging a field from the field list, a text box control (not a command button) is created. You must draw the rectangle or drag a macro to create a command button.

The Command Button Wizard displays the dialog box shown in Figure 32-3. You can select from several categories of tasks. As you choose each category, the list of actions under the header When button is pressed changes.

Chapter 32: Creating Switchboards, Menus, and Dialogs

In addition, the sample picture changes as you move from action to action. In Figure 32-3, the specified category is Form Operations, and the desired action is Open Form.

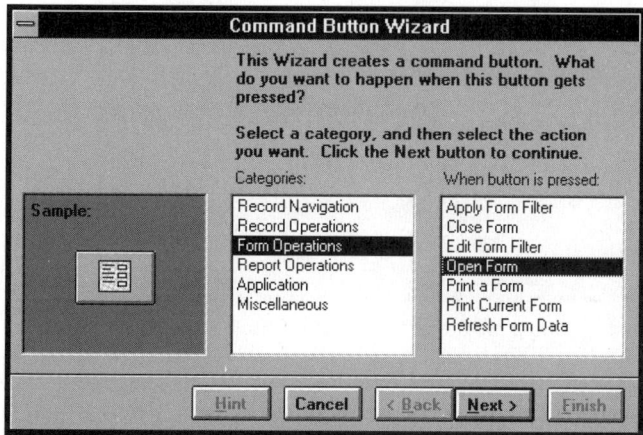

Figure 32-3: The Command Button Wizard's Category and Action dialog box.

Step 5. Choose the Form Operations category and the Open Form action.

Step 6. Press the Next > button to move to the next screen.

The wizard displays a list of the MTNANHSP database's forms.

Step 7. Select the Customer form and press the Next > button to move to the next wizard screen.

The next screen lets you decide what you want to appear on the button. You can display text or a picture on the button. The button can be resized to accommodate any size text. The default is to place a picture on the button. You can choose from the default button for the selected action, or you can click the Show all pictures checkbox to select from over 100 pictures. You also can press the Browse button to select an icon (.ICO) or bitmap (.BMP) file from your disk. For this example, simply display the text Customer on the button.

Step 8. Select the Text option button and type **Customer** into the text box.

The sample button displays the text instead of the picture (see Figure 32-4). Later, you can resize the button to properly display the text on the button.

Step 9. Press the Next > button to move to the final wizard screen, which lets you enter a name for the button and then display the button on the form.

Part V: Applications in Access

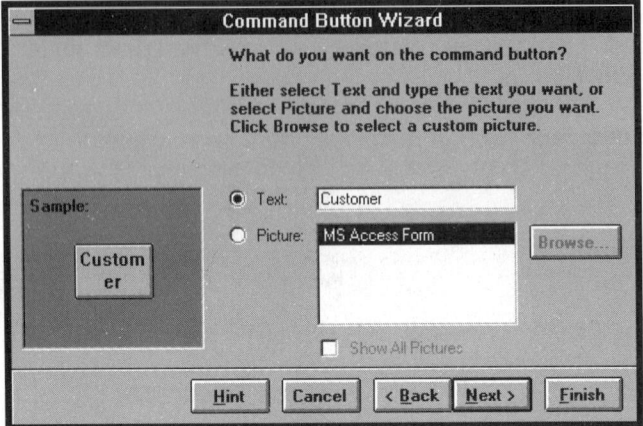

Figure 32-4: Selecting a picture or text for the button.

Step 10. Enter **Customer Button** as the name of the button. Press **F**inish. The button appears on the form design screen as shown in Figure 32-5.

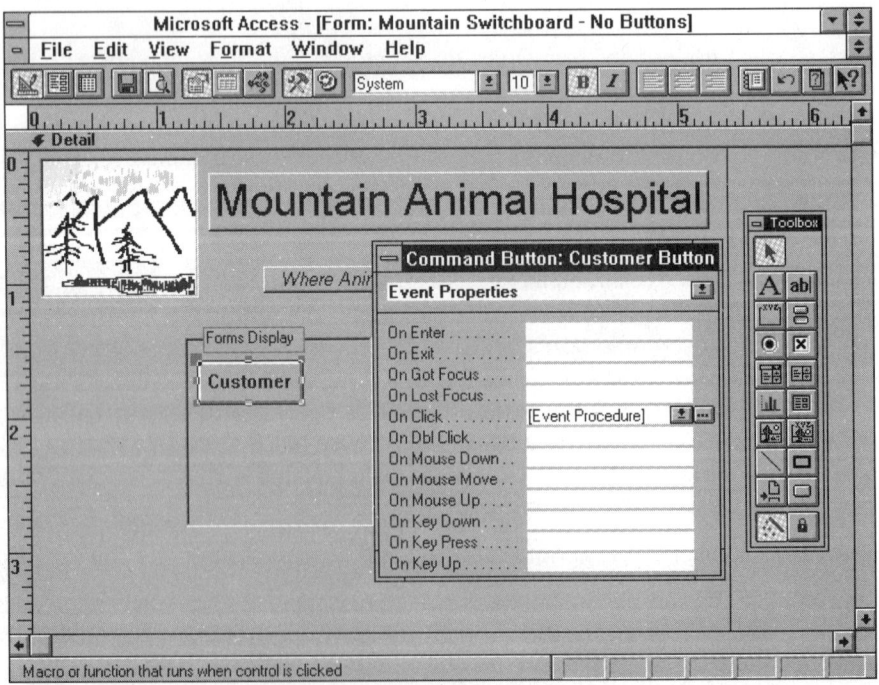

Figure 32-5: Adding a button to the form design.

Notice the property sheet displayed in Figure 32-5. The On Click property displays Event Procedure, which means that a module is stored *behind* the form. The only way to see this module library is to press the builder button (three dots) next to the [Event Procedure] text. When the button is clicked, the Access BASIC program is run and the Customer form is opened.

A module window appears with the specific Access BASIC code that's necessary to open the customer form (see Figure 32-6). There is no need to look at this code unless you plan to change the program.

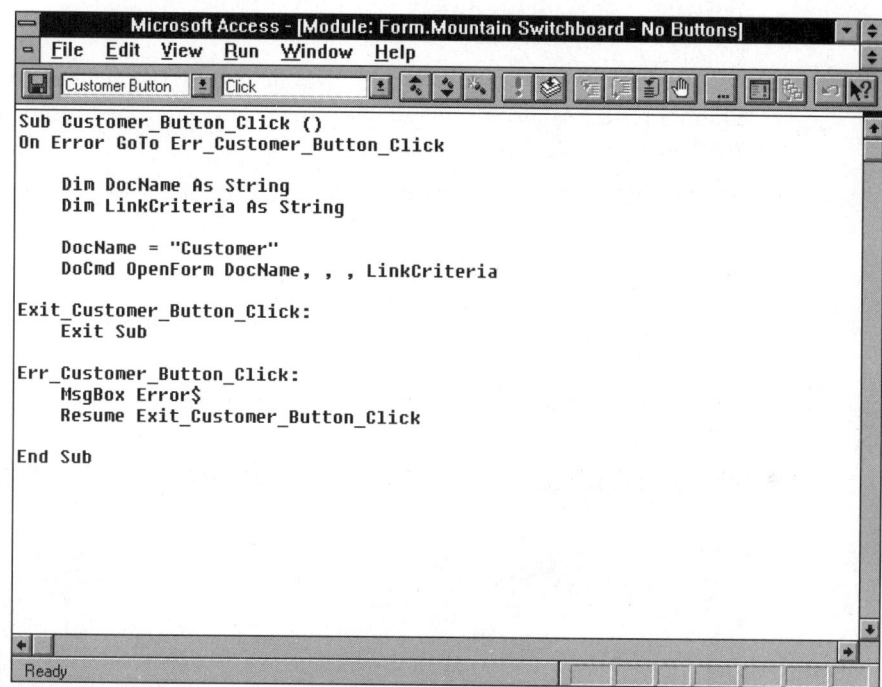

Figure 32-6: The Event Procedure Module for opening the Customer form.

We do not cover Access BASIC in this book. We devote the rest of this chapter to describing how to use macros to carry out actions.

You can create a command button and attach a macro very easily without using the wizard. You also can attach pictures without the wizard. In fact, if you don't want to dabble in Access BASIC, you should ignore the Command Button Wizard.

You can add new pictures to the list of pictures by using the File⇨Add-ins⇨Add-in manager. When the dialog box appears, select Control and Property Wizards and then press the Customize button. Then select Customize Command Button and press OK. A list of all the pictures appears. As you select each picture caption, the sample picture changes. You can press the Add button and then select from a standard Windows directory dialog box and select any bitmap (.BMP) or icon (.ICO) file.

If the bitmap is larger than 32 x 32 pixels, it will not fit on a standard button.

Steps: Creating a Command Button without Using the Wizard

Step 1. Display the Form Mountain Switchboard - No Buttons in design view.

Step 2. Make sure that the Control Wizard icon is toggled off.

Step 3. Select the Command Button icon in the toolbox.

Step 4. Place the cursor on the form under the Customer button in the Form Display rectangle and draw a small rectangle.

The command button appears with a name inside (begins with **Button**) and a number. Access also deselects Command button in the toolbox and highlights the selection pointer.

Step 5. Double-click on the button and change the caption name from Button# to Pets.

Step 6. Repeat Steps 2 through 5 for the form buttons Visits and Visit Details.

Step 7. Repeat Steps 2 through 5 for the report buttons Customer and Pets, Hospital Report, and Customer Labels.

With all the buttons displayed, your screen should look like Figure 32-7.

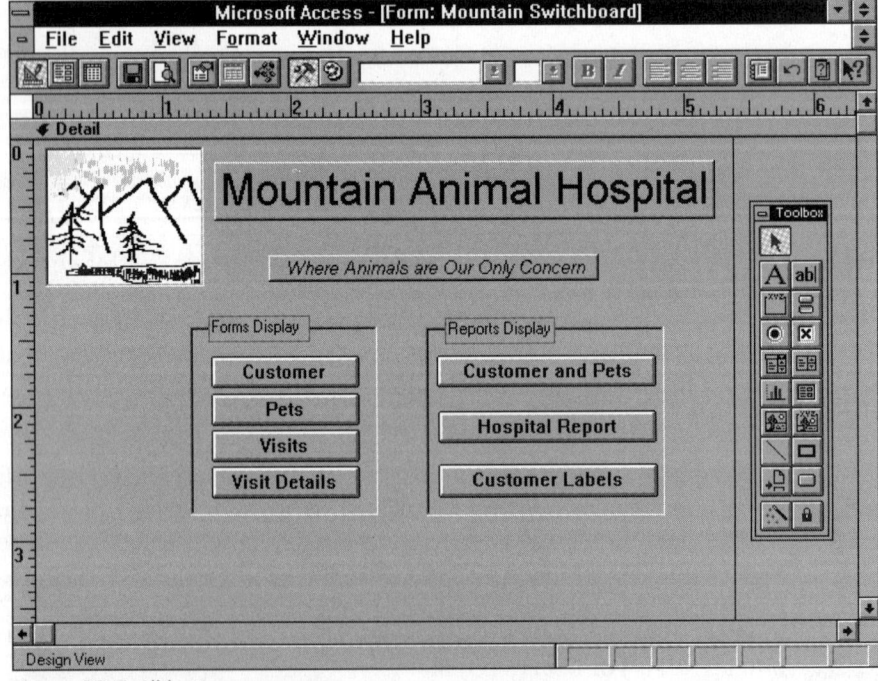

Figure 32-7: All buttons on-screen.

Linking a command button to a macro

As soon as you create a command button in the Design window, it is already active. You can push it, although it doesn't perform any action unless you created it with the wizard. If you switch to the Form window by selecting the Form button on the toolbar, you'll see the switchboard. You can push any of the seven buttons that you created in the design mode. Every time you select a button, it graphically pushes down, showing that it has been selected. However, except for the Customer button, nothing else occurs; only the button movement happens. By switching back to the design mode and selecting the Design button on the toolbar, you can link a macro to the button.

To link a command button to a macro, you enter the macro name into the property cell of one of the command button's event properties. To see the property sheet for a command button, follow these steps:

Steps: Activating the Property Sheet for a Command Button

Step 1. In design mode, select the Pets command button by clicking it.

Step 2. Click on the Properties button on the toolbar or select View⇨Properties....

A property sheet similar to the one in Figure 32-2 should be visible on your screen. Notice the event properties that begin with the word *On* in the property sheet.

The property most commonly used to link a command button to a macro is On Click. This property runs a macro whenever a user selects the button. When the button is selected, the On Click property becomes true and the macro specified is run. To associate the macro named Pets in the macro group Mountain Switchboard, follow these steps:

Steps: Linking a Macro to the On Click Property of a Command Button

Step 1. Click the Customer command button.

Step 2. Click the On Click property cell in the property sheet for the command button.

Step 3. Type **Mountain Switchboard.Pets** in the cell and press Enter.

Make sure that you type both the macro group name and then the macro name separated by a period.

 When you enter a macro name, the macro does not have to exist. You can enter the name of a macro that you create later. In this way, you can create the switchboard first and the macros later. However, if the macro name you enter in the On Click cell does not exist when you open the form and select the button, Access displays an error message.

Using these methods, you can now complete all seven buttons properties, assigning a macro for each button based on the On click property. Table 32-1 shows each button name and the macro it will call.

Table 32-1
The Seven Buttons and Their Macro Names

In Rectangle	Button Name	Macro for On Push
Form	Customer	Event Property (created by Button Wizard)
Form	Pets	Mountain Switchboard.Pets
Form	Visits	Mountain Switchboard.Visits
Form	Visit Details	Mountain Switchboard.Visit Details
Report	Customer and Pets	Mountain Switchboard.Customer and Pets
Report	Hospital Report	Mountain Switchboard.Hospital Report
Report	Customer Labels	Mountain Switchboard.Customer Labels

The macros for the Mountain Switchboard

In this example, each command button opens either a form or a report by using the OpenForm or OpenReport macro actions. The Exit button closes the form with the Quit macro action.

You can create each of the macros and its actions by following these general steps:

1. Enter a macro name in the Macro Name column.

2. Enter a macro action in the Action column (such as OpenForm, OpenReport, or Close) or select the macro action from the drop-down list box.

3. Enter a macro argument (name of form or report) for each action.

4. Optionally, enter a remark (as a reminder) in the Comment Column.

Chapter 32: Creating Switchboards, Menus, and Dialogs

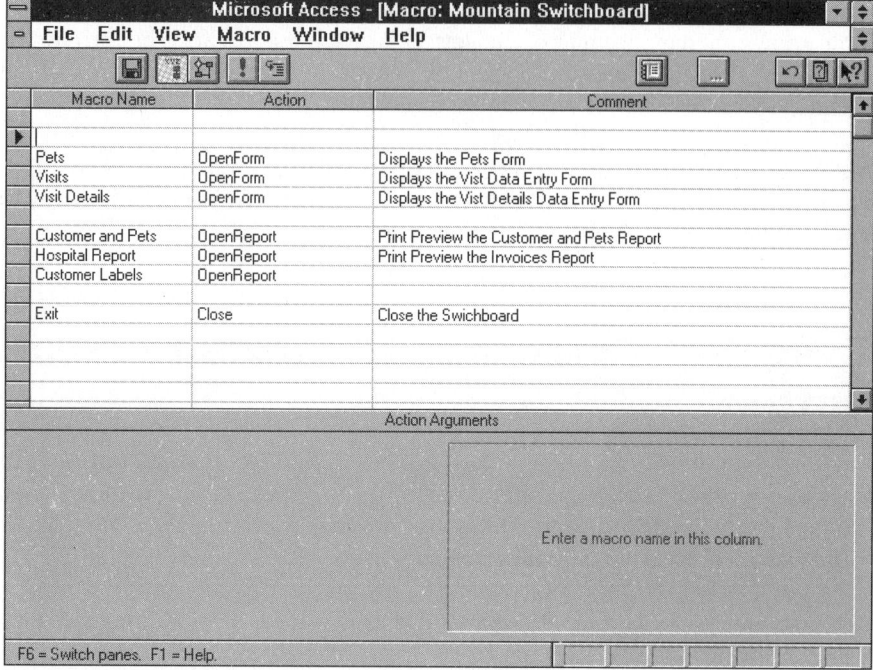

Figure 32-8: The seven macros used for Mountain Switchboard.

Another way to add a macro action and argument is to drag the form or report from the Database window to the macro's Action column. Access automatically adds the correct action in the Action column, which is OpenForm or OpenReport. Access also adds the correct argument in the Name cell of the arguments.

Table 32-2
Macros Used in the Group Macro

Macro Name	Action	Argument Name (Form, Report, Object)
Pets	OpenForm	Pets
Visits	OpenForm	Adding General Pet Visit Info
Visit Details	OpenForm	Adding Visit Details
Customer and Pets	OpenReport	Pets & Owners
Hospital Report	OpenReport	Invoices
Customer Label	OpenReport	Customer By State (three snaking columns)
Exit	Close	Mountain Switchboard

If you want to create the group macro for this chapter, you can follow Table 32-2. This table shows each macro name, the action for each macro, and the form or report name. (These are shown in Figure 32-8.) The macro Mountain Switchboard should already exist in the macro object list of the Database window.

Notice that Table 32-2 shows that the action Close will close the form named Mountain Switchboard. These macros work with the actual form named Mountain Switchboard. The Exit command button will be created next.

Dragging a macro to the form to create a button

The form Mountain Switchboard does not have an Exit command button. You already learned one way to add a command button in the Form Design window. Another way to create a command button is by dragging and dropping a macro name from the macro Database window to a position on the switchboard.

For example, to create an Exit command button for the form Mountain Switchboard by using the drag-and-drop method, follow these steps:

Steps:	Dragging a Macro to a Switchboard to Create a Button
Step 1.	Enter the design mode for the form Mountain Switchboard.
Step 2.	Activate the Database window by pressing F11 or Alt+F1.
Step 3.	In the Database window, select the Macro object button to display all macros.
Step 4.	Highlight the Mountain Switchboard in the macro object list.
Step 5.	Click and then drag and drop the macro Mountain Switchboard onto the form below the rectangles.
Step 6.	Click the button name and change it to **Exit**.
Step 7.	Click in the cell of the On Click property of the Exit button.
Step 8.	Move to the end of the macro group name and type **.Exit**.

Your screen should now look similar to Figure 32-9. Notice that when you added the macro to the form by the drag-and-drop method, Access automatically created a command button, named it the same as the macro, and placed the macro name (in this case, a group name) in the On Click property of the button.

Figure 32-9:
The new button created by dragging and dropping a macro onto the form.

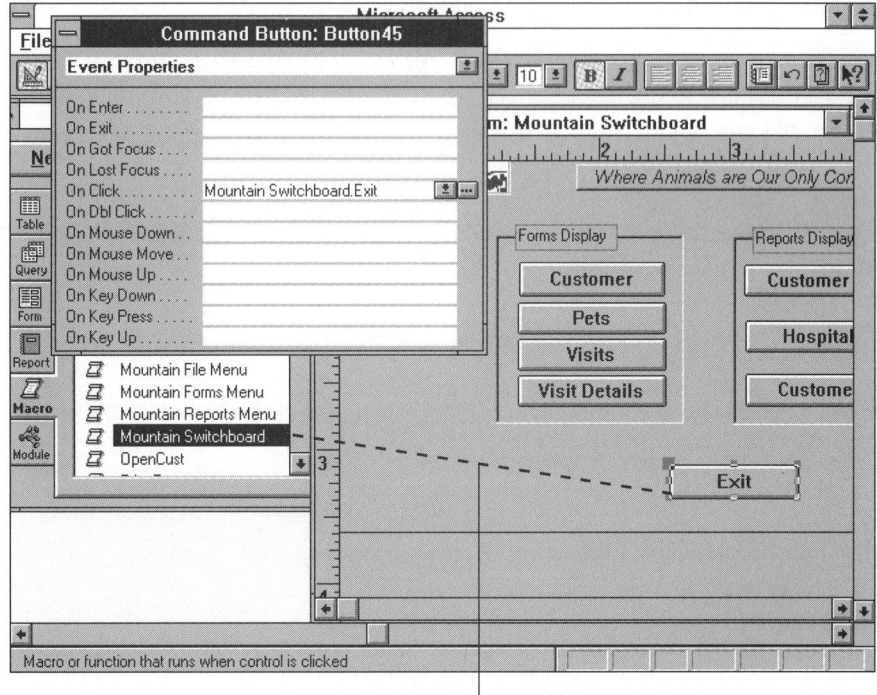

Drag and drop the macro name to the form.

When you added the macro name to the On Click property, you did not have to add the macro group name. Rather, you moved to the end and placed a period after the group name and then the macro name. Access automatically brought the group name into the On Click property for you.

 If you drag and drop a macro that is not a group macro, Access correctly places the macro name in the On Click property and names the button the same as the macro.

 If you drag a macro group, as you did in this example, and do not add a macro name to the On Click property, Access runs the first macro in the macro group.

Adding a picture to a command button

 **Following Along In This Chapter**
All the command buttons you have created contained text in the caption property of the button. However, you can have the button display a picture instead. For example, the disk in the back of the book contains a file named EXIT.BMP, which is a bitmap of an exit sign. You can have the Exit command button show the picture EXIT.BMP rather than the word *Exit*.

To change a command button to a picture button, you can

- Type the name of the bitmap (.BMP) containing the picture into the Picture property of the button.
- Use the Picture Builder to select from an icon list that comes with Access.
- Specify the name of an icon or bitmap file.

To change the Exit command button to the picture button, EXIT.BMP, follow these steps:

Steps: Creating a Picture Button by Using the Picture Builder

Step 1. In the Mountain Switchboard form, select the Exit command button.

Step 2. Display the property window.

Step 3. Click the *Picture* property for the Exit button.

Step 4. Click the Builder button (three dots on a little button).

The Picture Builder dialog box appears. No picture appears because the button you are modifying has no picture. Because you are adding a picture for an exit button, you may want to see if there is an exit button in Access 2.0. You can scroll down the list of Available Pictures, as shown in Figure 32-10. Access has an Exit picture, but it may not be what you want. You can select any bitmap or icon file on your disk.

Step 5. Click the Browse button.

The Select Bitmap dialog box shows a standard Windows directory list. Select the directory that contains your file.

Step 6. Select the directory that houses the file EXIT.BMP, select the file, and press OK.

The bitmap appears in the sample area. Though it doesn't fit in the sample, it should fit on the button when it is displayed.

Step 7. Press OK to accept the bitmap.

Access places the word *[bitmap]* in the Picture property of the command button.

Step 8. Resize the button so that the picture only shows the word Exit.

Your form should look like Figure 32-11. Notice that Access added the word (bitmap) to the Picture cell for the button Exit.

Chapter 32: Creating Switchboards, Menus, and Dialogs

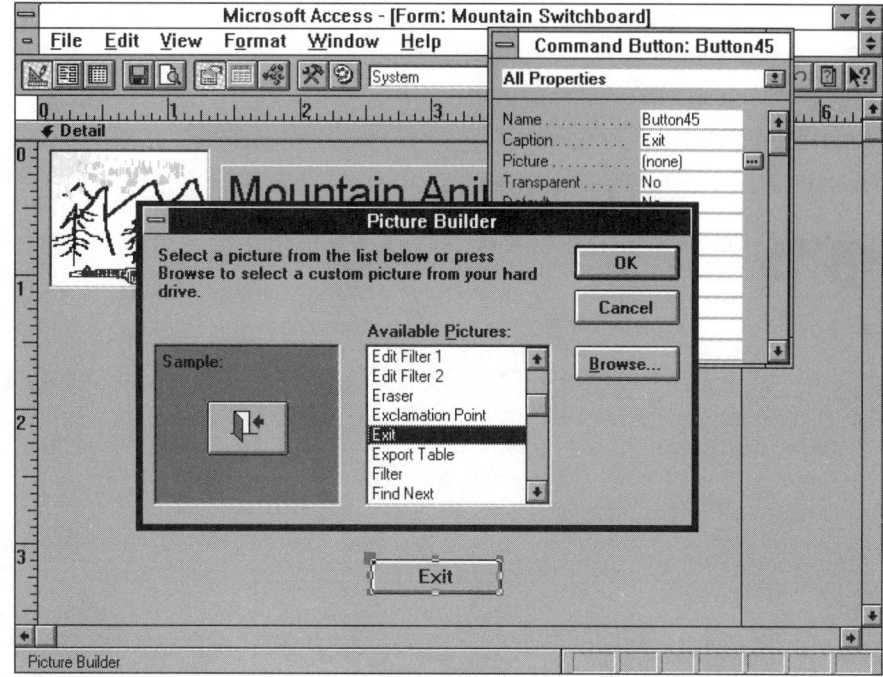

Figure 32-10: The Picture Builder.

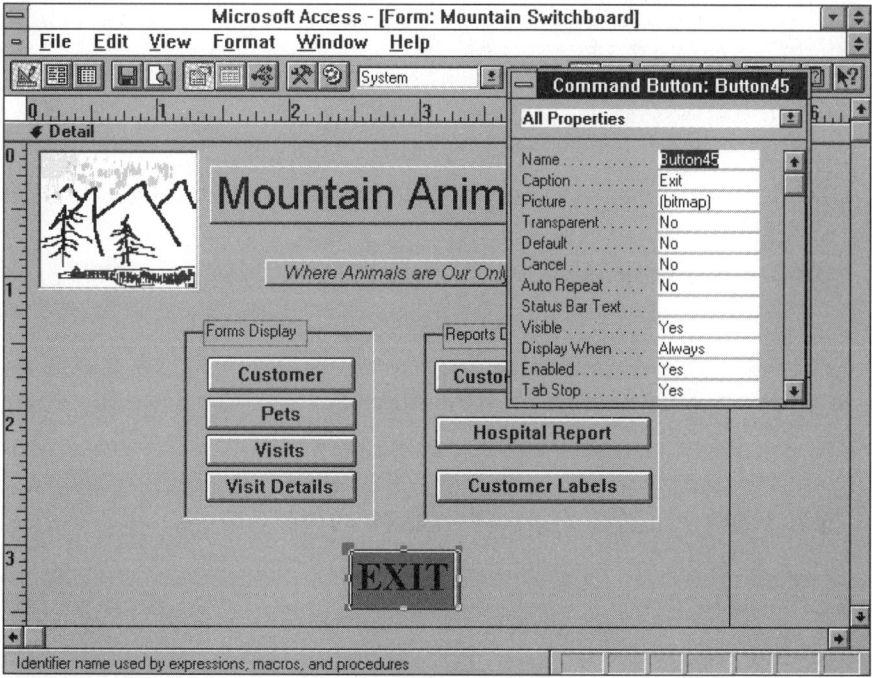

Figure 32-11: The final form with a picture button added.

You also can directly type the filename into the Picture property. If Access cannot find the picture file, it displays a dialog box stating that it couldn't find your file. If you know the drive and directory where the file is located, enter them in the picture cell with the filename (for example, C:\ACCESS\EXIT.BMP).

This action completes the Mountain Switchboard. Save your switchboard. The next task is to customize the menu bar to correspond to the buttons on the switchboard so that the choices can be made from the menu or the buttons.

Creating Customized Bar Menus

Besides creating switchboards with Access, you can create a custom drop-down menu bar that adds functionality to your system. You can add commands to this menu that are appropriate for your application. These commands may be the actions specified in your switchboard command buttons. When you create a custom drop-down menu bar, the new bar will replace the Access menu bar.

The menu bar is referenced only by a form; therefore, you can create a single menu bar and use it for several forms.

Figure 32-12 shows the Mountain Switchboard with a custom drop-down menu bar attached. Notice that each of the three choices on the bar menu, File, Forms, and Reports, has a drop-down menu attached.

You can use Access macros to create a menu bar and its attached drop-down menus. To create a drop-down menu bar, you follow these three basic steps:

1. Define each drop-down menu choice and its commands (actions) in a macro group.
2. Create the menu bar in a macro by using the AddMenu action.
3. Attach the menu bar to a form by setting the On Menu property for the form.

Another way to create a menu bar is to use the Menu Builder, which we cover later in this chapter.

Defining the drop-down menus

To create a drop-down menu, you must create a separate macro group for the menu. This macro will contain a separate macro name for each command (choice) in the menu. Access uses the macro name for the command name in the menu.

Chapter 32: Creating Switchboards, Menus, and Dialogs 955

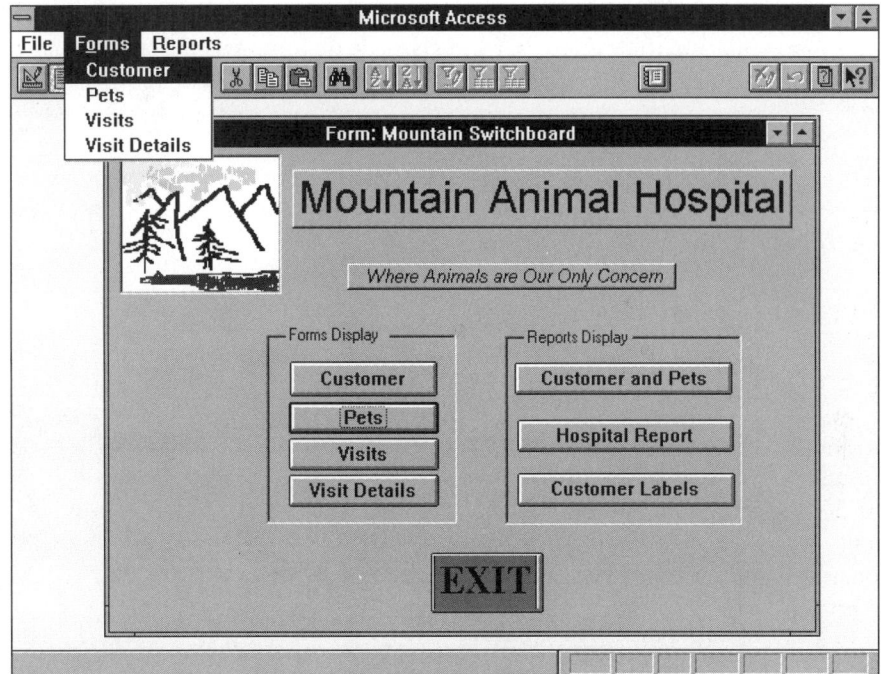

Figure 32-12: The custom drop-down menu bar.

Defining a single-bar drop-down menu

To create a drop-down menu for the bar menu prompt File, which has the single command Exit, follow these steps:

Steps:	Creating a Single-Choice Drop-Down Menu
Step 1.	Create a new macro.
Step 2.	Activate the Macro Name column by selecting the Macro Names button on the toolbar.
Step 3.	Type **Exit** in the first empty Macro Name cell.
Step 4.	Type **Close** in the Action cell or select the Close action from the pull-down menu.
Step 5.	Type **Form** in the Object Type action argument for the Close action or select Form from the pull-down menu.
Step 6.	Select Mountain Switchboard from the pull-down list in the Object Name action argument.

At the completion of these steps, your macro should look like the one in Figure 32-13.

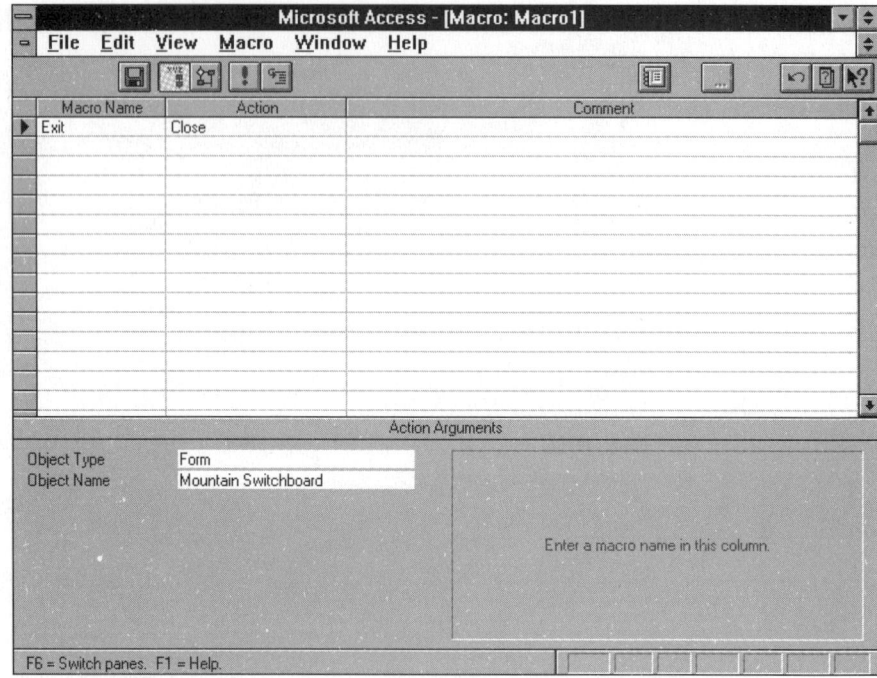

Figure 32-13: A group macro with a single macro to be used as a drop-down menu.

The macro in Figure 32-13 can now be saved to a macro file. For this example, save it to a macro file named Mountain File Menu.

Defining a multiple-bar drop-down menu

To create a drop-down menu with multiple bars, you also create a group macro. However, instead of creating a single macro in the macro group, you create a macro for each menu command (choice) of the drop-down menu. For example, to create the four-command drop-down menu for the menu bar prompt called Forms, follow these steps:

Steps:	Creating a Multiple-Bar Drop-Down Menu
Step 1.	Create a new macro and activate the Macro Name column.
Step 2.	Type **Customer** in the first empty Macro Name cell.
Step 3.	Type **OpenForm** in the Action cell or select the OpenForm action from the pull-down menu.
Step 4.	Type **Customer** in the Form Name action argument or select Customer from the pull-down menu.
Step 5.	Type **Pets** in the next empty Macro Name cell.

Chapter 32: Creating Switchboards, Menus, and Dialogs   **957**

Step 6. Type **OpenForm** in the Action cell or select the OpenForm action from the pull-down menu.

Step 7. Type **Pets** in the Form Name action argument or select Pets from the pull-down menu.

Repeat Steps 5 through 7 for the macro named Visits and the form named Adding General Pet Visit Info. Then repeat these steps for the macro named Visit Details and the form named Adding Visit Details. At the completion of these steps, your macro should look like the one in Figure 32-14.

Save the macro you just created with the name Mountain Forms Menu. You can now create the macro named Mountain Reports Menu, which will be used for the Reports prompt.

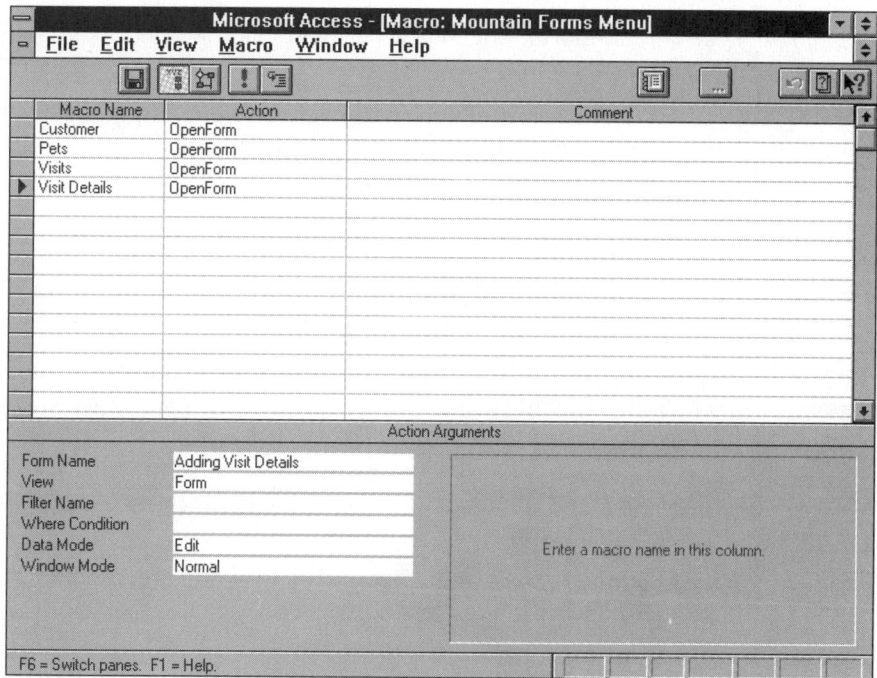

Figure 32-14: A group macro for a drop-down menu.

Adding options to a drop-down menu

As you work with macros for use in your custom drop-down menus, you'll want to take advantage of the special options for these menus. Access offers these two options for your drop-down menu:

- Separator lines — Lines separating the menu choices
- User-defined access keys — Mnemonic characters that you can assign

With the first of these options, you can place a line between two menu commands. The second option lets you define a letter from the menu prompt name that you select to access the menu. A typical example of this is the use of F to access the File menu in the Windows menu system. Note that the Windows method for identifying this key is to underline the letter within the menu name.

Next you create a drop-down menu for the menu bar prompt named Reports. You will add an access key for each prompt, and you'll add a line to separate the first command from the second. Follow these steps to complete this menu:

Steps: Creating a Drop-Down Menu with Options

Step 1. Create a new macro and activate the Macro Name column.

Step 2. Type **&Customers and Pets** in the first empty Macro Name cell.

Step 3. Type **OpenReport** in the Action cell or select the OpenReport action from the pull-down menu.

Step 4. Type **All Customers and Pets** in the Report Name action argument or select All Customers and Pets from the pull-down menu.

Step 5. Type **-** (hyphen) in the next empty Macro Name cell.

Step 6. Type **&Hospital Report** in the next empty Macro Name cell.

Step 7. Type **OpenReport** in the Action cell or select the OpenReport action from the pull-down menu.

Step 8. Type **Invoices** in the Report Name action argument or select Invoices from the pull-down menu.

Step 9. Type **Customer &Labels** in the next empty Macro Name cell.

Step 10. Type **OpenReport** in the Action cell or select the OpenReport action from the pull-down menu.

Step 11. Type **Customer Labels** in the Report Name action argument or select Customer Labels from the pull-down menu.

If you followed all 11 steps, your macro should look similar to the one in Figure 32-15. You should save this macro to a macro file named Mountain Reports Menu.

The macro group in Figure 32-15 will create a drop-down menu that should look similar to Figure 32-16. Notice that the letter C is underlined in the menu command Customer and Pets. Also notice that the two top choices are separated by a line.

Figure 32-15: Creating a macro that will display a menu with separating lines and access keys.

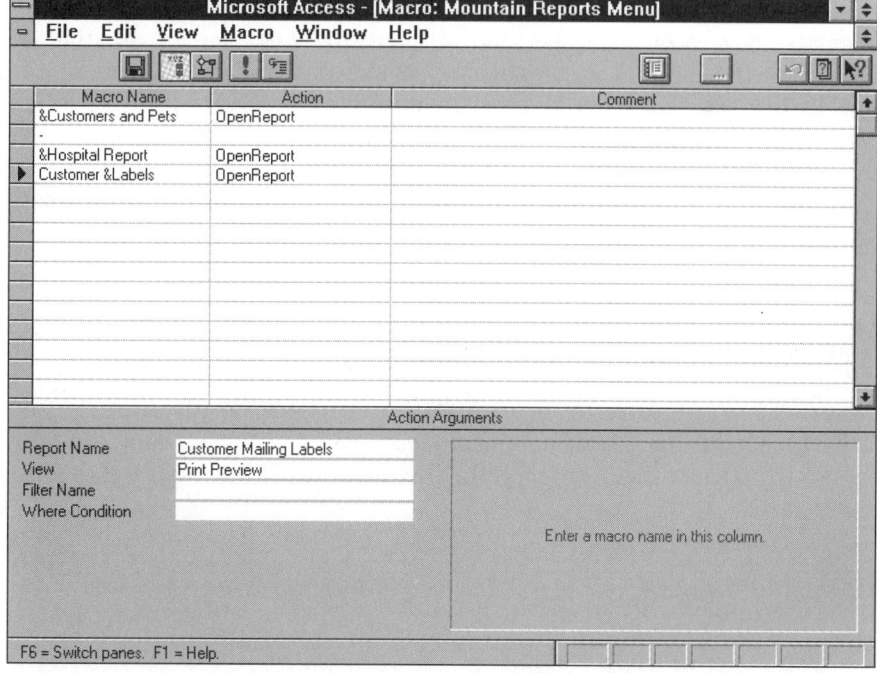

Figure 32-16: The drop-down menu with the options of separator lines and access keys.

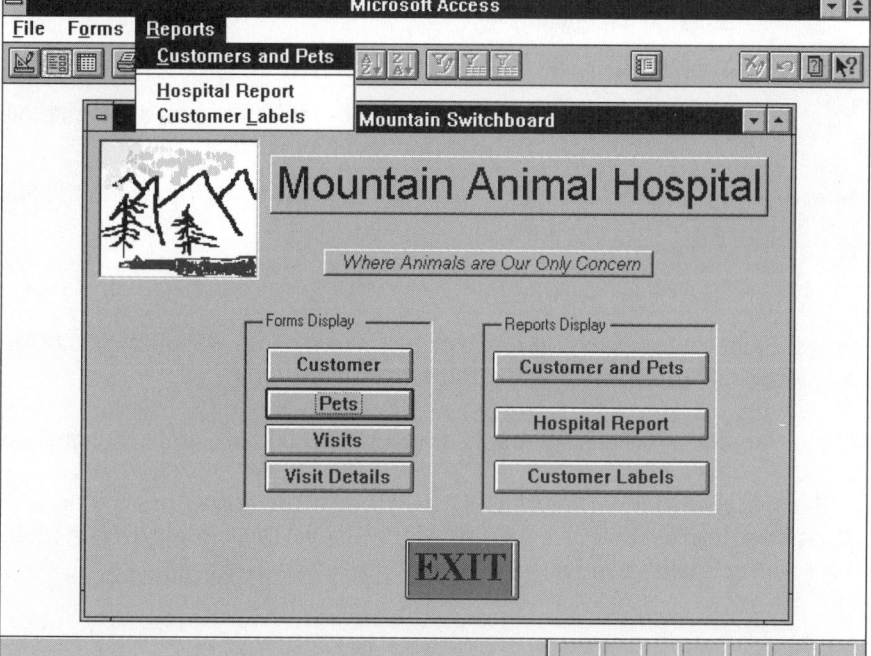

When you created the macro names in the preceding steps, you specified a letter as the access key by placing the ampersand (&) before the letter. Step 9 shows that the access key will be the letter *L* because the ampersand is immediately in front of this letter. To specify that you want a line between menu commands, you placed a hyphen (-) in the Macro Name cell in Step 5.

You can go back and add separator lines or access keys to your other menu commands by using these techniques.

Defining a menu bar

Now that you've created the drop-down menus, you are ready to create a macro that will be the menu bar. This menu macro will have an action for each drop-down menu macro. To create a menu bar with the three choices File, Forms, and Reports, follow these steps:

Steps:	Creating a Menu Bar for the Drop-Down Menus
Step 1.	Create a new macro.
Step 2.	Type **AddMenu** in the Action cell or select the AddMenu action from the pull-down menu.
Step 3.	Type **&File** in the Menu Name cell in the action arguments pane.
Step 4.	Select the Mountain File Menu macro from the pull-down menu in the Menu Macro Name cell in the action arguments pane.
Step 5.	Type **Select the Exit Choice to Close the Switchboard** in the Status Bar Text cell of the action arguments pane.

Repeat Steps 2 through 5 first for F&orms (macro name Mountain Forms Menu) and &Reports (macro name Mountain Reports Menu).

At the completion of these steps, your macro should look similar to Figure 32-17.

Notice that the macro in Figure 32-17 has three actions, one for each drop-down menu. Also notice that the action is the same for all three choices, which is AddMenu. The AddMenu action is used for building an Access menu bar.

Figure 32-17:
The macro for a menu bar.

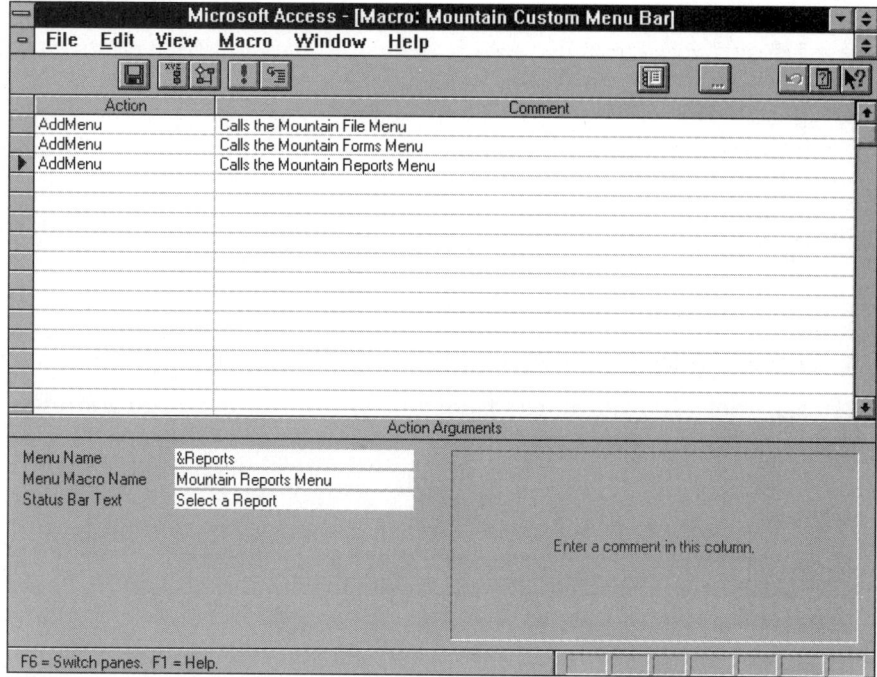

 You can also specify an access key for menu prompts. The user can select this access key just as all menu *hotkeys* are selected — by pressing the Alt key with the access key. For example, pressing Alt+F activates the File menu.

Save the macro you just created under the name Mountain Custom Menu Bar.

Attaching the menu bar to a form

You have now completed the drop-down menus and the menu bar named Mountain Custom Menu Bar to attach the drop-down menus to. You are now ready to attach the menu bar to a form.

To attach a menu bar to a form, open the form in design mode and set the On Menu property of the form to the menu bar macro name. To attach the menu bar named Mountain Custom Menu Bar to the switchboard form Mountain Switchboard, follow these steps:

Steps:	**Attaching a Menu Bar to a Form**
Step 1.	Open the form Mountain Switchboard in design mode.
Step 2.	Activate the property sheet by selecting the Properties button on the toolbar.
Step 3.	Click the small blank box to the left of the ruler (immediately below the toolbar).
	Access displays the title "Form" for the property sheet.
Step 4.	Click the Menu Bar event property of the property sheet.
Step 5.	Select the Mountain Customer Menu Bar from the pull-down menu (or type the menu bar name).

By following these steps, you have just attached the menu bar named Mountain Customer Menu Bar with its drop-down menus to the form. You should have a design screen similar to the one in Figure 32-18.

You are now ready to save the form and open it to see how the menus tie together.

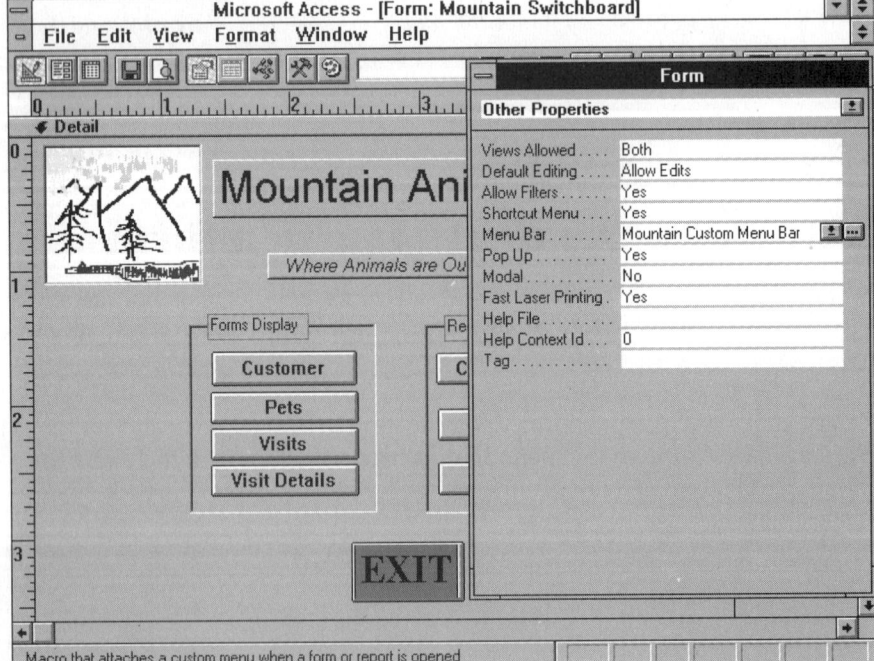

Figure 32-18: Attaching a menu bar to the form using the On Menu property.

The Access 2.0 Menu Builder

Until now, you have created the menu by hand. Access 2.0, though, has a Menu Builder that can help you create menus, drop-down menus, write (and save) the underlying macros, and attach the menu to a form. If you need to create a menu and attach it to a form, the Menu Builder enables you to do so automatically.

To run the Menu Builder and have it automatically attach the new menu to a form, activate the Property sheet for the form you want to attach a menu to, select Other properties, and then go to the menu bar property. In the Menu Bar field, *right* mouse click and select the Build button. Access starts the Menu Builder.

You can modify or add to existing menu bars in Access or create completely new menu bars for your custom applications. You can define the text for each pull-down menu and even define submenus or dialog box calls. You create each menu as a hierarchy. Figure 32-19 shows the menu bar that you just created typed into the Menu Builder.

As you define each menu item, you enter the text for the menu in the Caption text box. To designate hotkeys, precede the appropriate letter with an ampersand (&); the letter will appear underlined in the menu.

Figure 32-19: The Menu Builder screen.

Using the arrow buttons, you can rearrange or change the menu level. In other words, you can create various levels of pull-down submenus or top-level bar menu items. You can even enter a line separator by entering a single hyphen (-) on a line.

In the Action text box, you enter the type of action, such as DoMenuItem, RunCode, or RunMacro. The DoMenuItem has several arguments (see Figure 32-20) that, when entered, help determine which menu item to run when an item is selected: You pick the standard Access menu bar and the submenu command. When you want Access to perform an action other than drop down a subordinate menu (which requires no action) or enact a menu item, you code it in a module or enter it in a macro. (You simply enter the macro name as you would in any event property.)

When you are finished, the Menu Builder creates a series of macros: one for the menu bar and a separate macro for each pull-down menu in the menu bar hierarchy. Figure 32-21 shows the database container displaying these macros and the Forms macro open.

Figure 32-20: Entering actions for a menu item.

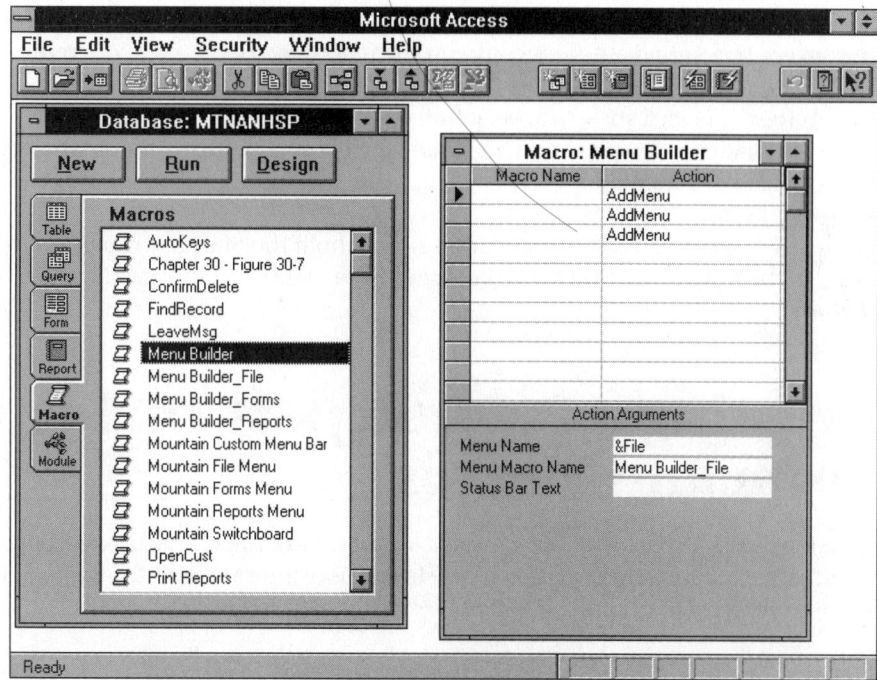

Figure 32-21:
The final macros.

Running a macro automatically on starting Access

After you create the switchboard, a menu bar, and the associated drop-down menu, you may want Access to open the form automatically every time you open the database. You can create an automatic macro named AutoExec that performs the actions necessary to accomplish this. To create an AutoExec macro to open the switchboard automatically, follow these steps:

Steps:	**Creating an AutoExec Macro**
Step 1.	Create a new macro (you'll name it AutoExec later).
Step 2.	Type **Hourglass** (or select the action) in the first empty Action cell.
Step 3.	Type **Minimize** (or select the action) in the next empty Action cell.
Step 4.	Type **OpenForm** (or select the action) in the next empty Action cell.
Step 5.	Type **Mountain Switchboard** (or select the switchboard form name) in the Form name cell in the action arguments pane.

Save the macro with the name Autoexec. After you save this macro with the name Autoexec, Access will automatically run the macro every time you open the database.

The Autoexec macro shows three actions. The Hourglass action displays an hourglass while the macro is processing. The Minimize action minimizes the Database window. The OpenForm action opens the switchboard.

To bypass an Autoexec macro, simply hold the Shift key down while selecting the database name from the Access File menu.

Creating a Print Report Dialog Box Form and Macros

A dialog box is also a form, but, unlike a switchboard, the dialog box usually displays information, captures a user entry, or lets the user interact with the system. In this section, you create a complex dialog box that prints reports and labels.

By using a form and some macros, you can create a dialog box that controls printing of your reports. This dialog box can even display a list of pets and their owners (see Figure 32-22), so you can print only a single page of the Pets Directory without having to change the query.

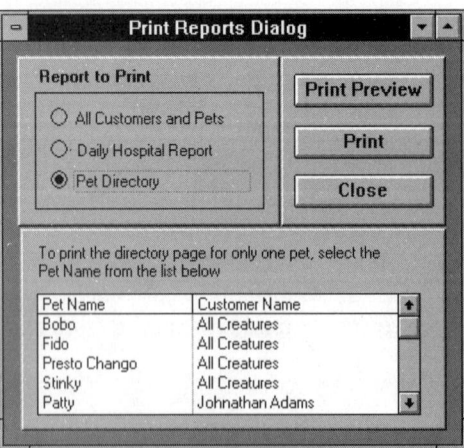

Figure 32-22: A Print Reports dialog box.

This dialog box is more complex than a switchboard but uses the same types of Access objects, which include the following:

- A form
- Form controls and properties
- Macros

Creating a form for a macro

The form you use in this example displays the various controls. There are three basic sections to the form.

The upper left corner of the form contains three option buttons, which are placed within an option group. The option buttons let you select one of the three listed reports. Each of the reports is already created and can be seen in the Database window. If you select All Customers and Pets or the Daily Hospital Report, you can print or print preview that report. If you select Pet Directory, as shown in Figure 32-22, you see a list box of pets and their owners. You can then choose a pet name for a printout from the Pet Directory report for only that one pet. If you don't choose a pet name, records for all pets are printed from the Pet Directory report.

The upper right corner of the form contains three buttons. Each of these buttons runs a different macro in the Print Report macro library. The first option button, Print Preview, runs a macro that opens the selected report in a Print Preview window. The second option button, Print, runs a macro that will print the selected report to the default printer. The last button, Close, simply closes the form without printing any reports.

The first step is to create a blank form. You can create the form and properly size it by following these steps:

Steps:	Creating, Sizing, and Coloring a New Blank Form
Step 1.	Create a new blank form unbound to any table or query.
Step 2.	Resize the form to 3½ inches x 3 inches.
Step 3.	Change the Back color to dark grey.

Three rectangles are placed on the form to give it a distinctive look. You can create the three rectangles, as shown in Figure 32-22, by following these steps:

Steps:	Creating Three Rectangles on the Form
Step 1.	Select the Rectangle button on the toolbox and click the Lock button.
Step 2.	Using Figure 32-22 as a guide, create three separate rectangles.
	Each rectangle in this example is shown with the raised special effect. To create this effect, follow these steps:
Step 3.	Select a rectangle.
Step 4.	Change the Back color to light grey.
Step 5.	Click the Raised special effect button.
Step 6.	Click the Clear button for Border color.
Step 7.	Repeat Steps 3 through 6 for the second and third rectangles.
	Finally, to enhance the raised special effect, drag each rectangle away from the adjacent rectangles so that the darker background of the form shows between the rectangle borders. You may need to resize one of the rectangles to line up the edges.

Creating the option group

After you create the form and the special effects, you can then create the necessary controls. The first set of controls is the option group. In Chapter 19, we described how to use the Option Group Wizard to create option buttons. To create the option group and option buttons, follow the following steps and use Figure 32-22 as a guide. In this example, the option group buttons are not bound to a field — they are used for the dialog box selection, not to enter data.

Steps:	Creating an Option Group and Option Buttons by Using the Wizard
Step 1.	Select the Option Group button from the toolbox, making sure that the Control Wizard icon is on.
Step 2.	Draw an option group rectangle within the upper left rectangle, as shown in Figure 32-23.
Step 3.	Enter **All Customers and Pets**, **Daily Hospital Report**, and **Pet Directory** as three separate labels in the first Option Group Wizard.

Chapter 32: Creating Switchboards, Menus, and Dialogs

Step 4. Click the Finish button to go to the last wizard screen.

Step 5. Click the Finish button again.

Your option buttons and the option group appear in the first rectangle. You may need to move or resize the option group box to fit properly (see Figure 32-23).

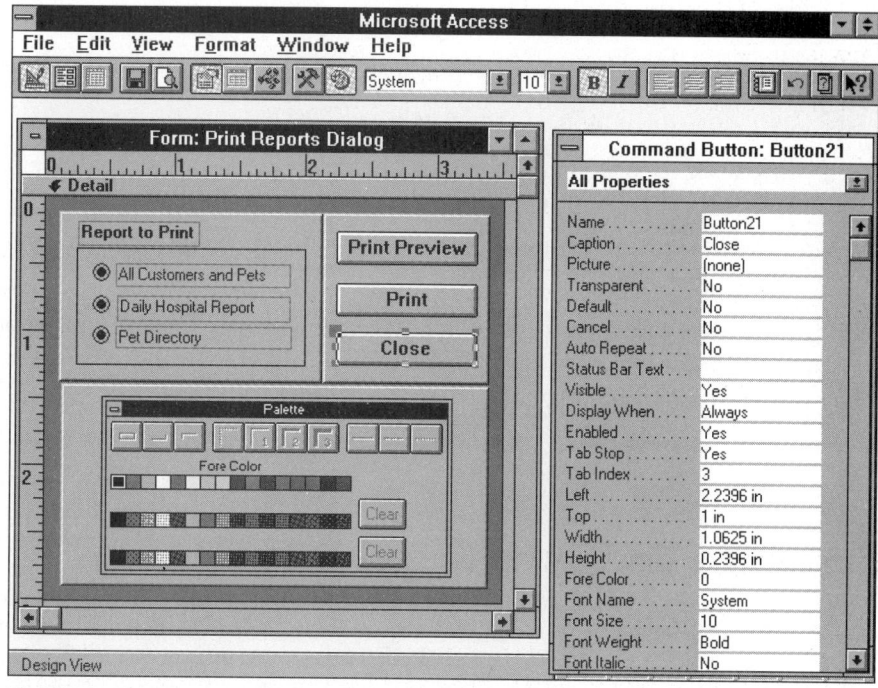

Figure 32-23: The command buttons in the Print dialog box.

Creating command buttons

After you complete the option group and the option buttons, you can create the command buttons. These are the pushbuttons that trigger the actions for your dialog box. As you can see in Figure 32-23, there are three buttons:

- Print Preview — Displays the selected report in the Print Preview window
- Print — Prints the selected report to the default print device
- Close — Closes the dialog box

To create each command button, follow the next steps. Remember that the command button icon is the last button in the toolbox. Because each button will be the same size, you will duplicate the second and third buttons from the first.

Steps: Creating Three Command Buttons and Changing Their Captions

Step 1. Select the Command Button in the toolbox.

Step 2. Create the first command button as shown in Figure 32-23.

Step 3. Select Edit⇨Duplicate to duplicate the first command button.

Step 4. Move the button as shown in Figure 32-23.

Step 5. Select Edit⇨Duplicate to duplicate the second command button.

Step 6. Move the button as shown in Figure 32-23.

You now need to change the command button captions. The remaining steps show how to make these changes.

Step 7. Select the first command button and change the caption property to **Print Preview**.

Step 8. Select the second command button and change the Caption property to **Print**.

Step 9. Select the third command button and change the Caption property to **Close**.

Creating a list box on the print report form

The last control that you need in the dialog box is the list box that displays the pet name and customer name when the Pet Directory option button is selected. To create the list box, follow these steps, using Figure 32-24 as a guide. In this example, You'll create the list box without the wizard.

Steps: Creating a List Box

Step 1. Select the List Box button from the toolbox. Make sure that the Control Wizard icon is off.

Step 2. Using Figure 32-24 as a guide, create the list box rectangle.

Step 3. Move the label control to a position above the list box.

Step 4. Resize the label control so that the bottom right corner is just above the list box, as shown in Figure 32-24.

Step 5. Using the palette, change the Back color of the label to light grey to match the background of the bottom rectangle.

Chapter 32: Creating Switchboards, Menus, and Dialogs   971

Step 6. Change the Caption property for the list box by clicking label the field caption in the label itself and typing **To print the directory page for only one pet, select the Pet Name from the list below.** The text in the label will automatically word wrap as you type.

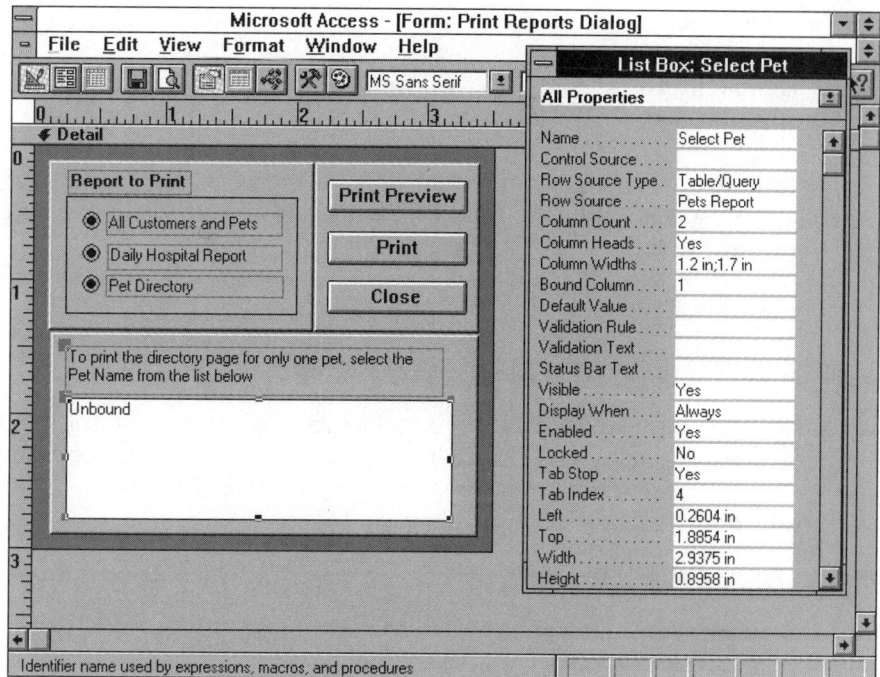

Figure 32-24: The completed form.

After the list box and label are created, you must define the columns of the list box. To define the columns and data source for the list box, follow these steps, using Figure 32-24 as a guide:

Steps: Defining the List Box Columns

Step 1. Change the Name property to **Select Pet.**

Step 2. Make sure that the Row Source Type indicates Table/Query.

Step 3. Change the Row Source to **Pets Report.**

The Pets Report must be created before you try to run this form. The Pets Report is a simple query that requires an interesting technique to create (see the sidebar "The Pets Report Query for the Print Report Form List Box" for more information).

Step 4.	Change the Column Count to **2**.
Step 5.	Change Column Heads to **Yes**.
Step 6.	Change the Column Widths to **1.2, 1.7**.
Step 7.	Make sure that the Bound Column property indicates 1.

Before continuing, you should save the form. Save the file but leave the form on-screen by selecting the menu option File⇒Save. Name the form Print Reports Dialog.

When the form is completed, you are half done. The next task is to create each of the macros you need and create the macro library. When you complete that task, you can add the macros to the correct event properties in the form.

Creating the print macros

As you've learned, macros are attached to the events of controls or objects. These events include entering, exiting, updating, or selecting a control. In this example, macros are attached to several controls and objects. Table 32-3 shows the macros that you create for this example and how they will be run.

Table 32-3
Macros for the Print Reports Form

Macro Name	Attached to Control/Object	Attached to Property	Description
Show List	Form	On Open	Displays list box if the third option button is on
Show List	Option group	After Update	Displays list box if the third button is selected
Print Preview	Print Preview button	On Click	Displays selected report in print preview mode when Print Preview button is selected
Print	Print button	On Click	Prints selected report if Print button is selected
Close	Close button	On Click	Closes form if Close button is selected

The Pets Report Query for the PrintReport Form List Box

The Pets Report is a simple query that has the Customer and Pets tables related by the Customer Number field. The query has two fields displayed: Pet Name from the Pets table and Customer Name from the Customer table. The data is sorted first by Customer Number and second by Pet Name. Figure 32-25 shows the partial datasheet for this list box.

You can see in Figure 32-25 that the Pet Name field is in the first column and the Customer Name field is in the second column. The data is sorted first by the customer number and second by the pet name. As you learned previously, to sort data by two fields, you must place the fields in the Query Design window in the order you want the two fields sorted in. To sort by the customer number first and then by the pet name, you must place the Customer Number field first in the query but not select it. You then place the Customer Name field third in the query and select it. The query would place Customer Name first in the datasheet. The query design is shown in Figure 32-26.

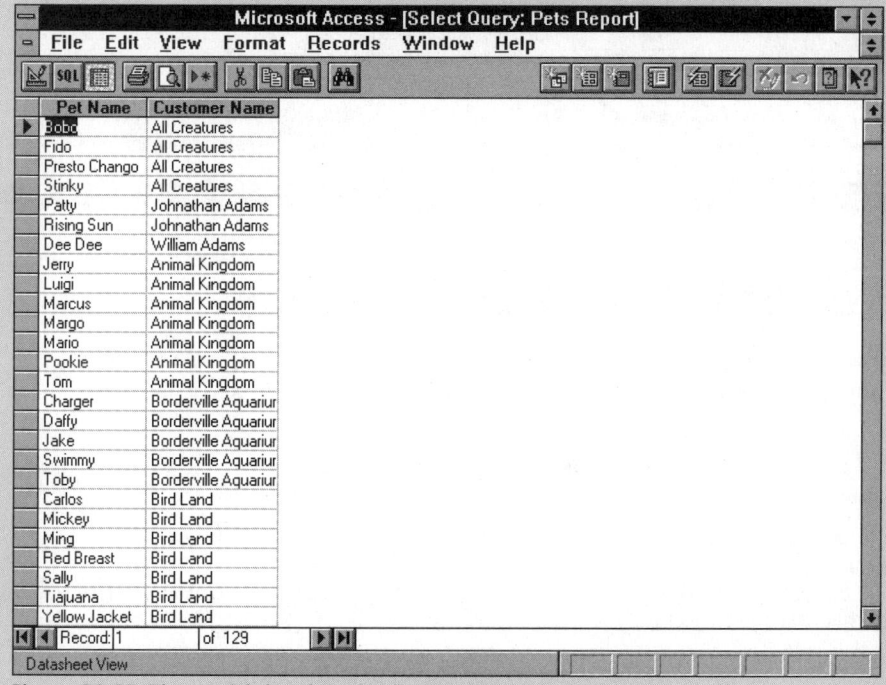

Figure 32-25: The partial datasheet for the Pets Report query.

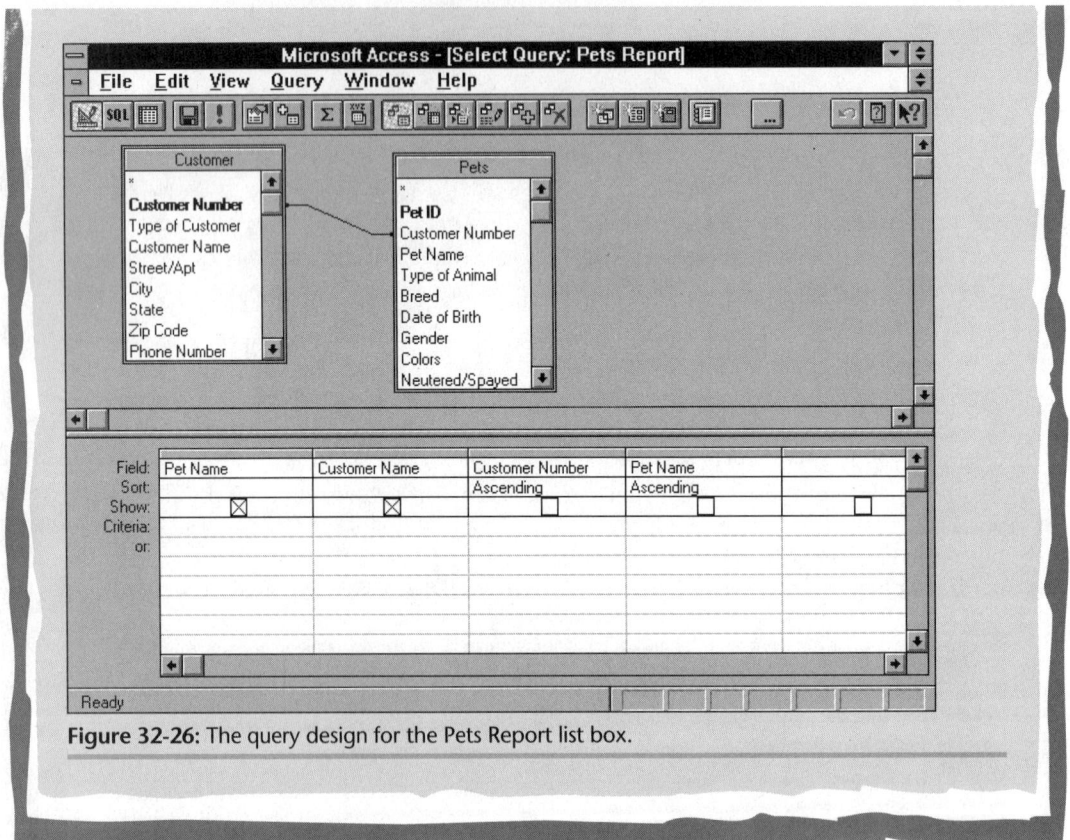

Figure 32-26: The query design for the Pets Report list box.

Creating the Print Macro Library

In the last two chapters, you learned that creating a macro library is the same as creating any macro. You can create this macro library by following these steps:

Steps:	Defining the Macro Library
Step 1.	From the Form window, select File⇒New⇒Macro to create a new macro.
Step 2.	Select View⇒Macro Names or select the Macro Names button in the toolbar, to display the Macro Names column.
Step 3.	Select View⇒Conditions or select the Conditions button in the toolbar, to display the Condition column.

Chapter 32: Creating Switchboards, Menus, and Dialogs

The Macro Names and Conditions menu options add two columns to the basic Macro window. You will use these columns to enter more parameters into the macro. The Macro Name column is used for creating the individual macro entry points in a macro library. The Condition column is used for determining whether the action in the Action column should be run, based on the condition. To create the macro, follow these steps:

Steps: Defining the Macro Library

Step 1. In the second row of the Macro Name column, type **Show List.**

Step 2. In the fifth row of the Macro Name column, type **Print Preview.**

Step 3. In the eighth row of the Macro Name column, type **Print.**

Step 4. In the eleventh row of the Macro Name column, type **Close.**

Step 5. Select File⇨Save As and name the macro **Print Reports.**

You can see these macros correctly created in Figure 32-27.

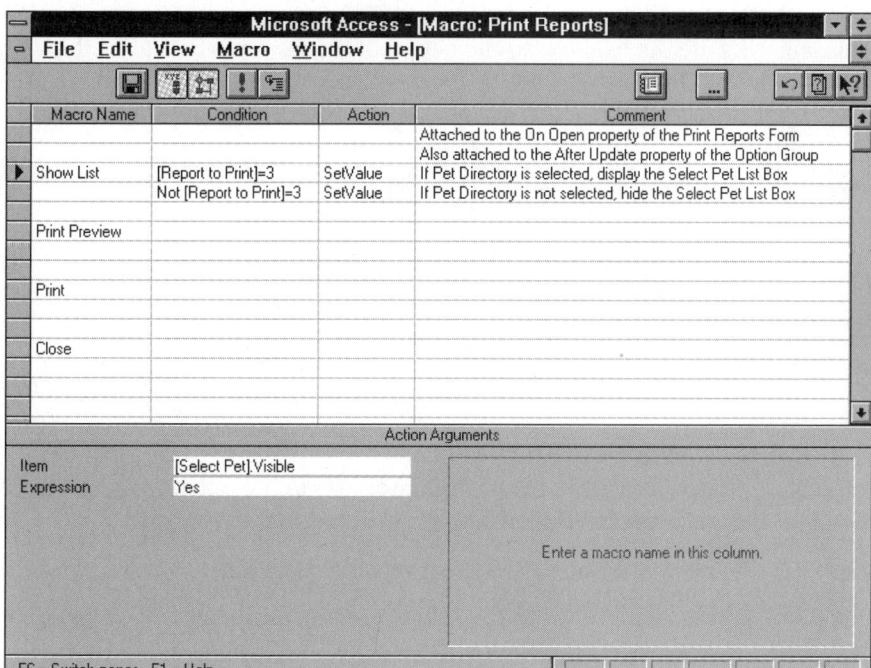

Figure 32-27: The Show List macro.

Creating the Show List macro

The Show List macro either displays or hides the list box that lists the pet names and customer names. This macro is triggered from both the form object and the option group control through use of the SetValue macro command. The SetValue macro command lets you set a property of a control in the form. In this example, the list box is named Select Pet. The Visible action argument is set to Yes to display the list box or No to hide the list box.

There will need to be two conditions for the Show List macro — the first condition if the third option button has been selected and the second condition if it has not been selected. The Macro Name column has already been set to Show List.

In the first line of the Show List macro, you will set the Condition column to [Report to Print]=3 to reflect the third option button being chosen from the option group. This line will display the list box, so the action of the macro is set to SetValue, the Item action argument is set to [Select Pet].Visible, and the Expression action argument is set to Yes. Figure 32-27 displays these settings.

You can also see the second line of the Show List macro and comments in Figure 32-27. Notice in the second line that the Condition column indicates that the third option button in the option group not chosen and is therefore set to Not [Report to Print]=3. This line will hide the list box, so the action of the macro is SetValue, the Item property is set to [Select Pet].Visible, and the Expression property is set to No. To create the macro, follow these steps:

Steps:	Creating the Show List Macro
Step 1.	Type the first two lines in the Comment column, as shown at the top of Figure 32-27.
Step 2.	Move the cursor to the first line of the Show List macro row.
Step 3.	Place the cursor in the Condition column and type **[Report to Print]=3**.
Step 4.	Place the cursor in the Action column and either select or type **SetValue**.
Step 5.	Press F6 to move to the Item property in the Action Arguments pane and type **[Select Pet].Visible**.
Step 6.	Move to the Expression property and type **Yes**.
Step 7.	Press F6 to return to the Action column and then move to the Comments column.
Step 8.	Enter the comments in the Comment column, as shown in Figure 32-27.
Step 9.	Move your cursor to the second line of the Show List macro row.

Chapter 32: Creating Switchboards, Menus, and Dialogs

Step 10.	In the Condition column, type **Not [Report to Print]=3**.
Step 11.	In the Action column, type (or select) **SetValue**.
Step 12.	Press F6 to move to the Item box in the Action Arguments pane and type **[Select Pet].Visible**.
Step 13.	Move to the Expression property and type **No**.
Step 14.	Press F6 to return to the Action column and then move to the Comments column.
Step 15.	Enter the comments in the Comment column, as shown in Figure 32-27.

When you complete the Show List macro, you can enter the calls to the macro in the form events properties. After this task is completed, you can test the macro. Before continuing, select File⇨Save to save the Print Reports macro library and leave it open on-screen.

Entering the Show List macro calls

You are now ready to enter the macro calls for the Show List macro. This macro is called from two places:

- The On Open property of the form object
- The After Update property of the option group control

As you've learned, these properties are found in the property sheet of the form. To enter the two macro calls, follow these steps:

Steps:	Entering the Show List Macro Calls
Step 1.	From the Print Reports Macro window, select Window⇨2 Form: Print Reports Dialog.
Step 2.	Make sure that the property sheet is displayed. If not, click on the Properties button in the toolbar.
Step 3.	Display the form's property sheet by clicking on the white square next to the ruler's 0 mark.
Step 4.	Enter **Print Reports.Show List** into the On Open property of the Form property sheet.
Step 5.	Click the Option Group control.
Step 6.	Enter **Print Reports.Show List** in the After Update property of the Option Group property sheet, as shown in Figure 32-28.

Part V: Applications in Access

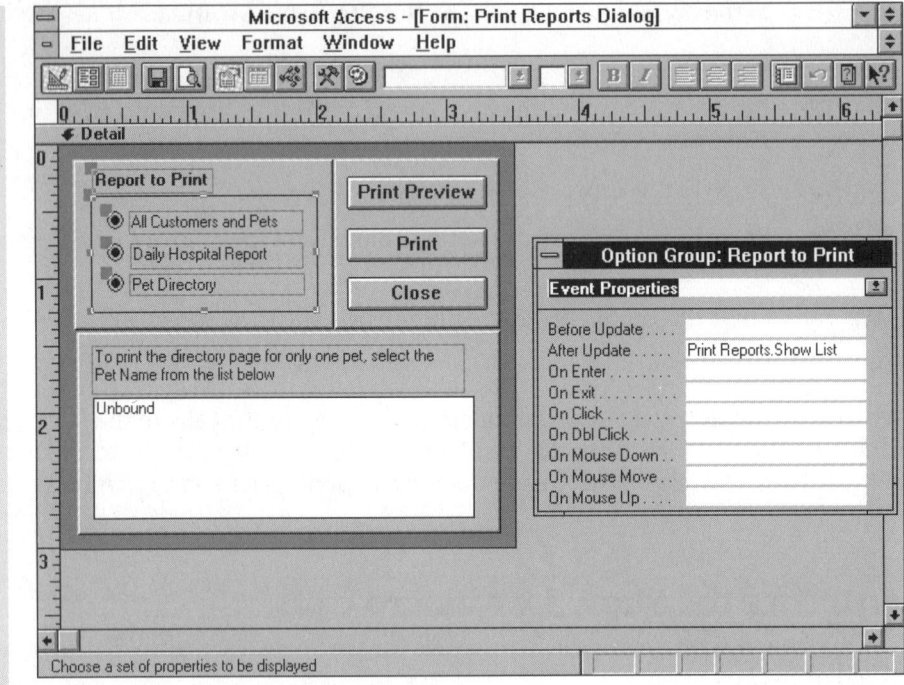

Figure 32-28: Entering the macro call.

You can test this macro by clicking the Form button in the toolbar. As you click the first and second option buttons, the list box should become invisible. When you select the third option button, the list box should appear. Return to the Design window before continuing.

Creating the Print Preview macro

The Print Preview macro is the next macro you need to create. You can switch to the Macro window by selecting Window⇨3 Macro: Print Reports. This macro is fairly complicated, although it uses only three different macro commands. As you enter the macro commands, you may need to add more lines to the Macro window. Select Edit⇨Insert Row whenever you need to add a new row to the Macro window.

 You must first select a row to add a new row.

Figure 32-29 shows the completed Print Preview, Print, and Close macros in the Macro window. You can enter all the comments and create the first macro row by following these steps:

Figure 32-29: Creating the Print Preview macro.

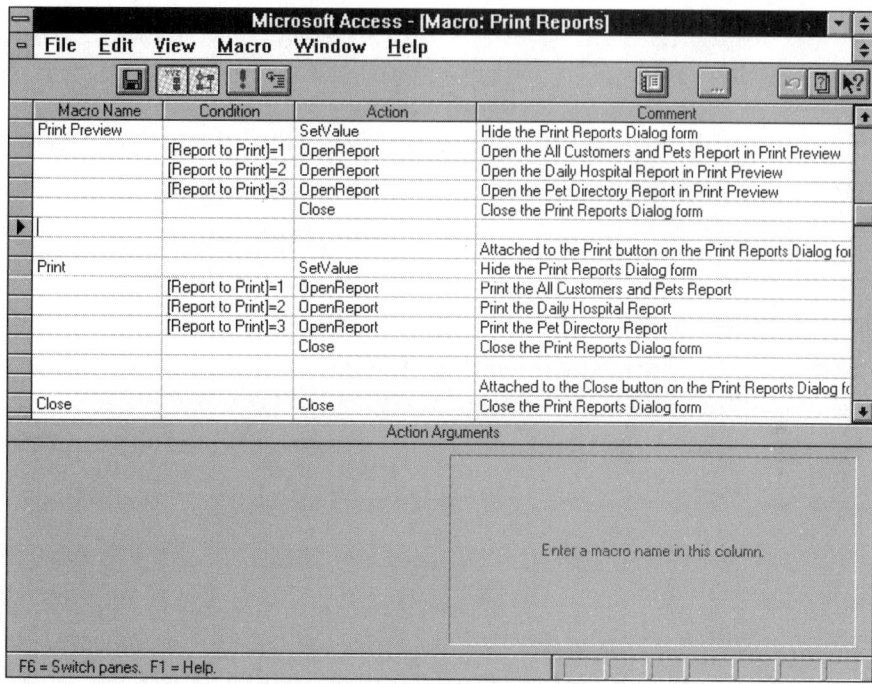

Steps: Creating the First Print Preview Macro Row

Step 1. Type all the lines in the Comment colum, as shown in Figure 32-29.

Step 2. Move the cursor to the first line of the Print Preview macro row.

Step 3. In the Action column, type (or select) **SetValue**.

Step 4. Press F6 to move to the Item property of the Action Arguments pane and type **Visible**.

Step 5. Move to the Expression box in the Action Arguments pane and type **No**.

Because no control is specified, it defaults to the form itself. This will hide the entire Form window when the Print Reports macro is started.

The next three lines of the macro determine the actions to be taken when the Print Preview button is selected for each of the possible option button choices. The first two choices simply display the selected report in a print preview mode. The third choice displays a report by selecting the pet name chosen from the list box. To create the next row, follow these steps:

Steps: Creating the First OpenReport Row of the Print Preview Macro

Step 1. Move your cursor to the second row of the Print Preview macro.

Step 2. In the Condition column, type **[Report to Print]=1.**

Step 3. In the Action column, type (or select) **OpenReport.**

The OpenReport macro command opens the report specified in the Action Arguments pane of the Macro window.

Step 4. Press F6 to move to the Report Name box in the Action Arguments pane of the Print Preview macro and type **All Customers and Pets.**

Step 5. Move to the View box in the Action Arguments pane and type **Print Preview.**

Step 6. Press F6 to return to the Action column.

These action arguments specify to open the report named All Customers and Pets in a Print Preview window. The second Print row of the Print Preview macro is very similar to the first, except that you must reference the second option button being selected. To create the next row, follow these steps:

Steps: Creating the Second OpenReport Row of the Print Preview Macro

Step 1. Move the cursor to the third row of the Print Preview macro.

Step 2. In the Condition column, type **[Report to Print]=2.**

Step3. In the Action column, type (or select) **OpenReport.**

Step 4. Press F6 to move to the Report Name box in the Action Arguments pane and type **Daily Hospital Report.**

Step 5. Move to the View box in the Action Arguments pane and type **Print Preview.**

Step 6. Press F6 to return to the Action column.

The third OpenReport row contains an extra action argument that the first two rows do not use. The Pet Directory report must use the results of the List Box selection to determine whether to print the entire Pets Directory report or print only the report for the specific pet selected. To create the next row, follow these steps:

Chapter 32: Creating Switchboards, Menus, and Dialogs

Steps: Creating the Third OpenReport Row of the Print Preview Macro

Step 1. Move the cursor to the fourth row of the Print Preview macro.

Step 2. In the Condition column, type **[Report to Print]=3**.

Step 3. In the Action column, type (or select) **OpenReport**.

Step 4. Press F6 to move to the Report Name box in the Action Arguments pane and type **Pet Directory**.

Step 5. Move to the View box in the Action Arguments pane and type **Print Preview**.

Step 6. Move to the Where Condition and type **=IIF(Forms![Print Reports Dialog]![Select Pet]Is Null,"","[Pet Name] = Forms![Print Reports Dialog]![Select Pet]")**. This entry is shown in Figure 32-30 in a Zoom box.

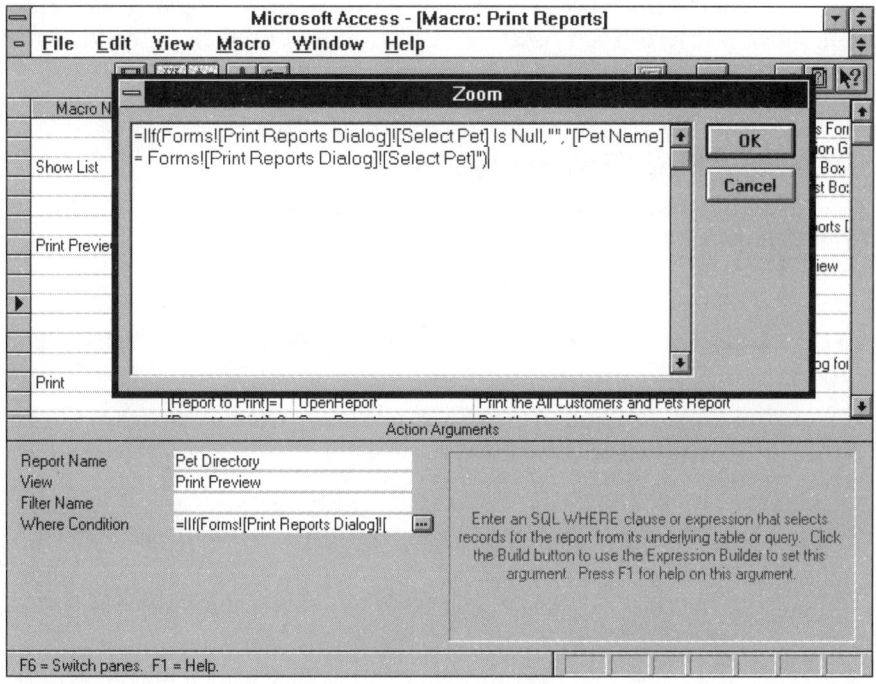

Figure 32-30: Using the Where Condition action argument.

The Where Condition specifies the condition when the pet name is selected. The condition has two parts. The first part of the IIF function handles the condition when no pet name is selected. The first part of the IIF forms the object hierarchy. The hierarchy is as follows:

Object	Forms
Form name	Print Reports Dialog
Control name	Select Pet (the list box)
Selection	Is Null

 Each of the hierarchy objects is separated with an exclamation mark (!).

If there is no selection, all the pet records are used. The second half of the IIF function is used when a pet name is selected. The second half of the function sets the value of Pet Name to the value chosen in the list box control.

Creating the Print macro

You can create all the macro code for the Print macro by copying each line from the Print Preview macro. Then substitute **Print** for Print Preview in the View box of the Action Arguments pane for each Open Report action.

Creating the Close macro

The Close macro simply uses Close for the action. Enter **Form** for the Object Type and **Print Reports Dialog** for the Action Arguments.

Entering the Print Preview, Print, and Close macro calls

You use the command buttons to trigger an action. Each uses the On Click property. To enter the three macro calls, follow these steps:

Steps:	Entering the Print Preview, Print, and Close Macro Calls
Step 1.	From the Print Reports Macro window, select Window⇨2 Form: Print Reports Dialog.
Step 2.	Make sure that the property sheet is displayed. If not, click the Properties button in the toolbar.
Step 3.	Display the Print Preview command button property by clicking the Print Preview button.
Step 4.	Enter **Print Reports.Print Preview** in the On Click property of the button's property sheet, as shown in Figure 32-31.

Chapter 32: Creating Switchboards, Menus, and Dialogs

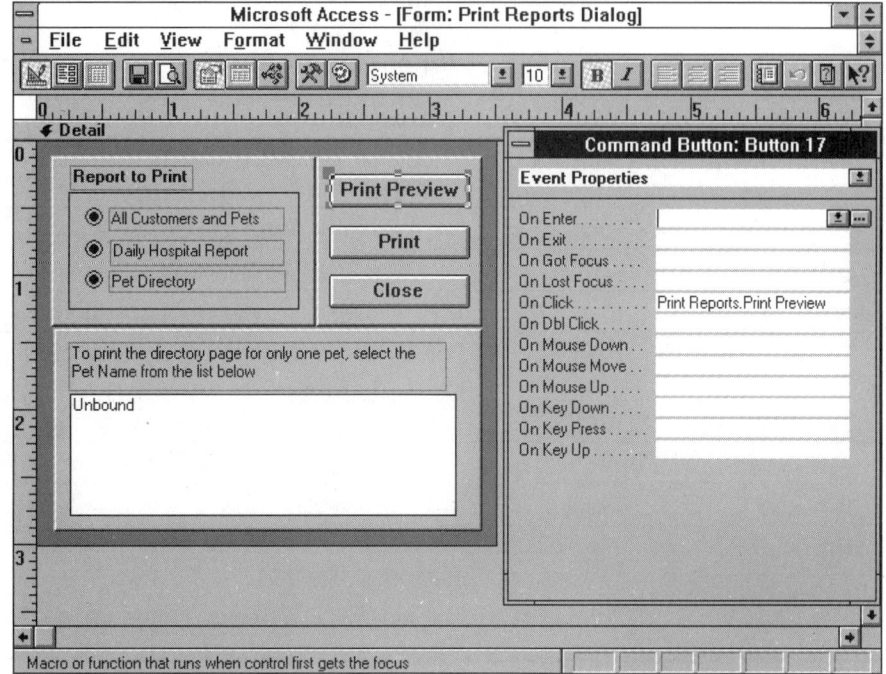

Figure 32-31: Entering the Print Preview macro call into the command button's property sheet.

Step 5. Display the Print command button property sheet by clicking the Print button.

Step 6. Enter **Print Reports.Print** in the On Click property of the button's property sheet.

Step 7. Display the Close command button property sheet by clicking the Close button.

Step 8. Enter **Print Reports.Close** into the On Click property of the button's property sheet.

Sizing the dialog and changing form properties

The last step in creating a dialog box is to change the Form window properties and size and place the window. You need to set several form properties. The list of properties and their explanations are shown in Table 32-4.

Table 32-4
Properties for a Form Dialog Box

Property	Value	Description
Default View	Single Form	Displays the form as a single form. This value is necessary for forms that take up less than half a page.
Views Allowed	Form	The user cannot switch into datasheet mode.
Scroll Bars	Neither	Scroll bars should be omitted in a dialog box.
Navigation Buttons	No	Does not display record navigation buttons.
Record Selectors	No	Does not display the standard record selectors at the bottom left of the form.
Auto Resize	Yes	Automatically resizes the form when opened.
Auto Center	Yes	Automatically centers the form when opened.
Border Style	Dialog	Makes border nonsizable.
Pop Up	Yes	Allows the form to be displayed on top of other windows as a pop-up dialog box.
Modal	Yes	The user must make a choice before leaving the dialog box.

The Form property sheet is shown in Figure 32-32, while the final form is shown in Figure 32-33.

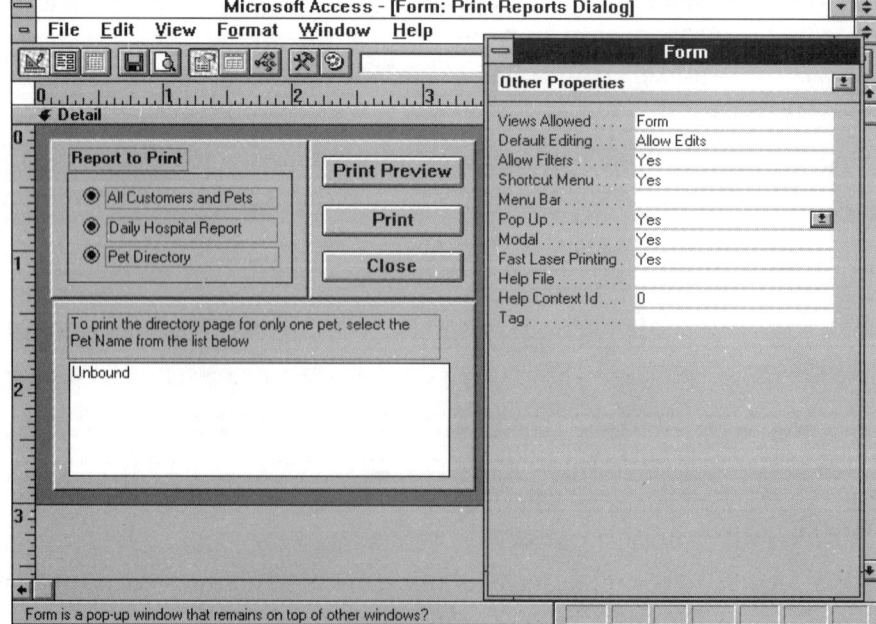

Figure 32-32: The Form property sheet with properties entered for a pop-up dialog box.

Chapter 32: Creating Switchboards, Menus, and Dialogs

 You should set the Pop Up property to No if the dialog will call any other windows. If this property is set to Yes, the dialog box is always displayed on top and you can't get to other windows without first closing the dialog box.

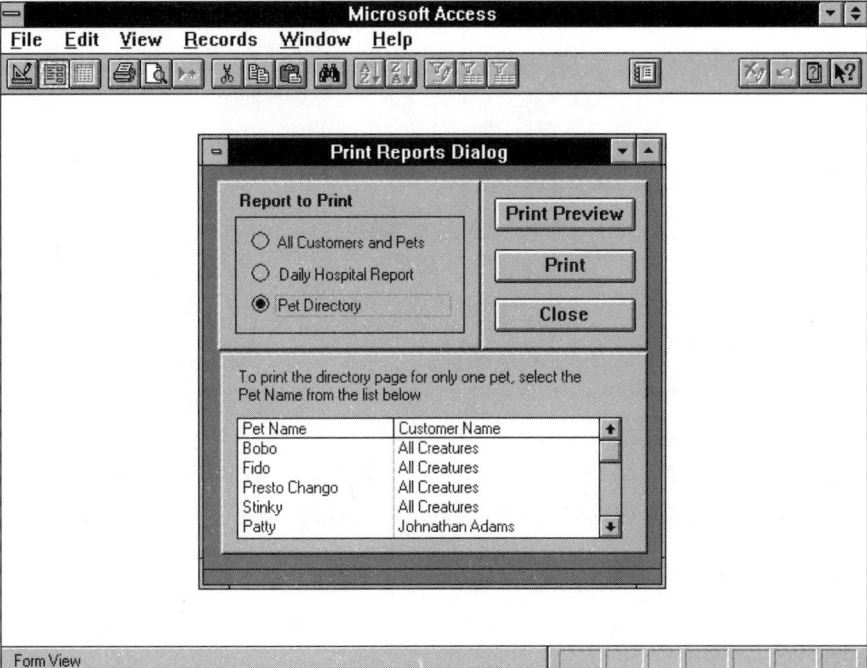

Figure 32-33: Displaying the final Print Reports dialog box.

- -

Summary

In this chapter, you learned how to create switchboards and dialog boxes, using an Access form. You also learned how to create your own custom menu. The following points were discussed:

- Switchboards are forms that usually contain command buttons.
- Switchboards are used as menus to help you navigate within your system.
- You can create command buttons by using the toolbox, by dragging a macro onto a form, or by using the Command Button Wizard.
- Command buttons trigger macros through several properties.
- The best way to create multiple command buttons that are all the same size is by duplicating the first button you created.
- You link a command button to a macro by entering the macro name in the proper event (On) property.

- You can create macro actions by entering them into the Macro window, by selecting them from the action pull-down menu, or by dragging a form or report into a macro action cell.

- You can have a command button display a picture instead of a text caption by entering the bitmap name into the command button's Picture property or by using the Picture Builder.

- Access lets you create custom bar menus through the use of macros.

- Each drop-down menu must be a separate macro. You can specify bar separators and hotkeys in a menu.

- You can activate a custom bar menu by entering a macro name in the On Menu property of a form or report.

- The Access 2.0 Menu Builder simplifies creating a menu.

- You can create a macro that runs automatically when you open a database by naming the macro Autoexec.

- You can bypass a macro that runs automatically by holding down the Shift key when you open the database window.

- A dialog box is nothing more than a form that is used as a pop-up window and usually contains various controls, such as option buttons, list boxes, and command buttons.

- A dialog box's pop-up property should be set to No if you are going to open any other windows from the dialog box.

As you have seen in the last few chapters, macros provide powerful alternatives to programming. In the next and final chapter in this book, you will get a quick introduction to modules and Access Basic.

Next Steps — Modules and Access Basic

CHAPTER 33

In This Chapter

- About the Module window
- Capabilities of modules
- How to create a module
- How to run a module

Occasionally, with the forms, reports, controls, and macros that you create, you can't do exactly what you have in mind. But with Access Basic, a powerful language, you can write programming code to accomplish everything you want to do.

Although this book is not intended to teach Access Basic, Access does offer a programming environment. And this environment can be used for creating modules.

Access Basic Programming

Access is a productive environment for working with your databases. It has ample tools to let you create and use tables, forms, queries, and reports. It even has a rich array of commands and functions that you can use when working with objects such as queries and forms.

Access offers flexible and powerful macro abilities, letting you automate many of the processes within your database. You can create menus, switchboards, and dialog boxes that tie all your objects together.

Added to all this power is Access Basic, a programming language. Access Basic, designed to extend the capabilities of Access, offers power beyond the scope of macros.

Access Basic is a true structured language that gives you the added ability to perform conditional and repetitive constraints. You can create routines and functions by using familiar programming syntax, such as If ... Then ... ElseIf ..., For ... Next, and Do While ... Loop.

Why Use Modules?

At times, you need to perform some action or use a function that cannot be done through the user interface, even with macros. You may find yourself saying, "Boy, I wish I had a function that would . . ." or "There just has to be a function that will let me. . . ."

At other times, you find that you are continually putting the same formula or expression into a query or filter. You may find yourself saying, "I'm tired of typing this formula into . . ." or "Doggone it, I typed the wrong formula in this. . . ."

Both of these scenarios sound like good examples of when to use Access modules. By using Access to create modules, you can accomplish these tasks:

- Write your own functions
- Build sophisticated database applications
- Further automate interaction between objects

Modules and Procedures

Using the last Database window object discussed in this book — the module — you can create and store Access Basic code.

You can create *procedures* in Access Basic code, also known as ABC or simply *code*. Each procedure is a series of code statements that perform an operation or calculation.

There are two types of procedures:

- Subs
- Functions

These procedures are collectively grouped and stored in modules, with each module being composed of two or more sections:

- A single declarations section
- A section for each procedure

You can store each procedure as a separate module. On the other hand, you can store all your procedures in a single module. Realistically, you'll probably want to store your procedures in logical groupings, with each group stored in a separate module.

Sub procedures

A *sub procedure* is code that does not return a value. Because it doesn't return a value, it cannot be used in an expression or called by assigning it to a variable.

You can use a sub to perform actions when you don't want to return a value. This may happen, for example, when you want to move or resize a form.

A sub can be called by another sub or a function and can be called with parameters.

Function procedures

A *function procedure* does return a value. The value can be a Null, but the procedure always returns a value. The function procedure can be used in expressions or called by assigning it to a variable.

Writing your own functions, also known as *user-defined functions,* or *UDFs,* can make using Access much easier. If you continually perform the same complex expression, you should create a small UDF and store it as a procedure. After it's created, you can use the function just as you do any Access function.

Like subs, functions can be called by other functions or other subs. The function can also have parameters passed to it when it is called.

Creating a Procedure

To create your own procedure, follow these steps:

Steps:	Creating a New Procedure
Step 1.	Click the Module button in the Database window.
Step 2.	Click the New button.

Access opens a new module, named Module1, in a Module window. This new module should look like the one in Figure 33-1. In this figure, notice that Access places a line of text on the first line in the window, beginning with Option Compare Database.

Referring to Figure 33-1, notice the section on the toolbar titled Procedure, with a pull-down combo box alongside it. This combo box indicates (declarations) because you are currently in the declarations part of the module.

As stated earlier, the module is composed of at least two parts — the declarations section and each individual procedure (sub or function).

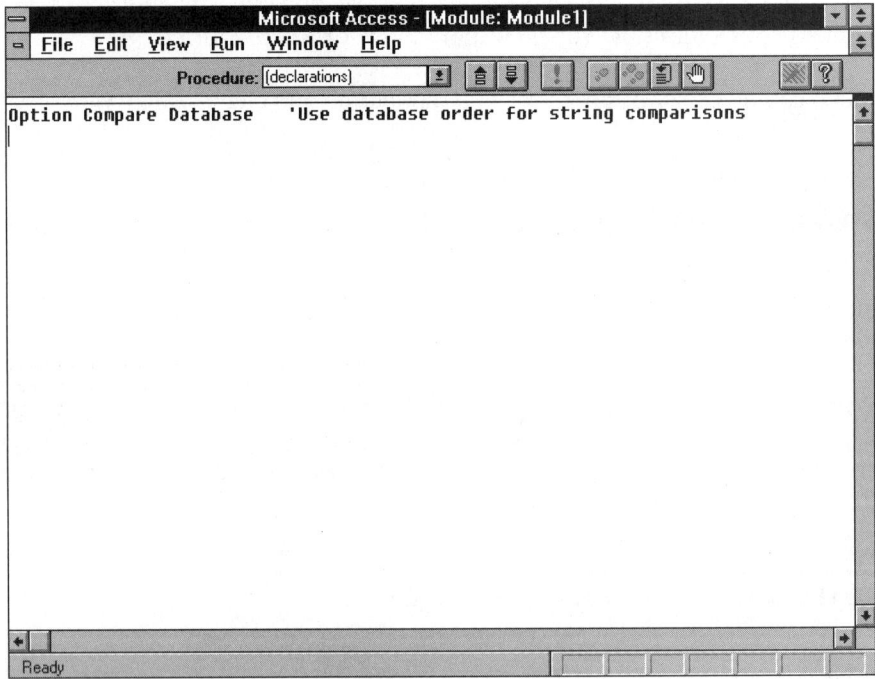

Figure 33-1: The newly opened Module window.

The declaration section

You can use the declaration section to *declare*, or *define*, variables that you want available to the procedures. You can declare variables that will be used only by the procedures in a module or all procedures across all modules within a database.

You are not required to declare variables in this section, as variables can also be declared in the individual procedures. In fact, you don't have to declare a variable at all. Access allows *implicit* variable declarations — that is, declarations on the fly. If you enter a variable name in an expression and it hasn't previously been declared, Access will accept it and declare it for you.

 If you are going to write Access Basic procedures, you may want to enter a single declaration in this section, which is Option Explicit. The statement Option Explicit forces you to declare any variables that you will use when creating procedures. If you need further information, refer to the Access documentation.

Creating a new function

Now that you are in the declarations section of a module, you need to be able to create a function. Access makes creating a procedure (function) easy. For example, to create a new function named DayOfWeek, follow these steps:

Steps: Creating a New Function

Step 1.   Go to any empty line in the Module window.

Step 2.   Type **Function DayOfWeek.** Your Module window should look similar to Figure 33-2.

Step 3.   Press Enter.

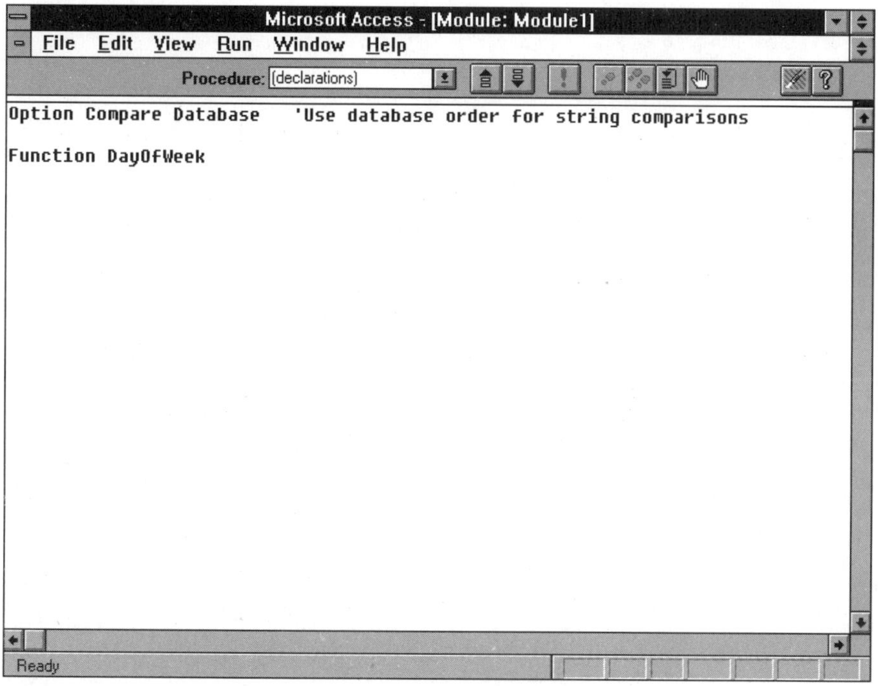

Figure 33-2: Entering a new function in the Module window.

 If you enter the name of a function that you had previously created in this module or another module within the database, Access informs you that it already exists. Access does not let you create another procedure with the same name.

Your Module window should look like Figure 33-3. Notice that when you pressed Enter, Access automatically did two things:

1. Placed the function named DayOfWeek in the Procedure combo box on the toolbar
2. Placed parentheses at the end of the function name and entered the End Function line to the function

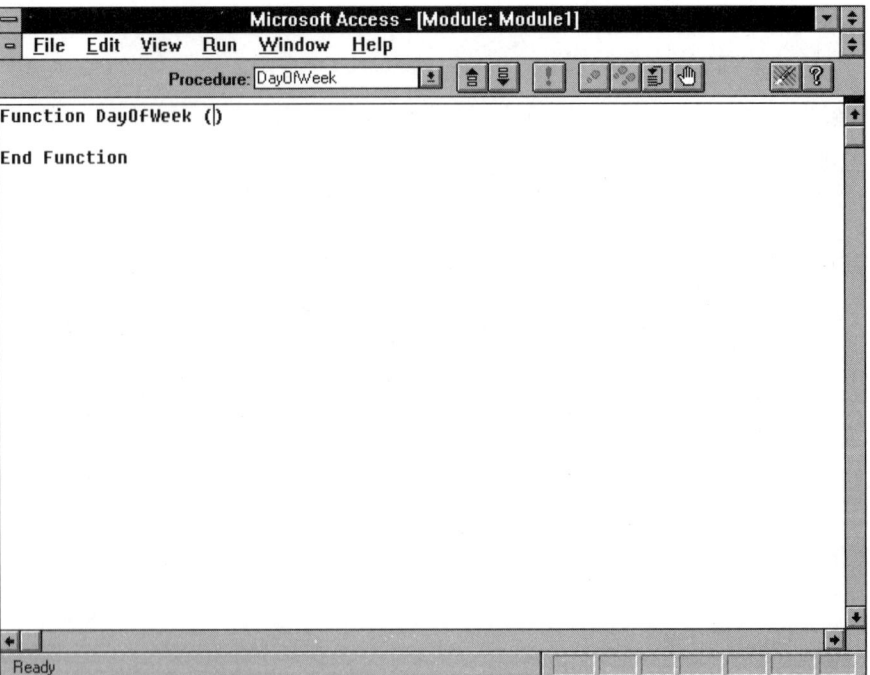

Figure 33-3: The Module window displaying a new function.

Now you can enter the lines of code needed for your function. In this case, you are passing a variable date to the function as a parameter, so you'll need to place a parameter name between the parentheses on the function name line. Your finished function should look like the one in Figure 33-4.

Figure 33-4:
The DayOfWeek function completed.

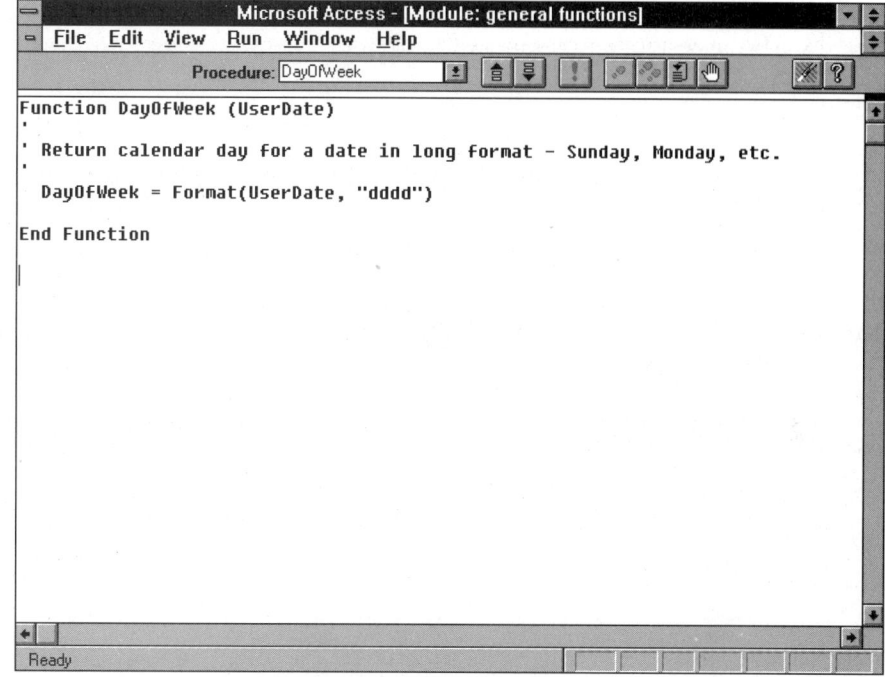

Saving a procedure

Access automatically stores the procedure in the module; however, it does not save it until you leave the module and *save* the module.

After you create the procedure, you can immediately create another procedure by going to a blank line below the End Function line and typing the keyword **Function** with a new function name.

Compiling the procedures

After you create all the functions, you should compile them by selecting Run⇨Compile All from the module menu. However, Access will compile an uncompiled procedure when run.

Saving a module

When you are finished creating your procedures, you should save them by saving the module. As with any other Access object, you can save the module by selecting File⇨Save, pressing F12 or Alt+F2, or saving it when you close the window.

994 Part V: Applications in Access

 You should consider saving the module every time you complete a procedure. The easiest way is to press F12 or Alt+F2.

Editing an Existing Procedure

To edit an existing procedure, follow these steps:

Steps:	Editing an Existing Procedure
Step 1.	Click the Module button in the Database window.
Step 2.	Double-click the module name that contains the procedure. You are taken into the declaration portion of the module.
Step 3.	Select View⇨Procedures... or press F2. Access displays the View Procedures dialog box, shown in Figure 33-5.

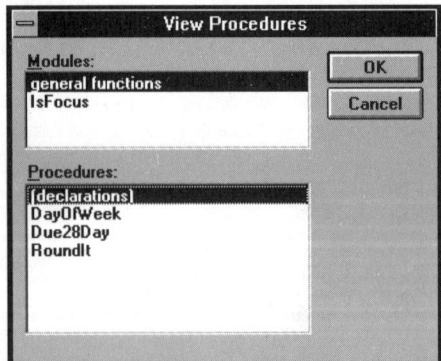

Figure 33-5: Selecting a procedure to edit.

Step 4.	Select the procedure you want to edit.

 After you are in a module, you can quickly select any procedure in another module by pressing F2 and highlighting a different module name in the Modules section of the View Properties dialog box. You'll see the names of all procedures in the new module.

Editing two procedures simultaneously

There are times when you want to edit two procedures at the same time. Perhaps you need to copy part of one into another. To work on two procedures simultaneously, simply click and drag the split bar (immediately under the title of the Module window and above the function name) or select View⇨Split Window from the module menu.

You can resize the window by moving the split bar up and down. Figure 33-6 shows two procedures open.

Now you can work with both procedures at the same time. To switch between windows, either press the F6 key or use your mouse.

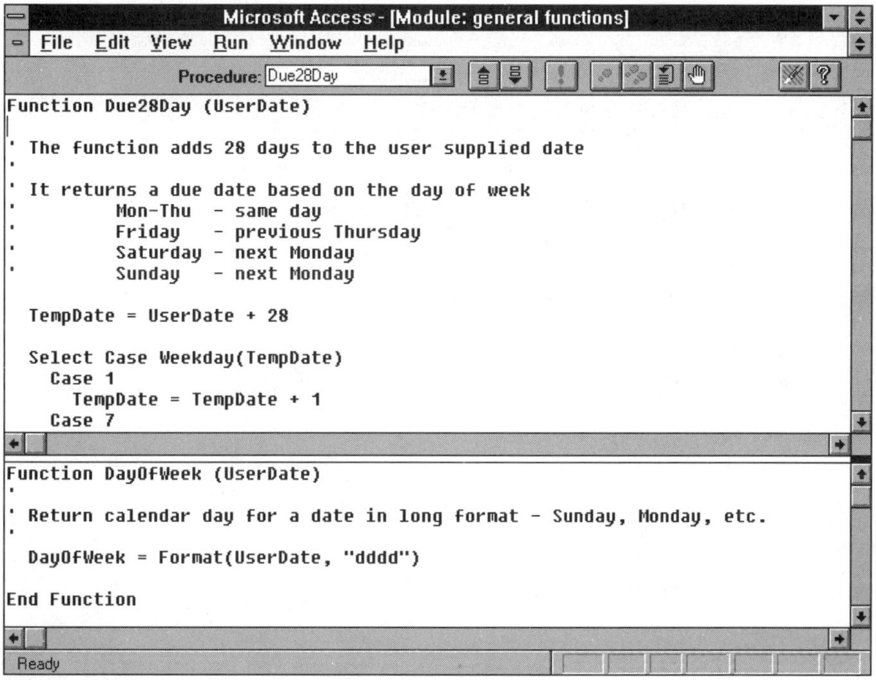
Microsoft Access - [Module: general functions]
File Edit View Run Window Help
Procedure: Due28Day
Function Due28Day (UserDate)
'
' The function adds 28 days to the user supplied date
'
' It returns a due date based on the day of week
'   Mon-Thu - same day
'   Friday   - previous Thursday
'   Saturday - next Monday
'   Sunday   - next Monday
TempDate = UserDate + 28
Select Case Weekday(TempDate)
Case 1
TempDate = TempDate + 1
Case 7
Function DayOfWeek (UserDate)
'
' Return calendar day for a date in long format - Sunday, Monday, etc.
'
DayOfWeek = Format(UserDate, "dddd")
End Function
Ready

Figure 33-6: Splitting the window to display two procedures simultaneously.

The immediate window

When you write code for functions, sometimes you want to try the function while you are in the module. The immediate window lets you try your functions without having to leave the module.

To view the immediate window, select View⇨Immediate Window from the module menu. Access opens a smaller window titled Immediate Window with the name of the module. Figure 33-7 shows the immediate window active.

With the immediate window open, you can use it to test your function. For example, to test the function Due28Day( ) with today's date, you type the following in the window:

? Due28Day(Date())

When you press Enter, Access executes the function Due28Day(.) and displays the answer in the immediate window. For example, if the date is December 31, 1992, and you enter the syntax just shown, the immediate window displays an answer similar to the one in Figure 33-8.

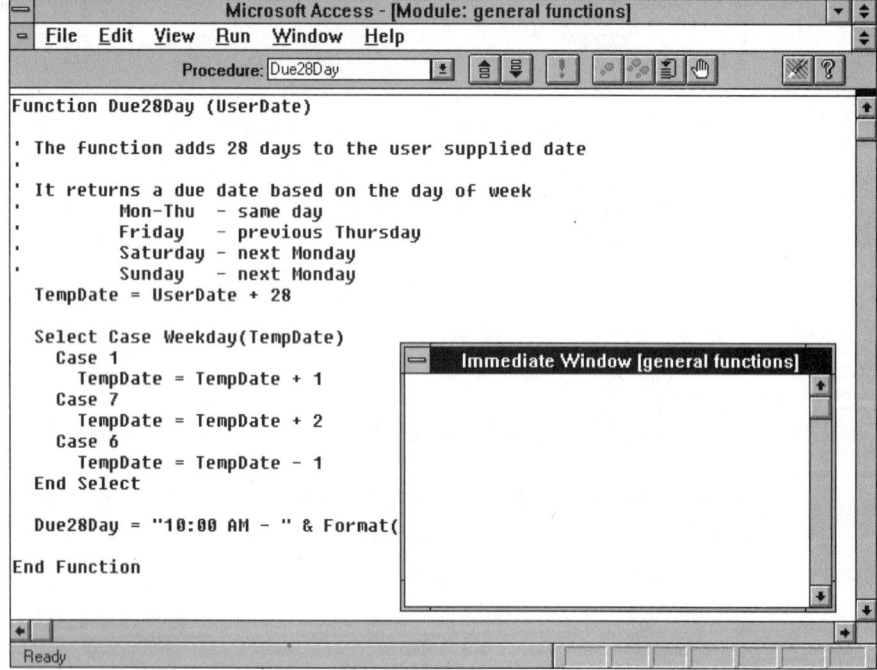

Figure 33-7: The immediate window open.

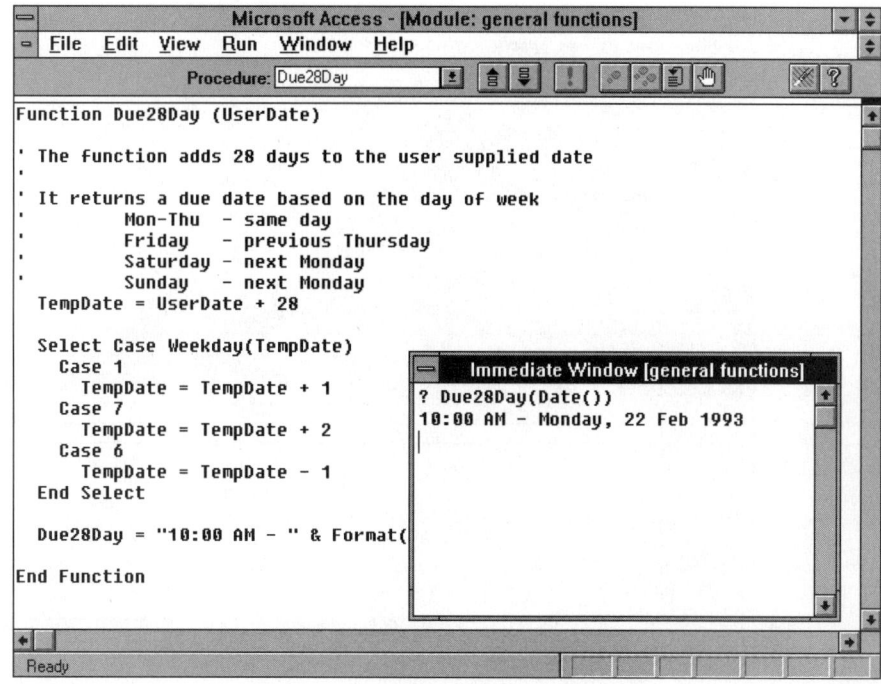

Figure 33-8: The immediate window with an answer set for the function Due28Day().

Using a Function Procedure

To use a function that you created in the module container of Access, simply use it like any other Access function — in queries, forms, or reports. Just type the name of the function where you want to use it. Figure 33-9 shows the use of the Due28Day( ) function in a query.

Notice that you don't have to reference the module name where the function is located. Access makes all functions in the database available to you for use. Therefore, you simply use your functions by typing in their name and any parameters they require, just as with any other Access function.

Running this function, with the query property Unique Values Only set, you get a datasheet similar to the one in Figure 33-10.

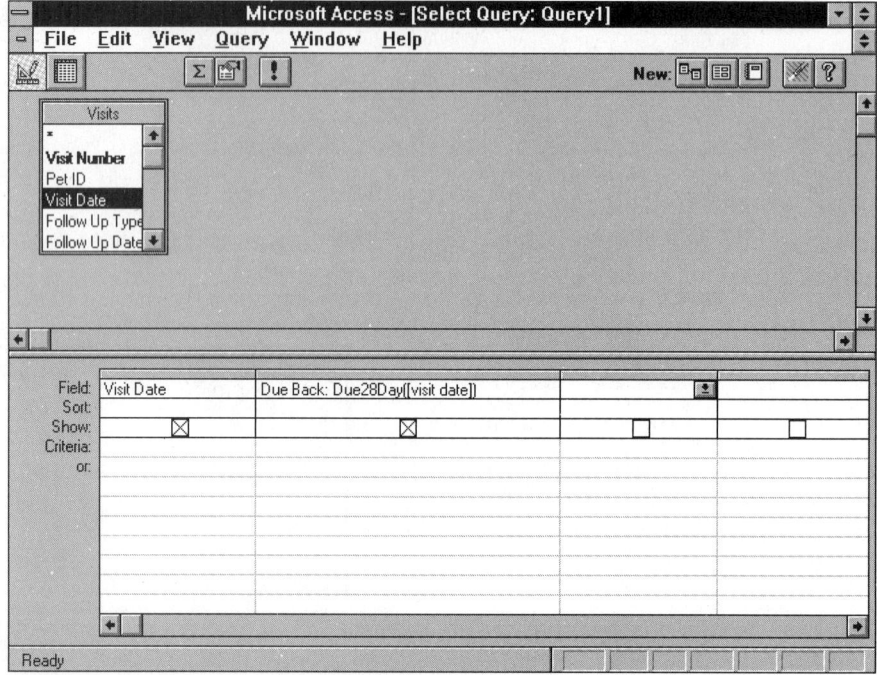

Figure 33-9: Using the Due28Day() function in a query.

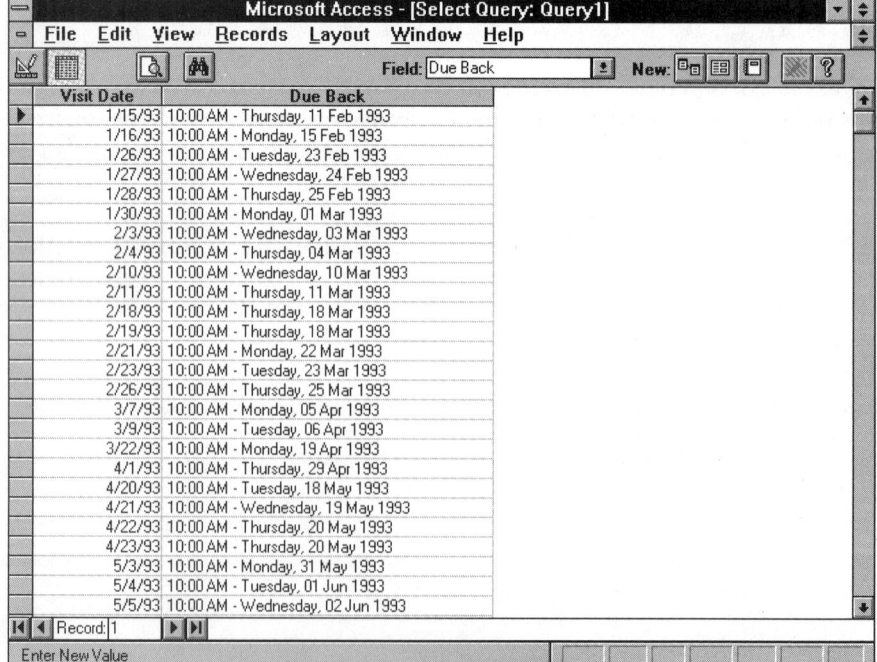

Figure 33-10: The datasheet produced by the query in Figure 33-9.

Where Do You Go from Here?

This chapter is a very short introduction to the Access modules and Access Basic. It demonstrates what programming code can do for you.

The point is that Access has an excellent variety of tools that let you work with databases and their tables, queries, forms, and reports, without ever having to write a single line of code. However, if the need arises for you to do something that can be better served by writing a small procedure or function, do it.

To learn more about Access Basic, you can refer to the *Introduction to Programming* guide or the *Language Reference* manual that comes with Access.

Summary

This chapter introduced you to modules and creating your own functions. These main points were explained:

- You create your own procedures, like functions, using Access Basic and store them in modules.

- A module has at least two parts — the declaration section and a section for each procedure stored in it. A procedure can be a sub or function.

- Access lets you edit two procedures simultaneously by splitting the window into two panes.

- If you need to test your function while in modules, simply open the immediate window and test the function using the ? statement.

- After you create functions and save them in a module, you use them just as you do any other Access function. To use the functions, simply refer to them by name.

- Access makes all functions and procedures available to all objects in the database. Therefore, you don't need to reference the module name when accessing a function that you created.

Microsoft Access Specifications

This appendix shows the limits of Microsoft Access databases, tables, queries, forms, reports, and macros.

Databases	
Attribute	*Maximum*
MDB file size	1GB for Access 1.1 and 2.0 and 128MB for Access 1.0 (Because your database can include attached tables in multiple files, its total size is limited only by available storage capacity.)
Number of objects in a database	32,768
Number of characters in object names	64
Number of characters in a password	14
Number of characters in a user name or group name	20
Number of concurrent users	255

Tables

Attribute	Maximum
Number of characters in a table name	64
Number of characters in a field name	64
Number of fields in a record or table	255
Table size	1GB
Number of characters in a Text field	255
Number of characters in a Memo field	64,000
Size of OLE object field	1GB
Number of indexes in a record or table	32
Number of fields in an index	10
Number of characters in a validation message	255
Number of characters in a table description	255
Number of characters in a field description	255

Queries

Attribute	Maximum
Number of tables in a query	32
Number of fields in a dynaset	255
Dynaset size	1GB
Number of sorted fields in a query	10
Number of levels of nested queries	50

Forms and Reports

Attribute	Maximum
Number of characters in a label	2,048
Number of characters in a text box	64,000
Form or report width	22 inches (55.87 cm)
Section height	22 inches (55.87 cm)
Height of all sections plus section headers (Design view)	200 inches (508 cm)
Number of levels of nested forms or reports	3 (form-subform-subform)
Number of fields/expressions you can sort or group on (reports only)	10
Number of headers and footers in a report	1 report header/footer; 1 page header/footer; 10 group headers/footers
Number of printed pages in a report	65,536

Macros

Attribute	Maximum
Number of actions in a macro	999
Number of characters in a comment	255
Number of characters in an action argument	255

Mountain Animal Hospital Tables

APPENDIX B

The Mountain Animal Hospital Database file (MTNANHSP) is made up of eight tables. There are four main tables and four lookup tables. The main tables are Customer, Pets, Visits, and Visit Details. The four lookup tables are States, Animals, Treatments, and Medications. This appendix displays a database diagram of all eight tables and the relations between them. Screen figures of each of the eight tables are shown in the Table Design window.

Figure B-1: The database diagram.

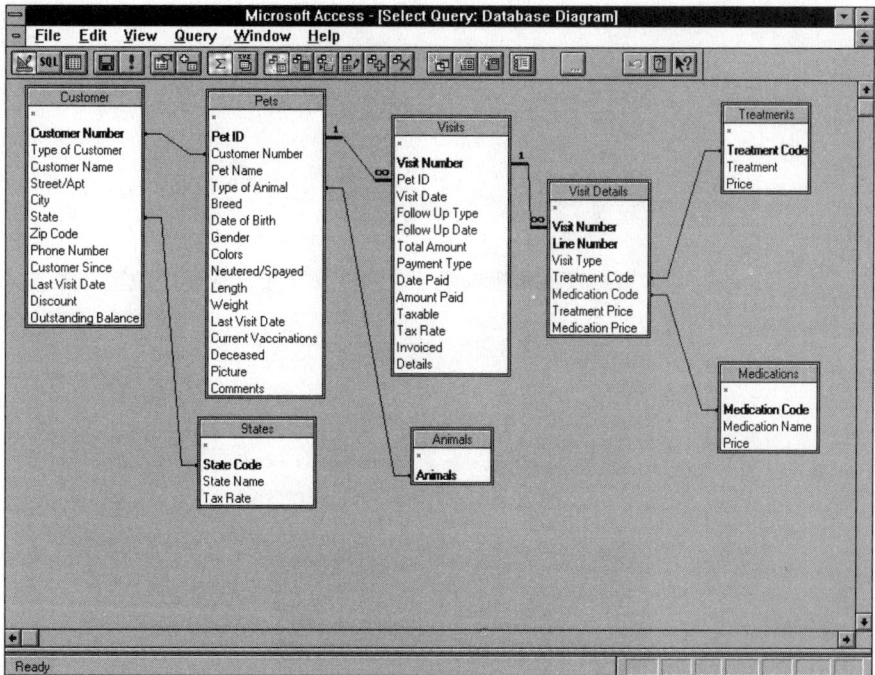

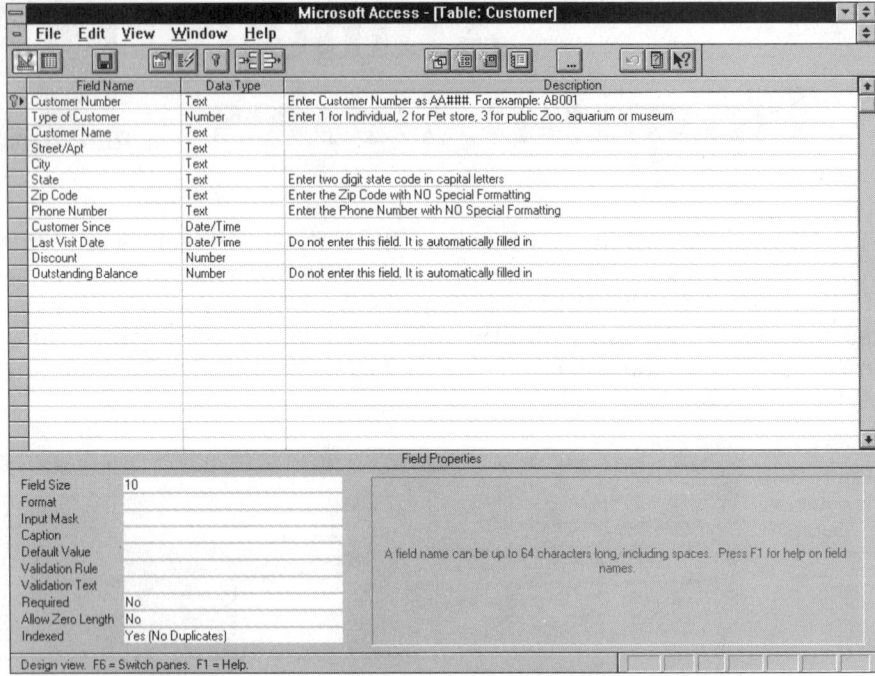

Figure B-2: The Customer table.

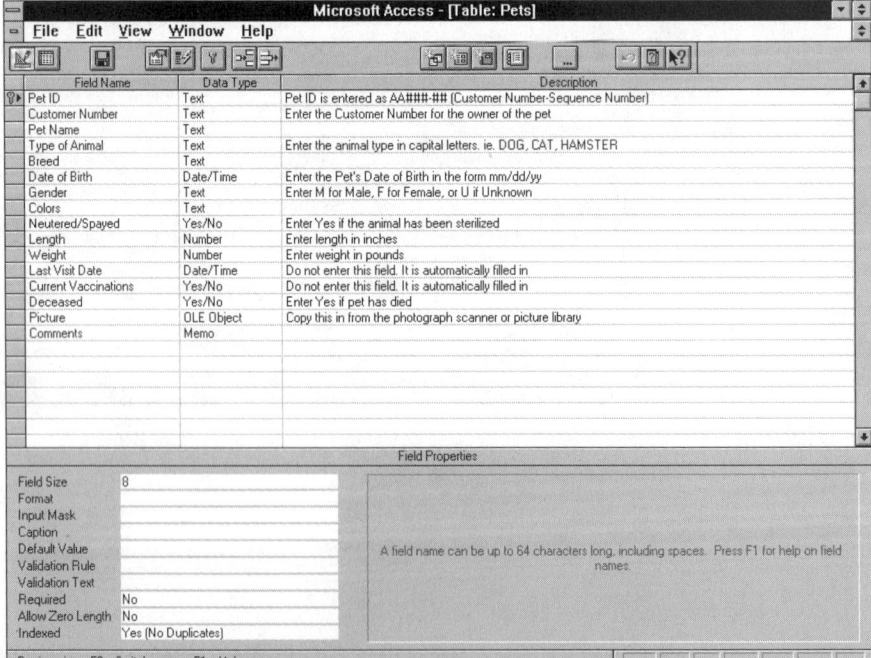

Figure B-3: The Pets table.

Appendix B: Mountain Animal Hospital Tables

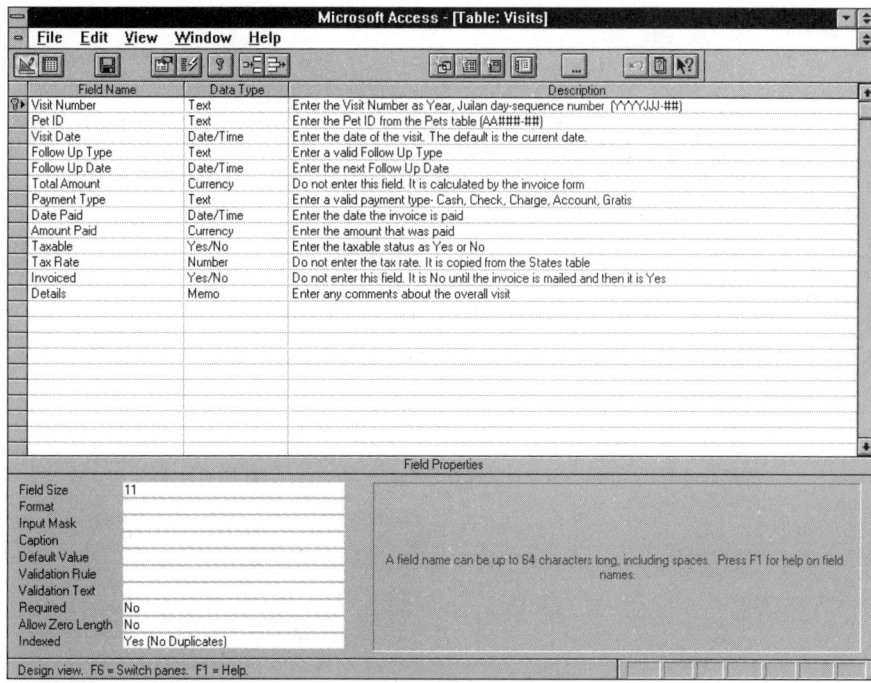

Figure B-4: The Visits table.

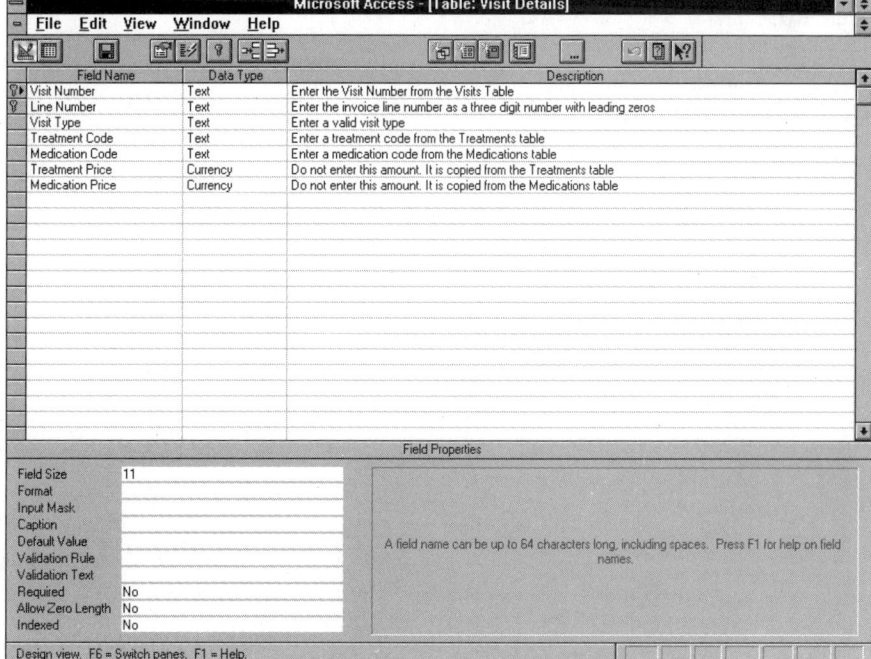

Figure B-5: The Visit Details table.

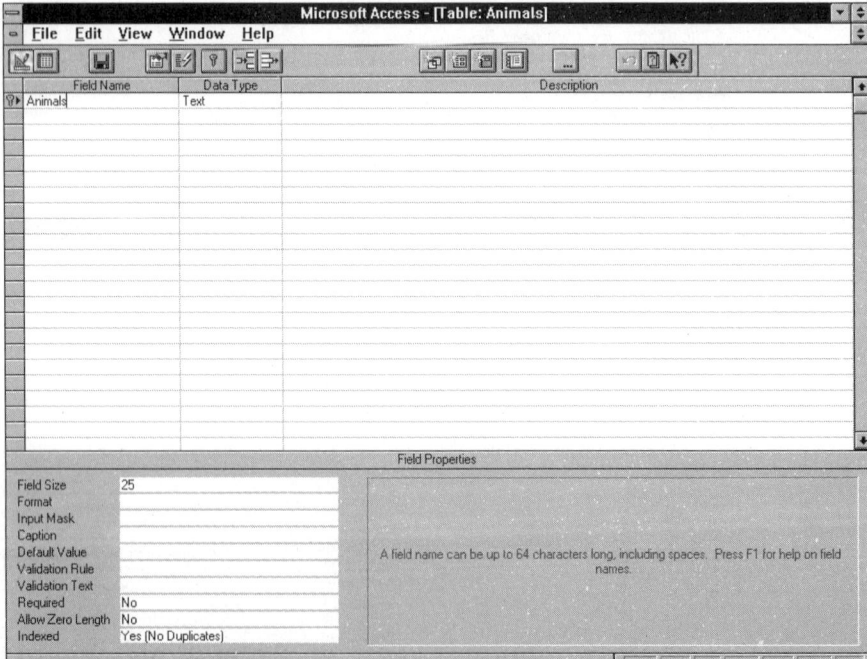

Figure B-6: The States table.

Figure B-7: The Animals table.

Appendix B: Mountain Animal Hospital Tables

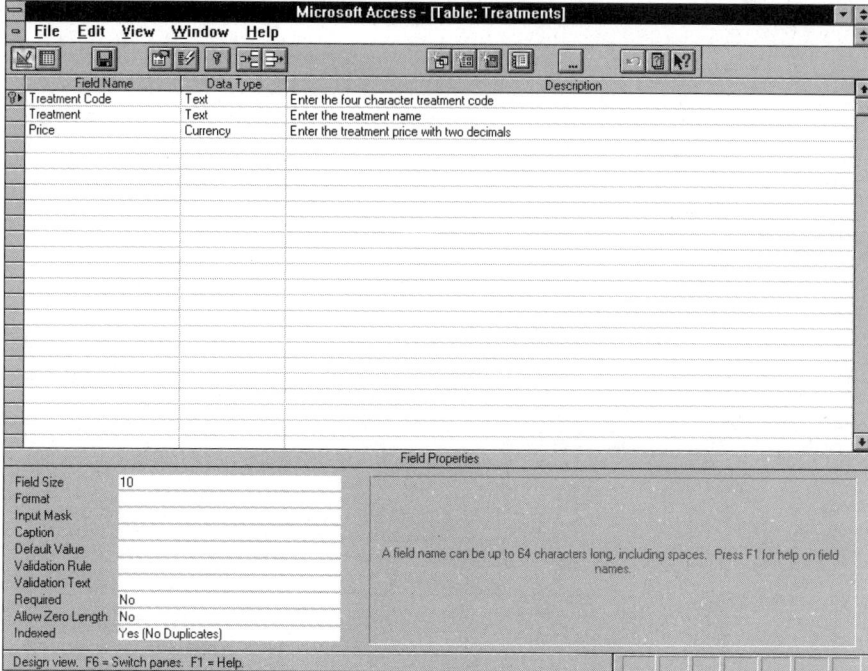

Figure B-8: The Treatments table.

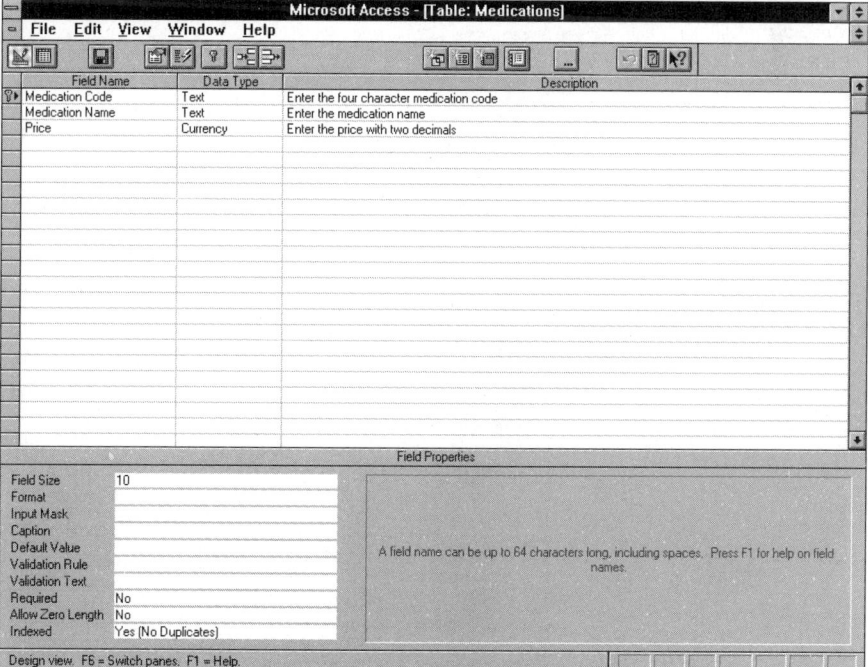

Figure B-9: The Medications table.

Index

• Symbols •

\# (pound sign)
  delimiting dates, 123, 228
  in expressions, 299
  in input masks, 121
  as wildcard, 150, 285, 344
^ (caret), as exponentiation operator, 281
& (ampersand)
  as format symbol, 116
  in input masks, 121
  as string concatenation operator, 283–284
* (asterisk)
  as all-field reference tag, 214, 216–217
  as multiplication operator, 279
  as new-record pointer, 143
  as wildcard, 150, 285, 344
+ (equal sign), as relational operator, 281
+ (plus sign), as addition operator, 279
<> (greater/less than signs)
  as format symbol, 116
  in input masks, 121
  as query comparison operators, 228
  as relational operators, 282
= (equal sign), as query comparison operator, 228
\ (backslash)
  in input masks, 120, 121
  as integer division operator, 280
? (question mark)
  in input masks, 121
  as wildcard, 150, 285, 344
@ (at sign), as format symbol, 116
' (backquote character), in database conversions from version 1.x, 28

[ ] (brackets)
  in control names after version 1.x-to-2.0 conversions, 28
  in expressions, 299
  for field references in select queries, 341
  as list "wildcard," 285, 344
! (exclamation point), in input masks, 120, 121
– (minus sign), as subtraction operator, 279
( ) (parentheses), with functions, 293
" " (quotation marks)
  in expressions, 299
  in input masks, 120
  in select queries, 343
/ (slash), as division operator, 279
_ (underscore), in input masks, 120

• A •

ABC (Access Basic Code) *See* Access Basic (programming language)
About Help command (Help menu), 41
Access 2.0 for Windows
  advantages, 1
  basic concept and terminology summary, 54
  exiting, 36
  multiple occurrences of, 34
  navigating screens, 55–60
  overview of features, 12–19
  reducing to icon, 57
  as relational database manager, 10, 12
  sample first session, 60–72
  See also help; navigating; starting Access
Access Basic (programming language), 987–988
  as ABC (Access Basic Code), 10, 988

  See also modules; procedures
Access features new to version 2.0
  Attachment Manager Add-In tool, 676–677
  control selection/spacing options, 385, 386, 389
  Expression Builder, 300
  multiple-table queries and updateability, 206, 317–320
  Option Group control wizard, 468
  properties and property window, 393
  shortcut menus, 36–37
Access icon, 31–32
Access installation, 23–26
  on networks, 21
  troubleshooting, 28
  for upgrades to version 2.0, 21, 23, 27–28
Access window, 56–57, 61
Action Failed dialog box, 883
Action pane of Macro window, 865
action queries, 202
actions in macros, 862, 868–872
Add-Ins/Attachment Manager command (File menu), 677
addition operator, 279
Add Table command (Edit menu/Relationships option), 264
Add Table command (Query menu), 206
Add Table tool, 210, 265
ad hoc queries, 203, 861
After Insert property, 894
After Update property, 895, 910
aggregate function, 709
Aggregate option of Total:row, 711, 719–720

Alias property, 792
aligning
   controls, 387–389
   graph titles, 520
   text in controls, 451
all-field reference tag (*), 214, 216–217, 316–317, 624
Allow Editing command (Records menu), 153–154
Allow Editing property, 409
Allow Filters property, 409
Allow Updating property, 409
Alpha Four, 2
Alt+F4 for Exit command, 36
Always on Top command (Help menu), 41
ampersand (&)
   as format symbol, 116
   in input masks, 121
   as string concatenation operator, 283–284
Analyze it with MS Excel tool, 105, 171
And operator, 286, 352–354, 356–359
annotating help topic text, 41
ANSI file imports, 660
APPEND (dBASE command). *See* data entry command
appending records with action queries, 755–761
Append Query tool, 210
application development, 11
applications
   exiting, 57
   launching with clicks on embedded objects, 496, 497
   Microsoft Graph (applet), 507
   See also exporting files; importing files; software

ApplyFilter action, 921
Apply Filter/Sort Tool, 141
Archive Records Wizard, 765–766
archiving records with action queries, 765–766
Argument pane of Macro window, 865–866
arrow keys, 65, 140, 153
arrows (triangles). *See* Maximize button; Minimize button
ASCII file imports, 13, 660
asterisk (*)
   as all-field reference tag, 214, 216–217, 316–317, 624
   as multiplication operator, 279
   as new-record pointer, 143
   as wildcard, 150, 285, 344
at sign (@), as format symbol, 116
attached (compound) controls, 432
attached macros
   for control events, 909–911
   for forms, 897–900
attached menu bars for forms, 961–962
attached text, 519
attaching files
   advantages, 14, 661–664
   with Attachment Manager Add-In tool, 676–677
   from dBASE and FoxPro, 667–669
   deleting links, 676
   optimizing tables, 675–676
   other Access tables, 665
   See also importing files
Attach Table command (File menu), 665–667
Attach Table tool, 105
Auto Center property, 409, 984
AutoColon property, 432
AutoExec macros, 35, 875–876, 965–966

AutoForm tool, 105, 179–180
AutoLabel property, 432
AutoLookup, 320
automatic data type validation, 145
AutoReport tool, 105, 240, 249–250
Auto Resize property, 409, 984
averages (function for returning), 296
Avery label stock, 833–834
Avg( ) function, 295
axes on graphs, 524, 526–527

• **B** •

Back Color property, 451
backgrounds
   colors for, 446–447, 456–457
   reverse video effects, 449–450
   shading, 607–608
backquote character ('), in database conversions from version 1.x, 28
backslash (\)
   in input masks, 120, 121
   as integer division operator, 280
Back Style property, 451
backups, 762
bands on reports, 532
bar menus. *See* menu bars; menus
Basic. *See* Access Basic (programming language)
Before Del Confirm property, 895
Before Insert property, 894
Before Update property, 894, 910
Between...And operator, 289, 354
billing forms. *See* invoices
bitmap pictures
   adding to command buttons, 945, 951–954

adding to toggle buttons, 476–476
in bound object frames, 502–503
enhancing form backgrounds with, 459–460
in MTN.BMP file, 603
in OLE fields, 147
suppressing printing of, 615
"black boxes," 43
blanks. *See* spaces
boldface
as used in this book, 3
See also fonts
Bookmark menu, Define command, 41
bookmarks, entering in help screens, 41
Boolean operators, 285–289
Border Color property, 451
Border Line Style property, 451
borders
choosing thickness from palette, 443–444, 586–587
on boxes, 446, 451
Border Style property, 410, 451, 984
Border Width property, 451
Borland dBASE. *See* dBASE
Borland Paradox. *See* Paradox
Both property, 409
bound objects
adding frames to forms, 423–426, 452–454
changing properties, 567
described, 494
embedding, 497–501
frames for, 368–369
linking, 505–507
in reports, 602–605
boxes
checkboxes, 367, 370, 372–373, 600–602
combo boxes, 367, 370, 376–377, 477, 484–490

enhancing with special effects, 444–446
See also combo boxes; label controls; list boxes; option groups; rectangles; text boxes
brackets ([ ])
in control names after version 1.x-to-2.0 conversions, 28
in expressions, 299
for field references in select queries, 341
as list "wildcard," 285, 344
BROWSE command (dBASE). *See* datasheets
browse screens or browse tables. *See* datasheets
Btrieve
file attaching, 663, 670–671
file exports, 702–703
file imports, 13, 660, 677, 681–682
Build tool, 110, 210
built-in functions, 17
buttons
for navigating datasheets, 140
in rectangles, 374–376
See also command buttons; toggle buttons; toolbars
byte (numeric field type), 116

• C •

calculated controls, 368–369, 597–600, 631–632
calculated fields
creating in select queries, 361–363
creating on forms, 430–431
described, 154
updateability in queries, 318
calculations
performing with queries, 203, 776–780

with Total:row, 708–722
CancelEvent action, 917
Can Grow/Shrink property, 568, 569, 590–592
"Can't create relationship to enforce referential integrity. Existing data..." message, 269, 270
CAPS indicator, 57
Caption property, 408, 792
captions, 115, 122
caret (^), as exponentiation operator, 281
carriage returns with Ctrl+Enter, 189
Cartesian products, 321
cascading delete queries, 763–764
case-sensitivity
for database filenames, 103
for field names, 111
forcing lower/uppercase in table fields, 117
in searches, 151
"C" as input mask character, 121
catalogs. *See* databases
~.CDX extensions, 667
cells. *See* values
chain links, 89
changing focus (expressions), 299
character data type. *See* text data type
charts. *See* graphs
checkboxes, 367, 370, 372–373, 600–602
child-parent table relationships, 263
chiseled boxes, 446
Clear Grid command (Edit menu), 214
Clear Grid command (Query Design menu/Edit option), 214
clicking the mouse, 3
clip art, 459

with Picture Builder, 476
Clipboard
  copying help topic text to, 41
  cutting controls to, 389
  pasting OLE objects to/from, 147, 190, 459
Close command (File menu), 66, 68, 193
closed sections (bands) on reports, 646
closing
  cue card screen, 38
  forms with macros, 902–904
  help windows, 42
  Query window, 229
  See also exiting
Code tool, 105, 531
colons, auto-placing after text in labels, 432
color printers, 584
colors
  choosing from palette, 443–444, 586–587
  on forms, 444, 446–447, 451, 456–457
  on graphs, 524
Column Heading property, 793
column reports, 233
  snaked, 840–845
columns
  described, 46
  display width/height adjustments, 158–160
  freezing, 162
  hiding or showing, 161–162
Column Width command (Format menu), 158
combo boxes, 367, 370, 376–377, 477, 484–490
  See also list boxes
Combo Box Wizard, 485
command buttons
  adding bitmap pictures to, 951–954
  creating, 911
  creating with Command Button Wizard, 942–945

creating with dragged macros, 950–951
described, 58, 104, 106, 368, 370
for opening forms, 911–916
Command Button Wizard, 942–945
command line options for starting Access, 35
commands
  selecting, 3
  See also boxes; buttons; controls; dialog boxes; macros; menus; moving; navigating; operators; switchboards; toolbars; Wizards
comments. *See* memo fields
compacting databases, 35
comparisons
  with Boolean operators, 285–289, 291
  with queries, 228
  with relational operators, 281–282, 291
  in select queries, 336–341
compiling procedures, 993
compound (attached) controls, 432, 557–558
computers
  caution on turning off, 36
  hardware requirements for Access, 22
concatenation operators, 283–284, 635–637, 641–642
conditional actions in macros, 878–882
Conditions tool, 867
connectivity of databases, 663
constants in expressions, 298
context-sensitive help, 12, 39
Control Box property, 410
control breaks
  in grouping/sorts, 571
  in totals, 715–718
control buttons for navigating datasheets, 140

control events, 891, 909–916
control menu button, 56, 57
controls
  adding to forms, 592–604
  advantages, 67, 93, 367–369
  aligning, 387–389
  changing type, 391
  compound (attached), 432
  copying, 391
  creating, 378–383
  deleting, 389–390
  enhancing with special effects, 443–446, 447, 450–452, 454–458
  as fields, 60, 411, 547
  formatting text in, 552–553
  moving, 386–387
  names for, 301
  navigation buttons, 149, 150
  placing in forms, 411–414
  referencing in macros, 879
  selecting, 383–385
  sinking or raising, 608
  sizing, 385–386
  specifying for use, 302
  triggering macros upon activation of, 891, 909–916
  See also combo boxes; commands; label controls; list boxes; menus; operators; option groups; properties; toggle buttons; toolbars; Yes/No (logical) criteria
control sources, 411, 547
Control Wizard icon, 368
conversion functions, 294–295
Convert Database command (File menu), 27–28
ConvertErrors table, 28
converting
  databases from Access 1.x to 2.0, 27–28, 35
  data types, 129–131
  data types for imported files, 680–681, 682

Copy and Paste options (Edit menu), 133–134
Copy command (Edit menu), 133–124, 155
copying
  controls, 391
  help topic text to Clipboard, 41
  macros, 873
  tables, 133–134
  values, 155
  See also exporting files; importing files
copyright information for Windows, 41
Copy tool, 105
counter data type, 111, 112, 125
counter fields, 154
Count( ) function, 780–781
counts
  function for returning, 296, 780–781
  obtaining for records, 712–714
  See also totals
cover pages/letters, 535
C programmers and advantages of Access to, 10, 11
Cross Reference icons, 4
crosstab queries, 202, 318, 722–734
Crosstab Query tool, 210
Crosstab Query Wizard, 733–734
Ctrl+key combinations
  Ctrl+Alt+spacebar for replacement with default value, 152
  Ctrl+End for navigating, 65, 140
  Ctrl+Enter for adding new lines in text or memo fields, 146, 189
  Ctrl+" for repeating value from preceding record, 153
  Ctrl+Home for navigating, 65, 140

Ctrl+PgUp/PgDn for navigating records in forms, 188
Cue Cards, 12, 13, 37–39
  See also help
Cue Cards command (Help menu), 38
Cue Cards tool, 105
cumulative totals, 652
currency data type, 111, 112, 130, 145
currency type formats (field properties), 117
current record pointer, 143
cursor
  changing focus of, 299
  moving. *See* navigating
customizing
  Access installation, 24–25
  drop-down menu bars, 954–961
  forms for data input, 185
  graphs, 517–527
  with options for starting Access, 34–35
  toolbars by adding icons, 106
Cut command (Edit menu), 155
Cut tool, 105

• D •

data. *See* database design considerations; queries; reports
database connectivity, 663
database design considerations
  creating overall concepts, 77
  data, 82–87
  fields, data entry and validation, 89–92
  forms for data input, 93–96
  menus, 97
  overview, 76–77, 98
  reports, 78–82
  tables, and relationships, 88–89

Database Documenter utility, 131
database management systems (DBMSs)
  Access as, 9, 18
  attaching, 663–673
  described, 44
  working with attached tables, 673–677
database publishing, 584–585
databases
  compacting, 35
  converting from Access 1.x to 2.0, 27–28, 35
  creating, 102–104
  described, 43–45
  diagrams of, 312–313
  maximums and limitations, 1001
  naming, 103
  opening, 62–63
  opening for read-only access, 35
  opening upon startup of Access, 32, 34, 35
  starting Access by selecting, 33
  See also attaching files; database design considerations; exporting files; files; importing files; saving; tables
Database windows, 56, 57–58, 59, 104–106
Database Window tool, 105, 210
data definition queries, 786
Dataease, 2
data entry. *See* datasheets; fields; forms for data entry/edits
Data Entry command (Records menu), 156
data series on graphs with patterns, 524
datasheets
  described, 19, 46, 49, 138–139

displaying, 64–65
entering data, 142–144
exporting to MS Word or
 Excel, 171–172
navigating, 64–65, 139–140,
 149–150
opening, 142
saving, 162
See also graphs; records;
 sorting
datasheet toolbar, 141–142
Datasheet View tool, 110,
 141, 210
Datasheet windows, 139–142
data types
 changing, 129–131
 conversion function for, 294
 conversion of imported
  data, 680–681, 682
 specifying for table fields,
  111–113
data validation
 advantages, 90, 123–124
 automatic, 145
 with combo boxes, 477,
  484–490
 with expressions, 464–466
 with list boxes, 477–484
 with macros, 916–919
 with option buttons,
  467–472
 with properties, 115
 with Yes/No options,
  472–476
 See also expressions; forms
  for data entry/edits
Date( ) function, 647–649
dates
 inserting into form fields, 189
 pound signs (#) delimiting,
  123, 228
date/time information
 data type, 111, 112, 129,
  130, 145
 in expressions, 300
 fields, 101
 formats (field properties),
  117–119

functions, 295
 inserting with Date( )
  function, 647–649
DAvg( ) function, 296
DayOfWeek procedure in
 Access Basic, 991–998
DB1.MDB, as default
 database name, 103
dBASE
 caution to users of, 2, 18
 file attaching (linking), 10,
  14, 663, 664, 667–669
 file exports, 700
 file imports, 13, 661, 677,
  679–681
 terminological equivalents
  for Access, 18
 ~.DBF extensions, 667, 668
DBMS. *See* database man-
  agement systems
  (DBMSs)
DCount( ) function, 296
DDB( ) function, 295
DDE (Dynamic Data
 Exchange), 17, 494
Decimal Place property, 792
decimal places, 115, 116,
 117, 122
declarations of variables in
 procedures, 990–991
Default Editing property, 409
defaults
 for attached label positioning, 432
 for control properties,
  395–397
 replacing existing values
  with, 152, 189
 setting for table fields, 123
 for text field record size, 115
 for units of measurement
  in inches, 546
 as values for table fields,
  115, 123
 for views of forms/
  datasheets, 408–411
Default View property, 408,
 984

Define command (Bookmark
 menu), 41
defining variables in procedures, 990–991
Delete All command (Query
 Design menu/Edit
 option), 217
Delete command (Edit
 menu), 133, 156
Delete Query tool, 210
Delete Row command (Edit
 menu), 127, 128
Delete Row tool, 110
deleting
 actions from macros, 872
 attached label controls, 429
 fields, 127, 128
 joins for table queries, 324
 label controls, 557
 records, 156, 189
 records with action
  queries, 761–764
 report headers/footers, 576
 tables, 133
 tables from queries, 311
 text boxes, 557
 values or characters in
  records, 152
delimited text files, importing, 677, 686, 687–688,
  691–692
depreciation function
 (DDB( )), 295
Description property, 792, 793
designing. *See* database
 design considerations;
 reports
Design tool, 531
Design view, 65
Design View tool, 110, 141, 210
design windows, 58
desktop publishing, 584
Dest Connect Str property,
 793
Destination DB property, 793
Destination table property, 793
detail controls, 559–560
detail records, 532, 536

Index 1017

testing, 632–633
dialog boxes
  advantages, 966–967
  creating form for macro, 967–968
  creating list box, 970–972
  creating macros for closing, 982–983
  creating macros for printing, 972, 982
  creating macros for print previews, 978–982
  creating macros for showing list boxes, 976–978
  creating option group and option buttons, 968–970
  creating print macro library, 974–975
  properties, 983–984
  sizing, 983
directories for Access file installation, 24
disks accompanying this manual, 4
disk space requirement for Access, 22, 24, 28
display forms, 51
  See also forms
displaying
  data with forms, 189–192
  dynasets, 217
  field lists, 411–412
  Field List window, 411–412
  forms, 66–68
  with frozen columns, 162
  graph type, 522–524
  gridlines, 162
  mailing labels, 836
  pictures/OLE objects in forms, 189–190, 452–454, 459–460
  records, 156–169
  reports, 71–72, 610–612
division operator, 279
DLookUp( ) function, 774–775
DOS
  starting Access from, 34

version for Access and Windows, 22
dot (.) identifier operator, 300–301, 303, 339
dot-matrix printers, 544, 546
double-clicking the mouse, 3
double (numeric field type), 116
dragging the mouse, 3
DR-DOS version for Access and Windows, 22
drop-down menus. *See* menus
Dynamic Data Exchange. *See* DDE (Dynamic Data Exchange)
dynasets
  described, 50, 71, 200, 204, 235–236
  displaying, 217
  editing, 218
  hiding fields in, 787–788
  maximums and limitations, 1002
  printing, 228–229

• E •

Edit/Clear Grid command (Query Design menu), 214
Edit/Delete All command (Query Design menu), 217
Edit Filter/Sort command (Records menu), 164–169
Edit Filter/Sort Tool, 141
editing
  dynasets, 218
  embedded objects, 504
  embedded OLE objects with their own applications, 496, 497, 504
  forms, 189, 192–193
  macros, 871–873
  mailing label designs, 836–839
  procedures, 994–995

records, 152–154
sound or video objects, 504
Edit menu
  Copy and Paste options, 133
  Copy command, 133–134, 155
  Cut command, 155
  Delete command, 133, 156
  Delete Row command, 127, 128
  Find command, 150–152
  Insert Object command, 147
  Insert Row command, 127
  Paste Append command, 147
  Paste command, 147, 155
  Paste Special command, 147
  Relationships/Add Table command, 264
  Relationships command, 320
  Replace...command, 155
  Set Primary Key command, 125
  Tab Order command, 420–421
  Undo Current Field command, 154
  Undo Current Record command, 154
  Undo Saved Record command, 154
  Undo Typing command, 154
EGA monitor requirement for Access, 22
elevation for three-dimensional effects on graphs, 525
embedding
  graphs in forms, 508–517
  objects, 494–504
  See also linking
embossed boxes, 446
End key, 65, 140, 188
Enter key for navigating in forms, 188
entity integrity, 124, 255
equal sign (=)

as query comparison
    operator, 228
as relational operator, 281
equi-joins, 325–326, 770, 772
Eqv operator, 287–288
error messages
    in ConvertErrors table, 28
    designing for violations of
        data validation rules,
        465
Esc key to undo changes to
    records, 154
events
    canceling with macros, 917
    control-level, 891, 909–916
    form-level, 891–893,
        894–909
    report and report section
        level, 893, 925–931
    for triggering macros, 861,
        884–886, 890
    See also macros
Excel. See Microsoft Excel
exclamation point (!)
    as identifier operator,
        300–301, 302
    in input masks, 120, 121
Exit command (File menu), 36
exiting
    Access, 36
    applications, 57
    help, 42
    See also closing
exponentiation operator, 281
exporting files
    to Btrieve, 702–703
    creating setups for reuse,
        688–698
    to dBASE, FoxPro or
        Paradox, 700
    described, 13, 698
    macros for, 893–894,
        931–932
    to MS Word or Excel,
        171–172, 701–702
    to other Access databases,
        699
    to spreadsheets, 699–700

to SQL servers, 703–704
as text files, 700
between Windows
    applications with DDE,
    704
to word processors, 701
See also importing files
Export tool, 105
Expression Builder, 300,
    777–780
Expression option of
    Total:row, 711, 721–722
expressions
    advantages, 10, 297
    creating, 299–300
    for data validation, 464–466
    parts, 298
    special identifier opera-
        tors, 300–303
    in text boxes, 553
    See also operators
extensions
    ~.CDX, 667
    ~.DBF, 667, 668
    described, 33
    ~.IDX, 667
    ~.INF, 667, 668, 669
    ~.MDB, 33, 103
    ~.MDX, 667
    ~.NDX, 667
    ~.PX, 669, 670
external data. See importing
    files

• F •

F1 key, for help, 12, 39
F2 key, for selecting entire
    field, 153
F5 key, for GoTo record, 149,
    150
F6 key, for switching
    between window
    panes, 109, 114
F7 key, for Find command,
    150
F12 key, for saving, 229
Fast Laser Printing property,
    410

Field command (Edit menu/
    Undo Current Record
    option), 141, 144, 154
field entry area, 109
Field List tool, 531
Field List window, 58, 59,
    378–381, 411–412
fields in datasheets
    changing display width or
        height, 158–160
    creating, 110–113
    data type changes, 129–131
    data type specification,
        111–113
    date/time type, 101
    deleting, 127, 128
    described, 46–47
    design considerations,
        88–90
    entering descriptions, 113
    inserting, 127
    memo type, 102
    moving, 127, 128
    naming, 110–111
    naming with captions, 122
    OLE type, 102
    properties of, 114–124
    rearranging, 156–158
    referencing in select
        queries, 341
    renaming, 129
    size properties, 115–116
    sizing, 129
    text type, 101
    uneditable, 153–154
    validating data upon
        entry, 90, 115, 123–124
    Yes/No type, 102
    See also formats (field
        properties); queries;
        reports
fields in tables, 46–47
    See also queries
fields on forms
    choosing, 182–183
    as controls, 60
fields on reports
    as controls, 60, 547

Index 1019

design considerations, 78
selecting and positioning, 547–551
specifying, 240–242
File Manager for starting Access, 33–34
File menu
  Add-Ins/Attachment Manager command, 677
  Attach Table command, 665–667
  Close command, 66, 68, 193
  Convert Database command, 27–28
  Exit command, 36
  Imp/Exp Setup command, 690–695
  New Database command, 102–103
  New/Form command, 179, 180–186
  New/Query command, 205
  New/Report command, 238–245, 543
  New/Table command, 107
  Open Database command, 62
  Print command, 169–170, 195, 248
  Print Definition command, 131, 196, 616
  Print Preview command, 170–172, 195
  Print Setup command, 544–545
  Rename command, 132
  Run command, 32
  Sample Preview command, 612
  Save As Report command, 439
  Save command, 131–132, 193
  Save Layout command, 162
  Save Record command, 145

filename extensions. *See* extensions
files
  converting from Access version 1.0, 23, 27–28
  display of current subdirectory contents, 103
  See also attaching files; databases; exporting files; extensions; importing files; saving
File/Save command (Query Design menu), 229
File Selector box, 103
file sharing and Access version considerations, 23
file transfers, 13–14
  See also exporting files; importing files
filling (populating) databases, 92
filtering
  criteria for, 167–168
  records with macros, 920–925
  report data with macro, 931
financial (monetary) functions, 295
financial (SQL) functions, 295
Find command (Edit menu), 150–152
Find Duplicate Records Wizard, 765
finding
  with DLookUp( ) function, 774–775
  duplicate records with action queries, 765, 766
  records with macros, 922–925
  specific values in records, 150–152
  unmatched records with action queries, 765
  See also lookup tables; queries; searching

FindRecord action, 922
Find Tool, 141
Find Unmatched Records Wizard, 765
fixed-width text file imports, 677, 686–687, 688, 695–696
Fix( ) function, 296
floppy disks/drives, 26, 28
  accompanying this book, 61
focus, 941
  and On Got Focus property, 895, 910, 940
  and On Lost Focus property, 910, 940
Font command (Format menu), 160–161
Font Italic property, 451
Font Name property, 451
fonts
  customizing on data input forms, 185–186
  for label and text box controls, 447–449, 588
  for mailing labels, 834–835
  on datasheets, 160–161
  on graphs, 519–520
Font Selection box, 531
Font Size property, 451
Font Size Selection box, 531
Font Underline property, 451
Font Weight property, 451
footers. *See* headers and footers
Fore Color property, 451
foreign keys, 255, 258, 260
Format Count property, 927
Format( ) function, 295
Format menu
  Column Width command, 158
  Font command, 160–161
  Freeze columns command, 162
  Gridlines command, 162
  Header/Footer command, 437

Hide Columns command, 161
Row Height command, 159–160
Send to Back command, 448
Show Columns command, 158, 161
Size command, 389
Snap to Grid option, 388
UnFreeze columns command, 162
Format property, 792
formats (field properties)
   date/time, 117–119
   described, 115, 116
   entering, 119–120
   number and currency type, 117
   text and memo type, 116–117
   yes/no type, 119
Form command (View menu), 191
Form design windows, 58, 59, 192–193
form events, 891
form letters, 845–853
Form Object button, 104
form objects' names, 302
form reports, 233
forms for data entry/edits
   adding controls (fields), 411–414
   adding/deleting labels and text controls, 428–429
   adding fields from second table, 426–428
   adding headers and footers, 435–438
   converting to reports, 439
   creating and binding to queries, 402–405
   creating multiple-page, 433–435
   creating with AutoForm, 179–180
   creating with Form Wizards, 180–186

   creating with queries, 204
   as database objects, 48
   for data entry, 44, 93–96, 402
   described, 51, 175–178
   design/display through queries, 49
   displaying, 66–68
   displaying data with, 189–192
   editing, 189, 192–193
   enhancing with color, 444, 446–447, 456–457
   enhancing with pictures/ OLE objects, 189–190, 452–454, 459–460, 493–494
   enhancing with special controls effects, 443–446, 447, 450–452, 454–458
   enhancing with special text effects, 447–452
   macros for, 891–893, 894–909
   maximums and limitations, 1003
   opening, 185–186
   opening with command buttons, 911–916
   opening with macros, 896–897
   previewing before printing, 195
   printing, 195, 438
   printing definitions of, 196
   samples of, 10, 94, 95, 96, 177, 178
   sizing, 405–407
   templates for, 397–398
   updatability, 431, 433
   versus reports, 235
   See also data validation; graphs; OLE objects; reports; subforms; switchboards
forms for reports
   column (form) reports, 233

   See also reports
Form View tool, 187
Form windows, 186–188
Form Wizard, 13, 180–186, 799–808
FoxPro
   attaching files, 18, 663, 667–669
   file exports, 700
   file imports, 13, 660, 677, 679–681
free-form (unattached) text, 521
Freeze columns command (Format menu), 162
freezing columns, 162
full-screen forms, 176, 177
functions
   advantages, 17, 292–293
   aggregate, 709
   in expressions, 298
   in select queries, 341
   types of, 294–296
   See also values

• **G** •

GoTo command (Records menu), 64
GoToControl action, 917, 919
GoToPage action, 920
GoToRecord action, 919
GQBEs (Graphical Queries by Example), 14, 16, 208
Graph (applet). *See* Microsoft Graph (applet)
graphics effects. *See* bitmap pictures; OLE objects
graphs
   advantages, 15
   as controls, 368
   creating with queries, 204
   customizing, 517–527
   embedding in forms, 508–517
   forms as, 176, 181

Index 1021

with Graph Wizard, 508
with Microsoft Graph
    (applet), 507–508
in OLE fields, 147, 508
Graph Wizard, 508, 510–517
grayed-out filenames, 103
grayed-out icons, 106
greater/less than signs (<>)
    as format symbol, 116
    in input masks, 121
    as query comparison
        operators, 228
    as relational operators,
        282
Grid command (View
    menu), 388
gridlines
    displaying, 158, 159, 162
    on graphs, 525
    printing, 169
Gridlines command (Format
    menu), 162
Gridlines command (Insert
    menu), 525
grids, 211
Grid X/Y properties, 410
group boxes, 370
group by: fields for reports,
    241–242
Group By option of
    Total:row, 711,
    715–718, 719, 723–724
group headers and footers.
    See headers and
    footers
grouping
    and carrying running
        sums, 652
    controls, 374–376
    with forced page breaks,
        579
    macros, 876–878
    report data, 532–537,
        570–580
    selections of controls, 558
    See also totals
groups/totals reports, 232,
    240

• H •

handles, 383, 385, 558
hard carriage return insertion
    with Ctrl+Enter, 189
hardcopy reports. *See*
    printing; reports
hardware requirements for
    Access, 22
Header/Footer command
    (Format menu), 437
headers and footers
    maximums and limita-
        tions, 1003
    on forms, 435–438
    on reports, 532–537,
        573–575, 576, 633–635,
        639–650, 654
Height property, 451
height/width adjustments
    for display columns,
        158–160
help
    context-sensitive, 12
    exiting, 42
    for icon functions, 105
    on-line, 39–40
    searching for topics, 40–42
    with Tool Tips, 105
    See also cue cards
Help Context ID property, 410
Help File property, 410
Help menu
    About Help command, 41
    Always on Top command,
        41
    Cue Cards command, 38
    How to Use Help com-
        mand, 41
Help tool, 105
Hide Columns command
    (Format menu), 161
hiding
    columns in datasheets,
        161–162
    columns in list boxes, 484
    columns in QBE panes,
        789–790

query fields in QBE pane,
    787–788
report data with macro,
    931
sections (bands) on
    reports, 577
Home key, 65, 140, 188
hotkey macros, 893, 932–934
How to Use Help command
    (Help menu), 41

• I •

IBM and IBM clone comput-
    ers for Access, 22
icons
    adding to toolbars, 106
    Control Wizard, 368
    for creating databases, 102
    for help, 39
    help with functions of, 105
    in Microsoft Access
        program group, 32
    paper clips for annotated
        help topics, 41
    QuickSort, 141
    reducing Access to, 57
    selecting program group
        for Access, 24
    for starting Access, 31–32
    as used in this book, 3–4
    See also toolbars
IDE (Integrated Develop-
    ment Environment), 17
identifier operators, 300
identifiers, unique, 87
~.IDX extensions, 667
images. *See* bitmap pictures;
    OLE objects
immediate window, 995–996
Imp/Exp Setup command
    (File menu), 690–695
Import Errors table, 698
importing files
    advantages and types
        of files, 13, 559,
        660–661
    from Btrieve, 13, 660, 677,
        681–682

creating setups for reuse, 688–698
from dBASE, 13, 661, 677, 679–681
from FoxPro, 13, 660, 677, 679–681
from Lotus 1-2-3, 660, 677, 683–685
macros for, 893–894, 931–932
from Microsoft Excel, 13, 660, 677, 683–685
OLE objects, 494–504
other Access databases, tables or objects, 662, 678–679
from Paradox, 13, 660, 677, 679–681
from SQL server, 13, 660, 677, 682–683
text files, 677, 685–688
versus attaching, 661–662
from word processor applications, 685
See also attaching files; bitmap pictures; embedding; exporting files
Import tool, 105
Indexes tool, 110
Indexes windows, 125–126
index files, 667
Index property, 126
~.INF extensions, 667, 668, 669
infinity symbol, 272
inner (equi-) joins, 325–326, 327–328, 770, 772
In operator, 289–290, 352
Input Mask property, 792
input masks, 115, 120–122
Input Mask Wizard, 121–122
inserting
 fields in tables, 127
 OLE objects in datasheets, 147
 records in forms, 189
 time/date into form fields, 189

Insert menu, Gridlines command, 525
Insert mode, 153
Insert Object command (Edit menu), 147
Insert Row command (Edit menu), 127
Insert Row tool, 110
integer division operator, 280
integer (numeric field type), 116
integers
 defined, 280
 functions for returning, 296
Integrated Development Environment. *See* IDE (Integrated Development Environment)
Int( ) function, 296
invoices
 creating and binding to query, 627
 designing, 620–625
 detail section and controls, 629–631
 header/footer and group summaries sections, 633–650
 percentage calculations, 650–651
 printer setup settings, 627–628
 sample, 80–82
 setting sort orders, 628–629
Is Null operator, 290, 357
italics
 for text in controls, 451
 as used in this book, 3
 See also fonts

• **J** •

Join Properties dialog box, 327
joins
 creating, 320–324
 creating for lookup tables, 772

deleting, 324
as lines indicating table relationships, 267, 271–272, 307–308
properties of, 326–327
of tables from other database sources, 674
of tables in queries, 321–323
types of, 324–333
See also queries; tables

• **K** •

keyboard
 Alt+F4 for Exit command, 36
 how to implement key combinations, 2
 See also Ctrl+key combinations; navigating; Shift+key combinations
key fields. *See* primary keys
keys
 foreign, 255, 258, 260
 primary, 124–126, 255, 256–259, 318, 767
 primary and unique, 124–126
key violations, 766, 767
key words, entering in help topics searches, 40–41

• **L** •

L, in input masks, 121
label controls
 adding, 562–563
 attaching labels, 390
 creating, 414–415
 creating unattached, 552
 defaults for positioning, 432
 deleting, 557
 described, 367, 370–371
 modifying appearance, 418–420
 modifying text, 415–416, 563, 588–589

moving, 417–418, 557–561
property options, 450–451, 566–567
sizing, 416–417
tab settings, 420–421
See also controls
labels
  advantages on forms, 93
  for mailing, 234
  on controls, 390
  on graph axes, 524
  See also mailing labels
Label X/Y properties, 432
landscape orientation, for reports, 243, 614
laser printers, 449, 544
launching. *See* starting
Layout for Printing property, 410
layouts. *See* reports
Lcase( ) function, 296
Left property, 451
Len( ) function, 296
length of strings, function for returning, 296
less than. *See* greater/less than signs (<>)
Like operator, 344–346
Like (similar to...) operator, 284–285
lines
  choosing thickness from palette, 443–444, 586–587
  on forms, 368, 454–456
  on reports, 605
linking
  command buttons to macros, 947–948
  graphs with forms, 15, 16
  objects, 494–495, 504–507
  tables, 266–267, 307
  See also attaching files; embedding; joins
list boxes, 367, 370, 376, 377, 477–484
  See also combo boxes; controls

List Box Wizard, 478–480
literal values
  in expressions, 298
  in select queries, 343
Locate and Seek (dBASE command). *See* Find command
locked/disabled fields, 154
  updateability, 318
locked records, 767
logical (Boolean) operators, 285–289
logos, 459
long integer (numeric field type), 116
Lookup (Paradox command). *See* List boxes
lookup tables
  design considerations, 89, 91–92
  examples, 255
  using in queries, 769–775
Lotus 1-2-3, file imports, 660, 677, 683–685
lowercase, function for returning, 296

• M •

maccros, stopping with actions, 917
macro design toolbar, 862–863, 867
Macro Names tool, 867
Macro Object button, 104
macros
  adding actions, 862, 868–872
  adding conditional actions, 878–882
  advantages, 10, 11, 17, 861–863, 889–890
  automatic execution of, 35
  copying, 873
  creating from Macro window, 864
  as database objects, 48
  for data validation, 916–919

deleting actions, 872
described, 44
editing, 871–873
for filtering records, 920–922
for finding records, 922–925
grouping, 876–878
maximums and limitations, 1003
for opening/synchronizing additional forms, 912–915
renaming, 873
running, 874–876, 877–878
running upon startup of Access, 35, 965–966
sample switchboard and custom menu, 11
saving, 872
triggering for control events, 909–916
triggering for form-level events, 891–893, 894–909
triggering for hotkeys, 893, 932–934
triggering for importing and exporting, 893–894, 931–932
triggering for report/report section events, 893, 925–931
triggering with events, 861, 884–886
troubleshooting, 882–883
See also commands; dialog boxes; events; modules
Macro window, 864
Mailing Label Report Wizard, 234, 240, 829–835
mailing labels
  creating with Mailing Label Report Wizard, 829–835
  displaying in Print Preview window, 836

modifying, 836–839
printing, 839
See also labels
Mail It tool, 171
mail merge operations
  with Mail Merge for Word for Windows Wizard, 853–856
  with Microsoft Word, 240, 701–702
  reports/form letters, 845–853
main/subforms, 176, 178, 181
Make Table command (Query menu), 753
Make-Table Query tool, 210
many-to-many relationship of tables, 262–263
many-to-one relationship of tables, 262
margins, for reports, 545–546
mathematical operations
  functions for, 296
  operators for, 278–281, 291
  precedence order of, 292
Max Button property, 410
Maximize button, 56, 57, 60
maximizing/minimizing. *See* sizing; zooming
~.MDB extensions, 33, 103
~.MDX extensions, 667
measurement units in inches, 546
memo data type, 111, 112, 131, 148
memo fields, 102, 145, 191
  maximums and limitations, 1002
  text box controls for, 421–423, 591–592
memory
  considerations for attaching to external files, 664
  RAM requirements for Access, 22
  See also disk space requirement for Access
memory variables, 369
memo type formats (field properties), 116–117
Menu Bar property, 409
menu bars, 56, 57
  attaching to forms, 961–962
  customizing drop-down, 954–961
  of Macro window, 866
Menu Builder, 963–965
menus
  creating with Menu Builder, 963–965
  design considerations, 97
  Query Design, 209–212
  selecting, 3
  See also Bookmark menu; commands; Edit menu; File menu; Format menu; Help menu; macros; Query menu; Records menu; shortcut menus; View menu
Merge It tool, 105, 171
messages
  issuing with macros, 908–909, 916
  See also error messages; status line
Microsoft Excel
  copying datasheets to, 172
  file imports, 13, 660, 677, 683–685
  similarities to Access, 19
Microsoft Graph (applet), 507–508, 517–527
Microsoft SQL server
  file attaching, 14, 663, 671–673
  file exports, 703–704
  file imports, 13, 660, 677, 682–683
Microsoft technical support, 73
Microsoft Windows
  advantage of familiarity with, 18
  copyright information, 41
  exporting files to other applications with DDE, 704
  version for Access, 22
  See also windows
Microsoft Windows Draw, 496
Microsoft Word
  copying datasheets to, 172
  exporting files for mail merge operations, 701–702
  exporting reports for mail merge operations, 240
  wizard for mail merge file creation, 853–856
Min Button property, 410
Minimize button, 56, 57, 60
minus sign (-), as subtraction operator, 279
miscellaneous operators, 289–290
Modal property, 410, 984
Modify DataEntry (Paradox command). *See* data entry command
Module Object button, 104
modules
  advantages, 17, 44, 988
  as database objects, 48
  saving, 993–994
monetary (financial) functions, 295
monetary formats. *See* Currency data type
monitors, requirement for Access, 22
Mountain Animal Hospital, 75, 77
  tables used in, 88, 254, 261, 272–273
mouse
  requirement for Access, 22, 55–56
  See also navigating

mouse buttons, right for shortcut menus, 36
move handles, 383, 385, 558
moving
  controls, 386–387
  Field List window, 412
  fields in datasheets, 156–158
  fields in forms, 192
  fields in tables, 127
  label controls, 417–418, 557–561
  text boxes, 417–418, 557–561
  toolbars, 106
  See also navigating
MS-DOS, version for Access and Windows, 22
MsgBox() function, 908–909
MTNANHSP.MDB file, 57, 61, 62, 254
MTNANIML file, 104
MTN.BMP file, 603
MTNSTART.MDB file, 61, 254
multiple files/records. See subforms
multiplication operator, 279
multiuser locked records, 154

• N •

naming
  controls, 301
  databases, 103
  fields, 110–111
  fields with captions, 122
  macros, 873
  reports, 248
  tables, 131–132
navigating
  in datasheets, 64–65, 139–140, 149–150
  fields/records on data input forms, 187–188
  with macros, 919–920
  in Query Design window, 207–208
  See also moving

Navigation Buttons property, 409, 984
~.NDX extensions, 667
networks, See also file sharing
New command, for creating queries, 69
New Database command (File menu), 102–103
New Database tool, 105
New/Form command (File menu), 179, 180–186
New Form tool, 105, 141, 210
New/Query command (File menu), 205
New Query tool, 105, 141, 210
New Record tool, 141
New/Report command (File menu), 238–245, 543
New Report tool, 105, 141, 210, 238, 543
newspaper-style columns, in snaked column reports, 840–845
New/Table command (File menu), 107
nine, in input masks, 121
normalization, 86
North Winds sample files, 1
NOTE icons, 3
Not operator, 288–289
Now() function, 295
NPV() function, 295
Null values
  Boolean operators, 286–289
  with controls, 372–374
  with Is Null operator, 290
  Like (similar to...) operator, 284
  searches using select queries, 340, 354–355
number data type, 111, 112, 129, 130, 145
number sign. See pound sign (#)
number type formats (field properties), 117

• O •

object buttons, 58, 104, 105
Object Linking and Embedding. See OLE (Object Linking and Embedding)
object list area, 104
object lists, 58
object names, in expressions, 298, 299
objects
  advantages, 493
  in databases, 48
  databases as, 45
  embedding, 494–504
  handling with command buttons, 106
  linking, 494–495, 504–507
  name length, 103
  positioning with properties, 451
  types, 494
  version 1.x to 2.0 considerations, 27
ODBC tables
  importing, 682–683
  updateability, 318
ODBC Timeout property, 793
OLE controls, 549
OLE data type, 111, 113, 130, 147
OLE fields, 102
  adding to forms, 423–426
OLE (Object Linking and Embedding), advantages, 17, 493, 494
OLE objects
  as criteria in select queries, 349
  displaying in forms, 189–190
  embedding, 494–504
  enhancing form backgrounds with, 452–454
  in reports, 602–605
  See also graphs

On Activate property, 895
On Change property, 910
On Click property, 895, 910, 940, 947–948
On Close property, 895, 904–905
On Current property, 894, 900–902
On Dbl Click property, 895, 910, 915–916, 940
On Deactivate property, 895
On Delete property, 895, 905–907
On Enter property, 910, 940, 941
On Error property, 895
one-to-many relationship of tables, 262, 317–318, 319, 320
one-to-one relationship of tables, 262, 318
On Exit property, 910, 940, 941
On Format property, 926
On Got Focus property, 895, 910, 940
On Key Down property, 895, 910, 940
On Key Press property, 895, 910, 940
On Key Up property, 895, 910, 940
on-line help, 39–40
On Load property, 895
On Lost Focus property, 910, 940
On Mouse Down property, 895, 910, 940
On Mouse Move property, 895, 940
On Mouse Up property, 895, 940
OnNotInLst property, 910
On Open property, 895, 931
On Print property, 926
On Resize property, 895
On Timer property, 895
On Unload property, 895

On Update property, 910
Open command, 63
Open Database command (File menu), 62
Open Database tool, 105
opening
 databases, 62–63
 datasheets, 142
 Design view, 65
 forms, 185–186
 forms with command buttons, 911–916
 forms with macros, 896–897
 reports with macros, 925
 tables, 63–64
opening programs. *See* starting
operators
 advantages, 277–278
 Boolean (logical), 285–289
 in expressions, 298
 identifiers (. and !), 300
 mathematical, 278–281
 miscellaneous, 289–290
 precedence of operations, 290–292
 relational, 281–282
 string, 283–285
 See also expressions
option buttons, 367, 370, 372–373, 467–472
 creating for dialog boxes, 968–970
option groups, 367, 374
 creating for dialog boxes, 968–970
 creating with calculated controls, 597–600
 creating with Option Group Wizard, 593–596
Option Group Wizard, 593–596
Options/Category command (View menu), 397, 398
Oracle, file imports, 13
order of operations with operators, 290–292
orientation (portrait or landscape)

for graph titles, 520
for reports, 243, 545, 614
Or operator, 287, 349–351, 356–359
orphans in table relationships, 263
OS/2, version for Access and Windows, 2
outer joins, 327, 328–331
 creating for lookup tables, 772
Output All Fields property, 793
overstrike mode, 153

• **P** •

page breaks
 control for forms, 368, 434–435
 on reports, 578–580
Page function, 553–554
page headers and footers, on reports, 536, 537, 559
page numbers
 function for returning, 553
 in report page footers, 537, 649–650
Paintbrush files, embedding, 498–500
palette, 59, 443–444, 531, 586–587
Palette command (View menu), 444
panes, 109, 211
 table and QBE, 165
paper clip icons, 41
paper source, 615
Paradox, 2, 10, 18
 file attaching, 14, 663
 file exports, 700
 file imports, 13, 660, 677, 679–681
 table updateability, 318
 terminological equivalents for Access, 18
parameter queries, 734–739
parameters in functions, 293

parent-child table relationships, 263
parentheses (( )), with functions, 293
pass-through queries, 784–785
passwords, requiring upon startup of Access, 35
Paste Append command (Edit menu), 147
Paste command (Edit menu), 147, 155
Paste Special command (Edit menu), 147
Paste tool, 105
pasting, values, 155
PC DOS, version for Access and Windows, 22
pencil symbol, 143, 144
percentages, 117, 650–651
period, as dot (.) identifier operator, 300–301, 303, 339
permissions denied fields, updateability, 318
perspective, on three-dimensional graphs, 525–526
PgUp/PgDn keys, 65, 140, 188
Picture Builder dialog box, 476
pictures. *See* bitmap pictures; OLE objects
plus sign (+), as addition operator, 279
pointing the mouse, 3
populating databases, 92
Pop Up property, 409, 984
portrait orientation, for reports, 243, 545, 614
pound sign (#)
   delimiting dates, 123, 228
   in expressions, 299
   in input masks, 121
   as wildcard, 150, 285, 344
Powerbase, 2
precedence of operations
   mathematical operations, 292
   with operators, 290–291

Preview button, 72
previews, samples, 612
primary keys, 124–126, 255, 256–259, 318, 767
primary tables, 268
Print command (File menu), 169–170, 195, 248
Print Count property, 927–928
Print Definition command (File menu), 131, 196, 616
printer drivers, 616
printers
   color, 584
   considerations for report design, 544
   dot-matrix, 544, 546
   laser, 449, 544
   requirement for Access, 22
printing
   form definitions, 196
   forms, 195, 438
   help topics, 41
   mailing labels, 839
   query results/dynasets, 228–229
   records, 169–172
   report definitions, 616
   reports, 243–244, 248, 530, 612–616
   suppressing for bitmap pictures, 615
   table designs, 131
Print Preview command (File menu), 170–172, 195
Print Preview tool, 141, 195, 531
Print Preview window, 245–246, 611–612
Print Setup command (File menu), 544–545
Print Setup dialog box, 614–616
Print tool, 105, 141, 171, 195
procedures
   compiling, 993

creating, 989–991
editing, 994–995
and function procedures, 989, 991–993, 997–998
saving, 993
storable in modules, 988
testing functions, 995–997
Procedures command (View menu), 994
program files. *See* modules
Program Manager for starting Access, 32–33
programming language. *See* ABC (Access Basic Code)
programs, 294
   See also applications; macros; modules; procedures
properties
   for attached external files, 673
   for controls, 392–395, 396–397, 450–452, 566–567
   for customized dialog boxes, 983–984
   described, 391–392
   displaying for controls, 589–590
   of events triggering macros, 890
   of fields, 114–124
   for forms, 407–411
   for group headers/footers, 574–575
   of joins, 326–327
   of list boxes, 480–482
   of objects, 301
   of queries, 791, 792–793
   of reports, 391
   See also controls
Properties command (View menu), 392
Properties tool, 110, 531
property area, 109
property sheets, 391, 392
property window, 59, 60, 391

push buttons, 368
pushing fields down, 127
~.PX extensions, 669, 670

• Q •

QBE panes/grids
  adding fields to, 165–166
  described, 207, 211–212
  hiding columns in, 789–790
  hiding query fields from dynasets, 787–788
  select queries from or: cell, 338, 351–352
  as SQL statements, 794–795
  Total:row in, 708–713
QBE (Query By Example), 50
queries
  adding fields, 212–217
  adding fields from attached tables, 674
  adding fields from multiple tables, 313–317
  adding tables, 305–312
  ad hoc, 203, 861
  advantages, 14, 49–50, 199–204
  binding to reports, 538, 542, 543
  calculated fields with, 776–780
  creating, 68–71, 205–212
  crosstab, 202, 318, 722–734
  as database objects, 48
  data definition, 786
  designing for invoice reports, 622–625
  displaying dynasets, 217–218
  of external files, 664
  GQBEs (Graphical Queries by Example), 14, 16, 208
  hiding fields in QBE pane, 787–788
  limitations of multiple-table, 317–320
  lookup tables with, 769–775
  maximums and limitations, 1002
  moving/deleting/rearranging fields in, 219–222
  parameter, 734–739
  pass-through, 784–785
  printing results/dynasets, 228–229
  properties of, 791, 792–793
  removing tables from, 311
  renaming fields in, 788–789
  running, 71
  saving, 229, 787–788
  setting record selection criteria, 224–228
  sorting results of, 223–224
  SQL, 202, 318, 784–786
  tips on updating fields, 320
  union, 784
  See also finding; joins; reports; searching
queries, action
  advantages, 741–743
  to append records, 755–761
  to archive records, 765–766
  to change values, 745–749
  to delete records, 761–764
  to find duplicate records, 765, 766
  to find unmatched records, 765
  to make new tables, 750–755
  running and troubleshooting, 766–767
  saving, 766
  viewing results, 744–745
queries, select
  advantages, 202, 336, 707–708
  with And and Or operators across fields, 356–359
  with And operator, 352–354
  with Between...And operator, 354
  with character (text or memo) criteria, 343
  with comparison operators, 336–341
  creating calculated fields, 361–363, 708–722
  field referencing, 341
  with functions, 341
  with In operator and list of values, 352
  with Like operator and wildcards, 344–346
  for nonmatching values, 346–347
  with Null data searches, 354–355
  with numeric criteria, 347–348
  with OLE object criteria, 349
  on different lines or same line, 360–361
  with or: cell of QBE pane, 351–352
  with Or operator, 349–351
  with yes/no (logical) criteria, 348
  See also totals
Query/Add Table command (Query Design menu), 307, 311–312
Query Design menu, 209–212
  Edit/Clear Grid command, 214
  Edit/Delete All command, 217
  File/Save command, 229
  Query/Add Table command, 307
Query Design toolbar, 208–209
Query Design window, 308–313
Query menu
  Add Table command, 206
  Make Table command, 753

Remove Table command, 206
View/Query Properties command, 791, 792–793
View SQL command, 794–795
View/Table Names command, 791
Query Object button, 104, 205
Query Properties command (Query menu/View option), 791, 792–793
Query window, 69, 206–207
 design mode, 206, 207–212
Query Wizards, 205, 764–766
question mark (?)
 in input masks, 121
 as wildcard, 150, 285, 344
Question mark toolbar button, for help, 39
QuickSort Ascending tool, 141, 163
QuickSort Descending tool, 141, 163
quotation marks (" ")
 in expressions, 299
 in input masks, 120
 in select queries, 343

• R •

R:Base, 2
radio buttons, 367, 467
raising controls, 445, 457, 608
RAM requirements for Access, 22
README files, 73
read-only access to databases, 35, 318
rearranging. See moving
record criteria for queries, 224
Record Lock property, 409, 793
records
 adding, 155–156

appending with action queries, 755–761
archiving with action queries, 765–766
counting, 296, 712–714, 780–781
creating, 142–144
deleting, 156, 189
deleting with action queries, 761–764
described, 46, 47
displaying, 156–169
editing, 152–154
filtering with macros, 920–925
finding duplicate or unmatched with action queries, 765, 766
finding first/top (n) with queries, 782–783
finding specific values, 150–152
finding with macros, 922–925
inserting, 189
locked, 767
navigating on forms, 188
navigating to, 64, 149–150
printing, 169–172
saving, 144–145, 163, 189
See also datasheets; sorting records
Record Selectors property, 409, 984
Records menu
 Allow Editing command, 153–154
 Data Entry command, 156
 Edit Filter/Sort command, 164–169
 GoTo command, 64, 149, 150
 Show All Records command, 156, 168
rectangles
 choosing thickness from palette, 443–444, 586–587

control buttons in, 374–376
 on forms, 368, 454–456
 on reports, 605–606, 609
referential integrity in table relationships, 263, 268–271, 308
 with external tables, 662
relational database managers
 Access as, 10, 12
 described, 44
relational operators, 281–282
relationship lines, 254
 for attached tables, 673
Relationships command (Edit menu), 320
 Add Table command, 264
Relationships tool, 105
Remove Table command (Query menu), 206
Rename command (File menu), 132
renaming fields, 129
Replace...command (Edit menu), 155
 form values, 189
replacing datasheet values, 152–153, 155
report and report section events, 893
Report Design window, 246–248, 530
Report Object button, 104
reports
 binding to queries, 538, 542, 543
 converting from forms, 439
 cover pages/letters, 535
 creating with AutoReport, 249–250
 creating with queries, 49, 204
 creating with Report Design window, 529–538, 542–570
 creating with Report Wizards, 238–248
 as database objects, 48

described, 44, 52–53, 231–235
design considerations, 78–82, 235–238, 539–542, 620–625
displaying, 71–72
as form letters, 845–853
headers and footers, 532–537, 573–575, 576
lines and rectangles, 605–607
macros for, 893
naming, 248
opening with macros, 925
page breaks, 578–580
printing, 243–244, 248, 530, 612–616
printing definitions of, 616
saving, 248–249, 580
sorting and grouping data for, 532–537, 570–580
templates for, 397–398
testing, 565, 625–626, 632–633
viewing, 530
See also forms for reports; invoices; mail merge operations; sections (bands) on reports
Report Wizards, 239–245
report writer, 584–586
resizing. *See* sizing
Restore button, 56, 57
reverse video effects, 449–450, 609–610
Right( ) function, 296
rotating on three-dimensional graphs, 525–526
Row Height command (Format menu), 159–160
rows described, 46, 47
Run command (File menu), 32
running sums, 652
Run Permissions property, 793
Run tool, 867

• S •

sample files, disks accompanying this manual, 4
Sample Preview command (File menu), 612
sample previews, 612
Sample Preview tool, 171, 531
Save As Report command (File menu), 439
Save command (File menu), 131–132, 193
Save Layout command (File menu), 162
Save Record command (File menu), 145
Save tool, 110
saving
 importance of, 36
 macros, 872
 modules, 993–994
 procedures, 993
 queries, 229, 787–788
 queries, action, 766
 records, 144–145, 163, 189
 report designs, 248–249
 reports, 248–249, 580
 table relationships, 271
 tables, 131–132
 upon exiting Access, 36
scaling property of bound object frames, 424
scientific notation, 117, 281
scoping criteria for action queries, 745
screens. *See* forms for data entry/edits
scripts (Paradox term). *See* modules
scroll bars in text boxes, 422
Scroll Bars property, 409, 984
scrolling
 in datasheets, 49, 139
 memo fields, 191
 on forms, 188
searching
 for help topics, 40–42

See also finding; queries
SECRET icons, 4
sections (bands) on reports
 closed, 646
 described, 532
 with forced page breaks, 579
 growing or shrinking, 568–569
 hiding, 577
 macros for, 926
 sizing, 577–578
security issues and database conversion from version 1.x, 28
selecting
 controls, 383–385
 entire field, 153
 form fields, 189
 groups of controls, 558
 values or characters in records, 152
 See also commands; finding; menus; queries; searching
Selection Behavior global property, 385
select queries. *See* queries, select
Select Query tool, 210
self-joins, 331–333
Send to Back command (Format menu), 448
Set Primary Key command (Edit menu), 125
Set Primary Key tool, 110
SetValue action, 917, 918
shading of backgrounds, 607–608
shadowing
 of boxes, 446
 of rectangles in forms, 458
 of text, 448–449, 588–589
sharing files. *See* exporting files; importing files
Shift+key combinations
 Shift+Enter to save records, 163, 193

Shift+F1 for help access, 39
Shift+F2 for Zoom box, 148
Shift+Tab for navigating, 65, 140, 188
shortcut menus
　described, 36–37
　for help, 39
Shortcut Menus property, 409
ShowAllRecords action, 922
Show All Records command (Records menu), 156, 168
Show All Records tool, 141
Show All Relationships tool, 265
Show Columns command (Format menu), 158, 161
Show Direct Relationships tool, 265
showing columns, 161–162
sidebars as used in this book, 4
Sigma (Totals button), 708
single-column forms, 181
single-column reports, 240
single (numeric field type), 116
single-step mode of troubleshooting macros, 882–883
sinking controls, 457, 608
Size command (Format menu), 389
size limitations
　of databases, 1001
　of forms and reports, 1003
　of macros, 1003
　of queries, 1002
　of table fields, 115–116
　of tables, 1002
sizing
　controls, 383, 385–386
　fields, 129
　fonts in controls, 451, 588
　forms, 405–407
　graphs, 522

label controls, 416–417, 554–556
OLE objects in unbound object frames, 500–501
report sections, 549–550
sections (bands) on reports, 577–578
table designs in table/query panes, 312
text boxes, 416–417, 554–555
toolbars, 106
See also zooming
slash (/) as division operator, 279
snaked column reports, 840–845
snapshots, 317
Snap to Grid option (Format menu), 388–389
software
　requirements for Access, 22
　See also applications; Microsoft
Sort command (Records menu/Edit Filter option), 164–169
sorting
　database records with Edit Filter/Sort options, 164–169
　database records with QuickSort, 163–164
　dynasets (query results), 203, 223–224
　and grouping data for reports, 570–580
　mailing labels, 832–833
　report fields, 242–243
Sorting and Grouping tool, 531
sound files in OLE fields, 147
sound objects, 504
Source Connect Str property, 793
Source Database property, 793
Source property, 792

spaces
　disallowed in field names, 111
　in input masks, 120
special characters
　disallowed in field names, 111
　for mathematical operators, 278
　See also front of index
Special Effect property, 451
special effects on forms, 441–452, 454–458
Split Window command (View menu), 995
spreadsheets
　exporting to, 699–700
　importing, 683–685
　See also datasheets; importing files
SQL (financial) functions, 295
SQL queries, 202, 318, 784–786
SQL server. *See* Microsoft SQL server
SQL statements, Queries By Example as, 794–795
SQL View tool, 210
Sqr( ) function, 296
square root function, 296
starting Access
　from Access icon, 31–32
　with customized options, 34–35
　from DOS, 34
　from File Manager, 33–34
　from Program Manager, 32–33
　and reactivating, 57
status line, 56, 57, 139, 464–465
StopMacro action, 917
stopping. *See* exiting; suppressing
Str( ) function, 294
string handling
　functions for, 296

operators for, 283–285
Style Step tool, 867
subforms
  adding lookup tables, 816–824
  adding to main forms, 813–815
  as controls, 368
  creating, 808–813
  creating with FormWizard, 799–807
  described, 96, 176, 797–799
  linking to forms, 815–816
  with subtotals, 824–826
  See also forms
sub procedures, 989
subtraction operator, 279
Sum( ) function, 295, 637–638
summary reports, 240, 637–638
sunken boxes, 446
suppressing
  appearance of Welcome screen, 26, 38
  printing of bitmap pictures, 615
  running of AutoExec macros, 35
switchboards
  adding command buttons, 939–946, 950–951
  adding pictures to command buttons, 951–954
  advantages, 97, 937–938
  creating basic form, 939
  linking command buttons to macros, 947–948
  macros for, 948–950
  sample, 97

• T •

Tab key
  for navigating in datasheets, 140
  for navigating in forms, 188
  for navigating in windows, 65
  setting order of fields for progress of (tab order), 420–421
Table Design window, 308
Table Names command (Query menu/View option), 791
Table Names command (View menu), 314–315
Table Names tool, 210
table panes, 165
Table properties windows, 126–127
table relationships
  adding or deleting, 271
  creating with links, 266–267
  creating with queries, 273
  creating with relationships builder tool, 264–265
  join lines, 271–272
  one-to-many, 87
  overview, 88–89, 260–263
  and referential integrity, 263, 268–271
  saving, 271
  specifying options, 268–271
tables
  attaching and converting from version 1.x, 28
  attaching from other applications, 662
  as "black boxes," 43
  changing structure of, 127–131
  copying, 133–134
  creating, 107–110
  creating or changing through queries, 202, 203, 750–755
  as database objects, 48
  deleting, 133
  described, 44, 45, 46, 47–48
  design considerations, 53, 85–89, 464–465
  foreign keys for, 255, 258, 260
  maximums and limitations, 1002
  naming or renaming, 131–132
  opening, 63–64
  primary, 268
  primary keys for, 124–126, 255, 256–259
  printing definitions, 131
  saving, 131–132
  snapshots (virtual tables), 317
  viewing, 65–66
  See also attaching files; datasheets; exporting files; importing files; joins; lookup tables; queries; reports
table views. *See* datasheets
Table windows, 109–110
Table Wizard, 108
Tab Order command (Edit menu), 420–421
tabular forms, 176, 177, 181
tabular reports, 232, 240
Task List/End Task button, 36
technical support for Access, 73
templates for forms and reports, 397–398
terms. *See* expressions
testing
  Access installation, 26
  data for validity upon input, 90
  function procedures, 995–997
  macros, 882–883
  reports, 565, 625–626, 632–633
text
  attached, 519
  in expressions, 300
  formatting in controls, 552–553
  free-form (unattached), 521
  requiring in table fields, 116

shadowing, 448–449, 588–589
Text Align property, 451
text boxes
  advantages in data entry forms, 93
  creating, 553–554
  deleting, 557
  described, 367, 370, 371–372
  enhancing forms with special effects, 447–452
  for memo fields, 421–423
  modifying appearance, 418–420, 563–564, 567–570
  modifying text, 415–416
  moving, 417–418, 557–561
  multiple line, 590–592
  property options, 450–451, 566–567
  sizing, growing or shrinking, 416–417, 554–555, 568–569, 590–592
  See also controls
text data type, 111, 112, 129, 130, 131
text fields, 101, 146, 1002
text files
  exporting, 700, 701–702
  importing, 677, 685–688, 695–696
  See also importing files
text type formats (field properties), 116–117
three-dimensional effects
  choosing thickness from palette, 443–444, 586–587
  for control boxes/rectangles on forms, 445–446, 457–458
  on graphs, 514–515, 522, 525–527
time
  inserting into form fields, 189
  See also dates

Time( ) function, 295
Timer Interval property, 895
TIP icons, 3
title bars, 56, 408
title pages, 652, 654
titles
  for data input forms, 184–185
  See also labels
toggle buttons, 367, 372–373, 474–476, 602
toolbars, 56, 57
  adding icons, 106
  controlling, 106
  in Database window, 104, 105
  datasheet, 141–142
  macro design, 862–863, 867
  moving, 106
  Query Design, 208–209
  in Report Design window, 530–532
  Table window, 110
  See also commands; icons
toolboxes, 67
Toolbox tool, 531
toolbox windows, 58–59
Tool Tips, 105
tool usability, 10
top(n) queries, 203
Top property, 451
Top Value property, 793
Total:row, 708–722
Total Field Record Limit option of Total:row, 711
total queries, 202, 318, 712
totals
  calculating for reports, 232, 537
  cumulative, 652
  on subforms, 824–826
  summary reports, 240, 637–638
  with Total:row in QBE pane, 708–722
  See also counts; grouping
Totals button, 708

Totals tool, 210
transferring files. *See* exporting files; importing files
triangles (arrows)
  Maximize and Minimize buttons, 56, 57, 60
  record pointer, 142, 144
troubleshooting. *See* testing
True/False values
  Boolean operators, 286–289
  with controls, 372–374
  Like (similar to...) operator, 284–285
  relational operators, 281–282
  in select queries, 340–341
tutorials. *See* Cue Cards; help
two-pass report writers, 537, 650

• U •

UDFs (user-defined functions), 292, 989
unattached (free-form) text, 521
unbound objects
  described, 494
  embedding, 497–501
  frames/controls for, 368–369, 381–383, 452–454
  in reports, 602–605
underlining
  report data with macro, 929–931
  text in controls, 451
  See also fonts
underscore character (_), in input masks, 120
Undo Current Record/Field command (Edit menu), 141, 144, 154
undoing changes to records with Undo button or Esc key, 154, 189

Undo Saved Record command (Edit menu), 154
Undo tool, 105
Undo Typing command (Edit menu), 154
UnFreeze columns command (Format menu), 162
union queries, 784
unique keys, 124–126, 318
Unique Records property, 793
Unique Value property, 793
units of measurement defaults (inches), 546
updateability of forms, 431, 433
Update Query tool, 210
upgrades to Access version 2.0, 21, 23
uppercase conversion with macros, 918
user-defined functions (UDFs), 292, 989
user name requirement upon startup of Access, 35

• V •

ValChecks (Paradox command). *See* validation rules
Val( ) function, 294
validating data. *See* data validation
values
  changing in datasheet records, 152–154
  changing with action queries, 745–749
  copying and pasting, 155
  described, 47
  editing in forms, 189
  in expressions, 298
  finding in datasheet records, 150–152
  nonmatching in select queries, 346–347

of object properties, 303
repeating from preceding record, 153
setting with macros, 917–919
See also functions
"The value you entered isn't appropriate for this field" message, 145
variables, 369
  defining in procedures, 990–991
VCR buttons, 64
VERSION 2.0 icons, 4
version information
  for Access with OS/2, 2
  for DOS with Windows, 22
  upgrades to Access version 2.0, 21, 23, 27–28
  See also Access features new to version 2.0
VGA monitor recommendation for Access, 22
video, reverse, 449–450, 609–610
video card requirements for Access, 22
video objects, 504
viewing
  reports, 530
  results of action queries, 744–745
  table names in QBE pane, 314–315
  table names in queries, 791
  tables, 65–66
View menu
  Field List command, 378
  Form command, 191
  Grid command, 388
  Options/Category command, 397, 398
  Palette command, 444
  Procedures command, 994
  Properties command, 392
  Split Window command, 995

Table Names command, 314–315
View/Query Properties command (Query menu), 791, 792–793
views
  setting for forms, 408–411
  See also queries
Views Allowed property, 409, 984
View SQL command (Query menu), 794–795
View/Table Names command (Query menu), 791
virtual tables (snapshots), 317
Visible property, 929, 931
Visual Basic language, 2

• W •

WARNING icons, 3
Welcome screen suppression, 26, 38
width/height adjustments
  for display columns, 158–160
  for reports, 546–547
Width property, 410, 451
wildcards
  with Like operator, 285
  in searches, 150–151
  in select queries, 344–346
windows
  Access, 56–57, 61
  database, 56, 57–58, 59, 104–106
  Datasheet, 139–142
  for design of forms/reports/queries, 58
  Field List, 58, 59, 378–381, 411–412
  Form, 186–188
  Form Design, 405, 406
  immediate, 995–996
  Indexes, 125–126
  Macro, 864
  palette, 59

Index

Print Preview, 245–246, 611–612
property, 59, 391
Query, 69
Query Design, 308–313
Report Design, 246–248, 530
switching between panes, 109
Table, 109–110
Table Design, 308
Table properties, 126–127
toolbox, 58–59
See also Microsoft Windows Wizards
advantages, 12
Archive Records, 765–766
Combo Box, 485
Command Button, 942–945
Crosstab Query, 733–734
Find Duplicate Records, 765
Find Unmatched Records, 765
Form, 13, 180–186, 799–808
Graph, 508, 510–517
Input Mask, 121–122
List Box, 478–480
Mailing Label Report, 234, 240, 829–835
Mail Merge for Word for Windows, 853–856
Option Group, 468, 593–596
Query, 205, 764–766
Report, 239–245
Table, 108
See also commands
Word. *See* Microsoft Word
word processor file imports, 685
workspace on forms, 405
WYSIWYG environment, 14, 442–443, 565, 585–586

• **Y** •

Yes/No data type, 111, 112–113, 130, 145
Yes/No fields, 102, 348
Yes/No (logical) criteria
  in checkbox controls, 600–602
  as options for data validation, 472–476
  with queries, select, 348
Yes/No type formats (field properties), 119

• **Z** •

zero as input character, 121
zooming
  pictures in forms, 424
  report print previews, 245, 246
  views, 72
Zoom tool, 171

IDG BOOKS' ... FOR DUMMIES™ SERIES

Find out why over 6 million computer users love IDG'S ...FOR DUMMIES BOOKS!

"I laughed and learned..."
Arlene J. Peterson, Rapid City, South Dakota

DOS FOR DUMMIES,™ 2nd EDITION
by Dan Gookin

This fun and easy DOS primer has taught millions of readers how to learn DOS! A #1 bestseller for over 56 weeks!

ISBN: 1-878058-75-4
$16.95 USA/$21.95 Canada
£14.99 UK and Eire

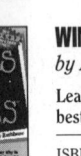  INTERNATIONAL BESTSELLER!

UPGRADING AND FIXING PCs FOR DUMMIES™
by Andy Rathbone

Here's the complete, easy-to-follow reference for upgrading and repairing PCs yourself.

ISBN: 1-56884-002-0
$19.95 USA/$26.95 Canada

  NATIONAL BESTSELLER!

WINDOWS FOR DUMMIES™
by Andy Rathbone

Learn the Windows interface with this bestselling reference.

ISBN: 1-878058-61-4
$16.95 USA/$21.95 Canada
£14.99 UK and Eire

 #1 BESTSELLER!

WORD FOR WINDOWS FOR DUMMIES™
by Dan Gookin

Learn Word for Windows basics the fun and easy way. Covers Version 2.

ISBN: 1-878058-86-X
$16.95 USA/$21.95 Canada
£14.99 UK and Eire

  NATIONAL BESTSELLER!

THE INTERNET FOR DUMMIES™
by John Levine

Surf the Internet with this simple reference to command, service and linking basics. For DOS, Windows, UNIX, and Mac users.

ISBN: 1-56884-024-1
$19.95 USA/$26.95 Canada
£17.99 UK and Eire

 NATIONAL BESTSELLER!

WORDPERFECT 6 FOR DUMMIES™
by Dan Gookin

WordPerfect 6 commands and functions, presented in the friendly ...For Dummies style.

ISBN: 1-878058-77-0
$16.95 USA/$21.95 Canada
£14.99 UK and Eire

  NATIONAL BESTSELLER!

PCs FOR DUMMIES,™ 2nd EDITION
by Dan Gookin & Andy Rathbone

This #1 bestselling reference is the perfect companion for the computer phobic.

ISBN: 1-56884-078-0
$16.95 USA/$21.95 Canada
£14.99 UK and Eire

  NATIONAL BESTSELLER!

1-2-3 FOR DUMMIES™
by Greg Harvey

Spreadsheet guru Greg Harvey's fast and friendly reference covers 1-2-3 Releases 2 - 2.4.

ISBN: 1-878058-60-6
$16.95 USA/$21.95 Canada
£14.99 UK and Eire

  NATIONAL BESTSELLER!

MACs FOR DUMMIES,™ 2nd Edition
by David Pogue

The #1 Mac book, totally revised and updated. Get the most from your Mac!

ISBN: 1-56884-051-9
$19.95 USA/$26.95 Canada
£17.99 UK and Eire

 #1 MAC BOOK

EXCEL FOR DUMMIES,™ 2nd EDITION
by Greg Harvey

Updated, expanded—The easy-to-use reference to Excel 5 features and commands.

ISBN: 1-56884-050-0
$16.95 USA/$21.95 Canada
£14.99 UK and Eire

  NATIONAL BESTSELLER!

WORDPERFECT FOR DUMMIES™
by Dan Gookin

Bestseller Dan Gookin teaches all the basics in this fun reference that covers WordPerfect 4.2 - 5.1.

ISBN: 1-878058-52-5
$16.95 USA/$21.95 Canada/£14.99 UK and Eire

 NATIONAL BESTSELLER!

UNIX FOR DUMMIES™
by John R. Levine & Margaret Levine Young

This enjoyable reference gets novice UNIX users up and running—fast.

ISBN: 1-878058-58-4
$19.95 USA/$26.95 Canada/ £17.99 UK and Eire

  NATIONAL BESTSELLER!

For more information or to order by mail, call 1-800-762-2974. Call for a free catalog! For volume discounts and special orders, please call Tony Real, Special Sales, at 415-312-0644. For International sales and distribution information, please call our authorized distributors:

CANADA Macmillan Canada
416-293-8141

UNITED KINGDOM Transworld
44-81-231-6661

AUSTRALIA Woodslane Pty Ltd.
61-2-979-5944

IDG BOOKS' ... FOR DUMMIES™ SERIES

"DOS For Dummies is the ideal book for anyone who's just bought a PC and is too shy to ask friends stupid questions."

MTV, Computer Book of the Year, *United Kingdom*

"This book allows me to get the answers to questions I am too embarrassed to ask."

Amanda Kelly, Doylestown, PA on Gookin and Rathbone's PCs For Dummies

"If it wasn't for this book, I would have turned in my computer for a stereo."

Experanza Andrade, Enfield, CT

CORELDRAW! FOR DUMMIES™
by Deke McClelland

This bestselling author leads designers through the drawing features of Versions 3 & 4.

ISBN: 1-56884-042-X
$19.95 USA/$26.95 Canada/17.99 UK & Eire

QUICKEN FOR WINDOWS FOR DUMMIES™
by Steve Nelson

Manage finances like a pro with Steve Nelson's friendly help. Covers Version 3.

ISBN: 1-56884-005-5
$16.95 USA/$21.95 Canada
£14.99 UK & Eire

NATIONAL BESTSELLER!

QUATTRO PRO FOR DOS FOR DUMMIES™
by John Walkenbach

This friendly guide makes Quattro Pro fun and easy and covers the basics of Version 5.

ISBN: 1-56884-023-3
$16.95 USA/$21.95 Canada/14.99 UK & Eire

MODEMS FOR DUMMIES™
by Tina Rathbone

Learn how to communicate with and get the most out of your modem — includes basics for DOS, Windows, and Mac users.

ISBN: 1-56884-001-2
$19.95 USA/$26.95 Canada
14.99 UK & Eire

1-2-3 FOR WINDOWS FOR DUMMIES™
by John Walkenbach

Learn the basics of 1-2-3 for Windows from this spreadsheet expert (covers release 4).

ISBN: 1-56884-052-7
$16.95 USA/$21.95 Canada/14.99 UK & Eire

NETWARE FOR DUMMIES™
by Ed Tittel & Denni Connor

Learn to install, use, and manage a NetWare network with this straightforward reference.

ISBN: 1-56884-003-9
$19.95 USA/$26.95 Canada/17.99 UK & Eire

OS/2 FOR DUMMIES™
by Andy Rathbone

This fun and easy OS/2 survival guide is perfect for beginning and intermediate users.

ISBN: 1-878058-76-2
$19.95 USA/$26.95 Canada/17.99 UK & Eire

QUICKEN FOR DOS FOR DUMMIES™
by Steve Nelson

Manage your own finances with this enjoyable reference that covers Version 7.

ISBN: 1-56884-006-3
$16.95 USA/$21.95 Canada/14.99 UK & Eire

WORD 6 FOR DOS FOR DUMMIES™
by Beth Slick

This friendly reference teaches novice Word users all the basics of Word 6 for DOS

ISBN: 1-56884-000-4
$16.95 USA/$21.95 Canada/14.99 UK & Eire

AMI PRO FOR DUMMIES™
by Jim Meade

Learn Ami Pro Version 3 with this friendly reference to the popular Lotus word processor.

ISBN: 1-56884-049-7
$16.95 USA/$21.95 Canada/14.99 UK & Eire

WORDPERFECT FOR WINDOWS FOR DUMMIES™
by Margaret Levine Young

Here's a fun and friendly reference that teaches novice users features and commands of WordPerfect For Windows Version 6.

ISBN: 1-56884-032-2
$16.95 USA/$21.95 Canada/14.99 UK & Eire

For more information or to order by mail, call 1-800-762-2974. Call for a free catalog! For volume discounts and special orders, please call Tony Real, Special Sales, at 415-312-0644. For International sales and distribution information, please call our authorized distributors:

CANADA	UNITED KINGDOM	AUSTRALIA
Macmillan Canada	Transworld	Woodslane Pty Ltd.
416-293-8141	44-81-231-6661	61-2-979-5944

IDG BOOKS' ...FOR DUMMIES QUICK REFERENCE SERIES

IDG's bestselling ...For Dummies Quick Reference Series provides a quick and simple way to remember software commands and functions, written in our down-to-earth, plain English style that guides beginners and experts alike through important commands and hidden troublespots.

Fun, Fast & Cheap!

"Thanks for coming up with the simplest idea ever, a reference that you really can use and understand."
Allison J. O'Neill, Edison, NJ

WORDPERFECT FOR DOS FOR DUMMIES™ QUICK REFERENCE
by Greg Harvey

With this guide you'll never have to worry about deciphering cryptic WordPerfect commands again!

ISBN: 1-56884-009-8
$8.95 USA/$11.95 Canada
£7.99 UK & Eire

WORD FOR WINDOWS FOR DUMMIES™ QUICK REFERENCE
by George Lynch

End your stress over style sheets, mail merge, and other pesky Word features with this quick reference. Covers Word 2.

ISBN: 1-56884-029-2
$8.95 USA/$11.95 Canada

ILLUSTRATED COMPUTER DICTIONARY FOR DUMMIES™
by Dan Gookin, Wally Wang, & Chris Van Buren

This plain English guide to computer jargon helps with even the most techie terms.

ISBN: 1-56884-004-7
$12.95 USA/$16.95 Canada
£11.99 UK & Eire

1-2-3 FOR DUMMIES™ QUICK REFERENCE
by John Walkenbach

Keep this quick and easy reference by your desk and you'll never have to worry about forgetting tricky 1-2-3 commands again!

ISBN: 1-56884-027-6
$8.95 USA/$11.95 Canada
£7.99 UK & Eire

WINDOWS FOR DUMMIES™ QUICK REFERENCE
by Greg Harvey

The quick and friendly way to remember Windows tasks & features.

ISBN: 1-56884-008-X
$8.95 USA/$11.95 Canada
£7.99 UK & Eire

EXCEL FOR DUMMIES™ QUICK REFERENCE
by John Walkenbach

A fast, fun and cheap way to remember bothersome Excel commands.

ISBN: 1-56884-028-4
$8.95 USA/$11.95 Canada
£7.99 UK & Eire

DOS FOR DUMMIES™ QUICK REFERENCE
by Greg Harvey

A fast, fun, and cheap way to remember DOS commands.

ISBN: 1-56884-007-1
$8.95 USA/$11.95 Canada
£7.99 UK & Eire

WORDPERFECT FOR WINDOWS FOR DUMMIES™ QUICK REFERENCE
by Greg Harvey

The quick and friendly "look-it-up" guide to the leading Windows word processor.

ISBN: 1-56884-039-X
$8.95 USA/$11.95 Canada/£7.99 UK & Eire

For more information or to order by mail, call 1-800-762-2974. Call for a free catalog! For volume discounts and special orders, please call Tony Real, Special Sales, at 415-312-0644. For International sales and distribution information, please call our authorized distributors:

CANADA Macmillan Canada
416-293-8141

UNITED KINGDOM Transworld
44-81-231-6661

AUSTRALIA Woodslane Pty Ltd.
61-2-979-5944

IDG BOOKS' PC WORLD SERIES

"I rely on your publication extensively to help me over stumbling blocks that are created by my lack of experience."

Fred Carney, Louisville, KY on
PC World DOS 6 Handbook

PC WORLD MICROSOFT ACCESS BIBLE
by Cary N. Prague & Michael R. Irwin

Easy-to-understand reference that covers the ins and outs of Access features and provides hundreds of tips, secrets and shortcuts for fast database development. Complete with disk of Access templates. Covers versions 1.0 & 1.1.

ISBN: 1-878058-81-9
$39.95 USA/$52.95 Canada
£35.95 incl. VAT UK & Eire

PC WORLD WORD FOR WINDOWS 6 HANDBOOK
by Brent Heslop & David Angell

Details all the features of Word for Windows 6, from formatting to desktop publishing and graphics. A 3-in-1 value (tutorial, reference, and software) for users of all levels.

ISBN: 1-56884-054-3
$34.95 USA/$44.95 Canada
£29.99 incl. VAT UK & Eire

PC WORLD DOS 6 COMMAND REFERENCE AND PROBLEM SOLVER
by John Socha & Devra Hall

The only book that combines a DOS 6 Command Reference with a comprehensive Problem Solving Guide. Shows when, why and how to use the key features of DOS 6/6.2.

ISBN: 1-56884-055-1
$24.95 USA/$32.95 Canada
£22.99 UK & Eire

PC WORLD WORDPERFECT 6 HANDBOOK
by Greg Harvey, author of IDG's bestselling 1-2-3 For Dummies

Here's the ultimate WordPerfect 6 tutorial and reference. Complete with handy templates, macros, and tools.

ISBN: 1-878058-80-0
$34.95 USA/$44.95 Canada
£29.99 incl. VAT UK & Eire

PC WORLD EXCEL 5 FOR WINDOWS HANDBOOK, 2nd EDITION
by John Walkenbach & Dave Maguiness

Covers all the latest Excel features, plus contains disk with examples of the spreadsheets referenced in the book, custom ToolBars, hot macros, and demos.

ISBN: 1-56884-056-X
$34.95 USA/$44.95 Canada /£29.99 incl. VAT UK & Eire

PC WORLD DOS 6 HANDBOOK, 2nd EDITION
by John Socha, Clint Hicks & Devra Hall

Includes the exciting new features of DOS 6, a 300+ page DOS command reference, plus a bonus disk of the Norton Commander Special Edition, and over a dozen DOS utilities.

ISBN: 1-878058-79-7
$34.95 USA/$44.95 Canada/£29.99 incl. VAT UK & Eire

QUARKXPRESS FOR WINDOWS DESIGNER HANDBOOK
by Barbara Assadi & Galen Gruman

ISBN: 1-878058-45-2
$29.95 USA/$39.95 Canada/£26.99 UK & Eire

OFFICIAL XTREE COMPANION, 3RD EDITION
by Beth Slick

ISBN: 1-878058-57-6
$19.95 USA/$26.95 Canada/£17.99 UK & Eire

For more information or to order by mail, call 1-800-762-2974. Call for a free catalog! For volume discounts and special orders, please call Tony Real, Special Sales, at 415-312-0644. For International sales and distribution information, please call our authorized distributors:

CANADA Macmillan Canada 416-293-8141   UNITED KINGDOM Transworld 44-81-231-6661   AUSTRALIA Woodslane Pty Ltd. 61-2-979-5944

IDG BOOKS' INFOWORLD SECRETS™ SERIES

...SECRETS

"Livingston is a Windows consultant, and it is hard to imagine any tricks or tips he has ommitted from these 990 pages. True to the name, there are lots of undocumented hints that can make life easier for the intermediate and advanced user."

Peter H. Lewis, New York Times *on Brian Livingston's* Windows 3.1 SECRETS

"Brian Livingston has worked his magic once again. *More Windows 3.1 SECRETS* is well worth any serious Windows user's time and money."

Stewart Alsop, Editor in Chief, InfoWorld

"...Probably the most valuable book on computers I've ever seen, and I work in a library."

Jacques Bourgeios, Longueuil, Quebec,
on *Brian Livingston's* Windows 3.1 SECRETS

"David Vaskevitch knows where client/server is going and he tells it all."

Dr. Robert Metcalfe, Publisher/CEO,
InfoWorld *on David Vaskevitch's* Client/Server Strategies

Over 750,000 SECRETS Books In Prints

WORDPERFECT 6 SECRETS™
by Roger C. Parker and David A. Holzgang

Bestselling desktop publishing wizard Roger C. Parker shows how to create great-looking documents with WordPerfect 6. Includes 2 disks with Bitstream fonts, clip art, and custom macros.

ISBN: 1-56884-040-3; $39.95 USA/
$52.95 Canada/£ 35.99 incl. VAT UK & Eire

DOS 6 SECRETS™
by Robert D. Ainsbury

Unleash the power of DOS 6 with secret work- arounds and hands-on solutions. Features "Bob's Better Than DOS" shareware Collection with over 25 programs.

ISBN: 1-878058-70-3; $39.95 USA/
$52.95 Canada/£ 35.99 incl. VAT UK & Eire

MORE WINDOWS 3.1 SECRETS™
by Brian Livingston   **BESTSELLER!**

IDG's Windows guru, Brian Livingston, reveals a host of valuable, previously undocumented, and hard-to-find Windows features in this sequel to the #1 bestseller.

ISBN: 1-56884-019-5
$39.95 USA/$52.95 Canada
£ 35.99 incl. VAT UK & Eire

PC SECRETS™
by Caroline M. Halliday   **BESTSELLER!**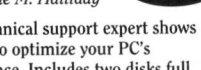

IDG's technical support expert shows you how to optimize your PC's performance. Includes two disks full of valuable utilities.

ISBN: 1-878058-49-5; $39.95 USA/
$52.95 Canada/£ 35.99 incl. VAT UK & Eire

WINDOWS 3.1 SECRETS™
by Brian Livingston   **BESTSELLER!**

The #1 bestselling Windows book/ disk by the renowned *InfoWorld* and *Windows Magazine* columnist. Over 250,000 in print! A must-have!

ISBN: 1-878058-43-6
$39.95 USA/$52.95 Canada
£35.99 incl. VAT UK & Eire

HARD DISK SECRETS™
by John M. Goodman, Ph.D.

Prevent hard disk problems altogether with the insider's guide. Covers DOS 6 and SpinRite 3.1. Includes a disk of hard disk tune-up software.

ISBN: 1-878058-64-9; $39.95 USA/
$52.95 Canada/£ 37.99 incl. VAT UK & Eire

NETWORK SECURITY SECRETS™
by David Stang & Sylvia Moon

Top computer security experts show today's network administrators how to protect their valuable data from theft and destruction by hackers, viruses, corporate spies, and more!

ISBN: 1-56884-021-7;
$49.95 USA/$64.95 Canada
£ 44.99 incl. VAT UK & Eire

WINDOWS GIZMOS™
by Brian Livingston and Margie Livingston   **BESTSELLER!**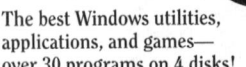

The best Windows utilities, applications, and games— over 30 programs on 4 disks!

ISBN: 1-878058-66-5
$39.95 USA/$52.95 Canada
£35.99 incl. VAT UK & Eire

CLIENT/SERVER STRATEGIES: A SURVIVAL GUIDE FOR CORPORATE REENGINEERS
by David Vaskevitch

An essential read for anyone trying to understand the data highways that will drive successful businesses through the '90s and beyond.

ISBN: 1-56884-064-0; $29.95 USA/$39.95 Canada
£ 26.99 incl. VAT UK & Eire

For more information or to order by mail, call 1-800-762-2974. Call for a free catalog! For volume discounts and special orders, please call Tony Real, Special Sales, at 415-312-0644. For International sales and distribution information, please call our authorized distributors:

CANADA Macmillan Canada   UNITED KINGDOM Transworld   AUSTRALIA Woodslane Pty Ltd.
         416-293-8141   44-81-231-6661   61-2-979-5944

Order Form

Order Center: (800) 762-2974 (8 a.m.-5 p.m., PST, weekdays) or (415) 312-0650

For Fastest Service: Photocopy This Order Form and FAX it to: (415) 358-1260

Quantity	ISBN	Title	Price	Total

Shipping & Handling Charges

Subtotal	U.S.	Canada & International	International Air Mail
Up to $20.00	Add $3.00	Add $4.00	Add $10.00
$20.01-40.00	$4.00	$5.00	$20.00
$40.01-60.00	$5.00	$6.00	$25.00
$60.01-80.00	$6.00	$8.00	$35.00
Over $80.00	$7.00	$10.00	$50.00

In U.S. and Canada, shipping is UPS ground or equivalent.
For Rush shipping call (800) 762-2974.

Subtotal _____
CA residents add applicable sales tax
IN and MA residents add 5% sales tax
IL residents add 6.25% sales tax
RI residents add 7% sales tax
Shipping _____
Total _____

Ship to:
Name _____
Company _____
Address _____
City/State/Zip _____
Daytime Phone _____

Payment: ❑ Check to IDG Books (US Funds Only)   ❑ Visa   ❑ Mastercard   ❑ American Express
Card# _____ Exp. _____ Signature _____

Please send this order form to: IDG Books, 155 Bovet Road, Suite 310, San Mateo, CA 94402.
Allow up to 3 weeks for delivery. Thank you!

Disclaimer and Copyright Notice

Note

IDG Books Worldwide, Inc., warrants that the disk that accompanies this book is free from defects in materials and workmanship for a period of 60 days from the date of purchase of this book. If IDG Books receives notification within the warranty period of defects in material or workmanship, IDG Books will replace the defective disk. The remedy for the breach of this warranty will be limited to replacement and will not encompass any other damages, including but not limited to loss of profit and special, incidental, consequential, or other claims.

5 ¼" Disk Format Available. The enclosed disk is in 3 ½" 1.44MB format. If you don't have a drive that size or format, and cannot arrange to transfer the data to the disk size you need, you can obtain the data on a 1.2MB 5 ¼" disk by writing: IDG Books Worldwide, Attn: PC World Microsoft Access 2 Bible 2nd Edition Disk, IDG Books, 155 Bovet Rd., Suite 310, San Mateo, CA 94402, or call 800-762-2974. Please allow 2-3 weeks for delivery.

IDG Books Worldwide, PCW Communications, Inc., and the authors specifically disclaim all other warranties, express or implied, including but not limited to implied warranties of merchantability and fitness for a particular purpose with respect to defects in the disk, the files, and source code contained therein, and/or the techniques described in the book, and in no event shall IDG Books Worldwide, PCW Communications, and/or the authors be liable for any loss of profit or any other commercial damage, including but not limited to special, incidental, consequential, or other damages.

Licensing Agreement

Do not open the accompanying disk package until you have read and unless you agree with the terms of this licensing agreement. If you disagree and do not wish to be bound by the terms of this licensing agreement, return the book for refund to the source from which you purchased it.

The entire contents of this disk are copyrighted and protected by both U.S. copyright law and international copyright treaty provisions. The individual files on this disk are copyrighted by the authors. You may copy any or all of these files to your computer system. To copy the files, you must follow the "Installation Instructions for the *PC World Microsoft Access 2 Bible, 2nd Edition* Companion Disk," included on the last pages of this book. Absolutely none of the material on this disk or listed in this book may ever be distributed, in original or modified form, for commercial purposes.

Installation Instructions for the PC World Microsoft Access 2 Bible, 2nd Edition Companion Disk

Attention: Before installing any of the files from the companion disk, read the Disclaimer and Copyright Notice on the preceding page.

The companion disk contains the example files that are used and created in this book. The files appear in their completed form so you can avoid a lot of typing if you only want to see how certain forms, reports, or queries work. Also included are files that were created as starting points for some of the more complicated examples in the chapters. There are five Access database files and many external files.

The five Access database files included on the disk are

MTNSTART.MDB	Contains only the tables used in the examples in the book
MTNANHSP.MDB	Contains all completed tables, queries, forms, reports, macros, and modules
ATCIMPEX.MDB	Contains several tables and is used to teach attaching, importing, and exporting files
SAMPLBTN.MDB	Contains sample picture buttons from the add-on product The Button Bundle. Adds pictures to your Access command buttons.
ABFORMS.MDB	Contains three forms from the highly acclaimed add-on product The Access Business Forms Library

The external files included on the disk include Paintbrush bitmaps, Excel, dBASE, Paradox, and text files used in various chapters throughout this book.

One file on the disk, named ACCESSBI.EXE, is a self-extracting archive file. When properly run, the file will create the five Access database files as well as the external files. We strongly recommend that you install the file in a sub-directory other than the main Access directory. It is assumed that Access is already installed.

The disk is in high-density 3½-inch format with approximately 1MB used. The instructions for installing the companion disk follow.

We have assumed that you installed Access on drive C using the subdirectory ACCESS and that your default 3½-inch floppy drive is drive A. If this isn't your setup, substitute your floppy or hard disk drive letters or directories in place of the default. You will need 3.3MB free to extract the files on your hard disk.

Steps:	**Installing from DOS**
Step 1.	Insert the companion disk into your default floppy drive.
Step 2.	Type **C:** and press Enter to make drive C active.
Step 3.	Type **MD ACCESS\ACCESSBI** and press Enter to create a subdirectory named ACCESSBI under your default ACCESS subdirectory on your hard disk.
Step 4.	Type **CD \ACCESS\ACCESSBI** and press Enter to go to the new subdirectory.
Step 5.	Type **COPY A:\ACCESSBI.EXE** and press Enter to copy the example file to your C:\ACCESS\ACCESSBI directory.
Step 6.	Type **ACCESSBI** and press Enter to extract the files. Each file will be extracted.
Step 7.	Type **DIR** and press Enter to check the files. You will see five Access databases with MDB file extensions and 20 other external files.
Step 8.	Remove the floppy disk, start Windows, and get into Access.

Steps:	**Installing from Windows**
Step 1.	Insert the companion disk into your default floppy drive.
Step 2.	Using Windows File Manager, create a new subdirectory named C:\ACCESS\ACCESSBI.
Step 3.	Using Windows File Manager, copy the file A:\ACCESSBI.EXE to C:\ACCESS\ACCESSBI.
Step 4.	From the Windows File menu, select Run; then type **ACCESSBI** and press Enter to extract the files. Each file will be extracted.
Step 5.	Using Windows File Manager, check the contents of the C:\ACCESS\ACCESSBI directory. You will see five Access databases with MDB file extensions and 20 other external files.
Step 6.	Remove the floppy disk and get into Access.

You can now use these files with the *PC World Microsoft Access 2 Bible,* 2nd Edition examples. Remember, when you open one of the example databases, you will find them in the C:\ACCESS\ACCESSBI subdirectory.